A to Z

of Pharmaceutical Marketing

World's First and Only Encyclopedia

Set of 2 Volumes

Volume - I

A to Z

of Pharmaceutical Marketing

World's First and Only Encyclopedia

Set of 2 Volumes

Volume - I

Subba Rao Chaganti

PharmaMed Press

An imprint of BSP Books pvt. Ltd

4-4-309/316, Giriraj Lane,

Sultan Bazar, Hyderabad - 500 095

A to Z of Pharmaceutical Marketing: World's First and Only Encyclopedia, Set of 2 Volumes
Volume - I
by Subba Rao Chaganti

Published by:

PharmaMed Press
An imprint of BSP Books Pvt. Ltd.
4-4-309/316, Giriraj Lane, Sultan Bazar, Hyderabad - 500 095.
Phone: 040-23445688; Fax: 91+40-23445611
e-mail: info@pharmamedpress.com
www.pharmamedpress.com/pharmamedpress.net

ISBN

Volume I : **978-81-972520-0-6 (Perfect Bound)**
Volume II : **978-81-972520-3-7 (Perfect Bound)**

Dedication

The *A to Z of Pharmaceutical Marketing* is dedicated to all the scholars, professionals, scientists, and technologists whose unwavering dedication and contributions have shaped the landscape of pharma marketing over the years. As we unveil the pages of this compendium, we acknowledge the collective wisdom and tireless efforts of those who have elevated pharma marketing to the dynamic discipline it is today.

To the marketing scholars whose intellect and curiosity have driven the exploration of innovative strategies, theories, and frameworks, this work is a tribute to your intellectual pursuits.

To the marketing professionals who have navigated the ever-evolving terrain of regulations, market dynamics, and ethical considerations, your practical insights have paved the way for effective and responsible pharmaceutical marketing.

To the scientists whose research and discoveries have propelled pharmaceutical advancements, this encyclopedia acknowledges your pivotal role in shaping the narrative of healthcare and influencing marketing strategies.

To the technologists who have harnessed the power of cutting-edge technologies, from data analytics to artificial intelligence, your contributions have transformed how we approach marketing in the pharmaceutical industry.

As we express our gratitude, we recognize that this encyclopedia is a tapestry woven with the threads of collaboration, knowledge-sharing, and a shared commitment to advance the field. May this compilation serve as a testament to the collective brilliance that has shaped the present and will undoubtedly shape the future of pharmaceutical marketing.

In honoring the past, we also look to the future, where continued collaboration and innovation will further people's pharmaceutical marketing into uncharted territories. May this dedication stand as a symbol of appreciation for those who have come before us and as an inspiration for those who will carry the torch forward.

With deepest gratitude,
Subba Rao Chaganti

Preface

The *A to Z of Pharmaceutical Marketing* emerges as an ambitious and pioneering endeavor in the dynamic landscape where healthcare intersects with marketing. As a compiler of this comprehensive encyclopedia, I am thrilled to introduce a compendium that spans the intricacies of an industry at the crossroads of science, commerce, and human well-being.

This volume, comprising over 1,464 entries in 7,25,000 plus words, is a testament to the collective expertise and dedication of professionals, researchers, and academics in pharmaceutical marketing over the years. A deeper understanding of this multifaceted domain is vital for navigating the challenges and embracing the opportunities that define the pharmaceutical landscape.

My goal has been to create an authentic and comprehensive resource that transcends the traditional boundaries of reference works. The *A to Z of Pharmaceutical Marketing* isn't just an assembly of entries; it is a journey through the strategies, ethics, innovations, and nuances that shape how pharmaceutical products are brought to market.

My endeavor from the beginning has been to create a collection that reflects the diversity of perspectives within the industry. The entries in this encyclopedia cover all the facets and the entire gamut of pharmaceutical marketing, enriching this encyclopedia immeasurably.

The entries synthesize great contributions from eminent pharmaceutical marketers, researchers, and technologists from various fields that have impacted pharmaceutical marketing over time.

This book is more than a static compilation; It is a living document that reflects the ever-evolving nature of pharmaceutical marketing. I invite you, the reader, to explore topics ranging from traditional strategies to cutting-edge innovations, ethical considerations to regulatory landscapes, and global perspectives to local nuances.

Here is an invitation to you, the reader, to embark on this intellectual journey with an open mind and a thirst for knowledge. Whether you are a seasoned professional, a student entering the field, or an academic seeking insights, I hope this encyclopedia serves as a source of inspiration, fostering a deeper appreciation for the complexities of pharmaceutical marketing.

The *A to Z of Pharmaceutical Marketing* is a collaborative achievement as it draws inspiration from numerous contributors over the past years. I am truly honored to present this work to you. May it be a source of enlightenment, exploration, and continued dialogue with the ever-evolving landscape of pharmaceutical marketing.

I sincerely believe you will be as excited to dive or dig deeply into it as I have been while compiling it.

Sincerely,

Subba Rao Chaganti

Acknowledgements

This monumental undertaking, A to Z of Pharmaceutical Marketing, has been a work of passion, dedication, and collaborative effort. As we present this comprehensive encyclopedia to the world, we extend our deepest gratitude to those whose contributions to the body of knowledge in pharmaceutical marketing have made this endeavor possible.

First and foremost, my heartfelt thanks go to the industry leaders, academics, and practitioners who generously shared their knowledge, insights, and experiences over the years making the field of pharmaceutical marketing an exciting field as it is today. Their commitment to excellence has enriched every page of this encyclopedia, providing a valuable resource for Pharma marketers, students, and researchers.

I extend my deepest thanks to the publishers and all those behind the scenes who worked tirelessly to bring this project to fruition.

A special thanks to the few individuals who helped me bring this book. Without their physical, intellectual, and moral support, this book would still be in the concept stage. I sincerely thank:

- J. Sivaprasad, managing director of Amitha Designs, for a great cover design
- Anil Shah, the most enthusiastic publisher with a passion for publishing
- Nikunjesh Shah for making the digital versions of this book available
- Naresh Davergave and his team at PharmaMed Press for designing this book

Last but not least, I thank Mahalakshmi, my better half, literally and figuratively, for supporting me throughout this book project. I must also thank my three children and their spouses—Srinivasa Phanindra, Geetha, Lavanya, Aditya, Soumya, and Chaitanya for their appreciation and feedback throughout this project.

More importantly, I thank my grand children— Aditi, Eesha, Surya, and Shriya. They have been a constant source of joy, happiness, and inspiration, contributing greatly to writing this book. The sparkle in their eyes when they saw their names, as I mentioned them in acknowledgments, gave me immense satisfaction.

Above all, I thank the readers—students, marketing practitioners, academics, researchers, and enthusiastic for embarking on this journey. I believe that A to Z of Pharmaceutical Marketing becomes a valuable companion, sparking curiosity, fostering learning, and inspiring a deeper understanding of the dynamic field of pharmaceutical marketing.

Finally, this encyclopedia is a collective achievement, a testament to the power of collaboration, knowledge-sharing, and the pursuit of excellence. Thank you to everyone who played a role, big or small, in making this ambitious project a reality.

Sincerely,

Subba Rao Chaganti

Disclaimer

The *A to Z of Pharmaceutical Marketing* is an expansive encyclopedia that provides insights, information, and perspectives on various aspects of pharmaceutical marketing. While every effort has been made to ensure the content's accuracy, relevance, and timeliness, it is important to note the following disclaimer.

1. **Accuracy of Information:** The content of this encyclopedia is intended to serve as a reference guide and informational resource. However, the pharmaceutical industry is dynamic and subject to constant evolution, regulatory changes, and scientific advancements. Therefore, the information provided in this book may become outdated, and readers are encouraged to verify critical details independently.
2. **Professional Advice**: This encyclopedia does not substitute for professional advice. The information presented is not intended to replace consultation with qualified healthcare professionals, legal experts, or other specialists. Readers should seek professional guidance relevant to their specific situations or concerns.
3. **Authorship and Perspective**: Entries in this encyclopedia are contributions from various sources, each presenting their perspectives and experiences. The views expressed within individual entries are those of the contributors and do not necessarily reflect those of the compiler, publisher, or affiliated institutions.
4. **Industry Variability**: The pharmaceutical industry operates in diverse global contexts, each with its regulatory frameworks, cultural nuances, and market dynamics. While efforts have been made to offer a broad understanding, readers are advised to consider the specificities of their regions or areas of interest.
5. **Continual Updates**: The field of pharmaceutical marketing is subject to continual change. New regulations, technologies, and market trends may emerge after the publication of this encyclopedia. Readers are encouraged to stay informed about the latest developments in the industry.
6. **Copyright and Usage:** This encyclopedia is protected by copyright laws, and unauthorized reproduction or distribution of content is prohibited. Any external references, quotes, or citations should be appropriately credited.

Readers are advised to approach the information in this encyclopedia with a critical mindset, supplementing their understanding with additional research, consultation, and verification as needed. The author and publisher disclaim any liability arising from using the information provided herein.

Sincerely,
Subba Rao Chaganti

Contents

Volume - I

Contents

Volume - II

List of Abbreviations

ADHD	Attention Deficit Hyperactivity Disorder
AHT	Average Handling Time
AI	Artificial Intelligence
AKS	Anti-Kickback Statute
AMEC	International Association for Measurement and Evaluation of Communication
AMP	Average Manufacturer Price
ANDA	Abbreviated New Drug Application
API	Active Pharmaceutical Ingredient
APRN	Advanced Practice Registered Nurse
AR	Augmented Reality
ASP	Average Selling Price
AUC	Area Under the Curve
B2B	Business-to-Business
B2C	Business-to-Consumer
BCG	Boston Consulting Group
BE	Bioequivalence
BI	Business Intelligence
BLE	Bluetooth for Energy
BVA	Brand Value Added
CAC	Customer Acquisition Cost
CAR-T	Chimeric Antigen Receptor-T
CBA	Cost-Benefit Analysis
CBT	Cognitive Behavioral Therapy
CCPA	California Consumer Privacy Act
CDC	Category Development Index
CDC	Centers for Disease Control and Prevention
CDP	Customer Data Platform
CDSCO	Central Drugs Standards Control Organization
CDSS	Clinical Decision Support System
CF	Cystic Fibrosis
ChatGPT	Conversational Generative Pre-Trained Transformer
CLM	Closed-Loop Marketing
Cmax	Maximum Concentration
CME	Continuing Medical Education
COGS	Cost of Goods Sold
COPD	Chronic Obstructive Pulmonary Disease
CPC	Cost-Per-Click

CPC	Cost-Per-Conversion
CPI	Consumer Price Index
CRM	Customer Relationship Management
CRO	Contract Research Organization
CT	Computed Tomography
CTA	Call to Action
CTC	Click-Through-Rate
CX	Customer Experience
DMD	Duchenne Muscular Dystrophy
DMF	Drug Master File
DMP	Data Management Platform
DOL	Digital Opinion Leader
DSS	Decision Support System
DTC	Direct-to-Consumer
DTCA	Direct-to-Consumer Advertising
DTx	Digital Therapeutics
EBIT	Earnings Before Interest and Tax
EEG	Electro Encephalograph
EFPIA	The European Federation of Pharmaceutical Industries and Associations
EMA	European Medicines Agency
eMSL	Electronic Medical Sales Liaison
EQ	Emotional Intelligence
EVA	Economic Value Added
eWOM	Electronic Word of Mouth
FCA	The False Claims Act
FCPA	Foreign Corrupt Practices Act
FCR	First Contact Resolution
FDA	Food and Drug Administration
fMRI	Functional Magnetic Resonance Imaging
FTC	Federal Trade Commission
GATT	General Agreement on Trade and Tariffs
GCP	Good Clinical Practice
GDP	Good Distribution Practices
GDP	Gross Domestic Product
GDPR	General Data Protection and Regulation
GM	Gross Margin
GMP	Good Management Principles
GMP	Good Manufacturing Practices
GMP	Good Marketing Practices
GPP	Good Promotional Practices

HCP	Healthcare Professional
HCP	Healthcare Provider
HEOR	Health Economics and Outcomes Research
HHS	Department of Health and Human Services
HIPAA	Health Insurance Portability and Accountability Act
HMO	Health Maintenance Organization
HON	Health on the Net Foundation
IND	Investigative New Drug
IPR	Intellectual Property Rights
ISMPP	The International Society for Medical Publication Professionals
KAM	Key Account Management
KOL	Key Opinion Leader
KPI	Key Performance Indicator
KSF	Key Success Factor
LCA	Life Cycle Assessment
LCM	Life Cycle Management
LMS	Learning Management Systems
LTV	Lifetime Value
M&A	Mergers and Acquisitions
MAA	Marketing Authorization Application
MAUT	Multi-Attribute Utility Theory
MBO	Management by Objectives
MCO	Managed Care Organization
MDS	Multi-Dimensional Scaling
mHealth	Mobile Health
MIS	Management Information Systems
ML	Machine Learning
MLC	Market Life Cycle
MLR	Medical, Legal and Regulatory
MOA	Market Opportunity Analysis
MOT	Moment of Truth
MR	Mixed Reality
MRI	Magnetic Resonance Imagery
MSL	Medical Science Liaison
MSRP	Manufacturer's Suggested Retail Price
NASDAQ	National Association of Securities Dealers Automated Quotations
NDA	New Drug Application
NDA	Non-Disclosure Agreement
NDDS	Novel Drug Delivery Systems
NGO	Non-Governmental Organization

NIH	National Institutes of Health
NLA	Natural Language Analysis
NLP	Natural Language Processing
NMPA	The National Medical Products Administration
NP	Nurse Practitioner
NPS	Net Promoter Score
NPV	Net Present Value
OCR	Optical Character Recognition
OIG	Office of the Inspector General
PA	Physician Assistant
PA	Prior Authorization
PAG	Patient Advocacy Group
PBM	Pharmacy Benefit Manager
PD	Pharmacodynamics
PESTEL	Political, Economic, Social, Technological, Legal, and Environment
PET	Positron Emission Tomography
PhRMA	Pharmaceutical Research and Manufacturers of America
PK	Pharmacokinetics
PKU	Phenyl Ketonuria
PLC	Product Life Cycle
PMI	Purchasing Managers' Index
PMS	Post-Marketing Surveillance
PPC	Pay-Per-Click
PR	Public Relations
PROMS	Patient-oriented Outcomes Measures
PSA	Public Service Announcement
PSP	Patient Support Program
R&D	Research and Development
RLD	Reference Listed Drug
ROI	Return on Investment
RWD	Real World Data
RWE	Real World Evidence
SEM	Search Engine Marketing
SEO	Search Engine Optimization
SFE	Sales Force Effectiveness
SFE	Sales Force Excellence
STP	Segmentation, Targeting, Positioning
SWOT	Strengths, Weaknesses, Opportunities, Threats
TDCS	Trans-cranial Direct Current Stimulation
TGA	Therapeutic Goods Administration (Australia)

TMS	Trans-cranial Magnetic Stimulation
UAT	User Acceptance Testing
UGC	User-Generated Content
UI	User Interface
UX	User Experience
VR	Virtual Reality
WOM	Word of Mouth
WTO	World Trade Organization
WWW	World Wide Web
XAI	Explainable Artificial Intelligence
XR	Extended Reality
ZBB	Zero-Based Budgeting
ZMOT	Zero Moment of Truth

A

1. A/B Testing
2. Abandonment
3. ABC (Always Be Closing)
4. Absolute Advantage
5. Acceptance
6. Acceptance Testing
7. Account Management
8. Account Planning
9. Account Care Organization (ACO)
10. Accreditation
11. Acquiescence Bias
12. Acquisition
13. Active Pharmaceutical Ingredient (API)
14. Activity Sampling
15. Adaptation
16. Added Value
17. Adoption
18. Adopter Categories
19. Ad Recall
20. Adverse Reactions
21. Advertising
22. Advertising Elasticity
23. Advertising Plan
24. Advertising Research
25. AdSense
26. Advertising Strategy
27. Advertorial
28. Advocacy Advertising
29. AdWords
30. Affiliate Marketing
31. Affinity Marketing
32. Affordable Care Act (ACA)
33. Aggregate Demand
34. Agile Marketing
35. AIDA
36. Aided Recall
37. Algorithms
38. Alignment
39. Amazon
40. Ambush Marketing
41. Analog Research
42. Ansoff Matrix
43. ANDA
44. Anonymization of Data
45. Anthropology
46. Anthropomorphic Marketing
47. Anthropomorphic Marketing Research
48. Anti-competitive Practice
49. Anti-corporatism
50. Anti-Kickback Statute
51. Apple
52. Application Programming Interface (API)
53. Archetypes
54. Artificial Intelligence
55. Asset-led Branding
56. Asset-led Marketing
57. Atomization
58. Attention
59. Attitudinal Research
60. Attitudinal Scaling
61. Attitudinal Surveys
62. Attribute Positioning
63. Attribution Modeling
64. Audience
65. Audience Fatigue
66. Audience Profiling
67. Audience Research
68. Augmentation
69. Augmented Intelligence
70. Augmented Reality (AR)
71. Authorized Generics
72. Awareness
73. Awareness-Trial-Reinforcement Process

A/B Testing

A/B testing, at its most basic, is a way to compare two versions of something to figure out which performs better. According to Kaiser Fung, the founder of the applied analytics program at Columbia University, the method is almost 100 years old.

Ronald Fisher, a statistician and biologist in the 1920s, discovered the principles behind A/B testing and randomized experiments in general. Then, in the early 1950s, many scientists started running clinical trials in medicine using these principles behind A/B testing. Later in the 1960s and 1970s, marketers started adapting the concept to evaluate direct response campaigns, such as which one — a postcard or a letter to target customers, resulted in more sales.

A/B testing first emerged as we know it in the 1990s. Although its origin dates back over one hundred years ago, its concept remains much the same except now it takes place online in real-time environments with different numbers of participants and experiments performed over time.

How to Do A/B Testing

Here are the essential steps for conducting A/B testing:

1. *Select Your Sample*: Once your target demographic and size have been defined, determine an adequate sample to achieve statistical significance during testing.
2. *Randomize Samples*: Assign each version of an ad randomly to different samples to ensure any differences in performance do not stem from differences among them.
3. *Monitor the Results*: Track the performance of each ad version, monitoring the KPI you identified. You could do this with the tracking tools, such as tracking or marketing pixels, Google Analytics, or other tracking tools.
4. *Analyze the Results*: Compare the results of each version of the ad and look for statistically significant differences. If one version significantly outperforms the other, you should select that version for wider use.
5. *Repeat the Process*: If the A/B test significantly improves performance, consider testing other variations to optimize performance further. If the version doesn't perform better, continue testing until a version does.

Please keep A/B testing a part of a continuous process; by constantly optimizing messaging to increase engagement and conversion rates, enhancing marketing campaign results, and making them more successful overall.

Abandonment

Abandonment in pharmaceutical marketing refers to patients who discontinue taking or refilling their prescriptions as directed by healthcare providers for various reasons, including side effects or high costs associated with medication use. This may occur for various reasons, such as experiencing side effects from taking such a drug and possible cost considerations being too great.

Abandonment of medication by both patients and pharmaceutical companies can have lasting repercussions for all parties involved, from worsening symptoms or complications for patients not taking prescribed doses to lost revenue for pharmaceutical firms when patients stop refilling prescriptions on time; plus facing challenges in demonstrating product efficacy if their users don't use their products properly.

Pharma marketers can implement several strategies to combat abandonment. Companies could provide educational material about the importance of adherence, financial aid for medication costs through patient assistance programs, or create products with easier dosing schedules, such as once-daily dosing or extended-release formulations.

Healthcare providers play an essential part in helping their patients avoid medication discontinuation by discussing potential side effects and emphasizing the necessity of adhering to prescribed dosage plans. Furthermore, they may help develop manageable regimens.

Pharmaceutical Companies Approach Abandonment

Pharmaceutical companies utilize many strategies to address abandonment. Here are a few examples:

1. *Patient Education Programs*: Companies may offer educational materials about the importance of taking medications as prescribed, including any consequences of not following instructions properly and the potential repercussions for failing to do so. These materials could be distributed via healthcare providers, patient support groups, or online channels.
2. *Patient Assistance Programs*: Companies may offer financial assistance programs to assist individuals in affording their medications, including coupons or copay cards, and programs offering eligible individuals free or reduced-cost medication.
3. *Packaging and Dosing Innovations*: Companies may implement inventive packaging and dosing solutions that make taking medication simpler

for patients, like extended-release formulations that need less frequent dosing, as well as pre-filled syringes that make taking medicines for certain medical conditions simpler than before.

4. *Adherence-Tracking Technologies*: Companies may develop adherence-tracking technologies, such as mobile apps, wearable devices, or electronic pill dispensers that assist patients in monitoring their medication use and receiving reminders to take them.
5. *Healthcare Provider Engagement*: Pharmaceutical companies may work with healthcare professionals to promote medication adherence and help patients manage side effects or complications, providing training or educational resources and supportive services such as nurse educators or patient advocates.

Pharmaceutical companies and patients can suffer when they stop taking their prescribed medication as directed, leading to more serious symptoms or complications. Meanwhile, pharmaceutical companies could lose revenue when patients don't refill their prescriptions on time, and also find it difficult to demonstrate effectiveness if their products are not used as prescribed.

Pharma marketers can employ various strategies to combat abandonment. Such measures include offering educational material on adherence and financial assistance for patients needing medication costs.

Healthcare providers can aid patients in staying compliant by explaining any possible side effects and emphasizing their importance, along with developing an individual medication plan which is both manageable and effective.

ABC (Always Be Closing)

ABC is the acronym for the popular sales mantra—*Always Be Closing*. Successful closing of the sale is vital for every salesperson, for his sales success depends on it. While closing is essentially a technique, Always Be Closing (ABC) is used more as a motivational phrase.

The Origin

The origin of the phrase and its popularity can be traced back to the famous 1992 movie *Glengarry Glen Ross*. The movie was based on a play by David Mamet that won the Pulitzer Prize in 1984.

In a scene from the film, an intimidating Alec Baldwin, the central character, playing the role of Blake, criticized a group of disheartened salesmen from his partitioned blackboard with the phrase—ABC: A-*Always*, B-*Be*, C-*Closing*, and AIDA: A-Attention, I-Interest, D-Desire, A-Action. The phrase has become very popular since the movie became a big success.

Closing Techniques

Closing the sale is used when a salesperson achieves a desired outcome by either a commitment by a prospect's signature or by exchanging goods and services for money. In the case of pharma selling, it is a commitment to prescribe or place an order by the physician or hospital for the company's products.

For a salesperson to *Always Be Closing* the sales, he needs to look at new prospects (General Leads), Pitch products or services to those prospects, and ultimately complete (Close).

Closing Techniques in Pharma Selling

Here are five commonly used closing techniques used in pharmaceutical selling.

1. Alternative Choice Closing
2. Assumptive Closing
3. Benefit Close
4. Time-based Close
5. Summary Close

Detailed descriptions of these closing techniques are presented under Closing Techniques under 'C.'

Closing to Helping!

Times have since changed since Glengarry Glen Ross! While Blake would never give up control of the sales process to a prospect, the excessive emphasis on closing the sale at any cost won't work in today's changed marketing environment. Research also confirms that customers are most motivated to purchase when they see a sales rep as a trusted advisor and don't like aggressive and pushy sales reps. Therefore, it's time to move from *Always Be Closing* to *Always Be Helping*!

Absolute Advantage

Absolute and comparative advantages are concepts used in international trade theory to describe the benefits of specialization and trade.

The noted 18th-century economist Adam Smith, in his book, The Wealth of Nations, described absolute advantage as the ability of an individual, company, region, or country to produce a greater quantity of a good or service with the same quantity of inputs per unit of time.

Later, David Ricardo, of British political economist fame, expanded upon Smith's concepts by developing the comparative advantage theory, which states that countries can still benefit from trade even when their absolute advantage in producing everything lies somewhere else.

However, in pharmaceutical marketing terms, absolute advantage refers to situations in which one company holds an unparalleled advantage over its rivals in producing and marketing pharmaceutical products. Such advantages could arise due to various factors, including:

1. *Strengthened Research and Development Capabilities*: Businesses that invest heavily in R&D may produce drugs more rapidly and with greater efficacy, giving them a distinct competitive edge over rival companies.
2. *Exclusive Intellectual Property Rights*: Companies with exclusive patents or other IP (Intellectual Property) rights for a particular drug can prevent competitors from entering the market for a certain period, giving them a monopoly.
3. *Strong Marketing and Distribution Channels*: Companies with robust marketing and distribution capacities can effectively reach more potential customers and promote their drugs more successfully.
4. *Regulatory Competencies*: Companies that possess stronger regulatory competencies often enjoy stronger relationships with regulatory authorities and may be able to get their drugs approved faster by regulatory bodies, giving them an early edge in the market.

Absolute advantage in pharmaceutical marketing is a great asset and crucial for companies to succeed in a highly competitive and regulated industry.

Acceptance

In pharmaceutical marketing, acceptance refers to a patient's willingness and ability to accept a new treatment or medication. It also includes its adoption and uptake by healthcare providers. Because it can impact the drug's revenue potential and improve patient outcomes, acceptance is critical to the success of any new drug.

To increase acceptance of their products, pharmaceutical companies may use a variety of strategies. Examples include:

1. *Clinical trial data*: Companies can use it to persuade healthcare professionals and patients about their product's benefits and safety, building trust.
2. *Key Opinion Leader (KOL) Engagement*: Companies can partner with KOLs, such as top physicians and researchers, to promote the medication and increase awareness among healthcare providers. KOLs can provide valuable insight and endorsements that could increase the drug's acceptance.
3. *Patient Advocacy Groups*: Companies may partner with patient advocacy groups to increase patient acceptance and medication awareness. These groups offer education and support to their members, creating a sense of community around the medication.
4. *Marketing and Advertising*: Companies may invest in advertising and marketing campaigns to increase medication acceptance and awareness. Targeting healthcare professionals through publications, conferences, and other channels, and direct-to-consumer advertisements can increase patient interest in the product.
5. *Patient Access Programs*: Companies may offer free trials or financial assistance programs to encourage patients to try the medication. These programs remove financial barriers that could hinder people from trying the drug and increase adoption and acceptance rates.

Acceptance Testing

In pharmaceutical marketing, acceptance testing refers to testing a new medication to meet patients' and healthcare providers' expectations.

Product development is incomplete without acceptance testing. It helps identify potential problems or areas for improvement and allows the product team to make changes before the medication goes into production. In addition, acceptance testing can involve key stakeholders like healthcare providers, patients, or other decision-makers. Here are a few examples of acceptance testing used in pharmaceutical marketing:

1. *Focus Groups and Surveys*: Companies may hold focus groups or surveys with patients and healthcare professionals to get feedback about a medication. These sessions can identify potential problems with the drug and areas for improvement.
2. *Analyzing Clinical Trial Data* can help companies to uncover trends or patterns in medication safety and efficacy, helping them

make important decisions regarding potential uses for their data while pinpointing areas that need improvement.

3. *Feedback from Key Opinion Leaders (KOLs)*: Companies might seek feedback from KOLs, such as top physicians and researchers, about medication to gain their perspective. KOLs can provide valuable insight and support for the use of medication and can help build support.
4. *User Acceptance Testing (UAT)*: Companies can conduct user acceptance testing in a controlled environment with a group to test the medication. UAT helps to identify any potential issues in the usability of the medication and areas that may not be suitable for patients or healthcare professionals.
5. *Pre-Launch Testing*: Companies can conduct pre-launch testing to test a medication's effectiveness in a controlled setting. This allows for identifying potential medication issues and helps inform marketing strategies and decisions regarding its launch.

The acceptance testing stage is an essential part of the pharmaceutical marketing process. Companies can gather feedback from different stakeholders to identify potential problems with medication before launch and make improvements, increasing its acceptance by healthcare providers and patients.

Account Management

Account management in pharmaceutical marketing is building and maintaining relationships with key accounts like hospitals, pharmacies, healthcare providers, and pharmacies. It is crucial in this industry because it ensures that products are effectively promoted and sold to the target audience.

Pharma marketing usually includes many activities, such as account management. Consider, for example, the following account management activities:

1. *Planning and Execution of Account Plans*: Companies can create plans outlining the strategies and tactics required to market their products to key customers effectively. These plans may include timelines and budgets tailored to each account's needs.
2. *Building Relationships with Key Stakeholders*: Account managers might establish connections with key stakeholders such as hospital administrators, pharmacists, and healthcare providers. This can increase trust and loyalty in these accounts and help to increase product adoption.
3. *Conducting Market Research*: Account managers can conduct market research to learn about the preferences and needs of key accounts. These data can be used for marketing strategies and tactics specific to each account.
4. *Creating Marketing Materials*: Account managers can work with marketing teams to develop customized marketing materials such as presentations and brochures to meet each client's needs.
5. *Managing Product Launches*: Account Managers may be integral to product launches. They work closely with key accounts to increase awareness and encourage product adoption.

Account Planning

Account planning is a strategy for engaging with key customers or accounts in the pharmaceutical industry. This involves deeply understanding the customer's goals, challenges, and competitive landscape.

Account planning in pharmaceutical marketing seeks to develop an inclusive plan that engages customers, builds meaningful relationships, and boosts sales. This involves identifying key stakeholder contacts for each account, understanding their priorities and challenges, and developing messaging strategies tailored to meet those requirements.

Pharma marketers utilizing account planning often rely on various tools and resources such as market research, competitive analysis, and customer profiling to implement an account planning strategy.

To ensure their message resonates with key stakeholders, they employ various communication channels such as email, social media, and in-person meetings to deliver it effectively. Account Planning involves a strong focus on these areas:

1. *Identifying Key Opinion Leaders (KOLs)*: Pharma companies often depend on KOLs to increase awareness and acceptance of products in specific therapeutic areas. Therefore, account planning involves identifying and engaging with the most influential KOLs in key accounts.
2. *Creating Customer Personas*: Pharma marketers might create customer personas to better understand their customers' needs and challenges. These personas will help identify key stakeholders in each account. Marketers can use these personas to tailor their marketing strategies and messaging to each customer's needs and challenges.

3. *Conducting Market Research*: Pharma companies can conduct market research to understand their customer's preferences and needs better. This research can be used to identify new product development opportunities and targeted marketing campaigns.
4. *Market Research and Customer Profiling*: Pharma marketers can create tailored messaging and marketing strategies based on customer profiles and market research. They may send targeted promotional materials or educational resources through email campaigns or social media.
5. *Data Analytics*: Pharma companies can use data analytics to measure the effectiveness and performance of their account planning strategies. These data can inform future account planning and identify areas that need improvement.

Account planning is, in summary, a crucial component of pharma marketing. It allows companies to build stronger relationships, increase brand loyalty, drive business growth, and also helps them to improve their customer service.

Accountable Care Organization (ACO)

An Accountable Care Organization (ACO) is a network of doctors, hospitals, and other healthcare providers who voluntarily come together to deliver coordinated, high-quality care to their Medicare patients. The aim is to avoid unnecessary duplication of services and prevent medical errors, thereby improving patient outcomes and reducing costs.

Role of ACOs

1. *Coordinated Care*: ACOs ensure that patients, especially those with chronic diseases, get the right care at the right time with minimal waste, repetition, or miscommunication.
2. *Quality Metrics*: ACOs are judged on specific performance metrics related to the quality of patient care and must report these to the Centers for Medicare & Medicaid Services (CMS). This includes patient satisfaction, timely care, and preventive health measures.
3. *Shared Savings*: If ACOs deliver care more efficiently and meet specific quality benchmarks, they can share the savings they generate for the Medicare Program.

Implications for Pharma Marketers

1. *Shift to Value-Based Medicine*: ACOs emphasize value over volume. Pharma marketers need to demonstrate the value and cost-effectiveness of their products rather than merely promoting them.
2. *Emphasis on Outcomes*: ACOs are focused on patient outcomes. So, the efficacy and safety profile of a drug becomes critical. Marketers may need to rely more on real-world evidence and patient outcomes data.
3. *Partnerships and Collaborations*: Pharma companies can become partners in the care process by collaborating with the ACOs. This can be through shared data, patient education, or joint initiatives to improve patient adherence and outcomes.
4. *Targeted Marketing*: Knowing the priorities of ACOs can help craft more relevant and impactful messaging. For instance, if an ACO is focused on reducing hospital readmissions, a drug with evidence of reducing these readmissions can be positioned in that light.
5. *Patient-Centered Approach*: With ACOs aiming to deliver a more patient-centric care model, pharma marketers should look at tools, services, or solutions that enhance the patient experience. This includes apps, adherence programs, or patient support services.
6. *Understanding Formularies and Treatment Protocols*: ACOs may adopt specific formularies or treatment protocols to ensure standardized care. Pharma marketers should be well-acquired with these to ensure their drugs are accessible and preferred in those settings.

In summary, the rise of ACOs represents a significant shift in how healthcare is delivered in the US, emphasizing outcomes, efficiency, and value. For pharma marketers, understanding this environment and adapting their strategies is essential for success.

Accreditation

Accreditation in Pharmaceutical Marketing is when a pharmaceutical company receives recognition or certification from an outside or regulatory agency. This allows them to adhere to industry standards, guidelines, and best practices. Accreditations are integral in pharmaceutical marketing, as they show customers, stakeholders, and regulators your dedication to quality, safety, and ethical marketing practices.

1. *GMP Certification*: This certification is required by regulatory agencies to ensure that pharmaceutical products are manufactured and distributed following good manufacturing practices (GMP).
2. *Certification Under ISO 9001*: The ISO 9001 standard provides an international quality management system and method for implementing quality systems across industries, including pharmaceuticals.
3. *Accreditation Council for Continuing Medical Education (ACCME)*: Voluntary accreditation with ACCME ensures that continuing medical education programs adhere to established quality standards.
4. *Health on the Net Foundation Certification (HON)*: This voluntary certification certifies that health-related websites meet established standards of accuracy, transparency, and ethical marketing.
5. *International Society of Medical Publication Professionals (ISMPP)*: ISMPP certification, which is voluntary, ensures that medical publication professionals follow established ethical and transparent publishing practices.

Accreditation is crucial for pharmaceutical marketing because it shows a company's commitment to quality, safety, and ethical marketing. Accreditation from recognized agencies and organizations can also be used to demonstrate excellence and build trust with regulators, customers, and stakeholders.

Acquiescence Bias

Acquiescence bias refers to a cognitive bias where respondents to questionnaires or surveys agree with certain statements or questions, regardless of their opinions or experiences. This bias can be particularly prevalent in pharma marketing research, where respondents might feel pressured to give positive feedback about a product.

Here are some examples of Acquiescence Biases in Pharma:

1. *Patient Satisfaction Surveys*: Pharmaceutical companies conduct surveys of patients to obtain feedback about a product or service. Patients may agree more positively if the questions are asked positively, regardless of their actual experiences.
2. *Surveys of Key Opinion Leaders*: Pharma companies might conduct surveys of key opinion leaders in a specific field to get feedback about a product or service. Key opinion leaders will be more inclined to agree with positive-framed statements, which could lead to biased feedback.
3. *Focus Groups*: This is a common method of gathering feedback from the target audience. Let's say the moderator or another member comments positively about a product; others may be more inclined than you to agree, even though they do not believe those statements.
4. *Customer feedback from Sales Representatives*: Representatives of pharmaceutical companies may be asked to give their opinion on a product or service. Sales representatives might be more inclined to give biased feedback if asked positive questions.
5. *Social Media Feedback*: Pharma companies might monitor social media channels to get customer feedback about a product or service. If they focus only on positive feedback, they may miss out on negative comments and have an inaccurate perception of a product's effectiveness.

Acquiescence bias in marketing pharmaceuticals can cause inaccurate data and biased results. While this can lead to poor decision-making and ineffective marketing strategies, there are several strategies that pharmaceutical marketing professionals can use to mitigate the effects of this bias:

A. Respondents will not feel pressured to answer a survey question or statement if presented with neutral or objective language.

B. To balance potential biases, ask questions about negative experiences.

C. Multiple survey methods, including interviews and focus groups, are used to get different perspectives and feedback.

D. To reduce bias potentials, blind or double-masked research is conducted where the respondents are unaware of the identity or product being evaluated.

E. Use statistical techniques such as reverse coding and factor analysis to identify and correct acquiescence bias in data analysis.

There can be an acquiescence bias in research on pharmaceutical marketing. However, it can be reduced by thoughtful survey design and data analysis techniques. Also, the emphasis on objective feedback from multiple sources is important.

Acquisition

Acquisition in pharmaceutical marketing refers to the process by which one pharmaceutical company acquires another company or particular products/portfolio to boost market presence, expand product offerings or gain competitive advantages. Pharma firms frequently pursue acquisitions as strategic growth initiatives designed to strengthen research and development capabilities, expand market shares, or open access to new markets.

Pharmaceutical companies might consider an acquisition about marketing for various reasons:

1. *Expanded Product Portfolio*: Acquiring another company allows a pharmaceutical firm to increase product offerings and diversify revenue streams by filling any existing gaps within its current portfolio, expanding patient or therapeutic coverage, and more efficiently servicing patient groups across therapeutic areas or populations.
2. *Gain Access to New Markets*: Acquiring an established company in a particular geographic region can give a pharmaceutical firm immediate entry to these markets and reduce both time and resources required for new market entry efforts.
3. *Enhance Research and Development Capabilities*: Acquiring a company with innovative drugs or advanced research capabilities can greatly strengthen a pharmaceutical company's research and development efforts by tapping into new technologies, intellectual property, or expertise that accelerate the development of new drugs or therapies.
4. *Acquisitions Can Provide an Edge*: In an increasingly competitive pharmaceutical market, acquisitions are an effective strategy to gain an advantage against rivals. By purchasing competitors or complementary products from rivals, a company can gain an edge by eliminating competition, increasing market share, and consolidating its position within the industry.
5. *Acquiring Specialized Expertise*: Acquiring a company that boasts expertise in specific therapeutic areas or technologies can bring valuable insights and talent into a pharmaceutical company, aiding its marketing strategies by giving them more options on how best to position and market its products.

Note that acquisition in pharmaceutical marketing involves several stages, from due diligence and negotiation through legal approvals and integration, with each transaction differing in motivations and strategies depending on which companies are involved and their long-term goals.

Active Pharmaceutical Ingredient (API)

Active Pharmaceutical Ingredient (API) refers to the substance in a drug that is biologically active, the component that provides the intended therapeutic effect. In contrast, the other drug components, which are inactive and are used primarily to deliver or stabilize the API, are known as excipients.

APIs: Implications and Uses in Pharma Marketing

1. *Efficacy and Safety Messaging*: The API is central to a drug's efficacy and safety profile. Pharma marketers leverage clinical data, real-world evidence, and other studies to create messaging around how effective and safe the API is in treating the targeted condition.
2. *Differentiation*: If a pharma company has a unique API or a novel mechanism of action, this can be a significant differentiating factor in the market, especially if competing treatments are less effective, have more side effects, or use older mechanisms of action.
3. *Branding*: The API's name, especially in the case of biologics or specialty drugs, often becomes synonymous with the brand, especially before generics or biosimilars enter the market.
4. *Educational Initiatives*: Pharma marketers often invest in educational campaigns to inform healthcare professionals about the benefits, risks, and mechanisms of action of a new API, especially if it represents a novel class or a significant advancement in treatment.

Implications for Pharma Marketers

1. *Patent Expiry and Generics*: Once the patent for an API expires, generic manufacturers can produce and market their versions. This can lead to a significant loss of market share for the original brand. Marketers often anticipate this by diversifying their portfolio, launching extended-release versions, or focusing on other differentiators beyond just the API.
2. *Regulatory Challenges*: Any claims made by marketers regarding the API's efficacy or safety must be backed by solid evidence and presented in a balanced way, considering both benefits and potential risks. Misrepresentation can lead to severe consequences, including legal ramifications and damage to the brand's reputation.
3. *Pricing and Market Access*: The cost of developing, manufacturing, and ensuring the consistent quality of the API can influence a

drug's price. Marketers need to communicate the value proposition of their drug, especially if it is priced higher than competitors.

4. *Supply Chain Concerns*: Many APIs are sourced or manufactured internationally. Any disruption in the supply chain (due to geopolitical issues, pandemics, or regulatory changes) can impact drug availability. Marketers need to manage the narrative around such disruptions to maintain trust among stakeholders.
5. *Biosimilars and Biologics*: In biological drugs (larger and more complex than traditional small molecule drugs), the API is often a protein or other large molecule. Here, marketers face challenges from biosimilars (similar but not identical versions of biologics) once the original biologic's patent expires. Communicating the uniqueness and value of the original biologic becomes crucial.
6. *Transparency and Quality*: There is a growing demand from stakeholders, including patients and healthcare professionals, for transparency around the sourcing, manufacturing, and quality control of APIs. Marketers must be prepared to address these concerns and use them as a trust-building strategy.

While the API is a technical and scientific component of pharmaceuticals, it plays a crucial role in shaping marketing strategies. Understanding the science, regulatory landscape, and market dynamics surrounding the API is essential for pharma marketers to create effective campaigns and navigate challenges.

Activity Sampling

Activity sampling in pharmaceutical marketing is a way of measuring the effectiveness of sales representatives by observing and recording their activities over a given period. This involves randomly choosing a group to observe their interactions with healthcare professionals like pharmacists or physicians.

Recording the activities and duration of a representative is called activity sampling. This includes recording their interactions with healthcare professionals or providing product information. These data are then analyzed to identify trends and patterns in the representative's performance and determine their success with sales strategies.

Pharma companies can use activity sampling to gain valuable insights about the effectiveness of their sales reps and optimize their marketing strategies. For example, companies can identify areas in which reps would benefit from additional support or training by analyzing data collected during activity sampling.

Pharma companies can also use activity sampling to recognize and reward top performers for their achievements. For example, companies can reward top performers for motivating their sales team and improving overall performance.

Activity sampling is a great way to gain insights into representatives' activities and performance, as it helps pharma companies optimize their effectiveness and improve performance.

Adaptation

Adaptation is changing an organism or its parts to make them better suited for existence, making life more convenient. Pharmaceutical marketers use adaption strategies as part of their pharmaceutical marketing approach to meet healthcare professionals' and patients' changing needs and preferences. This involves keeping up to date with new technologies and regulations and adapting your efforts accordingly. Here are some areas where pharmaceutical marketing needs to adapt:

1. *Digital Marketing*: Pharmaceutical companies must adapt their marketing strategies to reach patients and healthcare professionals online. This includes creating digital content and using social media platforms. Data and analytics are also used to optimize campaigns.
2. *Personalization*: Patients and healthcare professionals increasingly seek personalized solutions. This could include targeted messaging and content, segmenting people based on their preferences and behavior, and creating customized treatment plans.
3. *Regulatory-Compliant Marketing Strategies*: The pharmaceutical industry must adapt its marketing strategies to comply with all regulations and guidelines.
4. *Patient Engagement*: Patient engagement is more important than ever as patients become more involved in healthcare decisions. Therefore, Companies should create patient-centric marketing campaigns and provide educational resources and support, and use patient feedback to improve their strategies.

Pharma companies must adapt to keep up with the latest trends and technologies to remain competitive in a constantly evolving marketplace and tailor their marketing efforts to meet the changing needs of patients and healthcare professionals to remain competitive.

Added Value

Added value in pharma marketing is about the additional benefits or services that pharmaceutical companies offer their customers. This includes services or products that are not core products or services. Some examples of added-value services are customer education programs, ongoing support services, and training initiatives.

The goal of pharmaceutical marketing is to add value. This means that their products and services are different from other competitors. It creates a positive customer experience. Pharmaceutical companies can also increase customer loyalty and retention by offering additional services or benefits, ultimately increasing sales and revenue.

Here are some examples of added value in marketing pharmaceuticals:

1. *Patient Education*: Pharmaceutical companies may offer educational programs to patients online or in seminars to help them understand and manage their conditions better. They may even provide them with printed materials explaining the symptoms, treatment options of the condition, and the benefits and side effects of their products.
2. *Healthcare Professional Training*: Some companies offer training programs specifically targeted to healthcare professionals to enable them to more fully comprehend how the products they sell can enhance patient outcomes and contribute to improving the healthcare process overall.
3. *Disease Management Programs*: Pharmaceutical companies may offer support programs to patients suffering from chronic diseases to assist them in better managing their conditions.
4. *Compliance Programs*: Pharmaceutical companies might develop programs that help patients adhere to their medication regimens and avoid potential side effects.
5. *Customer Support and Service*: Some companies offer support and technical assistance to clients.

The added value of pharmaceutical marketing can make a company stand apart from its competitors and create a pleasant customer experience.

Adoption

Adoption in pharmaceutical marketing refers to the rate at which healthcare providers, patients, and patients takeup new medication or treatment approaches. Adoption includes becoming familiar with a product or treatment approach before considering its potential advantages and drawbacks, trying it on a small-scale test basis before finally adopting it into standard practice.

Pharmaceutical companies dedicate significant resources and energy to researching, creating, and marketing innovative new treatments to increase adoption by healthcare providers and patients alike. Aspects influencing adoption include evidence supporting its use, cost-effectiveness analysis, competition in the marketplace, and perceived benefits/drawbacks compared to existing treatments.

Adopting a new product or treatment approach can bring several significant advantages for patients, healthcare providers, and payers, including improved health outcomes, increased patient satisfaction, and decreased healthcare costs. Understanding this process and devising effective marketing strategies designed to drive adoption are, therefore, integral parts of pharmaceutical marketing strategy.

The adoption process typically encompasses five stages: Awareness, Interest, Evaluation, Trial period, and ultimately Adoption.

Pharmaceutical companies utilize various marketing strategies and tactics to increase product adoption. This may involve educational campaigns geared toward healthcare providers and patients, direct-to-consumer advertising campaigns, clinical trials, or medical conferences and events sponsorship.

One key element of pharmaceutical marketing that facilitates adoption is understanding the needs and preferences of stakeholders such as healthcare providers, patients, and payers. By tailoring their messages and tactics towards these groups, pharmaceutical companies can increase the odds that their product will successfully take hold.

Adoption hinges upon evidence and data supporting its safety and efficacy. Thus, pharmaceutical companies invest heavily in clinical trials to generate high-quality data that supports their products' adoption by healthcare providers and patients alike.

Adoption Process

Adoption occurs when healthcare providers or patients use a new drug or medical technology. It involves several stages: awareness, interest, evaluation, trial, and adoption.

1. *Awareness*: Awareness is the initial stage in any adoption process and occurs when potential users learn of an innovative product or technology through various sources like advertising, word of mouth, or any other form of promotion.

2. *Interest*: Once potential users become familiar with a product or technology, they may take an interest. They gather more information at this stage to see if it meets their requirements and needs.
3. *Evaluation*: After developing an interest in a product or technology, potential users will evaluate it by considering its features, benefits, and drawbacks; then compare this product or technology with similar offerings on the market.
4. *Trial*: Potential users who are satisfied with the evaluation should test the product or technology. This may involve trying it for free through trial versions or in real-world environments.
5. *Adoption*: Customers satisfied with a trial product or technology may become regular adopters and use it continuously.

One can observe these steps of adoption when looking at pharmaceutical marketing of new therapies and technologies like vaccines, digital health technologies, and oncology therapies. Healthcare providers and patients need to become knowledgeable of its benefits before becoming sufficiently intrigued with its safety and efficacy for further analysis; then evaluate further as part of a pilot trial on smaller patient populations before eventually adopting them as standard treatment protocols.

Adoption can be an intricate process requiring consideration of multiple aspects, such as patient needs, healthcare provider preferences, and regulatory compliance obligations. Pharma marketers should take note of such considerations to establish trust with target audiences to facilitate the adoption of new drugs or medical technologies.

Adopter Categories

The stages of Adoption in pharma marketing are often described using the innovation adoption curve, which is a model that describes the rate at which different groups of people adopt new products or ideas. Based on the level of Adoption, there are five adopter categories:

1. *Innovators*: *Innovators* represent the earliest adopters of those willing to test new products or ideas as soon as they become available, typically representing only a small portion (2.5 percent). Key Opinion Leaders and early Adopters might, for instance, participate in clinical trials for newly prescribed medication before becoming widely adopted by others in society.
2. *Early Adopters* are among the first people to try something new; often influential and respected figures in their communities, these Adopters take risks to be among the first to experiment. Physicians, for instance, are among this cohort, willing to prescribing new medication shortly after regulatory authorities approve it.
3. *Early Majority*: This group tends to be less adventurous than their early adopter counterparts, yet still open to trying a product or idea if there's evidence it works and is safe and efficacious. Healthcare professionals who prescribe new medication after it has been on the market for some time and established its safety and efficacy would fit this category nicely.
4. *Late Majority*: This group is even more cautious than the early majority and tends to adopt new products or ideas only after establishing themselves well in the market. Healthcare providers willing to prescribe a new medication only after it has been widely adopted and has become the standard of care belong to this category.
5. *Laggards* are the last group to adopt a new product or idea, often out of habit or reluctance to change. Likewise, healthcare providers in this category resist prescribing new medication because they are comfortable with existing treatments and are hesitant to change.

Understanding these stages and the characteristics of each adopter category can help pharmaceutical companies develop targeted marketing strategies to increase the Adoption of their products.

Adopter Categories and Communication Strategies

Pharmaceutical communication strategies can vary based on the target audience and their strategy of adopting a particular product or technology. Here are some possible strategies for different adopter categories.

1. *Innovators*: Innovators are the first 2.5 percent to adopt a new product or technology. To communicate with this group, pharmaceutical companies should highlight their product's unique features and benefits and emphasize its potential to transform healthcare, with expert endorsements, scientific data, or early adopter experiences serving as evidence that proves its efficacy or safety.
2. *Early Adopters*: Early Adopters represent 13.5 percent of those who adopt new technologies or products within weeks after initial release, becoming opinion leaders or influencers within their social circles. Pharmaceutical companies should cultivate relationships with opinion leaders such as physicians, pharmacists, and patient advocates. Social media can be an excellent platform to reach this group by

encouraging early adopters to share their experience with others.

3. *Early Majority*: To effectively reach this audience, pharmaceutical firms must present clear and concise information regarding product benefits, safety, efficacy, patient case studies, or testimonials as real-world examples of how new technology or products improve patient outcomes. Pharmaceutical firms may use case studies or testimonials as communication vehicles that engage their target group effectively.
4. *Late Majority*: To communicate effectively with this group (34 percent), pharmaceutical companies should address any concerns or objections they might have about the product, such as its safety or efficacy, using evidence-based messaging such as clinical trial data to demonstrate them effectively; they can also offer training programs so healthcare providers and patients understand how best to utilize the product.
5. *Laggards*: Laggards are the last group (16 percent) to adopt new products or technologies, often resisting change and needing considerable persuasion to try something different. To reach this group effectively, pharmaceutical companies need to present compelling reasons as to why the new treatment is superior compared to existing therapies; use persuasive messaging such as cost savings or quality of life improvements; leverage peer pressure or social proof as a way of encouraging laggards to try it themselves.

Improving the Rate of Adoption

Improving the adoption rate in pharmaceutical marketing can be challenging, but several strategies can help increase the likelihood of success. Some of these strategies are:

1. *Building a Strong Evidence Base*: A key factor in Adoption is the evidence and data supporting the safety and efficacy of a new medication or treatment approach. By conducting robust clinical trials and generating high-quality data, pharmaceutical companies can increase confidence in their products and encourage Adoption among healthcare providers, patients, and payers.
2. *Tailoring Marketing Messages*: Different stakeholders have different needs and preferences, and tailoring marketing messages to these groups can improve the chances of successful Adoption. For example, a marketing message that emphasizes the cost-effectiveness of a new medication may be more effective for payers. In contrast, a message that emphasizes patient outcomes may be more effective for healthcare providers.
3. *Providing Education and Training*: Healthcare providers may be more likely to adopt a new medication or a treatment approach if they feel comfortable and confident using it. Providing education and training on using a new product can help build this confidence and encourage adoption.
4. *Offering Support Services*: Patients may be more likely to adhere to a new medication regimen if they can access support services such as patient education materials, disease management programs, and financial assistance programs.
5. *Engaging with Key Opinion Leaders*: Key opinion leaders (KOLs) are influential healthcare providers who can help drive adoption among their peers. Engaging with KOLs and providing them with the latest clinical data and other resources help build their support for new products and encourage adoption among their networks.
6. *Addressing Barriers to Adoption*: Identifying and addressing barriers can help overcome resistance and increase the adoption rate. For example, if a new medication has a complex dosing regimen, providing tools and resources to help patients manage their medication schedule may improve adherence and encourage Adoption.

Pharma's Adoption Strategies

Here are some specific examples of how pharma has been implementing adoption strategies:

1. Pfizer implemented an aggressive marketing plan for Viagra (Sildenafil), targeting both urologists and primary care physicians as its target audience for this erectile dysfunction medication. They provided educational materials tailored towards HCPs and events to increase awareness about this medication's benefits for treating patients suffering from ED.
2. Novartis conducted clinical trials to demonstrate the safety and efficacy of Kymriah, its CAR (Chimeric Antigen Receptor)-T cell therapy for treating certain types of leukemia and lymphoma. The trials involved hundreds of patients and demonstrated the drug's ability to induce many remissions.
3. At a medical conference, Amgen implemented a thought leader endorsement strategy by engaging oncologist Dr. John Marshall to speak about its colorectal cancer drug Vectibix (Panitumumab). Dr. Marshall highlighted the drug's benefits for patients and the need for personalized treatment options in cancer care.

4. Eli Lilly created a Continuing Medical Education (CME) course for physicians about its diabetes drug Trulicity (Dulaglutide), providing information about the drug's mechanism of action, dosing, and clinical trial data to help physicians understand how to use the drug effectively in their practice.
5. Biogen created a website for patients and caregivers about its Alzheimer's drug Aduhelm (Aducanumab). The site offered information regarding the disease, the drug's mechanism of action, and patient selection criteria for treatment. Ultimately, the company aimed to increase HCP adoption while simultaneously creating demand by providing education about drugs to both patients and families affected by Alzheimer's disease.

Adopter Categories

Everett Rogers, a professor of communication studies, popularized the theory of *Diffusion of Innovation* in his book of the same name, published in 1962. He described in the book that diffusion manifests the type of adopters and innovation-decision process in different ways, the criterion for the adopter categorization being innovativeness. He defined innovativeness as the degree to which an individual adopts a new idea. These adopter categories are universally applicable across industries. For example, in pharma marketing, adopter categories refer to different types of customers or users who adopt a new product or technology.

The five adopter categories are:

1. *Innovators*: Innovators are risk-takers and, therefore, the first individuals willing to try new things and are often motivated by the potential for a competitive advantage or recognition. Innovators are the first to prescribe new medications or treatment options in pharma marketing.
2. *Early Adopters*: Early adopters are also willing to take risks but tend to be more deliberate and cautious than innovators. They are typically opinion leaders and influential within their social networks and are often motivated by the potential for gaining a competitive advantage or achieving social recognition.
3. *Early Majority*: The early majority comprises the majority of users who adopt a new product or technology. They tend to be more skeptical and require more evidence of the benefits of the product or technology before adopting it. In pharma marketing, the early majority may be the healthcare providers who require evidence-based research and clinical trial data before prescribing a new medication.
4. *Late Majority*: These adopters are more skeptical and resistant to change, often requiring significant social pressure or incentives to adopt a new product or technology. In pharma marketing, the late majority may be healthcare providers who require a significant amount of peer-reviewed publications and clinical evidence before adopting a new medication.
5. *Laggards*: Laggards are the last to adopt a new product or technology and tend to resist change. Traditions often motivate them, and they may be skeptical of new technologies or products. In pharma marketing, laggards may be healthcare providers who rely heavily on traditional treatment methods and resist new medications and technologies.

Distribution of Adopter Categories

The criterion for adopter categorization, as described earlier, is innovativeness. Rogers defines innovativeness as the degree to which an individual is relatively early in adopting a new idea than others. Adopter distributions closely resemble a normal, continuous probability distribution in which most data points cluster toward the middle of the range. The rest taper off, symmetrically toward either extreme in the figure showing how the five adopter categories follow the normal frequency distribution.

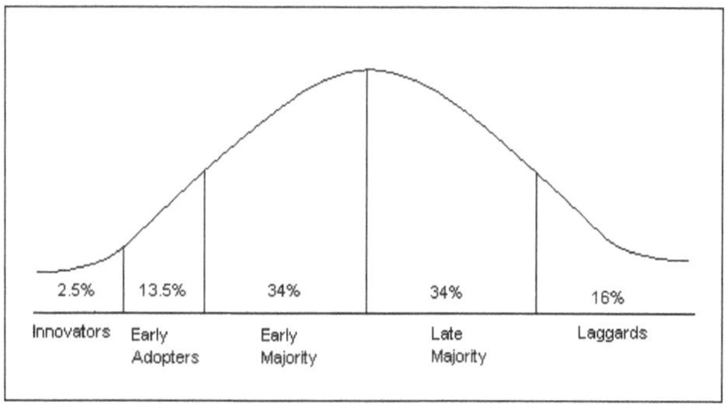

Figure. Distribution of Adopter Categories

1. As shown in the figure, Innovators are the first 2.5 percent of a group to adopt a new idea. The early majority are the next 13.5 percent, with the late adopters of 34 percent following them. The 34 percent of the group to the right of the mean is called the late majority, and the last 16 percent are laggards.
2. Pharma marketers should understand the different adopter categories to effectively target and communicate with different customer segments and tailor their marketing strategies to meet customers' specific needs and preferences based on their relative stages in the adoption process.

Ad Recall

Ad recall refers to the audience's ability to recall an advertisement after seeing or hearing it. This recall measure is used in pharmaceutical marketing to evaluate the effectiveness of an advertisement campaign. It is a sign that the ad successfully conveyed its message. If viewers can recall the message or content in an ad, they can remember it.

To measure the effectiveness of their ads among their target audience, pharma companies often conduct recall studies. These studies typically involve showing an advertisement to a group of people and then asking them specific questions after a certain period. Companies can use the study results to assess the effectiveness and make necessary adjustments for increased impact.

Here are three examples of how pharma companies used and benefited from ad recall studies:

1. For instance, a pharmaceutical company created an over-the-counter pain relief product TV commercial. After showing it to consumers and asking for specific details after one week, 60% remembered its name while 40% didn't recall its unique selling proposition (USP). Based on these statistics, they revised their advertisement to effectively convey product usage benefits to the audience.
2. A medical device company created an online advertisement for its new glucose monitoring system. After a month, they conducted an ad recall survey in which they showed the advertisement to participants and asked them to recall details about the product. The results showed that 70% of participants remembered the product's name correctly, while only 30% remembered its key benefits. This data was used to modify future advertisements that included product benefits.
3. A pharmaceutical company created a print advertisement for a new prescription medication for high cholesterol. They conducted a recall study of the ad by showing it to healthcare professionals, asking for details about the drug, and presenting it to them after two weeks. The results showed that 80 percent of participants correctly identified the medication's name, while only half remembered the dosing instructions. With this information in mind, the company made changes to make the dosing instructions easier to remember and more visible.

How does Pharma Measure Ad Recall?

How does a pharmaceutical company measure ad recall in its marketing research? Here are some tools and techniques they use for measuring an ad recall:

1. *Unaided Recall Surveys*: Participants in the unaided recall surveys are asked to recall any pharma ads they have seen or heard recently without prompting. This technique helps measure an advertisement's effectiveness in making a lasting impression on its target market.
2. *Aided Recall Surveys*: Participants are given prompts or cues to help them recall specific advertisements from Pharma. This provides additional information on which elements of the ads resonate strongly with the target audience.
3. *Eye-tracking Studies*: Participants' visual attention can be measured to different elements of a drug advertisement. This includes brand names, product features, or calls to action. This gives insight into the most effective components of advertisements that engage target audiences.
4. *Social Media Monitoring*: You can monitor mentions and engagement on social media platforms related to pharma advertisements. This provides real-time feedback about an advertisement's effectiveness in stimulating interest and activity among its target audience.
5. *Brand Recognition Surveys*: Participants are asked to identify the product or company they represent by identifying the brand name or logo. This measures the effectiveness of advertising in creating brand recognition and the association between products or companies.

Here are some examples of how pharmaceutical companies have measured advertising recall:

1. Pfizer ran an unaided recall study to assess the effectiveness of their Lyrica (Pregabalin) advertising campaign. This drug is used to treat nerve pain. This survey showed high recall rates among nerve pain patients targeted by the campaign.
2. Merck did eye-tracking studies to evaluate the effectiveness of its advertisement for Gardasil, the HPV vaccine. Results showed that visual elements such as images of happy and healthy young women were the most effective at engaging parents and healthcare professionals.
3. GlaxoSmithKline (GSK) used social media monitoring tools on Twitter to monitor the engagement with their advertisement campaign for the asthma drug Advair. As a result, they were able to track high participation rates, including mentions and retweets from healthcare

professionals and patients targeted by the campaign.

4. Sanofi carried out aided recall surveys to assess the effectiveness of its advertising campaign for Lantus (insulin glargine). According to Sanofi's findings, the survey showed that it had achieved brand recognition and recall among diabetes patients.
5. Novartis carried out brand recognition surveys to assess the success of its advertising campaign for Diovan (Valsartan), a blood pressure medication. The results showed that high blood pressure patients responded positively to the campaign. This demonstrated strong association and recognition of the brand among those targeted.

Adverse Reactions

Adverse reactions are negative side effects that can occur as a result of taking medication or using a medical device. Therefore, Pharma marketers should communicate adverse reactions to patients so they are fully informed about the potential risks.

Pharmaceutical companies must disclose any adverse reactions to their products as per regulatory mandate, usually via product packaging, literature, and promotional material. To help patients and healthcare providers easily comprehend this data, companies must present it concisely. Pharmaceutical companies may find it difficult to communicate adverse reactions in marketing materials. This is especially true when there are economic incentives to minimize such effects or emphasize product benefits. Pharmaceutical companies must balance providing accurate information about side effects and promoting accurate information regarding their product's benefits.

Advertising

Advertising is an essential part of pharmaceutical marketing. Advertising is a key component of pharmaceutical marketing. It allows pharma companies to promote their products and increase brand awareness among healthcare providers and consumers. Advertising in the pharma industry is tightly regulated to ensure accurate product claims that are not misleading. Here are the most common types of advertising in pharma marketing:

1. *Detailing*: This is the main method of selling and communicating information to healthcare professionals (HCPs). This involves representatives from pharmaceutical sales visiting HCPs to discuss their products and persuade them to prescribe them. Pharmaceutical marketing is all about detailing their products to their target audience. Therefore, companies invest heavily in training their staff to convey its benefits efficiently.
2. *Direct-to-Consumer Advertising (DTCA)*, as its name suggests, targets consumers directly through various media channels, such as television, radio, print media, and digital content. However, DTCA in pharmaceutical advertising has been restricted and can only be practiced within New Zealand and United States jurisdictions.
3. *Conferences and Events*: Pharmaceutical companies sponsor or participate in many healthcare-related conferences. This allows them to show their products, increase brand awareness, and connect with healthcare providers. In addition, these events enable companies to meet potential customers and exchange product information.
4. *Digital Marketing*: Pharmaceutical companies utilize digital platforms, including social media, email marketing, and search engine optimization (SEO), to reach their desired audiences more efficiently at reduced costs. Pharmaceutical firms benefit greatly from employing this form of promotion as it allows for maximum reach while keeping costs under control.
5. *Patient Education*: Another critical part of pharmaceutical marketing involves creating educational materials to assist patients in understanding their conditions and the products available to treat them, with copies distributed via healthcare providers, patient groups, or online channels.

How Pharma Companies Advertise

Pharmaceutical companies use multiple channels to reach customers and promote their products, including television, print, internet, and social media. Each campaign's message and creative execution varies based on the patient's condition. Here are just a few examples of pharmaceutical company advertising strategies:

1. Amgen launched several Direct-to-Consumer (DTC) advertising campaigns, such as TV commercials that featured people doing activities like dancing and hiking, with the tagline *See Me*, to promote their Otezla (Apremilast) medication, which is used to treat psoriasis.
2. Pfizer launched several Direct-to-Consumer (DTC) campaigns to promote its erectile dysfunction drug Viagra (Sildenafil). These TV

commercials featured middle-aged men discussing their struggles with ED and how Viagra (Sildenafil) helped them regain intimacy and confidence.

3. Merck has launched several Direct-to-Physician (DTP) advertising campaigns. These include print ads in medical journals for Keytruda, a medication that treats various types of cancer, like lung cancer and melanoma.
4. Bayer has launched multiple Direct-to-Consumer (DTC) ads for their Xarelto (Rivaroxaban), which reduces stroke risk in certain patients and prevents blood clots. With the tagline *Less risk of stroke, more enjoyment in life*, the television ads featured people living their normal lives while taking the drug.

Pharmaceutical companies gain a competitive edge through creative advertising and communication techniques. However, they must follow stringent regulations to ensure their communication remains accurate and balanced and does not mislead consumers.

Advertising Elasticity

Advertising elasticity in Pharma Marketing refers to how changes in advertising spend affect customer demand for a particular pharmaceutical product. Advertising Elasticity is simply a measure of how responsive customers are to changes in advertising messages.

Pharmaceutical companies use advertising elasticity to refine their strategies and determine the best level of spending for particular products or services. Companies can calculate an optimal budget to maximize sales and revenue by measuring product elasticity.

Advertising Elasticity in Pharma Marketing may depend on factors like perceived product value, the competitive landscape, and changes in consumer behavior. For example, advertising Elasticity could increase when a pharmaceutical company launches a new drug; initially, it may be lower, but over time, as people become familiar with its benefits, it may rise gradually.

Pharmaceutical companies can utilize advertising elasticity to maximize their advertising budget and inform their marketing strategies. Advertising elasticity can be used to optimize marketing spending and increase sales. Conversely, companies might reduce spending if they see low advertising elasticity to minimize spending and maximize profits.

Advertising elasticity is an essential concept in pharmaceutical marketing. It helps companies optimize their advertising strategies to increase sales and revenue. Pharmaceutical firms can improve their marketing campaigns by measuring and understanding advertising elasticity.

Advertising Plan

A pharmaceutical advertising plan is a detailed strategic document outlining a company's strategies and tactics to market its products to the right audience.

An effective plan for pharmaceutical advertising requires a deep understanding of your product, target audience, regulatory environment, and how to create it. The following are the steps you should consider when creating such a plan.

1. *Identify Your Target Audience*. Identifying your target audience before you can tailor your advertising message is crucial. For example, if your product targets older consumers, the message and channel might differ from the one you use for younger customers.
2. *Understanding the Regulatory Environment* is crucial. Pharmaceutical advertising is highly regulated. Therefore, you must know your target market's legal and regulatory restrictions. To avoid legal problems, you should ensure that your advertising adheres to the strict guidelines for prescription drug advertising in that country.
3. *Set Your Advertising Objectives*. What goals do you have? Are you looking to increase brand awareness? Or sales? These will help you craft an effective message and choose the right channels.
4. *Develop a Messaging Strategy*. A messaging strategy is needed. Your messaging strategy must align with the target audience and advertising goals while being clear, compelling, appealing, and simple for people to understand easily.
5. *Choose Your Advertising Channels Carefully*. A Pharma marketing has many advertising channels. Consider what strategies would work best to achieve the desired outcomes with your target audience when choosing an advertising strategy.

Once your advertising efforts have begun, their effectiveness can be evaluated by tracking sales, website traffic, and engagement on social media channels such as Twitter or Instagram. This provides a straightforward method for measuring their efficacy. In addition, this data can be used to improve your advertising strategy for future campaigns.

Pharma Advertising Plan: An Example

Here's an example of an advertising plan for a new drug targeted at middle-aged adults:

A. Objective:

- Within six months of its launch, to increase awareness and acceptance of the new medication by middle-aged adults.

B. Target Audience:

- Adults between 40-60 who are suffering from arthritis or chronic pain in their middle-age years

C. Messaging Strategy:

- This messaging strategy will highlight this medication's main benefits, including decreased pain and inflammation, better mobility and flexibility, and fewer side effects than similar medications.

D. Channels:

- Google Ads, and social media platforms like Facebook, Instagram, and Twitter, allow digital advertising to reach individuals interested in pain management, healthcare, arthritis, and other topics.
- To reach a wider audience, print ads can be placed in publications such as Arthritis Today and Pain Management News.
- Direct mail marketing to pain management specialists and physicians.

E. Regulatory Considerations:

Advertisements must comply with FDA regulations regarding pharmaceutical marketing. Advertisements must comply with certain measurements set by FDA

F. Measurement:

The metrics for measuring the success of the advertising campaign are:

- Sales of the new medication
- Website Traffic and engagement
- Reach and engagement via social media
- Patient and physician feedback
- Data will be collected and analyzed to optimize campaign efficiency

Advertising Research

Advertising research is a tool that helps companies understand and measure their advertising campaigns' effectiveness and devise strategies for improving them. Pharma marketers use it to measure and track this efficiently. Here are some important areas of advertising research in the pharmaceutical industry:

1. Marketers must identify their target audience and understand their motivations and behaviors before they can tailor their messaging and tactics to them.
2. Companies can use advertising research to refine and experiment with the branding and messaging of products. This can include testing different brand names, logos, taglines, and product positioning.
3. Companies often conduct pre-testing research before launching an advertisement campaign. This includes surveys, focus groups, or other methods that gauge the audience's response to the new drug ad. For example, pharmaceutical companies may pre-test to determine how their target audience views their new ad.
4. After a campaign is completed, post-test it to determine its effectiveness. For example, pharmaceutical companies may conduct post-testing research to assess the effect of an advertisement on the sales of a specific drug.
5. Do media research to determine the reach and frequency of ads across media channels. Also, you can measure their impact and identify emerging trends in media consumption. For example, pharmaceutical companies could use this data to determine the most effective channel-mix strategy to reach their target audience.
6. You can conduct tracking studies to monitor changes in consumer behavior or attitudes. For example, pharma companies might conduct tracking studies to determine how their campaigns affect brand awareness and purchase intent over time.
7. Pharma companies can use research to test different creative concepts. Pharma companies often use research to test creative concepts. For instance, Companies test different headlines, copy, and calls to action to find which resonates best with their target audiences.
8. Brain imaging techniques can be utilized for neuroscience research as well as studying the effects of advertising. In addition, Pharma companies may utilize Functional Magnetic Resonance Image technology (fMRI) to

communicate best the benefits associated with their drug products.

9. Pharmaceutical companies rely on advertising to measure the success of their campaigns and calculate return on investment (ROI). This allows them to determine which campaigns effectively drive sales while others might require tweaking or ending altogether.

Advertising research is crucial in helping pharmaceutical marketers identify how their campaigns resonate with their target audience. They can then test different advertising strategies to create campaigns that promote products and increase sales.

AdSense

Google AdSense is a platform that allows website owners to place ads on their websites and make revenue from clicks and impressions. AdSense is primarily used for website monetization but can also benefit pharmaceutical marketing. Let's take, for example:

1. *Reach*: You can reach many potential customers interested in your products and services with AdSense ads placed on relevant websites that will reach everyone looking for health and wellness information.
2. *Targeting*: AdSense lets you target specific audiences based on location, language, and interests.
3. *Cost-effective*: AdSense only charges you when someone views or clicks on your ad. Therefore. You can set a budget and maximize your effectiveness in reaching your target audience.
4. *Measurable Results*: AdSense provides comprehensive analytics and reporting capabilities that enable you to track the performance of your ads in real-time.

Advertising Strategy

Given its highly regulated environment and fiercely competitive market, formulating an effective advertising strategy for pharmaceutical marketing is imperative. Here's how you can develop one:

1. *Understand the Regulatory Environment*: First and foremost, familiarize yourself with Pharma regulations. Before getting involved with marketing strategies for pharmaceutical products or services, ensure you fully comprehend all applicable regulations within each country's laws regarding advertising to consumers and healthcare professionals. Gaining this insight is vital in creating legal and ethical marketing plans.
2. *Target Your Audience*: Deliberate on who your target audience will be. You may wish to consider marketing to doctors, healthcare professionals, patients, or even patients' family members, depending on the product or service being sold. Gain a deep understanding of their needs, challenges, and decision-making processes before selecting an audience for marketing efforts.
3. *Establish Clear Objectives*: What do you hope to accomplish with your marketing strategy? This could include anything from raising awareness for a new drug to increasing market share or driving the adoption of a novel therapy, etc.
4. *Unique Selling Proposition (USP)*: Every product offers distinctive qualities; in the pharmaceutical world, this could mean anything from efficacy or safety profile to mode of action, etc. The feature that sets you apart from competitors should be highlighted prominently to attract consumers and ensure success for you and the product!
5. *Choose Appropriate Channels*: When targeting doctors choose channels like medical journals, conferences, and digital marketing. If you target patients and their families, TV advertising or print media may best suit them. You have to choose the appropriate channels depending on the target audience.
6. *Establish Compelling Content*: Content must be developed considering its intended audience and should be educational, engaging, and compliant with applicable regulations. The content for healthcare professionals should include clinical evidence in highlighting patient benefits or how your product improves lives; at the same time, the content for consumers should be easy to comprehend and focus on how it helps them get better and manage their conditions effectively.
7. *Build Relationships*: Fostering strong relationships with healthcare professionals can play an integral role in pharmaceutical marketing efforts; sponsoring educational events, providing useful resources, or hosting webinars can all go a long way toward engaging them effectively with pharmaceutical marketing initiatives.
8. *Measure and Optimize*: Monitor your campaigns' performance by measuring reach, engagement, and conversion rates. Based on insights gained through measurement and optimization of campaigns for optimal

performance, whether this involves tweaking messages, using different channels, or targeting an alternate audience.

9. *Pharmacovigilance*: Ensure an effective system for recording adverse events reported through social media or interaction with healthcare professionals or patients.

Remember that transparency and ethical considerations are pivotal in pharmaceutical marketing. Misleading or unethical advertising can have serious repercussions, including reputational damage and penalties.

Not least of all, keep up-to-date on all of the newest trends and innovations in pharmaceutical marketing (particularly digital) to remain competitive and ensure success.

Advertorial

An advertorial is paid content that appears as an editorial or news article but is paid advertising to promote a product or service. For instance, in the pharmaceutical industry, advertorials are frequently utilized as marketing strategies to highlight new drugs and medical devices.

Advertorials offer subtler yet informative messages about the advantages and features of a drug or medical device than direct advertising does. As such, advertorials can help build trust with potential customers by offering useful information and positioning your brand as an authoritative source for such knowledge. Here are some examples of advertorials in pharma marketing:

A. *The Future of Diabetes Treatment* was an advertisement in a medical journal that provided details on the mechanism and potential benefits of a novel diabetes drug.

B. An advertorial, *Finding Relief for Joint Pain*, promoted a new medical device designed to provide relief.

C. Another, *Understanding Migraine Triggers*, promoted a migraine medication and appeared in Women's Health magazine.

Thus, advertorials can be an effective way for pharmaceutical companies to promote their products more subtly and informally and build trust with potential customers. However, pharmaceutical marketers should abide by pharmaceutical promotion rules and regulations while creating advertorials for their company or products.

Advocacy Advertising

Advocacy advertising refers to advertisements that use advocacy campaigns to raise awareness, persuade viewers, or advocate against an issue rather than directly selling products and services. Advocacy ads should inform, raise awareness, or persuade the viewer to support an issue, such as political candidates or points of view that viewers share.

Advocacy advertising is used by non-profits, interest groups, and organizations to raise public awareness on crucial issues while simultaneously promoting their causes. For example, ads may feature statistics and emotional appeals to inspire viewers to take action on pressing topics.

How Pharma Can Use Advocacy Advertising

Pharmaceutical companies can use advocacy in their advertising in many ways. Consider the following, for example:

1. *Disease Awareness Campaigns*: Pharmaceutical marketers can leverage advocacy advertising to raise awareness for health issues, educate patients on disease prevalence and encourage treatment seeking.
2. *Public Health Campaigns*: Pharmaceutical companies can use advocacy advertising to promote public health initiatives such as flu vaccinations, healthy lifestyle habits, regular checkups, and healthcare checks. These campaigns can target seniors and parents.
3. *Patient Education*: Advocacy advertising is a way to educate patients about medications' benefits and side effects. This advertising also helps to reduce the stigma associated with certain medical conditions, such as mental health disorders.
4. *Advocate for Access*: Pharmaceutical companies can leverage advocacy advertising to increase access to medication and treatment for rural residents or low-income people.

Pharma and Advocacy Advertising

Here are some examples of advocacy advertising used by pharmaceutical companies:

1. Pfizer's *Get Old Campaign* promoted healthy aging. The campaign featured print and TV ads and a website that provided resources and information about age-related health issues.
2. Gilead's *HIV Advocacy Campaign* used advocacy advertising to increase HIV awareness and encourage testing. To reach a larger audience, the campaign featured print and online ads and partnerships with community organizations.

3. Novartis' *Take on Migraine Campaign* represents a good example of patient education in advocacy advertising. This campaign offered information to patients via TV and online about migraine symptoms and encouraged them to talk to their doctors about possible treatment options.
4. AstraZeneca's *Forxiga Hearts Campaign* by AstraZeneca is an example of advocacy advertising that aims to increase access. The campaign included TV and online ads and partnerships with patient advocacy groups to increase access to Forxiga, a type 2 diabetes medication.

Pharma companies can use advocacy advertising to promote awareness, education, access, and accessibility to treatment. These campaigns can be a powerful tool for increasing public awareness and influencing positive healthcare changes. However, pharma marketers must ensure their campaigns are honest, transparent, and compliant with all industry regulations.

AdWords

AdWords (now known as Google Ads) are a valuable tool in pharmaceutical marketing. They allow you to target ads, track results, optimize campaigns for maximum impact and reach the right audience. Here are some of the key ways Google Ads can help pharma marketers:

1. *Targeting*: Google Ads allows you to target specific audiences based on location, demographics, and interests, helping you to reach those most interested in your products or services.
2. *Measurable Results*: Google Ads provides powerful analytics and reporting features that enable you to assess ad performance live and adjust accordingly so that you can measure their success for optimal outcomes. This feature makes the Google Ads platform highly measurable and results-focused, allowing for real-time monitoring and measurement. For example, Google Ads help you assess whether each campaign produces expected outcomes, and adjusts as necessary for maximum impactful success.
3. *Cost-Efficient*: Google Ads' cost-efficient model only charges when someone clicks your ad, giving you greater budgetary control while reaching more targeted audiences with your ads.
4. *Remarketing*: Google Ads allows you to target ads at visitors who have previously visited your website, or utilized your mobile application, reinforcing your brand and message among those who already demonstrated an interest in it. This way, you can strengthen loyalty among potential buyers for products already showing some degree of engagement from past visitors or app users.
5. *Flexibility*: You can create ads with Google Ads in various formats, such as text or display ads.

Affiliate Marketing

Affiliate marketing, also called performance-based marketing, utilizes an external partner who receives compensation in return for promoting products or services offered by an advertiser through commission-based models. Affiliate marketing has proven highly effective for increasing brand recognition and sales growth in the pharmaceutical industry.

Here are several examples that demonstrate how affiliate marketing can provide pharmaceutical companies with benefits:

1. *Health Affiliates* work with pharmaceutical companies to market their products directly to target audiences. For example, health bloggers, nutritionists, and fitness influencers may promote dietary supplements or related items on websites, social channels, or email lists. Healthline, for instance, provides comprehensive medical conditions, treatment, and product information and has an affiliate program, allowing website owners or bloggers to earn commission by promoting its vitamins, supplements or over-the-counter medication products like Healthline does.
2. *GoodRx* works with pharmacies to offer discounted prescription drugs at a discount for customers using coupon codes provided on its site, earning a commission when customers redeem those coupon codes when buying their medications. WebMD, another well-recognized health and wellness site, provides information regarding medical conditions and treatment solutions. WebMD also offers an affiliate program that allows website owners and bloggers to promote their products, including vitamins and supplements.
3. *Online Pharmacies*: Online pharmacies such as HealthWarehouse work with pharmaceutical companies online to sell their products. Some may work with doctors and other medical professionals to write prescriptions for certain

medications. Affiliate links can earn you a commission.

4. *Patient Support Groups*: Many patient support groups work with pharmaceutical companies to market their products to their members. A diabetes support group may partner with an insulin manufacturer to offer members discounted insulin products.
5. *Sites Devoted to Specific Diseases*: Websites that provide support and information for people with certain medical conditions can partner with pharmaceutical companies that make medications. A website that provides information on multiple sclerosis (MS) might partner with a company that makes MS-specific medication.
6. *Influencer Marketing*: Pharma companies might partner with doctors and other healthcare professionals to promote products via social media. These influencers could be compensated for any sales they generate through their promotion.

Remember that pharmaceutical companies and affiliate marketers should comply with the rules, regulations, and ethical standards that govern pharmaceutical promotion. These regulations ensure promotional materials are truthful, accurate, and not misleading, protecting customers against deceptive advertising practices that mislead.

Affinity Marketing

Affinity marketing is when a brand or organization has the same target audience as others and joins forces with it to promote its products or services. Affinity marketing allows brands to leverage the trust and loyalty of customers for increased brand awareness and sales.

Pharma can reap the benefits of affinity marketing by reaching more patients, healthcare professionals, and other relevant audiences.

Here are a few examples of affinity marketing employed by pharmaceutical companies:

1. Sanofi and the American Heart Association joined forces in an initiative called *Go Red for Women* that raises awareness about heart disease among women. With educational materials, resources, special events, promotions, and incentives designed to reduce participants' risks of contracting heart conditions, these campaigns aim to make women aware and take steps toward mitigating such conditions.
2. Pfizer and the National Psoriasis Foundation collaborated to offer educational resources and advocacy services to people affected by psoriasis to help them manage their condition better. They used online tools, advocacy campaigns, patient support programs, and patient education services.
3. GSK collaborated with the American Lung Association on an educational campaign and raised awareness about Chronic Obstructive Pulmonary Disease (COPD), patient support programs, and online resources.

Pharma companies can leverage affinity marketing to reach their target audience, build trust, and loyalty, drive sales, and improve patient outcomes.

Affordable Care Act (ACA)

The Affordable Care Act, commonly called Obamacare, has had an enormously lasting effect on various stakeholders within healthcare in America, specifically pharmaceutical companies and marketers. The primary purpose of ACA was to increase insured individuals and thereby their ability to afford medications, consequently increasing pharmaceutical companies' market opportunity.

However, the Affordable Care Act also brought new requirements, modifications, and implications for pharmaceutical marketers, such as:

1. *Greater Transparency*: Under the Affordable Care Act (ACA), pharmaceutical companies must disclose any financial relationships they may have with physicians and teaching hospitals that affect marketing to healthcare providers; this makes the marketing process more transparent but may necessitate additional compliance efforts by pharmaceutical firms.
2. *Focus on Outcomes and Value*: Under the Affordable Care Act (ACA), healthcare organizations are encouraged to transition away from fee-for-service models towards value-based care models, meaning pharmaceutical companies must demonstrate cost-effectiveness and health benefits of their drugs more clearly than ever before, placing more focus on real-world evidence and health outcome research when marketing pharmaceutical products.
3. *More Insured Customers*: With more people accessing insurance policies, prescription medication sales have experienced exponential growth. This presents new opportunities for pharmaceutical companies looking to reach wider audiences while at the same time getting

their products included in formularies to get medications covered by insurers.

4. *Increase in Generic Drugs and Biosimilars*: Under the Affordable Care Act (ACA), cheaper generic and biosimilar pharmaceuticals may become increasingly used to keep healthcare costs under control, increasing competition with branded pharmaceutical products while compelling marketers of these drugs to emphasize the unique qualities and advantages of their offerings. This trend presents marketers with new challenges when marketing their pharmaceutical products to consumers.
5. *Focused On Preventive Healthcare*: The Affordable Care Act has placed considerable importance on preventive healthcare to help stave off more serious and expensive treatments in the future. This could change how pharmaceutical markets develop products tailored toward preventative healthcare solutions.
6. *Healthcare Exchanges and Direct-to-Consumer Marketing*: With individuals now able to purchase health insurance through open exchanges, there's no direct interaction between healthcare consumers and providers, leading to possible increases in direct-to-consumer pharmaceutical marketing strategies.

To adapt to these changes, pharma marketers must become more transparent, demonstrate real-world value, appeal to a broader market, contend with increased competition while possibly shifting focus toward preventive healthcare, and alter their strategies for direct-to-consumer marketing.

Aggregate Demand

Aggregate demand refers to the total demand for drugs or services across an entire market or nation over some period. It includes demand from all segments, such as hospitals and clinics, pharmacies, and patients seeking treatments.

Demographics, disease prevalence, economic conditions, and government policies are all integral in driving demand for pharmaceutical products. Higher demand could lead to greater production and sales of drugs, resulting in greater revenues for pharmaceutical companies; conversely, a decrease could translate into decreased revenues and reduced profitability in this industry.

Pharmaceutical companies employ various marketing strategies to increase product demand. Direct-to-consumer advertising, physician education programs, and promotional events are just some of the tactics pharmaceutical firms utilize to increase awareness about their product's benefits among potential users. In addition, factors like patient demographics and disease prevalence rates can also affect consumer demand, and all these should be carefully considered when developing strategies tailored toward meeting market requirements.

Agile Marketing

Agile marketing emphasizes adaptability and flexibility in marketing to meet changing market conditions and customer needs. Agile marketing is the application of agile principles and methods to pharmaceutical industry campaigns and strategies.

Agile marketing in pharmaceuticals can help companies adapt faster to changing market dynamics and customer needs and increase the effectiveness and efficiency of their marketing campaigns. The following are key features of agile marketing for pharma:

1. *Cross-functional Teams*: Agile marketing teams in pharmaceuticals often include representatives from various departments such as sales, marketing, R&D, and medical affairs. This ensures that all parties are on the same page about goals and priorities.
2. *Iterative Approach*: Pharma's agile marketing teams typically work in short cycles or sprints. Each Sprint is focused on delivering results. This allows the team to refine and test their approach based on feedback from customers and stakeholders.
3. *Data-Driven Decision Making*: Pharma marketing teams rely heavily on data and analytics. This includes real-time data to track campaign progress and customer insights that optimize messaging and targeting.
4. *Continuous Learning*: Pharma's agile marketing teams prioritize continuous learning, continuously improving their capabilities and skills. This involves reviewing campaign performance regularly and looking for industry best practices.

Pharma companies can adapt to changing industry landscapes more efficiently and effectively by using agile marketing. In addition, companies can increase their marketing ROI and foster better customer relationships by adopting an interactive, data-driven strategy. This will allow them to grow sustainably.

Agile marketing can be difficult in the pharmaceutical industry as it is highly regulated. However, pharma marketers must adopt agile practices in their marketing efforts considering the many benefits of agile marketing. Here are some important things to consider while implementing agile ways:

Agile marketing offers many benefits, including faster time to market, greater customer satisfaction, and efficient resource use. Here are some things to consider when implementing agile pharmaceutical marketing:

1. *Define Your Goals*: Establishing your goals before you start agile marketing is important. What are you planning to achieve with agile marketing? Is it reducing costs, speeding up the time to market, or improving customer experience? By setting goals, you can better focus your efforts and track progress.
2. *Collaboration Between Functions and Teams* is key to agile marketing. Break down organizational silos and create an interdepartmental team, including sales, marketing, R&D, and regulatory affairs representatives. The legal team can also be included. This team will work together to develop and execute agile marketing strategies.
3. *Agile Marketing*: Scrum and Kanban are two examples of agile methodologies you should adopt. These methods promote team collaboration, break down silos and speed up project delivery. Please choose the best method for you and train your employees to use it effectively.
4. *Plan Sprint Meetings*: Sprints are agile marketing projects lasting two to four weeks. Teams should meet at the beginning of every Sprint, to plan, prioritize, assign roles, and establish goals for the next period.
5. *Use Data for Decision-Making*: Agile marketing relies heavily on data for decision-making purposes. Specifically, agile marketers utilize this information to track progress, evaluate marketing campaigns' success, and make any necessary modifications or adaptations.
6. *Encourage Experimentation*: Agile marketing is all about testing and iterating. Accept failures and learn from them. Iterate quickly based on feedback.
7. *Continuous Improvement*: Agile Marketing is an ongoing journey toward perfection. Regular retrospectives are a good way to evaluate progress and identify improvement areas. Then, adjust your strategy accordingly.

AIDA

AIDA is an acronym for *Attention*, *Interest*, *Desire*, and *Action*. It is a popular marketing concept. The AIDA model forms the core of successful email, social media, and promotional material distribution campaigns.

Over one century of AIDA's success speaks for itself—engaging consumers by drawing them in, increasing interest in your product or service, and encouraging action on consumers' part.

Attention is the starting point of AIDA. Marketers need to captivate the attention of their target audiences through compelling marketing communications that stand out in a competitive market; creating eye-catching visuals and persuasive copy is crucial in reaching this stage of development.

Once marketers have captured consumers' attention, AIDA's second stage is creating interest. Once marketing professionals have gained consumers' interest, the marketer needs to highlight its benefits as a differentiating factor from others in the marketplace answering this key question of *What's In It for Me?* Every buyer asks themselves this same question before purchasing.

Desire is the third stage in AIDA. Once consumers express an interest in your product or service, marketers must cultivate strong desires within them, using emotional appeals to influence people's behaviors at this step.

Action is the final stage in AIDA's marketing strategy, where marketers must persuade customers to act by buying their product or writing prescriptions. Therefore, their message should include an irresistibly compelling call to action.

AIDA has been a trusted marketing formula for more than 100 years. It is still relevant today in digital marketing.

Aided Recall

Aided recall measures how easily consumers can remember or recognize a brand if presented with certain prompts or cues, such as a logo, slogan, or brand name. This aided recall is used in pharmaceutical marketing to assess the effectiveness of a particular marketing campaign or promotional activity.

A pharmaceutical company may ask customers about their health conditions. This would be an effective aided recall if the consumers can recall the brand or treatment option or provide cues such as the drug's benefits, packaging design, or the medication's cost.

Pharmaceutical companies might use aided recall in marketing campaigns to increase brand recognition and awareness among their target audience. For example, companies can increase the chances that patients will choose their product over that of a competitor by providing cues and prompts to help them recall their brand.

Remember that aided recall can only be one factor in determining the success of a marketing campaign. To accurately evaluate the performance of your campaign, you should consider other metrics such as customer satisfaction surveys or sales figures.

Algorithms

An algorithm is a set of instructions designed to solve problems or carry out specific tasks and used both by humans and machines alike. An algorithm provides step-by-step solutions for specific issues or can perform specific functions.

Algorithms, the foundational elements of computer sciences, help solve problems by creating programs to implement them. Algorithms have numerous applications, such as data analysis, sorting, searching, pattern recognition, and machine learning, making them essential components in software development, data science, and other disciplines.

Digital transformation has revolutionized how pharmaceutical companies market their products over recent years, providing algorithms with invaluable aid in reaching target audiences and optimizing campaigns to maximize effectiveness.

Pharma companies use algorithms to get insight into the preferences and behavior of their target audience. This information allows them to create more relevant and effective marketing strategies. For example, algorithms can use online searches to identify the most common medical conditions and treatments. Pharmaceutical companies can target patients searching for specific products or treatments with this data.

Algorithms are also available to optimize the delivery and timing of marketing messages. For example, companies can optimize the timing and delivery of marketing messages by analyzing customer behavior data such as their online habits or devices.

Algorithms in pharmaceutical marketing have the potential to improve patient outcomes. Algorithms can quickly identify high-risk patients by analyzing patient data such as current medical conditions and history. With this data, targeted marketing campaigns that encourage seeking medical treatment or getting care can be created to encourage those at risk of illness.

Pharmaceutical companies can also analyze patient needs and offer treatment options to determine market gaps. Then, they develop new products to address those gaps.

Alignment

Aligning all aspects of pharmaceutical marketing strategy and execution ensures they work towards similar goals, leading to consistent efforts across the board. Alignment must occur at multiple levels:

1. *Align with Company Mission and Vision*: For maximum effectiveness, pharmaceutical marketing strategies must reflect on their vision and mission statements to contribute towards their organization's long-term goals.
2. *Align with the Brand*: Marketing activities should align with a brand's identity, positioning, and messaging to build an identifiable, memorable image that resonates with its intended target audiences.
3. *Align with Sales-Marketing*: Marketing and sales teams should communicate clearly and set clear, mutual objectives harmoniously. This ensures that marketing initiatives support sales effectively while the sales teams can use marketing materials and strategies effectively to achieve its goals.
4. *Cross-Channel Alignment*: When marketing through multiple channels, alignment between their message and strategy and ensuring that they are consistent across all channels is critical. This includes digital channels like social media, email, and websites, as well as traditional channels like print ads, television, and direct sales.
5. *Align with Regulatory Compliance*: Pharmaceutical marketing must adhere to various regulatory requirements to promote products responsibly and ethically. Also, marketing strategies and tactics must align with these regulations to avoid legal complications and uphold the company's reputation.
6. *Align with Market Needs and Trends*: Effective pharmaceutical marketing requires aligning itself with market needs and trends, including understanding patients' and healthcare providers' needs, staying current on scientific developments, and adapting to changes within healthcare environments.

7. *Align with Customer Journey*: Marketing strategies should take account of customer journey stages from awareness, consideration, and decision to recommendation and advocacy, to ensure the relevant message reaches its intended recipient at exactly the right moment in time.

Pharmaceutical marketers can develop more successful marketing strategies that drive results while contributing to overall company objectives by aligning at all levels. Conversely, failure to do this may result in inconsistencies, confusion, and missed opportunities resulting in less-than-optimal performance from marketing initiatives.

Amazon

Amazon, founded by Jeff Bezos in 1994 in Seattle, Washington, in the United States, is a multinational technology company rapidly evolved into the largest e-commerce platform globally. Starting as an online bookstore, it quickly expanded into offering products in numerous categories, becoming the biggest global e-commerce platform.

Amazon is exploring opportunities in the healthcare and pharmaceutical industries, with major implications for pharmaceutical marketers and distributors:

1. *Amazon Explores Online Pharmacy Platform*: Amazon has begun investigating whether they could establish an online pharmacy platform where customers could purchase prescription and over-the-counter drugs through their website, potentially disrupting traditional pharmaceutical retail markets while giving Amazon access to an impressive customer base.
2. *Acquisitions*: Amazon has expressed interest in making acquisitions within the pharmaceutical industry to speed up its entry. Acquired businesses could provide Amazon with established customer bases, supply chains, and regulatory compliance capabilities that simplify navigating this sector.
3. *Data Analytics*: Amazon excels at data analysis. Their analytics expertise allows them to develop personalized marketing strategies for pharmaceutical products by examining customer purchase patterns and customer data analysis, thus targeting specific consumer groups more effectively and increasing marketing effectiveness.
4. *Prime Membership Integral to Pharmaceutical Market Entry*: If Amazon enters the pharmaceutical market, it could incorporate pharmaceutical benefits into its Prime membership program to offer discounted prescription medication to Prime members as an incentive to purchase pharmaceutical products on Amazon.
5. *Distribution and Logistics*: Amazon could have an enormously positive effect on the pharmaceutical supply chain, thanks to their vast distribution network and proven expertise with efficient delivery methods with same or next-day service for pharmaceutical items!
6. *Pricing Transparency*: Amazon's entry into the pharmaceutical market could increase price transparency and competition, leading to more competitive pricing strategies and practices in Pharma marketing departments. Pharma marketers must pay special attention when setting pricing strategies according to price sensitivity factors in their campaigns.
7. *Consumer Convenience*: Amazon's focus on customer experience could change patient expectations in the pharmaceutical industry, making marketers accountable for providing seamless and user-friendly experiences to retain customer loyalty.
8. *Pharmacy Benefit Managers (PBMs)*: Amazon's entry into the pharmaceutical supply chain may alter how pharmacy benefit managers (PBMs) negotiate drug prices and contracts and disrupt Pharma partnerships within an ever-evolving distribution landscape.
9. *Direct-to-consumer Marketing on Amazon*: Marketers may use Amazon as a direct-to-consumer channel for pharmaceutical products by exploring advertising and promotional opportunities to reach wider audiences with over-the-counter (OTC) items they sell.
10. *Trust and Safety*: With Amazon expanding its presence within the pharmaceutical industry, ensuring customer trust and product safety becomes increasingly vital. Pharma marketers should focus on providing accurate information while meeting high-quality standards.
11. *Amazon Web Services (AWS)*: As one of the leaders in cloud services, AWS is an indispensable provider. Their cloud computing platform offers various solutions and services tailored specifically for businesses, including pharmaceutical ones. AWS can assist pharmaceutical companies by helping them use customer data to develop targeted marketing campaigns. In addition, AWS facilitates the development of robust yet user-friendly websites, applications, or portals that create

exceptional online customer experiences. Pharma companies can utilize AWS' cloud services to lower IT infrastructure costs more efficiently while investing more effectively in other aspects of their businesses. Pharma marketers can use AWS' machine learning and artificial intelligence (AI) capabilities to automate aspects of their marketing campaigns, such as ad targeting and content personalization, with AWS' range of security features and compliance certifications helping pharmaceutical companies meet regulatory compliance and safeguard customer privacy.

12. *Obstacles and Regulations*: Amazon faces rigorous regulations in its pharmaceutical business, so Amazon must successfully navigate a myriad of legal and regulatory hurdles to comply with healthcare laws, patient privacy standards, and prescription handling processes.

Amazon's entry into the pharmaceutical market could lead to greater competition, changing market dynamics, and forcing marketers to differentiate their products and services to stay afloat.

Recognizing that healthcare and pharmaceutical industries are extremely complex and heavily regulated is vital for successfully marketing these industries. Amazon's involvement presents both challenges and opportunities for marketers of pharmaceuticals. It is necessary to stay abreast of all developments, regulatory changes, market trends, and innovations to remain successful as time progresses and markets evolve.

Ambush Marketing

Ambush marketing is when a company or brand tries to associate itself with an event or property without official sponsorship or authorization. This tactic allows the company to gain exposure and create an impression of being affiliated with the event, often at a lower cost than official sponsors. Here are a few examples of ambush marketing:

1. *Nike and the 2012 London Olympics*: Nike, a major competitor of official Olympic sponsor Adidas, launched an advertising campaign featuring athletes training in various locations around London. Although Nike was not an official sponsor, the campaign created an association between the brand and the Olympics by showcasing London landmarks and using slogans such as *Find Your Greatness*.
2. *Bavaria Beer and the 2010 FIFA World Cup*: Bavaria Beer, a Dutch brewery, orchestrated a large-scale ambush marketing campaign in South Africa during the FIFA World Cup. A group of attractive women wearing orange dresses (the Dutch national color) attended a match, capturing significant media attention. FIFA, protecting its official beer sponsor Budweiser, considered it an unauthorized marketing ploy and ejected the women from the stadium.
3. *Beats by Dre and the 2012 Olympics*: Beats by Dre, a popular headphone brand, launched a campaign called The Game Before The Game just before the 2012 London Olympics. The campaign featured athletes wearing Beats headphones during pre-game rituals, including footballer Neymar, Jr. This association with top athletes indirectly linked the brand to the Olympics, even though it wasn't an official sponsor.
4. *Pepsi and the 1996 Super Bowl*: In 1996, Pepsi launched a clever ambush marketing campaign during the Super Bowl, which was sponsored by a rival brand Coca-Cola. Pepsi ran a television commercial featuring a group of Coca-Cola deliverymen secretly switching to Pepsi while the rival company's truck was parked. The commercial generated significant buzz and effectively undermined Coca-Cola's sponsorship.
5. *Red Bull and 2014 FIFA World Cup*: Red Bull, known for its energy drinks, used a creative ambush marketing technique during the 2014 World Cup in Brazil. The company organized a soccer tournament in a Rio de Janeiro slum named The Neymar Jr.'s Five. Although Red Bull was not an official sponsor of the World Cup, the association with Brazilian football star Neymar Jr, caught the attention and created a link between Red Bull and the event.

It is important to note that while ambush marketing can be seen as a clever and attention-grabbing tactic, it is often viewed negatively by event organizers and official sponsors who invest significant resources in securing exclusive rights and benefits. Ambush marketing campaigns can sometimes lead to legal action if they infringe upon trademark rights or breach advertising regulations.

Ambush Marketing in Pharma

Due to strict regulations and ethical considerations, Ambush marketing is uncommon in the pharmaceutical industry. Pharmaceutical industries are heavily regulated to safeguard patient safety and ensure fair competition, with the marketing of pharmaceutical products subject to stringent guidelines imposed by regulatory bodies such as the Food and Drug Administration in the US, or comparable bodies in other nations.

Given these restrictions, pharmaceutical industries do not commonly practice ambush marketing tactics by associating themselves with an event or property without authorization.

Analog Research

Analog research is creating new drugs or compounds by modifying existing ones. Modifying an existing drug's chemical structure to produce new molecules with novel biological activities and properties.

Analog research can be utilized to enhance the safety and efficacy of existing drugs while creating innovative therapies to treat various conditions and diseases. This strategy may prove helpful when an effective medication against one disorder fails to have suitable bioavailability and toxicity properties.

Researchers can alter the chemical structure of existing drugs to create an analog with better therapeutic benefits. This is due to altered absorption and distribution, metabolism, and elimination.

Analog research is a growing trend in pharmaceutical companies. This is due to its many advantages. Examples include:

1. *Patent Protection*: Pharmaceutical companies recognize that developing new drugs from scratch is costly and time-consuming; to increase patent protection on existing medications, they often modify existing versions to create analogs of existing medication. This allows the company to obtain another patent by creating analogous molecules which further delay generic competition for longer.
2. *Increased Safety and Efficiency*: Analogs can be made to improve the safety and efficacy of drugs.
3. *Cost Savings*: It can be very expensive to develop a new drug. Pharma companies might opt for an analog approach as a cost-saving measure.
4. *Competitive Advantage*: Pharmaceutical companies can create a product that is different from other products by creating analogs of existing drugs.

Ansoff Matrix

H. Igor Ansoff, a mathematician and business manager, created the Ansoff Matrix and described it in the Harvard Business Review article *Strategies for Diversification* in 1957. This strategic planning tool aids companies in defining their product and market strategy. As illustrated in the figure below, it includes four categories: market penetration (market development), product development (diversification), and product development (product development).

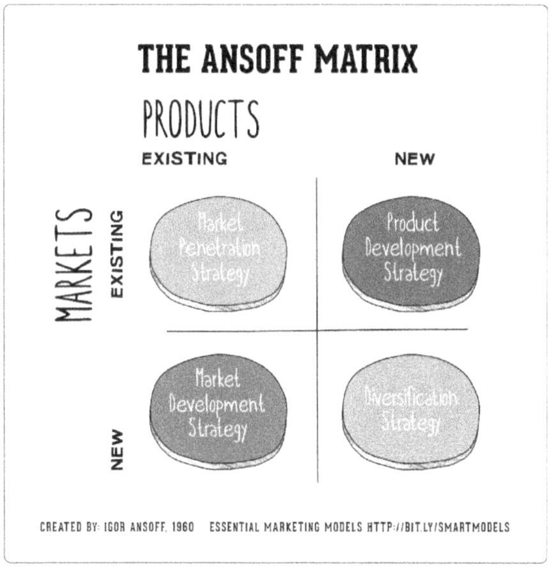

Pharma companies can reap the benefits of the Ansoff Matrix, which identifies and assesses product growth opportunities.

1. *Market penetration* is expanding existing products' market share in established markets. This could be expanding the use of an existing drug, targeting new patient groups, or creating novel formulations and delivery methods within the pharmaceutical industry.
2. *Market development* is the process of entering new markets using existing products. This could include expanding the indications of an existing drug to address new diseases in the pharmaceutical industry or launching a drug in a new geographic area.
3. *Product development* is the creation of new products for existing markets. This could include creating new drugs for existing diseases or developing novel formulations and delivery methods for drugs already used in the pharmaceutical industry.
4. *Diversification* strategies are the introduction of new products to new markets. This could be done in the pharmaceutical sector, for example, by expanding into new areas, such as diagnostics and medical devices, or creating new drugs for completely different disease types.

The Ansoff Matrix is a tool pharmaceutical companies can use to identify growth opportunities and assess the risks and benefits of different strategies. To bring new drugs to market, they must navigate the complex regulatory landscapes and lengthy clinical trials.

ANDA

Abbreviated New Drug Application (ANDA) is a regulatory pathway in the US used to approve generic versions of previously approved brand-name medications, providing generic manufacturers an avenue to demonstrate bioequivalence with existing drugs.

The ANDA approval process involves multiple steps.

1. *Submit an ANDA Application*: When filing their ANDA with the FDA for ANDA approval, generic drug manufacturers provide information regarding active ingredients, intended uses, and labeling specifications of their new drug product.
2. *Review of ANDAs by FDA*: To ensure similarity in safety, effectiveness, and quality between proposed generic versions and brand name drugs, this review typically lasts several months before coming to a final verdict.
3. *Inspection of Manufacturing Facility*: To ensure compliance with Good Manufacturing Practices (GMP), the FDA inspects every manufacturing facility producing generic drugs by GMPs.
4. *Approval or Rejection of ANDAs*: When reviewing an ANDA submitted by a generic drug, the FDA determines its bioequivalence to brand name drugs and regulatory compliance requirements before accepting or rejecting. If deficiencies exist with either application or manufacturing facility facilities, it could reject ANDA with more information requested to address deficiencies identified during the review process.

Once their ANDA application has been accepted, generic drug manufacturers can market and sell their product as an inexpensive generic equivalent of brand-name medications. This typically offers greater cost-savings to consumers as generics tend to have significantly reduced price tags than their brand-name counterparts.

ANDA approvals are an integral component of pharmaceutical marketing as they foster market competition while offering cost-cutting options to consumers.

Cost of Formulating an ANDA

The costs of creating an Abbreviated New Drug Application (ANDA) can vary considerably based on its complexity and regulatory requirements. Yet, it is typically cheaper than creating new medications from scratch since a generic manufacturer can rely on safety and efficacy data from brand-name medications to support an ANDA submission. However, there can still be significant expenses involved with creating an ANDA; some potential expenses include the following:

1. *Bioequivalence Studies*: Generic drug manufacturers must conduct bioequivalence studies to demonstrate that their product meets all safety and efficacy parameters for brand-name drugs; these studies must demonstrate bioequivalence.
2. *Manufacturing Costs*: When producing generic drugs, their manufacturing process must be established and validated to ensure consistent, high-quality production, often at significant upfront costs for equipment, raw materials, and facility upgrades. This may incur substantial upfront expenses from equipment purchase/rentals/leasing and facility upgrades/modifications.
3. *Regulatory Fees*: Generic drug manufacturers must pay regulatory fees to the FDA to have their ANDA reviewed by them, the amounts depending upon both company size and application type submitted for review.
4. *Legal Fees*: Generic drug manufacturers may incur legal expenses related to patent litigation as brand-name drug companies may challenge the validity of their patents to delay generic competitors entering the market.

Depending on its complexity and regulatory requirements, cost estimates for developing an ANDA range from several hundred thousand to several million dollars. While developing an ANDA may be cheaper than starting from scratch with new drug development, developing an ANDA still involves significant upfront expenses and can pose higher-than-usual risk levels.

What would it cost to develop generic medicines in the US? According to research by Generic Pharmaceutical Association, an estimate indicates that developing a generic drug could cost approximately USD 2.6 Million, including research & development expenses, bioequivalence studies, regulatory fees, and legal expenses.

But the cost of creating an ANDA may depend on its unique circumstances; for instance, generic drugs that do not necessitate extensive bioequivalence studies or complex manufacturing processes could require less money than more complex medicines that need additional clinical trials or costly equipment to create.

Developing an ANDA may require significant upfront investments. But when successful, an it could provide consumers with cost-cutting alternatives while helping promote competition in the marketplace.

Anonymization of Data

Anonymizing data in pharmaceutical marketing involves processing personal information so it cannot be linked back to specific individuals. Given the sensitive nature of health-related data and strict data privacy regulations (GDPR in Europe or HIPAA in the US), anonymization is pivotal in pharmaceutical data handling practices.

Implications for Pharma Marketers

Anonymizing data has many ramifications for pharmaceutical marketers. Here are the primary ones:

1. *Pharma marketers must comply with regulations*: When managing data processing and anonymization practices for pharmaceutical marketers must ensure compliance with relevant data privacy regulations to avoid severe fines and reputational damage.
2. *Data Use*: Anonymized data can be leveraged for many marketing uses, including understanding market trends, customer behavior patterns, and campaign performance analyses without infringing upon privacy rights.
3. *Customer Trust*: Pharmaceutical companies can build customer trust by ensuring all data is appropriately anonymized since individuals tend to engage with companies that respect their privacy more readily.
4. *Data Sharing and Collaboration*: With anonymized data being more easily shared between departments within an organization or between partners, collaborative projects, aggregating insights, and improving marketing strategies may become possible more freely.
5. *Data Analysis and Insights*: Anonymized data can generate valuable insights that support marketing strategies without jeopardizing individual privacy.
6. *Anonymization as part of data security*: Anonymization can form part of an effective data security plan to safeguard sensitive personal data against breaches that might compromise it.

On the other hand, however, anonymization must be executed properly to safeguard privacy. Improper anonymization could allow individuals or datasets to re-identify through combined linkage or inference techniques. Therefore, pharmaceutical companies must collaborate closely with data privacy and security experts to ensure their anonymization practices meet relevant regulations and standards.

Anthropology

Anthropology, the study of human societies and cultures can play an essential role in pharmaceutical marketing. Pharmaceutical companies can develop more efficient marketing strategies while improving patient outcomes by understanding cultural, psychological, and social factors affecting consumer behavior. Here are a few ways that anthropology may apply in pharmaceutical marketing:

1. *Cultural Analysis*: Anthropologists can conduct extensive research to gain an in-depth knowledge of how pharmaceutical products are utilized within various cultures, exploring beliefs, values, and practices related to health, illness, and treatment in distinct communities. With this information, pharmaceutical companies can tailor marketing messages and campaigns targeted toward specific cultural groups for improved engagement and adherence during therapy.
2. *Patient Journey Mapping*: Anthropologists can explore patients' journeys from initial diagnosis through completion of treatment by studying experiences, emotions, and challenges experienced during this process. By understanding pain points at each step in this path to wellness, pharmaceutical companies can develop solutions to address them, such as improving patient education or access, streamlining medication access, or augmenting support programs to address them effectively.
3. *Ethnographic Research*: Anthropologists conduct ethnographic research by immersing themselves in patients' everyday lives, which allows them to gain a deep insight into patient needs, motivations, and decision-making processes. By watching patients interact in their natural settings, pharmaceutical companies may identify opportunities to increase medication adherence rates by developing user-friendly packaging or designing patient-centric solutions.
4. *Cultural Sensitivity*: Anthropologists provide pharmaceutical companies with invaluable assistance as they navigate the various cultural environments found throughout global markets. Anthropologists can offer insight into cultural norms, beliefs, and sensitivities to ensure marketing materials are culturally appropriate without accidentally alienating specific communities. This knowledge is essential in successfully launching and marketing pharmaceutical products in different regions worldwide.

5. *Social Media Analysis*: Anthropologists can conduct social media and online community analyses to understand how patients and healthcare professionals discuss pharmaceutical products online, providing pharmaceutical companies with valuable data they can use when crafting targeted marketing and communications campaigns that resonate with their target audiences.
6. *Market Expansion*: Anthropological research can assist pharmaceutical marketers in recognizing opportunities for market expansion by understanding different regions' cultural and social dynamics. With this insight, pharmaceutical companies can tailor marketing strategies for different cultures to enter unchartered territories effectively while reaching untapped patient populations.
7. *Ethical Considerations*: Anthropology advocates ethical research practices that respect the studied communities. Pharma marketers can apply this principle by adhering to ethical marketing practices that uphold patients' rights and privacy. This involves gathering informed consent, protecting patient data, or refraining from manipulative or misleading marketing tactics.

Anthropology offers invaluable insights for pharmaceutical marketing by increasing understanding of patient cultures, societies, and psychological backgrounds. By tapping this insight, pharmaceutical companies can develop more efficient marketing strategies while improving the engagement and adherence of their target patients to provide enhanced patient experiences.

Implications for Pharma Marketers

Anthropology offers numerous implications for pharmaceutical marketers. By applying anthropological insights in their marketing campaigns and strategies, pharmaceutical companies may achieve several key results:

A. *Targeted Marketing*: Anthropological research gives pharmaceutical marketers insight into various cultural nuances and beliefs within different communities, which allows them to develop targeted campaigns that resonate with specific cultural groups. Marketers can increase effectiveness by adapting messages, visuals, channels, etc., to cultural preferences and values within target audience segments while improving product engagement.

B. *Patient-Centric Approach*: Anthropology emphasizes understanding patients' needs, experiences, and perspectives. By adopting a patient-centric approach in marketing initiatives for pharmaceutical products, pharmaceutical marketers can develop strategies to prioritize patient well-being, education, and empowerment, including creating understandable educational materials or user-friendly packaging designs to address patient challenges directly.

C. *Improved Patient Engagement*: Anthropology provides marketers with insight into patients' decision-making processes, motivations, and barriers to treatment. Marketers can then devise strategies to encourage patient engagement and boost treatment adherence by understanding individual behavior factors, such as creating personalized communication channels or using social media platforms like LinkedIn for patient support groups.

Anthropology highlights the need for cultural sensitivity when marketing pharmaceutical products and services. Pharma marketers need to have an in-depth knowledge of cultural norms, beliefs, and practices of different populations they will interact with; by including insights gained through anthropological studies in their marketing materials, they can ensure they resonate positively across diverse audience demographics.

Anthropology offers significant implications for pharmaceutical marketers, enabling them to devise culturally sensitive patient-focused marketing strategies that improve patient engagement and extend market reach. By employing insights gained through anthropological studies, pharmaceutical companies can increase marketing efficiency while strengthening patient relationships and ultimately improving outcomes for all their patients.

Anthropomorphic Marketing

Anthropomorphic marketing uses human traits on non-human entities such as animals, objects, or abstract concepts to increase sales or engage customers more deeply with your product, service, or brand. This tactic creates relatable connections with consumers for maximum sales results and engagement.

Here are a few examples of anthropomorphic marketing:

A. *Mascots*: Many companies and brands use mascots as their anthropomorphic representatives. These mascots can be animals, fictional characters, or even inanimate objects brought to life. For example, Tony the Tiger for

Kellogg's Frosted Flakes cereal, and the Michelin Man for Michelin tires.

B. *Animated Characters*: Animated characters, often with human-like qualities, are frequently employed in marketing campaigns. These characters can star in commercials, appear on packaging, or be used in digital marketing efforts. One notable example is the Gecko in GEICO. An anthropomorphic Gecko that serves as the brand spokesperson for GEICO Insurance.

C. *Social Media Profiles*: Brands may create anthropomorphic profiles on social media platforms to interact with consumers in a more engaging and relatable way. These profiles often feature a fictional character or mascot representing the brand, engaging in conversations, and sharing content on behalf of the company.

D. *Emotional Appeals*: Anthropomorphic marketing can tap into human emotions by assigning emotions or expressions to non-human entities. For instance, advertisements may depict animals or objects exhibiting happiness, excitement, or empathy, creating an emotional connection with the audience.

By leveraging human-like characteristics, anthropomorphic marketing makes a brand more memorable, relatable, and appealing to consumers. Companies hope to enhance brand loyalty and drive consumer engagement by creating an emotional connection and fostering positive associations. However, it is important to note that the effectiveness of anthropomorphic marketing can vary depending on the target audience, cultural considerations, and overall brand strategy.

Anthropomorphic Marketing in Pharma

Anthropomorphic marketing can be applied to pharma marketing in many ways to create engaging and relatable connections with consumers. Here are some possible approaches:

1. *Mascots and Characters*: Pharmaceutical companies can create mascots or characters representing their brand or specific medications. These characters can be human-like or anthropomorphized versions of organs, cells, or disease-fighting entities. The character can serve as a spokesperson or educator, delivering information about the medication in a friendly and relatable manner. For example, a character representing a medication for allergies could be an anthropomorphic bee.
2. *Animated Videos and Infographics*: Pharma companies can use animated videos or infographics featuring anthropomorphic characters to explain complex medical concepts or showcase the benefits of their medications. These characters can personify diseases, symptoms, or the process of drug action, making it easier for patients to understand and engage with the information.
3. *Social Media Engagement*: Pharma companies can create anthropomorphic profiles on social media platforms to engage with patients and healthcare providers. These profiles can feature characters that represent different medical conditions or medication benefits, providing educational content, support and answering questions in a relatable manner.
4. *Emotional Appeals and Storytelling*: Anthropomorphic marketing can evoke emotions and tell compelling stories about health conditions and medication usage. By assigning human-like traits and emotions to characters, pharma companies can create narratives that resonate with patients and highlight the impact of their medications on individuals' lives.
5. *Packaging and Branding*: Anthropomorphic elements can be incorporated into pharmaceutical product packaging and branding. By using characters or illustrations that evoke a sense of empathy and connection, companies can create a more approachable and patient-friendly image for their medications.

How Pharma Uses Anthropomorphic Marketing

Though pharmaceutical companies utilize anthropomorphic marketing less often than companies in other sectors, some firms have begun including anthropomorphic elements in their marketing initiatives. Here are a few examples showing how some pharmaceutical companies have used them:

1. *Flonase's Sensimist Allergy Relief Bee*: GlaxoSmithKline's Flonase, a nasal spray for allergy relief, introduced an anthropomorphic bee character in their marketing campaigns. The character represents the irritating allergy symptoms, showcasing how Flonase provides relief. The bee character appeared in TV commercials, online advertisements, and on product packaging, making the brand more relatable and memorable for consumers.
2. *Mucinex's Mr. Mucus*: Reckitt Benckiser's Mucinex, a brand known for its over-the-counter medications for cold and flu symptoms, introduced Mr. Mucus, an anthropomorphic representation of mucus. Mr. Mucus appears in the brand's advertising campaigns as a slimy, green, and snarky character. The

anthropomorphic representation of mucus helps to personify the discomfort caused by congestion and presents Mucinex as a solution to alleviate those symptoms.

3. *Osphena's Butterfly Campaign*: Duchesnay's Osphena, a medication for postmenopausal women with dyspareunia (painful intercourse), launched a campaign featuring an anthropomorphic butterfly named "O." The butterfly symbolizes the freedom and transformation that Osphena can provide to women experiencing sexual discomfort. The campaign aimed to create awareness and start conversations about this sensitive topic, using the butterfly as a relatable and empathetic character.
4. *Alli's Alligator Campaign*: GlaxoSmithKline's Alli, a weight loss medication, introduced an anthropomorphic alligator character in its marketing campaigns. The alligator represented the potential negative consequences of overeating and unhealthy habits. The campaign emphasized the alligators' urge to eat everything in sight, highlighting the importance of making healthier choices and using Alli as a tool for weight management.

Creating Anthropomorphic Marketing Campaigns

To incorporate anthropomorphic marketing into your pharmaceutical marketing efforts, here are some steps you can follow:

1. *Define Your Objective*: Establish your marketing objective and identify how anthropomorphic elements can support your goal. Determine, for example, if you want to increase awareness, enhance patient education, promote medication adherence, or create an emotional connection with your target audience.
2. *Understand Your Audience*: Conduct market research to understand your target audiences' preferences, needs, and behaviors. Identify their pain points, motivations, and communication preferences to ensure your anthropomorphic approach resonates with them.
3. *Choose the Right Character of Mascot*: Select a character or mascot that aligns with your brand identity, medication, and target audience. Consider creating a character that represents your medication, health condition, symptoms, or benefits in a relatable and engaging manner. Ensure the character is likable, memorable and communicates the desired message effectively.
4. *Develop a Compelling Story*: Craft a compelling narrative that integrates the anthropomorphic character into your marketing campaign. Create first, a backstory, personality traits, and experiences that resonate with your audience. Then, develop a story highlighting the character's journey and how your medication or healthcare solution plays a role in addressing their needs.
5. *Use Visual and Multimedia Elements*: Utilize visual elements such as illustrations, animations, or videos to bring your anthropomorphic character to life. Design marketing materials, packaging, and digital content that feature the character prominently and communicate your message effectively.
6. *Communicate Benefits and Information*: Ensure that your anthropomorphic marketing approach effectively communicates the benefits and information about your medication or healthcare solution. Use the character to explain complex medical concepts in a simple and relatable manner. Keep the messaging clear, concise, and aligned with regulatory guidelines.
7. *Leverage Multiple Marketing Channels*: Deploy your anthropomorphic marketing campaign across various channels, including TV, digital platforms, social media, print, and packaging. Tailor your messaging and creative assets to suit each channel and engage with your target audience where they are most active.
8. *Measure and Optimize*: Continuously monitor and evaluate the impact of your anthropomorphic marketing efforts. First, measure key performance indicators (KPIs), such as brand awareness, engagement, website traffic, or medication uptake. Then, analyze the results and make necessary adjustments to optimize your campaign's effectiveness.

These examples demonstrate how anthropomorphic marketing techniques are utilized within the pharmaceutical industry to engage and educate consumers about specific medications or conditions. It should be noted, however, that pharmaceutical marketing falls under strict regulatory constraints to guarantee patient safety and promote ethical promotion practices. Therefore, any anthropomorphic marketing approach must adhere to these guidelines and prioritize accurate information dissemination over entertainment value. Therefore, pharmaceutical companies should consult legal and compliance teams to ensure their marketing strategies align with industry standards and regulations.

Anthropomorphic Marketing Research

As defined by the dictionary, *Anthropomorphism* refers to ascribing human characteristics or behavior to animals, objects, or even Gods.

Anthropomorphic marketing research (AMPR) is an approach used to understand consumer behavior through personifying brands and products, drawing inspiration from humans' tendency to assign human-like qualities to non-living entities like animals, objects, and brands. According to this approach, it is about attributing human qualities like emotion or intelligence or personality traits or characteristics like intelligence to nonhuman beings such as animals. This approach is used in anthropomorphic marketing research to gain insight into consumers' perceptions of brands and products when they purchase.

Anthropomorphic marketing research has many advantages. First, it provides insights into the motivations and feelings of consumers. Researchers can understand consumers' feelings about brands and products better by associating them with human-like characteristics. Pharma marketers can then identify the key attributes that resonate with their target audience and create more effective marketing campaigns and appealing product strategies.

There are limitations to anthropomorphic studies. One limitation is that brands and products may not reflect consumers' perceptions. For example, a product might be friendly, but others perceive it as impersonal or cold. In addition, some consumers might view anthropomorphic market research as manipulative and deceptive if done wrongly. Pharma marketers must know these issues when developing campaign strategies and tactics.

What Pharma Can Do

How can pharmaceutical companies use anthropomorphic research in marketing strategies and tactics to promote their products and services? This approach allows pharma marketers to build a closer, more human connection with their patients. Here are some examples of how it might be used by pharma:

1. *Mascots and Characters*: Pharma companies often create anthropomorphic characters, or mascots, to represent their products. Zyrtec is a prescription drug with *Zyrtec Mole*, a cartoon character explaining how it works. This makes it easier to understand the medication.
2. *Patients' Personas*: Pharmaceutical companies sometimes create fictional representations of patients who might use their products to understand their customers better. These personas can include information about the demographics, medical history, and lifestyle of each patient, which allows companies to tailor their marketing messages to suit each audience's needs.
3. *Virtual Assistants*: Virtual assistants are created by some Pharma companies that use artificial intelligence to provide personalized patient support and information. These virtual assistants, like Eli Lilly's *LillyBot*, are friendly and approachable. They provide patients with a more human-like experience.
4. *Patient Communities*: Pharma companies might also set up online forums or communities where patients can share their experiences with a specific medication. These forums foster a sense of belonging and allow patients to voice their opinions about the drug. In addition, these spaces promote understanding and support among fellow users.

How to Conduct Anthropomorphic Marketing Research

Conducting anthropomorphic marketing research in the pharmaceutical industry involves studying and understanding the behaviors, needs, and preferences of human-like characters of personas as potential customers. While anthropomorphism is not traditionally applied to the pharmaceutical industry, it can be used to gain insights into consumer behavior and improve marketing strategies. Here are some steps to conduct anthropomorphic marketing research in the pharma sector:

1. *Define the Research Objectives*: Clearly outline what you aim to achieve through anthropomorphic marketing research. Determine the specific areas you want to explore, such as consumer perceptions, emotional connections, decision-making processes, or brand loyalty.
2. *Identify Target Personas*: Create human-like personas that represent different segments of your target audience. These personals should embody specific characteristics, motivations, and preferences that align with your target customers.
3. *Develop Qualitative Research Methods*: Use qualitative research techniques to gather insights from your target personas. This can include in-depth interviews, focus groups, or observational studies. Tailor your research methods to understand how these personas perceive pharmaceutical products, make purchasing decisions, and interact with brands.

4. *Design Quantitative Research Tools*: Develop surveys, questionnaires, or online polls to collect quantitative data. This data can help you measure and analyze attitudes, preferences, and behavior patterns across a larger sample size. Ensure your questions capture anthropomorphic aspects, such as emotional responses or personal associations.
5. *Gather Data and Analysis*: Use qualitative and quantitative research methods to gather relevant data. Then, analyze the data collected, looking for patterns, trends, and insights related to the personas' behaviors and attitudes toward pharmaceutical products and brands.
6. *Interpret Findings and Create Profiles*: Analyze the data to identify common themes and key findings. Then, use these insights to create detailed profiles for each persona, outlining their preferences, motivations, pain points, and behaviors. These profiles will help you understand the anthropomorphic aspects that influence their decision-making.
7. *Apply Findings to Marketing Strategies*: Utilize the personas' profiles and insights to develop targeted marketing strategies. Tailor your messaging, branding, and communication channels to resonate with the anthropomorphic traits of your personas. Consider emotional appeals, storytelling, and personalization in your marketing campaigns.
8. *Test and Refine*: Implement your revised marketing strategies and track their effectiveness. Monitor metrics such as customer engagement, brand awareness, and conversion rates to evaluate the impact of your anthropomorphic approach. Make adjustments as needed to optimize your marketing efforts.

Remember that anthropomorphic marketing research in the pharmaceutical industry may require creativity and out-of-the-box thinking, as this field is not widely explored. Ensure you respect ethical considerations and privacy regulations when researching and handling customer data.

Anthropomorphic marketing research can help pharmaceutical companies build patient trust and loyalty. This ultimately leads to better patient outcomes.

Anti-competitive Practices

Anticompetitive practices are tactical actions in pharmaceutical marketing taken by pharmaceutical companies to limit competition, gain unfair advantages over their competitors and ultimately increase their profits. Anticompetitive tactics include:

1. *Pay-for-Delay*: A pharmaceutical company can be paid to hold off on releasing generic drugs. Pay-for-delay agreements were legal before an antitrust ruling from the US Supreme Court in 2013 declared them illegal. These contracts may give an unfair edge and hinder competition, but their existence may now be illegal following an antitrust decision issued in 2013. This ruling prohibits pay-for-delay agreements from being made between generic and brand-name drug manufacturers. One notable example is Provigil (Modafinil), in which Cephalon, the brand-name pharmaceutical manufacturer, paid generic manufacturers to delay generics' introduction.
2. *Exclusive Dealing Agreements*: Many pharmaceutical companies enter into exclusive dealing arrangements that restrict competition by appointing select distributors or pharmacies exclusively to sell their products. These arrangements are now legally prohibited. For example, Aspen Pharmaceuticals was fined €5·3 million by the European Commission for engaging in anticompetitive practices, such as high prices and exclusive deals with hospitals.
3. *Price Fixing*: Many pharmaceutical companies agree to set a fixed price, which allows them to keep high prices and prevents competition. Many countries are investigating price-fixing allegations; for example, 44 US states filed suit in 2019, alleging 20 generic drug manufacturers participated in price-fixing and market allocation schemes to limit competition and raise generic drug costs.
4. *Misleading Advertising*: Pharmaceutical companies engaged in misleading advertising are subject to criminal sanctions in most countries for engaging in this practice. A case in point is Australia's Competition and Consumer Commission fining Reckitt Benckiser $1.7 Million for falsifying product claims related to Neurofen (Ibuprofen).
5. *Rebate Schemes*: Pharmaceutical companies often offer healthcare providers and insurers rebates for exclusive coverage or preferential treatment. This can restrict competition and increase consumer prices. For example, Indivior engaged in rebate schemes as anti-competitive practices when they offered kickbacks to healthcare providers to get them to prescribe its opioid addiction treatment product, according to investigations by the United States Department of Justice in 2020. The DOJ launched its investigation as the kickback scheme was an antitrust violation and potentially breached antitrust rules.

Consumers often experience higher prices, reduced access to medication, and a lack of innovation due to anti-competitive practices by pharmaceutical companies. Therefore, many countries have created regulatory bodies to monitor such activities within their pharmaceutical sectors and avoid adverse consumer outcomes.

Anti-corporatism

Anti-corporatism is a critique of the influence of corporations in the pharmaceutical industry and drug market. This perspective challenges their motives and ethics, arguing that they place profit above patient welfare.

Critics of pharmaceutical marketing corporatism claim that pharmaceutical companies use their power to influence medical research, doctors, and other healthcare professionals and manipulate public perception to sell their products. They also claim that corporations prioritize expensive patentable drugs over cheaper, more accessible options, even though the former may be more effective.

These concerns have led some anti-corporatism advocates to promote transparency in drug pricing and clinical trials. They also advocate stronger regulation to stop corporate influence on medical research and prescribing practices. Some support alternative distribution and drug development models prioritizing patient needs over corporate profits.

Here are some examples illustrating anti-corporatism within pharmaceutical marketing.

1. *Criticism of Drug Pricing*: One example of anti-corporatism within pharmaceutical marketing is the criticisms of drug pricing. Critics claim that drug pricing is problematic because corporations charge high medicine prices, making it unaffordable for many people who need it. In addition, some argue that corporations prioritize maximizing profits over providing affordable healthcare to all.
2. *Opposition to Direct to Consumer Advertising (DTCA)*: This is another example of anti-corporatism within pharmaceutical marketing. Critics claim that DTCA permits corporations to influence public perceptions and create demand for drugs that might not be needed or effective.
3. *Concerns about Corporate Influence on Medical Research*: Many anti-corporatist views question the role played by pharmaceutical companies in medical research. Critics claim corporations might manipulate or suppress research results that are not in their favor and use their financial power to influence research priorities.
4. *Anti-corporatism in Pharmaceutical Marketing*: The anti-corporatists advocate greater transparency and what regulations should be to prevent corporate influence on medical research and prescription practices. Some advocate disclosing financial ties between doctors and pharmaceutical companies. Furthermore, they want tighter drug pricing and marketing practices regulations.
5. *Alternative Drug Development and Distribution Models*: Some anti-corporatist views advocate alternative drug development models and distribution models that place patient needs above corporate profits. Some advocate public funding for drug research and non-profit drug development agencies. Others advocate more generic drugs and developing medicines less dependent upon corporate funding.

However, not all views on the pharmaceutical industry are anti-corporatist. Others believe that corporations are essential for driving innovation and improving patient outcomes.

A well-regulated corporate environment can be beneficial to both patients and society. The debate over anti-corporatism, in the end, is multifaceted and complex, reflecting healthcare's diverse values and interests.

Anti-Kickback Statute

The Anti-Kickback Statute (AKS) is a United States federal law prohibiting exchanges of any value exchanged in return for federal healthcare program business referrals. This federal regulation applies directly to pharmaceutical marketers and can have significant implications on their activities; here are a few key takeaways from AKS:

1. *Prohibition of Kickbacks and Bribes*: Under AKS guidelines, pharmaceutical marketers cannot offer, pay, solicit, or receive any remuneration in exchange for referrals or business generated through federal healthcare program business, including payments, gifts, discounts, rebates or any other incentives that might influence healthcare providers to prescribe or purchase specific drugs.
2. *Penalties and Enforcement*: Violating the Affordable Care Act can result in harsh punishment, such as criminal fines, imprisonment, and civil monetary penalties; exclusion from federal healthcare programs as

well as potential damage claims filed against companies who break it can also incur serious sanctions from HHS' Office of Inspector General (OIG), who oversees its implementation and enforce it accordingly.

3. *Safe Harbors*: The Anti-Kickback Statute (AKS) includes safe harbor provisions to identify activities that do not fall under its definition of kickbacks and illegality, thus safeguarding AKS enforcement actions. Pharma marketers should ensure their business arrangements, such as discounts or rebates with healthcare providers or financial relationships with providers, meet these safe harbor criteria outlined by AKS' safe harbor provisions.
4. *Comply with Law*: Pharma marketers face serious risks and consequences; due to this fact, they should develop comprehensive compliance programs to abide by all relevant laws and regulations, including AKS and local ones. Such plans include policies, procedures, training sessions, monitoring, and auditing to prevent violations against AKS; regular education/training sessions should also occur for sales reps and relevant personnel to ensure understanding and compliance.
5. *Relationship with Healthcare Providers*: The AKS affects relationships between pharma marketers and healthcare providers by prohibiting improper financial inducements that might influence prescribing decisions. Marketers must ensure their interactions with providers focus on an educational or scientific exchange of information rather than offering any incentives related to prescribing or purchasing decisions.
6. *Fair Market Value*: Under AKS regulations, payments or compensation provided to healthcare providers must meet fair market value for legitimate services or items provided. Pharma marketers should create transparent compensation arrangements based on industry standards and documented services offered.
7. *Compliance with Other Laws*: The AKS interweaves with other regulations, such as the False Claims Act (FCA). Any violation of AKS could also trigger FCA liability if claims submitted for federal healthcare programs contain illegal kickbacks; pharmaceutical marketers must understand all possible connections and ensure compliance with applicable laws and regulations.

Pharma marketers must thoroughly comprehend and comply with the Anti-Kickback Statute (AKS). Compliance requires meticulous tracking, documentation, and ongoing audit of marketing practices that comply with AKS laws. Consulting legal or compliance experts for guidance in specific situations and developing compliance plans to prevent AKS violations is recommended to avoid potential legal ramifications.

Apple

Apple, known for its iconic products such as iPhones, iPads, and Mac computers, has recently explored different avenues into the healthcare and medical industries. Below are key initiatives and potential involvement with pharmaceutical marketing:

1. *Health and Fitness Tracking*: Apple has invested significantly in health and fitness tracking through devices such as its Apple Watch and iPhone, featuring built-in health sensors which enable users to keep an eye on their heart rate, activity levels, sleep cycles, and more. Such data could prove immensely helpful to users and healthcare providers as a basis for targeted marketing of pharmaceuticals related to specific conditions or wellness aspects of living well.
2. *Health App and Research Kit*: Apple's iOS-only Health app enables users to store and manage all their health data in one central place, while ResearchKit, an open-source platform developed by Apple specifically for medical researchers, allows researchers to design apps for clinical studies by collecting health information from willing participants who provide consent; the data can then be anonymized before analysis for research purposes or used later for targeted pharma marketing efforts.
3. *Apple's Partnerships With Healthcare Providers*: Apple has collaborated with multiple healthcare institutions and providers to integrate its technology into patient care, for instance, by working with hospitals and health systems on data exchange and telemedicine services. These relationships could potentially result in targeted marketing initiatives in this space.
4. *Apple Health Records*: Apple recently unveiled the Health Records feature to allow users to gain access to medical records from participating healthcare providers directly on their devices, improving patient engagement and helping users better manage their care. Pharmaceutical companies could potentially deliver relevant drug information or marketing messages within this app as a marketing channel.
5. *Wearable Tech for Clinical Trials*: Apple has experimented with wearable technology such as its Apple Watch in clinical trials to gather real-

time health data from trial participants for analysis; clinical trial sponsors could potentially gain invaluable insights into drug efficacy and safety based on this data gathered during real-time health monitoring; it may even prove valuable in future marketing activities.

Apple may not directly venture into the pharmaceutical industry; however, its strong presence within the healthcare and medical sectors, and its vast user base, offer potential avenues for future collaborations or partnerships between pharmaceutical firms, healthcare providers, and Apple.

Application Programing Interface (API)

In a digital context, API can refer to the Application Programming Interface, a set of tools and protocols for building and interacting with software applications.

API (Application Programming Interface) has some implications even in the pharmaceutical industry:

1. *Data Integration*: APIs (Application Programming Interfaces) allow pharma companies to integrate data from multiple sources, like patient records, clinical trials, and other databases. This can be leveraged for more targeted marketing strategies.
2. *Interactivity with Healthcare Platforms*: Through APIs, pharmaceutical companies can create tools and apps that integrate with electronic health record systems, providing valuable resources for healthcare providers.
3. *Digital Health Ecosystem*: APIs allow pharma companies to join the broader digital health ecosystem, connecting with wearable devices, telehealth platforms, and other digital health tools.
4. *Personalization*: With access to data through APIs, pharma marketers can create more personalized and relevant content for healthcare professionals and patients.
5. *Compliance and Security*: Handling data, especially patient data, requires stringent compliance with regulations like GDPR or HIPAA. Any breach can have serious reputational and legal implications.
6. *Rapid Evolution*: The digital landscape evolves rapidly. Marketers must be agile, ensuring that developed tools or platforms remain compatible with changing API standards and integrations.

Archetypes

The collective unconscious of all humans, across all cultures and periods, contains timeless symbols or patterns called archetypes are mental images or ideas inherited from ancestors that often unconsciously shape our thoughts, feelings, and behavior.

Carl Jung, a Swiss psychiatrist who founded analytical psychology, was the first to propose the idea of archetypes. According to Jung, these symbols were fundamental human experiences such as mother-child relationships, wise older men, and hero journeys.

Literature and art have many archetypes, including characters, symbols, and themes. For example, the hero archetype is found in many cultures, including the Greek myth of Hercules and the Hindu epic Ramayana.

Archetypes provide insights and perspectives into our emotions and behavior by connecting us to the human experience. Recognizing and working with archetypes can increase self-awareness, insight, and understanding about ourselves and life.

Marketing archetypes can create memorable and relatable brand personalities based on these universal symbols or characters that represent typical human behavior. Pharma marketing reaps the benefits of archetypes' ability to create a unique brand identity and communicate their advantages to their target audiences.

Here are some of the most common archetypes in pharmaceutical marketing:

1. *The Caregiver* archetype is a nurturing, caring, and supportive brand. This archetype is often associated with companies focusing on patient care, wellness, and disease management. Pfizer's *Get Old Campaign* best illustrates this caregiver archetype. It emphasizes healthy aging and motivates patients to take control of their health. Pfizer's commitment to patient health is evident in this campaign.
2. *The Hero* archetype represents a strong, bold, innovative brand. This archetype is often used by companies that offer breakthrough treatments, lifesaving technologies, or cutting-edge technology. For example, this archetype is used by Novartis in its *Breakthrough Campaign* to promote its groundbreaking treatments for cancer and diabetes. This campaign highlights Novartis' commitment to developing lifesaving therapies while taking risks in searching for solutions.
3. *The Sage* archetype represents a trustworthy, wise, and knowledgeable brand. It is often

associated with research institutions, educational institutions, and evidence-based medical companies like Merck, where their *Science Will Win Campaign* highlights their commitment to scientific discovery. Merck's use of this sage archetype shows its credibility, trustworthiness, and expertise.

4. *The Rebel* archetype represents a disruptive and unconventional brand. This archetype often describes companies that challenge established practices and offer alternatives. For example, Allergan's *Real Women Campaign* features real women telling their stories about aging and encouraging them to accept their imperfections. This rebel archetype challenges conventional beauty standards and encourages body positivity.
5. *The Explorer* archetype represents a forward-thinking, curious brand. This archetype is often associated with companies exploring new medical frontiers or advancing medical research. This archetype is best illustrated in pharma marketing by Gilead's *Forward Campaign*. It emphasizes Gilead's commitment to finding cures for HIV/AIDS and other diseases through exploration. Through its innovative approach to medicine, Gilead embraces risk-taking.
6. *The Lover Archetype*: symbolizes passion, sensuality, and relationship intimacy. The lover archetype is often used by brands focused on sexual health and fertility, such as Viagra or fertility clinics. This archetype emphasizes the importance of intimacy and passion in romantic relationships. Bayer Pharmaceuticals, for example, used the lover archetype to market Yaz contraceptive pills with the tagline *Freedom to Be Yourself*. This promoted sexual freedom and choice, while Yaz was positioned as a brand that empowers women to manage their sexual health.
7. *The Magician Archetype*: is an archetype that transforms, creates magic, and remains mysterious. Companies can use it to offer innovative therapies or treatments that appear magical to patients. In addition, the magician archetype may emphasize the brand's revolutionary treatment of an incurable disease, such as immunotherapy or gene therapy. For example, Gilead Sciences used a magician archetype to promote Sovaldi, their treatment for hepatitis C. They also announced it with the tagline *A New Day in Hep C*. This campaign showcased how transformative this treatment can be, and established Gilead Sciences as an innovator in developing novel therapies for previously incurable diseases.
8. *The Jester Archetype*: is a playful, irreverent, and humorous archetype. Brands can use this archetype to ease tension over serious health issues and appeal to patients looking for fun in their healthcare experience. In addition, they might use the jester archetype to make their brand more approachable to patients looking for humor and lightheartedness in healthcare marketing. For example, Pfizer's OTC pain relief brand Advil used the Jester archetype to market their product with the tagline *When Pain Happens, Advil is There*. The campaign used humor and lightheartedness to make the brand more relatable to people looking for an easy yet effective solution to their everyday discomforts.
9. *The Everyman Archetype*: symbolizes a relatable and down-to-earth brand that wants to connect personally with its patients and show dedication to meeting their daily healthcare needs. This archetype can be used by brands who want to build personal connections with their customers and reinforce their commitment to excellent patient care. A brand that provides everyday healthcare products like OTC pain relief or multivitamins may use the Everyman archetype to highlight accessibility and affordability and position their products as essential for everyone's well-being and health. Vicks, an OTC cold and cough remedy brand, used the Everyman archetype to market its products. With *What you and your family deserve* tagline, Vicks was positioned as a brand that is accessible, affordable, and essential for everyday people's healthcare needs. This campaign highlighted the importance of family health.
10. *The Mentor* archetype is a wise, supportive brand offering guidance. This archetype can be used by brands that promote patient education, disease management, and self-care initiatives. The mentor archetype can be used by companies that offer self-care and patient education, such as mental health apps or diabetes management tools. This will position them as trusted companions in patients' healthcare journeys and show their commitment to giving patients control of their well-being. For example, Headspace, a mental-health app, used the mentor archetype to market its app with the tagline, *Meditation Made Simple*. Headspace was positioned as an authority ally and guide to users who want to improve their mental well-being through the campaign, highlighting mental health and self-care.

Pharma marketers can use archetypes to create a brand personality that is appealing to their target audience and sets them apart from their competitors.

However, it is important to choose archetypes compatible with the company's values, tone of voice, and messaging applicable to the target disease area and patient population.

Artificial Intelligence

AI stands for artificial intelligence. Artificial Intelligence (AI) in computer science works by building algorithms and systems capable of mimicking tasks that humans do commonly, such as speech recognition, visual perception, decision-making, and language translation. The difference is that AI uses machines instead. AI operates under the theory that machines can learn like people and then apply this knowledge more efficiently than humans to complete specific tasks more rapidly and cost-efficiently than humans could alone. AI encompasses numerous sub-disciplines like machine learning, natural language processing, and robotics, among many others.

Artificial Intelligence (AI), which can alter how pharmaceutical firms approach marketing strategies, could prove to be transformative technology for pharmaceutical firms. They could leverage it to gain insight into customer preferences and behaviors while streamlining sales and marketing efforts and personalizing messaging for individual customers — potentially increasing customer acquisition while decreasing marketing communications costs.

Customer data analysis is one of the primary applications of AI for pharmaceutical marketing. Pharma companies can utilize AI to quickly assess customer records, identify trends and predict the likelihood of customer responses during marketing campaigns or identify which marketing messages resonate best with certain customer segments.

Artificial intelligence can help automate certain marketing tasks, such as segmentation and lead scoring, to save time and increase efficiency. Furthermore, AI-powered chatbots provide customer support 24/7, allowing sales and marketing teams to focus on more complex tasks.

AI has the potential to make pharma marketing more personal. Pharma companies can use AI-powered algorithms to create customized customer messaging based on their preferences and behavior. This will increase customer engagement and improve the chances of receiving positive responses to marketing campaigns.

AI in Pharma Marketing

Here are a few examples of how artificial Intelligence (AI) can assist pharmaceutical marketers:

1. *Predictive Analytics*: AI can quickly and efficiently process large volumes of customer data to detect patterns and trends that can help inform marketing strategies. A pharmaceutical company could utilize predictive analytics to predict whether customers would purchase its product before targeting them with tailored marketing messages.
2. *Chatbots*: AI-powered chatbots can provide customer support and answer common queries, allowing sales and marketing teams to concentrate on more difficult tasks. A pharmaceutical company can use a chatbot to answer customer questions and explain where to buy it.
3. *Personalization*: AI allows you to create customized customer marketing messages based on their preferences and behaviors. A pharma company might use AI to target customers who have purchased a product in the past or expressed interest in a certain health condition.
4. *Voice Assistants*: AI-powered voice assistants like Amazon's Alexa and Google Home can inform customers about products and treatments. For example, a pharma company might develop an Alexa skill to inform customers about side effects and treatment options.
5. *Digital Ad Optimization*: Artificial intelligence can be used for optimizing digital ads to maximize effectiveness. A pharma company might use AI to test various ad variants and determine which is most effective in driving customer engagement and sales.
6. *Targeted Marketing*: AI algorithms can process vast quantities of information about patient demographics, prescription history, and social media activity to quickly identify likely customers for any drug being promoted by pharmaceutical companies — this allows pharma firms to tailor marketing campaigns more precisely toward specific customer requirements.
7. *Personalized Marketing*: AI can also assist in crafting personalized marketing materials such as emails, ads, and other content. By analyzing data on each customer, AI can identify which types of messaging and communication methods are most likely to resonate with that individual.
8. *Sales Analytics*: AI can analyze sales data to provide insights on which drugs and territories are performing well and provide key performance indicators, making data-driven decisions on sales strategies, resource allocation, etc. This knowledge may enable more informed business decisions regarding resource allocation or sales strategies.

9. *Drug Development*: Artificial intelligence can also aid the drug development process by helping identify possible new targets for discovery, forecasting the efficacy and safety of new compounds developed, and streamlining this step-by-step endeavor.

AI can assist pharmaceutical companies with streamlining their sales and marketing processes, improving targeting and personalization techniques, driving higher revenues, and ultimately expanding revenues.

AI in pharmaceutical marketing must meet ethical and regulatory considerations; companies should ensure customer data is collected responsibly and transparently in compliance with all applicable laws and regulations. AI-powered marketing campaigns may also raise issues around bias or fairness issues-just like any new technology would.

Although AI can transform marketing by offering insights into customer behavior, automating certain tasks, and personalizing messaging, pharmaceutical companies must be cautious about using AI in marketing and address ethical or regulatory concerns.

Asset-Led Branding

Asset-led Branding (ALB) is a marketing strategy that emphasizes a company's unique assets or resources as the basis for its branding efforts. These assets could include physical facilities, equipment, technology, and intangible assets like intellectual property rights, expertise, or reputation.

Asset-led Branding involves companies using their assets to develop a unique value proposition and brand identity, differentiating themselves from competitors and communicating it to target audiences. Companies showcase their assets to develop customer trust while positioning themselves as solution providers to satisfy customers' needs.

Asset-led branding is especially effective for companies operating in highly competitive industries or where customers have multiple choices. By emphasizing their unique assets and creating a strong brand identity in a crowded marketplace, companies can create an unforgettable brand image and stand out in the crowd over time while building customer loyalty and increasing market share.

Asset-Led Branding in Pharma

Asset-led Branding is an integral strategy for pharmaceutical companies, helping them differentiate themselves from competitors and establish an engaging brand image with their target audiences. Here are a few examples of how pharmaceutical firms have used assets in their branding efforts:

1. *Intellectual Property*: Patents, trademarks, and copyrights associated with products can be used as an asset-led branding strategy that helps a company establish itself as a leader in innovation and research. Pfizer is one company whose brand strength can be directly traced back to strong intellectual property like their patent protection for Viagra, which gave the company an exclusive source for this blockbuster drug for several years, creating significant competitive advantages in the marketplace.
2. *Manufacturing Capabilities*: Manufacturing capabilities can also be vital in asset-led branding strategies. A well-developed manufacturing process ensures product quality and consistency, building customer trust in your company's offerings. Roche Pharmaceuticals of Switzerland is an example of an organization that has successfully used its manufacturing abilities to establish itself as a leader within their industry by producing top-quality cancer drugs at competitive costs, something they do thanks to its robust manufacturing capability.
3. *Research and Development*: Research and development can also play a vital role in asset-led branding. By continuously creating new and innovative products, businesses can establish themselves at the forefront of their industry, as demonstrated by Novartis (another Swiss multinational), which has built its strong brand through continuous R&D investments across oncology and ophthalmology, leading to numerous innovative drugs reaching the market, thus becoming leaders in these fields.
4. *Distribution Networks*: Distribution networks can also serve as an invaluable branding asset. A well-established distribution network can ensure that products from any given company are widely available and accessible for customers, something Johnson & Johnson, an American multinational pharmaceutical company, has done by building its strong global distribution network to reach over 60 countries where partnerships with local distributors help make its products widely accessible to customers.
5. *Brand Reputation*: Reputation can also play an essential role in asset-led branding. A positive reputation helps establish customer trust and loyalty, which drives sales and revenue growth. Pfizer, for instance, has created a powerful brand identity through consistent messaging around innovation, quality patient care, and commitment, helping it become one of the industry's most admired names.

Asset-Led Marketing

Asset-led marketing refers to any strategy that uses a company's assets or resources as the focal point for its promotional messages. Such assets could be physical, like facilities, equipment, and technology; intangible, like intellectual property rights and expertise, or reputation.

Asset-led marketing entails companies emphasizing their strengths and capabilities to distinguish themselves from their competition and offer customers something special. By emphasizing assets as differentiators against rival firms and positioning themselves as solution providers for customer problems, companies hope to achieve trust from target audiences customers' needs.

Asset-led Marketing in Pharma has become an integral component of pharmaceutical businesses, with firms using asset-led strategies to define their unique value proposition for healthcare providers, patients, and other stakeholders. Here are a few examples of how asset-led marketing is used within this sector:

1. *R&D Expertise*: Companies such as Pfizer and Moderna showcase their strength in research and development as a key asset, positioning themselves as leaders in oncology and infectious disease therapy development.
2. *Manufacturing Capabilities*: Companies like Johnson & Johnson and Sanofi emphasize showcasing their manufacturing capabilities as core assets. By showing that they can consistently manufacture high-quality drugs at scale, these firms establish themselves as reliable partners to healthcare providers and their patients.
3. *Intellectual Property*: Gilead Sciences and Roche have long recognized intellectual property as an asset that protects their market position against competitors producing similar products while showing customers they invest in cutting-edge research and development efforts.
4. *Clinical Expertise*: Companies such as Novartis and Merck leverage their clinical expertise as an asset, positioning them as trusted partners among healthcare providers and patients who prioritize evidence-based treatments and clinical data.

Asset-led marketing offers pharmaceutical companies an effective means of standing out and communicating their unique value proposition to target audiences. By emphasizing their strengths and capabilities, companies can build credibility among stakeholders as they position themselves for long-term success in an otherwise challenging industry.

Atomization

Atomization refers to the fragmentation of a marketing message into smaller, more targeted pieces that can be distributed through multiple channels. Pharma marketers use atomization to create personalized, engaging content that responds to customers' needs and wants when they are most needed. The following are just a few examples of how pharmaceutical companies use atomization in marketing:

1. *Social Media*: Pharma companies use social media to reach specific audiences. Novo Nordisk, for example, created the Facebook page *Levemir FlexTouch* to offer information and support for patients who use their insulin brand Levemir. This page features videos, infographics, and testimonials from customers that are tailored to Levemir users.
2. *Email Marketing*: Pharma companies use email marketing to send personalized content to their customers' inboxes. Pfizer's monthly newsletter, *Living*, is sent by the company. It provides information and resources that may assist patients suffering from chronic conditions like arthritis or psoriasis.
3. *Webinars*: Pharma companies host webinars to educate customers and healthcare professionals on their products and services. GlaxoSmithKline hosts numerous such webinars through GSK *Health Partner*; such topics include HIV, COPD, asthma, and more.
4. *Mobile Apps*: Pharma companies have created personalized content and tools for patients and healthcare providers. Novartis created an app called *Living Like You* that provides support and resources for multiple sclerosis (MS) patients, educational materials, and an online community.
5. *Content Marketing*: Pharma companies employ content marketing to create targeted messages that resonate with a specific audience. Amgen, for example, created a blog called *Biosimilars: The Way to Access* that provides useful information and resources on biosimilars.

Atomization of content helps pharma companies communicate the right message to the right audiences at the right moment. This leads to better customer engagement and improved business results.

Attention

Pharmaceutical marketing is a complex process that requires "attention." It refers to the company's ability to attract patients and healthcare professionals to promote its products. Attention drives sales and market share in this highly competitive market.

Pharmaceutical companies use many strategies to draw the attention of their target audience. Some of these strategies include:

1. *Traditional Advertising*: Pharma companies use advertising channels like television, print, and online to attract potential customers. These ads often feature compelling visuals or messages to increase interest in a drug or disease.
2. *Sponsored Content* is another common strategy. This includes articles and videos that give information about a disease or drug. This material can be shared via social media and other online platforms to increase its reach.
3. *Events and Conferences*: Pharmaceutical companies sponsor and host conferences and events to attract attention from patients and healthcare professionals. These events may include presentations by keynote speakers or educational sessions. They also provide networking opportunities for companies to meet potential customers.
4. *Sales Representatives*: Pharma companies might employ sales representatives to attract the attention of healthcare professionals. They visit hospitals and clinics to inform HCPs and patients about their products.
5. *Patient Education*: Pharma companies might prioritize patient education to attract attention. This could include creating educational materials and support programs that give detailed information on specific disease treatments to help patients better understand their options.

Recently, attention-grabbing strategies in pharmaceutical advertising have been under increased scrutiny. These techniques could be misleading or manipulative, leading to inappropriate or overuse of certain drugs. As a result, there is much debate over the proper use of attention-grabbing techniques in pharma marketing. It also raises questions about balancing marketing needs and responsible, ethical promotion of drugs and treatments.

Attitudinal Research

Attitudinal market research attempts to understand customers' attitudes and opinions about a product or service. It can be used to gain insight into HCPs' and patients' perceptions of drugs or medical devices and provide feedback on marketing communications. Here are some examples of how some pharmaceutical companies have used attitudinal research:

1. *Bayer's Xarelto*: Bayer conducted attitudinal studies to understand better the attitudes of patients and healthcare providers towards its anticoagulant drug, Xarelto (Rivaroxaban).
2. *Sanofi's Toujeo*: Sanofi conducted more attitudinal research to understand the preferences and needs of diabetic patients better. Patients wanted a long-lasting treatment option for blood sugar control. As a result, Sanofi developed Toujeo, an insulin product that delivers insulin glargine conveniently and efficiently.
3. *Novartis' Cosentyx*: Novartis conducted attitudinal studies to understand better the attitudes of patients and healthcare providers towards its psoriasis drug Cosentyx (Secukinumab). The study revealed that patients wanted clear skin and a better quality of life. This led Novartis to highlighting these benefits in its marketing messaging.
4. *Roche's Ocrevus*: Roche did attitudinal research to understand better the attitudes of patients and healthcare providers towards its multiple sclerosis drug Ocrevus (Ocrelizumab). Roche identified that patients wanted a long-term treatment that provided safety and efficacy benefits. This led Roche to emphasize these benefits in its marketing messaging.

These examples show how attitudinal research provides valuable insights into customer perceptions, preferences, and needs that pharmaceutical marketers can use to create marketing and communication strategies that resonate, and improve business results.

Attitudinal Scaling

Attitudinal scaling is a technique commonly employed in pharmaceutical marketing to gauge the attitudes of healthcare professionals or patients toward a drug or treatment. Attitudinal scaling involves collecting data on various attitudes, opinions, beliefs, and perceptions related to the medication or treatment in question and then using this data to create an overall scale representing their collective opinion or attitude towards it.

Pharma marketing may employ several types of attitude scales, such as:

1. *Likert Scales*: Likert scales are a widely used attitudinal tool in pharmaceutical marketing. On these scales, respondents rate their agreement or disagreement with various statements about the drug or treatment they are considering. For example, Pfizer, one of the world's largest pharmaceutical companies, utilized this scale to assess healthcare professionals' attitudes toward certain products, such as its COVID-19 vaccine.
2. *Semantic Differential Scales*: Semantic differential scales allow respondents to rate their opinion of a drug or treatment based on several bipolar adjectives, such as effective-ineffective or safe-unsafe.
3. *Visual Analogue Scales*: Visual analog scales use a line or bar with endpoints representing opposing attitudes, such as very good or bad. Respondents are asked to mark their responses on the line or bar to express their opinion of a drug or treatment. For example, an international pharmaceutical major, Roche, used Visual Analogue Scales to measure patient satisfaction with cancer treatments.
4. *Ranking Scales*: Ranking scales require respondents to rank various items or attributes related to a drug or treatment in order of importance or preference.

Once data has been collected using attitudinal scaling techniques, it can be analyzed to gauge the overall attitude of your target audience towards a drug or treatment. This insight can inform marketing strategies, such as tailoring messaging to address specific concerns or misconceptions or emphasizing its positive attributes.

It is important to remember that attitudinal scaling is just one tool used in pharmaceutical marketing research. It often works with other quantitative and qualitative techniques to gain a comprehensive insight into the attitudes and behaviors of your target market.

Attitudinal Surveys

Attitudinal surveys are market research studies that measure people's attitudes and beliefs toward products or services. Attitudinal surveys can be an extremely valuable asset for pharmaceutical marketing as they allow pharmaceutical marketers to assess patients' and healthcare professionals' views of drugs or medical devices; the information gained can then be utilized as the foundation of marketing or communication strategies and plans. Here are just a few ways attitudinal surveys can benefit pharma marketers:

A. Pharmaceutical companies might conduct an attitudinal study to gain insight into patients' perceptions of specific medications. Such surveys could include questions regarding experiences related to conditions treated, clinician expectations, willingness to test it, etc.

B. Pharmaceutical companies seeking insight into healthcare provider perceptions about certain drugs' potential benefits and risks may conduct an attitudinal study with healthcare providers to gain more information regarding side effects, interactions, or the influence on patient outcomes. For example, such surveys could ask about side effects and possible adverse reactions affecting outcomes for patient treatment plans.

Conducting Attitudinal Studies

Here are the basic steps to conduct attitudinal studies in pharmaceutical marketing:

- Define your research goals.
- Construct a survey questionnaire.
- Recruit survey participants.
- Analyze and accumulate survey data.

After survey data has been analyzed and collected, it can be used to refine or create marketing and communication strategies.

Attribute Positioning

Attribute positioning refers to a marketing strategy emphasizing certain attributes about a product or service that differentiate it from competitors, for instance, in medical device or drug marketing campaigns. Pharmaceutical companies commonly utilize attribute positioning strategies in their advertising strategies by emphasizing specific features of medical devices or drugs as opposed to generic options; here are a few examples from pharmaceutical marketing campaigns using attribute positioning:

1. *Lyrica by Pfizer*: Pfizer has widely promoted Lyrica (Pregabalin) as a prescription medication to relieve nerve pain related to diabetic neuropathy, post-herpetic neuralgia, and fibromyalgia. Lyrica's main characteristic is relieving nerve discomfort highlighted in its marketing messaging; furthermore, it boasts low potential risks of abuse or dependence and safe usage with few side effects.

2. *Symbicort by AstraZeneca*: Symbicort (Budesonide and Formoterol) is an inhaler by AstraZeneca for treating asthma and chronic obstructive pulmonary disease (COPD). Symbicort's distinguishing feature lies in its rapid relieving capabilities that quickly relieve asthma symptoms while providing long-term control, as AstraZeneca emphasizes in their marketing messaging; Symbicort as being both an affordable and effective treatment option is highlighted prominently in AstraZeneca's marketing materials.
3. *Medtronic Insulin Pumps*: Medtronic insulin pumps offer an easy, precise alternative to multiple injections with their convenient dose delivery feature, saving enough time each day without multiple visits for administering precise doses via these convenient pumps.

Attribution Modeling

'Attribution Modeling' in pharmaceutical marketing is like putting together puzzle pieces. It involves assessing the impact of various marketing touchpoints on a customer's journey and determining which channels or activities contribute most to a desired outcome, such as the sale or a prescription.

In the pharmaceutical industry, where the customer journey can be complex and involve multiple touchpoints, attribution modeling becomes crucial. It helps marketers allocate resources effectively, optimize campaigns, and understand the overall impact of their marketing efforts.

There are several attribution models, each with its own approach to assigning value to touchpoints. Some common models include:

1. *Last Touch Attribution*: This gives all the credit to the last interaction before a conversion. It is simple but might not reflect the entire customer journey.
2. *First Touch Attribution*: This attributes the conversion to the first interaction in the customer journey. Again, it oversimplifies the process but can be insightful.
3. *Linear Attribution*: This model distributes credit equally across all touchpoints in the customer journey. It is more balanced but does not account for the varying impact of interactions.
4. *Time Decay Attribution*: It gives more credit to touchpoints closer to the conversion. This recognizes that interactions closer in time to the outcome might be more influential.
5. *Algorithmic Attribution*: Using machine learning algorithms, this model considers various factors to dynamically assign credit based on the historical performance of touchpoints.

In pharma marketing, a combination of these models or a custom model tailored to the specificities of the industry might be necessary. For instance, interactions with healthcare professionals, online information searches, and patient testimonials could all be part of the customer journey, and attributing value to each touchpoint accurately is essential.

Remember, attribution modeling is an ongoing process. As consumer behavior evolves and new channels emerge, adapting the attribution model ensures it stays relevant and effective in guiding marketing strategies.

Implications for Pharma Marketing

Attribution modeling in pharmaceutical marketing is crucial for several reasons, and its implications are far-reaching:

1. *Optimizing Marketing Budgets*: By understanding which marketing channels and activities contribute most to desired outcomes, pharma companies can allocate their budgets more effectively. This ensures that resources are directed towards strategies with a higher impact, improving overall ROI.
2. *Improving Campaign Effectiveness*: Attribution modeling helps identify the most effective touchpoints in the customer journey. This insight allows marketers to optimize campaigns in real time, focusing on elements that resonate with the audience and drive desired actions.
3. *Enhancing Customer Experience*: Understanding the customer journey through attribution modeling allows pharma marketers to tailor their messaging and engagement strategies. This personalization improves the overall customer experience, fostering stronger relationships and loyalty.
4. *Data-Driven Decision Making*: Attribution modeling relies on data analysis and insights. This data-driven approach enables marketers to make informed decisions based on actual performance metrics rather than assumptions. It promotes a culture of continuous improvement and adaptability.
5. *Patient Engagement*: In pharma marketing, patient education and engagement are critical. Attribution modeling helps identify touchpoints where patients seek information, enabling marketers to develop targeted educational campaigns and support programs.

6. *Compliance and Regulation*: The pharmaceutical industry operates within a highly regulated environment. Attribution modeling can help ensure marketing activities comply with regulatory standards by providing transparency into how marketing efforts influence customer behavior.
7. *Long-Term Strategic Planning*: Understanding the customer journey over the long term is essential for strategic planning. Attribution modeling provides insights into trends and patterns, helping pharma companies adapt their long-term strategies to changing market dynamics.
8. *Cross-Channel Coordination*: Pharma marketing often involves multiple channels, including online and offline platforms. Attribution modeling facilitates coordination across these channels, ensuring a cohesive and integrated marketing approach.

Despite these benefits, it is important to acknowledge the challenges associated with attribution modeling in pharma marketing, such as the complexity of the customer journey, data privacy concerns, and the need for accurate and reliable data. Overcoming these challenges requires a thoughtful and strategic approach to attribution modeling implementation.

Finally, attribution modeling is not just a tool for tracking marketing effectiveness; it is a strategic imperative for pharma companies looking to navigate the industry's complexities, engage effectively with healthcare professionals and patients, and deliver positive health outcomes.

Audience

Audience in pharmaceutical marketing refers to the target group that pharmaceutical companies reach with their advertising messages and promotional campaigns, for instance, healthcare professionals like pharmacists, doctors, nurses, and patients and caregivers.

Pharma companies segment customers based on various criteria, including demographics, geographical location, medical specializations, and disease areas. With this data, pharmaceutical firms can determine prescribing behaviors and treatment preferences, creating more efficient marketing strategies by pinpointing their target market.

Hierarchy of Audience

The following structure may help organize the pharma marketing audience hierarchy:

1. *Healthcare Practitioners (HCPs)*: HCPs include doctors, nurses, pharmacists, and other licensed healthcare providers tasked with prescribing or dispensing pharmaceutical products directly to patients — making this group the primary audience for pharmaceutical marketing efforts.
2. *Key Opinion leaders (KOLs)*: These influential HCPs are recognized as experts in their fields and are frequently sought for their advice and recommendations. In addition, KOLs have a significant impact on the prescribing behavior of their peers and are, therefore, an important audience for pharma companies.
3. *Patients*: While patients may not be the primary target audience of pharma marketing campaigns, they are increasingly important thanks to direct-to-consumer advertising (DTCA) and increasing patient-centric healthcare. Patients are the end-users and can influence HCP prescribing decisions through advocacy and research.
4. *Payers*: These are insurance companies, government agencies, or other organizations that pay for products and services in healthcare. As healthcare becomes more value-based, payers become increasingly influential in pharma marketing. Products are evaluated on their cost-effectiveness and outcomes.
5. *Regulators*: Regulatory bodies like the FDA play an important role in approving and overseeing pharmaceutical products. Although they are not often seen as a marketing audience for pharmaceutical companies, they must maintain positive relationships with regulators to ensure compliance with regulations to bring their products to market.

Audience Engagement Strategy

These are some strategies that pharma companies could use to effectively reach each audience within the hierarchy.

1. Healthcare Professionals

- *Conferences and Meetings*: Pharma companies may sponsor medical conferences and meetings. This allows them to meet with HCPs, share product information, and establish relationships with top opinion leaders.
- *Direct mail and Email Campaigns*: Pharma companies can use targeted direct mail or email campaigns to send information to HCPs about their products and services.
- *Sales Representatives*: Pharma companies employ representatives who will visit HCPs to give information and answer questions about their products.

2. Key opinion leaders

Partnerships with Thought Leaders: Pharma companies may form partnerships with KOLs to collaborate on research and development, fund research, or support their educational endeavors.

- *Advisory Boards*: Pharma companies can create advisory boards consisting of KOLs. These boards can help with product development, clinical trials, and marketing strategies.
- *Speaker Programs*: Pharma companies may invite KOLs for talks at events or conferences to share their knowledge and insight on relevant topics.

3. Patients

- *DTC advertising*: Pharma companies may use DTC marketing to reach patients directly with information about products and benefits.
- *Patient Education*: Pharma companies often produce patient education materials like videos and brochures to inform patients of diseases, treatment options, and benefits offered by their products. These educational pieces may serve as valuable learning resources.
- *Patient Support Programs*: Pharma companies may provide assistance programs, including helplines, online communities, and financial aid packages, to make accessing products simpler for patients.

4. Payers

- *Outcomes Data*: Pharma companies can use outcomes data to show the value of their products to justify their costs to payers.
- *Health Economics Research and Outcomes (HEOR)*: Pharma companies can do HEOR studies to evaluate their products' clinical and economic impact. This can help to guide reimbursement decisions.
- *Value-based Agreements*: Pharma companies can enter into value-based deals with payers that tie their product prices to patient outcomes.

5. Regulators

- *Compliance*: Pharma companies must ensure their products and marketing materials meet regulatory requirements.
- *Transparency*: Pharma companies must be transparent with regulators and provide complete and accurate information about their products.
- *Early Engagement*: Pharma companies can interact with regulators at an early stage of development to better understand their needs and ensure that their products comply with regulatory standards.

Audience Fatigue

Audience fatigue in pharmaceutical marketing refers to the phenomenon where healthcare professionals (HCPs) become overwhelmed or disengaged from the vast amount of promotional materials sent out by pharmaceutical companies. This may lead them to ignore or disregard these materials or opt out of further communications altogether.

Pharma marketers must be aware of audience fatigue and take proactive measures to avoid it. Here are some effective strategies pharma companies can utilize to prevent audience fatigue:

1. *Personalization*: Pharma marketers can improve engagement by tailoring their marketing materials to each HCP's individual needs and interests, decreasing the likelihood of fatigue among HCPs.
2. *Timing*: Pharma marketers must be strategic with the timing and frequency of their communications, avoid sending too many messages quickly, and consider when HCPs may be busy or unavailable.
3. *Relevance*: Marketing materials must be of value and relevance to healthcare practitioners (HCPs) who receive them, providing useful and actionable information to assist their clinical practice.
4. *Multichannel Approach*: Combining different communication channels such as email, social media, and in-person events can help reduce audience fatigue by offering HCPs a more diverse and captivating experience.
5. *Opt-in or Opt-out*: Giving HCPs the option to opt in or opt out of future communications can help reduce audience fatigue, as it puts the control back in their hands.

Pharma marketers must be aware of audience fatigue and take measures to prevent it from maintaining engagement and trust with their target audience. By creating personalized, relevant, and diverse communication strategies with healthcare professionals, they can build stronger connections, resulting in improved patient outcomes.

Audience Profiling

The process of audience profiling is to identify and assess individuals who are likely to show interest in your message or product. You can gain a deeper understanding of your audience by using audience profiling. This includes demographics, psychological characteristics, and communication preferences.

Businesses can more efficiently reach businesses by creating tailored messages and better understanding these demographics. It increases your chances of achieving your objectives, like increased sales, brand recognition, and traffic on your website. It involves collecting information on a particular audience segment, such as demographics, psychographics, and needs, to develop targeted campaigns and messages.

Here is how to profile your audience in pharmaceutical marketing. Pharma companies may use patient profiling to identify patients most likely to benefit from their products. The information they gather could include the gender, age and ethnicity, treatment history, and symptoms of patients with a certain medical condition. Then, the data collected can be used to create targeted messages addressing these patients' specific needs and issues.

Audience Profiling in Pharma

1. *Patient Profiling*: Pharmaceutical companies may employ audience profiling to target products to those most likely to benefit. Information such as the age, gender, and ethnicity of those affected by certain medical conditions and treatment histories, symptoms, and preferences might all be used to target messaging for each patient individually. This data allows companies to tailor messaging that addresses these patients' issues and needs directly.
2. *Profiling Physicians*: Pharma companies might use audience profiling to create profiles of the most likely healthcare professionals to prescribe their products. They might gather information about the practice setting, patient volume, prescribing patterns, and specialty of doctors who treat a specific medical condition. These data can be used to create tailored messaging that addresses the needs and preferences of these doctors.
3. *Payer Profiling*: Pharma companies often utilize audience profiling techniques to develop detailed profiles of payers (i.e., insurance companies) likely to cover their products. Information such as insurance policies, formularies, and reimbursement policies used by payers that cover particular medical conditions are collected to create targeted messaging that addresses the concerns and needs of these payers.

Pharma companies can use audience profiling to understand their customers better and create successful marketing strategies. For example, pharmaceutical companies can create targeted messaging that addresses customers' needs and desires by collecting information about their demographics, psychographics, preferences, and needs.

Audience Research

Pharmaceutical marketing is based on audience research. This helps companies better understand their target audience and develop more effective marketing strategies. Audience research gathers information about a segment, such as demographics and psychographics. It also involves understanding their needs and preferences. Here are some examples of audience research that might be used in pharma marketing:

1. *Research with Patients*: Pharma companies often conduct patient research to gain a more in-depth knowledge of those most likely to benefit from their products, which could include gathering information on gender, age, income, ethnicity, education level, and treatment history among their target group of individuals with specific medical conditions. Pharmaceutical firms use patient research in this way to create messaging tailored specifically for this segment of patients with the aim of better meeting their needs and preferences.
2. *Physician Research*: Pharmaceutical companies may conduct physician research to gain more insights into the needs and preferences of healthcare professionals (HCPs) likely to prescribe their products through data collection on physicians' prescribing patterns or practice settings for certain medical conditions. Through such investigations, pharmaceutical companies may tailor their messaging to physicians' demands and desires.
3. *Payer Research*: Pharma companies may conduct payer research to understand better the needs and preferences of insurance companies that are likely to pay for their products. This could include gathering information about the plans, formularies, and reimbursement policies that payers use to cover a particular medical condition. In addition, pharmaceutical companies can use payer research to help them tailor their messaging to address the concerns and issues of these payers.

Pharma companies can use audience research to create messaging that addresses their customer's needs and wants, resulting in campaigns with higher success rates.

Augmentation

Augmentation in the pharmaceutical industry refers to any effort to enhance or improve various aspects of pharmaceutical products, processes, or services by making changes or additions that produce better outcomes or meet specific needs. It may involve making structural modifications as part of this effort as well.

Augmentation can take different forms in the pharmaceutical industry, including the following:

1. *Product Augmentation*: Enhancing pharmaceutical products by introducing new features, formulations, or technologies. This could involve developing new dosage forms, improving drug delivery systems, or combining multiple drugs into a single product for improved efficacy.
2. *Process Augmentation*: Optimizing manufacturing processes to increase efficiency, reduce costs, or improve quality. This may involve adopting advanced automation technologies, implementing lean manufacturing principles, or introducing innovative process controls.
3. *Technology Augmentation*: Leveraging new technologies to enhance various aspects of pharmaceutical research, development, manufacturing, or distribution. Examples include using artificial intelligence (AI) and machine learning algorithms for drug discovery, implementing digital solutions for supply chain management, or employing advanced analytics for pharmacovigilance.
4. *Service Augmentation*: Providing additional services or support to healthcare professionals, patients, or other stakeholders, in the pharmaceutical ecosystem. This could include offering educational resources, patient adherence programs, remote monitoring solutions, or personalized healthcare services.
5. *Regulatory Augmentation*: Implementing regulatory frameworks and standards changes to improve drug safety, streamline approval processes, or facilitate innovation. Implementation may include adopting new guidelines, harmonizing regulations across regions, or taking risk-based approaches to regulatory oversight.

Augmentation within the pharmaceutical industry seeks to drive innovation, enhance patient outcomes and elevate overall product and service value. Through adopting cutting-edge technologies and processes while meeting unmet needs and meeting patient and healthcare professional demands more effectively, augmentation plays an essential role in providing healthcare advancement that keeps up with evolving expectations and demands.

Augmented Intelligence

Augmented Intelligence refers to integrating Artificial Intelligence (AI) technologies and human intelligence to enhance decision-making abilities and is sometimes known as Intelligence Augmentation (IA). Augmented intelligence strives to foster an idealized partnership between humans and machines, in which humans provide context, insight, and critical thought. In contrast, machines perform data processing, pattern recognition, and predictive capabilities.

Augmented intelligence (AI) seeks to enhance human productivity and decision-making rather than replace humans with machines through machine learning, natural language processing, and data analytics tools which assist humans with processing large volumes of data more efficiently and making more informed choices based on that analysis. To this end, artificial intelligence tools like machine learning techniques or natural language processing facilitate more effective human analysis while aiding more informed choices made from that analysis.

Augmented intelligence applications range from chatbots that assist customer service reps, data analysis tools that offer business insight, and virtual assistants that offer tailored recommendations based on user behavior to virtual assistants that offer tailored user recommendations based on AI technology integration with human intelligence — revolutionizing multiple industries such as healthcare, finance and education alike.

Augmented Intelligence in Pharma Marketing

Augmented intelligence holds great promise as a game-changing innovation in pharmaceutical marketing by providing insights and recommendations derived from data analysis that allow more personalized and targeted messages to healthcare providers and patients alike. Here are a few ways augmented intelligence is revolutionizing pharma marketing:

1. *Augmented intelligence* provides tailored messaging by assessing patient medical histories, demographics, and other pertinent factors to provide more tailored messaging for every individual customer. For instance, pharmaceutical companies might employ AI-enhanced software to evaluate each patient's

medical records to ascertain which medications might work for their specific condition— leading to more targeted marketing messages that resonate more strongly.

2. *Predictive Analytics*: Augmented intelligence allows pharma companies to identify market opportunities by using prescribing patterns and patient behavior data analysis to predict which drugs may become popular prescription choices shortly. By employing predictive analytics on prescribing patterns and patient data analytics, they could identify new market niches and predict new trends that would emerge later. For instance, companies might utilize augmented intelligence technology for market analyses of which prescriptions might become most prescribed over time.
3. *Digital Marketing*: Augmented intelligence can assist pharmaceutical companies with optimizing their digital marketing campaigns by analyzing user behavior and preferences data from social media or forums to determine which messaging resonates most effectively with patients and healthcare providers.
4. *Recruitment of Clinical Trial Participants*: Augmented intelligence can assist pharmaceutical companies in recruiting potential clinical trial participants more quickly and efficiently by analyzing patient demographics, medical history, and other factors contributing to patient recruitment for clinical studies. This allows more efficient recruitment efforts.

Augmented intelligence offers pharmaceutical companies new insights into their target audiences and more effective marketing strategies. These firms can deliver more tailored messaging directly to patients and healthcare providers by employing data analytics and machine learning technology.

Augmented Reality (AR)

Augmented Reality (AR) refers to a technology that superimposes computer-generated images or videos over real-world environments— for instance, images, videos, and 3D models. AR devices like smartphones or tablets typically support augmented reality experiences due to sensors and cameras used for tracking environments around them.

AR technology creates a greater relationship between users and their environments. It allows pharma companies to use AR to offer customers engaging experiences that allow them to learn about products and services better. Here are a few key ways they are utilizing AR for marketing efforts:

1. *Augmented Reality (AR) and Product Visualization*: Customers can view 3D visuals from products on their smartphones or tablets. This gives them an immersive experience that is impossible with traditional marketing materials. Likewise, customers can interact with products which is not possible with traditional marketing materials.
2. *Education*: AR can be used to create interactive educational materials for healthcare providers that simplify complex medical concepts.
3. *Training*: AR can provide immersive training experiences to healthcare providers. They can practice procedures and techniques in a virtual environment without surgical assistance.
4. *Marketing Campaigns*: Pharma marketers can use AR to create engaging and persuasive campaigns that increase brand awareness and customer loyalty and drive sales.
5. *Patient Engagement*: AR technology can also engage patients.

How Pharma Uses AR

The following are just a few examples of AR used by pharmaceutical companies in marketing campaigns:

1. Pfizer Developed an AR app called *RANarRAtive*, specifically designed for patients with rheumatoid arthritis (RA). AR technology allows users to see and learn about RA's effects and track their progress.
2. Merck developed an AR/VR (Virtual Reality) campaign called *MS Inside Out* to raise awareness about multiple sclerosis and its impact on patients. An AR book was created with interactive visuals and animations to educate the public about MS. A Virtual Reality (VR) experience allowed users to explore the brain and learn more about this degenerative condition.
3. Bayer created the *Xray Vision AR App* for surgeons to prepare for knee replacement surgery. AR technology allows surgeons to see and practice knee joint replacement surgery independently before performing it on patients.
4. Sanofi has recently launched an AR marketing campaign for their allergy product, Nasacort (Triamcinolone). The AR game lets users interact with virtual pollen particles to learn more about the product's advantages.

Augmented Reality (AR), a powerful tool for marketers, can create immersive customer experiences that will increase brand awareness and customer loyalty and improve patient outcomes. AR technology offers many possibilities to create these kinds of customer experiences.

Authorized Generics

Authorized generic drugs are produced and distributed by brand-name pharmaceutical companies under their generic labels, offering identical ingredients, dosage form strength, quality standards, manufacturing processes but priced lower as they do not carry brand labels or marketing expenses associated with brand label drugs.

Brand-name companies may authorize other companies to launch generics under their names. These authorized generics include any generic version of brand-name drugs produced and marketed under license from either a brand-name manufacturer or third-party manufacturer with permission from said brand-name manufacturer – hence their moniker as authorized generics.

Authorized generics typically enter the market when their brand-name counterpart's patent is set to lapse as their manufacturer attempts to capture market share from other generic makers and prevent any significant market disruption from them.

Authorized generics offer cost-cutting alternatives for consumers but can also have anticompetitive ramifications. For instance, introducing an authorized generic could reduce incentives for other generic manufacturers to enter the market as they face tough competition from their brand-name company's authorized generic. This may ultimately limit competition and drive prices up for all customers.

Also, brand-name companies introduce an authorized generic to slow the entry of other generic manufacturers into the market and extend their monopoly, restricting consumer choices while driving up prices.

Not all brand-name companies opt to launch authorized generic versions; some prefer relying on brand recognition and patent protection to maintain market exclusivity and high product prices. Therefore, whether a generic version will be authorized depends solely on each brand-name company's business strategy and market dynamics.

Authorized generics offer cost-cutting alternatives for consumers; however, their introduction can have anticompetitive impacts; regulatory bodies must monitor these practices carefully to promote competition while safeguarding consumers interests.

Awareness

According to the dictionary, awareness is simply being aware or informed about something. Therefore, awareness is essential to pharmaceutical marketing success. Patients, healthcare providers, and other stakeholders must accurately understand a drug or medical device's benefits and potential uses for sales figures, market shares, and patient outcomes to increase accordingly. Increased awareness can result in higher sales figures, greater market shares, and better patient outcomes.

Here are the essential steps necessary for reaching and raising awareness among your target audiences, be they patients, healthcare professionals, or any other stakeholder group:

1. *Establish Your Target Audience*: As a first step, one should establish who will benefit most from your drug/device, whether patients, healthcare professionals, or investors. For instance, pharmaceutical companies could market breast cancer drugs directly to oncologists and individuals living with breast cancer.
2. *An Effective Message Is Necessary*: After identifying your target audience, the next step should be crafting an impactful message about the benefits of your drug's usage – one which should be easy for potential recipients to comprehend, perhaps emphasizing its safety and efficacy for women diagnosed with breast cancer, for example.
3. *Multichannel Reach*: Use multiple channels, including medical journals, conferences, and social media. Collaborations with patient advocacy groups helps you to reach your target audience.
4. *Increase Awareness Through Educational Materials*: Offering educational materials such as patient brochures, videos, and online resources to patients and healthcare providers is another way to increase awareness about your product or service.
5. *Monitor and Measure Awareness*: It is crucial to monitor and measure the success of a marketing campaign. This can be done through surveys or social media metrics.

Pharma companies have developed strategies to increase product awareness and improve business results. Here are some examples of awareness campaigns that pharma companies have conducted:

1. Pfizer launched a marketing campaign to promote their cholesterol-lowering drug Lipitor (Atorvastatin). This included medical journal advertisements, medical conference

participation, direct-to-consumer advertising (DTCA), television, and educational materials for patients and healthcare professionals.

2. Eli Lilly's marketing campaign to raise awareness for Trulicity (Dulaglutide), its diabetes drug, was focused on education and participation in medical journal advertising and conferences. As a result, Trulicity was made more familiar to healthcare professionals (HCPs), increasing sales.
3. Roche's marketing campaign to raise awareness for Herceptin (Trastuzumab), a breast cancer drug, involved collaboration with patient advocacy groups and providing educational materials to patients. This increased brand recognition and sales significantly.

Awareness-Trial-Reinforcement Process

The Awareness-Trial-Reinforcement (ATR) process, also known as Ehrenberg's Process, is a marketing framework created by marketing scientist Andrew Ehrenberg. Pharmaceutical marketing often employs it to help companies build brand loyalty and boost sales. The ATR process consists of three phases:

1. *Awareness*: The initial step of the ATR process is creating brand awareness among potential customers. This involves cultivating a strong brand identity and communicating its unique value proposition through advertising, public relations, and other marketing channels. In addition, the objective is to foster an emotional connection between the brand and whatever medical condition it treats and the benefits it provides.
2. *Trial*: The second stage of the ATR process is to entice customers to try the brand. This could involve offering free samples, patient education materials, or other incentives to incentivize people to try the brand. Again, the goal is to demonstrate its effectiveness and persuade people to switch from their current medication or treatment to this brand.
3. *Reinforcement*: The final stage of the ATR process ensures that customers feel supported and educated about using the brand, providing them with ongoing support, education, and resources to help them stay engaged with it and achieve optimal results. This step aims to foster customer loyalty and promote repeat purchases.

The ATR process is an effective tool for cultivating brand loyalty and increasing sales in pharmaceutical marketing. Pharma companies can foster long-lasting customer relationships by crafting a strong brand identity, offering incentives to encourage trials, and providing ongoing support and resources.

B

1. Balanced Score Card
2. Balance Sheet
3. Banner Ads
4. Banner Blindness
5. Barcelona Principles
6. Barriers to Entry
7. Bayesian Theorem
8. BCG Matrix
9. Beaconing
10. Benchmarking
11. Benefit Positioning
12. Benefit Segmentation
13. Best Practices
14. Big Data
15. Big Tech
16. Billboard
17. Bioavailability
18. Bioengineering
19. Bioequivalence
20. Bioinformatics
21. Biologic Licence Application (BLA)
22. Biologicals
23. Biometrics
24. Bionsensors
25. Biosimilars
26. Biotechnology
27. Biotech
28. Bipolar Scale
29. Bivariate Data
30. Bivariate Analysis
31. Blanket Coverage
32. Blitzkrieg Advertising
33. Blockbuster
34. Blockchain
35. Blog
36. Body Language
37. Boomerang Effect
38. Bounce Rate
39. Bradford Hill Guidelines
40. Brand
41. Brand Advocacy
42. Brand Advocates
43. Brand Ambassador
44. Brand Archetypes
45. Brand Architecture
46. Brand Assets
47. Brand Associations
48. Brand Audit
49. Brand Awareness Metrics
50. Brand Book
51. Brand Building
52. Brand Cannibalization
53. Brand Character
54. Brand Collaboration
55. Brand Communications
56. Brand Community
57. Brand Differentiation
58. Branding Effectiveness
59. Brand Environment
60. Brand Equity
61. Brand Essence
62. Brand Evangelism
63. Brand Evangelists
64. Brand Experience
65. Brand Extension
66. Brand Financials
67. Brand Focus
68. Brand Habits
69. Branding & Hierarchy of Needs
70. Brand Identity
71. Brand Image
72. Brand Integrity

73. Brand Interactive
74. Brand Journalism
75. Brand Loyalty
76. Brand Makeover
77. Brand Management
78. Brand Manager
79. Brand Mapping
80. Brand Marks
81. Brand Meaning
82. Brand Metrics
83. Brand Mindset
84. Brand Mission
85. Brand Morphology
86. Brand Name
87. Brand Outreach
88. Brand Performance Metrics
89. Brand Performance Review
90. Brand Persona
91. Brand Personality
92. Brand Planning
93. Brand Plan
94. Brand Plan in the Digital Age
95. Brand Portfolio
96. Brand Positioning
97. Brand Positioning in the Digital Age
98. Brand Positioning Statement
99. Brand Presence
100. Brand Profile
101. Brand Presentation
102. Brand Profitability
103. Brand Profitability Metrics
104. Brand Promise
105. Brand Psychology
106. Brand Purpose
107. Brand Rationalization
108. Brand Reinforcement
109. Brand Relevance
110. Brand Reputation
111. Brand Reputation Management
112. Brand Resilience
113. Brand Review
114. Brand Revitalization
115. Brand Salience
116. Brand Scape
117. Brand Scope
118. Brand Sense
119. Brand Sentiment
120. Brand's Share of Voice (SOV)
121. Brand Story
122. Brand Strategy
123. Brand Sustainability
124. Brand Switching
125. Brand Touchpoints
126. Brand Tracking
127. Brand Values
128. Brand Value
129. Brand Value Added (BVA)
130. Brand Value
131. Brand Valuation Measures
132. Brand Valuation Metrics
133. Brand Value Proposition
134. Brand Vision
135. Brand Voice
136. Brand Pyramid
137. Breakeven Analysis
138. Bribery
139. Business-to-Business (B2B) Model
140. Business-to-Consumer (B2C) Model
141. Built-in Obsolescence
142. Bundling
143. Business Case
144. Business Ecology
145. Business Ethics
146. Business Model Canvas
147. Business Plan
148. Business Presentation
149. Burst Campaign
150. Buyer Behavior
151. Buzz

Balanced Score Card

Dr. Robert Kaplan and David Norton developed the Balanced Scorecard in the early 1990s to help organizations monitor and measure their performance from different angles. For example, the pharmaceutical industry uses a balanced scorecard to monitor marketing efforts and ensure they align with organizational goals.

A balanced scorecard usually includes four perspectives: customer, financial, internal business processes, and learning and development.

1. *The Financial Perspective* measures marketing initiatives' financial success by measuring revenue, return on investment (ROI), market share, and revenue. This method ensures that all initiatives are financially viable and contribute to organizational success.
2. *The Customer Perspective* focuses on the customer's needs and preferences, using metrics like customer satisfaction, retention rates, and loyalty. This approach ensures that marketing initiatives address these needs and create customer value.
3. *The Internal Business Processes Perspective* looks at the marketing systems and processes, measuring metrics like time to market, success rates with product launches, and campaign efficiency. This ensures that marketing initiatives can be implemented efficiently and effectively.
4. *The Learning and Growth Perspective* is focused on developing the marketing team and organization, measuring employee satisfaction and retention rates, and creating new marketing initiatives. This approach ensures that marketing staff continually improves existing programs and creates new ones to contribute to overall organizational success.

The Balanced Scorecard is a powerful tool for organizations to create performance measures that align with their vision and mission. These are used to monitor progress and make strategic decisions. The Balanced Score Card provides a comprehensive view of an organization's performance and ensures that all areas work towards the same goals.

Balance Sheet

The balance sheet, a vital financial document, summarizes the company's assets and liabilities. This statement is used in pharmaceutical marketing to monitor a company's financial health and evaluate its ability to meet obligations.

A. Assets

Assets are all a company's resources that have economic value and can produce future benefits. Pharmaceutical companies generally own several categories of assets:

1. *Intellectual Property*, for instance includes trademarks, patents, copyrights, and trade secrets. These assets protect a company's innovations by giving them exclusive access to the use of and licensing them.
2. *Manufacturing Facilities* are physical assets for manufacturing drug products, such as equipment and plants.
3. *Research and Development*: All assets used in research and development, such as lab equipment, experimental drugs, and research data, are included.
4. *Inventory* is the finished goods, raw materials, and work-in-progress a company has for sale or use during manufacturing.
5. *Property, Plant, and Equipment*: To support business operations, companies own and use physical structures like buildings and equipment for operations and investments in other companies, such as joint ventures, or financial instruments like stocks or bonds.
6. *Goodwill* is an intangible asset. It represents the value of its reputation, customer relationships, and goodwill.

The assets of a pharmaceutical firm include physical assets, intellectual properties, and intangible resources essential for its success in developing and marketing new drugs.

B. Liabilities

The following are the categories of liabilities in a pharmaceutical company:

1. *Long-Term Debt*: All outstanding long-term obligations due in the next 12 months, such as bonds or loans, can be classified as long-term debt. Accounts Payable is any unpaid monies owed to suppliers from goods and services received that remain outstanding on the invoice.
2. *Accrued Expenses* are those costs that have been incurred but not yet remitted. These include salaries, wages, rent, and utilities.
3. *Deferred Revenue* is a company's receipt of payments for goods or services yet to be delivered.
4. *Deferred Liabilities*: Deferred liabilities may include legal, warranty, and product liability claims that have yet to be satisfied by a company.

5. *Income Tax Payable*: Income taxes due are called "income tax payable."
6. *Other Liabilities* include obligations not covered by these categories, such as leases, pensions, or deferred compensation.

A pharmaceutical company's short-term and long-term liabilities are due to its complex financial structure and regulatory requirements.

C. Equity

Equity refers to the ownership interest in a company its shareholders own. There are many ways to break down equity, including:

1. *Common Stock* is the most basic type of equity within a company. Common stockholders can vote and receive dividends if the company so declares.
2. *Preferred Stock* refers to the equity that is treated preferentially over Common Stock. Preferred stockholders may receive fixed dividend payments and be given priority over common stockholders in the event of liquidation or bankruptcy.
3. *Retained Earnings* are the company's cumulative earnings that haven't been distributed as dividends. These profits are instead reinvested in the business to finance future development and growth.
4. *Treasury Stock* is a share of company stock that has been repurchased. Therefore, purchasing Treasury stock will enable you to reduce the total number of outstanding shares while simultaneously increasing their value.

Equity refers to a company's long-term value and ability to generate profit over time. The company's market competition, drug pipelines, and regulatory approvals can impact this value.

Banner Ads

Banner ads, or display ads, are very similar to digital billboards. Banner ads use imagery (hence their name) to attract attention and direct traffic toward an advertiser's website.

Banner ads are an important digital format used in pharmaceutical marketing to reach patients and healthcare professionals online. Here are some examples of pharmaceutical companies using banner ads:

1. *Product Ads* are banner advertisements that promote drugs or medications. They typically feature the name of the drug, its advantages, and a call to action for patients to talk with their healthcare provider.
2. *Disease Awareness Ads* inform the public about a condition, its symptoms, and possible treatment options. These ads do not usually promote any drug or medication.
3. *HCP Education Ad* is a banner ad targeting healthcare providers that advertises educational resources like webinars, medical conferences, or online courses.
4. *A Clinical Trial Ad* is a banner ad designed to draw participants to clinical trials. It details the study's requirements and objectives and how to get involved.
5. *A Branded Patient Support Ad* is a banner advertisement promoting a pharmaceutical company's patient support program. These programs may provide financial aid, education, and other support for those taking medication.

Pharmaceutical marketing falls under stringent regulation by both FDA and other governing bodies and must therefore abide by their requirements regarding compliance with regulations. This could impact the format and content of banner ads in this sector. Pharma marketers must comply with all regulatory requirements and provide accurate product information.

Banner Blindness

Banner blindness refers to the inability to see banner ads on websites due to their repeated and often unrelated placement. This can be a major obstacle in pharma marketing for companies trying to reach their target audience.

Here are some possible causes of banner blindness when it comes to pharmaceutical marketing:

A. *Overexposure to Banner Ads*: People may get used to seeing them and begin ignoring them. Users quickly adapt to sites with many pop-ups or advertisements and don't see them anymore due to conditioning.

B. *Relevance*: An irrelevant banner ad may quickly be ignored by users; an example would be advertising cholesterol-reducing drugs on websites for young adults, where its recipients could easily ignore this message.

C. *Ad-blocking Software*: Many individuals have adopted AdBlocker on their browsers to reduce ads from being shown. This automatically hides or removes banner ads from websites. As a result, pharma companies cannot reach the right audience with traditional banner ads alone.

Pharma companies might benefit from exploring other advertising methods like influencer marketing or sponsored content to reach their target audiences better. Furthermore, companies could create more engaging banner ads tailored to meet the target audience needs and interests.

Barcelona Principles

The Barcelona Principles provide guidelines for measuring success in public relations and communication campaigns. Thirty-three public relations (PR) professionals developed these Principles from 33 countries during an International Association for the Measurement of Communication (AMEC) summit in Barcelona, Spain, in 2010. They serve as an overarching framework for measuring PR effectiveness.

These principles are crucial in pharmaceutical marketing to assess how marketing campaigns affect patients, healthcare providers, and other stakeholders. Here are just a few examples of how the Barcelona Principles can be applied to pharma marketing:

1. *Setting Measurable Goals*: The Barcelona Principles stress the importance of setting measurable goals for communication campaigns. Pharma marketing is about setting goals, such as increasing awareness of a specific disease or improving patient compliance with medication. For example, a pharmaceutical company may aim to raise awareness of rare diseases by a specific percentage in a specified period.
2. *Measuring Outputs and Outcomes*: The Barcelona Principles stress measuring outputs (media mentions and social media shares) and other outcomes (changes to patient behavior, improved health outcomes) for communications campaigns. Pharma marketing often tracks reach (the number of people visiting websites or following social media) and its effect on patient behavior and outcomes. In addition, pharmaceutical companies may measure the impact of patient education campaigns on medication adherence rates.
3. *Use Valid and Trustworthy Metrics*: The Barcelona Principles stress the importance of using reliable and valid metrics to measure the success of communication campaigns. Pharma marketing needs metrics relevant to the objectives and based on sound scientific research methods. For example, when measuring the effectiveness of a campaign, pharmaceutical companies may use data from clinical trials or patient surveys.
4. *Transparency and Replicability in Communications Measurement*: The Barcelona Principles stress the importance of transparency and replication. Pharma marketing companies should be transparent about measuring campaign effectiveness and making results available to all stakeholders. For example, pharmaceutical companies may publish results from patient education campaigns on their website or in a medical journal so that healthcare professionals and other interested parties can access them.

The Barcelona Principles are fundamental to pharmaceutical marketing. They provide a framework for assessing the effectiveness of marketing campaigns for patients, healthcare providers, and other stakeholders. Pharma companies can use these guidelines to ensure that their marketing efforts are based on accurate data and focused on meeting business targets. This will result in more effective and influential campaigns that meet the needs of patients and healthcare providers.

Barriers to Entry

Barriers to entry are conditions that make it expensive or difficult for new businesses or industries to enter a market or industry. Several factors, including economies of scale, high fixed costs, brand recognition, and legal regulations, can create significant hurdles and prevent new businesses from competing effectively against established ones. As a result, monopolies or oligopolies may form where only one or a few firms hold large market shares, limiting competition's advantages such as lower prices, innovation advancement, and decreases competition. Here are the major entry barriers in any given industry, including pharmaceuticals:

1. *High Costs of Entry*: There are many barriers to entry in the pharmaceutical industry. This field is not for everyone. High research and development costs, clinical trials, and regulatory compliance obligations are major deterrents for new entrants.
2. *Complex Regulatory Environment*: The pharmaceutical industry is highly regulated. There are multiple laws and regulations surrounding drug marketing, approval, and sales that can make complying with their requirements complicated and time-consuming, thus requiring specific knowledge and abilities for success.

3. *Patent Protection*: Pharmaceutical companies often depend on patents to protect their intellectual property and recover research and development investment. New entrants may find it difficult to enter the market as they may not have patents or have access to existing patents.
4. *Strong Brand Recognition*: Established pharmaceutical companies have a strong brand reputation, making it a difficult market for newcomers to compete. Healthcare professionals and consumers may trust well-known brands more and will prescribe medications from them.
5. *Distribution Networks*: Pharmaceutical companies rely on large distribution networks to bring their products to the market. Established companies typically form relationships with distributors, making it difficult for newcomers to gain entry.

How can you overcome the entry barriers to enter the pharmaceutical industry? These strategies may help you overcome these barriers:

1. *Industry Knowledge and Expertise*: Being well-informed about the industry, its regulatory environment, and drug development processes is essential. This knowledge can be gained through networking, education, and research to help new entrants overcome any challenges the complex regulatory environment may present.
2. *Compelling Value Proposition*: New players in the market must establish an attractive value proposition that sets them apart from their competition, such as developing innovative marketing strategies, offering unique products or services, or using technology for better customer experiences. This may involve developing creative marketing plans and offering products or services with unique value.
3. *Make Strategic Partnerships*: Partnering with established industry players can help newcomers overcome costs and create intricate distribution channels. In addition, newcomers can benefit from established players' expertise and resources by joining hands to bring their products to the market more efficiently.
4. *Focus on Niche Markets*: For newcomers in an industry, entering can be made simpler by targeting niche market segments where established players are not present. By meeting customers' needs with products and services tailored specifically for them, newcomers may establish themselves as innovators of customer satisfaction and achieve lasting success in business.
5. *Utilize Digital Marketing Effectively*: Small businesses looking to break in can leverage digital marketing to reach customers and expand brand recognition without needing an expensive sales force or extensive distribution networks. Social media, search engine optimization (SEO), and other online promotion forms allow small businesses to connect directly with target markets without incurring extra expenses due to limited distribution channels or large sales force responsibilities.

Bayesian Theorem

Bayes' Theorem is named after the 18th-century British mathematician Thomas Bayes. It is a mathematical formula that calculates conditional probability. Conditional probability measures the likelihood of an outcome occurring based on past outcomes under similar conditions. This allows you to update probabilities or revise theories or predictions (update probabilities) based on new evidence or information.

Conditional probability is an essential concept of probability theory with wide application across disciplines such as statistics, machine learning, and decision-making. It measures the chances of something happening based on other events already happening — helping users calculate how likely an occurrence might be while accounting for extra information available to them.

Put simply, conditional probabilities refer to the likelihood that an event will happen if another event has occurred. Conditional probabilities, for example, measure the likelihood of someone developing diabetes based on their body weight and composition.

Pharma marketing can predict the success of a campaign based on past data, new insights, and other information.

Pharma companies may use the Bayesian Theorem, for example, to predict the likelihood that a marketing campaign will lead to certain prescriptions and sales. They can improve their estimates and make better decisions about marketing budget allocation by incorporating previous data from similar campaigns and new information on customer behavior and market trends.

The Bayesian Theorem is a tool that can be used in pharmaceutical marketing to optimize marketing campaigns and aid drug development and clinical trial design. Pharmaceutical companies can better predict their success rates for clinical trials of drugs by combining data from previous studies on similar drugs and patient populations with information from ongoing trials or real-world evidence.

The Bayesian Theorem, in general, is an indispensable tool for pharmaceutical marketers. It allows them to make informed decisions and improve their campaigns' return on investment (ROI). However, it requires careful analysis of past data, assumptions, and validation with ongoing evidence.

Bayesian Theorem in Pharma Marketing

Here are some examples of how pharmaceutical companies have used the Bayesian Theorem to market their products:

1. Novartis used the Bayesian Theorem 2017 to optimize direct-to-consumer marketing campaigns for Entresto (sacubitril) and Valsartan (valsartan). They analyzed past data from DTC campaigns to gain insights into market trends and customer behavior. This helped improve the efficiency of these campaigns and increased patient interest in Entresto.
2. Pfizer used the Bayesian Theorem 2018 to calculate the likelihood of success for its clinical trials for a rare form of lung cancer treatment. As a result, they improved the trial design and increased success rates by considering previous data on similar drugs, patient populations, and new information about biomarkers, disease progression, and other factors.
3. AstraZeneca used the Bayesian Theorem in 2019 to optimize its marketing campaigns for the diabetes drug Farxiga (Dapagliflozin). AstraZeneca increased campaign effectiveness by analyzing past campaigns and adding new insights about patient behavior and market trends. This helped to boost Farxiga's popularity and patient interest.
4. Roche used the Bayesian Theorem in 2020 to design a clinical study for a new cancer drug. They could optimize the trial design and improve the chance of success by considering previous data on similar drugs, patient populations, and new data about biomarkers.

These examples show how the Bayesian Theorem is applicable across the pharmaceutical industry. As a result, it can be used to optimize marketing campaigns, support clinical trial designs, and make drug development decisions.

BCG Matrix

Boston Consulting Group's (BCG) Product Portfolio Analysis tool has long been employed in pharmaceutical marketing to assess company performance and allocate resources accordingly. First introduced by them in 1970, its popularity has since expanded across various industries and market sectors.

The BCG matrix comprises four categories: Star, Cash Cows, Question Marks, and Dogs. These are determined using market growth and relative market shares, as shown in the figure below.

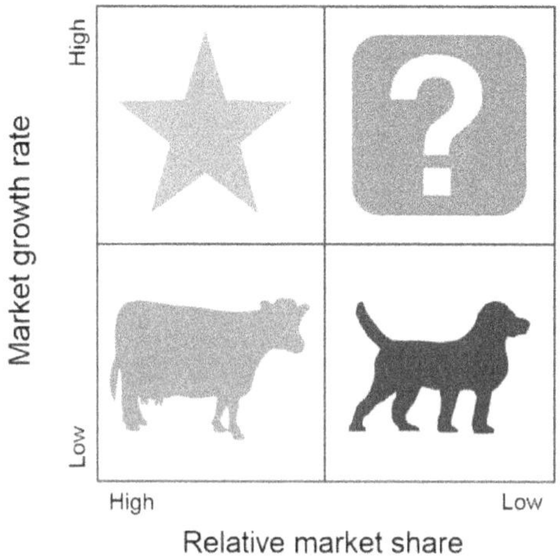

Figure: BCG Matrix

1. *Stars*: These products have high market share and growth rates. They are industry leaders, generating significant revenue for the company.
2. *Cash Cows*: Products with a high market share and slow growth rate generate significant revenue for companies, requiring very little investment.
3. *Question Marks*: These products have low market share but high growth rates. These products have the potential to be stars, but they require substantial investment to achieve this status.
4. *Dogs*: Products with a low market share and growth rates can generate very little revenue. They may need to be discontinued or divested.

Companies can use the BCG matrix to evaluate the performance of their product portfolio and allocate resources accordingly. Stars, for example, require investment to keep their position, while question marks for growth require investment. Cash Cows generate income without investing significant resources, but Dogs can be subject to discontinuation or divestiture.

The BCG matrix provides a framework for strategic decision-making in pharmaceutical marketing. It helps companies to focus on the most profitable products and allocate their resources efficiently.

BCG Matrix in Pharma

Pharma companies use BCG product portfolio analysis for strategic decision-making and to maintain competitiveness.

1. Pfizer has several products with varied market growth rates and relative market shares. For example, Lipitor (Atorvastatin), a cholesterol-lowering drug, enjoyed strong market growth for several years, but its market share began declining as prices decreased and competition intensified. Other products, such as Prevnar (Pneumonia vaccination) and Lyrica (Pregabalin), which treat neuropathic pain, were also successful in growing their market share. Pfizer's BCG matrix analysis allows them to allocate resources to their most promising products or business units.
2. Roche's product folio includes a variety of oncology drugs, each with its market growth rates and relative market share. For instance, the cancer drug Avastin (Bevacizumab) was an outstanding performer; however, its growth has since become stagnant as increased competition and decreased market share have reduced its growth rate and relative market share. By comparison, Perjeta (Pertuzumab), Herceptin (Trastuzumab), and Perjeta experienced rapid expansion with market share gains as quickly as three or more times faster growth than Avastin respectively. As a result, Roche can use BCG analysis to determine the most promising products and business units.
3. Novartis has a variety of products in its portfolio with different market growth rates and market shares. For example, Gilenya (Fingolimod), a drug for multiple sclerosis, experienced high growth, but its market share declined as competition increased. Entresto (Sacubitril and valsartan), and Cosentyx (Secukinumab), also saw high-growth potential. Novartis can use BCG analysis to determine the most promising products and business units.
4. Sanofi has a variety of products in its portfolio with different market growth rates and relative market shares. For example, Lantus, an insulin drug, was a product that had a high market share and high growth for many years. However, prices fell, and competition increased, so its relative market share dropped. Conversely, other high-growth products, like Dupixent (Dupilumab) and Aubagio (Teriflunomide), saw rapid increases in respective share sizes. As a result, Sanofi can use BCG analysis to determine which products and business units will most likely succeed.

Beaconing

Beaconing in pharmaceutical marketing refers to using beacon technology to promote products or services to potential customers or patients. Beacon technology utilizing Bluetooth Low Energy (BLE) signals has become popular within numerous industries — pharmaceutical firms included — to bolster marketing initiatives.

Beacon technology uses small wireless devices known as beacons to transmit messages or notifications directly to mobile phones nearby. Beacons may also be placed strategically within pharmacies, hospitals, clinics, or anywhere they'd benefit most; for instance, in pharma marketing, where beacons may deliver targeted promotions to individuals who opt-in by placing beacons near pharmacies, hospitals, or clinics.

A pharmaceutical company could utilize beacons in pharmacies to send notifications about new product releases, discounts, or educational resources directly to customers who have downloaded its mobile app and opted-in.

Beaconing allows pharmaceutical companies to monitor customer behavior and preferences and deliver customized marketing messages based on customers' interests and needs. By analyzing beacon data, pharmaceutical firms gain invaluable insight into customer preferences that allow them to refine marketing strategies for more successful campaigns and enhance campaign outcomes.

Pharmaceutical marketers must comply with relevant regulations and guidelines related to patient privacy and data protection while implementing beaconing technology to ensure that is ethical and legal.

Beaconing in Pharma Marketing

Here are some examples of pharmaceutical companies using beaconing technology to augment their marketing efforts:

1. Pfizer partnered with the startup Proximiti to implement beacon technology in a mobile app called *Quitter's Circle* in 2017. This app aims to assist smokers in quitting by providing motivational messages, medication reminders, and relevant health information. Beacons were placed in public places like shopping malls, triggering notifications on users' smartphones when they came within range. These notifications

encouraged users to engage with the app and offered support in their quit-smoking journey.

2. Novartis collaborated with Qualcomm Life to employ beacon technology for their clinical trials. They used wearable devices equipped with beacons to monitor patients' adherence to the study protocol and collect real-time data. The beacons sent signals to remind patients to take their medication, attend appointments, or perform certain activities. The collected data helped researchers understand patient behavior and improve clinical trial outcomes.
3. GlaxoSmithKline (GSK) partnered with a beacon technology provider to enhance the shopping experience for pharmacy customers. By placing beacons in GSK's product displays, they could trigger relevant information and promotions on customers' smartphones as they approached the display. For example, when a customer was in the cold and flu aisle, a beacon would activate and push notifications about GSK's cough syrup or cold relief products, offering discounts and product details.
4. Sanofi utilized beacon technology in its marketing campaign for the insulin product Toujeo in 2016. They placed beacons in select pharmacies, and when a customer used the Toujeo mobile app and entered one of these pharmacies, they received personalized messages, reminders, and exclusive offers related to Toujeo. This approach aimed to increase brand awareness and encourage medication adherence among diabetes patients.

However, it is important to note that beaconing in pharmaceutical marketers must comply with relevant regulations and guidelines, such as those related to patient privacy and data protection, to ensure that it is ethical and legal.

Benchmarking

Benchmarking compares the products and services of one organization with those offered by industry leaders or "best-in-class" to identify areas for internal improvement and any opportunities for advancement within an organization.

Benchmarking in pharmaceutical marketing refers to comparing your company's marketing practices and performance with similar businesses. Here are a few examples:

1. *Benchmarking Sales Force*: Companies may compare their sales team to determine the effectiveness of their strategies. This could include comparing the size, structure, and conversion rates of leads into sales.
2. *Digital Marketing Benchmarking*: Companies may compare their digital strategies to competitors to assess their online presence. This could include comparing website traffic and search engine rankings, social networking engagement, and email marketing results.
3. *Market Research Benchmarking*: To assess the quality and relevancy of their market research strategies, companies may use this method to compare them with competitors. This could include comparing the study scope, methodology, data collection, and insights generated.
4. *Product Launch Benchmarking*: To assess the success of their campaigns, companies may compare their product launches with other competitors. This could include comparing launch timings and plans, marketing messages, and promotional activities.
5. *Benchmarking the Pricing*: To assess their pricing competitiveness, companies may compare their marketing strategies to other competitors. This could include comparing product prices and pricing strategies and evaluating promotional effectiveness.

Benchmarking can give valuable insights into a company's marketing practices and help identify improvement opportunities. Companies can compare their marketing performance to identify success strategies and implement those to increase their marketing efficiency and drive growth.

Benchmarking Process

Here are some important steps in the benchmarking process in pharmaceutical marketing:

1. *Establishing the Process to Benchmark*: The first step in benchmarking involves identifying the process or area to be evaluated. This could be a marketing activity such as product launches or digital marketing or a marketing aspect like market research or sales force effectiveness.
2. *Identifying Benchmarking Partners*: The next step is identifying potential partners after selecting a benchmarking strategy. This could involve selecting companies or competitors with better marketing practices in similar industries.
3. *Collect Data*: This is the next step in the benchmarking process. The benchmarking partner and the organization being benchmarked need to provide data about the benchmarked process. For instance, this could involve collecting key performance indicators, including

sales figures, market shares, website visits, social media engagement, and prices.

4. *Analyzing Data*: Once all the collected information has been reviewed and analyzed, the next step should be identifying gaps between your organization and those being benchmarked — areas where things may be working well and areas for potential improvements requiring attention.
5. *Create Improvement Plans*: Create plans to fix gaps using data analysis. This could include creating new marketing strategies, streamlining existing processes, or introducing new technologies and tools.
6. *Implement Your Improvement Plan*: It is time to put them into practice after they have been created. This could include training employees, changing marketing processes, or introducing new marketing tools.
7. *Monitor and Assess the Results*: This is the final step of the benchmarking process. It involves monitoring and assessing the results of improvement plans. This could include collecting data about key performance indicators and comparing these with benchmarking partners. These strategies can improve your company's performance if implemented well.

Benefit Positioning

Benefit positioning is a marketing strategy where pharmaceutical companies emphasize the benefits of their product over other products. It may include highlighting its unique features and benefits or outperforming similar products. Here are a few examples that show how some pharma majors have used benefit positioning for their brands:

1. AbbVie's biological drug, Humira (Adalimumab), treats Crohn's disease and rheumatoid arthritis. AbbVie has promoted Humira as a comprehensive care solution, promising relief of multiple conditions with only once-weekly administration.
2. AstraZeneca has promoted Crestor (Rosuvastatin) as a cholesterol-lowering drug. Crestor (Rosuvastatin) can reduce LDL cholesterol by 52 percent, considerably more than the other statins.
3. GlaxoSmithKline's Advair inhaler provides effective asthma and chronic obstructive pulmonary diseases (COPD) therapy and has become the go-to option among others available today. Its marketing message emphasizes the drug's convenience and efficacy versus alternatives currently on the market.
4. Merck's Gardasil vaccine protects from several strains of Human Papilloma Virus (HPV), known to increase cancer risks among both males and females, according to clinical studies conducted over time. In addition, clinical evidence supports its safety and efficacy against HPV.
5. Bayer's blood thinner Xarelto was developed to address blood clot prevention for those experiencing atrial fibrillation more quickly and conveniently; Bayer claims Xarelto provides up to 21 percent less stroke reduction than warfarin.

How to craft a benefit positioning

Here are the steps to follow when creating a benefit positioning strategy:

1. *Identify Your Target Audience*: Understanding and identifying the needs and preferences of your target audience is key to creating a successful benefit positioning campaign. Therefore, it is important to identify your product's target audience and expectations. This identification should help create the positioning strategy.
2. *Identify Your Unique Selling Proposition (USP)*: First, identify the benefits and features that make your product stand out. Then, explain why they should choose your product. Finally, your USP should address their needs and show why your solution is better than others.
3. *Analyze Your Competition*: Evaluate and assess your competition to better understand their strengths and weaknesses and how best to position your product within the market. This evaluation process should help provide key insight for positioning products successfully within their respective niche.
4. *Define Your Benefit Statement*: Consider your USP and target audience. Create a concise but powerful statement highlighting your product's key benefits. It should be consistent across all marketing materials and convey the product's value to them.
5. *Communicate Your Benefit Statement*: Include it in all marketing communications, including packaging, advertising, social media platforms, and websites. Make sure that your messaging is consistent across all channels. It should also reinforce the key benefits of the product.
6. *Assess and Adjust*: Evaluate the effectiveness of your benefit positioning strategy, and make adjustments as needed. Also, assess the impact of your messaging by considering customer feedback and market changes.

These steps will help you craft a benefit positioning strategy to effectively communicate the benefits of your product to your target market and set it apart from its competitors.

Benefit Segmentation

Benefit segmentation is a marketing strategy that divides a market into segments based on the specific benefits or values customers seek from a product or service. Instead of focusing on traditional demographic or psychographic characteristics, benefit segmentation looks at customers' desired functional, emotional, or social advantages. The primary objective of benefit segmentation is to understand and cater to different customer groups' diverse needs and preferences. Employing benefit segmentation techniques allows businesses to craft tailored marketing messages and offerings that resonate more closely with their target audiences, giving them an advantage against rival businesses while improving customer satisfaction levels. Here are a few key points about benefit segmentation:

1. *Identification of Benefits*: The initial step of benefit segmentation involves recognizing what benefits customers seek. This could range from tangible items, like cost savings and product safety or efficacy, to intangible benefits, like status or self-expression.
2. *Segmentation Based on Benefits*: Customers with similar preferences are grouped into segments once the benefits are identified. Each segment represents a distinct group of customers who value a specific set of benefits.
3. *Developing Marketing Strategies*: After segmenting the market based on benefits, companies can tailor their marketing strategies to address the unique needs of each segment. This may involve creating targeted advertising campaigns, developing product features that align with desired benefits, or offering specialized services.
4. *Benefit Segmentation Can Increase Customer Satisfaction*: Companies using benefit segmentation can tailor offerings according to different customer segments' individual needs and preferences, increasing customer satisfaction while building long-term loyalty by offering products or services that fulfill desired benefits for these customer groups.
5. *Benefit Segmentation Can Give Businesses an Edge*: Benefit segmentation gives businesses a competitive advantage by helping them identify unexploited market opportunities. By understanding which benefits their customers appreciate most, businesses can create innovative products or services which address unmet market needs more effectively.

Benefit segmentation allows companies to develop deeper customer insights, enabling them to formulate targeted marketing strategies tailored toward specific customer groups. Aligning products, services, and messaging with desired benefits helps businesses increase customer satisfaction, strengthen brand loyalty, and gain competitive advantages over rival businesses.

Benefit Segmentation in Pharma

Benefit segmentation is a marketing strategy that allows pharmaceutical companies to divide the market into segments based on customer needs and wants. Here are a few examples of benefit segmentation in the pharmaceutical industry:

1. *Pain Management*: Many pharmaceutical companies place pain management as a top priority. Benefit segmentation may target specific markets, such as athletes or people with chronic pain. In addition, different pain types may offer different benefits, such as short-acting relief and long-lasting comfort.
2. *Cancer Treatment*: One area where benefit segmentation is commonly applied is cancer treatment. Some pharmaceutical companies may focus on specific forms, like breast and lung cancer, with products designed to offer reduced side effects or improved survival rates for their products.
3. *Segmentation of Benefits in Mental Health*: With products offering benefits like improved mood or reduced symptoms, pharmaceutical companies may target specific market segments to address certain market issues.
4. *Diabetes Management*: Focusing on specific market segments related to diabetes management could involve targeting those requiring exercise and diet for managing their blood sugar or those needing insulin injections to control it in terms of product offerings with ease of use and glucose regulation as primary benefits.
5. *Cardiovascular Health*: Market segmentation could help identify segments at high risk of heart disease or elevated blood pressure and offer products that might offer potential solutions to their ailments, like decreasing their chances of heart attack or lowering cholesterol levels.

Pharma companies can use benefit segmentation to create targeted marketing campaigns tailored to specific market segments' needs. This strategy allows firms to reach more people and improve the effectiveness of their promotional activities.

How Pharma Uses Benefit Segmentation

Here are a few examples of how top pharmaceutical companies have used benefit segmentation in marketing strategies:

1. Roche's Herceptin is a targeted therapy for HER2-positive breast carcinoma, an aggressive form of cancer affecting approximately 20 percent of patients. Roche used benefit segmentation to target this patient population. In addition, an advertising campaign spotlighted Herceptin's ability to extend survival and reduce cancer recurrence risks.
2. Pfizer's Celebrex, a non-steroidal anti-inflammatory drug (NSAID) is used to manage pain associated with osteoarthritis, rheumatoid arthritis, and other conditions. Pfizer employed benefit segmentation to target specific patient groups with specific messaging for Celebrex, ultimately positioning Celebrex as the ideal non-NSAID alternative for those seeking pain relief while seeking to minimize potential side effects.
3. Cymbalta by Eli Lilly is an antidepressant medication designed to relieve anxiety and chronic back pain, targeting various forms of depression, such as major depressive disorder and generalized anxiety disorder, while offering benefits such as improved mood. Eli Lilly utilized benefit segmentation techniques in its marketing of Cymbalta.
4. Crestor from AstraZeneca is designed to reduce cholesterol and the risk of stroke or heart attack, using benefit segmentation techniques that target patients with different cholesterol levels and cardiovascular risks. As such, its numerous advantages include lowered cholesterol and decreased cardiovascular events.
5. GlaxoSmithKline's Advair inhaler relieves asthmatics and people suffering from chronic obstructive pulmonary disease (COPD). To reach customers affected by either condition, benefit segmentation was used. Also, the company highlighted Advair's key benefits, such as improved lung function and decreased exacerbations, in advertisements and marketing communications.

These pharmaceutical companies demonstrate how benefit segmentation allows them to develop targeted marketing campaigns catering to different patient populations' needs and preferences, increasing effectiveness while reaching more people with their campaigns.

Best Practices

Best practices refer to guidelines, methods, or techniques generally accepted as efficient means of reaching a particular goal or objective. They are widely employed across industries that need standard approaches to success; for instance, in marketing, there could be target audience segmentation, data-driven decision-making, customer relationship management, and regular performance-tracking being considered best practices. Similarly, for customer service, active listening is considered crucial along with prompt response times, empathy, problem-solving skills, and follow-up.

Best Practices in Pharma Marketing

Here are some best practices in pharma branding:

1. *Understanding Your Target Audience*: Successful pharma branding starts with deeply understanding your target audience. Pharma companies should conduct market research to understand the needs, preferences, and behaviors of their target patients, HCPs, and other stakeholders. This research effort allows companies to create messaging that resonates with their target patients and stakeholders, driving engagement.
2. *Develop a Strong Value Proposition*: As soon as you understand your target audience, craft a compelling value proposition directly addressing their needs and wants. A good value proposition should help distinguish your brand from competitors while communicating the benefits of your products or services to them.
3. *Maintain Consistency*: Consistency is of utmost importance in pharmaceutical branding. Create and sustain a single brand identity across all marketing channels, including your website and social media, product packaging and labeling materials, packaging material, etc.
4. *Build Trust and Credibility*: Trust is essential for pharma branding. Be transparent about your products, services, and business practices while providing high-quality, evidence-based information and data that back up any claims you make about yourself or your products or services.
5. *Use Digital and Social Media*: Pharma companies can leverage digital and social media as powerful channels for engaging their

audiences, including targeted messaging and building brand advocates. By taking advantage of these channels to engage your target audiences directly, this strategy will help deliver tailored messaging directly where your target audiences are.

6. *Stay Compliant*: Pharma companies must abide by stringent regulatory requirements when branding and marketing their products. Stay informed on regulations and guidelines, so your branding materials comply with regulatory authorities such as FDA in the US, EMA in the European Union, and regulatory agencies in other countries.
7. *Offer Value-Added Services*: Provide value-added services such as patient education, disease management tools, and other resources that enable patients and healthcare providers to manage their conditions more effectively, helping to foster loyalty and trust among your target audience. Doing this will build loyalty and trust.
8. *Foster Relationships with Healthcare Providers (HCPs)*: Establish relationships with HCPs to increase brand recognition and influence prescribing behavior, through physician education programs, speaker programs, or any other activity which helps establish meaningful bonds with healthcare providers.
9. *Monitor and Measure Results*: Finally, assess and track the outcomes of your branding and marketing initiatives using data analytics and other metrics to gauge their success and make changes as necessary.

These best practices can assist pharmaceutical companies in creating marketing strategies that foster engagement, increase brand recognition, and generate more prescriptions from HCPs.

Big Data

Big data refers to large volumes of structured and unstructured information gathered from diverse sources like social media, electronic health records, and others collected over time and made accessible for analysis by businesses in multiple sectors, including pharmaceutical industry. Big data analysis allows pharmaceutical manufacturers to enhance drug development, patient outcomes, marketing strategies, and other aspects of business operations.

Big data in pharmaceutical marketing doesn't just serve these few purposes. Consider these other applications of big data as examples:

1. *Targeted Marketing*: Pharma companies can leverage patient data to identify which demographics, behavior patterns, and medical conditions would most benefit from their products. With this insight, pharma companies can develop targeted marketing campaigns to reach those most likely to prescribe or purchase them.
2. *Predictive Analytics*: Pharma companies can predict trends and patterns in patient behavior, treatment outcomes, and other factors by analyzing large data sets. These data can improve patient outcomes and create more effective marketing strategies.
3. *Drug Discovery*: Pharmaceutical companies use Big Data to identify new drug targets, decode disease mechanisms and develop more effective drugs. Companies can identify potential drug targets by analyzing large amounts of genetic, genomic, and proteomic data and then create personalized medications for specific patient populations. Merck, for example, uses big data to develop more effective drugs.
4. *Clinical Trials*: Pharma companies use big data to optimize clinical trials. Companies can analyze patient data to identify the right patient population, monitor patient safety, and optimize study design to improve success rates. This is what Pfizer does with its big-data-driven clinical trials.
5. *Personalized Medicine*: Pharma companies use big data to create more personalized medicine. They analyze patient records to determine how environmental and genetic factors affect treatment outcomes. This allows them to develop more appropriate drugs for certain patient populations while reducing the chance of adverse events. Novartis, for example, uses big data to develop personalized cancer medicine.
6. *Real World Evidence*: Pharma companies utilize big data analytics to produce objective evidence that can be used in regulatory approvals, reimbursement decisions, and clinical practice guidelines. Companies analyze large amounts of patient data in search of patterns that could inform clinical decision-making; for instance, Sanofi uses big data analysis to develop more effective treatments while decreasing adverse events risk.
7. *Marketing and Sales*: Pharma companies use big data for targeted marketing campaigns, customer analysis, and behavior tracking, as well as to optimize sales strategies. Pharma firms utilize patient records, social media data, and other data sources to analyze demographics,

behavior, and medical conditions that would most benefit from their products. With that information in hand, they can develop targeted marketing strategies to reach the right audiences; AstraZeneca uses big data in this manner, for example, in creating targeted campaigns, using targeted strategies utilizing big data for targeted marketing purposes.

Big Tech

Big Tech companies like Google, Amazon, Apple, and Microsoft are exploring healthcare and pharmaceutical marketing opportunities as part of their growth plans. Here are a few ways big tech has already participated or could potentially get involved:

1. *Data Analytics and Personalization*: Tech companies possess access to vast quantities of user information, such as search patterns, browsing behavior, and preferences, that they can leverage into targeted and customized marketing campaigns for pharmaceutical products that address users' health interests and needs.
2. *Digital Ad Platforms*: Google and Microsoft operate robust digital ad platforms that pharmaceutical companies can use to promote their products to wider audiences. These platforms feature various ad formats like display ads, search ads, and video ads for maximum flexibility in marketing strategies for pharmaceutical businesses.
3. *Wearable Tech and Health Devices*: Tech companies like Apple and Google have introduced wearable devices that monitor various health metrics. Their data provide valuable insight into users' medical conditions, habits, and treatment requirements so pharmaceutical marketers can target certain patient populations with effective medications or therapies.
4. *Telemedicine and Healthcare Services*: Amazon recently ventured into telemedicine services via virtual consultation platforms that facilitate virtual consultations between patients and healthcare providers. This allows personalized pharmaceutical recommendations and marketing within digital healthcare sectors.
5. *Health Apps and Ecosystems*: Companies like Apple have created health apps and ecosystems for users to manage their data and access relevant health information. In these ecosystems, pharmaceutical companies may find opportunities for providing targeted marketing materials about specific conditions or treatments to users enrolled within them.
6. *Clinical Trials and Real-World Data Collection*: Big Tech companies' advanced analytics and large user bases make them invaluable resources when conducting clinical trials or gathering real-world data. Their data analytics capabilities could assist pharmaceutical companies with recruiting trial participants and provide insight into medication's efficacy or safety.

As the pharmaceutical industry is highly regulated, big tech companies entering these spaces must comply with stringent legal and ethical regulations, such as data privacy and security, and transparency in their marketing practices.

Billboard

As a traditional form of outdoor advertising, billboards have been used for decades to promote various products and services, including pharmaceuticals. The use of billboards in pharma marketing carries unique implications and challenges due to the specific nature of the industry, its regulatory environment, and the complexities of communicating medical information to the public. Below are some implications and considerations for pharma marketing:

1. *Regulatory Restrictions*: Pharmaceutical advertising is subject to strict regulations in many countries. Information must be accurate, non-misleading, and often include a balanced presentation of benefits and risks. This can be a challenge on a billboard where space is limited.
2. *Direct-to-Consumer (DTC) Advertising*: In some countries, such as the US, DTC advertising of prescription drugs is permitted but must meet specific guidelines. In other countries, DTC advertising of prescription drugs might be completely banned.
3. *Simplicity vs. Information*: Billboards quickly convey messages to passing motorists or pedestrians. Pharma marketers must balance simplicity and provide enough information about the medication, its uses, and potential side effects.
4. *Public Perception*: The public may have mixed feelings about seeing drugs advertised in such a public and direct manner, especially if they feel it promotes over-prescription or trivializes health decisions.
5. *Branding*: Pharma companies often invest heavily in branding their products. Billboards

can be crucial in increasing brand awareness, especially in competitive markets.

6. *Digital Integration*: Modern billboards, especially digital ones, can integrate with other digital marketing efforts. QR Codes, URLs, or app promotions can bridge the gap between offline and online engagement.
7. *Targeted Challenges*: Unlike digital ads that can be narrowly targeted based on user behavior, billboards are seen by a broad audience. This can be an advantage (wide-spread visibility) and a disadvantage (less specific targeting).
8. *Location Considerations*: The placement of a billboard can greatly affect its efficacy. Billboards near hospitals, clinics, or pharmacies may be more effective for pharma products than those in unrelated areas.
9. *Ethical Considerations*: Using billboards to promote certain medications or treatments can raise ethical questions, especially if the advertising targets vulnerable populations or promotes treatments for non-life-threatening conditions.
10. *Cost*: Billboards, especially in prime locations, can be expensive. Pharma companies need to weigh the cost against potential returns in terms of increased brand visibility and sales.

Implications for Pharma Marketers

- Understanding the local regulations related to pharmaceutical advertising is crucial.
- Collaborating with legal and medical teams to ensure accurate and compliant messaging is essential.
- Testing and measuring the effectiveness of billboard campaigns can help optimize spending and messaging in their future campaigns.
- Keeping the patient's best interest in mind and ensuring transparent and ethical communications will help maintain public trust.

While billboards can offer substantial visibility and can be a component of an integrated marketing strategy for pharma companies, they come with unique challenges and considerations that must be thoughtfully addressed.

Billboard Advertising by Pharma Companies: Some Examples

Over the years, various pharmaceutical companies have utilized billboard advertising to promote their products to raise awareness about specific conditions. Here are some examples of pharma companies and the nature of their billboard campaigns:

1. *Pfizer and Moderna for COVID-19 Vaccines*: With the emergence of the COVID-19 pandemic, companies like Pfizer and Moderna used billboard advertising in various locations to promote the benefits of their vaccines, encourage vaccination, and provide information about vaccine availability.
2. *Gilead Sciences for Truvada*: Gilead Sciences has used billboards to promote Truvada for PrEP (Pre-Exposure Prophylaxis) as a preventative measure against HIV.
3. *Allergan for BOTOX*: Allergan has used billboard advertising to promote Botox for cosmetic purposes and medical uses like migraine prevention.
4. *Eli Lilly for Cialis*: Eli Lilly used billboards to promote Cialis, a drug for erectile dysfunction. Their advertisements often showcased couples and highlighted the of the drug's longer duration of action.
5. *Novartis for Takhzyro*: In some regions, Novartis used billboards to promote Takhzyro, a treatment for hereditary angioedema.
6. *Awareness Campaigns*: Beyond specific drugs, many pharma companies use billboards for disease awareness campaigns. For example, a company might promote awareness about conditions like rheumatoid arthritis, depression, or diabetes without necessarily naming a specific drug.
7. *Local Campaigns*: It is not uncommon for regional or local healthcare systems to use billboards to promote a new available treatment, often backed by a pharmaceutical company. For example, if a new oncology drug becomes available, a local hospital might promote its cancer center along with the availability of that treatment.
8. *Disease Awareness and Over-the-counter (OTC) Drugs*: Companies like Johnson & Johnson or Procter & Gamble might use billboards to advertise OTC drugs or products, from pain relievers to heartburn medications.

Bioavailability

Bioavailability refers to the proportion of a drug or other substance that enters the bloodstream when it is introduced into the body and is made available for use or storage. It is a key factor in drug development because it determines the effective dosage, frequency, and route of administration for the drug. Higher bioavailability means more of the drug reaches its intended target, potentially resulting in greater efficacy or the need for lower doses.

For pharma marketers, the concept of bioavailability has several implications:

1. *Differentiation*: A drug with superior bioavailability compared to competitor drugs can be a strong differentiator in the market. It suggests patients might achieve desired therapeutic effects with lower doses or fewer side effects.
2. *Dosage Forms*: Different forms or formulations of a drug (oral tablet vs. liquid vs. sublingual strip) can have different bioavailability profiles. Marketers can emphasize the benefits of one form over another based on this.
3. *Pricing and Value Proposition*: A drug with higher bioavailability might justify a higher price point because patients could need less of the drug to achieve the desired effects. Marketers can communicate this value proposition to both healthcare providers and payers.
4. *Patient Compliance*: Drugs with better bioavailability might be taken less frequently or in smaller doses. This can improve patient compliance, as taking medications becomes more convenient, and improved compliance can be a key marketing message.
5. *Educational Initiatives*: Pharma marketers can launch educational campaigns to inform healthcare professionals about the bioavailability advantages of their products. Understanding bioavailability can influence prescribing decisions.
6. *Reformulations*: Pharma companies often develop new formulations of existing drugs to improve their bioavailability. This can extend the lifecycle of a drug, especially if the original is going off-patent. Marketers can promote these new formulations as superior alternatives.
7. *Regulatory Implications*: Changes in bioavailability may require additional clinical trials and regulatory approvals. Marketers must coordinate with the R&D and regulatory departments to ensure accurate and compliant communication.
8. *Comparison with Generics*: When a drug goes off-patent and generics enter the market, the original branded drug might still have a bioavailability advantage if the generics do not match it perfectly. Marketers can emphasize this difference to maintain market share.
9. *Safety and Side Effects*: Enhanced bioavailability can also affect the drug's safety profile. While more of the drug is available to exert a therapeutic effect, there might also be a higher risk of side effects. This balance needs to be communicated clearly.
10. *Global Considerations*: Different populations might metabolize drugs differently, affecting bioavailability. Marketers must be aware of these nuances when launching campaigns in various regions.

Bioavailability, thus, is a critical factor in the pharmaceutics of a drug and holds significant implications for its marketing. By effectively communicating the benefits and implications of a drug's bioavailability, pharma marketers can influence perceptions, prescribing decisions, and patient outcomes.

Bioengineering

Bioengineering encompasses an expansive spectrum of sub-disciplines, such as Tissue Engineering. Tissue engineering creates biological replacement tissues or organs using cells, biomaterials, and chemical factors combining three-dimensional structures that mimic natural tissue to promote the regeneration of damaged organs or tissues or repair replacement organs or tissues.

1. *Genetic Engineering*: Genetic engineering refers to manipulating living organisms' DNA for therapeutic or industrial product development purposes, such as creating medical therapies or agricultural process optimization software programs, optimizing agricultural process efficiency, or creating novel items through gene editing technology (gene editing/recombinant DNA technology/synbio), or synthetic biology.
2. *Biomedical Imaging*: Biomedical imaging uses various imaging technologies to create detailed images of biological structures and processes within an individual's body.
3. *Biomaterials* are biocompatible materials designed for biological systems to replace existing tissues with implants that replace or augment them, such as stem cell transplantation techniques. Bioengineers typically select biocompatible, mechanical-strength materials with controlled drug-release capabilities as part of bioengineering projects.
4. *Bioinformatics*: Bioinformatics combines biological science with computer science and statistics to interpret biological data such as DNA sequences, protein structures, or gene expression profiles. Bioinformatics encompasses creating algorithms, databases, and software tools

targeted toward genomics, proteomics, or systems biology research projects.

5. *Biomechanics*: Biomechanics is the study of biological systems' physical properties and behaviors, such as cells, tissues, and organs, and their interactions - such as muscles - including mechanical forces exerted from within them, such as internal forces in cells or tissues by bioengineers who utilize concepts from mechanics and engineering principles to understand forces or stresses exerted upon cells or tissues that affect them - knowledge they apply when crafting medical devices such as prosthetics or orthopedic implants.

Bioengineering's applications span multiple fields, such as healthcare delivery and diagnosis, regenerative medicine research, understanding biological systems, and overall wellness promotion. Bioengineers collaborate closely with medical professionals, scientists, and industry specialists in translating scientific knowledge into tangible solutions that promote people's well-being and lead to improved healthcare outcomes with implications for Pharma Marketing.

Bioengineering plays an integral part in pharmaceutical marketing. Here are a few ways bioengineering influences this area:

1. *Advanced Pharmaceutical Products*: Bioengineering has enabled the creation of advanced pharmaceutical products such as targeted drug delivery systems, novel formulations, and personalized medicine that boast increased efficacy with decreased side effects for enhanced patient experiences. Pharma marketers must understand these products' scientific and technical features to market and effectively differentiate these new offerings from existing alternatives.
2. *Scientific Expertise*: Bioengineering requires extensive scientific knowledge and technical know-how, which pharma marketers must possess to effectively market pharmaceutical products with bioengineered components to healthcare providers and patients. Their understanding of its underlying principles must allow them to convey scientific advancements and benefits via compelling messages about complex scientific information in a clear manner.
3. *Educational Initiatives*: Bioengineering breakthroughs often necessitate educational efforts to inform healthcare providers and patients of new treatment options and technologies. Pharma marketers play an essential role in creating educational materials, organizing scientific symposiums, and working closely with medical societies and healthcare institutions in spreading bioengineering-related advancements; such initiatives help build awareness, trust, and credibility of pharmaceutical products among healthcare providers and patients alike.
4. *Engagement With Key Opinion Leaders (KOLs)*: In bioengineering, influential researchers and clinicians known as Key Opinion Leaders (KOLs), can significantly shape opinions and prescription practices. Pharma marketers should identify relevant KOLs specializing in this area for collaboration purposes. This can include creating educational materials, clinical trials under their watch, or even endorsements supporting marketing campaigns.
5. *Market Segmentation*: Bioengineering advances are frequently tailored toward specific patient populations or medical conditions, necessitating pharmaceutical marketers to understand these niche markets and adapt their marketing strategies accordingly. Pharma marketers can create tailored campaigns by segmenting target audiences based on disease profiles, genetic characteristics, or responsiveness to therapies, creating tailored campaigns that reach individuals most suitable to them with tailored messaging campaigns, and reaching relevant individuals with tailored campaigns.
6. *Digital Marketing and Communication*: Due to their intricate nature, bioengineering-related advances often need further explanation. Digital platforms like websites, social media, and online forums present great opportunities to provide this detailed knowledge about bioengineered pharmaceutical products. Pharma marketers can utilize channels, such as websites and forums, in particular as platforms where healthcare professionals and patients can be engaged by pharmaceutical marketers who share scientific content, address queries, or form communities around specific medical conditions or treatment approaches.
7. *Market Differentiation*: Innovations in bioengineering can differentiate pharmaceutical products from competitors' offerings. This allows marketers to highlight unique features and benefits of bioengineered products in promotional activities to drive market penetration and create a competitive advantage. Highlighting improved drug delivery mechanisms, therapeutic outcomes, or side effect reduction may create a competitive edge and promote market expansion.

Bioengineering's implications for pharmaceutical marketing center around understanding and effectively communicating its scientific advancements, benefits, and differentiation of pharmaceutical products through bioengineering innovations. Pharma marketers must remain abreast of bioengineering breakthroughs; collaborate with scientific experts; engage key opinion leaders; and formulate targeted marketing strategies to position and market these products effectively.

Bioequivalence

Bioequivalence, as described in pharmacology and pharmaceutical sciences, refers to the rate and extent of absorption of an active pharmaceutical ingredient (API) from one pharmaceutical product when administered at an equal dosage to that of its reference product; simply put, this measures whether different formulations of drugs produce similar effects in the body.

Generic drugs must demonstrate bioequivalence to their reference products (brand-name drugs) for approval, meaning that when taken, their active ingredients enter your bloodstream at roughly equivalent times and in similar doses, to ensure they provide equivalent therapeutic outcomes.

Bioequivalence studies compare the pharmacokinetic properties of generic and reference products. To conduct such an evaluation, both products must be administered to healthy volunteers before monitoring their blood concentration over time. The parameters typically evaluated include the maximum concentration (Cmax) reached in the blood and the total amount of drug absorbed (area under the curve, or AUC). In addition, the generic product must show that the Cmax and AUC fall within an acceptable range ; the acceptance range being 90% confidence interval of difference in the average values of logarithmic parameters to be assessed between test and reference product is within the range of log(0.80) - log (1.25) compared to the reference product.

Establishing bioequivalence is essential for generic drugs to gain regulatory approval. In addition, healthcare providers and patients need the assurance that generic products can replace brand-name alternatives without reducing therapeutic effects.

It is important to note that bioequivalence refers specifically to the pharmacokinetic properties of drugs; that is, their properties are related to how they are absorbed, distributed, metabolized, and excreted from the body. Therefore it does not guarantee identical formulation, excipients, and manufacturing processes between generic and reference products despite meeting quality standards.

Implications for Pharma Marketers

Bioequivalence has several implications for pharma marketers, particularly in promoting generic pharmaceutical products. Here are some key implications:

1. *Educational Messaging:* Pharma marketers must educate healthcare professionals and patients about bioequivalence. They should explain that generic products are bioequivalent to the reference products, meaning they deliver the same therapeutic effects. This messaging helps build trust and confidence in the efficacy and safety of generic drugs.
2. *Cost Savings:* Bioequivalence studies demonstrate that generic products are equivalent in effectiveness but are often available at a lower cost than branded products. Pharma marketers can emphasize the cost savings associated with generic options to healthcare professionals, payers, and patients. This messaging can be particularly relevant in cost-conscious healthcare systems and when targeting price-sensitive markets.
3. *Formulary Inclusion:* Demonstrating bioequivalence is crucial for generic drugs to be included in formularies, which are lists of medications covered by insurance plans and healthcare systems. Pharma marketers should work with payers, formulary committees, and healthcare organizations to provide evidence of bioequivalence and promote the inclusion of their generic products in formularies. This can increase access and utilization of the generic product.
4. *Generic Substitution:* Bioequivalence is essential for facilitating generic substitution. Pharma marketers can inform healthcare professionals and pharmacists about their generic products' regulatory approval and bioequivalence. They can also provide educational materials and resources on therapeutic interchangeability, encouraging the use of generic alternatives when appropriate. Such efforts can support the acceptance and adoption of generic substitution practices.
5. *Branding and Differentiation:* Generic pharmaceutical manufacturers can differentiate their products based on factors beyond bioequivalence. Marketers can focus on product packaging, brand reputation, manufacturing quality, and customer service to create a distinct brand identity for their generic products. Effective branding and differentiation strategies can help build customer loyalty and preference.

6. *Patient Education:* Pharma marketers should develop patient education materials that explain the concept of bioequivalence and the benefits of using generic drugs. Emphasizing generics' comparable efficacy and safety can help overcome patients' concerns or misconceptions about switching from branded products. In addition, clear and concise messages can empower patients to make informed decisions and choose cost-effective treatment options.
7. *Market Access and Competition:* Bioequivalence is a regulatory requirement for generic products to enter the market. Pharma marketers must navigate the regulatory landscape, obtain the necessary approvals, and meet bioequivalence criteria to ensure market access. Additionally, understanding the competitive landscape and conducting market research can help marketers position their generic products effectively and differentiate them from other generic alternatives.

By effectively communicating the concept of bioequivalence, emphasizing cost savings, and addressing concerns, pharma marketers can promote the acceptance and adoption of generic pharmaceutical products, leading to increased market share and improved patient access to affordable medications.

Bioinformatics

Bioinformatics, the intersection of biology and computational science, involves using software and mathematical models to make sense of biological data. The rise of this field has vast implications for various sectors, including the pharmaceutical industry. For pharma marketers, understanding the potential and implications of bioinformatics can provide a competitive edge. Here are the details:

1. Drug Discovery and Personalized Medicine

- *Faster Drug Discovery*: Bioinformatics tools can analyze massive biological datasets, helping researchers identify potential drug targets more efficiently.
- *Personalized Medicine*: With the ability to analyze an individual's genetic makeup, it is possible to design or prescribe drugs tailored for specific populations or individuals, ensuring higher efficacy and reduced adverse effects.
- *Implication for Marketers*: Marketers can highlight the precision and efficiency of their company's drugs, targeting niche populations and building trust with healthcare professionals.

2. Disease Prediction and Prevention

- Using bioinformatics, researchers can predict susceptibility to certain diseases based on genetic markers.
- *Implication for Marketers*: This opens doors for marketing preventive treatments or early intervention drugs.

3. Data Management and Cloud Services

- The sheer volume of genomic and proteomic data demands robust data storage and management solutions.
- *Implication for Marketers*: Pharma companies can form partnerships with tech firms, offering combined solutions or tools that simplify data management for researchers.

4. Enhanced Clinical Trials

- With a better understanding of genetics, pharma companies can select trial participants more likely to benefit from the drug, reducing costs and improving trial outcomes.
- *Implication for Marketers*: Such clinical trials can be marketed as more ethical and efficient, appealing to healthcare professionals and the public.

5. Ethical Considerations

- The more we delve into genetics, the more ethical questions arise regarding data privacy, genetic discrimination, and the cost of personalized medicine.
- *Implication for Marketers*: Pharma marketers should be ready to address these concerns in their campaigns, ensuring that the company's stance on these issues is clear and aligns with public sentiment.

6. Educational Initiatives

- There is a growing demand for professionals skilled in bioinformatics.
- *Implication for Marketers*: Pharma companies can sponsor or offer educational initiatives, courses, or tools to help foster the next generation of researchers, which also acts as a branding effort.

7. Collaborations and Mergers

- The overlap between computational tech and biology leads to new partnerships, mergers, and acquisitions.
- *Implication for Marketers*: These collaborations can be promoted to showcase a pharma company's innovative and interdisciplinary nature.

8. Enhanced Drug Repurposing

- Bioinformatics can identify new uses for existing drugs.

- *Implication for Marketers*: This can lead to new marketing opportunities for old drugs, extending their product lifecycle.

9. Regulatory Engagement

- Regulatory bodies are increasingly demanding digital analyses for drug approval processes.
- *Implication for Marketers*: By highlighting a company's proficiency in bioinformatics, marketers can assure stakeholders of smoother regulatory processes.

Bioinformatics is revolutionizing the pharmaceutical landscape, and pharma marketers must adapt. By understanding the potential of this field, marketers can craft compelling narratives, forge fruitful partnerships, and pave the way for the next generation of innovative pharmaceutical solutions.

Biologic License Application (BLA)

BLA stands for Biologics License Application in a pharmaceutical marketing context. Submittal to US Food and Drug Administration (FDA), include specific details regarding manufacturing processes, chemistry, pharmacology, clinical pharmacological effects, and potential medical uses of biological products. Once this application meets FDA standards, it can be approved, with license issued enabling firms to market the product.

Biologic products encompass vaccines, blood, components, allergenic compounds, somatic cells, gene therapy treatments, tissues, and recombinant therapeutic proteins, and biosimilars are similar but non identical copies of an innovator product.

Marketing biologics can be an intricate task. To be effective, one needs an in-depth knowledge of the product, the disease state being treated, and a narrow target market (often more so than traditional pharmaceutical products). Furthermore, marketing often includes informing healthcare providers and patients alike of both benefits and risks of the biologic since many new and novel therapies require education about them before being adopted into treatment regimens.

Additionally, marketing must comply with FDA regulations, such as advertising and promotional labeling, and post-market surveillance requirements for post-launch safety of products on the market. Furthermore, pharmaceutical companies must often address payor and reimbursement issues in their marketing strategies since biological drugs are significantly more costly.

Approval Process

Biologics License Application (BLA) processing can be complex. Below is an outline of all its phases to facilitate ease of completion and all approval processes that may be necessary.

1. *Preclinical Testing*: Before human clinical testing, laboratory and animal experiments must show whether a product is safe enough for human trials and provide preliminary efficacy data. Once their findings have been submitted for FDA review in an Investigational New Drug (IND) application and approved before beginning human trials.
2. *Clinical Trials*: These take place over various phases. Phase I tests measure safety and dosage. Phases II and III tests look into efficacy, side effects, and additional safety and effectiveness information gained through studies with different populations and doses comparing competing products. When complete, data are collated together for submission as part of BLA filing to the FDA for consideration.
3. *BLA Submission*: To submit a BLA with the FDA, data should include preclinical and clinical study information as well as details from manufacturing processes, packaging specifications, and labeling for your products, with proposed labeling proposals as well as user fees due.
4. *FDA Review*: Once submitted for consideration by the FDA, BLAs may be further reviewed or rejected as incomplete. Once accepted for filing by FDA reviewers, they usually take up to 60 days to decide whether the BLA can be filed for further review or to refuse to file the BLA if it is incomplete. If the FDA accepts the BLA for filing, they will review the BLA to make the final approval decision. The FDA may require additional studies or may convene an advisory committee of outside experts for their advice and recommendations needed for making the final approval decision.
5. *FDA Approval*: If the Food and Drug Administration finds your product safe and effective and outweighs its associated risks, they will approve its marketing in the US.
6. *Post-Market Surveillance*: The FDA continues to monitor the products released for commercial distribution for their safety and efficacy. Companies must submit regular updates regarding safety incidents for review by the FDA.

Approval processes vary significantly based on the product (vaccines, blood products, or cell therapy therapies) and their intended use.

Marketing Biologics

Selling biologics within the pharmaceutical industry poses unique marketing challenges and obstacles; here are a few key points for pharmaceutical marketers:

1. *Scientific Complexity*: Due to biologics' greater scientific complexity than small-molecule drugs, marketing teams need to take extra care in understanding its science and how it will treat disease. Once this information has been accumulated, healthcare providers, patients, and researchers all require accessing it easily for treatment.
2. *Education and Awareness*: Like other novel medications, biologic therapies typically necessitate education and awareness campaigns to raise public awareness regarding their use as treatments and any possible benefits or risks of biological therapies used by healthcare practitioners. This may require promotion campaigns and details regarding their products, diseases being treated, or potential benefits and risks from biologic therapy regimens.
3. *Pricing and Reimbursement*: Since biologic drugs tend to be significantly more costly to produce than their traditional equivalents, marketers of biologic medications must not only convince healthcare providers about their advantages but also demonstrate cost-effectiveness to payors (insurance companies or government bodies) to guarantee patient access.
4. *Compliance With FDA Requirements and Post-Market Surveillance Requirements*: Compliance is key in all communications and promotional activities undertaken for pharmaceutical sales due to stringent pharmaceutical marketing regulations. This means adhering to FDA advertising and promotion guidelines and meeting post-market surveillance requirements.
5. *Patient Support Programs*: Marketers need to provide extensive patient support programs when marketing biologics to treat serious and persistent conditions. This may include education about treatment as prescribed, assistance navigating insurance reimbursement issues, and even adherence programs that ensure patients adhere to therapy per physician orders.
6. *Market Exclusivity*: For biosimilars (biologically similar products already approved by regulators), marketers must successfully differentiate their product in the marketplace from its reference product. It can be challenging as biosimilars do not usually have clinically meaningful distinctions from the reference product.
7. *Long-Term Relationship Building*: Developing lasting relationships is essential with biological treatments, typically for chronic diseases. This requires ongoing engagement and support that goes beyond typical product promotion efforts.

Given these hurdles and implications, marketing in the biologics field requires a distinct strategy from traditional pharmaceutical marketing: deep scientific knowledge combined with patient centricity is paramount; additional challenges lie within complex regulatory and reimbursement landscapes that must be navigated effectively.

Biologicals

Biologicals refer to drugs derived from living organisms, including monoclonal antibodies, vaccines, genes, and cell therapies. These are distinct from traditional small molecule drugs in that they are often larger, more complex molecules or even cells. The emergence and growth of biologicals in the pharmaceutical landscape have brought about significant implications for pharma marketers:

1. Complex Manufacturing and Quality Control

- Biologicals often require more intricate manufacturing processes and quality control measures than traditional drugs.
- *Implication for Marketers*: Marketers need to communicate the unique value, safety, and efficacy of these products, especially given the intricate production methods.

2. Higher Costs

- Due to the complexities in research, development, and manufacturing, biologicals often come with higher costs.
- *Implication for Marketers*: There is a need to justify these costs to healthcare providers, payers, and patients, emphasizing the unique benefits or long-term savings like fewer hospitalizations.

3. Personalized Medicine

- Some biologicals, especially gene and cell therapies, can be tailored for individual patients.
- *Implication for Marketers*: Marketing campaigns can emphasize the personalized nature of these treatments, suggesting better efficacy and fewer side effects.

4. Cold Chain Logistics

- Many biologicals require stringent temperature-controlled logistics.

- *Implication for Marketers*: It is crucial to highlight the company's capability to ensure product integrity during transportation and storage.

5. **Regulatory Hurdles**

- Due to their complexity and novelty, biologicals often face more challenging regulatory pathways.
- *Implication for Marketers*: Building trust is essential. Emphasizing rigorous testing, safety protocols, and post-market surveillance can help.

6. **Patient Education**

- The mechanisms of action of biologicals can be complex and may be unfamiliar to patients.
- *Implication for Marketers*: There is an increased need for patient education tools, such as brochures, videos, or interactive apps, explaining how the treatment works and its benefits.

7. **Biosimilars**

- Just as generics are to small molecule drugs, biosimilars are to biologicals. They are similar but not identical versions of the original biological product.
- *Implication for Marketers*: Originator companies might need to differentiate their products from biosimilars, emphasizing original research, consistent quality, or patient support programs.

8. **New Treatment Modalities**

- Biologicals can address diseases previously deemed untreatable or provide more effective treatments with fewer side effects.
- *Implication for Marketers*: Marketing can focus on the groundbreaking nature of these therapies and the hope they bring to patients.

9. **Collaborations**

- The development and distribution of biologicals often involve collaborations between multiple entities, including academic institutions, biotech startups, and larger pharma companies.
- *Implication for Marketers*: Showcasing collaborations can bolster a company's image as innovative and forward-thinking.

10. **Ethical and Societal Implications**

- Especially with gene therapies, there are broader ethical and societal implications.
- *Implication for Marketers*: Companies should be prepared to address these concerns transparently and engage in dialogues with stakeholders, including patient advocacy groups and ethicists.

In summary, while biologicals present unique challenges for pharma marketers, they offer unparalleled opportunities. Marketers can craft compelling narratives around the innovative nature of these treatments, the science behind them, and the tangible benefits they bring to patients.

Biometrics

Biometrics measures and analyzes biological data such as physiological or behavioral characteristics to identify individuals or evaluate responses from them. While biometrics is typically associated with areas like security or authentication, biometrics also has applications within pharmaceutical marketing research. Here are a few ways biometrics could be implemented in pharma marketing research:

1. *Targeted Marketing*: Biometric data can assist pharmaceutical companies in better comprehending their target audiences by measuring physiological reactions to marketing materials and advertisements. Marketers can gain valuable insight into consumers' emotional and cognitive responses by measuring heart rate, skin conductance, and facial expressions when exposed to ads or promotional campaigns. This knowledge allows marketers to tailor messaging that resonates better with each specific group in the target audience.
2. *User Experience Testing*: Biometrics can measure user experiences of pharmaceutical products or medical devices. By measuring biometric data such as eye movement, facial expressions, or brain activity of users interacting with these products and tracking biometric information of consumers using them, marketers can assess user interactions, pinpoint pain points and make improvements based on this collected information. Thus creating products that are user-friendly while increasing overall customer satisfaction.
3. *Clinical Trials*: Biometrics can be instrumental in pharmaceutical marketing by improving clinical trials' efficiency. By collecting and analyzing biometric data from participants, researchers gain insight into the efficacy and safety of any particular medication or therapy; then use this information in marketing efforts that illustrate its value to healthcare providers, regulatory bodies, or potential consumers.
4. *Personalized Medicine*: Biometric data can be integral to creating personalized medicine approaches. By assessing individuals' genetic

makeup, physiological characteristics, and behavioral data to identify those that would gain the most from particular drugs or treatments, pharmaceutical marketers can more efficiently market to those likely to benefit most and deliver tailored messages about available bespoke options for treatment options to the correct patient segments.

5. *Compliance and Adherence*: Biometrics can be employed to measure patient compliance with prescribed medications and increase adherence through wearable devices or mobile applications that collect biometric information such as heart rate variability or medication intake patterns to measure levels of compliance or adherence. Pharmaceutical marketers can leverage this data by designing targeted interventions, reminders, or incentives to encourage patients to follow through with prescribed treatment plans.

However, biometrics use in pharmaceutical marketing raises ethical and privacy issues. Collecting personal biometric information must be done with informed consent from individuals involved, by applicable regulations, and safeguarded with robust data security measures to maintain privacy and confidentiality for individual users and pharmaceutical marketers.

Biometrics in Pharma Marketing Research

Biometrics can play a valuable role in pharmaceutical marketing research by providing objective data regarding participants' physiological and behavioral responses. Here are a few ways biometrics may be utilized:

1. *Emotional Response Analysis*: Biometric measurements such as facial expressions, skin conductance, or heart rate variability can provide researchers valuable insight into participants' emotional reactions to pharmaceutical products, advertisements, or marketing messages. Tracking these physiological indicators gives them greater insights into different stimuli, enabling them to craft more engaging and persuasive campaigns by optimizing messaging.
2. *Attention and Engagement Measurement*: Eye-tracking technology combined with biometrics is an invaluable way to monitor participants' visual attention and engagement with marketing materials. By tracking eye movement patterns and pupil dilation rates, researchers can pinpoint which ads or packaging elements garner most of our participants' visual focus and trigger strong emotional reactions. This information allows marketers to design future promotional materials better to increase their efficacy.
3. *Brand Perception and Recall*: Biometrics can assess participants' brand perception and recall. Furthermore, researchers may use electroencephalography (EEG) measurements to analyze neural responses associated with brand recognition and memory; such measurements could reveal insights into branding strategy effectiveness while helping create memorable marketing campaigns that stand out.
4. *Usability Testing*: Biometrics can be integral in usability testing for pharmaceutical websites, mobile applications, and medical devices. By tracking participants' biometric responses during interaction with these digital platforms or devices, researchers can quickly pinpoint usability issues, such as bottlenecks or confusion, to enhance user experience and optimize digital marketing assets. This data assists marketers and developers alike.
5. *Neuromarketing Studies*: Neuromarketing utilizes biometric measurements and traditional market research methods to gain insights into customer decision-making processes. By monitoring brain activity and biometric responses, researchers can uncover subconscious reactions, preferences, and motivations influencing purchase decisions; such knowledge can inform pharmaceutical marketing strategies related to positioning, messaging, and pricing.

Complying with ethical guidelines when conducting pharmaceutical marketing research using biometrics is essential. Participants must provide informed consent, with their privacy and confidentiality protected. Likewise, studies must comply with relevant data gathering, storage, and analysis regulations.

Biopharmaceuticals

Biopharmaceuticals are medical drugs produced through biotechnology. This includes proteins (including antibodies) and nucleic acids such as DNA, RNA, or antisense oligonucleotides that have therapeutic, or in vivo diagnostic uses but are produced, using means other than direct extraction from non-engineered biological sources; examples include monoclonal antibodies, vaccines, gene therapy drugs recombinant proteins cell and tissue-based products produced through this process.

Marketing Biopharmaceuticals

Promoting biopharmaceuticals requires an individualized strategy due to their distinctive properties. Here are a few key differences and considerations when compared with conventional pharmaceutical marketing:

1. *Scientific Complexity*: Biopharmaceuticals, or "biologics," are composed of molecules derived from living organisms and can often be quite complicated in their structure and mechanism of action. Marketing these products requires in-depth knowledge of this science, including target diseases, mechanisms of action, and potential patient benefits, and knowing where best to market these products.
2. *Regulatory Compliance*: Biopharmaceuticals must conform to strict regulatory requirements. Marketers must navigate these complex guidelines while adhering to specific ones for promoting biologics accurately, like conveying approved indications, risks, and benefits for each biologic.
3. *Target Audience*: Biopharmaceuticals are typically prescribed by specialists such as oncologists, rheumatologists, or immunologists. Therefore, effective marketing requires cultivating relationships with these key opinion leaders (KOLs) to gain insight and understand their treatment preferences, needs, and potential challenges.
4. *Clinical Evidence*: To establish product safety and efficacy, successful biopharmaceutical marketing relies heavily on scientific evidence such as clinical trial results, real-world data collection, and post-marketing studies. Marketers must effectively communicate this evidence to healthcare professionals, payers, and patients.
5. *Market Access*: Biopharmaceuticals can sometimes face reimbursement challenges due to their higher costs and more complicated administration, so marketers need to work closely with payers, health authorities, and reimbursement agencies to demonstrate their cost-effectiveness and ensure market access.
6. *Patient Support*: Biopharmaceutical marketing typically entails providing patients with support throughout their treatment journey, whether providing educational materials, access programs, financial assistance, and patient services to increase adherence and outcomes.
7. *Competitive Landscape*: Biopharmaceuticals can face unique competition in the form of biosimilars or innovative biologics; marketers must keep tabs on this space, distinguish their product's distinctive features, and explain any advantages over rival therapies.
8. *Digital Engagement and Educational Content*: As with pharmaceutical marketing, biopharmaceutical marketing relies heavily on digital channels; but due to the scientific complexity and specialist audience involved, strategies should be tailored specifically for biopharmaceuticals, delivering targeted educational content through relevant platforms, like medical conferences, webinars or online communities.

Marketing biopharmaceuticals requires an in-depth knowledge of their scientific and regulatory landscape, effective communication of clinical evidence, cooperation among key stakeholders and patient support programs, plus strategic marketing approaches combined with scientific expertise for product launches and successful market penetration.

Biosensors

Biosensors are analytical devices that convert a biological response into an electrical signal. They have been increasingly integrated into healthcare solutions to monitor, diagnose, and manage various conditions. Introducing and promoting biosensors can reshape the industry in various ways when considering pharma marketing:

Applications of Biosensors in Pharma

1. *Drug Monitoring*: Biosensors can monitor the level of a drug in a patient's system, ensuring the drug remains within therapeutic levels and helping prevent toxicities.
2. *Disease Monitoring*: Biosensors can track markers or conditions related to diseases, such as glucose levels in diabetes or INR (International Normalized Ratio) levels for patients on anticoagulants.
3. *Drug Delivery*: Some advanced systems can monitor levels and administer medications in response to the reading, ensuring optimal drug dosing.
4. *Clinical Trials*: Biosensors can collect real-time patient data during clinical trials, providing a

richer data set to understand drug effects and side effects.

Implications for Pharma Marketers

1. *Value Proposition*: Biosensors can elevate the value proposition of a pharmaceutical product by offering more than just the drug. For instance, an insulin product paired with a biosensor that provides real-time glucose monitoring can offer significant advantages over competitors.
2. *Patient Engagement and Adherence*: By offering tools that allow patients to be more engaged with their health and treatments, there is a potential to improve medication adherence. Better adherence can lead to improved outcomes, reinforcing the value of the medication and leading to better brand loyalty.
3. *Data Collection and Insights*: Biosensors can provide pharma companies with a wealth of data (with proper patient consent) that can be analyzed for insights, leading to better patient segmentation, personalized medicine approaches, or understanding of patient behavior.
4. *Regulatory Considerations*: Marketing a drug-device combo may come with additional regulatory hurdles. Marketers must know their target markets' regulatory framework for drugs and medical devices.
5. *Pricing and Reimbursement*: Integrating biosensors might justify premium pricing, but marketers must be prepared to demonstrate the added value to payers, healthcare providers, and patients. Payers will be particularly interested in evidence that the biosensor component leads to better outcomes or reduced healthcare costs.
6. *Educational Needs*: Healthcare professionals and patients may need training and education about using the biosensor component effectively, translating to a need for additional marketing materials, training programs, and possibly dedicated support teams.
7. *Competitive Differentiation*: As more Pharma companies integrate biosensors, simply having a sensor won't be enough. Marketers must emphasize their biosensors' unique features, accuracy, user-friendliness, or other differentiating factors.
8. *Collaborations and Partnerships*: Pharma companies might collaborate with tech companies specializing in biosensor technology. These partnerships can be highlighted in marketing campaigns, especially if the tech partner has a strong reputation.
9. *Data Privacy and Ethical Considerations*: Collecting data through biosensors can raise privacy concerns. Pharma marketers should prioritize and highlight data security measures and ethical data using, ensuring patients that their data is protected and used responsibly.

Integrating biosensors in pharma adds a layer of complexity but also offers numerous opportunities for marketers. By staying ahead of the curve and prioritizing patient value and safety, Pharma marketers can leverage biosensor technology to position their products more effectively in the market.

Biosimilars

Biosimilars are biological products that are highly similar to an already approved biological product, often referred to as the originator or reference product. However, unlike generic drugs, which are exact replicas of their reference products, biosimilars cannot be considered exact copies due to biological molecules' complexity and manufacturing processes.

Here are a few key points about biosimilars:

1. *Biological Nature*: These drugs come from living organisms like proteins, antibodies, or complex molecules produced within living cells that contain complex molecules. They are typically produced through recombinant DNA technology or other biotechnological processes.
2. *Reference Product*: Biosimilars are compared to a specific reference biological product that has already received regulatory approval and demonstrated safety and efficacy. The reference product serves as a benchmark for demonstrating similarity.
3. *High Similarity*: Biosimilars must demonstrate a high degree of similarity to the reference product in terms of structure, biological activity, efficacy, safety, and immunology.
4. *Regulatory Pathway*: Biosimilars undergo a distinct regulatory approval pathway, typically involving comprehensive comparability studies demonstrating similarity to the reference product. The regulatory requirements for biosimilars vary across countries and regions, but they generally involve demonstrating similar quality, efficacy, and safety profiles.
5. *Clinical Trials*: Biosimilar development may require comparative clinical studies to establish similarity in safety and efficacy. These studies compare the biosimilar to the reference product in a sensitive patient population, assessing factors such as pharmacokinetics, immunogenicity, and clinical outcomes.

6. *Cost Savings*: Biosimilars are intended to offer more affordable alternatives to reference biological products. By introducing competition into the market, biosimilars have the potential to reduce healthcare costs and improve patient access to essential therapies.
7. *Interchangeability*: Some biosimilars may meet additional regulatory requirements to be designated interchangeable with the reference product. Therefore, these can be easily substituted without involving healthcare providers or pharmacists to switch.

Biosimilar products must undergo post-marketing surveillance for their safety and effectiveness, such as using pharmacovigilance programs to gather adverse event reports and ongoing safety monitoring.

Biosimilar development and approval require an established scientific and regulatory framework to guarantee patient safety and therapeutic equivalence. As specific regulations and requirements may differ depending on where one resides, it is wise to contact local regulatory bodies for accurate and up-to-date information.

Biotechnology

Biotechnology or Biotech uses living organisms or biological systems to develop or create products. In the context of the pharmaceutical industry, biotechnology has been transformative, leading to the development of innovative drugs, therapies, and diagnostic tools. For pharma marketers, the rise of biotechnology presents both challenges and opportunities:

1. Innovative Therapies

- Biotechnology has enabled the creation of groundbreaking therapies, such as gene and cell therapies, monoclonal antibodies, and RNA interference.
- *Implication for Marketers*: The novelty of these therapies requires robust educational efforts to inform healthcare professionals, patients, and payers about their mechanisms, benefits, and potential risks.

2. Precision Medicine

- Biotech advancements have accelerated the move towards personalized medicine, where treatments are tailored based on individual genetic profiles.
- *Implication for Marketers*: Marketing campaigns can emphasize treatments' unique and tailored nature, suggesting higher efficacy and targeted outcomes.

3. Higher Costs

- Due to their complexity in research, development, and manufacturing, biotech drugs and therapies often carry higher price tags.
- *Implication for Marketers*: Justifying these costs becomes paramount. Marketers must communicate the long-term value, potential cost savings (like reduced hospital stays), and superior efficacy to stakeholders.

4. Biosimilars and Competition

- Similar to how generics compete with branded small molecule drugs, biosimilars (biotech equivalents of generics) pose competition to original biotech drugs.
- *Implication for Marketers*: It is essential to differentiate original products from biosimilars, highlighting aspects like original research, consistent manufacturing quality, or patient support programs.

5. Complex Regulatory Pathways

- Biotech products often face rigorous and intricate regulatory scrutiny due to their novel nature.
- *Implication for Marketers*: Building trust through transparency, showcasing rigorous clinical trials, and emphasizing post-market safety surveillance can assuage concerns.

6. Patient Engagement and Advocacy

- Biotech therapies often address rare or severe conditions, making patient advocacy groups vital stakeholders.
- *Implication for Marketers*: Building strong relationships with these groups, involving them in drug development processes, and supporting their initiatives can bolster the product's reputation and acceptance.

7. Ethical Considerations

- Biotech, especially in areas like gene editing, brings forth ethical dilemmas.
- *Implication for Marketers*: Engaging in ethical discussions, being transparent about the company's stance, and addressing societal concerns proactively is essential.

8. Advanced Diagnostics

- Biotech has enabled advanced diagnostic tools, allowing early and more precise disease detection.

- *Implication for Marketers*: There is an opportunity to market treatments, diagnostic tools, and kits, emphasizing their accuracy and importance in disease management.

9. Digital Integration and Data

- Biotech often intertwines with digital technologies, generating vast data from research and patient outcomes.
- *Implication for Marketers*: Highlighting data-driven insights and real-world evidence and integrating digital tools (like apps for patient monitoring) can enhance marketing strategies.

10. Global Reach

- Biotech therapies, especially for rare diseases, have a global patient base due to the rarity of the conditions.
- *Implication for Marketers*: Global marketing strategies, understanding regional regulatory and cultural differences, and ensuring broad access becomes crucial.

11. Continued Education

- The rapidly evolving nature of biotechnology means that new findings and therapies are continually emerging.
- *Implication for Marketers*: Marketers must stay updated and provide accurate and up-to-date information. This might involve regular training sessions, attending biotech conferences, and collaborating with R&D departments.

As biotechnology continues to shape the pharmaceutical landscape, marketers must adapt to its challenges and opportunities. With a nuanced understanding of biotech advancements and a patient-centric approach, pharma marketers can effectively communicate the benefits of these novel therapies to diverse stakeholders.

Biotech

Biotech, short for biotechnology, uses living organisms or their components to develop products or processes that benefit various industries, including healthcare, agriculture, and environmental sustainability. Biotechnology utilizes biological systems, such as cells, proteins, and genetic material, to create innovative solutions and technologies.

Biotechnology is crucial in discovering, developing, and producing new drugs and therapies to treat some difficult-to-treat chronic and rare diseases. It encompasses a wide range of applications, including:

1. *Drug Discovery*: Biotech tools and techniques help identify and study disease targets, such as specific genes, proteins, or cellular pathways. This knowledge helps researchers develop drugs that can interact with these targets by blocking or enhancing their activity to treat diseases.
2. *Genetic Engineering*: Biotech enables genetic engineering, which involves manipulating the genetic material of organisms, such as bacterial or mammalian cells, to produce therapeutic proteins or modify their properties. This process is commonly used to produce recombinant proteins, monoclonal antibodies, and gene therapies.
3. *Biopharmaceuticals*: Biopharmaceuticals are drugs derived from living organisms, such as vaccines, recombinant proteins, monoclonal antibodies, and cell and gene therapies. Biotech techniques revolutionized the manufacture of these biopharmaceuticals, allowing for the large-scale production of these complex molecules, ensuring consistent quality and purity.
4. *Diagnostics and Biomarkers*: Biotechnology plays a vital role in developing diagnostic tests and biomarkers that help in detecting, monitoring, and prognosis diseases. Techniques like polymerase chain reaction (PCR), immunoassays, and next-generation sequencing are widely used in diagnostics and personalized medicine.
5. *Personalized Medicine*: Biotech enables the development of personalized medicine approaches, where treatments are tailored to an individual's genetic makeup, lifestyle, or disease characteristics. This involves identifying genetic markers or biomarkers that indicate a patient's response to a particular treatment, allowing for more targeted and effective therapies.
6. *Regenerative Medicine*: Biotechnology advances regenerative medicine to repair or replace damaged tissues or organs. Stem cell research, tissue engineering, and gene editing techniques are utilized to develop innovative therapies for spinal cord injuries, cardiovascular diseases, and organ transplantation.
7. *Bioprocessing and Biomanufacturing*: Biotech is essential in optimizing the processes involved in manufacturing biopharmaceuticals. It includes developing cell culture techniques, bioreactors, purification methods, and downstream processing to ensure efficient and cost-effective production of therapeutic proteins and other biologics.

Overall, biotechnology profoundly impacts health care, enabling the development of new drugs, personalized therapies, diagnostic tools, and regenerative treatments. It continues to drive innovation and revolutionize various sectors by harnessing the power of living systems to address critical challenges and improve human health.

Role of Biotech in Pharma Marketing

Biotech plays a significant role in pharma marketing by enabling innovative strategies and providing new tools to pharmaceutical companies. Here are some ways biotech influences pharma marketing:

1. *Targeted Marketing*: Biotech allows for a deeper understanding of disease mechanisms and patient populations, enabling pharmaceutical companies to develop targeted therapies. This knowledge can be leveraged in marketing efforts to identify and reach the specific patient groups who would benefit from these therapies. Biotech tools like genetic testing and biomarker identification help identify and segment patient populations.
2. *Personalized Medicine*: Biotech advancements have led to the development of personalized medicine, where treatments are tailored to individual patients based on their genetic makeup or other specific characteristics. Thus, pharmaceutical marketers can communicate the value of personalized therapies to healthcare providers and patients, emphasizing the potential for improved outcomes and patient experiences.
3. *Digital Marketing and Data Analytics*: Biotech has also contributed to the rise of digital marketing strategies in the pharmaceutical industry. Companies can reach a broader audience through digital channels and engage more effectively with healthcare professionals and patients. Biotech tools, combined with data analytics, help pharmaceutical marketers gain insights into the behavior and preferences of their target audience, enabling them to develop personalized and data-driven marketing campaigns.
4. *Disease Awareness and Education*: Biotech innovations provide opportunities for pharmaceutical companies to educate healthcare professionals and the general public about diseases and treatment options. With advancements in biotechnology, companies can create interactive and engaging educational materials, such as virtual reality simulations and augmented reality experiences. Furthermore, mobile applications can improve disease awareness and enhance patient understanding of complex treatment processes.
5. *Clinical Trials and Real-World Evidence*: Biotech tools and technologies are vital in clinical trials and real-world evidence generation. These advancements help pharmaceutical companies collect and analyze data more efficiently, leading to faster drug development and regulatory approval processes. The ability to demonstrate the safety and efficacy of a product through robust clinical trials and real-world evidence strengthens marketing efforts, as companies can provide evidence-based information to healthcare professionals and patients.
6. *Health Tech Partnerships*: Biotech and pharmaceutical companies often collaborate with health tech startups and digital health platforms to enhance their marketing strategies. These partnerships can involve leveraging wearable devices, mobile apps, or telemedicine solutions to improve patient monitoring, medication adherence, and treatment outcomes. By integrating these technologies into their marketing campaigns, pharmaceutical companies can position themselves as innovative and patient-centric.

Biotech innovations have transformed pharmaceutical marketing by enabling targeted marketing, personalized medicine, digital marketing strategies, disease education, leveraging clinical trials and real-world evidence, and fostering collaborations with health tech companies. These advancements contribute to more effective and patient-centered marketing approaches in the pharmaceutical industry.

Bipolar Scale

The Bipolar Scale, a survey question used in pharmaceutical marketing, measures customer attitudes and perceptions toward a product or service. This scale usually has two opposing adjectives and a neutral middle point. Respondents are asked to identify where they fall on the scale. The following are some examples of bipolar scale questions used in pharmaceutical marketing research:

1. Which rating would you assign this medication's effectiveness to? Very Effective—Neither effective nor ineffective—Not at all effective?
2. What are your chances of recommending it to a friend? Very likely—Neither likely nor unlikely—Very unlikely?

3. How easy is this medication's dosing schedule for you? Very convenient— Neither convenient nor inconvenient – Not at all convenient?
4. What is your opinion on the importance of the drug's cost? Very important— Neither important nor unimportant—Not At all important?
5. What level of satisfaction do you feel about the product's overall experience? Very satisfied— Neither satisfied nor dissatisfied—Very dissatisfied?

Because they provide a deeper understanding of healthcare professionals' and customers' attitudes toward products or services, bipolar scale questions can be invaluable for pharmaceutical marketing research. These questions can be used to compare attitudes or perceptions between different groups or subgroups. This includes patients with different diseases or healthcare professionals with different experience levels.

Pharmaceutical companies can gain valuable insights about their target audience by asking bipolar scale questions. This allows them to create more effective marketing strategies.

Bivariate Data

Bivariate data is a collection of information that includes two variables. Bivariate data is used in pharmaceutical marketing research to study the relationship between two variables. Bivariate data is used in pharma marketing for the following:

A. *Correlation Studies*: Correlation studies look at the relationship between two variables to determine their relationship. Pharma companies might use bivariate data to examine patient age and medication compliance rates to see if there is a connection.
B. *Drug Efficacy Studies*: Bivariate data allows researchers to explore the relationship between drug dose and patient response rates to determine an ideal dosage based on medical conditions or other considerations.
C. *Patient Satisfaction Surveys*: Bivariate data can be analyzed to determine the relationship between patient satisfaction and elements such as medication side effects, ease of use, effectiveness, and overall effectiveness. This data helps pharmaceutical companies pinpoint areas for enhancing their products and services.

Bivariate data analysis can be a vital tool in pharmaceutical marketing research. It helps companies discover relationships between variables influencing their marketing strategies and product development.

Bivariate Analysis

Bivariate analysis is used in pharmaceutical marketing to analyze two variables and establish their relationship. In addition, this type of analysis is used by pharma marketers to understand how variables interact and impact sales and other marketing outcomes. Here are some examples showing how bivariate analysis can help pharma marketers:

1. *Sales and Promotion*: Pharmaceutical companies utilize bivariate analysis to examine the relationship between promotional activities and sales activities, like direct mail campaigns or email marketing efforts, to help assess their effect on sales to establish which strategies work most efficiently. For instance, they might assess the impact of various promotional tactics such as email or social media ads.
2. *Product Effectiveness and Patient Satisfaction*: Using bivariate analysis can give researchers invaluable insight into any correlations between product effectiveness and patient satisfaction; specifically, accumulating patient satisfaction data can reveal whether satisfied users of certain products tend to achieve superior health outcomes than less pleased counterparts.
3. *Sales and Market Share*: Bivariate Analysis can be utilized to examine the relationship between market share and an organization's sales data; in doing this, a firm could compare its sales data with its market share to determine if its position has increased or decreased over time, providing insight as to whether their business has gained or lost ground over time.
4. *Physician Prescribing Patterns*: Bivariate Analysis can be utilized to study physician prescribing patterns and patient demographics with prescription data as an indicator. For example, companies could utilize physician practices' prescription data as an indicator to see whether certain populations, like older individuals or people experiencing certain medical conditions, tend to receive medications from them more readily than others.
5. *Adverse Events and Product Safety*: To better comprehend the relationship between product safety and adverse events, companies may look at data about adverse events and see if they correlate with a product's safety profile.

Blanket Coverage

Blanket coverage is a marketing strategy targeting a broad audience without any segmentation. Broad coverage is a term used in pharmaceutical marketing to describe any message or campaign that reaches all patients, regardless of their medical conditions or demographic characteristics. Here are some examples of pharmaceutical marketing that has blanket coverage:

1. *Direct-to-Consumer Adverting (DTCA)*: Direct-to-Consumer Advertising (DTC Ads) promote prescription medications directly to consumers to raise awareness regarding their benefits in treating specific conditions and bring greater understanding about treatment effectiveness among all.
2. *Mass Media Advertising*: Pharma companies often utilize mass media channels like TV, radio, and print ads to reach a larger audience with their marketing messages. While these ads don't focus on specific demographics or medical conditions, they aim to increase brand recognition of a particular product or service and build awareness.
3. *Industry Events*: Pharma companies sometimes participate in large-scale industry events and conferences. This allows them to meet other healthcare professionals, researchers, and stakeholders. These events might not specifically target certain demographic groups or medical conditions, yet they can still help build brand recognition and foster business relationships.

Though blanket coverage can boost brand recognition and reach large audiences, it might not be the optimal use of marketing resources. Blanket coverage can have a lower return on investment than targeted marketing strategies that target specific audiences or medical conditions.

Blitzkrieg Advertising

According to The History Channel, Blitzkrieg refers to an offensive warfare strategy that uses mobile forces like armored tanks and air support to strike an enemy quickly. This attack usually results in quick victory and minimal casualties for soldiers or artillery.

Blitzkrieg's advertising was originally based on a strategic military concept. However, it is now a highly effective marketing tactic. This involves intense activity across multiple media channels simultaneously. For example, pharmaceutical companies commonly employ this strategy when conducting major product launches and marketing campaigns to create a lasting impression.

Here are some examples of blitzkrieg ads used in pharmaceutical marketing:

1. Pfizer launched Viagra in 1998 as the first oral medication to treat erectile dysfunction. They used aggressive advertising campaigns to build their brand and quickly generate demand. They used television, print, radio, and direct mail to promote Viagra. These campaigns proved extremely successful, making them a household name in months.
2. Gilead Sciences introduced Sovaldi as a groundbreaking treatment for hepatitis in 2013. To promote their product, they launched an impressive multichannel advertising campaign encompassing television commercials, print ads, online ads, social media posts, and public relations activities. Ultimately, this strategy proved highly successful as Sovaldi quickly became one of the top pharmaceutical products available on the market.
3. Novartis introduced Entresto in 2015 as a new treatment for heart disease. They launched a multichannel campaign to quickly build their brand and educate patients and healthcare professionals about the medication's benefits. This included TV, print media, direct mail pieces, educational events, and television. As a result, Entresto gained market share quickly in a highly competitive space for cardiovascular products.

Blitzkrieg advertising is a powerful strategy for pharmaceutical companies when launching new products and entering competitive markets. However, it can be costly and risky. Therefore, companies must plan and execute campaigns carefully to maximize their impact and return on investments.

Blockbuster

Blockbusters in pharmaceutical marketing refer to drugs that generate at least $1 billion in annual sales, typically used to treat chronic conditions that impact millions of patients, like hypertension, diabetes, high cholesterol, and high blood pressure.

A combination of factors is what makes blockbuster drugs successful. These include strong clinical trial results, marketing campaigns that work, and the lack of viable alternatives. In addition, pharmaceutical companies are known for investing heavily in research and development to create and distribute blockbuster drugs. This can prove extremely profitable.

Blockbuster drug marketing strategies include targeting healthcare professionals like doctors and pharmacists with persuasive messaging and educational materials to increase drug awareness and encourage patients and their doctors to ask about the drug. Sponsorships and celebrity endorsements may also help to promote the drugs and increase their visibility. But the marketing of blockbuster drugs has often been criticized as encouraging unnecessary or harmful treatments while driving up healthcare costs. Pharma companies, therefore, face greater scrutiny to ensure their marketing practices are transparent and ethical while communicating potential benefits/risks of their drugs to both patients and healthcare professionals.

Here are some examples of blockbuster drugs:

1. Pfizer, a pharmaceutical giant, succeeded with several blockbuster drugs. Lipitor (Atorvastatin), used to reduce cholesterol and decrease heart disease risks, reached peak sales at $13 billion in 2006.
2. Humira (Adalimumab), used for treating autoimmune conditions like arthritis and psoriasis, Crohn's, and ulcerative colitis, recorded over $19 billion for AbbVie in 2020 sales.
3. Amgen produced Enbrel (Etanercept), an anti-autoimmune drug used to treat rheumatoid and psoriatic arthritis, reached its peak sales of $7.2 billion in annual sales in 2019.
4. Sovaldi (Sofosbuvir), an effective drug to treat hepatitis C, has a remarkable cure rate of more than 90%. Gilead Sciences generated $10 billion in sales for Sovaldi (Sofosbuvir) 2014.
5. Roche's peak sales for Avastin (Bevacizumab), used to treat different types of cancer, was $7 billion in 2017.

Blockchain

Blockchain is a distributed digital ledger technology used by multiple participants to keep an updated record of transactions or information. Initially introduced as the foundation of cryptocurrency like Bitcoin, its applications now extend well beyond finance alone.

At its core, blockchain consists of interlinked blockchains containing lists of data transactions.

Blockchain in Pharma

Blockchain can be leveraged in the pharmaceutical sector to enhance supply chain management, drug traceability, clinical trials, data security, and operational excellence. Here is an overview of its use within this field:

A. *Distributed Ledger*: Blockchain utilizes a distributed ledger as its backbone. This decentralized and unalterable record can store details regarding drug manufacturing, distribution, and other relevant details within the pharmaceutical industry.

B. *Transaction Validation*: Anytime a transaction occurs within a pharmaceutical supply chain, such as when drugs move between parties, this event is recorded as a block and verified by multiple participants to be added to the blockchain network.

How Blockchain Works in Pharma

Blockchain technology is increasingly being applied in the pharmaceutical industry to enhance supply chain management, drug traceability, clinical trials, and data security. Here is an outline of its usage:

1. *Distributed Ledger*: Blockchain provides its core data storage solution through the distributed ledger, an immutable and decentralized record of drug production, distribution, sales transactions, and any relevant details from pharmaceutical industries around the globe. This ledger documents all relevant details.
2. *Validation*: Any time there is a transaction in the pharmaceutical supply chain, such as moving drugs between parties, this event record must first be validated by multiple nodes in the network before being added as a block into blockchain technology. This consensus mechanism ensures integrity and accuracy in recorded data.
3. *Smart Contracts*: Smart contracts are self-executing agreements that automatically enforce predefined rules or conditions. In the pharmaceutical industry, smart contracts can authorize processes like drug authentication, quality control, and compliance with regulatory requirements. These contracts help eliminate intermediaries and reduce the potential for errors or fraud.
4. *Supply Chain Management*: Blockchain can improve transparency and traceability in the pharmaceutical supply chain. Each drug unit can be assigned its unique identifier, such as a serial number or barcode, which will be recorded on the blockchain. It allows stakeholders to track all aspects of a drug, from its manufacture through

distribution, while guaranteeing its authenticity and quality.

5. *Data Security*: Blockchain technology uses cryptography and decentralized consensus mechanisms to enhance data security. Data stored on the blockchain is cryptographically secured, preventing unauthorized access or tampering. Additionally, blockchain's distributed nature ensures no single-point failure, making it more resilient to cyberattacks.
6. *Clinical Trials*: Blockchain can streamline conducting clinical trials by securely storing and sharing patient data. It enables efficient data management, consent tracking, and auditability. Patients can have more control over their data and grant access to researchers securely while maintaining privacy.
7. *Counterfeit Drug Prevention*: Blockchain helps combat the issue of counterfeit drugs by providing a secure and immutable record of drug transactions. The transparency and traceability offered by blockchain can help verify the authenticity of drugs, reducing the risk of counterfeit products entering the supply chain.

Thus, blockchain technology in the pharmaceutical industry aims to enhance transparency, data integrity, and security while optimizing various processes across the supply chain and clinical trials. It can potentially revolutionize the industry by fostering trust, reducing costs, and improving patient safety.

Blog

Blogs are websites that provide insight into a topic and are frequently updated. The blog is a combination of two words: *Web* and *Log*. Blogs were originally online diaries that allowed people to record their daily lives. Since then, they have become essential platforms for businesses and individuals to share updates and information.

Pharma companies can use blogs to share more information than is allowed on websites about their products and initiatives. In addition, it allows pharmaceutical companies to ensure compliance with regulatory requirements for its informational articles, as they have full control over their content. Pharma can create two types of blogs: Unbranded Blogs or Branded Blogs.

Branded blogs can be a great way to raise brand awareness and give voice to patients in a particular disease state. They can also educate patients about specific diseases or products. In addition, branded blogs allow influencers to post content in online communities and forums that brands might be unable to access.

Because there are no restrictions on content creation, *Unbranded blogs* offer greater value. Notable examples are Sanofi's *Discuss Diabetes,* and Lundbeck's *Your Partner In Epilepsy*, a well-known blog in the pharmaceutical industry.

Here are some examples showing how pharmaceutical companies use blogs to market:

1. *Health Education*: Blogs can inform patients and healthcare professionals about certain diseases and conditions. Novartis' *Living Like You* blog provides information and support to multiple sclerosis patients and their caregivers.
2. *Thought Leadership*: Blogs can help a company or person position themselves as experts in certain areas of healthcare. Pfizer's *The Catalyst* blog features articles written by executives, industry experts, and thought leaders about healthcare-related topics.
3. *Product Promotion*: Pharmaceutical companies can use blogs to promote their products and highlight the benefits of their products. AstraZeneca's *LabTalk* blog explains its products in oncology and how they are used in cancer treatment.
4. *Patient Engagement*: Patients can use blogs to stay informed, encouraging them to participate in clinical trials, and provide feedback about pharmaceutical products. *Janssen Health's* blog, for example, features stories from patients and their perspectives on chronic illness.

A blog helps readers trust you and your company as experts in your field. Blogs foster relationships and encourage readers to return for more information. In addition, blogs regularly add new content to your website, which can be shared on social media, increasing traffic and inbound links. Here are just a few benefits blogging can bring to your site:

1. Shareable content should resonate with your target audience.
2. Infographics can be an ideal way of providing complex data in a simple, easy-to-understand way.
3. Blogs can be seamlessly linked to social media platforms like Twitter and Facebook. Notifying your followers about blog posts published on these networks will increase traffic to those pages.
4. Engaging your target audience is possible by regularly adding content to your blog. Search engines prefer fresh content. Therefore, regular posts will help improve your page ranking.

Blogs provide pharmaceutical companies with a powerful platform to communicate more directly and authentically with patients and healthcare professionals. Companies can use blogs to build trust and credibility with their target audience and drive growth. In addition, they can educate about diseases, foster thought leadership and promote products.

Body Language

Body language refers to people's nonverbal signals and cues to express thoughts, emotions, and intentions through physical movements and gestures like facial expressions, hand gestures, posture, eye contact, body position, and more subtle acts or behaviors.

Body language is essential to human communication, often revealing information that may not be expressed explicitly through words. It can convey emotions, attitudes, confidence levels, and interest in a conversation. Observing and interpreting body language can gain insights into a person's feelings and intentions.

Here are some common examples of body language and their associated meanings:

1. *Facial Expressions*: Smiling, frowning, raising eyebrows, or wrinkling the forehead conveys happiness, surprise, anger, or confusion.
2. *Eye Contact*: Maintaining eye contact indicates attentiveness, interest, and confidence, while avoiding eye contact may suggest discomfort, shyness, or dishonesty.
3. *Posture*: Standing or sitting upright typically signifies confidence and attentiveness, while slouching or crossing arms may indicate defensiveness, disinterest, or discomfort.
4. *Hand Gestures*: Various hand movements, such as pointing, waving, or thumbs-up, can express agreement, disagreement, emphasis, or enthusiasm.
5. *Touch*: Touching or physical contact can convey affection, reassurance, or dominance, depending on the context and relationship between individuals.
6. *Personal Space*: People have different comfort levels regarding personal space. Invading someone's personal space may be seen as aggressive or intrusive while maintaining an appropriate distance respects their boundaries.
7. *Mirroring*: When two individuals adopt similar body language, such as matching postures or gestures, it often indicates rapport, empathy, and connection.

It is important to note that while these examples can provide general insights into body language, interpreting individual gestures accurately requires considering the context, cultural differences, and individual variations. Combining body language observations with other verbal and contextual cues is crucial for a more comprehensive understanding of a person's communication.

Body Language and Non-verbal Communication

Body language is just one element of nonverbal communication; non-verbal is the umbrella term covering all non-verbal cues outside spoken and written language, such as touch, proximity (use of space), paralinguistic (tone, pitch volume, etc.), appearance, clothing, grooming as well as artifacts or objects used as means to send and interpret messages without verbal communication being employed directly by either party involved in communicating. All non-verbal forms can help facilitate successful dialogue without using spoken or written language alone.

Body Language in Pharma Marketing

Body language is significant in pharmaceutical marketing, particularly face-to-face interactions between sales representatives and healthcare professionals (HCPs). Here are a few ways body language can impact pharma marketing:

1. *Establishing Rapport*: Effective body language helps build rapport and trust with HCPs. Maintaining eye contact, using open and relaxed postures, and mirroring the HCP's body language (to a certain extent) can help create a positive connection. It is essential to convey confidence, sincerity, and attentiveness through non-verbal cues.
2. *Active Listening*: Engaging in active listening is crucial in marketing conversations. Non-verbal cues like nodding, maintaining an open posture, and facing the person directly indicate attentiveness and interest. These gestures demonstrate your interest in the HCP's needs and concerns.
3. *Confidence and Professionalism*: Body language can convey confidence and professionalism, essential in pharmaceutical sales. Standing or sitting tall, maintaining appropriate personal space, and using purposeful and controlled gestures can project confidence and competence in the marketed products or services.
4. *Facial Expressions*: Facial expressions can be expressive and convey various emotions, and impact how your message is perceived. A friendly and genuine smile can create a positive

impression and foster a more receptive atmosphere. Avoiding facial expressions that might be perceived as disinterest, arrogance, or dishonesty is important.

5. *Adaptation to Cultural Norms*: In a globalized industry like pharmaceuticals, understanding and adapting to cultural differences in body language is crucial. Different cultures have distinct norms and interpretations of body language cues. Awareness of these differences can help prevent miscommunications or misunderstandings in marketing efforts.

It is important to note that body language should be used authentically and sensitively. Overdoing or manipulating body language can come across as insincere or manipulative, which can harm relationships with HCPs. Effective body language should support and enhance spoken communication, creating a positive and productive environment for marketing pharmaceutical products and services.

Boomerang Effect

The Boomerang Effect, more commonly referred to as Boomerang Principle or Backfire Effect, is a psychological phenomenon in which attempts at persuasion or influence result in exactly the opposite way, and resistance against change becomes even stronger; rather than becoming convinced or persuaded, an attempt leads them into strongly holding onto original beliefs or behavior patterns than before.

Boomerang effects often result from perceived threats to an individual's identity, beliefs, or values. When confronted with information or arguments contradicting these ideals, people may need to defend their sense of self by guarding against changing their opinions. Unfortunately, this may strengthen existing attitudes and behavior rather than bring about desired changes.

The boomerang effect takes its name from boomerangs, which are objects used for throwing that return to their use instead of hitting their intended targets, much as persuasive messages often do if sent unsuccessfully, without ever reaching their desired destinations.

Note that the boomerang effect may not apply in every situation or circumstance; factors like the strength of existing beliefs, the credibility of persuasion, and persuasive message composition could all play a part.

Boomerang Effect on Pharma Marketing

In pharmaceutical marketing, the boomerang effect refers to situations where attempts to promote a particular medication or healthcare intervention backfired, leading to unintended consequences such as resistance or skepticism from the target audience. This can occur when marketing messages or tactics are perceived as manipulative, misleading, or conflicting with the values and beliefs of the audience.

How Boomerang Effect Can Occur

What can lead to a boomerang effect in pharmaceutical marketing? Here are a few reasons:

1. While fear-based advertisements can help encourage patients to take their medication on time, they could backfire by alarming viewers of its potential risks if an advertisement focuses too heavily on its risks; people could then feel anxious or fearful and decide not to take their prescribed dose altogether.
2. Fake claims about medication's safety or efficacy can have serious adverse consequences, even when patients receive it as intended. Even when their drug is safe and effective, patients may remain skeptical.
3. Negative media attention about medications may have a devastating impact. Patients could become wary if news stories describe negative side effects or safety concerns as reported in the media; even without valid reasons to do so, they might eschew taking it altogether.
4. Boomerang effects may also result from aggressive sales tactics like pushy representatives or high-pressure pitches; healthcare professionals and patients may become annoyed and stop using or taking the medication even though it is safe and effective.

How to Prevent a Boomerang Effect

Dealing with the boomerang effect in pharmaceutical marketing requires a thoughtful and ethical approach. Here are some strategies that can help mitigate the risk of the boomerang effect and maintain trust with the target audience:

1. *Transparency and Honesty*: Be transparent about the limitations and potential side effects of the medication or intervention being promoted. Present the information honestly and rationally, acknowledging both the benefits and risks. Avoid exaggerated or misleading claims that may erode credibility.
2. *Education and Awareness*: Provide comprehensive educational resources to healthcare professionals and patients. Promote a deeper understanding of the condition being

treated, the available treatment options, and the evidence supporting the efficacy and safety of the promoted medication. Encourage open dialogue and address questions and concerns.

3. *Empathy and Patient-Centric Approach*: Understand the target audience's needs, perspectives, and concerns. Tailor marketing messages to resonate with their values and priorities. Emphasize the potential benefit to patients' quality of life and well-being.
4. *Key Opinion Leader Collaboration*: Engage respected healthcare professionals and key opinion leaders to endorse and communicate the benefits of the medication. Their credibility and expertise can help build trust and reduce resistance.
5. *Two-way Communication*: Encourage open dialogue and actively listen to healthcare professionals' and patients' feedback and concerns. Respond promptly and respectfully to questions or criticisms. This approach can help address misconceptions, correct misinformation, and foster trust.
6. *Ethical Marketing Practices*: Ethical marketing practices can play a crucial role in mitigating the boomerang effect by fostering trust, transparency, and genuine connections with healthcare professionals and patients. Therefore, adhere to industry regulations and ethical guidelines. Avoid aggressive or misleading marketing tactics perceived as manipulative or pushy. Maintain the highest possible standard of integrity and professionalism in all marketing activities.

Reducing the boomerang effect in pharmaceutical marketing takes persistent efforts and an unwavering dedication to building trust and credibility with healthcare professionals and patients. Open communication channels, ethical business practices, and patient-centricity play key roles in maintaining positive associations between healthcare providers, patients, and pharmaceutical companies.

Bounce Rate

The bounce rate is a measure of how many people leave a website without ever taking any action. For example, if many people visit Pharma marketing websites without taking any action, it could indicate that they are not converting to sales. High bounce rates could indicate that website visitors aren't finding the content interesting or relevant. Here are a few examples of how pharma marketing can use bounce rate:

1. *Landing Pages*: Pharmaceutical companies might use landing pages to market specific drugs or treatments. If a landing page has a high bounce rate, it could indicate that the site is not effectively communicating the benefits of the drug or treatment.
2. *Email Campaigns*: Pharmaceutical companies might send emails to promote their products. If the bounce rate is high and the link to a website is included in the email, this could mean that recipients did not fully engage with the content.
3. *Online Ad*: Pharma companies might use online ads to drive visitors to their website. If an advertisement's bounce rate is high, it could indicate that it was not directed toward its intended target market.
4. *Mobile Optimization*: Pharmaceutical companies must optimize their websites to be easily accessible on mobile devices as more people access them. A high bounce rate could indicate difficulty using or reading clearly on small screens.

Pharmaceutical companies should monitor the bounce rate of their website to identify areas for improvement, and make necessary modifications that engage target audiences more effectively.

Bradford Hill Guidelines

The Bradford Hill Criteria or Guidelines also referred to as Bradford Hill's Causality Considerations, were first proposed by British epidemiologist Sir Austin Bradford during the 1960s as a means of evaluating potential causal relationships between exposures (risk factors or interventions) and outcomes (disease/health conditions). These criteria assess the likelihood that such associations exist.

The Bradford Hill criteria do not provide conclusive proof of causality but instead serve as a framework to measure evidence supporting causal links commonly employed in epidemiology, public health, and other scientific fields. Here are nine criteria outlined by Bradford Hill that you may use:

1. *Strength of Association*: A strong association between exposure and outcome is more likely to increase a causal relationship.
2. *Consistency*: The relationship between exposure and outcome should be observed consistently across different studies and populations.
3. *Specificity*: The exposure should be specifically associated with the outcome rather than related to multiple outcomes.

4. *Temporality*: The exposure should precede the outcome in time, suggesting a causal relationship.
5. *Biological Gradient (Dose-response Relationship)*: There should be an apparent dose-response relationship in which an increase in exposure leads to an increased risk for certain outcomes.
6. *Plausibility*: Any proposed causal relationships must be biologically plausible based on current knowledge and understanding of disease processes.
7. *Coherence*: The causal relationship should be coherent with existing knowledge and not contradict other established facts.
8. *Experiment*: Evidence provided through experiments such as randomized controlled trials provides stronger proof of causality than observational studies alone.
9. *Analogy*: Similarities between studied relationships and known causes provide additional proof for causality.

Please note that all criteria must be satisfied to establish a causal relationship; their relative weights and importance depend on the specific context and research question being explored.

Researchers and scientists often employ these criteria in evaluating evidence and making informed judgments regarding causality. It should be remembered, though, that causality establishment can often be an extremely complex endeavor, and in certain instances, definitive results may not be achievable.

Implications for Pharma Marketers

The Bradford Hill criteria for causality have implications for pharma marketers regarding how they communicate and promote their products. Here are some key implications:

1. *Evidence*: Pharma marketers must ensure the evidence supporting the efficacy and safety of their products meets several criteria relating to the strength of association, consistency, temporality, etc. Utilize high-quality clinical studies like randomized controlled trials as part of this strategy to support the claims made about them.
2. *Dose-response Relationship*: Highlighting a dose-response relationship can be beneficial in marketing pharmaceutical products. If the product's effectiveness or safety improves with increasing the dosage or duration of use, this information can help strengthen the case for its use.
3. *Plausibility and Coherence*: Pharma marketers should strive to communicate the scientific plausibility of their product's mechanism of action and how it fits coherently within the existing knowledge and understanding of the disease. This can help build credibility and trust among healthcare professionals and patients.
4. *Comparative Effectiveness*: The analogy criterion suggests that similarities with other known causal relationships can support the case for causality. Pharma marketers can leverage comparative effectiveness data to show that their products perform better or are equivalent to treatment options. This can help differentiate their product and demonstrate its potential impact.
5. *Education and Transparency*: Pharma marketers should educate healthcare professionals and patients about the evidence behind their products. Transparently sharing information about clinical trials, study designs, and endpoints can help build trust and credibility.
6. *Regulatory Compliance*: Pharma marketers must ensure that their promotional activities adhere to regulatory guidelines and not overstate the evidence to make unsupported claims. Compliance with regulations helps maintain ethical marketing practices and protects patients, and the pharmaceutical company's reputation.
7. *Working With Healthcare Professionals*: Working closely with healthcare professionals allows pharma marketers to ensure their promotional activities match what scientific communities understand and expect, gathering real-world evidence that could support causal relationships between products and their outcomes.

Pharma marketers should prioritize accurately communicating the evidence supporting their products, aligning their messaging with scientific standards, and maintaining transparency in their promotional efforts. By doing so, they can enhance trust, credibility, and the adoption of their pharmaceutical products.

Brand

In the pharmaceutical industry, a brand refers to a specific product or medication a pharmaceutical company markets. Branding gives that product its identity in the marketplace and sets it apart from similar offerings on sale.

Pharmaceutical companies devote significant resources and effort toward promoting their brands among healthcare professionals, patients, and consumers. Branding involves creating an identifiable name, logo, packaging, and overall image for the product that sparks associations or perceptions in its target audiences.

Brand in pharma marketing is crucial in establishing product recognition, building trust, and influencing prescribing decisions. They convey information about the product's efficacy, safety, and therapeutic benefits. Additionally, brands can also communicate specific attributes of differentiating factors of the medication, such as extended-release formulations, unique delivery mechanisms, or specialized indications.

Branding in pharmaceutical marketing extends beyond just the product itself. It also encompasses the pharmaceutical company's reputation, values, and overall corporate identity. A strong brand can create customer loyalty, foster positive relationships, and contribute to a product's success and market positioning within the competitive pharmaceutical landscape.

Pharma companies must ensure their branding complies with legal and regulatory requirements such as trademark laws and FDA guidelines for pharmaceutical products that must undergo stringent safety and efficacy testing before being sold to the patients.

How do you develop a pharmaceutical brand?

An effective pharmaceutical brand requires creating an easily understood identity among patients, healthcare providers, and other stakeholders. Below are steps you can follow to develop one:

1. *Conduct Market Research*: Analyze your target audience, competition, and market trends to discover unmet needs and opportunities for differentiation.
2. *Define Brand Values*: Your brand's purpose, values, and mission should align with the aspirations and needs of your target audience.
3. *Create a Brand Identity*: Choose a name, logo, and visual identity that conveys your values to your ideal customer.
4. *Communicate the Brand*: Use advertising, public relations, and social media platforms to increase awareness and brand image.
5. *Establish Trust and Credibility* by positioning the brand as a trustworthy source of healthcare information through education and clinical data.

Here are some examples of successful Pharma Brands:

1. *Viagra* from Pfizer, used to treat erectile dysfunction, has long been recognized and has become synonymous with the condition it treats.
2. *Humira* from AbbVie is also well known, having established itself as an extremely successful medication used for autoimmune conditions like rheumatoid arthritis and psoriasis treatment with a great brand image.
3. *Otezla*: Celgene's brand for treating psoriasis and psoriatic arthritis has cultivated a passionate online community through its *Show More of You* campaign.
4. *Botox*: Allergan's Botox is the Go-to brand when it comes to treating wrinkles. Botox has enjoyed celebrity support and promotion via social media from prominent figures who endorse its products.
5. Gilead stands out with innovative HIV and Hepatitis C treatments like *Truvada* and *Harvoni*.

These brands have successfully created identities that resonate with their target audiences and stand out.

Brand Advocacy

In pharmaceutical marketing, brand advocacy refers to active promotion and support for a product or brand by people who have had a positive experience. Patients, healthcare professionals, and other stakeholders can become brand advocates and share their feelings.

Brand advocacy builds trust and raises brand awareness. A trusted source will increase the likelihood of people purchasing a product.

Here are some examples to show how pharmaceutical companies can use advocacy:

1. *Patient Testimonials*: Patients can share their positive experiences with medication online and face-to-face, such as in inpatient forums or support groups. You can inspire others to try the medication by sharing your stories!
2. *Key Opinion Leaders (KOLs)* are healthcare experts who have a great deal of influence on others' opinions and behavior. Pharmaceutical companies may invite KOLs to participate in marketing campaigns, speak at conferences, or write articles.
3. *Patient Advocacy Groups* represent patients affected by a specific illness or condition. These groups may be partnered with pharmaceutical

companies to provide support services and education for patients.

4. *Social Media Influencers*: These digital professionals have a large following that can promote products to their followers. These influential individuals on social media could help pharmaceutical companies market their products efficiently and effectively.
5. *Healthcare Providers*: Physicians, pharmacists, nurses, and others who prescribe or administer prescription drugs can be your brand ambassadors. In addition, pharmaceutical companies may offer information and resources for healthcare professionals to better comprehend and share their products' advantages with patients.

Pharmaceutical companies can leverage brand advocacy strategies to raise brand recognition and establish rapport among their target audiences. Brand advocates can help increase brand recognition and sales by sharing their personal experiences and word-of-mouth referrals. In addition, brand advocates should be able to communicate with pharmaceutical companies to discuss patient safety and ethical marketing strategies.

Brand Advocates

Brand Advocates actively support and promote a particular brand, product, or company voluntarily. They go beyond being satisfied customers and become enthusiastic and loyal advocates for the brand. Brand advocates may include customers, employees, influencers, or members of the general public who have developed an emotional attachment to your brand. Brand advocates share positive experiences about using it while advocating against criticism or competition. Furthermore, they frequently interact with it on social media as user-generated content is created, testimonials are given out, and online discussions about it occur.

Characteristics of Brand Advocates

Here are some of the prominent characteristics of brand advocates:

1. *Passion and Enthusiasm*: Brand advocates have a genuine passion and enthusiasm for the brand. They believe in its values, products, or services and are eager to share their positive experiences.
2. *Trustworthiness*: Brand advocates are seen as credible sources of information and recommendations. Their opinions and recommendations carry weight and influence others' brand perceptions.
3. *Engagement*: Brand advocates actively interact with their brand through various platforms such as social media, forums, or events, such as creating user-generated content for brand posts on various channels like social media or forums or attending brand-related events, creating user-generated posts related to that brand or sharing brand-related posts with fellow supporters and engaging other advocates as part of a network of support for that particular cause.
4. *Authenticity*: Brand advocates genuinely believe in the brand and its offerings. Incentives or ulterior motives do not drive their advocacy but stem from their personal experiences and satisfaction.
5. *Influence*: Brand advocates can influence the opinions, behaviors, and purchasing decisions of others. Their recommendations and endorsements can significantly impact brand perception and customer acquisition.

Importance of Brand Advocates

1. *Word-of-Marketing Marketing*: Brand advocates are crucial in spreading positive word-of-mouth about the brand. Their recommendations and testimonials can reach a wider audience and have a powerful impact on brand awareness and reputation.
2. *Increased Credibility*: Brand advocates are seen as unbiased and trustworthy sources of information. Their positive endorsement adds credibility to the brand's messaging and can help overcome skepticism or doubt among potential customers.
3. *Cost-Effective Promotion*: Brand advocates promote the brand voluntarily, reducing the need for extensive advertising and marketing efforts. Their advocacy can generate organic buzz and attract new customers without significant financial investment.
4. *Customer Retention and Loyalty*: Brand advocates are typically highly loyal customers themselves. By nurturing and engaging with brand advocates, companies can strengthen customer relationships and foster long-term loyalty.
5. *Feedback and Improvement*: Brand advocates often provide valuable feedback and suggestions for product improvement or innovation. They can act as a source of insights and ideas for the brand's continuous development.

Building and nurturing a community of brand advocates is a valuable marketing strategy for companies, as it can lead to increased brand visibility, customer trust, and business growth.

Brand Advocates in Pharma

While brand advocacy is more commonly associated with consumer products, it also applies to the pharmaceutical industry. Here are a few examples of brand advocates in pharmaceutical marketing:

1. *Support Patient Advocacy Groups*: Collaborate with patient advocacy groups that pertain to your therapeutic area and collaborate with them by offering support, education, and resources that enable them to meet their goals. In addition, working closely together allows patient advocates to promote your brand within their communities while creating awareness around it.
2. *Offer Exemplary Customer Service*: Make sure that patients, healthcare providers, and other stakeholders enjoy positive interaction with your brand when engaging. Offer personalized support services like timely inquiries, responses, and problem resolution efficiently while encouraging brand advocates share their positive experiences with others.
3. *Key Opinion Leaders (KOLs)*: KOLs are respected healthcare professionals, such as doctors, researchers, or specialists, with expertise in specific therapeutic areas. They often strongly influence their peers and patients through their professional reputation and knowledge. In addition, KOLs can act as brand advocates by endorsing and recommending certain pharmaceutical products, participating in clinical trials, or speaking at industry events. For example, a renowned oncologist specializing in breast cancer research may be a KOL for a pharmaceutical company that develops targeted therapies. The KOL could advocate for these therapies, participate in promotional events, or educate other healthcare professionals about their benefits.
4. *Influencers and Patient Bloggers*: With social media's rise, online influencers and patient bloggers have emerged as key representatives within the pharmaceutical industry. These individuals frequently possess a significant following that shares their experiences regarding various diseases, treatments, medications, and more. Furthermore, these advocates can represent particular pharmaceutical brands or products by sharing treatment options through positive stories shared from followers, or reviews posted about specific pharmaceutical brands or products. For example, a patient blogger with rheumatoid arthritis could collaborate with a pharmaceutical company producing a new biologic medication to raise awareness and provide insights about its effect on their condition. In addition, by writing blog posts or producing videos about this drug, their blog could raise awareness and provide a deeper understanding.
5. *Healthcare Professionals and Prescribers*: Physicians, pharmacists, and other healthcare professionals can also act as brand advocates for pharmaceutical products. Healthcare professionals with positive experiences of any medication or treatment often recommend it to patients, speak about it at medical conferences, and share what they know with colleagues. For instance, cardiologists could act as brand advocates for new cholesterol-reducing medication, sharing their positive experiences and teach other healthcare providers of its benefits while prescribing it to suitable patients.

Ethical rules and regulations must be observed regarding brand advocacy in the pharmaceutical industry, including transparency about any financial ties between the brand and its advocates. In addition, pharmaceutical companies must uphold integrity by prioritizing patient well-being with accurate and balanced information through advocacy initiatives.

Cultivating Brand Advocates

Cultivating brand advocates in the pharmaceutical industry involves building strong relationships with stakeholders, engaging with them effectively, and providing value to encourage advocacy. Here are some strategies to cultivate brand advocates in pharma:

1. *Prioritize Patient-Centricity*: Place patients at the center of your brand's efforts. Develop medications, services, and initiatives that address their needs and improve their quality of life. Demonstrating a genuine commitment to patient well-being can positively impact patients to become brand advocates.
2. *Build Relationships with Healthcare Professionals*: Engage and collaborate with healthcare professionals, including physicians, pharmacists, and nurses. Provide educational resources, conduct seminars, and facilitate scientific exchanges to establish trust and credibility. This can lead to healthcare professionals recommending and advocating for your brand.
3. *Support Patient Advocacy Groups*: Collaborate with patient advocacy groups that pertain to your

therapeutic area and help them by providing educational resources, and patient support programs that enable them to meet their goals. In addition, working closely together allows patient advocates to promote your brand within their communities while creating awareness.

4. *Offer Exemplary Customer Service*: Make sure that patients, healthcare providers, and other stakeholders enjoy positive interaction with your brand when engaging. Offer personalized support services like timely inquiries, responses, and problem resolution efficiently while encouraging brand advocates who will share positive experiences with others.
5. *Leverage Digital and Social Media*: Utilize digital and social media channels to engage with patients, healthcare professionals, and influencers. Share valuable content, educational resources, and updates about your brand. Encourage conversations, address queries, and actively participate in online discussions to foster brand advocacy.
6. *Share Success Stories and Testimonials*: Highlight patient success stories, testimonials, and case studies that demonstrate the positive impact of your brands and services. These real-life examples can inspire others and generate trust and credibility for your brand.
7. *Engage with Key Opinion Leaders (KOLs)*: Identify and engage with respected KOLs in therapeutic areas of your interest. Collaborate on research, clinical trials, and educational initiatives. Involve KOLs in advisory boards, speaker programs, and conferences to share their expertise and advocate for your brand.
8. *Provide Education and Training*: Offer educational programs, workshops, and training opportunities for healthcare professionals. By providing valuable knowledge and skills, you can position your brand as a trusted resource and cultivate brand advocates among professionals who appreciate your contribution.
9. *Seek and Act on Feedback*: Actively listen to the feedback and suggestions of patients, healthcare professionals, and other stakeholders. Incorporate their insights into product development, service enhancements, and communication strategies. You can foster a sense of partnership and loyalty by demonstrating responsiveness and acting on feedback.
10. *Recognize and Appreciate Advocates*: Show appreciation to brand advocates through acknowledgment, recognition, and rewards. Highlight their contributions on social media, in newsletters, or during events. Consider loyalty programs or partnerships that offer exclusive benefits of opportunities to advocates who actively promote your brand.

Remember, cultivating brand advocates require consistent efforts, transparency, and a genuine commitment to servicing the needs of patients and healthcare professionals. In addition, building strong relationships and providing value can foster brand advocacy and positively impact the pharmaceutical industry.

It is important to note that you should observe ethical rules and regulations while cultivating brand advocates in the pharmaceutical industry. You must be transparent about any financial ties between the brand and its advocates. Upholding integrity by prioritizing patient well-being with accurate and balanced information through advocacy initiatives can help you develop more advocates for your brand.

Brand Ambassadors

Brand ambassadors are people who promote a brand to potential customers. Brand ambassadors can be healthcare professionals, celebrities, patient advocates, or anyone who endorses a brand or a product.

Pharmaceutical marketing uses brand ambassadors to boost brand awareness and increase product interest. Healthcare professionals like pharmacists or doctors can lend credibility to a product's safety and effectiveness. Patient advocates can also give testimonials about how the product helped them. Celebrities can increase brand recognition by appealing to a broader audience.

Remembering to follow advertising and healthcare marketing regulations when hiring brand ambassadors for pharmaceutical marketing is vitally important. Companies should ensure all claims made by brand ambassadors for pharmaceutical advertising comply with all relevant laws and regulations as any violations could lead to fines as well as reputation damage for them.

Brand Ambassadors in Pharma Marketing

Here are some examples of brand ambassadors in Pharma marketing:

1. *Jennifer Aniston*, an American actress has served as brand ambassador for Aveeno skincare products such as creams, lotions and body washes for many years now. Aniston is prominently featured in numerous ads that promote Aveeno's products.
2. *Dr. Mehmet Oz* has become one of the best-known TV personalities and cardio-thoracic

surgeons, serving as brand ambassador of Pfizer Pharmaceutical Company of New Jersey, one of the largest pharmaceutical corporations globally. Dr. Mehmet Oz promoted various Pfizer products including Lipitor for cholesterol reduction.

3. *Michael Phelps* is a brand ambassador for Talkspace. Michael Phelps, the Olympic swimmer, has joined Talkspace, an online therapy site, to become a brand ambassador. Phelps spoke about his mental health struggles and encouraged others to use Talkspace's services.
4. *Jenny McCarthy* for Blincyto: Jenny McCarthy, actress, and activist, has joined forces to promote Amgen's Blincyto (a leukemia medication). McCarthy wishes for others to benefit from her experiences using Blincyto.
5. *Peyton Manning* for Eli Lilly: Former NFL quarterback Peyton Manning serves as brand ambassador of Eli Lilly, an international pharmaceutical company producing insulin-related medications. Manning shared his experience living with type 1 diabetes to encourage others in managing it with Eli Lilly products.

Brand Archetypes

Archetypes are universal personality traits and behavioral patterns rooted deep within human minds, serving as fundamental building blocks in stories, myths, symbols that span cultures across history. Carl Jung, a Swiss psychologist first suggested archetypes as manifestations in our collective unconscious that reflect fundamental experiences for humans.

Pharmaceutical companies can leverage archetypes as an aid for developing and communicating their brand values and personality to customers more effectively. By selecting an archetype that best encapsulates their company identity, pharmaceutical brands can create more relatable messaging that resonates well with target audiences, setting themselves apart from competitors while leaving lasting memories with customers.

Pharma companies might use the *caregiver* archetype as the cornerstone of their brand image, conveying compassion and concern for patient wellbeing. Furthermore, *innovators* could highlight their dedication to medical innovation.

Archetypes offer pharmaceutical companies an effective tool to establish brand identities based on fundamental patterns of human behavior, while building deeper customer relationships and increasing sales growth. Here are some archetypes commonly used for branding pharmaceutical products:

1. The *Caregiver* archetype embodies our desire to help others, providing comfort to others. Pharma branding for companies dedicated to patient care such as hospice or pediatric medicine may particularly benefit from employing this archetype; Johnson & Johnson's brand embraces it through its *Caring for the World One Person at a Time* initiative which emphasizes its dedication to wellness for patients worldwide.
2. *The Innovator Archetype*: Innovative companies tend to associate themselves with cutting-edge technology, pushing boundaries, and pioneering groundbreaking ideas. This can be particularly applicable in pharmaceutical R&D firms developing treatments. Pfizer has used this archetype of innovation as part of their brand identity to position themselves as leaders in pharmaceutical research; thus their slogan *Science Will Win* displays this commitment to cutting edge research.
3. The *Hero* archetype symbolizes strength, courage and the ability to overcome obstacles. This could be particularly applicable when marketing pharmaceutical drugs to treat serious conditions like HIV or cancer where patients need encouragement and support in fighting their illness and finding inner peace. Novartis for instance has built its brand around Heroism while emphasizing their dedication towards fighting serious illnesses like these through slogans like *We Reimagine Medicine* which illustrate this commitment to fighting serious illness such as HIV or cancer.
4. The *Innocent* archetype stands for simplicity, purity, honesty, and innocence, making it an excellent way for brands that wish to project an impression of simplicity and purity. Clorox's *Earth-friendly* American multinational brand Burt's Bees leverages this archetype effectively as they position themselves as using natural ingredients while prioritizing sustainable practices.
5. The *Explorer* archetype represents adventure, discovery and curiosity, three characteristics brands may use to foster innovative images; for instance, Novartis' Innovation for *Better Health Campaign* emphasizes this mission of providing cutting-edge treatment options to its patients.
6. The *Sage* archetype stands for wisdom and knowledge, making it a fitting symbol for companies providing educational materials to

patients or healthcare providers in the Pharma industry. Merck has utilized this archetype successfully as it positions them as leaders in medical education and research; their brand identity highlights this with their slogan *Inventing for Life,* as a further testament.

7. Pharma companies frequently utilize the *Regular Guy/Girl* archetype to present an approachable and relatable image for their brand campaigns, such as *Sanofi's Blood Sugar Basics* campaign which educates people with diabetes how best to manage their condition.
8. Pharmaceutical companies could employ the *Jester* archetype in order to add humor and lightheartedness into their marketing. Allergan's Restasis campaign uses *Dry Eye Lady* as part of its Jester archetype promotion of their product, Restasis.
9. The *Magician* archetype: Magicians have long been associated with transformation and making impossible things possible, which could provide valuable lessons for pharmaceutical companies that create treatments with profound impacts on patient lives, such as curating previously incurable conditions with drugs that transform lives for better. AbbVie, for instance, has made impossible things possible through breakthrough treatments. Its motto, *Advancing Possibilities Delivering Solutions*, stands as proof.

Pharmaceutical companies use brand archetypes to establish memorable brand images that resonate with their target markets and create lasting memories about themselves and the products.

Brand Architecture

Brand architecture is the organization and structure of brands within a company. It also includes how they relate to one another and the business. For example, pharmaceutical companies often use brand architecture when creating product portfolios that address specific patient needs. Here are a few examples of brand architecture that have been successful in pharma marketing:

1. *Branded House Strategy*: Branded house strategies represent an entire company or its products. Pharmaceutical companies often use this strategy with a large portfolio of items under a common brand. For example, Johnson & Johnson's pharmaceutical division uses Janssen as its umbrella brand for all the prescription drugs it makes.
2. *Endorsed Brand Strategy*: This is where a master brand endorses sub-brands. This is common in the pharmaceutical industry when companies seek to create product portfolios that address specific diseases or conditions. For example, Pfizer's vaccine portfolio for different illnesses is supported by its master brand.
3. *House of Brands*: This strategy uses distinct brands for each product. This strategy is used in the pharmaceutical industry to target different patient populations and conditions. GlaxoSmithKline, for example, has several brands, such as Advair and Trelegy, each targeting a different type of respiratory condition.
4. *Hybrid Brand*: This strategy combines elements from several brands. Pharmaceutical industries use this strategy to create a broad product portfolio with tailored therapies focused on specific patient populations. For example, AstraZeneca has a portfolio of generic drugs marketed under the AstraZeneca brand and targeted therapies sold under different brand names.

Pharma companies utilize various brand architecture strategies to develop portfolios that address the needs of different populations. This strategy is determined by company goals, product line-up and target audience.

How to Create and Use a Brand Architecture

Here are six steps essential for creating and leveraging brand architecture in pharmaceutical marketing:

1. *Make Sure Your Strategy is Defined*: Before beginning to create your brand architecture, your brand strategy must first be defined. This involves identifying your target audience, understanding their preferences, and developing an exclusive value proposition for your business.
2. *Do a Brand Audit*: Conducting a brand audit is a great way to evaluate your brand architecture, and find areas for improvement. This includes a review of your existing portfolio to identify any product gaps and strengths.
3. *Choose a Brand Architecture Model*: Decide which model best suits your strategy and business goals. It could be a house model with a brand name, an endorsed brand, or a hybrid.
4. *Develop Brand Guidelines*: Create guidelines that describe your brand architecture's visual and verbal elements and design. These include its name, logo, and color palette. These guidelines should be included in every aspect of development to maximize impact.
5. *Implement Your brand Architecture*: Implement your brand architecture across all your

touchpoints, including advertising, packaging, social media, and other promotional materials. This ensures your messaging is consistent and aligns with your business positioning.

6. *Measure and Optimize*: Evaluate the success of your brand architecture, and make adjustments as necessary. This involves analyzing customer feedback and tracking marketing initiatives.

These steps will help you create and leverage a brand structure that clearly communicates your products' benefits to your target market and sets you apart from your competitors. This will improve your brand equity and customer loyalty.

Brand Assets

Brand assets are the elements that define a brand's identity and set it apart from other brands. These may include tangible items such as logos, packaging designs, and product design; intangible assets like personality traits, tone of voice, and brand storytelling.

Brand assets are essential for cultivating brand recognition and loyalty and creating a consistent image across all marketing and communication channels. They help brands craft an identity that resonates with consumers and sets them apart from competitors. By using these assets effectively, brands can build a strong and recognizable market presence, ultimately driving awareness, sales volume, and customer loyalty.

Pharma marketing relies heavily on brand assets for building and maintaining identity, reputation, and customer loyalty. Common assets used in this sector include:

1. *Brand Name and Logo*: The brand name and logo are essential assets that help identify a company and its products. These elements are usually prominently displayed on packaging, marketing materials, and websites.
2. *Colors and Typography*: Colors and typography can create a distinct visual identity for a brand. Blue, for instance, is often used in healthcare marketing as it conveys trust and professionalism, while sans-serif fonts are often employed to convey modernity and simplicity.
3. *Slogans and Taglines*: Slogans and taglines are catchy phrases that convey a brand's values and positioning. For instance, Prizer's slogan *Working Together for a Healthier World*, conveys their commitment to improving global health outcomes.
4. *Packaging Design*: Packaging design is an invaluable brand asset in pharmaceutical marketing, helping to communicate a product's advantages and set it apart from similar items. For instance, Roche's Accu-Chek glucose meters stand out due to their distinctive shape and color, which make them instantly recognizable by consumers.
5. *Brand Ambassadors*: Brand ambassadors are individuals associated with a brand who help to spread its awareness to its audience. In the pharmaceutical industry, key opinion leaders (KOLs) often serve as brand ambassadors to give credibility to a product or company.

Brand Associations

Brand associations are the attributes and qualities a consumer associates with that brand. Brand associations are particularly important in the pharmaceutical industry because they influence how patients see medications and whether they trust them enough. Here are the key brand associations that are relevant to pharmaceutical marketing:

1. *Quality*: Pharmaceutical brands are keen to project a positive quality image through rigorous research and development processes. Viagra, by Pfizer, has been associated with excellence since it was the FDA's first approved medication for erectile dysfunction.
2. *Trust*: Another key component in pharmaceutical marketing is trust. Patients rely on medications to manage their medical conditions. For prompt pain relief, patients rely on Johnson & Johnson's Tylenol as it stands out as an exceptional pain relief product that is both safe and effective.
3. *Innovation*: Pharma companies often try to be seen as innovators through their innovative technology and ability to develop new treatments. For example, Roche's Avastin, a cancer drug, is often considered the first to target a protein that causes blood vessels to grow and feed tumors. This marks it as an early success.
4. *Safety*: Patients want to be sure their medication doesn't have unwanted side effects. Safety is an important brand association in pharmaceutical marketing. Sanofi's Lovenox is a beacon of safety because it has a lower risk of bleeding than other blood thinners.
5. *Convenience*: Many pharmaceutical brands aim to be synonymous with convenience, offering easy-to-use delivery mechanisms and requiring fewer dosages than other medications.

GlaxoSmithKline's Advair is an example of this. This inhaler combines two medications to make managing COPD or asthma much easier for patients.

It is important to understand that brand associations may vary depending on the market and patient population. Therefore, pharmaceutical companies can create marketing campaigns that communicate the benefits of their products by understanding the most important brand associations.

Brand Audit

A brand audit in pharmaceutical marketing evaluates the brand and perception of a pharmaceutical company. In addition, it examines the company's brand messaging, visual identity, and product offerings. It also evaluates competitive positioning. Here are the ten steps for conducting a brand audit in the pharmaceutical industry:

1. *Define the Scope of the Brand Audit*: First, determine the scope of the brand audit. This involves identifying key areas such as company strategy and messaging, product offerings, customer perceptions, and competitive and competitor positioning.
2. *Gather Data*: Gather all pertinent brand-related data such as company reports, market research studies, customer satisfaction forms and competitive analyses.
3. *Analyzing Data*: Conduct a data analysis in order to uncover key insights and trends about your brand. This includes evaluating strengths and weaknesses, pinpointing improvement opportunities and measuring whether or not your strategy is working.
4. *Evaluate the Brand Strategy*: Assess the company's target audience, positioning, and unique value proposition to determine its brand strategy. Align your brand strategy with your business goals to communicate effectively to your intended audiences.
5. *Assess Brand Messaging*: Evaluate the company's message across all touchpoints, including advertising, social media, and promotional materials. Ensuring consistency and clarity across all channels includes assessing tone, language, and message hierarchy.
6. *Assess the Brand's Visual identity*: Evaluate its logo, color palette, and typography to ensure they align with the brand strategy. This will help convey the company's value proposition.
7. *Assess the Product Portfolio*: To identify strengths and weaknesses in the company's product range, you must assess it. This includes a review of product offerings, quality control, and pricing strategy.
8. *Evaluate Customer Perception*: This is how customers perceive a brand. It includes loyalty, satisfaction, and awareness. This includes customer reviews and feedback, social media sentiment analysis, and market research.
9. *Assess Your Competitive Positioning*: Examine the competitive landscape to identify key players, strengths, and weaknesses and compare your brand with others on the market.
10. *Make Recommendations*: Based on the brand audit results, improve performance, positioning, and other factors, develop recommendations. This could include refining and optimizing messaging and visual identity and tweaking product offerings and customer loyalty.

A brand audit is a valuable tool for pharmaceutical companies to identify potential areas of improvement, improve their brand strategy, and strengthen their market position.

Brand Awareness Metrics

Brand awareness metrics are critical for measuring the success of Pharma marketing campaigns and determining the effectiveness of a company's efforts to increase brand recognition among its target audience. Some common brand awareness metrics used in Pharma marketing include the following:

1. *Reach*: This determines how many individuals were exposed to a brand via advertising, social media posts, in-person visits or any other promotional channels.
2. *Impressions*: This metric tracks how often prospective customers have seen your brand across various mediums, such as website visits, ad impressions, or social media engagement.
3. *Recall*: Recall measures how well a brand is remembered amongst its target audience and can be assessed through surveys or focus groups.
4. *Share of Voice*: This metric compares a pharma company's brand awareness to competitors within a specific market or industry.
5. *Net Promoter Score (NPS)*: NPS is an indicator of customer loyalty and satisfaction that measures whether people would recommend your pharmaceutical brand to others. It measures customer retention over time by

tracking how likely customers are to recommend your brand over time.

6. *Website Traffic*: This metric tracks how many visitors come to a pharmaceutical company website, what pages they view and for how long.

These metrics can assist pharmaceutical companies with measuring the success of their marketing initiatives and identify areas for enhancement of their brand outreach strategies.

How Pharma Measures Brand Awareness

Here are some common methods that pharmaceutical companies use for measuring brand awareness:

1. *Surveys*: Pharma companies can survey their target audience to measure their awareness and perception of the brand. Here are some example questions: Have you heard of our brand; What comes to mind when hearing our brand name etc.,
2. *Social Media Analytics*: Pharma companies can leverage social media analytics tools to track brand mentions, followers and engagement rates on social media channels related to their brand or competitors, in addition to tracking any conversations related to them on these same channels that discuss brand awareness levels between their brands and competitors.
3. *Website Analytics*: Pharma companies can utilize web analytics tools such as Google Analytics to monitor website traffic, including unique visitors, page views and bounce rate. In addition, these companies could track search engine ranking information regarding brand name or related keyword.
4. *Share of Voice Analysis*: Pharma companies can use the share of voice analysis tools to compare their brand awareness to competitors in the industry. They could also track the number of media mentions, press releases, and other content related to their brand.
5. *Net Promoter Score (NPS)*: Pharma companies can conduct NPS surveys to measure customer loyalty and satisfaction. They could also use customer feedback to improve their brand outreach strategies.
6. *Focus Groups*: Pharma companies can conduct focus groups to gather qualitative feedback from their target audience. They could ask questions about their brand perception, awareness, and engagement to identify opportunities for improvement.

Measuring brand awareness in pharma marketing requires a combination of quantitative and qualitative methods to help them better understand how well their brand resonates with their target audience and adjust their marketing strategies accordingly.

Brand Book

A brand book, also known as a brand style guide or brand guidelines, is a document that outlines the visual and messaging standards for a brand. It serves as a reference for employees, partners, and vendors to ensure the brand is represented consistently across all channels.

Pharma marketing requires a brand book that sets visual and messaging standards across all channels. This content typically comprises:

1. *Brand Overview*: This section introduces the brand, its history, mission statement, and values. Additionally, it includes details on its target audience, competitive landscape, and unique selling proposition.
2. *Brand Identity*: This section establishes the visual identity of a brand, such as its logo, typography, color palette and imagery. Additionally, this document details their utilization across various media such as print media platforms, digital platforms, and social networks.
3. *Brand Voice and Messaging*: This section outlines the brand's messaging across various contexts, such as marketing materials, customer service responses, and social media accounts. It may also contain examples of prohibited language, such as off-label claims.
4. *Regulatory Compliance*: Pharma marketing must abide by regulations from regulatory bodies like the Food and Drug Administration in the United States or the European Medicines Agency in the EU. Your brand book should include guidelines that comply with all these requirements.
5. *Brand Applications*: This section provides examples of how the brand should be applied across various channels, such as sales materials, websites, and social media profiles. It may also include guidelines for advertising, sponsorships, and partnerships.
6. *Brand Guidelines*: This section contains guidelines for using the brand in various contexts and details the approval process for new applications. It should also provide advice on managing adverse events or product recalls.

7. *Brand Assets*: This section offers downloadable brand assets such as logos, fonts, and imagery to ensure consistent brand representation.

A brand book in pharma marketing serves as a reference for ensuring a consistent and effective brand representation while complying with regulatory requirements. In addition, it provides visual and messaging standards guidelines so employees, partners, and vendors understand how to represent the brand accurately while complying with all regulatory requirements.

Brand Building

Brand building in pharmaceutical marketing refers to creating an easily identifiable and memorable brand for a pharmaceutical product or company. The brand building aims to differentiate it from competitors, increase recognition and awareness, and generate sales.

Brand Building Strategies

The Following are a few strategies for brand building in pharma marketing:

1. *Establish a Clear Brand Strategy*: Developing a clear brand strategy ensures consistent messaging and positioning across all channels.
2. *Establishing a Brand Identity*: A unique brand identity through logo design, color palette, and visual styling can help set apart and differentiate brands from their competition and increase recognition.
3. *Content Creation*: Producing appealing and informative blogs, articles, and social media posts that present an engaging narrative can position the brand as a thought leader within their industry and build trust and credibility among customers and HCPs alike.
4. *Nurturing Relationships with Key Opinion Leaders (KOLs)*: Cultivating relationships with KOLs can help your brand to increase brand recognition and credibility within an industry while providing valuable insights into customers' or HCPs' needs and preferences.
5. *Engaging in Sponsorship or Partnership Agreements*: By entering into sponsorship or partnership arrangements with relevant organizations or events, businesses can strengthen brand recognition while reaching new audiences.
6. *Investment in Digital Marketing*: Engaging various digital platforms like social media, email marketing and search engine optimization (SEO) to build brand visibility can significantly expand reach.
7. *Offer Outstanding Customer Support*: Delivering outstanding customer support can build trust with customers or HCPs and increase the likelihood of repeat prescriptions and business.

Brand building in pharmaceutical marketing requires an intensive strategy that addresses its specific needs and challenges. When implemented effectively, pharmaceutical companies can create a strong, recognizable brand identity while increasing brand recognition and sales revenue.

Brand Cannibalization

Brand cannibalization occurs when sales of a new or existing product from a company reduce the sales of another product within the company's portfolio. For example, in pharma marketing, this could happen when a company launches a new drug that competes with its existing drug, leading to a decline in sales of the other brand. Here are a few examples of brand cannibalization in the pharmaceutical industry, and what they must do to prevent it:

1. *Pfizer's Lipitor and Vytorin*: Pfizer's cholesterol-reducing drug Lipitor illustrates brand cannibalization. Pfizer's newer cholesterol-reducing drug Vytorin partially replaced Lipitor when it was released. Both drugs are in the same therapeutic category. Lipitor sales declined, while Vytorin saw an increase in demand. Companies should conduct extensive market research before releasing new drugs to avoid this. They should ensure the new medication does not compete directly with existing products.
2. *GlaxoSmithKline's Zyban and Wellbutrin*: First introduced as an antidepressant medication by GlaxoSmithKline in 1985, Wellbutrin quickly found use helping smokers quit and was later launched as Zyban in 1997. Zyban is a brand of smoking cessation drugs with the same active ingredient. However, Wellbutrin was prescribed by many doctors and patients who continued to use it even for smoking cessation. This led to cannibalization. To avoid this, companies must differentiate their products and highlight their unique benefits in marketing. They should also train their sales staff and educate healthcare professionals about the differences between their products.
3. *Roche's Perjeta and Herceptin*: Perjeta (Pertuzumab), a more recent, less expensive option for HER2-positive breast cancer, has been

on the market since 1998. Despite concerns about brand cannibalization, studies have not shown any significant differences in efficacy. To prevent this, companies should ensure that their value propositions and product pricing strategies are clear and transparent to avoid such an accident. They should also research to show the unique benefits of new drugs over older ones.

4. *Gilead Sciences' Hepatitis-C Drugs* offer a good example of pharmaceutical brand cannibalization can be observed through Sovaldi (Sofosbuvir) and Harvoni (Ledipasvir and Sofosbuvir) products from Gilead Sciences designed to treat Hepatitis C infection. Sovaldi, launched in 2013, quickly became a hugely successful drug, generating over $10 billion in revenue in its first year. Harvoni, however, quickly followed Sovaldi in 2014. It was more efficient and user-friendly and led to a decrease in Sovaldi's market share.

Pharmaceutical companies can face significant challenges due to brand cannibalization. Therefore, companies should conduct extensive marketing research and differentiate their products to prevent cannibalization.

Brand Character

Brand Character and Personality: What is the Distinction?

Two essential elements of pharmaceutical marketing are brand personality and character. These elements help brands differentiate themselves from competitors while building customer trust and creating a sense of identity within customers' heads. While sometimes used interchangeably, each has unique distinctions.

Brand personality describes a brand's human traits or characteristics, such as tone, values, voice, and visual identity. An organization's brand personality is how it speaks to customers and presents an image to them. For example, pharmaceutical brands may strive to project trustworthiness, reliability, and expertise.

A brand's character is, in fact, its ethical values and principles. It describes how the brand conducts itself on the market. The brand character is the combination of actions and behaviors taken. For example, pharmaceutical brands might want to portray a reputation for being ethical, responsible, and socially conscious.

The brand's personality can be defined as how it interacts and acts with customers. However, the brand's character is determined by its values and principles. These elements are essential to pharmaceutical marketing and help create a lasting brand image.

Brand Character

Brand character in pharmaceutical marketing refers to the distinct set of characteristics, values and traits embodied by an organization or brand that distinguish it from competitors and make it more desirable among prospective customers. These special touches help make a brand stand out among its rivals, and customers. The following examples show how pharmaceutical companies use brand character in their marketing:

1. Lipitor (Atorvastatin), a brand of by Pfizer, was promoted as a symbol of *intelligence* and *leadership*. The brand's marketing campaigns highlighted its ability to lower cholesterol levels and reduce heart disease risk. Lipitor consumers were also seen as proactive, intelligent individuals who take their health seriously.
2. GlaxoSmithKline promoted Advair (Fluticasone and Salmeterol) to be a brand that represented *freedom* and *empowerment*. The long-lasting relief of COPD symptoms and asthma was highlighted in their marketing campaigns. This allows people to live active lives without restrictions. The brand was also associated with people who wanted to control their lives and health.
3. Novartis promoted Diovan (Valsartan) to be a brand that represented *stability* and *dependability*. Marketing campaigns highlighted its ability to lower blood pressure, prevent stroke and heart attacks, and work with people who value stability and dependability.
4. Sanofi promoted Plavix (Clopidogrel) as an icon of *security* and *protection*. Its ability to prevent blood clots and reduce risks such as heart attack and stroke resonated strongly with individuals looking for assurance in both life and health.
5. Roche presented Tamiflu (Oseltamivir) to be a brand that embodied *resilience* and *preparedness*. The brand's ability to prevent and treat flu and keep people healthy meant that it was easily accessible and could be used in marketing campaigns. This person was associated with people who were prepared for any situation and could recover from setbacks.

How do Pharma Companies Create a Brand Character?

It takes careful planning and consideration to create a brand character in pharmaceutical marketing. Here are the steps that pharma companies usually take when creating their brand:

1. *Define your Brand's Purpose and Mission*: Creating a brand's character begins with clearly defining the brand's purpose and mission. This involves defining the brand's core values and principles and determining its market positioning and target audience.
2. *Conduct Market Research*: Pharma companies need to understand customers' needs, preferences, expectations, and perceptions of the company. Therefore, market research gives companies valuable insights into customer behavior and attitudes.
3. *Develop a Brand Personality*: Once the brand's mission and purpose have been established, pharmaceutical companies can create a brand personality that reflects these values. This includes creating the brand's tone of voice and visual identity.
4. *Communicate Your Brand Character*: Pharma companies must communicate their values and principles through all channels to build a strong brand image. This applies to marketing materials, sales presentations, and customer interactions.
5. *Foster A Culture of Responsibility*: Building a brand character is more than just what a company says. It also requires how the company behaves. Pharma companies can create this character by creating an environment that promotes responsibility, ethics, social consciousness, and teamwork.

Your pharmaceutical brand will be distinctive if you use a strategic and intentional approach that aligns with your company's mission, values, and purpose. In addition, companies can be distinguished from their competitors by creating strong brand character and establishing lasting customer relationships.

Brand Collaboration

In pharmaceutical marketing, brand collaboration involves two or more pharmaceutical companies working together to promote a product or service. Here are some examples of collaboration in pharmaceutical marketing:

1. *Co-promotion Agreements* are agreements where two or more pharmaceutical companies work together to market and sell a product. For example, Glaxo, a leading US antiulcerant manufacturer, made a similar arrangement to promote Zantac (Ranitidine) in the US with Roche. This has allowed them to maintain a strong position in this market, and Zantac became the world's first prescription drug brand to cross $4 billion in annual sales.
2. *License Agreements*: Pharmaceutical companies can license the right to market and sell products from other companies through licensing agreements. Takeda Pharmaceuticals, for instance, announced in 2021 that Ovid Therapeutics had licensed its Soticlestat to treat Dravet syndrome (formerly known as severe myoclonic epilepsy of infancy or SMEI), and Lennox-Gestaut syndrome, to them for marketing globally.
3. *Joint Ventures*: A joint venture is where two or more pharmaceutical companies form a separate entity to create and market a product. In 2021, Merck and Ridgeback Biotherapeutics merged to create Molnupiravir, an antiviral drug that treats COVID-19.
4. *Research Collaborations*: A research collaboration involves two or more pharmaceutical companies working together to develop new products and services. AstraZeneca announced in 2021 a partnership with Regeneron to develop and commercialize obesity treatments.

Companies can use brand collaboration to promote innovative products. But, first, companies must evaluate potential partners carefully and ensure that the collaboration matches their strategic goals and values.

Brand Communications

Brand communications in pharmaceutical marketing refer to various methods and channels pharmaceutical companies use to communicate their brand messages with their target audience. Communications can range from sales representatives to traditional advertising, digital marketing, and social media. Brand communications must deeply understand their target audience's needs, preferences, and tailor messages to appeal to them while highlighting the brand's unique advantages. Here are some of the most common brand communication strategies used in pharma marketing:

1. *Pharma Sales Representatives* offer virtual and in-person demonstrations to physicians about the unique features of their products and how they differ from competitors.
2. *Advertising*: Traditional media such as print ads and radio spots remain effective tools in

pharmaceutical marketing, particularly brand awareness campaigns.

3. *Digital Marketing*: Utilizing channels such as search engines, social networks, and email allows pharma companies to connect and interact directly with target audiences.
4. *Public Relations*: This includes media relations, events, and other tactics that generate positive coverage and awareness for the brand.
5. *Educational Resources*: Brochures, white papers, webinars, and other online resources can be used to provide information about a brand or relevant disease conditions.
6. *Patient Support Programs*: These programs offer education and financial assistance to eligible patients to help them through their treatment.

A strategic approach to pharmaceutical marketing requires brand communication focused on the target audience's needs. Pharma companies can create strong brand identities and increase engagement to improve patient outcomes. They can also tailor messaging and tactics to appeal to their target audiences.

Brand Community

In pharma marketing, brand community refers to people with a common interest in a pharmaceutical product or brand. For example, patients, caregivers, healthcare professionals, and other stakeholders who have emotional connections to the brand could be included.

Marketing tactics such as social media and patient support programs can help to nurture and strengthen brand communities. Pharmaceutical companies, for example, can increase brand loyalty and engagement, and improve patient outcomes by creating a sense of belonging that their customers are part of a shared value system. Pharmaceutical companies that produce rare disease medications can build a community of patients by hosting educational events and offering support programs. This supportive network of caregivers and patients can help the company to strengthen its brand and increase customer loyalty.

Brand communities also provide valuable feedback and insight to pharmaceutical companies. This helps them better understand customer preferences and needs. This feedback can improve products and marketing strategies, leading to increased sales.

Brand Differentiation

Differentiation sets a product or service apart from its competitors in the marketplace. Pharma marketers create distinctive features or benefits to make their brand even more desirable to customers and differentiate it from competitors.

Differentiation can be accomplished through various strategies, including product design, quality assurance, branding, pricing structure and customer service, or marketing tactics. The ultimate aim is to gain an advantage that stands out amongst its target market and appeals directly to it.

Brand differentiation is crucial in pharmaceutical marketing, enabling companies to set themselves apart from competitors while creating an exclusive identity among their target audiences. Here are a few strategies pharmaceutical firms can utilize in order to differentiate their brands:

1. *Highlight Unique Features and Benefits*: Define your product's unique characteristics and advantages, then emphasize them in marketing messages. Pharmaceutical companies might strive to differentiate their product through features that emphasize its efficacy, safety profile or ease of use.
2. *Concentrating on Target Audience*: Differentiation can be accomplished through satisfying the needs and preferences of particular target audiences. Pharmaceutical companies might differentiate their product by targeting either specific patient populations or healthcare provider segments.
3. *Investing in Innovation*: Companies investing heavily in research and development (R&D) may create innovative products that distinguish themselves from their competition, such as new drug formulations or delivery systems that reduce side effects improve efficacy and patient adherence, leading to better outcomes.
4. *Develop Strong Relationships with Healthcare Providers*: Companies can differentiate their brand by cultivating meaningful connections with healthcare providers. This could involve providing educational resources, sponsoring research studies, or offering support services.
5. *Leveraging Digital Marketing*: Digital marketing can be a valuable asset in the pharmaceutical industry. Businesses can utilize channels like social media and email marketing to engage customers while spreading product information and building brand recognition.

Effective brand differentiation can increase sales, customer retention and market share while ineffective or weak differentiation may reduce profits and diminish your position in the marketplace. Thus, businesses should prioritize this strategy to gain an edge over their competitors.

Branding Effectiveness

Branding effectiveness in the pharmaceutical industry refers to a company's brand creating an indelible impression in the minds of healthcare professionals, patients, and other key stakeholders. Branding is essential in differentiating products from competitors while building patient trust and fostering long-term adherence.

An effective pharmaceutical brand must be easily recognizable and memorable and communicate its value proposition clearly. Additionally, it should have a solid track record of quality, safety, and efficacy.

What Branding Effectiveness Can Do

Effective branding can have a dramatic effect on a pharmaceutical product and company. Here is what it can achieve:

1. *Building Trust and Credibility*: Effective branding can play an essential role in helping establish your company as a reliable source of information. It is particularly essential in the pharmaceutical industry, where patients and healthcare professionals need products they can depend on.
2. *Differentiation*: Branding can help differentiate products from competitors through distinctive branding elements like messaging, imagery, and product names. Differentiation also helps you stand out in an oversaturated market, drawing patients and healthcare providers to your company.
3. *Patient Engagement*: Branding that effectively engages patients can play an instrumental role in encouraging active involvement with healthcare decisions, be it through simple messaging, relatable imagery, and education materials, for example.
4. *Brand Loyalty*: Strong branding can help foster patient and healthcare provider brand loyalty when executed properly. Patients who experience positive interactions with a company's products are likely to become repeat buyers. Healthcare professionals who trust a given product line are more likely to recommend them to patients.
5. *Attracting Investors*: Strong brands can attract investors and support a company's expansion. Accordingly, investors tend to invest more readily in companies with powerful brands and positive reputations.

Key Steps to Branding Effectiveness

Branding Effectiveness is fundamental for business success. Here are a few steps pharmaceutical companies can take to achieve branding effectiveness:

1. *Develop a Clear Brand Strategy*: Companies need a well-developed brand strategy for successful branding. Companies should carefully outline their target audience, key messages and personality of their brand identity to create an engaging and distinctive presence in the market place.
2. *Conducting Market Research*: Companies seeking to gain insight into their target audiences' needs, preferences and behaviors must conduct market research to gain an accurate depiction of attitudes perceptions and behaviors of this target demographic.
3. *Create an Engaging Visual Identity*: Developing an impressive visual identity using logo, color palette, and typography can create an eye-catching brand image for any company or product.
4. *Maintain Consistent Messaging*: Consistency across channels, marketing materials, sales collateral and digital platforms is integral in creating an impactful brand identity.
5. *Establish an Engaging Online Presence*: In today's digital environment, businesses require an effective online presence to engage their target audiences and bolster brand recognition. Therefore, organizations should create robust websites, social media presence, and digital marketing channels designed to engage these target groups while building up brand recognition.
6. *Establishing Relationships with Key Stakeholders*: Cultivating relationships with key stakeholders like healthcare professionals, patients and advocacy groups is crucial in cultivating trust and building credibility to increase brand loyalty and foster success for any company.
7. *Measure and Adjust*: Proactively measuring brand performance metrics such as awareness, engagement, and perception can help companies pinpoint areas for improvement, and adapt their branding strategy accordingly.

Branding effectiveness in the pharmaceutical industry requires a sustained and focused commitment to building an identity, messaging, and positioning strategy that resonates with target customers.

Brand Environment

In pharma marketing, the brand environment refers to the general context within which a brand operates. This includes market conditions, competitors, and regulatory framework. It also affects brand perception and performance. Here are some examples of the brand environment in pharma marketing:

1. *Regulatory Environment*: This is an important part of creating a brand environment for pharmaceutical companies. Regulatory changes, for example, can significantly impact the approval process for new drugs, pricing strategies, and advertising rules.
2. *Competitive Landscape*: The brand environment is also affected by the competitive landscape. Companies competing in certain therapeutic areas of the pharmaceutical industry must remain cognizant of their competitive environment to develop effective marketing strategies that set themselves apart from their rivals and stand out.
3. *Understanding Patients' Needs and Preferences*: Understanding patient needs is central to the success of pharmaceutical brands, so in order to develop products and marketing strategies that appeal to target markets pharmaceutical companies must fully comprehend them.
4. *Healthcare Providers*: Doctors and other professionals in healthcare play an essential part in shaping a pharmaceutical company's brand image, so companies need to understand their needs and preferences in order to create successful marketing strategies and build relationships with key stakeholders.
5. *Social and Cultural Factors*: Pharma companies may be affected by social and cultural forces such as changing public attitudes toward health and wellness that alter consumer behaviors, and drive demand for certain products.

Pharma companies must understand their brand environment to create long-lasting and successful branding strategies. Companies can adapt to changing market conditions by carefully considering all factors influencing brand perception and performance to remain ahead of their competitors.

Brand Equity

Brand equity refers to the added value that a brand brings to a product or service beyond its functional benefits. Pharma marketing relies heavily on brand equity because it can influence physician and patient trust, loyalty, and willingness to pay for a product. Brand equity in the pharmaceutical industry is built on several key components.

1. *Brand Awareness* refers to how patients and healthcare professionals recognize a particular brand. Brand recognition can have an impact on its prescription rates, market share, and patient preference.
2. *Brand Loyalty* refers to how loyal patients and healthcare professionals are to a brand. Brands with high levels of loyalty are more likely to retain market share and sell more.
3. *Perceived Quality* is the customer's perception of the overall quality or superiority of a brand with respect to its intended purpose, relative to alternatives. Patients and healthcare professionals are more likely to trust high-quality brands, which could command higher prices.
4. *Brand Associations*: Healthcare professionals and patients have a connection to a specific brand. While positive associations can build trust and loyalty, negative ones can damage the company's reputation.
5. *Brand Identity* refers to a brand's visual imagery and messaging elements. Strong brand identities can make your company stand out in a crowded market and leave a lasting impression on patients and healthcare professionals.

Strong brands with strong brand equity

Here are a few powerful brands with strong brand equity in the pharmaceutical industry:

1. Botox, now owned by AbbVie has a great brand equity within its customer base thanks to innovation and high-quality standards that built a stellar reputation as an effective wrinkle treatment and cosmetic problem treatment. It has earned customer trust through cutting edge research.
2. Humira, owned by AbbVie and developed as an effective treatment of autoimmune conditions, such as Crohn's and rheumatoid arthritis, enjoys a strong brand equity. Humira's reputation is founded upon innovation, dependability, and an emphasis on patient outcomes.
3. Crestor, owned by AstraZeneca and known for being an effective treatment for high cholesterol levels, holds great equity with consumers and

healthcare professionls. Crestor stands out for innovation, quality patient outcomes and overall value to society.

4. Purdue Pharma's Oxycontin has recently come under scrutiny due to its involvement in the opioid crisis; yet many doctors and patients still consider it as an effective and reliable pain management option.

These brands have earned themselves an exceptional track record by producing products to meet both patient and physician requirements, building lasting reputations for reliability, innovation and patient outcomes.

Building Brand Equity

A holistic approach to pharmaceutical marketing is essential for building and protecting brand equity. The following steps are important as they help increase brand equity in this industry:

1. *Define Your Brand*: Creating and strengthening brand equity starts with clearly defining who you are as a brand. Understanding your unique value proposition, target audience, and key messages sets you apart from competitors is essential.Your core values should resonate with those you hope to attract as partners or customers.
2. *Develop a Brand Strategy*: After you've defined your brand, the next step should be creating an extensive brand strategy. This should outline how the brand will be communicated to and placed within its market environment. This may involve developing a messaging hierarchy, selecting key communication channels and setting overall company goals and objectives.
3. *Consistent Brand Communication*: For optimal branding results, it's crucial that all channels, including advertising, social media and your website, receive your brand message consistently. Doing this helps create an identity across channels while reinforcing core values.
4. *Build Brand Awareness*: In order to build brand equity, creating and increasing brand awareness must be at the top of your priority list. Advertising, public relations and other marketing techniques may help your brand increase visibility and reach. Social media and content marketing platforms such as Youtube or Vine can also be leveraged as tools to reach target audiences more directly while encouraging engagement with your target demographics.
5. *Focusing on Quality and Customer Service*: Customer experience can have an enormous impact on brand equity. In order to build long-lasting customer relationships, brands must offer services and products of superior quality that address customers' specific needs.
6. *Influencer Marketing and Partnerships to Expand Brand Equity*: Influencer marketing and strategic partnerships can be extremely useful tools in expanding brand equity. Brands can work together with influential industry figures or people from their target industry in order to expand reach, gain credibility and raise brand awareness.
7. *Measure and Refine*: Evaluating brand equity strategies is of vital importance and any necessary adjustments should be implemented as quickly as possible. Brands must use metrics such as brand recognition, customer loyalty and satisfaction levels as gauges of their impact; plus be open to customer feedback to adapt according to their needs and preferences.

Pharma companies can take these steps to build equity. Doing so may result in greater customer loyalty, higher revenues and an enhanced standing within their industry.

Brand Essence

The brand essence is a core identity that distinguishes it from its competitors and fosters emotional connections with its target audience. It concisely and memorably captures the company's values, mission, and purpose.

The brand essence is the foundation for all communications and activities, helping to establish a distinct image in the market. It should align with the company's overall business plan and appeal to the needs and wants of the target audience. The following are the most common elements of the brand essence in pharmaceutical marketing:

A. *Purpose*: What a brand does and what it means to patients and healthcare professionals.

B. *Personality*: A brand's personality resonates emotionally with its customers.

C. *Differentiation*: It has unique features or benefits that distinguish it from its competitors.

D. *Promise*: The commitment to delivering a quality outcome to patients and healthcare professionals.

E. *Story*: A narrative communicating the brand's history, values, and vision.

Brand Essence in Pharma: Some Examples

Here are some examples of brand essence in pharma marketing:

1. Pfizer's *Innovating for a Healthier World* embodies its brand essence, innovation

commitment, and mission to improve global healthcare. Their determination to find breakthroughs in medical science that will ultimately benefit humanity stands as a testimony to their passion and perseverance in improving outcomes for everyone.

2. Johnson & Johnson is an inspiration in medical sciences innovation that improves lives worldwide. Through the *Caring for the World, One Person at a Time* campaign, they demonstrate this dedication towards bettering lives through healthcare innovation. It also demonstrates their belief in universal access to quality healthcare regardless of income.
3. Roche's slogan, *Doing Now What Patients Need Next*, reflects their commitment to patients and the ability to find innovative solutions to unmet medical needs. It also demonstrates their commitment to keeping up with the latest medical developments and their belief in allowing all patients to access the best treatments.
4. Novartis' *Reimagining Medicine* perfectly captures the essence of its brand, reinforcing its commitment to innovation and faith in medical science's transformative powers. It also highlights the company's commitment to challenging the status quo and finding innovative ways to improve patient outcomes.
5. Sanofi's *Empowering Life* Campaign reflects its brand essence. It emphasizes Sanofi's commitment to improving the quality of patients' lives through innovative healthcare solutions. It also demonstrates their commitment to giving people the freedom to live fully and their belief in universal healthcare.

The essence of a successful pharmaceutical brand can help them stand out in a competitive market, foster trust with its audience, and drive business growth.

Brand Evangelism

Brand evangelism is creating passionate, dedicated customers or healthcare professionals (HCPs) who actively advocate for a brand, becoming brand evangelists who spread positive word-of-mouth and drive new business through their networks.

There are various strategies for developing brand evangelism in pharmaceutical marketing, such as:

1. *Building Trust*: Establishing relationships of trust between customers and HCPs a brand is essential in creating brand evangelists. This can be accomplished by offering high-quality products or services, exceptional customer support, and transparency and honesty in your communications.
2. *Delivering Value*: Offering customers and HCPs the right value through informative content, tools, resources, or personalized experiences can create strong bonds between brands and their audiences.
3. *Establish an Emotional Bond*: Establishing an emotional connection with customers or healthcare professionals (HCPs) can foster brand loyalty and passion for your product or service, build shared experiences through storytelling and showing empathy toward their needs and challenges.
4. *Encourage Engagement*: Engaging customers or HCPs with your brand through social media, forums, and other channels can foster a sense of belonging and community in your target market.
5. *Reward and Incentives*: Offering rewards and incentives such as discounts, loyalty programs, or exclusive access to products or services can encourage brand evangelism and cultivate customer and HCP loyalty. However, doing this in an industry with such stringent regulations may prove challenging; for this reason, pharma companies must develop innovative, non-financial, and emotional rewards while adhering to all regulatory guidelines and standards.

Brand evangelism can be invaluable in developing an iconic and recognizable brand identity in pharmaceutical marketing, yet its implementation can be extremely complex and time-consuming. By recruiting passionate brand evangelists who advocate for their products or services within a targeted community, pharmaceutical companies can increase brand recognition while driving new business growth and developing long-term connections with their target audiences.

Brand Evangelists

Brand evangelists are individuals who passionately promote a brand to others. Brand evangelists can be integral in marketing products and increasing brand recognition within the pharmaceutical industry. Here are some examples of brand evangelists in pharmaceutical marketing:

1. *Patients*: Individuals who have had positive experiences with certain medicines or treatments can act as brand evangelists for those products. For instance, patients who have successfully managed their diabetes through certain

medications may share their stories with others with diabetes.

2. *Healthcare Professionals (HCPs)*: Healthcare providers who prescribe or recommend certain drugs can act as brand evangelists for them, serving as brand advocates if they see positive results with that drug and recommend it to their peers. For instance, when doctors notice positive outcomes using certain treatments, they recommend it further to colleagues.
3. *Advocacy Groups*: Advocacy groups that represent patients with specific conditions can act as brand evangelists; for instance, American Diabetes Association may promote certain medications or treatments related to diabetes.
4. *Celebrities*: Influencers who have used particular medications or treatments themselves may act as brand evangelists for them. For instance, a celebrity who uses one medication successfully to manage her anxiety may share that information with her followers.
5. *Key Opinion Leaders (KOLs)* in the pharmaceutical industry can also serve as brand evangelists. These individuals possess significant influence and expertise in specific therapeutic areas. For instance, a KOL in cardiology may advocate a particular medication he uses to treat heart disease.

Brand evangelists can be invaluable in pharmaceutical marketing as they help create awareness and credibility around a particular brand or treatment.

Brand Experience

Brand experience is the sum of all interactions customers have with a brand. A positive brand experience is crucial in pharma marketing to build strong customer relationships and foster positive perceptions about a company. Brand experience in the pharmaceutical industry can include the following:

- Effectiveness of medication in treating a medical condition
- Easy access to information about the medication that is clear, concise, and easy to understand via websites and apps
- Customer service that is prompt, responsive, and helpful in answering queries about the drug.
- Consistency in messaging and tone across all marketing channels.

An Unbeatable Brand Experience

A comprehensive and strategic approach is required to create a memorable brand experience in pharmaceutical marketing. This includes taking into consideration the unique regulations and challenges of the industry. The following are the key steps to creating such an experience:

1. *Define the Brand*: Defining your brand is key to creating a superior brand. This includes identifying the brand's unique value proposition, target audience, key messages, and other important information that will set it apart from its competitors. In addition, make sure that the brand is built around core beliefs that resonate with all it seeks to serve.
2. *Develop a Brand Strategy*: After defining the brand, it's time to create it. This will outline how the brand will be communicated and position itself in the market. This involves creating a messaging hierarchy, choosing key communication channels, and setting goals and objectives for the business.
3. *Create Engaging Content*: For a memorable brand experience, create engaging content. Pharma marketers must create engaging and informative content that addresses the interests and needs of their target audience. These could include patient stories, expert insights, and educational resources.
4. *Optimize the Customer Journey*: Pharma marketers need to optimize this journey from brand awareness to purchase and beyond to ensure that every touchpoint is informative, engaging, and helpful. This could include using data to personalize experiences, providing easy access to information, and offering exceptional customer service.
5. *Use Technology*: Technology can be valuable when creating a memorable brand experience. Pharma marketers should use digital channels like social media, email, or mobile to engage with their target audience. They may also consider data analytics and artificial Intelligence to personalize customer journeys and improve outcomes.
6. *Measure and Refine*: Evaluating the brand experience's success and making any necessary adjustments is crucial. Pharma marketers can monitor key metrics such as engagement, conversion rates, and customer satisfaction. In addition, they should be open to feedback and adjust to changing customer preferences and needs.

These steps will help pharma marketers create a memorable brand experience that sets them apart from their competitors and foster trust with their target audience.

Brand Extension

In pharmaceutical marketing, brand extension refers to using an existing brand or product line to market new products related to the original offering. This strategy allows pharmaceutical companies to leverage their existing equity and recognition to launch innovative products and increase their market share. Here are some examples of brand extension in pharma marketing:

1. *Expanding the Product Line*: Pharmaceutical companies might introduce a new drug or medical device related to an existing product. For example, a company that produces medication for high blood pressure might introduce another medication to treat hypertension that targets another pathway in the body.
2. *Targeting New Patient Populations*: A company may use a brand name for marketing a prescription drug targeted at another patient population. For example, a company that makes adult medication might create a similar formulation or dosage for children with the same condition.
3. *Diversifying Product Portfolio*: Pharma companies might use an existing brand to enter a new therapeutic area or market segment. For example, a company that produces diabetes medication could launch a weight-management drug.
4. *Enhancing Brand Image*: Companies can use an existing brand name to launch a new product that improves their reputation or image. For example, companies that produce drugs for rare conditions might also offer treatments for common conditions. This can increase the visibility and reputation of the original drug.

Companies looking to increase their product range and market share can benefit from brand extension in pharmaceutical marketing. However, it takes careful planning and consideration to ensure the new product is compatible with the existing brand and protects its equity and reputation.

Brand Financials

Brand financials in pharmaceutical marketing refer to the financial aspects related to the branding and marketing of pharmaceutical products. These financials include the investment made by pharmaceutical companies in developing, promoting, and maintaining their brands and the revenue generated from branded product sales.

1. *Brand Development Costs*: Pharmaceutical companies invest significant resources in research and development to create new medications. This includes costs associated with conducting clinical trials, obtaining regulatory approvals, and formulating the product. These development costs contribute to the overall financials of the brand.
2. *Marketing and Promotion Expenses*: Once a pharmaceutical product is developed, companies allocate substantial budgets for marketing and promoting their brands. This includes advertising campaigns, physician education programs, direct-to-consumer advertising, sales force activities, medical conferences, and other promotional activities. These expenses help create awareness, generate demand, and influence prescribing behavior.
3. *Sales and Revenues*: Brand success can only be measured through revenue generated from product sales, with pharmaceutical companies striving to maximize this by targeting healthcare professionals, hospitals, pharmacies, and other distribution channels with their product or service offering. Market demand, pricing strategies, market access, competition, and patent exclusivity play key roles when measuring this success metric.
4. *Gross Profit and Margin*: Gross profit can be calculated by subtracting the Cost of Goods Sold (CGS) from Sales Revenue to arrive at Gross Profit (GP) and Margin figures. It represents the profit before deducting other operating expenses. Gross Margin (GM) is the gross profit expressed as a percentage of sales revenue. These metrics provide insights into the profitability of the brand's sales activities.
5. *Operating Expenses*: Operating expenses include marketing, sales, research & development, administrative functions, and any activities associated with brand management. They affect overall finances, including salaries, advertising budgets, research spending, and overhead expenses.
6. *Return on Investment (ROI)*: Return on investment (ROI) measures how well

investments have performed relative to what was originally invested in marketing and promoting your brand. ROI compares financial gain (revenue or profit) with investment costs to determine its efficiency and effectiveness and measure the financial success of brands.

7. *Market Share and Competitive Landscape*: Brand financials are influenced by a particular brand's market share within its therapeutic area. Companies often monitor and compare competitors' market shares to assess performance and tailor their marketing strategies accordingly.
8. *Brand Profitability*: Metrics such as gross profit, operating profit, net profit, and profit margins can help assess brand profitability by showing how its marketing and sales activities contribute financially towards viability and success.

Note that financial figures and details will differ greatly based on company, product, and market dynamics. Pharmaceutical companies, therefore, closely monitor brand financials to make informed decisions regarding resource allocation, marketing strategies, and overall brand management.

Brand Focus

Brand focus in pharmaceutical marketing is essential to its success. Aligning brand messaging, values, products, and services towards one clear purpose of improving patient health and well-being is what brand focus means in this space.

Here are a few examples that demonstrate why brand focus is essential in pharmaceutical marketing:

1. *Pfizer's Lipitor*: Pfizer's brand focus for Lipitor (Atorvastatin), a cholesterol-lowering medication, is improving patient outcomes and decreasing heart disease risk. Their messaging focused on the benefits of taking Lipitor, such as reduced cholesterol levels, better cardiovascular health, and longevity gains.
2. *Sanofi's Lantus (Insulin Glargine)*: Sanofi's focus with Lantus, a long-acting insulin used to treat diabetes, is to improve patient convenience and compliance. Their messaging highlighted the benefits of taking Lantus, such as fewer daily injections, greater dosing flexibility, and better blood sugar control.
3. *Roche's Herceptin (Trastuzumab)*: Roche's brand focus for Herceptin, a breast cancer medication, is to improve patient outcomes and quality of life by emphasizing its benefits, such as reduced tumor size, improved survival rates and fewer side effects. Their marketing messaging highlighted these advantages of taking Herceptin.

Brand focus in pharmaceutical marketing requires creating a clear and defined purpose for any given product, from creating differentiation from competitors, establishing loyal customer bases, and improving patient outcomes, all the way down to patient engagement. Successful brand focus in pharmaceutical marketing requires in-depth knowledge of target audiences, product benefits, and consistent messaging across marketing channels.

Brand Habits

Brand habits are behaviors or actions associated with a brand over time as customers become familiar with its offerings. Strong brand habits can lead to greater brand loyalty and repeat customer business.

Starbucks and Amazon have successfully developed positive brand associations by consistently offering products, services, and customer experiences that create lasting memories with their clients.

A. *Starbucks*: Many customers rely on Starbucks as part of their morning routine for a dose of caffeine, thanks to the brand's consistent delivery of high-quality coffee in an inviting setting and personalized customer service.

B. *Amazon*: Amazon customers rely heavily on Amazon as an online shopping source due to the brand's user-friendliness, quick delivery timeframes, and wide variety of products and services.

Brand habits are pivotal in pharmaceutical marketing as they establish brand loyalty among patients and healthcare providers. Here are some examples of brand habits in pharmaceutical marketing:

1. *Prescription Refills*: Patients taking medications for chronic conditions often refill their prescriptions at the same pharmacy or brand of medicine due to its reliability, effectiveness, and convenience. This practice often results in consistent refills of brands.
2. *Physician Prescribing Habits*: Healthcare providers may develop habits of prescribing certain brands of medication due to their efficacy and safety and the support or education provided to them. This practice often comes down to preferences.
3. *Patient Support Services*: Brands offering patient support services, such as medication adherence programs, disease education, or

financial assistance, can create an association between their services and personalized healthcare delivery, improving patient outcomes and satisfaction. This creates a habitual reliance that could increase patient outcomes and satisfaction.

Brand habits are crucial in creating and maintaining customer loyalty in healthcare marketing. Businesses that can establish positive brand habits through consistently providing high-quality products, customized customer experiences, and reliable support services will have greater chances of succeeding in today's highly competitive healthcare environment.

Study the Behavior of Highly Successful Brands

When studying the behavior of highly successful prescription brands and trying to identify common habits among them, you'll notice seven characteristics in common that define highly successful brands. So, following in Stephen Covey's tradition as the author of *7 Habits of Highly Effective People* book, here are the seven habits of highly successful brands:

1. *Consistency*: Successful brands strive for consistency in their messaging, design, and brand experience across all marketing channels. Doing this fosters brand recognition and builds customer trust.
2. *Differentiation*: Successful brands set themselves apart from competitors by providing unique value propositions or experiences that differentiate them in the marketplace. Successful brands stand out among industry competitors and as leaders by offering something distinct.
3. *Innovation*: Successful brands seek ways to remain at the cutting edge by constantly finding ways to develop innovative products, services, and customer experiences. They embrace new ideas and technologies while pushing beyond what was possible before.
4. *Customer Focus*: Successful brands place customer needs first and understand them fully before crafting products, services, and messaging tailored specifically for them.
5. *Authenticity*: Successful brands demonstrate authenticity and transparency in their communications and actions, being open about their values, mission statement, and business practices, to build customer trust.
6. *Adaptability*: Successful brands quickly adjust to changing market conditions, customer demands, and industry trends. They take necessary risks and don't hesitate to alter their strategies accordingly.
7. *Emotional Connection*: Successful brands create emotional connections with their customers by tapping into their values, aspirations, and desires. They understand that customers purchase both the product or service offered as well as buying into its story and purpose.

Highly successful brands consistently display these seven habits to build strong brand equity, customer loyalty, and competitive advantages in the marketplace.

Branding and Hierarchy of Needs

Abraham Maslow first proposed the Hierarchy of Needs theory in 1943 as a motivational theory that identified five levels of human needs that must be satisfied to attain personal growth and self-actualization. They include physiological, safety concerns, Love and Belonging, Esteem, and self-actualization needs. These are from the most basic to the most advanced.

Maslow believed that individuals should satisfy lower-level needs before progressing to more complex and fulfilling ones. Once basic needs are satisfied, individuals can focus on reaching more complex and fulfilling goals.

Maslow's Hierarchy of Needs can provide a useful framework for understanding patients' and healthcare professionals' motivations and behaviors when marketing pharmaceutical products.

Maslow's Hierarchy of Needs and Pharma Marketing

Maslow's Hierarchy of Needs suggests that human needs can be classified into five distinct tiers; these include:

1. *Physiological Needs*: These needs encompass necessities for survival, such as food, water, shelter, and clothing. Products designed to address physiological needs could include those used to relieve acute or chronic pain, such as inflammation or infection, and their effectiveness or safety in relieving customers of pain relief symptoms.
2. *Safety Needs*: Once physiological needs have been satisfied, individuals look to satisfy their sense of safety and security physically and emotionally. This includes seeking stability, order, and protection. For example, pharmaceutical products that address safety needs may include vaccines, anticoagulants, or cholesterol-reducing medications that prevent or

reduce the risk of serious health conditions. In addition, brands may promote these products to meet customers' safety needs more effectively.

3. *Love and Belonging Needs*: After meeting their basic safety needs, individuals seek to fulfill their needs for love, affection, and a sense of belonging from family, friends, and romantic partners. For instance, pharmaceutical products that address love and belonging needs might include products that treat conditions that impede social functioning (such as anxiety or depression). Brands can also help people feel more connected and involved in social life. Brands can emphasize these products' function in helping consumers feel more engaged with society.
4. *Esteem Needs*: After meeting their basic needs, individuals seek self-esteem and respect from others, including recognition, status, and achievement. Pharmaceutical products which address this need could include products designed to improve physical appearance or performance-enhancing drugs marketed to help users feel more confident while reaching personal goals. Brands may emphasize these products' impact in helping individuals feel empowered and achieve personal objectives.
5. *Self-Actualization Needs*: Maslow's Hierarchy of Needs emphasizes Self-Actualization Needs as one of his highest needs, covering personal growth, creativity, and fulfillment through creative pursuits such as personal development programs that help one to realize one's full potential while setting meaningful goals. Pharmaceutical products which satisfy these self-actualization needs may allow people to pursue passions or interests they care deeply about while meeting rare or hard-to-treat conditions. Brands can highlight how these products help individuals realize their full potential while reaching personal goals.

Implications for Pharma Marketers

Maslow's Hierarchy of Needs can assist pharma marketers in understanding patients' and healthcare professionals' motivations and behaviors in their marketing efforts. Here are some ways this theory may help them:

1. *Understanding Patients' Needs*: By understanding the hierarchy of needs, pharmaceutical marketers can more accurately recognize patients' requirements and create marketing campaigns tailored to meet those demands. For instance, an anti-cancer medication campaign might emphasize its ability to help cancer patients attain higher levels of self-actualization through living more fulfilling lives, giving pharmaceutical marketers the means to enable these patients to live better lives.
2. *Create Patient-Centric Messaging*: Pharma marketers can craft messaging that speaks directly to patients' needs. For instance, campaigns geared toward weight loss drugs might emphasize how losing weight increases self-esteem and confidence levels in individuals.
3. *Addressing Physicians' Needs*: Besides understanding patient needs, pharmaceutical marketers can leverage the hierarchy of needs model to understand healthcare professionals' needs. For example, a campaign for a new drug might focus on how it can assist physicians in achieving greater professional recognition and status.
4. *Uncovering Unmet Needs*: Pharma marketers can use an understanding of the hierarchy of needs to identify areas where existing drugs or therapies do not fulfill patient and physician needs, thus informing the development of new medications that better address the needs of patients and healthcare professionals.

Maslow's Hierarchy of Needs gives pharmaceutical marketers an effective framework to comprehend better patients' and healthcare professionals' motivations and behaviors while creating more targeted marketing strategies.

Brand Identity

Brand identity is the visual, verbal, and experiential elements defining a pharmaceutical company's brand and helping it stand out in the market. These elements differentiate the brand and shape its perception in the minds of stakeholders, including healthcare professionals, patients, and the general public.

The following components contribute to the brand identity in pharma:

1. *Name and Logo*: A pharmaceutical brand typically has a distinct name and logo visually representing the company or its products. These elements should be unique, memorable and convey the desired message or values.
2. *Tagline or Slogan*: A concise and meaningful tagline or slogan can further reinforce the brand's positioning, mission, or key benefits. It is often used in marketing materials and advertisements.

3. *Visual Identity*: This includes the design elements such as colors, typography, and imagery associated with the brand. Consistent use of these visual elements across various touchpoints helps create recognition and brand equity.
4. *Packaging*: Packaging plays a crucial role in brand identity in the pharmaceutical industry. The design, color schemes, and labeling on the product packaging should align with the overall brand image and communicate essential information about the product.
5. *The tone of Voice*: The language and communication style the brand uses in its marketing materials, website, educational content, and other channels contribute to its brand identity. The tone of voice should be consistent, reflecting the brand's values, expertise, and target audience.
6. *Corporate Culture and Values*: A brand's identity also encompasses the values and culture of the pharmaceutical company itself. This includes a commitment to quality, innovation, ethical practices, patient-centricity, and social responsibility.
7. *Patient Experience*: How a pharmaceutical brand interacts with patients and healthcare professionals shapes its identity. Customer service, patient support programs, educational resources, and online platforms contribute to the brand experience.

Pharmaceutical companies must establish a strong and consistent brand identity to differentiate themselves in a competitive market, build trust with stakeholders, and create a positive perception of their products and services.

Creating a Distinct Identity for Your Brand

Creating a distinct identity for a pharmaceutical brand involves several strategic steps and considerations. Here's an outline of the process:

1. *Establish Your Brand Strategy*: Write out and define your mission, vision, values, and unique selling proposition (USP). Understand the target audience, market dynamics, and competitive landscape. This strategic foundation will guide the development of your brand identity.
2. *Conduct Market Research*: Gain insights into your target audience's needs, preferences, and perceptions. Identify gaps in the market and understand what sets your brand apart. This research will inform your brand positioning and help you develop a differentiated identity.
3. *Develop Brand Messaging*: Craft compelling and consistent messaging that communicates your brand's value proposition and resonates with your target audience. Define key messages, taglines, and elevator pitches that convey the essence of your brand.
4. *Design Your Visual Elements*: Create a visual identity that reflects your brand's personality and resonates with your target audience. Design an original logo and select colors, typography, and imagery that communicate your brand values and positioning. Be consistent across all visual touch points to maintain continuity across brand communications.
5. *Establish Brand Guidelines*: Draw up clear rules outlining how your brand should be represented across platforms and mediums, from logo usage and color palette choices, typography, imagery, and tone of voice to set brand guidelines for logo usage and consistency of messaging across media platforms and mediums. Staying consistent across these elements can create a strong brand identity with lasting customer recognition.
6. *Build an Impactful Online Presence*: Establishing an effective digital footprint is increasingly crucial in today's digital era. Create an accessible website that showcases your brand while offering valuable information to target audiences, leverage social media platforms to connect with them via engaging content, educational resources, and interactive campaigns, and use these platforms to drive business growth.
7. *Consistent Communication*: Ensure your brand communicates consistently across all touch points, including marketing materials, packaging, advertising, and customer interactions. Maintain a cohesive tone of voice and messaging to reinforce your brand identity.
8. *Engage Key Stakeholders*: Engage with healthcare professionals, patients, and other stakeholders through educational initiatives, events, conferences, and patient support programs. This helps build trust, credibility, and loyalty toward your brand.
9. *Monitor and Adapt*: Continuously monitor the market, consumer trends, and competitor activities. Regularly evaluate and refine your brand identity to stay relevant and responsive to evolving market dynamics.

Remember, building a distinct brand identity takes time and effort. Consistency, authenticity, and delivering on your brand promises are essential to establishing a strong and memorable pharmaceutical brand identity.

Brand Image

Brand image refers to people's perceptions and impressions of a brand. It is the overall mental picture or reputation that individuals, consumers, and the general public associate with a particular brand. Brand image is shaped by various factors, including a brand's identity, messaging, product quality, customer experiences, marketing efforts, and public perception.

Brand Image in Pharma

Brand image is essential in how healthcare professionals, patients, payers, regulators, and the general public perceive pharmaceutical companies and their products. A positive brand perception helps create trust between healthcare providers and patients and builds credibility for market success. Here are some key considerations related to the brand image in the pharmaceutical sector:

1. *Reputation and Trust*: Pharmaceutical companies strive to build an image associated with quality, reliability, and ethical business practices. A strong brand image signifies trustworthiness, integrity, and commitment to patient safety and well-being.
2. *Product Efficacy and Safety*: Pharmaceutical products' efficacy and safety can directly affect their brand image. Positive clinical trial results, regulatory approvals, and adherence to rigorous quality standards are crucial for establishing a favorable brand image.
3. *Scientific Expertise and Innovation*: Pharmaceutical brands perceived as leaders in scientific expertise and innovation tend to have a positive brand image. Staying ahead in research and development, offering innovative treatments, and showing commitment to furthering healthcare can all contribute to building an outstanding brand image.
4. *Patient-Centric Approach*: Pharma companies recognize the significance of taking an approach that prioritizes patients' needs and experiences as integral elements. This type of patient-centric approach has become incredibly prevalent. Brands seen as genuinely caring for patients, providing support programs, and ensuring access to medicines can create a positive brand image.
5. *Corporate Social Responsibility (CSR)*: Pharmaceutical companies engaging in CSR initiatives, such as supporting public health campaigns, advocating for affordable access to medicines, or investing in community development, can enhance their brand image by demonstrating a commitment to societal well-being.
6. *Thought Leadership and Education*: Building a brand image as a thought leader involves sharing valuable insights, educational resources, and research findings. Being seen as a trusted source of information and expertise can contribute to a positive brand image.
7. *Regulatory Compliance and Transparency*: Complying with regulatory requirements and maintaining transparency in clinical trial data, product information, and marketing practices are crucial for building a trustworthy brand image in the pharmaceutical industry.
8. *Relationship with Healthcare Professionals*: Pharmaceutical brands often cultivate relationships with healthcare professionals (HCPs), key influencers, and prescribers of their products. A positive brand image among HCPs can increase product endorsements and recommendations.
9. *Crisis Management and Patient Safety*: How a pharmaceutical company responds to crises, product recalls, or safety concerns significantly impacts the brand image. Effective crisis management, promoting communication, and prioritizing patient safety can help mitigate damage to the brand image.

Pharmaceutical companies must proactively manage their brand image by aligning actions, messaging, and communications with desired perceptions among stakeholders. Establishing and upholding an excellent image requires long-term dedication to quality patient care and ethical business practices.

Brand Integrity

Brand Integrity refers to the consistency and authenticity of a brand's values, messaging, and overall image. Measuring how effectively a brand maintains its identity is integral for building trust among customers while creating long-term customer relationships. Here are key contributors to brand integrity:

1. *Consistent Brand Identity*: For any brand to remain with integrity, its identity should remain clear and consistent across all touchpoints. This includes its visual elements (logo, colors, typography), tone of voice, and brand personality. Consistency builds recognition while reinforcing the values and purpose of its mission statement or purpose statement. For instance, Coca-Cola has maintained its iconic red and white color scheme, distinctive logo, and classic

typography for decades, reinforcing its brand integrity and strengthening brand recognition over time.

2. *Authenticity*: Brands with integrity demonstrate authenticity by remaining genuine when engaging customers, aligning actions, messaging, and values to build trust and establish customer credibility. They abide by their mission, promises, and transparency and deliver customer expectations accordingly. For instance, Patagonia stands out in this respect by its dedication to environmental sustainability. Both its actions reduce the ecological footprint and encourage customers to reduce consumption or recycle clothing products!
3. *Ethical Business Practices*: Brands that operate ethically and responsibly enjoy strong brand integrity. Their businesses uphold high standards in product quality, customer service, fair labor practices, environmental sustainability, and social responsibility. These practices build trust between consumers and the brand itself. The Body Shop, for instance, advocates ethical sourcing of ingredients, fair trade agreements, and animal welfare, which aligns well with its core values, helping strengthen its integrity.
4. *Customer-Centric Approach*: Brands with integrity prioritize their customers and strive to meet their needs, actively listening and responding to feedback and addressing concerns as part of providing exceptional experiences that build loyalty while reinforcing integrity. For example, the leading online shoe and clothing retailer Zappos with outstanding customer service, hassle-free returns policy, and outstanding customer experiences, has earned its brand a stellar reputation in customer satisfaction and integrity.
5. *Adherence to Brand Guidelines*: Maintaining brand integrity requires following guidelines across all marketing and communication channels. Apple is known for adhering to its brand guidelines with its consistent use of its logo, minimalist design aesthetic, and precise typography. It is a classic example that illustrates its strong brand integrity.

By emphasizing brand integrity, companies can establish themselves as reliable, trustworthy, and authentic in the eyes of their target audiences. Brand integrity requires an ongoing effort for companies that want to maintain their strong and trustworthy image as brands.

Brand Integrity in Pharma

Pharma marketing places great value on brand integrity, as any other industry does. Pharmaceutical firms maintain strong and trusting brand images while adhering to ethical practices and upholding commitments to patients, healthcare professionals, and other stakeholders. Here's an example of brand integrity at work in pharmaceutical advertising:

1. *Compliance with Regulations*: To uphold brand integrity, Pharma marketing must abide by stringent regulatory bodies like the Food and Drug Administration (FDA) in the US, or European Medicines Agency (EMA) in Europe. Brand integrity implies ensuring promotional materials comply with these rules by accurately representing product information, avoiding false claims, adhering to advertising requirements and labeling specifications, etc.
2. *Transparent and Accurate Communication*: Pharma brands should maintain open, honest communication with stakeholders that delivers clear, evidence-based information regarding products' benefits, risks, and appropriate usage. This helps build trust while strengthening brand integrity.
3. *Ethical Marketing Practices*: Pharma marketing should prioritize ethical marketing practices to preserve brand integrity. This means avoiding misleading or deceptive tactics, respecting patient privacy and confidentiality, and ensuring fair and unbiased representation of products. Responsible and ethical marketing builds trust while strengthening brands.
4. *Patient Centricity*: Pharma brands must place patients at the core of their marketing initiatives to create strong brand images and ensure brand integrity. Brand integrity means understanding patient needs, offering pertinent and valuable information, prioritizing safety and well-being measures, and emphasizing safety over well-being concerns. Patient centricity shows a genuine dedication to serving them while building up your brand image.
5. *Building relationships with Healthcare Professionals*: Pharma brands need strong relationships with healthcare providers (HCPs). Engaging ethically and transparently with HCPs means providing accurate and up-to-date information, supporting their educational needs, and respecting their autonomy in prescribing decisions.
6. *Social Responsibility*: Pharma brands can demonstrate integrity through social responsibility initiatives that support healthcare access programs, contribute to public health

initiatives, or invest in research and development to address unmet medical needs. Such efforts align with brand values and increase brand integrity.

7. *Product Quality and Safety*: Pharmaceutical marketers maintain brand integrity by consistently offering products of superior quality while assuring patient safety. Pharma brands must implement stringent quality control measures, adhere to good manufacturing practices, and disclose product safety profiles openly. Delivering safe yet effective products will strengthen brand integrity over time.

By upholding brand integrity in pharmaceutical marketing, companies can establish themselves as trusted healthcare partners while building long-term relationships with stakeholders and differentiating themselves within a highly regulated and competitive industry. Doing this requires adhering to ethical practices, complying with regulations, and engaging in a patient-centric approach in all marketing activities.

Brand Interactive

Brand Interactive is how pharmaceutical companies interact with their audiences and build brand awareness. It also fosters loyalty and drives sales. Here are a few examples of brand interaction strategies used in pharma marketing:

1. *Social Media Marketing*: Businesses can reach their target audiences quickly in real-time , using social media platforms like Facebook, Instagram, or Twitter to provide educational material or address customer inquiries. This helps pharma companies build stronger relationships with their target audiences.
2. *Interactive Webinars* can be an excellent way to engage customers and raise brand recognition, and offer product education webinars to healthcare professionals.
3. *Augmented Reality (AR)*, a new way for pharmaceutical companies to engage with their customers, is a promising approach. AR allows companies to create virtual lab tours or show how their products work.
4. *Virtual Reality (VR)* goes one step beyond Augmented Reality (AR) to give users an immersive and unforgettable experience. For example, pharmaceutical companies could utilize VR technology to demonstrate the efficacy of their products or provide training sessions for healthcare providers.
5. *Gamification* is an interactive approach to training or learning that makes the experience more fun, interactive, and stimulating. For instance, pharma companies might employ this tactic to inform healthcare providers of product benefits while making learning experiences more pleasurable and stimulating.

Pharma companies can use Brand Interactive strategies to build deeper customer relationships, increase brand recognition and loyalty, and stimulate sales. Companies can be competitive in a highly competitive market by using cutting-edge technology and engaging their customers creatively to build lasting brands.

Brand Journalism

Brand Journalism is a marketing tactic used by pharmaceutical companies that creates and disseminates engaging content to attract and retain customers while at the same time informing healthcare providers, patients, and stakeholders about their products, values, and the company in general. Here are a few examples of how pharmaceutical companies utilize brand journalism:

1. *Pfizer's The Science of mRNA Series*: Pfizer is a global pharmaceutical giant that developed the COVID-19 vaccine. This series of articles and videos explain *The Science Behind mRNA Vaccinations*. This content written specifically for a general audience uses simple language and graphics to explain complex ideas, making the series easily digestible for readers of any age. You can find this series on Pfizer's website and social media channels.
2. *Janssen's Cancer Chronicles Podcast*: Janssen is a global pharmaceutical company that develops cancer treatments. *The Cancer Chronicles Podcast* shares the stories of cancer patients, caregivers, and other healthcare professionals. The program also features interviews with Janssen scientists, executives, and other professionals discussing their research and development efforts.
3. *Novartis' Living Proof Patient Stories*: Novartis is a pharmaceutical company that has developed treatments for many diseases. *The Living Proof* series explores the stories and accounts of individuals affected by multiple sclerosis, leukemia, and psoriasis to raise awareness of these conditions and their impacts.
4. *Sanofi's The Human Side of Health Blog*: Sanofi is a global healthcare company that created this blog to offer caregivers and patients support on

various health topics, including nutrition, mental well-being, and managing chronic conditions. In addition, the content is written by Sanofi employees and healthcare professionals to provide useful tips and tricks.

These are some examples of pharmaceutical companies using brand journalism to engage and inform their customers. Pharma companies can promote their products and services by creating quality content that inspires and informs.

Brand Loyalty

In pharmaceutical marketing, brand loyalty refers to customer attachment or preference for a particular pharmaceutical brand. This is an important factor in the longevity of a product's success, as loyal customers are more likely to continue using it and recommend it to others.

Here are some ways you can build and strengthen brand loyalty in the pharmaceutical industry:

1. A distinctive brand identity is essential to distinguish your product from its competitors. It can also help you build customer loyalty.
2. Quality products and services are key to building customer trust and increasing brand loyalty.
3. Communicate Frequently with Customers. Regular communication with customers via email newsletters and social media posts can help build relationships and keep them connected to your brand.
4. Loyalty programs are vital to a brand's success. For example, customers can be encouraged to reuse a product by offering discounts or rewards with repeat purchases, thus earning loyalty points and increasing customer retention. In addition, outstanding customer service is pivotal in building brands' reputation and increasing customer trust.
5. Healthcare professionals and patients can work together through educational programs, patient support services, and clinical trials to foster community support and enhance customer loyalty.
6. Customers may be satisfied by a brand's constant product improvement based on market trends and customer feedback.

Pharmaceutical marketing demands strong brand identities, high-quality products and services, regular customer communication, and loyalty programs that deliver excellent customer service, engaging patients and healthcare providers while improving products. These strategies enable pharmaceutical companies to build meaningful client relationships while assuring long-term success.

Brand Makeover

Brand makeover in pharmaceutical marketing refers to rebranding a pharmaceutical product or company to increase appeal and relevance among its target audience. A brand makeover should create a fresh and modern image that reflects customers' and healthcare professionals (HCPs) changing needs and preferences.

Here are a few common strategies used in pharmaceutical marketing to redesign or revamp their brand:

1. *Conduct Market Research*: Market research can help identify your target audience's needs and preferences and potential improvement opportunities.
2. *Reevaluating Your Brand Strategy*: Reassessing your brand strategy can ensure that its messaging and positioning align with the needs and preferences of target audiences.
3. *Rebranding Your Visual Identity*: Rebranding can involve updating a logo, color scheme, typography, and other visual components to give a modernized appearance to the brand.
4. *Updating Brand Messaging*: Revamping brand messaging involves revising its tagline, mission statement, and other key messaging points to reflect its values and positioning accuracy.
5. *Engaging with Digital Marketing*: Utilizing digital channels such as social media, email marketing, and search engine optimization (SEO) to advertise and expand brand exposure is one way to expand reach while reaching more prospects and customers.
6. *Launch New Products or Services*: Releasing new products or services can establish your brand as innovative and forward-thinking, drawing in customers or healthcare professionals (HCPs) who may find your offerings appealing.

Brand makeover in pharmaceutical marketing requires a targeted and strategic approach that considers each brand's requirements and challenges. By implementing the right strategies and tactics, pharmaceutical companies can create a fresh and modern image for the brand, improve its appeal and relevance to its target audience, and drive sales and revenue.

Brand Management

In pharmaceutical marketing, brand management involves the creation and execution of strategies to increase sales and promote specific prescription or over-the-counter (OTC) drug brands. This includes creating a brand identity and designing marketing campaigns.

Here are the key elements of brand management in pharmaceutical marketing:

1. *Brand Identity*: Establishing a distinct brand identity for medical or pharmaceutical product marketing is crucial. This requires creating a unique name, logo, and visual identity that distinguishes it from its competitors.
2. *Market Research*: This is crucial for understanding customer needs, recognizing market patterns, and gathering competitive intelligence. These data are essential in formulating successful marketing strategies.
3. *Marketing Campaigns*: Brand management in pharmaceutical marketing is essential to designing and executing successful marketing strategies and campaigns, such as flyers, brochures, and product samples distributed via different channels such as email marketing, social media, or conferences to reach target audiences.
4. *Budget Management*: Managing budgets for promotional materials and marketing campaigns is crucial to ensure the brand's financial viability.
5. *Compliance with Regulations*: Pharma marketing is all about following the rules. Marketing materials must meet FDA regulations, requirements, and any additional restrictions or guidelines set by regulators.
6. *Stakeholder Management*: Establishing relationships with key stakeholders such as patients, healthcare professionals, and advocacy groups is crucial in building and strengthening your brand to ensure its long-term success.

Brand management refers to developing strategies designed to increase sales of specific pharmaceutical or healthcare products and increase market awareness for them. To create effective marketing strategies that promote sales growth and expansion, it is necessary to have a deep understanding of the pharmaceutical market, customer needs, and regulations.

Brand Manager

The brand manager is responsible for developing and executing marketing strategies that increase the sales and reputation of a product or brand. For example, brand managers promote and advertise specific drugs or medical products in pharma marketing.

Brand managers in the pharmaceutical market must fulfill many responsibilities and duties to do their jobs successfully:

1. *Planning and Execution of Marketing Strategies*: Brand managers are responsible for devising marketing strategies that effectively communicate a product or drug's benefits and features to patients and healthcare professionals.
2. *Market Research*: Brand managers must conduct market research to understand customer needs and identify market trends. They also need to collect competitive intelligence to understand the moves of competitors better so that they can create winning strategies for their products.
3. *Design of Promotional Materials*: As a brand manager, your role is to design promotional material, such as brochures and flyers, that effectively outline product benefits and features. This may involve producing product samples and any necessary promotional collateral, such as brochures, and detail-aids.
4. *Maintaining Relationships With Key Stakeholders*: To promote and ensure their brand's success, brand managers must build and sustain strong relationships with key stakeholders such as patients and healthcare professionals.
5. *Budget Management*: The brand manager manages budgets for promotional materials and marketing campaigns to ensure profitability.
6. *Analyzing and Reporting Marketing Campaigns*: Brand managers are responsible for assessing the success of marketing campaigns and reporting back their findings to senior management.

Brand managers are essential in protecting and building the reputation of any drug or medical product under their stewardship. To develop and execute profitable marketing strategies, brand managers must understand the pharmaceutical market, and customer needs.

Brand Mapping

Brand mapping is a useful strategy in pharmaceutical marketing to visually represent where a particular brand stands relative to its competitors and provide insights into its competitive environment, helping the brand team identify opportunities and threats.

Pharmaceutical brand mapping typically depicts two key market dimensions, such as drug efficacy and safety profile. Then, brands are plotted onto the map according to where they fall along these dimensions, with the dot's size representing each brand's market share.

Brand maps can help identify underserved markets, allowing brands to differentiate themselves from rivals and increase market share gains. However, they may also reveal areas of overlap among bands where market share gains may occur.

Brand mapping can be invaluable to pharmaceutical marketers looking to understand the competitive landscape and develop effective brand strategies.

Key Steps

Here are some essential steps involved in creating a brand map in pharmaceutical marketing:

1. *Determine Key Dimensions*: Step one identifies key dimensions on the map, such as efficacy, safety, cost, convenience, or other factors that are important and relevant to the target audience.
2. *Select Brands*: Next, select the brands on the map, including your current project brand and potential competitors.
3. *Collect the Data*: Then, collect data on each brand for each dimension identified in step one. Once the data are in hand, use them to plot each brand on the map according to where it lands in each dimension, with each dot representing its market share.
4. *Analyze Results*: Analyze your results to identify areas of opportunity, and threats. For instance, look for areas where customers are underserved and where your brand can differentiate itself from competitors.
5. *Develop Strategies*: Once your analysis is complete, draft strategies addressing identified opportunities and threats. This could involve optimizing brand positioning, developing new products, or improving marketing tactics.
6. *Monitor and Adjust*: Lastly, be sure to monitor the market and adjust your strategies as necessary to remain competitive.

Brand Maps: Some Examples

Here are a few examples of brand maps used in pharmaceutical marketing. Of course, their dimensions and plotting will depend on your brand's goals and the competitive landscape in your market.

A. *Efficacy vs. Safety*: This brand map plots pharmaceutical brands along two dimensions—efficacy and safety. The goal is to help identify which brands are most effective and safe and where your brand may have opportunities. For example, marketing its safety benefits might be worthwhile if your product boasts high safety ratings but lower efficacy than competitors.

B. *Convenience vs. Cost*: This brand map compares brands along two dimensions— convenience and cost. This brand map aims to help identify which products are most convenient and affordable and any areas where opportunities might exist for your product. For instance, if it outshines competitors in convenience but costs more, focus on marketing its convenience benefits in marketing efforts.

C. *Patient Satisfaction vs. Physician Satisfaction*: This brand map displays brands along two dimensions, patient satisfaction and physician satisfaction, to identify which are most satisfying to patients and physicians and areas for potential growth for your brand. For instance, if your brand has higher patient satisfaction ratings but lower physician ratings than competitors, increasing physician education and training may increase your product's satisfaction among physicians.

Brand mapping can be a complex undertaking that involves input from numerous parties, such as market researchers, brand managers, and sales teams. Still, its insights can prove invaluable for crafting effective marketing strategies.

Brand Marks

Brand marks, logos, and trademarks are the visual components that distinguish a particular brand from others.

Brand marks may incorporate various elements, including symbols, icons, typography, colors, and graphic design elements. They are generally designed to be simple yet memorable and easily recognizable even in small sizes or from distances.

Brand marks serve to differentiate and identify products while simultaneously conveying meaning and associations associated with them. For example, Nike's swoosh logo has come to symbolize athleticism, motion, and speed, while Apple's iconic Apple logo stands for innovation, simplicity, and elegance.

Brand Marks in Pharma Marketing

Brand marks play an integral role in pharmaceutical marketing. They help establish and differentiate pharmaceutical products by creating their visual identity, becoming instantly recognizable symbols, and helping create brand loyalty among consumers. In addition, pharmaceutical brand marks may include elements that reflect their therapeutic area. For instance, colors are associated with conditions treated by that specific medicine while conveying safety, reliability, and trustworthiness, which is crucial when choosing healthcare products.

As pharmaceutical products are subject to stringent regulatory requirements, brand marks used in marketing them must comply with specific size, placement, and content guidelines. In addition, they should avoid confusion with other brands or products.

How to Develop Indelible Brand Marks in Pharma

Establishing unforgettable brand marks for pharmaceutical products takes careful consideration and execution. Here are a few steps that will enable you to craft truly impactful brand marks that endure throughout time.

1. *Carefully Consider Your Target Audience*: Understanding the needs and concerns of your target audience are vital in creating an enduring brand mark that resonates with them. Carefully explore demographics, psychographics, values, attitudes toward healthcare, and conditions being treated.
2. *Consider Your Product's Therapeutic Area*: To make the brand mark more memorable and relevant to its target audience, incorporate elements that evoke its therapeutic area into the mark, including symbols, colors, or typography related to treating specific conditions.
3. *Keep it Simple*: An easily recognizable design can make a brand mark more memorable and flexible across various mediums. Avoid including too many elements or details that might clutter or confuse the image.
4. *Assure Compliance With Regulatory Requirements*: Brand marks used in pharmaceutical marketing must conform with stringent regulatory requirements regarding size, placement, and content. Speak with regulatory specialists to make sure your design fulfills these criteria.
5. *Test and Refine the Design*: Conducting user tests with your target audience can help identify areas for improvement, ensuring the final design resonates with its intended target group.

Building an unmistakable brand mark in pharmaceuticals requires taking an in-depth and strategic approach that considers both the needs and preferences of target audiences and regulatory guidelines within the industry.

Brand Meaning

Brand meaning refers to consumers' emotional and psychological associations with a particular brand. This encompasses their thoughts, feelings, beliefs, and values associated with its functional benefits and any emotional attachments people might form with it beyond its functional benefits.

A brand's meaning can be determined by many different elements, such as its messaging, advertising, visual identity, customer experiences, and perceptions of those who use or encounter it. A strong and positive brand meaning sets it apart from competitors by connecting more deeply with consumers, leading to greater loyalty, customer engagement, and perceived value for your product or service.

Brand Meaning in Pharma Marketing

Pharmaceutical companies should work to establish a strong brand meaning by communicating its functional benefits, efficacy, safety, and trustworthiness to consumers. Pharma companies may also aim to position their products as solutions to specific health conditions or challenges, which helps define how consumers view them and further shape the meaning of their brand in consumers' minds.

Pharmaceutical brand meaning must match the values and needs of its target audience and healthcare professionals involved with prescribing or recommending the product.

Establishing a solid brand meaning is an integral component of a successful marketing strategy, helping companies establish credibility among target customers while differentiating themselves from the competition and growing loyal relationships with existing ones. Proper branding strategies also result in repeat customer business and positive word-of-mouth recommendations from existing ones.

There are many steps involved in creating brand meaning. Consider these, for example:

1. *Defining a Brand's Purpose and Values*: First, define its purpose, values, and vision, including

identifying its core beliefs and mission statement. These can help to inform messaging and positioning strategies.

2. *Market Research*: This involves understanding the needs, preferences, and perceptions of your target audience and those of its competitors.
3. *Developing a Brand Identity*: Conceiving a brand identity involves creating an iconic visual identity, such as a logo and color palette.
4. *Creating Brand Messaging*: Developing a brand messaging involves creating messages that effectively communicate the brand's unique benefits and value proposition to its target market.
5. *Building Brand Awareness*: This involves creating a marketing plan to increase brand awareness through advertising, public relations, and social media presence.

Brand Metrics

In the pharmaceutical industry, brand metrics assess pharmaceutical brands' perception, awareness, and reputation among various stakeholders, including healthcare professionals, patients, and payers. Here are some examples of brand metrics commonly used in the pharma sector:

1. *Brand Awareness*: Measures the level of recognition and familiarity that healthcare professionals and patients have with a pharmaceutical brand. This can be assessed through surveys, market research studies, or tracking metrics such as brand mentions in medical literature, social media, or online discussions.
2. *Brand Perception*: Evaluates how healthcare professionals and patients perceive a pharmaceutical brand in terms of its efficacy, safety, quality, and reputation. This can be measured through surveys or by analyzing the sentiment of online conversations, reviews, or ratings.
3. *Brand Differentiation*: Assesses a pharmaceutical brand's unique value proposition differentiated from competitors. This metric helps to understand if the brand stands out regarding therapeutic benefits, formulation, delivery mechanism, or other attributes that set it apart.
4. *Brand Loyalty*: Measures how healthcare professionals and patients remain committed to prescribing or using a specific pharmaceutical brand over alternatives. Repeated prescriptions, brand switching rates, or customer retention metrics can determine this.
5. *Prescription Share*: Indicates the market share of a pharmaceutical brand within a specific therapeutic area or among a targeted group of healthcare professionals. Prescription data and sales reports can help evaluate the brand's performance relative to competitors.
6. *Key Opinion Leader (KOL) Influence*: Assesses the impact and reach of key opinion leaders of influential healthcare professionals who support or endorse a pharmaceutical brand. This metric helps to understand the brand's thought leadership and advocacy within the medical community.
7. *Patient Satisfaction*: Measures patient satisfaction and overall experience with a pharmaceutical brand, including factors such as ease of use, adherence, side effects, and support services. Patient surveys, feedback, or patient-reported outcomes (PROs) can be used to gauge this metric.
8. *Brand Reputation*: Evaluates the overall reputation and trustworthiness of a pharmaceutical brand among stakeholders, including healthcare professionals, patients, and payers. This metric can be assessed through reputation surveys, corporate social responsibility initiatives, analysis of media coverage, and online sentiment.

These brand metrics help pharmaceutical companies understand the effectiveness of their marketing strategies, brand positioning, and the impact of their products on key stakeholders. In addition, they assist in making informed decisions and implementing targeted interventions to strengthen brand perception, loyalty, and market presence.

Brand Mindset

Brand Mindset refers to shared attitudes, beliefs, and values shaping how customers and the wider market perceive and interact with a brand. This encompasses everything from its mission statement and brand identity through marketing strategy implementation and customer experience management.

To succeed at pharmaceutical marketing, having a strong brand mindset means clearly and consistently communicating your company's brand to healthcare providers, patients, and other stakeholders. A positive brand mindset can also foster greater loyalty from patients and healthcare professionals, improving treatment adherence plans and patient outcomes.

Pharmaceutical companies must create an unmistakable product identity and value proposition, then effectively communicate that message across different channels, including sales representatives, websites, social media, advertising, etc. Messaging should focus on product features/benefits which affect patients' health and well-being; advertising helps raise brand recognition while visual identity helps establish an identifiable and consistent image; customer experiences also play a pivotal role in shaping customer mindset towards pharmaceutical brands, though to ensure messaging accuracy credibility, compliance is essential!

In addition to external communication, a brand mindset in pharma marketing also involves internal alignment among employees, from R&D to commercial teams. As with any brand, there should be an agreement about its vision, mission, values, target audience, and competitive landscape. This ensures all activities undertaken, from drug development through sales and marketing, align with its strategy, and must prioritize patient-centricity. It means placing patient needs and preferences first in all activities undertaken. This approach demands empathy, transparency, and working in concert with healthcare providers and patient advocates to meet their needs and improve health outcomes for patients.

Brand Mindset in Pharma: Some Examples

Here are some examples of brand mindset in pharma marketing:

1. *Advil*: Advil (Ibuprofen) is a pain reliever brand with a strong brand mindset of effectiveness and fast relief. Its branding efforts emphasize the product's speed and strength, with messaging, such as fast relief and the strength to get you through your day. This brand mindset is reinforced by customers' experiences who have found the product effective in relieving pain.
2. *Humira*: Humira (Adalimumab) is a biological medication to treat various autoimmune diseases. Its brand mindset focuses on the product's ability to help patients achieve remission and improve their quality of life. Humira's branding efforts emphasize the product's effectiveness and impact on patient's lives, with messaging, such as *turning the corner* and *moving toward remission*. This brand mindset is reinforced by the experiences of patients who have seen improvements in their symptoms and quality of life.
3. *Pfizer's* Science Will Win *Brand Mindset*: Pfizer's brand mindset focuses on its commitment to using scientific innovation to improve the health and well-being of people worldwide. This message was especially prominent during the COVID-19 pandemic, where Pfizer positioned itself as a leader in vaccine development.
4. *Novartis's* Reimagining Medicine *Brand Mindset*: Novartis' brand mindset is centered on its mission to discover, develop, and provide innovative medicines and therapies to help people live healthier and longer. The company focuses on patient needs and collaborating with healthcare providers to deliver meaningful outcomes.
5. *Roche* is Meeting Patients' Needs Now *Brand Mindset*: Roche has built their brand around patient centricity and innovation, striving to anticipate and meet patients' future needs by investing in research and development to produce breakthrough therapies that improve their outcomes.
6. *Johnson & Johnson's* Caring for the World, One Person at a Time *Brand Mindset*: Johnson & Johnson has adopted an ethical business framework and socially responsible strategies to improve people's health worldwide. Johnson & Johnson emphasizes ethical business practices, social responsibility initiatives, and sustainable solutions to meet global health challenges.

These examples demonstrate the significance of having an established brand mindset when marketing pharmaceutical products. By developing a distinct identity, companies can differentiate themselves from competitors, build stakeholder trust, and drive long-term growth.

Developing a Strong Brand Mindset

Developing a strong brand mindset in pharma marketing involves several steps, including:

1. *Define Your Brand Identity*: Carefully consider what makes your company distinctive among competitors and which key attributes it needs to communicate to its target audience. Step one in creating an identity for your business that resonates with stakeholders and customers is creating its name or slogan.
2. *Establish Your Target Audience*: Understanding Your Audience is central to pharmaceutical marketing; understanding the needs, preferences, and behaviors of healthcare providers, patients, payers, and other stakeholders is of vital importance in meeting marketing objectives successfully.
3. *Conducting Market Research* can provide invaluable insight and allow you to tailor messaging specifically for your target audience and creating strategies tailored for them.

4. *Conduct a Competitive Analysis*: To distinguish your brand from competitors, you must gain an in-depth knowledge of their strengths, weaknesses, and messaging strategies. An examination can uncover any gaps within the market or opportunities to position your brand uniquely.
5. *Create a Messaging Strategy*: Once you understand your brand identity, target audience, and competition effectively, the next step should be creating a messaging strategy to effectively communicate its value proposition across channels and satisfy stakeholder preferences. Your messaging must remain consistent throughout, meeting all stakeholder needs with precision.
6. *Train Your Employees*: A strong brand mindset requires alignment among employees, from R&D to commercial teams. Please bring all employees up to speed by providing training and resources so they understand your brand's vision, mission, and values and feel empowered to deliver its promise.
7. *Measure and Adapt*: It is also crucial to regularly evaluate your brand mindset strategy's success to adapt accordingly as your audience evolves and changes. Monitor key performance indicators, such as brand awareness, engagement, and loyalty, and gather feedback from stakeholders to continually improve your brand's messaging and positioning.

Brand Mission

A brand mission is a statement that defines a brand's purpose and what it seeks to achieve in the market. A mission statement should be short, clear, and compelling, aligning with the brand's vision and values.

Pharma marketing necessitates brands having an effectively written mission statement outlining their purpose and goals within the marketplace. A mission statement should be clear, straightforward, and compelling while respecting both vision and values of a brand.

A strategically created brand mission in pharma marketing can help differentiate a company from competitors, motivate employees and stakeholders, and foster an emotional connection with patients and healthcare providers. Here are some examples of brand missions used in pharma marketing:

Brand Mission Statements

1. *Bayer Aspirin*: To provide fast, effective pain relief and help prevent heart attacks and strokes.
2. *Crestor*: To reduce the risk of heart attacks and strokes by lowering cholesterol levels.
3. *Nexium*: To relieve acid reflux symptoms and heal the damage caused by the condition.
4. *Zyrtec*: To effectively relieve allergy symptoms and help people enjoy the outdoors without suffering.
5. *Advair*: To improve lung function and reduce asthma symptoms to help people breathe easier.
6. *Humira*: To relieve pain and inflammation caused by autoimmune diseases and improve the quality of life for patients.

Corporate Brand Mission Statements

1. *Pfizer's Brand Mission*: We combine science and global resources to bring therapies to people that extend and significantly improve their lives.
2. *Novartis' Brand Mission*: Our focus on science-based innovation enables us to address some of society's most intractable healthcare problems, from discovering groundbreaking treatments to finding ways to get them into as many hands as possible.
3. *Roche's Brand Mission*: We strive to improve lives by developing cutting-edge diagnostic and therapeutic products which promote earlier diagnosis, personalized therapy, and efficient disease management.
4. *Johnson & Johnson's Brand Mission*: We strive to be the world's healthiest workforce, dedicated to improving people's well-being of people everywhere.

How to Develop a Brand Mission Statement

Developing a brand mission statement in pharma marketing involves both creativity and strategy. A brand mission statement should outline the purpose, goals, and value offered to its customers by your brand. Here are a few steps that will assist in this process:

1. *Determine Your Target Audience*: Determine who the brand is intended to reach and their needs/desires; this could include patients, healthcare providers, payers and other stakeholders.
2. *Analyze the Market*: Conduct a market analysis of the pharmaceutical industry to understand current trends, challenges, and opportunities thoroughly. Having this insight will enable you to define the unique value proposition of your brand.

3. *Define Your Brand's Core Values*: Define the values that characterize your brand and align with those of your target audience, then incorporate these in your mission statement.
4. *Craft a distinctive Brand Promise*: Craft an identity-defining promise for your brand that resonates with its target audience and stands out from competitors. Make it specific, measurable, and relevant.
5. *Draft Your Mission Statement*: Draft an engaging mission statement that clearly and succinctly articulates your brand's purpose, goals, and value proposition for its customers. Make sure it aligns with your brand promise and core values.
6. *Refine and Finalize*: Utilize feedback from key stakeholders such as your team, customers, and partners to refine and finalize your mission statement. Once confirmed as part of your marketing activities, use it as the cornerstone for all future endeavors to ensure they align with brand purpose and values.

Brand mission statements in pharmaceutical marketing require constant revision and evolution to remain relevant and competitive.

Brand Morphology

Brand morphology is the study of how the structure and form of a brand name can influence its meaning and perception among customers. Pharma marketing requires companies to craft brand names that are easy to remember, pronounce, and identify as distinctive and stand out from competitors.

Here are some examples of how brand morphology can be utilized in pharmaceutical marketing:

A. *Portmanteau*: A brand name created by combining two or more words. For instance, Combivent, used for combination inhalers treating asthma and chronic obstructive pulmonary disease (COPD), is an example of this. Its name comes from combining and ventilator which is a machine that helps respiration.

B. *Acronym*: An acronym is a brand name created using the initial letters of words in a longer phrase.

C. Neologism: A neologism is an invented word used for branding purposes. For instance, "Xarelto," used for blood thinners, has no additional significance outside its use as a brand name.

D. *Descriptive Brand Names*: Descriptive brand names provide insight into what a product does or is used for, such as Claritin (an antihistamine used to treat allergies). For instance, Claritin includes the word Clarify in its name, which implies it helps alleviate allergy symptoms.

E. *Associative Brand Names*: A brand name links a product with an emotion or experience. For instance, Abilify, used as an antipsychotic medication, includes the word ability which implies it can help improve one's capacity for functioning.

Brand morphology is essential in pharmaceutical marketing, shaping how consumers perceive and remember a brand. Therefore, pharmaceutical companies must consider various elements when selecting a name for their brand, such as legal considerations, trademark availability, and cultural and linguistic traits.

Brand Name

A brand name in pharma marketing is a name that a company gives to a medication or medical product to differentiate it from other offerings. It fosters consumer loyalty and recognition. A brand name distinguishes a company's product and encourages loyalty.

Pharma companies invest significant resources in the promotion and creation of brand names. The brand name should be easy to remember, memorable, and clear about the product's benefits or intended use. In addition, patents and trademarks can help safeguard unique identities.

Pharmaceutical industries are famed for their brand names, such as Advil (Ibuprofen), Tylenol (Acetaminophen), Lipitor (Atorvastatin), and Viagra (Sildenafil), all recognized globally. These names serve as symbols that represent specific products for all users worldwide.

Arriving at a Brand Name

How can one select an effective brand name for a pharmaceutical product?

Naming a pharmaceutical product effectively is no simple task. This requires creativity, research, and legal considerations. However, here are the steps that pharmaceutical companies usually take when choosing their trademark:

1. *Brainstorming*: The first step is to brainstorm potential names for your product. This could involve brainstorming sessions or seeking ideas from outside sources like focus groups and surveys.

2. *Market Research*: After creating a list, the pharmaceutical company will conduct a market analysis to determine if each name resonates with its target audience. This could include conducting focus groups, surveys, or analyzing social media data.
3. *Legal Considerations*: Pharmaceutical companies should search for a trademark before choosing a name for their pharmaceutical brand names to check their availability. This ensures that no other company has the same name. They should also examine how patents and other legal mechanisms protect their chosen domain name.
4. *Final Selection*: Once all factors have been considered, a pharmaceutical company should select a name that best encapsulates its intended function and resonates with its targeted market. This name will then be utilized across marketing and promotional material.

Notably, selecting a brand name can be challenging and costly. That is why, many companies hire outside agencies to assist them in this endeavor. Nevertheless, investment in a strong brand name will pay off over time, increasing brand recognition, loyalty, differentiation, and market share within a crowded market.

Brand Outreach

Brand outreach refers to efforts undertaken by brands to grow and extend their presence and influence among potential customers, industry influencers, and other relevant stakeholders. It can involve social media engagement, influencer marketing, content marketing, public relations activities, community building, or similar strategies.

Brand outreach strives to build brand recognition, foster loyalty, and drive sales and revenue growth. This process involves targeting potential customers through relevant communities or online platforms while building relationships with influential individuals or organizations within your industry.

Brand Outreach in Pharma Marketing

In pharma marketing, brand outreach refers to strategies and tactics employed to market pharmaceutical products to healthcare professionals, patients, and other key audiences. Brand outreach seeks to build a greater understanding of an illness or treatment, enhance brand trustworthiness and drive sales of those particular brands.

Here are a few tactics pharmaceutical companies employ in their brand outreach initiatives:

1. *Medical Education Programs (MEPs)*: Pharmaceutical companies frequently organize educational events or workshops designed to educate healthcare providers on specific medications or treatments regarding features, benefits, and safety profiles of specific products or treatments offered by pharmaceutical firms. These can be events or online courses as part of MEPs.
2. *Patient Education Programs (PEPs)* offer resources to educate patients on their conditions, treatment options, and how particular medicines or therapies might benefit them.
3. Key Opinion Leader (KOL) Engagement: Engaging key experts within a field to promote and build credibility for a brand is crucial to a brand's success.
4. *Sales Force Engagement*: This involves training and supporting the sales force so they can effectively explain brands and their benefits to healthcare professionals.
5. *Digital Marketing*: Digital marketing refers to any promotion on digital channels like social media campaigns, SEO (search engine optimization), email marketing, or any other strategy to spread a brand or its message to a broader audience.

Pharmaceutical marketing is strictly governed, and its outreach initiatives must comply with legal and ethical principles. Pharmaceutical companies must disclose any potential conflicts of interest when working with KOLs or providing educational materials to healthcare professionals.

Brand Performance Metrics

Brand performance metrics in the pharmaceutical industry focus on evaluating pharmaceutical brands' tangible outcomes and business impact. These metrics help assess the success of marketing efforts, product performance, and overall business objectives. Here are some examples of brand performance metrics commonly used in the pharmaceutical industry:

1. *Sales Revenue*: Measures the financial performance of a pharmaceutical brand by tracking sales revenue generated from product sales. This metric directly indicates the brand's market success and overall commercial performance.

2. *Market Share*: Indicates a brand's total or specific market segment share and measures its position relative to competitors in the market. Market share assessments may involve tracking sales or prescription data or conducting market research studies on similar brands.
3. *Market Penetration*: Evaluates the brand's ability to penetrate and capture a specific market segment or geographical area. It measures the brand's presence and acceptance within a defined target market.
4. *Return on Investment (ROI)*: Assesses the financial returns generated from brand-related investments, such as marketing campaigns, sales force activities, or research and development efforts. ROI compares the costs incurred with the revenue or profit generated, providing insights into the effectiveness of investments.
5. *Patient Adherence*: Measures the extent to which patients adhere to prescribed medications of a specific pharmaceutical brand. This metric assesses patient compliance and persistence in using the brand, which can impact long-term revenue and market share.
6. *Key Performance Indicators (KPIs)*: Pharmaceutical companies often define specific KPIs that align with their business objectives and strategies. These could include metrics such as new customer acquisition, customer retention rates, average prescription size, and product launches.
7. *Customer Satisfaction*: Evaluates the satisfaction levels of healthcare professionals, patients, and other stakeholders with a pharmaceutical brand's products or services. Surveys or feedback mechanisms can be used to assess customer satisfaction and identify areas for improvement.
8. *Brand Value*: Evaluate and assess pharmaceutical brands' overall financial worth and value by considering market capitalization, brand equity, and intellectual property rights. Assessing brand value offers insight into pharmaceutical brands' long-term sustainability and growth potential.

These brand performance metrics enable pharmaceutical companies to track their brand's financial performance, market position, customer loyalty, and return on investment. In addition, they help evaluate the effectiveness of marketing strategies, identify improvement areas, and make data-driven decisions to drive brand growth and success.

Brand Performance Review

Pharma marketers conduct brand performance reviews to evaluate the success of a brand or pharmaceutical product on the market. The evaluation usually covers many factors, such as:

1. *Sales Performance*: This measures the brand's sales figures in volume, revenue, market share, and growth rate. This key metric determines a brand's success in sales performance.
2. *Competitive Landscape*: This is a way to assess the brand's competitive environment, including competitors' market shares, number of competitors, growth rates, pricing strategies, and marketing tactics.
3. *Brand Perception* refers to examining how customers and other stakeholders perceive your brand. This research can include market analysis, customer research, direct customer contact, social media tracking, and monitoring.
4. *Marketing Activities*: To evaluate the efficacy of marketing activities such as advertisements, promotions, and branding campaigns, it is necessary to assess their reach and impact on sales growth, and key performance indicators can assist here.
5. *Product Innovation* assesses a brand's ability to conceive new ideas or formulas that meet changing customer demands.

Pharma companies can utilize brand performance reviews to pinpoint areas for improvement and adjust marketing strategies accordingly, keeping ahead of their competition. They can also utilize them to make strategic decisions regarding product development, pricing, promotional activities, etc.

Brand Persona

Brand personas can be an invaluable tool in pharmaceutical marketing to create an easily recognizable brand identity among healthcare professionals (HCPs) and patients. A brand persona is a fictional character representing your brand's values, personality, and characteristics that can guide brand messaging, marketing strategy development, customer communication, and product evaluation. Here are a few ways they can be applied:

A. *HCP Personas*: Brands may create personas for primary care physicians that reflect empathy, patient focus, and knowledge about preventive healthcare measures like vaccinations and screenings. Their messaging for this persona may emphasize regular check-ups as part of preventive healthcare measures and vaccinations or screenings as needed. Similarly, they can create personas for physicians across the specialities to personalize their messaging.

B. *Patient Personas*: Brands may create personas for patients with chronic conditions representing proactive, informed, and supported characteristics. Their messaging could emphasize the significance of adhering to treatment, employing self-management strategies, and accessing support forums or educational materials as part of this persona's success story.

C. *Brand Personas*: For pharmaceutical products, marketers may create brand personas to convey innovative, reliable, and patient-centric values. Their messaging should highlight recent scientific research findings, clinical trial results, patient outcomes, and commitments from their brand to provide personalized support and resources for patients.

Brand personas can help pharmaceutical marketers develop more targeted and effective marketing strategies by tailoring messages and outreach efforts to particular customer segments. By reflecting on their desired characteristics and values that resonate with these customer segments, brands can foster lasting connections with their target audiences, creating more positive interactions.

Brand Personality

In pharmaceutical marketing, brand personality refers to a pharmaceutical product's human characteristics or qualities. It influences how customers see your brand in terms of personality, values, behavior, and other aspects.

Pharma companies often depend on their brand personality to differentiate their products from competitors and build an emotional connection with their customers. Businesses can build a more appealing brand image and resonate with their target audience by creating more engaging and relatable personality traits.

Here are some examples of brand personality traits used in pharmaceutical marketing:

1. *Caring*: Pharma products marketed as caring can be perceived as compassionate and sympathetic towards patients. This characteristic is often used when products are being developed to treat life-threatening or chronic illnesses. For example, pharmaceutical companies might use brand personalities to produce medications for rare conditions that currently do not have any treatment options. They may show compassion and understanding toward those with the condition. Companies could also highlight their support for patients and community outreach programs to show that they care about their customers.
2. *Trustworthy*: Pharmaceutical products marketed as trustworthy can be viewed as reliable and secure by healthcare professionals. For example, a pharmaceutical company that produces medication for chronic conditions might use a trustworthy brand personality. This could include a focus on safety and reliability. They might also display their extensive research and clinical trial data or endorsements by medical professionals to make themselves known as trusted treatment sources.
3. *Innovative*: Pharmaceutical products marketed as cutting-edge or technologically advanced are deemed innovative. This trait is often associated with products that address unmet medical needs or have a unique mechanism for action. Pharmaceutical companies producing complex drugs may choose an innovative brand personality, emphasizing cutting-edge technology or scientific breakthroughs. To demonstrate its leadership in medical innovation, the business may showcase its manufacturing processes and collaborations with top academic institutions.
4. *Expert*: Products marketed as experts in pharmaceutical marketing are viewed as having clinical and scientific data. This personality trait is often found in hospital products or medicines specialists prescribe. The expert brand personality may emphasize clinical and scientific knowledge, such as when pharmaceutical companies produce medication for specialized medical conditions. They might also highlight their relationships with experts in the field, scientific advisory boards, and professional associations to show their authority and credibility.
5. *Friendly*: Products marketed as friendly personality can be perceived as easy to use and approachable, especially for over-the-counter or home medications. Common illnesses medications companies may have a brand personality that stresses accessibility and convenience. This might include clear instructions, packaging, and patient education materials.

Brand personality plays an important role in pharma marketing. Companies using brand personality can differentiate their products and establish emotional connections with their target audiences through building a brand image. For example, businesses may identify and promote specific personality traits to develop an engaging brand image for target customers.

How Pharma Creates Brand Personality

Some pharmaceutical companies have taken the initiative and created brands with personalities. The following examples show how some pharmaceutical companies create distinctive personalities for their brands:

1. *Pfizer's Viagra*: Pfizer developed a brand personality for Viagra, their erectile dysfunction drug, emphasizing confidence, vitality, and masculinity. Advertisements featured strong men who could get back their sexual power with Viagra. This drug was seen as a symbol of male strength and masculinity.
2. *Johnson & Johnson's Tylenol*: Johnson & Johnson has designed their over-the-counter pain reliever Tylenol to emphasize being safe and effective, creating a trustworthy personality so consumers can rely on this effective medication for relieving their symptoms.
3. *Crestor by AstraZeneca*: To differentiate it, AstraZeneca created an innovative brand personality for their Crestor (Rosuvastatin), a cholesterol-reducing brand. The company highlighted scientific rigor and innovation. They used advertisements to highlight the unique mechanism of Crestor's action and its ability to lower cholesterol. This brand is presented as the result of rigorous scientific research and clinical data.
4. *Novartis' Excedrin*: Novartis developed a brand identity focused on reliability and quick relief. The product's ability to provide quick and effective headache relief was highlighted in the ads. It was also made easily accessible and easy to use.
5. *Sanofi's Lantus*: Sanofi developed a brand personality to represent Lantus, emphasizing compassion and support. Advertisements for the company highlighted how the product could help people with diabetes manage their condition and live healthy lives. In addition, this product has the support of a large network of healthcare professionals and patient support services to ensure maximum success.

Brand Plan

A brand plan is a detailed strategic blueprint outlining key objectives, target audience, messaging, and tactics over time (usually one to three years).

The brand team, including marketers, medical professionals, sales representatives, and other stakeholders creates the brand plan. This document is the foundation for all communications and marketing efforts that promote the product to patients, payers, and healthcare professionals.

The Pharma brand plan usually includes an assessment of the market and competitive landscape. The plan also includes key strategies, such as advertising, sales force engagement, medical education, and social media presence, to reach targeted audiences.

Pharma brand plans are dynamic documents that evolve according to customer feedback and performance metrics. With a strong brand plan, pharmaceutical companies can effectively promote their products and therapies, increase market share, and improve patient outcomes.

Here are the key components of a brand plan in pharmaceutical marketing:

1. *Situation Analysis*: This section comprehensively overviews the current market conditions. It includes patient demographics, regulatory environment, and other factors that could impact product success.
2. *Target Market*: This section describes which patient groups or healthcare providers the product is targeted and provides key attributes and characteristics for these groups.
3. *Objectives*: This section describes the brand's objectives, which include increasing market share, generating prescriptions, improving patient outcomes, and expanding into new geographical regions.
4. *Strategy*: This section describes the main tactics and approaches to achieve objectives, such as product positioning, pricing, and promotional strategies.
5. *Tactics*: This section describes the specific tactics used to implement the strategy. These include advertising campaigns, sales material, educational programs, and promotional events.
6. *Metrics*: This section describes the key performance indicators that will measure the success of the brand plan. These include sales revenue, market share, customer satisfaction, and product adoption rates.

A well-constructed brand plan in pharmaceutical marketing is crucial for companies looking to maximize the success of their products in a highly competitive and regulated market. It guides companies to achieve their marketing goals while keeping them focused on their target audience, strategies, and success metrics.

Brand Plans in a Digital Age

The digital age has profoundly impacted how pharmaceutical companies plan and execute their brand strategies. Here are the key points to remember when planning a pharma brand plan in the digital age:

1. *Embrace Digital Channels*: Every pharma brand plan must include digital channels. Email marketing, social media platforms such as Facebook or Twitter, websites, and mobile applications allow businesses to reach their target market directly.
2. *Utilize Data Analytics*: Companies looking to gain a greater insight into their customers, measure marketing initiatives more precisely and make data-driven decisions regarding brand image can use analytics as an invaluable asset.
3. *Utilize Influencers*: Social media influencers can be invaluable in promoting pharmaceutical brands. Companies can find influential people with a large relevant, engaged audience to help promote their brand. Pharma companies have unprecedented opportunities in the digital age to reach their target audience and increase awareness about their products and treatments. Pharma companies can create successful brand plans that are digitally compatible by leveraging digital channels, using data, creating relevant content, and tapping into influencers.
4. *Meet Compliance Requirements*: Using digital channels in pharma brand plans requires companies to consider and comply with regulatory requirements for advertising and promoting pharmaceutical products.

The digital age offers pharmaceutical companies new opportunities to engage with their target audience and drive awareness of their products and therapies. By embracing digital channels, leveraging data, developing relevant content, utilizing influencers, and addressing regulatory requirements, pharma companies can develop effective brand plans that drive success in the digital age.

Brand Planning

Brand Planning in pharma marketing involves the creation of a plan to promote and build the brand for a pharmaceutical product. The following are the key steps:

1. *Define the Target Audience*: The first step to brand planning is to define your target audience. This may involve analyzing market research data to determine healthcare professionals' and patients' needs and preferences.
2. *Develop the Brand Message*: Once you have identified your target audience, create a clear and persuasive message that resonates. This message should highlight the product's unique benefits and distinguish it from competitors.
3. *Choose the Marketing Channels*: Pharmaceutical companies have many marketing channel options, including direct mail, print and digital advertising, events, and social media. The target audience and budget will determine the channel selection.
4. *Set Objectives*: After your brand has established its objectives (such as increasing sales, market share, or building brand recognition), it is time to establish measurable objectives and time frames. These objectives should be specific and linked to specific outcomes.
5. *Implement the Plan*: Once your plan has been finalized, it's time to implement it. Hiring a marketing agency might help create campaigns and promotional materials and measure its success over time.
6. *Monitor and Adjust*: It's important to monitor and adjust the success of your brand plan over time and make any necessary changes. This could mean changing messaging, shifting marketing channels, or tweaking budgets to maximize performance.

Effective brand planning in pharmaceutical marketing requires a deep understanding of your target audience, a persuasive brand message, and a marketing strategy that can easily be modified based on performance data.

Brand Portfolio

A company's brand portfolio is its collection of brands and products. As healthcare products can range from prescription drugs, over-the-counter meds, medical devices, and other healthcare services provided, businesses must offer a wide selection of items that meet both patient needs and healthcare professionals' requirements while increasing revenue and profitability.

To build and protect their brand portfolio, pharmaceutical companies use various strategies. These strategies could include:

A. *Brand Extension* involves the launching of new products under an established brand name. For example, a company might produce a drug that reduces cholesterol and launch another product under the same brand name for a related condition.

B. *Line Extension* is the introduction of new products to an existing product line. For example, a pain reliever company might introduce a migraine-specific product.

C. *Brand Acquisition* refers to purchasing other brands or companies to expand a company's product ranges. An example is a producer of cancer treatments who might acquire another firm specializing in rare diseases.

D. *Brand Rationalization* is consolidating or eliminating unprofitable brands that do not align with company's strategic goals.

A well-managed portfolio of brands can help a pharmaceutical company to build a strong market position, grow its customer base and drive revenue growth. However, it takes careful planning, market research, regular evaluation, and monitoring to ensure that the brand portfolio meets the provider's and patients' needs, and company goals.

Brand Positioning

Brand positioning in pharmaceutical marketing involves creating a distinct and unique image of a brand among customers and stakeholders. By positioning the product, customers will recognize it as the ideal solution to their needs, wants, and preferences.

Pharma marketers must consider brand positioning when competition is fierce, and customers have a wide range of choices. To effectively position a pharmaceutical product, marketers should take into account factors like:

1. *Identification of Target Audience*: Marketers must identify their ideal customers, based on their needs, preferences, and behaviors.
2. *Decide the Unique Selling Proposition (USP)*: A pharmaceutical product's USP is the distinct benefit that sets it apart from similar items in the market.
3. *Competitive Analysis*: Assessing the competition allows marketers to identify their rivals' strengths and weaknesses and any market gaps their products can fill. This analysis is invaluable for developing a strategic marketing plan.
4. *Communicate Effectively*: To position their brand appropriately, marketers need to communicate their unique selling proposition (USP) clearly and consistently through various marketing channels such as advertising, social media platforms, and public relations efforts.
5. *Provide Evidence*: Pharmaceutical products undergo stringent testing and regulatory requirements. Therefore, marketers should use scientific evidence and clinical data to demonstrate the safety and effectiveness of their products.

Brand Positioning in Pharma: An Example

Take Advil, a brand of ibuprofen used to relieve pain, fever, and inflammation. Advil's brand positioning emphasizes fast relief that lasts longer than competing products. Advil's USP is its ability to provide relief in as little as 15 minutes, which sets it apart from other pain relievers that may take longer to work.

In summary, brand positioning is a crucial component of pharma marketing, and it requires careful consideration of the target audience through effective segmentation, identifying its unique selling proposition (USP), analyzing competition to differentiate the brand, and effectively communicating the value proposition with scientific evidence.

Brand Positioning in the Digital Age

Brand positioning within the pharmaceutical industry in today's digital era can be daunting and exciting. With evolving digital health innovations, pharmaceutical brands must adapt their strategies to meet expectations from healthcare professionals, patients, and stakeholders. Consider the following points for effectively positioning your brand in the digital age:

1. *Patient-Centric Approach*: Gone are the days when pharmaceutical companies were solely concerned with serving physicians and healthcare providers. With digital health apps and platforms becoming more widely adopted by users, more individuals than ever before are taking control of their healthcare decisions and

becoming informed. Pharma brands must become patient-oriented, offering information and assistance to help individuals better manage their conditions effectively.

2. *Leveraging Data and Analytics*: Pharma companies in today's digital era understand the power of data as the ultimate weapon against the competition, using it from various sources to analyze patient behavior, predict trends, and spot opportunities for business expansion. Furthermore, advanced analytics help pharmaceutical brands position themselves so that their services accurately meet customers' needs.
3. *Digital Presence and Engagement*: Consumers nowadays expect brands to have a robust digital footprint. Pharma brands should note that an effective website, engaging social media pages, providing informative articles online, and creating an excellent customer experience are essential for successful positioning.
4. *Telemedicine and Remote Healthcare*: The COVID-19 pandemic has significantly accelerated the adoption of telemedicine and remote healthcare services. Pharma brands must recognize this development and adapt their strategies accordingly through partnership agreements or the creation of digital health solutions.
5. *Personalized Marketing*: Digital technology makes for highly targeted and tailored advertising strategies, offering pharmaceutical brands an opportunity to use these tools and platforms in their personalized efforts to deliver targeted messaging directly to those they target at precisely the right moment, increasing engagement and customer loyalty while increasing engagement rates and satisfaction levels.
6. *Transparency and Trust*: In today's increasingly digital world, transparency has never been more essential to brand building and positioning success. Pharma brands must remain open about their products, services, and business practices to build consumer trust that aids brand positioning efforts.
7. *Collaboration with Tech Companies*: With so much overlap between healthcare and tech industries, pharma brands can find strength by joining tech firms in creating digital health apps or using AI and machine learning for drug discovery.
8. *Compliance with Regulation*: Digital marketing in the pharmaceutical industry is tightly regulated to protect consumers by assuring them of accurate information that does not mislead them. Pharma brands must ensure their digital strategies comply with relevant regulations for maximum impact and success.
9. *Digital Training for Sales Reps*: Digital technology has revolutionized how pharmaceutical brands interact with their target consumers and healthcare providers. Therefore, pharma brands should provide training programs for sales reps to navigate this changing digital terrain and engage effectively with healthcare providers.
10. *Investing in Emerging Technologies*: Technologies such as Artificial Intelligence (AI), blockchain, and virtual reality can transform healthcare delivery systems, and give a competitive edge.

Digital technology is dramatically revolutionizing the pharmaceutical industry, forcing brands to adapt to remain relevant. By adapting and taking advantage of its potential, pharma brands can improve their positioning while staying ahead of competitors in this digital era.

Implications for Pharma Marketers

Brand positioning within the pharmaceutical industry has become more complicated and challenging in today's digital environment, thanks to widespread internet use that gives access to consumers with vast amounts of healthcare-related data and empowers them to make healthcare decisions. Here are some implications of digitalization on brand positioning strategies in pharma:

1. *Digital Presence*: Pharma brands require an effective digital presence for successful marketing strategies, with marketers creating a user-friendly website that provides accurate product details. In addition, social media channels should be leveraged as platforms that engage target audiences while sharing educational materials, responding to customer inquiries, and solving problems.
2. *Patient-Centric Approach*: As the digital world has given patients more power over managing their health conditions, pharma marketers need to adopt an empathetic, patient-oriented strategy in providing resources and tools that empower individuals to make well-informed choices when making healthcare decisions. Educational materials, interactive apps, and online communities can provide useful support and engagement mechanisms.
3. *Content Marketing*: Producing high-quality, informative content is key to building brand authority and patient trust. Pharma marketers

should create material that informs patients about health conditions, treatment options, and product benefits as part of an educational approach to healthcare products today. Content can be distributed via blogs, videos, podcasts, or social media to reach a broader audience.

4. *Influencer Marketing*: Partnering with healthcare professionals and patient influencers to establish credibility and reach more audiences can be advantageous for pharmaceutical brands leveraging influencer marketing effectively. By teaming up with credible influencers with large online followings, pharmaceutical brands may find an ally willing to endorse pharmaceutical brands while simultaneously informing followers about relevant treatment options available to them.
5. *Data Privacy and Compliance*: With digital media's exponential expansion coming to an increase in privacy and compliance regulations like the General Data Protection Regulation (GDPR) and the Health Insurance Portability and Accountability Act of 1996 (HIPAA), marketers must remain mindful of compliance issues when collecting or using customer data. Following strict privacy policies is vital in building consumer trust.
6. *Personalization and Targeting*: Digital platforms allow marketers to tailor their messaging and target specific audience segments using data analytics and insights, tailoring communication for individual patient groups based on individual needs and preferences, increasing engagement and conversion rates.
7. *Monitoring and Reputation Management*: With today's rapidly evolved digital landscape, pharmaceutical brands should actively track online conversations, reviews, and social media mentions to address customer inquiries promptly while engaging in open dialogue to mitigate negative comments that surface online and protect their brand reputation.
8. *Collaboration with Healthcare Providers*: Pharma marketers must build meaningful relationships with healthcare professionals so that their marketing can assist their efforts by offering educational materials or providing valuable assistance when managing patient cases, ultimately benefitting both brand's reputation and market presence.

Digital platforms present opportunities and challenges to pharmaceutical brand positioning strategies. Marketers must adapt their tactics to engage and educate consumers while building trust between key players in the healthcare ecosystem and consumers alike.

Brand Positioning Statement

A brand positioning statement in pharmaceutical marketing is a concise and straightforward declaration that communicates the unique value proposition of a pharmaceutical brand. Generally, this consists of one sentence summarizing key differentiators, the target audience, and the overall promise of the brand.

Consider, for example, a brand positioning statement for AllergyRelief, a hypothetical allergy medication:

AllergyRelief is a fast-acting allergy medication that offers 24-hour relief to sufferers who want to feel better quickly. Unlike other allergy medications that cause drowsiness, AllergyRelief provides powerful relief without the side effects so you can get back to living your life normally quickly.

This brand positioning statement highlights the brand's unique benefit (fast-acting, non-drowsy relief), target audience (allergy sufferers who want immediate relief), and differentiator (lack of side effects compared to competitors). Furthermore, it positions the brand as a superior solution for people searching for an effective allergy medication without drowsiness or other side effects.

Brand Positioning Statements in Pharma Marketing: Some Examples

Here are a few examples of brand positioning statements used in pharmaceutical marketing:

1. *Tylenol*

   Tylenol provides fast and effective pain relief without upsetting the stomach—perfect for anyone needing fast relief without side effects such as an upset stomach. It's the ideal choice when fast relief without discomfort is desired.

2. *Nexium*

   Nexium is the Go-to medication for heartburn and acid reflux relief. Unlike other antacids, Nexium offers long-lasting relief from these symptoms so you can enjoy your favorite foods without worry.

   Nexium differentiates itself in this brand positioning statement because Nexium provides long-lasting relief from acid reflux unlike others, making it the best choice for people to enjoy their meals without the discomfort and pain of heartburn or acid reflux.

3. *Humira*

   Humira is the top treatment option for moderate to severe rheumatoid arthritis. Unlike other approaches, Humira targets inflammation's source, providing long-lasting relief and helping people resume active lives.

   Humira's positioning as an effective solution that targets the source of rheumatoid arthritis symptoms makes it a stand-out product among individuals looking for long-lasting relief while remaining active. This brand positioning statement highlights this feature.

4. *Lipitor*

   Lipitor is the leading medication for treating high cholesterol. Unlike other cholesterol reducers, Lipitor reduces the risk of heart attack and stroke, making it a superior choice for anyone looking to improve their heart health.

   Lipitor emphasizes its proven ability to lower heart attack and stroke risk to stand out in this brand positioning statement. In addition, it positions itself as an optimal choice for improving overall cardiovascular health.

5. *Advil*

   Advil provides fast and effective relief to anyone seeking an active lifestyle without pain. In addition, Advil works within 15 minutes to allow the quick return of activity—the ideal option for any individual wanting to resume active living quickly.

Advil is an effective pain-relief option that enables active people to remain pain-free for as long as possible. In this brand positioning statement, Advil emphasizes its fast-acting pain relief to promote its use as a product for keeping active without pain.

Brand Presence

Brand presence refers to a brand's overall visibility and recognition in the market, including its reputation, perception, and awareness among its target audience. It includes all customer interactions with a brand, such as advertising, social media platforms, and customer service operations. So it's essential for creating successful and sustainable brands.

In pharma marketing, brand presence is the visibility and reputation of a pharmaceutical brand among healthcare professionals, patients, and other stakeholders. Pharmaceutical companies typically employ various tactics for building their brand presence, such as:

1. *Advertising* includes placing advertisements in medical journals, conferences, and trade shows.
2. *Online Marketing*: Establishing a strong digital presence through websites, social media channels, and other digital media vehicles.
3. *Content Marketing*: This involves crafting and sharing valuable content like blog posts, white papers, and e-books to inform customers about the brand and its advantages.
4. *Thought Leadership*: Position the brand as an authority in its field by publishing research papers, attending industry events, and connecting with key opinion leaders.
5. *Patient Education*: This includes creating educational materials for patients to help them better comprehend their condition and treatment options.

Measuring Brand Presence

Measuring brand presence in pharmaceutical marketing can be challenging because it involves qualitative and quantitative aspects. However, there are several methods available for measuring and improving brand presence, such as:

1. *Conducting Surveys*: Surveys are an excellent way to collect information on brand awareness, perception, and reputation among healthcare professionals and patients. This data can assist companies in recognizing areas where they need to strengthen their brand presence.
2. *Analyzing Website Traffic and Engagement*: By studying website traffic and engagement metrics, companies can assess how effectively their websites attract and engage target audiences.
3. *Monitor Social Media Metrics*: Social media analytics offer insight into brand recognition, sentiment analysis, and follower engagement.
4. *Tracking Media Mentions*: Monitoring media mentions can provide companies with insights into how audiences perceive their brand and help identify opportunities to strengthen their presence in the market.
5. *Conduct Market Research*: Market research can assist companies in understanding their target audience's needs, preferences, and behaviors so that tailored marketing campaigns can increase brand presence.

How to Enhance Brand Presence

To enhance brand presence in pharmaceutical marketing, companies can:

1. *Start With a Solid Brand Strategy*: Pharma companies need a well-conceived brand strategy in place to craft an identity and message that resonates with their target audiences.
2. *Advertising and Promotion*: Utilizing advertisements and promotions as an integral

component of healthcare can increase brand recognition while stimulating patient engagement with healthcare providers about their services.

3. *Focus on Patient Education*: Creating patient educational materials can help foster trust and credibility, increasing brand visibility.
4. *Engaging With Key Opinion Leaders*: Building relationships with influential key opinion leaders can help companies establish themselves as thought leaders.
5. *Monitor and Respond to Feedback*: Companies should monitor feedback from healthcare professionals and patients and act upon it promptly and appropriately. Doing this can improve brand reputation and perception.

A strong brand presence in pharma marketing can help build trust among healthcare professionals and patients, differentiate the brand from competitors, and drive sales and revenue growth.

Brand Presentation

Brand presentation in pharmaceutical marketing is about how pharmaceutical companies present their brand visually. Here are a few examples of brand presentation strategies that pharmaceutical companies often use:

1. *Packaging* design is an important aspect of brand branding. Pharma companies should make packaging an integral component of their customer engagement efforts by employing colors, graphics, and typography to visually represent their product and brand identity, and attract their target customer base.
2. *Brands* can also communicate effectively with their target market through advertising campaigns. For example, companies can use print, TV, and digital advertising to communicate their brand's values and identity.
3. *Exhibits at Trade Shows*. Trade shows are a great way for pharmaceutical companies to showcase their products and interact directly with customers. They also create trade show exhibits that reflect the brand's values and identity.
4. *Brochures, Flyers:* Product brochures provide businesses with an effective means to present their brand image to prospective customers. Companies can leverage high-quality printing and design processes to develop sales materials that look appealing visually and communicate the benefits associated with their products.
5. *Website Design*: In today's digital environment, website often serves as customers' initial point of contact with brands and organizations. Pharma companies can utilize web design to showcase their values, identity, and product messaging through an appealing yet user-friendly website layout.

Brand presentation is an important element of pharmaceutical marketing. It helps to communicate the brand's values and messaging to the market. Through various design strategies and elements, pharma marketers can create an engaging brand image, connect with customers and drive sales.

Brand Profile

Brand profiles in pharmaceutical marketing serve to introduce and describe products by outlining their features, benefits, and value proposition. A brand profile conveys this distinctiveness to target audiences such as patients, physicians, other healthcare providers, and patients. An effective brand profile in pharmaceutical marketing requires several key elements:

1. *Brand Name*: When creating a brand name for products and services, ensure that it is unique and memorable for its target customer group. Involve an element that conveys some aspects of product benefits while building positive associations in customers' minds.
2. *Logo and Visual Elements*: For maximum impact, brand identities should feature distinct logos and visuals which reflect its brand message and therapeutic area.
3. *Unique Value Proposition (UVP)*: A brand's unique value proposition highlights those benefits which set it apart from its competition and differentiate its offering. In the case of pharmaceutical products these could be efficacy, side effect profile, cost-effectiveness, or ease of dosing, such as once-daily dosing.
4. *Target Audience*: Identifying your target audience is crucial to creating an effective brand profile. Your audience could include patients, physicians, pharmacists, healthcare providers, and payers. You need to address all their needs and concerns accordingly in your brand profile.
5. *Brand Personality*: Brand personality refers to human characteristics or traits associated with the brand, such as trustworthiness, innovation, care-taking, or reliability, that help create emotional connections with its target audiences.

6. *Key Messages of Your Brand*: These should provide key information about what the brand wants its target market to understand. The messages should remain consistent across marketing channels and be simple enough for their target demographic to comprehend.
7. *Brand Promise*: This represents what the brand hopes to do for its customers. This could be superior efficacy, improved quality of life, or reliable customer service for pharmaceutical brands.
8. *Evidence and Endorsements*: In the pharmaceutical industry, clinical evidence and endorsements from healthcare professionals are crucial in creating brand credibility and customer trust.
9. *Positioning Statement*: A positioning statement outlines your target market and how your brand stands out among rivals, outlining the unique benefits it brings customers.
10. *Compliance and Ethical Standards*: Pharma brand profiles should clearly illustrate compliance with regulatory guidelines and ethical marketing practices.

Pharmaceutical companies can create an engaging brand profile by outlining these elements for their target audiences and meeting their needs in an increasingly competitive marketplace.

Brand Profitability

Brand profitability in pharmaceutical marketing refers to the measure of a pharmaceutical brand's ability to generate financial gains. It assesses a brand's financial performance by considering the revenue generated from the sales of the branded product and the associated costs and expenses incurred in marketing and promoting the brand. Here are some key factors that contribute to brand profitability in pharma marketing:

1. *Revenue Generation*: The primary driver of band profitability is the revenue generated from the branded product sales. Market demand, pricing strategies, market access, competition, and patient exclusivity influence this revenue. Higher sales volumes and premium pricing can increase revenue and improve profitability.
2. *Cost of Goods Sold (COGS)*: The cost of goods sold represents the expenses incurred in manufacturing. The pharmaceutical product cost includes the cost of raw materials production, packaging, and quality control. Managing and optimizing the cost of goods (COGS) is essential for improving brand profitability.
3. *Marketing and Promotion Expenses*: Pharmaceutical companies allocate significant budgets for marketing and promoting their brands. These expenses include advertising campaigns, physician education programs, direct-to-consumer advertising, sales force activities, medical conferences, and other promotional initiatives. Managing and optimizing these expenses while ensuring effective marketing efforts can impact band profitability.
4. *Research and Development (R&D) Costs*: Pharmaceutical companies invest heavily in R&D to develop new medications. Research and development (R&D) costs occur during research, preclinical testing, clinical trials, and regulatory approval processes. Carefully managing R&D costs while creating an attractive product pipeline is key for sustained brand profitability in the long run.
5. *Patent Protection and Exclusivity*: Patents provide companies with exclusivity and protection for a defined period, allowing them to charge premium prices and maintain higher profitability, as generic competition after patent expiration can lead to lower prices and decreased profitability.
6. *Market Access and Reimbursement*: The ability to secure favorable market access and reimbursement from payers, such as insurance companies and government health programs, can impact brand profitability. Higher reimbursement rates and broad market coverage can increase sales and profitability.
7. *Lifecycle Management*: Effective lifecycle management strategies, such as line extensions, new indications, or reformulations, can help extend the patent life and profitability of a brand. Continuously evaluating and enhancing a brand's portfolio can positively impact profitability.
8. *Market Share and Competitive Landscape*: A brand's market share within its therapeutic area also influences brand profitability. Higher market share often translates into greater sales profitability. Proactively keeping up with and adapting to changes in the competitive environment are vital steps toward maintaining brand profitability.

Pharmaceutical companies use various financial metrics, including gross profit margin, operating profit margin, return on investment, and net profit, to assess the profitability of their brands. By increasing revenues while simultaneously controlling costs and strategically positioning them within an incredibly competitive pharmaceutical market, companies strive to maximize brand profitability to remain viable competitors in an extremely difficult business environment.

Brand Profitability Metrics

Brand profitability metrics in the pharmaceutical industry focus on assessing pharmaceutical brands' financial performance and profitability. These metrics help evaluate the effectiveness of marketing strategies, product pricing, and overall brand profitability. Here are some examples of brand profitability metrics commonly used in the pharma sector.

1. *Gross Margin (GM)*: Measured as the difference between the revenue generated from pharmaceutical product sales and the cost of goods sold (COGS), gross margin indicates the profitability of each unit sold, and provides insights into brands' pricing strategy and manufacturing efficiencies.
2. *Net Profit Margin (NPM)*: Used to assess a pharmaceutical brand's profitability by measuring the percentage of revenue remaining as profit after deducting all expenses (COGS), marketing expenses, research & development costs, and administrative), net profit margin measures whether their operations can generate profit for them.
3. *Contribution Margin*: This represents the portion of each pharmaceutical product's revenue that covers fixed costs and generates profit. It helps assess the profitability of individual products and their contribution to overall brand profitability.
4. *Return on Investment*: Assesses the financial returns generated from brand-related investments. ROI measures the relationship between expenses incurred (marketing, and research and development costs) and profits generated, giving insight into investment, and profitability, and how a brand generates return from those investments.
5. *Price Elasticity* indicates how responsive pharmaceutical demand is to changes in price. Price elasticity helps determine the optimal pricing strategy for maximizing profitability. Higher price elasticity may suggest more flexibility to adjust prices without significantly impacting demand.
6. *Customer Lifetime Value*: Assesses a customer's long-term value to a pharmaceutical brand over their lifetime. CLV considers factors such as the duration of the customer's relationship with the brand, purchase frequency, and the average revenue generated. It helps identify profitable customer segments and informs customer acquisition and retention strategies.
7. *Market Access and Reimbursement*: Evaluate the brand's ability to gain favorable market access and secure reimbursement from payers. Metrics such as reimbursement rates, formulary inclusion, and market coverage can impact the brand's profitability by ensuring wider market reach and adequate pricing.
8. *Cost of Customer Acquisition*: Measures the cost incurred by a pharmaceutical brand to acquire a new customer. It helps assess the efficiency and effectiveness of marketing and sales activities. The brand can determine the profitability of acquiring new customers by comparing the customer acquisition cost with the customer's lifetime value.

These brand profitability metrics assist pharmaceutical companies in evaluating the financial performance of their brands, optimizing pricing strategies, managing costs, and making informed decisions to maximize profitability.

Brand Promise

A brand promise is a company's unique value proposition to its customers. It is a statement that highlights the benefits patients can get from a specific drug or treatment.

The brand promise in pharma marketing can include various elements, such as:

1. *Efficacy*: Pharma marketing relies heavily on effectively selling their drugs, such as by emphasizing clinical trial results or other evidence supporting claims regarding the efficacy of particular treatments. Brand promises may highlight this aspect to emphasize a drug's efficacy in treating specific conditions.
2. *Safety*: Patients can feel comforted knowing their drug has undergone rigorous safety testing to ensure its efficacy and safety.
3. *Convenience*: Brand promises can emphasize how easy or few doses it requires than its competitors.
4. *Accessibility*: A brand promise might stress the affordability of the drug in comparison to other treatments.

5. *Patient Experience*: This promise could focus on the patient's experience with the drug, including reducing symptoms and improving mobility and overall health.

Here's an example of how a brand promise might look in pharmaceutical marketing:

You can trust our brand X for superior pain relief (show evidence)! Brand X provides fast, effective relief for arthritis symptoms so you can return to what you love most.

Brand Psychology

Brand psychology in pharmaceutical marketing is about creating a strong brand image and connecting with healthcare providers and patients. It examines the way brands engage their target audience using psychological principles. Here are some examples of brand psychology used in pharma marketing:

1. *Creating Emotional Connections*: Pharmaceutical companies use emotional messaging to communicate with patients and healthcare professionals. As a result, they can build trust and loyalty with their customers by creating emotional connections.
2. *Using Social Proof*: Social proof assumes that people trust others and will follow their lead. Pharmaceutical companies can use this concept to showcase positive reviews from patients, endorsements and testimonials of healthcare professionals, and other evidence that their product is safe and effective.
3. *Highlighting Science*: Pharma companies can use the science behind their products to enhance their brand identity. They will be recognized as an authority in the industry if they emphasize the research and development involved in creating these products.
4. *Establishing a Unique Brand Voice*: A unique brand voice can make pharma companies stand out from their competition. A unique voice that resonates with their target audience can help create a strong identity and increase recognition for their products or services.
5. *Using Colors and Imagery*: Colors, imagery, and branding can influence brand psychology. For example, pharmaceutical companies could use blue to communicate professionalism and trust or green for well-being and health. Images can also evoke emotions and establish connections with their audiences.

Brand psychology plays an important role in pharmaceutical marketing. It helps companies create an identity and emotionally connect with their target audience.

Brand Purpose

A brand's purpose is what makes it exist beyond its commercial goals. It shapes decisions and communicates brand messages, and is becoming increasingly important in pharmaceutical marketing.

Pharma companies need to do more than sell drugs. They must also contribute to society. Pharma companies must establish stronger connections with their customers, employees, stakeholders, and partners and foster greater collaborations.

Brand Purpose in pharma marketing can take many forms. Consider the following, for example:

1. *Enhancing Patient Outcomes*: One goal for brand objectives should be improving patient outcomes by developing innovative medications, providing education and resources, and investing in research to develop new products.
2. *Supporting Healthcare Professionals*: Pharma companies could support healthcare professionals by providing the tools and information necessary for effective patient care.
3. *Promotion of Public Health*: Pharma companies might want to help improve public health by supporting initiatives, increasing disease awareness, and advocating for policies that benefit patients.
4. *Promoting Sustainability*: Many pharmaceutical companies place a high priority on sustainability and reducing their environmental footprint. This can be a significant brand purpose for those who value sustainability.

A strong brand purpose in pharma marketing is a great way to help companies stand out among competitors, build trust with customers and stakeholders, and ultimately drive growth and positively impact society.

Brand Rationalization

In pharmaceutical marketing, brand rationalization refers to consolidating and eliminating brands that are not profitable or don't align with the company's strategic goals. In addition, companies aim to rationalize their product portfolio to reduce costs and focus on the products most likely to increase revenue and satisfy customer needs.

Pharma companies might choose to rationalize their brand portfolio for various reasons. However, here are the most important ones:

A. *Declining Sales*: A company might rationalize a brand if it has experienced a sudden decrease in sales or stopped producing significant revenue.
B. *Overlapping Product Lines*: If a company has many brands offering similar benefits or competing, it might make financial sense for them to merge to cut marketing and operational costs.
C. *Shifts of Market Demand*: A company might need to adapt its brand portfolio if there are any changes in the market demand for a specific product or treatment.

A pharmaceutical company must thoroughly analyze its brand portfolio to determine its profitability, market potential, and alignment with strategic goals. The company can then consolidate or remove certain brands and invest or create new products to fill the gaps in its product offering.

Pharma companies can rationalize their brands to improve product offerings, increase operational efficiency, and concentrate resources on the products most likely to generate revenue growth and satisfy customer needs. However, it requires careful planning and execution to ensure the business is competitive while adapting to changing market demands.

Brand Reinforcement

Brand reinforcement in pharmaceutical marketing involves strengthening and maintaining a pharmaceutical brand's relevance and appeal among its target audience. Brand reinforcement ensures it stays at the top of the mind and drives sales and revenue. Here are some effective strategies for brand reinforcement:

1. *Consistent Branding*: Ensuring a brand's messaging, visual identity, and tone remain consistent across all marketing channels and touchpoints can help build and reinforce brand recognition.
2. *Pharmaceutical Companies Should Conduct Ongoing Market Research*: Undergoing periodic market research can assist pharmaceutical companies in staying aware of their target audience's needs and preferences, which may reveal new growth opportunities or enhance the brand value.
3. *Digital Marketing*: Relying on creative digital marketing techniques like social media marketing, email marketing, and search engine optimization (SEO) can help brands remain relevant while expanding further.
4. *Educational Initiatives*: Engaging in educational initiatives such as webinars, conferences, or content development can strengthen a brand's thought leadership status and ensure they stay at the forefront.
5. *Strengthened Customer Support*: Offering customers and HCPs access to strong customer support services can help build brand trust while strengthening loyalty and satisfaction among the target demographics.
6. *Continuous Improvement*: Refining products, services, or relationships with HCPs continuously hold the key to reinforcing a company's dedication to quality and excellence.

Brand reinforcement in pharma marketing involves an active and ongoing approach considering each brand's requirements and challenges. By employing effective strategies, pharmaceutical companies can strengthen their brands while maintaining relevance, increasing sales revenue, and driving growth in sales and profitability.

Brand Relevance

Brand relevance refers to how meaningful, recognizable, and valuable an individual pharmaceutical brand is to its target audience. Brands relevant to their target audiences tend to be remembered more fondly; therefore, they are more often chosen over competitors.

Brand relevance in pharmaceutical marketing is vitally important for several reasons. First and foremost, in the pharmaceutical industry competition can be fierce; numerous products compete to gain market share. A relevant brand can differentiate a product and gain a competitive edge against its rivals; trust is also integral in healthcare settings, so having an identifiable, relevant brand that creates it helps build trust more easily among patients as well as healthcare professionals. Finally, it increases patient adherence since patients tend to trust and adhere to brands they perceive as relevant more easily than ones which don't come across their radar screen!

To achieve brand relevance in pharma marketing, companies must have a strategic approach that involves several key steps:

1. *Understand Your Target Audience*: Before creating a relevant brand message, you need to understand your target audience, their needs, concerns, and preferences. Conduct market research, engage patient groups, and interact

with healthcare professionals to fully understand your target audience.

2. *Determine Key Benefits*: Determine which features of your products or services are most relevant and compelling to the needs and desires of your target audience, then present these features and the benefits they offer clearly so they resonate.
3. *Create Your Brand Message*: Craft an effective message that communicates your product's key benefits appealingly and memorably and meets target audience preferences while setting you apart from the competition.
4. *Build A Strong Brand Identity*: Develop an easily recognizable and memorable brand identity. This includes creating a name, logo, and visual identity reflecting your brand's message and value.
5. *Engaging With Healthcare Community*: Involve yourself with healthcare professionals, patient groups, and other stakeholders to build positive associations between your brand and healthcare professionals and patient groups or other stakeholders to build brand recognition and establish positive associations between yourself and them. You could do this by attending conferences, sponsoring events, and participating in social media or online forums.
6. *Monitor and Adjust*: Monitor the effectiveness of your branding efforts and adjust your approach as needed. This involves tracking key metrics such as brand awareness, customer engagement, and patient adherence and making changes to your strategy based on these insights.
7. *Brand Relevance* in pharmaceutical marketing requires deep knowledge of your target audience, developing an eye-catching brand message, creating a memorable identity, and maintaining engagement with healthcare community members. Following these steps and constantly adapting based on feedback can create brands that resonate with patients and healthcare providers alike.

Brand Reputation

Brand reputation refers to how individuals perceive, evaluate and experience a brand among its target audiences, stakeholders, and the general public, including customers, employees, partners, and investors. It can be affected by various factors, including quality products/services provided, corporate behavior such as customer service levels, and an organization's public communications strategies. Branding reputation plays an indispensable part in the success of an organization.

Pharmaceutical marketing relies heavily on reputation. Various key elements can determine a brand's reputation:

1. *Product Efficacy and Safety*: Pharmaceutical companies place immense importance on ensuring their products work as intended without serious side effects undermining their brand's credibility. When drugs don't perform as promised or develop undesirable reactions, this can have devastating repercussions for brand reputation and loyalty.
2. *Transparency*: Pharmaceutical companies must act transparently when sharing clinical trial data or handling adverse event reports to maintain trust between patients and themselves and preserve their brand reputation. Failure to do so could result in mistrust, eroding consumer loyalty over time and possibly harming its brand name.
3. *Ethical Marketing Practices in Pharma*: Ethics are of utmost importance within the pharmaceutical industry. Ethical marketing practices are at their heart, from providing accurate drug information without prejudice or unduly impacting prescribing behaviors to respecting patient privacy and not influencing prescription decisions.
4. *Patient Centricity*: Businesses that prioritize patient needs and feedback, offer exceptional patient support services, and engage patients authentically can build an impeccable reputation amongst consumers.
5. *Corporate Social Responsibility (CSR)*: Businesses that demonstrate an active commitment to CSR initiatives, such as contributing to public health efforts, providing access to medicines, and engaging in environmentally sustainable practices, can significantly bolster their reputations.
6. *Compliance With Regulations*: Compliance with regulations is of utmost importance in the pharmaceutical industry. Any violations can lead to harsh fines that have lasting ramifications on brand image and business success.
7. *Crisis Management*: How a pharmaceutical company handles crises such as recalls or negative publicity can significantly affect its reputation, so an effective crisis management plan should help lessen potential damage.
8. *Quality Customer Service*: High-quality customer service can significantly boost a brand's image by efficiently responding to

inquiries and effectively handling complaints from its customer base.

Pharmaceutical marketers must follow ethical practices in shaping the messaging and communication of their brands to build and uphold brand identities. They should engage authentically with patients and healthcare providers, advocating the brand's dedication to patient health, safety, and well-being.

Brand Reputation Management

Brand reputation management involves overseeing how a brand is perceived. Maintaining a strong brand reputation within the pharmaceutical sector, where trust and credibility are at an absolute premium, is essential.

Here are a few key aspects of brand reputation management in pharmaceutical marketing:

1. *Transparency*: Pharmaceutical companies must exhibit transparency when providing clinical trial data, product efficacy, and safety information to potential investors or the general public. Failure to be up-front about these matters could create stakeholders' mistrust, negatively impacting brand recognition and credibility.
2. *Crisis Management*: Effective crisis management is crucial to maintaining a strong brand reputation. It should include an elaborate communications plan and be ready to quickly and appropriately address potential issues or crises, like recalls or adverse events.
3. *Compliance Regulation*: Adherence to all industry regulations and guidelines is crucial, with violations resulting in substantial fines and irreparable damage to a brand's image and credibility.
4. *Patient Engagement*: Pharmaceutical companies must prioritize patients' needs and feedback, as an authentic dialogue between the brand and patients is often beneficial in shaping its reputation. Patients will speak candidly about their experiences which could significantly boost or damage their standing with customers.
5. *Ethical Marketing*: Ethics-focused marketing practices are vital in maintaining brand integrity, providing accurate, balanced, and useful drug information. Pharmaceutical companies should honor patient privacy concerns and not exert undue pressure or influence over prescribing behavior.
6. *Product Quality and Safety*: A pharmaceutical brand's reputation hinges upon its products being perceived to have quality and safety characteristics that exceed expectations. Regular quality control checks, rigorous testing protocols, and taking proactive steps to manage side effects are critical components to its success.
7. *Corporate Social Responsibility (CSR)*: CSR activities such as participating in public health initiatives, adhering to responsible environmental practices, and improving access to medicines can significantly affect a pharmaceutical brand's reputation.
8. *Thought Leadership and Expertise*: Establishing your brand as a thought leader within its therapeutic area can greatly bolster its reputation. By offering valuable and trustworthy information in educational materials, scientific publications, conferences, or expert opinions, positioning it as a source of knowledge is paramount in building its brand recognition and trust with consumers.
9. *Stakeholder Engagement*: Establishing strong relationships with healthcare professionals, patient advocacy groups, regulatory authorities, and media members is crucial to building and upholding a positive brand reputation. Engaging in open dialogue while listening attentively and responding swiftly to feedback or any potential concerns can build trust and establish credibility over time.
10. *Patient-Centric Approach*: Engaging patients as key decision-makers and emphasizing a commitment to patient health can bolster a company's brand image positively. Initiatives like patient support programs, disease awareness campaigns, and advocacy groups all positively contribute to brand image.
11. *Monitoring Social Media and Online Presence*: Establishing and overseeing an effective brand presence online includes social media channels, review sites, and forum discussions. Doing this effectively will help manage the brand's reputation.

Brand reputation management in pharma marketing requires an inclusive, proactive, and reactive strategy, given its highly sensitive nature and regulatory compliance framework. Establishing trust over time while being prepared to respond swiftly when challenges arise is paramount.

Brand Resilience

Brand resilience refers to a brand's capacity to survive or quickly rebound from difficult situations such as crises, scandals, market fluctuations, competitive pressures, or negative publicity. A resilient brand can quickly recover from setbacks while protecting its reputation, customer loyalty, and market share.

Brand resilience in pharmaceutical marketing is of utmost importance due to the highly regulated nature of this sector. Pharmaceutical companies may face difficulties such as product recalls, adverse drug reactions, patent expiration dates and regulatory changes, and competition from generic drugs, and how a brand reacts can have lasting ramifications on long-term success and sustainability.

Here are several strategies pharmaceutical marketers can employ in building brand resilience:

1. *Trust*: At the core of brand resilience lies trust between customers and pharmaceutical brands, built through transparency, consistency, promise fulfillment, and dedication to patient well-being and safety. Establishing this bond ensures customers remain loyal during tough times.
2. *Crisis Management*: Being prepared with an effective crisis management plan can enable pharmaceutical brands to respond swiftly, and effectively in times of potential issues, whether that means having a dedicated crisis team in place, pre-loaded communication templates and strategies for engaging media outlets, regulators, healthcare providers, or members of the public.
3. *Diversification*: Diversifying product portfolios can be an effective strategy to strengthen brand resilience. If one product experiences a setback, other offerings from that brand can still rely on each other as backup. Market diversification also can play a part, with companies operating across various nations or regions to spread risk more evenly.
4. *Patient-Centric Approach*: Adopting a patient-centric approach can boost brand resilience by staying relevant and valuable to customers. This might involve prioritizing customer needs during product design or focus group testing, providing top-quality education and support, or engaging with patients through various channels.
5. *Continuous Innovation*: Innovation can help a brand stay competitive and resilient in today's healthcare environment, from developing new drugs or improving existing ones to innovating patient support programs or finding novel methods of engaging healthcare providers and patients.
6. *Compliance*: Compliance in the pharmaceutical industry is paramount in maintaining brand resilience. If left unaddressed, noncompliance can result in severe penalties, trust issues, and irreparable harm to a brand's reputation. To avoid such penalties and damage to reputation, companies should implement stringent compliance processes and invest in ongoing staff training to maintain brand resilience.
7. *Establish Strong Ties With Healthcare Providers*: Building strong relationships can strengthen brand resilience. If healthcare providers trust your product or brand, they may continue prescribing its products even during times of difficulty.

By emphasizing these areas, pharmaceutical marketers can develop brands that meet immediate success requirements and withstand inevitable market shifts and changes over the longer run.

Brand Review

Pharma marketing involves promoting and branding pharmaceutical products and services for healthcare providers and patients (consumers). Branding is integral to pharmaceutical company success as it differentiates their offerings from competitors, builds trust between patients and physicians, and creates positive associations in the marketplace. Below is an outline for reviewing brand effectiveness:

1. *Brand Identity*: Evaluate the brand identity's clarity and consistency by considering factors like name, logo, tagline, and overall visual representation of your business. Does its image communicate your company values, purpose, and USP effectively?
2. *Brand Positioning*: Evaluate how well-positioned a brand is within its market environment. Is its target audience well-defined? Does its messaging successfully communicate its positioning and differentiate it from competitors? Is there an appealing unique value proposition that resonates with its target demographic, etc?
3. *Brand Awareness*: Assess your target audience's awareness level regarding your brand through market research, surveys, or social media listening. Establish whether the brand remains visible across several relevant channels—both online and off.
4. *Brand Perception*: Assess how target audiences and stakeholders perceive your brand. Examine customer reviews to gauge perception. For

insight, examine strengths, weaknesses, opportunities, and threats within its market image.

5. *Messaging and Communication*: Evaluate the efficacy of your brand's messaging and communications strategy by considering whether its benefits, features, and safety messages reach different target audiences efficiently and clearly across various communication channels.
6. *Customer Experience*: Evaluate the overall customer experience provided by your brand and consider factors like ease of accessing information, product quality, customer support services, and engagement activities. Review feedback ratings and testimonials to assess customer satisfaction levels.
7. *Physician and Healthcare Provider Perception*: Investigate how physicians, healthcare providers, and key opinion leaders perceive your brand. Are they familiar with it and its products? Do they trust the band with recommending to their patients, etc? Acquire insight by surveying, interviewing, and medical conferences their perceptions.
8. *Compliance and Ethics*: Evaluate whether the brand adheres to industry compliance guidelines and ethical standards in pharmaceuticals and ascertain its commitment to relevant laws, codes of conduct, and best practices in terms of ethics. A strong commitment to compliance will increase the credibility and trustworthiness of your brand.
9. *Conduct a Competitive Analysis*: Evaluate how well your brand compares with its competition by examining market share, positioning, messaging, and customer perception. This allows for identifying opportunities for improvement or differentiation.
10. *Return of Investment (ROI)*: Assess the financial performance and return on investment (ROI) of your brand's marketing initiatives by reviewing sales data, market share, and customer acquisition costs to measure the effectiveness of marketing initiatives.

Pharmaceutical companies can conduct an in-depth assessment across these dimensions to gain valuable insights into their brand's strengths, weaknesses, and areas for improvement. With this knowledge, strategic decisions will become clearer to guide branding and marketing efforts more efficiently.

Brand Revitalization

Brand revitalization refers to reinstating the relevance and customer appeal of an outdated or disappointing brand to customers due to changes in market dynamics, shifting consumer preferences, or increased competition from competing products. Pharmaceutical companies can take several steps to bring back their brands:

1. *Do a Thorough Analysis of Your Brand*: Before embarking on any revitalization efforts, conduct a comprehensive analysis to identify the brand's core values, distinguishing factors, and areas that need improvement.
2. *Reevaluate Your Brand Positioning*: Companies should analyze and reevaluate their brand positioning. This involves identifying your target audience, your brand's unique selling proposition (USP), creating key messages, and communicating with them in a way that resonates with consumers.
3. *Develop Comprehensive Marketing Strategy*: After defining the brand positioning, companies should create an integrated marketing strategy that uses both digital and traditional channels. For example, targeted advertising, social media campaigns, and email marketing are all possible methods to reach the target audience.
4. *Enhance your Product Portfolio*: This is a way to revive a brand by adding new products or relevant features to current consumers. This could include investing in research and development to improve or create new products.
5. *Leverage Partnerships and Collaborations*: To help revive their brand, companies might consider partnering with other organizations or firms. This could include collaborating with experts or influencers in related fields, sponsoring events, or co-branding products and services with other companies.

A comprehensive strategy is required to revitalize a brand in the pharmaceutical sector. This includes analysis, reevaluating its positioning, creating a marketing plan, expanding your product portfolio, and taking advantage of partnerships and collaborations.

How Pharma Companies Revitalize Their Brands: Some Examples

1. *Pfizer*: When faced with increasing competition from generic drugmakers and declining Lipitor sales in 2000, Pfizer responded by reinventing itself as a biopharmaceutical company and developing therapies to treat cancer and other serious diseases to revitalize its brand name.

They made significant investments in research and development which led to the discovery of new drugs like Ibrance (Palbociclib), and Xeljanz, Tofacitinib.

2. *Novo Nordisk*, a Danish pharmaceutical company known for its insulins globally, has successfully repositioned itself by focusing on diabetes care. They have introduced Victoza (Liraglutide) and Ozempic (Semaglutide), which improve the lives of people with diabetes. Novo Nordisk also invested in digital health technologies such as wearables and mobile apps to improve patient care.
3. *GlaxoSmithKline (GSK)*, selling its blockbuster drug Advair (Fluticasone & Salmeterol), saw declining sales and faced increased competition from generic drugs. As a result, GSK restructured research and development to focus on HIV, oncology, and respiratory diseases. GSK also adopted new marketing strategies to improve customer perception, including a value-based pricing strategy.
4. *AstraZeneca* faced patent expirations, and sales decline for Crestor and Nexium, leading to declining revenues for these blockbuster drugs. As a result, AstraZeneca decided to shift focus, developing medicines in areas such as oncology, diabetes care, and respiratory disease treatment, investing heavily in digital health technologies like wearables and mobile apps in patient management, and running successful marketing campaigns such as its *Healthy Heart Africa Campaign* that focused on increasing the African cardiovascular health.

Reviving Pharma Brands

Here are two examples of how well-known brands were revived:

A. *Purdue Pharma's* prescription painkiller Oxycontin saw sales decrease due to negative publicity due to its association with the opioid crisis. As a result, Purdue changed the formulation to make it harder for individuals to abuse and launched a marketing campaign touting its pain management effectiveness. However, they were later hit with legal troubles for their involvement with the crisis and unethical marketing practices.

B. *Pfizer's* Viagra brand faced competition from generic medications and declining sales. To revive it, Pfizer launched an emotional awareness campaign featuring an older man discussing his experiences with erectile dysfunction. This helped remove the stigma related to the erectile dysfunction condition, while increasing knowledge about treatment options such as Viagra.

These examples show how pharmaceutical companies can revive their brands by investing in new drugs, digital health technology, marketing strategies, and adapting to changing market conditions.

Brand Salience

Brand salience refers to how customers remember or note one brand during a buying situation. In other words, brand salience is its prominence or visibility relative to competitors' brands in consumers' minds. Brand salience influences customer choices at point-of-sale and whether that brand even enters consideration during purchase decisions. It could influence choice at purchase time and future options considered before purchase decisions occur.

Brand Salience in Pharma

Brand salience in pharmaceutical marketing requires special consideration due to its unique industry nature. Here are a few key points:

1. *Raising Awareness*: Pharmaceutical brand salience can start by building awareness among healthcare professionals about its existence and benefits through medical conferences, published studies, information sessions, or other outreach methods.
2. *Educating Healthcare Professionals*: For prescription drugs, healthcare professionals (HCPs) often decide which brand is recommended or prescribed to patients. So, brand salience includes informing these HCPs about your drug's specific benefits, use cases, and any competitive advantages it might possess.
3. *Patient Awareness and Education*: With patients increasingly playing a more active role in healthcare decisions, direct-to-consumer advertising, and educational initiatives may play a pivotal role in building brand salience. Explaining its benefits, distinct features is essential.
4. *Consistent Messaging*: Maintaining consistent messaging across channels and touchpoints can bolster brand recognition. This includes visual (logo, color scheme) and messaging consistency (value proposition, brand voice, etc).
5. *Value Proposition*: An engaging value proposition is vital for creating brand salience. This involves clearly outlining and conveying your drug's advantages over competing options regarding its effectiveness, safety, ease of use, and cost comparisons.

6. *Reputation and Trust*: Trust is essential in healthcare, so building it up takes many forms, such as proven effectiveness, safety measures communicated transparently, and effective collaboration among medical practitioners and patients alike.

Remember, reaching high brand salience requires more than increasing brand recognition. It requires forging meaningful connections with target audiences so your brand becomes recognized, trusted, and preferred.

Brand Scape

The competitive environment in which a pharmaceutical company operates is called the Brandscape. This includes competitors, market conditions, regulatory environment, and others.

When formulating strategies for their brands, pharma marketers need to consider brandscape. Companies can identify their brandscape and devise strategies to win an edge over the competition by becoming familiar with it.

Pharma companies are competing fiercely to maintain market dominance. To stand out in an otherwise saturated field, businesses must highlight their unique benefits and features, such as superior efficacy, safety profiles, or other specific qualities, to distinguish themselves.

The brandscape also includes regulatory considerations such as approval processes for new drugs or limitations on marketing claims. Companies must understand these regulations to ensure that their marketing messages adhere to all guidelines.

A deep understanding of the brandscape is crucial for crafting effective marketing strategies in the pharmaceutical sector. By carefully assessing the regulatory and competitive environment, companies can position their products for success.

Brand Scope

Brand Scope is a brand's reach, extent, and influence in an industry or market. This encompasses its products and services offered under it, the target audiences it serves, and the geographic regions or markets it operates in.

The brand scope defines the parameters within which a brand operates, including its positioning, messaging, and marketing strategies. It sets the boundaries for the brand's expansion and helps maintain consistency in its offerings and communication. Key elements of brand scope include:

1. *Product or Service Range*: The brand's range of products or services. This could include different product lines, variations, or complementary offerings.
2. *Target Audience*: The specific group of customers or consumers the brand aims to serve and appeal to. Understanding the target audience is crucial for effective marketing and communication strategies.
3. *Market Presence*: The geographic regions or markets where the brand operates or plans to expand, locally, nationally, or internationally.
4. *Brand Positioning*: Brand positioning refers to the unique value proposition and differentiation factors that set a brand apart from its rivals, shaping customer perceptions and brand loyalty.
5. *Brand Promise*: The commitment or promise the brand makes to its customers regarding the benefits or solutions it provides.
6. *Brand Personality*: The set of human-like characteristics or traits associated with the brand helps create an emotional connection with customers.
7. *Marketing Strategies*: The approaches and tactics used to promote the brand, engage with customers, and build brand awareness.

The brand scope is a fundamental aspect of brand management as it guides strategic decisions and ensures consistency across all brand-related activities. It defines the brand's purpose and direction, enabling it to create a lasting and meaningful impact in the market.

Brand Scope in Pharma Marketing

In pharmaceutical marketing, Brand Scope refers to a pharmaceutical brand's overall reach, influence, and positioning within the market. It encompasses various aspects, including brand awareness, market share, target audience, competitive landscape, and marketing strategies. Here are some key considerations related to brand scope in pharma marketing:

1. *Target Audience*: Identifying the target audience is crucial for developing effective marketing strategies. Understanding the target audience's demographics, needs, and preferences helps tailor messages and promotional activities to reach and engage them effectively.
2. *Brand Positioning*: Brand positioning involves defining the unique value proposition of a pharmaceutical product within the market. It

includes identifying the key benefits, differentiators, and competitive advantages that set the brand apart. A clear and compelling brand positioning helps to establish a strong presence and attract customers.

3. *Market Research and Analysis*: Market research and analysis is vital to assess the market landscape, identify trends, and gather insights about competitors. It helps understand customer behaviors, market dynamics, and emerging opportunities or challenges that may impact the brand's scope.
4. *Brand Awareness and Visibility*: Building brand awareness is crucial for pharmaceutical companies. Various marketing channels and tactics, such as advertising, public relations, digital marketing, and medical conferences, can enhance brand visibility among healthcare professionals, patients, and other stakeholders.
5. *Thought Leadership and Education*: Establishing thought leadership by providing valuable educational content, conducting clinical trials, sponsoring research, and engaging in medical conferences helps build credibility and trust in the pharmaceutical brand. It also helps position the brand as an authority in the industry and build enduring relationships with healthcare professionals.
6. *Multichannel Marketing*: Adopting a multichannel approach enables companies to reach customers via various platforms, including online platforms, social media, email marketing campaigns, direct sales tactics, and traditional advertising methods. A multi-faceted campaign ensures consistent messaging while increasing brand exposure.
7. *Regulatory Compliance*: Pharma marketing operates under strict guidelines to ensure ethical practices and protect consumer interests. Complying with regulations while marketing pharmaceutical products is essential to maintain brand reputation and avoid legal consequences.
8. *Post-Marketing Strategies*: Monitoring the brand's performance post-launch is crucial. Collecting and analyzing data on sales, customer feedback, and market trends helps identify areas for improvement and refine marketing strategies accordingly.

How to Optimize Your Brand's Scope

To optimize the brand scope in pharmaceutical marketing, consider the following strategies:

1. *Define Clear Objectives*: Set specific and measurable goals for your brand scope, such as increasing market share, improving brand awareness, or targeting specific customer segments, and clearly defining objectives provides a roadmap for optimizing your marketing efforts.
2. *Conduct Market Research*: Continuously gather data and insights about the market, competitors, and target audience. Understand the evolving needs, preferences, and behaviors of healthcare professionals, patients, and other stakeholders. Analyze market trends and identify opportunities to differentiate your brand.
3. *Establish an Engaging Brand Positioning*: Outline and define your brand's distinct value proposition and differentiation factors, highlight benefits over competitors, and develop messaging which resonates with target audiences while conveying brand value.
4. *Utilize Targeted Marketing Channels*: Once your target audience has been established, determine the most efficient ways of reaching them using digital marketing, content marketing, social media, SEO (search engine optimization), email marketing, direct sales, or traditional ads as avenues. Personalize and tailor your marketing mix based on the preferences and behaviors of its members.
5. *Strengthen Your Online Presence*: Create an engaging digital experience through user-friendly website design, search engine optimization strategies, and social media engagement. Provide informative and entertaining content that educates your target audience. Use online platforms to promote thought leadership while building relationships between healthcare professionals and patients.
6. *Personalize Marketing Messages*: Tailor your marketing messages to resonate with different segments of your target audience. Segment your audience based on demographics, geographic location, behavior, or medical specialization. Develop customized messaging and content to address their specific needs and concerns.
7. *Establish Thought Leadership*: Position your brand as an authoritative industry information source. Publish educational content, white papers, or case studies highlighting your team's expertise. Engage with experts by attending medical conferences, seminars, and webinars, sharing knowledge while building networks!
8. *Leverage Data Analytics*: Leverage data analytics tools to track and assess the performance of your marketing initiatives by monitoring metrics like brand awareness, engagement rates, conversion rates, and sales conversion rates. Apply what insights have been

gleaned for optimizing strategies and making data-driven decisions.

9. *Collaborate with Key Stakeholders*: Build strong relationships with healthcare professionals, key opinion leaders, patient advocacy groups, and other stakeholders. Collaborate on research, educational initiatives, or community outreach programs. Leveraging partnerships can expand your brand's reach and enhance its reputation.
10. *Stay Compliant with Regulations*: Ensure all marketing activities adhere to regulatory guidelines and ethical standards. Stay updated with changes in regulations and guidelines governing pharmaceutical marketing. This helps maintain brand reputation, avoid legal issues, and builds customer trust.

Optimizing brand scope in pharmaceutical marketing requires a strategic approach, continuous evaluation, and adaptation to the evolving market landscape. By implementing these strategies and monitoring the results, you can enhance your brand's visibility, credibility, and market share.

Brand Sense

Brand sense is a marketing concept that utilizes all five senses, such as sight, sound, touch, taste, and smell, to create a sensory brand experience and increase recognition and brand loyalty. It draws from human nature's affinity with sensorial experiences over abstract ones; emotions and memories are tied more strongly with sensory memories than abstract ideas and are stronger drivers of recognition among consumers.

By appealing to multiple senses, brands can create a more immersive and lasting experience for their customers, increasing brand awareness, loyalty, and sales.

Brand sense is often tied to experiential marketing, which creates immersive brand experiences that appeal emotionally and physically to consumers.

Pharma marketers use brand sense to leverage sensory experiences to showcase pharmaceutical products and create an unforgettable brand experience for patients and healthcare professionals. This is particularly crucial in an industry with many similar products, where differentiation can be difficult.

Pharmaceutical companies may employ a range of sensory marketing tactics to cultivate brand perception, such as:

1. *Visual Branding* refers to the design of product packaging, logos, and other visual elements that help patients and healthcare professionals identify and remember a specific brand. For instance, Excedrin's bright purple packaging stands out among other pain relievers on the market, making it easily recognizable.
2. *Sound Branding* involves using music, jingles, and other sounds to elicit an emotional connection with the brand. For example, the Claritin jingle has become iconic and widely associated with its product.
3. *Touch Branding* refers to the tactile experience provided by product packaging or other brand-associated tactile experiences. For instance, GlaxoSmithKline's Ventolin asthma inhaler comes with a textured grip on its packaging that helps differentiate it from other inhalers and provides customers with a memorable tactile sensation.
4. *Taste branding* is less common in pharmaceutical marketing but can still be employed to promote products like cough syrups or dietary supplements. For instance, Pfizer's Emergen-C dietary supplement offers various fruit flavors for consumers to create a unique palate experience.
5. *Smell Branding* creates a sensory experience associated with the brand through scents or aromas. Some over-the-counter products like vapor rubs or nasal sprays use strong menthol scents that can help create this connection.

Pharmaceutical Companies Utilizing Sensory Branding

Here are some examples of pharmaceutical companies that utilize brand sense in their marketing initiatives:

1. Pfizer has taken a sensory marketing approach for their drug Chantix, used to help people quit smoking. In an *Experience Chantix* campaign, the company created a website with videos, virtual tours, and other interactive elements designed to engage patients' senses and enhance their brand experience.
2. Novartis has taken a visual branding approach for its eye care products, such as Alcon eye drops and contact lenses. The company employs vibrant packaging with eye-catching designs to differentiate its products from other eye-care brands.
3. GlaxoSmithKline (GSK) has adopted a touch branding approach for their asthma inhaler Ventolin. The inhaler features an ergonomic textured grip that helps patients hold it securely,

making it easier to use and providing patients with an enjoyable tactile experience that can help build strong brand associations.

4. Sanofi has taken a novel approach with its allergy medication Allegra. They used smell branding to help patients identify it and create an immersive sensory experience associated with the brand. For example, In 2011, Sanofi launched a marketing campaign for Allegra that focused on the sense of smell. The campaign featured a scratch-and-sniff advertisement in magazines, which allowed readers to experience the scent of the Allegra brand and highlighted how Allegra could restore the sense of smell by providing relief from respiratory allergies.
5. Johnson & Johnson has successfully used taste branding for over-the-counter products such as Children's Tylenol and Motrin, offering different flavors to provide customers with an authentic flavor experience and help differentiate themselves from similar offerings from competitors.

Brand Sentiment

Brand sentiment is the overall perception of a brand among its target audience. This measure of emotional tone associated with a brand can be positive, negative, or neutral. Measuring brand sentiment is crucial since it allows pharmaceutical companies to understand how their target audience perceives their product or service and can help improve the reputation and image of the company.

Here are some factors that may impact brand sentiment in pharmaceutical marketing:

1. *Product Quality*: A pharmaceutical product that successfully treats an illness or condition will likely elicit positive responses among patients, healthcare professionals, and other stakeholders.
2. *Patient Experience*: Patients who have had a positive experience while using a particular pharmaceutical product may harbor positive feelings toward the brand.
3. *Safety and Efficacy*: When a pharmaceutical product is deemed safe and effective, it can contribute to an upbeat brand sentiment among healthcare professionals and patients.
4. *Reputation and Trust*: A pharmaceutical company's reputation and history can influence brand sentiment. Companies with a positive reputation and track record of producing high-quality products may enjoy more favorable brand sentiment than those with negative perceptions.
5. *Marketing and Advertising*: The tone and messaging of pharmaceutical company's marketing and advertising campaigns can significantly impact brand sentiment. Genuine campaigns that provide accurate information can produce positive feelings toward the brand, while deceptive or misleading tactics may elicit negative responses.

Measuring Brand Sentiment

Pharmaceutical companies can measure brand sentiment using various methods. Here are some commonly used ones:

1. *Social Media Monitoring*: Monitoring social media platforms such as Twitter, Facebook, and LinkedIn provides companies with invaluable insights into customer conversations about a brand. By monitoring these conversations, pharmaceutical companies can determine the tone of voice associated with their brand.
2. *Online Surveys*: Conducting surveys to gather feedback from patients, healthcare professionals, and other stakeholders about a brand can provide valuable insights into brand sentiment. Surveys can ask open-ended questions to encourage respondents to provide their thoughts or use rating scales as sentiment indicators.
3. *Focus Groups*: Focus groups offer valuable qualitative insight into how a particular audience perceives a brand. During these sessions, participants are polled about their opinions of a brand and their experiences with its product.
4. *Net Promotion Score (NPS)*: Net Promoter Score measures customer loyalty by measuring how likely people are to refer a brand/business/service to others. A high NPS score suggests positive brand sentiment and can serve as an indication of overall brand sentiment.
5. *Online Review Analysis*: Online reviews on websites such as Yelp, Google, and HealthGrades offer valuable insight into how patients perceive a pharmaceutical product or brand.

Brand sentiment is an integral factor in pharmaceutical marketing, directly affecting a company's profitability and reputation. By understanding what factors contribute to positive or negative brand sentiment, companies can take steps to enhance their image and foster customer loyalty.

Brand's Share of Voice (SOV)

A brand's share of voice (SOV) refers to the percentage of total advertising or promotional activities within a therapeutic category or market attributed to that brand. Measuring a brand's SOV helps determine its level of competitiveness in the market and how it stacks up against its rivals.

Here are some steps to determine a brand's share of voice:

1. Identify first all advertising or promotional activities within an individual therapeutic category or market.
2. Determine the advertising or promotional activities of each brand within the market.
3. Calculate the percentage of advertising or promotional activities each brand has within the market.
4. Compare the percentage of advertising or promotional activities of each brand to arrive at their respective SOVs.

Let us consider a hypothetical example. A pharmaceutical company with a new drug for diabetes might want to assess its share of voice within the diabetes therapeutic category. They would first identify all promotional activities within the market and calculate what percentage of their drug received; they then compare this percentage with that of competitors to determine their Share of Voice.

Brands with a higher Share of Voice than their rivals tend to be considered more competitive and may enjoy stronger market positions; however, having a higher SOV does not ensure success; other elements like brand recognition, reputation management, and product quality must also be taken into consideration before making this determination.

Brand Story

Brand storytelling is a compelling narrative communicating its unique value proposition to its target audience. It is used in marketing to build emotional connections with customers, differentiate the brand from its competitors and foster customer loyalty.

There are five compelling reasons why telling a brand story in modern marketing is so important:

1. *Differentiation*: Brands' stories are what set them apart from their competitors. They emphasize the brand's unique qualities, values, and benefits. Companies can make their brand story unique and appeal to customers who share similar ideals.
2. *Emotional Connection*: Brand stories should be able to appeal to customers' emotions. They should instill feelings of trust, empathy, and motivation. Brands can create loyal customers and turn them into advocates by connecting emotionally with their customers.
3. *Memorable*: Customers can remember a well-crafted brand story long after encountering it. This builds recognition and allows customers to easily recall the provider when they need it.
4. *Authenticity*: The brand story should accurately reflect the company's beliefs and values. When the narrative is authentic to the company's mission, principles, and values, customers are likelier to trust and feel connected with the brand.
5. *Consistency*: Your brand story must be consistent across all touchpoints (advertising, customer service, and product design). This reinforces the message that you want customers to hear and builds trust.

Pharma marketing is heavily based on Brand stories. This is a story that conveys the benefits of a drug or treatment to its target audience. Successful brand stories create an emotional connection, help people understand its benefits, and distinguish it from competitors. Here are a few examples:

1. *Pfizer's Viagra* (sildenafil citrate) treats male erectile dysfunction by increasing blood flow to the penile area and relaxing muscle tone, leading to improved performance in sexual activities and intimacy. Its brand story revolves around breaking down barriers to intimacy. The slogan *Get back to mischief* highlights its ability to restore sexual function and deepen the relationship.
2. *AbbVie's Humira* is an anti-autoimmune medication that treats Crohn's disease and rheumatoid arthritis. Its brand story demonstrates its ability to treat these diseases and regain control of their lives. Therefore, the slogan *Go Further with Humira* encourages people to live a full life.
3. *Gilead's Sovaldi*: Sovaldi treats hepatitis C. The brand story of Sovaldi emphasizes the drug's transformative power and the patient's ability to overcome the disease. In addition, Sovaldi offers hope for a better future by promoting the slogan that *HepC can be cured*.
4. *Merck'a Gardasil*: Gardasil is a vaccine that protects against human papillomavirus HPV,

which can cause cervical cancer. Its brand story emphasizes prevention and the vaccine's ability to protect against this condition. Their slogan, *One Less*, aims to show that vaccination saves lives and slows the spread of viruses.

These examples show the power of compelling brand stories in pharmaceutical marketing. These brands stand out among their competitors by emphasizing the emotions of taking a drug, providing hope for a better future, and meeting patient needs.

Brand Strategy

A brand strategy in pharma marketing is a long-term plan describing how a pharmaceutical company plans to position and market its products to establish a strong brand identity.

There are three essential ingredients for a successful brand strategy:

A. Identify your target audience
B. Understand their preferences and needs
C. Tailor the marketing efforts to these needs.

This includes choosing the right channels and messages to communicate the brand's key attributes, value proposition, and competitive differentiation.

A successful brand strategy can significantly impact a product's market share in the pharmaceutical industry. This is because products compete based on efficacy, safety, pricing, and other factors. It also helps to build trust, loyalty, and recognition among patients and healthcare providers. This is important for product adoption and adherence.

Here are the key elements of a successful brand strategy:

1. *Positioning*: Identify and position your product's unique selling point to potential customers. Positioning should communicate the product's advantages to prospective consumers while setting it apart from competing offerings.
2. *Brand Identity*: Overall visual identities must remain constant to accurately express and reflect its personality and values across marketing materials, brand names, logos, and packaging designs.
3. *Target Audience Identification*: Deliberately selecting your target audience is vital to creating a winning brand strategy. Understanding their needs, preferences, behaviors, and how they respond will allow you to tailor marketing materials and messaging to your ideal customers.
4. *Messaging*: Effective messaging should clearly and succinctly convey your product or service's benefits and value proposition to its target market. It should be clear and concise but also expressive and evoke emotion.
5. *Communication Channels*: Identifying the most effective communication channels to reach different audiences via various media such as print, broadcast, digital, and events. Each channel must target the intended audience and effectively convey the brand message.
6. *Measuring Success*: It is crucial to evaluate the brand strategy's effectiveness. Measure brand recognition, market share, customer engagement levels, and sales metrics, as these data points will allow you to refine and optimize your strategy and ensure its success.

Pharmaceutical brand strategies must effectively communicate a product's unique selling points and value proposition, appealing to its target audience while setting itself apart from competitors. Periodic evaluation and refinements should take place to maintain consistency across marketing channels and materials.

Brand Sustainability

In pharmaceutical marketing, brand sustainability refers to using sustainable practices in producing and marketing pharmaceutical products. This means minimizing the environmental impact of manufacturing, sourcing ethical raw materials, and encouraging ethical and responsible marketing. A key element of brand sustainability in pharmaceutical marketing is ensuring that pharmaceutical products are produced and developed sustainably. This could include reducing energy consumption and reducing waste, using sustainable packaging, and implementing waste reduction or recycling programs.

Pharma companies can encourage ethical and responsible marketing by not making exaggerated or misleading claims about their products' efficacy, giving accurate information about side effects, and refraining from using aggressive or unprofessional tactics.

Another key element of brand sustainability in pharmaceutical marketing is sourcing ethically and sustainably the raw materials used to make pharmaceutical products. Responsible sourcing can include considering the production's economic, social, and environmental impacts.

In pharmaceutical marketing, brand sustainability is a holistic approach that ensures pharmaceutical products have minimal negative effects on society and are produced and promoted in a way that promotes safe and effective patient treatment.

Building sustainability

It takes many steps to achieve sustainability. Here are the key steps:

1. *Sustainability Goals*: Establishing sustainability goals is the cornerstone of sustainability efforts, so first, set sustainability goals that are quantifiable and time-bound so you can monitor the progress over time.
2. *Develop a Sustainability Strategy*: Once you have identified your sustainability goals, creating an action plan outlining their achievements is important. This document should also include specific timelines and targets.
3. *Implement Sustainable Practices*: You must implement sustainable practices in your company. This may involve adopting environmentally friendly methods, cutting waste and energy use, and utilizing sustainable sourcing practices.
4. *Monitor Progress*: Monitoring progress and meeting sustainability goals is important. Analyzing and reporting can be used to monitor progress and identify areas that require improvement.
5. *Continuously Improve Sustainability Performance*: Building sustainability is a continuous journey. Therefore, it is important to improve performance over time continuously. This could include setting new sustainability goals, implementing new practices, and engaging stakeholders to encourage sustainability in the organization.

These steps will help organizations foster sustainability, minimize the negative effects on society and the environment, and encourage long-term economic growth.

Brand Switching

Brand switching is a marketing tactic pharmaceutical companies use to encourage patients or healthcare providers to switch brands of medication, encouraging consumers to switch away from an existing treatment brand to another.

Companies can increase sales and revenues by convincing patients and healthcare providers to switch from competing products to theirs.

Brand switching can be an invaluable strategy in the pharmaceutical sector for various reasons:

1. *Increasing Market Share*: Patients and healthcare professionals can be persuaded to switch brands to increase their market share.
2. *Revenue Growth*: Brand switching can increase sales, translating into higher revenues.
3. *Increasing Profitability*: Increasing sales volumes can lead to economies of scale, lower production costs, and improve profitability.
4. *Brand Loyalty*: Patients and healthcare professionals with positive experiences with a new brand may be likelier to continue using its products.

Brand switching in the pharmaceutical industry is highly regulated. Companies must adhere to stringent guidelines to ensure their messages are truthful and non-misleading; patients should consult their healthcare provider before switching medications to ensure it's appropriate and safe for their specific situation.

Three Types of Switching

There are three general types of brand switching in the pharmaceutical industry. These are:

A. *Switching from Competitor's Brand*: Pfizer's Lipitor faced competition from generic Simvastatin and Atorvastatin. As a result, Pfizer offered incentives and discounts to providers who recommended Lipitor over generic versions. This was done to encourage patients to switch back to Lipitor.

B. *Switching From Own Brand in Case of Patent Expiry*: After Viagra's patent ran out, Pfizer released an Authorized Generic version with incentives and discounts to encourage patients to switch from its brand name Viagra product towards its generic version.

C. *Switching from Own Brand to a Product that had Improved Features*: Symbicort Turbuhaler was released by AstraZeneca when Symbicort's patent expired. AstraZeneca advised patients to switch from Symbicort to the Symbicort Turbuhaler.

Brand Switching: Key Elements

The key elements in brand switching include:

1. *Understanding the Target Audience*: To create compelling messaging and incentives that encourage brand switches, companies must first understand the needs and preferences of their target audience. This includes analyzing patient data and conducting market research.
2. *Communicating the Benefits of the Brand*: To persuade patients and healthcare providers to switch, companies should explain the benefits of the new brand. These benefits could include

improved efficacy and fewer side effects. They can also be easier to dose or less expensive.

3. *Addressing Concerns or Objections*: Healthcare providers and patients may have concerns about switching brands. They might be afraid of changing to the new brand or being loyal to it. These concerns must be addressed by companies so that they can assure patients that the product will work in their best interests.
4. *Offering Incentives*: Companies may offer incentives to encourage brand switchings, such as rebates, discounts, or coupons for free samples. These incentives can be used to cover the cost of switching and provide an advantage for patients or healthcare professionals.
5. *Ensuring Regulatory Compliance*: The pharmaceutical industry is very regulated. Companies must adhere to strict guidelines to ensure their messaging is accurate and not misleading. They must also ensure their marketing materials and incentives comply with all applicable regulations.

Brand Touchpoints

Brand touchpoints refer to interactions between pharmaceutical marketing campaigns and target audiences that occur via various channels and media. Examples may include but aren't limited to:

1. *Advertising*: Advertisements can be found in magazines, medical journals, and digital ads online.
2. *Sales Representatives*: Sales representatives liaise between healthcare professionals and their organization and inform them about its products and services.
3. *Company Website*: Your company website serves an essential function, connecting with potential customers while offering information, educational material, and other useful resources to potential consumers.
4. *Social Media*: Pharma companies can leverage social media channels like Facebook, Twitter, or LinkedIn to engage their target customers more closely while building brand recognition and efficiently marketing products and services.
5. *Patient Support Programs*: Patient support programs offer essential resources and information on treatments and their potential side effects.
6. *Events and Conferences*: Pharmaceutical companies may showcase their products at industry gatherings where healthcare professionals gather.
7. *Email Marketing* allows businesses to connect with appropriate audiences and effectively showcase their goods or services. Healthcare professionals and patients can receive targeted messages and information via direct mail campaigns.

Pharma companies can use these touchpoints to build a brand strategically, communicate with their target audience and promote products and services.

Leveraging the Brand Touchpoints

Pharmaceutical companies can take the following steps to use brand touchpoints effectively.

1. *Discover Your Target Audience*: Identify your audience to understand better their needs, preferences, behaviors, and how they act. This knowledge allows for more tailored touchpoints designed specifically for them.
2. *Establish a Consistent Brand Message*: Create an engaging, consistent message across all touchpoints. This will help to build trust and recognition for your business.
3. *Integrate Touchpoints*: Provide frictionless customer service by connecting all of your touchpoints. For example, you can use social media to drive traffic and email marketing campaigns.
4. *Personalize Touchpoints*: To increase engagement and drive sales, use customer data and behavior to tailor to each touchpoint.
5. *Measure and Analyze the Results*: Use data analytics to assess each touchpoint's effectiveness and identify improvement areas.
6. *Continuous Optimization*: Optimize customer touchpoints for superior customer experiences and better results.

Pharma companies can effectively leverage brand touchpoints to build a strong presence, engage with customers, and increase sales. Companies can maximize their marketing impact by following these steps.

Brand Tracking

Brand tracking is the core element of pharmaceutical marketing. This involves continuously monitoring and assessing the performance of a brand and its perceptions over time. This includes collecting data about brand awareness, loyalty, equity, and other metrics. The information is then used to make marketing decisions and strategies.

Pharma companies can track their brand with various tools and techniques, such as focus groups, surveys, social media listening, and data analytics. Then, companies can analyze this information to evaluate marketing campaigns' success, identify improvement areas, and adjust their strategies accordingly.

Because pharmaceutical marketing is highly regulated, brand tracking is crucial. Companies must adhere to strict guidelines and laws regarding product promotion. Pharmaceutical companies can ensure that their marketing efforts drive sales by monitoring and understanding their customers' perceptions.

How Do You Track the Brand?

You need to take the following steps to track the brand's marketing efforts in pharmaceutical marketing:

1. *Identify Key Performance Indicators (KPIs)*: The first step in tracking metrics relevant to your brand and business goals is identifying them. For example, common KPIs for pharmaceutical companies include brand awareness, recall, loyalty, equity, and customer satisfaction.
2. *Choose A Data Collection Method*: Once your KPIs have been determined, the next step should be selecting an effective data collection strategy. Your options might include surveys, focus groups, or social media listening; all have advantages and disadvantages, so you must select one best suited to your brand and budget.
3. *Make a Questionnaire or Discussion Guide*: Create a questionnaire or discussion guide that addresses your identified KPIs. For accurate data collection, ensure that the questions are objective and clear.
4. *Collect Data*: Once the questionnaire or discussion guide has been created, it's time to collect data. First, gather representative data that is statistically significant.
5. *Analyze The Data*: Once data have been compiled and analyzed, it's crucial to recognize any trends or insights within it. This can be accomplished via software packages for statistical analysis or data visualization.
6. *Interpret Your Findings*: Analyzing and making informed decisions based on your findings is paramount in successful marketing strategy and tactics implementation. For instance, if brand recognition levels are low, advertising or public relations activities might help raise brand visibility to boost awareness.

You should monitor your brand and evaluate its performance over time. This will ensure that your marketing efforts align with your business goals.

Brand Values

Brand values are the fundamental beliefs and principles that guide a brand's behavior, actions, and decision-making. They articulate the brand's purpose, vision, and mission and help create its distinct identity and reputation. Brand values are not simply words; they're actions that demonstrate your company's dedication to upholding those ideals.

Brand values can be communicated through messaging, visual identity, and marketing activities. They may include honesty, openness, social responsibility, innovation, customer-centricity, and quality, all of which should align with the target audience, industry, and overall brand business strategy.

Pharma marketing is driven by brand values and principles that direct a pharmaceutical company's behavior and actions toward customers, stakeholders, and the healthcare industry. Here are some commonly seen brand values within pharmaceutical marketing:

1. *Patient-Centricity*: A patient-centric approach is an essential brand value for many pharmaceutical companies. This involves placing patients' needs and well-being at the forefront of all activities, from product development to customer service. Novo Nordisk illustrates this philosophy through its *Changing Diabetes* campaign, which educates patients and healthcare professionals about diabetes while giving them tools for successful management.
2. *Integrity*: Integrity is a core brand value for pharmaceutical companies. This implies acting ethically, transparently, and responsibly in all business activities, such as research and development, manufacturing, and marketing. For example, Pfizer has demonstrated its commitment to transparency throughout its operations by publishing clinical trial data and disclosing payments to healthcare professionals.
3. *Innovation*: Innovation is a crucial brand value in pharmaceutical marketing. It means continually improving patient outcomes by developing novel therapies and treatments. Genentech, for instance, displays its dedication to innovation through its *Science in Service of Patients* campaign, showcasing its research and development efforts to find treatments for serious illnesses.

4. *Quality*: Quality is a paramount brand value in pharmaceutical marketing, impacting patient safety and well-being. Pharmaceutical companies must prioritize quality throughout all operations, such as manufacturing, testing, and distribution. Johnson & Johnson has proven its dedication to quality through its *Our Credo* program, setting high standards for product safety, efficacy, and compliance. Additionally, they employ an effective quality control system to guarantee this commitment.
5. *Sustainability in Pharmaceutical Manufacturing*: Sustainability has quickly become an increasing focus for pharmaceutical manufacturers, with companies adopting environmentally conscious practices as part of their brand value propositions. These practices include reducing waste, conserving resources, and supporting environmentally conscious initiatives like AstraZeneca's ambitious sustainability targets, including cutting carbon emissions and water usage, while encouraging sustainable packaging practices across their supply chains.

Pharmaceutical companies can leverage brand values into their marketing activities to foster trust and loyalty with customers and stakeholders, demonstrate their dedication to improving patient outcomes, and stand out from competitors.

Brand Value

Brand value refers to the perceived worth of a company's brand as judged by consumers, customers, stakeholders, and members of the general public. It encompasses tangible and intangible assets associated with it, such as reputation, trustworthiness, customer loyalty, and overall market perception. These are just a few examples of assets associated with brands that comprise brand value.

Brand value is crucial in convincing patients, healthcare providers, payers, and other stakeholders to choose one drug over the next. Therefore, pharmaceutical companies need to build strong brand value by cultivating a positive image and reputation for products in customers' minds.

Numerous Benefits

Companies in the pharmaceutical sector have many benefits from strong brand values, including:

- Increased trust and loyalty with customers and healthcare providers.
- Increased market share and an advantage over other firms.
- Patients and healthcare professionals will have greater brand recall and recognition.
- As a result, you can charge more for your products with higher pricing power.
- A better brand reputation leads to more word-of-mouth recommendations.

What It Takes

How can pharmaceutical companies increase brand value? To build brand value, companies must:

A. Firstly, invest in a strong brand image.
B. High-quality products stand out among competitors.
C. Building a positive reputation through ethical and responsible business practices creates a positive image in the marketplace.

They must also use effective branding and marketing strategies that resonate well with their target audience.

Brand Value Added (BVA)

Brand Value Added (BVA) refers to the additional value a brand-name product can command beyond its functional benefits. It's essentially the financial premium that a brand-name product can command over a generic equivalent because of the strength and reputation of the brand.

The pharmaceutical industry understands the concept of Branded Value-Added or BVA. With competition between brand-name drugs and generic versions rising, BVA can become especially pertinent as patents expire for one drug and generic versions become available at significantly reduced costs compared to their branded equivalent. Yet many patients and healthcare providers still prefer brand-name drugs over their generic versions, showing their added value and BVA.

Here's how pharmaceutical companies can add value to their brands:

1. *Building a Strong Reputation*: Pharmaceutical brands with strong, positive reputations have an edge when competing against generic competitors. Reputation-building requires proven efficacy, safety measures, positive interactions between healthcare professionals and patients, and corporate social responsibility initiatives to keep market shares growing.
2. *Innovation*: Pharmaceutical brands that foster continuous innovation through new drugs, improved formulations, novel drug delivery

mechanisms, or patient support services will find additional value within their brand portfolios.

3. *Brand Trust*: Trust is at the core of healthcare delivery. Pharmaceutical companies can build it through ethical conduct, transparent product information, and patient health and safety commitment.
4. *Patient-Centric Approach*: Brands that focus on meeting patients' needs can bring enormous value through support programs, educational materials, or personalized patient care services.
5. *Establish Strong Relations With Healthcare Providers*: Pharmaceutical brands that establish meaningful relationships with healthcare providers, such as physicians and pharmacists, can increase brand value by providing high-quality educational materials, responsive support services, and ongoing engagement opportunities for their target audiences. This may involve offering premium education resources, responsive assistance services, and high-quality support systems to enhance engagement with targeted audience segments.
6. *High-Quality Customer Service*: Delivering outstanding customer service, and handling queries and compliants effectively can greatly boost a pharmaceutical brand's value.
7. *Brand Consistency*: Maintaining consistent branding across all touchpoints and channels strengthens brand recognition and trust while adding to its value.

Pharmaceutical marketers who pay attention to these areas can increase the value of their brand, differentiate it from generic competitors and command a higher price, while creating customer loyalty and preference for it from generic competitors while creating customer loyalty and preference for it.

Brand Value Metrics

Brand value metrics in the pharmaceutical industry help assess pharmaceutical brands' overall value and financial worth. These metrics consider the market position, brand equity, intellectual property, and future growth potential. While the valuation of a brand can be complex and multidimensional, here are some commonly used brand value metrics in the pharma sector.

1. *Market Capitalization*: Representing the total value of outstanding shares held by pharmaceutical companies on the stock exchange, market capitalization reflects how consumers view and perceive a brand's worth and growth potential about competing brands.
2. *Brand Equity*: Measures the intangible value and strength of a pharmaceutical brand. Brand equity considers factors such as brand awareness, perception, customer loyalty, and associations with positive attributes. Brand equity can be assessed through market research, brand health studies, or band equity models.
3. *Licensing and Royalty Income*: Evaluate the revenue generated by a pharmaceutical brand through licensing agreements and royalties. This metric reflects the brand's ability to extend its value beyond its core products by leveraging intellectual property and entering into partnerships or collaborations.
4. *Pipeline Value*: Assesses the value of a pharmaceutical product pipeline, which includes drugs under development or clinical trials. Pipeline value considers the potential market size, clinical efficacy, regulatory prospects, and expected revenue from future product launches.
5. *Patents and Intellectual Property*: Considers the value of patents and other intellectual property assets owned by the pharmaceutical brand. This includes the exclusivity and market protection provided by patents, trademarks, and proprietary technologies, contributing to the brand's competitive advantage and future revenue potential.
6. *Market Positioning*: Evaluates the brand's positioning relative to competitors within a specific therapeutic area or market segment. Market share, customer loyalty, physician preference, and patient satisfaction contribute to the brand's market position and value.
7. *Brand Extension Opportunities*: Assesses the potential for the pharmaceutical brand to extend its presence into new product categories or therapeutic areas. The brand's reputation, customer trust, and market recognition can create opportunities for successful band extensions, which can increase brand value.
8. *Brand Recall and Recognition*: Measures the ability of healthcare professionals and patients to recall and recognize the brand. A strong brand recall indicates the brand's visibility, impact, and ability to stay top-of-mind among target audiences.
9. *Reputation and Trust* considers the brand's reputation and trustworthiness among stakeholders, including healthcare professionals, patients, payers, regulators, and investors. Positive brand reputation and trust can increase market acceptance, customer loyalty, and long-term value.

These brand value metrics help pharmaceutical companies understand their brands' financial worth and potential, inform strategic decisions, and drive brand growth and sustainability. It is important to note that brand value assessment often involves a combination of financial analysis, market research, and qualitative assessments to provide a comprehensive understanding of a pharmaceutical brand's value.

Brand Valuation

Brand valuation is an integral aspect of marketing in the pharmaceutical industry. This process measures the financial worth of a brand through its perceived market value, such as recognition, reputation, and customer loyalty.

Brand valuation in the pharmaceutical industry is essential as it allows companies to assess both intellectual property values and revenue generation potential of brands, identify possible areas for improvement within their structure, and determine the success of marketing campaigns.

Companies often consider several factors when valuing brands in pharmaceutical marketing:

- *Market share* is the percentage of total sales attributable to a brand in a market. Therefore, higher shares usually indicate stronger brand performance.
- *Brand Awareness* is measured by consumer recognition through surveys, focus groups, social media analytics, and surveys. Companies can utilize surveys, focus groups, and social media analytics to measure brand awareness. Reputation measures the brand's overall perception of quality, reliability, and trustworthiness in the marketplace.
- *Competitive Landscape Analysis* provides insight into a brand's strength relative to competitors.
- Sales and Revenue measure the financial performance of a brand or each business unit.

Arriving at the Brand Value

As part of a valuation exercise, all aspects affecting its value must be examined when assessing what makes up a brand's total worth. Here are the steps necessary for appraising a pharma company brand:

1. *Prioritize Brand Valuation Objectives and Goals*: Its purpose and goals must be clear before undertaking brand valuation. This may involve outlining what analysis will cover and the timeframe, assets, and liabilities of interest to you.
2. *Gather Data*: Gather information regarding a brand's financial performance and market standing by gathering financial statements, market research reports, customer surveys, and other necessary documents.
3. *Assess Your Brand's Financial Performance*: To assess a brand's financial performance, various metrics, including revenue, profitability, and growth rates, should be employed as analysis measures. Similar brands could also be considered when performing this comparison exercise.
4. *Assess a Brand's Market Position*: Market share, competitive landscape analysis, and trends can all help evaluate a brand's position within its respective industry. Furthermore, analyzing how similar brands fare within that same marketplace can also be beneficial for comparison purposes.
5. *Analyzing Customer Perception of the Brand*: Awareness, loyalty, and satisfaction can all serve to assess a brand's customer perception. This can be done by conducting customer surveys or conducting market research.
6. *Determine the Brand Value*: This involves considering financial performance, market position, and customer perception. You can use various valuation methods, such as market, income, and cost, to calculate the brand's value.
7. *Communicate the Results*: The valuation report must present and explain the assumptions and methodology used in the analysis.

Brand Valuation Measures

Pharmaceutical professionals use various valuation measures for brands to gauge their overall worth, quantify tangible and intangible assets of an enterprise and measure performance over time. Here are a few popular measures of valuation:

1. *Market Capitalization*: Market capitalization measures the total worth of all outstanding stock shares of an organization and includes their brand value. For example, if a pharmaceutical company had a market capitalization of $10 billion, and its brand could account for 20% of that total worth, the brand value would be approximately two billion USD.
2. *Brand Equity*: Brand equity measures the added value that a brand adds to a company's products and services, calculated through customer associations with it. Surveys or market research studies may help estimate this figure. For instance, one pharmaceutical company

estimated their brand equity as valued at $500 Million! This sum demonstrates their added brand value.

3. *Brand Value Added (BVA)*: BVA measures the added value that a brand brings to a company's financial performance. It subtracts the performance without the brand from the performance with it. For example, if a pharmaceutical company's financial performance is $1 billion without its brand and $1.5 billion with it, its BVA would equal $500 million.
4. *Royalty Relief*: This valuation method uses hypothetical royalties to determine the brand's value. This method is used in the valuations of pharmaceutical brands because many companies license their brand to third-party producers. An illustration would be: A pharmaceutical company owning a brand with a royalty rate of 5% on sales totaling $1 billion would have an approximate market value of $50 million.

Pharma companies can utilize brand valuation measures to ascertain their brands' worth and how they impact financial performance. These figures allow companies to make informed decisions about brand management and investment while optimizing the long-term value created by their brands.

Brand Valuation Metrics

Brand valuation in the pharmaceutical industry can be complex due to several unique factors. While there is no one-size-fits-all approach, the following are some commonly used brand valuation metrics in the pharma sector:

1. *Revenue-based Approach*: This method values a pharmaceutical brand based on its revenue-generating potential. It involves estimating the brand's future revenue streams, discounting them to present value, and calculating its net present value (NPV). The NPV represents the present value of the brand's future cash flows.
2. *Market-based Approach*: This approach assesses the brand value by comparing it to similar brands. It involves analyzing market transactions, such as mergers, acquisitions, or licensing deals, to derive a brand's value. Comparable brand valuations can be used as a benchmark to estimate the value of the pharmaceutical brand in question.
3. *Cost-based Approach*: This method estimates brand value by considering all costs of creating an equivalent brand from scratch, including research and development expenses, marketing expenditures, and time and resource requirements needed for recognition. Brand valuation estimates can then be reached by deducting these expenses from market valuation estimates of that brand.
4. *Royalty Relief Approach*: This methodology estimates a pharmaceutical brand's value by considering any hypothetical royalty payments it would require from companies licensing it from third parties. The value is calculated by discounting the estimated royalty payments to the present value.
5. *Multi-attribute Utility Theory*: MAUT is a more advanced approach that considers various brand attributes and assigns weights to each attribute based on their relative importance. This method involves market research to understand consumer preferences and perceptions of the brand's attributes. The brand value is then derived based on the utility generated by these attributes.

Brand valuation in the pharmaceutical industry depends upon many variables, including regulatory changes, patent expiration dates, and public perception. Therefore, metrics serve as a starting point; individual circumstances of each brand and industry must also be considered when conducting valuation analyses. Consulting with professionals experienced in brand valuations or financial analysis within the pharma sector is recommended for a more accurate assessment.

Brand Value Proposition

A brand value proposition is the unique benefit that a pharmaceutical brand offers its target audience in pharmaceutical marketing. This concise statement sums up a pharmaceutical brand's key advantages and distinguishing features in an attractive way that appeals directly to potential customers.

Typically, a brand value proposition includes the following elements:

1. *Target Audience*: The group of patients or healthcare professionals the brand aims to reach.
2. *Differentiation*: Brands with distinct advantages or features that distinguish them from competitors.
3. *Value*: Value is the specific benefits a brand offers its target audience regarding health outcomes, convenience, and cost efficiency.
4. *Proof*: These claims can be supported by examples or evidence distinguishing them from their competitors.

The brand value proposition for a new diabetes drug might, for example, be:

Our medication is easy to use and can be used by busy professionals with difficulty managing diabetes. A study has shown a 20% reduction in A1C after six months. There are no side effects.

Brand value propositions are an essential part of pharmaceutical marketing. They help brands stand out among competitors and communicate their unique benefits to potential customers. As a result, pharmaceutical companies can increase their customer base, retain existing customers, grow their sales, and improve patient outcomes by crafting a compelling value proposition.

Brand Vision

A brand vision is a statement that defines a brand's long-term aspirations and goals. It outlines the desired future state of the brand and provides direction for its strategy and activities.

Pharma marketing requires an aspirational, inspiring brand vision that aligns with the company's mission and values. In addition, it should communicate the brand's purpose and intended impact on society. A well-crafted vision can help differentiate a brand, encourage employee engagement, and foster strong emotional connections with stakeholders.

Here are some examples of brand visions in pharmaceutical marketing:

1. *Pfizer's Brand Vision*: Our goal is to become one of the world's most valued companies for patients, customers, colleagues, investors, business partners, and communities where we operate and live.
2. *Novartis' Brand Vision*: Our goal is to discover, develop, and commercially market innovative products designed to prevent or cure diseases while relieving suffering and improving the overall quality of life.
3. *Roche's Brand Vision*: We aim to become the leading provider of innovative healthcare solutions that enrich patients' and their families lives.
4. *Johnson & Johnson* has one clear mission: To promote global health and well-being by pioneering new ideas and technologies that deliver more accessible care services.

Pharma marketing requires creating an inspiring brand vision to engage employees, stakeholders, and the broader community with your mission and goals. A powerful brand vision will distinguish your product or service from competitors while leaving an indelible mark on patients' lives.

Brand Voice

In pharma marketing, brand voice refers to the tone, style, and language used to communicate its messaging to its target audience. In pharma marketing, brands must have a consistent voice across all channels, including advertising, sales materials, social media presences, and customer service interactions, for maximum impact.

Here are some key considerations when crafting a brand voice in pharmaceutical marketing:

1. *Clarity and Accuracy*: In pharmaceutical marketing, it's essential to convey complex information clearly and precisely. The brand voice should be straightforward and free from jargon or technical terms that might confuse your target audience.
2. *Empathy*: The brand voice should demonstrate empathy towards patients and healthcare professionals by showing an understanding of their needs, worries, and difficulties.
3. *Professionalism*: The brand voice should be professional and trustworthy. It should convey the brand's expertise and authority within healthcare.
4. *Compliance*: The brand voice should adhere to regulatory requirements, such as refraining from making off-label claims and providing balanced information about the product's benefits and risks.
5. *Differentiation*: The brand voice should set itself apart from competitors by clearly communicating its unique selling proposition and value proposition persuasively.
6. *Consistency*: The brand voice should be consistent across all channels, including advertising, sales materials, social media posts, and customer service interactions. Furthermore, this voice should align with the visual identity and messaging of the brand.

In conclusion, the brand voice in pharma marketing must be concise, accurate, empathetic, professional, compliant, differentiated, and consistent. Furthermore, it should communicate the brand's messaging to resonate with target audiences and set it apart from competitors.

Brand Pyramid

The Brand pyramid is a marketing framework that helps businesses build and communicate their brand identities to their target audiences. It serves as a tool for creating a consistent brand strategy across all communication channels and touchpoints, guaranteeing consistent brand perception among target audiences.

The brand pyramid typically comprises five levels, each representing an aspect of a brand. Here are some ways it can be utilized in pharmaceutical marketing:

1. *Physical Attributes*: Physical attributes of pharmaceutical products may include dosage form, formulation, packaging, and delivery method. Highlighting physical attributes can help distinguish your product from competitors while positioning it as the perfect option for specific patient populations.
2. *Functional Benefits*: In pharmaceutical marketing, functional benefits refer to efficacy, safety, tolerability, and ease of use of a product. It is vital to clearly and concisely communicate this information backed up with scientific data to build trust between HCPs and patients.
3. *Emotional Benefits*: When marketing pharmaceutical products to patients, their emotional benefits could include improved quality of life, symptom relief, and peace of mind. By emphasizing these emotional advantages over product features, marketers can form deeper connections and foster loyalty from patients.
4. *Brand Personality*: The brand personality of pharmaceutical products should reflect qualities like reliability, innovation, and patient focus. Communicating this consistently throughout all marketing materials is vital to brand recognition and trust among target audiences.
5. *Brand Culture*: In pharmaceutical marketing, brand culture refers to an organization's beliefs about patient education, empowerment, HCP engagement, and scientific innovation. Marketers can build long-term trust relationships by sharing their brand culture through effective communications with HCPs and patients.

The Brand Pyramid framework can provide pharmaceutical marketers with an effective strategy for creating an in-depth brand strategy. By considering physical attributes, functional benefits, emotional benefits, personality, and culture as they develop their strategy, they can create a winning brand that resonates with target audiences.

Breakeven Analysis

Breakeven analysis is a tool employed in pharmaceutical marketing to determine the minimum level of sales necessary to recoup all costs associated with producing and selling a pharmaceutical product. When total revenue equals total costs, we say we've reached breakeven. Here are some examples of breakeven analysis used in pharma marketing:

A. *New Drug Launch*: When a pharmaceutical company introduces a new drug, it must determine the minimum level of sales necessary to cover all costs related to development, clinical trials, regulatory approvals, marketing, and distribution. Breakeven analysis can assist the company in determining an optimal pricing strategy for the drug based on anticipated sales volume, variable costs per unit, and fixed expenses.

B. *Manufacturing Costs*: Break-even analysis can also identify the minimum level of sales needed to cover manufacturing expenses for a pharmaceutical product. This is especially pertinent when companies consider outsourcing production to a contract manufacturer or investing in new production capabilities. By understanding the breakeven point, companies can better make informed decisions about the profitability of different production scenarios.

C. *Product Line Optimization*: Breakeven analysis can also optimize a company's product line. By analyzing the breakeven points for each item in the lineup, companies can identify unprofitable products and potentially discontinue them while focusing on those that generate the most revenue and profitability.

Bribery

Bribery in pharmaceutical marketing refers to providing incentives or gifts to healthcare professionals (HCPs) as compensation for prescribing or promoting a drug or medical product. This unethical practice may be concealed behind legitimate marketing expenses such as sponsored trips, conferences, and meals.

Bribery in pharmaceutical marketing is illegal and considered a corrupt practice. In addition, bribes may lead to healthcare providers prescribing unnecessary or inappropriate medications, patients being adversely affected due to subpar healthcare, and harm being done to the pharmaceutical industry's reputation.

Many countries, like the US, have laws and regulations to curb bribery in pharmaceutical marketing. For instance, the Anti-Kickback Statute and Foreign A corrupt Practices Act forbids receiving anything valuable for healthcare referrals or contracts. In addition, the European Federation of Pharmaceutical Industries and Associations (EFPIA) has also implemented codes of conduct designed to combat unethical marketing strategies that pharmaceutical companies employ.

Pharmaceutical companies should ensure their marketing practices conform to all relevant laws and regulations and ethical standards in industry legislation while remaining transparent regarding activities undertaken and financial arrangements made with healthcare professionals. Doing this helps build trust within the industry while guaranteeing patient care remains top of mind.

What is Bribery in Pharma Marketing?

Here are a few examples of what constitutes bribery in pharmaceutical marketing:

1. Offering free drug samples to healthcare professionals in exchange for prescribing their products to patients.
2. Another common practice is offering extravagant rewards, such as luxurious vacations or electronics, to healthcare professionals who promote a specific drug or medical product.
3. Paying healthcare professionals to attend conferences or seminars sponsored by pharmaceutical companies with the expectation that they will prescribe or promote the company's products is also prohibited.
4. Offering meals or entertainment as incentives may also be employed to influence prescribing habits of healthcare professionals.
5. Offering financial rewards to healthcare professionals who enroll their patients in clinical trials sponsored by pharmaceutical companies.
6. Paying healthcare professionals to give lectures or presentations that promote a certain drug or product.

It is worth noting that not all gifts or incentives offered by pharmaceutical companies are considered bribes. For instance, providing educational materials or covering reasonable travel expenses to attend a conference may be acceptable. Nonetheless, any gift or incentive intending to influence a healthcare professional's prescribing habits would likely qualify as bribery.

Business-to-Business (B2B) Model

Business-to-business (B2B) marketing in the pharmaceutical industry refers to directly selling products and services to other businesses, such as hospitals, clinics, pharmacies, or distributors. Here are a few B2B models used for pharmaceutical marketing:

1. *Contract Manufacturing Organizations (CMOs)*: Contract manufacturing organizations offer pharmaceutical companies numerous services, including formulation development, production management, packaging, and labeling. For instance, Lonza--a Swiss-based CMO, offers custom manufacturing solutions for active pharmaceutical ingredients (APIs) and drug products to other pharmaceutical firms.
2. *Contract Research Organizations (CROs)*: CROs offer pharmaceutical companies various services, such as clinical trial design and management, data analysis, and regulatory assistance. For instance, Parexel, a global CRO, offers clinical research and consulting to other pharmaceutical companies.
3. *Pharmaceutical Distribution Companies* serve as intermediaries between drugmakers and healthcare providers such as hospitals, clinics, and pharmacies. One US-based distributor offering this service is McKesson Corporation which provides products and supply chain solutions to pharmaceutical firms and healthcare organizations such as McKesson Healthcare Logistics Solutions Inc (MCHLT).
4. *Healthcare IT Companies*: Healthcare IT firms specialize in creating technology solutions tailored specifically for pharmaceutical and healthcare providers, such as electronic health records (EHRs), clinical decision support systems (CDSS), and telemedicine platforms like Cerner Corporation provides in the US market.

Pharmaceutical firms looking to market and distribute their offerings among healthcare providers and patients via B2B partnerships should develop relationships with CMOs, CROs, distribution firms, and healthcare IT firms to efficiently promote, market, and disperse them while effectively fueling growth.

Business-to-Consumer (B2C) Model

Business-to-consumer (B2C) marketing in pharma marketing refers to selling directly to end users (patients or caregivers). Here are a few B2C models used in pharmaceutical advertising:

A. *Direct-to-consumer (DTC) Advertising*: Direct-to-consumer (DTC) advertising refers to any form of marketing directly targeting patients or caregivers through print, television, digital media, and other channels such as email. DTC ads may promote prescription medications or OTC products. Two such examples would include Pfizer's Viagra and AbbVie's Humira with advertisements targeting the consumer market directly.

B. *E-commerce Platforms* allow consumers to purchase pharmaceuticals and healthcare supplies online. For example, Amazon Pharmacy makes ordering prescription and over-the-counter items online easier for their customers and offers home delivery.

C. *Patient Support Programs*: Patient support programs provide resources and assistance for both patients and caregivers to meet better their healthcare needs, including educational materials, financial assistance, and medication adherence support services. For instance, Novartis offers its *Patient Assistance Now* program, which grants eligible individuals financial aid when accessing their medications.

D. *Disease Awareness Campaigns*: Disease awareness campaigns aim to heighten public understanding about an illness or condition through public campaigns that raise public awareness. Such campaigns may be organized by pharmaceutical companies, patient advocacy groups, or government organizations. For instance, Pfizer's *Get Old* campaign addresses age-related health concerns as part of healthy aging initiatives.

Pharmaceutical marketers utilizing the B2C model in pharmaceutical marketing are integral in connecting directly with patients and caregivers, offering information, resources, and assistance for managing healthcare needs. In addition, pharmaceutical firms can further optimize patient outcomes while driving growth using direct-to-consumer advertising (DTC), e-commerce platforms, patient support programs, and disease awareness campaigns—all integral to B2C pharmaceutical marketing strategies.

Built-in Obsolescence

Built-in or planned obsolescence is an intentional strategy manufacturers employ to produce goods with limited lifespans and, thus, lower production costs. Items are deliberately made obsolete after some period, prompting customers to upgrade by purchasing similar or identical versions from their manufacturer, an approach commonly employed across the electronics, fashion, and automobile industries.

Due to its highly regulated environment and stringent drug development, testing, and approval guidelines, built-in obsolescence is less prevalent within the pharmaceutical industry than in other sectors.

Certain practices in pharmaceutical marketing can be seen as deliberate obsolescence. Drug companies sometimes promote newer medications as superior, even though their effectiveness might only differ marginally from existing medicines. This creates the false perception that existing ones are outdated or inferior and prompts patients and healthcare providers alike to switch even when switching could cost more money.

One practice that could be seen as built-in obsolescence in pharmaceutical marketing is ever-greening. An attempt is made at this when a drug company makes minor modifications to an existing medicine, such as changing dosage form or delivery system, then submits for a patent extension application to lengthen its patent protection against generic versions entering the market at reduced prices and compete on price alone.

While these practices may not be outright examples of built-in obsolescence, they can still affect patient access to affordable medications and contribute to rising healthcare costs.

Bundling

Bundling is a marketing technique in which two or more products are offered at discounted rates to create an appealing bundle deal, proven effective within the pharmaceutical industry for driving sales growth. Here are just a few ways it could benefit your company:

1. *Combining Related Products*: Pharmaceutical companies can bundle related items, such as combining a drug with its related medical device or mixing commonly prescribed medicines.

2. *Discount Bundled Products*: Offering bundle discounts can encourage customers to buy more. Pharmaceutical companies could discount customers purchasing prescription and over-the-counter medicines from them. However, patients do not buy more prescription drugs as they have to use them as prescribed only.
3. *Bundling Can Save Customers Time and Hassle*: Bundling can provide customers with added convenience by giving them products they frequently use together at one discounted price, saving time and hassle by eliminating multiple purchases of each product separately.
4. *Targeting Specific Patient Groups*: Bundling can also target specific patient groups, such as offering products for those suffering from certain conditions.
5. *Brand Awareness*: Bundling helps raise awareness by offering products under one company's brand.

Bundling Strategies in Pharma

Here are some examples of bundling strategies in the pharmaceutical industry:

1. *Combination Drug Therapies*: Pharmaceutical companies can combine two or more drugs into a combination therapy. For instance, Gilead Sciences offers Harvoni, which includes two drugs to treat hepatitis C.
2. *Device and Drug Combinations*: Some pharmaceutical companies offer combinations of drugs with related medical devices. For instance, GlaxoSmithKline provides a bundle of its asthma medication Advair Diskus and a device to help patients inhale it more effectively.
3. *OTC and Prescription Drug Bundles*: Pharmaceutical companies often provide discounts when customers purchase prescription and over-the-counter medicines. For instance, Pfizer offers a package that includes its Lyrica prescription drug and Advil OTC pain relief tablet.
4. *Disease-specific Bundle Options*: Pharmaceutical companies can offer products tailored to a particular disease or condition. For instance, Novo Nordisk provides an insulin bundle specifically for patients with diabetes.
5. *Branded Bundles*: Pharmaceutical companies can package products together under one brand to raise brand awareness. For instance, Merck provides a bundle of its prescription drugs, Januvia and Janumet, branded with the Merck name to increase customer awareness.

Pharmaceutical companies must take great care to ensure their bundling strategies do not violate laws or regulations, such as anti-kickback laws or product promotion rules. Furthermore, companies should guarantee their bundling tactics are ethical and do not endanger patient safety or health.

Business Case

A business case is a written proposal that outlines a particular business project or investment's reasoning, justification, and financial feasibility. Your proposal provides a compelling argument supporting why certain business initiatives should be pursued and include relevant data and analysis to substantiate it.

Business cases inform decision-makers so they may make an informed decision regarding whether or not to continue with a particular project or investment. They typically involve conducting an in-depth cost/benefit analysis and examining any risks/challenges of any venture or proposal.

Pharmaceutical marketing business cases involve developing strategies and tactics for promoting and selling pharmaceutical products to customers. This plan must consider the unique challenges and regulations of marketing pharmaceutical products. Here are some essential elements of a business case:

1. *Market Analysis*: Define the target market for your pharmaceutical product, evaluate competitors and track industry trends. Conducting comprehensive market research can help you recognize opportunities and challenges related to this venture.
2. *Product Positioning*: Define the product's unique value proposition and how it stands out from competitors. Identify your target customer segments and craft a positioning message tailored towards them.
3. *Marketing Mix*: Create a comprehensive marketing mix incorporating all marketing elements, such as product, price, place, and promotion. Determine the most efficient channels for reaching your target audience and craft a messaging strategy that resonates with them.
4. *Regulatory Compliance*: Ensure all marketing initiatives adhere to regulations established by regulatory bodies like the FDA. This includes abiding by product labeling, advertising, and marketing communications guidelines.
5. *Sales Forecasting*: Create a sales forecast considering market demand, pricing, and promotional efforts. This can assist in planning

inventory management strategies and setting sales objectives.

6. *ROI Analysis*: Calculate the return on investment for marketing efforts and identify the most successful product promotion strategies. Doing this allows you to make data-driven decisions about future marketing initiatives.

Pharma marketing requires an in-depth comprehension of the target market, competitive landscape, and regulatory environment. By crafting a business case with an integrated marketing plan that considers these factors, pharmaceutical companies can successfully market and sell their products and projects while adhering to regulations and exceeding sales targets.

Business Ecology

Business ecology studies the interdependent relationship between businesses and their environment. It emphasizes how companies can operate sustainably, minimizing their environmental footprint while achieving economic success.

Business ecology emphasizes that businesses cannot operate in isolation from their environment and that maintaining natural systems' health is essential for long-term success. It emphasizes balancing economic, social, and environmental considerations with business decisions.

Business ecology emphasizes minimizing waste and pollution, conserving natural resources, and encouraging sustainable development. Businesses must adopt environmentally responsible practices and incorporate sustainability into their strategy and operations.

Business ecology in pharmaceutical marketing refers to applying ecological principles to marketing strategies and operations within the industry. The objective is to foster sustainable, environmentally friendly practices that enhance economic success for all involved.

Pharma marketing encompasses several facets of business ecology, such as:

A. Reduce waste

B. Encourage responsible sourcing of raw materials

C. Design environmentally friendly packaging and labeling.

These include using renewable energy sources, reducing carbon emissions, and using sustainable packaging materials.

Business ecology in pharmaceutical marketing also involves considering the effects of pharmaceuticals on the environment and public health. This requires ensuring products are secure for patients and the environment and designing biodegradable or easily recyclable items.

In conclusion, business ecology in pharma marketing strives to foster a more sustainable and responsible pharmaceutical industry that benefits it and the environment.

How Pharma Can Be Ecologically Responsible

Here are a few examples of how business ecology can be applied in pharma marketing:

1. *Sustainable Packaging*: Many pharmaceutical products come in plastic packaging, contributing to environmental pollution. Companies can utilize sustainable packaging materials like biodegradable or recyclable materials to reduce waste in production and minimize environmental impacts.
2. *Reduce Environmental Footprint*: Pharma companies can reduce their environmental footprint by investing in green energy solutions like solar or wind power to power operations and facilities.
3. *Responsible Sourcing*: Companies can ensure that all raw materials used for manufacturing come from sustainable sources like certified sustainable palm oil in manufacturing processes.
4. *Recycling Programs*: Companies often implement recycling programs to decrease waste created from their products. Pfizer offers inhaler recycling programs, while Novo Nordisk recycles plastic pen injectors.
5. *Environment Impact Analysis*: Pharmaceutical companies may conduct environmental impact analyses to gauge any negative consequences that their products, manufacturing processes, and packaging materials might pose on the environment.
6. *Establish a Sustainable Supply Chain*: Businesses can work closely with suppliers and distributors to ensure their supply chains are environmentally friendly and responsible, from procuring raw materials to shipping products directly to customers.

Pharma's Sustainability Initiatives

Pharmaceutical companies have taken various initiatives to advance sustainability and responsible practices within their operations and marketing activities. Below are some examples:

1. *Johnson & Johnson*: In 2020, Johnson & Johnson pledged to switch completely to 100 percent renewable energy by 2025 and achieve carbon neutrality by 2030. Furthermore, it launched Healthy Future 2030 as an initiative that seeks to simultaneously improve human and global well-being.
2. *Sanofi*: Sanofi's sustainability efforts include cutting greenhouse gas emissions, encouraging sustainable packaging practices, and investing in renewable energy sources. Furthermore, they've launched a circular economy initiative to minimize waste generation while encouraging recycling initiatives.
3. *Pfizer*: Pfizer has adopted a sustainability strategy called Pfizer's Green Journey that involves cutting carbon emissions, using renewable energy sources, and adopting sustainable packaging practices. Furthermore, the company offers a recycling program for used inhalers.
4. *AstraZeneca*: By 2025, AstraZeneca plans to become carbon neutral and utilize 100 percent renewable energy sources. Furthermore, the company has implemented sustainable packaging practices and used green chemistry principles in manufacturing processes to decrease environmental impacts.

These examples represent just some examples of pharmaceutical companies taking steps towards increasing sustainability initiatives in their operations and marketing practices. However, other firms in their sector have also implemented programs promoting environmental responsibility and sustainability.

Business Ethics

Business ethics refers to the moral principles and values guiding individuals and organizations operating within the business world. It encompasses making ethical decisions and taking actions that adhere to these standards and values.

Business ethics encompass a range of matters, such as Corporate Social Responsibility (CSR). Sustainable business practice means considering the effects of business decisions on society and the environment before taking steps to mitigate them.

1. *Fairness*: All stakeholders, such as employees, customers, suppliers, and investors should be treated fairly.
2. *Transparency* requires being open and forthcoming about business practices and decision-making processes. At the same time, Integrity involves adhering to moral and ethical principles, even if this may go against what might otherwise be best for a given business.
3. *Integrity*, open communication, and sound decision-making all go towards building trust between people.
4. Trust: *Trust* is earned by ethical behavior, open communication, and responsible decision-making.

Business Ethics in pharmaceutical marketing refers to the core moral principles and values that shape pharmaceutical companies' marketing initiatives. Here are some examples of ethical pharma marketing:

1. *Compliance With Regulations and Guidelines*: Pharmaceutical companies must abide by stringent rules when marketing their products, such as those set out by the US Food and Drug Administration (FDA) regarding accurate disclosure of benefits and risks concerning their products in promotional materials they distribute to healthcare professionals, patients and other stakeholders.
2. *Avoid Off-label Promotion*: Pharmaceutical companies should avoid marketing their products for uses not authorized by regulatory authorities. For example, promoting antidepressant medication to aid weight loss would constitute off-label promotion which is unethical.
3. *Respecting Patient Privacy*: Pharmaceutical companies should respect patient privacy when collecting and using personal data about them for marketing purposes, seeking consent before using patients' health data.
4. *Ensuring Transparency*: Pharmaceutical companies must disclose any financial relationships with healthcare professionals or organizations, including any payments or gifts given directly or through intermediaries to healthcare professionals or groups.
5. *Focusing on Patient Outcomes*: Pharmaceutical companies must place patients' needs above financial gain when marketing their products. For instance, companies shouldn't favor sales of more expensive medication over a less costly alternative if both medications are equally effective for patients.

Business ethics in pharmaceutical marketing are integral for developing trust between patients, healthcare professionals, and regulatory agencies. By complying with regulations, avoiding off-label promotions, respecting patient privacy rights, maintaining transparency, and prioritizing Patient outcomes, pharmaceutical companies can demonstrate their dedication to ethical marketing practices that promote public health.

Business Model Canvas

The Business Model Canvas is a strategic tool businesses use to define, visualize, and communicate their business model. It comprises nine key elements that help companies identify their value proposition, target market, revenue streams, key activities, resources, and partnerships. Here's how the Business Model Canvas can be applied in pharmaceutical marketing:

1. *Customer Segments*: The pharmaceutical industry caters to various customer segments, such as healthcare providers, patients, insurance companies, and regulators. Understanding their needs and preferences is essential for crafting effective marketing strategies that reach these target groups.
2. *Value Proposition*: A pharmaceutical company's value proposition differentiates them from competitors. This could include developing innovative drugs, providing superior quality products, or having a reputation for safety and efficacy.
3. *Channels*: Pharmaceutical companies utilize various channels, such as sales representatives, digital marketing, conferences, and medical publications to reach customers. The selection of channels depends on the target audience and stage in the drug development cycle.
4. *Customer Relationships*: Establishing strong customer relationships is paramount in the pharmaceutical industry, where trust and credibility are essential. Companies can utilize personal and digital communication methods to engage with customers and offer assistance.
5. *Revenue Streams*: The pharmaceutical industry primarily derives its revenue from drug sales. Companies may also generate profits through licensing agreements, partnerships, and royalties.
6. *Key Resources*: Pharma marketing requires several essential resources, including research and development capabilities, regulatory expertise, manufacturing facilities, and an experienced workforce. These assets are necessary for bringing new drugs to the market while maintaining a competitive advantage.
7. *Key Activities*: In pharmaceutical marketing, key activities include drug discovery, clinical trials, regulatory approval, manufacturing, and marketing. These processes are interrelated and necessitate collaboration across multiple departments and functions.
8. *Key Partnerships in Pharma*: Partnerships play an essential role in the pharmaceutical business, where innovation and expertise are shared among companies, academic institutions, and research organizations. Successful collaborations can reduce costs, speed up drug development processes, and expand market access further.
9. *Cost Structure*: Pharmaceutical costs can be determined by research and development expenses, regulatory compliance fees, manufacturing expenses, marketing expenditures, and sales expenses. Companies should weigh the potential revenue a sale would bring against development expenditures to find an approach that best serves their budget needs.

The Business Model Canvas can assist pharmaceutical companies in recognizing the key elements of their business model and creating successful marketing strategies. As a result, companies can optimize operations to achieve success in an increasingly competitive industry by understanding customers, value propositions, channels, relationships, revenue streams, resources allocated for marketing activities, partnerships, and cost structure.

Business Plan

Pharmaceutical marketing develops business plans outlining strategies and tactics to promote their products or services to healthcare professionals and patients. Here are the key elements of such plans:

1. *Market Analysis*: This section should provide an overview of the pharmaceutical market as a whole, and identify opportunities and challenges related to your products or services in it. For instance, a company creating a new cancer medication might research the size and growth of that sector, the competitive landscape, and unmet patient needs.
2. *Product Positioning*: This section should outline the company's product positioning strategy and pinpoint the unique selling points of its products. For instance, a company creating a new diabetes medication might position it as more efficient or user-friendly than existing treatments.
3. *Target Audience*: This section should identify the target audience for your company's products and specify which channels and tactics will be utilized to reach them. For instance, a company

developing a cardiovascular medication might target cardiologists by using conference sponsorships and scientific publications to reach them.

4. *Marketing Mix*: This section should present the company's product marketing mix, including pricing, promotion, and distribution strategies. For instance, a company developing a new dermatology medication may price its item higher than existing treatments to position it as a superior alternative and use tactics such as sales representatives, digital marketing, and patient education materials to promote it.
5. *Sales Forecasting*: This section should include sales forecasting for the company's products based on market size, competition, and other elements. For instance, a company developing a new respiratory medication may project sales based on the prevalence of respiratory conditions and its potential market share.
6. *Financial Analysis*: This section should contain a financial evaluation of the company's marketing plan, including costs and revenue projections. Assuming an oncology pharmaceutical manufacturer is developing its drug from start to finish, costs associated with clinical trials, regulatory approval processes, marketing efforts, potential revenue targets, and pricing strategies must be calculated before projecting costs associated with sales targets and pricing strategies are estimated.

Pharma marketing requires a business plan, which helps pharmaceutical companies develop and implement successful marketing strategies for their products and services. It should be built upon an in-depth market and target audience analysis and include an exhaustive marketing mix analysis and financial forecasting.

Business Presentation

Business presentations are an indispensable aspect of pharmaceutical marketing, used by companies to showcase their products and services to potential customers, investors, and other key constituents. Here are the essential components you must include to create a winning presentation:

1. *Introduce Your Company and the Topic*: Kickstart your presentation by briefly outlining the topic at hand and your organization in an introduction. This will give your audience an overview of what to expect as they prepare to hear more from your firm about its place within an interdisciplinary industry framework.
2. *Problem Statement*: Define the challenge your product or service will address so your target audience understands the significance of what is on offer and how it could improve patient outcomes and assist healthcare providers.
3. *Target Audience*: When setting out to market a product or service to healthcare providers, patients, or payers, these parties must understand who your product or service targets and its benefits for them.
4. *Product or Service Overview*: Give your audience an in-depth introduction to your offering by outlining its key features, benefits, and competitive advantages. Doing this will allow them to recognize what distinguishes it from competitors and better appreciate why your solution stands out.
5. *Clinical Evidence*: Display the clinical evidence supporting your product or service's safety and efficacy. This could include data from clinical trials, case studies, or any other sources that prove its utility.
6. *Market Opportunity*: Provide details about your offering's market opportunity by detailing its size, competitive landscape, and growth potential. This will allow your audience to understand why investing in it would generate revenues and how your offering can provide returns.
7. *Marketing Plan*: Draft a marketing strategy to effectively launch and promote your product or service, utilizing advertisements, direct mail promotions, or engaging key opinion leader (KOL) engagement strategies.
8. *Final Thoughts*: Conclude your presentation by restating the major points, and restating both your value proposition and product promise.

Pharmaceutical companies must ensure that their product value proposition and marketing claims adhere to ethical and regulatory requirements in the pharmaceutical industry.

Burst Campaign

A burst campaign in pharmaceutical marketing is a short-term, high-intensity effort designed to quickly increase awareness and interest in a pharmaceutical product or service. Here are some examples of burst campaigns:

1. *Disease Awareness Campaign*: Pharmaceutical companies may launch a burst campaign to raise awareness about a particular disease or condition and urge for improved treatments. For

instance, targeted digital ads, social media posts, and email marketing could be utilized to reach patients and healthcare professionals with information regarding symptoms, prevalence rates, and impacts associated with the condition.

2. *Product Launch Campaign*: A burst campaign can also be employed to publicize the launch of a new pharmaceutical product or service. This could use various channels such as email marketing, digital ads, and social media to reach healthcare professionals and patients and generate enthusiasm around this exciting new offering.
3. *Patient Education Campaign*: Pharmaceutical companies may use a burst campaign to inform patients about certain diseases or conditions and available treatments. For instance, this could involve targeted digital ads and social media posts providing tips on managing one's condition and how their product or service can benefit them.
4. *Conference and Event Campaign*: Pharma companies may launch a burst campaign to advertise their presence at medical conferences or events. This could involve targeted email marketing and social media promotion of the company's products/services, motivating healthcare professionals to visit the booth or attend presentations.
5. *Sales Promotion Campaign*: A burst campaign may also offer a short-term sales promotion for pharmaceutical products or services. For instance, targeted digital ads and email marketing could provide discounts or special deals to healthcare professionals or patients who purchase the item for a limited period.

In pharma marketing, burst campaigns raise awareness and interest in a pharmaceutical product or service. Pharmaceutical marketers must use multiple channels and tactics to reach their targeted audience quickly while creating urgency about the campaign's message. It should be remembered, though, that pharmaceutical marketing is highly regulated, with numerous rules regarding product promotion. Therefore, Pharma marketers should abide by these rules while planning promotional campaigns.

Buyer Behavior

In pharmaceutical marketing, *Buyer Behavior* refers to the customer or end-user actions, attitudes, and decision-making processes when prescribing or purchasing pharmaceutical products or services. Pharmaceutical companies must recognize buyer behavior to craft marketing strategies tailored to their target audience's needs and preferences. Here are some examples of buyer behavior within pharmaceutical marketing:

A. *Prescribing Behavior*: Physicians are key decision-makers in the pharmaceutical industry, prescribing medications to patients. Various factors influence prescription behavior, such as clinical efficacy, safety profile, cost efficiency, and patient preferences. Therefore, pharmaceutical companies need to comprehend how physicians make prescribing decisions so they can develop marketing strategies that effectively communicate product advantages to this audience.

B. *Patient Behavior*: Patients are an integral component of pharmaceutical marketing. Medical conditions, knowledge about available resources, finances, and personal preferences for various medications, ultimately dictate their treatment decisions. Therefore, pharmaceutical companies must understand how patients make treatment decisions to develop marketing strategies that effectively convey their products' advantages to this target market.

C. *Institutional Behavior*: Institutional buyers such as hospitals and health systems are an important target audience for pharmaceutical companies. Many factors influence institutional behavior, including clinical efficacy, safety profile, cost-efficiency, formulary decisions, and competitive landscape. Therefore, pharmaceutical companies need to understand how institutional buyers make purchasing decisions so they can develop strategies that effectively communicate the advantages of their products to this group.

Understanding buyer behavior is essential for pharmaceutical marketing campaigns to be successful. Companies can increase their campaigns' effectiveness and drive sales growth by developing an in-depth knowledge of their target audiences' purchasing patterns.

Buzz

Buzz is a term that describes the energy and interest generated around an issue, product, or event. It encompasses positive word-of-mouth advertising, online conversation, media coverage, and people's general interest in something.

In pharmaceutical marketing, buzz refers to the enthusiasm generated around a product or brand. This goal may involve various strategies such as advertising, public relations, social media platforms, and events.

Pharmaceutical companies create buzz around their products by engaging key opinion leaders (KOLs) and influencers who will speak positively of them and spark interest among followers. They may also utilize social media platforms to run targeted ad campaigns and interact with their target audience.

Generating buzz in pharmaceutical marketing can be particularly challenging due to stringent regulations governing the advertising and promotion of prescription drugs. But with careful planning and creative approaches, pharmaceutical companies can still generate excitement around their products while abiding by regulatory boundaries.

How Pharmaceutical Companies Create Buzz

Here are some examples of how pharmaceutical companies generate attention with their marketing initiatives:

1. *Celebrity Endorsements*: Pharmaceutical companies often partner with celebrities or influencers to generate product awareness. For instance, Pfizer joined forces with NFL player Terry Bradshaw to promote Celebrex (Celecoxib), a medication used for arthritis treatment.
2. *Disease Awareness Campaigns*: Pharmaceutical companies may also launch awareness campaigns to build anticipation around their products. For instance, Novartis launched the *Behind the Seizure* campaign to spread knowledge about epilepsy and promote its medication and anti-epileptic drugs.
3. *Social Media Campaigns*: Pharmaceutical companies can leverage social media platforms to build product awareness. For instance, Bristol-Myers Squibb created the *Ready. Raise. Rise* campaign on Twitter to raise cancer awareness and spur donations toward cancer research.
4. *Event Sponsorships*: Pharmaceutical companies may sponsor events to increase product awareness. For instance, AbbVie sponsored the Crohn's and Colitis Foundation's Annual Charity Walk to raise money and awareness about Crohn's disease while promoting Humira (Adalimumab).

Patient Testimonies: Patient testimonials can help build awareness for a pharmaceutical product. For instance, Roche created the *I'm not my cancer* campaign to promote Herceptin (Trastuzumab) campaign.

C

1. Call Planning
2. Canned Presentation
3. Call-to-Action
4. Carbon Foot Print
5. Carbon Neutrality
6. Caregivers
7. Catchphrases
8. Category Development Index
9. Category Positioning
10. Cause-Related Marketing
11. Causal Research
12. Celebrity Marketing
13. cGMP
14. Challenger Brand
15. Chatbot
16. Channels of Communication
17. Channel Conflict
18. Character Symbols
19. ChatGPT
20. Checklist
21. Churn Rate
22. Citizen Petition
23. Click Stream Analysis
24. Click-through Rate
25. Clinical Trials
26. Closed Loop Marketing
27. Closing Techniques
28. Cloud Computing
29. Cluster Analysis
30. Clutter
31. Co-creation
32. Co-development
33. Cognitive Dissonance
34. Collaboration
35. Collaborative Research
36. Color
37. Co-marketing
38. Commoditization
39. Company Culture
40. Companion Diagnostics
41. Comparative Advantage
42. Compliance
43. Competition
44. Competitive Advantage
45. Competitive Analysis
46. Competitive Intelligence
47. Competitiveness
48. Competitive Positioning
49. Competitive De-positioning
50. Competitive Forces
51. Competitor Analysis
52. Competitive Myopia
53. Concentrated Marketing
54. Concentric Diversification
55. Conditioning
56. Conjoint Analysis
57. Consumers
58. Consumerism
59. Content Marketing
60. Content Management System (CMS)
61. Continuing Medical Education (CME)
62. Contract Research
63. Contextual Advertising
64. Contextual Marketing
65. Continuous Glucose Monitoring (CGM)
66. Conversion
67. Conversion Metrics
68. Conversion Rates
69. Coopetition
70. Copay
71. Copycatting
72. Copyright

73. Copy Testing
74. Copywriting
75. Corporate Appraisal
76. Corporate Governance
77. Corporate Social Responsibility (CSR)
78. Cost-Benefit Analysis (CBA)
79. Cost-per-Click (CPC)
80. Cost-per-Conversion (CPC)
81. Cost-per-Lead (CPL)
82. Counterfeit Drugs
83. Crisis Communications
84. Cross Selling
85. Crowdsourcing
86. Culture
87. Cultural Environment
88. Cultural Environment Monitoring
89. Cultural Environment Scanning
90. Customers
91. Customer Acquisition
92. Customer Acquisition Rate
93. Customer-Centricity
94. Customer Effort Score (CES)
95. Customer Engagement
96. Customer Experience
97. Customer Experience Measurement
98. Customer Experience Metrics
99. Customer Feedback
100. Customer Focus
101. Customer Insights
102. Customer Journey
103. Customer Journey Mapping
104. Customer Lifetime Value (CLV)
105. Customer Obsession
106. Customer Relationship
107. Customer Relationship Management (CRM)
108. Customer Retention
109. Customer Retention Rate
110. Customer Reviews
111. Customer Satisfaction
112. Customer Satisfaction Measurement
113. Customer Satisfaction Research
114. Customer Satisfaction Score
115. Customer Touchpoints
116. Cybersecurity

Call Planning

Call Planning is a crucial element of pharmaceutical marketing that involves creating a strategy for how sales representatives should engage with healthcare professionals (HCPs) during visits. Call planning aims to maximize these interactions and achieve desired outcomes, such as increasing brand awareness, driving prescription volume, or securing a formulary placement.

Here are some key steps involved in effective call planning in pharma marketing:

1. *Identification of Your Target Audience*: Determine which healthcare professionals will most likely prescribe your product. This could involve analyzing prescription data, referral patterns, and other relevant metrics.
2. *Establish Specific Objectives*: Define specific goals for each call, such as introducing a new product, building brand awareness, or informing HCPs on the latest clinical data.
3. *Develop the Message*: Craft an engaging message that addresses the needs and concerns of your target audience. This may include emphasizing key product features, clinical advantages, and safety data.
4. *Scheduling Calls*: Determine the optimal frequency and timing of calls based on HCP availability and preferences. It is essential not to overwhelm HCPs with too many calls, which may lead to negative perceptions about your company and its products.
5. *Prepare the Sales Reps*: Make sure your sales representatives are educated on key messages, objections, and clinical data relevant to each call so they are well-equipped to have meaningful conversations with healthcare providers. This will guarantee they have adequate time to prepare for each conversation.
6. *Monitor and Evaluate Performance*: Track the sales representatives' performances and the outcome of calls to identify areas for improvement and adjust your call planning strategy accordingly.

Effective call planning is essential for optimizing pharmaceutical marketing initiatives and achieving desired business outcomes.

Canned Presentation

Canned presentations in pharmaceutical marketing refer to pre-prepared, standardized presentations used by sales representatives when engaging with healthcare professionals (HCPs). These presentations typically contain product details, clinical data, and key messages designed to showcase their benefits.

Canned presentations can be beneficial for ensuring key messages are consistently delivered to healthcare providers (HCPs), but they may also be perceived as impersonal and overly scripted. Here are some advantages and drawbacks of using canned presentations in pharmaceutical marketing.

Advantages

1. *Consistency*: Canned presentations guarantee consistent key messages are delivered to all healthcare providers, which can help build brand awareness and boost product knowledge.
2. *Efficiency*: Sales representatives can create and deliver canned presentations for each HCP more quickly and cost-effectively, saving time and resources.
3. *Control*: Canned presentations give companies greater control over the information presented to healthcare professionals, allowing them to guarantee accuracy and adherence to regulations.

Drawbacks

1. *Absence of Personalization*: Canned presentations can appear impersonal and generic, making it challenging for sales representatives to build relationships with healthcare providers.
2. *Inflexibility*: Canned presentations may not be tailored to healthcare practitioners' individual needs and concerns, which could limit their effectiveness.
3. *Boredom*: If listeners hear the same canned presentation repeatedly, they may become bored or disengaged and reduce attention spans, potentially decreasing the impact of the message delivered.

It is essential to balance consistency and personalization when creating canned presentations. This may involve developing multiple presentations tailored for different HCP segments or situations, allowing sales representatives to customize them according to each HCP's individual needs and interests. Furthermore, adding more interactive materials like case studies or videos may be beneficial in keeping HCPs interested and involved in the conversation.

Call-to-Action

A Call-to-Action (CTA) in pharmaceutical marketing refers to an explicit request or instruction designed to elicit a specific response or behavior from the target audience. CTAs motivate healthcare professionals (HCPs) to take action, such as prescribing medications, requesting more information, or attending product seminars. Here are some tips for creating successful CTAs:

1. *Be Specific and Clear*: CTAs should be concise, leaving no room for confusion or ambiguity. Utilize an action-oriented language that conveys what you want the HCP to do, such as *prescribe now* or *schedule a meeting* with our representative.
2. *Use Urgency*: Create a sense of urgency in your CTA and motivate HCPs to act quickly. Use language that suggests the opportunity is time-limited, or there could be negative repercussions if not taken advantage of, such as *limited time offer* or *don't miss out on this important information.*
3. *Highlight Benefits*: Highlight the advantages of taking your desired action to motivate HCPs to take it. For instance, you could emphasize the clinical advantages of prescribing your medication or the educational value of attending a product seminar.
4. *Make It Easier for HCPs to Take Action*: Provide clear instructions on how they can take the desired action, such as a registration page link or phone number to call. The simpler the process for HCPs is, the greater their likelihood of taking it.
5. *Utilize Multiple Channels*: Utilize various methods to deliver your CTA, such as email, direct mail, or social media. Doing this increases the likelihood that healthcare professionals (HCPs) will see your message and take the desired action.

A strong and persuasive call to action is essential for pharmaceutical marketing success. By crafting a concise yet compelling message and providing specific instructions on how to take action, you can increase the likelihood that healthcare practitioners (HCPs) will respond favorably to your message and take the desired action.

Carbon Foot Print

Carbon footprint is defined as the total greenhouse gases released into the atmosphere due to an individual, organization, event, or product and expressed as tons or kilograms equivalent emissions; its purpose is to raise awareness of human activities' environmental effects and draw attention toward those activities which generate carbon emissions such as transportation emissions; energy use (such as electricity or heating/cooling); food production and consumption as well as manufacturing activities that produce them.

Carbon Footprint in Pharma Marketing

The following are some factors which contribute to its environmental footprint in the pharmaceutical industry:

1. *Manufacturing*: Pharmaceutical marketing's carbon footprint can be extensive due to drug manufacturing, packaging, and transport, as well as marketing materials like brochures, advertisements, and samples being manufactured, distributed, and transported for promoting these products.
2. *Transportation*: Shipping drugs and marketing materials to pharmacies or hospitals can contribute to the carbon footprint associated with pharmaceutical marketing. This is particularly true for international shipments requiring air travel, which has a high environmental impact.
3. *Marketing Materials*: Producing and distributing marketing materials such as brochures, advertisements, and samples contribute to the carbon footprint of pharma marketing. Paper usage, printing processes, and shipping all play a role in contributing to these emissions.
4. *Events and Conferences*: Pharmaceutical companies often host and attend conferences to showcase their products and services, which requires travel, lodging, and creating marketing material production. These activities inevitably contribute to carbon emissions.

Pharmaceutical marketing's carbon footprint can be substantial due to drug manufacturing, packaging, transportation, and the production and distribution of marketing materials and services. However, pharmaceutical companies can reduce energy consumption, promote sustainable packaging and transportation methods, and shift marketing initiatives towards digital channels to reduce their carbon footprint and contribute towards a more sustainable future.

Carbon Neutrality

Carbon neutrality is creating an environmental footprint with zero greenhouse gas emissions, typically achieved through reforestation projects or renewable energy generation and carbon capture storage technologies that reduce atmospheric CO2.

Carbon neutrality has become an important goal for individuals, businesses, and governments as they work to minimize human activities' environmental effects and combat climate change. Attaining carbon neutrality allows these entities to drastically decrease emissions of greenhouse gases while creating more sustainable futures.

Carbon Neutrality in Pharma Marketing

Carbon neutrality in pharmaceutical marketing refers to the effort to offset carbon emissions from companies' marketing activities. Pharmaceutical manufacturing, packaging, and transportation contribute significantly to global carbon emissions. Companies can take steps such as shifting away from traditional print or television ads towards digital channels; adopting energy-saving practices within operations; supporting recycling programs to cut back waste production; supporting renewable energy initiatives to offset against their carbon footprint; or contributing projects and initiatives specifically created to offset their carbon emissions.

Pharmaceutical companies and their supply chain partners can join forces to reduce the environmental footprint of their operations by encouraging suppliers to adopt Eco-friendly practices, using Eco-friendly materials in packaging, and optimizing shipping routes with reduced carbon emissions.

Reaching carbon neutrality in pharmaceutical marketing takes an unyielding commitment to sustainability and investments in renewable energy projects and carbon offset programs. These actions enable pharmaceutical companies to reduce their environmental footprint and contribute towards creating a more sustainable future.

What Pharma Can Do to Achieve Carbon Neutrality

Here are some examples of how pharmaceutical companies can achieve carbon neutrality in their marketing initiatives:

1. *Utilize Digital Marketing Channels*: Instead of relying solely on print and television advertising, pharmaceutical companies can transition their marketing efforts into digital channels such as social media, email marketing, and online ads. Doing so reduces the need for paper production, leading to significant reductions in carbon emissions.
2. *Implementing Energy-Efficient Practices*: Pharmaceutical companies can reduce energy consumption through upgrades to energy-saving lighting and HVAC (Heating, Ventilation, and Air-conditioning) systems, optimizing heating/ cooling settings, or using renewable sources like solar or wind power.
3. *Reducing Waste and Promoting Recycling*: Pharmaceutical companies can considerably lower their carbon footprint through waste reduction and recycling initiatives, including using Eco-friendly packaging materials, creating recycling programs for paper, plastics, and other materials, eliminating single-use plastics, and adopting waste reduction tactics such as Eco-friendly transportation routes for medical supplies.
4. *Investing in Renewable Energy*: Pharmaceutical companies can reduce their carbon emissions by investing in renewable energy projects like wind farms, solar installations, or hydropower schemes to support sustainability in energy sectors such as wind power. By supporting renewable projects, they help lower emissions from these areas while creating more Eco-friendly environments to operate their business.
5. *Collaboration with Supply Chain Partners*: Pharmaceutical companies can collaborate with their suppliers to reduce their operations' environmental impact. This could include encouraging them to adopt sustainable practices, using sustainable materials in packaging, and optimizing shipping routes to reduce carbon emissions.

Pharma's Initiatives to Achieve Carbon Neutrality

Pharmaceutical companies have taken numerous initiatives to lower their carbon footprint and foster sustainability. Here are a few examples:

1. Pfizer has set itself an ambitious goal of becoming carbon neutral across its operations by 2030. To accomplish this goal, they invest in renewable and energy-saving technologies; decrease their waste output; encourage recycling practices; collaborate with suppliers on environmental solutions, and collaborate in mitigating any negative environmental impact that might exist with their operations.
2. Novartis has committed to reaching carbon neutrality across its operations by 2025 and has begun taking steps toward this end, such as adopting energy-saving practices, investing in

renewable sources for power, recycling programs, and Eco-friendly packaging to reach this objective.

3. Roche has set itself the goal of becoming carbon neutral by 2025 and is taking steps such as investing in renewable energy sources, adopting energy-saving practices, and striving to minimize supply chain environmental impacts.
4. Sanofi has pledged to reduce carbon emissions by 55% by 2025 by investing in renewable energy sources, encouraging sustainable packaging practices, decreasing waste production, and expanding recycling programs.
5. Merck has set itself the ambitious goal of being carbon neutral by 2025. To achieve it, it has implemented measures such as investing in renewable energy sources, practicing energy-saving measures, and recycling and Eco-friendly packaging practices.

These initiatives demonstrate how pharmaceutical companies are decreasing their carbon footprint and fostering sustainability. Through investing in renewable energy sources, energy-saving practices, and encouraging Eco-friendly packaging and recycling options, pharmaceutical businesses contribute directly to helping foster an environmentally friendly future.

Caregivers

Caregivers provide care and assistance to someone in need, often family or friends of people with chronic illness, disability, or another medical condition. In addition, caregivers may assist with tasks like personal care, medication administration, transportation needs, household duties, and emotional support, which is often needed.

Caregiving can be rewarding and challenging. Caregivers typically form close bonds with those they care for, while finding satisfaction in helping to preserve their independence and quality of life. Yet caregiving may also require significant time, resources, and provider sacrifice.

As part of healthcare delivery systems, caregivers provide essential help and care for patients and their families. Caregivers work closely with healthcare providers in managing patients' care by scheduling appointments or managing medications as necessary and communicating directly with healthcare teams on behalf of each patient.

As our population ages and chronic conditions become more widespread, caregivers' roles become more essential. Numerous organizations and advocacy groups provide resources and assistance, including training programs, respite care services, financial aid, to address this burgeoning demand for caregiving services.

Caregivers are integral to healthcare delivery systems, offering vital assistance and care to those in need while improving patient outcomes.

Catchphrases

Catchphrases are memorable phrases or expressions closely associated with a particular person, brand, product, or cultural reference. They are often repeated or quoted, becoming iconic or recognized as a distinctive slogan or tagline. Catchphrases are designed to be catchy and memorable, serving as a form of verbal branding that conveys messages in memorable ways and can easily identify them in various settings, such as advertising campaigns, movies, TV shows, sports teams, politics, and popular culture in general.

Catchphrases serve multiple functions including conveying specific messages while stirring emotions or advertising products or services or character encapsulation. They can deliver important information while being easily remembered, which serves multiple uses such as brand promotions or communicating specific ideas and emotions encapsulating characters' personalities within these settings as well as serving different functions. Catchphrases can often be found within commercials/TV shows/sport/politicized TV/Sport/politicized media shows as well as pop culture. Catchphrases can often be used throughout advertising/politicizing character; they can create messages and promote personality characteristics when used.

Catchphrases have long been used as an effective marketing tactic in advertising; no less so for pharmaceutical industry advertising! Catchphrases are memorable phrases with some form of wordplay or rhyme to draw in potential patients while raising brand recognition. In medical advertising, catchphrases are frequently used to market specific products, services, or procedures while raising patient brand awareness.

Pharmaceutical marketers frequently employ catchphrases or taglines as part of their promotional tactics to build brand recognition, convey important messages, and differentiate products from competitors. Here are a few catchphrases used in pharmaceutical marketing campaigns:

1. *Feel Better, Live Better* is popular slogan pharmaceutical companies use to advertise their products' ability to improve quality of life.
2. *Find the Cure with Us* is another phrase often employed to convey an organization's dedication to finding a cure for certain diseases.
3. The *Helping You Live Your Best Life* catchphrase expresses a company's dedication to improving customer health and well-being. In addition, companies use this slogan to endorse their products' effectiveness in treating various medical conditions.
4. Companies use the *Power to Heal* catchphrase to promote the effectiveness of their products in treating various medical conditions.
5. The *Innovation for Life* catchphrase demonstrates a company's dedication to discovering and developing novel treatments that can enhance patients' lives.
6. *Trusted by Doctors and Preferred by Patients* emphasizes a company's standing among healthcare professionals and its growing popularity with patients.
7. *Science for a Better Life* catchphrase emphasizes the significance of science in discovering treatments that can enhance people's lives.
8. *Healthy Living, Healthy You* catchphrase emphasizes that leading an active lifestyle is key to maintaining good health and preventing illness.
9. *Advancing Medicine, Improving Lives* is the tagline companies use to show their dedication to progress in medical science and developing treatments that improve patients' lives.
10. *Committed to Caring* encapsulates their commitment to providing high-quality healthcare and reinforces their focus on patients.

Category Development Index

The Category Development Index (CDI) is an industry-standard metric widely employed to gauge drug categories' performance within their markets. It gives insight into how one category fared compared to others by dividing local sales of one category by national sales and multiplying by 100; for example, if sales for an item totaled $10 million while national sales totaled $100 million, then its CDI would equal 10.

The CDI provides pharmaceutical companies with data they can use to pinpoint specific categories that are underperforming or outperforming compared with their national average so that their marketing strategies and tactics may be revised appropriately, leading to higher sales in certain markets.

How is CDI useful in pharmaceutical marketing? Here are some examples to demonstrate the application of the Category Development Index:

A. Let's say a pharmaceutical company produces an innovative medication to treat diabetes. They can use the CDI index to assess how well their drug performs in different markets relative to the national average, enabling them to focus their marketing efforts on underperforming areas to boost sales and overall market share.

B. A company produces a new drug to manage hypertension. They can use the CDI (Compare Drug Index) to compare drug sales in different geographic locations to the national average. If a particular location's CDI is low, it could indicate low awareness or limited access to the drug there. Therefore, they can devise targeted marketing strategies to increase awareness and access in that location.

C. Pharmaceutical companies produce various skincare products. Companies can utilize CDI (Category Development Index) to analyze market sales performance. If a CDI for a certain item is low in one area, this could indicate strong competition or low demand in that particular market. In such cases, companies can adjust their marketing strategies by offering promotions or introducing new product lines to boost sales in that region.

The Category Development Index (CDI) is an invaluable resource for pharmaceutical companies seeking insight into their market performance and making data-driven decisions to enhance marketing and sales tactics.

Category Positioning

Category positioning in pharmaceutical marketing refers to how a drug fits into an established therapeutic category or market segment. This process involves understanding your target audience's needs and crafting a unique value proposition that sets your product apart from competitors within that same category.

Category positioning typically begins with market research to understand the needs and preferences of your target audience and the competitive landscape within a therapeutic category. This analysis helps pinpoint key benefits and features that matter most to them, leading to creating a USP for your product.

Once a USP is defined, pharmaceutical companies will craft a marketing strategy to communicate the product's advantages and differentiators to their target audience. This may involve creating tailored messaging and advertising campaigns, creating sales collateral and promotional materials, and using digital channels to reach healthcare providers and patients.

Effective category positioning is essential for pharmaceutical companies as it helps ensure their products are differentiated from competitors and seen as the ideal solution for customers' needs. Doing this can boost market share, brand recognition, and overall business performance.

Effective Category Positioning

While the specific steps involved in category positioning may differ depending on your product and market, here are some commonly followed guidelines:

1. *Define the Therapeutic Category*: Define the therapeutic category in which your product will compete. Doing this requires understanding the market landscape and determining key characteristics such as patient demographics, market size, and treatment options.
2. *Identify Target Audience*: Define who the intended audience for your product is by researching patient needs, preferences, and behaviors, as well as healthcare providers who will prescribe or suggest it.
3. *Conduct Market Research*: Conduct market research to understand your target audience and competitive landscape. This includes collecting information on patient needs and preferences, physician prescribing patterns, and competitor products.
4. *Create a Unique Selling Proposition (USP)*: Based on market research, create a USP that sets your product apart from competitors and effectively meets target audience needs. Your USP should highlight product features, benefits, and advantages over rivals.
5. *Develop Marketing Strategy*: Craft a marketing plan that effectively conveys your USP to your target audience. This may involve crafting messaging and advertising campaigns, creating sales collateral and promotional materials, and using digital marketing channels.
6. *Implement and Monitor*: Monitor marketing strategy and track key performance metrics to assess its effectiveness. Continuously assess the market conditions and adjust your approach as necessary to maintain a competitive edge and meet evolving needs of your target audience.

Cause-Related Marketing

Cause-related marketing in pharmaceuticals refers to companies joining forces with non-profit organizations to support a social cause that aligns with their company's values and goals. This type of promotion may also be called cause marketing, social impact marketing, or corporate social responsibility (CSR).

Cause-related pharmaceutical marketing aims to build brand awareness, enhance the company's reputation and spur business growth while benefitting society. By aligning with a specific cause, pharmaceutical companies can demonstrate their dedication to social responsibility and connect with engaged customers about similar causes. Examples of cause-related marketing in pharmaceuticals include:

- Funding research and development efforts for a specific disease or condition
- Donating part of product sales to non-profit organizations to raise awareness about that condition or illness
- Offering complimentary products or services to patients or healthcare providers in underserved communities
- Sponsoring educational programs or events dedicated to disease prevention or management

Pharma's Cause-related Marketing Initiatives

Here are some examples of cause-related marketing initiatives implemented by some pharmaceutical companies:

1. *Novo Nordisk's Changing Diabetes Program*: Novo Nordisk, a global healthcare company, created the *Changing Diabetes Program* to raise awareness about diabetes and its devastating effects on individuals and communities. This program includes partnerships with the World Diabetes Foundation for disease prevention and management initiatives in low and middle-income countries as well as screening efforts worldwide in an attempt to detect undiagnosed cases of diabetes.
2. *Pfizer Global Health Innovation Grants*: As a leading global pharma major, Pfizer awards grants to non-profit organizations to increase healthcare access and outcomes among underserved communities worldwide, supporting initiatives ranging from community health to innovative digital solutions.
3. *Merck for Mothers Initiative* by Merck, the global pharmaceutical leader, partnered with governments, non-government organizations

(NGOs), healthcare providers, and others by providing access to quality maternal healthcare while simultaneously combatting to reduce maternal mortality.

4. *GlaxoSmithKline (GSK)*: A multinational healthcare company, partnered with *Save the Children*, a global leader among child-focused charities, to improve vaccine access and support maternal and child health in community-based health programs in developing nations.
5. *Sanofi*: An international pharmaceutical company, launched its *Dengue Vaccine Access Program*, pledging its contribution to eradicate Dengue globally. The company offered public sector organizations in countries with high dengue incidence their Dengue vaccine at an affordable cost to improve vaccine access.

Cause-related marketing in pharmaceutical companies can be an effective strategy to set themselves apart and build customer trust. But these initiatives must be true to the company's values and goals, as consumers increasingly scrutinize companies based on their social impact and ethical practices.

Causal Research

Causal research in pharmaceutical marketing is an analysis designed to establish a cause-and-effect relationship between two variables. Pharma companies employ causal research techniques to understand how different factors impact patient behavior, treatment outcomes, and other important metrics. Here are a few examples of how pharmaceutical companies leverage causal research in their marketing activity:

1. *Determining Effectiveness of New Drug*: Causal research can ascertain whether a particular medication can successfully treat particular illnesses or conditions. Researchers can create an effect-and-cause relationship by conducting clinical trials comparing outcomes among participants given new medicines versus those receiving placebo treatments or conventional remedies.
2. *Identification of Drivers Affecting Patient Adherence*: Causal research can be employed to uncover factors that prevent patients from adhering to treatment regimes as planned. By analyzing patient behavior and outcomes data, researchers can pinpoint which elements influence adherence rates most and create interventions designed to enhance them.
3. *Understanding Marketing Interventions*: Causal research can be used to measure the effects of marketing interventions like ads or sales promotions on patient behaviors and outcomes, like whether there was any causal connection between intervention and changes in patient behaviors or changes to outcomes. Researchers can compare outcomes before and after interventions are carried out to establish whether there has been a noticeable change.
4. *Analyzing Healthcare Policies' Effects*: Causal research can be employed to analyze how healthcare policies impact patient outcomes. For example, researchers can pinpoint the causal link between specific policies, patient behavior, and outcomes by comparing outcomes across different geographic areas or populations.

Causal research is essential for comprehending the complex factors influencing patient behavior and treatment outcomes in pharmaceutical marketing. In addition, it helps researchers create more effective interventions and strategies through causal research by establishing causal connections between variables.

Celebrity Marketing

Celebrity marketing is a strategy many industries, including the pharmaceutical industry, use to advertise and promote their goods and services. In pharmaceutical marketing, celebrity marketing involves using an iconic person to endorse a medication or medical device.

Celebrity marketing in the pharmaceutical industry can be controversial. Celebrities can serve a dual role by helping raise awareness for medications or medical conditions through personal connections; furthermore, celebrities often serve as role models who help remove the stigma around certain health concerns, encouraging people to seek treatment.

On the contrary, celebrity marketing in the pharmaceutical industry can be seen as unethical or exploitative. For example, some critics contend that celebrities may not have sufficient medical training or credibility to provide medical advice, with endorsements often driven more by financial incentives than a genuine belief in a product. Furthermore, there is concern that celebrity endorsements could encourage the overuse or misuse of medications if celebrities are unaware of potential hazards.

Here are some examples of pharma using celebrity marketing in their marketing efforts:

1. Brooke Shields, an established Hollywood actress, made headlines in 2005, after appearing in television commercials for GlaxoSmithKline's antidepressant medication Paxil (Paroxetine). Shields had been seen candidly discussing her postpartum depression experience after giving birth; some critics felt this personal story had been exploited commercially.
2. Montel Williams, an American television host with multiple sclerosis (MS), has been a spokesperson for several medications to combat MS, such as Teva's Copaxone. Furthermore, Williams has spoken openly about his experience with MS and how the medication has helped him manage its symptoms.
3. In 2018, tennis great Serena Williams became an ambassador for AbbVie's migraine medication Ubrelvy and shared her experiences with migraines, which have affected her both on and off the court.
4. Bob Dole, a former US Senator and spokesperson for Pfizer's erectile dysfunction drug Viagra in the late 1980s, became an advocate for this medication after having prostate cancer surgery. Dole openly discussed his struggles with ED and how taking Viagra helped him cope.
5. Michael Phelps, Olympic swimmer, has become a spokesperson for Takeda's ADHD medication Vyvanse. He claims the medication has helped him manage his symptoms and stay motivated during training sessions.

Celebrity marketing can be an effective tool to promote pharmaceutical products and raise awareness about medical conditions. However, pharma marketers should exercise caution and be sensitive to ethical concerns when employing this strategy.

cGMP

cGMP stands for Current Good Manufacturing Practice. cGMP regulations cover the design, monitoring, and control of manufacturing facilities and processes used in pharmaceutical industries. Enforced by regulatory agencies like the United States Food and Drug Administration (FDA), their purpose is to guarantee pharmaceutical products' safety, efficacy, and quality.

Although cGMP regulations mainly pertain to manufacturing quality control processes, they also have implications for pharmaceutical marketing. Consider the following, for example:

1. *Scientific Evidence to Support Claims in Pharmaceutical Marketing Materials*: Any claims made in pharmaceutical marketing materials must be accurate and supported with scientific data, including claims about safety, efficacy and quality.
2. *Tracking Adverse Events*: Pharmaceutical companies must establish monitoring and reporting systems to track adverse events related to their products. This includes adverse events reported through marketing channels, such as social media.
3. *Labeling Requirements*: Pharmaceutical products must be labeled following cGMP regulations, including requirements for accurate ingredient listing, dosage information, and warnings and precautions.
4. *Product Recalls*: In the event of a product recall, pharmaceutical companies must follow cGMP regulations for the recall process, including notifying regulatory agencies and customers, conducting investigations, and implementing corrective actions.

Pharma marketers should be familiar with cGMP regulations and ensure their marketing practices comply. This includes working closely with regulatory affairs and quality control departments to ensure that marketing materials are accurate and supported by scientific evidence and that adverse events are reported promptly.

Challenger Brand

Challenger brands in pharmaceutical marketing refer to brands that are relatively new to the market or hold lower market shares than existing brands yet aim to challenge the status quo and disrupt markets by offering innovative products or services that offer unique patient benefits.

Challenger brands in pharma marketing typically face significant challenges, such as limited budgets and resources, a lack of brand recognition, and regulatory barriers. However, they can overcome these challenges by developing a strong marketing strategy that builds brand awareness, differentiates them from competitors, and establishes credibility with healthcare professionals and patients.

Strategic Approaches

Here are some strategies that challenger brands can use in pharma marketing to succeed:

1. *Focusing on a Specific Niche*: By targeting a specific patient population, challenger brands can differentiate themselves from established

brands and build a loyal following among patients and healthcare professionals.

2. *Leveraging Digital Marketing*: Digital marketing can be cost-effective for challenger brands to reach a wider audience and engage with patients and healthcare professionals.
3. *Partnering with Patient Advocacy Groups*: Partnering with patient advocacy groups can help challenger brands build credibility and trust among patients, who are often more likely to try new treatments if trusted patient advocates recommend them.
4. *Providing Educational Content*: Providing educational content about the disease condition their products treat can help challenger brands establish themselves as experts and build trust with patients and healthcare professionals.

Challenger Brand in Pharma: An Example

Orkambi by Vertex Pharmaceuticals is a good example of a challenger brand. Orkambi (Lumacaftor/Ivacaftor) is a medication for cystic fibrosis (CF) that targets a specific genetic mutation. When it was first launched, it was a challenger brand competing against established treatments for cystic fibrosis. As a result, vertex Pharmaceuticals used a targeted marketing approach, focusing on educating physicians and patients about the unique benefits of Orkambi and partnering with patient advocacy groups to build awareness and credibility.

The key to success for challenger brands in pharma marketing is to be innovative, focused, and strategic while building trust and credibility with patients and healthcare professionals.

Chatbot

Chatbots are computer programs that employ artificial intelligence (AI) and natural language processing (NLP) to simulate human dialogues, providing automated support through messaging apps, websites, or any digital channel. They offer automated assistance to their users as they communicate.

Pharma marketing can benefit from chatbots offering personalized customer engagement and 24/7 support. Here are some ways in which chatbots are useful in pharma marketing:

1. *Providing Product Information*: Chatbots can offer customers detailed information about a company's products, such as their benefits, side effects, and usage instructions. This helps customers make educated decisions regarding their healthcare requirements.
2. *Conducting Market Research*: Chatbots can conduct surveys and collect customer feedback about their experiences with a company's products. This helps companies improve their products and services based on customer input.
3. *Supporting Patient Adherence*: Chatbots can play an instrumental role in supporting patient adherence by reminding patients when to take their medications on schedule and offering tailored guidance about managing conditions, leading to improved patient outcomes and lower healthcare costs.
4. *Customer Support*: Chatbots can quickly and effectively respond to customer queries while improving satisfaction and loyalty. This results in increased loyalty and satisfaction from users.

Here are some examples showing how pharmaceutical companies use chatbots:

1. *Woebot Health* is a chatbot that utilizes cognitive-behavioral therapy (CBT) techniques to assist people in managing their mental health. Stanford psychologists created it, and it is accessible through Facebook Messenger.
2. *YourMD* chatbot provides users with symptoms-checking and medical advice. It utilizes artificial intelligence (AI) to tailor recommendations based on individual user symptoms.
3. *Merck*, a global pharmaceutical giant, launched a chatbot on Facebook Messenger to provide information about their products— specifically contraceptive options. Furthermore, the chatbot provides personalized responses based on the user's age and location.
4. *HealthTap* is a chatbot that connects users with doctors and other healthcare professionals for virtual consultations. It utilizes AI technology to match users with the most suitable healthcare professionals.
5. *Sanofi*, a leading multinational pharmaceutical company, launched a chatbot on Facebook Messenger to provide diabetes management advice. The bot provides personalized diet, exercise, and medication advice based on the user's age, weight, and activity level.

Chatbots have proven invaluable in pharmaceutical marketing for providing personalized assistance and information directly to their target audiences. As such, chatbots offer companies an incredible tool for providing tailored customer care while increasing efficiency and cutting costs.

Channels of Communication

Pharmaceutical marketing employs multiple communication channels to reach its intended audiences, such as healthcare providers, patients, and other key constituents to reach its desired result. Here are the most frequently employed channels:

1. *Sales Representatives*: Sales representatives or medical reps are the most prevalent communication channel in pharma marketing. They visit healthcare professionals to promote and inform them about their products' advantages, potential risks, and recommended use.
2. *Conferences and Events*: Pharmaceutical companies regularly sponsor or take part in healthcare conferences and events as an avenue to showcase their products while offering educational resources for healthcare providers.
3. *Direct Mail*: Direct mailing can provide healthcare providers and patients with details on a product directly. Brochures or information packets sent directly can provide them with details that help decisions about their purchase or usage.
4. *Digital Marketing*: Pharmaceutical marketing now integrates many facets of digital marketing, from email campaigns and social media management to online ads to search engine optimization (SEO).
5. *Patient Advocacy Groups*: Pharmaceutical companies often partner with patient advocacy groups to raise awareness for their products while offering patient resources and assistance.
6. *Medical Journals and Publications*: Companies may place ads for their products in medical journals and publications or sponsor research studies, demonstrating the efficacy and safety of their products.

Pharmaceutical marketing is heavily regulated by government organizations like the Food and Drug Administration in the United States, with companies adhering to stringent guidelines when advertising and promoting their products.

Channel Conflict

Channel conflict in marketing refers to situations when there is disagreement or tension among different parties in distributing products or services. Customers, manufacturers, wholesalers, and retailers all could experience marketing conflicts through various means; price wars may arise between manufacturers, distributors, and retailers in terms of distribution conflicts; promotional wars can arise between product/service vendors as well as territories in conflict over marketing issues; pricing can lead to distribution disputes which are in turn affected by geography differences as well.

Pharma marketing can experience conflict in several ways, as the distribution chain for pharmaceutical products is intricate and involves multiple parties. Here are a few examples of how channels of conflict may arise in pharma marketing:

1. *Price Conflict*: Pharmaceutical products can be costly, leading to disagreements regarding pricing between manufacturers, wholesalers, retailers, and insurance companies. Manufacturers may want to raise prices to recoup R&D expenses; however, insurers and customers may oppose such increases.
2. *Distribution Conflict*: Pharma products can be distributed through various channels, such as hospitals, clinics, pharmacies, and online retailers. Manufacturers may sell directly to customers while retailers purchase from wholesalers; as a result, disagreements may arise regarding who holds the rights for certain items to be distributed.
3. *Promotional Conflicts*: Pharmaceutical manufacturers employ various promotional tactics such as ads, direct mailers, and sales reps to reach potential customers. This leads them into promotional conflicts when using these methods that may overlap or conflict. Unfortunately, there can be disagreements between manufacturers and retailers about the frequency of such activities. For instance, retailers may oppose direct mail campaigns encouraging customers to buy items online since this reduces foot traffic in their stores.
4. *Product or Service Conflict*: Pharmaceutical manufacturers often create new drugs or enhance existing ones, but disagreements about their value can exist. Retailers may resist stocking these medications if they are too costly or won't sell well.
5. *Territory Conflict*: Manufacturers may disagree about which regions to sell their products to. For instance, if an entrepreneur attempts to break into a new market, they may encounter resistance from established wholesalers or retailers with a significant presence there.

Pharma companies need effective communication and negotiation skills to manage potential channel conflicts. Furthermore, they should ensure all parties involved in the distribution chain are aware of their products' advantages and encouraged to work together towards common objectives. Doing this will guarantee their products reach those in need while fulfilling commercial targets.

Character Symbols

Character symbols are visual representations of a brand or product that use characters or mascots to create an emotional connection with their target audience. These images are often used in marketing and advertising campaigns for consumers to remember and identify a brand or product.

Pharma marketing often utilizes character symbols to showcase prescription drugs, medical devices, or healthcare services. For instance, a pharmaceutical company might utilize an animated character or mascot to advertise medication for children or an adorable animal character to market medications to pets.

Character symbols can help distinguish a brand or product from competitors, making it more memorable and appealing to customers. However, care must be taken that any character symbols used in marketing campaigns are appropriate and do not mislead or deceive customers.

How Pharma Uses Character Symbols

Here are some examples of pharmaceutical companies using character symbols in their marketing campaigns:

1. Pfizer uses the *Zoloft Blob* character to promote their antidepressant medication Zoloft. This character is meant to convey the positive feelings patients may experience when taking this medication.
2. AstraZeneca uses *the Character Turbuhaler* to promote their asthma medication, Symbicort. This character is designed to represent the inhaler device used for administering the drug and make the product more relatable and memorable for patients.
3. Roche uses *Tamiflu Man* to promote their antiviral medication, Tamiflu. This character is designed to represent the flu virus and make the product more relatable and engaging for customers.
4. Merck uses a character named *Gardasil Girl* to promote its HPV vaccine, Gardasil. She is meant to represent the target audience for this particular vaccine (young girls and women) and create an emotional connection with viewers.
5. Sanofi uses the character *Goulu* to promote their insulin medication Toujeo. The character is designed to represent a small bird that flies around and assists patients with managing their data.

It is worth noting that character symbols in pharmaceutical marketing can be controversial, with some criticizing their potential to mislead or minimize serious health conditions. On the other hand, when utilized correctly, character symbols help make pharmaceutical products more relatable and engaging for customers.

ChatGPT

ChatGPT stands for *Chatter Pre-trained Transformer,* an open platform AI application using natural language processing technology to simulate human conversations and mimic real-life dialogs.

ChatGPT is an AI-powered natural language processing tool designed to enable natural conversations between humans and chatbots, answering queries about language models or helping with tasks such as email drafting or essay composing. Furthermore, its language model supports answering related queries and tasks like writing emails, essays, or code.

ChatGPT can help pharma marketers in various ways. Consider the following, for instance:

1. *Offering Insights*: ChatGPT can deliver insights on industry trends, market analysis, and customer behavior using the data and information available.
2. *Content Creation*: ChatGPT can generate content for pharma marketing materials such as product descriptions, patient education materials, and social media posts.
3. *Customer Engagement*: ChatGPT can help pharma marketers engage with their customers through chatbots and conversational interfaces, providing real-time assistance and personalized recommendations.
4. *Regulatory Compliance*: ChatGPT can guide regulatory compliance, ensuring that pharma marketers follow the rules and guidelines set by regulatory bodies such as the FDA in the United States.
5. *Data Analytics*: ChatGPT can help pharma marketers analyze and interpret large amounts of data, providing insights into customer behavior, market trends, and product performance.
6. *Digital Marketing*: ChatGPT can assist pharma marketers in developing and executing digital marketing strategies, including social media

campaigns, email marketing, and online advertising.

7. *Language Translation*: ChatGPT can provide translation services for pharma marketers, helping them reach a global audience and communicate effectively in different languages.

As an AI (Artificial Intelligence) language model, ChatGPT can provide various services to help pharma marketing improve their marketing efforts, increase brand awareness, and ensure regulatory compliance.

Checklist

Checklists are useful tools to guarantee all necessary steps have been taken to complete a task or reach your goal. A checklist typically consists of items or tasks that must be accomplished, along with checkboxes or other indicators indicating completion.

Checklists can be useful in many contexts, from personal tasks like grocery shopping or packing for a trip to professional ones like project management or quality control. Not only do checklists ensure no missed steps, and simplify complex tasks by breaking them into manageable chunks.

In many industries, such as pharmaceuticals, checklists are commonly used to ensure compliance with regulators and guidelines and that all necessary steps have been taken for safety and efficacy. For instance, they could include ensuring all necessary documentation has been completed, approvals obtained, safety/quality measures implemented, and the list goes on!

Checklists can be created with tools like paper checklists, spreadsheets, and specialized software. In addition, many industries have developed standard checklists or templates to guarantee consistency and accuracy when completing complex tasks.

Checklists in Pharma Marketing

Here are some examples of how checklists can be utilized in pharmaceutical marketing:

1. *Compliance Checklists*: Compliance checklists guarantee all marketing materials adhere to industry regulations and guidelines. This includes verifying that claims made in promotional materials are backed up by scientific evidence, disclosures are included as required, and all materials have been reviewed and approved by appropriate regulatory authorities.
2. *Launch Checklists*: Launch checklists can be utilized to guarantee all necessary steps have been taken in preparation for launching a new product or marketing campaign. These may include ensuring all marketing materials comply with regulations, obtaining all necessary approvals, training sales representatives, and organizing logistics.
3. *Safety Checklists*: Safety checklists can be utilized to guarantee all necessary steps have been taken to guarantee the safety and efficacy of pharmaceutical products. This may include conducting clinical trials, reporting adverse events as required, and creating risk management plans.
4. *Social Media Checklists*: Social media checklists can help ensure all activities adhere to regulations and guidelines. These could ensure all disclosures are included in posts, duly reviewed by appropriate regulatory authorities, and provide training to social media managers.

Checklists can help guarantee all necessary steps have been taken to guarantee compliance and safety while streamlining marketing activities by providing a logical framework for planning execution. However, checklists must be regularly reviewed and updated according to changes in regulations or guidelines so that all necessary measures are taken to ensure safety and compliance.

Churn Rate

Churn rate is an integral metric within all industries, including pharmaceutical marketing.

Churn rate, used as an indicator in pharmaceutical marketing, refers to the rate at which patients or healthcare professionals (HCPs) stop using or prescribing certain medication from pharmaceutical companies for an extended period, usually one year, thus decreasing customer loyalty or satisfaction with such product or brand.

To calculate the churn rate in pharmaceutical marketing, set out your time frame (typically one year). Next, count all patients or healthcare professionals who stopped taking or prescribing your product during that period and divide by its initial usage figure.

An example would be a pharmaceutical company that started the year with 10,000 patients taking one medication but saw two thousand leave by year's end; this would indicate their churn rate is 20%.

Conversely, if a pharmaceutical company had 1,000 HCPs who prescribed one product at the beginning of the year and 150 of those prescribers stopped prescribing by year's end, their churn rate among HCPs would equal 15%.

A churn rate among HCPs is an important metric because it indicates their satisfaction and loyalty toward a particular medication or product from a pharmaceutical company. An increased churn rate among HCPs could result from numerous reasons, such as side effects, noncompliance with regulations, lack of efficacy, or better alternatives elsewhere. Pharmaceutical companies must identify what caused HCP churn and take appropriate actions such as improving product quality, offering better support and education programs, or developing products tailored to HCP needs and patients.

Pharmaceutical companies must focus on customer retention and acquisition to offset the effects of churn among HCPs. Maintaining strong relationships with HCPs, providing them with quality support and education, and engaging in continuous product improvement are all essential strategies for reducing churn and building long-term customer loyalty.

Citizen Petition

Citizen petitions are written requests submitted to the Food and Drug Administration (FDA) in the United States by individuals or organizations seeking changes in policies or regulations concerning drugs, medical devices, or any other products regulated by FDA.

Citizens may use petitions in pharmaceutical marketing to protest practices they disagree with or ask regulators for changes that affect drug promotion and sales regulations. For instance, they could demand that the FDA takes action against pharmaceutical companies engaging in deceptive or misleading tactics.

Submitting a citizen petition requires an in-depth description of the issue and supporting evidence and data. The FDA has specific guidelines for submitting citizen petitions; those that don't meet these standards may be rejected.

The FDA is usually required to respond to citizen petitions within 180 days. After that, they can grant the petition and take appropriate action, deny it with a justification, or take other appropriate actions.

Citizen Petitions in Pharma: Some Examples

Here are a few examples of citizen petitions related to pharmaceutical marketing:

1. In 2016, Public Citizen, a consumer advocacy group, submitted a citizen petition to the FDA to tighten regulations concerning opioid marketing. This petition asserted that pharmaceutical companies were using deceptive tactics by underplaying the risks of addiction and overdose associated with these drugs.
2. In 2019, a coalition of healthcare organizations and consumer advocates submitted a citizen petition to the FDA asking it to take action regarding insulin's high cost. The petition noted that prices had skyrocketed recently, making insulin unaffordable for many patients. At that time, they asked FDA to use its authority to increase competition and lower prices for prescription medicines.
3. In 2020, physicians and patient advocates had submitted an official petition to FDA regarding DTC advertising practices for pharmaceutical drugs. They claimed DTC advertising contributed to the overuse and overprescribing of certain medications, so stronger regulations should be implemented so such claims are accurate and not misleading.

Click Stream Analysis

Clickstream analysis tracks the sequence of clicks and other user interactions as users navigate websites or digital platforms. Clickstream data includes information such as which websites users accessed, the time users spent viewing each page, which links were clicked upon, and other user behaviors.

Clickstream analysis provides companies with valuable insight into user behaviors and preferences, which they can utilize to enhance website design, optimize marketing campaigns and elevate the overall user experience.

Analyzing clickstream data gives companies insight into which pages and products are the most viewed or purchased and which marketing messages work most efficiently.

Clickstream analysis typically involves using specialized software tools to collect, store and analyze large amounts of data. These instruments offer companies valuable insights into user behavior, help identify patterns and trends, and develop targeted strategies for optimizing website performance and increasing user engagement.

How Clickstream Analysis Can Benefit Pharma Marketing: Some Examples

Here are some examples of how clickstream analysis can be beneficial to pharma marketing:

1. *Identifying Popular Products and Pages*: By analyzing clickstream data, pharmaceutical companies can determine which products and

pages users most frequently visit. This data can then be used to create targeted marketing campaigns that highlight these popular items.

2. *Tracking Marketing Campaigns*: Clickstream analysis can assist companies in measuring the success of their marketing campaigns over time. By tracking changes in user behavior before and after campaigns, businesses can identify which tactics work most successfully at driving engagement, and adjust their strategies accordingly.
3. *Personalizing Marketing Messages*: Companies can gain insight into user preferences and behavior by analyzing clickstream data. This data allows companies to customize marketing messages for each user based on their interests and past activities.
4. *Identifying Opportunities for Optimization*: Clickstream analysis can assist companies in recognizing opportunities to enhance their websites and marketing campaigns by analyzing user behavior. For example, companies can identify areas on their sites or campaigns where users are dropping off or disengaging, so they can make targeted improvements to boost engagement levels and conversion rates.
5. *Understanding the Customer Journey*: Clickstream analysis can give companies a deeper comprehension of the customer journey, from initial awareness of a product or service to purchasing decisions. This knowledge can be used to craft more effective marketing strategies tailored for each stage in that journey.

Click-Through Rate

CTR (Click-Through Rate) in pharmaceutical marketing refers to the percentage of people who click on a particular link in an ad, or email related to pharmaceutical product promotion. CTR provides pharmaceutical companies and their marketing teams with an accurate measure of digital campaign effectiveness.

CTR (Click-Through Rate) can be measured for various digital marketing channels in pharmaceutical marketing, such as:

A. *Display Ads*: CTR can be measured for display ads placed on websites, social media platforms, and other digital channels. For instance, pharmaceutical companies often display ads targeting healthcare professionals (HCPs). CTR helps the marketing team understand how many HCPs are curious about the drug or potential prescribers; its CTR allows this insight.

B. *Search Ads*: Click-Through-Rate (CTR) can be measured for search engine ads that respond to specific keywords or queries. For instance, pharmaceutical ads target conditions related to specific diseases; using CTR measures of these ads helps companies understand how effectively they drive traffic back to their product websites or landing pages.

C. *Email Marketing*: Click-Through Rate can be measured for links within promotional emails that direct users to product websites or landing pages, such as HCP emails from pharmaceutical companies to promote new medications. Tracking how effective messaging and calls-to-action drive HCPs toward learning more about them through CTR analysis will provide insight into whether their efforts succeeded in engaging HCPs to learn more about the drug in question.

Measuring CTR can give pharma marketers insights into the effectiveness of specific digital marketing campaigns or tactics and help them make data-driven decisions to optimize their campaigns. For example, low CTR rates could indicate that messages or targeting should be changed to resonate more strongly with their intended audiences.

CTR may not be used alone in pharmaceutical marketing to assess digital marketing campaigns' success. Due to the highly regulated nature of pharma marketing, other metrics like engagement rate, conversion rate, and cost per acquisition may also be employed to provide a complete overview of a campaign's success.

Clinical Trials

Clinical trials are vital in pharmaceutical R&D as they test new medications' safety and efficacy before being released for market use. They provide critical feedback from regulatory bodies, healthcare providers, and patients about safety and efficacy before their introduction onto the market. Furthermore, they play an integral part in shaping pharmaceutical marketing strategies.

Pharmaceutical companies use clinical trial results as marketing strategies for selling drugs to healthcare providers and patients. For example, pharmaceutical companies highlight positive trial outcomes to show healthcare professionals and consumers why their drug is superior to competitors' products; companies may also utilize this information in advertisements and brochures produced for promotional use. Here are some ways in which pharmaceutical companies use clinical trial data to drive their marketing communication strategies:

1. *Pharmaceutical Companies Can Prove Drug Efficacy:* Pharmaceutical companies frequently rely on clinical trial data when marketing drugs to treat specific illnesses or conditions to demonstrate efficacy. For instance, companies can conduct trials demonstrating their medication is more effective than placebo or competitor treatments for treating specific ailments.
2. *Create Marketing Materials*: Clinical trial data can be utilized to create marketing materials such as brochures, advertisements, and websites promoting the benefits of drugs, featuring their mechanism of action, trial results, and patient testimonials.
3. *Sponsoring Clinical Trials*: Pharmaceutical companies regularly sponsor clinical trials as a source of market intelligence that supports their marketing initiatives. For instance, many conduct trials that compare their drug with those produced by competitors and use the results to showcase their superiority over competing drugs.
4. *Education of Healthcare Professionals*: Clinical trial data can be used to inform healthcare providers of the benefits and risks of their medications. Pharmaceutical companies may provide educational materials, such as slide decks or webinars, highlighting these results while giving guidance for prescribing them.
5. *Regulatory Submissions*: Clinical trial data must be submitted to regulatory agencies to secure approval for a drug, then utilized in marketing materials as proof of its efficacy to healthcare professionals and patients.

Clinical Trial Phases

Most clinical trials follow four distinct phases:

A. *Phase 1*: At this point, a drug is tested in small groups of healthy volunteers (typically 20 to 100) to evaluate its safety profile, dosage range, and any potential side effects. Phase I trials typically occur under controlled clinical settings, such as clinical trials for new cancer treatments, which involve testing their safety and tolerability with 20 to 100 healthy volunteers.

B. *Phase 2*: The drug is tested in larger groups (typically 100 to 300) of patients (such as Alzheimer's) to evaluate its efficacy and safety. For instance, testing an Alzheimer's drug requires conducting this phase 2 clinical trial among an expansive cohort.

C. *Phase 3*: Drugs are tested in large groups (typically several hundred to several thousand patients) to confirm efficacy and safety and assess potential side effects. Phase 3 trials often include multiple clinical sites. For example, testing the efficacy and safety of the new COVID-19 vaccine requires simultaneously testing its effects across many clinical sites.

D. *Phase 4*: Following approval for marketing, drugs are monitored after approval to evaluate their long-term safety, efficacy, and optimal use. Phase 4 trials typically involve large patient populations. For instance, monitoring long-term safety and efficacy for cholesterol-lowering drugs in such trials would involve monitoring this parameter over a prolonged period.

Clinical trials are an integral component of drug development. They ensure that drugs are safe and effective before being approved for marketing. Clinical trials in pharmaceutical marketing must adhere to regulations and guidelines and present data ethically and accurately.

Closed Loop Marketing

Closed-loop marketing (CLM) is a marketing approach that gathers and uses data to form an efficient loop between marketing and sales efforts. Within the pharmaceutical industry, CLM typically involves using digital technologies to gather and analyze healthcare professionals' preferences to develop tailored marketing strategies.

Pharmaceutical companies use Closed Loop Marketing (CLM) strategies to develop targeted and effective marketing campaigns while improving sales and marketing initiatives. CLM collects information from various sources like electronic medical records (EMRs), customer relationship management (CRM) systems, website visits, social media engagement, etc., to formulate targeted and successful campaigns and drive increased sales/marketing initiatives.

CLM data collection enables pharmaceutical companies to create customized marketing messages and tailor communications directly for individual healthcare professionals, building stronger relationships between themselves and healthcare professionals, leading to increased sales and improved patient outcomes.

CLM offers healthcare professionals more than personalized marketing messages. It also provides timely information regarding new drugs, treatment options, and clinical research that helps establish trust and increase loyalty towards a certain brand or product.

CLM software can be an invaluable resource for pharmaceutical firms that wish to bolster their marketing and sales strategies and strengthen relationships with healthcare professionals. Firms using CLM can create targeted and personalized marketing strategies to increase conversions and prescriptions.

How CLM Works

Closed Loop Marketing (CLM) works through several steps:

1. *Gathering Data*: The initial step involves gathering data about healthcare professionals from multiple sources, such as electronic medical records (EMRs), customer relationship management systems (CRMs), or digital interactions, such as tablet detailing, website visits or social media engagement.
2. *Data Analysis*: Once data collection has taken place, it must be carefully examined to uncover patterns and trends to reveal healthcare professionals' interests, preferences, and behaviors, helping create more targeted and personalized marketing messages and campaigns that resonate with customers (HCPs).
3. *Personalization*: Pharmaceutical companies can use data analysis to develop targeted marketing messages for individual healthcare professionals, tailoring emails or websites to reflect each healthcare professional's interests and preferences.
4. *Communication*: Once a personalized marketing message has been developed, it must be communicated to healthcare professionals in various forms, such as emailing, calling, or even visiting them directly.
5. *Feedback*: As part of CLM, the final step entails gathering feedback on your marketing message and overall campaign. Taking this feedback into consideration can help refine future campaigns as well as refine future marketing strategies.

How CLM Can Assist Pharma Marketers

CLM offers many ways for pharmaceutical marketers to enhance their campaign effectiveness. Here are a few examples:

1. *Personalized Email Campaigns*: Pharmaceutical companies can leverage CLM data to craft tailored email campaigns for healthcare professionals. For instance, using data on the prescription history of specific physicians could enable pharmaceutical companies to recommend drugs and treatment options relevant to that healthcare professional's specialty or patient population.
2. *Targeted Digital Ads*: CLM's custom digital ads use data on healthcare professionals' visits and search histories to deliver relevant ads about new drugs or treatments that meet their criteria. For instance, this might involve serving them ads about specific treatments available.
3. *Remote Detailing*: In response to the COVID-19 Pandemic, pharmaceutical companies have increasingly turned to remote detailing to communicate with healthcare professionals. CLM can help pharmaceutical sales representatives customize these interactions by providing data on healthcare professionals' interests and preferences to sales representatives.
4. *Social Media Engagement*: Pharmaceutical companies can also use CLM to engage healthcare professionals on social media. For instance, using data gathered about an individual healthcare professional's social media activity as an indicator; pharmaceutical companies could deliver relevant updates regarding clinical research or new drugs that might interest these healthcare providers on a specific social network page.

CLM allows pharmaceutical companies to develop more targeted and effective marketing strategies by using data to personalize communications with healthcare professionals and deliver relevant information. As a result, they can increase sales while simultaneously improving patient outcomes by building stronger relationships through CLM.

Closing Techniques

Closing techniques in pharmaceutical marketing refer to strategies and tactics designed to persuade healthcare professionals (HCPs) to prescribe or recommend pharmaceutical products. For example, closing techniques may be employed during the final stages of sales presentations to secure a commitment from HCPs for product use or prescription.

Here are some popular closing techniques used in pharmaceutical marketing:

1. *Trail Close*: When conducting HCP visits, trial close techniques may include testing whether they're ready to commit by asking or providing statements such as, for instance, *Based on what I've told you, do you believe our product could be suitable for your patients?*
2. *Assumptive Close*: An assumptive close is a technique where a sales representative assumes that an HCP will prescribe or recommend their product, for instance, by asking, *When would you like to begin using our product with your patients?*

3. *Urgency Close*: An urgency close is a sales technique in which sales representatives create an atmosphere of urgency or scarcity to persuade HCPs to act quickly. For instance, they could say, *Our product is in high demand right now; therefore, if you want to secure your supply quickly, act now.*
4. *Benefit Close*: Benefit close is a sales technique whereby sales representatives use product benefits to emphasize how it will enhance patient outcomes; for instance, *Our product has been shown to enhance patient outcomes by decreasing symptoms and improving quality of life.*
5. *Negotiation Close*: Negotiation Close is a technique wherein sales representatives collaborate with healthcare practitioners (HCP) to come to an agreeable solution together; *for instance, if the cost of products is an issue for HCPs, we may be able to work together towards finding one that better suits their needs. For instance*: If the cost of our product is an issue for you, we may be able to work out something satisfactory.

Closing techniques aim to convince healthcare providers (HCPs) to prescribe or recommend pharmaceutical products. However, sales representatives must use such tactics ethically and responsibly, ensuring their pitches contain accurate and trustworthy information.

Cloud Computing

Cloud computing enables users to access computing resources, such as servers, storage space, and applications over the Internet instead of depending on local hardware and software. When used for pharmaceutical marketing campaigns, cloud computing offers numerous advantages:

1. *Scalability*: Cloud computing enables pharma companies to scale up dynamically, or down their computing resources as necessary without investing in costly infrastructure investments.
2. *Cost Savings*: Cloud computing can save costs for pharma companies. With cloud computing, pharmaceutical companies can reduce IT expenses by forgoing investments in acquiring, and maintaining hardware and software infrastructure.
3. *Collaboration*: Cloud computing enables easy collaboration among different teams and departments within a pharma company, external partners, and stakeholders.
4. *Data Management*: Cloud computing can offer secure and reliable storage and management for data, such as clinical trial results, drug development information, and marketing data.
5. *Analytics*: Cloud computing enables pharmaceutical companies to leverage advanced analytics and machine learning tools for data analysis to gain insights that inform marketing strategies and decision-making processes.

Cloud computing holds enormous promise to revolutionize pharma marketing by providing access to powerful computing resources and advanced analytics tools, giving companies access to cutting-edge resources and an edge. However, Pharma companies using cloud computing in their marketing activities must abide by relevant regulations and standards related to data protection and privacy when doing so.

Cluster Analysis

Cluster analysis is a statistical technique commonly utilized in pharmaceutical marketing that allows pharmaceutical companies to break customer populations down into distinct groups based on shared characteristics. This allows pharmaceutical firms to target specific customer segments with tailored marketing strategies and product offerings.

In pharmaceutical marketing, cluster analysis is used in many ways, such as the following:

A. *Customer Segmentation*: Cluster analysis can be leveraged in various forms of pharmaceutical marketing, including customer segmentation. By clustering customers based on demographic data, behavioral patterns, or any other factor, pharma companies can create different customer segments with distinct needs and preferences that allow them to tailor marketing messages and product offerings accordingly, increasing the chances of success in each one.

B. *Product Development*: Cluster analysis can also identify new product opportunities based on customer needs and preferences. By categorizing customers according to health conditions, treatment preferences, or other variables, pharmaceutical companies can create products tailored specifically to individual customer segments.

C. *Sales and Distribution*: Pharmaceutical companies can optimize their sales and distribution strategies by segmenting customers based on buying behaviors. For instance, this can enable them to identify who is more likely to buy online or prefer direct interactions with sales representatives.

Cluster analysis gives pharmaceutical marketers an effective tool for better understanding their customers and creating tailored marketing strategies that boost business success.

Clutter

Clutter in pharmaceutical marketing refers to excess information, messaging, and branding that overwhelm and confuse target audiences. Clutter can make it more difficult for patients and healthcare providers to access relevant healthcare products and services information they require for informed decisions about healthcare products and services. Below are examples of clutter in pharma marketing:

1. *Overly Complex Product Messaging*: Pharma companies often seek to differentiate their products through complex features and benefits that stand out. Unfortunately, this often leads to confusing messaging, making it hard for patients and healthcare providers to comprehend.
2. *Overuse of Branding*: Pharma companies may overdo their branding in marketing materials, resulting in unnecessary visual noise that detracts from messaging. This may involve large logos, multiple brand colors, or taglines that don't pertain directly to the product being advertised.
3. *Information Overload*: Pharma companies may include too much information that makes it hard for patients and healthcare providers to locate what they require. This includes lengthy product descriptions, complex dosing instructions, and legal disclaimers that do not apply directly.
4. *Multiple Marketing Channels*: Pharmaceutical companies may employ multiple channels for their marketing initiatives, including television, print media, digital platforms, and social media, which may confuse target audiences and cause unnecessary repetition of messaging.

Declutter Your Communication

Here are a few strategies pharma companies can employ to manage clutter in their marketing communications:

1. *Focus on the Core Message*: Companies should pay special attention to communicating the core message they want to their target audience. They should clearly outline their product's benefits and communicate them as effectively and concisely as possible.
2. *Use Clear and Straightforward Language*: Companies should utilize clear and direct language when explaining the features and benefits of their product to patients and healthcare providers alike, making messaging more accessible. This approach may make their messages easier for individuals to comprehend as well.
3. *Prioritize Information*: Companies should prioritize the essential details for patients and healthcare providers. This will reduce clutter in marketing materials and make it simpler for target audiences to locate what they require.
4. *Employ Visuals Strategically*: Infographics and videos can effectively convey complex information clearly and succinctly, so companies should strategically utilize visuals like infographics and videos to break up dense text and make messaging more engaging.
5. *Streamline Branding*: Companies should streamline their branding to avoid overwhelming their target audience with multiple logos, brand colors, and taglines. A more focused branding approach may help to reduce clutter while developing an identifiable brand identity.
6. *Targeted Marketing*: Businesses should employ targeted marketing to target specific patient populations and healthcare providers, tailoring messaging according to each group's needs, and making messages more pertinent and engaging for all audiences. This approach can reduce clutter while making communication more meaningful and engaging for patients and healthcare providers.

Clutter in pharmaceutical marketing can have serious repercussions for companies and target audiences. Patients and healthcare providers may become disoriented by unfocused messaging, leading to frustration or distrust of products or brands. Companies should instead prioritize clear and concise messaging relevant to target audiences to reduce clutter in pharma marketing; prioritize important patient/healthcare provider information in branding and marketing channels carefully without overwhelming target audiences.

Co-creation

Co-creation is an interactive, collaborative process in which individuals or groups work together on developing something new with customers, employees, stakeholders, and other relevant parties, typically products, services, or solutions through active input from them all.

Co-creation has become essential to pharmaceutical marketing, helping pharmaceutical companies meet healthcare providers' and patients' needs and preferences more closely.

Pharma companies can use co-creation to gather feedback from healthcare professionals and patients regarding their products and services, then use this insight to enhance them. For instance, pharmaceutical companies could involve patients when developing educational materials or patient support programs to ensure they are engaging and effective.

Co-creation can also assist pharmaceutical companies with deepening relationships with healthcare professionals and patients by including them in product design processes, engaging them, giving them a voice, building trust, increasing engagement, and ultimately leading to improved health outcomes.

Co-creation can help pharmaceutical companies develop more effective and relevant strategies, products, and services while strengthening relationships with healthcare professionals and patients.

Opportunities for Co-creation in Pharma

Here are a few examples of co-creation in pharmaceutical marketing:

1. *Patient-centered Co-creation*: Pharma companies may partner with patient advocacy groups to co-create an appropriate patient support program for specific diseases. Patients can provide insights into their experiences with the disease while outlining what kind of support they require from the program, enabling pharma companies to tailor it specifically for their needs and preferences.
2. *Collaborative Product Development*: Pharma companies may collaborate with healthcare professionals to co-design a medical device or medication. Healthcare professionals can offer valuable feedback regarding its design and usability to ensure it fulfills patients' needs while being effective enough for treatment.
3. *Co-creation of Educational Materials*: Pharma companies may partner with healthcare professionals and patients to co-create educational materials like brochures, videos, or websites providing information about specific diseases or treatments. Professionals will review these documents to make sure the data provided is relevant, while patients will provide feedback about the usability and readability of these resources.
4. *Co-creation of Clinical Trial Design*: Pharma companies may involve patients and healthcare professionals in co-creating clinical trial designs. Patients can offer feedback regarding inclusion criteria and patient burden to ensure the trial meets patient needs. At the same time, healthcare providers can use patient input to tailor trials that fit within their practice or meet patient expectations.

Co-creation can be applied in pharmaceutical marketing in numerous ways; the possibilities are virtually limitless, and the key is engaging all relevant stakeholders to meet their needs and preferences.

Co-creation in Pharma: Examples

Here are a few examples of pharmaceutical companies co-creating:

1. Novo Nordisk collaborated with patients, healthcare professionals, and patient advocacy groups to co-design *NovoPen Echo*, an insulin pen designed to be small, easy to use, and discreet, utilizing input from patients and healthcare providers regarding design and usability.
2. Sanofi joined with patient advocacy groups and healthcare professionals to co-develop the *GoMeals App*, which helps those living with diabetes track their meals and blood glucose levels. Patients and healthcare providers were involved in designing this solution to ensure it met all their needs and preferences.
3. AstraZeneca joined forces with patients and healthcare professionals to co-develop *HealthyMinds Clinical Trial Platform*. The aim was to make it simpler for participants to enroll in trials for mental health conditions with input from both parties on its design and functionality.
4. Roche co-created the *Patient Partner Program* to engage patients in drug development processes and solicit feedback on drug development plans, clinical trial designs, patient information materials, and more. Their feedback ensures that the medications developed are relevant and effective for patients.

Co-development

Co-development is an iterative process in which two or more parties collaborate to develop a product, service, or technology. Co-developing involves sharing resources, knowledge, and expertise towards reaching one common goal— usually between companies, research institutes, or universities.

Co-development combines the strengths and abilities of each partner to produce products or technologies that exceed what either could have accomplished on its own, leading to faster development times, reduced costs, and enhanced innovation, saving both parties money along the way. Both sides can benefit from this approach.

Co-development can also help pharmaceutical marketers develop more successful marketing strategies, products, and services that resonate with target audiences. Co-development typically entails working closely with external partners, such as healthcare professionals, patient advocacy groups, marketing agencies, etc., to devise solutions that meet patient and healthcare provider preferences and needs.

Here are a few examples of co-development in pharmaceutical marketing:

1. *Co-Development of Patient Education Materials*: Pharmaceutical companies may collaborate with patient advocacy groups or healthcare professionals to co-develop patient education materials like brochures or videos that inform about specific diseases or treatments, with partners providing insight into what information patients require and how it should be presented.
2. *Co-Developing Digital Marketing Strategies*: Pharma companies may collaborate with marketing agencies to co-develop a digital marketing strategy geared toward healthcare professionals or patients. Working in tandem, both partners can produce engaging content and campaigns to reach their target audiences effectively.
3. *Co-development of Patient Support Programs*: Pharma companies may collaborate with patient advocacy groups or healthcare professionals to co-develop patient support programs that offer resources and assistance for those suffering from specific diseases. Partners can share insight into what patients need help with and any programs that would most assist.
4. *Co-creating Clinical Trial Recruitment Strategies*: Pharma companies may join patient advocacy groups or healthcare professionals to co-develop recruitment strategies targeting patients suffering from specific diseases. Partner organizations can collaborate to determine the most efficient methods of reaching prospective participants while ensuring the trial design remains patient-centric.

Co-Development in Pharma: Some Examples

Here are examples of pharmaceutical companies working collaboratively with external partners to co-develop innovative products, services, and technologies to increase patient outcomes while speeding up drug development.

1. Pfizer collaborated with IBM Watson Health on co-developing *Watson for Clinical Trial Matching*. This artificial intelligence-powered matching platform quickly matches eligible patients to clinical trials to reduce development times and costs.
2. GlaxoSmithKline (GSK) and Verily Life Sciences, an affiliate of Alphabet which owns Google, recently formed *Galvani Bioelectronics* as a joint venture to co-develop bioelectronic medicines. Bioelectronic medicines use electrical signals to stimulate natural bodily processes to treat diseases; GSK and Verily have come together to utilize this strategy and find innovative treatments using this approach.
3. Sanofi and Google collaborated to co-develop an artificial intelligence-powered innovation lab called *Onduo* that utilizes machine learning algorithms to analyze patient data and discover new targets for drug development, aiming to speed up drug discovery processes and improve patient outcomes.
4. Novartis and Qualcomm created a joint venture to co-develop mobile health solutions for those with asthma and other respiratory diseases. Novartis and Qualcomm aim to combine their expertise in respiratory medicine and wireless technology to develop tools to assist individuals in more easily managing their conditions while increasing their quality of life.

These are examples of pharmaceutical companies working collaboratively with external partners to co-develop innovative products, services, and technologies to increase patient outcomes while speeding up drug development.

Cognitive Dissonance

American social psychologist Leon Festinger first proposed cognitive dissonance at the beginning of the 1950s. Cognitive dissonance describes psychological discomfort experienced when encountering information that conflicts with their beliefs or values. For example, cognitive dissonance might arise when patients or healthcare professionals come across information that challenges their opinions about a certain drug or treatment option.

Healthcare professionals may experience cognitive dissonance when prescribing certain drugs to their patients based on the belief they provide optimal treatments, yet come across new evidence suggesting another medication could be more effective. Furthermore, patients taking certain medicines for an extended period can feel uncomfortable when new information suggests potential side effects or reduced effectiveness compared to what was thought previously.

Pharmaceutical companies frequently utilize marketing strategies to address cognitive dissonance among patients and healthcare professionals. For instance, pharmaceutical companies might employ social proof by emphasizing testimonials or case studies from other users with positive experiences with a drug; or use scientific data as proof of efficacy and safety, providing education or information regarding its benefits.

How Pharma Address Cognitive Dissonance

Pharmaceutical companies often employ one or more of the following approaches to combat cognitive dissonance among their patients and healthcare professionals:

1. *Education and Information*: Pharmaceutical companies often provide education and information to patients and HCPs regarding specific drugs to address any queries or concerns about potential side effects or risks of taking certain medications. A company could, for example, distribute patient education materials that outline both benefits and potential risks of each medicine in clear language.
2. *Scientific Evidence*: Pharma companies often present scientific evidence supporting their drugs' efficacy and safety, such as clinical trial results or studies conducted to investigate its mechanism of action, for instance, providing details about its actions within the body and the specific conditions they're used to treat.
3. *Social Proof*: Pharma companies may employ social proof to combat cognitive dissonance by featuring testimonials or case studies of patients or healthcare professionals who have had positive experiences with the drug. For instance, they could post patient or physician stories or testimonials in marketing materials and websites.
4. *Comparison Marketing*: Pharmaceutical companies may use comparison marketing to address cognitive dissonance by emphasizing how their drug compares with competitors regarding efficacy, safety, and side effects. A company could, for example, display side-by-side comparisons of their drug and competing medications to emphasize its advantages over the latter.
5. *Patient Support Programs*: Pharma companies may offer patient support programs to alleviate cognitive dissonance by offering extra resources and assistance to manage their condition more easily. For instance, they might offer access to a nurse hotline or other support services to assist their patients in navigating treatment options and managing potential side effects more easily.

Pharmaceutical companies may employ various strategies to combat cognitive dissonance among their target patients and healthcare professionals, offering accurate information that informs treatment decisions while diminishing cognitive dissonance.

Pharmaceutical companies must abide by ethical marketing practices when developing marketing strategies and avoid providing misleading or incorrect information that leads to cognitive dissonance. By being honest and providing accurate details, pharmaceutical companies can assist patients and healthcare professionals in making more informed decisions and reduce cognitive dissonance.

Collaboration

Collaboration is a core strategy in pharmaceutical marketing, helping companies establish themselves as market leaders while building meaningful relationships with patients, healthcare professionals, and other stakeholder groups such as healthcare organizations. Here are some examples of collaboration in pharma marketing:

1. *Partnership with Patient Advocacy Groups*: Pharmaceutical companies can leverage partnerships with patient advocacy groups to gain greater insight into patient needs and develop products to meet them more accurately. Companies may build patient trust through such efforts while improving overall patient outcomes.
2. *Working with Healthcare Professionals*: Engaging healthcare professionals like physicians, nurses, and pharmacists as partners on pharmaceuticals and treatments can foster relationships built upon trust and credibility, which will enhance product adoption rates and raise patient awareness of products offered by your company.
3. *Collaboration With Academic Institutions*: Pharmaceutical companies can reap many advantages by working with academic institutions like universities and research centers to remain at the cutting edge of scientific research and innovation, leading to new products or treatments designed specifically to benefit patients.

4. *Joint Ventures and Partnerships*: Joining forces with other pharmaceutical firms can allow pharmaceutical firms to pool resources and expertise, create new products faster or expand existing ones into new markets more easily while sharing risks more evenly for product development.
5. *Social Media Collaborations*: Pharmaceutical companies can tap the influencer or patient community on social media as partners to extend their reach further while building stronger brand relations directly and indirectly with patients and healthcare professionals alike.

Collaboration can be an invaluable asset in pharmaceutical marketing, helping companies foster relationships with stakeholders, expediting product adoption rates while staying at the cutting edge of scientific research and innovation.

Collaborative Research

Collaborative research in pharmaceutical marketing refers to partnerships among pharmaceutical companies and organizations, such as academic institutions or healthcare providers, that engage in joint studies regarding marketing strategies for pharmaceutical products. The objective is to find effective means of promoting and selling these drugs while guaranteeing patient safety and efficacy.

Collaborative research in pharmaceutical marketing encompasses various activities, such as market research, clinical trials, and health outcomes studies. For instance, pharmaceutical companies might partner with academic institutions or healthcare providers in conducting market research about patient preferences for different medications or clinical trials to test new ones. Benefits associated with collaborative research in pharma marketing could include the following:

1. *Enhance Understanding of Patient Needs*: Collaborative research can assist pharmaceutical companies in better comprehending patient preferences and needs, allowing them to create more efficient marketing strategies and products.
2. *Enhanced Credibility*: Partnering with respected institutions can give pharmaceutical companies and products greater credibility with healthcare providers and patients, further cementing their standing within healthcare environments.
3. *Access to Expertise and Resources*: Collaboration can open access to expertise and resources. Pharmaceutical companies collaborating with academic institutions or healthcare providers may gain access to expertise and resources they might not possess independently.
4. *Faster Product Development*: Collaborative research can assist pharmaceutical companies in speeding the development and commercialization of new products that benefit both themselves and those they might help, including patients.

However, collaborative research in pharmaceutical marketing does have its share of challenges. Some may include:

1. *Conflict of Interests*: Working with external organizations could result in potential conflicts of interest if those organizations hold financial vests in your research project's outcome.
2. *Cooperating with External Organizations May Limit Research Outcomes*: Collaborating with external organizations can sometimes involve ceding some control of research processes and outcomes to third parties, which can be problematic for pharmaceutical companies.
3. *Differences in Goals and Priorities*: Organizations participating in research may have conflicting goals and priorities, which may cause tension during the research process.
4. *Intellectual Property Issues*: Collaboration can sometimes present unique legal issues regarding intellectual property ownership and management for research results produced due to collaboration, particularly if this research creates new products or technologies through development.

Collaborative research can be an invaluable asset to pharmaceutical companies seeking greater insight into patient needs and creating more efficient marketing strategies. Still, companies must carefully evaluate potential benefits and risks before entering such partnerships.

Collaborative Research in Pharma: Some Examples

Here are a few examples of collaborative research in pharmaceutical marketing:

1. *Novartis and University of Pennsylvania Partnership*: Novartis collaborated with the University of Pennsylvania to study personalized cancer therapies using genetic biomarkers tailored specifically for individuals, allowing Novartis to devise more efficient marketing strategies for its cancer drugs.

2. *Pfizer and Mayo Clinic* collaborated in exploring innovative therapies for cardiovascular disease through clinical trials that assessed safety and efficacy. Their joint efforts helped Pfizer utilize research findings for more efficient marketing of its cardiovascular drugs.
3. *GlaxoSmithKline and the National Institutes of Health*: GlaxoSmithKline and the NIH joined forces in researching new therapies for HIV/AIDS patients through clinical trials which assessed both safety and effectiveness, in addition to helping GlaxoSmithKline create more successful marketing campaigns for its HIV/AIDS drugs.
4. *Collaboration Between Sanofi and Academic Institutions*: Sanofi joined with academic institutions to study diabetes management. As part of their partnership, mobile health platforms were developed to assist those living with the condition in managing it effectively. At the same time, Sanofi leveraged research findings to more efficiently market its diabetes treatments.
5. *Merck and Healthcare Providers Join Force*: Merck has collaborated with healthcare providers to find an anticancer vaccine against certain forms of cancer. This partnership included clinical trials assessing its safety and effectiveness and patient education programs to promote vaccination. Furthermore, this research may help Merck create more effective marketing strategies for its cancer vaccines.

Color

Color psychology examines how different hues influence our emotions, behaviors, and perceptions. Recognizing these connections can be invaluable when creating successful marketing campaigns in pharmaceutical marketing. Here are some colors commonly used and their associated psychological effects:

1. *Blue*: Blue is an uplifting, trustworthy hue commonly employed in healthcare and pharmaceutical branding. This color conveys reliability, professionalism, and competence. Also, blue symbolizes cleanliness, which is crucial in healthcare industries such as hospitals.
2. *Green*: Green has long been associated with health, nature, and balance. It can signify that an item is natural, Eco-friendly, or ecologically conscious. Furthermore, its soothing qualities make it popular in pharmaceutical marketing campaigns and packing designs.
3. *Red* is an eye-catching color that draws our focus quickly, creating an immediate sense of urgency or excitement. Red also signifies warmth and passion, making it perfect for products that promise to awaken or stimulate.
4. *Yellow*: Yellow is widely associated with happiness and optimism, creating an inviting and cheerful ambiance, and make it the ideal hue to use when designing products to uplift and inspire.
5. *Purple*: Purple is an elegant, luxurious hue that connotes quality and exclusivity and creates an air of calm and serenity. It is ideal for products designed to help people unwind and unburden themselves from stress.
6. *White*: White has long been associated with cleanliness, purity, and simplicity— attributes that help create a sense of calm and clarity, making it a popular choice in packaging and advertising for healthcare providers.

Color plays an integral role in pharmaceutical marketing, as it can dramatically affect how people view medications and treatments. Here are some strategies pharmaceutical companies use color in their advertising:

1. *Branding*: Colors play an essential part in branding for pharmaceutical companies and their products, such as blue for conveying trustworthiness and professionalism, while green is often used to represent natural, healthy products.
2. *Packaging*: The color of medication packaging can also affect patient perception. Bright and bold hues could imply the medication is powerful and effective, while soft pastel hues or muted tones could convey gentler approaches.
3. *Advertising*: In pharmaceutical advertising, color can create specific moods or associations. For instance, bright hues like red and orange may evoke energy and excitement, while cool shades like blue and green evoke calmness and relaxation.
4. *Labels*: Medication labels utilize color to convey crucial patient information such as dosage and side effects. Warning labels often feature bright red text to grab patients' attention and highlight their significance.

Pharmaceutical companies have increasingly employed color in their marketing communications and materials. Here are a few examples that show how pharma companies utilize colors strategically in their communications to elicit emotional responses in target audiences and differentiate themselves from competitors by building strong brand identities that resonate with customers.

1. *Pfizer's Blue Branding*: Pfizer, a global pharmaceutical company, uses blue as its main brand color; this hue stands for trustworthiness, professionalism, and dependability— traits associated with business success. Pfizer uses blue as part of their marketing materials, such as websites, packaging, and advertisement campaigns, such as website header images.
2. *Burt's Bees Green Packaging*: Burt's Bees is known for using Eco-friendly packaging, showcasing their commitment to environmental responsibility and sustainable business practices. Their natural products come packaged in green that represents this dedication. Its use exemplifies how it pledges support of sustainability through commitment.
3. *Red Packaging by Excedrin*: Excedrin Migraine is a pain relief medication known for using red packaging to convey its effectiveness and power. Red symbolizes strength, energy, and excitement, corresponding to Excedrin's promise of providing fast and powerful relief.
4. *Yellow in Advertising by Cymbalta*: Cymbalta, an antidepressant medication prescribed to treat depression and anxiety, employs yellow as part of its advertising campaign to project happiness and optimism as part of its promise to enhance mood and quality of life. The use of yellow creates an optimistic and sunny tone to complement its promise.
5. *Lush's Purple Packaging*: Lush Cosmetics, specializing in handmade and natural products, uses purple packaging to evoke luxury and exclusivity. In addition, purple often connotes sophistication and creativity— characteristics that align perfectly with Lush's commitment to using high-quality ingredients ethically sourced.

By understanding the psychological impacts of different colors, pharma companies can strategically use color in their marketing campaigns to evoke specific emotional responses in their target audience. However, cultural and individual differences can impact how people perceive various hues. Therefore, pharma companies should consider this factor when planning campaigns.

Co-marketing

Co-marketing occurs when two or more businesses collaborate to jointly market one product or service, sharing resources, knowledge, and expertise to form an overall joint campaign that benefits everyone involved. This allows businesses to reach wider audiences while increasing brand recognition and sales.

Co-marketing in Pharma

Co-marketing can also be applied in the pharmaceutical industry to promote products or services. When applied this way, two or more pharmaceutical companies partner in co-marketing an offer, leveraging each other's strengths and expertise for an enhanced campaign. Co-marketing in pharma often includes working closely with healthcare providers, advocacy groups, or other entities to reach wider audiences while improving patient care. Here are a few examples of co-marketing within pharmaceuticals:

1. *Pharmaceutical Companies Can Join Forces to Co-Promote Drugs*: Pharmaceutical companies may collaborate to promote drugs that treat similar conditions. By creating a joint marketing campaign highlighting both medications' advantages, pharmaceutical firms can make an effective partnership for marketing them together and emphasizing each drug's specific features and benefits.
2. *Co-branded Educational Programs*: Pharma companies may partner with patient advocacy groups and healthcare professionals to co-develop educational programs promoting disease awareness and patient education. These partners can craft programs tailored specifically for patients and healthcare providers by pooling their expertise.
3. *Co-sponsored Medical Conferences*: Pharma companies may collaborate to co-sponsor healthcare professional conferences. Companies working together can increase the reach and impact of an event while creating more opportunities to showcase products and services.
4. Co-*Marketing with Medical Devices*: Medical device firms may collaborate with pharmaceutical firms in co-marketing their products. For instance, one such partnership might include one whereby one produces medical devices used with medication produced by another firm so both companies could create an integrated marketing campaign that promotes the benefits of both products together.

Co-marketing in pharma can be a very beneficial way for pharmaceutical companies to expand their audience reach, improve patient care and increase sales. In addition, pharmaceutical firms can leverage each party's strengths for more impactful and successful marketing campaigns by working collaboratively with external partners.

Co-marketing in Pharma: Examples and Practices

Here are some examples of co-marketing within the pharmaceutical industry:

1. Pfizer and Bristol-Myers Squibb have collaborated to co-market Eliquis (Apixaban). Leveraging sales teams to promote the medication to healthcare professionals and creating an impressive marketing campaign highlighting its advantages over competing blood thinners, Pfizer and Bristol-Myers Squibb collaborated to co-market Eliquis (Apixaban).
2. Sanofi and Regeneron joined forces to co-market Dupixent (Dupilumab), an anti-eczema medication. Together they organized a joint marketing campaign featuring TV commercials, social media ads, targeted outreach to dermatologists and other healthcare providers, etc.
3. AstraZeneca and Bristol-Myers Squibb joined forces to co-market Onglyza (Saxagliptin), an oral diabetes medication. In addition, both companies conducted a joint marketing campaign highlighting its benefits as a blood sugar control solution.
4. Novartis and Eli Lilly collaborated to co-market Effient (Prasugrel), an anticoagulant medication used to prevent blood clots among heart disease patients. Furthermore, both companies launched a joint marketing campaign highlighting its advantages relative to other blood thinners while targeting healthcare practitioners treating such cases of heart disease.
5. GlaxoSmithKline and Merck announced an exclusive co-marketing agreement to market Cervarix and Gardasil HPV vaccines jointly, along with an integrated marketing campaign designed to raise awareness among young adults while increasing vaccination rates.

By joining forces with other businesses or organizations, pharma firms can harness each partner's strength for an impactful marketing effort.

Commoditization

Commoditization in pharmaceutical marketing refers to consumers viewing pharmaceutical products as interchangeable commodities with little distinction among competing brands regarding perceived benefits or value. This phenomenon often arises when markets become saturated with similar products or industries lack innovation. When this occurs, pharmaceutical companies may struggle to differentiate their offerings and be forced to compete mostly on price, leading to a race to the bottom in pricing, whereby competitors try to undercut each other for market share; unfortunately, this could also lead to decreased profitability and the loss of market share for certain companies.

One example of commoditization in pharmaceutical marketing is the market for generic drugs. Generic drugs are copies of brand-name products with similar active ingredients, dosage, and strength but sold at reduced costs. Therefore, consumers may view generic alternatives as interchangeable with brand-name versions and may choose the cheaper option without considering other factors like brand loyalty or perceived quality.

Pharmaceutical companies can combat commoditization by creating unique product offerings or value-added services that differentiate their offerings from competitors. This may involve investing in research and development efforts for creating drugs with unique benefits or providing additional services such as patient education or support services. Likewise, branding and marketing strategies may help create strong brand identities among customers that resonate strongly.

Company Culture

Company culture in pharma marketing refers to the collective values, beliefs, practices, and attitudes shared among employees that influence employee behaviors and shape the working environment within pharmaceutical marketing companies. Culture can tremendously affect the success of pharmaceutical companies, whether attracting top talent, encouraging innovation, or reaching business goals.

Here are some common elements of company culture in pharma marketing:

1. *Compliance and Ethical Behavior*: As part of its company culture in pharma marketing, companies must uphold stringent compliance with regulations. All employees are part of an effective compliance and ethics culture and should understand and abide by them.
2. *Innovation and Creativity*: With pharmaceutical industries constantly innovating and changing, businesses must foster an atmosphere that fosters innovation and creativity to remain at the cutting edge. An environment encouraging risk-taking could result in new products or marketing strategies that give your company a leg up on competitors.

3. *Collaboration and Teamwork*: Pharmaceutical marketing often includes cross-functional teams consisting of Medical and legal, regulatory (MLR), and marketing experts. A culture that fosters teamwork can facilitate better communication, faster decision-making processes, and more effective marketing campaigns.
4. *Customer Focus*: At the heart of it all lies the pharma marketing company's success in meeting customers' needs, including healthcare providers, patients, or payers. An organizational culture that prioritizes customer needs can result in better knowledge about individual customer preferences, leading to more successful marketing campaigns overall.
5. *Diversity, Equity, and Inclusion*: Diverse workplace environments can foster better decision-making processes, greater innovation, and improved employee engagement. Cultivating such environments also attracts and retains top talent with different backgrounds and perspectives, which are vital advantages in any competitive marketplace.

Effective company culture in pharmaceutical marketing is essential to success in an increasingly regulated environment. Cultivating a company culture that values compliance, innovation, collaboration, customer focus, and diversity and inclusion, companies can foster an environment that attracts top talent while driving business success.

Companion Diagnostics

Companion diagnostics are medical tests combined with a particular therapeutic product to assess whether it will benefit an individual. When applied in the pharmaceutical industry, companion diagnostics can serve as an invaluable marketing tool and promote certain drugs if validated as reliable predictors of response to that drug.

Pharmaceutical companies using companion diagnostics can quickly identify patients likely to benefit from their product and target their marketing efforts more effectively, leading to higher sales and revenue and improved patient outcomes.

Pharmaceutical companies can use companion diagnostics to differentiate their products from competitors, particularly if theirs provides distinct advantages over similar offerings.

As with all marketing practices, companion diagnostics used in pharmaceutical marketing must be used responsibly and with patient welfare in mind. Companies should avoid marketing products based on results of non-validated companion diagnostics, using companion diagnostics to overstate efficacy, or making unsupported claims about benefits.

Companion Diagnostics in Pharma Marketing: Examples

Below are a few examples of companion diagnostics' use in pharmaceutical marketing:

A. *Testing for Herceptin (Trastuzumab) in Breast Cancer*: Herceptin, designed to target HER-2 receptors, has proven successful against approximately 20% of breast cancer cases. Therefore, a companion diagnostic test has been implemented to ascertain which patients would qualify for Herceptin treatment and determine who is eligible for its use as a breast cancer therapy solution. Its success can be directly tied to this feature of its formulation as a cancer therapy option.

B. *BRAF Testing in Melanoma*: Zelboraf (Vemurafenib) targets a specific mutation of the BRAF gene found in about 50 percent of cases, making its companion diagnostic test essential in targeting those most likely to benefit from the treatment of melanoma with Zelboraf. By doing this, its manufacturer was able to effectively target patients who could best utilize its effectiveness against melanoma patients.

C. *Testing EGFR Gene in Non-Small Cell Lung Cancer*: Tarceva (Erlotnib) targets a specific mutation found in 10-15% of non-small cell lung cancer cases; its companion diagnostic test determines if an individual's tumor carries this mutation and thus qualifies for treatment with Tarceva. By employing this companion diagnostic, Tarceva's manufacturer was able to pinpoint those lung cancer patients most likely to benefit from taking this drug.

These are only a few examples of companion diagnostics in pharmaceutical marketing. Each time, they enabled drug manufacturers to target only those patients likely to benefit most from taking medicine, thus improving patient outcomes while increasing sales for themselves.

Comparative Advantage

Comparative advantage is an economic principle, which in simple terms, means that when different entities focus on producing the goods or services they can produce more efficiently (with lower costs or resources) and then trade with others who specialize in different goods or services, all parties can gain. It is based on the idea that by specializing in what they are relatively better at, entities can increase overall production and benefit from a diverse range of products and services available through trade.

Comparative Advantage in Pharma Marketing

Pharmaceutical marketing may offer comparative advantages due to various factors, including research and development capabilities, manufacturing capacity, marketing expertise, regulatory experience, and distribution networks. Companies with one or more advantages could use those advantages strategically during drug development and promotion activities, increasing profitability while growing market share.

Pharmaceutical companies with exceptional research and development capacities could create groundbreaking medicines to address medical needs that currently go unfulfilled. In contrast, those with strong manufacturing capacities might specialize in producing generic versions of existing medications at reduced costs.

Comparative advantage can also assist companies in devising global marketing strategies, utilizing their unique strengths to compete effectively across different regions and markets. For instance, an organization skilled at navigating regulatory environments in emerging markets might expand operations there.

Here are a few examples that demonstrate how pharmaceutical companies capitalize on their comparative advantage:

1. *Research and Development*: Pharmaceutical companies specializing in research and development specialize in creating new drugs to address unmet medical needs, thus offering their comparative advantage to competitors in this space. For instance, Roche subsidiary Genentech stands out in cancer research and development; their teams have created many effective cancer drugs.
2. *Manufacturing Capabilities*: Pharmaceutical companies with robust manufacturing capacities may specialize in producing generic versions of existing drugs for lower costs. Teva Pharmaceuticals stands out as an example of such an enterprise; Teva is considered an innovator in generics production.
3. *Marketing*: Pharmaceutical companies with superior marketing expertise may create engaging campaigns to reach patients and healthcare professionals. Pfizer has a considerable comparative advantage and has successfully promoted several blockbuster medications like Lipitor and Viagra over time.
4. *Regulatory Know-How*: Pharmaceutical companies with expertise in navigating regulatory landscapes could focus their expansion in emerging markets like China and India, using this expertise as a comparative advantage to expand operations successfully. Novartis boasts such expertise, having successfully expanded in countries like these.
5. *Distribution Networks*: Pharmaceutical companies with strong distribution networks may seek to expand their reach in various regions and markets worldwide. Johnson & Johnson boasts an unmatched comparative advantage in distribution and has successfully expanded operations into emerging markets worldwide.

Comparative advantage can play an instrumental role in shaping pharmaceutical companies' marketing strategies, helping them identify their areas of strength and potentially leading to greater success.

Compliance

Compliance in pharmaceutical marketing refers to adhering to legal and ethical regulations when marketing pharmaceutical products. The pharmaceutical industry must abide by numerous regulations and guidelines designed to ensure marketing practices are transparent and accurate and do not mislead healthcare professionals or members of the general public. Compliance plays an essential role in maintaining its integrity while guaranteeing patient safety. Here are some key aspects of compliance in pharma marketing:

1. *Regulatory Framework*: Pharmaceutical marketing is subject to various rules and guidelines that vary between countries. For instance, the Food and Drug Administration (FDA) oversees pharmaceutical advertising through the Federal Food, Drug, and Cosmetic Act in the US. Pharmaceutical companies must understand and abide by any local or regional requirements when marketing pharmaceutical products.
2. *Fair and Balanced Communication*: Pharmaceutical marketing must provide accurate, objective information that supports its products' efficacy, safety, or benefits objectively and transparently. Any claims about them that exaggerate these features must be avoided to preserve fair competition with similar offerings

from competitors, and approval by regulatory authorities is critical to product launches.

3. *Promotion to Healthcare Professionals*: Marketing activities targeting healthcare professionals such as doctors and pharmacists should be carried out ethically, providing objective information without conflicts of interest or sponsor arrangements that could influence prescribing or dispensing medication decisions.
4. *Direct-to-consumer (DTC) Advertising*: While some countries allow direct-to-consumer (DTC) advertisements of pharmaceutical products, others impose restrictions or bans. When DTC ads are allowed, pharmaceutical companies must adhere to certain guidelines regarding content presentation and disclosure that ensure they provide accurate and not misleading information to their audience.
5. *Adverse Event Reporting*: Pharmaceutical companies must promptly and accurately report any adverse reactions to their medications to monitor safety and efficacy, and take corrective actions if needed. Adverse event reporting serves the crucial purpose of monitoring safety and efficacy while taking necessary actions if required.
6. *Internal Compliance Programs*: Pharmaceutical companies should create comprehensive compliance programs to ensure they abide by applicable regulations and guidelines, with training, monitoring, auditing, and reviewing marketing activities to identify possible compliance concerns that could lead to compliance violations.

Noncompliance with pharmaceutical marketing regulations can have serious repercussions, including legal penalties and the erosion of public trust. Therefore, pharmaceutical companies must prioritize compliance and embrace ethical marketing practices to safeguard patient safety while upholding industry integrity.

Competition

Competition in the pharmaceutical industry refers to the rivalry and contest between pharmaceutical companies operating in the same market or therapeutic area. It encompasses various aspects of competition, including research and development, intellectual property, pricing and market access, marketing and promotion, regulatory compliance, global expansion, technological advancements, generics and biosimilars, and collaboration. Pharmaceutical companies compete to gain a competitive advantage by developing innovative drugs, securing patents, pricing their products competitively, accessing markets, effectively promoting their drugs, complying with regulations, expanding into new territories, adopting advanced technologies, and forming strategic partnerships. Competition within the pharmaceutical industry strives to capture market share, generate revenues, and enhance patient health outcomes with safe and effective medicines that improve outcomes.

Key Aspects

Competition in the pharmaceutical industry is intense and dynamic. Here are several key aspects of competition within this industry:

1. *Research and development (R&D)*: Pharmaceutical companies invest heavily in R&D efforts to discover and create new drugs, with competition among them for creating innovative and effective remedies to treat various conditions or illnesses. Companies strive to be the first to market with breakthrough therapies, which can lead to significant market advantages.
2. *Intellectual Property*: Patents play a central role in the pharmaceutical industry. Companies file patents to secure their drug discoveries and gain the exclusive right to manufacture and market these medications over an agreed-upon time frame. Competition often involves challenges to existing patents and the development of generic versions of drugs after patent expiration.
3. *Pricing and Market Access*: Pharmaceutical companies face competition in pricing their products and gaining market access. This includes negotiations with health insurance providers, government healthcare agencies, and other stakeholders to ensure their drugs are included in reimbursement lists and formularies. Price competition can be fierce, especially when multiple companies offer similar drugs or generics.
4. *Marketing and Promotion*: Companies compete to promote their drugs to healthcare professionals, hospitals, and patients. Marketing strategies such as direct-to-consumer ads, physician engagement programs, and educational initiatives can give companies an advantage and increase market share.
5. *Mergers and Acquisitions*: Pharmaceutical companies have undertaken mergers and acquisitions to strengthen their portfolios, expand market presence or gain access to cutting-edge technologies. Many deals involve mergers aimed at increasing R&D capabilities, broadening distribution networks, or tapping

new markets — often seeking competitive advantages through these deals.

6. *Regulatory Environment*: Compliance with strict regulatory requirements is crucial for pharmaceutical companies. The competition includes obtaining approvals from regulatory authorities for clinical trials and drug registrations. The speed and efficiency of navigating regulatory processes can impact a company's competitive position.
7. *Global Expansion*: Many pharmaceutical companies strive to expand into international markets to tap into growing demand and increase their customer base. Competing in diverse markets requires understanding local regulations, healthcare systems, and cultural differences and tailoring strategies accordingly.
8. *Technological Advancements*: Integrating technology and data analytics is transforming the pharmaceutical industry. Companies compete to adopt advanced technologies for drug discovery, clinical trials, manufacturing processes, and supply chain management. Artificial intelligence, machine learning, and genomics are among the prevalent areas of competition.
9. *Biosimilars and Generics*: When patents expire, pharmaceutical companies face competition from manufacturers producing generic versions of drugs or biosimilars (similar versions of biological drugs). This leads to price competition and market share battles, as multiple companies may offer interchangeable products. Additionally, marketing strategies such as direct-to-consumer ads, physician engagement programs, and educational initiatives can help companies expand their market share.

Competitive Advantage

Competitive advantage in pharmaceutical marketing refers to a company's ability to offer products or services with a superior value proposition for its customers compared to its rivals. Here are some examples of such advantages in pharmaceutical marketing:

1. *Patent Protection*: Companies with strong patent portfolios for innovative drugs enjoy an advantage in competing therapeutic areas, like the Hepatitis C drug Sovaldi by Gilead Sciences, which holds its patent protection, helping it retain a competitive advantage within its marketplace.
2. *First-Mover Advantage*: Companies that launch new drugs first often enjoy an advantage in a particular therapeutic area. For instance, Pfizer's Viagra was approved as the first treatment for treating erectile dysfunction, giving Pfizer a significant competitive edge within this market.
3. *Clinical Efficacy*: Drugs that demonstrate superior clinical efficacy over other drugs in their category hold an edge in the market, such as Roche's cancer drug Herceptin's superior efficacy at treating HER2-positive breast cancer, giving it a competitive advantage against similar products.
4. *Strong Brand and Reputation in the Market*: Companies with strong brands and reputations enjoy an edge over competing businesses in their respective industries. For example, Johnson & Johnson enjoys strong brand recognition within healthcare, giving it a significant competitive advantage over other competitors in this marketplace.
5. *Pricing Strategy*: Companies with competitive drug pricing strategies gain an edge in the marketplace. Teva Pharmaceuticals stands out by providing cheaper generic medications than its rivals do, to create this competitive edge in generic pricing.

Companies can derive competitive edge from several sources, such as patent protection, clinical efficacy, branding strength, and first-mover advantage. Effective utilization of first-mover advantage and pricing advantage can all provide distinct competitive advantages that enable them to take a leading role in the marketplace and maintain it over time. Companies that master this art can establish themselves as market leaders while keeping an edge that lasts.

Competitive Analysis

The competitive analysis involves identifying your company's strengths and weaknesses relative to the competition and opportunities and threats that might help or harm its success. Understanding your industry's landscape and using that information to build a strategic plan is to gain a competitive edge.

Key Steps

Here are the key steps of competitive analysis:

1. *Identify and Analyze Your Competitors*: First, identify direct and indirect competitors to understand better their products/service offerings, market shares, target customers, etc.

2. *Gather Information*: Research competitors through various sources, such as their websites, social media profiles, press releases, industry reports, and customer reviews. Analyze their strengths, weaknesses, marketing, pricing, and sales tactics.
3. *Analyzing Competition*: Use SWOT (Strengths, Weaknesses, Opportunities, Threats) analysis to gain an in-depth knowledge of your competition's strengths and weaknesses to identify areas where you can distinguish yourself and areas that require improvement. This can assist with strategic differentiation and any areas that should be improved.
4. *Recognizing Opportunities and Threats in the Market*: Recognizing opportunities and threats within your target market that could aid or hamper the success of your business is essential to its long-term viability, such as consumer behavior shifts, new technologies emerging on the market, regulatory updates, or economic trends that might influence its success.
5. *Create a Strategy*: Once your analysis has concluded, develop a plan that takes advantage of opportunities while mitigating threats. This might involve changing pricing, marketing, or product development strategies to stay ahead of the competition.
6. *Monitor Your Competitors*: Stay abreast of competitors' activities to adjust your strategy appropriately. Monitor them frequently!

Competitive analysis is an integral component of business strategies and can help identify new opportunities, keep ahead of competitors and meet business goals.

Competitive Intelligence

Competitive intelligence is gathering and analyzing competitors' strengths, weaknesses, strategies, and performance to make informed business decisions. It involves monitoring markets, industry trends, and the activities of competitors, then using this knowledge to identify opportunities or threats and develop strategies to gain a competitive advantage over them.

Competitive intelligence helps businesses better understand their competitors and use that information to make smarter decisions. By keeping up with competitors' actions and performances, businesses can adjust strategies, create new products/services, or improve operations to stay ahead of the competition.

Competitive intelligence involves multiple techniques, including:

- Monitoring competitors' websites and financial reports.
- Attending industry conferences and trade shows.
- Conducting surveys or interviews with industry experts.
- Using social media monitoring tools.
- Gathering intelligence about competitors' strengths and weaknesses, marketing tactics used, and customer bases understood and anticipating market trends for future market projections.

The information gathered can provide vital clues into competitors' strengths and weaknesses and future market developments.

Competitive Intelligence in Pharma Marketing

Pharmaceutical marketers recognize the critical nature of competitive intelligence for success, particularly as companies must navigate complex regulatory environments, rapidly evolving technologies, and intense competition. Pharma marketers use competitive intelligence to gain information on competitors' products, sales strategies, and marketing tactics; gathering this intelligence enables them to develop more efficient marketing campaigns while creating a competitive advantage.

Pharmaceutical companies use competitive intelligence to:

1. *Understand Market Opportunities*: Companies can use competitive intelligence to identify untapped market opportunities, potential customers, and unmet needs in the competitive landscape.
2. *Develop Effective Marketing Strategies*: Competitive intelligence helps companies create effective marketing strategies to reach their target audience and stand out.
3. *Monitor Pricing and Promotions*: Companies can use competitive intelligence to monitor and respond to competitors' pricing and promotional activities, adapting their pricing strategies accordingly.
4. *Examine Clinical Trial Results*: Pharmaceutical companies use competitive intelligence to monitor their competitors' clinical trial results and assess how these could impact product development plans.
5. *Anticipate Regulatory Changes*: Competitive intelligence can assist businesses in staying aware of regulatory updates that could affect their products or marketing strategies.

Competitive intelligence is an indispensable resource in the pharmaceutical industry, helping companies to remain competitive and identify new opportunities while devising effective marketing strategies.

How Pharma Collects Competitive Intelligence

There are multiple strategies available for collecting competitive intelligence within pharmaceutical marketing. Here are some of them:

1. *Monitor Competitor Websites*: By monitoring competitor websites, you can gather intelligence regarding new product releases, features, and prices that compete against your product offerings.
2. *Analyze Market Reports*: Market research reports can offer invaluable insight into the pharmaceutical industry, providing market sizes, growth rates, and trends analysis from firms like Evaluate Pharma, IQVIA, and Pharma Intelligence, among others.
3. *Conduct Surveys and Interviews*: Surveys and interviews with industry experts, physicians, and patients can offer valuable insights into product effectiveness, patient needs, and unfulfilled requirements.
4. *Social Media Monitoring*: By monitoring social media, pharmaceutical companies can gain insights into what patients and healthcare providers think of various products or brands.
5. *Examine Financial Reports*: Examining competitors' financial reports can provide invaluable insight into revenue growth, R&D spending, profitability, and strategies your competition uses.

Pharma companies utilize traditional and modern approaches to gather competitive intelligence, including attending conferences, monitoring competitors' websites and social media, conducting surveys with physicians, patients, and industry experts, and interviewing these stakeholders in-person or by phone. Such insights help businesses make informed decisions and stay ahead of competitors.

Competitive intelligence gathering must be carried out ethically and legally. For instance, acquiring confidential information or trade secrets through unlawful means is illegal. Therefore, it is vital to focus on publicly available data instead of unethical methods of gathering intelligence.

Competitiveness

Competitiveness in pharmaceutical marketing refers to a company's ability to compete effectively by understanding the market landscape; identifying key competitors; creating strategic marketing plans with competitive advantages in mind, and devising marketing plans accordingly. Here are a few factors that contribute to competitiveness:

1. *Product Differentiation*: Offering innovative goods or services can give any business an advantage in the marketplace, such as creating innovative drugs, medical devices, or healthcare services that address unmet medical needs.
2. *Pricing*: Pricing is essential to pharmaceutical marketing as it determines a company's ability to attract and keep customers. Companies must find an equilibrium between making profits while keeping prices affordable for patients.
3. *Marketing Strategies*: Strategic marketing approaches are integral in pharmaceutical marketing, helping companies connect and engage with customers more effectively. These may involve devising targeted advertising campaigns, employing social media to reach patients directly, or partnering with patient advocacy groups.
4. *Regulatory Compliance*: The pharmaceutical industry is highly regulated, and companies must abide by various regulations and standards to operate efficiently. Companies that demonstrate their dedication to regulatory compliance will likely win patients' and healthcare providers' trust.
5. *Innovation*: Innovation is crucial to remaining competitive in pharmaceutical marketing, as it allows companies to outpace competitors by creating products and services to address evolving medical needs.

Pharmaceutical marketing relies heavily on competition in today's highly aggressive environment to be effective and successful. Companies can gain an edge and thrive by closely studying market conditions and competitors and creating successful marketing strategies.

Competitive Positioning

Competitive positioning involves identifying and analyzing how a company compares to its competitors regarding market share, target audience demographics, product offerings, pricing strategies, and other pertinent aspects. This requires understanding the strengths and weaknesses of a business relative to competitors to devise strategies that give an edge against them.

Competitive positioning seeks to distinguish a company's products or services from its rivals in an appealing manner for customers by targeting specific niche markets, emphasizing quality and performance, providing more value than its rivals, or any other means.

Companies can utilize competitive positioning analysis to make informed decisions regarding product development, marketing, pricing, and other key business areas. Doing so allows them to build stronger brands while increasing market share and customer retention.

Here are a few steps that will assist with conducting a competitive positioning analysis:

1. *Identification of Competitors in Your Target Market*: You must recognize competitors offering products or services similar to your target market. These direct competitors offer similar products or services directly as you, and indirect ones could be substitutes.
2. *Analyzing Competitors*: Once you've identified your competitors, the next step should be analyzing their strengths and weaknesses. When doing this, factors like market share, customer base, product offerings, pricing strategies, marketing plans, and distribution channels could all prove extremely helpful. Collecting this data through market research reports or online sources could prove especially advantageous.
3. *Uncover Your Unique Selling Proposition (USP)*: By researching competitors, identify your unique selling proposition (USP). Your USP should set your product or service apart, making them more appealing to customers, such as superior quality, lower prices, or offering unique features or benefits that set them apart.
4. *Develop a Competitive Strategy*: With your newly acquired information, devise a competitive strategy to give your company an edge against its rivals. This could involve targeting niche markets, improving product quality or pricing strategies, or building stronger brand recognition.
5. *Monitor and Adjust Your Strategy*: Competitive positioning is a continuous process, so keeping an eye on competitors and the market as a whole is important for maintaining an edge over your competition. Be ready to make necessary changes to keep an edge over them and maintain your advantage.

Remember that competitive positioning is an ongoing process that requires constant examination and adjustment. By staying vigilant about focusing on your unique selling proposition (USP), you can stay ahead of competitors and build a successful business.

Competitive Positioning in Pharma

Positioning is a cornerstone of pharma marketing, as it helps companies differentiate their products or services from rivals and gain an edge. Here are the steps involved in creating a competitive positioning strategy in pharma marketing:

1. *Identify Your Target Customers*: The initial step in developing a competitive positioning strategy is identifying your company's ideal customers for its products or services. This may involve targeting specific patient demographics, healthcare providers, or key stakeholders as your audience.
2. *Evaluate Competition*: The next step is to evaluate the competition to identify its strengths and weaknesses, such as products, pricing strategies, marketing tactics, or other relevant factors. This may involve studying their products, pricing strategies, marketing tactics, and other relevant considerations.
3. *Create a Unique Value Proposition*: By conducting a thorough analysis of its competitors, companies can develop an original value proposition that differentiates their products or services from those of competitors. This may involve emphasizing product efficacy, safety, convenience, or cost-effectiveness as differentiating factors.
4. *Communicate Your Unique Value Proposition*: Once a unique value proposition has been developed, it must be effectively communicated to customers to remain competitive. This may involve using targeted marketing campaigns, social media, or any other channels to effectively engage and reach target customers.
5. *Monitor and Adjust*: Successful competitive positioning requires constant vigilance and adjustment of strategies as necessary. This may involve adapting to market changes, responding to new competitors, or adapting marketing tactics to reach target audiences more effectively.

Competitive Positioning in Pharma: Some Examples

Here are some examples of how some pharmaceutical companies positioned themselves competitively:

1. *Pfizer* has become a global pharmaceutical powerhouse by creating innovative drugs to address various medical conditions. As the leader of its industry, their competitive positioning includes research and development, strategic acquisitions of smaller firms with potential, and strong brand recognition.
2. *Roche* is a leader in oncology, offering an expansive array of cancer treatments. Their competitive advantage rests in their expertise in personalized medicine, thus enabling highly targeted cancer treatments for their patients. Further, it has become an industry leader in diagnostics to strengthen its pharmaceutical business.
3. *Novartis* offers an impressive portfolio of medications to treat cardiovascular and respiratory ailments and cancer. Their unsurpassed competitive advantage stems from advanced research and development capabilities, allowing them to create treatments specifically targeted toward meeting unmet medical needs in emerging markets, thus giving them an unmatched competitive edge against rival pharmaceutical firms.
4. *Johnson & Johnson*, an integrated healthcare company, operates three main divisions—pharmaceuticals, medical devices, and consumer health products. Johnson & Johnson's competitive advantage rests with its ability to leverage extensive resources across these markets to develop and market products effectively. Furthermore, it enjoys strong brand recognition with numerous successful acquisitions that have broadened its product portfolio.
5. *Merck* is widely respected for their research and development work in oncology, infectious disease, and vaccines. Their competitive edge lies in innovation. They develop treatments to meet unmet medical needs while remaining a strong presence in emerging markets, giving them an unmistakable competitive advantage.

Competitive De-positioning

Competitive de-positioning is a marketing strategy used to decrease customer perception of competitor offerings, making them less appealing and less likely to be chosen by potential customers. This tactic creates negative associations and thus lessening customer preference for them.

There are various strategies for competitive de-positioning, including:

A. *Highlighting Weaknesses of Competitor Products or Services*: By drawing attention to flaws or shortcomings within competitors' offerings, businesses can create doubt among potential customers and reduce the likelihood of choosing them.

B. *Emphasizing the Strengths of the Company's Product or Service*: By emphasizing its advantages and benefits, companies can make their offering seem more desirable than those offered by competitors.

C. *Offering Incentives or Promotions*: Companies can use discounts, free trials, or other incentives to lure customers away from competing products or services and toward their products or services.

Competitive De-positioning in Pharma

Competitive de-positioning strategies are used in pharmaceutical marketing to gain market share by persuading customers to switch from competing products and use yours instead. Here are some examples of competitive de-positioning:

1. *Comparative Clinical Studies*: Companies conduct comparative clinical studies to prove their product outshines competitors in efficacy, safety, or tolerability. They then use the findings from these studies as part of their marketing campaigns to persuade doctors and patients to switch over.
2. *Price Undercutting*: Companies may attempt to displace competitors by offering their products at a cheaper price. Generic drug manufacturers often employ this strategy to gain market share from branded drugs.
3. *Negative Advertising*: Companies may employ negative advertising tactics against competing products by emphasizing their drawbacks or negative features and positioning one's product as the superior alternative.
4. *Patent Challenges*: Companies may challenge an opponent's drug patent to bring generic versions to market and cause price wars that force customers to switch to cheaper generic options. This strategy may lead customers to opt for these alternative versions over the original ones.
5. *Direct-to-Consumer Advertising*: Companies may use direct-to-consumer advertising to differentiate their product from competitors by targeting patients directly with advertisements emphasizing its benefits over those offered by competitors.

How Pharma Employs Competitive De-positioning

Here are a few examples of pharmaceutical companies engaging in competitive de-positioning:

1. *Pfizer's Lipitor Vs. Merck's Zocor*: In the early 2000s, Pfizer employed comparative clinical studies to show that Lipitor was superior in cholesterol-lowering to Merck's Zocor. They then used these findings in marketing campaigns to persuade doctors and patients to switch. Pfizer even engaged in price undercutting by offering Lipitor at lower costs than Zocor.
2. *Gilead's Harvoni Versus AbbVie's Viekira Pak*: Gilead launched its treatment for hepatitis C in 2014 under the brand name Harvoni and used direct-to-consumer advertising to position it as an attractive alternative to AbbVie's Viekira Pak, using direct advertising targeting consumers with messages that highlighted how its one-pill daily treatment was more effective and had fewer side effects compared with Viekira Pak. In addition, price undercutting was used so consumers would make up their minds about what to choose between these products!
3. *AstraZeneca vs. Pfizer Lipitor*: In 2003, AstraZeneca unveiled Crestor as a cholesterol-lowering medication. Comparative clinical studies demonstrated its superior effectiveness over Pfizer Lipitor. AstraZeneca then utilized these results in its marketing campaigns to convince doctors and patients alike to switch over. They even engaged in price undercutting by offering Crestor at a lower cost than Lipitor.
4. *Sanofi Lantus Vs. Novo Nordisk Levemir*: Sanofi introduced Lantus, a long-acting insulin used for treating diabetes, in 2009. Using comparative clinical studies to prove Lantus's superiority over Novo Nordisk Levemir, marketing studies were conducted to persuade doctors and patients alike to switch. Furthermore, Sanofi utilized price-undercutting tactics when offering Lantus at lower prices than Levemir.

Certain de-positioning practices and examples can involve controversial and illegal acts, such as price fixing or false advertising. Therefore, companies must adhere to regulations and ethical guidelines when de-positioning competitively.

Competitive Forces

Competitive Forces are those elements that could impede or help an organization's market standing or ability to compete against rival companies effectively.

Michael Porter, an expert on competitive strategy and economics, first introduced competitive forces analysis in his 1980 book *Competitive Strategy: Techniques for Analyzing Industries and Competitors*. Within this work, he explained his theory of industry structure and five forces that drive competition within an industry. Understanding this information is crucial to creating effective strategies and gaining a competitive advantage.

Here are the five competitive forces proposed by Micheal Porter in pharma marketing that may impact its performance:

1. *Rivalry among Existing Competitors*: Competition between existing pharma companies can enormously affect their ability to thrive in the market. Companies with larger market shares may enjoy an edge over smaller or newer competitors. However, these larger entities may face fiercer opposition from other large pharma firms.
2. *The Threat of New Entrants*: New companies entering a market can pose significant threats, particularly those offering innovative products and services which attract customers.
3. *Bargaining Power of Suppliers*: Supplier bargaining power enormously affects a company's position in the market. More powerful suppliers may demand higher prices for goods and services, ultimately hindering profits.
4. *Bargaining Power of Buyers*: Buyers such as healthcare providers or patients have significant bargaining power that can drastically change a company's standing in its target market. Buyers with more leverage may demand lower prices or better terms from businesses, impacting profitability negatively.
5. *The Threat of Substitutes*: Substitutes such as generic drugs and alternative therapies may threaten a company's market position and make maintaining a competitive edge more challenging. However, if many substitutions are available, companies may struggle to maintain an edge against competitors and remain viable businesses.

Understanding the competitive forces in the pharma market is essential for companies looking to develop effective marketing strategies and gain a competitive advantage. By understanding and responding to these forces, businesses can enhance their market position and survive even in the most demanding environments.

Competitor Analysis

Competitor analysis involves identifying and assessing your competitors' strengths and weaknesses to develop strategies to gain a competitive advantage against them. Assimilation involves developing an in-depth knowledge of rival strategies, resources, capabilities, and vulnerabilities for refining your business plan.

Pharmaceutical companies must gain an in-depth knowledge of their competitors' marketing strategies to devise an effective plan and gain a competitive advantage.

Important Steps

The following are the important steps of competitor analysis for pharmaceutical marketing:

1. *Locate Competitors*: Recognizing direct and indirect competitors is key for business growth, including companies offering similar products/services or targeting similar customer bases.
2. *Gather Information*: Gain knowledge about your competitors' marketing strategies by consulting various sources such as their websites, social media profiles, press releases, industry reports, and advertisements. Examine their messaging, target audience, and promotion techniques to gain a competitive edge over them.
3. *Analyzing Competitors*: Assess your competitors' strengths and weaknesses by reviewing market share, reputation, product offerings, pricing strategies, distribution channels, and sales tactics. Conduct a SWOT (Strengths, Weaknesses, Opportunities, Threats) analysis on them to compare your company with them, discovering ways to distinguish yourself.
4. *Identify Gaps*: Uncover any market gaps your competitors aren't filling, such as meeting the unmet needs of target audiences who don't currently receive such products from competitors.
5. *Create a Marketing Strategy*: Once your analysis is complete, craft a marketing strategy using its findings to develop an action plan to address competitors by altering pricing, messaging, product development, or sales strategies as necessary.
6. *Keep an Eye on Your Competitors*: Keep tabs on your competitors' marketing activities and adapt your strategies accordingly to stay ahead.

Competitor Analysis is vital to pharmaceutical companies for thriving in an increasingly competitive market. By understanding their competitors' marketing strategies and finding ways to differentiate themselves, pharmaceutical firms can develop successful marketing plans to gain an edge against rival pharma companies and gain an edge themselves.

Competitive Myopia

Myopia (nearsightedness) is a visual condition in which near objects appear clear while further away objects appear blurry. Myopia, as applied to marketing, refers to an approach that prioritizes selling products or services over satisfying customer needs and wants. Theodore Levitt of Harvard Business School introduced this concept and term in his 1960 article titled *Marketing Myopia*.

Levitt suggests that many businesses fail to achieve long-term success because they focus too heavily on products rather than understanding customers' broader needs and desires. When businesses fall into this trap, they exhibit marketing myopia, focusing on short-term gains rather than sustainable long-term growth.

To avoid marketing myopia, companies should prioritize understanding customer needs and creating products and services to fulfill them. In addition, they must be open to adapting to market changes while continuously innovating to remain ahead of their competition.

Marketing myopia reminds businesses to place customers first and adapt quickly to changing market conditions to ensure long-term success.

Competitive Myopia

Competitive myopia refers to a business or organizational mindset prioritizing short-term competitive advantages over longer-term goals and sustainability. Such myopic thinking often results in companies prioritizing short-term gains such as market share, revenue, or profits over investments such as research & development, employee training, or customer service that could offer greater long-term gains.

At times, companies may become too focused on beating immediate competitors that they lose sight of the larger picture, including customer needs and preferences, emerging technologies, or market shifts that provide opportunities for innovation and growth, jeopardizing long-term success.

Competitive myopia contrasts sharply with an approach focused on cultivating long-term customer relationships, innovating continuously, and building sustainable competitive advantages.

Competitive Myopia in Pharma Marketing

Pharmaceutical marketing firms often suffer from competitive myopia. For instance, companies may spend too much time and resources promoting existing products to capture market share from competitors rather than investing in research and development to produce drugs that more closely meet patients' needs. This can result in reduced innovation and failure to address unmet medical needs, ultimately decreasing market share and profitability for the companies involved.

Competitive myopia can erode pharmaceutical marketing in another way. Companies may erroneously prioritize short-term sales over patients' long-term interests leading them to prioritize short-term profits over long-term well-being, and safety concerns. This can result in aggressive or misleading tactics prioritizing sales targets over patient safety and wellbeing. For instance, some firms push sales representatives to promote drugs for uses not approved by regulatory agencies to boost sales or downplay risks associated with them to boost earnings.

To avoid competitive myopia in pharmaceutical marketing, companies must adopt a customer-centric strategy that places patient needs and long-term success ahead of short-term sales goals. The investment must also take place in research and development while adhering to ethical marketing practices, with initiatives intended to support patient health and well-being initiatives. Finally, companies should collaborate with healthcare providers, patient advocacy groups, regulatory agencies, so that products meet safety, effectiveness, and requirements for patient use.

Below are a few examples of competitive myopia in the pharmaceutical industry:

A. *Blockbuster Drugs*: Pharmaceutical companies may become too dependent on their blockbuster drugs and fail to invest in research and development of new therapies or alternative options, leaving themselves susceptible to competition from other companies or alternative solutions.

B. *Patent Protection*: Pharmaceutical companies often place too much importance on defending their patents and maintaining market exclusivity for their products, which inhibits partnerships or developing therapies with improved effectiveness or reduced side effects.

C. *Biologic Drugs*: Pharmaceutical companies may become too focused on biotech drug development and neglect investing in research and development of other therapies, such as small molecule or gene therapies, leaving themselves open to competition from companies investing in these areas.

Pharmaceutical companies need a broad market perspective to avoid competitive myopia and keep abreast of threats posed by new and emerging competitors or alternative therapies. Therefore, pharmaceutical firms must consider the following to avoid competitive myopia:

- Invest in the research and development of new drugs or therapies
- Collaborate with other companies on new ideas
- Be open-minded about different ideas or approaches
- Be aware of changing market conditions, and
- Adapt their strategies accordingly

Competitive Myopia in Pharma: Some Examples

These examples from pharmaceutical companies that were subjected to competitive myopia illustrate and reinforce why we must remain aware of competitive myopia and develop long-term sustainability and growth goals within our strategic thinking:

1. Pfizer experienced competitive myopia when it failed to invest in new drugs and relied too heavily on Lipitor for revenue generation. When the patent for Lipitor expired, revenues suffered, Pfizer experienced difficulty coming up with replacement products to fill this void.
2. Johnson & Johnson was accused of competitive myopia when they aggressively promoted Risperdal for use off-label in treating children with ADHD, even though there could be serious side effects associated with taking it. As a result, Johnson & Johnson was fined billions in fines for its marketing practices and causing significant damage to its reputation.
3. Valeant Pharmaceuticals fell prey to competitive myopia when they acquired several smaller pharmaceutical companies and raised prices without investing in R&D or improving efficacy, leading to public outrage, regulatory investigations, and ultimately a drop in stock price and profitability.
4. Mylan (now Viatris) experienced competitive myopia when they increased the price of EpiPen allergy treatment by over 400% without investing in R&D or improving the product's efficacy, an act widely criticized as prioritizing profits over patient needs and leading to congressional investigations and widespread outrage.

These examples illustrate how competitive myopia can threaten pharmaceutical companies' long-term success and reputation, negatively affecting patients and public health.

Concentrated Marketing

Concentrated marketing refers to an approach by which a company dedicates all of its efforts and resources to targeting one clearly delineated market niche or segment. Instead of trying to appeal to as wide an audience as possible, concentrated promotion targets customers with specific needs or characteristics.

Companies can tailor marketing messages, products, and promotions to specific customer segments to address customer preferences and meet customer needs. This approach results in more effective campaigns, higher customer loyalty, and profits.

Concentrated marketing can be particularly useful for companies with limited resources or facing stiff competition in an oversaturated marketplace. By targeting one niche specifically and creating a stronger brand identity, these firms can stand out from their competition and differentiate themselves.

Concentrated Marketing in Pharma

Concentrated marketing can also be found within the pharmaceutical industry, where companies target specific patient populations or disease areas with their products. This approach allows pharmaceutical firms to develop customized treatments tailored to meet the needs of various patient populations or disease areas.

Orphan drug development provides one example of concentrated pharmaceutical marketing, targeting diseases or conditions affecting only a limited patient population. Larger pharmaceutical companies often neglect these diseases, and there is an unmet need for treatments. Orphan drug developers can focus their efforts on an exclusive target market.

Pharmaceutical companies can create highly targeted treatments with fewer side effects and fewer efficacy issues than conventional chemotherapy by targeting specific genetic mutations associated with certain cancer types. By developing drugs for these mutations, pharmaceutical companies can develop highly targeted drugs that provide more targeted care and improve patient outcomes than standard chemotherapy.

Pharma and Concentrated Marketing

Below are examples of pharmaceutical companies using concentrated marketing tactics:

1. *Vertex Pharmaceuticals*: Vertex Pharmaceuticals' core mission is to find treatments for cystic fibrosis, an uncommon genetic disease affecting an estimated 30,000 Americans. They have produced various drugs targeting specific mutations associated with this disorder. Their marketing initiatives target healthcare professionals who treat cystic fibrosis patients and those directly living with the disorder themselves.
2. *Novo Nordisk*: Novo Nordisk is a pharmaceutical company dedicated to diabetes care, offering treatments like insulin and other remedies specifically targeted toward those with the condition. Their marketing strategies focus on creating targeted strategies and treatments.
3. *Genentech*: Genentech is a biotechnology company dedicated to producing cancer medications and other serious illnesses, with specific marketing efforts targeting healthcare providers and individuals with specific cancer types such as breast and lung. Genentech has developed tailored drugs specifically designed for these patient populations.
4. *Takeda Pharmaceuticals* has made its mark by producing drugs to treat rare conditions like hereditary angioedema and Crohn's disease, targeting healthcare providers and their respective patients with marketing initiatives.
5. *Biogen* is a biotechnology company that treats neurological conditions like multiple sclerosis and Alzheimer's. Their marketing campaigns target healthcare providers who treat these conditions, and patients living with these disorders. Biogen has produced tailored medications for specific patient populations.

Concentrated marketing in the pharmaceutical industry can give companies an edge against rivals. By targeting specific market segments, pharmaceutical firms can gain greater insight into patient population needs, tailor their efforts accordingly, increase patient engagement rates, and ultimately achieve improved patient outcomes.

Concentric Diversification

Concentric diversification in pharmaceuticals is where a company expands its product lines or services into related areas that complement existing ones, using existing knowledge, resources, and expertise to enter new markets related to its core business.

Concentric diversification in the pharmaceutical industry involves expanding into related healthcare markets such as medical devices, diagnostics, and services. For example, an oncology drug company might diversify into cancer diagnostics or radiation therapy equipment to tap its existing knowledge and expand its market share while creating new revenue streams and increasing market share.

Concentric diversification in pharmaceutical marketing may also involve expanding into related therapeutic areas. For instance, a pharmaceutical company that specializes in diabetes drugs might expand into related therapeutic areas like obesity or cardiovascular disease. This would allow it to leverage its existing expertise with metabolic disorders to create products and services which address related health conditions.

Let's consider some examples of concentric diversification in pharmaceutical marketing:

1. Johnson & Johnson is an international pharmaceutical company with businesses specializing in various healthcare markets. For example, its medical device division produces surgical instruments, care products, and orthopedic devices; its consumer health division offers over-the-counter (OTC) drugs and personal care items.
2. Roche is an innovative global healthcare company recognized for developing and manufacturing pharmaceuticals and diagnostic tests. Their therapeutic specialty areas include oncology, neuroscience, and rare diseases. Their diagnostics division offers products like blood glucose monitors and laboratory instruments.
3. Novo Nordisk is a Danish pharmaceutical company specializing in diabetes care but also has expanded into related therapeutic areas such as obesity treatment and rare diseases. For example, Novo Nordisk manufactures the Saxenda (Liraglutide) designed to combat obesity.
4. Sanofi is a French pharmaceutical company with global operations that has successfully expanded into multiple healthcare markets, such as vaccines, consumer health, and rare diseases. Furthermore, they have acquired companies specializing in these areas. For instance, Kadmon is an example of such an acquisition.

Concentric diversification in pharmaceutical marketing is a useful strategy for companies to expand their product lines and enter new markets by capitalizing on existing expertise, knowledge, and resources. But for it to work properly, it requires meticulous planning and execution to ensure any new offerings fit perfectly into an established business and target market.

Conditioning

Conditioning in pharmaceutical marketing refers to associating one product or brand with specific reactions or outcomes in consumers' minds through various means such as advertisements, packaging, or promotions.

Conditioning in pharmaceutical marketing aims at building positive associations between product or brand usage and specific responses or outcomes, such as pain relief, symptom relief, or improved health outcomes. Through conditioning efforts, pharmaceutical companies can increase brand recognition, build customer loyalty and drive sales by creating this positive association between themselves and desired responses or outcomes.

Here are some examples of conditioning in pharma marketing:

A. *Advertising*: Pharmaceutical companies may use advertising to condition consumers to associate their product with specific outcomes. For instance, an ad for pain relievers might show someone experiencing relief after taking medicine, thus creating an association between it and pain reduction.
B. *Packaging*: Pharmaceutical companies use packaging to condition consumers to associate their product with an outcome. For instance, a cough syrup may feature an image of someone coughing on its label to create an association between its use and cough relief.
C. *Promotional Activities*: Pharmaceutical companies may use promotional activities to condition consumers to associate their product with certain outcomes. For instance, by sponsoring health fairs with free product samples to create positive associations between their product and improved health outcomes.

Conditioning in Pharma Marketing: An Example

One example of a pharmaceutical company using conditioning in its marketing is the pain reliever brand Advil (Ibuprofen). Advil's advertising campaigns have historically focused on creating a positive association between the brand and pain relief, with slogans like *Advil: Advanced Medicine for Pain and Relief don't get any better than this.* In addition, the company's ads often feature people engaging in activities that may cause pain, such as running or playing sports and taking

Advil to alleviate their pain and continue their activity.

Advil also uses packaging to condition consumers to associate the product with pain relief. The product packaging features the Advil logo along with phrases such as Pain Relief and Fast Relief, which creates a positive association in the minds of consumers between the product and pain relief.

Furthermore, Advil uses promotional activities to condition consumers to associate the product with pain relief. For example, the company may offer coupons or free product samples at healthcare fairs or other events to positively associate the brand with pain relief, which has helped it establish itself as a leading pain relief brand.

Conditioning in pharmaceutical marketing refers to associating one product or brand with specific reactions or outcomes in consumers' minds through various means such as advertisements, packaging, or promotions.

Conditioning in pharmaceutical marketing aims at building positive associations between product or brand usage and specific responses or outcomes, such as pain relief, symptom relief, or improved health outcomes. However, as conditioning could potentially be seen as manipulative or deceptive tactics by customers, pharmaceutical firms must ensure ethical and transparent marketing practices.

Conjoint Analysis

Conjoint analysis is an established statistical method in market research used to understand how consumers view various characteristics or attributes of a product or service and how it is perceived by its target consumers.

Conjoint analysis can be particularly effective for pharmaceutical marketing, providing researchers insight into how patients and healthcare providers assess treatments or interventions based on benefits vs. risks evaluations.

Researchers conducting a conjoint analysis study on a new drug could present participants with different hypothetical drug versions that differ in dosage, side effects, and effectiveness before asking them which version they would most likely prescribe or take themselves.

By studying patient and provider preferences for pharmaceutical features, researchers can gain valuable insight into which groups most appreciate features, and any willingness to compromise between features that might otherwise conflict. Such data could guide product design, pricing, and marketing strategies.

The conjoint analysis allows healthcare providers to quickly understand patient preferences for treatments like surgery, medication, or lifestyle modifications and tailor treatment plans more precisely according to individual needs and preferences by understanding which factors matter most for patients.

Conjoint Analysis in Pharma Marketing

Here are a few examples of how conjoint analysis can be utilized in pharmaceutical marketing:

1. *Determining the Optimal Dosage for a New Drug*: Researchers could use conjoint analysis to explore how patients and providers weigh the benefits and risks of various dosage options for new drugs, providing insight into dosing recommendations that are both effective and well-accepted by patients and healthcare professionals.
2. *Understanding Patient Preferences for Different Treatment Options*: Conjoint analysis can explore patient preferences regarding healthcare treatment options such as medication, surgery, or lifestyle modifications. As a result, healthcare providers can more efficiently create patient-centric plans by understanding which factors are most crucial.
3. *Estimating the Value of New Drug Features*: Conjoint analysis can be used to ascertain what patients and providers are willing to pay for various features of a new drug, such as improved efficacy, decreased side effects, or convenience features. This data could then inform pricing decisions as well as marketing strategies.
4. *Evaluating the Impact of Different Promotional Messages*: Conjoint analysis can measure the effectiveness of different promotional messages on patient and provider preferences for any drug, helping pharma companies create more targeted and persuasive marketing campaigns by understanding which messages work most efficiently.

How Pharma Companies Apply Conjoint Analysis

Many pharmaceutical companies utilize conjoint analysis as a market research tool to gain insight into patient and provider product preferences. Below are some examples:

1. Pfizer used conjoint analysis to understand how patients and providers rated different attributes of its new drug for treating overactive bladder. The study enabled Pfizer to optimize dosing and formulation to meet patient needs more closely.

2. Merck used conjoint analysis to understand how physicians and patients prioritize different outcomes in treating type 2 diabetes. This enabled the pharmaceutical giant to develop a more patient-centric treatment approach to decrease the treatment burden.
3. Novo Nordisk employed conjoint analysis to measure patient preferences for different insulin pen designs. As a result of this research, Novo Nordisk optimized its designs to best meet patient needs and preferences.
4. Sanofi utilized conjoint analysis to understand how patients and providers valued different attributes of a new drug for multiple sclerosis. The findings allowed Sanofi to optimize formulation and dosing to increase patient outcomes.

Consumerism

Consumerism in healthcare refers to patients taking an increasingly active role in making healthcare decisions and engaging in their health management. Many factors contribute to this trend, including rising healthcare literacy levels, increased access to information, rising healthcare costs, more accessible options, and an emphasis on personalized patient-centric care solutions.

Consumer-centric healthcare systems allow individuals more freedom in selecting healthcare providers and treatments, from choosing healthcare plans and physicians to researching treatments and managing health records.

Consumerist healthcare practices have brought with them various tools and technologies designed to empower patients and facilitate managing their healthcare, such as online health portals, mobile health apps, telemedicine services, and digital health tools which allow patients to gain access to vital information regarding their conditions as well as communicate directly with doctors while monitoring progress over time.

Critics of consumerism in healthcare note how it puts profits before the patient's needs, potentially prompting unnecessary treatments or procedures. Meanwhile, supporters emphasize how consumerism in healthcare can lead to greater patient satisfaction, better health outcomes, and reduced healthcare costs over time.

Consumer-driven healthcare systems give individuals more control in selecting healthcare providers and treatments, from selecting healthcare plans and providers to researching treatment options and managing health records.

Consumption in healthcare has inspired various tools and technologies designed to empower patients and simplify managing their health, including online health portals, mobile health apps, telemedicine services, and digital tools that enable accessing data while communicating with doctors and tracking progress over time.

Critics of consumerism in healthcare point out that it could result in unnecessary procedures by prioritizing profit over patient welfare too heavily. In contrast, supporters point out it can improve patient satisfaction, enhance health outcomes, and lower healthcare costs in the long term.

Consumerism in healthcare represents an exciting development, providing patients with more control of their treatment while driving greater innovation across the sector.

Consumerism Impacts Pharma Marketing

Here are a few examples of how consumerism has revolutionized pharmaceutical marketing:

1. *Direct-to-Consumer (DTC) Advertising*: One powerful illustration of consumerism's effect on pharmaceutical marketing are DTC advertising campaigns from Pfizer, Johnson & Johnson, and Merck for medications like Viagra, Xarelto, and Gardasil.
2. *Patient Support Programs*: Pharma companies have increasingly pledged their dedication to supporting patient programs providing information, resources, and assistance for people living with multiple sclerosis. For instance, the Novartis' *Living Like You* program provides resources and assistance specifically targeted to this condition.
3. *Social Media Engagement*: Many pharma companies use social media to engage patients and offer valuable resources and information. Sanofi uses Facebook pages for this purpose, such as its page dedicated to Sanofi products while simultaneously sharing news updates about them and engaging with patients.
4. *Patient-Centric Messaging*: Companies like Roche and AstraZeneca are shifting their messaging towards patients and their needs, such as through Roche's Personalized Healthcare strategy, which emphasizes tailoring treatments to each patient.
5. *Digital Health Solutions*: Consumerism has led to an explosion of digital health solutions like mobile apps and wearable devices that empower patients to manage their healthcare more easily.

Companies such as Novartis and Pfizer are developing such tools so patients can monitor their well-being more closely while more easily tracking medications.

These are only some examples of how consumerism has transformed pharmaceutical marketing. With patients becoming increasingly involved in healthcare decisions, pharma companies must adapt their marketing strategies to accommodate their needs and preferences.

Consumers

Consumers are essential in pharmaceutical marketing, choosing which pharmaceutical products to purchase. Yet their behavior differs considerably from other industries due to several reasons, including:

A. *Pharmaceutical Products are Different from Consumer Goods*: Pharmaceutical products differ significantly from other consumer goods in that consumers usually only purchase them if they have a health issue to treat, as most pharmaceutical products require a valid prescription from healthcare professionals and thus limit consumers from selecting exactly which product they desire.

B. *Information Sources*: Pharmaceutical industry consumers rely heavily on healthcare professionals as sources for product information rather than advertisements or traditional marketing channels, so pharmaceutical companies aim to build strong relationships with healthcare professionals so that doctors can prescribe their products to patients.

C. *Ethical Considerations*: Pharmaceutical marketing is heavily regulated, and companies must abide by certain ethical considerations when marketing pharmaceutical products like prescription drugs. Companies cannot advertise directly to consumers for these medications but must use more subtle promotional techniques instead.

Consumers in Pharma Marketing

Pharmaceutical marketing targets consumers seeking treatment for specific health problems. Consumers in this segment can generally be divided into two groups.

A. *Patients*: Pharmaceutical products are designed for people suffering from health conditions requiring medication and treatments; individuals taking them themselves and using them directly constitute the ultimate users. Patients can be classified based on age, gender, medical condition and any relevant variables.

B. *Caregivers:* Monitoring patient health and welfare include family, friends, and healthcare professionals providing medication or direct support. These people play an essential part in making treatment decisions and setting priorities. Caregivers may also serve as targets of pharmaceutical marketing efforts as their decisions are vital in treatment decision-making processes. Besides patients and caregivers, healthcare professionals such as doctors, nurses, and pharmacists also serve as consumers within pharma marketing; these healthcare providers prescribe and recommend treatments directly to patients, making them ideal targets within marketing efforts.

Consumers play a part in pharmaceutical marketing; however, due to its unique nature, companies must build relationships with healthcare professionals and adhere to ethical considerations when marketing products.

Patients as Consumers

Patients as consumers is the concept that patients are active participants in their healthcare decisions and should have access to information to make informed choices for healthcare services and alternatives. Recently, this concept has gained momentum as more patients gain greater knowledge and engagement with healthcare due to accessing it online and prioritizing patient-centric care. As such, they are more likely to ask questions, seek second opinions, and compare treatment options than before.

As more consumers transition into patients as consumers, healthcare providers are emphasizing patient-centric care and experience as they look to meet patients' needs and expectations — from improving communication with them and engaging them, offering tailored care plans, to creating more patient-friendly environments.

Patients' role as consumers has dramatically affected the healthcare industry, leading to a greater emphasis on personalized patient care and the development of innovative tools and technologies that assist individuals in making more informed decisions regarding their healthcare.

As patients are integral to pharmaceutical products and treatments, pharmaceutical companies employ various strategies and tactics to reach them effectively. These may include:

1. Pharma companies use Direct-to-Consumer Advertising (DTCA) to reach patients via print, television and online media to raise awareness for specific medications or diseases and

encourage patients ask their physicians about their products.

2. Pharmaceutical companies can use patient education materials, such as brochures, pamphlets, or websites which provide details about a medication's potential benefits and any side effects it might cause.
3. Pharmaceutical companies are increasingly using social media campaigns to connect with patients, patient advocacy groups and to disseminate education and advertise their products.
4. Patient advocacy programs are created to assist patients in accessing medications and support those living with an illness or condition. Such programs may offer educational resources, support groups, and financial aid for medications that these individuals cannot afford.

Content Marketing

Content marketing in the pharmaceutical industry refers to using educational and informative material to engage patients and healthcare providers, build brand recognition, establish credibility and trustworthiness, and strengthen relationships between pharma companies and patients, healthcare professionals, and other stakeholders.

Pharmaceutical companies use content marketing strategies, such as blog posts, social media updates, email newsletters, white papers, infographics, and videos to reach their target audiences. Their content may address topics related to disease education, available treatment options for their patient's conditions, clinical trial updates, and lifestyle tips that benefit patients.

Content marketing can be particularly helpful in the pharmaceutical industry, where trust between patients and healthcare professionals is integral to its success. By creating valuable, accurate, and engaging content, pharmaceutical companies can establish themselves as thought leaders and reliable resources of information in their areas of expertise.

Content Marketing in Pharma: Examples and Implications

Here are a few examples of content marketing in Pharma:

1. *Disease Education*: Pharmaceutical companies often create content to educate patients and healthcare providers about certain diseases or conditions, like Pfizer's *Get Healthy Stay Healthy website* offering articles and videos on heart health, cancer, and infectious diseases.
2. *Treatment Options*: Pharmaceutical companies create content to inform readers about different treatment options, including medications and therapies, how they work, and what lifestyle tips might help their patients make informed decisions. For example, Novartis' *Living Like You website* features multiple sclerosis treatment options and lifestyle tips.
3. *Clinical Trial Updates*: Pharma companies may provide updates on clinical trial results and ongoing research. For example, Roche's Genentech subsidiary offers information regarding cancer trials on its website.
4. *Lifestyle Tips*: Pharma companies create content to give patients tips and information for managing their condition and leading a healthy lifestyle. Sanofi *Diabetes Stories website* features abundant content about managing diabetes, such as healthy eating tips and exercise advice.
5. *Interactive Tools*: Pharma companies may create interactive tools that enable patients and healthcare professionals to explore various topics about healthcare. For instance, Merck's *Know Your Risk website* features an interactive tool allowing patients to assess their individual risk for various diseases based on age, gender and lifestyle considerations.

Content marketing can be an invaluable asset to pharmaceutical and healthcare companies seeking to engage with patients, build their brands, and connect with patients via engaging content. However, content marketing in pharma is subject to stringent regulations around promoting prescription drugs; pharmaceutical companies must ensure their messages are truthful, not misleading, and follow regulations regarding disclosing risks or side effects associated with their products.

Content Management System (CMS)

Content Management Systems (CMSs) are software platforms enabling users to produce, organize and publish digital content easily. CMSs help organize, deliver, and track that content through various channels and stakeholders into pharmaceutical marketing campaigns. Here are a few benefits a CMS may bring:

1. *Centralized Content Repository*: CMSs offer an ideal way of organizing all marketing content, such as product info, promotional materials, clinical data, educational resources, and multimedia assets, into one easily accessible repository that ensures version control across teams and departments, content consistency across platforms, and seamless use by end-users.
2. *Content Creation and Collaboration*: CMS allows marketing teams to author, edit, and review content collaboratively. Features like authoring tools, workflow management features, and approval processes facilitate seamless coordination among internal stakeholders, such as medical, regulatory, legal, and marketing teams.
3. *Personalization and Targeting*: CMS enables personalized content production and delivery by using user segmentation features to deliver tailored messages directly to specific audiences such as healthcare providers, patients, or payers, increasing engagement while supporting tailored communication strategies.
4. *Multichannel Publishing*: With a CMS, marketers can publish content across various channels like websites, social media platforms, email campaigns, and mobile apps with consistent messaging while meeting any particular channel requirements. CMS tools offer templates, integrations, and templates designed specifically to optimize this type of publishing across channels, ensuring brand consistency while meeting specific channel specifications.
5. *Compliance*: Pharma marketing relies heavily on adhering to regulatory requirements, so having a CMS can assist in this area by offering features like audit trails, content approvals, and controlled access to sensitive material. A CMS also helps maintain records related to compliance while encouraging efficient collaboration between marketing and regulatory teams.
6. *Content Performance Tracking*: CMS typically comes equipped with analytics and reporting features that enable marketers to track the effectiveness of their content through metrics like page views, downloads, engagement rates, and conversion rates, providing marketers with valuable data-based decisions for optimizing marketing strategies and making strategic marketing decisions based on hard facts.
7. *Content Localization and Globalization*: CMS enables pharmaceutical companies operating across multiple regions or countries to customize content localized for each language, culture, and regulatory requirement, creating consistency while meeting multiple market requirements simultaneously.

Content Management Systems are invaluable tools for pharmaceutical marketing, offering capabilities like centralized content collaboration and personalization across multichannel publishing sites, regulatory compliance tracking, performance measurement capabilities, and global content administration. Utilizing CMS allows pharmaceutical companies to streamline marketing operations while simultaneously creating targeted content delivery for multiple channels with increased compliance standards and measurement metrics for measuring the effectiveness of marketing efforts.

Continuing Medical Education (CME)

CME (Continuing Medical Education) programs provide opportunities for pharmaceutical companies to educate healthcare professionals about new drugs, treatments, and technologies. They help pharmaceutical companies position themselves as reliable information sources and create relationships, driving prescriptions and sales of their products. Here are some CME opportunities for pharmaceutical companies:

1. *Live Events*: Pharmaceutical companies may host conferences or symposiums to provide healthcare professionals with up-to-date information about their products and therapeutic areas. Such events might feature keynote addresses, panel discussions, and workshops.
2. *Online Courses*: Pharmaceutical companies can create online courses for healthcare professionals to access at their own pace, assessed through the company website or learning management system (LMS).
3. *Webinars*: Pharmaceutical companies can utilize webinars as a cost-effective method for reaching large audiences online. Pharma companies can reach a broader target market without breaking the bank by hosting such sessions on specific topics or products.
4. *Medical Publications*: Pharmaceutical companies may publish articles and white papers in medical publications to inform healthcare professionals of their products or therapeutic areas. Healthcare professionals may access these articles online in medical libraries or in print forms.

5. *Medical Education Grants*: Pharmaceutical companies may provide medical education grants to academic institutions or societies to create continuing medical education (CME) programs. These grants may cover the funding of live events, online courses, or any other CME opportunities available.

CME opportunities allow pharmaceutical companies to connect with healthcare professionals and establish themselves as reliable information sources. Furthermore, pharmaceutical companies can strengthen relationships with healthcare professionals by providing educational support services while increasing sales for their products.

Pharma and CMEs

Pharmaceutical companies provide continuing medical education programs covering various therapeutic areas to reach and engage healthcare professionals. Consider the following, for example:

1. *Janssen Pharmaceuticals*, a division of Johnson & Johnson, provides various CME programs, such as webinars, online courses and in-person events to educate healthcare professionals across various therapeutic areas such as mental health, infectious disease and cardiovascular health.
2. *Novartis Pharmaceuticals* provides healthcare professionals with various continuing medical education (CME) programs including live events, webinars and online courses, covering therapeutic areas like neurology, dermatology and cardiology.
3. *Pfizer's* CME programs for healthcare professionals span live events, webinars and online courses covering oncology, cardiology and infectious disease therapeutic areas.
4. *AbbVie's* continuing medical education (CME) programs include live events, webinars and online courses in therapeutic areas like rheumatology, gastroenterology and dermatology to healthcare professionals.
5. *Merck* provides healthcare professionals live events, webinars and online courses covering vaccines, oncology and infectious disease topics as part of the CME programs.

These examples demonstrate how pharmaceutical companies utilize CME programs to educate healthcare providers about the latest treatments and technologies. As a result, pharmaceutical companies can enhance patient care while strengthening relationships between healthcare providers through accessing the most up-to-date information.

Contract Research

Contract research in pharmaceutical marketing is a business model where pharmaceutical companies contract out some or all of their research and development (R&D) activities to organizations engaged in conducting research. These organizations are known as Contract Research Organizations (CROs). CROs, offer research and development services to pharmaceutical and biotech companies. Contract research aims to streamline drug development processes, lower costs, and rapidly bring new products to market. Contract research allows pharmaceutical companies to outsource various parts of the drug development process to CROs, such as preclinical and clinical research, data management, and regulatory compliance. CROs specialize in these services using their staff and facilities allowing pharmaceutical companies to focus on core competencies like marketing, sales, and distribution.

Several Benefits

Contract Research can bring several advantages to pharma marketing:

1. *Cost Savings*: By outsourcing their R&D activities to CROs, pharmaceutical companies can reduce operating costs while increasing efficiency.
2. *Access to Expertise*: CROs provide pharmaceutical companies with access to specialized expertise, such as clinical research, data management, and regulatory compliance. By outsourcing these activities directly to CROs instead of investing their resources, pharmaceutical companies can access this specialized knowledge without investing as heavily in them.
3. *Faster Time to Market*: Contract research organizations (CROs) can speed drug development by conducting clinical trials more quickly and efficiently than traditional academic institutions. In addition, CROs offer the expertise and resources necessary for expedited drug research.
4. *Risk Mitigation*: Contract research allows pharmaceutical companies to share the risks associated with drug development with CROs, who will then be responsible for providing contracted services and mitigating those risks on their behalf.

Examples of pharmaceutical CROs include IQVIA, Parexel, and LabCorp. These companies provide pharmaceutical companies with research and development services ranging from preclinical research to post-marketing surveillance.

Contextual Advertising

Contextual advertising in pharmaceutical marketing refers to placing targeted ads directly in front of healthcare providers and patients based on specific contextual and behavioral factors. This approach utilizes real-time data analytics tools to accurately pinpoint an audience's needs, interests, and preferences before serving up ads that meet them.

Contextual advertising in pharmaceutical marketing typically means targeting healthcare providers or treating physicians who treat patients with specific medical conditions with particular medications or devices. Contextual ads could also target those searching for information about those devices or conditions related to them.

Examples of Contextual Advertising in Pharma

Here are a few examples of what pharmaceutical companies can do when it comes to contextual advertising:

1. *Google Ads*: Pharmaceutical companies may use Google Ads to target potential patients searching for information about specific medical conditions or treatments. For instance, companies manufacturing type 2 diabetes medications might use this platform to place ads at the top of search engine results in pages when patients search for related medications.
2. *Social Media Ads*: Pharmaceutical companies may utilize social media ads to reach patients searching for information regarding a specific medical condition or treatment. For instance, a company manufacturing migraine medications may place ads on platforms like Facebook and Twitter to reach users looking for details.
3. *Display Ads*: Pharmaceutical companies may use ads to reach healthcare providers who prescribe similar medicines or treat patients for specific medical conditions. For instance, companies producing blood pressure medication might display ads on websites frequently visited by cardiologists.
4. *In-App Advertising*: Pharmaceutical Companies often utilize in-app advertising to market certain medications or medical devices within mobile apps used by patients or healthcare providers, such as apps designed for asthma patients that feature ads for inhalers or medications that help manage asthma symptoms.
5. *Programmatic Advertising*: Pharmaceutical companies may employ programmatic advertising to reach healthcare providers and patients based on contextual and behavioral considerations. This strategy uses real-time data analytics to target specific groups across digital channels before placing ads directly before those individuals.

Companies must collect and analyze data from various sources, including electronic health records, social media platforms, and search engines, to implement contextual advertising in pharmaceutical marketing. Furthermore, they must adhere to stringent patient privacy and data security regulations.

Contextual advertising in pharmaceutical marketing can help companies deliver more targeted and relevant ads to healthcare providers and patients, improving patient care and better overall results.

Contextual Marketing

Contextual marketing in pharmaceuticals refers to providing personalized messages and content to healthcare providers and patients based on their unique contextual and behavioral factors. This approach utilizes real-time data analytics to accurately identify target audience needs, interests, and preferences before tailoring marketing messages accordingly. For example, contextual marketing could target physicians who recently prescribed certain medications, treat certain medical conditions, or may target newly diagnosed patients looking for information regarding available treatment options.

Companies must collect and analyze data from various sources, including electronic health records, social media platforms, and search engines, to effectively implement contextual marketing in Pharma. Furthermore, they must adhere to stringent patient privacy and data security regulations.

Contextual Marketing in Pharma: Some Examples

Here are some examples of contextual marketing in pharmaceuticals:

1. *Targeted Email Campaigns*: Pharmaceutical companies may implement email campaigns specifically targeted to healthcare providers who recently prescribed or treated patients for particular medical conditions with particular medications, providing information regarding efficacy, safety, dosing instructions, etc. These emails could also contain details about these drugs' efficacy and dosing details.
2. *Social Media Advertising*: Pharmaceutical companies may use social media ads to reach patients searching for information on a certain

medical condition or treatment, providing educational materials, patient testimonials, or product details from the pharmaceutical company.

3. *Search Engine Optimization*: Pharmaceutical companies may employ Search Engine Optimization (SEO) techniques to ensure their website and digital content will appear at the top of search engine results when patients or healthcare providers search for specific medical conditions or treatments to reach their target audiences with relevant and useful content. This will enable the pharmaceutical company to deliver relevant and informative messages.
4. *In-App Advertising*: Pharmaceutical companies can market their products through mobile apps that are widely used by both patients and healthcare providers. For example, an app designed for managing blood sugar may feature advertisements for medications that help manage diabetes.
5. *Personalized Content*: Pharmaceutical companies may utilize data and analytics to personalize content for individual patients and healthcare providers. For instance, those diagnosed with rare diseases may receive tailored emails or educational resources about treatment options and clinical trials.

Contextual marketing in pharma can help companies deliver more relevant and targeted messages to healthcare providers and patients, leading to improved patient care outcomes and increased efficiency.

Continuous Glucose Monitoring (CGM)

Continuous Glucose Monitoring (CGM) is an innovative technology that continuously measures glucose levels throughout the day and night. It uses an under-skin sensor that transmits them back to a monitoring device or smartphone app for display.

In pharmaceutical marketing, CGM can play a role in promoting diabetes-related products or medications. Here are a few ways CGM can be leveraged in pharma marketing:

1. *Product Promotion*: Pharmaceutical companies that produce diabetes medications or devices may incorporate CGM into their marketing strategies. They can highlight how their products complement or integrate with CGM technology, emphasizing the benefits of accurate and continuous glucose monitoring for diabetes management.
2. *Education and Awareness*: CGM can educate healthcare providers and patients on the significance of glucose monitoring in diabetes management. Pharma companies may offer educational materials, seminars, or webinars which outline its uses and advantages in helping achieve improved glycemic control for better overall healthcare management.
3. *Patient Support Programs*: Pharma companies can develop patient support programs that include CGM as a component. These programs can offer discounted or subsidized CGM devices, provide training on device usage and interpretation of data, and offer ongoing support to patients using CGM technology alongside their medications.
4. *Data-driven Insights*: CGM generates a wealth of data on glucose patterns and trends. Pharmaceutical companies can utilize patient data to gain insights into patient behaviors, treatment effectiveness, and medication adherence. With this insight, they can refine marketing strategies, create customized messaging, and tailor products/services better to their patients' needs.

It is important to note that marketing strategies involving medical devices, such as CGM, should comply with relevant regulations and ethical guidelines to ensure accurate and responsible promotion. The specific implementation of CGM in pharma marketing will depend on the products, target audience, and regional regulations in place.

Conversion

Conversion in pharmaceutical marketing refers to turning potential customers or leads into actual buyers by persuading them to prescribe, purchase leading to greater sales and brand loyalty for both parties. Conversion should create an enjoyable customer journey while leading to increased revenues and brand equity.

Conversion in pharmaceutical marketing occurs through various channels, including online advertising, email marketing, social media marketing, SEO optimization, and direct mail campaigns. Typical steps involved in conversion include drawing customers in by engaging them with targeted messaging that engages them as potential customers; providing relevant product or service information and encouraging them to take the desired actions like purchasing it or asking for further details about.

Improve Conversion Rates

As you might imagine, improving conversion rates in pharmaceutical marketing takes several steps. Consider these examples:

1. *Establish Your Target Audience*: As part of the initial steps for any product or service launch, you must identify your intended audience, including their demographics, interests, behaviors, and pain points.
2. *Create Appealing Content*: After identifying your target audience, generate content that resonates with them. This could include blog posts, social media updates, videos, and infographics that provide useful information that meets their needs and address these.
3. *Optimizing Your Website*: Your website should offer users a seamless user experience and encourage visitors to take action, including optimizing landing pages, making checkout easier, and being mobile-friendly.
4. *Use Targeted Calls-to-Action (CTAs) that are Relevant and Engage*: To entice visitors, use targeted CTAs that are relevant and engaging, such as signing up for your mailing list, downloading white papers, or making purchases. These CTAs should include signing up, downloading white papers, or purchasing products/services from you.
5. *Provide Social Proof*: Leveraging social proof through customer reviews, testimonials, and case studies to build trust with target customers can lead to higher conversions and revenue gains.
6. *Testing and Refining*: Finally, it's vitally important that you continually evaluate and refine your conversion rates by conducting A/B tests on various content, CTAs, and landing page versions to find what resonates most effectively with your target audience.

Improving conversion rates in pharmaceutical marketing requires having a deep knowledge of your target audience and being open-minded enough to test and refine strategies to obtain optimal results.

Conversion Metrics

In pharmaceutical marketing, "Conversion Metrics" are used to measure the effectiveness in turning potential interest into desired actions. Some key conversion metrics in pharma marketing include:

1. *Prescription Conversion Rate*: Measures the percentage of healthcare professionals prescribing a particular drug after exposure to the marketing campaign.
2. *Patient Conversion Rate*: Tracks the percentage of patients who receive a prescription for a specific medication after engaging with marketing materials or campaigns.
3. *Lead-to-Prescriber Conversion Rate*: Assesses how many leads generated through marketing efforts eventually result in healthcare professionals prescribing the promoted pharmaceutical product.
4. *Engagement-to-Sale Conversion Rate*: Analyzes the journey from initial engagement, such as attending a medical conference or accessing online resources, to the ultimate prescription or sale.
5. *Adherence Rate*: Focuses on how well patients adhere to prescribed medications over time, which is critical for patient outcomes and the pharmaceutical product's success.
6. *Healthcare Professional Awareness and Knowledge Metrics*: Measures the impact of marketing efforts in increasing awareness and knowledge of a pharmaceutical product among healthcare professionals.
7. *Market Share Growth*: Examines the growth in market share for a particular drug compared to competitors, which effective marketing strategies can influence.
8. *Return on Investment (ROI)*: Evaluates the financial returns compared to the cost of marketing campaigns, providing an overall measure of campaign effectiveness.
9. *Digital Engagement Metrics*: For online campaigns, metrics such as click-through rates, website conversions, and social media interactions can indicate the success of digital marketing efforts.
10. *Sales Metrics*: Traditional sales metrics, such as total sales revenue, sales volume, and average transaction value, provide an overall indication of product success resulting from marketing initiatives.

These metrics help pharmaceutical marketers assess the impact of their strategies, refine campaigns, and allocate resources effectively to maximize the conversion of interest into desired actions, whether prescriptions, sales, or other relevant outcomes.

Conversion Rates

Conversion rates in pharmaceutical marketing refer to the percentage of individuals who take desired actions after being exposed to marketing campaigns or promotional material, such as purchasing an item or signing up for services, or subscribing for something. Conversion rates in the pharmaceutical industry tend to be measured using prescription fulfillment, meaning how often patients fill their prescription after seeing healthcare professionals (HCPs) recommend certain medication.

Pharma companies utilize numerous marketing channels and tactics to reach potential patients and healthcare providers, including digital advertising, direct mail, in-person sales visits, educational events, targeted messaging, personalized outreach strategies and value added services such as patient education/support programs. To optimize conversion rates they may employ targeted messaging, personalized outreach efforts as well as value added services like patient education/support programs.

Pharma companies track prescription fulfillment rates as one of many key performance indicators (KPIs). Pharma companies may also measure and analyze other KPIs such as reach (the total number of people exposed to marketing messages), engagement (how often people interact with these messages), customer satisfaction, and reach/engagement ratio. By studying these metrics closely, companies gain valuable insights into the success of marketing campaigns while adapting their strategies accordingly.

Measuring Customer Conversion Rates

In pharmaceutical marketing, companies typically rely on data sources and analytical tools to measure customer conversion rates. Here are a few steps in measuring them:

1. *First Step in Conversion Goal Development*: Establish your conversion goal as soon as a marketing campaign launches by outlining an action you want patients and HCPs to take as a result of it. For instance, filling a prescription, signing up for patient support programs, attending educational events, etc are examples of such actions that should result from marketing initiatives.
2. *Track Conversions*: Once conversion goals have been defined, pharmaceutical companies can easily monitor conversions using various data sources including prescription data, website analytics and call center records. They could track how many patients fill a prescription within a specified period after being exposed to marketing messages or advertisements.
3. *Calculating Conversion Rate*: Calculating conversion rates can be accomplished by dividing the number of conversions by total exposures to marketing message. For example, if 500 patients were exposed and 100 converted; the conversion rate would be 20 percent.
4. *Analysis and Optimization*: After calculating their conversion rates, pharmaceutical companies can utilize data analytics techniques to pinpoint areas for optimization. They might identify particular marketing channels or messages which have proven more successful and allocate additional resources accordingly.
5. *Monitoring and Tuning Marketing Campaigns to Maintain or Increase Conversion Rates*: Conversion rates fluctuate over time, making it essential to continue monitoring and refining marketing strategies in order to maintain or increase conversion rates.

Measuring conversion rates in pharmaceutical marketing requires meticulous planning, data gathering and analysis as well as ongoing optimization to ensure successful campaigns.

Coopetition

Coopetition is the term used to refer to companies that operate both as competitors and collaborators at once, meaning they may operate as competitors within certain business areas while simultaneously working together on certain projects within that same market. For example, co-optition can often occur among larger corporations competing over certain business areas while working on joint initiatives within that same market.

Coopetition offers several advantages for companies, including:

1. *Accessing New Markets*: Through collaboration with other firms within an industry, firms may gain entry to markets they might otherwise not have been able to enter alone.
2. *Shared Costs*: Joining forces with other companies can also help reduce expenses associated with research and development, marketing, and other business operations.
3. *Innovation*: Coopetition can lead to increased innovation as businesses collaborate on developing products or services, they may have had difficulty creating independently.
4. *Risk Sharing*: Partnering with other businesses can also help spread risk across multiple

organizations and reduce any one company's failure's impact.

Coopetition in the pharmaceutical industry includes collaborative projects between companies to develop new drugs or medical technologies, partnerships between pharmaceutical companies and healthcare providers to enhance patient care, and alliances between companies to expand into new markets or regions. Coopetition allows companies to gain competitive advantages and add value for all stakeholders.

Coopetition in Pharma

The following examples show how some pharmaceutical companies have engaged in coopetition:

1. *Pfizer and BioNTech*: Although Pfizer and BioNTech were competitors in developing COVID-19 vaccines, they joined forces in producing and manufacturing the Pfizer-BioNTech COVID-19 vaccine in partnership. Leveraging their strengths enabled both companies to bring it to market rapidly.
2. *Merck and Bristol-Myers Squibb*: Merck and Bristol-Myers Squibb, two rival cancer drug developers, collaborated on Keytruda/Opdivo combination therapy which FDA approved to treat melanoma.
3. *Roche and Illumina*: Roche and Illumina are competitors in genomic sequencing; however, they came together to develop BaseSpace as a next-generation sequencing platform, helping both companies expand their presence in this market.
4. *Novartis and Sanofi*: Though these companies competed in the vaccines sector, they jointly developed MenHibrix to protect against meningococcal and HiB diseases. This partnership allowed both companies to offer patients greater protection by pooling their expertise.

Pharmaceutical companies engaging in co-optition offer several examples of working with competitors to leverage strengths and create value for all stakeholders.

Copay

Copay is a term commonly used in pharmaceutical marketing to refer to a portion of a prescription's cost that patients must cover themselves. An insurance plan usually determines co-pays and can differ depending on factors like drug type, coverage, and the pharmacy from where it was filled.

Pharmaceutical companies may provide copay assistance programs as part of their marketing initiatives to assist patients in affording their medications. These programs offer reduced or waived co-pays, making the drug more accessible and increasing the likelihood that patients will continue taking it.

Here are a few examples of copay assistance programs used in pharmaceutical marketing:

1. *Copay Cards*: Pharmaceutical companies may provide their patients with co-pay cards that reduce out-of-pocket drug costs when filling prescriptions from participating pharmacies. The patient presents the card when filling their order and pays an adjusted co-pay amount when picking up their prescription from them.
2. *Copay Foundations*: Some pharmaceutical companies and nonprofit organizations collaborate to establish co-pay foundations that offer financial aid for patients who can't afford their prescription drug co-payment.
3. *Copay Coupons*: Pharmaceutical companies may provide co-pay coupons that offer reduced co-pay amounts when prescriptions are filled, and when presented to their pharmacist for filling, patients present their coupons to receive reduced co-pay amounts.
4. *Copay Assistance Programs* can effectively allow pharmaceutical companies to set themselves apart from competitors and increase patient adherence. Still, companies must ensure that these programs comply with applicable regulations and industry standards to avoid potential legal or ethical repercussions.

Copays in Pharma Marketing

Here are a few examples of copay assistance programs in pharma marketing:

1. *GoodRx*: For example, GoodRx in the US provides copay assistance programs to assist patients in finding lower prices for their medications. The website and app tools allow patients to compare prescription prices and locate coupons to reduce out-of-pocket expenses.
2. *Novo Nordisk*: Novo Nordisk provides a copay assistance program for users of its insulin products. Eligible patients may receive financial aid to cover their copays.
3. *Pfizer*: Pfizer offers a copay assistance program to eligible patients for using its medications with copays, deductibles, and coinsurance premiums.
4. *AbbVie*: AbbVie offers a copay assistance program to patients with conditions like rheumatoid arthritis or psoriasis by providing

financial assistance that allows eligible patients to meet copays and out-of-pocket costs easily.

5. *Merck* offers a copay assistance program for eligible patients living with conditions, such as diabetes and HIV who take its medications and need financial help covering copayments and deductibles.

Copycatting

Copycatting refers to the practice of mimicking or recreating someone else's actions, ideas or behaviors without their prior authorization and approval. Copycatting can have both positive and negative connotations depending on its intended usage by those practicing this act of mimicry.

Copycatting can be seen as an act of flattery or admiration; an artist might create work similar to another they adore as an act of flattery and admiration.

Copycatting in an unfair context may constitute plagiarism or theft. For instance, students submit stolen essays as their work; in other cases, it can be used fraudulently, and intellectual property theft cases.

Copycatting in Marketing

In marketing, copycatting refers to imitating the strategies or tactics of competitors or another company as a strategy or tactic to gain market share or remain competitive. Copycatting can help gain ground over those that want to copycatting by mimicking what works and copying tactics of what has worked previously.

Legal copycatting involves employing marketing techniques not protected by intellectual property rights or patent laws; for instance, if one company executes a successful social media campaign and other companies adopt similar approaches in their marketing plans it would be legal for other organizations to imitate them legally.

Illegal copycatting occurs when marketers copy marketing materials protected by intellectual property rights or patent laws. For instance if one company copies another company's logo, branding and slogan, then this could constitute illegal copycatting.

Copycatting can be an effective marketing strategy, helping companies learn from competitors without repeating their errors. But to remain within legal bounds and avoid engaging in illegal copycatting is of utmost importance as engaging in such activity can damage both their reputation and result in legal ramifications for both parties involved.

Copycatting in pharma marketing refers to marketing a generic version of an original branded drug from another company. Generic drugs contain identical active ingredients, strengths, dosage forms and routes of administration as their counterpart brand-name drugs.

Generic drugs are generally seen as more cost-effective alternatives to brand name pharmaceuticals and are frequently sold at lower prices. This is likely because companies that produce generics don't need to invest as heavily in research and development or marketing since they essentially copy an already successful drug's formulation and ingredients.

However, generic drugs must adhere to the same quality, safety and efficacy standards set by original brand-name drugs. According to US Food and Drug Administration requirements, generic equivalents of brand name medications must meet standards regarding ingredients, dosage strength, route of administration, bioequivalence, and intended purpose.

Copycat marketing in pharma is legal and provides consumers with cost-cutting alternatives; however, companies must abide by all relevant regulations and standards to maintain safety and efficacy for drugs produced.

Copyright

Copyright in pharmaceutical marketing refers to the protection of Intellectual Property Rights (IPR) associated with marketing materials used by pharmaceutical companies for advertising campaigns or promotions, such as product descriptions, packaging designs, promotions or advertisements.

Pharmaceutical companies invest substantial resources in creating marketing materials to promote their products and services, so it is critical that any reproduction without consent be prevented from unapproved uses or reproduction. Furthermore, copyright law gives pharmaceutical companies exclusive control of how these materials are utilized and distributed.

Here are several key aspects of copyright in pharmaceutical marketing:

1. *Copyright Ownership*: When it comes to ownership, marketing materials produced for pharmaceutical companies or their agencies typically belong to those involved with creating

them and therefore their rights belong to those involved in creating them.

2. *Copyright Protection*: Under copyright law, original works of literary, artistic and intellectual content, such as literary texts and artwork created by writers are safeguarded. Even marketing material created by pharmaceutical companies are protected by copyright.
3. *Duration of Copyright Protection*: The duration of copyright protection varies by jurisdiction but usually covers both a creator's lifetime as well as some amount of years after they pass away.
4. *Fair Use*: Fair use is a legal concept which permits limited copyrighted material usage for specific reasons such as criticism, commentary, news reporting, teaching scholarship and research without specific prior consent from its right holders.
5. *Infringement*: Any unauthorized reproduction or use of copyrighted materials without authorization constitutes copyright infringement and could lead to legal actions for damages and injunctive relief.

Pharmaceutical companies must protect their copyright in marketing materials carefully to safeguard investments while assuring ethical product promotion. This may necessitate seeking legal advice, registering their copyright with relevant authorities and monitoring for possible infringements.

Copy Testing

Copy testing is a research methodology commonly employed in advertising to evaluate the effectiveness of messaging and creativity before its launch. For pharmaceutical marketing purposes, copy testing ensures compliance with regulatory guidelines, connects with target audiences, and effectively communicates the benefits/risks of prescription drugs. Here are some key aspects of copy testing used in pharmaceutical marketing:

1. *Compliance*: Pharma companies must ensure their advertising complies with regulatory guidelines, such as requirements for fair balance, truthful and non-misleading messaging, and appropriate disclosures. Copy testing can help pharma companies identify any compliance issues before launching advertisements.
2. *Research Design*: Copy testing typically uses surveys, focus groups, or other research methodologies to gather feedback on advertising messaging and creativity. Care must be taken when developing this method of inquiry to ensure that samples accurately reflect target audiences while questions are structured for actionable insights.
3. *Metrics*: Metrics used in copy testing may vary depending on the research design and campaign goals; for instance, some testing may focus on measuring recall or recognition of key messaging points, while others may explore their emotional impact.
4. *Copy Testing and Iteration*: Pharma companies can utilize copy testing to detect potential issues with their ad copy and creatives before launch. This enables them to make necessary modifications until reaching an optimal solution.
5. *Regulatory Review*: Once their messaging and creative have been approved, pharmaceutical companies must submit their ads for regulatory review to ensure compliance with guidelines. Again, copy testing can help detect compliance issues early in the process and save time and resources.

Here are a few examples of how copy testing has been utilized in pharmaceutical marketing:

A. *Recall Testing*: Before launching its print ad campaign to promote a new prescription drug, one pharma company conducted recall testing to gauge how well its target audience remembered key messages. When recall testing revealed that some aspects failed to resonate with audience members, changes were made before rolling out their campaign.

B. *Emotional Impact Testing*: A pharmaceutical company developed a TV ad campaign for chronic conditions to promote prescription medication, then conducted emotional impact testing to measure how it made viewers feel. Unfortunately, the tests revealed that it wasn't emotionally engaging enough, leading the company to adjust the ad creative and increase emotional impact before launching it on air.

C. *Comprehension Testing*: A pharmaceutical company created a website to promote a new prescription drug. Before launching the site, comprehension testing was conducted to measure how well the target audience understood what was presented. Results revealed that it was too technical and complex for them to comprehend easily, prompting the company to change website content to simplify messaging and increase comprehension.

These examples demonstrate how copy testing can assist pharmaceutical companies in identifying any issues with ad messaging and creatives before launching campaigns and making necessary modifications to increase advertising campaigns' effectiveness.

Copy testing is an integral component of pharmaceutical marketing that ensures advertising meets regulatory guidelines, resonates with target audiences, and accurately conveys the benefits and risks associated with prescription medicines. By gathering feedback on ad messaging and creatives through research methodologies, pharma companies can make data-driven decisions to optimize the performance of their advertising campaigns.

Copy Testing Methods

There are various copy-testing strategies you can employ to assess the efficacy of pharmaceutical marketing materials; here are a few commonly utilized ones:

1. *Focus Groups*: Focus groups involve gathering a small group representing your target audience to see marketing materials and engage in a facilitated dialogue where participants share their opinions, perceptions, and reactions. This method offers in-depth qualitative feedback that provides deeper insights into participants' thoughts, emotions, and perceptions.
2. *Surveys and Questionnaires*: Surveys and questionnaires can be conducted online, by email, or in-person to gather quantitative data efficiently from larger samples. They often incorporate rating scales, multiple choice questions, or open-ended inquiries that gather feedback regarding specific aspects of copy, such as clarity, credibility, relevance, or impact, providing efficient data collection from this method.
3. *Interviews*: Conducting one-on-one interviews with participants allows for an in-depth exploration of their perceptions and experiences with a copy, giving interviewees a chance to provide detailed feedback on their decision-making processes and preferences. This method is especially effective at understanding individual perspectives and collecting qualitative data.
4. *Eye Tracking* technology measures where participants' eyes focus while viewing marketing materials, providing invaluable insights into visual hierarchy, attention-grabbing elements, and navigation patterns within the copy. Analyzing eye movement data reveals areas of potential improvement for design or layout improvements.
5. *Online Panels*: An online panel comprises individuals regularly participating in market research activities. Participants gain access to marketing materials and provide feedback through an online platform. This method offers convenience, wider geographical coverage, and the capacity for data collection from diverse respondents.
6. *A/B Testing*: An A/B test involves creating two versions (A and B) of marketing copy and randomly assigning participants into either group; their responses to either version (A or B) will then be compared to establish which version performs better; this technique can help compare messages, visuals or calls-to-action to identify those which perform best and determine which are more successful overall.
7. *Neuromarketing Techniques*: Neuromarketing is an approach combining neuroscience and market research that seeks to uncover the subconscious reactions of consumers when exposed to marketing stimuli. Techniques such as electroencephalography (EEG), functional magnetic resonance imaging (fMRI), or biometrics (heart rate or skin conductance measurements) may be utilized as ways of monitoring participants' physiological and neurologic responses to copy. Such measures provide valuable insight into emotional engagement, attention span, and memory activation processes.

Select copy-testing methods that fit with your objectives, budget, and resources available to you. Combining multiple approaches may give a deeper insight into marketing materials' effectiveness while increasing the accuracy of insights gained.

Copy Testing in Pharmaceutical Marketing: Step by Step

Here is a step-by-step guide on conducting copy testing in pharmaceutical marketing:

A. Step 1: Define Objectives

Objective: Assess the clarity and impact of a print advertisement promoting a new prescription medication.

B. Step 2: Identify the Target Audience

Target Audience: Adult patients suffering from chronic migraines.

C. Step 3: Select the Testing Method

Testing Method: Qualitative research using focus groups.

D. Step 4: Develop Test Materials

Test Material: Prepare a print advertisement with key messaging about the medication, its benefits, and a call to action.

E. Step 5: Recruit Participants

Recruit participants who fit the target audience profile, such as patients diagnosed with chronic migraines. Aim for a diverse group to gather a range of perspectives.

F. Step 6: Conduct the Copy Test

Gather the focus group participants in a controlled environment. Present the print advertisement and facilitate a discussion using the following prompts:

- *Overall Impression*: What are your initial thoughts and feelings about the ad?

  Example Response: *The ad grabs* attention with its vibrant colors and large font.
- *Clarity of Messaging*: How well does the ad communicate the key information about the medication?

  Example Response: *The headline and* subheadings clearly highlight the benefits of the medication.
- *Relevance to the Target Audience*: Does the ad resonate with your experiences as chronic migraine sufferers?

  Example Response: *The testimonials* from patients who have experienced relief are relatable and compelling.
- *Call-to-Action*: Does the ad effectively prompt you to take action, such as speaking to your healthcare provider?

  Example Response: *The Call-to-Action* is clear and provides a toll-free number for further information.

G. Step 7: Analyze Results

Analyze the feedback from focus group participants to identify common themes, strengths, weaknesses, and areas for improvement. Look for patterns in responses related to clarity, relevance, and impact.

Example Analysis: *Most participants found the ad visually appealing and felt that the messaging was clear and relevant to their experience as chronic migraine sufferers. However, a few participants suggested including more information about potential side effects and highlighting the medication's efficacy compared to competitors.*

H. Step 8: Draw Conclusions and Take Action

Based on the analysis, we conclude that the print advertisement generally resonates with the target audience. However, determine the need to address the feedback regarding side effect information and comparative efficacy. Plan to revise the copy accordingly.

I. Step 9: Iterate and Refine

Update the print advertisement to incorporate the feedback received. Include additional information about potential side effects and highlight the medication's comparative advantages. Implement these changes in subsequent iterations of the ad.

J. Step10. Monitor Performance

Track the performance of the revised advertisement through metrics such as patient inquiries, prescription rates, or brand perception surveys. Monitor any changes in these metrics to assess the impact of the refined copy.

By following these steps, you can systematically evaluate the effectiveness of your pharmaceutical marketing copy and make informed decisions to optimize its impact on the target audience.

Copywriting

Copywriting refers to creating written content for marketing and advertising purposes. Copywriters aim to persuade their readers to take certain actions, such as purchasing something or signing up for services. Therefore, a great copywriter must craft compelling, persuasive messages that resonate with their target audience.

Copywriting plays an essential role in healthcare marketing by providing engaging and informative messaging for healthcare providers and patients alike. Pharmaceutical copywriting aims to inform healthcare professionals and patients alike of the advantages and side effects of prescription medications, medical devices, or other healthcare products or services they use or purchase.

Pharmaceutical copywriting comes in many forms, such as:

1. *Sales Collateral*: Pharmaceutical copywriters often create copy for sales collateral such as brochures, leaflets, or detail aids that inform healthcare providers about the benefits of specific drugs or medical devices.
2. *Product Websites*: Copywriters create copy for product websites that offers comprehensive information about drugs or medical devices, including dosage, side effects, and clinical trials.
3. *Patient Education Materials*: Copywriters create material such as brochures and websites for patients to help them better understand their condition and treatment options.
4. *Medical Journal Articles*: Copywriters specialize in crafting medical journal articles to report

clinical trials or studies that establish the efficacy or safety of drugs or medical devices.

5. *Advertising Campaigns*: Copywriters create copy for advertisements designed to promote pharmaceutical or healthcare services to healthcare professionals and patients.

Pharmaceutical copywriting requires an in-depth knowledge of scientific and medical concepts and an ability to communicate complex ideas clearly and concisely. In addition, pharma marketers must ensure adherence to all messaging by being accurate and not misleading to the regulatory guidelines. Effective copywriting can educate healthcare providers and patients, improving patient outcomes.

Corporate Appraisal

Corporate appraisal in pharma marketing refers to assessing a pharmaceutical company's overall performance and strategic direction. Internal stakeholders such as senior management, the board of directors, external consultants, and investors may conduct this appraisal process.

Here are the essential aspects of corporate appraisal in pharmaceutical marketing:

1. *Financial Performance*: Corporate appraisal involves an examination of a company's financial performance, such as revenue, profits, and return on investments. In addition, an assessment may also include its financial stability and liquidity.
2. *Market Position*: Corporate appraisal may also involve an analysis of a company's market position, including its share, competitive landscape, and growth potential. Furthermore, this evaluation could take into account wider trends within healthcare as well as regulatory considerations.
3. *Product Portfolio*: Pharmaceutical company appraisal requires an evaluation of their product portfolio, from pipeline strength and existing product performance, as well as potential for future product developments.
4. *Marketing and Sales Effectiveness*: Corporate appraisal can also assess the success of a company's marketing and sales strategies, including promotional material quality, the effectiveness of sales force personnel, and online digital marketing initiatives.
5. *Corporate Governance*: Finally, an appraisal may examine the quality of corporate governance at an organization, including leadership structure and board membership, as well as compliance with ethics and legal standards.

Corporate appraisal in pharmaceutical marketing is an indispensable way of assessing a pharmaceutical company's performance and strategic direction. By analyzing key metrics related to financial performance, market position, product portfolio management effectiveness, sales effectiveness, and corporate governance, companies can identify areas for improvement and craft long-term strategies to drive long-term success.

Corporate Governance

Corporate governance refers to the rules, practices and processes by which companies are directed and controlled. This encompasses structures and processes for decision-making, accountability, control and resource allocation management. Corporate governance exists primarily to ensure companies operate ethically while adding value for stakeholders such as employees, customers, suppliers and wider society.

Key Elements in Corporate Governance

Corporate governance includes several essential components. Consider the following, for example:

1. *Board of Directors*: The board of directors oversees and directs a company's overall direction and management, oversees management team performance, and sets goals and objectives while making major decisions regarding operations and the direction of the company.
2. *Executive Management*: The executive management team oversees day-to-day operations of the company's business, implements strategy set forth by the board of directors and oversees company resources.
3. *Shareholders*: Shareholders are the ultimate owners of their company and have an important say in major decisions like electing the board of directors and authorizing major transactions.
4. *Transparency*: Corporate governance calls for complete and open financial reporting and disclosure practices that foster trust with shareholders and other stakeholders.
5. *Ethics and Compliance*: Companies must observe ethical and legal standards set out by industry regulations as well as have systems in place to detect fraudulent activities and misconduct.
6. *Risk Management*: Corporate governance involves identifying and mitigating any threats to

an organization's operations or reputation that threaten its viability, as well as informing key board members on which risks exist and their means of management. Developing plans to mitigate those threats requires planning meetings where key risks will be disclosed to board members as part of effective corporate governance practice.

7. *Corporate Social Responsibility*: Corporate governance encompasses an organization's social responsibilities to its wider community, which may include environmental impact assessment and mitigation; diversity/inclusion initiatives, and ethical sourcing activities.

Corporate governance is essential to a company's long-term success by setting clear structures, processes, and accountability mechanisms that facilitate value creation while meeting stakeholder expectations and providing support in its community.

Corporate Governance in Pharma Marketing

Proper governance standards in pharmaceutical marketing are vitally important to ensure pharmaceutical companies operate ethically when advertising their products, given their potential impact on public health and other factors. Pharma companies must abide by stringent governance requirements to maintain public trust.

Here are a few key components of corporate governance in pharmaceutical marketing:

1. *Compliance*: Pharma companies must abide by laws and regulations concerning their promotion of pharmaceutical products, adhering to codes of conduct set by regulatory bodies such as FDA (Food and Drug Administration) in the United States or EMA (European Medicines Agency) in the European Union, and industry groups like PhRMA (Pharmaceutical Research and Manufacturers of America).
2. *Transparency*: Pharma companies must maintain transparency when conducting marketing practices and provide accurate product information that includes potential risks or side effects. Healthcare professionals and patients need access to data-backed recommendations from pharmaceutical companies.
3. *Ethics*: Pharmaceutical companies must uphold ethical standards in their marketing practices to maintain patient privacy, avoid deceptive advertising and thwart conflicts of interests.
4. *Monitoring and Oversight*: Pharma companies must establish effective monitoring and oversight mechanisms to ensure compliance with governance standards, such as conducting regular audits on marketing practices or creating independent review boards to oversee promotional activities.
5. *Patient Safety*: Pharma companies should place patient safety as the core focus in their marketing practices, including providing accurate information regarding potential side effects and contraindications, promptly reporting adverse events to regulatory bodies, and providing accurate advice regarding potential side effects or contraindications of medications prescribed.
6. *Corporate Social Responsibility*: Pharma companies should recognize their social responsibilities, including considering how marketing practices impact wider society, by creating accessible products at reasonable costs for all patients, regardless of financial means.

Corporate governance standards within pharmaceutical marketing are crucial in building and upholding public trust in this industry. By adhering to strict compliance measures, pharmaceutical companies can promote their products ethically while simultaneously increasing patient safety and enhancing public health outcomes.

Corporate Social Responsibility (CSR)

Corporate Social Responsibility (CSR) in pharmaceutical marketing refers to ethical and responsible marketing practices employed by pharmaceutical companies when selling their products to healthcare professionals and patients, such as providing accurate product information with no false claims made for it and refraining from engaging in promotional activities that might jeopardize patient safety or compromise public health in any way. Pharma companies must ensure their activities do not risk patient well-being or diminish public well-being.

Pharmaceutical companies typically participate in various CSR initiatives as part of their marketing practices, including:

1. *Access to Medicines*: Pharmaceutical companies have instituted access programs designed to make essential medications accessible at an affordable cost for underserved populations, like Novartis' Access Program which makes essential drugs available in low and middle income countries at no-profit pricing.

2. *Community Outreach*: Many pharmaceutical companies implement community outreach programs to foster health and well-being in underserved regions. Pfizer employees through its *Global Health Fellows Program* and then partners with nongovernmental organizations (NGOs) and government agencies to improve healthcare provision to these underserved regions.
3. *Environmental Sustainability*: Pharma companies help foster sustainable development by minimizing environmental footprints. For example, Sanofi has set ambitious environmental targets, such as cutting CO emissions, water usage, and waste production for 2025.
4. *Clinical Trial Transparency*: Many pharmaceutical companies have committed to transparency with clinical trial data by making results publicly available. Roche's policy on data sharing ensures that their clinical trial information can be made accessible for researchers and members of the public alike.
5. *Employee Health and Wellbeing*: Pharmaceutical companies prioritize employee well-being by providing wellness programs, mental health support services, and flexible work arrangements for their staff. Johnson & Johnson's Employee Wellness Program includes fitness classes, mental health support services, and stress management techniques.
6. *Disease Awareness*: Pharma companies engage in disease awareness campaigns to inform the public and facilitate early diagnosis and treatment of disease. For example, *Merck for Mothers* strives to decrease maternal mortality worldwide by equipping healthcare workers with training, education, and supplies necessary for maternal healthcare delivery.

These are just a few examples of CSR activities undertaken by pharmaceutical companies. By taking steps towards sustainable development, access to medicines, clinical trial transparency, and employee health initiatives, they can contribute to society's well-being.

Cost-Benefit Analysis (CBA)

Cost-benefit analysis (CBA) is an invaluable decision-making technique utilized by businesses, governments and other entities to examine both potential benefits and costs before making their determination regarding whether an undertaking merits proceeding further or not.

Cost-benefit analysis plays an essential role in pharmaceutical marketing, helping companies determine potential returns on investment (ROI). Cost-benefit analysis evaluates various marketing initiatives like:

1. *Size and Structure of Sales Force*: Utilizing cost-benefit analyses can assist companies in selecting an optimal size and structure of salesforce based on factors like target market size, complexity of offerings and competition levels.
2. *Advertising Campaigns*: Cost-benefit analysis can assist companies in assessing the potential return on investment (ROI) of advertising campaigns by considering target audience size, reach, frequency of campaign communications and expected impact on sales.
3. *Sampling Programs*: Cost-benefit analysis can assist companies in gauging the potential returns from sampling programs by considering factors like cost per sample distributed and potential impact on sales.
4. *Medical Education Programs*: Cost-benefit analyses can assist companies with calculating the potential ROI of medical education programs by taking into account costs, number of healthcare professionals reached, and expected effect on sales.

Before proceeding, a pharmaceutical company would assess the costs and expected benefits of any marketing initiative, such as increased sales, brand recognition improvement, and enhanced relationships with healthcare professionals in each instance.

Cost-per-Click (CPC)

Cost-per-Click (CPC) advertising in pharmaceutical marketing refers to the fee an advertiser pays each time someone clicks their online ad for pharmaceutical products. CPC ads use pay-per-click (PPC) models where advertisers bid on keywords, then only pay when someone clicks their ad.

Pharma marketing presents unique challenges and regulations compared to other industries, thus resulting in higher CPC rates than in other sectors due to this extra scrutiny and regulations. Pharma advertisers may need to adhere to stringent rules regarding the content and message of their ads which can limit content delivery, impressions, and click-through rates (CTR).

Pharma is an extremely competitive industry, which drives up CPC rates further. Advertisers must compete for ad space across search engines, social media platforms, and other channels, with bidding on popular keywords may prove expensive.

CPC rates in pharmaceutical marketing can fluctuate depending on several variables, including product, target audience, the platform used to advertise, and competition for space available to the advertiser.

Here are some examples of CPC rates in pharma marketing:

1. According to research by AdEspresso, pharmaceutical ads on Facebook averaged an average CPC cost of $1.72, higher than the overall average CPC costs.
2. Google Ads estimates the Cost per Click (CPC) for different keywords, with cholesterol medication costing an estimated CPC of $3.33 and insomnia medication estimated to cost only $2.54 as of 2021.
3. In 2021, the Healthcare Marketing Report conducted research that indicated an average cost per lead for pharmaceutical and healthcare ads on LinkedIn of $5.26.

Please note that these rates are averages and may differ depending on factors like product, target audience, and competition for advertising space.

Cost-per-Conversion (CPC)

Cost per conversion (CPC) in pharmaceutical marketing refers to the fee an advertiser pays each time someone completes an action related to their online ad for a pharmaceutical product (such as filling out a form or making a purchase) via their clickbait ads.

Cost per conversion in pharmaceutical marketing varies depending on campaign goals and desired actions, such as encouraging users to fill out forms requesting more information about drugs or registering for clinical trials; here, the conversion would equal each completed form or sign-up, thus becoming one cost per conversion in this instance.

Like CPC rates for pharmaceutical marketing, industry-specific challenges, and regulations can affect the cost per conversion rate, advertisers must ensure their ads adhere to regulations established by regulatory bodies such as Food and Drug Administration (FDA) or Federal Trade Commission (FTC) in the United States, which could result in limited ad impressions and reduced conversion rates resulting in an increased CPC rate.

Additionally, the competitive nature of the pharmaceutical industry can affect the cost per conversion rates. Advertisers must vie for advertising space on search engines, social media platforms, and other online channels, thus, bidding on popular keywords or targeting specific audiences can become costly.

Cost-per-Lead (CPL)

Cost per lead (CPL) is a marketing metric that quantifies the costs of generating one lead or potential customer for any product or service. A lead refers to someone interested in something by providing contact details such as name, email address, or phone number in response to marketing campaigns.

Cost per lead calculations are easily done by dividing the total marketing campaign costs by the number of leads generated during it; so for a campaign costing $1,000 that generated 50 leads, cost per lead would equal $20.

CPL (cost per lead) is an integral metric in marketing because it helps businesses evaluate their campaigns' efficacy and ROI (Return on Investment). By assessing cost per lead data, businesses can identify which marketing channels, tactics, or messages are most successful at generating leads, and adjust their strategies to optimize budget and resource allocation.

Cost Per Lead in Pharma Marketing

The cost per lead (CPL) in pharmaceutical marketing varies greatly, depending on product type, target audience demographics, marketing channel selection, and competition. Below are examples of average CPL rates found across various pharma marketing initiatives:

1. *Email Marketing*: Pharmaceutical companies may send targeted email campaigns to physicians and healthcare providers to promote a new medication or treatment. Typical CPL rates in the pharmaceutical industry range between $20-50 per lead for email marketing campaigns.
2. *Social Media Advertising*: Pharmaceutical companies may utilize Facebook or LinkedIn-targeted ad campaigns to reach healthcare professionals or patients interested in specific drugs or treatments. The average Cost Per Lead (CPL) of social media ads within the pharma industry averages between $30-50 per lead.
3. *Search Engine Marketing*: Pharmaceutical companies may use Search Engine Marketing (SEM) to bid on keywords associated with specific conditions or treatments to ensure they appear at the top of search results when patients

or healthcare professionals search for that topic online. On average, search engine marketing costs around $50-$100 per lead for pharmaceutical industries.

4. *Webinars*: Pharmaceutical companies may host webinars featuring key opinion leaders or specialists from certain fields to discuss potential treatments or therapies, with an average cost per lead between $50-$150 for such webinars in the pharmaceutical industry.

It is important to note that these are general examples and that the cost per lead may differ based on your specific campaign, target audience, and other considerations. Furthermore, regulatory restrictions within the pharmaceutical industry may limit what marketing activities can take place, impacting this cost.

Counterfeit Drugs

Counterfeit drugs are illegal copies of genuine medications produced without regard for quality or safety standards, in an effort to deceive and defraud consumers, potentially containing harmful ingredients that pose significant threats to public health.

Counterfeit drugs represent a global challenge that can be hard to identify due to online sales or illicit channels. Furthermore, counterfeit products often look identical to genuine ones and come packaged with convincing labeling or branding features to confuse authorities and the general public alike.

Counterfeit drugs have an enormous financial and reputational cost on the pharmaceutical industry. Losses due to fraudulent drugs include lost revenues and damaged brand equity; compliance costs increases for regulatory compliance measures and supply chain protection will rise exponentially as counterfeit medicines enter circulation.

Estimating the financial loss from counterfeit drugs to the pharmaceutical industry can be challenging. The Organization for Economic Cooperation and Development (OECD) estimates counterfeit drug sales are around ten percent of global pharmaceutical sales.

Counterfeit medicines pose both financial and health threats to both industries and patients. Counterfeit medications contain potentially hazardous or ineffective ingredients which could prove fatal for patients using them to treat themselves.

Pharmaceutical companies and regulatory agencies around the globe work diligently to combat counterfeit medicine production and sale. They strive to raise public awareness to stop the manufacture and distribution of counterfeit drugs.

Pharmaceutical companies can combat counterfeit drug trafficking by taking steps to verify the authenticity of their products, using track-and-trace technologies to monitor supply chains and detect counterfeit drugs before entering the market. In addition, certain regulatory bodies require unique product identifiers or tamper-evident packaging features as additional safeguards against counterfeiting.

Ways to Combat Counterfeit Drugs

There are various approaches available for combatting counterfeit drugs, including raising public awareness on its risks and how to recognize counterfeit medications. Doing this may reduce unknowingly purchasing and taking fake medications from pharmacies or online sources. Here are some ways that can help prevent the spread of counterfeit drugs:

1. *Implement Regulatory Measures*: Governments and regulatory agencies can implement measures to combat counterfeit drugs, such as mandating unique product identifiers, tamper-evident packaging materials and track-and-trace technologies.
2. *Strengthen Supply Chains*: Strengthening supply chains to source medications from reliable manufacturers and distributors can help prevent counterfeit drugs from entering the market.
3. *Conduct Regular Inspections*: Performing periodic inspections at manufacturing facilities, distribution centers, and pharmacies can help detect and prevent counterfeit drug production and sale.
4. *Use of Authentication Technologies*: Utilizing authentication technologies like holograms, QR codes and serial numbers can assist in verifying the authenticity of medicines to avoid counterfeiting and prevent abuse by patients.
5. *Cooperation*: Working closely together between pharmaceutical companies, regulatory bodies, law enforcement authorities, and other relevant parties can assist in detecting and stopping counterfeit drug production and sales.

Combatting counterfeit drugs is a complex issue requiring multiple approaches; by working together we can ensure patients receive safe and effective medications while safeguarding public health.

Crisis Communications

Crisis communications in pharma marketing refer to communicating with stakeholders such as healthcare providers, patients, regulators, and the general public during an incident or crisis affecting pharmaceutical industries. Crisis communications aim to provide timely and accurate information addressing concerns while maintaining credibility among these stakeholder groups.

Essential Elements

Here are the core elements of crisis communication that pharmaceutical companies should remember and act on:

1. *Proactive Planning*: Pharmaceutical companies should prepare an emergency communication plan before any crisis arises, including roles, responsibilities, communication channels, key messages, and crisis response procedures.
2. *Timely and Accurate Communication*: In a crisis, stakeholders must receive timely, accurate company communication. Companies should use multiple forms of communication, such as social media posts, press releases, and emails to reach all their stakeholders quickly and keep them updated.
3. *Empathy and Transparency*: Companies should show empathy and transparency during a crisis by acknowledging stakeholders' needs, communicating openly and honestly, and offering trustworthy communication channels to build trust with those impacted. Doing this will build credibility with stakeholders.
4. *Collaboration*: Crisis communication in pharmaceutical marketing often necessitates working closely with regulators and patient advocacy groups, so companies must collaborate closely with these parties to develop an integrated response and ensure all parties involved are informed and included.

Crisis Communications in Pharma Marketing: Examples and Implications

The following three examples show how these pharmaceutical companies communicated effectively to overcome a crisis:

1. Johnson & Johnson's response to the Tylenol poisoning crisis in the 1980s stands out as an outstanding example of effective communication during an emergency, swiftly informing and responding to stakeholders while recalling and reformulating the product quickly, maintaining stakeholder trust and credibility through prompt action taken during that crisis.
2. Merck implemented an intensive crisis communication plan following the Vioxx recall in 2004. This included timely and accurate communications with stakeholders and commitments to transparency and collaboration with regulators and patient advocacy groups.
3. Moderna quickly responded to COVID-19 vaccine safety concerns by communicating directly with regulators and the public to address safety issues quickly and providing transparent information on its safety and efficacy.

Cross Selling

Cross-selling in pharmaceutical marketing refers to promoting or recommending additional products or services to customers who have already purchased medication or treatments from pharmaceutical companies to increase revenue and customer retention. Pharmaceutical companies employ this strategy to increase both revenue and customer loyalty.

Pharmaceutical companies use cross-selling in various ways. One approach involves offering additional medications or treatments to those already prescribed a specific drug. For instance, if someone was taking medication to control high blood pressure, pharmaceutical companies might offer medications or supplements to lower cholesterol or improve cardiovascular health as a form of cross-selling.

Cross-selling in pharmaceutical marketing also involves directly offering related products or services to healthcare providers who prescribe their medication, such as educational resources, training programs, or consulting services.

Cross-selling in pharmaceutical marketing must adhere to stringent regulations and guidelines; otherwise, it risks breaching patient safety or privacy. Therefore, pharmaceutical companies must ensure their cross-selling practices adhere to ethical principles without endangering patient well-being or security.

Cross-selling in Pharma Marketing

Here are some examples of cross-selling used by pharmaceutical companies in their marketing:

A. *Promoting Related Medications*: Pharmaceutical companies provide promoting similar medications offering educational resources or training sessions. Pharma companies frequently offer educational resources or training sessions for healthcare providers prescribing their medication such as online courses, webinars or in-person training sessions that detail its potential side effects and implications more comprehensively.

B. *Promoting Supplements*: Pharmaceutical companies may cross-sell vitamin supplements to patients taking certain medications that deplete essential vitamins or minerals to provide replenishment. For instance, they might promote one that can replenish them.

C. *Consulting Services*: Pharmaceutical companies may offer consulting services to healthcare providers to enhance patient care. This may involve helping with medication dosing or monitoring or providing guidance for managing specific populations.

However, it must be remembered that these examples must comply with stringent regulations and guidelines set by the pharmaceutical industry and regulatory bodies.

Crowdsourcing

Crowdsourcing is a practice where a company gathers ideas, opinions, or services from an undefined pool of individuals via the Internet. Crowdsourcing can be an extremely efficient tool for pharmaceutical marketing as it leverages collective intelligence from patients, physicians and stakeholders within the healthcare ecosystem.

Crowdsourcing can play an important role in pharmaceutical marketing in many ways:

A. *Idea Generation*: Crowdsourcing helps companies access fresh ideas for products, services, and marketing campaigns they might otherwise struggle to develop independently. By collecting input from patients and healthcare providers on what features should be included in an innovative drug or treatment or the most efficient ways to market products or services and conduct campaigns, crowdsourcing methods can yield useful ideas leading to their products/services or campaigns being developed and launched successfully.

B. *Patient Education*: Crowdsourcing can assist pharmaceutical companies with creating patient education materials. For example, patients and caregivers may be asked about their experiences managing certain conditions or taking certain medicines; the collected feedback could be used to create more effective educational resources.

C. *Social Media Campaigns*: Crowdsourcing can help organizations develop and execute social media campaigns that engage patients and healthcare providers alike. For example, companies may request user-generated content like patient testimonials or stories and use this material to develop more authentic marketing efforts.

How Pharma Uses Crowdsourcing

Pharmaceutical companies have increasingly used crowdsource to engage with customers, developing ideas for projects and understanding target audience needs and preferences. Here are a few examples:

1. Pfizer launched the *Get Old* campaign in 2013 to address the challenges associated with aging. For this initiative, they utilized crowdsourcing as part of the *Get Old* initiative and received over 1,200 submissions to use as content development for their campaign.
2. Johnson & Johnson launched its *Donate a Photo* campaign in 2014, encouraging people to post their pictures online and share them. For each picture shared, Johnson & Johnson donated one dollar directly to a charity of their user's choosing; over 1 million photos were submitted during this initiative and raised over one million for charity!
3. Novartis launched *Dare to Change Diabetes* as a crowdsourcing campaign to uncover innovative solutions to help those with Diabetes. They invited ideas from patients, caregivers, healthcare providers, and other stakeholders. Over 150 submissions were received, with one winning idea for a mobile app designed to assist people in managing their condition.
4. Roche launched the *My Cancer Voices* initiative in 2019 to give cancer patients and their loved ones a voice. Crowdsourcing enabled Roche to collect patient and caregiver stories, experiences, and insights gathered through *My Cancer Voices*; then, this data was used to create videos showcasing cancer's human side.
5. In 2020, AstraZeneca unveiled its COVID-19 vaccine with *Our Best Shot* campaign to promote its COVID-19 vaccine. As part of this promotional campaign, crowdsourcing was used to collect stories from those who had received it and use this footage in creating an inspiring video that encourages others to get immunized against COVID.

Crowdsourcing can be an invaluable asset to pharma marketers, but they must use it ethically and transparently. Patient privacy must always come first, and companies must ensure they do not exploit patients or healthcare providers for personal gain.

Culture

Culture refers to the collective beliefs, values, customs, behaviors, and artifacts that define a group or society. This encompasses shared knowledge, experiences, and practices that influence how individuals think, feel, and act within a particular social setting. Culture may manifest through art forms like painting, language, music, religion, cuisine, clothing, architecture, etc., and be affected by historical, economic, political, and environmental forces continuously shifting their shape over time. Culture also provides individuals with a sense of identity and belonging as well as serving as an intermediary in communication among groups or societies by serving as an intermediary platform between different groups or societies by serving as means for communication and interaction between groups and societies, providing individuals a sense of identity while providing them a means to connect across various social settings and interactions between various social contexts.

Culture's Importance for Pharma Marketing

Culture plays a central role in shaping people's attitudes, beliefs and behaviors regarding health and medicine; therefore understanding its cultural context is integral to crafting effective marketing strategies that resonate with your target audience.

Cultural factors, such as language, social norms, and beliefs about health and illness, can greatly impact how people perceive and respond to pharmaceutical products. In some cultures, traditional remedies and alternative medicines may be preferred over Western medicines, while prescription drugs may be more prevalent elsewhere. Understanding these nuances is vital when developing marketing messages that effectively communicate product benefits while meeting cultural sensitivities and preferences.

Culture plays an essential role in how pharmaceutical companies conduct business across various regions. Gaining an insight into a region's cultural norms and values can assist pharmaceutical firms with complying with local regulations, creating relationships with key stakeholders, and building brand recognition.

Understanding the cultural environment within which pharmaceutical products are marketed is crucial to developing successful marketing strategies that resonate with target audiences and drive sales.

Culture's Impact on Pharma Marketing

Here are a few examples of how culture impacts pharmaceutical marketing:

1. *Language*: Pharmaceutical companies operating in countries with multiple languages must ensure their marketing materials are available in each of those languages. For instance in India where over 20 languages are spoken, marketing materials must be translated accordingly in order to effectively reach target audiences.
2. *Social Norms*: Discussing personal health issues may be taboo in certain cultures. Thus, marketing messages addressing sensitive health topics must be carefully designed to avoid offending or alienating audiences. For example, in some conservative Middle Eastern countries, pharmaceutical companies may only target women when marketing products that address health concerns that solely concern women.
3. *Beliefs About Health and Illness*: Traditional or alternative remedies may be considered more natural and less invasive in some cultures than Western medicine. Traditional Chinese medicine, for instance, is widely utilized there and could benefit from pharmaceutical companies emphasizing their products' compatibility with this treatment style or offering scientific evidence of efficacy for each product they sell.
4. *Local Regulations*: Different countries and regions have various regulations concerning pharmaceutical marketing practices. While direct-to-consumer advertising may be prohibited in some markets, others allow direct-to consumer ads. Understanding each market's regulatory environment is critical in creating compliant marketing strategies for pharmaceutical companies.

Culture can greatly impact pharma marketing. By understanding the cultural environment in which their products are being promoted, pharmaceutical companies can develop marketing strategies that better reach their target audiences.

How Pharma Uses Cultural Insights

Here are a few examples of how pharmaceutical companies have leveraged cultural insights in their marketing strategies:

1. *Pfizer* in China understood the significance of building trust among healthcare providers and patients alike, so they collaborated with Chinese medical associations, sponsored medical conferences, conducted clinical trials locally, created patient education materials in Chinese languages, and hired Chinese-speaking staff members to facilitate communication between healthcare providers and patients.

2. *GlaxoSmithKline (GSK)*: GlaxoSmithKline has launched an awareness-raising initiative in India designed to bring greater rotavirus vaccine awareness among parents living in rural areas where access to healthcare may be limited. GSK recognized the significance of cultural sensitivity and engaged local health workers to educate parents on its benefits, while culturally appropriate communication channels like radio broadcasts and community meetings were used effectively reach out to target audiences.
3. *Novartis*: To gain market access in Brazil, Novartis recognized the significance of developing relationships with local stakeholders to gain market access. They established partnerships with healthcare providers and patient organizations to gain insights into patients' needs and preferences. Furthermore, they engaged in social responsibility initiatives like providing free medication or sponsoring educational programs to build goodwill amongst the Brazilian healthcare ecosystem and establish themselves as trusted partners.

Cultural Environment

Cultural environment refers to the collective beliefs, values, customs, behaviors, and artifacts that characterize a society or a specific group within society. This includes everything from language and religion through art and music to societal norms, political systems, and historical traditions.

Culture plays a very important role in shaping how individuals think, act, and interact with one another. It can influence everything from individual choices and preferences to economic and political systems.

Culture and Pharma Marketing

Culture is essential in pharmaceutical marketing as it influences how people perceive and use pharmaceutical products. Influencers such as language, religion, social norms, historical traditions, and healthcare delivery systems can affect how individuals approach health and wellness and interact with the healthcare system.

Understanding these cultural factors is integral for pharmaceutical companies in creating marketing strategies that resonate with target audiences and meet their needs and preferences.

Cultural factors also considerably influence how pharmaceutical products are regulated and marketed across different countries, with approval, advertising, and pricing regulations differing significantly depending on local contexts. Therefore, businesses must remain aware of cultural differences within each geographical location to ensure compliance with local laws and regulations.

Understanding the cultural environment is vital for pharmaceutical companies when developing marketing strategies and building relationships with their target audiences, such as healthcare providers, patients, payers, and regulatory authorities.

Cultural Factors that Impact Pharma Marketing

Cultural factors can vary significantly across countries and regions, potentially affecting the success of pharmaceutical company marketing initiatives. Here are a few examples of how cultural environment can affect pharma marketing:

1. *Attitudes Towards Health and Medicine*: Health and medicine differ greatly between cultures. Some societies may prefer traditional remedies over pharmaceutical products like herbal remedies and acupuncture (especially valued in China and Japan). Pharma companies may need to adjust their marketing strategies accordingly to emphasize both benefits of their products and address potential side effects.
2. *Perception of Authority and Expertise*: In some cultures, healthcare professionals, such as physicians, are highly regarded and trusted. For instance, physicians are particularly esteemed in the United States. Therefore, pharmaceutical companies marketing in this market may focus on building relationships with healthcare professionals (HCPs) by offering scientific evidence and educational material supporting their use of their products.
3. *Regulatory Environment*: Regulatory environments vary considerably across different countries and regions, such as Europe, where marketing regulations for pharmaceutical products can be more stringent than in the US, forcing European pharmaceutical companies to adapt their marketing strategies to local requirements.
4. *Language and Communication*: Pharma marketing relies heavily on language and communication styles. China differs significantly from Western nations regarding its language and communication styles; therefore, pharmaceutical companies that target China as their market may need to translate marketing materials into Mandarin and consider cultural nuances and communication styles when communicating to their targeted audiences in this market.
5. *Social and Cultural Norms*: Pharma marketing must consider social and cultural norms when

marketing their product or service to potential patients and healthcare professionals. For instance, in certain cultures discussing health matters openly may be considered offensive. Companies, therefore, must find alternative means of communicating with both patients and healthcare professionals alike. For instance, in India, pharmaceutical companies may use community health workers or social media platforms to reach their target audiences more easily.

Understanding cultural factors is paramount for effective pharma marketing; pharmaceutical companies must incorporate them when formulating marketing strategies to reach their target audiences successfully.

How Pharma Companies Can Adapt

Pharmaceutical companies can adjust to a cultural environment in multiple ways to develop effective marketing strategies and form close ties with their target audiences. Here are a few examples:

1. *Conduct Cultural Research*: Pharma companies should conduct cultural research to understand their operating regions' cultural environments. This may involve studying local populations' language, customs, beliefs, and behaviors to identify cultural influences that might impact how customers perceive or use their products.
2. *Create Culturally Sensitive Marketing Campaigns*: Pharma companies can tailor marketing campaigns to their target audiences' cultural environments by employing appropriate language, imagery, and messaging that resonates with local customs and beliefs.
3. *Collaborate With Local Partners*: Pharma companies should form relationships with local organizations and healthcare providers to strengthen relationships within their community and gain an in-depth knowledge of its cultural environment through collaborative efforts with these local partners, gaining invaluable insights and creating effective marketing strategies.
4. *Ensure Regulatory Compliance*: To comply with regulatory standards in different cultural environments, Pharma companies should be sensitive to cultural differences when it comes to drug approvals, advertising, and pricing regulations. They should work closely with local authorities in their region to comply with local laws and regulations.
5. *Culturally Appropriate Patient Education*: Pharmaceutical companies must deliver culturally responsive patient education to build trust with patients and improve health outcomes. This involves providing information in their native language and considering cultural factors that might impact how patients approach health and wellness issues.

Adapting to cultural environments is key for pharmaceutical companies looking to develop effective marketing strategies and form lasting relationships with their target audiences. By taking an adaptable and culturally sensitive approach, these businesses can better understand their customers, provide better health outcomes and achieve long-term success.

Cultural Environment Monitoring

Monitoring the cultural environment for pharmaceutical marketing means staying abreast of all social and cultural influences that might impede sales in specific regions or countries. Here are some steps pharmaceutical companies can take to monitor this element:

1. *Stay Informed*: Pharmaceutical companies should stay abreast of cultural trends and developments in regions where they sell their products, which may require monitoring local media and news sources, attending industry conferences and events, or engaging with local experts.
2. *Social Media Monitoring*: Pharmaceutical companies can gain invaluable insight from monitoring social media to understand better patient and healthcare professional attitudes and behaviors in different regions or countries. Pharmaceutical companies can identify emerging trends or concerns by monitoring social media platforms and learning how their target audiences view their products.
3. *Collect Feedback* : Collecting feedback from patients and healthcare professionals can provide invaluable insight into cultural factors influencing pharma marketing. This may involve conducting surveys and focus groups and gathering opinions through social media and other channels.
4. *Engage Local Experts*: Engaging with local experts such as healthcare professionals, patient advocacy groups, and regulatory authorities can offer valuable insights into cultural factors affecting pharma marketing efforts. In addition, by cultivating relationships with these local experts, pharmaceutical companies can stay abreast of developments within their region and

learn best practices for marketing their products effectively there.

5. *Analyze Sales Data*: Analyzing sales data can offer valuable insight into how cultural factors affect pharmaceutical product success in various countries or regions. Pharmaceutical companies can track sales trends to identify areas where their marketing strategies may need to change to better align with local preferences and attitudes.

Monitoring the cultural environment is essential for effective pharmaceutical marketing. Pharmaceutical companies can develop targeted and effective marketing campaigns by staying abreast of social and cultural factors that might impede marketing strategies.

Cultural Environment Scanning

Scanning the cultural environment for pharmaceutical marketing means identifying and assessing any social and cultural influences that could impede its promotion in a country or region. Here are some steps pharmaceutical companies can take to scan cultural environments effectively.

1. *Conduct Market Research*: Market research can be invaluable in understanding cultural influences that could impede pharmaceutical product marketing in any particular country or region. This may involve surveys, focus groups, or other data collection methods to gather insights about patient and healthcare professional attitudes toward medicine and social norms that might impact its marketing in that place.
2. *Examining Local Media and Communication Channels*: By studying local media and communication channels, pharmaceutical companies can better understand the language and communication styles used in each country or region they're operating in. This will allow them to tailor marketing messages and strategies effectively toward reaching their target audiences.
3. *Consult Local Experts*: Consulting local experts such as healthcare professionals, patient advocacy groups, and regulatory authorities, can be extremely valuable when seeking insight into cultural factors that may impact pharma marketing strategies. Furthermore, local experts may offer guidance regarding regulations, social and cultural norms, and other factors hindering successful marketing strategies.
4. *Monitoring Local Trends and News*: Pharmaceutical companies should closely follow local news and trends that could effectively affect their marketing efforts, such as healthcare policy changes, attitudes about medicine, and other factors that impact its marketing. Monitoring may include tracking changes that affect healthcare policies or social attitudes toward medicine that could influence marketing activities in their area.
5. *Evaluate Competitor Strategies*: Examining competitor strategies provides valuable insight into how other pharmaceutical companies approach cultural environments in specific countries or regions, helping pharmaceutical firms identify best practices and potential differentiation opportunities.

Scanning the cultural environment for pharmaceutical marketing requires an in-depth knowledge of all social and cultural influences that could alter marketing strategies. By gathering and analyzing relevant data and insights, pharmaceutical companies can develop marketing plans that resonate with target audiences for maximum success.

Customers

Pharmaceutical marketing involves directly marketing medications and medical products to healthcare professionals, patients, and other stakeholders. Pharma's customers typically comprise two groups: healthcare professionals (HCPs) and patients. Pharma marketers employ various strategies to reach their customers. Consider the following, for example:

A. *Targeting Healthcare Professionals*: Pharmaceutical companies aim to reach healthcare professionals such as doctors, nurses, and pharmacists through various channels such as sales representatives, conferences, journals and online resources. By educating healthcare professionals on the advantages and safety features of their drugs, and providing access to up-to-date clinical studies, and research data, pharmaceutical companies can build strong relationships and positively influence the prescribing behavior of healthcare professionals.

B. *Connecting with Patients*: Pharmaceutical companies connect directly with patients via direct-to-consumer (DTC) advertising campaigns, education programs, and support groups. Pharmaceutical companies aim to reach their customers to enhance brand recognition while informing patients about diseases and treatment options and inspiring them to contact healthcare professionals with inquiries about medication choices.

Pharma marketing typically targets healthcare professionals, patients, and payers. They may also include stakeholders such as government agencies or advocacy groups to ensure patients obtain safe, effective medications that enhance health outcomes.

Customer Hierarchy in Pharma Marketing

In pharma marketing, customer hierarchy refers to all levels of decision-makers involved with purchasing and prescribing pharmaceutical products. A typical hierarchy consists of five tiers:

1. *Primary Care Physicians (PCPs)*: Primary care physicians serve as first-line medical providers, prescribing pharmaceutical products directly and thus playing an essential role in any successful drug launch.
2. *Specialists*: Medical doctors specializing in specific areas such as oncology, cardiology, or neurology may possess additional training and expertise to prescribe drugs tailored to specific patient populations or diseases.
3. *Pharmacists*: Pharmacists are healthcare professionals who dispense medications and advise on their proper usage. Pharmacists may be able to influence physician choices through recommendations of generic versions of brand drugs for substitution purposes.
4. *Payers*: Payers refer to insurance companies, government agencies, or other organizations that fund healthcare services and drugs. Depending on their contract with them, payers may create formularies, or preferred drug lists, which influence prescribing practices and use.
5. *Patients*: Pharmaceutical products are designed for patients who are the end users. Furthermore, patients can significantly influence prescribing decisions if they are informed and active participants in their treatment decisions.

Pharmaceutical companies must understand the decision-making processes and influencers at every level of the customer hierarchy and use this understanding to adapt their marketing strategies accordingly. Pharmaceutical firms can increase product adoption by targeting appropriate decision-makers with relevant messaging and resources.

Customer Acquisition

Gaining new customers for pharmaceutical marketing can be difficult, as it requires navigating complex regulations and building trust between potential clients and your brand. Several strategies have proven successful at helping to secure more customers:

1. *Targeted Advertising*: By understanding the demographics and behaviors of your target audience, you can develop targeted advertising campaigns designed to reach potential customers where they are most likely to respond. For instance, pharmaceutical companies selling medications for heart disease might use targeted ads directed toward those with prior diagnoses of cardiovascular conditions, or at high risk. In addition, they could use data such as electronic health records or health insurance claims data in targeting these ads at specific individuals.
2. *Thought Leadership Content*: Generating thought leadership content, such as blog posts, white papers, and webinars is an effective way to establish your company as a trusted authority within an industry while drawing in potential customers who need information or solutions related to that industry. For example, an oncology company might create a white paper on recent advances in cancer treatment or host a webinar discussing managing side effects from chemotherapy treatments and then share these resources via their website or social media channels to bring new customers seeking answers or solutions related to cancer treatment.
3. *Influencer Marketing*: Partnering with key opinion leaders in your industry can be a great way to establish credibility and trust among prospective customers who value these influencers' opinions. Take, for instance a biotech company that has recently developed new gene therapy treatments partnering with opinion leaders from genetics to promote it; or inviting those influencers to speak at industry events, share content via social media channels, or collaborate on research studies with them, which further helps build credibility and build customer trust with potential buyers.
4. *Events and Conferences*: Industry events and conferences provide an ideal setting to connect directly with potential customers face-to-face and form lasting relationships. A pharmaceutical company selling medical devices might attend an industry event to showcase its devices while networking with potential buyers; alternatively, the same pharma company might host an informal dinner or reception to discuss products and services with healthcare professionals casually.
5. *Referral Programs*: Encouraging existing customers to refer other individuals can help

your products and services effectively acquire new ones through word-of-mouth marketing. A biotech startup, for instance, might use social media channels such as Twitter, LinkedIn, and Facebook to share updates on research progress while engaging potential customers interested in its technology. They could even use paid ads targeted towards investors or potential collaborators, an effective method of reaching more potential clients than word-of-mouth alone can do!

6. *Email Marketing*: Targeted email campaigns to promote products or services to potential customers who have subscribed can effectively drive leads and cultivate relationships. Take, for instance, the example of a pharmaceutical company that creates targeted emails, promoting new drugs to healthcare professionals who have previously prescribed similar medication; their emails could contain information regarding efficacy, safety profile, and pricing, as well as links for additional information, or samples if appropriate.

Although any of these strategies can be highly effective, pharma marketers must comply with the regulations and guidelines of the pharmaceutical industry in promoting their products fairly, transparently, and responsibly without misleading customers.

Customer Acquisition Rate

Customer Acquisition Rate is an essential metric in every industry, measuring how quickly new customers are acquired during a given time.

Customer acquisition rate, in pharmaceutical marketing terms, refers to the rate at which new patients or healthcare professionals (HCPs) start prescribing or using specific medication from pharmaceutical companies. It serves as an important metric because it quantifies a company's marketing and promotional efforts in drawing in new customers.

To calculate customer acquisition rate in pharmaceutical marketing, first set an appropriate measurement period (usually one year). Next, count up all new patients or healthcare professionals who began using your medication or product during that time and divide that total number by total use or prescription at start of period. For instance if there were 1,000 users taking that particular medicine at beginning and 300 new users starting by end of year then your customer acquisition rate would be 30 percent.

Assuming 1,000 HCPs were prescribing your product at the start of 2018, with 200 additional physicians starting to do so over time, your customer acquisition rate would be 20 percent.

An effective customer acquisition rate among HCPs is essential as an indicator of marketing and promotional success; it reveals the effectiveness of efforts used to attract HCPs as new prescribers of products produced by your company. Additionally it can show where competitors stand within the pharmaceutical sector.

Higher customer acquisition among HCPs can translate to increased patient acquisition, better outcomes and satisfaction among their patients, and consequently stronger patient retention and satisfaction rates. Therefore it is critical for pharmaceutical companies to periodically assess their marketing and promotional activities to make sure that they are effectively targeting, reaching out, acquiring new HCPs, patients as well as keeping existing ones engaged and satisfied.

Customer-Centricity

Customer centricity is a business strategy that places customer needs and preferences at the center of all decisions made, aiming to build and maintain long-term customer relationships by offering exceptional value and experiences to their target customer base.

Customer-centric companies prioritize developing relationships with their customers by learning their needs, wants, preferences, behaviors, and feedback in depth. From this data gathering and analysis come products, services, and marketing strategies that meet or surpass customer expectations and deliver maximum value to them.

Customer-centric organizations ensure the focus of all departments and employees on meeting customer needs and expectations in every interaction with their organization, such as pre-sales, sales, post-sales interactions, customer service interactions, product development initiatives, and marketing activities. This ensures a consistently positive customer journey across every touch point, such as pre-sales interactions; sales transactions; post-sales interactions; customer service interactions; product development efforts, and marketing activities.

Customer-centricity has become an increasingly crucial aspect of pharmaceutical marketing as the industry shifts toward a more patient-oriented model. Pharmaceutical companies used to rely heavily on healthcare professionals for prescribing decisions. However, patients becoming more involved and informed in healthcare decisions, preferences, and needs have become integral to pharma marketing efforts.

Pharma marketing must be customer-centric to be effective. Companies must fully comprehend the needs and preferences of their customers at every step, from pre-diagnosis through post-treatment. This involves understanding patients' experiences with the disease, their concerns, and its effect on daily life; companies can then use this data to develop educational or support programs to assist patients in managing their conditions effectively.

Healthcare professionals continue to be an essential target audience in pharma marketing. Companies must provide HCPs with up-to-date clinical data, educational resources, and support so they feel confident when prescribing. Pharma companies should also listen closely for feedback from HCPs and patients to continually enhance their products and services.

Customer Centricity

Achieving customer-centricity in pharmaceutical marketing takes effort, strategy, and dedication over time. Below are several key steps pharmaceutical companies can take to become more customer-centric:

1. *Learn About Your Customers*: Conduct market research to gain an in-depth knowledge of customers' needs, preferences, behaviors and feedback. Use this insight to develop customer personas, and map their journey for improvement opportunities.
2. *Align Your Organization*: Establish a company culture that places customers' needs at the core of all decision-making processes, encouraging cross-functional collaboration and communication to ensure all members of your organization understand them, and are aligned with customer requirements.
3. *Develop Customer-Focused Products and Services*: Leverage customer insights to inform the product development team that addresses their needs and preferences while including feedback in your development process to create products that provide tangible benefits for them.
4. *Personalize Your Messaging and Marketing Efforts*: Employ customer data to customize your messaging and marketing initiatives according to each customer segment's needs and preferences, such as healthcare professionals, patients, and other stakeholders' requirements. Tailor marketing channels to meet them.
5. *Provide Exemplary Customer Service and Support*: Ensure your customer service and support teams have everything needed to provide an exceptional experience, including resources to assist patients and healthcare professionals in effectively using your products and services.
6. *Continuously Measure and Improve*: Use customer data and feedback to measure your marketing initiatives' success, identify improvement areas, and continuously revise and alter them to meet customers' needs more closely.

Pharmaceutical firms are beginning to adopt more customer-oriented marketing approaches for their marketing campaigns, building stronger customer relationships while strengthening loyalty and trust between themselves and customers. Furthermore, this strategy may enable pharmaceutical firms to offer tailored solutions, which better fulfill patient, healthcare professional, and other stakeholders needs.

Customer Effort Score (CES)

Customer Effort Score (CES) is a metric designed to gauge how simple a customer's experience of engaging with a business has been. CES measurements typically involve survey questions that ask customers to rate how easy or difficult it was to complete a specific task or resolve an issue, for example.

The Customer Effort Score (CES) metric is founded on the idea that customers who make more effort than necessary to complete tasks or address an issue will form negative associations between themselves and your products or services and any perceived effort they expend completing it or solving it, and how likely they are to perceive you negatively as an organization. Businesses can identify areas for improving customer experiences and decreasing client frustration levels by measuring and tracking CES.

Customer Effort Scores are typically evaluated on a scale from 1-7, with 1 indicating difficulty and seven being extremely simple. Scores of five or higher are generally considered satisfactory, while scores below three may indicate serious issues that must be addressed immediately.

Customer Effort Score in Pharma Marketing

In pharmaceutical marketing, customer effort score (CES) surveys can accurately measure the customer experience when engaging with pharmaceutical products or services. For example, these surveys can determine how easy it is to obtain prescription medication or schedule appointments with healthcare providers.

Measuring the Customer Experience Score (CES) in Pharma marketing can enable businesses to identify areas for improving the customer experience and decreasing patient frustration, and increase satisfaction, loyalty, and patient health outcomes.

However, companies should remember that measuring customer experience scores in pharmaceutical marketing presents unique challenges, including privacy considerations and regulations about prescription medication sales. Therefore, when designing and implementing customer experience surveys in the pharmaceutical industry, companies should ensure compliance with the relevant laws and regulations.

How CES Can be Used in Pharma Marketing

Here are a few examples of how the Customer Effort Score (CES) can be utilized in pharmaceutical marketing:

1. *Prescription Medication Access*: Pharmaceutical companies may use CES surveys to ask healthcare providers for feedback about the ease of acquiring prescription medications for their patients. This may help identify areas where company processes may create difficulties for healthcare providers, such as prior authorization requests, or understanding coverage information.
2. *Patient Support Programs*: Pharmaceutical companies may conduct CES surveys to gather feedback from their patient base about how easy enrolling into one of their patient support programs is, providing insight into any areas where enrollment may cause confusion or create barriers for patients. This helps identify areas that could present barriers during the enrollment process.
3. *Experiences at Medical Conferences*: Pharmaceutical companies may conduct surveys with healthcare professionals at medical conferences to gauge how easily healthcare professionals were able to navigate their booth or access information at it to identify areas in which booth design or materials may be causing confusion, making accessing information harder, or simply adding another layer of complexity for HCPs. This helps identify any areas where HCPs struggled to access relevant data quickly.
4. *Adverse Event Reporting*: Pharmaceutical companies may use CES surveys to survey healthcare providers on the ease of reporting adverse reactions associated with medications they are prescribing, which can reveal areas in their reporting process that cause difficulty, such as complex forms or unclear requirements.

Pharmaceutical companies can utilize the Customer Experience Score (CES) as a useful tool to identify areas where they can enhance customer experiences for healthcare providers and patients. By eliminating barriers to care and streamlining interactions with products/services offered, companies can increase customer satisfaction and enhance patient health outcomes.

Customer Engagement

Customer engagement in pharmaceutical marketing refers to creating and nurturing meaningful relationships between pharmaceutical manufacturers and their target customers, such as healthcare professionals, patients, caregivers, and other key constituents. Engagement may take many forms, from educational initiatives and disease awareness campaigns through social media outreach efforts and patient support programs and other services.

Here are the key aspects of customer engagement for pharmaceutical marketers.

1. *Engaging Customers*: The key to successful customer engagement lies in understanding your target audience's needs and preferences through market research, customer data analytics or direct interactions to gain a deep insight into their challenges, priorities and goals.
2. *Providing Relevant Information*: Once you understand their needs and they receive information pertinent to their health, that allows them to make well-informed choices about their well-being. This may include educational resources, product details, or clinical studies.
3. *Building Trust*: Trust is essential in customer engagement, so pharmaceutical companies must work to build and keep it with their customers. This may involve being transparent about product information, adhering to ethical marketing practices, and keeping promises made to customers.
4. *Providing Customer Support*: Customers require support in managing their health, whether that means patient assistance programs, disease management resources, or accessing healthcare professionals. Offering such support helps build long-term customer relationships while improving overall health outcomes.
5. *Engaging Customers by Building Community*: Finally, customer engagement in pharmaceutical

marketing may involve creating an environment of community among customers through social media groups, online forums, or in-person events. This can allow customers to meet others who share similar experiences and foster feelings of belongingness among members.

Customer engagement in pharmaceutical marketing requires a careful approach that considers customers' needs and preferences. By creating meaningful relationships between pharmaceutical companies and their customers, providing pertinent information and support services, and improving health outcomes while cultivating long-term trust, pharmaceutical firms can drive long-term business success and achieve increased health benefits, and build stronger customer bonds.

Customer Engagement in Pharma

Pharmaceutical companies have several effective means for engaging meaningfully with their customers. Consider these examples of such engagement:

1. *Content Marketing*: Pharmaceutical companies can use content marketing to engage their target customers by producing and sharing valuable blog posts, white papers, and educational resources related to products, industry trends, and healthcare issues.
2. *Social Media*: Pharma companies using social media can utilize it as an invaluable platform for customer engagement and relationship management. By sharing product-related updates on these platforms, responding to customers' inquiries, or responding to any customer issues raised directly on those platforms, and engaging customers directly, companies can quickly connect with potential clients and engage in conversations about products with customers.
3. *Events and Conferences*: Pharmaceutical companies can leverage events and conferences as an excellent way to connect directly with their target customers, showcase products, provide knowledge transfer opportunities, and build customer relationships.
4. *Patient and Healthcare Professional Portals*: Establishing patient and HCP (Healthcare Professional) portals can be an easy and accessible hub for customers to find information regarding products, treatments, and disease management strategies and connect with other patients or healthcare professionals.
5. *Gamification*: Gamification refers to adding game-like elements, such as challenges, rewards, and leaderboards, into marketing strategies for pharmaceutical companies. By engaging customers through fun and interactive experiences with their products and services, pharmaceutical companies can use gamification to encourage customer engagement with their offerings more enjoyably and memorably.

Pharmaceutical companies can implement customer engagement strategies that are beneficial to them to engage their customers effectively. However, first and foremost, companies must follow all regulations and guidelines applicable to the pharmaceutical industry when developing and implementing customer engagement strategies.

Customer Experience

Customer experience in pharmaceutical marketing encompasses every interaction that a customer (patient or healthcare professional) has when engaging with pharmaceutical products or services, from initial awareness of a drug or treatment through prescription and administration of medications to ongoing support and follow-up.

Here are a few strategies pharma companies use to enhance customer experience:

1. *Education and Awareness*: Pharma companies offer educational materials and resources that help patients better understand their conditions and treatment options.
2. *Patient-centric Care*: Focusing on patient needs in every interaction by putting patients needs and preferences at the center of all activities.
3. *Digital Platforms*: Develop digital platforms to enable easier access to information, connect with healthcare providers, and help them achieve better patient outcomes.
4. *Personalization*: Individualized treatment plans and support tailored to patients' needs and preferences.
5. *Post-Treatment Support*: Offering ongoing follow-up helps keep patients engaged with and motivated through treatment.

How Pharma Improves Customer Experiences

Pharmaceutical companies have taken numerous steps to enhance patient experiences. Consider, for instance:

1. Pfizer has launched the *Pfizer Meds* mobile app, enabling patients to monitor their medication schedule and receive reminders when it's time to take their medicine. Additionally, this resource also offers educational materials as well as access to healthcare providers.
2. Novartis' *Patient Support* offers services to assist patients in managing their medications and navigating the healthcare journey, including accessing personalized support from healthcare professionals, financial assistance, and educational resources.
3. Roche has developed *mySugar* mobile app to assist patients living with diabetes. It enables individuals to track their blood sugar levels, receive personalized coaching, and join a community of diabetic patients.
4. Sanofi recently developed the *iBGStar* program, featuring an iPhone-connected blood glucose monitoring system to allow patients to track their levels, share this information with healthcare providers and receive tailored coaching and educational resources.
5. *Merck Helps* provides financial assistance, insurance claims support, and free medication access to help those struggling to afford their medications.

Pharmaceutical companies have recently put more effort into creating an enhanced customer experience to improve patient outcomes and foster brand loyalty, which is particularly important when treating chronic diseases requiring ongoing medication and support.

Customer Experience Measurement

Customer experience measurement in pharmaceutical marketing involves gauging interactions and experiences between patients, healthcare professionals, and other stakeholders of a pharmaceutical company and its products, services, and marketing efforts. Here are some steps pharmaceutical companies can take to measure customer experience:

1. *Establish the Customer Journey*: Pharmaceutical companies should create an overview of customer interactions with their products and services, from touchpoint identification to journey mapping from start to finish.
2. *Develop Metrics*: Pharmaceutical companies should track customer experience at each touchpoint along the customer journey, with metrics such as net promoter score, customer satisfaction, and customer effort score.
3. *Collect Data*: Pharmaceutical companies should collect customer experience data through various means, including surveys, focus groups, and customer feedback forms. Social media monitoring tools can also help pharmaceutical firms gain patient and healthcare professionals' feedback.
4. *Analysis*: Pharmaceutical companies should analyze customer experience data to identify trends and areas for improvement, including common customer pain points or issues, and areas in which their performance stands out positively.
5. *Take Action*: Pharmaceutical companies should use customer experience analysis data to inform actions designed to enhance customer experience. This may include making design modifications, improving service levels, and creating targeted marketing campaigns.
6. *Monitor Progress*: Pharmaceutical companies should regularly track metrics and analyze customer experience improvement efforts by continuously tracking metrics and examining data. This can help them identify areas where changes need to be made, or evaluate the impact of their efforts.

Measuring Customer Experience in Pharma Marketing

Below are examples of customer experience measurement within pharmaceutical marketing:

1. *Customer Satisfaction Surveys*: Pharmaceutical companies can utilize customer satisfaction surveys to gather feedback from patients and healthcare professionals regarding their experiences with their products and services. For instance, companies could survey patients recently using one of their medications about its effectiveness, ease of use, side effects experienced, and overall satisfaction level.
2. *Net Promoter Score (NPS)*: NPS surveys offer pharmaceutical companies an effective means of measuring customer loyalty and finding ways to enhance the customer experience, offering valuable data that allows for continuous customer relationship management (CRM).
3. *Social Media Monitoring*: Pharmaceutical companies can utilize social media monitoring tools to gather feedback from patients and healthcare professionals on their experiences with their products and services, including potential patients who will use them. A company

could, for instance, monitor social media channels for feedback trends and areas for improvement from its constituents.

4. *Focus Groups*: Pharmaceutical companies may utilize focus groups with patients and healthcare professionals to gain more in-depth feedback about the company's products and services, which will give the business an understanding of its customer journey and help identify areas for potential improvement.
5. *Customer Feedback Forms*: Pharmaceutical companies can give customers feedback forms to collect feedback about their experiences with their products and services. For instance, one may include such forms with medication that prompt patients to rate their experience and suggest possible improvements.

Customer Experience measurement is an integral component of pharmaceutical marketing, helping companies better understand the needs and preferences of their target audiences, as well as identify areas for improving customer experiences.

Customer Experience Metrics

Pharmaceutical companies utilize several customer experience metrics in order to measure customer experience:

1. *Net Promoter Score (NPS)*: NPS measures customer propensity to recommend products or services of an organization to others, from those rating themselves from zero (not likely at all up to 10 (extremely likely). NPS calculations involve subtracting detractors (those giving scores 0-6 from promoters (those giving scores 9 to 10) before arriving at their final result.
2. *Customer Satisfaction (CSAT)*: CSAT measures customer satisfaction with products or services offered by an organization, typically asking customers to rate themselves from 1-10 on scales. Higher scores signify increased levels of contentment from customers.
3. *Customer Effort Score (CES)*: The Customer Effort Score measures how easy or difficult it is for customers to interact with a company, with higher scores signifying reduced effort on behalf of its customer base. Customers rate their experience using either 1-5, or 1-10 scales.
4. *Churn Rate*: Churn rates measure the percentage of customers that stop purchasing goods or services offered by an enterprise over an agreed-upon time frame, thus signaling an unsatisfied experience for these clients. A high churn rate could signal to companies that their customer experience needs improvement.
5. *FCR (First Contact Resolution):* This indicator measures how often customer issues are resolved during initial interactions. A high FCR indicates effective and efficient customer support services provided to the customers.
6. *Average Handle Time (AHT)*: This measurement indicates how quickly and efficiently customer support agents resolve customer inquiries and requests for help. A shorter AHT indicates better support to customers.
7. *Customer Retention Rate*: Customer retention rate measures the percentage of customers who continue using products or services from one business over time, which indicates customer satisfaction with said company. A high retention rate indicates satisfied customers.

These metrics provide companies with valuable tools for understanding the customer experience and pinpointing improvement areas. Furthermore, by monitoring these metrics over time and monitoring progress made towards improving it, they can monitor progress, and make data-driven decisions to enhance it further.

Customer Feedback

Customer feedback can be an effective marketing strategy tool for pharmaceutical companies. It gives insights into how patients and healthcare professionals perceive a medication's efficacy, safety, and overall patient experience.

Pharmaceutical companies may collect several different kinds of feedback from patients and HCPs. Here are some examples include:

1. *Product feedback* focuses on the effectiveness and safety of the medication and potential side effects or adverse reactions that patients might experience. Patients can provide feedback regarding, whether medication helped manage symptoms effectively while reporting side effects like nausea or dizziness.
2. *Customer service feedback* focuses on the level of service patients receive from companies, such as interactions between customer service representatives, educational materials provided, or ease of medication access. A patient may provide feedback regarding the helpfulness of customer service representatives in resolving an issue related to her medication, or she could

evaluate the clarity of educational materials offered by pharmaceutical firms.

3. *Patient experience feedback* focuses on the overall experience with medication for the individual patient, from its convenience and ease of use to its impact on quality of life. Patients may provide input regarding whether taking their medicine has helped with daily activities like performing daily chores more easily or how it has affected relationships in their social circle.
4. *Healthcare professional (HCPs) feedback* centers on their experiences with medication, such as its effectiveness, safety, and ease of use. HCPs may give feedback regarding support offered by pharmaceutical companies when managing patients' treatments, or on its effects on health outcomes for these individuals.

Pharma companies must collect feedback logically and organize to collect meaningful, and actionable insights to inform product development and marketing strategies. This may involve gathering responses through surveys, focus groups, or online forums and using tools like sentiment analysis to analyze and categorize it all effectively.

How Pharma Companies Leverage Feedback

Here are a few strategies pharmaceutical companies can utilize customer feedback in their marketing:

1. *Use Feedback for Product Development*: Pharmaceutical companies can utilize customer feedback to identify areas for improvement and inform the development of new products. Patient surveys might reveal an urgent need for a different dosing regimen or formulation, which informs the development of entirely new medications or modifications of an existing medicine.
2. *Use Feedback in Promo Materials*: Utilizing positive patient and HCP comments as testimonials in promotional materials such as print ads, social media posts, and website content can build trust and credibility for a medication, encouraging both to consider it for treatment options.
3. *Integrate Patient Feedback into Patient Education Materials*: Utilizing patient feedback can demonstrate how medications have assisted with managing conditions, improving quality of life, or meeting treatment goals in real-time, helping reinforce medication adherence's importance while encouraging patients to continue with prescribed treatment plans.
4. *Engaging Customers Through Feedback*: Pharma companies can engage customers who provide feedback by responding to their comments, offering additional information or support, addressing concerns or issues they might be raising, and developing positive relationships that demonstrate commitment to health and well-being for their customer base. This approach may lead to long-term customer loyalty while building customer engagement strategies within an organization.

Importantly, customer feedback in pharmaceutical marketing must adhere to strict regulatory guidelines to ensure it provides accurate, balanced information that does not distort reality or mislead consumers. Feedback must also be collected transparently and objectively before being presented for review by pharmaceutical sales reps. This may disclose potential risks or side effects associated with medications prescribed to customers.

Customer Focus

Customer focus is an approach to doing business that emphasizes prioritizing customers over all other activities performed by an organization— from product design and development, through marketing campaigns and support services, right up until product retirement, and support services. Simply stated: this business philosophy prioritizes customers in everything it does!

Customer-focused organizations understand the significance of customer satisfaction to long-term success and competitive advantage. Thus their mission to develop products and services which meet customers' needs, surpass their expectations, and offer extraordinary value is critical for long-term success and competitive edge.

Organizations seeking to be customer-focused must first gather customer insights and feedback, use this data to inform decisions, design products and services with customer-centricity in mind, and measure and improve the experience continuously over time.

Customer focus is indispensable in today's business environment, where customer preferences and needs continually change. Organizations prioritizing customer focus can build stronger relationships, increase loyalty and retention rates, enhance brand image, and strengthen reputations more rapidly.

Customer focus in pharmaceutical marketing is essential to developing strong relationships between patients, healthcare professionals (HCPs), and other stakeholders. As the pharmaceutical industry increasingly adopts a patient-centric approach where patients play more of an active role in healthcare decisions, and have more input into treatment plans, pharmaceutical companies must prioritize customer's needs and preferences to be successful. To achieve customer focus, companies must do the following:

1. *Understand the Needs and Preferences of Customers*: Companies looking to establish customer-driven pharma marketing must first understand the needs and preferences of their target customers, conduct market research to gain insight into the patient journey, understand the impact of disease on the daily lives and concerns of healthcare professionals, and create personas to suit customer requirements and tailor their marketing messages accordingly.
2. *Develop Customer-Focused Products and Services*: Use customer insights to inform product development, designing solutions that meet the needs of patients and healthcare providers. Ensure your products and services are simple for users to use effectively and provide maximum value to your customers.
3. *Communicate Effectively*: Utilize clear and direct language when communicating the benefits of your products and services to patients and healthcare professionals. In addition, provide educational resources and support so they understand how best to utilize your offerings.
4. *Deliver Superior Customer Service and Support*: Ensure your customer service and support teams have everything necessary to provide customers with an outstanding experience, including resources to assist patients and healthcare professionals in navigating your products and services successfully.
5. *Constantly Measure and Improve*: Utilizing customer feedback as an evaluation mechanism will allow you to accurately assess your marketing initiatives' success and pinpoint improvement areas. After which, continuously iterate on and update your strategies to meet customers' needs more closely.

By catering to their customer's needs and preferences, pharmaceutical companies can build stronger relationships with patients and healthcare professionals while increasing customer retention rates and driving business growth.

Customer Insights

Customer insights in pharmaceutical marketing refer to an in-depth knowledge of healthcare providers' and patients' needs, motivations, behaviors, and preferences. Customer insights may be gained via various means, such as market research studies, customer surveys, social media listening techniques, or data analytics can provide this level of understanding of healthcare consumers and providers alike.

Customer insights are critical in developing effective pharmaceutical marketing strategies that effectively engage and target their customers. By understanding HCPs' needs and preferences and patients', pharmaceutical companies can create messaging and campaigns that resonate with their target audiences and reach them more effectively than before.

Customer insights provide pharmaceutical companies with valuable tools for reaching customers effectively, such as online forums, or social media platforms. Customer insights also inform product development decisions so that drugs designed by these firms meet the needs of their target customers.

Customer Insights: Examples

Pharmaceutical companies can gain customer insights through various research and analysis methodologies:

1. *Demographic Data*: By analyzing demographic information such as age, gender, and geographic location, companies can better understand customer groups with various needs and preferences.
2. *Customer Preferences*: Through surveys, focus groups, and other forms of research, companies can gain valuable insights into customer preferences regarding product features, pricing, packaging, and other factors.
3. *Customer Behavior*: Companies can gain valuable insights into customer behaviors such as purchasing patterns, product usage, and loyalty through data derived from sales transactions and interactions.
4. *Customer Pain Points*: By gathering customer feedback, companies can gain insights into areas in which customers may be experiencing difficulties or frustration regarding their products or services.
5. *Customer Satisfaction*: Through surveys and other forms of research, companies can gain insights into customer satisfaction levels. By doing this, they can also identify improvement areas that would enhance the overall customer experience.

How To Gain Customer Insights

Gaining customer insights is vital in pharmaceutical marketing, allowing companies to understand their target customers better and devise more effective marketing strategies. Here are a few ways customer insights can be achieved in pharma marketing:

1. *Surveys*: Surveys can help pharmaceutical marketers gain customer insight. Companies can use surveys to ask customers about their experiences with products, their likes or dislikes and any areas for improvement that should be prioritized. Surveys may be administered either online, via telephone or face to face.
2. *Focus Groups*: Focus groups provide businesses with invaluable insight into customer needs and preferences by gathering customers for discussions about products or services offered, led by an impartial moderator who directs discussions amongst attendees.
3. *Social Media Listening*: Social media platforms like Twitter, Facebook and Instagram provide companies with access to an abundance of customer data that allows them to understand customer needs and preferences more precisely. By tracking conversations about their products on these social networks, companies gain important insights into customer sentiment.
4. *Data Analysis*: Companies can utilize data analytics to gain a deep insight into customer behaviors, preferences and needs. This may involve conducting research into sales transactions, or gathering customer interactions data to detect patterns or trends among customer records.
5. *Customer Feedback*: Businesses can utilize various channels like email, telephone and social media to gather customer feedback to identify areas for improvement and create more efficient marketing strategies.

Customer insight lies at the center of successful pharmaceutical marketing strategies and companies who invest in understanding their target demographic are more likely to meet their marketing objective.

Customer Journey

The customer journey in pharmaceutical marketing refers to all the interactions a patient or healthcare professional has with pharmaceutical products and services, from initial awareness through purchase, post-purchase follow-up, and beyond.

Here are the typical stages of the customer journey in pharmaceutical marketing:

1. *Awareness*: At this stage, customers become aware of your pharmaceutical company through either advertising, social media channels, or word of mouth.
2. *Consideration*: At this stage, customers begin researching more in-depth the products and services provided by pharmaceutical companies, evaluating their features, benefits, and potential side effects.
3. *Decision*: Customers make purchases based on research and their preferences when buying from pharmaceutical companies.
4. *Post-Purchase*: Pharmaceutical companies should remain engaged once the customer purchases to ensure they are completely satisfied, and offer additional support and resources as required.
5. *Advocacy*: At this stage, the customer becomes an advocate for the pharmaceutical company's products and services by recommending them to others and sharing positive experiences on social media or through other channels.

Optimizing customer journeys in pharmaceutical marketing means providing positive customer experiences at each journey stage, such as offering helpful resources and personalized recommendations and continually collecting customer feedback to enhance products and services. Pharmaceutical companies can increase customer satisfaction by prioritizing customer journeys while strengthening relationships and increasing business by prioritizing this journey.

Customer Journey Mapping

Customer journey mapping in pharmaceutical marketing is an approach to understanding and visually representing the steps and touchpoints customers encounter when engaging with pharmaceutical products or companies. It is an effective tool for pharmaceutical firms looking to engage and serve their customers effectively throughout their journeys.

Here are the steps involved in customer journey mapping for pharmaceutical marketing. These steps include: defining the customer journey, including its stages, various touchpoints they experience during their travels with a pharmaceutical company, and product interactions.

1. *Conduct Customer Research*: Research to understand the needs, goals, pain points, and behaviors of target customer segments at each stage of the customer journey.
2. *Recognizing Touchpoints*: Determine the touchpoints where customers interact with your company or product. This could include social

media, websites, patient portals, customer service, or sales representatives.

3. *Map the Customer Journey*: Use a visual tool such as a journey map to plot each step in the customer journey and the touchpoints associated with each stage to identify areas where customers may encounter difficulty, delays, or confusion. This will enable businesses to address such potential challenges better.
4. *Analyze the Customer Journey*: Analyzing customer journeys helps identify pain points and areas for improvement, helping prioritize improvement efforts while discovering opportunities for innovation.
5. *Implement Changes*: Make adjustments to enhance the customer journey by changing touchpoints, processes, and technologies. This could involve redesigning websites, improving customer service processes, or offering new products or services.
6. *Monitor and Measure Success*: Keep track of changes made to the customer journey to assess their impact on customer satisfaction, loyalty, and business results.

Pharmaceutical Companies Leverage Customer Journey Maps

Many pharmaceutical companies have implemented customer journey mapping to enhance customer experiences. Here are a few examples of how pharma companies accomplish this:

1. Novartis used customer journey mapping to gain an in-depth understanding of patient experiences related to certain drugs, including their challenges and where interactions took place with Novartis. Leveraging these insights gained from customer journey mapping, changes were implemented to enhance patient journey experiences by developing mobile applications that assist patients in managing their treatments more easily.
2. Roche utilized customer journey mapping to understand customer experiences for laboratory tests thoroughly. As a result, Roche discovered that customers experienced significant delays in receiving test results, negatively impacting customer satisfaction. Roche then implemented changes that reduced turnaround times for test results and enhanced communication between staff members and customers.
3. Sanofi utilized customer journey mapping to understand patient experiences for a specific drug comprehensively. Based on this insight, they discovered that patients experienced difficulty accessing information about it, which led to confusion and frustration; as a result, Sanofi implemented changes designed to enhance education and communication for its patient base by developing educational materials, and creating a support program for this particular drug.
4. Pfizer utilized customer journey mapping to analyze its customers' journey for one disease state. Through this insight, they learned that customers had difficulty accessing information regarding this condition and treatment options. Pfizer then made changes to improve the availability of this knowledge, such as creating a patient education website and a patient advocacy program.

Customer journey mapping is an effective tool for pharmaceutical companies looking to enhance customer experiences. By understanding each stage and pinpointing pain points, they can craft more customer-centric approaches that spur business expansion and growth.

Customer Lifetime Value (CLV)

Customer Lifetime Value (CLV) is an integral concept in marketing that refers to the estimated total revenue each customer is projected to bring a company over time. CLV analysis can be particularly significant when applied to pharmaceutical marketing because many medications must be taken over an extended period, and customers may require ongoing medical treatments; thus, calculating CLV requires an estimation of total customer lifetime sales generated from that medication or treatment in terms of frequency of purchases, duration, and potential repeat business.

Here are a few key benefits of CLV in pharmaceutical marketing:

A. *Targeted Marketing*: Understanding customer lifetime values can assist pharmaceutical companies with more accurately targeting their marketing efforts, targeting those with higher CLV to increase return on investment and maximize revenues.

B. *Improved Customer Service*: Understanding CLV can assist companies in providing superior customer service. By recognizing high-value customers, companies can provide more personalized assistance that meets customers' needs more precisely.

C. *Product Development*: CLV can also be used as a product development basis. By understanding the needs and preferences of high-value customers, companies can develop medications and treatments more tailored toward them.

How Pharma Can Apply CLV

Pharmaceutical companies can utilize CLV concepts in many different ways when devising their marketing strategies, including:

1. *Targeted Advertising*: Pharmaceutical companies can use customer data to calculate customer lifetime value (CLV) to target their advertising campaigns at higher-value customers better. For instance, they might advertise certain medications or treatments more aggressively to customers who have purchased related products or show promise as repeat buyers.
2. *Loyalty Programs*: CLV can also be utilized to design and incentivize loyalty programs. Businesses can promote repeat business by offering high-value customers discounts, rewards, or other perks in exchange for repeat purchases.
3. *Treatment Plans*: Understanding customer lifetime value (CLV) is key to developing more efficient healthcare treatment plans. By considering each patient's potential lifetime value, doctors can make more informed decisions about which medications or treatments should be prescribed and when.
4. *Personalized Service*: High-value customers often require additional personalized assistance, and companies can use CLV data to identify these individuals and offer tailored assistance accordingly. They might offer additional educational resources, access to specialist support teams, or priority access to new products or treatments.

Customer Lifetime Value (CLV) can be an effective tool in pharmaceutical marketing as it allows companies to make data-driven decisions that increase customer satisfaction while growing revenues.

Customer Obsession

Customer obsession is a critical element of marketing that refers to an organization's insistence on meeting customers' needs and exceeding their expectations. Customer obsession in pharmaceutical marketing can profoundly affect patient outcomes while driving business success.

Pharma companies must focus on customer orientation to remain competitive and meet the evolving needs of healthcare providers and patients. Doing this requires having an in-depth knowledge of the customer's journey from diagnosis through treatment; in other words, customer obsession requires:

1. *Listening to Customer Feedback*: Customer feedback can give pharma companies invaluable insight into what patients and healthcare providers want and need, helping to refine products, services, and marketing messages to meet customer requirements more closely.
2. *Use Data to Drive Decision-making*: Data can assist pharma companies in understanding customer behaviors and preferences and pinpoint areas for improvement, leading to more effective marketing campaigns, targeting audiences more accurately, and better patient outcomes.
3. *Focus on Patient-centricity*: Pharma companies should prioritize patient-centricity, which means placing patients at the core of all they do. Assuring patient well-being may involve providing educational materials, support services and products tailored specifically for each individual's requirements.
4. *Collaborate With Healthcare Providers*: Pharma companies should work collaboratively with healthcare providers to understand their needs and preferences to design more effective products and services that fulfill healthcare providers' and patients' requirements.

Customer obsession is an important concept in pharmaceutical marketing. By prioritizing patient and healthcare provider needs, pharma companies can increase business success while improving patient outcomes.

Customer-Obsessed Pharma Companies: Exemplars

Pharmaceutical companies increasingly prioritize customer focus in their marketing strategies. Consider the following examples:

1. Novo Nordisk is an innovative global healthcare company focused on diabetes care. Renowned for their customer-first approach that involves working closely with healthcare providers and patients to understand individual needs and preferences, Novo Nordisk offers various products and services designed to support those living with the condition, such as educational resources, mobile apps and support programs.
2. Pfizer, a leading pharmaceutical company, has made customer obsession a core value. To realize

this goal, they have implemented various customer-driven initiatives, such as their Assistance Program for uninsured and underinsured patients to access Pfizer medicines, using data analytics to understand better patient needs and preferences and craft targeted marketing campaigns.

3. Roche is an international healthcare company, specializing in oncology, immunology and other areas. Roche offers customer-centric approaches, working closely with healthcare providers and patients alike to develop products and services specifically tailored for them and offering patient support programs with expert guidance as well as educational resources.
4. Sanofi is a world-class pharmaceutical company dedicated to customer excellence. Through various initiatives designed to support patients, such as its *Patient Connection Program*, which assists those in accessing Sanofi medicine while offering financial aid when necessary, and working alongside healthcare providers on creating products and services more suitable to patient needs, Sanofi stands out as an industry leader that puts customers first.

Customer Relationship

Pharma marketing refers to customer relationships as interactions, communications, and experiences between pharmaceutical companies and their customers, such as patients and healthcare professionals. Strong customer relations can help pharmaceutical firms build customer loyalty while driving revenue growth and increasing the standing of their products and services.

Here are the keys to building strong customer relationships in pharmaceutical marketing:

1. *Communication*: Communication is vital in building strong customer relationships. Pharmaceutical companies should use various channels, email, social media, and customer service, to engage customers and provide helpful information regarding their products and services.
2. *Personalization*: Tailoring communications and marketing messages based on customers' needs and preferences can create stronger customer relationships. Companies can leverage data analytics to gain a clearer picture of customer tastes and tailor marketing strategies accordingly.
3. *Educational Resources and Support*: Offering customers educational materials related to your products will allow them to fully comprehend all their advantages while developing long-lasting customer relationships.
4. *Customer Service*: Providing exceptional customer service is key to developing long-term relationships and winning over loyal customer bases. Businesses should make it simple for their customers to access support whenever needed and respond swiftly and helpfully when inquiries or complaints come their way.
5. *Feedback and Improvement*: Establishing strong customer relationships by inviting customer input on products/services offered. Pharmaceutical companies should actively solicit customer reviews to identify areas for enhancement.

By prioritizing these elements, pharmaceutical companies can create strong customer relationships, increase customer satisfaction, and drive business growth.

Customer Relationship Management (CRM)

CRM, an acronym for Customer Relationship Management, is a business strategy focused on cultivating long-term customer relationships to increase customer satisfaction, boost sales growth and boost profits for an organization.

CRM combines technology, processes, and people. CRM systems use CRM databases to manage customer data and interactions, track customer behavior, automate various marketing and sales activities, and monitor the preferences and behaviors of their target audiences.

CRM involves devising and executing strategies for customer engagement, such as personalized marketing and service delivery, and skilled individuals, using the technology effectively to implement strategies. CRM can be found across many industries, such as healthcare, finance, retail, and manufacturing, while pharmaceutical companies are especially using CRM to manage healthcare professional (HCP) and patient relations, to enhance outcomes and drive growth for pharmaceutical and healthcare organizations.

CRM in Pharma Marketing

Customer Relationship Management (CRM) is an essential aspect of pharmaceutical marketing, helping businesses cultivate long-term relationships with their customers and ultimately drive sales. Here are examples of CRM's use in pharmaceutical marketing:

1. *Personalized Communication*: Pharma companies use CRM to communicate with their customers in an interactive, tailored and personalized way based on their needs and preferences. For instance, an HCPs may receive targeted emails regarding specific drugs pertinent to their practice area.
2. *Data-Driven Decision-Making*: CRM systems offer pharmaceutical companies valuable insight into their customers, such as their prescribing patterns, preferences, and behavior. With this data, decisions regarding product development, marketing strategies, and sales efforts can be made more informed.
3. *Customer Service and Support*: CRM software allows companies to provide excellent customer service and support. If an HCP needs answers about a drug, they can contact the company through their CRM system and receive immediate replies.
4. *Sales Force Automation*: CRM systems can assist pharma companies in managing their sales force more effectively. A company could use CRM to monitor the performance of its sales reps and identify areas in which they need additional training or support.
5. *Patient Engagement*: CRM systems can help companies engage with patients and assist them with managing their health. For instance, companies could utilize such software to send reminders about taking medications on time and provide educational materials about specific conditions that affect them.

CRM is essential to pharmaceutical marketing, helping companies cultivate customer relationships, drive sales and ensure positive patient outcomes.

Customer Retention

Customer retention in pharmaceutical marketing refers to companies' strategies and efforts to maintain existing customers as loyal clients. Customer retention strategies help these organizations build loyal customer bases, drive revenue growth and enhance the reputation of their products and services.

Here are a few strategies pharmaceutical companies can employ to increase customer retention in pharma marketing:

1. *Offer High-Quality Products and Services*: One of the key aspects of customer retention lies within the quality of products and services provided by your company. In addition, offering products that satisfy patient and healthcare professional needs is critical to creating customer loyalty.
2. *Build Strong Relationships with Customers*: Establishing strong customer relationships is vital for maintaining retention. Companies can engage their customers through multiple communication channels such as email, social media, and customer service channels. In contrast, tailoring conversations according to customers' preferences and needs can foster stronger bonds between the company and its customer base.
3. *Provide Excellent Customer Service*: Exceptional customer service is key to keeping customers. Companies should make it easy for customers to access support when necessary and provide timely, helpful responses for any issues or complaints that arise.
4. *Reward Customer Loyalty*: Pharmaceutical companies can leverage loyalty programs such as discounts or loyalty incentives to reward those customers who use their products and services over time. This may include discounts, loyalty programs, or any other incentive which rewards loyal users.
5. *Educational Resources and Support*: Pharmaceutical companies can help customers understand the advantages and appropriate use of their products by providing educational resources and support. It will help companies achieve higher customer satisfaction and retention rates.

Pharmaceutical companies can use these strategies to increase customer retention, form stronger bonds with their customer base and drive business growth.

Customer Retention Rate

Customer retention rate in pharmaceutical marketing, is an invaluable metric. It indicates the percentage of customers that continue purchasing from an organization over an established timeframe.

Customer retention rate, in pharmaceutical marketing terms, refers to the percentage of patients or healthcare professionals (HCPs) who continue prescribing or purchasing from one specific pharmaceutical company over time. It is an essential metric which measures customer loyalty and satisfaction with an offering.

Assuming a pharmaceutical company had 10,000 patients taking its medication at the beginning of a given year and 8,000 continued taking it at year's end, their customer retention rate would be 80 percent.

Likewise, if a pharmaceutical company had 1,000 HCPs who prescribed their product at the start of the year and 900 continued prescribing by year's end, their customer retention rate among HCPs would be 90%.

Retention rates among HCPs are essential indicators of their satisfaction with products they've tried, and of the effectiveness of marketing or promotional efforts directed toward HCPs.

Customer Reviews

Customer reviews can be an essential tool in pharmaceutical marketing strategies, providing invaluable feedback from patients and healthcare professionals (HCPs) about medication's efficacy, safety, patient experience with its usage or treatments, etc.

Here are a few strategies pharma companies can utilize customer reviews in their marketing:

1. *Use Reviews in Promotional Materials*: Positive reviews can be utilized in promotional materials like print ads, social media posts and website content to highlight the advantages and safety features of medications while building trust among both patients and HCPs.
2. *Integrate Reviews into Patient Education Materials*: Reviews can serve to demonstrate how medications have assisted with managing conditions, improving quality of life and reaching treatment goals for individual patients. By doing this, reviews reinforce medication adherence's importance while simultaneously encouraging patients to adhere to their treatment plans as prescribed.
3. *Collect and Analyze Reviews to Enhance Products and Services*: Pharmaceutical companies can utilize customer reviews as an opportunity to collect feedback on their products and services and identify areas for improvement, providing insights that could inform development of new products as well as patient support programs or educational resources.
4. *Engaging Customers Through Reviews*: Pharma companies can engage customers who leave reviews by responding to them with relevant feedback, offering informational resources or support services, and building positive relationships that demonstrate commitment to customers' health and well-being. This strategy may prove particularly fruitful in building stronger customer relations as well as showing commitment towards supporting good health outcomes for them all.

However, customer reviews in pharma marketing must comply with strict regulatory standards to ensure accurate, balanced information without bias or misrepresentation. Reviews should also be collected transparently and objectively with any risks or side effects disclosed proactively.

How Pharma Companies Leverage Customer Reviews: Some Examples

Here are several examples of how pharmaceutical companies may leverage customer reviews as part of their marketing:

1. *Novartis*: Novartis created *Living Like You*, an online community designed to bring those living with multiple sclerosis (MS) together to share stories and experiences. There's even an *MS Life Hacks* section where those managing their condition share tips from their daily experiences, and product reviews of medications or medical devices used for managing it.
2. *Pfizer*: Pfizer's Lyrica (Pregabalin) medication for fibromyalgia features its own dedicated website with patient reviews organized around symptoms associated with this illness. These insights into how Lyrica (Pregabalin) helped its recipients manage pain, fatigue and other associated fibromyalgia symptoms are accessible here.
3. *Eli Lilly*: On their *Real Stories* section of their website for Trulicity (Dulaglutide), patients have posted video testimonials that showcase how well this medication has helped manage their type 2 diabetes and patient reviews of Trulicity medication.
4. *Sanofi*: Sanofi offers its Toujeo (Insulin Glargine Injection) medication for managing diabetes with video testimonials of real patients who successfully used Toujeo to reduce complications while managing blood sugar levels effectively and reduce risks. Their website includes an additional section for patient reviews which provides more insights into how Toujeo helps users control blood sugar and minimize risks related to its use.

Pharma companies utilize customer reviews as an opportunity for valuable customer insights while developing trust among patients and healthcare providers.

Customer Satisfaction

Customer Satisfaction in pharmaceutical marketing refers to the level of satisfaction among patients and healthcare professionals with pharmaceutical companies' products, services and experiences, thus serving as an indicator for measuring marketing strategies' success and their products/services' offerings.

Pharmaceutical companies can measure customer satisfaction using various tools, including surveys, focus groups and feedback mechanisms on their websites or social media channels. Such techniques provide invaluable insight into customer perceptions of products and services provided by pharmaceutical companies as well as levels of satisfaction among target demographics.

Companies looking to improve customer satisfaction with pharmaceutical marketing should pay particular attention to:

1. *Quality Products and Services*: Ensuring high-quality products that satisfy both patients and healthcare providers is vital in creating customer loyalty; products must be safe, effective and user-friendly to do this effectively.
2. *Effective Communication*: Communicating clearly and precisely about the products and services your company provides is vital in building trust with customers and creating credibility with potential investors. Effective communication helps customers better comprehend how products benefit them as well as how best to use them effectively.
3. *Customer Service and Support*: By providing exceptional customer service and support, companies can make customers feel valued during their healthcare journey. This may include offering resources or guidance about products or services offered by your organization.
4. *Personalization*: Tailoring marketing messages and strategies specifically to satisfy each customer's individual needs and preferences is one way to increase satisfaction, such as developing customer personas or mapping the customer journey to identify opportunities for personalization.

Pharmaceutical companies can increase customer satisfaction by prioritizing these areas, strengthening relationships with customers and providers and driving business expansion.

Customer Satisfaction Measurement

Customer satisfaction measurement in pharmaceutical marketing involves various techniques to assess customer and patient satisfaction with pharmaceutical products and services. This practice helps pharma companies understand customer needs and preferences while pinpointing areas for improvement that could increase loyalty and retention rates.

Here are a few methods used for measuring customer satisfaction in pharmaceutical marketing:

1. *Surveys*: Surveys provide direct feedback from patients and healthcare providers regarding their experiences with specific medications or treatments. They can also be conducted online, over the phone, or in person.
2. *Net Promotion Score (NPS)*: NPS is a popular customer satisfaction and loyalty metric, asking customers to rate the likelihood of recommending products or services they use on a ten-point scale, scoring from 0-10, with scores above nine being considered promoters. At the same time, anything under six may be detractors.
3. *Focus Groups*: Focus groups are an effective qualitative research methodology involving gathering a small group of customers or patients together for in-depth discussions about their experiences with a product or service, which can reveal key insight into what factors drive customer satisfaction or dissatisfaction.
4. *Social Media Monitoring*: Platforms such as Twitter and Facebook provide real-time insight into customer feedback and sentiment about a specific drug or treatment, providing real-time insight into customer satisfaction levels while helping pharmaceutical companies identify any issues or potential concerns that arise from customer engagement on these channels.
5. *Customer Service Feedback*: Gathering customer service feedback can be done through various means such as phone, email, and chat. Doing this will give insight into customer service quality and potential improvement areas.

How Pharma Measures Customer Satisfaction

Pharmaceutical companies have implemented various techniques to assess customer satisfaction and enhance the customer experience. Here are some examples:

1. Johnson & Johnson uses surveys and focus groups to solicit feedback from patients and healthcare providers regarding their experience with its products and services, and gain an in-depth knowledge of customer preferences and needs.
2. GlaxoSmithKline (GSK) uses Net Promoter Score (NPS) as an objective means of measuring customer loyalty, while gathering feedback through social media monitoring and customer service responses.
3. Novartis utilizes surveys and focus groups to collect patient feedback on its products and services, while social media monitoring keeps an eye on customer sentiment analysis.
4. Pfizer utilizes multiple strategies for measuring customer satisfaction, such as surveys, focus groups, and customer service feedback. In addition, data analytics help them identify improvement areas and drive continuous customer experience enhancement.
5. Roche utilizes the Net Promoter Score (NPS) to measure customer satisfaction and loyalty, and gathers feedback through surveys and social media monitoring.

Measuring customer satisfaction is a core component of pharmaceutical marketing. By gathering feedback and insights from their customers and patients, pharma companies can make data-driven decisions to increase customer satisfaction while increasing performance.

Customer Satisfaction Research

Customer satisfaction research can provide pharmaceutical companies insight into how their customers perceive their products and services. Here are some steps they can take to conduct this important endeavor:

1. *Establish Research Objectives*: The first step should be clearly defining your research objectives, whether that means identifying areas for improvement, measuring customer loyalty, or determining the effectiveness of marketing campaigns.
2. *Identify the Target Audiences*: Pharmaceutical companies should identify which customer segments they wish to survey, such as healthcare professionals, patients, or caregivers.
3. *Choose Your Research Methodology*: Various research methodologies, such as surveys, focus groups, and interviews, should be selected based on the objectives and target audience of the research study.
4. *Design a Questionnaire*: Pharma companies selecting to conduct surveys should create a questionnaire with relevant questions to gather insights that meet their desired outcomes. Its questions should be clear, concise, and unbiased.
5. *Gathering Data*: Pharmaceutical companies can gather data through several channels, such as online surveys, focus groups, and phone, or in-person interviews.
6. *Analyzing Data*: Pharmaceutical companies must examine data to detect trends and patterns collected, which may involve quantitative methods like coding or thematic analysis as well as qualitative techniques like content analysis.
7. *Develop Insights and Action Plans*: Pharma companies can utilize analysis results to develop insights and action plans to address any areas of concern or potential areas for improvement.

Examples of Customer Satisfaction Research in Pharma

Here are examples that demonstrate how pharmaceutical companies conduct customer satisfaction research:

1. Pfizer conducted a customer satisfaction survey in 2020 to obtain feedback about its products and services, such as quality, usability and delivery. A questionnaire was distributed in this regard covering aspects like product quality, usability and service provision.
2. Novartis conducted a customer satisfaction survey in 2019 to gather customer input on its pharmaceutical products, with questions concerning aspects like effectiveness, usability and side effects.
3. Merck conducted a customer satisfaction survey in 2018 to gather feedback on their vaccines. This questionnaire focused on various aspects of customer experience, such as effectiveness, ease of administration, and service quality.
4. AstraZeneca conducted a customer satisfaction survey to collect feedback on their cardiovascular drugs. The survey asked about various aspects of customer experience, such as drug effectiveness, side effects, and customer support.
5. Roche conducted a customer satisfaction survey in 2016 to obtain feedback on its cancer drugs. This questionnaire addressed various elements of customer experience, such as drug effectiveness, side effects and satisfaction surveys.

Pharma companies can benefit greatly from conducting customer satisfaction studies to gain invaluable insights that will allow them to enhance their products and services, create customer loyalty, and advance business expansion.

Customer Satisfaction Score

Customer Satisfaction (CSAT) surveys provide pharmaceutical companies with an essential tool to measure customer satisfaction with their products and services, including patients, healthcare providers, and other stakeholders within their pharmaceutical ecosystems. CSAT can be administered in every aspect of customer experience.

An example would be for a pharmaceutical company to conduct a (Customer Satisfaction (CSAT) survey with patients who recently started taking their medication to gather feedback regarding effectiveness, ease of use, and any side effects, as well as questions about customer service experiences such as accessibility of customer support representatives.

Pharma companies may conduct customer satisfaction surveys with healthcare providers to collect feedback about the effectiveness of their educational materials, ease of prescribing medication, and overall experience working with the company.

By tracking customer satisfaction ratings over time, pharmaceutical companies can identify areas for improvement and take appropriate actions to address customer issues. If a low CSAT score can be linked with difficulty accessing customer service, for example, perhaps investing in more customer services will improve it further.

CSAT is an important metric pharmaceutical companies use to monitor customer satisfaction and enhance the customer experience. By gathering feedback from patients, healthcare providers, and other stakeholders on customer experiences provided, pharma companies identify areas for improvement while taking proactive steps toward increased satisfaction from all stakeholders.

Customer Touchpoints

Customer touchpoints in pharmaceutical marketing refer to any interaction between an existing customer or potential customer and your products or services, whether through different online or offline channels.

1. *Pharmaceutical Sales Reps (PSRs)*: Pharmaceutical sales representatives serve as key figures within their respective fields, engaging healthcare providers (HCPs) to share product knowledge, answer any inquiries they might have, and solicit feedback.
2. *Websites* help pharmaceutical companies inform patients and healthcare practitioners (HCPs) of their services and educational materials on these pages.
3. *Social Media*: Pharma companies use social media like Twitter, Facebook, and LinkedIn to engage with patients and healthcare providers (HCPs). Pharma companies share updates about new products or services and educational content about them through these avenues.
4. *Events*: Conferences and trade shows provide pharmaceutical companies valuable opportunities to showcase their products and engage with HCPs and key stakeholders.
5. *Direct Mail Campaigns*: Direct mailing campaigns can provide pharmaceutical companies with effective touchpoints targeting specific population segments such as HCPs or patients with certain conditions.
6. *Email marketing*: Email is another popular avenue of engagement between pharmaceutical companies and HCPs/patients, using it to market products/services, share educational material, and engage them. Companies often utilize emails in this capacity.

Customer touchpoints play a pivotal role in pharmaceutical marketing. They enable companies to build strong relationships with existing and prospective customers, effectively marketing their products and services to both parties.

Maximizing Impact

Enhancing customer experiences at each touchpoint is vitally important in pharmaceutical marketing, as this can enhance engagement with existing customers while driving sales growth. Consider the following strategies to deliver exceptional customer experiences:

1. *Understanding Your Customers*: To have maximum impact at every touchpoint with customers, we must gain an in-depth knowledge of their needs, preferences, and behaviors through market research or other means such as customer surveys or consumer focus groups. You can do this via market research studies or customer satisfaction questionnaires.
2. *Personalize the Experience*: Personalization is at the heart of all successful interactions between brands and customers, using customer data to tailor messaging, and content specific to each touchpoint.

3. *Provide Value*: Customers will engage more actively with your offer if they perceive value in it.
4. *Apply Multiple Channels*: Customers engage with brands through various channels; therefore, brands must maintain a presence across each relevant platform, such as social media, email marketing campaigns, and direct mailing.
5. *Optimize for Mobile*: With mobile phones becoming increasingly prevalent, optimizing touchpoints to accommodate them is paramount. This involves ensuring websites and digital assets such as apps are mobile-friendly so users can navigate easily on smaller screens.
6. *Measure and Analyze*: To make each touchpoint as effective as possible, measuring and analyzing results is vital. Analytical tools allow tracking customer engagement as you use this data to refine your approach over time.

By following these tips, pharma marketing campaigns can maximize each customer touchpoint's effect, increasing engagement while driving sales growth.

Cybersecurity

Cybersecurity in pharmaceutical marketing refers to protecting digital assets, systems, and data from unauthorized access, theft, or damage. Because pharmaceutical industries handle sensitive research information for drug research development and distribution purposes, they make them prime targets for cyberattacks, with serious repercussions such as intellectual property loss, reputational damage, and legal and financial penalties if data breaches or cyberattacks occur.

Here are the key aspects of cybersecurity in pharmaceutical marketing:

1. *Data Protection*: The primary goals of cybersecurity in pharmaceutical marketing are safeguarding sensitive data, such as the personal information of patients and healthcare providers, and intellectual property related to drug development.
2. *Cyber Threat Intelligence*: Pharmaceutical companies must remain aware of potential cyberattacks and vulnerabilities to defend themselves effectively, which means gathering threat intelligence from various sources like government agencies, cybersecurity vendors, and industry associations.
3. *Employee Training*: Cybersecurity should not only be the domain of IT specialists; all pharmaceutical company employees must receive adequate cybersecurity training to recognize and report potential security threats. This includes training on safe browsing habits, password administration, and phishing prevention.
4. *Secure Networks and Devices*: Protecting all networks and devices used by pharma marketing is also an integral component of cybersecurity, including firewalls, antivirus software, intrusion detection systems, and encryption solutions.
5. *Incident Response Planning*: Unfortunately, cyberattacks still happen despite our best efforts at prevention. Therefore, companies must have incident response plan protocols outlining steps to take if a breach occurs, for containing the breach, communicating with affected parties, and conducting forensic analyses to determine its sources.

Cybersecurity is an ongoing process requiring constant monitoring, updating, and training. Pharmaceutical companies can safeguard their digital assets while protecting sensitive information by adopting proactive cybersecurity measures that monitor emerging threats.

D

1. Daily Sales Plan
2. Dashboard
3. Data Analytics
4. Data Integrity
5. Database Marketing
6. Data-Driven Marketing
7. Data Privacy
8. Data Protection
9. Data Visualization
10. Deductibles
11. Defensive Marketing
12. De-identification of Data
13. Delphi Technique
14. Demand
15. Demand Planning
16. Demarketing
17. Demographics
18. Demographic Segmentation
19. Dependent Variables
20. Depth Interview
21. Design Thinking
22. Desire
23. Detailing
24. Differentiation
25. Differentiated Marketing
26. Differentiating Variables
27. Diffusion of Innovation
28. Digital Assets
29. Digital Branding
30. Digital Darwinism
31. Digital Divide
32. Digital Health
33. Digital Immigrants
34. Digital Intelligence
35. Digitilization
36. Digital Landscape
37. Digital Marketing
38. Digital Maturity
39. Digital Maturity Analysis
40. Digital Maturity Stages
41. Digital Medicine
42. Digital Natives
43. Digital Opinion Leader (DOL)
44. Digital Pill
45. Digital Therapeutics
46. Digital Transformation
47. Digital Twins
48. Diminishing Returns, The Law of
49. Dirichlet Model
50. Direct-to-Consumer Advertising
51. Direct-to-Consumer Marketing
52. Discretionary Analysis
53. Discretionary Variables
54. Discriminant Analysis
55. Discriminating Variables
56. Disintermediaries
57. Disease Management
58. Disparaging Copy
59. Display Advertising
60. Disruption
61. Disruptive Marketing
62. Dissonance Attribution Model
63. Dissonance Hierarchy
64. Distribution
65. Diversification
66. Diversity
67. Dogs
68. Domino Effect
69. Dosage Form
70. Double Jeopardy
71. Drip Capaigns
72. Drug Development
73. Drug Discovery
74. Drug Laws
75. Drug Master File (DMFs)
76. Drug Price Control
77. Drug Recall
78. Drug Repositioning
79. Drug Repurposing
80. Drug-Drug Interaction (DDI)

Daily Sales Plan

A daily sales plan in pharma marketing is a plan that outlines the specific sales targets and activities that a sales representative or team should focus on during a given day. The plan is typically based on the company's sales objectives, the market conditions, and the specific needs and preferences of the targeted healthcare professionals or customers.

A typical daily sales plan in pharma marketing may include the following components:

1. *Establish Daily Sales Targets*: Setting daily sales goals involves setting specific, measurable objectives that sales representatives or teams strive to meet daily.
2. *Target Healthcare Professionals or Customers*: Identifying likely healthcare professionals or customers interested in your product/service involves selecting those most likely interested.
3. *Planning Sales Activities*: Planning sales activities to reach targeted healthcare professionals or customers involves scheduling specific phone calls, emails, visits, or other necessary means.
4. *Develop an Effective Sales Pitch*: In this step, healthcare professionals or customers targeted as customers or audiences are provided with persuasive sales pitches tailored to their needs and interests.
5. *Tracking Progress*: This involves tracking progress against the daily sales targets and adjusting the sales plan to meet the targets.

A daily sales plan in pharma marketing is essential for ensuring sales representatives and teams are focused and productive and can promptly and efficiently achieve their sales objectives.

Dashboard

Dashboards are visual displays of data that offer an easily understandable summary of key information, metrics, and performance indicators in an easily consumable form. Dashboards are widely utilized by businesses, technology firms, and data analysts for monitoring data, tracking progress, and making informed decisions.

Dashboards typically consist of widgets such as charts, graphs, tables, gauges, or maps to display relevant information to viewers. These components offer data in either graphical or tabular forms to quickly reveal trends, patterns, and insights for a quick grasp by users. Dashboards provide users with an interactive way to present complex data in an easily understandable and visually stimulating format, making it possible to monitor important metrics, identify outliers and trends quickly, and drill into details when necessary. They're also usually customizable, giving users control over layout, data selection, and any special interactive features such as filters or features they might include in their display.

Dashboards in Pharma Marketing

Pharmaceutical marketers rely heavily on dashboards to track key performance indicators (KPIs) that measure campaign and strategy success. Here are a few examples of dashboard use in pharmaceutical marketing:

1. *Sales Performance*: Dashboards allow marketers to easily monitor sales performance with real-time dashboard data like product sales, volume, revenue, market share, and growth rates to help make better-informed decisions. Dashboards present this data in real-time so marketers can compare how various products compare with one another while simultaneously identifying patterns or trends which assist decision-making processes.
2. *Campaign Metrics*: Dashboards give marketers an overview of marketing campaign metrics like reach, impressions, click-through rates (CTRs), conversion rates, and return on investment (ROI). Marketers can utilize this data to assess campaigns or tactics and optimize strategies accordingly.
3. *Physician Engagement*: Pharma companies often engage with healthcare professionals, such as physicians, through various activities like conferences, webinars, or educational programs. Dashboards can track physician engagement metrics, such as event attendance, feedback, interactions, and prescription rates, to measure the impact of these initiatives.
4. *Digital Marketing Analytics*: Dashboards can integrate data from different digital marketing channels, such as websites, social media platforms, email campaigns, and online advertising. Marketers can monitor website traffic, engagement metrics, social media interactions, and campaign performance in a centralized dashboard, enabling them to assess the effectiveness of their digital marketing efforts.
5. *Market Research and Competitive Analysis*: Dashboards can display market research data and competitive intelligence, including market size, patient demographics, competitor sales, and physician preferences. These insights help marketers understand the market landscape,

identify opportunities, and make informed decisions about positioning, targeting, and product development.

6. *Compliance and Regulatory Monitoring*: Pharma marketing is subject to various regulations and compliance requirements. Dashboards can track compliance metrics, such as adherence to promotional guidelines, adverse event reporting, or regulatory submissions, ensuring that marketing activities align with legal and ethical standards.

By leveraging dashboards, pharma marketers can gain valuable insights into their marketing initiatives, assess their performance, identify areas for improvement, and make data-driven decisions to optimize their strategies and achieve their marketing objectives.

Data Analytics

Data analytics examines large and complex datasets to uncover insights, trends, and patterns, which allow businesses to make more informed decisions. In the pharmaceutical industry, data analytics may be utilized for clinical trial data evaluation and patient records or sales figures to gain an edge in drug discovery processes, disease management, or market trends.

Data analytics involves several steps: collection, cleaning, preparation, modeling, and visualization. First, data are compiled from various sources such as electronic health records (EHR), clinical trial data, social media posts, wearable devices, and then it needs to be cleaned to make it accurate, complete, and consistent. Following that comes data modeling which involves utilizing statistical and machine learning algorithms to conduct data analyses and reveal patterns clearly and succinctly, utilizing charts, graphs, and other forms of visualization.

The pharmaceutical industry increasingly utilizes data analytics in its drug development and commercialization strategies. Data analysis allows pharmaceutical companies to identify new drug targets, predict efficacy and safety levels of existing treatments, and optimize drug development processes; data can also aid pharmaceutical firms with marketing campaign optimization, identify market trends, track sales performance, and optimize marketing plans.

Here are a few examples of data analytics being employed within the pharmaceutical industry:

1. *Drug Development*: Pharmaceutical companies utilize data analytics to identify new drug targets, predict efficacy and safety profiles of drugs under development, optimize drug development processes, and streamline drug production operations. Machine learning algorithms have become powerful tools in this regard. For instance, they can analyze large-scale genomic data sets to detect possible drug targets associated with specific diseases.
2. *Clinical Trials*: Data analytics provides invaluable assistance in designing and conducting clinical trials, from optimizing sample sizes and decreasing dropout rates to cutting the time and costs of conducting trials. For instance, statistical models can optimize sample sizes while decreasing dropout rates to shorten trial runs by cutting costs by up to 40%.
3. *Personalization*: Today, data analytics is being utilized in medicine to develop tailored healthcare solutions based on an individual's genetic makeup and other variables. Machine learning algorithms effectively analyze patient data to provide personalized treatment plans to specific populations.
4. *Marketing and Sales*: Data analytics is widely used to optimize marketing campaigns, identify market trends, and track sales performance. Data analysis can also identify customer segments for targeted product positioning or measure the campaigns' effectiveness.
5. *Supply Chain Management*: Data analytics is being increasingly leveraged in the pharmaceutical industry to enhance supply chain management processes, such as optimizing inventory levels, cutting wasteful spending, and increasing visibility and efficiency throughout their supply chains.

These are only some examples of how data analytics is applied within the pharmaceutical industry; its applications continue to expand as new technologies and sources become available.

Data analytics promises to revolutionize the pharmaceutical industry by helping organizations make data-driven decisions and devise innovative solutions that enhance patient health while driving business success.

Data Integrity

Data integrity assures accurate, complete, and consistent information throughout its lifespan. When applied to pharmaceutical marketing efforts, data integrity guarantees reliable marketing messages and materials for pharmaceutical marketing campaigns.

Here are some best practices regarding data integrity for pharma marketing:

1. *Document and Validate Data Processes*: Pharmaceutical companies should carefully document and validate all their data processes, from collection through storage, analysis, and reporting. This ensures data is handled consistently while any problems can be identified quickly and addressed accordingly.
2. *Establish Data Quality Checks*: Companies should establish quality checks to ensure their data is complete, accurate, and consistent with business needs. Such measures could include validation checks, range checks, and consistency tests.
3. *Implement Version Control*: Companies should implement version control measures across their marketing materials to maintain accurate information that reflects current events, including keeping an archive of version histories and recording any modifications made to materials.
4. *Ensure Data Accuracy Through Training*: Companies should ensure all employees involved with data collection, analysis, and reporting receive proper training on its integrity, such as quality checks, validation processes, or documentation practices. This may involve offering training programs focusing on data quality monitoring or validation practices as appropriate.
5. *Use Data Management Software*: Firms should implement data management software to protect data integrity. Such solutions provide validation checks, visualization tools, and the capacity for tracking changes made to them.
6. *Conduct Regular Audits of Data Processes*: Companies should perform routine audits on their data processes to detect any vulnerabilities and ensure that data integrity remains intact over time.

Pharmaceutical companies that employ these best practices can ensure their marketing materials are built upon accurate and trustworthy information, thus increasing the effectiveness of marketing strategies while building customer trust.

Database Marketing

Database marketing can help pharmaceutical companies target potential customers such as healthcare professionals and patients by using data analytics for targeted campaigns and customer identification. Here are a few examples of database marketing's use in pharmaceuticals:

1. *Physician Outreach*: Pharmaceutical companies can leverage healthcare professional databases to quickly and accurately identify physicians likely to prescribe their drugs, then using targeted marketing campaigns, reach out with educational materials, product details, or any other relevant content for these potential prescribers.
2. *Patient Education*: Pharmaceutical companies can leverage patient information databases to offer targeted educational resources and assistance for patients taking medications, including personalized emails and newsletters with details regarding benefits, side effects, and dosing instructions of these drugs.
3. *Compliance Support*: Using databases with patient information, pharmaceutical companies can identify patients at risk of noncompliance and provide targeted support through automatic reminders or appointment scheduling with healthcare providers.
4. *Adverse Event Monitoring*: Pharmaceutical companies can leverage databases of patient information to keep an eye out for any possible side effects caused by their products, including monitoring patient-reported adverse event data, which might signal potential safety issues.

Database marketing allows companies to enhance customer engagement, build loyalty and enhance marketing performance by understanding their target audiences better. In pharmaceuticals, database marketing uses data analytics and targeted campaigns to engage healthcare providers and their patients effectively and personally.

Data-Driven Marketing

Data-driven marketing uses data to drive marketing decisions and strategies by analyzing customer behavior. Customer behavior analytics involves collecting, analyzing, and using customer interactions on websites or social media platforms as sources for customer insights into target markets' needs and preferences.

Data-driven marketing employs cutting-edge technologies like artificial intelligence, machine learning, and predictive analytics to interpret large volumes of customer data to detect patterns and trends that enable tailored experiences for individual customers, optimize campaigns and outreach initiatives and boost overall business performance.

Here are some important applications of data-driven marketing in the pharmaceutical industry:

1. *Targeted Advertising*: Leveraging customer data to deliver tailored ads directly to certain customer segments.
2. *Content Personalization*: Tailoring website or email content based on customer behavior and preferences.
3. *A/B Testing* involves testing different marketing messages or designs to see which are more effective and successful.
4. *Predictive Analytics* utilizes data to predict customer behaviors, preferences, purchases in the future, and more.
5. *Data-Driven Marketing:* Pharmaceutical companies increasingly rely on data-driven marketing as an essential strategy to effectively reach healthcare providers and patients and promote their products. Data-driven marketing involves collecting information from various sources like electronic medical records (EMR), patient databases, clinical trials, or surveys to gain insight into patient and provider behavior and preferences.

Here are a few examples of data-driven marketing's use in the pharmaceutical industry:

1. *Targeted Advertising*: Pharmaceutical companies use data to deliver targeted ads based on prescription behavior, special needs, and location factors of healthcare providers.
2. *Patient Engagement*: Pharma companies can leverage patient data analysis to develop targeted campaigns aimed at patients who meet particular conditions or criteria, such as age, gender, or geographic location, including tailored messaging and educational material to increase awareness about drugs or treatments that might interest patients.
3. *Sales Force Optimization*: Data analytics can also assist with optimizing sales force activities by identifying high-value prescribers and targeting them with customized messages and marketing collateral.
4. *Recruitment Strategies for Clinical Trials*: Pharmaceutical companies can identify prospective trial participants through patient data and behavior analysis and devise tailored recruitment plans designed to increase enrollment rates in clinical trials.
5. *Health Outcomes Research*: Data analytics allows pharmaceutical companies to quickly detect trends and patterns in patient outcomes, helping them gain greater insights into product efficacy and safety while creating tailored marketing and educational campaigns for specific products or campaigns.

Data-driven marketing can be an essential asset to pharmaceutical companies looking to engage healthcare providers and patients, improve patient outcomes and drive business expansion. Companies can use analytics data for targeted, personalized strategies to increase customer engagement while improving bottom-line growth.

Data Privacy

Data privacy is vital in pharmaceutical marketing since pharmaceutical companies often collect and utilize sensitive patient information as the foundation of their marketing plans. Here are some best practices for data privacy when marketing pharmaceutical drugs:

1. *Obtain Patient Consent*: Pharmaceutical companies should obtain patient consent before collecting or utilizing data. Before collecting, storing, or using patient data in any capacity, pharmaceutical companies must gain consent through either an opt-in form on their website, or mobile app, or an opt-in form in writing.
2. *Use De-identified Data*: Companies should employ de-identified data to protect patient privacy, concealing identifiable details such as names, addresses, or social security numbers from patient data.
3. *Limit Data Collection and Utilization*: Companies should only gather and utilize patient information as necessary for their marketing strategies, communicating clearly to patients how and who will access it.
4. *Implement Comprehensive Data Security Measures*: Companies should employ robust measures for protecting patient information against unintended access, including encryption, access controls, and performing regular security audits.
5. *Ensure Transparency and Control*: Companies should give patients complete and transparent control and access to their data, giving them full freedom and authority over their collection and usage practices. Patients must have full authority and freedom of their data. They may review, amend, or opt-out anytime necessary.
6. *Compliance with Regulations*: Pharmaceutical companies operating within the US should abide by any data protection regulations, such as California Consumer Privacy Act (CCPA), or the European General Data Protection Regulation (GDPR) in the European Union.

Pharmaceutical companies who adopt best practices can protect patient data while adhering to regulations, which ultimately helps build trust between themselves and patients and increase marketing strategies' efficacy.

Data Protection

Data protection in pharmaceutical marketing is paramount, as pharmaceutical companies deal with sensitive patient data such as medical records and prescription histories. Here are some best practices for data security within this area:

1. *Compliance with Relevant Regulations*: In the US, HIPAA (Health Insurance Portability and Accountability Act) regulates healthcare providers' handling of patient information by their business associates, including pharmaceutical companies. Therefore, companies should adhere to HIPAA and any relevant regulations, such as data security requirements or rules about patient consent.
2. *Limit Access to Patient Data*: Companies should ensure only authorized personnel have access to patient data, with access restricted as much as necessary for job performance. Access controls, user authentication, and data encryption all facilitate this goal.
3. *Use Secure Technologies*: Companies should safeguard patient information, by using secure technologies including firewalls, antivirus software, and data encryption tools. They should also implement safe data storage and backup procedures to prevent data loss or unauthorized access.
4. *Provide Employee Training*: Companies should offer employees training on data protection best practices, including how to handle patient records safely, detect data breaches swiftly, and ensure regulatory compliance.
5. *Conduct Regular Risk Evaluations*: Organizations should perform risk evaluations to detect vulnerabilities within their data protection practices and implement necessary mitigation steps, including regular security audits, vulnerability, and penetration tests.
6. *Establish a Data Breach Response Plan*: Businesses should establish a plan outlining how they would react in the event of a data breach, including who should be informed, steps taken to contain the breach, communication to patients and stakeholders, and more.

Pharma marketing requires effective data protection through regulatory compliance, secure technologies, employee training, risk assessments, and an actionable breach response plan to safeguard patients' data effectively and ensure its protection and confidentiality. By following the best practices pharmaceutical companies can guarantee patient data is kept private and safe from outside intrusions.

Data Visualization

Data visualization refers to the visual presentation of data and information. It uses visual elements like charts, graphs and maps to easily communicate complex datasets in an understandable and pleasing format for their audiences. Data visualization's primary aim is helping individuals make sense of data quickly and efficiently. Using visual elements allows us to spot patterns, trends or outliers not evident through raw data alone.

Examples of common data visualization techniques include:

- Line charts are commonly used to illustrate trends over time and plotted relationship between two variables
- Scatter plots show correlation between variables
- Maps display geographical details and patterns

Data visualization can be created with various tools, from spreadsheet programs and dedicated visualization software, such as R or Python programming languages, all the way up to spreadsheets themselves. When choosing visualization for any given information set, the key element is selecting appropriate graphics with accurate, legible visual elements that make sense of its presentation and are pleasing visually.

Data Visualization in Pharma Marketing

Pharma marketers increasingly rely on data visualization as a powerful means to convey complex data on drugs, disease states and patient populations in an easy and aesthetically appealing way.

Here are a few examples of data visualization's application in pharmaceutical marketing:

A. *Graphs and Charts*: Graphs and charts can be an excellent way of visually representing data on drug efficacy, safety and tolerability as well as comparing their performances with similar medications or treatments. A bar chart might show the reduction of symptoms among patients taking one drug vs placebo treatment.

B. *Heat Maps*: These show spatial patterns of disease prevalence, drug sales or other metrics.

Pharma marketers can use heat maps to quickly identify areas with greater demand for certain medicines or where disease burden is particularly high.

C. *Interactive Visualizations*: Interactive visualizations have quickly become a trendy tactic in pharma marketing, providing users with engaging ways to explore complex data sets in an engaging manner. An example might include exploring a drug's molecular structure or viewing how different patient subgroups respond to treatment options.

How Pharma Can Utilize Data Visualization

Here are some examples that show how data visualization can be effectively employed in pharmaceutical marketing:

1. *Comparative Efficacy Chart*: Data visualization techniques can help produce a chart which compares the efficacy of various drugs used to treat an illness or condition. Such charts may show which percentage of patients experienced reduced symptoms with each medicine and use different colors or symbols to differentiate among drug classes.
2. *Patient Journey Map*: A patient journey map is an interactive data visualization used to illustrate all of a patient's interaction points with various healthcare systems or treatment regimens. Pharma marketers can utilize such maps as part of their marketing strategies in order to better engage patients while understanding how patients move through healthcare systems.
3. *Geographic Heat Map*: A heat map can demonstrate geographical patterns related to disease prevalence, drug sales or other metrics. For instance, such maps could show where specific diseases or medications are most frequently prescribed or sold.
4. *Interactive Molecular Visualization*: Interactive visualization that allows users to explore the molecular structure of drugs can help communicate complex scientific ideas visually, which makes for engaging data visualization that may be utilized by pharmaceutical marketers to inform healthcare providers or patients of how certain drugs function on a molecular level. Such data visualization could potentially serve as part of marketing campaigns to demonstrate this point to healthcare professionals or patients alike.
5. *Social Media Sentiment Analysis*: Data visualization techniques can help analyze social media data to uncover user sentiment for any given drug or condition, providing invaluable insight into how patients and healthcare providers discuss such treatments and opportunities to enhance messaging or engagement strategies.

Data visualization can be an indispensable asset to pharmaceutical marketers, providing an accessible method for communicating complex information to their target audiences in an engaging manner. Effective use of data visualization by marketers can contribute significantly to better patient outcomes, sales increases and overall business performance enhancement.

Deductibles

Deductibles in health insurance refer to the amount of money an individual must pay out of pocket for covered healthcare services before their insurance plan starts to cover the costs. The insured person must pay a fixed amount annually before the insurance company begins contributing to the expenses.

For example, if a health insurance plan has a $1,000 deductible, the policyholder must personally pay the first $1,000 of the covered medical expenses in a given year. After reaching this deductible, the insurance coverage typically kicks in, and the individual is responsible for only the specified copayment or coinsurance for covered services.

Deductibles vary widely among insurance plans; higher deductibles often correspond to lower monthly premiums. They serve as a way to share healthcare costs between the insurance company and the insured individual.

Implications for Pharma Marketers

Deductibles in healthcare plans can have implications for pharmaceutical marketers in several ways:

1. *Affordability Challenges*: High deductibles can pose affordability challenges for patients, making them more cost-conscious about their healthcare expenses, including prescription medications,. This may influence their choice of drugs and willingness to adhere to prescribed treatments.
2. *Price Sensitivity*: Pharma marketers need to know patients' price sensitivity with high deductibles. Patient assistance programs, copay assistance, or discounts can address this sensitivity and improve medication access.
3. *Formulary Placement*: Health plans often structure their formularies with different cost-sharing tiers. Pharma marketers may need to

negotiate with insurers to secure favorable formulary placement, reducing out-of-pocket patient costs and potentially increasing market share.

4. *Communication Strategies*: Marketers must develop communication strategies that address the cost concerns associated with high deductibles. This might involve emphasizing medication's long-term value or cost-effectiveness and providing clear information about available financial assistance programs.
5. *Generic Competition*: Patients with high deductibles may be more inclined to choose generic alternatives if available. Pharma marketers should consider the competitive landscape, including generic options, and position their products effectively.
6. *Patient Education*: Educating patients about the benefits and value of a particular medication and available financial assistance programs can help improve adherence and acceptance despite high deductibles.
7. *Market Access Strategies*: Understanding the dynamics of insurance plans and their deductibles is crucial for market access strategies. It may involve negotiating pricing agreements with payers that align with patients' financial situations.

In essence, deductibles can influence patients' purchasing behaviors and their choices regarding prescription medications. Pharma marketers must navigate these dynamics by addressing affordability concerns, optimizing formulary placement, and employing effective communication strategies to ensure product access to patients.

Defensive Marketing

Defensive marketing can help pharmaceutical companies protect their market share against competitive threats by protecting themselves with defensive strategies such as:

1. *Patent Protection*: Pharmaceutical companies can safeguard their market share by obtaining patents on their drugs, effectively banning competitors from creating and selling similar drugs during an allotted timeframe.
2. *Strategic Pricing*: Companies can utilize pricing strategies to defend their market share by setting prices that prevent competitors from undercutting their offer and taking market share away.
3. *Brand Reputation*: Establishing a positive brand reputation within the pharmaceutical industry can help set products apart and foster customer loyalty.
4. *Advertising and Promotion*: Launching targeted advertisements and promotions highlighting the unique characteristics and advantages of your products can help shield them against competitive threats.
5. *Superior Customer Service*: Delivering exceptional customer service can help build customer loyalty and satisfaction while simultaneously guarding them against competitive threats.
6. *Partnerships and Collaborations*: Forming strategic alliances and collaborations with other businesses or organizations is an invaluable way of expanding a company's network while giving an advantage against competitors.
7. *Continuous Innovation*: Pharmaceutical companies can protect their market share by constantly innovating and improving their products to stay ahead of competitors and meet shifting customer requirements.

De-identification of Data

Data de-identification is crucial in safeguarding privacy and compliance across many fields, such as the pharmaceutical industry. De-identified information is information without personal identifiers, so it cannot be traced back to a person.

Pharmaceutical industries use patient data such as treatment outcomes, drug reactions, or demographics for better drug development strategies or patient care approaches that meet regulatory compliance. This allows pharmaceutical firms to use this information effectively while remaining compliant.

Here are the key steps of de-identifying data in pharmaceutical marketing:

1. *Data Minimization*: Collecting only necessary information as this reduces any risks related to privacy breaches.
2. *Anonymization of data* removes any identifiable details that could identify individuals from data. Such details could include names, addresses, social security numbers, or anything allowing someone to identify someone directly.
3. *Pseudonymization* involves replacing identifiable data with artificial identifiers to reduce risk and preserve privacy. Although such measures don't completely eradicate any chance of an individual being identified with sufficient

other sources, pseudonymization techniques significantly minimize that risk.

4. *Data Masking*: Data masking protects sensitive information in datasets by replacing it with identical but inauthentic information. This technique is commonly employed when testing or training requires using real data that users cannot see directly.
5. *Data Swapping*: This involves altering data slightly to protect individuals in a dataset without altering its integrity. Noise addition adds random amounts of statistical noise into it. And yet, both processes seek to prevent identifications within datasets.
6. *Aggregation*: Aggregation is a method of adding data together so that individual entries cannot be identified. This could be in the form of averages, sums, or other statistical measures.

All these steps ensure the data remains useful to its intended use, especially de-identified health information, which could still be re-identified if combined with other data sets. Therefore, safeguards must be implemented to avoid this possibility.

These practices must adhere to any data protection legislation, such as GDPR in Europe or HIPAA in America, that regulates how personal or health data can be handled. For instance, GDPR and HIPAA laws have stringent restrictions regarding how data must be managed.

Impact on Marketers

De-identification has various implications for pharmaceutical marketing professionals, offering challenges and opportunities:

1. *Compliance With Regulatory Requirements*: De-identification is a legal mandate under GDPR (General Data Protection Regulations), HIPAA (Health Insurance Portability and Accountability Act), and similar laws in other countries. So adopting proper de-identification processes helps marketers comply with both laws to avoid fines or reputational damage.
2. *Balance Privacy with Utility*: With de-identification techniques potentially altering data quality and utility, marketers face an uphill climb in balancing its usefulness with privacy considerations. Too much generalization or noise addition may render detailed analysis and segmentation less useful.
3. *Public Trust and Reputation*: De-identified data can increase customer and public trust when handled appropriately and is likely to increase patient trust in pharmaceutical companies as their privacy is protected.
4. *The Potential of Larger Datasets*: With proper de-identification techniques in place, marketers can access and use larger datasets without fear of violating privacy standards, leading to greater insights than before.
5. *Analytical Capabilities*: De-identified data can still be examined for patterns, trends, and insights which could assist marketing strategies, such as market segmentation, patient journey analysis, or marketing ROI analysis. This may prove valuable during market segmentation analyses or ROI estimation.
6. *Limitations on Personalized Marketing*: De-identified data does not lend itself well to personalized or targeted advertising on an individual level, as all Personally Identifiable Information (PII) has been removed from it. Marketers must rely more heavily on aggregated segments than individually targeted messages when marketing de-identified datasets.
7. *Security Requirements*: Marketers must implement stringent security measures to prevent unwarranted access or data breaches. These measures could include technological solutions, employee training programs, and possibly appointing a Data Protection Officer.
8. *Ethical Considerations*: Regardless of its legality, ethical considerations must always come first when using de-identified data. Misuse can lead to loss of trust and backlash against an institution even though, technically, they remain anonymous.
9. *Partnerships and Third Parties*: Marketers collaborating with third-party companies must take precautionary steps to ensure these partners adhere to similar privacy standards, creating robust data handling protocols to avoid privacy violations and subsequent infringements.

Delphi Technique

The Delphi technique is a qualitative research method used to gather and analyze opinions from a panel of experts. In Pharma marketing, the Delphi technique can gain insights from healthcare professionals and other experts to inform marketing strategies and product development. Here's how the Delphi technique works in pharma marketing:

1. *Establish an Expert Panel*: Gather together healthcare professionals, researchers and other specialists who will participate in the Delphi technique.
2. *Design a Questionnaire*: A series of open-ended questions is created in order to elicit opinions

from a panel of experts on various healthcare and pharmaceutical related subjects such as patient needs, treatment options available to them, market trends, etc.

3. *Collect and Analyze Responses*: After asking experts to fill out a questionnaire anonymously, their answers are then collected, analyzed, summarized and presented back for review by all experts involved in the survey.
4. *Repeat the Process*: Experts are invited to review and assess results as part of an iteration of Delphi technique questionnaire development; feedback received is used to create another round. The cycle continues until all experts reach consensus among themselves.

The Delphi technique can be an invaluable asset in pharmaceutical marketing, providing pharmaceutical companies with an efficient means to gather expert opinions and insights in an organized fashion. This helps pharmaceutical firms make more informed decisions regarding product development, marketing strategies and other areas of their businesses.

Examples of Pharma Companies Utilizing Delphi Technique

Here are a few pharmaceutical companies using Delphi method as part of their marketing research:

1. *Novartis*: Novartis used the Delphi technique to gain insights from an international panel of healthcare experts on the future of healthcare, composed of physicians, researchers, and healthcare providers from around the globe. By using Delphi analysis on emerging trends and technologies that would impact future developments of healthcare services and products, this process enabled Novartis to devise strategies for new product development initiatives.
2. *Pfizer*: Pfizer used the Delphi technique to collect insights from healthcare professionals about unmet patient needs related to chronic pain. They then utilized this information in developing products which met those specific patient requirements.
3. *Merck* used the Delphi technique to collect insights from an advisory panel of clinical trial experts about using new technologies in clinical trials. These specialists included clinicians, statisticians and others specializing in trial design. Merck utilized this process to identify technologies with great promise for increasing efficiency and accuracy during clinical trials; ultimately this helped the company take new approaches for both design and execution of clinical trials.

These are just a few ways Pharma companies can utilize the Delphi technique to gain key insights from an expert panel. By collecting and assessing expert opinions systematically, companies can make more informed decisions regarding product development, marketing strategies, or any aspect of their business operations.

Demand

Demand in economics refers to the quantity of a good or service that consumers are willing to purchase at an agreed upon price, over an agreed upon period of time. Demand represents consumers' desire or intent of buying at that particular price point.

Demand can be affected by various factors, including price of products/services offered, consumer income levels, availability of alternative offerings from competitors, preferences amongst consumers and changes to economic climate conditions.

Demand is an essential economic concept as it helps businesses and policymakers analyze consumer behavior to inform pricing, production and marketing decisions. By studying demand data, businesses can determine their optimal product/service prices as well as identify opportunities for increased sales growth and profits.

Demand in Pharma Marketing

In pharmaceutical marketing, demand refers to healthcare providers and patients' interest or desire for particular drugs or treatments. Demand can be affected by various factors including their effectiveness and safety as well as prevalence, severity or availability of alternative options for treatment.

Pharmaceutical companies employ various strategies to stimulate demand for their products. These may include conducting clinical trials that demonstrate its efficacy and safety; engaging key opinion leaders as advocates to healthcare providers; or investing in direct-to-consumer advertising strategies in order to raise patient awareness.

External factors, including demographic and economic fluctuations, also impact demand for pharmaceuticals. Changes to insurance or reimbursement policies may alter patient usage patterns while economic downturns could lessen patients' ability to afford medications.

Understanding demand is vital for pharmaceutical companies in creating successful marketing strategies that cater to patients and healthcare providers. By tracking trends closely and adapting marketing efforts accordingly, pharmaceutical firms can increase sales while improving patient outcomes and increase profits.

Demand Planning

Demand planning is an integral element of supply chain management. It entails anticipating consumer needs so products can be manufactured and distributed efficiently and promptly. It is especially relevant in the pharmaceutical industry due to the potentially devastating ramifications associated with shortages or surpluses of medication.

Here are a few key aspects of demand planning in pharmaceutical marketing:

1. *Accurate Demand Forecasting*: Demand forecasting involves accurately anticipating future drug demand using sales data from past sales data, market research, and trend analysis, among other sources. Inaccurate forecasts could result in either shortage, potentially having serious ramifications for patient health consequences, or overstock, which leads to waste due to expiration.
2. *Cooperation With Supply Chain*: Marketers must collaborate with supply chain managers to accurately anticipate demand forecasting. Marketers may provide input regarding forthcoming marketing campaigns, changes in market conditions, or anticipated fluctuations due to new clinical guidelines or competitor activities that impact demand projection.
3. *New Product Launches*: Marketers need to estimate expected demand to inform production levels when launching new drugs to inform production. Doing this effectively requires in-depth knowledge of the target market, competition, and drug's value proposition.
4. *Seasonal Demand Fluctuations*: Certain drugs, such as flu medication, may experience seasonal fluctuations that should be factored into demand planning strategies.
5. *Integrating Real-Time Data*: With sophisticated data analytics tools, real-time data can create more accurate demand forecasts. These data sources may include electronic health records, pharmacy sales data, or social media sentiment analysis data.
6. *Understanding Market Dynamics*: Marketers must remain mindful of market dynamics that could alter demand, including changes to healthcare policies, competitive activities, and trends in disease prevalence.
7. *Contingency Planning*: Demand planning must also include planning for unexpected fluctuations in demand due to disease outbreak, competitor drug withdrawal, or recall.
8. *Balancing Patient Needs and Business Objectives*: Demand planning in the pharmaceutical industry must balance business objectives and provide adequate patient access to the medicines they require.

Accurately forecasting demand for their products allows pharmaceutical marketers to ensure efficient supply chain management, reduce waste, prevent drug shortages, and provide patients with access to necessary medication. Doing this requires a deep knowledge of market dynamics, close cooperation between supply chain partners, and advanced data analytics tools.

Impact on Pharma Marketers

Demand planning holds substantial significance for pharmaceutical marketers. It could significantly boost revenues while decreasing inventory levels. Here are the key implications of demand planning for pharma marketers:

1. *Inventory Management*: By accurately forecasting demand, marketers can ensure the ideal inventory is always on hand; this helps avoid shortages that might impact patient health or trust in a brand while at the same time minimizing or avoiding overstock that could cause wastage and financial losses.
2. *Supply Chain Efficiency*: By working collaboratively between marketing and supply chain teams, efficiency in the supply chain can be increased significantly, decreasing costs while improving customer satisfaction.
3. *Competitive Advantage*: Strategic demand planning can give pharmaceutical companies an advantage in meeting customer demand while competing companies fail. Pharmaceutical firms could gain market share more easily than their rivals by continually meeting consumer needs while other businesses cannot.
4. *Profitability*: Businesses can increase profitability by ensuring the appropriate products are available when and where needed and not spending unnecessary funds on excess inventory.
5. *Reputation Management*: Pharma marketers must meet customer demand efficiently as it helps build and uphold an impressive brand image. Shortages could damage it, while efficient delivery could increase it.
6. *Customer Satisfaction*: Careful demand planning ensures medicines are available

whenever patients require them, increasing customer trust and satisfaction.

7. *Launch of New Product Success*: Effective demand planning is crucial for new product launches as it can make or break its success. Guaranteeing the supply to meet the initial demand is vital for new product success.
8. *Risk Mitigation*: Proper demand planning can help companies address unexpected fluctuations in demand by being well-prepared to face and manage them head-on.

Pharmaceutical marketers must actively engage in demand planning processes to remain effective demand planners. Their unique insights into market trends, customer behavior, and competitive dynamics are invaluable when forecasting demand accurately. Collaboration among marketing and supply chain teams and using sophisticated data analytics is vital for successful demand planning.

Demarketing

Demarketing in the pharmaceutical industry refers to any marketing strategy designed to reduce demand for an overused or inappropriately prescribed or consumed product or service resulting in negative health impacts or increased costs to healthcare providers. Demarketing can often be seen used by pharmaceutical firms when overuse leads to undesirable health outcomes or costs for healthcare providers.

Here are a few strategies used by pharmaceutical companies when demarketing products:

1. *Reducing Advertising*: Pharmaceutical companies may restrict advertising for certain products or services to reduce demand. For instance, companies producing highly addictive pain medication might attempt to limit advertising as one strategy to limit prescriptions written.
2. *Pharmaceutical Companies May Raise Prices to Decrease Demand*: Pharmaceutical companies often raise prices of certain products or services to curb demand for them. For instance, by raising the cost of certain medications used to treat conditions that do not pose immediate danger, in an attempt to curtail overuse of medications produced. For instance, companies producing medications for non-life threatening conditions might raise prices as an indirect way of discouraging overuse of such treatments.
3. *Pharmaceutical Companies Can Assist Patients and Healthcare Providers in Education*: Pharmaceutical companies may offer educational materials to both patients and healthcare providers to promote more responsible usage of specific products or services, for instance a company producing medication to manage conditions through lifestyle modifications may supply materials focusing on diet and exercise's significance in managing them.
4. *Pharmaceutical Companies Can Develop Alternative Products*: Pharmaceutical companies may create substitute products and services to replace an existing one, for instance if their painkiller product becomes highly addictive they could create non-addictive alternatives instead.

Demarketing can be a challenging strategy for pharmaceutical companies, since it may involve decreasing demand for an otherwise profitable product or service. Yet demarketing can also serve as an effective strategy to promote responsible use of healthcare products and services, leading to improved patient health outcomes while simultaneously decreasing healthcare provider expenses.

Demarketing in Pharma

Here are some examples showing how pharmaceutical companies employed demarketing strategies:

1. *Purdue Pharma*: Responding to the opioid epidemic, Purdue Pharma, the manufacturer of Oxycontin, agreed to stop promoting its opioid medications to doctors. The company also paid $600 million in fines for indulging in unethical marketing practices. Furthermore the company agreed to contribute $3 billion to address the opioid crisis and declared bankruptcy. It is an action seen as demarketing strategies designed to lower demand for highly addictive pain medications.
2. *GlaxoSmithKline*: In 2014, GlaxoSmithKline made an unprecedented announcement by declaring it would no longer pay doctors to promote its products as part of a wider effort to increase transparency and reduce conflicts of interest in the pharmaceutical industry. This move can be seen as demarketing strategy designed to limit sales representatives' influence over doctors' prescribing patterns.
3. *Pfizer* announced in 2021 that they were no longer marketing Chantix to US residents due to concerns surrounding its potential side effects, including suicidal thoughts and behavior. This act can be seen as demarketing strategy designed to decrease demand for an medication with potential dangers.

Pharmaceutical companies use demarketing strategies to encourage the responsible use of their products and services, with demarketing tactics that are often challenging but ultimately essential in improving public health and lowering healthcare costs.

Demographics

Demographics in pharmaceutical marketing refers to the characteristics of the population, such as age, gender, income, education level, or occupation type, or geographic location, that pharmaceutical companies target with their marketing initiatives.

Pharmaceutical companies can ascertain which demographics would most benefit from their products by conducting market research. For instance, companies marketing treatments for chronic conditions like diabetes often target older adults while those promoting genetic disorders target younger individuals.

Demographic information can also help businesses tailor marketing messages and strategies more precisely. For example, a company targeting older adults may use different communication channels, such as print ads, newspapers, or direct mail campaigns. In contrast, a company targeting younger individuals may focus more on social media and digital advertising.

However, pharmaceutical companies must consider ethical and legal considerations when targeting specific demographics. In addition, marketing efforts should be truthful and not misleading and comply with regulations governing the promotion of prescription drugs.

Demographic Segmentation

Demographic segmentation in pharmaceutical marketing refers to dividing an audience into smaller subpopulations according to demographic characteristics such as age, gender, income level and education level. This segmentation technique allows pharmaceutical companies to tailor their marketing initiatives toward certain groups that may have differing healthcare needs or preferences.

How Pharma Can Leverage Demographic Segmentation

Here are a few examples of how pharmaceutical companies may utilize demographic segmentation in their marketing initiatives:

1. *Age*: Pharmaceutical companies may target different age groups based on which health conditions are more prevalent within those populations, for instance a company offering medications for osteoporosis may target postmenopausal women at greater risk for this condition.
2. *Gender*: Pharmaceutical companies may use gender segmentation for medications targeted towards specific genders, such as hormonal contraceptives or treatments for prostate cancer. Furthermore, pharmaceutical firms can target health concerns that disproportionately impact one gender such as breast cancer in women or erectile dysfunction in men.
3. *Income*: Income segmentation can be utilized when targeting more expensive pharmaceuticals or conditions that tend to occur more commonly among higher-income individuals. Pharmaceutical companies could utilize income segmentation for targeted marketing of health insurance plans, or out-of-pocket expenses that they might cover with income segmentation targeting consumers more likely to have adequate out-of-pocket expenses, and less likely to require out-of-pocket payments for treatment costs.
4. *Education*: Education segmentation can be particularly effective for pharmaceutical products requiring greater levels of comprehension or compliance, like complex treatments for chronic conditions. Pharmaceutical companies could target consumers with higher educational backgrounds who would likely understand both benefits and risks when making these choices.

Demographic Segmentation in Pharma: Some Examples

Here are a few examples of pharmaceutical companies using demographic segmentation as part of their marketing initiatives:

1. *Pfizer's Viagra*: Pfizer's Viagra medication is used to treat erectile dysfunction in men. Pfizer, its manufacturer, has used demographic segmentation targeting older male consumers who may experience more difficulty. They have also targeted gender specific messaging as well as higher income consumers more likely to purchase the medicine.
2. *Johnson & Johnson Baby Shampoo*: Johnson & Johnson has utilized demographic segmentation to target parents concerned about the safety of products they choose for their children. Johnson & Johnson markets its baby shampoo as being gentle and safe, appealing specifically to these

parents who may have more reasons to be wary about ingredients present in other products.

3. *Merck's Gardasil*: Gardasil is a vaccine that prevents some human papillomavirus (HPV) strains, which may lead to cervical cancer. Merck, the manufacturer, uses demographic segmentation to reach young women and their parents as well as healthcare providers who may recommend its use more likely.
4. *GlaxoSmithKline's Advair*: GlaxoSmithKline developed its asthma and COPD medication Advair specifically to target consumers with higher incomes who may more likely have health insurance that covers its cost.

These examples demonstrate how pharmaceutical companies may utilize demographic segmentation to tailor their marketing messages and outreach efforts specifically towards certain groups of consumers, improving relevance and efficacy while potentially leading to greater sales or better patient health outcomes.

Pharmaceutical companies can utilize demographic segmentation to gain greater insight into their target audiences and craft more targeted and effective marketing campaigns using this technique. Tailoring messaging and outreach efforts directly towards particular groups of consumers may increase relevance and efficacy, potentially leading to greater sales, and better health outcomes for patients.

Dependent Variables

The psychology-Lexicon website defines a *Dependent Variable* as any variable measured during an experiment that responds directly to its independent variable, hence the name. Dependent variables can only exist with their accompanying independent variable in scientific experiments. Here is an example**:** You are interested in how stress affects the heart rate in humans. In this case, the stress would be the independent variable, and the heart rate would be the dependent variable. You can directly control stress levels, measure how they change the heart rate in your human subjects, and measure how those stress levels change the heart rate.

The dependent variable (DV) is just like the name sounds. It depends upon some factor that you, the researcher, control. For example:

- How well you perform in a race *depends* on your training
- How much you weigh *depends* on your diet
- How much you earn *depends* upon the number of hours you work

Whatever event you are expecting to change is always the dependent variable. In the first example above, performance is the variable you would expect to change if you changed your training, so that's the dependent variable. In the second example, the dependent variable is the weight; in the third, the dependent variable is the amount earned.

A simple way to figure out which of your variables is the independent one and which is the dependent one, try inserting the variables into the following sentence:

(Independent Variable) causes a change in (dependent Variable), and it is not possible that (Dependent Variable) could cause a change in (Independent Variable).

Dependent Variables in Pharma Marketing

Dependent variables refer to outcomes or metrics marketers aim to influence or measure with their marketing initiatives, providing insight into how well a marketing plan and strategy perform in various aspects of a pharmaceutical business.

Here are a few common dependent variables used in pharmaceutical marketing and their potential implications for marketers:

1. *Sales or Revenue*: Pharmaceutical marketers' primary objective is often increasing product sales and revenue. Sales data serves as the cornerstone of successful marketing campaigns. Marketers can analyze patterns and trends of sales to measure the effectiveness of various strategies used and optimize efforts accordingly.
2. *Prescription Volume*: Prescription volume is an invaluable metric in the pharmaceutical industry as it indicates how much and how often healthcare professionals prescribe certain drugs. Pharma marketers can evaluate how their marketing initiatives, such as brand recognition, physician engagement, and promotional activities (dependent variables), affect the prescription volume (independent variable) and prescribing behavior.
3. *Brand Awareness and Recognition*: Brand awareness refers to how familiar target audiences are with pharmaceutical brands, measured via surveys, market research, or social media analytics. Marketers monitor brand awareness as a dependent variable to evaluate whether marketing campaigns increase brand recognition and adapt their strategies to strengthen the visibility of the brands they wish to market.
4. *Engagement with Healthcare Providers or Patients*: Pharmaceutical marketers recognize the value of cultivating strong relationships and engaging effectively with physicians and patients

in pharmaceutical marketing campaigns. Marketers use metrics like physician interactions at medical conferences or patient engagement through educational materials to measure engagement initiatives that have worked effectively. These measurements help refine marketing strategies to reach healthcare professionals more efficiently while engaging patients more deeply.

5. *Patient Adherence*: Patient adherence refers to how closely patients follow prescribed medication regimens. Marketers play an integral part in supporting medication adherence through educational campaigns, reminders, and support programs. Marketers can measure impactful interventions by tracking adherence rates over time and making necessary changes accordingly.
6. *Market Share*: Market share refers to the proportion of the total pharmaceutical market that one brand or product owns; this represents its position within its industry and allows marketers to evaluate the impact of marketing activities compared with competitors, Using this information helps establish positioning, pricing, and promotional strategies accordingly.

By considering these dependent variables, pharmaceutical marketers can gain greater insight into the efficacy of their marketing activities and make data-driven decisions to optimize their strategies. By understanding their efforts' effect on sales, brand perception, physician and patient engagement, and market position, they can ensure more successful campaigns with improved business results.

Depth Interview

Depth interviews are qualitative research methods that involve in-depth conversations between an interviewer and respondent, typically followed by structured questioning of respondents' attitudes, beliefs, values, experiences, and perceptions.

An interviewer conducting depth interviews will usually present open-ended questions that allow respondents to freely express their thoughts and opinions, with probes to elicit more specific or complex responses or clarify respondent answers. Such interviews can be found across market research, sociology, and psychology to understand a phenomenon or issue further. In-depth interviews can be especially useful when exploring sensitive subjects or complex matters that cannot be quantified.

Depth interviews aim to obtain an in-depth and rich understanding of respondents' perspectives on an issue and use that understanding for decision-making or further research purposes.

Depth Interviews in Pharma Marketing

Depth interviews can be an efficient qualitative research method in the pharmaceutical industry for gathering insights about patients, healthcare providers, and stakeholders' attitudes, beliefs, and behaviors. Here are some ways pharma companies can use depth interviews in their marketing efforts:

1. *Understand Patient and Provider Needs*: Depth interviews can play an integral part in pharmaceutical marketing by helping pharma companies better understand patient and healthcare provider needs. Companies can use that insight to develop more impactful marketing messages and educational materials for target audiences.
2. *Explore Patient Journeys*: Depth interviews can effectively uncover patient experiences from diagnosis through to treatment and beyond, allowing pharmaceutical companies to develop more patient-centric solutions that improve outcomes and patient experiences.
3. *Identify Key Influencers*: Depth interviews can also identify influential healthcare opinion leaders and influencers within an industry, providing pharmaceutical companies insight into these stakeholders for more targeted marketing strategies and strong relationships with influencers.
4. *Develop Insights into Competitive Landscape*: Interviews can give Pharma companies deep insight into their competitors' strategies and understand how they position their products in the market. This gives them the insight to refine marketing strategies or develop more effective competitive positioning. This knowledge may then be utilized in refining marketing plans or formulating more powerful competitive positioning approaches.

How to Conduct a Depth Interview

Here are some general steps to follow when conducting a depth interview:

1. *Determine the Purpose and Scope of the Interview*: Clearly define the objectives of the interview and determine the scope of the discussion.
2. *Select and Recruit Participants*: Identify the target populations for the interview and recruit participants who fit the criteria. This may involve contacting individuals directly or working with a recruiting agency.

3. *Develop the Interview Guide*: Develop a structured interview guide with open-ended questions that will help to elicit detailed responses from the participants. Consider using probes to encourage participants to elaborate on their responses.
4. *Conduct the Interview*: Schedule a time and location for the interview and begin by introducing yourself and explaining the purpose of the interview. Use the interview guide as a framework for the discussion, but be flexible in allowing participants to lead the conversation.
5. *Record the Interview*: Record the interview using an audio or video recorder or take detailed notes to accurately capture the participant's responses.
6. *Analyze the Data*: Transcribe and examine your interview to analyze its data by noting themes and patterns among responses, using that knowledge to provide insights that could inform decision-making processes.
7. *Report the Findings*: Create a report or presentation outlining your findings from in-depth interviewing and recommendations for further action.

How to Develop an Interview Guide

Here are some steps to develop an interview guide for a depth interview:

1. *Define Your Research Question*: As soon as the interview starts, clearly state its objective or research question: what you hope to gain from conducting it, or which information do you require to complete it successfully?
2. *Determine Your Target Audience*: Establish who the interviewees will be. These could include patients, healthcare providers, or any other stakeholders you would like to interview. Keep this target audience's demographics, experience level, and expertise in mind as part of this analysis process.
3. *Conduct a Literature Review*: To conduct an effective literature review, review existing studies that address your research question to identify key concepts and themes related to its topic. This will help you to develop relevant and targeted questions.
4. *Develop an Initial List of Questions*: Based on the research question and literature review, develop a list of open-ended questions that elicit detailed participant responses. Start with broad, general questions and refine them to be more specific and targeted.
5. *Group Questions into Themes*: Group related questions into themes or topics. This will help you structure the interview guide and ensure all relevant topics are covered.
6. *Refine and Pilot the Interview Guide*: Review the interview guide and refine the wording and order of questions. Pilot the interview guide with a small group of participants to identify any issues or areas for improvement.
7. *Finalize the Interview Guide*: Make any necessary revisions based on feedback from the pilot group and finalize the interview guide.

An interview guide requires careful preparation and attention to detail. Following these steps, you can craft an interview guide that allows for structured questioning that leads participants to respond thoroughly and appropriately.

The Art of Asking Questions: Some Examples

Asking the right questions will elicit relevant and appropriate responses; therefore, it should be both a science and an art in equal measure. Questions to consider in in-depth interviews fall into categories, Including background, attitude, opinion, experience, perception, behavioral and future-oriented queries. Here are some sample questions in each category:

1. *Background Questions*:

   Can you tell me more about yourself and the experience with (topic of interest) that led you to this area of inquiry? Likewise, why and how did it catch your interest initially?
2. *Attitude and Opinion Questions*:

   How do you feel about (product/service/topic of interest)?

   What are your thoughts on (related topic or issue)?
3. *Experience Questions*:

   Can you describe your recent experience (product/service/topic of interest)?

   What challenges have you encountered when using (product/service/topic of interest)?
4. *Perception Questions*:

   How do others view (product/service/topic of interest)?

   What are the most important factors when using (product/service/topic of interest)?
5. *Behavioral Questions*:

   How often do you use (product/service/topic of interest)?

   What factors influence your decision to use (product/service/topic of interest)?
6. *Future-oriented Questions*:

   How do you see (product/service/topic of interest) evolving?

What changes would you like to see in (product/service/topic of interest)?

These are just some questions that could be included in an interview guide. The specific questions will depend on the research questions and target audience. Assuring your questions are open-ended and tailored toward eliciting detailed and pertinent responses is paramount.

Overall, depth interviews offer valuable insights into the needs and perspectives of patients, healthcare providers, and other key players in the pharmaceutical industry, helping pharma companies create more effective marketing strategies while improving patient outcomes.

Design Thinking

Design Thinking is an approach to problem-solving that prioritizes creativity, empathy, and experimentation. Human-centered design processes aim to understand people's needs, experiences, and perspectives using products or services; design thinking seeks innovative solutions that address complex problems while improving user experiences.

Design thinking involves several stages that should include:

1. *Engage*: Designers strive to understand the needs and experiences of people using the product or service through user research, observational data collection, or direct conversation with users. This may involve conducting user tests, monitoring behaviors, or conversing directly with users.
2. *Define*: At this phase, designers analyze research findings to clearly define the problem, or opportunity that needs to be solved. Reframing problems or opportunities might provide more creative approaches that enable rapid solutions.
3. *Ideate*: At this step, designers brainstorm solutions for their defined problem or opportunity using creative techniques like brainstorming or sketching.
4. *Prototype Development and Testing*: At this step, designers create and test physical or digital prototypes of their ideas to visualize them for testing purposes. This may involve building physical or digital prototypes, storyboards, or other visualization techniques.
5. *Test*: At this step, designers put their prototypes through an evaluation with end users to gather feedback and fine-tune their ideas. This may involve user testing sessions, surveys, or other feedback mechanisms.

Design Thinking can tackle numerous problems and opportunities, from product design to business strategy. It offers an efficient yet iterative process emphasizing collaboration and experimentation to encourage designers to take risks while learning from failure. There have been various applications of this methodology within pharma marketing as well.

Design Thinking in Pharma Marketing

How can design thinking be applied in pharmaceutical marketing? Here are a few examples of its usage within this space:

1. *Patient-Centric Drug Development*: Pharmaceutical companies can employ design thinking as an approach for developing drugs that are both more effective and easier for their users to use, using empathy-informed insight from interviews or surveys with potential patients as a basis for designing drug delivery systems that are less painful, less intrusive, or more convenient than current practices.
2. *Digital Health Solutions*: Design thinking can be used to develop more engaging and user-friendly digital health solutions, like mobile apps or online portals that help patients manage their conditions more effectively, or provide healthcare professionals with more useful patient data. Companies using user-centered design principles could use design thinking techniques like user-centricity to make such offerings.
3. *Patient Education and Support*: Design thinking can be used to create patient education and support materials that are both engaging and efficient. Companies may utilize insights from patient interviews, or surveys to create visually appealing educational material that more closely meets patients' specific needs.
4. *Clinical Trial Design*: Design thinking techniques can be utilized to design more patient-centric clinical trials using empathy-informed interviews or to generate useful data for healthcare providers. For example, companies can employ design thinking to reduce burdensome trials while providing more useful data for healthcare decisions.
5. *Packaging and Labeling*: Design thinking can transform pharmaceutical packaging and labeling into more user-friendly and user-centric, providing more information to patients and healthcare providers about products' packaging or labeling. Businesses could employ user-centric design principles to create easier-to-open packaging or provide additional useful details about medical treatments to patients or healthcare professionals.

Design thinking offers pharmaceutical marketers a powerful strategy for marketing pharmaceutical products and services more effectively and engagingly, meeting patients' care and healthcare professionals' needs with an iterative, patient-centric approach to problem-solving; pharmaceutical companies can develop more engaging offerings that meet those of patients and healthcare providers.

Pharmaceutical Companies Utilizing Design Thinking

Here are some examples of pharmaceutical companies using design thinking techniques to develop more patient-centric products and services:

1. Pfizer has taken steps to use design thinking in their products and services to offer more patient-oriented options. As part of one project, they collaborated with patients on co-creating an app that helps patients more efficiently manage their medications, using user-generated design principles to create an engaging patient experience.
2. Novo Nordisk utilized design thinking to develop an insulin pen for people with visual impairment. After conducting extensive user research to understand their needs and experiences, Novo Nordisk took this information and created an insulin pen with larger buttons, clearer labeling, and other features designed to make it simpler for these patients.
3. Roche utilized design thinking to develop an advanced diagnostic test for breast cancer. Working closely with patients, healthcare providers, and other stakeholders, Roche used design thinking techniques to understand patients' needs and overcome any hurdles to diagnosing. With this understanding, the company developed a faster, more accurate, and less invasive test than existing diagnostic options.
4. Merck utilized design thinking to develop an online platform providing education and support for chronic disease patients, using user-centric design principles for an engaging patient experience and offering tools and resources to assist in managing their conditions more efficiently.
5. Sanofi utilized design thinking to develop an insulin delivery device that is easier for those with limited dexterity. Working closely with patients and healthcare professionals, the company conducted in-depth discussions regarding the needs and challenges associated with insulin administration. The company then used this insight to design an intuitive device that anyone can manage.

Pharma companies utilize design thinking principles to develop more innovative, user-centered products and services for their patients. Design thinking enables these organizations to better comprehend users' needs while crafting solutions that effectively meet those demands.

Desire

Desire is essential to pharmaceutical marketing as it motivates patients to improve their health. Desire can refer to any desire that motivates a patient to take steps toward improved well-being, such as managing symptoms or reaching remission through prescribed treatment or medications.

Pharma companies can create a desire for their medications and treatments through marketing campaigns by emphasizing their benefits, using emotional appeals, testimonials from satisfied patients, or educational material that outlines how the medicine works and its potential advantages.

Pharma companies can make people desire positive health outcomes beyond medications by emphasizing the advantages of healthy lifestyle choices, such as regular exercise and balanced nutrition, which positively influence overall well-being. This strategy works because pharma companies focus on showing how important healthy lifestyle decisions can be to overall well-being and can create desire among their target audiences for such solutions.

Pharmaceutical companies must engage in ethical marketing practices and not make false or misleading claims regarding their medications and treatments. Companies should strive to craft messages that provide patients with enough information to make well-informed healthcare decisions.

Here are some examples of how pharma companies use desire in their marketing:

1. *Highlight Benefits*: Companies marketing medication to treat chronic pain may use marketing to demonstrate its benefits, including reduced pain and improved mobility, as emotional hooks to create desire. Showing chronic pain patients can resume activities they previously enjoyed after taking medicine is another effective technique for marketing medications that treat it.
2. *Testimonials*: Pharma companies often utilize testimonials from patients as a marketing technique for their medications. For example, a company marketing a depression treatment may feature one where someone was able to improve

their quality of life and return to work after taking this particular pill.

3. *Educational Content*: Pharma companies often produce educational videos about how their medications work and any potential benefits to users. For example, companies marketing medications to treat high cholesterol may create videos to show how these pills lower cholesterol levels while decreasing heart disease risks.
4. *Lifestyle Choices*: Pharma companies may also foster positive health outcomes by emphasizing lifestyle choices that foster well-being. For instance, companies marketing type 2 diabetes medication might develop campaigns that urge their target patients to incorporate healthier eating and physical exercise choices alongside taking their prescribed dose and medications, as this demonstrates potential advantages associated with doing so.

Although creating desire is an effective marketing technique for pharmaceutical companies, they should do it ethically and according to regulatory requirements. Furthermore, marketing messages must be truthful, accurate, and not misleading to be effective.

The following examples demonstrate how pharmaceutical companies leverage the desire to create positive associations between their medications and healthy behaviors:

1. *Pfizer's* Get Old *Campaign*: Pfizer launched an ambitious marketing initiative called *Get Old* to foster healthy aging among older adults, featuring inspiring stories about those able to maintain fulfilling lives by making healthy decisions as they age. The *Get Old* campaign included websites, social media accounts, and events designed to motivate individuals to improve their health and well-being.
2. *Novo Nordisk's* Loose the Weight *Campaign*: in 2018, Novo Nordisk introduced their *Loose the Weight campaign* to raise awareness for Saxenda (Liraglutide). This marketing initiative featured testimonials of patients who successfully lost weight with Saxenda and educational material regarding its function and benefits.
3. *AbbVie's* Feel More Like You *Campaign*: In 2018, AbbVie unveiled its marketing campaign *Feel More Like You* to increase consumer desire for oncology medications from AbbVie. This effort focused on emotional impacts associated with cancer treatment while depicting stories about patients able to maintain a sense of themselves during treatment through AbbVie medications. Additionally, it provided resources such as makeup and wig tips so patients and caregivers felt like themselves during this difficult journey.
4. *GlaxoSmithKline's* Breathless *Campaign*: In 2019, GlaxoSmithKline introduced their *Breathless* marketing campaign to raise interest and awareness around Relvar (Fluticasone and Vilanterol inhaler). Television commercials featured patients struggling to breathe before taking Relvar and experiencing relief afterward. In addition, an educational website provided details regarding Relvar's operation and potential advantages over competing medications.

Although these examples demonstrate how pharmaceutical companies employ marketing messages designed to encourage healthy behavior change, it should be remembered that such messages must always be truthful, accurate, and non-misleading. Furthermore, patients should consult their healthcare provider before making treatment decisions independently.

Detailing

Pharmaceutical marketing utilizes detailing to promote specific prescription drugs to healthcare professionals like doctors, nurses, and pharmacists. Detailers (pharmaceutical sales representatives) arrange meetings with healthcare professionals (HCPs) during which information regarding benefits, risks, and any relevant details about each drug being detailed is presented by them to HCPs face-to-face.

Pharmaceutical companies use detailing to increase awareness and usage of their products among healthcare professionals. Detailers are trained to present information compellingly yet casually about each drug being discussed, answering any queries from healthcare providers and providing supporting material, such as clinical studies or patient information leaflets as needed.

Detailing has traditionally been conducted face-to-face. However, with the proliferation of digital technologies, some pharmaceutical companies have begun using digital detailing (or "e-detailing") as an avenue to market their products and drive revenue growth. E-detailing involves communicating directly with healthcare professionals via digital channels like video conferencing, and mobile applications.

Detailing is subject to regulation by regulatory bodies like the Food and Drug Administration in America and the European Union's European Medicines Agency. Pharmaceutical companies must abide by specific protocols when dealing with healthcare professionals.

How to Improve the Effectiveness of Detailing

Here are some ways to improve the effectiveness of detailing in pharmaceutical marketing:

1. *Develop Strong Relationships*: Building strong relationships with healthcare professionals is key to effective detailing. Detailers should focus on understanding the healthcare professional's needs and providing tailored information that meets those needs.
2. *Provide Evidence-based Information*: Healthcare professionals rely on evidence-based information when making treatment decisions. Detailers should be well-informed about the clinical studies, safety data, and other relevant information about the drugs they promote.
3. *Use Multimedia Resources*: Detailers can use multimedia resources such as videos, animations, and interactive tools to present information more engagingly and memorably.
4. *Provide Clear and Concise Information*: Healthcare professionals are often pressed for time, so it's important to present information clearly and concisely, highlighting the drug's key benefits.
5. *Follow-up*: Following up with healthcare professionals after a detailing session can help reinforce the information presented and address any additional questions or concerns they may have.
6. *Leverage Digital Channels*: Digital detailing, or e-detailing, can be a highly effective way to reach healthcare professionals, especially those geographically dispersed. E-detailing can also provide more flexibility and convenience for both the detailer and the healthcare professional,
7. *Provide Ongoing Education*: Healthcare professionals need ongoing education about the latest developments in their field. Pharmaceutical companies can provide ongoing education through webinars, seminars, and other training programs to keep healthcare professionals up-to-date on the latest advances in treatments and drugs.

Differentiation

Differentiation is a marketing strategy designed to create a distinct image for a product or service and set it apart from the competition. Differentiation aims at giving products or services an advantage by making them more appealing than comparable offerings from rival companies.

Differentiation strategies in pharmaceutical marketing are particularly vital given the highly competitive industry and availability of multiple treatments for similar medical ailments. Pharma companies utilize differentiation strategies to establish unique identities for their products that differentiate them from rival offerings to perusuade healthcare providers and patients that theirs should be chosen instead.

Some examples of differentiation strategies that pharma companies use include:

1. *Product Features*: Pharma companies may differentiate their products by developing new formulations, dosages, or delivery methods. For example, a company may develop a long-acting version of an existing medication or a more convenient method of administration.
2. *Clinical Outcomes*: Pharma companies may differentiate their products by highlighting their efficacy and safety profiles, particularly compared to competitors. This can involve conducting clinical trials and publishing data demonstrating their products' superiority.
3. *Patient Support Services*: Pharma companies may differentiate themselves by offering additional support services, such as educational materials, patient assistance programs, or personalized support from healthcare professionals.
4. *Branding and Marketing*: Pharma companies may differentiate themselves by creating a unique brand image and marketing message that sets them apart from competitors. This can involve developing memorable logos, advertising campaigns, and building a strong online and social media presence.

Effective differentiation in pharma marketing can increase market share, greater patient and healthcare professional loyalty, and higher profits. By creating a unique and distinctive image for their products, pharma companies can compete in a crowded marketplace and deliver better patient outcomes.

Differentiated Marketing

Differentiated marketing is a strategy that targets specific segments of customers with tailored approaches or marketing mixes that cater to their unique needs, preferences, behaviors, and characteristics. The purpose is to appeal to different customer groups while increasing sales and profits through differentiated offerings of similar product/service versions.

Differentiated marketing recognizes that all customers differ and that using one approach to reach and engage all may not always be effective. Instead, differentiated marketing involves identifying various customer segments and crafting tailored marketing mixes to those segments based on product features, pricing strategies, promotion tactics, and distribution models that best appeal.

Cosmetics companies could use differentiated marketing to market product lines to distinct age groups or skin types. For instance, anti-aging creams for older customers and oil-free solutions for customers with oily complexions are examples of differentiated offerings from cosmetic companies.

Differentiated marketing can effectively increase customer satisfaction, strengthen brand loyalty and boost sales and profits. But successfully doing so requires careful market research and segmentation analysis to accurately identify customer segments with distinct needs and preferences, and satisfy them through targeted promotion.

Differentiated Marketing in Pharma

Here are a few examples demonstrating how pharmaceutical companies implement differentiated marketing:

1. *Disease-Specific Marketing*: Pharmaceutical companies develop strategies tailored to certain diseases or conditions, such as cancer, diabetes, and multiple sclerosis. Novo Nordisk followed such an approach for their diabetes drug Victoza. It featured television commercials, social media promotions, and educational materials for those with type 2 diabetes.
2. *Geographic Marketing*: Pharmaceutical companies also create marketing strategies to target customers in specific regions or countries. For example, Roche targeted the Chinese market by launching a marketing campaign for its cancer drug Avastin, which included a website, social media, and educational materials in Chinese.
3. *Age-specific Marketing*: Pharmaceutical companies create marketing strategies to target different age groups. For example, Pfizer launched a marketing campaign for its vaccine against pneumococcal disease, Prevnar 13, targeting adults over 65.
4. *Gender-Specific Marketing*: Pharmaceutical companies employ gender-based strategies in marketing their medications for men and women, such as Pfizer's marketing of its erectile dysfunction drug Viagra directed solely toward male users.
5. *Marketing to Healthcare Providers*: Pharmaceutical companies typically create marketing strategies targeting healthcare providers like doctors, nurses, and pharmacists. For instance, Pfizer ran an impressive primary care physician promotion for its cholesterol-reducing drug Lipitor as part of its market growth strategy.

Differentiated marketing allows pharmaceutical companies to tailor their marketing efforts towards different customer segments, increasing effectiveness and efficiency. However, the marketing of prescription drugs must adhere to stringent FDA regulations regarding promotion.

Differentiating Variables

Differentiating variables are essential in pharmaceutical marketing as they help distinguish one product from its competition within the same therapeutic category and create a unique selling proposition (USP) to emphasize benefits over the competition in the market.

Here are a few differentiating variables used in pharmaceutical marketing:

1. *Mechanism of Action*: This term refers to how drugs treat specific conditions. Each medication, although targets similar conditions or diseases in a given therapeutic category could have its distinct mode of action that sets it apart from its competitors. By emphasizing such features of a medicine's mechanism of action, pharma marketers can differentiate it from others.
2. *Dosage Form*: Drugs come in various forms, from tablets and capsules to liquids or injections, that offer advantages to patients in terms of increased absorption, convenience, or ease of administration. These alternatives could provide greater benefits.
3. *Effectiveness*: Regarding medication efficacy, effectiveness describes how well they treat specific disease states. Different drugs may have different efficacy levels that help set one product apart.
4. *Safety Profile of Drugs*: A drug's safety profile refers to its side effect profile and potential adverse events, and healthcare providers and patients often prefer medications with more favorable safety profiles as differentiators when choosing these drugs.

5. *Price:* Price can be an important consideration in pharmaceutical marketing, with some drugs priced higher or lower than others in their therapeutic category. Asserting that value proposition at each price point may be an effective marketing tactic.

These are some examples of differentiating variables used in pharmaceutical marketing, with the key ones being targeting patients and healthcare professionals to whom customized marketing messages highlight product benefits that stand out in the market.

Diffusion of Innovation

Diffusion of innovation is the process by which new ideas, products, or technologies spread through a population over time. Sociologist Everett Rogers introduced the concept in his 1962 book, *Diffusion of Innovations* which has since been applied to several fields, including marketing, technology, and public health.

The diffusion of innovation theory is a popular framework used in marketing to explain how a market adopts new ideas, products, and technologies. For example, the diffusion of innovation theory can be used in pharmaceutical marketing to understand how healthcare providers and patients adopt new drugs.

The diffusion of innovation theory distinguishes five categories of adopters: innovators, early adopters, early majority, late majority, and laggards.

Innovators are the first to adopt new products or technologies first, while laggards follow the suit later. However, other adopters segments fall some where between these extremes.

Pharma marketing relies heavily on various influencing factors determining how people adopt a new medication. These factors include its perceived benefits, potential side effects, and cost; in addition to this, marketing strategy also plays a pivotal role.

Marketing strategies to promote new drugs typically include advertising, direct-to-consumer (DTC) advertising, and personal selling to healthcare providers. Advertising may take the form of television, print media, and the web, providing companies with a great platform to directly reach target customers and build awareness for new treatments. DTC advertising is controversial but effectively increases patient demand for certain drugs. Personal selling to healthcare providers involves pharmaceutical representatives visiting healthcare providers and promoting the drug through educational materials and other means.

The diffusion of innovation theory suggests that adopting a new drug is a gradual process, and the marketing strategy should be tailored to different categories of adopters. For example, innovators and early adopters are more likely to respond to personal selling. In contrast, the early and late majority are more likely to respond to advertising and other mass communication channels.

Thus, the diffusion of innovation theory can be a useful framework for understanding how new drugs are adopted in the market and for developing effective marketing strategies to promote them.

Applying the theory of the Diffusion of Innovation Theory in Pharma Marketing

Everett Rogers proposed five categories of adopters in his diffusion of innovation theory, and understanding these and how they adopt any new product or idea is essential for pharmaceutical marketers. The following are the adopter categories:

1. *Innovators*: Innovators are the first to adopt new drugs. In pharma marketing, they are typically the healthcare providers who are the earliest adopters of new therapies. Pharmaceutical companies often target these healthcare providers through personal selling, conferences, and other forms of communication to create buzz and excitement about the new drug.
2. *Early Adopters*: Early adopters are healthcare providers receptive to new drugs but require additional information before adopting them. Early adopters are targeted in pharmaceutical marketing through peer-to-peer communication, scientific conferences, and educational materials.
3. *Early Majority*: The Early Majority are healthcare providers who adopt new drugs after they have been widely tested and proven effective. In pharma marketing, the early majority is often targeted through advertising and other mass communication channels.
4. *Late Majority*: The Late Majority are healthcare providers who are skeptical of new drugs but eventually adopt them once they have become the standard of care. In pharma marketing, the late majority are often targeted through educational materials, clinical trial data, and other evidence-based communication.
5. *Laggards*: Laggards are healthcare providers who resist new drugs and often only adopt them when required. In pharma marketing, laggards are often targeted through educational campaigns, demonstration of clear benefits, and peer-to-peer communication.

By understanding the different categories of adopters and tailoring marketing strategies accordingly, pharmaceutical companies can effectively promote new drugs and increase their adoption in the market.

Implications for Pharma Marketers

The diffusion of innovation theory has several implications for pharma marketers. Here are some important ones:

1. *Identify the Target Audience*: Marketers should identify the target audience for the new drug and segment them based on their willingness to adopt new drugs. By understanding the different categories of adopters, marketers can tailor their marketing strategies and tactics to each group to increase the adoption of the new drug.
2. *Create a Compelling Value Proposition*: Marketers of new drugs must craft an engaging value proposition that effectively communicates its benefits while assuaging potential adopter concerns; this can be accomplished using educational materials, clinical trial data, or any form of evidence-based communication.
3. *Marketers Should Take Advantage of Multichannel Approach*: Marketers can reach potential adopters through various media outlets, such as advertising, direct mail, email marketing, and social media that will increase awareness about a new drug while creating interest among potential adopters. This strategy may increase awareness about your drug while sparking curiosity from prospective adopters.
4. *Develop Key Opinion Leaders*: Marketers should identify and engage with key opinion leaders in the healthcare industry who can help promote the new drug and influence the adoption rate. Key opinion leaders can be healthcare providers, patient advocates, or other influencers with a significant following in the healthcare community.
5. *Monitor and Adjust Marketing Strategies*: Marketers should continually track the adoption rates of a new drug and adapt their marketing strategies accordingly, including reviewing data from sales and marketing campaigns, conducting market research studies, engaging key stakeholders for feedback purposes, and seeking feedback and insights from key players in healthcare.

Pharma marketers who understand these repercussions and take appropriate actions are better equipped to promote new drugs, increase adoption by healthcare providers and patients, and realize improved patient health outcomes and increased revenue growth for their company.

Digital Assets

Digital assets are digital resources businesses use to directly market and communicate their products or services with target customer bases.

Here are a few ways pharmaceutical companies are making use of digital assets in their marketing initiatives:

1. *Websites*: Pharmaceutical companies utilize their websites as communication channels with customers and healthcare providers. Websites may also collect customer data for analysis and generate sales team leads.
2. *Social Media*: Pharma companies often utilize platforms like Facebook, Twitter, and LinkedIn for connecting with customers, marketing products, and providing healthcare-related updates to visitors. Social media also creates leads and can drive sales.
3. *Mobile Apps*: Pharma companies can utilize mobile apps as an efficient and interactive means to provide information to their customers, collect customer preferences data and deliver targeted marketing messages that promote customer engagement.
4. *Email Newsletters*: Email Newsletters provide customers with timely updates regarding new products, clinical trials, and relevant information that could influence sales decisions. They also serve as effective promotional vehicles which help drive product awareness.
5. *Videos*: Pharma companies can utilize videos as a powerful marketing and sales tool by producing informative product videos and educational healthcare awareness videos for customers and staff. Furthermore, videos create engaging marketing content, which increases customer engagement and sales.

Digital assets have become an indispensable element of pharmaceutical marketing, allowing companies to communicate more engagingly and directly with customers. Pharmaceutical firms can therefore utilize various digital assets in their campaigns and drive revenue growth using them effectively.

Digital Assets in Pharma Marketing

Here are a few examples of how pharmaceutical companies are employing digital assets in their marketing:

1. Pfizer recently developed an interactive mobile application called *Pfizer Meds*. It helps customers manage their medications, track symptoms, receive appointment reminders, and

gain information about Pfizer products and services.

2. Novartis has launched the *Living Like You* website as an invaluable support and education source for individuals with multiple sclerosis. It features articles, videos, and other forms of content to educate and encourage patients and healthcare professionals.
3. Sanofi recently created a Twitter account called *Diabetes Heroes* that offers guidance and assistance for people with diabetes. Tweets address management strategies, healthy diet, exercise, and the physical effects of the condition.
4. Merck has launched *Your Cancer Story* as a website designed to give cancer patients the space and platform to share their cancer experiences and receive emotional support. Videos, blog posts, and other forms of content provide users with ways to connect emotionally.
5. Johnson & Johnson has launched its YouTube channel, *JNJ Health*, with information regarding various health concerns and topics like healthy living, disease prevention, and medical research. This channel includes videos about healthy lifestyle choices and medical research advancement.

These are only some examples of how pharmaceutical companies utilize digital assets to engage their customers and market their products, with more innovative uses of digital tech expected as time progresses in this sector.

Digital Branding

Digital branding refers to creating an identity through various digital channels like websites, social media accounts, email marketing campaigns, and online advertising. The goal is to establish an accessible online presence representing company values, messaging, and imagery to its target market.

Digital branding encompasses your company's logo, website design, user experience, social media presence, content marketing efforts, online advertising strategies, and search engine optimization (SEO), among other elements that work together to establish an identifiable and memorable digital brand that stands out in an oversaturated digital marketplace.

Digital branding seeks to establish an engaging online presence that draws and keeps customers, fosters brand recognition and loyalty among target consumers, and boosts company revenue streams. A successful digital branding strategy can enable firms to distinguish themselves from rival businesses while creating an identity that resonates with target markets.

Digital Branding in Pharma Marketing

Pharmaceutical marketing has seen digital branding take on greater significance as more individuals rely on the web for research and purchasing products. The goal of digital branding in pharma marketing is to establish an authoritative digital presence that conveys its benefits directly to patients and healthcare providers.

Key Strategies

Here are a few key strategies for digital branding in pharmaceutical marketing:

1. *Build a User-Friendly Website*: A website designed with easy navigation is paramount in offering accurate information on your product or service, making the experience smooth and straightforward for visitors. Ensure all data presented easily enables people to understand its significance quickly.
2. *Optimize Your Content for Search Engines*: SEO (search engine optimization) refers to optimizing a website to be higher up in search engines' results pages like Google or Bing by including relevant keywords in its content creation process, creating high-quality writing pieces, and building reliable backlinks from reliable sources.
3. *Utilize Social Media Effectively*: Facebook, Twitter, and LinkedIn are powerful tools for increasing brand recognition while engaging patients and healthcare providers in active dialogue about your healthcare brand. Ensure your online presence stays vibrant by regularly uploading high-quality content via these channels.
4. *Utilize Email Marketing*: Email marketing is an efficient and powerful way of reaching patients and healthcare providers with relevant updates regarding your product or service.
5. *Create Engaging Content*: Content marketing expands brand recognition and engages your target audience through blog posts, infographics, videos, or other mediums that bring them value.
6. *Monitor and Analyze Results*: Analyzing your digital branding efforts and their outcomes is key to seeing which efforts work and which don't. To assess this, utilize analytics tools such as web traffic tracking tools, social media engagement tracking, email open/click-through rates monitoring tools, etc.

By employing these strategies, pharmaceutical companies can develop an impactful digital brand that resonates with patients and healthcare providers, driving sales and revenues forward.

Digital Darwinism

Digital Darwinism refers to the idea that businesses and organizations must adapt quickly to an ever-evolving digital environment or risk becoming extinct. The term is inspired by Charles Darwin's concept of natural selection as expressed through evolution theory; species that successfully adapt to their changing environments tend to thrive longer; this principle can also apply in digital technology, where new tools, platforms, and trends constantly appear that businesses need to navigate to remain relevant and competitive; failing this, companies could potentially fall behind their more innovative competitors who adapt more readily.

Digital Darwinism serves as a reminder that businesses cannot remain complacent or depend on outdated strategies and technologies to remain competitive in today's business climate. Instead, to remain successful, they must embrace change, test out different approaches, and continually adapt to customer preferences and the digital ecosystem.

Digital Darwinism in Pharma Marketing

Digital Darwinism has had an immense effect on pharmaceutical marketing strategies. Consider, for instance:

A. Pharma marketing traditionally relied on conventional means, including print ads and direct mail, and face-to-face sales interactions between reps and healthcare professionals. But with digital technology's evolution comes an entirely different way of marketing products by pharmaceutical companies.

B. Digital channels such as social media, email marketing, and search engine marketing have increasingly become effective platforms to connect healthcare professionals and patients with each other. Pharma companies utilize big data analytics tools to gain insight into target audiences and optimize marketing campaigns accordingly.

These opportunities come with unique challenges; due to their highly regulated nature, pharmaceutical industries present particular hurdles in digital marketing. Pharma companies must adhere to stringent advertising regulations, such as disclosing risks and adverse reactions.

Due to digital channels' prevalence, pharmaceutical companies may find it increasingly challenging to differentiate themselves. With all the advertising on digital platforms competing for target audience attention, pharma companies may struggle to engage their target customers effectively.

Pharma companies looking to thrive in today's digital pharma era must adopt agile, and innovative marketing strategies to thrive in this era of digital Darwinism. If they fail to evolve and embrace digital transformation, they could be left behind, and their market share will erode over time.

How Pharma is Responding

Here are a few strategies pharmaceutical companies have employed to adapt to an ever-evolving environment and stay relevant and competitive during this era of digital Darwinism:

1. *Social Media Marketing*: Pharmaceutical companies often utilize popular social media platforms like Facebook, Twitter, and LinkedIn to reach healthcare professionals and patients. A company might use Facebook to market a new drug directly to patients suffering from certain medical conditions; at the same time, LinkedIn connects healthcare professionals while sharing relevant details regarding efficacy and safety data on this medication.
2. *Search Engine Optimization (SEO)*: Pharma companies utilize search engine optimization (SEO) techniques to increase their presence in search engine results pages (SERPs). By optimizing the website content and targeting relevant keywords, pharmaceutical firms can increase their ranking in SERPs while expanding visibility among potential customers.
3. *Mobile Applications*: Pharma companies increasingly use mobile apps as informational and promotional mediums for their products and services. For instance, diabetes drug makers might develop apps to track patients' blood glucose levels while reminding them when to take their medicine.
4. *Wearable Technology*: Pharma companies are taking to wearable technologies such as fitness trackers and smartwatches to collect patient health information, assess drug efficacy, and collect more precise metrics on health.
5. *Data Analytics*: Pharma companies often utilize data analytics to gain insight into their target audiences and optimize marketing campaigns. For instance, data analysis might identify which marketing channels work most effectively when trying to reach healthcare professionals and patients.

Pharma Companies Adopt Digital Transformation

Here are some examples of pharmaceutical companies taking steps to embrace digital technologies by adopting cutting-edge marketing strategies:

1. Novartis has developed an Android and iPhone mobile application called *MS LifeLines* which offers support and resources for people with multiple sclerosis, such as medication reminders, symptom-tracking features, and educational materials. The app features medication reminders and educational content.
2. Pfizer has used social media channels like Twitter and Facebook to market its products while engaging with patients, healthcare professionals, and caregivers. For instance, Pfizer created an oncology Twitter account dedicated to this division to share cancer drug updates while supporting caregivers and patients.
3. Roche has developed *mySugr*, a wearable device to assist those living with diabetes manage their condition more effectively. The device offers blood glucose monitoring capabilities, an insulin calculator, and a carb counting functionality; its connected mobile app also delivers personalized insights and coaching services.
4. Sanofi has used data analytics to optimize its marketing campaigns and increase targeting. For instance, they employ predictive modeling to identify healthcare professionals likely to prescribe their products before sending targeted promotional communications directly.
5. Johnson & Johnson has developed *The Johnson & Johnson Institute Virtual Reality Experience*, which provides medical professionals with education on surgical techniques and procedures via mobile app access or VR headset use. The VR experience can also be utilized anywhere with proper permission and without restrictions from its mobile app user base.

Digital Divide

A digital divide refers to unequal access to digital technologies and the internet among different groups or regions, including unequal distribution of hardware (computers, smartphones, or other devices), software applications, or internet connectivity services to specific groups or areas.

Socio-economic status, geographic location, age, ethnicity, and education level all create digital divides that separate populations; those in remote or rural areas may only have access to slow internet due to infrastructure limitations; those from lower socio-economic backgrounds might lack digital devices and internet services altogether.

The digital divide has emerged as a serious challenge due to digital technologies' ever-increasing role in education, work, and social integration. Without access to digital technologies, inequalities may worsen further, restricting economic mobility opportunities. Governments and private organizations are working toward closing this divide by increasing internet accessibility for underserved communities and broadening digital technology use among them.

Digital Divide in Pharma Marketing

The digital divide can immensely impact pharmaceutical marketing, particularly regarding access to information and resources. Healthcare providers and patients who lack digital access may find it harder to receive updates regarding pharmaceutical products, clinical trials, medical education courses, etc.

Rural healthcare providers may lack access to digital resources like online medical journals, continuing medical education (CME) courses, or telemedicine tools that may allow them to stay abreast of medical news and treatment options, hindering their ability to offer patients superior care. This may impede them in providing optimal healthcare to them all.

Patients without access to digital technologies may also find themselves less informed of pharmaceutical products, treatment options, and clinical trials available— something which may limit their ability to make informed decisions regarding their health care, negatively influencing patient health outcomes and impacting overall healthcare costs.

Pharmaceutical companies can aid healthcare providers and patients facing limited access by offering digital resources and information that enable informed healthcare decision-making. This might involve creating educational materials in various formats (print, online video), partnering with organizations working within underserved communities, or investing in digital infrastructure in those same communities, helping to ensure all healthcare providers and patients have access to all needed knowledge about health issues to make well-informed health choices. By doing this, pharmaceutical companies ensure all healthcare providers and patients have access to make well-informed health decisions!

Digital Health

Digital health uses digital technologies such as software, mobile phones, wearable sensors, or artificial intelligence. These technologies help enhance healthcare delivery and patient outcomes. Digital health technologies can be used in many healthcare settings, such as hospitals, clinics, and home-care services.

Here are some examples of digital health technologies:

1. *Electronic Health Records (EHRs)*: EHRs are digital records of patient health information stored and shared among healthcare providers. They help enhance patient safety, reduce medical errors, and improve care coordination, improving patient outcomes.
2. *Telemedicine*: Telemedicine uses digital communications technologies like videoconferencing and remote monitoring to provide healthcare services remotely. It helps increase patient access, lowers healthcare costs, and improves outcomes.
3. *Wearable Devices*: Wearable devices such as fitness trackers and smartwatches can gather vital statistics on an individual's activity level, heart rate, and other vital signs. This data is very useful as it helps monitor health or detect early warning signs of health concerns.
4. *Mobile Health (mHealth) Apps*: Mobile health apps provide patients access to health-related resources like information on chronic conditions and treatment plans, medication reminders, and symptom-tracking tools. With such apps in their arsenal, patients may better manage their conditions.
5. *Artificial Intelligence (AI)*: AI datasets such as medical images and patient health records can spot abnormalities and make predictions that help healthcare providers make more accurate diagnoses, create personalized treatment plans for individual patients, and ultimately enhance patient outcomes.

Digital health technologies promise to radically alter healthcare delivery and patient outcomes by offering better access to care, streamlining coordination practices, and offering tailored and efficient care solutions.

Digital Immigrants

Marck Prensky, an American writer, and speaker on education, coined the term *Digital Immigrants* in 2001 to describe individuals born or growing up before widespread digital technology adoption and then having to adjust later. These digital immigrants may include older individuals who were never exposed to computers, the internet, or similar digital technologies as integral parts of daily life.

Notably, D*igital Immigrants* is an umbrella term and does not apply equally across older generations. Many older individuals have successfully embraced digital technology and are proficient users. However, the term can help highlight the potential generation gap in technology adoption and individuals' different experiences regarding digital literacy.

Pharmaceutical companies can engage digital immigrants through various strategies, including:

1. *Pharmaceutical Companies Can Train Healthcare Professionals on Digital Tools and Technologies*: Pharmaceutical companies may train healthcare professionals on digital tools and technologies used in practice, such as electronic medical records, telemedicine platforms, and patient portals.
2. *Pharmaceutical Companies Can Create User-Friendly Digital Tools*: Pharmaceutical companies should develop user-friendly digital tools that simplify life for healthcare professionals, such as apps or online platforms that deliver information regarding medications, treatment options, and patient care. This may include apps or platforms with important patient resources that offer additional value.
3. *Utilizing Traditional Marketing Strategies*: While digital strategies continue to play an increasing role, traditional tactics offer pharmaceutical companies an effective means of reaching digital immigrants. They could use print advertisements, mailings, or in-person events to reach healthcare professionals unfamiliar with digital channels.
4. *Engaging Healthcare Professionals on Social Media*: Healthcare professionals can often be active on platforms like LinkedIn and Twitter, making digital engagement easy for pharmaceutical companies by sharing vital product and service insights through these networks.
5. *Offering Online Resources*: Pharmaceutical companies could create an easily navigable website or resource center that gives healthcare professionals access to valuable product information, such as clinical trial data, prescribing information, and patient support resources. Such an interface would ensure clear and concise presentations with easily understood text suited for user consumption.

Reaching digital immigrants requires an integrated marketing approach incorporating traditional and digital strategies. Pharmaceutical companies can effectively reach this important target audience through education programs, user-friendly digital tools development, and engaging healthcare providers on social media.

Digital Intelligence

Digital intelligence refers to the capacity of an entity, such as a computer system or artificial intelligence algorithm, to understand, process and produce digitally created information in digital environments. This involves gathering and analyzing data for learning purposes before taking informed actions based on that knowledge.

Digital intelligence can encompass various aspects, including:

1. *Data Processing and Analysis*: Data intelligence involves the capability to process large volumes of data quickly and efficiently. This may involve data mining, pattern recognition, and statistical analysis to extract meaningful insights.
2. *Machine Learning and AI*: Digital intelligence often incorporates machine learning algorithms and AI technologies to enable systems to learn from data and improve their performance over time. This allows them to make predictions, identify patterns, and adapt it to changing circumstances.
3. *Natural Language Processing*: Digital intelligence can involve understanding and generating human language. Natural language processing (NLP) techniques enable systems to interpret and respond to written or spoken language, facilitating tasks such as chatbots, voice assistants, and language translation.
4. *Decision-making and Automation*: Digital intelligence systems can be designed to make autonomous decisions based on available data and predetermined rules. They can automate routine tasks, optimize processes, and provides recommendations or suggestions to humans.
5. *Cognitive Computing*: Digital intelligence can encompass elements of cognitive computing, which aims to mimic human thought processes. These abilities encompass perception, reasoning, problem-solving, and learning from experience.

Digital intelligence finds various uses across numerous fields, such as business analytics, cybersecurity, healthcare management, and personalized marketing. Digital intelligence empowers systems to interpret complex digital environments while improving efficiency, accuracy, and user experiences.

Here are a few ways pharmaceutical companies use digital intelligence in their marketing:

1. *Customer Data Analysis*: Pharmaceutical companies use digital intelligence to collect customer information from various channels such as social media platforms, website interactions, and mobile app usage to analyze customer behaviors and preferences in-depth. This allows companies to develop more tailored marketing campaigns for each customer.
2. *Predictive Modeling*: Pharmaceutical companies can use predictive modeling techniques to analyze customer data to detect patterns and anticipate customer behavior, creating targeted marketing campaigns while increasing engagement levels with their customer base.
3. *Artificial Intelligence (AI)*: AI technology allows marketers to sift through large volumes of customer information to gain greater insights into customer behaviors and preferences, leading to targeted campaigns with higher engagement for greater customer success.
4. *Real-Time Analytics*: Real-time analytics tools allow companies to track real-time customer responses for digital marketing campaigns and instantly adjust and optimize them for maximum effectiveness.
5. *Marketing Automation*: Marketing automation tools allow pharma marketers to streamline the processes of creating, executing, and measuring marketing campaigns more easily, saving time and resources while improving accuracy and boosting efficiency in marketing efforts.

Digital Intelligence in Pharma Marketing

Digital intelligence has become an invaluable asset in pharmaceutical marketing, allowing pharmaceutical companies to develop more customized and targeted campaigns while measuring their impact in real time. Pharmaceutical firms can then analyze data for increased customer engagement and revenue growth.

Examples of How Pharma Companies Utilize Digital Intelligence

Here are a few examples of how pharmaceutical companies employ digital intelligence in their marketing initiatives:

1. Pfizer uses digital intelligence to personalize its marketing campaigns for its products. For instance, they leveraged data analysis to identify highly engaged super-consumers with its products; Pfizer then implemented targeted

marketing initiatives to engage these consumers and increase sales.

2. GlaxoSmithKline has launched AI-powered chatbots to enhance customer engagement and support services, using natural language processing (NLP) technology to understand customer requests for products or services by understanding any queries that come in using natural language analysis (NLA) capabilities and provide relevant answers about them.
3. Merck uses predictive modeling to target its products to those most likely to benefit. Data analytics detect patterns within patient records and predict those most likely to respond positively, using this knowledge for targeted marketing campaigns that promote improved patient outcomes.
4. Novartis utilizes real-time analytics to gauge the success of its digital marketing campaigns. Through various tools, such as web analytics and social media monitoring, Novartis tracks customer interaction in real-time with its campaigns to provide real-time customer intelligence that allows it to make adjustments that optimize campaigns to achieve maximum effectiveness.
5. Roche uses marketing automation tools to streamline and enhance its marketing efforts and efficiency, saving both time and resources while improving the accuracy and efficacy of its efforts. By automating campaign creation and execution and measuring the effectiveness of campaigns created and executed through them, this strategy enables Roche to save both resources while improving the efficiency of its efforts.

These are a few examples of how digital intelligence is applied in pharmaceutical marketing. As this field evolves, pharmaceutical companies should expect to leverage data and analytics to increase customer engagement and stimulate revenue growth.

Digital Landscape

The digital landscape encompasses all digital technologies, platforms, and services operating today, such as the internet, websites, social media pages, online communication tools like Skype or MSN Messenger, and emerging technologies like blockchain, or VR/AR devices. Below are key aspects of today's digital world:

1. *Internet*: The Internet is the foundation of our digital ecosystem, connecting billions of devices globally to exchange information and online services for communication purposes.
2. *Websites and Apps*: Websites and apps serve as digital platforms that enable businesses, organizations, and individuals to showcase their goods, services, content, or offers for e-commerce sales or entertainment, or productivity gains. Their primary function may include information sharing or productivity improvement.
3. *Social Media*: Platforms like Facebook, Twitter, Instagram, and LinkedIn have become essential parts of digital life, where individuals and communities can interact online by connecting, exchanging information, and communicating globally.
4. *E-commerce* platforms have revolutionized how people shop and conduct business online, providing individuals and enterprises with convenience when transacting business online.
5. *Digital Marketing*: As digital environments progress, marketing strategies have increasingly relied upon digital channels, such as SEO (Search Engine Optimization), content marketing, social media marketing, email marketing, and paid advertisements to reach target audiences and engage them effectively.
6. *Data and Analytics*: Businesses use analytics tools to harness vast quantities of digital information for strategic decision-making purposes, which allows them to comprehend customer behavior better, refine strategies, and boost overall performance. Utilizing data-driven decision-making allows businesses to glean customer insight while improving strategies, optimizing them further, and driving overall performance.
7. *Mobile and Connected Devices*: With so many smartphone owners now carrying connected devices like smartphones and other connected devices, smartphones have made an immense mark on digital spaces. Businesses must utilize mobile-optimized apps as a comprehensive strategy to effectively reach mobile users via apps or responsive web design strategies.
8. *Artificial Intelligence (AI) and Automation*: Artificial intelligence technologies, such as machine learning and natural language processing are rapidly revolutionizing digital environments. AI-powered automation streamlines processes, enhances personalization capabilities and powers intelligent systems across industries.
9. *Cybersecurity*: With an increasingly digital landscape comes an increasing need for robust cybersecurity measures that safeguard sensitive information, prevent data breaches, and ensure

online privacy— three vital concerns in an interconnected digital sphere.

10. *Emerging Technologies*: As technology rapidly develops in digital spaces, emerging technologies such as blockchain, VR/AR technology, IoT (Internet of Things) connectivity, and 5G connectivity continue to change and disrupt industries while creating new opportunities.

Overall, the digital environment is ever-evolving and impacts how individuals, businesses, and societies engage with one another while conducting activities within it.

Digital Landscape in Pharma Marketing

The digital landscape has had a significant impact on pharmaceutical marketing. Here are some key aspects of the digital landscape in pharma marketing:

1. *Online Presence*: Pharmaceutical companies have recognized the importance of establishing a strong online presence. They create websites about their products, services, and disease areas. These websites are a hub for healthcare professionals, patients, and other stakeholders to access educational resources, product information, clinical data, and support materials.
2. *Digital Advertising*: Digital advertising plays a crucial role in pharma marketing. Companies utilize targeted online advertisements to reach specific audiences, such as healthcare professionals or patients with certain conditions. Digital advertising platforms allow precise targeting based on demographics, interests, and online behavior.
3. *Social Media Engagement*: Pharma companies engage with healthcare professionals and patients through social media platforms. They share educational content, provide updates on medical breakthroughs, and respond to inquiries. Social media also offers opportunities for patient support communities, where individuals can connect and share experiences.
4. *Content Marketing*: Content marketing provides valuable and educational content, such as articles, blog posts, videos, infographics, and interactive tools, to healthcare professionals, patients, and caregivers. Pharma companies aim to establish thought leadership and build trust by offering informative and innovative content.
5. *Mobile Apps and Wearables*: Mobile and wearable devices have gained prominence in healthcare. Pharma companies develop apps that offer medication reminders, disease management tools, treatment trackers, and patient support resources. These apps enhance patient engagement and promote adherence to treatment plans.
6. *Virtual Meetings and Webinars*: The digital landscape has facilitated the pharma industry's virtual meetings, conferences, and webinars. Healthcare professionals can participate in medical education programs, conferences, and workshops remotely, allowing for global collaboration and knowledge exchange.
7. *Regulatory Compliance*: The digital landscape presents unique challenges in terms of regulatory compliance for pharmaceutical marketing. Companies must adhere to regulations regarding the promotion of prescription drugs, patient privacy, adverse event reporting, and fair balance of product information. Pharma marketers need to navigate these regulations while utilizing digital platforms effectively.
8. *Data Analytics and Personalization*: The digital landscape allows for collecting and analyzing vast data. Pharma companies can leverage data analytics to gain insights into customer behavior, target audience segmentation, and measure campaign effectiveness. Personalization techniques enable tailored messaging and engagement, improving the overall impact of marketing efforts.
9. *Telemedicine and Remote Patient Monitoring*: The digital landscape has accelerated the rise of telemedicine and remote patient monitoring. Pharma companies can integrate their products and services with digital health platforms, enabling remote consultations, virtual follow-ups, and real-time monitoring of patient's health conditions.
10. *Influencer Marketing and Advocacy*: Pharma companies collaborate with healthcare influencers, patient advocates, and key opinion leaders to amplify their messages and promote their products. Influencer marketing in the pharma industry involves partnering with credible individuals with a strong online presence and influence within specific disease areas.
11. The digital landscape in pharma marketing offers numerous opportunities to reach and engage with healthcare professionals, patients, and other stakeholders. However, it also requires a deep understanding of regulatory guidelines, privacy considerations, and ethical practices to ensure responsible and effective digital marketing strategies.

Digitalization

Digitalization involves employing digital technologies to digitize analog information or analog content from paper into an electronic format for easier storage, access, sharing, and analysis. Digitizing has become an indispensable aspect of modern life, revolutionizing how we work, learn, and interact with one another and inspiring innovative new technologies like artificial intelligence (AI), IoT (Internet of Things) devices, and blockchain with potentially vast positive ramifications across society.

Digitalization has Changed Pharma Marketing

Digital technology has transformed pharma marketing, opening new opportunities for pharmaceutical companies to engage their target audiences more directly while increasing the efficiency and effectiveness of marketing initiatives. Some ways digitalization has affected this field include:

1. *Big Data and Analytics*: Pharma companies can take advantage of big data by employing analytics to gain valuable insight into customer behavior and preferences, helping them target their marketing efforts more successfully and create tailored campaigns for maximum impact.
2. *Social Media and Online Advertising*: Pharma companies can use social media and online advertising channels as new ways of connecting with their target customers and building lasting relationships with them. Targeted ads or campaigns on these platforms allow pharma firms to promote products or services to specific demographics more efficiently than before.
3. *Telemedicine*: With the rise in prevalence of the COVID-19 pandemic, telemedicine has become more prominent, offering pharmaceutical companies new opportunities for customer engagement via virtual consultations and remote monitoring, which they can integrate into their marketing initiatives.
4. *Mobile Apps and Wearables*: Pharma companies have begun developing mobile applications and wearables designed to assist their customers in managing their conditions and medication regimens and collect data that could improve marketing campaigns. These digital tools may also serve to track customers who take prescriptions.
5. *Digital Content*: Pharma companies often create digital content such as blog posts, videos, and infographics to educate customers about their products and services. This content can be shared across social media channels to raise brand recognition and engagement with target customers.

Digitalization has transformed pharmaceutical marketing, offering companies targeted, personalized and cost-efficient campaigns to reach specific customer groups more precisely while creating opportunities to engage customers and enhance product/service experiences for them.

Digitization

Digitization refers to digitizing information or physical objects into digital formats that can be stored, accessed, and modified using electronic devices and computer systems. Digitizing involves turning analog information into formats computers can read and process. Digitizing involves techniques like scanning, OCR (Optical Character Recognition), and digital imaging, which have become integral in many industries' transformation journeys, yielding vast quantities of digital data which can then be utilized to inform decision-making processes or enhance business practices.

Digitized Pharma Marketing

Digitization has had an immense effect on pharmaceutical marketing, revolutionizing how pharmaceutical companies reach out to, and interact with their target markets. Some examples of how digitization is used in pharma marketing include:

1. *Online Advertising*: Pharma companies increasingly turn to digital channels like social media, search engines, and email to reach targeted customers cost-effectively. Social media, search engines, and email are popular channels for quickly targeting product ads at customers while reaching many potential clients.
2. *Virtual Events*: Due to the pandemic, many in-person events had to be canceled or postponed, prompting pharmaceutical companies to host virtual events like webinars, conferences, and meetings to engage customers and educate them on their products.
3. *Mobile Applications*: Pharmaceutical companies have begun creating mobile apps to inform customers about their products while helping them more easily manage conditions or medication regimens.
4. *Patient Data Management*: Digitization has allowed pharmaceutical companies to collect and analyze patient information that can help drive product development, customer engagement strategies, and marketing plans forward.

5. *Telemedicine*: With the rapid proliferation of telemedicine technology, pharmaceutical companies are joining with healthcare providers to offer virtual consultations, treatment and educate patients about their products.

Digitization has enabled pharmaceutical companies to enhance the efficiency and effectiveness of their marketing initiatives while offering increased value to customers.

Digital Marketing

Digital marketing in pharma is defined as using various digital channels and technologies, such as social media, email marketing, mobile applications, or other digital assets to market pharmaceutical products directly to consumers and healthcare professionals.

Below are a few ways digital marketing has been utilized in the pharmaceutical industry:

1. *Social Media*: Pharma companies use popular social media platforms like Facebook, Twitter, and LinkedIn to engage their target customer groups and healthcare professionals. Businesses utilize these networks to share product details and educational material and answer customer inquiries.
2. *Email Marketing*: This form of communication between customers and healthcare professionals informs them about new products, clinical trials, and any relevant news or updates regarding health.
3. *Search Engine Optimization (SEO)*: SEO increases the visibility of pharmaceutical products and services within search engine results pages, with companies employing techniques designed to optimize websites and digital content to boost search rankings and visibility in results pages.
4. *Search Engine Marketing (SEM)*: SEM draws customers directly to websites through paid advertisements like Google Ads that target specific keywords and audiences.
5. *Mobile Apps*: Mobile applications provide customers and healthcare providers with information about products and services while collecting customer behavioral and preference data.

Digital marketing has become an essential aspect of pharmaceutical sales as customers and healthcare professionals increasingly rely on digital channels for accessing information and engaging with companies. Pharmaceutical firms can use various digital tactics to create more effective campaigns, increase customer engagement, and drive revenue growth.

Digital Maturity

Digital maturity refers to the degree to which organizations or individuals use digital technologies for business processes, process improvement, and innovation. It measures how effectively an organization uses these digital assets in achieving its goals and objectives using various channels. These may include:

1. *Strategy*: Is digital technology being integrated into the organization's overall strategy? A mature organization would make digital technology central to their business plans.
2. *Culture*: Does the culture support digital technology within an organization? Established digital enterprises typically foster environments open to change and innovation.
3. *Organization*: What organizational structures, processes, and governance mechanisms exist to facilitate digital transformation? Digitally mature businesses tend to possess flexible organizational structures which facilitate quick decision-making and execution processes.
4. *Capabilities*: What capabilities does your organization possess regarding digital technology? This may involve technical skills like data analytics or machine learning and soft skills like employees' digital literacy.
5. *Technology*: Assess your organization's level of digital maturity. Organizations utilizing cutting-edge digital tools like AI (Artificial Intelligence), IoT (Internet of Things), and cloud computing are more advanced in their approach. Such technologies help drive their business processes.

These dimensions of digital maturity are interdependent; progress made on one often leads to improvements in others. Reaching digital maturity is a journey; maturity stages typically progress as organizations continue integrating more digital technology into their operations.

Digital Maturity in Pharma Marketing

Pharma companies increasingly leverage digital technologies in their marketing strategies and campaigns, using it as part of digital maturity in pharma marketing, to improve their results and customer interactions.

Digital maturity in pharmaceutical marketing entails the following:

1. *Customer Centricity*: A digitally mature pharmaceutical company uses digital channels to gain greater insights into its customers, such as doctors, patients, and other key constituents. It uses cutting-edge tools and analytics to segment and profile customers and delivers relevant, personalized content.
2. *Data Analytics*: More established organizations employ data analytics in their marketing decisions, using techniques like predictive modeling to anticipate market trends or patient needs.
3. *Digital Channels*: Utilizing digital channels like websites, social media accounts, email marketing campaigns, and mobile applications to reach and engage with customers is one of the core aspects of digital maturity. These channels can deliver information in novel ways, such as interactive presentations or virtual reality experiences that ensure optimal engagement between companies and their target customers.
4. *Technology Integration*: Companies with high digital maturity typically utilize marketing technologies (MarTech), including customer relationship management (CRM) systems, content management systems (CMSs), and marketing automation platforms that connect, offering a holistic view of customers while supporting seamless multichannel marketing efforts.
5. *Compliance and Digital Ethics*: Digitally mature companies in the heavily regulated pharmaceutical industry manage to innovate while remaining compliant with all relevant regulations by respecting digital ethics such as data privacy and security while using customer data to drive tailored marketing messages to their customer bases.
6. *Agility and Innovation*: Digitally mature pharmaceutical companies possess the agility to quickly adapt their marketing strategies in response to changes in the digital environment while encouraging innovation by exploring and testing new digital tools and techniques.
7. *Digital Skills*: Digitally mature organizations invest in cultivating digital capabilities within their marketing teams by training staff in data analysis, digital content production, SEO/SEM techniques, and social media promotion.

All these aspects are vitally important, yet digital maturity should go beyond simply using digital technology for its own sake. Instead, digital maturity involves strategically harnessing its benefits to enhance marketing effectiveness and efficiency, bring customers value, and drive business expansion.

Digital Maturity Analysis

Digital maturity analysis involves assessing an organization's readiness and effectiveness in leveraging digital technologies for its business processes, including marketing, operations, customer service, and overall strategy. Here's a broad process for performing a digital maturity analysis:

1. *Identify Key Areas*: Identify key areas of your organization where digital technology plays a significant role or has the potential to do so. These might include things like marketing, customer service, operations, data analytics, etc.,
2. *Develop Assessment Criteria*: Develop a set of criteria for each area to assess digital maturity. These criteria will typically be related to the extent of digital technology use, the degree of integration of digital technology into business processes, the level of digital skills and culture, and the degree of innovation in using digital technology.
3. *Collect Data*: Collect data to assess the organization against the criteria. This could involve surveys, interviews, observations, or other methods. The data could be quantitative (percentage of digital processes) or qualitative (how well digital technology is integrated into the culture).
4. *Analyze Data*: Analyze the data to assess the organization's digital maturity. This might involve scoring the organization against each criterion and then aggregating the scores to provide an overall digital maturity assessment.
5. *Benchmark*: Compare your organization's digital maturity to industry benchmarks or competitors' digital maturity.
6. *Identify Gaps and Opportunities*: Based on the analysis, identify gaps in the organization's digital maturity and opportunities for improvement.
7. *Develop Action Plans*: Develop action plans to address the gaps and seize the opportunities. These plans should be specific, measurable, achievable, relevant, and time-bound (SMART).
8. *Implement and Monitor*: Implement the action plans and monitor progress toward improving digital maturity.

Digital maturity analysis is not a one-off process. Given the rapidly changing digital environment, organizations should regularly reassess their digital maturity to keep up with changes and continually improve their digital technology use. It's also important to note that the goal of digital maturity is not just about technology adoption. It's about leveraging technology to achieve strategic objectives, improve performance, and create value.

Digital Maturity Analysis in Pharma Marketing

Digital maturity analysis in pharma marketing involves assessing how much a pharmaceutical company effectively utilizes digital technology in its marketing practices. This analysis can help a company understand its current state, identify gaps and opportunities for improvement, and develop strategies for enhancing its digital capabilities.

Here are some key areas to consider when conducting a digital maturity analysis in pharma marketing:

1. *Customer Engagement*: How effectively does the company use digital channels to engage with customers, such as physicians, patients, pharmacists, and other stakeholders? This includes assessing the use of social media, email marketing, webinars, mobile apps, virtual reality, etc.,
2. *Data and Analytics*: Does the company use data analytics to drive marketing decisions? This includes collecting, analyzing, and acting on data from various sources, such as market research, social media analytics, and customer behavior data.
3. *Marketing Technology*: What marketing technologies (MarTech) does the company use? How integrated are these technologies? For example, is there seamless integration between the company's customer relationship management (CRM) system, marketing automation platform, and content management system (CMS)?
4. *Digital Compliance*: Given the heavily regulated nature of the pharma industry, how well does the company ensure compliance in its digital marketing activities? This includes issues like data privacy, online advertising regulations, etc.,
5. *Digital Skills and Culture*: How digitally literate are the company's marketing staff? Does the company's culture support digital innovation and change?
6. *Strategic Alignment*: How well are digital marketing activities aligned with the company's business strategy? Is digital marketing seen as a strategic tool for achieving business objectives?

You could use a combination of surveys, interviews, observation, and document analysis to assess these areas. Based on the assessment, you can identify gaps, develop action plans for improvement, and monitor progress toward enhanced digital maturity.

Comparing your company's digital maturity with industry benchmarks or competitors can provide additional insights.

Remember that the ultimate goal of improving digital maturity is to adopt and use more digital technology to deliver value, enhance marketing effectiveness, and drive business growth.

Digital Maturity Stages

Digital maturity in Pharma marketing digital maturity stages resemble those found in other industries but with some key differences due to some specific aspects unique to pharmaceutical marketing, such as regulations, physician roles, considerations for drug discovery and development processes, and patient care considerations. Here are the digital maturity stages specific to pharmaceutical marketing:

1. *Digital Denial*: At first, pharma companies fail to acknowledge the significance of digital technologies for marketing strategies. Instead, traditional marketing methods remain predominant, while digital tools may only be implemented partially or not at all!
2. *Digital Experimentation*: At this stage, a company explores digital marketing channels, be they social media platforms, email newsletters, or content strategies, such as digital content creation, with no clear strategy or goals.
3. *Digital Literacy*: Pharma companies begin to comprehend the impact of digital marketing. There may even be the development of an integrated digital strategy using tools from across the digital landscape to increase marketing efficiency and expand customer reach. Online campaigns, content marketing strategy, and digital ad campaigns have become more sophisticated and targeted as part of this initiative.
4. *Digital Integration*: At this stage, digital marketing fully integrates into a company's overall marketing strategy and practice. Advanced tools like data analytics, artificial intelligence (AI), machine learning (ML), customer relationship management (CRM) systems, and personalized targeting technologies help enhance personalized campaigns while measuring marketing performance, plus compliance becomes second nature when communicating digitally!
5. *Digital Mastery*: The pharmaceutical company excels at digital marketing within its industry. The company leverages cutting-edge digital technologies and data-driven insights to deliver

an exceptional customer experience. Their marketing is highly personalized across multiple digital channels, and they use this medium to form strong relationships between physicians, patients, and stakeholders.

Pharmaceutical companies face unique industry-related challenges, from stringent regulations and scientific accuracy requirements to protecting patient confidentiality. All while keeping pace with growing expectations from doctors and patients who are increasingly digitally literate.

The COVID-19 pandemic has hastened digital transformation in pharmaceutical marketing as traditional in-person activities have been disrupted, and digital channels have become essential in reaching and engaging with customers.

Digital Medicine

Digital medicine is an emerging field that integrates technology, medicine, and data for improved patient outcomes. Wearable devices, sensors, and mobile apps may monitor health conditions remotely while offering personalized treatment plans tailored to individual patients.

Digital medicine can play an invaluable role in pharmaceutical marketing. Pharma companies may utilize digital tools and applications that assist patients in managing their health conditions while providing information about products and services. Furthermore, this data collection tool may assist future marketing strategies with better targeting patient needs and outcomes.

Digital medicine offers pharmaceutical companies another effective tool to connect with healthcare professionals and develop relationships with key opinion leaders. Through digital resources such as e-learning modules, webinars, and virtual conferences, they can share their expertise and foster opportunities for collaboration or partnership between pharma companies and healthcare professionals.

Digital medicine presents pharmaceutical companies with an invaluable opportunity to improve patient outcomes, increase engagement among healthcare providers, and enhance marketing initiatives. However, before diving in, they must ensure all digital marketing practices comply with regulations and ethical standards and that patient privacy and data security are ensured.

Exploit Digital Medicine Opportunities in Pharma

Pharmaceutical companies have many ways of capitalizing on digital medicine opportunities. Here are some examples:

1. *Digital Therapeutics*: Pharma companies can create digital therapeutics, which are software treatments using digital tools and technologies as part of their treatment strategies to prevent, manage or treat diseases such as depression. Digital therapeutics may be combined with conventional drugs or used alone as standalone solutions. For instance, an app utilizing cognitive behavioral therapy techniques may be developed as one form of digital therapy treatment.
2. *Provide Patient Education and Support*: Pharma companies can utilize digital resources to educate and support patients. For instance, creating a mobile app could offer information about disease or condition and symptom management techniques while connecting patients to support groups or resources may help the company deliver education services and offer additional help for managing them.
3. *Building Relationships with Healthcare Professionals*: Pharma companies can utilize digital tools and platforms to engage healthcare professionals and form meaningful relationships with key opinion leaders. For instance, offering e-learning modules, webinars, or virtual conferences to share their expertise could prove highly successful in engaging healthcare professionals and creating productive working environments.
4. *Collecting and Analyzing Patient Data*: Pharma companies can utilize digital tools to collect and analyze patient information that informs drug development, clinical trials, marketing strategies, and wearable or sensor technology for patient monitoring on medication adherence or symptom management. For instance, wearable sensors could collect such information.
5. *Enhancing Marketing Efforts*: Pharma companies can effectively employ digital marketing strategies such as social media, email marketing, or SEO to reach, engage, and promote their products to their target audiences.

Digital Natives

Digital natives refer to those born and raised during an era of digital technology who exhibit a natural aptitude with various digital tools from an early age, typically younger generations who were immersed in its applications; digital natives may possess inherent understandings regarding its usage, which give them a competitive advantage; as a result, digital natives could be considered more tech-savvy than their older counterparts who must slowly acquire this expertise over time.

However, it should be remembered that not all young people are digital natives, as older individuals might also possess IT knowledge and capabilities. Additionally, this term cannot be generalized; individuals may possess differing levels of familiarity and comfort with digital technologies depending on factors like socioeconomic background, education level, and exposure to tech devices.

Digital Natives in Pharma Marketing

Pharma companies must take note that digital natives represent an essential demographic when targeting Gen Z and Millennial audiences with marketing campaigns since this group has grown up using technology and digital platforms themselves. To effectively reach digital natives, companies must understand their preferences before creating tailored campaigns to reach them effectively.

Here are a few strategies pharma companies can use to reach digital natives:

1. *Leverage Social Media*: Digital natives often spend significant amounts of time engaging on various social media platforms like Instagram, Facebook, Twitter, and TikTok; pharmaceutical companies should leverage these platforms by posting engaging videos, infographics or user-generated content to connect with digital natives on these social networks.
2. *Targeted Digital Ads*: Digital natives have grown accustomed to personalized content and respond favorably when ads are tailored specifically to them. Pharma companies can leverage data-based targeting techniques for digital ads targeted to specific demographics and interests. For instance, birth control ads targeted toward young women.
3. *Emphasize Convenience*: Digital natives have come to expect instant, on-demand services like telemedicine or home delivery of medications as their go-to service providers, so pharmaceutical companies should capitalize on that expectation by emphasizing convenience when marketing products and services such as home delivery of medication, or telemedicine services.
4. *Focus on Values*: Digital natives tend to be socially aware and appreciate brands that align with their ideals, and principles. Pharma companies should emphasize social responsibility, sustainability, and ethical conduct through marketing.
5. *Provide Educational Content*: Digital natives have grown accustomed to accessing information online and finding valuable educational material, like blog posts, webinars, and e-books about health and wellbeing online. Pharma companies should utilize this opportunity by creating educational material, such as blog posts, webinars, and e-books with valuable health and wellbeing-oriented information for digital natives.

How Pharma Engages Digital Natives

The following are examples of pharmaceutical companies successfully engaging digital natives through their marketing initiatives:

1. *Nurx*, a telemedicine company offering birth control and other medications, has successfully targeted digital natives through social media channels like Instagram and Twitter. Nurx created engaging content targeting this demographic, such as humorous videos or user-generated posts that appealed to them; additionally, they have collaborated with influencers and celebrities in promoting their services to reach a broader audience.
2. *Blink Health*, an online prescription drug price comparison website, has launched digital advertising targeting digital natives using data mining techniques to reach them directly. Their ads target specific demographics and interests, such as advertising medications to people searching for related items online.
3. *Hims*, a telemedicine company offering treatments for conditions including hair loss and erectile dysfunction, has used targeted digital advertising on Instagram and Snapchat to reach digital natives with humorous yet relatable messaging that appeals to this demographic.
4. *Johnson & Johnson* is a pharmaceutical company that has used educational content such as blog posts and videos on health and well-being to reach digital natives through platforms like Facebook and Twitter.
5. *Ro*, a digital health clinic providing telemedicine services, has used social media channels like Instagram and TikTok to raise awareness among digital natives for its offerings. They've produced engaging content targeted towards this demographic, such as humorous videos highlighting its convenience.

Pharma companies should adjust their marketing strategies to engage digital natives effectively. Pharma firms can do so by tapping social media channels, employing targeted digital ads, highlighting convenience while emphasizing values, and offering educational content.

Digital Opinion Leader (DOL)

Digital Opinion Leaders (DOLs) are influential individuals with demonstrated credibility and expertise in one field who use digital platforms, including social media, blogs, podcasts, and webinars, to share their opinions with a broader audience. DOLs play an instrumental role in shaping attitudes and behaviors among healthcare professionals, patients, and other key players within the pharmaceutical industry. Leading pharmaceutical companies increasingly employ them as part of their marketing strategies; for example, the following examples reveal some DOL-driven pharmaceutical company marketing activities:

1. *Pharmaceutical Companies Are Partnering With DOLs to Develop Thought Leadership*: Pharmaceutical companies are teaming up with DOLs to produce thought leadership content for distribution among their target audiences, such as guest blog posts, podcast episodes, or webinars that cover relevant products or disease areas within their product portfolios, or areas of specialty.
2. *Social Media Marketing*: Pharmaceutical companies employ DOLs to boost their social media campaigns and expand reach and engagement among target audiences. DOLs may share social media posts, retweet or share company content, or participate in online chats or discussions.
3. *Influencer Marketing*: Pharmaceutical companies partner with DOLs with a large social media following to promote their products or services to their audience. This may include sponsored posts or product reviews on social media platforms or blogs.
4. *Advocacy and Patient Engagement*: Pharmaceutical companies are partnering with patient advocates and DOLs to raise awareness of specific diseases or conditions and improve patient engagement. DOLs may participate in patient forums, write patient education materials, or share their experiences and insights with patients and their families.
5. *Medical Education*: Pharmaceutical companies are partnering with DOLs to develop and deliver medical education programs to healthcare professionals. DOLs may serve as speakers, trainers, or content creators for these programs.

How to Identify DOLs

Identification of Digital Opinion Leaders (DOLs) in the pharmaceutical industry can be challenging; many individuals could have strong followings and influence within various fields. Below are a few approaches pharmaceutical companies can employ to identify DOLs:

1. *Social Media Monitoring*: Pharmaceutical companies can utilize social media monitoring tools to quickly identify individuals actively engaging with their brand or discussing product portfolio or disease-related topics, then analyze these individuals' social media profiles to gauge their level of influence and engagement.
2. *Online Communities and Forums*: Pharmaceutical companies can participate in online communities and forums related to their product portfolio or disease areas, identify active members within these forums, and develop relationships to establish credibility among other members.
3. *Industry Conferences and Events*: Pharmaceutical companies may attend industry conferences and events, and identify individuals presenting, speaking, or participating on panels that relate to their product portfolio or disease areas.
4. *Professional Associations and Societies*: Pharmaceutical companies can identify individuals who are members of professional associations and societies related to their product portfolio, or disease areas, and who have established credibility and influence among their peers.
5. *Google Search and Media Mentions*: Pharmaceutical companies can perform a search and media mentions analysis to identify individuals frequently mentioned in news articles, blog posts, or other online publications related to their product portfolio or disease areas.

Pharmaceutical companies must approach DOL identification critically and ensure that the individuals they identify are credible, trustworthy, and aligned with their brand values and messaging.

Digital opinion leaders (DOLs) are increasingly integral to pharmaceutical marketing strategies. DOLs help pharmaceutical companies connect more directly with and engage their target audiences more easily while increasing brand recognition, trustworthiness, sales revenue growth, and maximization. Companies should remain transparent regarding relationships formed with DOLs while adhering to all regulatory requirements governing pharmaceutical marketing activities and disclosing any financial ties with them.

Digital Pill

A digital pill, smart pill, or digital medicine contains an ingestible sensor that communicates with a wearable device or smartphone app to track medication adherence, and provide other health-related data.

The ingestible sensor is usually made of a tiny chip and a sensor integrated into a pill, or other medication. Once a pill is consumed, its digestive fluids activate its sensor and send data directly to a wearable device or smartphone app containing time/date stamps, heart rate information, activity level data, and sleep patterns.

Digital pills offer revolutionary solutions to medication adherence for those living with chronic illnesses who must follow stringent medication schedules. Their data transmission feature allows healthcare providers to track medication adherence and adjust treatment plans as necessary; additionally, they may reduce healthcare costs by eliminating medication errors and hospital admissions.

Concerns have also been expressed over the privacy and security of health data collected through digital pills, with patients potentially unwilling to use these medicines if their information is inadequately safeguarded. There may also be ethical considerations related to using digital pills for monitoring medication adherence if the data collected can be used for punitive or coercive means.

Digital Pills: Some Examples

Here are a few examples of digital pills:

1. *Abilify MyCite*: *Abilify MyCite* is an FDA-approved digital pill used to treat schizophrenia, bipolar disorders, and depression. It contains an ingestible sensor that sends a signal to a wearable patch when the pill is swallowed, and the patch then transmits data to a mobile app.
2. *Proteus Discover*: *Proteus Discover* is a digital medicine platform with an ingestible sensor, wearable patch, and mobile app. The sensor is embedded in the medication, and the patch collects data about medication adherence, activity, and sleep.
3. *ID-Cap System*: The *ID-Cap System* is a digital pill that uses radio waves to detect when a patient has taken their medication. The pill contains an ingestible sensor that sends a signal to a wearable receiver, then sends data to a cloud-based platform.
4. *Pillsy*: *Pillsy* is a digital pill bottle that reminds patients to take their medication and tracks medication adherence. The pill bottle connects to a smartphone app and sends reminders when it's time to take medication.
5. *Otsuka's Digital Medicine System*: *Otsuka's Digital Medicine System* is an ingestion sensor, wearable patch, and mobile app system designed to increase medication adherence among those with serious mental illnesses.

In summary, digital pill development remains an active area of research and development with various advantages and drawbacks that should be carefully considered before selecting one among the available options.

Digital Therapeutics

Digital Therapeutics (DTXs) are software-based interventions used to treat or manage various health conditions alongside traditional medications, or standalone therapies. Digital therapeutics may be delivered via mobile apps, wearable devices, or web platforms.

Pharmaceutical companies are increasingly turning to digital therapeutics as part of their marketing strategies to complement traditional pharmaceutical products and reap its many advantages for marketing purposes. Here are a few benefits associated with digital therapeutics in pharmaceutical marketing:

1. *Improved Patient Outcomes*: Digital therapeutics provides patients with personalized and evidence-based interventions to manage their health conditions better, enhancing patient outcomes and greater patient satisfaction.
2. *Increased Patient Engagement*: Digital therapeutics can assist patients in becoming more involved with their healthcare by offering tools and resources to monitor progress and manage conditions more efficiently.
3. *Enhanced Data Collection*: Digital therapeutics offer pharmaceutical companies access to abundant patient behavior data and health outcomes analysis they can use for product innovation or improving existing ones.
4. *Differentiation from Competitors*: Pharmaceutical companies that incorporate digital therapeutics into their marketing strategies can distinguish themselves from competitors while offering additional value to customers.

5. *New Revenue Streams*: Digital therapeutics offer pharmaceutical companies new revenue streams; these products can either be stand-alone or become part of an overall product offering.

Digital therapeutics is an exciting addition to pharmaceutical marketing strategies as they can deliver tangible advantages to patients and pharmaceutical companies. By including digital therapeutics in their marketing plans, pharmaceutical companies can enhance patient outcomes, boost engagement among their target patients and generate useful data that inform future product development efforts. Here are examples of digital therapeutics being utilized in pharmaceutical marketing:

1. *Pear Therapeutics*: Pear Therapeutics is a company that creates digital therapeutics for various health conditions, with products like *ReSET-O* and its predecessor *ReSET* available to treat substance use disorders.
2. *Akili Interactive*: Akili Interactive is a company developing video game-based digital therapeutics for treating cognitive disorders like ADHD. Their flagship product, *Akili*, is prescribed digital treatment specifically designed for ADHD (Attention Deficit Hyperactivity Disorder).
3. *Novartis and Pear Therapeutics* have joined hands to produce digital therapeutic solutions to treat schizophrenia and multiple sclerosis.
4. *Otsuka Pharmaceutical* has created *Abilify MyCite* as an electronic medication designed to combat depression; each pill has sensors tracking patients' medication adherence to improve compliance.
5. *Sanofi recently allied with Happify Health* to develop digital therapeutics for treating mental health conditions like depression. Their first product, an antidepressant digital therapeutic currently under development could become available soon.

As technology and medicine progress, more pharmaceutical companies may include digital therapeutics in their marketing strategies to augment traditional pharmaceutical products as more evidence emerges of digital therapeutics' usefulness in healthcare marketing strategies.

Digital Transformation

Digital transformation refers to using digital technologies to transform how organizations operate fundamentally, deliver value to customers, and compete in the market. Implementing digital tools across every aspect of an organization's operations involves employing these digital solutions for its processes, customer interactions, and internal communications.

Digital transformation involves adopting cutting-edge technologies like artificial intelligence (AI), big data analytics (BDA), and cloud computing platforms like Azure, IoT or mobile phones to increase operational efficiencies, strengthen customer relationships and foster innovation. These innovations often improve operational efficiencies and customer engagement while fueling future innovation efforts.

Transformation involves altering one's mindset, culture, and business strategy fundamentally. Implementing new technologies does not constitute true digital transformation. Rather, successful transformation requires strong leadership with clear goals, an innovative culture committed to continuous learning, continuous innovation efforts, and ongoing improvement plans.

Digital transformation has become ever more crucial to businesses looking to compete effectively in an age of rapid technological change. By adopting digital transformation strategies, organizations can open up new growth opportunities, enhance customer satisfaction, and propel company expansion.

Digital Transformation in Pharma Marketing

A digital transformation approach in pharmaceutical marketing integrates digital tools and strategies across all aspects of its operations, from understanding customer needs more accurately through to personalization campaigns to improving overall customer experiences across touchpoints. Here are a few ways pharmaceutical companies are taking advantage of digital transformation in their marketing initiatives:

1. *Big Data Analytics*: Businesses use big data analytics to better understand customer needs, preferences, and behavior. They use these insights to craft tailor-made marketing campaigns and improve the customer experience.
2. *Artificial Intelligence and Machine Learning*: Artificial intelligence and machine learning technologies enable marketers to analyze customer data more precisely, thus leading to targeted marketing campaigns with improved customer experiences and relationships.
3. *Customer Engagement Platforms*: Many organizations are now developing platforms that combine data from various sources into an in-depth view of customer behavior, providing more targeted marketing efforts and

strengthening engagement between service providers and their clients.

4. *Digital Content Creation*: Businesses have developed digital content such as videos, blog posts, and social media updates to engage their target audiences online and boost website visits and visibility with search engines and social networks. Content is optimized specifically for each channel to gain maximum exposure for the business website while increasing website visits and exposure for the brand itself.
5. *Customer Relationship Management (CRM)*: Businesses employ CRM tools to facilitate customer interactions across various channels and monitor customer preferences for tailored marketing initiatives. By monitoring behavior more precisely and tracking preferences over time, CRM allows companies to gauge customers better and develop relevant campaigns more quickly.

Digital transformation is driving dramatic transformation within pharmaceutical marketing strategies and campaigns. By capitalizing on digital technologies and strategies, companies create more effective campaigns, improve customer experiences, and drive business expansion.

Digital Transformation Journey: Key Steps

Undergoing digital transformation can be an arduous, multi-stage process requiring careful planning, implementation, and ongoing refinement. Here are six essential steps organizations should follow to embark upon their digital transformation journeys successfully:

1. *Define Your Vision and Strategy for Digital Transformation*: Develop an Organization's Vision and Strategy for Digital Transformation by outlining key objectives, opportunities, challenges, resources required, and capabilities required to accomplish desired results.
2. *Assess the Current State*: Conduct an in-depth evaluation of your organization's digital capabilities to identify gaps or restrictions, which may involve conducting a digital maturity evaluation, benchmarking against industry best practices, or engaging with organizational stakeholders.
3. *Create a Roadmap*: Create a digital transformation roadmap detailing all key initiatives, milestones, and timelines to reach organizational goals. Align this plan with the overall vision and strategy and prioritize initiatives with greater impact than others.
4. *Engage Stakeholders*: Engage all relevant stakeholders across an organization— executives, employees, customers, and partners alike, to garner support and obtain alignment for a digital transformation initiative. This may mean sharing vision and strategy documents, gathering feedback and ideas from them, and including them in the planning and execution process of such initiative.
5. *Build Digital Capabilities*: Establish the necessary digital capabilities that support a digital transformation initiative by investing in new technologies, developing skillsets and competencies, and designing processes and workflows to support it.
6. *Implement and Iterate*: Create the digital transformation roadmap, implement it according to feedback and results, iterate on it with feedback received, refine as required based on customer input and results, as well as test or pilot new initiatives if applicable, monitor progress against key performance indicators, make necessary adjustments as required, ensuring success!

Digital transformation requires an integrative approach across every facet of an organization's operations and culture, from operations management to strategy execution and culture change. These general steps can help organizations successfully navigate this challenging journey toward their desired results.

Digital Twins

Digital twins are digital replicas of physical objects, systems, or processes created using sensors, data collection methods, and algorithms to develop digital models replicating real-world behavior, performance characteristics, and an entity's real-time characteristics.

Digital twins can be invaluable in manufacturing, engineering, and industrial settings to optimize operations, predict maintenance needs and increase efficiencies. For example, a digital twin of a wind turbine could be used to monitor its performance, detect potential problems, and optimize its maintenance schedule.

Digital Twins in Pharma Marketing

In pharma marketing, digital twins can be used to simulate the behavior of drugs and medical devices in a virtual environment, which can help marketers better to understand their products and their potential impact on patients.

One application of digital twins in pharma marketing is developing personalized marketing strategies. By creating virtual replicas of patients, marketers can stimulate how different patients may respond to a particular drug or treatment and tailor their marketing messages accordingly.

Another application of digital twins in pharma marketing is real-world data analysis. By creating virtual replicas of clinical trials, marketers can analyze the data in a more controlled environment that helps them to understand their products' efficacy and safety.

Digital twins can revolutionize pharma marketing by providing more accurate and comprehensive insights into the behavior of drugs and medical devices, ultimately leading to better patient outcomes.

How Pharma Can Use Digital Twins: A Few Examples

Here are a few examples of how digital twins are being used in pharma marketing:

1. *Stimulating Drug Behaviors*: Digital twins can help pharmaceutical companies better understand how their products function and any possible interactions with other medications or medical conditions by simulating how drugs behave under virtual conditions. This information could assist pharma companies with increasing their understanding of how their products work and potential interactions among products to expand understanding.
2. *Personalizing Marketing Messages*: Pharma companies can personalize marketing messages by creating virtual replicas of patients to simulate how different populations may react to particular drugs or treatments, helping them tailor marketing messages directly to specific patient populations.
3. *Analyzing Real-World Data*: Digital twins provide pharmaceutical companies with an effective tool for analyzing real-world data in an easily controlled environment, helping them better comprehend product efficacy and safety issues.
4. *Predictive Modeling*: Digital twins can help pharma companies create predictive models of patient outcomes, helping identify those likely to benefit most from their products and create marketing plans that reach these patients effectively.
5. *Virtual Product Demonstrations*: Digital Twins can create virtual product demonstrations to provide pharmaceutical companies showing their products more engagingly and interactively to healthcare providers. This feature may prove particularly helpful when marketing medical device products.

How Pharma Companies Use Digital Twins

Here are a few examples of pharma companies that are using digital twins in their marketing efforts:

1. Roche uses digital twins to simulate cancer cells' behavior and predict how cancer treatments affect patients. Using digital twins to model patient outcomes, Roche can develop personalized treatment plans and create targeted marketing messages.
2. Novartis has turned to digital twins as an innovative approach for understanding how its medicines affect immune cells in their attempt to develop more effective treatments for diseases like cancer and multiple sclerosis. By simulating immune cell behavior using virtual replicas created from real ones, Novartis hopes to gain better insight into their interactions and develop more targeted medications against such ailments.
3. AstraZeneca is using digital twins to simulate the behavior of patient populations. AstraZeneca can develop more targeted marketing strategies tailored to specific patient needs by creating virtual replicas of different patient groups.
4. Pfizer uses digital twins to create virtual product demonstrations for its medical devices. Using digital twins to showcase the functionality and benefits of its products, Pfizer can provide healthcare providers with a more engaging and interactive experience.
5. GlaxoSmithKline is using digital twins to simulate the behavior of drugs to predict how they will interact with different patient populations. By using digital twins to model patient outcomes, GlaxoSmithKline can develop personalized treatment plans and targeted marketing messages.

Diminishing Returns, The Law of

The Law of Diminishing Returns also referred to as Diminishing Marginal Returns, is an economic principle that states that as more units of variable inputs are added onto fixed ones, their marginal output decreases after reaching a certain point; each additional unit of variable input produces less additional output with each addition; therefore it provides insight into an optimal amount of variable inputs for maximum output and efficiency. Too many variable inputs could decrease production, leading to inefficiency.

The Law of Diminishing Returns in Pharma Marketing

Pharmaceutical marketing also follows this law of diminishing returns: as companies increase their marketing efforts, marginal benefits decrease at some point due to increasing efforts.

An illustration would be the launch of a pharmaceutical drug product by an established pharmaceutical company; early sales increases can result from marketing initiatives; however, marginal returns of additional efforts may diminish as time progresses. Several factors, including market saturation, competition from similar products, or consumer skepticism, could cause this.

Direct-to-consumer advertising (DTCA) also displays diminishing returns in pharmaceutical marketing. Direct to Consumer Advertising refers to direct promotion by pharmaceutical companies of their products through media platforms directly targeted towards customers, with awareness raised and demand created with every impression; its marginal benefit may decrease over time as repeat viewings lead to a lessened reaction by customers, as soon as multiple ads for one product come along at once, their response might no longer be so immediate, and they become less responsive than before when more ads come around.

Therefore, pharmaceutical companies must carefully track and assess their marketing initiatives to optimize return on investment and identify an ideal level of marketing investment that will yield maximum benefits.

Dirichlet Model

The Dirichlet Model is an extremely useful statistical model in marketing research, particularly pharmaceutical marketing. The Dirichlet Model analyzes market share statistics of multiple brands where each is competing to take a slice of the overall market.

The Dirichlet model can help pharmaceutical marketers analyze drug market shares within various therapeutic categories or disease areas and understand which factors influence those shares, including efficacy, safety profile, price promotion, and distribution strategies of various drugs within those therapeutic categories or disease areas.

The Dirichlet model assumes that market shares of each brand correspond with a Dirichlet distribution, a multivariate probability distribution describing the customer selection of each brand. Based on historical market share data, it estimates the parameters of this distribution and uses these figures to predict its future evolution and market shares of individual brands.

Pharmaceutical companies can utilize the Dirichlet model to gain valuable insight into their competitors, gain strategic decisions for product development, pricing, and marketing decisions, identify effective channels for reaching different patient segments, or anticipate which drugs may capture market shares based on the clinical profile or price point.

The Dirichlet analysis provides pharmaceutical marketers a valuable tool for examining market share data in pharmaceutical marketing. It enables them to make data-based decisions to optimize their commercial strategies and increase market share.

Direct-to-Consumer Advertising

Direct-to-Consumer (DTC) Advertising refers to any strategy by which companies promote their products directly to consumers rather than through intermediaries like healthcare providers or pharmacists. DTC strategies in pharmaceutical advertising often consist of directly advertising prescription medicines or medical devices to patients, for example.

DTC advertising within the pharmaceutical industry takes many forms, from television and print ads to online and social media campaigns. DTC ads aim to raise product awareness among potential consumers while encouraging them to talk to their healthcare professionals about these products, leading them to request prescriptions. There are two types of DTC advertising:

A. *Product-claim Advertising*: DTC advertising includes specific information about a product's indications, benefits, and risks. This type of advertising must include a list of possible side effects and contraindications.

B. *Reminder Advertising*: This type of DTC advertising includes only the product's name and reminds patients to talk to their healthcare providers about their product.

DTC advertising is legal only in a few countries, including the United States and New Zealand. In other countries, DTC advertising is prohibited or highly regulated.

Direct-to-consumer (DTC) advertising advocates assert that it can educate patients about medical conditions and treatments available and empower patients to play an active role in healthcare decision-making. Critics of DTC advertising argue that it increases sales of prescription medications, medical devices and drug products sold over-the-counter (OTC), and raises healthcare costs by creating pressure on healthcare providers to prescribe certain products. They also contend that DTC advertising can misinform consumers or provide misleading or incomplete data regarding risks and benefits information while forcing healthcare providers into prescribing products, causing pressure contributing directly to out-of-pocket costs rising considerably faster.

DTC advertising remains controversial in the pharmaceutical industry, and ongoing debates exist about its benefits and drawbacks.

Direct-to-Consumer Marketing

Direct-to-Consumer (DTC) Marketing is a marketing strategy in which companies promote their products directly to consumers rather than through intermediaries such as healthcare providers or pharmacists. DTC marketing typically applies in the pharmaceutical industry as it directly advertises prescription medicines and medical devices to patients.

DTC marketing in the pharmaceutical industry takes many forms, from television and print ads to online and social media campaigns. DTC aims to raise product awareness among potential customers while encouraging them to contact their healthcare provider about this product and request a prescription.

DTC marketing in the pharmaceutical industry offers both advantages and drawbacks. Some benefits may include:

A. *Increased Patient Awareness*: DTC marketing may increase patient awareness about healthcare conditions and treatment options that leads to earlier diagnoses and treatments.

B. *Patient Empowerment*: DTC marketing can empower patients to take an active role in their healthcare decisions and to ask their healthcare providers about specific products.

C. *Increased Sales*: DTC marketing can help increase sales of prescription drugs and medical devices, benefiting pharmaceutical companies and their shareholders.

However, there are also several criticisms associated with DTC marketing in the pharmaceutical industry, including:

1. *Increased Healthcare Costs*: DTC marketing can increase demand for prescription drugs and medical devices, contributing to rising healthcare costs.
2. *Misleading or Incomplete Information*: Some critics argue that DTC marketing can be misleading or provide incomplete information about a product's risks and benefits.
3. *Pressure on Healthcare Providers*: DTC marketing can put pressure on healthcare providers to prescribe specific products, even if they may not be the best option for a patient.

DTC marketing in the pharmaceutical industry remains controversial and is prohibited or highly regulated in most countries except in the United States and New Zealand.

Discretionary Analysis

Analysis of discretionary spending patterns within the pharmaceutical industry requires studying and comparing discretionary expenditure patterns. Discretionary spending refers to any portion of a company's budget which can be allocated or reduced at management's discretion, unlike essential or fixed items, which cannot be altered at will.

In pharmaceutical marketing, discretionary analysis focuses on understanding and optimizing the allocation of resources for marketing activities that are not mandatory or directly tied to regulatory requirements. These discretionary marketing expenditures may include promotional campaigns, advertising, sponsorships, market research, digital marketing initiatives, and sales force activities.

Here are several aspects of discretionary analysis in pharmaceutical marketing:

- *Budget Allocation*: Pharmaceutical companies can use discretionary analysis to allocate budgets to various marketing initiatives based on expected returns on investments (ROI). It helps marketers analyze marketing activities' respective ROI potential and make informed resource allocation decisions based on the expected impacts of promotional activities. The discretionary analysis, thus, provides pharmaceutical firms with a tool for budget allocation decisions that make sense in light of expected impact and return.
- *Marketing Effectiveness Evaluation*: Discretionary analysis provides companies with an effective means of measuring the efficiency and success of different marketing strategies and tactics. A company can assess its marketing initiatives' success and efficiency by measuring

how discretionary marketing expenditure impacts key performance indicators (KPIs) such as sales, market share, brand recognition, and customer engagement.

- *ROI Evaluation*: The discretionary analysis involves measuring the return on investment for various marketing activities undertaken by pharmaceutical companies, providing insights into which ones generate maximum return and contribute most effectively towards meeting overall business objectives.
- *Resource Optimization*: Pharmaceutical companies that utilize discretionary analysis can pinpoint areas where marketing resources may have been over or under-allocated. This allows them to optimize resource allocation by reallocating budgets to more effective initiatives or terminating activities that do not generate desired outcomes.
- *Market Trends and Competitive Analysis*: Pharmaceutical companies often conduct discretionary analysis as part of a strategic marketing initiative to study market trends, monitor competitor activities, and identify emerging opportunities or threats to make informed decisions regarding discretionary marketing expenditures and remain competitive within a rapidly shifting healthcare environment. This approach helps them make strategic marketing investments to stay on the leading edge and remain at the top of their game.

The discretionary analysis in pharmaceutical marketing involves evaluating and optimizing resource allocation to non-essential marketing activities. This process encompasses analyzing various marketing initiatives to assess their impacts and effectiveness while optimizing resource allocation to reach business goals more effectively.

Discretionary Variables

In pharmaceutical marketing, discretionary variables refer to all factors or elements under the control or discretion of marketing teams or management, which can be modified according to marketing strategies, goals or market conditions. Here are a few examples of discretionary variables used for pharmaceutical marketing:

1. *Marketing Budget Allocation*: The marketing budget allocation is a discretionary variable. It involves deciding how much funding should be allocated to marketing activities such as advertising, promotional campaigns, market research, digital marketing, physician education, or patient support programs. The marketing team has discretion in determining the allocation of resources to these various initiatives.
2. *Promoting Channels*: Pharmaceutical marketers have considerable flexibility when selecting promotional channels to advertise their products, such as print media, television, radio, online advertising, social media, direct mail, and physician detailing services. Channel selection will depend upon factors like target audience, budget considerations, marketing objectives, and their effectiveness in reaching the desired audience.
3. *Marketing Message or Creative Content Development*: Marketing messages and creative content development are left up to each marketing team's discretion, with them devising messaging strategies, positioning plans, branding techniques, and promotional material designs tailored specifically for healthcare providers and patients. They may use visuals, language, or imagery that showcase benefits while underscoring the safety features of pharmaceutical products as an additional form of differentiation between them and competitors.
4. *Target Market Segmentation*: Target market segmentation is a discretionary variable. Pharmaceutical marketers can define and segment the market based on demographics, geographical location, disease conditions, treatment preferences, or physician specialties. The selection of target segments influences the development of marketing strategies and the allocation of resources to reach specific customer groups.
5. *Sales Force Deployment*: The sales force deployment is a discretionary variable. Pharmaceutical companies can decide how many sales representatives to assign to different territories, which healthcare providers to target, and the frequency and duration of sales visits. These decisions are based on market potential, prescribing patterns, competition, and strategic priorities.
6. *Key Opinion Leader (KOL) Engagement*: Pharmaceutical companies may identify and engage influential healthcare professionals like KOLs to advocate for their products or participate in advisory boards or educational sessions. Selection and level of engagement of KOLs will be based on the discretion of their marketing team, making it a discretionary variable.

These discretionary variables enable pharmaceutical marketers to adapt their strategies, tactics, and resource allocation according to market dynamics, business goals, and competitive landscape. They offer flexibility when reacting to market shifts and optimizing marketing efforts to maximize impactful promotional activities.

Implications for Pharma Marketers

Knowing and effectively using discretionary variables in pharmaceutical marketing can help marketers significantly. Here are a few key implications:

1. *Strategical Decision-Making*: Pharma marketers can utilize discretionary variables to make strategic decisions aligning with their marketing goals and strategic direction. Marketers can customize strategies based on market dynamics, competitive landscape considerations, and specific customer segments by controlling budget allocation, promotional channels used, target market segmentation criteria, or any other variable they deem important for making effective strategic decisions.
2. *Resource Optimization*: Marketers use discretionary variables to optimize resource allocation, ensuring budgets go toward activities with maximum return on investment (ROI). By studying the ROIs of different initiatives, marketers can ensure resources are directed at high-impact strategies to maximize results while optimizing the marketing mix to achieve desired results.
3. *Agility and Adaptability*: Marketers using discretionary variables can adapt their strategies and tactics as market conditions shift in response to customer feedback, emerging trends, or competitor activities, helping them remain responsive in today's evolving healthcare environment. This ensures agile marketing.
4. *Personalized and Targeted Marketing*: Pharma marketers can utilize discretionary variables to customize marketing efforts and target specific customer segments. By segmenting based on demographics, disease conditions, or treatment preferences, marketers can tailor messaging, content creation, and promotional activities to resonate with individual customer groups resulting in more successful campaigns.
5. *Improved Return On Investment and Performance Measurement*: Thanks to control over discretionary variables, marketers can effectively measure and assess the success of various marketing initiatives. Analyzing how different strategies affect KPIs, such as sales volume, market share, customer engagement, or brand awareness helps marketers assess ROI while refining marketing plans accordingly.
6. *Enhance Customer Engagement*: Pharma marketers can boost customer engagement through discretionary variables by employing personalized messaging, targeted campaigns, and tailored educational programs to engage target audiences while building stronger relationships between healthcare providers and patients. Such practices foster brand loyalty and lead to a better understanding and adoption of pharmaceutical products.

Overall, understanding and managing discretionary variables in pharmaceutical marketing enables marketers to make more informed decisions and optimize resource allocation more accurately in line with market dynamics and customer requirements. This leads to more agile resource allocation practices and creates innovative customer solutions that align better with market requirements, leading to enhanced marketing performance and business results.

Discriminant Analysis

Discriminant analysis is a statistical technique commonly utilized in pharmaceutical marketing to differentiate among different groups of patients or healthcare providers. As part of predictive analytics, discriminant analysis allows companies to determine which variables play the greatest role in accurately forecasting desired outcomes.

Discriminant analysis can be applied in pharmaceutical marketing to determine which patients or healthcare providers are more likely to respond positively to specific drugs or treatments so targeted marketing campaigns that resonate more easily with this audience can be developed accordingly.

Here are a few examples of how discriminant analysis can be used in pharmaceutical marketing:

A. *Patient Segmentation*: Pharmaceutical companies frequently use discriminant analysis for patient segmentation by grouping them based on age, gender, medical history, and lifestyle considerations. With this data, pharmaceutical firms can tailor marketing messages and campaigns toward each group of patients.

B. *Predicting Treatment Outcomes*: Discriminant analysis can identify factors most predictive of treatment outcomes, such as drug efficacy, adverse effects, and patient satisfaction. With this data, marketing campaigns highlighting benefits while simultaneously addressing concerns or side effects can be launched utilizing discriminant analysis as the tool of choice.

C. *Identifying Key Opinion Leaders*: The discriminant analysis allows healthcare providers to identify key opinion leaders based on specialty, research experience, and publications. With this data, marketing campaigns targeting key opinion leaders and forming relationships can be implemented effectively.

The discriminant analysis provides pharmaceutical companies with a powerful way of better understanding their target audiences and creating targeted marketing campaigns that are more likely successful. By identifying factors that distinguish different patient or healthcare provider groups, discriminant analysis enables pharmaceutical firms to create tailored messaging to increase effectiveness for both patient and provider outcomes.

How Pharma Companies Utilize Discriminant Analysis

Here are several examples of pharmaceutical companies using discriminant analysis as part of their marketing initiatives:

A. *Novartis*: Novartis used discriminant analysis to divide patients with heart failure into distinct groups according to age, gender, medical history, and symptoms. With this data, targeted messaging was sent directly to these patient segments about Entresto's benefits, increasing market share for the company's heart failure drug.

B. *Pfizer* used discriminant analysis to identify factors most indicative of patient adherence for treating rheumatoid arthritis medication regimens. Their analysis indicated that those with strong relationships between themselves and healthcare providers tended to adhere more readily. Pfizer applied this data towards creating an advertising campaign focused on communicating between these parties.

C. *GlaxoSmithKline* used discriminant analysis to identify characteristics of physicians most likely to prescribe their asthma medication Advair and found that physicians with more experience treating severe asthma are more likely to prescribe it than others. With this insight, GlaxoSmithKline developed targeted marketing messages highlighting its benefits to these patient segments.

Pharmaceutical companies can leverage discriminant analysis to understand their target audiences better and craft targeted marketing campaigns more effectively. Furthermore, by identifying factors most predictive of patient behaviors, such as drug efficacy or healthcare provider preferences, they can create personalized, relevant messaging that leads to improved patient experiences. This ultimately can result in improved health outcomes for patients and providers and sales increases for pharmaceutical manufacturers.

Discriminating Variables

Discriminating variables (also referred to as discriminant variables) are used in statistical analysis for differentiating between classes or groups of data, often being utilized during discriminant analysis— an approach often utilized during machine learning and pattern recognition that utilizes statistical techniques like discriminant analysis to identify which variables play the key role in differentiating among various classes or groups.

The discriminant analysis utilizes discriminating variables with high predictive power to differentiate or identify between data groups. For instance, medical researchers studying patients who either do or don't suffer from certain medical conditions might employ discriminant variables like age, gender, and blood pressure levels as effective ways of discriminating between these two categories of people.

Discriminating variables are used extensively in other statistical analysis techniques, including regression and cluster analyses. Here they serve two functions: they either predict or explain variations in dependent variables; or group them into clusters according to similarities and differences among values for certain variables.

Discriminating variables are vital tools in statistical analysis, as they help identify key elements that distinguish different groups and enable predictions or decisions based on those differences.

Discriminating Variables in Pharma Marketing

Within pharmaceutical marketing, discriminating variables are used to identify factors that distinguish among customers or patients and develop tailored marketing strategies tailored specifically towards each group's individual needs and preferences. Here are a few discriminating variables used in pharmaceutical marketing:

1. *Demographic Variables* like age, gender, income level, and education level can help distinguish different groups of customers and patients. For instance, a pharmaceutical company might develop different marketing messages and strategies for younger or older patients and those from differing income brackets.
2. *Disease-Related Variables*: Disease-related variables like the severity of illness, comorbidities, and disease stage can help

identify patients who require different healthcare needs and preferences. A pharmaceutical company might use disease-related variables such as these when developing marketing strategies aimed at early-stage cancer patients or those suffering from different comorbidities that limit treatment options for each type of cancer or comorbidity patients with differential results.

3. *Behavioral Variables*: Behavior variables like treatment adherence, healthcare provider preferences, and health-related beliefs can be used to differentiate patients with varied attitudes and behaviors regarding healthcare. A pharmaceutical company could implement different marketing strategies targeting highly engaged healthcare consumers who adhere well to treatment regimens about those less involved who may need additional support or education services.
4. *Geographic Variables*: Geographic variables like region, population density, and socioeconomic status can help pharmaceutical companies differentiate customers or patients within different demographic groups or locations. For instance, their marketing strategy might target urban versus rural customers or those from regions with different cultural or socioeconomic backgrounds.

Pharmaceutical companies can utilize various discriminating variables and target marketing strategies accordingly to gain greater insight into customer preferences and develop more targeted marketing campaigns that improve patient outcomes while driving business expansion.

Disintermediation

Disintermediation means avoiding transactional intermediaries like healthcare providers, pharmacies, or insurance companies to market pharmaceuticals directly to consumers. Digital channels like social media platforms, ad networks, and e-commerce platforms have simplified disintermediation for pharmaceutical firms looking to reach target demographics quickly and cost-effectively.

1. *Direct-to-Consumer Advertising (DTC)*: Pharmaceutical companies increasingly turn to direct-to-consumer (DTC) ads to efficiently reach their products directly to customers without depending on healthcare providers or pharmacies to distribute or prescribe those goods themselves. DTC ads come in various forms, such as TV commercials, print ads, online ads, and social media campaigns, each reaching consumers directly for greater awareness and demand generation without needing a prescription from healthcare providers or pharmacies first.
2. *Online Pharmacies*: Online pharmacies allow customers to directly purchase pharmaceutical products from manufacturers or distributors for cost savings and increased sales for pharmaceutical companies.
3. *Telemedicine*: Telemedicine platforms allow patients to connect with healthcare providers remotely without visiting an office, increasing convenience while cutting costs. Some pharmaceutical companies have even partnered with these telemedicine providers for virtual consultations and product prescriptions.

While disintermediation presents pharmaceutical companies with new opportunities for direct consumer engagement, it also presents unique challenges. Direct-to-consumer advertising of prescription drugs has been widely criticized as potentially leading to overuse or misuse due to reduced reliance on healthcare professionals, as individuals may start new medications without consulting first with them beforehand. Furthermore, disintermediation disrupts traditional healthcare models and may leave unknown who is ultimately accountable for patient safety and care.

Disease Management

Disease management programs typically encompass an integrated, multidisciplinary approach that brings healthcare providers, patients, and families together to manage a disease effectively. Such programs also utilize evidence-based guidelines or protocols to ensure patients receive appropriate care and treatments.

Disease management programs typically incorporate interventions and services, including patient education and self-management support; medication monitoring; lifestyle interventions like exercise or diet modifications; regular check-ins with healthcare providers; or care coordination between healthcare providers. Patient monitoring and tracking through devices or telemedicine services may also help.

Disease management programs offer great advantages to those suffering from chronic conditions that need ongoing medical care and support by improving education, monitoring, and support of their conditions. Disease management programs allow these patients to control their conditions better while avoiding complications and improving their quality of life.

Disease Management in Pharma Marketing

Pharma marketers use products and services designed to aid patients in managing chronic diseases effectively to enhance health outcomes, including medication management, lifestyle modifications, patient education programs, and support services. Disease management programs typically take an integrative approach with medication, lifestyle modification plans, patient education classes as well as additional support services being included as components.

Pharma companies are essential in disease management by producing medications to treat chronic illnesses like diabetes, cardiovascular disease, and cancer. Furthermore, pharmaceutical firms may offer additional disease-management services like patient education sessions with nurses and remote monitoring capabilities.

What Pharma Can Do

Pharmaceutical companies can play an invaluable role in disease management by creating programs and services to assist patients with chronic condition in managing their illnesses effectively, offering support and resources, and increasing patient satisfaction while building brand loyalty with patients. Here are a few strategies pharmaceutical companies can utilize in disease management:

1. *Create Disease-Specific Education and Support Programs*: Pharmaceutical companies are well suited to create disease-specific education and support programs designed to equip their patients with more efficient knowledge of managing their conditions. They include patient education materials, online support groups, and mobile apps that allow patients to monitor symptoms and treatment progress.
2. *Partner with Healthcare Providers*: Pharmaceutical companies should collaborate closely with healthcare providers when developing and implementing disease management programs to ensure these are evidence-based and follow clinical guidelines.
3. *Utilize Technology*: Pharmaceutical companies should utilize technology as an invaluable asset in disease management. They can leverage it by creating innovative solutions, such as wearables, telemedicine services, and mobile apps that enable patients to monitor symptoms while communicating with healthcare providers about them.
4. *Medication Adherence Support*: Adherence is vital when managing chronic conditions and pharmaceutical companies may provide medication adherence support services like reminder apps, calendars, and patient education materials to their customers.
5. *Monitor and Analyze Patient Data*: By collecting and analyzing patient data, pharmaceutical companies can uncover insights that inform disease management programs as well as track outcomes of treatments over time, and gauge the effectiveness of disease management programs over time.

Pharmaceutical companies can increase patient outcomes, enhance satisfaction, and build brand loyalty by effectively helping patients manage their illnesses or conditions.

What Pharma is Doing

Below are examples of how pharmaceutical companies are employing disease management programs as part of their marketing initiatives:

1. *Novo Nordisk* has developed *Cornerstones4Care* as an integrated disease management program for individuals with diabetes. The website and mobile app feature resources to aid healthcare providers and patients, while the latter allows patients to track blood sugar levels, medications, and health data continuously.
2. *Pfizer* offers the *RA Navigate* disease management program as part of support services to assist people living with rheumatoid arthritis in managing their conditions more easily and enhancing their quality of life. Support services offered include nurse counseling, educational resources, and financial aid to eligible patients, all aimed at helping manage symptoms more effectively and improving the quality-of-life for these individuals.
3. *Merck* offers *The Heart Truth* disease management program as part of their treatment for cardiovascular conditions. It features educational resources, patient support services, and mobile applications designed to assist individuals in managing their conditions more effectively while decreasing risk of complications.
4. *Sanofi* offers its disease management program for cancer patients called *iCAN* to provide customized support services like nurse counseling and assistance, managing treatment side effects.

These are just a few examples of how pharmaceutical companies employ disease management programs as marketing strategies. By offering comprehensive patient support, these pharma firms can improve patient outcomes, raise patient satisfaction levels and differentiate themselves from competitors by offering better patient support programs.

Disparaging Copy

Disparaging copy in pharmaceutical marketing refers to using disparaging language against competitors' products or services to gain market share or advantage in an unethical and damaging fashion. Such statements could compromise both reputations of those doing the criticizing as well as those being targeted with this tactic.

Examples of disparaging copy in pharmaceutical marketing include companies emphasizing potential adverse side effects of competing medications in their marketing materials rather than emphasizing their product's benefits. While such advertising might make consumers wary of competing brands, but also cause anxiety surrounding medication use generally; thus, it may not always be effective as an advertising tactic.

Disparaging copy in pharmaceutical marketing occurs when companies make false or misleading claims against rival products in their advertisements, violating advertising regulations and risking legal ramifications for breaking them.

Negative language should generally not be employed when marketing pharmaceutical products; doing so can damage a company's reputation and may not increase market share. Instead, businesses should promote the benefits of their product offerings while developing strong brands with reputations based on trust and reliability.

Display Advertising

Display advertising is a type of online advertising that involves creating visual ads on websites, social media platforms, and other digital channels. In pharma marketing, display advertising can effectively reach and engage with target audiences, including healthcare providers and patients. Here are some key aspects of display advertising in pharma marketing:

1. *Compliance*: Pharmaceutical companies must adhere to strict regulatory guidelines when creating display ads. Ads must be truthful and not misleading, including certain disclosures and safety information. Pharma companies usually work closely with regulatory experts to ensure their ads comply with all relevant regulations.
2. *Targeting*: Display ads are designed to reach specific audiences based on several variables such as their geographic location, demographics, interests, and behaviors. This allows pharma companies to reach those most likely to engage with their messages while increasing engagement rates.
3. *Creative*: Display ads' visual design and messaging can significantly impact their effectiveness. Pharma marketing ads may feature medication images, lifestyle imagery, or educational graphics, depending on the campaign goals and audience. The message may focus on the benefits of the medication or the importance of disease management.
4. *Tracking and Optimization*: Display advertising provides data on impressions, clicks, conversions, and ROI that pharma companies can utilize to adjust campaigns over time and enhance targeting, creativity, and messaging for more successful ads.
5. *Ad Formats*: Display ads can take many forms, from banner and interstitial ads to native ads and video ads. Each format offers advantages and disadvantages. Finding the ideal solution depends on campaign goals and target audience considerations.

Display advertising can be an effective tool in pharma marketing when done correctly. Pharma companies can create engaging and effective display ad campaigns by following regulatory guidelines, targeting the right audiences, creating compelling creatives, and tracking and optimizing the right ad formats.

Disruption

Until recently, pharmaceutical marketing relied heavily on in-person sales visits and conventions as traditional channels to reach target audiences. However, new digital technologies and changing consumer tastes have altered this model and presented opportunities for pharmaceutical firms to reach them more directly.

One major development in pharmaceutical marketing has been its move toward digital and online channels. Pharma companies now use social media, email marketing, and other digital channels to connect with healthcare professionals and patients, which has allowed them to reach wider audiences while providing more targeted messaging.

One major disruption has been the surge in patient-centric care. Today's patients are becoming more involved and informed in making healthcare decisions. Pharmaceutical companies have responded by creating patient-oriented marketing strategies intended to equip individuals with information so that they may make well-informed decisions when making healthcare choices.

Telemedicine and remote healthcare have provided pharmaceutical companies with opportunities to interact directly with patients and healthcare providers by offering virtual education/training programs or remote patient monitoring support services.

Disruption in pharmaceutical marketing has driven companies to be more innovative and flexible with their marketing strategies and focus on meeting the needs and preferences of target audiences.

Disruption in pharmaceutical marketing refers to introducing innovative ideas or technologies that alter an industry's operations, like using new marketing strategies, emerging technologies, or innovative drug development and distribution approaches. Some examples of disruption include:

1. *Direct-to-Consumer Advertising (DTCA)*: In the past, pharmaceutical companies marketed their products to healthcare providers, who then prescribed them to patients. Now DTCA campaigns are emerging as an avenue of advertising for these pharmaceutical products, directly targeting individuals through TV commercials, online ads, or any other relevant medium.
2. *Digital Health Technologies*: With the proliferation of wearables, mobile apps, and telemedicine technology, revolutionary healthcare delivery methods like wearables have emerged. Pharmaceutical companies are turning to these innovative platforms to increase patient outcomes while increasing engagement levels and offering personalized treatment plans.
3. *Precision Medicine*: Precision medicine involves tailoring medical treatments specifically to each individual. This strategy uses genetic tests and other diagnostic tools to pinpoint which therapies would provide the optimal treatments. Pharmaceutical companies invest heavily in precision medicine to create targeted therapies for certain patient populations.
4. *Artificial Intelligence*: Artificial intelligence and machine learning (ML) have proven instrumental to the operations of pharmaceutical companies, with AI analyzing large datasets, recognizing new drug targets quickly, and speeding development timeframes significantly faster.
5. *Value-based Pricing*: Under value-based pricing, drug pricing decisions are determined based on how effective they are at improving patient outcomes, rather than traditional models that account for costs related to developing and producing the drug. Value-based pricing has quickly gained ground as an approach to managing healthcare expenses while expanding patient access to innovative treatments.
6. *Digital Therapeutics*: Digital therapeutics is an emerging healthcare technology using software programs and wearable devices to treat various medical conditions, like mobile apps. Pharmaceutical firms such as Novartis are collaborating with digital therapeutics companies to collaborate and develop novel treatments.
7. *Blockchain Technology*: As an efficient method to store and share data safely, blockchain provides an ideal way for supply chain management, combatting drug counterfeiting, and increasing patient data privacy. These benefits are currently under evaluation by pharmaceutical companies like Pfizer.

Pharma's Disruptive Moves

Below are a few examples of disruptive practices among pharmaceutical companies:

1. *Pfizer's Viagra* was revolutionary when first released for commercial sale in 1998 and transformed sexual health and well-being conversation worldwide.
2. *Gilead Sciences' Sovaldi*: Since Sovaldi became available for treating hepatitis C in 2013, its impactful release caused waves throughout the healthcare industry and revolutionized how pharmaceutical companies approached drug development for chronic illnesses. It even led to some government regulations being adjusted accordingly!
3. *Novartis CAR-T Therapy*: Novartis' CAR-T Therapy is a groundbreaking cancer therapy solution, making significant strides toward curing certain blood cancers with remarkable success. CAR-T therapy extracts immune cells from patients' blood, modifies them to recognize and destroy cancerous cells, then re-infusing back into them. The US FDA approved CAR-T therapy in 2017 after showing remarkable success against previously incurable forms.
4. *Roche's Avastin*: One of the earliest drugs designed to target blood vessels that feed tumors, Avastin first gained FDA approval for use against colon cancer but has been expanded for use against numerous forms. Avastin offered an unconventional cancer therapy solution by targeting its blood supply rather than targeting cancerous cells directly.
5. *Amgen's Enbrel*: Enbrel is an FDA-approved biological medication for treating autoimmune conditions like rheumatoid arthritis and psoriasis, becoming one of the most frequently prescribed treatments against such ailments,

surpassing traditional approaches which relied upon nonspecific immunosuppressant medicines as an immuno-modulatory solution.

Disruptive Marketing

Disruptive marketing in the pharmaceutical industry involves employing novel and unconventional strategies to set one company's products or services apart from competitors and capture target audiences' interest. Here are a few examples of disruptive marketing:

1. *Social Media Marketing*: Pharmaceutical companies increasingly rely upon platforms like Facebook, Twitter, LinkedIn, or Instagram as channels of engagement between themselves and patients, as well as healthcare professionals and general audiences, leveraging these platforms to connect with patients, healthcare professionals, and other stakeholders.
2. *Influencer Marketing*: Influencer marketing refers to partnering with social media influencers (patient advocates or healthcare influencers) to market your product or service and reach a wider audience. Pharma companies partnering with influential bloggers or patient advocacy networks is another form of influencer marketing they may utilize to reach broader audiences with their offerings.
3. *Content Marketing*: Content marketing involves producing and sharing educational and engaging content such as blog posts, videos, and infographics to spread information about pharma products and services with healthcare providers and patients and establish them as thought leaders in their respective industries. Pharma companies utilize content marketing to build awareness among patients and healthcare providers about them, positioning themselves as thought leaders within those fields and improving patient care through continued awareness campaigns.
4. *Gamification* refers to using game mechanics like points, rewards, and leaderboards to engage users and motivate them to take action. Pharmaceutical companies employ this tactic to encourage patients to adhere to their medication regimen and promote healthier behaviors amongst patients.
5. *Virtual and Augmented Reality Technologies*: Pharma companies use virtual and augmented reality technologies to provide engaging experiences for patients and healthcare providers. Pharma firms may use VR simulation to simulate medical procedures or train healthcare staff on various tasks.

Disruptive Marketing By Pharma: Some Examples

Below are examples of pharmaceutical companies employing disruptive marketing to engage their audiences more directly while distinguishing themselves from their competition:

1. *Social Media Marketing*: Pfizer's Twitter (@pfizer) accounts are regularly updated with news, educational material, and research updates about its products and initiatives. Pfizer also uses Facebook Live for virtual events, online webinars, and real-time updates about clinical trials or studies at its facilities.
2. *Influencer Marketing*: Roche Diabetes Care collaborated with various influencers across social media to market its AccuCheck blood glucose meters, including working closely with an influential diabetes blogger to create blog posts and videos about monitoring blood glucose levels.
3. *Content Marketing*: Novartis Oncology provides educational resources, news updates, and support services for cancer patients and caregivers through the *My Oncology Coach* website. My Oncology Coach features videos, articles, and infographics to help visitors better comprehend their condition and potential treatment plans.
4. *Gamification*: Novartis developed *My PKU Life*, a mobile application that uses gamification to help patients with Phenylketonuria (PKU) adhere to their dietary restrictions. The app tracks food intake daily while offering incentives and rewards for following the prescribed regimen.
5. *Merck* has developed a virtual reality training program for healthcare professionals that uses virtual reality simulation to demonstrate cancer's mechanisms and chemotherapy's effects, helping them better comprehend both. Healthcare workers can practice administering chemotherapy safely in this safe, controlled environment.

Disruptive marketing in pharma entails employing novel and creative strategies to reach and engage target audiences more meaningfully and positively, thus differentiating themselves from competitors while forging stronger connections with their audiences. By adopting such initiatives, companies can differentiate themselves and establish lasting relationships.

Dissonance Attribution Model

The dissonance attribution model is a theoretical framework used in psychology and marketing to understand how individuals make sense of conflicting information or experiences. Pharmaceutical marketers employing the dissonance attribution model believe that when consumers encounter information or experiences undermining their beliefs about medication and treatments, they may experience psychological discomfort, otherwise known as dissonance.

Consumers can employ various strategies to decrease this dissonance, such as reframing information to reflect existing beliefs, seeking further details to support or refute conflicting information, or altering attitudes or beliefs. Hence, they are in line with the new data.

Dissonance Attribution Model in the Pharma Industry

When presented with conflicting information regarding the safety or efficacy of medication, the dissonance attribution model becomes especially relevant as consumers experience confusion between the belief that certain drugs are safe and effective when news reports containing adverse reaction data suggest otherwise; such information includes news stories of adverse reactions as well as clinical trial results that don't support initial impression. The dissonance attribution model suggests that the consumer may experience psychological discomfort of dissonance and may then engage in strategies to reduce this discomfort and resolve conflicting information.

Pharmaceutical marketers may seek to influence consumers' attribution of dissonance by framing information to minimize the potential for conflicting information or by providing additional information to support the safety and efficacy of their products. Additionally, they may attempt to anticipate and address potential sources of dissonance in their marketing materials by acknowledging their products' potential side effects or limitations and providing strategies to mitigate these concerns.

Dissonance Attribution Model in Pharma: Some Examples

The following examples show how the dissonance attribution model might be applied in pharmaceutical marketing:

A. A consumer sees a commercial for a medication that claims it is safe and effective for treating a certain condition. However, the consumer has previously heard negative news reports about the medication's side effects. The dissonance attribution model suggests that the consumer may experience psychological discomfort or dissonance as their beliefs about the medications are challenged. The pharmaceutical marketer may seek to address this dissonance by providing additional information supporting the medication's safety and efficacy, such as clinical trial data or expert comments.

B. A consumer is prescribed a medication by the doctor but later learns from a friend that the medication caused negative side effects in their friend's experience. The dissonance attribution suggests that the consumer may experience dissonance as their initial beliefs about the safety and efficacy of the medication are challenged. Pharmaceutical marketers may address this dissonance by providing educational materials outlining potential adverse reactions of medication and strategies to alleviate them, such as taking it with food or at different times during the day.

C. A consumer sees an advertisement for a new medication that claims to be more effective than existing treatments. However, the consumer has previously been skeptical of new medications and prefers to stick with tried-and-true treatments. The dissonance attribution model suggests that the consumer may experience dissonance as their beliefs about the effectiveness are challenged. The pharmaceutical marketer may seek to address this dissonance by providing additional information about the research and development process behind the new medication and emphasizing the benefits it offers over existing treatments.

Consumers respond to ads promoting new medications which claim to be more effective than existing treatments, yet have previously been wary of such claims and tend to opt for established options instead of potentially risky newcomers. According to the dissonance attribution model, they could experience dissonance as their beliefs regarding effectiveness are challenged; to alleviate such dissonance, pharmaceutical marketers may provide further details regarding research and development processes related to the new medication in question, emphasizing its advantages over older forms.

Dissonance Hierarchy

In pharmaceutical marketing, the Dissonance Hierarchy is a theoretical framework that describes three levels of cognitive dissonance experienced by customers when exposed to information that conflicts with their existing beliefs, attitudes, or behaviors associated with certain medications or treatments. Each level represents different degrees of psychological discomfort:

A. *Post-Purchase Dissonance*: After customers purchase medication or treatments, post-purchase dissonance can occur as they question whether their decision was correct because the information challenges their belief. They could encounter information that contradicts the perception that this medication was ideal for addressing post-purchasing dissonance effectively; pharmaceutical marketers may seek ways to strengthen consumer decisions by providing more details of benefits, such as patient testimonials or clinical trial data to reinforce customers' decisions about buying it.
B. *Pre-Purchase Dissonance*: Consumers may experience pre-purchase dissonance when considering various treatment and medication options and may encounter conflicting information regarding safety, efficacy, or cost-effectiveness between options. To address pre-purchase dissonance effectively, pharmaceutical marketers could provide consumers with additional details of the benefits/risks of each option and resources to assist in making more informed decisions.
C. *Dissonance Avoidance*: This level of dissonance occurs when a consumer actively avoids information that challenges their beliefs or attitudes about a medication or treatment. They may avoid information that conflicts with their beliefs to avoid experiencing dissonance. To address dissonance avoidance, pharmaceutical marketers may seek to provide information consistent with the consumer's beliefs and attitudes while acknowledging potential concerns or limitations of the medication or treatment. This approach may help build trust with the consumer and reduce the likelihood that they will avoid information that challenges their beliefs.

Distribution

Distribution in pharmaceutical marketing refers to moving pharmaceutical products from their manufacturers directly to end users, typically patients or healthcare providers, via an intricate network of wholesalers, distributors, pharmacies, and hospitals collaborating to make sure the appropriate pharmaceutical products reach them when and where they want.

Pharmaceutical marketing relies heavily on effective distribution to reach end-users when needed. Here are a few essential points about distribution in pharma marketing:

1. *Supply Chain Management*: Efficient supply chain management is key for timely pharmaceutical product deliveries. This involves optimizing inventory levels and distribution routes while working closely with intermediaries along the supply chain.
2. *Distribution Channels*: Pharmaceutical companies can choose among various distribution channels for pharmaceutical products, including wholesalers, distributors, pharmacies, and hospitals, to meet their distribution requirements. Each has different strengths and weaknesses; choosing one may depend on which products must first be distributed.
3. *Compliance Issues*: Pharmaceutical distribution is heavily regulated to protect patient safety. Pharmaceutical companies must abide by guidelines such as Good Distribution Practices (GDP) and Good Manufacturing Practices (GMP) when selling pharmaceuticals.
4. *Logistics*: Successful logistics management is essential to timely pharmaceutical product deliveries. This involves overseeing transportation, storage, and inventory levels to guarantee products reach customers efficiently and quickly.
5. *Sales Forecasting*: Sales forecasting is essential to meeting consumer demands accurately and optimizing supply chains accordingly. Pharmaceutical companies must use data and analytics to accurately anticipate customer requirements to forecast demand accurately and maximize profits accordingly.

Distribution Channels

There are various distribution channels used in pharmaceutical marketing:

1. *Wholesalers*: Wholesalers purchase pharmaceutical products directly from manufacturers and resell them to distributors, pharmacies, or hospitals for distribution or sale to end-users. Sometimes, they also provide storage management and inventory tracking or delivery services.
2. *Distributors*: Distributors deliver pharmaceutical products to pharmacies, hospitals, and other healthcare facilities for distribution. Most specialize in certain product categories or geographical regions.

3. *Pharmacies*: Pharmacies serve as primary suppliers of pharmaceutical products to end-users such as patients. Retail and mail-order pharmacies may both sell pharmaceutical items directly.
4. *Hospitals*: Hospitals generally purchase large volumes of pharmaceuticals through distribution systems or directly from manufacturers or wholesalers to meet patients' healthcare needs, often via direct contracts with these organizations.
5. *Group Purchasing Organizations (GPOs)*: GPOs offer healthcare facilities the chance to purchase discounted pharmaceuticals by negotiating directly with manufacturers on their behalf and taking advantage of group rates with them. They do this for hospitals and clinics so their facilities can purchase pharmaceuticals at reduced rates.
6. *Specialty Distributors*: Specialty distributors specialize in dispensing complex medications used for oncology or rare disease treatment at competitive costs, often offering storage and handling services as part of the package deal.
7. *Direct-to-Patient Distribution*: Direct-to-patient distribution entails shipping pharmaceutical products directly from online pharmacies or mail-order services to patients.

Pharmaceutical companies must carefully choose their distribution channels based on product type, target market, and geographical location to ensure customers can find their product when and where needed. They should implement strategies designed to satisfy end-user demands at every opportunity.

Diversification

Diversification is an innovative marketing approach in which pharmaceutical companies expand their product portfolio with complementary but different offerings that differentiate from those already offered. Diversification can help pharmaceutical firms tap new customer segments while expanding into new markets, and decreasing reliance on only one product or market segment.

Here are a few examples of pharmaceutical companies' successful diversification marketing strategies:

1. Novartis Pharmaceuticals Corporation is a global pharmaceutical company with an expansive product portfolio in healthcare products and services, such as diagnostic tools, eye care items, animal health solutions, and animal-health items. Novartis was originally formed to develop pharmaceutical drugs; today, its portfolio encompasses numerous healthcare-related offerings, from diagnostic tools and eye care to animal healthcare products.
2. Pfizer, another pharmaceutical giant that has leveraged diversification to broaden its product offering, offers pharmaceutical products and consumer healthcare items like over-the-counter medicine and vitamins.
3. GlaxoSmithKline (GSK), an international pharmaceutical company with offices worldwide and over 300 products on offer, including vaccines and consumer healthcare items like toothpaste and pain relievers, has expanded its product offering through diversifying into vaccine development, manufacturing, and consumer healthcare items.
4. Johnson & Johnson is an innovative healthcare company that offers pharmaceuticals, medical devices, and consumer healthcare products across a wide spectrum. Johnson & Johnson develops and manufactures drugs targeted to treat specific conditions, while their portfolio also encompasses surgical instruments and diagnostic equipment for use by hospitals worldwide.

Diversification can be an effective marketing strategy for pharmaceutical companies seeking to broaden their product offering and access new customer segments. By diversifying into multiple product and service lines, businesses can diversify revenue streams while decreasing dependency on any one product or market segment.

Diversity

Diversity refers to differences and variations among people, such as race, ethnicity, gender, age, culture, religion, language, socioeconomic status, physical and mental ability, and sexual orientation, among many other characteristics. Diversity is an integral aspect of human society that provides richness and strength by teaching us new perspectives while appreciating different experiences. Diversity promotes innovation and creativity in workplace settings by gathering individuals with disparate backgrounds and different ideas, allowing greater innovation and creative decision-making from these unique viewpoints.

Diversity is increasingly significant across many aspects of modern business, from pharmaceutical marketing to recruitment practices. With our world becoming ever more diverse, companies must ensure their marketing initiatives reflect all parts of society.

Pharmaceutical companies who prioritize diversity in their marketing initiatives stand to gain from prioritizing diversity as part of their efforts, such as reaching a wider audience, strengthening customer relations, and creating an identity as an inclusive and socially responsible organization.

How Pharma Can Promote Diversity

Pharmaceutical companies can advance diversity within their marketing initiatives in several ways. Consider the following, for instance:

1. *Inclusive Advertising*: Pharmaceutical companies should incorporate images of people of diverse racial and ethnic backgrounds, age ranges, and gender identities into their advertising and marketing materials for more inclusive healthcare marketing efforts. This can create more inclusive campaigns.
2. *Tailored Marketing Messages*: Businesses should try to understand different communities' healthcare needs and concerns and craft tailored marketing messages accordingly, creating campaigns tailored specifically towards ethnic or racial groups' concerns.
3. *Forge Partnerships with Diverse Organizations*: Pharmaceutical companies have an opportunity to partner with diverse organizations and communities to advance health in underrepresented communities through sponsoring health fairs or supporting initiatives designed to meet the healthcare needs of underserved populations.
4. *Diversity Hiring*: Companies can increase diversity in marketing by hiring employees from diverse backgrounds and ensuring that teams represent the communities they serve to ensure marketing messages address the needs and concerns of diverse populations.
5. *Accessibility*: Companies can ensure accessibility in their marketing initiatives by creating promotional materials in multiple languages and formats that are easily accessible for those with disabilities. This helps ensure everyone can access and understand the information needed to make informed healthcare decisions. This way, everyone has equal access and understanding.

Promoting diversity in pharmaceutical marketing is more than a social statement; it's also an intelligent business tactic, helping companies connect with a wider audience and forge stronger customer relationships.

Dogs

The BCG Matrix or Boston Consulting Group Matrix, as it is commonly known, is an analytical management tool created by Bruce D. Henderson, the founder of Boston Consulting Group, in early 1970s to analyze product portfolios based on market growth rate and relative market share. It's been utilized successfully ever since its inception!

The BCG Matrix categorizes products produced by companies into four quadrants--Stars, Cash Cows, Question Marks, and Dogs— representing different strategic positions within an organization.

Under the BCG Matrix, "Dogs" refers to business units or products with low market shares in a slow-growth industry. *Dogs* typically give minimal returns when money is put into them. They often constitute cash traps where investment yields no real dividends in return.

A *Dog* in the pharmaceutical industry could be a drug that once had high sales but has since fallen behind as new, more effective versions from competitors, or its patent has expired, and generic versions are now available. A Dog still requires investments for production, marketing, and supply management purposes, yet profitability would be low.

Recognizing "Dogs" within their product portfolio for pharmaceutical marketers is paramount to successfully managing their product portfolio. Marketers might choose to sell off these items or discontinue them completely. However, in certain instances, they might keep these offerings if they still meet the unique needs of specific patient populations or support brand reputation or relationships among healthcare professionals.

Managing *Dogs* effectively avoids wasting resources and instead invests them in better, more promising products (Stars or Cash Cows in BCG matrix terminology).

Implications for Marketers

Strategic Decisions on *Dogs* within pharmaceutical product portfolios have many repercussions for marketers:

1. *Resource Allocation*: Recognizing products as Dogs allows marketers to make more informed decisions regarding resource allocation. Spending heavily on marketing products with low market shares and growth potential may not justify investing heavily; resources would likely be better utilized by targeting Stars (high market shares, fast growth potential) or Cash Cows (low market shares, slow growth).

2. *Strategic Deliberations*: Discontinuation may make sense strategically; however, any decisions must be carefully considered, assessing the impact on patients who still use "Dog" products, potential effects on relationships with healthcare providers, and possible financial implications of discontinuation.
3. *Diversifying Your Portfolio*: Understanding where each product falls on the BCG matrix can assist marketers in creating more diversified portfolios to minimize risks related to over reliance on certain items while assuring steady cash flows and steady sales streams.
4. *Market Positioning*: Dogs may be repositioned into niche markets to become cash cows for smaller market niches. Doing this requires in-depth knowledge of their target audience and individual patient groups' unique requirements.
5. *Innovation and Development*: Recognizing a product as a *Dog* can also spur innovation. It can trigger the development of improved versions of the product or new products that better meet the needs of patients and healthcare providers.
6. *Communication Strategy*: When communicating the discontinuation of products deemed as *Dogs*, healthcare providers and patients must be fully informed. If necessary, communication must also include possible alternative products which might replace discontinued ones.

Pharmaceutical marketers need a firm grasp on portfolio analysis tools like the BCG matrix for effective strategic decision-making and to direct marketing efforts towards products with greater investment returns.

Domino Effect

The domino effect refers to situations in which one action or event leads to a series of further reactions, often as the result of dominoes' gameplay: one falling domino can trigger another domino's fall until all have fallen! Its name comes from this chain reaction effect of events.

Real-world examples of domino effects include closing down due to economic issues causing employees to lose jobs, the closure of related companies reliant on its services, and an overall reduction in the local economy. A natural disaster like an earthquake or hurricane may create similar results, with infrastructure damage, power outages, transportation disruptions, and social and economic ramifications being experienced as ripple effects.

The domino effect can also be observed in complex systems like global economies, where financial crises in one nation may cause ripples and have far-reaching economic implications worldwide.

Domino Effect in Pharma Marketing

Pharma marketers may observe a domino effect in many forms when marketing new drugs, such as when new medications hit the market and spark chain reactions that impact healthcare providers, patients, and pharmaceutical industries.

Imagine that patients and healthcare providers will receive a successful new drug; demand may increase, leading to greater production and sales for its pharmaceutical company and similar drugs being developed by competing firms to compete on the market.

However, when new medications produce unexpected side effects or fail to meet patient or healthcare provider satisfaction levels, sales could decline or lead to recall action being taken against it, potentially damaging its manufacturer and prompting increased scrutiny by regulatory bodies as well as possibly having negative repercussions for similar drug development by other firms.

When it comes to drug pricing, we see similar dominoes falling. When pharmaceutical companies raise drug costs, this often sparks events affecting patients, healthcare providers, and insurers, ultimately leading to greater scrutiny against the pharmaceutical industry overall and potential changes to pricing policy/regulation measures.

These examples demonstrate how decisions and actions in pharmaceutical marketing can have far-reaching ramifications that influence various stakeholders and the industry as a whole.

The domino effect illustrates how events and decisions in pharmaceutical marketing are interdependent and emphasizes the significance of considering any possible ripple effects from decisions or actions taken.

Dosage Form

Dosage forms refer to the different ways medications are formulated for patient administration. Some common dosage forms include:

1. *Tablets and Capsules*: These are solid dosage forms that are taken orally and contain medication in a compressed or powdered form. Aspirin, ibuprofen, and paracetamol are among the many medications commonly available as tablets; antibiotics like amoxicillin and

supplements like fish oil may come packaged as capsules.

2. *Solutions and Syrups*: These liquid dosage forms used for oral administration contain a medication solution mixed with water and other solvents. Cough syrups, oral rehydration solutions, and some liquid antibiotics are examples of solutions.
3. *Suspensions*: These are liquid dosage forms containing insoluble medication particles suspended in a liquid. Calamine lotion for external use and some cough syrups for oral use are available as suspensions.
4. *Injectable Forms*: Dosages administered via injection include intravenous (IV), intramuscular (IM), and subcutaneous (SC). Common injection-based dosage forms include vaccines, insulin injections, and many antibiotics.
5. *Topical Forms*: These dosage forms applied directly to the skin include creams, ointments, gels, and transdermal patches like hydrocortisone cream. Other examples are neomycin ointment or nicotine patches as topical forms of treatment.
6. *Suppositories* are dosage forms inserted into the rectum or vagina and contain the medication in a solid form that melts at body temperature. Medications for constipation, like bisacodyl and promethazine for nausea, are available in suppository form.
7. *Inhalation Forms*: Dosages delivered into the lungs through various inhalation devices like nebulizers, inhalers, and nasal sprays may include salbutamol for bronchodilatory use as well as corticosteroids like Budesonide for corticosteroid treatment and nasal decongestants like Oxymetazoline decongestant for nasal decongestion purposes. These forms may also provide other advantages over oral medication forms like capsules.

Double Jeopardy

Double jeopardy is a legal concept designed to prevent individuals found not guilty or sentenced for an offense from being tried again, thus avoiding multiple prosecutions or penalties for their crime. Based on this principle, once someone is no longer facing additional legal proceedings for that same crime, they cannot be subjected to another trial for it again.

Double jeopardy can be traced back to the Fifth Amendment of the US Constitution, which stipulates: No person shall be subject to being twice put in jeopardy of life or limb for the same offense, thus ensuring once an individual has been found innocent of a specific crime they cannot be tried again for it.

Double jeopardy was developed to protect individuals from harassment, abuse, and multiple prosecutions by the government. This ensures that legal processes end quickly without the government repeatedly using its power against an individual until a desired result has been attained.

Double Jeopardy in Pharma Marketing

In pharmaceutical marketing, double jeopardy refers to instances when an organization faces multiple penalties or legal actions for marketing activities that violate federal guidelines or ethical codes. This situation arises when multiple regulatory or legal bodies, such as government agencies or law enforcement, bring multiple actions against one company for marketing and promotion activities to ensure safety and accuracy for healthcare providers and patients. Violating these regulations, such as off-label promotion (promoting drugs for uses not approved by regulatory authorities), misleading advertising, or failing to provide safety information, could result in fines or legal actions against violators.

At times, different regulatory bodies like the Food and Drug Administration (FDA) and the Department of Justice (DOJ) in the US and similar law-enforcing organizations elsewhere may possess jurisdiction to investigate or prosecute misconduct independently. This could lead to potential multiple enforcement actions for one violation by pharmaceutical companies, potentially resulting in multiple penalties or legal ramifications being levied upon them for each one of their offenses.

However, it must be pointed out that double jeopardy protections in legal systems generally refer to criminal prosecutions where individuals cannot be tried multiple times for one offense. When applied to pharmaceutical marketing violations, enforcement actions are usually civil rather than criminal and therefore do not fall within this concept of double jeopardy.

Pharmaceutical companies are highly regulated, and violations of marketing regulations may lead to severe consequences for companies. Avoid multiple enforcement actions and maintain transparency and accuracy in product communication strategies.

Double Jeopardy in Pharma Marketing: Some Examples

Here are a few examples to illustrate double jeopardy in pharmaceutical marketing:

1. *Off-Label Promotion*: When pharmaceutical companies engage in off-label promotions by marketing drugs for uses that do not have regulatory approval, violations could result in enforcement actions from multiple regulatory bodies, such as the FDA, DOJ, or state attorney general among them— all at once for one off-label promotion campaign. Each regulatory body could conduct its investigations and enforce penalties accordingly, leading to multiple actions being brought against the same off-label promotion activity by this pharmaceutical company.
2. *False Advertising*: When pharmaceutical companies run marketing campaigns that include false or misleading claims about the effectiveness or safety of their product, violating advertising regulations; this could bring penalties from various regulatory bodies such as the Federal Trade Commission (FTC) and FDA, who possess the authority to investigate false advertising claims that may lead to individual enforcement actions against the same violations, resulting in separate penalties being enforced by each regulatory agency.
3. *Failure to Disclose Safety Information*: If a pharmaceutical company fails to appropriately disclose important safety information about its products, endangering public health in the process, they could face legal actions from regulatory bodies like FDA as well as civil suits from affected patients claiming harm due to this violation; regulatory bodies could potentially impose fines and other penalties, while civil suits seek damages for the injuries caused. Thus, the company could face multiple legal actions for failing to disclose safety info.

It is important to note that every case's circumstances and outcomes will differ.

Double Jeopardy in Pharma Marketing: Some Examples

Pharma companies may experience double jeopardy due to multiple penalties or legal actions for their marketing practices that resulted in multiple penalties or legal actions from authorities:

1. *Purdue Pharma*: Purdue Pharma, the manufacturer of Oxycontin, faced multiple legal actions and penalties related to its marketing practices. In 2007, the company and three executives pleaded guilty to criminal charges of misbranding the drug and paid over $600 million in fines. However, in later years, they faced additional legal actions from states, municipalities, and individuals who alleged deceptive marketing practices, contributing to the opioid crisis. These cases involved various settlements, fines, and ongoing litigation.
2. *Johnson & Johnson*: Johnson & Johnson has faced multiple legal actions and penalties for different products and marketing practices. For example, in 2019, an Oklahoma judge ordered the company to pay $572 million for its role in the state's opioid crisis. Additionally, Johnson & Johnson has faced lawsuits and settlements related to allegations of deceptive marketing for drugs such as Risperdal and Xarelto.
3. *GlaxoSmithKline (GSK)*: GSK has faced enforcement actions and penalties for various marketing-related violations. In 2012, the company agreed to pay $3 billion to settle criminal and civil charges related to unlawful promotion and failure to report safety data for several drugs, including Paxil and Wellbutrin. This settlement involved multiple government agencies, including the DOJ and the FDA.

These examples show instances in which pharmaceutical companies have experienced severe penalties or legal actions due to their marketing practices, leading to multiple penalties or legal actions being brought against them. However, it's important to research specific cases and refer to up-to-date information for the latest developments and outcomes.

Drip Campaigns

Drip campaign in pharma marketing is a type of email marketing campaign that involves sending automated, pre-written emails to targeted recipients over some time. In pharmaceutical marketing, these campaigns are typically used to educate and engage healthcare professionals (HCPs) about a specific drug or treatment.

Drip campaigns are effective because they allow marketers to deliver relevant and timely information to HCPs in a structured and automated way. This can help build brand awareness and credibility, nurture leads, and encourage conversions.

As part of pharmaceutical marketing strategies, content should always be tailored to its target audience. This may involve information such as a drug's mechanisms of action, clinical trial data, and patient case studies. When designing drip campaigns in this fashion for pharmaceutical marketing purposes, ensure the content provided to target groups is pertinent and valuable to them.

Notably, it is also imperative that any campaign adheres to relevant regulations and guidelines established by regulatory agencies like US FDA or European Medicines Agency (EMA). Pharma marketers should seek approval from medical/legal review teams, with emails containing appropriate disclaimers/warnings, and ensure implementation of opt-in/opt-out procedures.

Drip campaigns can be a highly effective tool for pharma marketers looking to engage and educate HCPs about their products. Still, ensuring they are designed, executed, compliant, and ethical is important.

How Pharma Can Use Drip Campaigns

Here are some examples of how pharmaceutical companies can use drip campaigns in their marketing efforts:

1. *New Product Launch*: Drip campaigns provide healthcare professionals with information about new medications through email notifications of their launch, followed by more in-depth emails providing details, such as the mechanism of action, clinical trial results, safety profile information, and dosing guidance.
2. *Disease Awareness*: Drip campaigns may raise awareness for specific conditions or diseases to increase available treatment options. Emails could provide educational content about symptoms, prevalence, and impact on patient lives, and follow-up emails could offer advantages of specific drugs for treating said diseases.
3. *Continuing Medical Education (CME)*: A drip campaign could provide healthcare professionals with educational content about a particular disease or condition. The campaign might include a series of emails with links to webinars, online courses, or other resources that can help HCPs stay current on the latest research and best practices in the field.
4. *Patient Support*: A drip campaign could support patients using a particular drug or treatment. The campaign might include a series of emails that provide information about managing side effects, coping with the emotional impact of the disease, and accessing resources and support groups.

How Pharma Uses Drip Campaigns

The following examples illustrate how some pharmaceutical companies used drip campaigns in their marketing efforts:

1. *Pfizer* used a drip campaign to promote their Prevnar 13 pneumococcal vaccine to healthcare professionals. The campaign consisted of emails that provided educational content about the vaccine, including its mechanism of action, clinical trial data, and dosing information.
2. *Novartis* used an email-drip campaign to market Cosentyx psoriasis treatment to healthcare professionals. Each email provided information regarding disease symptoms and benefits associated with treatment and links to webinars or other educational materials.
3. *Sanofi* utilized emails to raise awareness for their Auvi-Q autoinjector for treating severe allergic reactions as part of a drip campaign to create greater visibility for this device. They provided details regarding benefits, features, and how the autoinjector worked through email updates sent throughout their campaign period.
4. *Boehringer Ingelheim* used an email-driven drip campaign to market their Spiriva Respimat inhaler as an effective treatment option for chronic obstructive pulmonary disease (COPD). Each email included educational material about COPD, its treatment benefits, and proper usage instructions for their Spiriva Respimat inhaler.

These examples demonstrate how pharmaceutical companies utilize drip campaigns to inform healthcare professionals of their products, raise brand recognition and build credibility. By offering informative yet valuable content in an automated and systematic fashion, drip campaigns help drive leads and conversions and improve patient outcomes.

Drug Development

Pharma marketing involves promoting pharmaceutical products to healthcare professionals, patients, and other stakeholders. Pharma marketing strives to raise awareness of new treatments while informing healthcare providers and patients of their benefits and risks and encouraging clinical use of such products.

Thus, drug development and pharmaceutical marketing are integral to the pharmaceutical industry, bringing patients new treatments while improving overall health outcomes. Although each may pursue individual objectives and goals, both are crucial in driving medical science forward while benefiting patient health outcomes.

Drug Development

Drug development involves conducting extensive research, development, and trials of new pharmaceutical medications to ensure they are safe and effective for their intended patient populations. Drug development typically follows several steps, which include:

1. *Discovery and Preclinical Research*: At this phase, scientists identify potential drug targets. Candidate compounds with therapeutic potential are tested on laboratory animals and human volunteers to ensure safety and efficacy.
2. *Investigative New Drug Application (IND)*: When preclinical trials for an investigational new drug (IND) demonstrate promising results, regulatory bodies such as the Food and Drug Administration (FDA) usually receive an Investigatory New Drug Application describing its clinical development plan for approval by these agencies.
3. *Clinical Trials*: Clinical trials involve giving medications or treatments to human volunteers under strict control in an experiment designed to assess safety, efficacy, and optimal dosage regimen for any therapy or treatment regimen. Most trials typically include three steps; in phase one, the drug will be tested on healthy volunteers, while phase two will typically test it against larger patient populations with target diseases to establish efficacy and an optimum dosing regime. Finally, Phase 3 tests the drug with larger groups to ascertain safety and efficacy against existing treatments or placebo.
4. *New Drug Application (NDA)*: When clinical trials reveal the safety and efficacy of a medication, a New Drug Application (NDA) must be filed with regulatory agencies such as the FDA for consideration. An NDA includes preclinical and clinical study data and the drug's production, labeling, and potential uses information.
5. *Post-Market Surveillance (PMS)*: After an approved and commercialized drug has been distributed for sale, post-marketing surveillance must take place to assess its safety and efficacy under real-world conditions.

Low Success Rate

Drug development success is quite low, with many drug candidates failing to reach the market. A study by the Tufts Center for the Study of Drug Development indicated an approximate 11% success rate among drugs entering clinical development, meaning only one will be approved by regulatory bodies such as the US FDA or EMA (European Medicines Agency) per every ten drug candidates entering trials. Some important reasons for the high failure rate in drug development are:

1. *Safety and Efficacy Concerns*: Many new drugs fail to demonstrate sufficient safety during clinical trials, often leading to their suspension from clinical development programs and discontinuation.
2. *Technical Challenges*: Due to the rigorous nature of drug development, many projects fail due to technical obstacles like manufacturing issues or delivery challenges.
3. *Lack of Commercial Viability*: Even though a drug shows promise in clinical trials, its commercial viability could still be threatened due to competition with existing treatments, limited patient populations, or high development costs.
4. *Regulatory Concerns*: Drugs may fail to gain regulatory approval due to issues surrounding safety, efficacy, or manufacturing processes.

Cost of Drug Development

Drug development costs vary dramatically based on factors like drug type, disease complexity, and stage. The cost of developing a single new drug can be very high. Here is what it would cost according to recent estimates:

1. *Drug Development Cost*: According to estimates from 2020 by the Tufts Center for the Study of Drug Development, new drug development costs approximately $2.6 billion per drug. The cost includes research & development costs, such as conducting preclinical and clinical research studies, and regulatory costs.
2. *Regulatory Costs* include obtaining regulatory approval from the US regulators like FDA or EMA and global bodies like WHO. Manufacturing and distribution costs include manufacturing, packaging, and distributing the drug to patients and healthcare providers.
3. *Intellectual Property Costs* include patents and other forms of intellectual property.
4. *Failed Drug Candidates*: Because drug development often results in failed candidates that never enter the market, much of R&D expenses go toward these unsuccessful drug candidates that never reach the market.

Note that drug development costs do not always correspond with their final market prices once on sale. Rather they depend on competition, market demand, and insurance coverage as factors determining their actual costs. Drug development requires significant resources and investments,

While drug development success rates tend to be low, those that make it to market can significantly impact patient health outcomes and quality of life, so pharmaceutical companies must continue investing in this area to bring new treatments into the market and enhance patient care.

Drug Discovery

Drug discovery entails discovering new medications to treat diseases or improve health outcomes, but its scope also has significant ramifications for pharmaceutical marketing. Here are just a few ways that drug discovery intersects with pharmaceutical marketing:

1. *Targeted Discovery*: Drug discovery often begins by identifying specific biological pathways or mechanisms involved with disease; this knowledge allows pharmaceutical companies to design drugs that address its causes rather than only treating its symptoms. Targeted marketing helps pharmaceutical firms reach patients most likely to benefit from such medicines.
2. *Patent Protection*: Pharmaceutical marketing relies heavily on patent protection. Patents grant pharmaceutical companies exclusive rights to sell newly developed medications until the patent expires, so drug discovery is integral to securing patents, and companies must show how their medication provides meaningful therapeutic benefit and stands apart from competitors.
3. *Competitive Positioning*: Drug discovery can enable pharmaceutical companies to develop drugs with distinct market positions. For instance, companies that create new medications with reduced side effects or extended duration of action may establish themselves as leaders within a therapeutic field.
4. *Patient Education*: With drug discovery comes new medications that patients may be unfamiliar with. Pharmaceutical companies must invest in patient education efforts so patients understand both benefits and risks when considering new medication regimens.

Drug discovery is a critical element of pharmaceutical marketing, enabling companies to discover medicines with enhanced health outcomes that distinguish themselves from competitors and offer competitive differentiation. Pharmaceutical firms can successfully launch new medications into the market through targeted marketing efforts such as patent protection, competitive positioning strategies, and patient education efforts.

Drug Laws

Laws and regulations surrounding pharmaceutical products govern prescription and over-the-counter (OTC) medication to ensure their safety, efficacy, and quality. Some examples of laws related to pharmaceuticals could include:

1. *Approval Process*: Pharmaceutical companies must obtain approval from regulatory agencies like the Food and Drug Administration (FDA) in the United States before marketing a new drug. The approval process typically involves extensive testing and clinical trials to establish the safety and efficacy of the drug.
2. *Good Manufacturing Practices*: Drug manufacturers must adhere to good manufacturing practices (GMP) to ensure the quality and consistency of their products. This includes regulations governing the equipment and facilities used in drug manufacturing and standards for testing and quality control.
3. *Labeling and Packaging*: Drug laws require that pharmaceutical products are labeled and packaged in a way that provides clear and accurate information about the drug, its uses, and potential side effects. This includes requirements for package inserts, warning labels, and dosing information.
4. *Prescription Requirements*: Many pharmaceuticals are only available with a prescription from a licensed healthcare provider. This helps ensure that drugs are only used by people who need them and are used safely and appropriately.
5. *Adverse Event Reporting*: Pharmaceutical companies must report any adverse events, such as side effects or complications, in people using their products. This helps identify potential drug safety issues and can lead to changes in labeling or manufacturing practices.
6. *Drug Enforcement*: Drug laws also include provisions for enforcing pharmaceutical regulations, including investigating and prosecuting companies and individuals who violate drug laws.

Drug laws exist to ensure medications are safe, effective, and of superior quality, protecting both consumers from harm as well as society from potential health concerns. Consider the following examples of laws governing pharmaceuticals in select countries worldwide:

1. The Federal Food, Drug, and Cosmetic Act (FD&C Act) in the United States regulates the safety and efficacy of drugs, medical devices, and cosmetics. It establishes the approval process for new drugs, drug labeling and packaging requirements, and guidelines for clinical trials and manufacturing practices.

2. The Medicines Act in the United Kingdom regulates medicines' safety, efficacy, and quality. It requires pharmaceutical companies to obtain product licenses and adhere to good manufacturing practices and labeling requirements.
3. The Therapeutic Goods Act in Australia regulates therapeutic goods' safety, quality, and efficacy, including prescription and over-the-counter medicines. It establishes product labeling, packaging requirements, and guidelines for clinical trials and manufacturing practices.
4. The Pharmaceutical Affairs Act in Japan regulates the manufacture, sale, and import/export of drugs and medical devices. It establishes requirements for clinical trials, manufacturing practices, and product labeling and packaging.
5. India's Drugs and Cosmetics Act regulates the safety, efficacy, and quality of pharmaceuticals and cosmetics sold in the country. It sets requirements for drug approval, labeling, and packaging processes while outlining guidelines regarding clinical trials and manufacturing practices.

These are some examples of drug laws from various nations governing pharmaceutical products. However, specifics will depend upon your region and may need updating or amending according to new drug research or regulatory developments.

(DMF) Drug Master File

DMF stands for Drug Master File (DMF). It is a document that contains detailed information regarding the production, process, packaging, and testing procedures of active pharmaceutical ingredients (APIs) and excipients the pharmaceutical companies manufacture to obtain approval from regulatory bodies like the FDA in the United States to market their product.

Here are a few key points about Drug Master Files (DMFs):

1. *Purpose*: A DMF aims to inform regulatory authorities regarding the manufacturing process and quality control measures associated with producing or manufacturing the substance or product without disclosing sensitive or confidential details to third parties.
2. *Confidentiality*: The DMF must remain confidential, accessible only by regulatory agencies during drug approval procedures, and not accessible by members of the general public.
3. *Contents of DMF*: The Drug Master File typically provides details regarding the manufacturing process used, including facilities, equipment, and specifications used to ensure quality drug substances or products, as well as test methods to guarantee this quality.
4. *Access*: Drug manufacturers may cite their DMF when applying for FDA drug approval; regulatory authorities may review it during product assessments. However, its information remains hidden from the general public and will never be made part of an application or publicly available.
5. *Types*: There are three different DMF types; Type 1 contains information regarding a drug substance; Type II provides details regarding a drug product; and, finally, Type III contains details concerning packaging materials or excipients utilized within that drug product.

Role of DMF

A Drug Master File, more commonly referred to as a DMF, does not directly facilitate the manufacturers' marketing of a drug product; however, it can indirectly assist their efforts by helping obtain regulatory approval for their drug product and documentation of manufacturing processes that meet regulatory standards.

Regulators often inspect the facilities of DMF applicants as part of the review process to confirm the information provided in their DMFs and ensure manufacturing facilities and processes comply with applicable regulations and standards. These inspections serve to validate the information in DMF applications as well as to validate whether manufacturing processes meet relevant regulations and standards.

At an inspection, regulatory authorities review recorded procedures and other documents related to manufacturing operations, observe manufacturing operations first-hand, and interview facility personnel before recording results in an inspection report with observations, findings, and suggestions for corrective actions.

The regulatory authority may use inspection results to assess whether manufacturing facilities and processes are suitable for producing drug products/substances and review DMF or drug application submissions.

FDA approval of a DMF is an integral component of regulatory approval processes and essential for marketing products.

The FDA can authorize drug manufacturing facilities if they comply with Good Manufacturing Practices (GMP) and regulatory requirements, giving this approval an indication of compliance to meet consistent, high-quality product manufacturing.

FDA approval of drug manufacturing facilities is vital to marketing drug products that rely on them since this indicates they were produced according to regulatory requirements and will be safe and effective for their intended uses. Without FDA approval of their DMF and manufacturing facility, drug products could never be marketed legally in the US market. Similar procedures apply in many other countries; inspectors inspect applicant DMF manufacturing facilities before authorizing importation into their countries of products containing active pharmaceutical ingredients manufactured only within facilities approved by regulatory bodies of respective nations.

DMFs are widely used within the pharmaceutical industry as they aid communication between drug makers and regulatory authorities while simultaneously providing them with a way of sharing confidential product data while safeguarding intellectual property rights.

Drug Price Control

Drug Price Control refers to government efforts to control prescription drug costs to make them affordable and accessible to the general population. By controlling pricing on essential medication at manageable levels, drug price control helps patients prevent paying inflated prices for essential medicines while helping keep healthcare costs in check. Here are a few examples of drug price control measures:

1. *Reference Pricing*: The government sets an upper benchmark price for an individual drug in reference pricing based on other countries where that drug sells at a lower cost than domestically. Manufacturers must price their products below this price.
2. *Price Negotiation*: In healthcare systems such as Medicare in the US, governments directly negotiate with pharmaceutical companies to negotiate lower drug prices and achieve savings for taxpayers. This approach has proven highly successful.
3. *International Price Index (IPI)*: To lower drug costs in America, President Trump proposed creating the International Price Index (IPI), which would have linked certain Medicare drugs with those available elsewhere around the globe and tied their prices together as one index figure.
4. *Patent Laws*: Governments can modify patent laws to promote competition among pharmaceutical companies and prevent them from cornering the market monopolistically. As one example, India recently promoted generic versions of patented drugs, significantly decreasing the prices of these medications.
5. *Medicaid Drug Rebates in the US*: Under the Medicaid Drug Rebates Program, manufacturers must offer rebates to state Medicaid programs when products purchased by Medicaid beneficiaries from manufacturers are purchased at average manufacturer price (AMP). The rebate amount depends upon AMP.

Drug Price Control in Global Context

Price controls vary significantly among countries worldwide. Some have implemented stringent regulations to guarantee affordable medicine prices, while others take an unrestrictive approach to pricing their prescription medicines.

Here are a few examples of drug price control measures across various regions:

1. *Europe*: European nations employ various measures to regulate drug prices. Some EU member countries, like France and Germany, set their prices through legislation; others, such as the UK negotiate them directly with manufacturers. Additionally, the European Medicines Agency (EMA) can guide pricing and reimbursement policies.
2. *United States*: The US has an intricate drug pricing system that manufacturers, insurers, and pharmacy benefit managers determine. There are no federal regulations regarding drug pricing practices, but certain states have implemented measures such as price transparency laws to regulate prices more closely.
3. *Canada*: Canada's national healthcare system negotiates drug prices directly with manufacturers. Prices tend to be significantly less expensive than their US counterparts. However, some have criticized Canada's national system as it restricts access to certain medications.
4. *India*: India has instituted stringent regulations regarding drug prices, setting price caps on essential medications. Furthermore, their government supports producing generic versions of patented drugs to further lower prices and increase competitiveness in the global marketplace.
5. *Australia*: Prescription drug prices in Australia are determined and reviewed continuously. At the same time, subsidies from the Pharmaceutical Benefits Scheme (PBS) help decrease out-of-pocket patient costs for certain drugs.

Drug price control measures greatly influence pharmaceutical companies and individuals relying on prescription medicines. Supporters believe price controls help ensure lifesaving medications remain accessible; opponents contend they stifle innovation by restricting investment into research and development projects. Global trends reflect this tension as some nations employ stringent controls while others take an incremental market approach.

Drug Recall

Recalls in the pharmaceutical industry involve recalling prescription or over-the-counter (OTC) drugs from the market individually or voluntarily by their manufacturer when health risks associated with their use arise. Drug recalls often fall under regulatory oversight, such as that by Food and Drug Administration (FDA).

Recalls can be divided into various classes according to their level of risk for public safety:

A. *Class I recalls* are classified as those with a high probability that their use or exposure could result in severe adverse health impacts severe adverse physical symptoms and death.

B. *Class II products*: Exposing or using one may cause temporary, medically reversible adverse health impacts that will likely decrease in time; serious ill effects are unlikely.

C. *Class III Recalls*: Drugs that do not meet FDA labeling or manufacturing standards but are deemed unlikely to cause adverse health consequences.

Impact on Company

Recalls have significant marketing ramifications. Consider the following, for example:

1. *Brand Reputation*: Recalls often harm brand image; trust is essential in healthcare, and recalls can impact trust among patients and healthcare companies.
2. *Financial Impact*: Recalls may lead to severe financial ramifications. Costs incurred as part of the recall process, loss of sales due to recall actions, potential litigation action, and regulatory fines all add up quickly.
3. *Communication*: The company must effectively communicate about the recall to regulatory authorities, healthcare professionals, and the public. This communication strategy is crucial to mitigate the negative impact of the recall.
4. *Market Strategy*: After experiencing a recall, companies must rebuild their market strategy in response to it. Depending on its severity, an organization may need to spend significant resources rebuilding trust by relaunching the product once again, if considered safe, or advertising alternative products to address customer demands.
5. *Competitive Dynamics*: Recalls may allow competitors to capture market share if they offer similar products with better safety profiles.

Pharmaceutical companies frequently devise risk management plans to prevent recalls and manage them proactively and effectively, if they occur. Such plans often consist of rigorous quality control processes, strong surveillance systems for post-marketing safety monitoring, and clear communication strategies.

Drug Recalls: Some Examples

Here are a few instances of significant drug recalls which have taken place over time:

1. *Vioxx (Rofecoxib)* was a widely prescribed pain reliever until voluntary withdrawal by Merck, following a study that demonstrated increased risks for heart attack and stroke among long-term users. It remains one of the largest drug recalls ever, impacting millions of patients worldwide.
2. *Zantac (Ranitidine)*: In April 2020, the FDA immediately requested the removal of all prescriptions and over-the-counter ranitidine drugs from the market. This was because they found an impurity called N-Nitrosodimethylamine (NDMA) at low levels in samples of ranitidine. NDMA is a probable human carcinogen (a substance that could cause cancer).
3. *Darvon and Darvocet*: (Propoxyphene) In 2010, Xanodyne Pharmaceuticals withdrew both Darvon and Darvocet following studies showing they could potentially cause fatal heart rhythm abnormalities for millions of patients who used these pain relievers over decades.
4. *Phenylpropanalomine (PPA)*: PPA was once widely used in OTC cold and weight loss products. However, due to concerns that PPA might increase hemorrhagic stroke risk, the FDA public health advisory issued in 2000 banning it. It forced companies that used PPA products voluntarily withdraw them.
5. *Pfizer discontinued Bextra (Valdecoxib)* due to safety concerns regarding increased risks for heart attack, stroke, and serious skin reactions.
6. *Baycol (Cerivastatin)*: Manufactured by Bayer, this cholesterol-reducing drug was removed from the market due to links with serious and

possibly lethal muscle conditions known as Rhabdomyolysis.

These examples demonstrate the significance of post-marketing surveillance and taking prompt action if safety concerns emerge. Even after extensive clinical testing and trials have taken place, adverse side effects may not become noticeable until being taken by larger and more diverse populations than were included in initial trials.

Drug Repositioning

Drug Repositioning, or *repurposing*, involves finding new therapeutic uses for existing prescription medications that were originally meant for another purpose or disease/condition than originally anticipated. Repurposing can identify new avenues of investigation into which an existing pharmaceutical product can potentially treat.

Repositioning prescription drugs may bring many advantages, including:

1. *Reduced Development Time and Cost*: Repositioning can significantly decrease development costs as its safety and efficacy have already been validated for one indication, shortening development timelines.
2. *Expanded Patient Populations*: Repositioning can expand patient populations for your drug, creating additional revenue streams for pharmaceutical companies.
3. *Improved Market Access*: Since a drug already approved can enter the market more quickly and smoothly, patients can access therapy sooner.
4. *Increased Lifespan and Patents*: Repositioning can extend a drug's lifecycle and open up possibilities of additional patents for it, giving pharmaceutical companies more time to market and sell the drug exclusively. Repositioning may even give pharmaceutical firms exclusive distribution rights over it for longer.

Here are a few examples of repurposing prescription drugs:

1. *Propranolol* was initially developed to treat hypertension, but later it was found useful in treating many other conditions, such as migraines, and anxiety disorders, to control tremors.
2. *Rituximab*: Rituximab was initially approved to treat B-cell lymphomas. However, its use has expanded beyond B-cells to treat other conditions, such as rheumatoid arthritis, granulomatosis with polyangiitis, and MPA (Microscopic Polyantitis).
3. *Duloxetine*: Duloxetine has long been prescribed to manage depression and anxiety disorders. More recently, however, the Food and Drug Administration approved Duloxetine to aid against chronic muscle and joint pain conditions, such as Fibromyalgia.

Repositioning prescription drugs can be an invaluable strategy for pharmaceutical companies looking to broaden their product offering and enhance patient care. However, Repositioning requires extensive research and clinical testing on new indications before receiving regulatory approval.

Drug Repurposing

Drug Repurposing or Drug Repositioning refers to finding new therapeutic uses for existing drugs that have grown increasingly popular over time, saving time and money compared to conventional drug development processes. When used strategically for pharmaceutical marketing purposes, drug repositioning offers several distinct advantages, including:

1. *Repurposing Drugs to Unlock New Revenue Streams*: Repurposing existing pharmaceutical drugs to address new indications can open up new revenue streams for pharmaceutical companies and help offset research and development expenses while diversifying product lines. This practice could generate much-needed new revenue streams while broadening product lines further.
2. *Reducing Development Costs*: Repurposing can often be cheaper than developing entirely new drugs as much of the research and development has already been completed, helping reduce financial risks associated with new drug development.
3. *Shortened Development Time*: Repurposing can reduce development times significantly for drugs already approved by regulatory agencies for other indications. This strategy may prove particularly advantageous.
4. *Improved Market Access*: Repurposing drugs to meet new indications can greatly enhance market access, as their safety and efficacy profiles may already have been established. Repurposing can speed up regulatory approval processes, making them more appealing to healthcare providers and patients.

Drug repurposing can be an important strategy for pharmaceutical companies seeking to broaden their product offerings and capitalize on existing research efforts. Repurposing an old medication to fit new indications still requires extensive clinical testing for safety and effectiveness. Additionally, companies must follow regulations related to marketing to ensure accurate marketing materials that won't mislead patients about their true risk.

Repurposing Drugs: Two Examples

Here are three examples of drug repurposing in pharmaceutical marketing:

A. Viagra was initially developed to treat high blood pressure and angina. After a research scientist serendipitously identified that it is useful for erectile dysfunction, Pfizer's marketing division adopted it as an ED (Erectile Dysfunction) treatment. The rest was history. Sales increased, leading to significant revenue gains for the company.

B. Thalidomide was initially developed in the 1950s to treat morning sickness symptoms and reduce anxiety. However, after marketing, the drug showed it contained teratogenic properties, resulting in birth abnormalities among its babies, prompting its global withdrawal. Research later identified that it has anti-inflammatory and immuno-modulatory properties useful in treating multiple myeloma, leprosy, and certain autoimmune disorders.

C. The Food and Drug Administration initially approved botulinum toxin to treat involuntary blinking; since its approval, however, its versatility has made it suitable for cosmetic treatments and therapeutic remedies like wrinkle treatments, migraine relief, excess sweating relief, or headache relief.

Drug-Drug Interaction (DDI)

Drug-drug interactions (DDIs) refer to the effects of altering one drug by the concomitant use of another drug. These interactions can result in reduced effectiveness of one or both drugs or an increased risk of adverse effects. DDIs can be categorized into different types based on their underlying mechanisms:

1. Pharmacodynamic Interactions

This involves the effects of the drugs on the body. When two drugs produce similar effects, the combined effect might be additive or synergistic. If they have opposite effects, one drug might counteract or reduce the effect of the other.

- *Example*: Using alcohol with sedative medications can have additive sedative effects, increasing the risk of respiratory depression, overdose, or death.

2. Pharmacokinetic Interactions

This involves how the body processes the drugs. Interactions can occur at various stages:

- *Absorption*: Some drugs can affect the absorption of others. For instance, antacids might reduce the absorption of certain antibiotics.
- *Distribution*: Some drugs can displace others from protein-binding sites, increasing free concentrations of the displaced drugs.
- *Metabolism*: Many DDIs involve the cytochrome P450 enzyme system in the liver. Some drugs inhibit the action of these enzymes, while others induce them. This can lead to increased or decreased levels of another drug.
- *Excretion*: Some drugs can affect the renal excretion of others, altering their levels in the bloodstream.
- *Example*: Fluoxetine, an SSRI (Selective Serotonin Reuptake Inhibitor) antidepressant, can inhibit the CYP2D6 enzyme, which might increase the levels of other drugs metabolized by this enzyme.

3. Pharmaceutical Interactions

These occur when two drugs interact in a solution, leading to precipitation or changes in solubility.

- *Example*: Combining a drug in solution with another solution containing an incompatible drug can precipitate one or both drugs.

Implications of Drug-Drug Interactions

1. *Decreased Therapeutic Effect*: One drug might reduce the effectiveness of another, leading to suboptimal treatment outcomes.
2. *Increased Risk of Adverse Effects*: Some interactions can result in toxic levels of a drug or an increased risk of side effects.
3. *Serious Health Threats*: Some DDIs can lead to life-threatening conditions like serotonin syndrome, severe hypotension, or fatal arrhythmia.
4. *Alterations in Drug Monitoring*: Drugs monitored through blood levels (like warfarin or digoxin) might need dose adjustments and closer monitoring when used with interacting drugs.
5. *Increased Healthcare Costs*: DDIs can lead to hospitalizations, longer hospital stays, or additional medical interventions.

Prevention and Management

1. *Medication Reviews*: Review all medications, including over-the-counter drugs and supplements, for potential interactions.
2. *Electronic Health Records and Decision Support Systems*: These tools can alert healthcare providers to potential DDIs.
3. *Patient Education*: Inform patients about the risks of DDIs and encourage them to always disclose all medications they take to all healthcare professionals.

To prevent adverse outcomes related to DDIs, healthcare providers and patients must be vigilant and communicate effectively. Always consult a pharmacist or another healthcare professional when starting or stopping medication.

DDIs: Implications for Pharma Marketers

Pharma marketers must recognize drug-drug interactions (DDIs) for several reasons. The implications of DDIs can directly and indirectly impact pharmaceutical marketing strategies, positioning, and even brand reputation. Here are some considerations for pharma marketers:

1. *Ethical Responsibility*: The primary responsibility of pharma marketers is to ensure that healthcare professionals and patients are aware of the potential risks associated with their products, including DDIs. Ethical marketing ensures that all claims are supported by robust scientific evidence and that potential risks are clearly communicated.
2. *Regulatory Compliance*: Regulatory bodies worldwide are stringent about how pharmaceuticals are promoted. False or misleading marketing, especially if it omits information about serious DDIs, can lead to heavy fines, warnings, or even product recalls.
3. *Brand Reputation*: Negative patient outcomes resulting from DDIs can harm the reputation of a drug brand, especially if it is perceived that the manufacturer did not provide adequate warning. Pharma marketers need to maintain trust by being transparent about the full risk profile of their products.
4. *Education and Training*: Pharma marketers often engage in educational campaigns, webinars, seminars, and training sessions for healthcare professionals. A significant aspect of this education is highlighting potential DDIs to ensure prescribers can make informed decisions.
5. *Competitive Positioning*: Knowledge about DDIs can also be a strategic advantage. If a new drug has fewer interactions than existing drugs in the market, this can be positioned as a unique selling point. However, such claims must be made responsibly and based on robust scientific evidence.
6. *Monitoring and Reporting*: Marketers must proactively monitor reports of adverse reactions related to DDIs. Pharma companies usually have pharmacovigilance departments that track adverse events. Collaborating closely with these departments can give marketers insights into emerging issues that may need to be addressed in marketing materials.
7. *Direct-to-Consumer Marketing*: In regions where direct-to-consumer (DTC) advertising is allowed, it is crucial to ensure that potential DDIs are communicated clearly. Patients might not always be aware of the complexities of DDIs, so messages should be crafted carefully to be easily understood.
8. *Digital Marketing and Social Listening*: With the rise of digital channels, pharma marketers have new platforms to spread awareness about their products. However, these channels also allow for real-time feedback and reviews. Utilizing social listening tools can help marketers identify concerns or misinformation related to DDIs and address them proactively.
9. *Collaboration with Pharmacies*: Pharmacies often have software that alerts them to potential DDIs when dispensing medications. Collaborating with pharmacies can offer an additional layer of safety and an opportunity for co-marketing and educational initiatives.
10. *Patient Support Programs*: Pharma companies often offer support programs for patients on their medications. These can serve as platforms to educate patients about DDIs, especially if they are on multiple medications.

While DDIs pose challenges for pharma marketers, they also offer opportunities to build trust, provide genuine value to healthcare professionals and patients, and position products effectively.

E

1. Early Adopters
2. E-Detailing
3. e-Learning
4. email Marketing
5. e-MSL
6. E-Pharmacy
7. Early Majority
8. Earned Media
9. Ecological Environment
10. Econometric Analysis
11. Economic Environment
12. Economic Value Added (EVA)
13. Educational Advertising
14. Educational Marketing
15. Effective Frequency
16. Efficiency
17. Effectiveness
18. Electroncephalography (EEG)
19. Electronic Health Record (EHR)
20. Electronic Media
21. Electronic Word-of-Mouth (eWOM)
22. European Medicines Agency (EMA)
23. Emotional Branding
24. Emotional Engagement
25. Emotional Intelligence (EI)
26. Emotional Marketing
27. Emotional Model
28. Empathy
29. Empirical Research
30. Employee Communication
31. Employee Value Proposition
32. Empowerment
33. Encryption
34. Endogenous Attention
35. Engagement Metrics
36. Engel's Laws
37. Enlightened Marketing
38. Entrepreneurial Marketing
39. Enterprise Resource Planning (ERP)
40. Environmental Scanning
41. Environmentalism
42. Ethics
43. Ethical Codes
44. Ethical Incentive Plan
45. Ethical Marketing
46. Ethnic Marketing
47. Ethnocentrism
48. Ethnography
49. Ethnographic Research
50. Event Marketing
51. Ever-greening
52. Evidence-based Marketing
53. Exclusivity
54. Exhibition Marketing
55. Exogenous Attention
56. Experiential Marketing
57. Experience Curve
58. Exploratory Research
59. Export Marketing
60. Eye-Tracking

Early Adopters

Everett M. Rogers first proposed the Diffusion of Innovations Theory. This theory divides consumers into five groups according to their willingness and capacity to adopt innovations: *Innovators, Early Adopters, Early Majority, Late Majority, and Laggards.*

Early Adopters are one of the fastest categories of individuals to adopt innovations after innovators themselves, often acting as opinion leaders and engaging with other members more frequently than most. Their endorsement often helps convince others in an *Early Majority* group to accept innovation or technology more readily; their role can also play an essential part in pharmaceutical marketing.

Targeting Early Adopters

Pharmaceutical marketers can employ various strategies to reach early adopters:

1. *Education and Information*: Provide comprehensive information about the drug or treatment, including its benefits, how it works, clinical trial results, etc.
2. *Engaging Early Adopters*: Work closely with Early Adopters through medical conferences, professional networks, or one-on-one meetings to receive their input and make them feel involved with the process. Listen carefully to their comments while receiving feedback, and make them part of it all!
3. *Incentivization*: Offering incentives such as free trial periods, discounts, or access to special programs as incentives can encourage adoption.
4. *Promoting through KOLs*: Working closely with key opinion leaders (KOLs) to promote your products will increase their exposure and adoption of your drugs or treatments among Early Adopters.

Remember that while early adopters may be key for rapid adoption, a strategy that includes all categories of adopters is equally essential to long-term market viability.

Implications for Pharma Marketers

Marketing to early adopters has some very important implications. Consider the following, for example:

1. *Targeting Strategy*: Pharmaceutical marketers should effectively identify and target early adopters, as early adopters are vital to product diffusion. Doctors considered thought leaders or influencers within their specialties might make for good early adopters, while patient groups actively searching out innovative therapies could also make great targets.
2. *Feedback Mechanism*: Early adopters provide invaluable feedback that marketers must utilize. Their perspectives offer firsthand knowledge of product efficacy, safety, and potential improvements. So marketers must establish avenues for collecting, analyzing, and acting upon this group of early adopters' comments for product and marketing strategy improvements accordingly.
3. *Relationship Building*: Early adopters play an invaluable role for marketers in expanding market reach and awareness of products or services they support. By building lasting relationships, marketers can use early adopters as ambassadors who promote them with consistent support, education, and value. Marketers should keep these early adopters loyal and build trust within this group.
4. *Risk Management*: Early adopters tend to tolerate risks when testing new products. Nevertheless, marketers should ensure these risks are communicated, managed, and minimized effectively through rigorous pre-launch testing, open discussion about potential adverse side effects or challenges, and swift post-launch support services.
5. *Innovation and Strategy*: Early adopters give marketers invaluable feedback regarding future innovations. Their responses can provide insights into market trends and consumer behavior, informing future product development strategies and innovation adoption plans.

Early adopters in pharmaceutical marketing play an essential part in successfully introducing and disseminating information on medications or healthcare services to wider acceptance. By sharing valuable feedback, early adopters influence their peer's product adoption.

Understanding the characteristics and motivations of early adopters is vitally important to marketers. Understanding them allows you to create effective targeting, communication, and relationship strategies; build strong relationships; manage potential risks; inform future innovation strategies, as well as increase product success rates, driving sustained growth. By targeting influential early adopters, pharmaceutical marketers can increase product success rates and sustain growth in this ever-competitive healthcare market.

Remember that while early adopters may be key for rapid adoption, a strategy that includes all categories of adopters is equally essential to long-term market viability.

E-Detailing

E-detailing, or electronic or remote detailing, uses digital technology to remotely promote and educate healthcare professionals about pharmaceutical products or medical devices. E-detailing involves using various electronic platforms like webinars, video conferencing sessions, online presentations, and multimedia interactivity to deliver product details, clinical data, and marketing messages directly to healthcare professionals.

E-detailing has quickly grown increasingly popular due to its ability to reach a wider audience while cutting costs and offering greater scheduling/location flexibility. Furthermore, this method provides invaluable data regarding healthcare professionals' engagement preferences that can help tailor future marketing efforts accordingly. However, e-detailing also presents challenges, such as strong digital infrastructure, potential technological barriers, and effective communication and relationship-building with healthcare professionals in a remote setting.

Key Steps

E-detailing typically involves a few key steps, including the following:

1. *Identifying the Target Audience*: The pharmaceutical or medical device company identifies the healthcare professionals they want to target based on specialty, location, and prescribing habits.
2. *Inviting Healthcare Professionals to Participate*: The company may reach out to healthcare professionals directly via email, social media, or other digital channels, inviting them to participate in an e-detailing session.
3. *Scheduling the Session*: Once healthcare professionals express interest in participating, the company schedules a specific time and date for the e-detailing session. This may involve coordinating schedules across multiple time zones and locations,
4. *Conducting the E-detailing Session*: The e-detailing session can take various forms, such as a live video conference with a sales representative, a pre-recorded video presentation with interactive elements, or an online interactive module that healthcare professionals can complete at their own pace. During the session, the company presents information about the product or device, including its features, benefits, and clinical data.
5. *Follow-up and Tracking*: After the e-detailing session, the company may follow up with healthcare professionals to answer additional questions or provide further information. They may also track engagement metrics, such as how long healthcare professionals spent on each slide or which features were most commonly accessed, to improve future e-detailing sessions.

How to Make it More Effective

To make e-detailing more effective, consider the following tips:

1. *Personalize the Content*: Healthcare professionals are likelier to engage with e-detailing if the content is tailored to their interests and needs. Consider using data on healthcare professionals' prescribing habits or areas of specialization to create personalized content that resonates with them.
2. *Use Interactive Elements*: Interactive elements such as quizzes, polls, and surveys can make e-detailing sessions more engaging and encourage active participation. These elements can also help companies gather valuable feedback on healthcare professionals' preferences and opinions.
3. *Provide High-quality Visuals*: Using high-quality visuals such as graphics, images, and videos can help convey complex information more easily. Visuals can also help to keep healthcare professionals engaged and interested in the presentation.
4. *Follow-up Promptly*: After the e-detailing session, it is important to follow up with healthcare professionals promptly to answer any additional questions or provide additional information. This can help to build trust and credibility with healthcare professionals.
5. *Gather Feedback and Adjust Accordingly*: Collect feedback from healthcare professionals after e-detailing sessions to understand what worked well and what could be improved. Use this feedback to adjust future e-detailing sessions and make them more effective.

E-detailing can be a powerful tool for educating and engaging healthcare professionals. Still, it's important to approach it strategically and continually to improve the e-detailing sessions' effectiveness.

eLearning

eLearning has become an increasingly popular method for training and educating professionals in the pharmaceutical industry. Here are some ways e-learning is being used in pharma marketing:

1. *Sales Training*: eLearning is being used to provide sales reps with the knowledge and skills

needed to promote pharmaceutical products effectively. This includes training on the science behind the products, disease states, and market trends.

2. *Product Knowledge Training*: eLearning is being used to provide employees with in-depth knowledge about pharma products, including their features, benefits, indications, and side effects. This helps employees communicate with healthcare providers and patients and promote their products more effectively.
3. *Compliance Training*: eLearning helps train employees on compliance regulations, such as FDA regulations and the PhRMA (The Pharmaceutical Research and Manufacturers of America) Ethical Code. This helps ensure that all employees understand their role in maintaining compliance.
4. *Product Training*: Healthcare professionals such as physicians and nurses can utilize eLearning for in-depth product training to comprehend better its features, benefits, and administration techniques for products prescribed or administered under their care. This aids them in understanding these products more fully while prescribing them appropriately and administering them correctly.
5. *Virtual Training*: Pharma companies using eLearning can use virtual training sessions for healthcare professionals through conferences or webinars online to reach a broader audience and connect with them directly. It can provide convenient yet cost-effective means of reaching more healthcare professionals, such as physicians, nurses, pharmacists and others, engaging them effectively in training activities.
6. *Customer Education*: eLearning serves to inform healthcare providers (HCPs) and patients of products, disease conditions, and treatment options, including their medications as well as tips to manage symptoms and maintain health. In addition, pharmaceutical companies can create digital resources like videos or interactive tools which allow patients to comprehend their condition better while increasing adherence.
7. *Customer Relationship Management*: eLearning can support customer relationship management by offering healthcare professionals an easy platform to track educational progress, access digital resources, and engage with pharmaceutical companies.

E-learning offers pharmaceutical companies an effective, flexible way of providing employee training and customer education on pharmaceutical marketing practices and strategies at a lower cost and with greater accessibility across any device imaginable. Companies using eLearning are discovering their power. E-learning allows pharma firms to provide high-quality educational materials that customers and employees can access at any time from any device with internet connectivity, giving their staff and customers a great learning experience at any point in time!

Email Marketing

Email marketing is an online strategy that utilizes emails sent out to targeted recipients, such as customers, subscribers, and prospects to promote a product or service, build relationships or encourage engagement with an audience. Here are some examples of what email marketing can do to make your marketing more effective:

1. Email marketing is used mainly to strengthen brand recognition, nurture leads, and make conversions. Businesses may utilize email marketing for several other reasons, including to market new products or services; announce special offers or promotions; provide valuable content or information; or invite customers to events or webinars.
2. Email marketing campaigns can be tailored specifically for specific customer demographics, interests, or past behaviors, allowing companies to tailor messaging directly toward specific audiences.
3. Email marketing campaigns typically include newsletters, promotional material, and welcome messages.
4. Email marketing offers companies an efficient and cost-effective way to engage customers and prospects, build loyalty, and drive conversions.

Email Marketing in Pharma

Many pharmaceutical companies employ email marketing as part of their overall marketing strategy. The following examples illustrate what you can achieve with email marketing:

1. *Product Promotions*: Pharmaceutical companies use email marketing to advertise new drug launches directly to healthcare professionals via email marketing campaigns. Email can also be used to market existing products, share clinical trial data, or information about additional indications for existing drugs.

2. *Educational Content*: Some pharmaceutical companies utilize email marketing to share educational material with healthcare professionals or patients regarding disease management, treatment options available, or new research findings. This may include information such as disease progression tracking or new scientific findings.
3. *Event Invitations*: Pharmaceutical companies use email marketing to invite healthcare professionals to conferences, webinars, and other events they organize, helping raise brand recognition while creating opportunities for face-to-face engagement with healthcare professionals. This strategy has proven extremely successful at increasing engagement.
4. *Newsletters*: Pharma companies may utilize email marketing to send regular newsletters with company updates, new product offerings, or educational material directly to healthcare professionals and patients. These messages could include updates on company happenings as well as educational articles.
5. *Patient Support*: Some pharmaceutical companies utilize email marketing as part of their support strategy for patients using their products, whether reminders to take medication on time, tips on managing side effects effectively, or information regarding patient assistance programs.

Effective Email Campaigns

Pharmaceutical companies use email marketing differently depending on their goals, target audience, and marketing objectives. Consider the following strategies to make your email campaigns more effective:

1. *Establish Your Target Audience*: As part of your email strategy, start by compiling an updated email list for your targeted audience, including healthcare professionals, patients, or any other relevant parties, such as stakeholders or government representatives. Get their permission before sending any emails out, if possible.
2. *Segment Your Audience*: Divide your email list into smaller segments according to interest, location, or any other relevant criterion to customize messaging and increase engagement for each group. This approach should allow for targeted messaging for optimal engagement among recipients in everyone.
3. *Compelling Subject Lines*: Your mail subject lines are the first impression recipients get of you, so ensure they're engaging and relevant to their interests. Be wary of using overtly promotional language or misleading claims, as this could cause recipients to unsubscribe from your list.
4. *Content that is Valuable to Your Audience*: Ensure your email content provides value to your target audience. This could include educational material, product details, or updates about industry trends. Use text, images, and videos in combination to keep emails engaging and visually pleasing for maximum impact.
5. *Use Personalization*: Personalizing emails will increase engagement by engaging recipients directly based on their interests or preferences. Use personalization features like using recipients' names in subject lines or email content or tailoring it based on interests to make the experience more relevant and interesting to all recipients.
6. *Optimize for Mobile Devices*: With many people accessing email on mobile phones and other small screens, ensure your emails are optimized to be easily read on such small displays. Use mobile-friendly designs, making the content easily readable on small displays.
7. *Test and Measure*: Experiment with different email strategies and evaluate their effects to find what resonates best with your target audience. This could involve testing various subject lines and content types or sending times before compiling data that helps optimize email campaigns over time.

e-MSL

An electronic Medical Science Liaison, or e-MSL, is an emerging role in the pharmaceutical industry that emphasizes creating relationships between pharmaceutical companies and healthcare professionals such as physicians and pharmacists.

e-MSLs play an invaluable role in pharmaceutical marketing by disseminating scientific and medical information to healthcare professionals about new drugs' risks, benefits, and safety aspects and answering queries regarding usage or safety concerns. Furthermore, these e-MSLs identify prospective clinical trial investigations while offering assistance during ongoing ones.

E-MSLs utilize various channels to engage healthcare professionals, including email, video conferencing, and social media. In addition, e-MSLs may attend medical conferences and scientific meetings to stay abreast of industry research trends and developments.

Role and Responsibilities

The roles and responsibilities of an electronic Medical Sales Liaison (e-MSL) in pharmaceutical marketing will vary based on each company and its individual needs, although some common responsibilities might include the following:

1. *Establish and Maintain Relationships*: e-MSLs are responsible for building and maintaining relationships with healthcare professionals such as doctors, pharmacists, and key opinion leaders in healthcare organizations. This involves frequent communications to provide scientific or medical information as needed to answer queries or address concerns raised.
2. *Provide Accurate Scientific and Medical Data*: Electronic Medical Science Liaisons provide up-to-date scientific and medical data about the products they represent, such as their mode of action, clinical trial results, safety information, and dosing guidelines.
3. *Provide Digital Access to Information*: E-MSLs utilize digital tools to offer healthcare professionals easy and quick access to scientific and medical knowledge, including content delivery, virtual events management, and customer relationship management services.
4. *Conducting Market Research*: E-MSLs may conduct market research to discover new business opportunities, understand customer requirements, and inform marketing strategies.
5. *Support of Clinical Trials*: e-MSLs frequently identify potential investigators for clinical trials and provide services, often working alongside healthcare professionals to recruit suitable patients to participate. Furthermore, training and support services may also be offered during each step of a trial process.
6. *Educating Healthcare Professionals*: e-MSLs are responsible for informing healthcare professionals of their company's products and diseases they treat through presentations, educational programs, or providing written materials or other resources.
7. *Staying Current on Scientific and Industry Developments*: e-MSLs must remain informed on scientific and industry advancements to provide healthcare professionals with accurate medical information. This may involve attending medical conferences or scientific meetings and reading up-to-date medical literature.
8. *Collaborating with Cross-Functional Teams*: Electronic Medical Sales Liaisons can collaborate with cross-functional teams like marketing, sales, and medical affairs in developing and executing marketing strategies for their company's products; however, they will only educate these groups regarding product knowledge and clinical trial data rather than promote or sell the company's offerings directly.
9. *Data Analytics*: e-MSLs may use data analytics tools to track customer engagement metrics such as content consumption, email open rates, and website visits. This data can then be used to inform marketing strategies and enhance customer relationships.

E-MSLs play an invaluable role in pharmaceutical marketing. They ensure healthcare providers access accurate and up-to-date information regarding new drugs and treatments, ultimately benefitting patients by increasing quality care delivery.

E-Pharmacy

E-pharmacy refers to selling pharmaceutical products online through either an independent online retailer or as an extension of an established pharmacy. E-pharmacies have become more common over time, and pharma companies can leverage this trend when marketing themselves and their products online.

Here are some ways e-pharmacies can support marketing initiatives by pharmaceutical companies:

1. *Strategic Promotions and Discounts*: Offering promotions or discounts through an e-pharmacy can attract new customers while encouraging existing ones to shop more frequently, thus helping increase sales while building brand loyalty.
2. *Educational Content*: E-pharmacies enable pharmaceutical companies to educate customers about their products and the conditions they treat through educational content such as articles, videos, or interactive tools that inform customers on benefits, risks, and how best to use their products safely and effectively.
3. *Personalized Messaging*: E-pharmacy platforms allow pharmaceutical companies to tailor messaging based on customer behavior and preferences, providing data for increased relevance and impact of marketing efforts. Pharma companies can use these platforms' targeted messaging to personalize messaging for specific customer segments by using this data as part of personalized promotions.
4. *Data Analysis*: E-pharmacy platforms provide valuable data on customer behaviors and preferences that can help pharma companies optimize marketing initiatives and product

development efforts. With access to this valuable insight into customer needs and preferences, pharma companies can utilize this data for more informed product and marketing strategy development decisions.

E-pharmacy provides pharmaceutical companies an invaluable opportunity to reach and engage customers via targeted messaging, promotions, and educational content. By creating strategic partnerships, offering online discounts and promotions, creating educational material, personalizing messaging, and using data analytics, pharma companies can use e-pharmacy in their marketing strategies for maximum effect.

How Pharma Leverages E-Pharmacy Platforms

Here are a few examples of pharmaceutical companies employing e-pharmacy platforms as part of their marketing initiatives:

1. *Pfizer and Amazon Partner for Over-The-Counter Sales*: Pfizer joined Amazon Pharmacies' online pharmacy platform in 2018 to sell OTC medications such as Advil (ibuprofen OTC) and Centrum (multivitamin supplement). Through this partnership, Pfizer could increase visibility, accessibility, and sales through one major retailer online.
2. *GlaxoSmithKline (GSK) Utilizing Online Promotions*: GSK has utilized various promotions and discounts through e-pharmacies platforms to market their products. Through these channels, GSK provided discounts for Nicorette products (Nicotine gum and lozenges for quitting smoking) to encourage smokers to quit while increasing sales.
3. *Merck Created Educational Content for Customers*: Merck developed educational videos and articles designed to inform customers about their products and the conditions they treat, such as its *Breaking Migraine* video series providing information about migraine prevention and treatment as well as promoting Emgality (Galcanezumab).
4. *Sanofi Uses Personalized Messaging* based on customer behavior and preferences to promote their products via e-pharmacy platforms, for instance, using data analytics to target allergy medication purchasers with personalized messaging about Allegra (Fexofenadine).
5. *Novartis Utilizing Data Analytics*: Novartis has used data analytics to enhance its marketing and product development efforts. They use customer information gleaned from online pharmacies such as E-Pharmacy platforms to better understand customer preferences for its heart failure medication Entresto (Sacubitril/Valsartan), then modify marketing/product strategies accordingly.

These are just a few ways pharmaceutical companies use e-pharmacy platforms to enhance their marketing initiatives. By creating partnerships, offering promotions, creating educational content, personalizing messaging, and taking advantage of data analytics solutions, pharma companies are effectively reaching and engaging with their target customers online.

Early Majority

Everett Roger's Diffusion of Innovation Theory defines "early majority" as the collective group of adopters that has a significant bearing on a product's widespread adoption and success. In pharmaceutical marketing, stringent regulations and high stakes make early majority's role particularly crucial to marketers. Therefore, the early majority has significant implications for Pharma marketers.

Early Majority Group in Pharmaceutical Marketing

The early majority group represents approximately 34% of the potential market. They typically adopt new drugs or medical devices after innovators and early adopters. Their decisions often reflect previous experiences from early adopters before making up their minds about innovations. They are encouraged to adopt new products by seeing innovators and early adopters using them successfully. The adoption by this large segment of early adopters signifies acceptance by mainstream markets, marking its transition from an innovation used only by early adopters into widely accepted treatments or products.

Implications for Pharma Marketers

Here are the key implication for pharmaceutical marketers:

1. *Product Positioning*: Marketers should promote products according to proven results and advantages since most consumers (the early majority) favor tried-and-tested solutions over newer innovations. Therefore, evidence-based marketing becomes key to assure this group about the product's safety and efficacy.
2. *Communication Strategy*: Transparent communication is of utmost importance when marketing any product or service to potential consumers, especially early majority decision-makers who rely on comprehensive and trustworthy information before making their final choice. Therefore, marketers should communicate

concisely, transparently, and balancingly by giving details of benefits, side effects, and potential risks.

3. *Building Trust*: The early majority generally adopt products when they see others, mainly opinion leaders or early adopters, using and benefiting from them. Marketers must leverage testimonials, case studies, and other social proof from innovators and early adopters to build it quickly and effectively.
4. *Education and Support Services*: Educating the early majority of consumers is paramount for sales growth. Webinars, seminars, product demonstrations, and training can all play an instrumental role in helping the early majority understand and appreciate products' advantages.
5. *Distribution Channels*: Ensuring broad accessibility for their product is essential to reaching the early majority of consumers, so marketers must develop strong partnerships with pharmacies, hospitals, and healthcare providers for the distribution process to run smoothly.

Establishing trust with early majority audiences in pharmaceutical marketing is crucial to reaching widespread market penetration and product success. Achieving this requires adopting an evidence-based product positioning, clear communication channels, trust building through social proof mechanisms, comprehensive education, and wide product accessibility. Pharmaceutical marketers that understand and meet early majority needs can drive long-term product adoption and gain mainstream acceptance more smoothly.

Earned Media

Earned Media refers to the publicity that a company or brand receives through media coverage or other third-party sources rather than paid advertising or promotion. In pharma marketing, earned media can be important for building credibility and trust with healthcare professionals and patients.

Earned media can take many forms, such as positive reviews or mentions in medical journals, news articles highlighting a pharmaceutical company's research or initiatives, or social media posts from healthcare professionals or patients sharing positive experiences with a particular medication or medical device. To leverage earned media effectively in pharma marketing, companies can:

1. *Develop Strong Relationships with Key Influencers*: Influencers such as journalists, bloggers, and social media personalities can significantly impact how a pharmaceutical company is perceived in the media and among healthcare professionals and patients. Building relationships with these influencers and providing them with accurate and engaging information can help to generate positive earned media coverage.
2. *Monitor Media Coverage and Respond Promptly*: Monitoring and responding promptly and appropriately can help pharmaceutical companies address any negative coverage or misinformation and reinforce positive messaging.
3. *Encourage Patient Advocacy and Engagement*: Engaging with patient advocacy groups and encouraging patients to share positive experiences with medications or medical devices can help generate positive earned media coverage and build trust with healthcare professionals and patients.
4. *Focus on Educational Content*: Rather than solely promoting a particular product, pharmaceutical companies can generate earned media by producing educational content that provides value to healthcare professionals and patients. This content can include research findings, disease education materials, or expert insights.

In summary, earned media can be an effective way for pharmaceutical companies to build credibility and trust with healthcare professionals and patients. By developing relationships with influencers, monitoring media coverage, encouraging patient advocacy, and producing educational content, companies can leverage earned media to their advantage in pharma marketing.

Ecological Environment

The ecological environment in pharma marketing refers to the external factors and conditions related to the natural environment, such as climate change, pollution, and sustainability, that may impact pharmaceutical companies' marketing strategies and operations. Here are some ways that the ecological environment can impact pharma marketing:

1. *Sustainable Practices*: Consumers have become more concerned with how their purchases impact the environment, so pharmaceutical companies should incorporate sustainable practices into their marketing strategies, including using Eco-friendly packaging, cutting waste production, and supporting sustainable supply chain practices.
2. *Environmental Regulations*: Pharma companies' operations may be negatively impacted by environmental regulations that restrict certain chemicals' usage during drug production, which

can influence pharmaceutical product availability and pricing strategies, potentially impacting marketing strategies.

3. *Product Labeling*: Compliance with product labeling regulations may necessitate that pharmaceutical companies disclose any environmental impacts related to the production and disposal of their pharmaceutical products. Hence, marketers need to bear this consideration when marketing their products.
4. *Climate Change*: Climate change can significantly exacerbate disease outbreaks and drive sales for specific pharmaceutical products, so pharmaceutical companies must carefully consider its possible impact and adapt marketing plans accordingly.
5. *Reputation Management*: The ecological environment can impact the reputation of pharma companies. Companies that engage in sustainable practices and promote environmental awareness may be viewed more positively by customers and stakeholders.

The ecological environment can have a significant impact on pharma marketing. By considering the environmental impact of their products and incorporating sustainable practices into their marketing strategies, pharma companies can demonstrate their commitment to social responsibility and improve their reputation with customers and stakeholders.

Monitoring the Ecological Environment

Monitoring the ecological environment in the pharmaceutical industry can be challenging, as it involves tracking a wide range of external factors and conditions related to the natural environment. However, here are some ways pharma companies can monitor the ecological environment:

1. *Stay Informed*: Pharma companies should stay informed about the latest developments in environmental regulations, climate change, and other environmental factors that may impact their marketing strategies. This can be done by following relevant news sources, attending industry conferences, and engaging with environmental organizations.
2. *Conduct Environmental Impact Assessments*: Pharma companies can conduct environmental impact analyses to understand potential environmental consequences related to their products and manufacturing processes and assess any negative environmental impacts they might be creating. By doing this, companies may identify areas for improving environmental performance and ways to lessen environmental impact through effective mitigation strategies.
3. *Measure and Track Environmental Metrics*: Pharma companies can track various environmental metrics, such as energy consumption, water usage, and waste generation, to monitor their environmental performance over time. This can help companies identify areas for improvement and demonstrate their commitment to sustainability to customers and stakeholders.
4. *Engage with Stakeholders*: Pharma companies should engage with stakeholders, such as customers, environmental organizations, and regulators, to understand their concerns and expectations related to the ecological marketing strategies aligned with stakeholder expectations and demonstrate their commitment to environmental responsibility.
5. *Use Data Analytics*: Pharma companies can use data analytics to monitor and analyze environmental trends and develop insights into the potential impact of environmental factors on their marketing strategies. This can help companies develop more effective marketing strategies tailored to the changing environmental landscape.

Monitoring the ecological environment in pharma marketing requires a proactive and comprehensive approach incorporating various monitoring techniques and engaging with several stakeholders. By monitoring the ecological environment, pharmaceutical companies can develop more effective marketing strategies aligned with the needs and expectations of customers and stakeholders while contributing to environmental sustainability.

Econometric Analysis

Econometric Analysis is like the Sherlock Holmes of Economics. It investigates the relationships between different economic variables. Imagine you have a puzzle, and each piece represents a different economic factor. Econometrics helps you figure out how these pieces fit together. It uses statistical methods to analyze and quantify the relationship among variables, making it possible to test economic theories and make predictions.

Econometricians take real-world economic data, apply statistical techniques, and build models to understand and predict economic phenomena. It is like peering into a crystal ball, but it is all about numbers and patterns instead of magic.

Econometric Analysis in Pharma Marketing

Econometric Analysis in pharmaceutical marketing is like having a crystal ball that helps you understand the economic forces at play in the market and predict how changes will impact your business.

Implications for Pharma Marketing

Econometric analysis in pharma marketing holds immense importance and has far-reaching implications for the industry. Here is why it is a game-changer:

1. *Informed Decision-Making*: Pharma companies operate in a dynamic and complex environment. The econometric analysis provides valuable insights into the factors influencing the market, enabling companies to make informed decisions about pricing, marketing strategies, and resource allocation.
2. *Optimizing Resource Allocation*: Limited resources, especially in research and development, marketing, and production, need to be allocated efficiently. Econometric models help determine the most effective use of resources, ensuring that investments yield the highest returns.
3. *Market Forecasting and Planning*: Econometric models assist in forecasting demand for pharmaceutical products. This is crucial for production planning, inventory management, and ensuring that medications are available when and where needed.
4. *Price Optimization*: Determining the optimal pricing for pharmaceutical products is complex. Econometric analysis helps understand price elasticity and the impact of pricing on demand, allowing companies to set competitive and profitable prices.
5. *Marketing Effectiveness*: Pharma marketing involves various channels and strategies. Econometric models assess the effectiveness of marketing initiatives, helping companies identify which channels and activities contribute most to sales and brand awareness.
6. *Risk Management*: The pharmaceutical industry is exposed to various risks, including regulatory changes, market competition, and economic fluctuations. Econometric analysis enables companies to assess and mitigate these risks by understanding how different variables interact and impact business outcomes.
7. *Policy Compliance*: Healthcare is subject to stringent regulations. Econometric models assist in ensuring that marketing practices comply with regulatory requirements. This is essential for avoiding legal issues and maintaining the trust of healthcare professionals and consumers.
8. *Competitive Advantage*: Companies that leverage econometric analysis effectively gain a competitive advantage. By understanding market dynamics and consumer behavior, they can stay ahead of competitors, adapt quickly to changes, and position themselves strategically in the market.
9. *Patient-Centric Approaches*: Econometric analysis allows a deeper understanding of patient behavior and preferences. This insight is invaluable for tailoring marketing strategies to meet the needs of patients, improving patient engagement, and fostering better health outcomes.
10. *Adapting to Industry Trends*: The healthcare landscape constantly evolves with technological advancements, demographic changes, and shifts in consumer behavior. Econometric analysis helps pharma companies adapt to these needs, ensuring they remain relevant and responsive to the market's changing needs.

While the importance of econometric analysis in pharma marketing is clear, it is important to note that successful implementation requires skilled analysts, high-quality data, and a commitment to continuous refinement of models. The implications of effective econometric analysis include sustained growth, improved market positioning, and a stronger ability to navigate the complexities of the pharmaceutical industry. It is not just about analyzing data; It is about shaping the future of the pharma landscape.

Economic Environment

The economic environment is the general condition of an economy in a certain region or country. It includes various aspects, including its level of development, the degree of market competition, resources available and government policies and regulations that impact it, inflation rates, and unemployment levels, among others.

Economic environments influence individuals' and organizations' business and investment decisions. A favorable economy provides opportunities for growth and profit, while unfavorable ones present challenges and risks; hence understanding your economic environment is integral in making informed business and investment decisions.

Implications for Pharma Marketers

The economic environment can significantly impact pharma marketers. Some key implications could include the following:

1. *Pricing Strategies for Pharmaceutical Products*: Economic considerations can influence pharmaceutical pricing strategies. A recession or economic downturn leaves people less willing to pay high medication prices, so pharmaceutical marketers may need to adjust their strategies in response to such trends.
2. *Access to Healthcare*: The economic environment can also impact access to healthcare, which can impact the demand for pharmaceutical products. In countries where healthcare is publicly funded, changes in government spending on healthcare can impact access to pharmaceutical products.
3. *Regulatory Environment*: The economic environment can impact the regulatory environment for pharmaceutical products. In times of economic downturn, governments may introduce new regulations or cut funding for regulatory bodies, which can impact the regulatory approval and launch of new products.
4. *Investment*: The economic environment can impact investment in research and development for pharmaceutical products. In times of economic recession, companies may cut back on R&D spending, which can impact the pipeline of new products.

Pharma marketers must know the economic environment and its product and strategy implications. They can position their products for success in any economic environment by monitoring economic trends and adjusting their strategies.

Monitoring the Economic Environment

Pharma marketers can use the following for tracking economic conditions and making informed business decisions:

1. *Economics Indicators*: Keep tabs on key economic indicators like GDP, inflation, employment rates, consumer confidence, and government spending, as these can provide key insights into the health of an economy and its impact on the healthcare industry.
2. *Market Research*: Pharma marketers conducting market research will conduct market studies better to understand consumer behavior, attitudes, and preferences as they are affected by economic factors to tailor products and messages according to changing consumer needs.
3. *Staying Up-To-Date With Regulatory Developments*: Pharma marketers can stay informed on any regulatory updates or changes which impact the pharmaceutical industry, helping them anticipate any shifts and adapt their strategies accordingly.
4. *Stay Up-to-Date on Industry News and Reports*: It is beneficial for pharma marketers to remain current on industry news from credible sources like trade publications, industry associations, and market research firms to understand market trends and emerging opportunities better. This can assist pharma marketers with creating tailored campaigns.
5. *Expert Analysis*: Securing expert analysis from economists, industry specialists, or financial analysts may provide additional perspectives on how the healthcare economy affects itself and impacts healthcare practitioners.

By monitoring these sources and staying abreast of economic conditions, pharmaceutical marketers can make well-informed decisions and adjust strategies as required for success in any economic climate.

Economic Value Added (EVA)

Economic value added (EVA) measures a company's financial performance based on the residual wealth calculated, deducting its cost of capital from its operating profit, adjusted for taxes on a cash basis. It can also be described as the value produced from funded operations during a specific period in pharmaceutical marketing. EVA can measure the effectiveness of marketing strategies by evaluating whether they generate a return that exceeds the company's cost of capital. This involves calculating the net operating profit after taxes attributed to a marketing initiative and subtracting the associated capital costs

Here are a few applications of EVA in pharmaceutical marketing:

1. *Measuring Campaign Effectiveness*: EVA can measure the economic value generated from marketing campaigns by tracking sales and profitability compared with its associated direct and allocated costs.
2. *Resource Allocation*: EVA can serve as a valuable guideline when allocating resources. Marketing initiatives with positive EVA should be pursued further, while any initiatives producing negative

returns should be reconsidered for improvement or cancellation.

3. *Strategic Planning*: Economic Value-added (EVA) analysis can gauge the potential financial repercussions of various marketing strategies, helping companies make informed decisions regarding which will likely create the greatest economic benefit.
4. *Performance Evaluation*: EVA can measure the success of marketing teams or managers by comparing the economic value generated with the costs incurred.
5. *Pricing Decisions*: EVA can aid pricing decisions by helping to identify a price at which a product would generate maximum value over and above its cost of capital.

While EVA can be an extremely valuable performance indicator for pharmaceutical marketing, it should be combined with other metrics that reflect strategic and operational goals, such as market share, brand recognition, patient outcomes, etc. Additionally, as EVA measures financial data, it may not accurately depict investments made over a longer period in areas like brand building, patient relationship building, or innovation.

Implications for Marketers

Utilizing Economic Value Added as a performance metric has profound ramifications for marketers in the pharmaceutical industry, particularly within its marketing arena. Consider the following, for example:

1. *Justifying Marketing Spend*: EVA provides a quantitative basis for justifying marketing expenditure by showing its economic value created through various initiatives, making budget discussions, and advocating for investment in marketing easier and more convincing.
2. *Informing Strategy*: EVA can help inform strategy development by measuring the potential economic impact of various marketing strategies, leading to more informed decision-making that aligns marketing tactics with financial goals.
3. *Enhancing Resource Allocation*: Marketers can make more effective resource allocation decisions by recognizing which marketing initiatives generate positive EVA (economic value added). This allows marketers to optimize marketing expenditure while improving the efficiency and effectiveness of operations.
4. *EVA Drives Accountability*: Connecting marketing performance to financial metrics through EVA allows marketing teams to take greater accountability for its results-focused approach and focus on value creation.
5. *Evaluating Pricing Strategy*: EVA can assist pharmaceutical marketers in creating effective pricing strategies. Marketers can identify an optimum price point to bring maximum returns while considering capital costs.

EVA can be an extremely helpful metric, yet marketers must remember to balance short-term financial performance and invest in long-term brand building and customer relationship management. Furthermore, as EVA is only an indicator of financial outcomes, its full effect may not necessarily reflect what EVA indicates about non-financial objectives like improving patient outcomes or customer loyalty.

Marketers must remember that EVA does not account for risks related to specific investments or initiatives, for instance, regulatory risks in pharmaceutical marketing . Thus, it should be used alongside other performance metrics and risk assessment tools to obtain an overall picture of performance and value creation.

Educational Advertising

Educational advertising is a type of pharmaceutical marketing that provides information about medical conditions, treatments, and healthcare resources. Educational advertising aims to educate patients and healthcare providers about a particular condition or treatment while promoting the pharmaceutical company's products.

One way to create effective educational advertising in pharma marketing is to provide clear, accurate, and engaging information about the condition or treatment. This can include explaining the causes, symptoms, and risk factors of the condition, as well as the treatment's benefits and potential side effects. Educational advertising should be based on sound medical evidence and should avoid making exaggerated or unsupported claims.

Another approach is to provide educational resources that go beyond traditional advertising messages. For example, a pharmaceutical company might create a website that provides patients with resources on managing their condition, including diet, exercise, and stress management tips. The website could also include information on support groups and other resources that patients can access to help them cope with their condition.

Here are a few examples of pharmaceutical companies that have used educational advertising to connect with patients and healthcare providers:

1. *AbbVie's* Understanding Crohn's & Colitis *Campaign*: AbbVie created a campaign to educate patients

and healthcare providers about Crohn's disease, ulcerative colitis, the two chronic inflammatory bowel diseases. The campaign included a website with resources on managing the condition and a video series featuring patients talking about their experiences with the disease.

2. *Merck's* Your Health Matters *Campaign*: Merck created a campaign to encourage patients to participate actively in their healthcare. The campaign included a website with resources on different health conditions and tips on staying healthy and managing chronic conditions.
3. *Pfizer's* Quit Smoking *Campaign*: Pfizer created a campaign to help smokers quit, featuring information on the health risks of smoking and tips on how to quit. The campaign included TV commercials, print ads, and a website with resources on quitting smoking.

Pharmaceutical companies can build trust with patients and healthcare providers by providing educational resources and information, ultimately leading to better health outcomes. First, however, it's important to ensure that educational advertising is based on sound medical evidence and delivered clearly and engagingly.

Educational Marketing

Educational marketing in pharma refers to using educational materials and resources to promote pharmaceutical products while informing healthcare providers and patients about disease states, treatment options, and the advantages and benefits of specific pharmaceutical products. Educational marketing's main goal is to provide valuable knowledge for making informed decisions regarding treatment options, improving patient outcomes, and ultimately creating better healthcare experiences.

Here are a few educational marketing strategies used in pharmaceuticals:

1. *Medical Education Programs*: Pharma companies may provide healthcare professionals with courses on disease states and treatment options through continuing medical education (CME) courses or self-paced learning modules. These can be delivered online, in person, or self-paced learning modules.
2. *Educational Resources*: Pharmaceutical companies may offer educational materials such as brochures, videos, websites, and apps that contain specific diseases, treatment options, and product information for healthcare providers and patients. These may cover issues like specific disease treatments as well as product details.
3. *Disease Awareness Campaigns*: Pharmaceutical companies may host awareness campaigns to educate members of the general public and healthcare providers on specific illnesses and their early detection and treatment benefits through events, social media promotions, or online resources. These can include events or social media strategies.
4. *Patient Support Programs*: Pharma companies may offer patient support programs, including educational materials, counseling services, and financial aid for treatment plans and medications. Furthermore, access may also be given to specialty pharmacy services that help individuals manage medications effectively and stay compliant with prescribed regimens.

Educational marketing for pharmaceutical products can build relationships between healthcare professionals and patients, promote pharmaceutical products, and ultimately enhance patient outcomes.

Effective Frequency

Effective frequency in pharmaceutical marketing refers to the number of times an audience must see or hear a message before seeing or hearing its desired response or impact. Effective frequency can provide desired effects or responses to targeted messaging campaigns based on repeated exposure of messages, such as increasing brand recognition or product sales.

Finding an optimal frequency for pharma marketing campaigns can be challenging, depending on variables such as target audience demographics and message complexity, competitive landscape issues, etc. Here are some general guidelines you can follow when setting an optimal frequency:

1. *Establish the Target Audience*: Pharma companies should develop an in-depth knowledge of their target audience's behaviors, preferences, and attitudes about healthcare products and services. This can help to inform the messaging and determine an appropriate, effective frequency strategy.
2. *Test and Measure*: Pharma companies should test different effective frequency strategies and measure their impact on key performance indicators, such as brand awareness and product sales. This can help to identify the most effective strategy for a given campaign.
3. *Consider the Competitive Landscape*: Pharma companies should consider the market

competition level and adjust their frequency strategy accordingly. A higher effective frequency may be necessary for a crowded market to stand out.

4. *Balance Frequency with Relevance*: Pharma companies should balance the effective frequency of their messaging with its relevance to the target audience. Too much messaging can lead to audience fatigue, while too little can result in a lack of impact.

Effective Frequency Strategies in Pharma

Here are some examples of effective frequency strategies that pharmaceutical companies could use:

1. *Reminder Ads*: Pharma companies often use reminder ads to reinforce brand messaging and increase patient awareness. For example, a company could create advertisements targeting patients suffering from certain medical conditions with frequent prescription drug ads, and serve to remind physicians and patients alike about its brand when discussing treatment options with healthcare providers. By running such advertisements repeatedly, the company can increase the odds that physicians and patients will remember its brand when discussing options with healthcare providers.
2. *Drip Campaigns*: Drip Campaigns are an email marketing technique that involves sending incremental messages over an extended period to reach targeted audiences. Pharma companies might utilize drip campaigns as an educational initiative or reminder for healthcare providers and patients about medication adherence.
3. *Retargeting Ads*: Retargeting ads are an online advertising format used by pharmaceutical companies that target visitors who have already visited or engaged with a website in some manner, whether to remind patients about an option they viewed earlier on their site or engage healthcare providers about an emerging treatment option. Retargeting Ads are typically shown within 24 hours after users interact with content from that website, making these advertisements ideal for reminding patients or healthcare providers about medications or therapies they have already seen advertised through other channels, such as display advertising.
4. *Disease Awareness Campaigns*: Disease awareness campaigns educate the public about a medical condition or disease. By running these campaigns repeatedly, pharma companies can increase public awareness and understanding of a condition, ultimately driving demand for treatment options.

An effective frequency strategy is an important consideration for Pharma companies looking to maximize the impact of their marketing campaigns. By understanding the target audience, testing and measuring different strategies, and balancing frequency with relevance, companies can optimize their messaging and achieve the desired outcomes for their campaigns.

Efficiency

Efficiency, in simple terms, is doing things the right way by optimizing resources, minimizing waste, and maximizing return on investment (ROI) of marketing activities. This means developing streamlined and effective processes for executing marketing campaigns, leveraging technology to automate tasks and increase productivity, and allocating resources to maximize the impact of marketing efforts.

Campaign management also involves continuous monitoring and evaluation to make adjustments as necessary to ensure it achieves its desired goals.

Companies can ensure their marketing initiatives are efficient and effective by following proper procedures to plan, execute and optimize marketing strategies that generate positive returns while driving business expansion. Doing this properly involves careful planning, implementation, and ongoing evaluation so they produce their intended outcomes. Companies use marketing automation tools such as *Salesforce Marketing Cloud* to quickly produce and distribute materials to utilize their resources on higher-value activities.

Companies can reduce costs, improve productivity and drive improved business results by doing things correctly and becoming more efficient. Doing this requires continuous improvement initiatives and being ready to adapt marketing strategies according to changing market conditions, and customer demands over time.

Efficiency in pharma marketing can be measured in several ways, including:

1. *Cost per Customer Reach*: This measures the cost of reaching each healthcare provider with the company's marketing message. A lower cost per customer reach indicates that the company uses resources more efficiently to reach its target audience.
2. *Sales per Representative*: This metric measures the sales generated by each sales representative. A higher sales per representative indicates that the company's sales force is more efficient in converting healthcare providers into customers.

3. *Return on Investment (ROI)*: Return on Investment is an indicator of financial return from marketing investments made by an enterprise, measuring how profitable their marketing investments have been per dollar spent on marketing activities. A higher ROI indicates greater revenue generated as a result.

Companies seeking to improve efficiency in pharma marketing may employ various strategies and tools, including:

1. *Targeted marketing*: Companies can maximize efficiency by targeting their marketing efforts to healthcare providers likely to prescribe their products, thereby optimizing efforts while decreasing wasteful expenditures.
2. *Sales Force Automation*: By automating tasks that have become routine and providing sales representatives with better data and tools, companies can increase productivity while decreasing costs associated with selling.
3. *Multichannel Marketing*: Companies using various marketing channels like email, social media, and direct visits can reach healthcare providers with customized messages through their preferred channels to optimize customer reach and build meaningful customer relationships.

Efficiency in pharmaceutical marketing is vital to reaching business objectives and realizing maximum returns on investments. Companies can optimize their sales and marketing activities by efficiently using all available resources and tools to get maximum results with limited resources.

Effectiveness

In simple terms, effectiveness is doing the right things, while efficiency means doing things the right way.

Effective pharmaceutical marketing means doing what's necessary to reach desired outcomes and goals of any marketing strategy or campaign, which means creating a detailed marketing plan tailored specifically to target audiences' needs and preferences. Effective pharma marketing involves:

- Identifying the most appropriate marketing channels and tactics to reach the target audience
- Developing compelling messaging that resonates with the audience
- Executing the plan with precision and consistency

Constant monitoring and evaluation ensure the campaign remains on course toward reaching its goals.

Attaining success requires companies to put forth effort in every aspect of marketing activities; from planning and execution through evaluation and optimization; to ensure they deliver desired outcomes and drive business expansion. This necessitates careful consideration during each phase.

Electroencephalography (EEG)

EEG (Electroencephalography) can provide insights into consumers' neurophysiological responses and enable marketers to assess cognitive and emotional reactions to marketing stimuli. Here are a few applications of EEG technology in pharmaceutical marketing:

1. *Ad Content Testing*: EEG can measure brain activity to evaluate the efficacy of pharmaceutical ads, promotional content, or educational materials. By analyzing EEG data, researchers can isolate those moments or elements which elicit strong emotional reactions or engagement and pinpoint them for further examination. This helps optimize marketing content by prioritizing what matters.
2. *Brand Perception and Recall*: EEG can offer valuable insight into how consumers perceive and recall pharmaceutical brands. By studying brain activity patterns, researchers can measure neural responses associated with brand recognition, recall, and association. This data allows the evaluation of branding strategies and identification of ways to increase brand recall in marketing campaigns.
3. *EEG Can Assess Pharmaceutical Marketing Strategies Effectiveness*: EEG provides researchers a means of measuring the impact of various messages or slogans used for pharmaceutical marketing campaigns by measuring brain activity levels in consumers who respond most strongly. With this data in hand, they can develop powerful and persuasive messages.
4. *Product Positioning and Differentiation*: EEG can assist marketers with understanding how consumers perceive and differentiate pharmaceutical products. Through analysis of brain activity patterns, researchers can detect neural responses associated with features, benefits, or claims associated with various

pharmaceutical offerings, providing valuable data that allows better product positioning and differentiation strategies to be executed by marketers.

5. *Usability Testing*: EEG can be used to measure usability and user experience on pharmaceutical websites, mobile apps, or digital platforms. Researchers can measure cognitive load, frustration, or engagement levels during user interactions using EEG to measure brain activity levels, providing data that helps pinpoint improvement areas. These can help marketers optimize the user experiences of their digital marketing assets.

EEG research in pharmaceutical marketing must be careful and follow ethical guidelines and obtain participant consent. Furthermore, pharma marketers should comply with regulations and guidelines regarding data collection and analysis to protect participant privacy.

Electronic Health Record (EHR)

Electronic Health Records (EHRs) are digital records created and maintained by healthcare providers that contain patient health data, such as their medical history, diagnoses, medications prescribed to them, laboratory test results, or imaging studies. EHRs aim to enhance patient care and communication between healthcare providers by digitizing this vital information.

EHRs in Pharma Marketing

Electronic Health Records can play an invaluable role in pharma marketing by offering insights into patient and healthcare provider behavior that inform targeted advertising efforts. Below are a few ways EHRs are being leveraged:

1. *Targeting Individual Patients*: Pharmaceutical companies can use EHRs to target patients diagnosed with specific conditions, or prescribed certain drugs; then send these patients using relevant marketing messages and educational resources about available treatment options.
2. *Physician Outreach*: EHRs allow pharmaceutical companies to identify providers who frequently prescribe certain medicines or treat specific medical conditions with specific treatments, providing pharmaceutical firms with valuable intelligence on which to tailor marketing messages and education materials about their products to reach these providers.
3. *Clinical Trial Recruitment*: EHRs can help pharmaceutical companies identify eligible patients for clinical trials by looking at their past and current medical histories, providing them with vital data for improving recruitment efforts and participation rates.
4. *Real-Time Monitoring*: Electronic Health Records can enable pharmaceutical companies to track patient outcomes instantly, giving them real-time insight into their products' effectiveness and making necessary adjustments in marketing strategy and implementation.
5. *Post-Market Surveillance*: EHRs can monitor adverse events and other safety concerns related to pharmaceutical products after approval and release for sale, providing valuable data that informs ongoing marketing initiatives and product development strategies. This data could inform ongoing product sales strategies.

EHRs offer great insights into patient and healthcare provider behavior that can inform targeted marketing efforts and enhance patient care. Yet, pharmaceutical companies must abide by applicable privacy and data security regulations when employing EHRs for marketing purposes.

How Pharma Companies Can Engage with EHRs

Electronic health records for pharmaceutical marketing purposes are highly regulated, and pharmaceutical companies must abide by certain strict guidelines when using EHRs to market their products. Pharma companies using EHRs as part of their engagement programs must adhere to privacy laws and regulations when conveying marketing messages through electronic medical records to healthcare providers to engage them successfully.

Here are several examples of pharmaceutical companies leveraging electronic health records (EHRs) for marketing purposes:

1. In 2018, Pfizer announced in its partnership with Komodo Health to identify patients that could benefit from its products. Pfizer planned on using data from Komodo's EHR network to target marketing messages at these patients likely to respond well to its products and use that as its starting point.
2. Novartis announced a partnership with Science 37, a clinical research solutions company, to use EHR data for clinical trial recruitment purposes, using Science 37's platform to target patients interested in participating in clinical trials for its products via ads or marketing messages.
3. In 2019, Merck announced its partnership with Human Longevity, the genomics-based health

intelligence company, to use EHR data to identify patients likely to benefit from its products, develop targeted marketing campaigns, and identify individuals interested in clinical trials.

However, pharmaceutical companies must use EHRs transparently and without deception to identify patients who might benefit from their products. Patients have an absolute right to control their healthcare information, and healthcare providers must always respect patient privacy and confidentiality.

At the same time, healthcare providers must remain mindful of any possible pharma marketing activities through EHRs and be wary about any information received. When making clinical decisions and disclosing potential conflicts of interest, healthcare providers should keep patients' best interests in mind and be honest and transparent when discussing any possible conflicts of interest.

Electronic Media

Electronic media is news and entertainment created through televisions, radios, computers, smartphones, or the Internet. This term includes traditional broadcast forms like television and radio and newer forms like websites, social media platforms streaming services, etc., that enable global content distribution and consumption, revolutionizing how people connect and interact worldwide.

Electronic Media in Pharma Marketing

Digital technology has given pharmaceutical companies new ways to use electronic media in marketing more effectively to reach and directly engage with target audiences. To reach this objective, pharmaceutical electronic marketing campaigns may use various channels like websites, social media accounts, email campaigns, mobile applications, or advertising.

Pharmaceutical companies can utilize electronic media to effectively promote and engage customers for product promotion and customer engagement. They could, for instance, develop interactive websites providing educational materials about their products, mobile apps to monitor patient medications or symptoms, targeted social media campaigns directed towards specific patient groups, or to distribute marketing material, such as product brochures or videos online and provide customer support through chat, or email services.

Electronic media in pharmaceutical marketing presents many distinct advantages, with electronic platforms helping companies engage with a wider audience more quickly and reach customers more efficiently. Electronic platforms also enable pharmaceutical firms to send personalized and targeted messages directly to patients, healthcare professionals, or other interested stakeholders and collect insights that help optimize marketing strategies over time.

Electronic media in pharmaceutical marketing presents unique challenges, including compliance and data privacy considerations. Therefore, pharmaceutical companies using electronic media must abide by strict guidelines and regulations when marketing their products; furthermore, they should strive for transparency and ethics to create trust among their target audiences.

Example of How Pharma Uses Electronic Media

Here are a few pharmaceutical companies using electronic media as part of their marketing initiatives:

1. Pfizer recently unveiled an iPhone application called *Quitter's Circle* designed to assist smokers in quitting smoking. This tool provides resources such as tips for quitting, motivational messages, and an option allowing users to track their progress.
2. Novartis developed the *Heart Partner* digital health platform specifically tailored for those living with heart failure. The mobile app tracks symptoms and gives personalized feedback, while the web portal allows patients to connect with healthcare teams directly.
3. Merck launched a social media campaign called *Type 2 Diabetes Time* to increase awareness about type 2 diabetes and encourage patients to manage it independently. It consisted of posts across social media platforms and providing resources and information about managing this condition.
4. Sanofi recently unveiled its digital health platform, *My Dose Coach*, specifically tailored for patients living with diabetes. This platform includes mobile phone apps that provide personalized insulin dosage recommendations, reminders, and web portals, allowing patients to track progress and communicate with healthcare teams.
5. Roche developed the *Cervical Cancer Risk* website to educate patients on the risk factors for cancer and encourage them to speak to healthcare providers about screening guidelines. Resources provided on the site include an interactive cancer risk quiz and information regarding screening guidelines.

These examples demonstrate how pharmaceutical companies utilize electronic media to reach and engage their target audiences, provide valuable resources, and improve patient outcomes.

Electronic Word-of-Mouth (eWOM)

Electronic Word-of-Mouth (eWOM) refers to sharing opinions or information about products, services, or brands via electronic channels like social media platforms and social networks such as Twitter or Facebook, online forums, blogs, or review websites—often initiated by consumers who have firsthand experience of a service/product and wish to express their thoughts. It could either be positive or negative and can significantly change consumer behaviors, brand reputation, and sales figures. This form of marketing now represents an indispensable asset in businesses looking for growth online. eWOM can build customer bases while increasing online presences!

Electronic Word-of-Mouth (eWOM) marketing can be an extremely powerful asset to pharmaceutical marketing campaigns, reaching wide audiences and affecting consumer purchases. Furthermore, positive reviews or endorsements from patients or healthcare providers can build brand recognition. At the same time, negative comments provide opportunities to address areas for improvement or identify problems within a product's lifespan.

But electronic Word-of-Mouth Marketing (eWOM) also has its share of challenges for pharmaceutical marketers. Regulatory agencies such as the FDA monitor the online promotion of pharmaceutical products and services to ensure accuracy. Companies should also pay careful attention when collecting or sharing eWOM with patients not to compromise patient privacy.

Companies looking to leverage electronic word-of-mouth (eWOM) marketing may utilize social media and other online channels to engage with patients and healthcare providers, share product/service details, receive feedback, and answer any queries or address comments and inquiries. They could also employ influencer marketing strategies with key opinion leaders and influential individuals or agencies to promote products/services and increase brand awareness and reputation development efforts.

How Pharma Companies Utilize Electronic Word-of-Mouth (eWOM)

Pharmaceutical companies increasingly use electronic word-of-mouth (eWOM) marketing strategies to reach wider audiences and build brand recognition. Here are a few examples of eWOM implementation by pharmaceutical organizations:

1. With Facebook and Twitter accounts, Pfizer has leveraged social media and other online channels to engage patients and healthcare providers and share information about its products and services. They regularly post updates regarding Pfizer products and respond to patient inquiries or suggestions through these mediums.
2. Novartis has established partnerships with online patient communities, such as PatientsLikeMe, to market its products and services and engage patients directly by tapping into such communities' insights about patient experiences and preferences and developing innovative therapies or services more rapidly.
3. Merck has leveraged influencer marketing strategies to form partnerships with key opinion leaders and other influential stakeholders to promote its products and services. One such influencer campaign involves joining forces with Dr. Mehmet Oz, a well-known television personality and physician in promoting diabetes medication and raising awareness for this condition.

Electronic word-of-mouth (eWOM) can be an invaluable asset to pharmaceutical companies looking to increase brand recognition, engage patients and healthcare providers, promote products or services and build loyalty from existing customers. However, when considering this marketing technique, companies must comply with regulatory guidelines and safeguard patient privacy when developing strategies that incorporate this strategy.

European Medicines Agency (EMA)

The European Medicines Agency (EMA) is a decentralized agency charged with reviewing, supervising, and regulating medicinal products available within the European Union markets to protect patient safety and efficacy while assuring market access for new medications.

Key functions of the European Medicines Agency include:

Evaluation of Medicines: The European Medicines Agency reviews applications for marketing approval of new human and veterinary drugs in the Europian Union. To do this effectively, it evaluates clinical trial data, safety profiles, and quality controls before deciding if its benefits exceed any risks of using such medicine.

Pharmacovigilance: The agency actively oversees the safety of approved medicines through an efficient system known as pharmacovigilance. They collect, evaluate, and take appropriate regulatory action on any reported potential side effects or safety concerns arising with any drug.

Scientific Advice: The European Medicines Agency provides scientific advice to pharmaceutical companies regarding all aspects of medicine development, including study designs, data requirements, and regulatory procedures.

Harmonization: The European Medicines Agency works towards harmonizing regulations across European member states so patients can access high-quality and safe medicines across Europe.

Collaboration: The EMA collaborates with regulatory authorities outside the European Union and international organizations to foster global cooperation on medicine regulation and safety issues.

With its headquarters in Amsterdam, the Netherlands, the European Medicines Agency safeguards public health by promoting quality, safety, and efficacy standards for medicinal products sold in the European Union.

Emotional Branding

Emotional branding is a marketing strategy which seeks to establish an emotional bond between brands and their target audiences, to foster brand loyalty and advocacy by tapping into consumer emotions and values that resonate.

Emotional Branding involves developing a brand personality to reflect the emotional benefits and values of the product or service, aiming to establish positive associations between users of that brand and promote it. This association aims to form positive emotional associations between consumers' use of and support of product/service and emotional branding efforts.

Emotional branding has proven particularly successful for pharmaceutical companies when it comes to building trust among patients seeking solutions for sensitive health concerns. Here are some examples of emotional branding in the pharmaceutical industry:

1. Johnson & Johnson's *Caring for the World, One Person at a Time* campaign builds a strong emotional connection with consumers by emphasizing its values of trust, reliability, and care. It focuses on its commitment to caring for people's health and well-being.
2. Pfizer's *Working Together for a Healthier World* campaign emphasizes its commitment to working collaboratively to find new solutions for healthcare challenges. In addition, the company's messaging is designed to create a sense of optimism and hope around the future of healthcare.
3. Roche focuses on its commitment to innovation and finding new solutions for patients' health challenges in their *Doing Now What Patients Need Next* campaign, creating a sense of excitement and anticipation around the future of health.

Emotional Branding can be an invaluable asset to pharmaceutical companies looking to build trust and loyalty among patients and healthcare providers. By tapping into emotions that resonate with their target audiences, pharmaceutical firms can craft brand personalities that foster lasting commitment from patients and healthcare providers alike.

How to Create an Emotional Branding Strategy

How can pharma companies create emotional branding strategies? Here are some important steps to create it:

1. *Define Your Brand Personality*: Your brand personality is the traits and characteristics defining your brand. It's important to identify your brand's emotional benefits and values and how they align with your target audience. For example, a pharmaceutical company might focus on empathy, innovation, and hope as key emotional benefits.
2. *Conduct Market Research*: Understanding your target audience's emotional needs and preferences is important. Market research can help you identify the emotional triggers that can resonate with your target audience.
3. *Develop Emotional Messaging*: Once you have identified your brand personality and emotional triggers, it's time to develop messaging that speaks to your target audience's emotional needs. This might include creating taglines, brand statements, and advertising campaigns emphasizing your brand's emotional benefits and values.

4. *Use Emotional Imagery*: Visuals can evoke emotions and create a strong emotional connection with your target audience. Consider using emotional imagery, such as photographs or videos, to convey your brand's benefits and values.
5. *Consistency Across all Touchpoints*: It's important to maintain consistency across all touchpoints., including your website, social media channels, advertising, and customer service. Ensure your emotional messaging and imagery are consistent across all channels to reinforce your brand personality and create a unified brand experience.
6. *Measure Success*: Finally, measuring the success of your emotional branding strategy is important. Use metrics such as brand awareness, customer loyalty, and customer satisfaction to evaluate the effectiveness of your strategy and make adjustments as needed.

Emotional branding strategy can help pharmaceutical companies build trust and loyalty with their target audience by tapping into their emotional needs and preferences. In addition, these steps can help companies to create a strong brand personality that resonates with their audience and inspires long-term brand advocacy.

Emotional Engagement

Emotional engagement is essential to pharmaceutical marketing as it creates bonds between audiences and the brands or products they consume. Here are a few strategies for encouraging emotional connection in pharmaceutical advertising campaigns:

1. *Storytelling*: Employ techniques to depict how pharmaceutical products or treatments have helped patients, caregivers, or healthcare professionals. Tell their experiences using personal narratives which elicit empathy while creating emotional ties that compel audiences to engage more closely with your brand.
2. *Empathy and Understanding*: Showcase patient centricity, compassion and support in your marketing materials. This helps you demonstrate empathy towards patients' and families' challenges and struggles, generating emotional resonance with your brand. It helps build trust and increase loyalty.
3. *Authenticity and Transparency*: Communicate in an authentic, honest, and straightforward manner when communicating the benefits, risks, and limitations of a pharmaceutical product or treatment to healthcare professionals, patients and other stakeholders. Being truthful with them will build credibility and trust, fostering emotional engagement.
4. *Visual and Emotional Appeal*: Engage consumers using visually captivating imagery, videos, or graphics that create positive associations or generate hopefulness or feelings of well-being. Include images depicting healthy individuals or vivid scenes that produce the desired emotional responses on websites, social media accounts, or advertisements. These visuals could be utilized across marketing channels, including websites, social media, and advertisements.
5. *Patient Support Programs*: Offer comprehensive patient support programs beyond pharmaceutical products, such as resources, educational materials, counseling services, or online communities to support both patients and their families. Doing this can foster stronger emotional connections to your brand while increasing loyalty among your audience.
6. *Emotional Testimonials*: Include emotional testimonials from patients, caregivers, or healthcare professionals who have seen positive outcomes or significant interactions with your product or treatment. Hearing personal stories demonstrating their emotional impact will resonate with audiences and strengthen emotional engagement.
7. *Social Impact and Corporate Social Responsibility*: Emphasize your company's dedication to social impact and corporate social responsibility initiatives, such as improving healthcare access, community welfare, or supporting charitable causes. Demonstrating genuine commitment can foster an emotional bond with its audience.

Emotional engagement in pharmaceutical marketing must always remain ethical, respectful, and considerate of patients' needs and privacy. Compliance with relevant regulations and guidelines regarding patient data or testimonials should always come first.

Emotional Intelligence (EQ)

Emotional intelligence refers to the capacity for understanding, processing, and controlling one's emotions and those of others. It encompasses empathy, self-awareness, self-motivation, and social abilities.

Pharmaceutical marketing relies heavily on emotional intelligence for building meaningful relationships with healthcare professionals, patients, and other key stakeholders. Sales representatives with high emotional IQ can better recognize and respond to people's emotions and needs, leading them towards building more trusting and genuine rapport-filled interactions with patients, healthcare providers and other stakeholders.

Here are several ways emotional intelligence can play an essential role in pharmaceutical marketing:

1. *Fostering Relationships*: Sales representatives who possess high emotional intelligence are better at understanding the needs and preferences of healthcare providers and patients and forging stronger, long-lasting relationships with them.
2. *Effective Communication*: Emotional intelligence is integral for successful sales communication, with sales reps who possess it more likely to convey their messages effectively and establish rapport.
3. *Conflict Resolution*: Pharmaceutical marketing can be an inherently high-pressure environment and disagreements may arise between sales representatives, healthcare providers and other stakeholders. Representatives who possess strong emotional intelligence are better prepared to manage and resolve conflicts constructively.
4. *Leadership*: Emotional intelligence is an integral aspect of successful sales management, and managers with superior emotional IQ have an advantage when motivating and engaging their teams, creating a productive culture within their sales departments.

Emotional intelligence (EQ) is an indispensable skill set for sales representatives and managers in pharmaceutical marketing, helping to foster strong relationships, communicate efficiently, and meet sales targets successfully.

Emotional Marketing

Emotional Marketing (or Affective Marketing) is an approach to advertising that seeks to tap into consumers on an emotional level rather than focus on just advertising its features and benefits. The idea is to create an unforgettable and positive experience that resonates with customers intimately and eventually builds brand loyalty and advocacy among its consumers.

Emotional marketing refers to businesses' attempts at tapping into the emotions and desires of their target audiences to generate belonging, excitement, or happiness in them. This can be accomplished using different techniques, such as storytelling, visual imagery, or music, as examples that elicit emotional responses; thus producing optimal marketing campaigns that reach target markets with strong emotional messages.

Emotional marketing has proven particularly effective for pharmaceutical products and services designed to improve health and well-being, such as medications that ease discomfort or enhance the quality of life. A campaign that emphasizes emotional benefits, such as relieving pain, can often prove more successful than one which emphasizes features or benefits alone.

Here are a few examples of emotional marketing within the pharmaceutical industry:

1. *Disease Awareness Campaigns*: These campaigns aim to bring attention to particular health concerns by emphasizing their emotional toll, such as Pfizer's *Get Old* campaign which features phrases like *It is not about adding years but life.*
2. *Patient Testimonials*: By featuring real-life stories of how real patients have benefitted from medication or treatments offered by companies, emotional connections with consumers can be created that showcase the positive influence their products can have. AbbVie's *It Takes Guts* campaign strives to raise awareness about IBD and its effect on patients. Real patients share their stories and experiences, with a particular focus on the emotional burden of living with chronic conditions like IBD. Novartis' *Heart to Heart* campaign offers another example of using testimonials in an emotionally engaging way to increase awareness about heart failure and encourage patients to manage it themselves. Real patients share their accounts of living with this condition, showing its emotional impact on daily living.
3. *Visual Images*: Photos or videos that successfully illustrate consumer emotions can have an incredible effect. For example, a campaign showing happy, active people enjoying life after taking a medication may be more effective than simply showing the product itself. Roche's *The Moment* campaign is a good example of visual imagery of emotions as it is focused on raising awareness of breast cancer and the importance of early detection. The emotional campaign features real women who have been affected by breast cancer, sharing their stories and encouraging others to take action.

These campaigns demonstrate how emotional marketing can build connections with consumers and raise awareness of important health issues while promoting a brand's offerings.

Emotional marketing can be a powerful tool for pharmaceutical companies looking to build brand loyalty and connect with their target audience meaningfully.

Emotional Model

Emotional Model is a marketing approach targeting customers emotionally rather than simply touting its features or benefits. Emotional marketing in pharmaceutical marketing can help foster relationships on an intimate level with patients and healthcare providers by tapping into their values, fears, and desires and building trust and loyalty by tapping into those relationships on a deeper level.

One approach for pharmaceutical marketing that creates emotional resonance with consumers is emphasizing patient experiences. This could involve featuring real-life patient narratives, providing educational resources to understand conditions and treatment options, and offering supportive communities for patients and caregivers. Another strategy could include emphasizing how medication improves patients' quality of life. For instance, a pharmaceutical company might launch a campaign showing how certain treatments help regain independence, fully enjoy favorite activities, or spend more time with loved ones. The company can create a strong emotional connection with patients and careers by focusing on these benefits, increasing brand loyalty and advocacy.

It's important to note that emotional marketing in pharma must be handled carefully, as it involves promoting products that can have serious health consequences. Marketers must be transparent and ethical in their messaging, avoiding claims not supported by clinical evidence and providing clear information about potential side effects and risks. Using emotional marketing responsibly, pharmaceutical companies can build deeper connections with patients and healthcare providers, ultimately leading to better health outcomes.

How Pharma Uses the Emotional Model

Here are a few examples of pharmaceutical companies that have used emotional marketing to connect with patients and healthcare providers:

1. *Pfizer's Get Old Campaign*: Pfizer created the *Get Old* campaign to help older adults embrace aging and take control of their health. The campaign included a website with resources like staying active, managing chronic conditions, and maintaining social connections. The website also featured real-life stories of older adults overcoming health challenges and living fulfilling lives.
2. *Novo Nordisk's* Changing Diabetes *Campaign*: Novo Nordisk created the *Changing Diabetes* campaign to raise awareness of the global diabetes epidemic and the importance of early detection and treatment. The campaign featured a website with resources and a series of videos highlighting the impact of diabetes on patients' lives for patients, caregivers, and healthcare providers.
3. *Roche's Know Your Cancer Campaign*: Roche created the *Know Your Cancer* campaign to help patients understand their cancer diagnosis and treatment options. The campaign included a website with resources on different types of cancer and patient stories and videos showing how Roche's treatments had helped patients overcome their cancer.
4. *Sanofi's Toujeo Campaign*: Sanofi created a campaign to promote its insulin product, Toujeo, designed to help patients with diabetes better manage their blood sugar levels. Campaign advertisements featured patients discussing the challenges associated with diabetes and how Toujeo had helped them feel in charge of their healthcare.

Pharmaceutical companies have successfully used the emotional model of marketing to connect with patients and healthcare providers. By emphasizing patient experience and products' emotional impact, these pharmaceutical firms have formed stronger bonds with their target audiences, resulting in better overall health outcomes.

Empathy

Empathy in pharmaceutical marketing (and any marketing, for that matter) means understanding and catering to customer emotions, needs, and perspectives. Empathy also involves connecting with an audience by showing companies understand their experiences and issues.

Empathy becomes especially crucial in pharmaceutical marketing due to the nature of health and wellness industries. They directly connect with patients' struggles, pain, and aspirations. So empathy plays a fundamental role here:

1. *Patient-Centric Approach to Marketing*: Empathy is essential in creating a patient-centric approach to marketing, placing patients' needs

above any company's agendas or pushing what the business has on sale. Understanding patient journeys, struggles, needs, and hopes helps create this empathetic approach for effective patient engagement.

2. *Trust Building*: Health care can be a dynamic experience for most. An empathic approach helps build patient trust by showing that a company cares more for its well-being than selling its products.
3. *Product Development and Promotion*: Empathy provides invaluable guidance in marketing campaigns and product creation processes. By understanding patients' needs and struggles, companies can produce more effective, beneficial products. Furthermore, empathy informs how a product should be presented to appeal directly to its user's feelings and needs.
4. *Communication Strategy*: For any company to effectively engage patients and prospects in its communications strategy, an empathic approach must drive its strategy. That means using language and messages that show an understanding of care without alienating or confounding patients is imperative.
5. *Educational Content*: Pharmaceutical companies often create educational material on diseases and treatments for their customers so they can manage their conditions better. Empathy in designing this information ensures that patients understand and resonate with it.
6. *Digital and Social Media Presence*: Social media is ideal for companies to interact empathetically with patients. Companies can utilize these platforms to offer support, answer inquiries, and participate in conversations that show they care.
7. *Relationship with Healthcare Professionals*: Empathy extends far beyond just patient relationships. It is also integral to an organization's interactions with healthcare providers. Understanding their needs, challenges, and perspectives will improve collaboration and results.

As much as empathy may be beneficial, it must not be used to manipulate. Companies should genuinely care for their patients instead of just appearing concerned about selling products.

Implications for Marketers

Marketers need to recognize that empathy plays a pivotal role in pharmaceutical marketing. Here are a few points they should keep in mind when conducting their campaigns:

1. *Understanding Audience*: Marketers must thoroughly understand their audiences, such as patients, families, and healthcare professionals. Exploring each patient's journey, pain points, challenges, and emotional aspects related to health conditions. It is critical in creating effective marketing materials and patient support services. Marketers need more than demographic knowledge; they should also understand psychographics (values, fears, desires).
2. *Content Creation*: Marketers must craft messages that speak directly to the audience's understanding. Medical terminology or complex sentences should be replaced by plain-speaking communication in a format easily understood by customers, providing educational value while being warm-hearted.
3. *Digital and Social Media Presence*: Social and digital marketing platforms should be utilized to authentically engage their target audiences, answering queries, offering support, sharing patient stories, and offering an avenue for users to interact and exchange experiences.
4. *Building Trust*: Empathic marketing aims to establish relationships of trust with its audience by being transparent, honest and showing genuine concern for them as individuals. Involve yourself during difficult periods such as disease outbreaks or drug recalls; remain there when problems arise so your audience knows you care for their well-being and are there when times get difficult for your target demographic.
5. *Empathetic Product Design*: Marketers must work alongside product development teams to design products empathetically, meeting patients' specific needs and simplifying their lives. This may involve packaging that allows people with physical limitations or dosage instructions that are easy to comprehend and adhere to.
6. *Training and Education*: Marketers and other customer-facing staff may require training on empathy to better communicate empathetically with customers and patients. Such classes might focus on communication skills development and understanding different patient perspectives.
7. *Measure and Iterate*: Like with any marketing strategy, measuring the efficacy of an empathic approach should be at the core of its design. You can use customer satisfaction scores, engagement data on social media, or feedback forms from customers or sales figures as indicators to iterate upon and optimize this method of engagement. With such information at your fingertips, use this data to modify and refine it for maximum impact!

Remind your employees that empathy should not just be used as a marketing tactic. Rather it should form the company's core value and be applied across every facet of the business, from product development and customer service to employee training and recruitment. Consumers will quickly recognize if your empathetic approach is genuine or simply marketing-speak.

Empirical Research

Empirical research is an observational investigation utilizing observations, experiments, or other systematic means of data collection for its goal, gathering objective evidence that can be used to test theories or hypotheses and draw inferences about the world at large.

Empirical research takes various forms depending on its subject matter and methods for collecting data, from surveys or questionnaires designed to gather information on people's attitudes, opinions, and behavior to focus groups conducted over an extended period.

Studies, experiments, and case analyses can yield fruitful answers about human behavior in real-world situations. Observational studies entail watching and recording behavior within natural settings while experimentation measures their effect on an outcome of interest (like health status or wellbeing). Experiments involve manipulating one or more variables before measuring how they affect an outcome of interest. Finally, case studies offer an in-depth examination of one individual or group to gain new understandings.

Content analysis allows organizations and their management teams to assess their communication material, such as speeches, news articles, or social media posts, for evaluation purposes.

Empirical research can be invaluable in many fields, from psychology and sociology to economics and biology. Empirical studies allow scientists to test their theories against real-world data for testing purposes as they make evidence-based statements regarding the phenomena they study.

Empirical Research in Pharma Marketing

Empirical research can assist pharmaceutical companies by using scientific methods to collect and evaluate data to gain insight into the success of various marketing strategies and tactics, giving them better knowledge for making more effective marketing decisions for their products and services. Such empirical research can also aid them in making strategic business decisions regarding product or service marketing more efficiently.

Pharmaceutical marketing research can be carried out across various areas, such as:

1. *Patient Behavior and Preferences*: Empirical research has been undertaken to gain insight into patient behaviors and preferences, such as their preferred channels for receiving medication information, how they make health-related decisions, or their response patterns to various marketing messages.
2. *Healthcare Provider Behavior*: Empirical research has also been done on healthcare provider behavior to understand better how they make treatment decisions and respond to various marketing messages, including detailing visits, medical conferences, and promotional events.
3. *Pricing and Access*: Empirical studies have examined the effects of pricing and access strategies such as copay cards or patient assistance programs on patient behavior and medication adherence.
4. *Digital Marketing*: Researchers have conducted empirical studies to gauge the efficacy of various digital marketing strategies, such as social media advertising, search engine marketing, and email marketing, on patient and healthcare provider behavior.

Empirical research can assist pharmaceutical companies in making more informed decisions about allocating marketing resources, creating effective messaging, engaging patients ethically and successfully, and allocating the marketing budget responsibly.

Empirical Studies in Pharma Marketing: Examples and Considerations

Below are examples of empirical research in pharmaceutical marketing:

1. *Patient Studies*: These studies utilize surveys and focus groups to understand better how patients prefer receiving information about medications and treatments, for instance, through print materials, digital channels, or interactive websites, or websites with educational videos or websites.
2. *Detailing Effectiveness Studies*: These research studies evaluate the effect of detailing visits on healthcare provider behavior, such as prescribing habits or medication adherence. A typical comparison may involve in-person visits vs. virtual visits or promotional activities as a basis for comparison.
3. *Studies of Copay Cards*: Copay card studies aim to understand how patient assistance programs such as copay cards influence patient behaviors such as medication adherence or treatment

initiation. A typical research question would investigate whether offering copay cards improve medication adherence rates and users' health outcomes.

4. *Digital Marketing Studies*: These studies examine the effect of various digital marketing strategies, such as social media advertising or email marketing campaigns, on patient and healthcare provider behaviors. For instance, such studies might evaluate whether targeted social media ads increase patient engagement with pharmaceutical brands or whether tailored email campaigns increase prescribing habits among healthcare professionals.

As empirical research is central to pharmaceutical marketing, empirical investigations must take place to understand patient and healthcare provider behavior and measure marketing strategies' effectiveness to make informed decisions regarding allocating marketing resources.

Employee Communication

Employee communication in pharmaceutical marketing refers to strategies pharmaceutical companies use to inform and engage employees regarding products, services, and business-related information. Effective employee communications are essential in improving employee engagement, motivation, and productivity to achieve better business results.

Pharmaceutical companies employ different strategies and channels for communicating with their employees, such as:

1. *Internal Newsletters and Publications*: Companies often produce internal newsletters and publications to inform employees about new products, services, or business developments.
2. *Intranet and Social Media*: Companies may utilize intranet sites and social media platforms to provide news and updates to employees and encourage collaboration and communication within their workplaces.
3. *Employee Events and Training Sessions*: Companies may host training and educational events about products, services, and business operations.
4. *Executive Communications*: Businesses may utilize executive communications strategies like town hall meetings and other meetings with top management to inform employees of company strategies, goals, and other relevant business information.

Effective employee communication in the pharmaceutical industry is particularly essential, given that employees play such an integral part in creating new drugs and treatments for patients' use. By keeping employees up-to-date and engaged, companies can foster an environment conducive to innovation and collaboration, ultimately leading to enhanced patient outcomes.

Employee Value Proposition

Employee Value Proposition (EVP) in pharmaceutical marketing refers to a combination of benefits, rewards, and opportunities offered to employees as compensation for their expertise, experience, and dedication to work at that pharmaceutical company. An EVP represents how much an organization will give back for an employee's time, such as tangible compensation benefits and opportunities such as career advancement or a positive work culture.

Pharmaceutical companies typically provide employees with competitive salaries and packages, career advancement opportunities, professional development programs, work-life balance initiatives, and supportive and inclusive work environments as part of their Employee Value Proposition (EVP). Furthermore, some pharmaceutical companies may provide unique perks like on-site wellness facilities, flexible work schedules, or employee stock ownership plans as part of the EVP.

Pharmaceutical companies need a compelling EVP to attract and retain talent in an increasingly competitive job market. Organizations can separate themselves from competitors by offering desirable benefits and opportunities while showing they care about employees' professional growth and development. A strong EVP also helps improve employee engagement and productivity, leading to superior business results and patient care outcomes.

Empowerment

Empowerment in pharmaceutical marketing refers to providing patients with all the resources and tools required to take an active part in making healthcare decisions by equipping them with information regarding treatments available and any associated benefits or risks. It entails helping patients make educated choices when selecting treatments.

One way pharma marketers can empower patients is with patient education materials like brochures, websites, and videos that provide patients with information about their condition, treatment options available, and possible outcomes of each one. By making such information easily available to patients, they are better empowered to make treatment decisions themselves.

Patient support programs offer another means of empowering patients. Giving access to resources like patient advocates, support groups, and financial assistance programs, these programs help patients feel supported throughout their healthcare journey while having greater influence in decision-making regarding treatments they decide upon.

Pharmaceutical companies may provide digital tools, such as apps and online platforms, to empower patients. Such tools could inform patients about their condition, help track symptoms and medication consumption, and connect patients to healthcare providers and fellow patients, all while increasing access to care.

Pharmaceutical companies may create marketing campaigns focusing on patient experience. Such efforts could feature patient testimonials or support programs to encourage active involvement from patients in their healthcare decisions.

Pharma companies can support healthcare providers by arming them with the resources and training to communicate with patients effectively. This may involve offering access to patient education materials, communication training courses, or assistance in creating patient support programs.

Empowerment in pharmaceutical marketing is an integral aspect that empowers patients to play an active part in their healthcare decisions, leading to enhanced results and patient satisfaction.

Encryption

Encryption plays an essential role in pharmaceutical marketing, protecting patient data while upholding privacy regulations and complying with them. Here are several areas in which encryption plays a part:

1. *Data Privacy*: Pharmaceutical companies often gain access to sensitive patient data, such as health records, for various uses, including research, targeted marketing, and patient outreach. Encryption provides essential protection of this sensitive information during storage and transmission, protecting patients and companies against the legal issues stemming from any data breach incidents.
2. *Email Marketing*: If pharmaceutical companies send sensitive health or financial data via email, these communications should be encrypted for maximum protection and ensure only those designated can read its content.
3. *Website Security*: Pharmaceutical companies often create websites where patients can learn more about medications, get support in managing diseases and directly order medications online. Such websites frequently require users to disclose sensitive data related to health or payment. Encryption, usually through HTTPS, is crucial in protecting this sensitive data from being misused or breached.
4. *HIPAA Compliance*: In the US, laws such as Health Insurance Portability and Accountability Act (HIPAA) set stringent encryption standards that must be observed for health information stored by pharmaceutical companies dealing with patient records in this market. Therefore, pharmaceutical companies should follow HIPAA-compliant encryption when they deal with patient information in the US.
5. *Cloud Storage and Transfer*: Pharmaceutical companies frequently rely on cloud services to store and transfer marketing-related data securely in the cloud, with all access restricted accordingly to prevent unapproved access by outsiders. All such data should be encrypted for maximum protection from unwelcome readers.

Pharmaceutical companies using encryption in these areas can protect privacy, secure sensitive data, and meet legal and ethical standards more easily. Failing to do so may result in legal sanctions, financial losses, and irreparable damage to the company's reputation.

Endogenous Attention

Endogenous Attention refers to the voluntary, intentional allocation of attention to specific stimuli or regions of the environment based on internal goals, expectations, or task demands. In simpler terms, it is when you consciously focus on something because it aligns with your current intentions or objectives. For example, if you are reading a book and actively paying attention to the words on the page, your attention is endogenously focused on the task. It contrasts with exogenous attention, which is more reflexive and automatic, driven by external stimuli that capture your attention without conscious control.

In psychology and neuroscience, understanding endogenous attention helps researchers explore how our cognitive processes influence where we direct our focus and how we prioritize information based on our goals and expectations.

Endogenous Attention in Pharma Marketing

Endogenous Attention in pharmaceutical marketing involves strategies that focus on capturing the attention of individuals within the healthcare and medical community. These approaches target healthcare professionals, patients seeking information about a specific condition, or other stakeholders within the industry. Here are some examples:

1. *Continuing Medical Education (CME)*: Developing educational programs for healthcare professionals to keep them informed about the latest pharmaceutical advancements. This can involve workshops, seminars, and online courses that provide in-depth information about specific medications or treatment protocols.
2. *Medical Conferences and Symposia*: Participation in medical conferences and symposia to present scientific data, clinical trial results, and new research findings. These events provide a platform for pharmaceutical companies to showcase their products to healthcare professionals.
3. *Publications in Medical Journals*: Publishing research studies, clinical trial results, and articles in reputable journals. This helps establish credibility within the medical community and ensures that healthcare professionals can access accurate, detailed information about a pharmaceutical product.
4. *Key Opinion Leader (KOL) Engagement*: Collaborating with key opinion leaders in the medical field who can endorse and speak positively about a pharmaceutical product. These influencers can significantly impact the opinions and decisions of other healthcare professionals.
5. *Targeted Direct-to-Healthcare Professional DTHCP) Marketing*: Implementing targeted marketing campaigns specifically directed at healthcare professionals. This can include direct mailings, emails, and digital advertising on platforms frequented by doctors, nurses, and other medical professionals.
6. *Patient Support Programs*: Developing programs that provide support and information directly to patients. This can include patient starter kits, helplines, and educational materials distributed through healthcare providers.
7. *Detailing to Healthcare Providers*: Utilizing pharmaceutical representatives to detail healthcare providers about the benefits, mechanisms, and clinical evidence supporting a particular medication. These representatives engage in one-on-one discussions with healthcare professionals to provide detailed information.
8. *Disease Awareness Campaigns*: Launching campaigns to raise awareness about specific medical conditions and available treatment options. These campaigns target healthcare professionals and patients, providing information about the disease landscape and potential solutions.

Endogenous attention strategies aim to build trust and credibility within the healthcare community by providing accurate and relevant information to professionals and patients involved in healthcare decision-making.

Engagement Metrics

Engagement metrics in pharmaceutical marketing provide insights into consumer engagement with content created for marketing purposes. Engagement metrics provide quantified success measurements and information to optimize future marketing endeavors by measuring consumer interaction with campaigns or strategies implemented for pharmaceutical marketers. Here are some commonly utilized engagement metrics in pharmaceutical industry marketing campaigns:

1. *Website Traffic*: Website traffic measures the total number of visits to a company website from various sources (organic, paid, referral, and direct) along with pages visited, duration on site and bounce rates.
2. *Social Media Engagement*: Social media engagement includes *likes, shares, comments*, and *follows* on platforms like Facebook, Twitter, Instagram, and LinkedIn. Video views can be measured using platforms like YouTube to measure average watch time.
3. *Email Engagement* includes open rates, click-through rates (CTR), bounce rates, and unsubscribe rates of emails sent from an address.
4. *Content Engagement* measures how users respond to different forms of media content, such as blogs, infographics, and videos, through metrics such as views, shares, likes, comments, and time spent per piece.
5. *Conversion Rate*: This metric indicates the percentage of visitors completing a desired action, such as filling out a form, downloading white papers, or purchasing from all site visitors.
6. *Return on Investment (ROI)*: Return on Investment is used to measure the efficiency of

investments. When applied to pharmaceutical marketing campaigns, it could be determined by comparing profits generated with costs incurred for running these campaigns.

7. *Net Promoter Score (NPS)* assesses customer loyalty by asking how likely they would be to refer a product or service they experienced to friends or coworkers.
8. *Patient Adherence* is a key metric for pharmaceutical marketers. It looks at whether patients take their medicines as prescribed. This metric can be affected through marketing and educational campaigns.

Remember these metrics do not work independently. Their relevance and utility vary based on the specifics of a marketing campaign, product being promoted, or target audience. Thus, selecting appropriate metrics according to marketing goals and objectives is important.

Engel's Laws

Engel's laws represent empirical observations related to consumer spending habits. First introduced by German statistician Ernst Engel in the 19th century and still widely applied today as a framework for understanding how income changes influence spending patterns. These laws include the following:

1. *The Law of Demand* states that as income rises, so too does its proportional expenditure for necessities like food, meaning people tend to spend a smaller proportion of their earnings on eating as their earnings rise.
2. *The Law of Constant Proportion*: As income grows, people spend the same percentage on non-essentials such as leisure activities or luxury goods regardless of income levels. This ensures a constant spend ratio regarding non-necessities like entertainment costs or luxury purchases.
3. *Income Elasticity*: With increased income comes greater demand for luxurious goods and services at the expense of necessities, meaning people tend to use any additional earnings on purchasing these luxurious products over necessities.

Engel's laws indicate that as income rises, people spend less of it on necessities and more of it on non-necessities; this has profound ramifications for policymakers and businesses as it suggests economic expansion may come about from increased demand for luxury items rather than necessities alone.

How Pharmaceutical Companies Can Apply Engel's Laws

Below are examples of how pharmaceutical companies can employ Engel's laws in their marketing initiatives:

A. *Necessities*: Prescription drugs and services are considered necessities, increasing incomes and driving people towards purchasing them. Pharma companies should direct their marketing efforts toward essential medications for chronic conditions like diabetes or heart disease and medical services that include routine check-ups, diagnostic testing, or lab analysis.

B. *Comforts*: When income levels increase, people often increase spending on non-essential comfort items like brand medications or health products that might not be considered essential. For instance, a pharmaceutical company marketing a high-end multivitamin supplement might target higher income groups by emphasizing its premium quality ingredients and extra health benefits beyond basic nutritional needs.

C. *Luxuries*: As income rises, people may spend more on luxury healthcare items, such as cosmetic surgery and other elective medical procedures. For example, a pharma company marketing a new aesthetic treatment or cosmetic procedure can target affluent consumers by highlighting its unique features, advanced technology, and personalized approach.

In summary, Engel's laws suggest that pharma companies can target their marketing efforts to different income groups based on their products or services' necessity, comfort, or luxury level. By understanding their target audience's income and expenditure patterns, pharma companies can develop effective marketing strategies that appeal to their customer's needs and preferences.

Enlightened Marketing

Enlightened marketing considers consumers, society, and the environment in its holistic consideration of products or services sold to them. It goes beyond traditional models focused on profits and sales and considers their greater societal ramifications.

Four Core Principles

1. *Consumer-oriented Marketing*: Focusing on meeting consumers' needs while respecting and safeguarding their rights is at the core.
2. *Innovative Marketing*: Employing creative and disruptive marketing techniques that benefit both the company and society. For instance,

developing sustainable products, decreasing waste levels, and supporting social causes.

3. *Value-driven Marketing*: Focusing on creating value for customers, society, and the environment rather than simply increasing profits is called value-driven marketing.
4. *Marketing with Purpose and Social Responsibility*: Integrating purpose, social responsibility, and sustainability into their marketing strategy to enhance society and environmental wellbeing.

Enlightened marketing includes ethical and socially responsible business practices that are transparent, fair, and accountable. Businesses recognize they must create value for all stakeholders: customers, employees, investors, communities, and the environment alike.

Enlightened marketing is a philosophy that prioritizes society and the environment's well-being while still creating value for customers and the company. Furthermore, this approach recognizes businesses' interdependence with society to foster sustainable futures for both.

Enlightened Marketing in Pharma

An enlightened approach can be utilized in several aspects of pharmaceutical marketing. Consider:

1. *Design Socially Responsive Products*: Pharma companies can develop socially and environmentally responsible products that satisfy patient needs while contributing to social and environmental sustainability. For instance, Eco-friendly packaging materials or waste reduction measures could be utilized.
2. *Provide Value-added Services*: Pharma companies can offer value-added services that help patients and healthcare providers manage their conditions more effectively, such as educational resources, support groups, or patient advocacy programs.
3. *Promoting Social Causes*: Pharma companies can leverage their marketing platforms to support philanthropic initiatives that contribute to society, like sponsoring charity events or giving some of their profits to various social causes.
4. *Practice Ethical Marketing*: Pharma companies can engage in ethical marketing practices by being transparent, honest, and fair in their marketing practices. This means disclosing all relevant product information, refraining from misleading advertising practices that mislead patients, and respecting patient privacy.
5. *Collaboration With Stakeholders*: Pharmaceutical companies must collaborate closely with all relevant stakeholders, such as patient groups, healthcare providers, and regulatory agencies, to craft marketing strategies that simultaneously address all their needs, such as creating campaigns focused on evidence-based and culturally aware patients.

Pharma companies who abide by ethical marketing principles in their marketing strategies can build stronger relationships between patients, healthcare providers, and society while contributing to its welfare and creating shareholder value for themselves.

Entrepreneurial Marketing

Entrepreneurial marketing in the pharmaceutical industry refers to applying entrepreneurial principles and strategies to marketing activities. It involves a proactive, innovative, and agile approach to navigating the complex and highly regulated pharmaceutical landscape. Here are some key aspects and implications of entrepreneurial marketing in pharma:

1. *Identifying Opportunities*: Entrepreneurial marketing in pharma involves actively seeking and identifying market opportunities. This could include identifying unmet medical needs, gaps in existing treatment options, emerging trends, or untapped patient populations. By continuously monitoring the market, competitive landscape, and patient insights, pharmaceutical entrepreneurs can discover new areas where their products or services can make a difference.
2. *Innovation and Differentiation*: Pharmaceutical entrepreneurs focus on innovation and developing unique value propositions that differentiate their offerings from competitors. This could involve developing novel drugs, therapeutic approaches, or medical devices. Differentiation can also be achieved through innovative packaging, delivery mechanisms, patient support programs, or personalized medicine approaches. Entrepreneurial pharmaceutical companies can attract attention and gain a competitive edge by offering something distinct and valuable.
3. *Agility and Adaptability*: Entrepreneurial marketing in pharma requires agility and adaptability to respond quickly to changing market dynamics. This involves staying informed about evolving regulations, scientific advancements, and healthcare trends.

Entrepreneurs need to be flexible in adjusting their marketing strategies and tactics to align with the ever-changing landscape, enabling them to seize opportunities and overcome challenges.

4. *Targeted Marketing Strategies*: Entrepreneurs in Pharma understand the importance of targeted marketing strategies to reach specific patient populations or healthcare providers. Instead of employing mass marketing approaches, they focus on identifying key customer segments and tailoring their messages and channels to engage those audiences effectively. This could involve utilizing digital marketing techniques, social media, targeted advertising, or partnering with patient advocacy groups or healthcare professionals to reach the intended audience.
5. *Patient-centric Approach*: Entrepreneurial marketing in pharma emphasizes a patient-centric mindset. It involves understanding the needs, preferences, challenges of patients and developing marketing strategies addressing their concerns. This could include educational campaigns, patient support programs, or initiatives that enhance patient adherence and empowerment. Pharmaceutical entrepreneurs can build strong relationships and loyalty by prioritizing the patient experience and delivering value to patients.
6. *Strategic Partnerships and Collaborations*: Entrepreneurial marketing in pharma often involves forging strategic partnerships and collaborations with various stakeholders, including academic institutions, research organizations, healthcare providers, patient advocacy groups, or technology companies. These collaborations can bring together complementary expertise and resources and enhance the overall value proposition of the entrepreneurial venture.
7. *Regulatory Compliance*: While entrepreneurial marketing embraces innovation and agility, it is important to maintain regulatory compliance in the pharmaceutical industry. Entrepreneurs need to navigate complex regulatory frameworks, such as FDA regulations in the United States or EMA regulations in the European Union, ensuring that their marketing activities adhere to ethical standards, promote patient safety, and meet the requirements for product approvals, labeling, and promotional practices.

It is important to note that entrepreneurship in the pharmaceutical industry is not without challenges. The sector is highly regulated, with long development timelines, stringent safety requirements, and substantial investment needs. However, entrepreneurial marketing can still play a vital role in driving innovation, bringing novel solutions to patients, and disrupting traditional practices to improve healthcare outcomes.

Enterprise Resource Planning (ERP)

Enterprise Resource Planning (ERP) software solutions integrate key business functions and processes, such as finance, human resources, inventory management, production planning, and marketing into one streamlined software system for greater Pharma company efficiency, accuracy, and collaboration across departments. ERP can assist Pharma firms by streamlining operations while increasing efficiency, accuracy, and collaboration within different teams of employees.

Many Advantages

ERP systems offer several benefits in pharmaceutical marketing, such as improved data management. Pharmaceutical companies can use an ERP system to collect and organize customer and sales information into one centralized database for easier decision-making and operational analysis. This enables more holistic analysis and enhanced decision-making across their marketing operations.

1. *Streamlined Processes*: An ERP system can streamline many marketing processes, such as campaign planning, budgeting, and reporting to streamline these efforts while increasing efficiency and decreasing the effort required to complete them.
2. *Better Collaboration*: ERP systems enable better collaboration among marketing teams such as sales, advertising, and public relations, helping ensure everyone works towards similar goals while sharing information efficiently.
3. *Customer Relationship Management Improvement*: ERP systems offer companies a full view of customers, from preferences and purchase history to interactions across marketing channels, sales channels, and marketing departments. This insight allows pharma firms to tailor marketing efforts more specifically and increase customer engagement.
4. *Better Compliance*: An ERP system can assist pharma companies with meeting regulatory compliance, including reporting and record-keeping obligations, by automating these

processes and guaranteeing accurate and complete information.

An ERP system offers many advantages to pharmaceutical marketing, from data management and streamlining processes, collaboration enhancement, customer relationship management enhancements, and better compliance to increasing marketing operation efficiency, accuracy, and profit. By adopting such technology, Pharma companies can use ERP solutions to enhance the efficiency, accuracy, and profitability of marketing operations.

Environmental Scanning

Environmental scanning is the practice of tracking and evaluating internal and external factors that might hinder an organization from meeting its goals, including political, economic, social, technological, and legal influences. Environmental scans involve gathering and analyzing information regarding an organization's business environment, such as political considerations, sociological developments, and legal considerations, to inform strategic decision-making processes.

Environmental scanning allows businesses to recognize opportunities and threats within the business environment and adapt accordingly, staying ahead of market changes, anticipating trends for the future, and responding proactively to emerging challenges.

Environmental scanning can be achieved through various techniques, such as market research, industry reports, publications analysis, trade shows, conference attendance, or monitoring news and social media sources. Environmental scanning should be conducted regularly and when specific events or changes arise within your business environment.

Environmental scanning has become indispensable in today's dynamic business climate. It gives organizations an advantage by keeping abreast of trends and developments that directly affect them, improving decision-making processes, and positioning themselves for long-term success.

Environmental Scanning in Pharma Marketing

Environmental scanning in pharmaceutical marketing refers to tracking trends, developments, and challenges within external environments that might impede or modify pharmaceutical industries, healthcare systems, or patient behavior. Here are some examples of how Pharma companies can use environmental scanning:

1. *Regulatory Environment*: Pharma companies must keep abreast of changes to regulatory environments in their markets, specifically drug approvals, clinical trial protocols, pricing strategies, and marketing that could affect product development, promotion, and sales activities. Environmental scanning helps companies detect changes that might affect these areas, specifically those concerning approval, clinical trial protocols, pricing strategies, or marketing communications that impact product development, promotion, or sales activities.
2. *Competitive Landscape*: Pharma companies must monitor competitors' activities and strategies to remain competitive. Environmental scanning helps pharma firms identify new competitors, track product development pipelines and analyze rival businesses' marketing and sales strategies.
3. *Healthcare System*: Pharma companies must remain aware of changes within the healthcare system to adapt their strategies accordingly. Environmental scanning helps pharma firms look for shifts in policies, reimbursement models, and patient care models, which could affect the demand for their products or services.
4. *Technology Trends*: With technology rapidly revolutionizing healthcare, pharmaceutical companies must stay abreast of emerging digital health, telemedicine, and wearable tech developments to maximize patient engagement while improving outcomes and engagement rates. Environmental scanning helps these organizations keep abreast of the innovations for continuous monitoring. Environmental scanning helps monitor digital health technologies like wearable technologies that could enhance outcomes or engagement for better patient outcomes and engagement purposes.

Environmental scanning is essential for pharmaceutical companies to keep informed of external factors that could impede business operations and strategies. By keeping tabs on these external influences and their ramifications, companies can identify opportunities or challenges related to changing market conditions, develop more efficient marketing plans to meet them more quickly or adapt them according to changing market needs more easily.

Conducting Environmental Scanning in Pharma Marketing

1. *Define the Scope*: Before initiating environmental scanning in pharma marketing, define its scope by identifying markets, regions, and segments relevant to your business and

gathering appropriate information about them. Doing this will allow researchers to focus their research efforts more efficiently while gathering pertinent details needed by business operations.

2. *Gather Data*: Assemble information from various sources, including industry reports, government publications, news articles, social media channels, and online resources such as surveys. You could conduct interviews or focus groups with key stakeholders, including patients, doctors, payers, and others, to glean insights into your findings.
3. *Analyze the Data*: Once your information has been compiled, take some time to study its implications on business operations and marketing strategies. Keep an eye out for common themes or patterns emerging in your data that could affect them and assess the possible repercussions for you and your firm.
4. *Develop Action Plans*: Based on the insights from analysis, create action plans addressing opportunities and challenges identified within your data. Consider capitalizing on emerging trends to develop new products or services, improve patient engagement or distinguish yourself from competitors.
5. *Monitor and Update*: Environmental scanning should be an ongoing practice; as such, it's vitally important that data analysis be regularly revised and kept current with emerging trends, technologies, or regulatory changes that might impact your business to be prepared when adjusting marketing strategy accordingly.

Environmental scanning is essential for pharmaceutical companies to stay aware of external factors that could negatively influence their business operations and strategies. By tracking these external influences and their ramifications, companies can better recognize opportunities and challenges and create marketing plans tailored to changing market conditions.

Environmentalism

Environmentalism is a social and political movement that seeks to preserve, improve and conserve natural environments, such as air, water, land, and all their constituents, with sustainable resource usage practices. Environmentalism's core belief lies in protecting nature as something sacred for its own sake and future generations.

Environmentalism takes many forms, from lobbying for policy changes and conversation efforts to supporting sustainable practices in industry and agriculture while covering topics like climate change, pollution, biodiversity conservation, and environmental justice. The environmental movement spans these various arenas as a whole.

Environmentalism strives to build healthier and more sustainable relationships between humans and nature and ensure future generations enjoy all the same advantages as we do now.

Environmentalism in Pharma Marketing

Environmentalism can play a pivotal role in pharmaceutical marketing by emphasizing environmental benefits and sustainable practices associated with pharmaceutical companies and their products to stand out from competitors, create brand loyalty among environmentally minded customers, and contribute to a greener tomorrow. Here are a few ways environmental consideration can be integrated into pharma marketing:

1. *Green Packaging*: Pharmaceutical companies can utilize Eco-friendly packaging materials, including recycled paper, biodegradable plastics, or reusable containers, to reduce waste generated from their products while improving their environmental footprint. Labeling that indicates recycling or biodegradability helps educate customers to dispose of them responsibly and encourages responsible disposal practices.
2. *Sustainable Production*: Pharma companies can incorporate sustainable production practices, such as using renewable energy sources and decreasing water consumption and waste generation. Companies could also implement Eco-friendly manufacturing technologies and processes like green chemistry that help minimize their products' environmental footprints.
3. *Promoting Environmental Initiatives*: Pharmaceutical companies can increase public trust in them as environmental stewardship efforts by publicizing environmental initiatives and partnerships with environmental groups, which helps demonstrate commitment to sustainability for customers who value such actions.
4. *Green Marketing Messages*: Pharma companies can employ marketing messages emphasizing their environmental and sustainability commitment. Companies could, for example, use slogans like *Preserving Health, Protecting the Planet*, or *Green Solutions for Better Health* to communicate these initiatives and values to their audience.

Integrating environmental messaging into pharmaceutical marketing campaigns is an excellent way for companies to build positive brand images, attract environmentally aware consumers, and contribute towards creating a more sustainable future.

Ethics

Ethics are principles or values which guide individual or collective behavior, actions, and decision-making. Ethics provide a basis for deciding right from wrong, fairness from injustice, or why a moral value should be upheld over immoral values.

Ethics are applied in numerous fields, from business and healthcare to politics and personal relationships. Though ethical principles differ depending on the context, generally, they consist of honesty, respect for others, responsibility, fairness, and compassion as core tenets of ethics.

Ethics play an integral part in business operations. They help organizations understand how their interactions impact customers, employees, suppliers, and the broader community, from customers and employees to suppliers and the larger world. Ethical considerations could encompass social responsibility, sustainability, and corporate governance practices.

Ethics guide healthcare professionals' interactions with their patients, families, and communities. Ethical considerations could include patient confidentiality, informed consent, and appropriate use of medical resources.

Ethics in Pharmaceutical Marketing and Their Implications for Pharma Marketers

Ethics in pharmaceutical marketing refers to applying ethical principles when marketing pharmaceutical products to public health consumers, making this industry especially sensitive regarding ethical considerations in advertising practices. Some key implications of ethics for pharma marketers may include:

1. *Truthfulness and Transparency*: Pharma marketers should remain truthful and transparent when communicating about their products, making no false or misleading claims regarding their safety or efficacy.
2. *Patient Welfare*: At the core of any pharma marketing initiative lies patient welfare. Marketers must ensure their promotional activities don't compromise patient safety or promote inappropriate medication usage practices.
3. *Fairness and Respect*: Marketers must treat healthcare professionals and patients fairly, adhering to ethical principles by not engaging in unethical activities like bribery or kickback schemes.
4. *Regulatory Compliance*: Marketers must adhere to all pharmaceutical marketing regulatory guidelines, such as advertisements, promotions, and labeling practices.
5. *Social Responsibility*: Pharma marketers must act with social responsibility when conducting marketing activities related to pharmaceutical products, considering access and affordability.

Failing to comply with ethical marketing principles can have serious repercussions for companies, including damage to reputations and legal liabilities and harm to public health. Pharma marketers must incorporate ethical considerations into marketing strategies and adhere to relevant regulations and guidelines.

Ethical Codes

Pharmaceutical marketing is subject to several ethical codes and guidelines that ensure companies market their products responsibly and transparently. Here are some important ethical codes governing the pharmaceutical industry worldwide:

1. *International Federation of Pharmaceutical Manufacturers & Associations (IFPMA) Code of Practice*: The IFPMA code serves as an industrywide code of ethics governing global pharmaceutical product marketing and promotion, including product claims, advertising and promotion strategies, and interactions between healthcare professionals.
2. *Pharmaceutical Research and Manufacturers of America (PhRMA) Code on Interactions with Healthcare Professionals*: These voluntary guidelines cover interactions between pharmaceutical companies and healthcare providers, such as gifts or incentives, education or research conducted, or conference or meeting support.
3. *European Federation of Pharmaceutical Industries and Associations (EFPIA) Code of Practice*: This set of ethical principles covers European marketing and promotion for pharmaceutical products, such as advertising, promotion, interactions with healthcare professionals, and disclosing financial relationships.

4. *Canadian Code of Ethics for Pharmaceutical Marketing*: This voluntary set of guidelines regulates and guides pharmaceutical marketing efforts across Canada, such as advertising and promotion campaigns, interactions among healthcare professionals, and use of social media. It contains provisions related to advertising and promotion tactics, interactions among healthcare providers, and social media usage.
5. *World Health Organization (WHO) Ethical Criteria for Drug Promotions*: These WHO guidelines establish ethical criteria to promote drugs and pharmaceuticals responsibly, prioritizing patient safety and well-being when marketing activities involve patients. Their regulations cover product claims, advertisements, promotions, and interactions with healthcare professionals.

Ethical Codes in India and China

India and China are two of the world's biggest pharmaceutical markets, each having established ethical codes to guide pharmaceutical products' marketing and promotion activities. Here is an overview of their codes of ethics:

1. Ethical Codes in India

The Indian Pharmaceutical Alliance has devised an ethical code of practice for India's pharmaceutical industry modeled on that established by the International Federation of Pharmaceutical Manufacturers and Associations (IFPMA). This includes advertising and promotion practices, interactions with healthcare professionals, compliance with relevant laws and regulations, and setting forth reporting and investigating systems and penalties in case of non-compliance with its requirements.

Additionally, the Medical Council of India (now the National Medical Council) has developed guidelines regulating interactions between healthcare professionals and pharmaceutical industry representatives. These regulations ensure interactions prioritizing patient care without conflicts of interest arising between professionals and companies.

In 2014, India's Department of Pharmaceuticals issued a voluntary ethical code known as Uniform Pharmaceutical Code (UCPMP) for Marketing Practices as guidelines for drug promotion by pharmaceutical companies operating in India. Since then, it has been updated in 2015 and 2018, respectively, to set forth promotional practices regarding promotional materials, gifts, and incentives, sponsorship of medical conferences, events, and interaction with healthcare professionals in terms of transparency and ethics aimed at patient safety as well as responsible use.

2. Ethical Code in China

China has adopted regulations governing the marketing and promotion of pharmaceutical products, with enforcement falling primarily upon the China Food and Drug Administration (CFDA), which oversees approval, registration, compliance, and monitoring with applicable laws, regulators, and relevant compliance issues.

China Association for Pharmaceutical Research and Development (CAPRD) has implemented an ethical code of conduct for Chinese pharmaceutical industries that addresses issues like advertising and promotion, interaction between healthcare professionals, compliance with applicable laws and regulations, timely reporting violations, and sanctions in case noncompliance occurs. Furthermore, this code establishes a system to report violations swiftly and sanctions/penalties should noncompliance occur.

Ethical Incentive Plan

Incentive plans for pharma sales reps are typically focused on sales and prescription volumes, as these are key performance indicators (KPIs) that directly impact a company's revenue and profitability. Sales reps are often given targets for the number of prescriptions they should generate or the revenue they should bring in. The incentive plan may be structured so that the sales rep receives a higher commission or bonus as they meet or exceed their targets.

But in recent years, pharmaceutical industry leaders more widely recognize the need to balance financial incentives with an eye on patient outcomes and ethical behavior. Incentive plans may include metrics related to patient satisfaction, adherence, treatment protocols adherence, or other measurements which reflect how a drug impacts patient health; additionally, pharmaceutical companies are investing more resources in training programs that aid sales reps in building strong relationships with healthcare providers while offering accurate product information.

GlaxoSmithKline's Pioneering Steps

GlaxoSmithKline (GSK) pioneered ethical incentives plans in Pharma, with their 2010 implementation of an ethical selling model intended to address some ethical concerns associated with pharmaceutical sales practices. Their sales reps provided accurate and balanced information regarding the benefits and risks of their products rather than simply increasing sales numbers alone.

The new model included several changes to GSK's incentive structure, such as eliminating individual sales targets for reps and tying their compensation to overall company performance. In addition, GSK's new ethical model is pathbreaking. Consider the following initiatives the company has taken to promote ethical behavior and culture in its sales and marketing operations:

1. *Decoupling Sales Force Incentives from Prescriptions*: GSK decoupled its sales force incentives from its sales and prescription targets to reduce ethical dilemmas and deepen customer relationships.
2. *Selling Competency*: Reps are evaluated on scientific knowledge, proficiency, understanding of the drug, technical skills, quality of service delivered to physicians, and business planning skills and execution.
3. *Customer Evaluations*: The company randomly collects customers' feedback to assess each sales rep's in-clinic performance and the quality of dialogue they maintain with the physician.
4. *Greater Investment in People and Transparency Measures*: The company has invested heavily in up-skilling its medical, sales, and marketing teams to deliver superior customer service. The company has also invested in improved multichannel, particularly digital capabilities, to help strengthen its engagement competencies with doctors.

Will the GSK's new ethical incentive plan work? While the jury is still out on GSK, some industry experts believe it is right. It's a top-down change, and it shows commitment. Even if it is not an overnight success, they will likely attract talent and build trust that has a lasting impact.

As Christopher Bowe, a leading healthcare expert, says: By changing the skills and aligning a sales force with health goals instead of pill volume, a company might create a new and sorely needed value for their customers by having a public health army out there in the field, which are helping to drive goals beneficial to society.

Ethical Incentive Plan in the Future

The future incentive plan for pharma sales reps will likely continue to evolve as the industry faces increasing scrutiny and regulation around ethical behavior and transparency. However, an ethical incentive plan for the future is likely to focus on several key principles:

1. *Patient Outcomes*: Incentive plans should incentivize sales reps to emphasize patient outcomes rather than sales targets, including metrics like patient satisfaction and clinical results that reflect treatment success.
2. *Transparency*: The incentive plan should be transparent and easy to understand. Sales reps should know exactly how their performance is evaluated, what they need to do to earn their incentives, and how they are calculated.
3. *Ethical Behavior*: The incentive plan should promote ethical behavior, such as reporting adverse events promptly or following up with healthcare providers after a sale. It should also discourage unethical behavior, such as offering bribes or kickbacks.
4. *Compliance*: The incentive plan should be tied to compliance with industry regulations and company policies. This can include compliance training, company code of conduct adherence, and other compliance-related metrics.
5. *Non-Financial Incentives*: Besides monetary incentives, non-financial incentives such as recognition, promotions, and career development opportunities can effectively motivate sales reps. For example, companies could recognize sales reps who excel in ethical behavior and patient outcomes.
6. *Continuous Feedback*: Regular feedback on performance can help sales reps understand how they are progressing toward their targets and can help them stay motivated. The feedback should be tied to patient outcomes and ethical behavior rather than just sales targets.
7. *Alignment with Company's Values*: The incentive plan should align with the company's values, such as patient focus and ethical behavior. Incentives that align with the company's values can help create a culture that promotes these values.

In summary, an ethical incentive plan for pharma sales reps in the future will need to prioritize patient outcomes, ethical behavior, compliance, and transparency. By promoting these principles and offering financial and non-financial incentives, companies can create a culture of transparency and ethical behavior that benefits patients and the industry.

Ethical Marketing

The ethical marketing approach prioritizes honesty, transparency, and social responsibility. In addition, ethical marketers aim to build long-term customer relationships based on trust, respect, and mutual benefit.

Some key principles of ethical marketing include:

1. *Honesty and Transparency:* Ethical marketers demonstrate this value through open communications with customers and providing accurate, truthful information regarding their products or services.
2. *Ethical Marketers Strive for Social Responsibility*: Ethical marketers strive to limit any harmful consequences of their marketing activities on society or the environment by mitigating any detrimental outcomes caused by marketing activity.
3. *Respect for Privacy:* Ethical marketers respect the privacy of their customers and do not engage in practices such as spamming or selling customer data without their consent.
4. *Fairness:* Ethical marketers treat all customers fairly and equally, avoiding discrimination or exploitation.
5. *Empathy:* Ethical marketers aim to understand their customers' needs, wants, and values so that their marketing initiatives reflect those.
6. *Compliance With All Applicable Laws and Regulations:* Ethical marketers comply with all marketing-related laws and regulations, such as those related to data privacy or truth in advertising.

Ethical Marketing in Pharma

Ethical marketing is particularly important in the pharmaceutical industry, where marketing activities can significantly impact patient health and well-being. Some key principles of ethical marketing in pharma are:

1. *Accurate and Truthful Communication*: Ethical marketers in pharma provide accurate and truthful information about their products without exaggeration or misleading claims.
2. *Promotion of Patient Health*: Ethical pharma marketers prioritize patients' health and well-being and do not engage in practices that could harm patient health or safety.
3. *Compliance with Regulations*: Ethical marketers in pharma comply with all relevant regulations related to marketing, such as those related to drug approval, labeling, and advertising.
4. *Respect for Privacy*: Ethical marketers in pharma respect the privacy of patients and healthcare professionals and do not engage in practices such as spamming or selling customer data without their consent.
5. *Transparency*: Ethical marketers in pharma are transparent in their communication with patients and healthcare professionals, providing information about the risks and benefits of their products clearly and understandably.
6. *Collaboration With Healthcare Professionals*: Ethical marketers in pharma collaborate with healthcare providers in providing education and information regarding their products without conflict of interest or undue influences.

Ethical marketing in the pharmaceutical industry requires a commitment to improving patient health and well-being while providing accurate and truthful information in line with all regulations and ethical standards.

Ethnic Marketing

Ethnic marketing is a form of targeted marketing approach designed to reach specific ethnic or cultural groups with messages tailored for them. Ethnic marketers recognize that different cultural groups possess distinct ways of thinking, behaving, and communicating and strive to craft campaigns that resonate with these diverse cultural communities.

Ethnic marketing can involve:

- Using language or imagery specific to a particular culture.
- Highlighting cultural values or traditions in advertising or branding.
- Developing products specifically designed for a particular ethnic group.

Ethnic marketing can effectively reach and engage with diverse consumer populations, particularly in markets where different ethnic groups have significant purchasing power.

Ethnic Marketing in Pharma

Ethnic marketing in pharma involves developing marketing strategies and campaigns tailored to specific ethnic or cultural groups to improve patient outcomes and engagement. Ethnic marketing in pharma recognizes that different cultural groups may have unique health needs, beliefs, and preferences and seeks to develop marketing messages and products that resonate with these groups.

One example of ethnic marketing is developing marketing messages and educational materials available in multiple languages to reach diverse patient populations. This might involve providing patient education materials in languages other than English or developing culturally sensitive messaging tailored to specific ethnic groups.

Another form of ethnic marketing within pharmaceuticals is creating products targeted toward specific ethnic groups. Some pharmaceutical companies have even designed medications tailored specifically for different genetic profiles within certain ethnicities to optimize treatment results and minimize side effects.

Here are some ways in which pharmaceutical companies may approach ethnic marketing:

1. *Multilingual Packaging*: Pharmaceutical companies may include information on drug packaging in multiple languages to make it easier for patients from diverse backgrounds to understand and use the medication.
2. *Cultural Sensitivity in Advertising*: Advertisements for pharmaceuticals may feature actors or models from specified ethnic or racial groups to help patients from those groups feel more represented and connected to the product. Additionally, ads may include cultural nuances or references that resonate with specific groups.
3. *Community Outreach*: Pharmaceutical companies may partner with community organizations or healthcare providers that serve specific ethnic or racial groups to provide education and support related to certain health conditions.
4. *Disease Awareness Campaigns*: Pharmaceutical companies may launch disease awareness campaigns targeting certain ethnic or racial groups at higher risk for certain health conditions. These campaigns may feature targeted messaging and educational materials considering cultural differences and language barriers.
5. *Personalized Medicine*: Some pharmaceutical companies are developing medications tailored to specific genetic variations more common in certain ethnic or racial groups. These medications may be marketed specifically to patients from the groups that benefit most from the treatment.

How Pharma Engages Ethnic Marketing

The following examples show how some pharmaceutical companies are engaging in ethnic marketing:

1. *Pfizer*: Pfizer has launched various initiatives to improve health outcomes for underserved communities, including ethnic and racial minorities. Pfizer's *Get Old* campaign provides resources and information about age-related health conditions, specifically targeting African American, Hispanic, and Asian American communities.
2. *AstraZeneca*: To address healthcare disparities for underserved populations such as ethnic and racial minorities, AstraZeneca created its *Health Equity Initiatives* program. This includes initiatives designed to expand access to care, clinical trials, and partnerships with community organizations that provide education about certain health conditions as resources for education.
3. *Novo Nordisk*: Novo Nordisk has designed programs to advance health outcomes among diverse populations, such as its *Cities Changing Diabetes* initiative. This effort addresses the increasing incidence of diabetes among urban dwellers by engaging local communities and tailoring interventions specifically designed to fit cultural and linguistic contexts.
4. *Eli Lilly* and Company has designed an initiative called *Taking Diabetes to Heart* to address the high prevalence of diabetes and cardiovascular diseases among Asian populations. These comprehensive educational materials, resources, and tools tailored specifically for Asian patients are offered within this initiative.
5. *GlaxoSmithKline (GSK)* has initiated several programs to expand access to healthcare and medications among underserved populations, particularly ethnic and racial minorities. One such initiative, the *Orange Card* program by GSK, offers free or discounted medication to eligible patients who might otherwise struggle to afford them, including resources tailored to individual participants' cultural or linguistic needs.

There are several reasons why pharmaceutical companies might engage in ethnic marketing. For example, certain ethnic or racial groups may be more susceptible to certain medical conditions. Targeting these groups with specific marketing efforts can help raise awareness of relevant medications and treatments. Additionally, marketing efforts considering cultural differences may be more effective in reaching these groups and encouraging them to seek medical treatment

Ethnocentrism

Ethnocentrism refers to viewing one's culture or ethnic group as superior. This may manifest in various forms, from believing their culture is superior in terms of civilizedness or sophistication to discrimination based on cultural standards.

Ethnocentrism in global business and marketing can be problematic; it may lead to miscommunication, biases, and discrimination against different cultures. For example, a company that assumes its products or marketing messages will be universally appealing without considering cultural differences or preferences may find its efforts ineffective or offensive in certain markets.

To avoid ethnocentrism in global marketing, companies should take a culturally sensitive and inclusive approach to their activities. This might involve researching different markets' cultural norms and preferences, adapting marketing messages and strategies to be culturally appropriate, and engaging with local stakeholders to build relationships and trust.

In addition, companies should ensure that their marketing activities are consistent with ethical and legal standards in different markets and avoid using stereotypes or assumptions based on cultural biases.

Ethnocentrism in Pharma Marketing: Key Implications

The implications of ethnocentrism for pharma marketers are significant, particularly as companies seek to expand into new markets and engage with diverse patient populations. Some key implications include the following:

1. *Need for Cultural Sensitivity*: Pharma marketers must be sensitive to the target audience's cultural norms, beliefs, and preferences to develop effective marketing messages and strategies. This might involve adapting marketing materials to be culturally appropriate, using local language, or incorporating cultural symbols and values into marketing campaigns.
2. *Regulatory Compliance*: Pharma marketers must know different markets' regulatory and legal frameworks to ensure their marketing activities follow these guidelines. This might involve working closely with local regulatory agencies, understanding local advertising and promotional regulations, and avoiding any activities that could be viewed as unethical or illegal.
3. *Building Relationships*: Pharma marketers must strive to build meaningful relationships and establish trust between diverse patient populations, healthcare providers, and other key stakeholders. This may involve engaging with local communities or working closely with patient advocacy groups, or perhaps working alongside healthcare organizations that specialize in patient outcomes to create partnerships to enhance them.
4. *Avoid Stereotypes*: Pharma marketers must strive to avoid stereotypes or assumptions based on cultural biases when creating marketing messages catering to diverse patient populations.

By adopting an approach to pharmaceutical marketing that considers culture and includes diversity-sensitive marketing practices, companies can ensure success in an increasingly global healthcare industry and form strong bonds among diverse populations.

Ethnography

Ethnography is a qualitative research method that studies human cultures and social interactions. This process typically entails deep immersion within a particular group, community, or society by an ethnographer who actively takes part in the everyday lives of their subjects.

Anthropology seeks to gain an in-depth knowledge of a culture's beliefs, values, and practices by studying its members; then compiling this understanding in an organized fashion. Ethnography typically involves participant observation, interviews, and document analysis spanning an extended period for maximum insight into the subject's culture.

Anthropology, sociology, and cultural studies typically utilize ethnography as a research method to gain insight into different social groups' ways of life and functioning. Business professionals also utilize ethnography in business development efforts by gathering data for marketing campaigns or product design efforts; It is often an efficient means of gathering consumer behavior data to design more culturally sensitive interventions in healthcare and education settings.

Ethnography as a Tool in Pharma Marketing

When applied to pharmaceutical marketing, ethnography can be invaluable for gaining insight into patients, healthcare providers, and other stakeholders' behaviors, attitudes, and experiences within healthcare industries.

Pharmaceutical companies can utilize ethnographic research methods such as observations, interviews, and participant observation to understand better how their products are utilized, cultural influences on healthcare decisions, and unmet patient and healthcare provider needs.

Ethnographic research can assist pharmaceutical companies in understanding patients' decision-making processes when selecting medications, how patients navigate healthcare systems, and social and cultural influences that impede treatment adherence.

Ethnography offers key insights into the provider-patient relationship in healthcare settings, including how healthcare providers communicate with their patients, challenges in providing care, and factors influencing prescribing behavior.

Ethnography can assist pharmaceutical companies in creating more patient-centric and culturally sensitive marketing strategies to meet better patient and healthcare provider needs. Nonetheless, ethnographic research must be conducted ethically with informed consent obtained and respect shown for research participants' privacy and confidentiality.

Below are examples of ethnography being employed within pharmaceutical marketing:

1. *Understanding the Patient Journey*: A pharmaceutical company may employ ethnography as part of their healthcare journey research strategy to thoroughly understand patient experiences— from initial symptoms through diagnosis and treatment options selection. This data allows pharmaceutical firms to uncover any obstacles patients encounter when accessing care, emotional or social impacts associated with illness, and decisions when selecting treatment options.
2. *Identification of Cultural Factors*: Ethnographic research can assist pharmaceutical companies in understanding how cultural factors play a part in healthcare decision-making, including beliefs regarding illness and disability, family and community participation in decision-making processes, and potential language barriers between patients and healthcare providers.
3. *Examining Healthcare Provider-Patient Interactions*: Ethnography can also offer unique insight into healthcare provider-patient relationships, including communication styles used by healthcare providers, challenges associated with providing care, and any cultural factors which affect interactions with their patients.
4. *Evaluating Treatment Adherence:* Ethnography can provide valuable insight into factors impacting patient adherence, including beliefs about medication, available social support, and daily routine.

Ethnography provides a complete picture of patient experience and cultural and socioeconomic influences on healthcare decision-making, helping pharma companies create more targeted marketing strategies with patients in mind.

Ethnographic Research

Ethnographic research in pharmaceutical marketing employs qualitative methodologies to understand better patient behaviors, attitudes, and beliefs about healthcare and medication. Observing patients in their natural environments, such as homes or communities, and conducting in-depth interviews or focus groups, provides key insights.

Ethnographic research can give pharmaceutical companies invaluable insights into patient needs and preferences, allowing them to create more targeted marketing strategies and interventions. By studying patients as they navigate their healthcare journey, companies can identify areas of difficulty where patients might encounter barriers in meeting healthcare needs or staying on schedule with medication regimens.

Ethnographic research can assist pharmaceutical companies with creating targeted messaging and marketing campaigns that resonate with patients. By understanding patient beliefs and values as well as their attitudes about healthcare providers and medication, companies can develop communication strategies that are both culturally responsive and successful.

Ethnographic Research in Pharmaceutical Marketing

Here are a few examples of ethnographic research's use in pharma marketing:

A. *Understanding Medication Adherence*: One pharmaceutical company conducted ethnographic research to understand what influences medication adherence among chronic disease patients. Researchers observed patients in their homes and communities to understand their daily routines, social support networks, beliefs about medication, and beliefs associated with medication usage before conducting in-depth interviews. Based on the findings, pharma companies created medication adherence interventions that addressed specific challenges different patient groups face.

B. *Developing Culturally Sensitive Messaging*: An ethnographic research approach was employed by one pharmaceutical company to create culturally sensitive messaging for a new medication. Researchers conducted in-depth interviews and focus groups with patients from diverse cultural backgrounds to assess their beliefs and attitudes regarding healthcare and medication before tailoring messaging for individual patient groups that improved marketing campaign success.

C. *Identification of Unmet Patient Needs*: A pharmaceutical company conducted ethnographic research to understand unmet patient needs among those with rare diseases. Researchers observed patients in their homes and communities and conducted in-depth interviews to gain insight into their experiences and needs. Based on these results, a patient support program was created specifically for this population, addressing its challenges while increasing satisfaction levels among these individuals.

How to Conduct Ethnographic Research

Here are several key steps for conducting ethnographic research in pharmaceutical marketing:

1. *Establish the Research Question*: To create a more focused ethnographic research agenda, identify what question or problem this research hopes to tackle and the methods it intends to employ. Doing this will guide the research project's design and a selection of suitable methodologies.
2. *Select the Study Population*: When researching patients suffering from specific ailments or diseases, determine which population it will focus on regarding geography, age, gender, and cultural diversity.
3. *Conduct Background Research*: Review existing literature and data sources to fully understand your research question and pinpoint any gaps in current knowledge.
4. *Create the Research Plan*: Determine which research methods, such as observation, interviews, or focus groups, will be employed, as well as an appropriate sample size and study duration for this plan.
5. *Recruiting Participants*: Researchers must select participants who meet the criteria set for a study population, secure informed consent from them, and protect their privacy and confidentiality.
6. *Collect Data*: Use one or more research methods to collect the desired information. For instance, ethnographic research may entail watching patients interact in their natural settings such as homes, workplaces, or communities; it might also involve in-depth interviews or focus groups to gather their experiences and attitudes.
7. *Analyzing Data*: Using qualitative research methods such as coding and thematic analysis to examine your data. You'll want to look for patterns, themes, and insights emerging from it all.
8. *Draw Conclusions from Data Analysis*: From your analysis, draw conclusions based on patient needs and preferences and use these to develop recommendations for marketing strategies or interventions that meet those requirements.
9. *Communicate Findings*: Present research findings to pharmaceutical companies, healthcare providers, and patient advocacy groups to inform decision-making and enhance patient outcomes.

Ethnographic research involves:

- Gathering informed consent from participants
- Protecting their privacy and confidentiality
- Assuring cultural sensitivity in conducting the research and ensuring its conduct respectfully

Ethnographic research can offer pharmaceutical companies valuable insights into patient behaviors and needs that they can use to craft more successful marketing strategies and interventions designed to improve patient outcomes. However, it must be conducted ethically without compromising patient needs over marketing objectives.

Event Marketing

Event marketing in pharmaceuticals involves using events, such as conferences, symposiums, and trade shows to market pharmaceutical products to healthcare professionals, patients, and other key audiences. Event marketing provides pharmaceutical companies with an effective means to build brand recognition, generate leads and form lasting relationships.

Here are a few key considerations when planning event marketing within the pharmaceutical industry:

1. *Identification of Appropriate Events*: When selecting events to attend, companies must consider factors like target audiences and relevance of each event to their product or therapy area, size, scope, location, timing, budget, and resources required for participation.
2. *Develop a Plan*: Before attending any event, companies should develop an in-depth strategy outlining their goals, target audience, messaging strategy, and tactics for engaging attendees. The strategy should also include a plan for measuring the event's success through lead-generation or attendee feedback.
3. *Engage with Attendees*: Companies should focus on engaging with attendees meaningfully to make the most of an event. This can include providing interactive exhibits or demos, hosting education sessions or workshops, and offering opportunities for one-on-one meetings with key stakeholders.

4. *Provide Valuable Content*: To capture the attention of attendees and establish thought leadership, companies should provide valuable content, such as research findings, case studies, or expert insights. This can help position the company as a trusted source of information and build relationships with healthcare professionals and patients.
5. *Follow up After the Event*: Following up with attendees after the event is essential to continue building relationships and capturing leads. Companies should have a clear plan for following up with attendees, such as through personalized emails or phone calls, and should track the effectiveness of their follow-up efforts.

Event marketing can be an effective tool for pharmaceutical companies to market products, build relationships with key stakeholders, and establish thought leadership in their therapy areas. Companies can maximize the impact of their event marketing efforts by selecting the right events, developing a clear strategy, engaging with attendees, providing valuable content, and following up effectively.

Ever-greening

Ever-greening refers to extending the life of pharmaceutical patents by making small modifications or developing a different formulation for existing drugs to maintain market exclusivity and keep competition at bay. This technique may extend patent life beyond its typical 20 years (from the filing date), keep generic versions under control and maintain market exclusivity for longer than expected.

Ever-greening in pharmaceutical marketing involves developing new marketing strategies and campaigns for an updated or reformulated drug that bears only minor differences from its original version, even if these differences initially seem minor. Examples may include emphasizing the benefits of the updated formulation or emphasizing how important brand name drugs are regardless of minor variations between versions of the medication.

Ever-greening may be a widely practiced tactic within the pharmaceutical industry, yet it is also divisive and controversial. Critics claim it limits competition by keeping drug prices artificially high while delaying more low-priced generic alternatives from becoming available sooner. Furthermore, ever-greening may raise ethical concerns when advertised as offering significant innovations or breakthroughs when there may only be minor benefits over its original formulation.

As such, many countries have introduced regulations and laws designed to combat ever-greening in pharmaceutical marketing to foster competition within this sector. Some nations have implemented shorter patent terms for additional patents on an approved drug or stricter criteria for patentability to prevent companies from ever-greening patents. Additionally, companies should be transparent when marketing updated or reformulated drugs and avoid making misleading or exaggerated claims about their effectiveness or innovation in marketing communications.

Ever-Greening in Pharma: Examples

Below are two instances that show how pharmaceutical companies have utilized ever-greening to extend their patents:

1. Nexium (Esomeprazole) is a proton pump inhibitor commonly prescribed to treat acid reflux and heartburn. When AstraZeneca's patent on another proton pump inhibitor called Prilosec was set to expire in 2001, AstraZeneca developed Nexium as a slightly modified version. Although effectiveness wasn't substantially different between Nexium and Prilosec, AstraZeneca maintained market exclusivity in the antiulcerant market while charging higher prices for their drug.
2. GlaxoSmithKline has been accused of ever-greening for their asthma drug Advair. In 2010, GlaxoSmithKline developed the Ellipta Inhaler device, which it claimed would offer significant improvements over existing inhalers; critics of GlaxoSmithKline claimed this change wasn't significantly different, and the company tried to extend their patent rights through it.

Ever-greening may be controversial, but pharmaceutical companies frequently utilize this tactic to maintain market exclusivity and increase profits. Therefore, regulators, healthcare providers, and patients must remain aware of such practices to foster competition and transparency within the pharmaceutical industry.

Evidence-based Marketing

Evidence-based marketing in the pharmaceutical industry involves using data and scientific evidence to make informed decisions about marketing strategies. This approach relies on clinical trial data, real-world evidence, and other scientific information to support the efficacy and safety of pharmaceutical products. It helps build trust with healthcare professionals and patients by providing transparent and credible information. Additionally, evidence-based marketing enables companies to tailor their messages more effectively, ensuring that marketing efforts align with the scientific evidence supporting their products.

Opportunities and Challenges

Pharma marketers adopting evidence-based strategies face both opportunities and challenges. On the positive side, leveraging scientific evidence enhances credibility and fosters trust among healthcare professionals and patients. It allows marketers to craft messages that resonate with specific audiences, leading to more effective communication. This, in turn, can contribute to better market positioning and increased adoption of pharmaceutical products.

However, challenges arise in managing the complexities of interpreting scientific data for non-expert audiences. Striking a balance between compliance with regulations and engaging marketing practices is crucial. Moreover, staying abreast of evolving scientific developments and adjusting marketing strategies is essential in this dynamic industry.

In summary, while evidence-based marketing offers substantial benefits, pharma marketers must skillfully integrate scientific rigor into their communication strategies, ensuring a delicate balance between transparency, compliance, and effective messaging.

Exclusivity

Exclusivity is when drug manufacturers gain exclusive marketing rights for specific medications or medical products. Regulators like the Food and Drug Administration typically grant this exclusivity period to support drug development and innovation.

Two main forms of exclusivity exist that drug manufacturers can be granted:

A. *Patent Exclusivity*: Manufacturers who successfully file for drug or medical product patents receive exclusive rights to manufacture, market, and sell the product within an allotted timeframe, typically 20 years from the filing date, protecting its exclusivity provisions.

B. *Regulatory Exclusivity*: Manufacturers who have completed an new drug application (NDA),or biological application (BLA) filing with the FDA can receive this type of exclusivity, lasting from three to seven years, depending on its terms.

Exclusivity provides pharmaceutical manufacturers with a window to recoup research and development expenses and maximize profit. However, exclusivity also raises drug prices, restricting patient access to affordable medication management tools, which is particularly problematic when relied upon to treat chronic conditions.

Exclusivity in Pharma

There are many types of exclusivity that regulatory agencies, such as the Food and Drug Administration (FDA) in the United States may grant pharmaceutical products:

1. *New Chemical Entity (NCE) Exclusivity*: NCE exclusivity applies to manufacturers that have created an entirely new drug compound not previously approved by the FDA, providing five years' exclusivity starting when approval was given by FDA and prohibiting other manufacturers from applying for approval of similar drugs during that timeframe.
2. *New Clinical Investigation Exclusivity*: Manufacturers who conduct new clinical investigations for already approved drugs that result in significant new uses or indications will receive New Clinical Investigation Exclusivity up to three years from FDA approval.
3. *Orphan Drug Exclusivity*: The US FDA grants a seven-year orphan drug exclusivity to manufacturers who develop drugs to treat rare conditions (affecting fewer than 200,000 individuals), during which no other manufacturer can gain approval to market similar treatments to treat the same conditions.
4. *Pediatric Exclusivity*: In addition, the US FDA grants a six-month pediatric exclusivity to manufacturers conducting pediatric trials for drugs approved for adult use. No other company may obtain approval to sell it as children's medication during this time.

Exhibition Marketing

Exhibition Marketing refers to using exhibitions or trade shows as part of a company's promotional plan to showcase its products or services and reach a larger target market. Exhibitions give businesses an ideal venue to show potential customers their offerings while networking with industry peers and gaining wider visibility from customers and professionals alike.

Exhibition marketing involves creating and executing an exhibition booth or display that draws in visitors while effectively communicating your company's message. This may involve product demonstrations, interactive displays, giveaways, or promotional materials like brochures or flyers to do this effectively.

Exhibition marketing can be especially useful for companies in healthcare, pharmaceuticals, and medical devices, as it provides direct interactions that build customer trust and credibility.

Here are the advantages of exhibition marketing:

1. *Increase Brand Recognition and Awareness*: Exhibitions provide businesses with an ideal venue to present their products or services directly to an international audience and raise brand recognition and awareness.
2. *Lead Generation*: Exhibitions give businesses an excellent way to meet potential customers and generate leads they can follow up on after attending an exhibition event.
3. *Networking*: Exhibitions enable businesses to meet with other industry professionals and form relationships that could result in future partnerships or collaborations.
4. *Market Research*: Displaying at exhibitions provides businesses an excellent way to collect customer insights and conduct market research that can inform future product design and marketing strategies.

Exhibition marketing can provide businesses with a cost-effective means of advertising their product or service offerings, creating leads for growth, and developing relationships with clients and industry professionals.

How Pharma Can Leverage Exhibition Marketing

Pharma marketers can use exhibition marketing to cultivate relationships with customers and industry professionals through various approaches, including exhibitions. Consider the following, for example:

1. *Exhibiting at Medical Conferences*: Pharma companies may exhibit at medical conferences and events to present their products and interact with healthcare professionals, creating the opportunity to promote them further, give demonstrations and generate leads. This gives them an invaluable chance for promotion, demonstration, and lead generation.
2. *Hosting Educational Events*: Pharma companies can host educational events for healthcare professionals to increase awareness and educate them on treatment options for diseases or conditions they want to promote and create relationships with key opinion leaders that generate leads for sales opportunities.
3. *Exhibiting at Patient Events*: Pharma companies should participate in patient events to connect with patients and caregivers while offering educational resources and showcasing their products, providing an ideal oppotyunity to raise brand recognition and generate leads.
4. *Participating in Industry Exhibitions*: Pharma companies should participate in exhibitions to network with industry professionals, showcase their products, and discover emerging developments within their sector. By joining exhibitions, they can build relationships while remaining up-to-date with market trends and keeping an edge over their competition.
5. *Showcasing Clinical Trial Data*: Pharma companies can utilize exhibitions to display clinical trial data demonstrating their products' efficacy and safety, building credibility among healthcare providers and potential customers.

Exhibition marketing can be an efficient and effective means for pharma companies to promote their products, foster customer relations with industry professionals, and stay abreast of industry trends. Furthermore, by participating in relevant events and offering educational resources at exhibition booths, they can build trust and credibility among healthcare providers and patients, driving sales growth while improving patient outcomes.

Exogenous Attention

Exogenous Attention is when a sudden movement or a bright color catches your eye, even if you focus on something else. It is like the attention-grabbing you rather than you choosing to pay attention to something. It is the involuntary, automatic aspect of attention.

Here is an example of exogenous attention: Imagine reading a book in a quiet room, and suddenly, a loud noise outside attracts you. That distraction is an example of exogenous attention; it is something external grabbing your focus with you intending it.

Another example could be when you are walking down the street, and a flashy billboard or sudden movement in your peripheral vision captures your attention, diverting it from your original path or thoughts. These are instances where external stimuli involuntarily draw your attention.

Exogenous Attention in Marketing

Understanding exogenous attention is crucial for creative, effective advertisements and campaigns in marketing. Marketers aim to capture the audience's attention amidst a sea of information and stimuli. Here are a few ways exogenous attention plays a role:

1. *Eye-Catching Designs*: Bright colors, bold fonts, and visually striking designs can be exogenous

attention triggers. A visually appealing ad can quickly grab attention in a crowded advertising space.

2. *Unexpected Elements*: Incorporating unexpected or surprising elements in advertisements can trigger exogenous attention. This might include unexpected humor, a plot twist, or a unique visual that stands out.
3. *Intriguing Visuals*: Using visuals that naturally attract attention, such as high-contrast images or motion graphics, can engage viewers and hold their focus.
4. *Sensory Appeals*: Ads that engage multiple senses, like sight and sound, have a better chance of capturing exogenous attention. This might include jingles, catchy tunes, or immersive visuals.
5. *Limited-Time Offers*: Urgency and scarcity are known to grab attention. Marketing strategies highlighting limited-time offers or exclusive deals trigger a sense of urgency, compelling consumers to pay attention.

Understanding the principles of exogenous attention allows marketers to design campaigns that stand out in a world full of distractions, increasing the likelihood that the target audience will notice and remember their message.

Exogenous Attention in Pharma Marketing

Exogenous attention in pharma marketing refers to strategies and tactics that draw attention to a product or brand outside the typical healthcare or pharmaceutical context. It involves capturing the interest of individuals who may not be actively seeking information about a specific drug or medical condition. Here are a few examples:

1. *Celebrity Endorsement*: Engaging celebrities to endorse a pharmaceutical product or raise awareness about a particular health issue can attract attention from a broader audience. For instance, a well-known personality sharing their experience with a medication or health concern can generate widespread interest.
2. *Social Media Campaigns*: Creating attention-grabbing social media campaigns beyond traditional medical platforms. For example, a pharmaceutical company might develop a viral marketing campaign on platforms like Instagram or TikTok to increase brand visibility and reach a younger demographic.
3. *Partnerships with Non-Health Brands*: Collaborating with non-health-related brands to promote pharmaceutical products can bring attention from diverse consumer groups. For instance, partnering with a fitness brand to promote a medication related to a health condition might attract individuals interested in wellness.
4. *Interactive Educational Initiatives*: Developing interactive and engaging educational initiatives beyond standard medical information. This could include virtual reality experiences, interactive websites, or mobile apps that provide information in an entertaining and accessible manner.
5. *Community Events and Sponsorships*: Sponsoring or organizing events in the community, such as health fairs, workshops, or sports events. This can help the pharmaceutical company establish a positive presence and engage with the community directly.
6. *Innovative Advertising*: Creating attention-grabbing and innovative advertising campaigns that stand out from traditional healthcare advertisements. For example, using creative visuals, storytelling, or humor to capture the audience's interest.
7. *Influencer Marketing*: Leveraging influencers in non-health sectors to promote pharmaceutical products. Influencers with a large following in lifestyle, travel, or other niches can introduce healthcare messages to a diverse audience.

Pharma marketers must be mindful of ethical considerations and regulatory guidelines when implementing exogenous attention strategies to ensure that information is accurate, balanced, and compliant with industry standards.

Experiential Marketing

Experiential marketing in the pharmaceutical industry refers to creating unique experiences for patients, healthcare professionals and other key stakeholder groups that engage emotionally, build positive associations between brands and customers and strengthen customer loyalty and advocacy. Here are a few examples of experiential marketing in the pharmaceutical industry.

1. *Virtual Reality Simulations*: Pfizer created virtual reality experiences to educate healthcare providers on the effects of rheumatoid arthritis on body systems. This allowed healthcare workers to interact with virtual patients to better comprehend its effect.
2. *Interactive Exhibits*: Organizing interactive exhibits at medical conferences, trade shows and other events which demonstrate the features and benefits of particular drugs or treatments is

becoming an increasing trend. Sanofi for instance developed *IBGStar Blood Glucose Monitoring System* allowing visitors at conferences to try it themselves while learning more about diabetes management.

3. *Patient Education Programs*: Employing storytelling, videos, and multimedia tools to educate patients about certain diseases or treatments. Novo Nordisk developed an interactive diabetes education program with videos, quizzes, and games for patients to help manage their condition effectively and support networks to assist.
4. *Patient Support Programs*: Johnson & Johnson has designed an app to offer resources, guidance, and emotional support during patients' treatment journeys. Reminders, alerts and educational materials help keep patients up-to-date, and engaged throughout treatment plans.
5. *Live Events*: Organizing live events, such as patient forums, support groups, educational seminars, or healthcare professional summits that bring patients and healthcare professionals together to share experiences, insights, and knowledge, is increasingly common. AbbVie hosted an event dubbed a patient summit about Crohn's disease or ulcerative colitis, which included workshops, panels, and interactive exhibits designed to educate participants while creating a sense of community among attendees.

These examples demonstrate how pharmaceutical companies employ experiential marketing techniques to inform, engage and empower both patients and healthcare providers while building brand loyalty and improving patient outcomes.

Pharma companies using experiential marketing in their marketing strategy will gain greater insights into customers' needs and preferences and can customize products and services more closely, distinguishing themselves from their rivals in the process.

Experience Curve

The Experience Curve, or Learning Curve, is a concept originating in manufacturing that has since spread into other fields, including pharmaceuticals, with promising implications. The Experience Curve indicates that as companies gain experience producing and selling a product, associated production and sale costs decrease while improving product quality and the efficiency of the processes involved.

Experience curves are used extensively in pharmaceutical marketing, providing various strategies and applications of this concept. As companies gain more practice promoting particular drugs, their effectiveness may increase at targeting physicians and patients for promotion or sales calls; creating promotional material; conducting sales calls more efficiently; as a result, costs decrease while their resources can be better allocated by managing marketing effectively.

Experience curves can also play an essential part in the pharmaceutical industry by streamlining drug development processes for faster time frames and reduced costs.

The experience curve is useful in pharma marketing as it encourages companies to focus on continuous improvement and learning, leading to increased efficiency and profitability.

Experience Curve in Pharma Marketing: Some Examples

Here are some examples of how the experience curve can be applied in pharma marketing:

1. *Sales Force Efficiency*: As a pharmaceutical company gains experience promoting a drug, its sales representatives become more efficient at targeting the right physicians and patients, making sales calls, and delivering key messages. This leads to increased sales and lower marketing costs.
2. *Manufacturing Efficiency*: With experience comes increased production efficiency that yields better-quality drugs at reduced costs.
3. *Clinical Trial Efficiency*: As companies gain more experience designing and conducting clinical trials, they may be able to streamline the processes, leading to faster development times at reduced costs.
4. *Marketing Strategy*: Once a company gains experience promoting drugs in one therapeutic area, its knowledge of market dynamics and healthcare provider and patient requirements may improve and result in more efficient marketing and sales efforts. This could enable more successful strategies.
5. *Drug Development*: With experience comes an ability to identify new targets and create more potency-boosting compounds resulting in greater success for drug development programs.

Exploratory Research

Exploratory research in pharmaceutical marketing refers to initial investigations conducted into topics, ideas or problems to gain insight, generate hypotheses and discover opportunities for further investigation. Exploratory studies often take place before marketing campaigns or product releases as this type of investigation provides invaluable intelligence about consumers needs as well as potential barriers that might impede adoption.

Here are a few examples of exploratory research in pharma marketing:

1. *Focus Groups*: Convene focus groups with patients, healthcare providers or other key stakeholders in order to gain an in-depth understanding of their perceptions, attitudes and behaviors regarding an issue, or drug treatment.
2. *Case Studies*: Examining real cases involving patients who have used specific medicines or therapies to recognize common patterns, challenges, and outcomes for each drug therapy used by these individuals.
3. *Secondary Data Analysis*: Examining existing sources, like medical journals, databases and market reports to detect trends, gaps, and opportunities within the marketplace.
4. *Conduct In-Depth Interviews*: Conduct individual one-on-one interviews with key opinion leaders, thought leaders and industry experts to gain their perspectives about specific drugs or treatments.
5. *Online Surveys*: Conduct online surveys with patients or healthcare professionals to collect data regarding their preferences, behaviors and perceptions regarding certain drugs or treatments.

Exploratory research can give pharmaceutical companies valuable insights into the market, identify unfulfilled needs and create strategies to differentiate themselves from competitors.

Export Marketing

Export Marketing in pharma refers to selling pharmaceutical products in foreign markets. This involves identifying, and targeting potential customers in different countries, complying with local regulations, and adapting marketing strategies to fit different regions' cultural and economic contexts.

Export Marketing Strategy: Key Factors

Here are a few key considerations when creating an export marketing strategy in pharmaceuticals:

1. *Compliance Requirements*: Pharmaceutical companies must follow local regulatory requirements wherever their products are sold, which may involve securing any required licenses, adhering to labeling rules, and assuring product quality and safety.
2. *Market Research*: Pharma companies should conduct market research to identify target customers, understand local market trends and create customized marketing strategies tailored for each region's preferences and requirements.
3. *Distribution Channels*: Pharmaceutical firms must identify appropriate channels of distribution in each country they sell products in, such as distributors or agents who will serve as local agents for selling the drugs they produce.
4. *Pricing Strategy*: Pharma companies must develop a pricing strategy considering local market conditions, including competition and regulations.
5. *Cultural and Language Considerations*: Pharma companies must consider cultural and language differences when developing marketing materials and communications strategies for different markets.
6. *Training the Staff*: Pharma companies should train staff on cultural and regulatory differences in each target market to ensure compliance and effective communication.
7. *Monitoring*: Pharmaceutical companies should also monitor sales, customer feedback, and regulatory compliance in each market after launching their products.

Export marketing in pharma requires careful planning and execution to ensure compliance with regulatory requirements and successful entry into new markets. By conducting thorough market research, developing strong distribution channels, and adapting marketing strategies to fit local contexts, pharma companies can successfully expand their reach and improve patient outcomes on a global scale.

Eye-Tracking

Eye-tracking can be very useful in marketing research, particularly in the pharmaceutical sector. By giving insight into consumer visual engagement with marketing materials and campaigns, this tool allows companies to optimize strategies and increase campaign effectiveness.

Eye-tracking may involve the visual engagement of patients or potential clients with marketing materials or ads.

Eye-tracking can serve both of these purposes in different contexts. For example, it can be used for gaining insights about consumer visual interaction with material so companies can optimize strategies related to improving campaign effectiveness

1. *Attention and Engagement*: Eye-tracking helps researchers assess which elements of marketing messages or advertisements engage viewers and for how long. By studying eye movement patterns, researchers identify focal points, understand which components viewers may ignore, and make educated decisions to increase engagement with a marketing message or advertisement.
2. *Visual Hierarchy in Marketing Materials*: These eye tracking studies can reveal a visual hierarchy in marketing materials by showing which parts viewers focus on first in an advertisement or packaging piece. With this knowledge, content can be structured accordingly to ensure all vital pieces receive their due consideration and deserve sufficient attention from viewers.
3. *Branding and Logos*: Eye-tracking studies can assess the effect of logos and branding elements on viewers. Researchers can measure whether viewers easily notice, recognize and associate them with an intended brand identity, enabling companies to optimize visual branding strategies more effectively.
4. *Labeling and Packaging Design* : By studying how people engage with labels and packaging elements, eye-tracking allows companies to assess how effective these are at improving product visibility, emphasizing important information, and offering users an enhanced user experience.
5. *Print and Digital Ads*: Eye-tracking studies help companies assess the efficacy of print and digital advertisements through eye movement analysis. Researchers can use eye-tracking studies to ascertain which elements attract most of a viewer's focus while pinpointing potential distractions or unnoticed areas, providing companies with valuable data to optimize ad designs and placement.
6. *Website and Digital Experience*: Eye-tracking provides invaluable data for understanding user experiences on websites and digital platforms, from determining which elements garner the most focus to measuring the navigation efficiency or the performance of call-to-action buttons and optimizing content layout to increase engagement and conversion rates.

Eye-tracking provides invaluable insights into customer behavior for pharmaceutical marketers conducting marketing research. It allows them to optimize strategies to engage their target audiences efficiently, increase brand recognition, and enhance user experiences.

F

1. Face-to-face Detailing
2. Facebook
3. Factor Analysis
4. False Claims Act (FCA)
5. Family Brands
6. Family Lifecycle
7. FDA
8. Feedback
9. Field Marketing
10. Field Sales Management
11. Field Research
12. Field Sales Manager
13. Field work
14. Fighter Brand
15. Findability
16. First-mover Advantage
17. Five Forces Model
18. Flagship Brand
19. Flanker Brand
20. Flexible Pricing Models
21. fMRI
22. Focus Group
23. Folksonomy
24. Foot-in-the-Door Technique (FDIT)
25. Forecasting
26. Foresight
27. Foreign Corrupt Practices Act (FCPA)
28. Foresight
29. Formulary
30. Forum
31. Framing
32. Franchising
33. Free Drug Coupons
34. Frequency
35. Free Standing Insert (FSI)
36. Freemium
37. Free Website Promotion
38. Funnel

Face-to-Face Detailing

Face-to-face detailing is a widely employed strategy in pharmaceutical marketing where sales representatives meet directly with healthcare providers to present and educate them about their company's offerings.

During these meetings with healthcare providers, sales representatives provide extensive details regarding products, such as their indications, dosages, and possible side effects. Samples may also be given out so their patients can try them themselves.

Face-to-face detailing can be an extremely powerful marketing strategy, enabling sales representatives to form personal relationships with healthcare professionals and increasing brand recognition, loyalty, sales, and prescriptions of your company's products.

The COVID-19 pandemic has led many companies to switch to virtual detailing or remote detailing, where sales representatives use video conferencing or other digital platforms like WeChat for communication with healthcare professionals instead of face-to-face detailing, which has proven very popular and may continue even once this pandemic ends.

Improving the Effectiveness of Face-to-face Detailing

Here are some useful tips to improve the effectiveness of face-to-face detailing in pharma marketing:

1. *Develop a Strong Product Knowledge*: Sales representatives should deeply understand the products they are promoting, including their benefits, side effects, and how they compare to competitors' products. This will help them answer any healthcare professionals' questions and build credibility.
2. *Tailor the Message to the Audience*: Healthcare professionals have different levels of expertise and different patient populations. Therefore, sales representatives should customize their messaging to meet the needs of each healthcare professional they are speaking with.
3. *Use Visual Aids*: Visual aids such as brochures, infographics, and videos can be powerful tools to help sales representatives convey complex information about the products they are promoting. These aids can also help healthcare professionals remember key points after the meeting.
4. *Build Relationships*: Sales representatives should focus on building relationships with healthcare professionals rather than just making a sales pitch. This can involve following up with them after the meeting, providing ongoing education, and demonstrating a commitment to helping them provide the best care for their patients.
5. *Stay Abreast*: Sales representatives should remain abreast of the most up-to-date research and clinical guidelines related to their field to position their products effectively against current best practices while creating trust among healthcare professionals.
6. *Measure Success*: Tracking metrics like prescription writing rates and market share is critical to gauge the efficacy of face-to-face detailing services. Doing this allows us to identify areas for improvement while honing our approach over time.

Face-to-face Detailing: Future Outlook

One trend likely to continue is using digital technology in sales and marketing. The COVID-19 pandemic accelerated the adoption of virtual detailing and remote communication, and many companies are likely to continue using these methods even as in-person interactions resume.

However, face-to-face detailing will likely remain an important part of pharma marketing, particularly for more complex products or situations where personal relationships are important. In addition, many healthcare professionals value discussing in person with sales representatives. As a result, they may be more likely to prescribe products from companies that invest in these interactions.

Regulatory changes may also impact the future of face-to-face detailing. For example, some countries and regions have restricted interactions between pharmaceutical companies and healthcare professionals regarding gifts, meals, or travel. As these restrictions spread further, their influence could reduce the effectiveness of face-to-face detailing services and force companies to consider alternative marketing strategies for marketing their goods or services.

Overall, face-to-face detailing in pharmaceutical marketing will likely consist of physical and digital interactions, with companies tailoring their strategy according to healthcare professionals' preferences and regulatory guidelines.

Facebook

Recently, Facebook has emerged as an essential social media tool for pharmaceutical marketing. Pharma companies can use it as a channel to engage patients and healthcare providers (HCPs), share product and service information directly through this social networking tool and increase brand recognition among these groups.

Here are a few ways pharma companies use Facebook for marketing:

1. *Disease Awareness Campaigns*: Firms may utilize this social network platform to spread knowledge of an illness or condition among their target demographic, share stories from affected patients and offer information regarding available treatments.
2. *Patient Education*: Companies may provide educational materials and resources on Facebook that help patients better comprehend their condition and treatment options.
3. *Advertising*: Facebook allows pharmaceutical companies to target specific audiences using paid sponsored posts and newsfeed ads.
4. *Engagement with Patients and HCPs*: Companies can leverage Facebook to engage patients and HCPs via comments, messages, and other forms of social interaction. This helps build trust while developing relationships.
5. *Clinical Trial Recruitment*: Facebook can be an excellent platform to recruit patients for clinical trials by targeting specific demographics and geographic areas with targeted ads.

Learn How Pharma Uses Facebook

Here are a few examples of pharmaceutical companies using Facebook for marketing:

1. Pfizer utilizes Facebook as a marketing channel by sharing information about its products and services, offering resources and support to patients, HCPs, and HCAs (Health Care Assistants) on its products/services/resources, conducting disease awareness campaigns, and recruiting clinical trial candidates.
2. Novartis maintains a Facebook page to raise Multiple Sclerosis (MS) awareness and education, sharing relevant product details and engaging directly with patients and healthcare providers.
3. Sanofi uses Facebook to educate patients and healthcare practitioners (HCPs) on its products and services, engage them and raise disease awareness of different illnesses or conditions. They share educational materials on this platform as well.
4. Roche utilizes Facebook as an information-sharing and resource-providing platform, as well as for disease awareness campaigns and clinical trial recruitment purposes.
5. GlaxoSmithKline (GSK) maintains an asthma education and awareness page on Facebook to share knowledge about products for people living with asthma while connecting with HCPs and patients.

These are some examples of pharmaceutical companies using Facebook as part of their marketing initiatives. However, regulations surrounding their practices change, and companies must remain aware of all current guidelines to avoid legal or ethical ramifications.

Factor Analysis

Factor analysis is a statistical technique to uncover factors or dimensions which explain variations among observed variables, often used for data analysis in fields like psychology, sociology, marketing, and finance.

Factor analysis involves identifying factors or dimensions which account for correlation patterns within a set of observed variables and uncovering any intercorrelations. Its goal is to discover as few underlying causes as possible that can explain them. The goal of factor analysis is to minimize variance across observed variables by finding their strongest predictors.

There are two main types of factor analyses: Exploratory Factor Analysis (EFA) and Confirmatory Factor Analysis (CFA). EFA identifies unknown or unclear data structures when exploring data sets for factors or dimensions to explore, while CFA validates hypothesized structures based on prior research or knowledge.

Factor analysis serves several useful purposes. Consider the following, for example:

1. *Data Complexity*: By highlighting key underlying elements within data, factor analysis helps researchers focus on what are truly the essential parts.
2. *Validation of Constructs*: Factor analysis can be an invaluable way of validating the construct validity of any measurement instrument. Construct validity is *the degree to which the measured variables used in the study represent the hypothesized constructs.*
3. *Marketing Research*: Factor analysis can provide invaluable insight into consumer preferences or product features which drive purchase behavior, providing marketers with crucial intelligence about consumers and purchase behavior.

4. *Financial Analysis*: Factor analysis can be utilized in finance to identify underlying economic forces responsible for variations in stock prices or other variables of financial significance.

Factor Analysis in Pharma Marketing

Pharma marketers use factor analysis to gain a deep insight into what factors drive patient and healthcare provider (HCP) behavior, for instance, identifying key drivers such as medication adherence, patient satisfaction, or physician prescribing behavior.

Here are a few examples of how factor analysis is applied in pharmaceutical marketing:

A. *Identification of Patient Preferences*: Pharmaceutical companies often perform factor analyses on survey data collected from patient interviews to understand which factors strongly influence individual preferences for medication attributes like ease of use, side effect profile, and price.

B. *Understanding Physician Prescribing Behavior*: Pharmaceutical companies may conduct factor analyses of physician prescribing data to uncover underlying factors influencing physician prescribing behavior, including patient demographics, clinical characteristics, and medication safety concerns.

C. *Segmenting Patient Populations*: Pharmaceutical companies may utilize factor analysis of patient survey data to uncover factors that differentiate patient subgroups based on medication preferences or adherence behaviors, helping the company develop marketing messages and interventions tailored specifically toward certain patient segments.

How to Conduct Factor Analysis

Here is an outline of how to conduct factor analysis:

1. *Establish Your Research Question or Objective*: The first step in conducting factor analysis involves clearly outlining its research question or objective. This will assist the analyst with selecting an appropriate data set and statistical method.
2. *Select the Data Set*: Factor analysis requires collecting multiple observed variables into one data set gathered via surveys, interviews, or other research methods.
3. *Determine Sample Size for Factor Analysis*: The sample size needed for factor analysis depends on several variables, including their number and degree of intercorrelation among themselves. A larger sample size should generally be chosen to ensure stability and reliability within its results.
4. *Select the Factor Extraction Method*: Various techniques for extracting factors from data sets, including principal component analysis (PCA) or Maximum likelihood estimation (MLE), that could work to your advantage when extracting factors; you should base your decision on its nature as well as what questions your research poses.
5. *Determine the Number of Factors*: Once this step has been taken, the next step involves extracting factors from your data set using various criteria, such as scatter plot analysis, Eigenvalue calculations, or Parallel analysis may all play an essential part here.
6. *Interpret Factors*: Once factors have been extracted, they must be interpreted for meaning by examining factor loadings, which indicate how closely each observed variable is associated with each factor.
7. *Name and Label Factors*: Once all factors have been assessed, their names and labels should be determined based on the interpretation of their underlying meaning through consultation with subject matter experts and developing a theoretical framework to aid interpretation.

Factor analysis provides pharmaceutical companies an invaluable opportunity to comprehend better the complex factors affecting patient and healthcare professional behaviors, thus helping inform marketing and product development strategies and efforts.

Factor analysis requires statistical analysis and interpretation expertise, understanding your research question, data set, and extraction method to achieve meaningful and accurate results.

False Claims Act (FCA)

The False Claims Act (FCA) is a federal law in the United States that imposes liability on individuals or companies that knowingly submit false or fraudulent claims for payment to the federal government. The FCA significantly impacts pharma marketers' interactions with federal healthcare programs. Here are some key implications of the False Claims Act for pharma marketers:

1. *Prohibition of False Claims*: The FCA prohibits pharma marketers from knowingly submitting or causing the submission of false or fraudulent claims to federal healthcare programs, such as Medicare or Medicaid. Claims can include reimbursement requests for purchased drugs, services, and healthcare-related items.

2. *Liability for False Claims*: Violators of the FCA can face significant penalties, such as fines and triple damages (three times what was suffered), as well as potential exclusion from federal healthcare programs. Furthermore, this statute permits private individuals known as whistleblowers or *Qui tam* relators to sue on behalf of the government and receive part of any recovered damages as compensation for filing legal actions on its behalf and recovering them themselves.
3. *Anti-Kickback Implications*: The FCA and Anti-Kickback Statute (AKS) often overlap; violations of either statute may lead to FCA liability. Pharma marketers must ensure their business arrangements and relationships with healthcare providers comply with both acts to avoid penalties and potential liability issues.
4. *Off-label Promotion*: The FCA has been used to pursue cases against pharmaceutical companies for off-label promotion, which refers to promoting a drug for uses not approved by the US Food and Drug Administration (FDA). If a marketer engages in off-label promotion and the government determines that false claims were submitted to those off-label users, it may trigger FCA liability.
5. *Compliance Programs*: Pharma marketers should establish comprehensive compliance programs to prevent and detect potential violations of the FCA. These programs typically include policies, procedures, training, monitoring, and auditing to ensure the law's adherence and identify potential false claims. Regular education and training sessions should be conducted for sales representatives and other relevant personnel to ensure understanding and compliance with the FCA.
6. *Whistleblower Lawsuits*: Under the False Claims Act (FCA), private individuals may file suit on behalf of the government to recover any incurred damages and share in any recoveries made possible. Pharma marketers should recognize this potential threat of whistleblower lawsuits and take proactive measures to address concerns or potential violations before they escalate into legal proceedings, such as promptly investigating any internal reports of misconduct and taking appropriate corrective actions immediately.
7. *Compliance with Other Laws*: The FCA intersects with other laws and regulations, such as the Anti-Kickback Statute and the Stark Law. Violations of these laws can trigger FCA liability if false claims are submitted to federal healthcare programs due to illegal conduct. Pharma marketers must ensure compliance with all applicable laws and regulations to mitigate the risk of FCA violations.

Pharma marketers should consult legal counsel or compliance experts to ensure a thorough understanding of the False Claims Act and its implications. Implementing effective compliance strategies, conducting regular compliance audits, and fostering a culture of ethical conduct can help mitigate the risk of FCA violations and promote responsible marketing practices.

Family Brands

Family or umbrella brands are an approach to branding whereby companies use one brand for marketing a group of related products or services under its name, thus capitalizing on one brand name's recognition across multiple products or services. This strategy gives companies leverage in terms of cost reduction as they increase brand recognition across products or services while improving reputation management across a company's brand portfolio.

Family brands are an increasingly common strategy used by consumer product companies to market a selection of related items under one brand name. For instance, Proctor & Gamble uses Tide as its umbrella family brand name to market laundry detergent, fabric softener, and stain remover products under its Tide brand umbrella. By using the Tide brand name across these related products, P&G can benefit from the brand recognition and reputation of the Tide name. As a result, consumers are more likely to trust and purchase new products that fall under the Tide family brand.

Family Branding in Pharma

Family branding refers to a marketing technique in which companies utilize their corporate or brand name to market multiple products or services under one umbrella brand name. This tactic has proven popular with pharmaceutical marketers who utilize family brands to increase product portfolio exposure. Here are a few examples of family brands used within pharmaceutical marketing:

1. *Tylenol*: Tylenol is an iconic brand synonymous with relieving pain and fever. Their products include Extra Strength Tylenol, Tylenol PM, and Tylenol Cold & Flu.
2. *Advil*: Advil is another popular pain reliever brand offering various products under the Advil® family brand. These products include Advil Liqui-Gels, Advil PM, Advil Migraine, and more.

3. *Allegra* is an allergy medication brand offering various products under the Allegra® family brand. These products include Allegra-D, Children's Allegra, and more.
4. *Motrin* is a brand that relieves pain and reduces fever, offering a range of products under the Motrin family brand. These products include Motrin® IB, Motrin® PM, and more.
5. *Nexium* is a brand of proton pump inhibitors used to treat acid reflux and heartburn. The brand offers several products under the Nexium® family brand, including Nexium 24 HR, Nexium Control, and more.

While these are just a few examples of family brands in the pharmaceutical industry, family branding is an increasingly popular practice employed by numerous pharmaceutical firms to build brand recognition for their product portfolio and expand sales.

Family Lifecycle

The family lifecycle is a concept used in marketing that describes the stages a typical family goes through as it evolves. Each stage of the family lifecycle presents unique opportunities and challenges for marketers who want to target specific products or services to families.

The typical stages of the family lifecycle are:

1. *Bachelor/Bachelorette*: This is the stage before marriage and children, where young adults may be focused on building their careers, social lives, and independence.
2. *Newlyweds*: This stage occurs after marriage but before the arrival of children. Newlyweds may be focused on establishing their household, building their careers, and enjoying their newfound partnership.
3. *Full Nest I* occurs when young children require significant care and attention. Marketers targeting families in this stage may focus on products and services related to child care, education, and family-friendly activities.
4. *Full Nest II*: This stage occurs as children grow older and become more independent. Marketers targeting families in this stage may focus on products and services related to education, extracurricular activities, and family travel.
5. *Empty Nest I*: This stage occurs when children leave home for the first time, typically for college or other pursuits. Marketers targeting families in this stage may focus on products and services related to travel, hobbies, and retirement planning.
6. *Empty Nest II*: This stage occurs as parents age and retire from their careers. Marketers targeting families in this stage may focus on products and services related to healthcare, financial planning, and retirement living.

Thus, the family lifecycle can be useful for marketers who want to tailor their products and services to specific stages of family development and target their advertising and promotional efforts accordingly.

Implications for Pharma Marketers

The family lifecycle concept can have several implications for pharma marketers.

A. First, it can help pharmaceutical companies understand the need and behaviors of their target audiences at different stages of the family lifecycle. For example, marketers targeting families in the *Full Nest I stage* may focus on promoting products related to children's health and well-being, such as vaccines and medications for common childhood illnesses. Marketers targeting families in the *Empty Nest II* stage may focus on promoting products related to aging and health, such as medications for chronic conditions and supplements for overall wellness.

B. Second, using the family lifecycle concept can assist pharma marketers with crafting targeted marketing campaigns and messaging that resonate with target audiences. For instance, pharmaceutical companies targeting families in the *Full Nest II* stages might develop campaigns emphasizing maintaining healthy lifestyle habits to meet demands associated with active family life; similarly, *Empty Nest I* stage families may receive campaigns emphasizing staying healthy during retirement years.

Family lifecycle concepts provide pharmaceutical companies with an effective means for identifying emerging trends and opportunities in the market. The Baby Boomer generation members age and require products related to senior care or aging-related conditions, such as care for people with dementia. Understanding family lifecycle concepts helps pharmaceutical marketers anticipate these trends so that products or marketing strategies successfully meet these emerging demands of target audiences.

FDA

The Food and Drug Administration, commonly referred to by its acronym FDA, is a regulatory agency in the US government responsible for protecting public health by monitoring food products, drugs, medical devices, vaccines, and biological products.

Role and Responsibilities of the FDA

The role and responsibilities of the Food and Drug Administration (FDA) in the United States include the following:

1. *Ensuring Product Safety and Effectiveness*: The FDA implements standards regulating product safety, effectiveness, and quality before products enter the market. Before becoming commercialized for sale or use in consumer environments, these must meet approval or clearance of food, prescription, and over-the-counter drugs, medical devices, and other products.
2. *Regulating, Distributing, and Labeling Products*: The FDA regulates and oversees the production, distribution, and labeling of products, such as foods, drugs, and medical devices, to comply with relevant laws and regulations.
3. *Conducting Research and Collecting Data*: The FDA researches to support its regulatory decisions, address public health concerns effectively, evaluate products' safety and efficacy, and support them by continuous monitoring.
4. *Collaboration With Other Organizations*: To advance public health and safety, the FDA works with numerous organizations from industry, academia, and other government agencies that work towards this common goal.
5. *Responding to Emergencies and Outbreaks*: In times of an emergency or outbreak, such as food-borne illness outbreaks or pandemics like COVID-19, the FDA takes swift and decisive actions to safeguard public health by offering guidance and oversight of any regulatory activity required.

FDA and Pharma Marketing

The Food and Drug Administration regulates pharmaceutical marketing materials in the US to ensure they are accurate, truthful, balanced, and not misleading for patients.

The FDA reviews all promotional materials before pharmaceutical companies use them to promote their products. The review ensures that these marketing materials are unbiased and provide balanced information regarding the drug's benefits and risks.

Pharmaceutical companies must abide by stringent rules when advertising prescription medications. For instance, advertisements must fully disclose risks and side effects without falsely claiming efficacy.

Recently, the FDA has taken an aggressive stance towards pharmaceutical marketing regulation by targeting companies making false or deceptive statements about their products, increasing focus on digital channels like social media and mobile apps that allow pharmaceutical firms to reach customers directly.

The FDA is essential in ensuring that pharmaceutical marketing practices are truthful, accurate, and non-misleading so consumers can make informed healthcare decisions. They ensure that customers (HCPs) and consumers (patients) can access accurate data to make educated choices regarding their well-being.

Pharmaceutical companies, therefore, must abide by stringent regulations when advertising prescription medications. For instance, their advertisements must fully disclose risks and side effects and avoid false or misleading claims regarding efficacy.

Feedback

Feedback in pharmaceutical marketing refers to gathering information regarding the success of campaigns or initiatives undertaken; gathering this feedback can come from customers, sales representatives, healthcare professionals, or market researchers, among many other sources.

Feedback in pharmaceutical marketing is vitally important because it allows companies to understand how well their marketing efforts connect with target audiences and help identify improvement areas to adjust strategies and generate better business results.

Here are a few examples of feedback in pharmaceutical marketing:

1. *Customer Feedback*: Companies can gather customer feedback by conducting surveys, focus groups, or other methods. This feedback allows the business to understand better customer needs, preferences, and opinions regarding its products, marketing campaigns, or related offerings.
2. *Sales Representative Feedback*: Sales representatives provide invaluable insights into the success of marketing materials like brochures or presentations used for communicating with healthcare providers. At the same time, they may also gain knowledge of customer needs through interactions with healthcare professionals.
3. *Feedback From Healthcare Professionals (HCPs)*: HCPs such as physicians or nurses can offer vital feedback about marketing campaigns or educational programs designed to reach patients and insight into their patients' needs and preferences.

4. *Market Research*: Businesses may conduct market research to gather feedback about their products or marketing initiatives from potential target audiences, using surveys or focus groups to gather it.

Feedback can help pharmaceutical companies improve their marketing strategies, better comprehend their target audiences, and increase business results.

Field Marketing

Field marketing in the pharmaceutical industry involves pharmaceutical companies' activities and strategies to market and promote their products directly to healthcare professionals such as doctors and pharmacists. It involves engaging in face-to-face interactions, educational initiatives, and promotional campaigns to build awareness for pharmaceutical products while increasing prescriptions and driving sales of their medications.

Here are some key aspects and strategies involved in field marketing in the pharmaceutical industry:

1. *Product Education*: Field marketing teams provide comprehensive product information to healthcare professionals. They conduct in-person meetings, seminars, and training sessions to educate healthcare providers about pharmaceutical products' features, benefits, and indications.
2. *Relationship Building*: Building strong relationships with healthcare professionals is crucial in the pharmaceutical industry. Field marketers aim to establish trust and credibility by engaging in one-on-one interactions, addressing concerns, and supporting healthcare providers. This helps in fostering loyalty and influencing prescribing decisions.
3. *Key Opinion Leader (KOL) Management*: KOLs are influential healthcare professionals whose opinions and recommendations carry weight in the medical community. Field marketing teams identify and engage with KOLs, involving them in advisory boards, speaker programs, and clinical research initiatives. KOLs help create awareness, influence peers, and improve brand reputation.
4. *Territory Management*: Field marketers typically work in specific geographical regions or territories. They develop and execute marketing plans tailored to their assigned areas, considering local market dynamics, competitor activities, and healthcare provider preferences. Territory management involves regular visits, relationship maintenance, and tracking performance metrics.
5. *Promotional Activities*: Field marketing teams organize promotional activities such as medical conferences, symposiums, and healthcare exhibitions. These events provide opportunities to showcase pharmaceutical products, present scientific data, and engage with healthcare professionals in a larger gathering.
6. *Compliance and Regulatory Guidelines*: The pharmaceutical industry is subject to strict compliance and regulatory guidelines. Field marketers must ensure their activities adhere to legal and ethical standards, including proper documentation, fair promotional practices, and compliance with regulations governing interactions with healthcare professionals.
7. *Market Research and Intelligence*: Field marketing teams are crucial in gathering market intelligence, collecting feedback from healthcare professionals, and monitoring competitor activities. This information helps pharmaceutical companies make informed marketing and sales decisions.
8. *Digital and Remote Engagement*: With technological advancements, field marketing strategies often incorporate digital and remote engagement methods. This includes webinars, online training sessions, virtual conferences, and remote detailing through video calls. These approaches allow for wider reach, cost-effectiveness, and flexibility in engaging healthcare professionals.

Filed marketing in the pharmaceutical industry requires a deep understanding of the medical landscape, strong interpersonal skills, and a balance between educational initiatives and promotional activities. By effectively engaging healthcare professionals, field marketers contribute to the success of pharmaceutical products.

Implications for Pharma Marketers

Field marketing in the pharmaceutical industry has several implications for pharma marketers. Here are some key implications to consider:

1. *Targeted Marketing*: Field marketing allows pharma marketers to target specific healthcare professionals most relevant to their products. Marketers can tailor their messaging and promotional activities to address these target audiences' specific needs and interests by focusing on physicians, specialists, pharmacists, and other healthcare providers.

2. *Relationship Building*: Field marketing emphasizes building and nurturing relationships with healthcare professionals. This personal interaction helps establish trust and credibility, which can influence prescribing decisions. Pharma marketers must prioritize relationship building and invest in strategies fostering long-term partnerships with healthcare providers.
3. *Product Education*: Field marketing allows pharma marketers to educate healthcare professionals about their products. By effectively communicating their products' features, benefits, and clinical evidence, marketers can increase awareness, address any concerns, and promote the appropriate use of their products.
4. *Brand Awareness and Reputation*: Field marketing initiatives contribute to building brand awareness and reputation within the medical community. By organizing and participating in industry conferences, seminars, and events, pharma marketers can create a presence for their brands and establish themselves as thought leaders in their respective therapeutic areas.
5. *KOL Influence*: Key Opinion Leaders (KOLs) play a significant role in the pharmaceutical industry. Field marketing teams work closely with KOLs, engaging them in various activities to leverage their influence and expertise. Pharma marketers must identify and collaborate with relevant KOLs to enhance brand visibility, gain endorsements, and influence peer recommendations.
6. *Compliance and Ethics*: The pharmaceutical industry is highly regulated, and pharma marketers must ensure compliance with ethical standards and legal guidelines. Field marketing activities must align with regulations governing interactions with healthcare professionals, including fair and balanced product promotion, accurate data dissemination, and proper documentation.
7. *Market Research and Competitor Analysis*: Field marketing teams have the opportunity to gather valuable market insights and competitive intelligence. Pharma markets can leverage this information to understand market trends, identify unmet needs, evaluate competitor strategies, and adjust their marketing plans accordingly.
8. *Integration of Digital Strategies*: With the advancement of digital technologies, pharma marketers should consider integrating digital strategies into their field marketing efforts. This includes utilizing digital channels for remote engagement, conducting virtual events and webinars, and leveraging data analytics to optimize marketing campaigns and track performance.
9. *Measuring Effectiveness*: Pharma marketers need to establish key performance indicators (KPIs) to measure the effectiveness of their field marketing initiatives. These may include metrics such as sales growth, prescription rates, brand awareness, customer satisfaction, and return on investment (ROI). Marketers can regularly assess and analyze these metrics to refine their strategies and maximize their impact.

Overall, field marketing in the pharmaceutical industry provides pharma marketers with an opportunity to establish strong relationships, educate healthcare professionals, build brand awareness, and gain a competitive edge. By understanding the implications and leveraging effective strategies, marketers can drive successful product launches, increase market share, and improve patient outcomes.

Field Sales Manager

Field Sales Managers in pharmaceutical marketing oversee a team of pharmaceutical sales representatives promoting company products to healthcare professionals such as doctors, pharmacists, and hospital staff. Furthermore, this position requires managing, coaching, and motivating their representatives to successfully reach their sales targets and objectives.

Key Responsibilities

A field sales manager's key responsibilities include:

1. *Developing and implementing sales strategies*: Working with his sales team, the field sales manager develops strategies and plans aligned with company-wide marketing and sales goals.
2. *Training and Coaching*: A field sales manager's primary responsibility is training and coaching the sales team so they can improve their selling techniques and product knowledge and comply with any relevant governmental requirements.
3. *Management and Motivation of Sales Team*: A field sales manager oversees his sales team's performance by giving regular feedback, motivating them, and managing performance goals to reach sales targets.
4. *Analyzing Sales Data*: A field sales manager must examine the sales data of his representatives to spot trends, opportunities,

and areas for improvement in their sales territories.

5. *Building Relationships with Key Customers*: A field sales manager's job involves cultivating and nurturing key customer relationships, such as opinion leaders and healthcare providers, to promote his company's products and services.
6. *Ensuring Compliance With Regulations*: A field sales manager ensures his sales team abides by all laws, regulations, and industry guidelines applicable to them.
7. *Budget and Forecast*: As the field sales manager, your responsibilities lie in budgeting and forecasting sales targets for managing the expenses and resources of your sales team.

Field Sales Managers are essential in pharmaceutical marketing and sales, ensuring their sales teams are adequately motivated, trained, and equipped to promote company products to healthcare professionals.

Field Sales Management

Field Sales Management in Pharma is fundamental to any pharmaceutical company's success, overseeing a team of sales representatives responsible for marketing and selling the company's products to healthcare providers. Successful field Sales Management requires excellent leadership, communication, strategic planning, and data analysis skills.

Field Sales Management

A field sales manager is essential in driving revenue growth and creating strong relationships with healthcare providers. Their duties typically include:

- Leading a team of sales representatives in setting targets.
- Formulating strategies.
- Tracking sales performance while offering coaching support and opportunities within their sales teams.

Field sales managers are invaluable in communicating with key stakeholders such as healthcare professionals, distributors, and internal teams such as marketing, product development, and customer service. A field sales manager must effectively convey the value proposition of their products or services while responding to customer inquiries or feedback and contributing their expertise toward product development or marketing strategies.

Steps involved in Field Sales Management in Pharma

1. *Recruiting and Hiring*: Field Sales Management in Pharma begins by recruiting qualified sales reps that fulfill specific skills and experience criteria while creating job descriptions, interviewing questions, and evaluating candidates against qualifications and company culture criteria.
2. *Training and Development*: Once your sales team is assembled, the next step should be training and development to equip them with all the skills and knowledge required for success. This may involve providing product training, sales training, communication skills training, and ongoing mentoring for all team members.
3. *Sales Planning*: A field sales manager's primary task is designing sales plans aligning with their company's overall marketing and sales strategies, such as setting targets, identifying key customer segments, devising sales strategies to support them, and devising plans to help reach sales goals.
4. *Monitoring Sales Performance in Pharma*: Monitoring sales performance is a fundamental aspect of field sales management of Pharma companies. A sales manager must analyze data regularly, identify trends, coach their team to achieve optimal performance, meet sales targets, and set incentives as part of employee motivation strategies.
5. *Customer Relationship Management*: Developing strong relationships with healthcare providers is paramount for pharmaceutical sales to succeed. A field sales manager must work closely with their sales team to identify key customer needs and create tailored sales messages for individual accounts while offering exceptional service that builds long-lasting bonds between sales reps, HCPs, pharmacists, and other stakeholders.

Field Research

Field research in pharmaceutical marketing can provide vital insights about healthcare professionals, patients, and other key participants within the healthcare industry. Here are a few important considerations when conducting field research:

1. *Objectives*: The first step in conducting field research in pharma marketing is to define the research objectives. The research objectives should clearly define and align with the overall marketing strategy. Examples of research

objectives may include understanding prescribing patterns, evaluating the effectiveness of a marketing campaign, or assessing the patient experience.

2. *Sampling*: The sampling strategy for field research in pharma marketing should be carefully considered. The sample should be representative of the target population and be large enough to provide meaningful insights. For example, the sampling strategy may involve randomly selecting participants or targeting specific groups of healthcare professionals or patients.
3. *Methodology*: The methodology for field research in pharma marketing may vary depending on the research objectives and the target population. Field researchers should select their methodology based on research objectives and feasibility. Surveys, interviews, focus groups, and observational studies are commonly used.
4. *Data Collection*: When conducting field research in pharmaceutical marketing, data collection must be carefully planned to guarantee its accuracy and reliability. Methods may include paper surveys, online surveys, phone interviews, or in-person interviews as part of this process; standardization will help ensure consistency for participants involved in this data acquisition step.
5. *Data Analysis*: The data from field research in pharma marketing should be carefully analyzed to identify key insights and trends. The analysis may involve statistical analysis, content analysis, or other methods. Experienced researchers should conduct the analysis and be aligned with the research objectives.
6. *Reporting*: Findings from field research for pharmaceutical marketing must be reported clearly and concisely, including an outline of research objectives, methodology, sample size selection criteria, data collection process details, and key findings derived from analysis. Reports must also address their intended audiences while offering recommendations for future marketing strategies if applicable.

Field Research Methods in Pharma: Some Examples

Here are some examples of field research methods used in pharmaceutical marketing:

1. *Surveys*: Pharmaceutical companies often conduct surveys among healthcare professionals to gain insight into their prescribing patterns and attitudes regarding specific medications. Such polls often cover aspects like effectiveness, side effects, and ease of use—factors pharmaceutical firms consider during research projects.
2. *Interviews*: Interviews involve patients taking certain medicines to assess their experience with their medications, asking about effectiveness, adverse side effects, and overall perceptions about the medications.
3. *Focus Groups*: Pharmaceutical companies may conduct focus groups with healthcare professionals to gain perspectives about new medications they're developing or planning to launch, including potential benefits, target population considerations, and any barriers or challenges involved with prescribing them.
4. *Observational Studies*: Pharmaceutical companies may conduct observational studies to understand better how healthcare professionals interact with patients in clinical environments. For instance, such research could involve monitoring how healthcare practitioners diagnose and treat their patients; also gathering insights about attitudes regarding the medication prescribed.
5. *Online Analytics*: A pharmaceutical company may analyze online data to understand patient behavior and preferences. This may include analyzing search engine queries, social media activity, and website analytics to identify trends and insights about patient behavior.

These are some examples of field research used for pharmaceutical marketing. The method chosen depends on your objectives, target population, and available resources.

Field research in pharmaceutical marketing can be essential to gather insights from healthcare professionals, patients, and other key stakeholders. Therefore, when planning field research objectives, sampling strategies, methodologies, data collection and, analysis processes, reporting protocols and structures should all be carefully considered to ensure accurate and reliable data and reveal insights that may inform future marketing strategies.

Field Work

Fieldwork in Pharma marketing refers to pharmaceutical sales representatives' activities when they visit healthcare professionals (HCPs) in person. Fieldwork aims to promote pharmaceutical products, provide information about the products, and increase prescriptions and sales.

Here are some examples of fieldwork activities that pharmaceutical sales representatives may undertake:

1. *Detailing*: This involves providing in-depth information about a specific drug product's features, benefits, and clinical data to HCPs. Sales representatives use various tools and materials to support their detailing efforts, such as brochures, clinical studies, and samples.
2. *Relationship Building*: Sales representatives aim to establish and maintain relationships with HCPs. They may also discuss non-work related topics like hobbies or sports to build rapport and trust.
3. *Product Demonstrations*: Sales representatives may demonstrate how to use a medical device or administer a drug product to HCPs.
4. *Conference Attendance*: Sales representatives may attend medical conferences and trade shows to network with HCPs, showcase their products, and learn about industry trends.
5. *Territory Management*: Sales representatives typically manage a specific geographic area or territory. They may prioritize their visits to HCPs based on factors such as prescription volume, prescribing behavior, and potential for future sales.

Fieldwork in pharma marketing requires strong interpersonal and communication skills and knowledge of medical terminology, clinical data, and pharmaceutical regulations. It also involves significant travel and requires working independently and managing time effectively.

Fighter Brand

Fighter brand strategies in pharmaceutical marketing represent an effective defensive measure, where companies introduce lower-priced products or brands to compete against generic or biosimilar counterparts.

Once a drug's patent expires, generic or biosimilar competitors can enter the market with lower-priced alternatives threatening its market share. A pharmaceutical company may introduce *fighter brands*, which are lower-priced versions of an original brand designed to capture some market share away from generic competitors by offering similar benefits at reduced cost while maintaining the same quality elements from the original product.

Fighter brand strategies aim to preserve market share and revenue for their branded drug, seizing some market shares that might otherwise go to generic or biosimilar competitors.

Fighter brand strategies in pharmaceutical marketing represent an effective defensive measure designed to defend an incumbent company against generic or biosimilar competitors that threaten its market share. Such an approach is an immediate response when faced with potential competition in its existing marketplace.

Findability

Findability refers to the ease with which something can be discovered or located. In digital marketing, findability refers to how easily users can locate websites or specific pages through search engines or other means.

Websites and digital media must be optimized to attract search engines while remaining user-friendly and easily discoverable online. This requires techniques like Search Engine Optimization (SEO), which entails improving website content to rank higher on Search Engine Results Pages (SERPs), as well as User Experience Design (UXD), which involves designing user-friendly navigational and usage experiences on sites and digital media.

Digital marketers recognize the significance of findability as key in digital marketing; it determines visibility and accessibility for customers of a company's site and content. When websites or pieces of content are hard to locate, user engagement suffers severely, resulting in decreased website traffic, brand recognition, sales revenue, and profit.

Findability in Pharma Marketing

Pharma marketers recognize the significance of findability as it impacts how easily patients, healthcare providers, and other stakeholders can find information related to pharmaceutical products and services. In pharmaceutical marketing, findability optimization involves making websites, content, or digital assets highly visible within search engine result pages (SERPs) while remaining easily accessible to users.

Pharmaceutical companies looking to boost search engine rankings with search engine optimization (SEO) techniques like keyword research, meta descriptions, and backlinks may increase findability on search engines like Google. Furthermore, optimizing website design and content may improve user experience (UX), making finding what visitors are searching for easier than before.

Pharma companies can optimize websites and content while improving findability via social media marketing, email marketing, and other digital channels. By doing this, they can gain more exposure while reaching more potential customers with their offerings.

Findability is integral to pharmaceutical marketing, determining how easily users can locate information about pharmaceutical products and services. By optimizing digital assets and employing various digital marketing channels effectively, pharmaceutical companies can improve findability while expanding customer bases and improving findability.

First-mover Advantage

First-mover advantage (FMA) is a term commonly used in marketing and business strategy that refers to any advantage gained by being first to enter or introduce something into a new market, product, or service. Being first can often establish brand recognition, customer loyalty, and an authoritative position for yourself that's difficult for competitors to dislodge.

Becoming the pioneer in entering or introducing products or services into a new market or introducing innovations can establish the company with impressive brand recognition and customer retention, which could prove difficult for competitors to overshadow.

First-mover advantage can be especially advantageous in pharmaceutical marketing due to the industry's stringent regulations that can take years for new drugs to reach the marketplace. Companies able to get new medicines out before competitors may establish dominant positions and capture significant market shares before competitors enter.

First-mover advantage comes with its share of risks, however. Development costs could become prohibitively expensive; regulatory hurdles might stand in your way, or there could even be the chance that an innovative product or service introduced does not meet market acceptance.

Overall, first-mover advantage can be an influential factor in pharmaceutical marketing and business strategies, yet companies should carefully weigh its risks and benefits before embarking on this course.

Five Forces Model

The Five Forces Model, also called Porter's Five Forces Framework, is an innovative method of evaluating competitive industry environments, created by Michael E. Porter of Harvard Business School in 1979.

This model identifies five forces that impact competitive intensity and profitability within any industry:

1. *The Threat of New Entrants*: This refers to the possibility that new companies enter an industry and compete against existing firms. Factors influencing this include barriers such as economies of scale, regulatory restrictions, and brand recognition among established firms. Additionally, firmly entrenched competitors may make the availability of distribution channels for expansion difficult.
2. *Bargaining Power of Suppliers*: Supplier bargaining power refers to their influence over input costs within an industry, including input prices for firms within that field. Factors impacting this include their number, unique products offered, and provider switching costs.
3. *Bargaining Power of Buyers*: Buyer bargaining power refers to their influence over the pricing of products or services firms offer within an industry. Factors influencing this include buyer volume, the importance of products within an industry to buyers, and the cost associated with switching away.
4. *The Threat of Substitute Products or Services* refers to the possibility that customers might switch to alternative offerings from firms outside the industry. Factors that influence this threat of substitute products include availability, price, and differentiation between them and comparable alternatives within an industry's products or services.
5. *Rivalry among Existing Firms*: Rivalry refers to the intensity of competition among firms within an industry, including factors like the number and size of competitors, product differentiation levels, and pricing strategies. Rivalries between existing firms vary based on several criteria, including number and size, levels of differentiation of products offered, and degree of price competition among them.

By studying these five forces, companies can gain more insights into the competitive environment of their industry and develop strategies to compete more successfully.

Implications for Pharma Marketers

The Five Forces Model can help pharma marketers understand the industry's competitive environment and develop strategies effectively. Here are some ways that they can analyze these five forces and develop strategies to gain a competitive advantage:

1. *The Threat of New Entrants*: The pharma industry is highly regulated, creating entry

barriers for new firms. However, technological advances and the rise of new healthcare models may create opportunities for new entrants. Pharma marketers must monitor these trends and develop strategies to compete with new entrants.

2. *Bargaining Power of Suppliers*: Pharma marketers need to be aware of the bargaining power of suppliers, such as manufacturers of active pharmaceutical ingredients (APIs) and distributors. They should develop strong relationships with suppliers to ensure reliable supply chains and manage costs.
3. *Bargaining Power of Buyers*: Pharma marketers must understand and anticipate healthcare providers' and patients' needs and preferences to create marketing strategies to satisfy those demands and set themselves apart from the competition.
4. *Substitute Products*: Pharma marketers must carefully track any emerging alternative treatments or generics that threaten to displace their offerings as possible replacements and devise plans to separate their product offerings from any substitutes that might come onto the market.
5. *Rivalry Among Existing Firms*: The pharma industry is highly competitive, with many players vying for market share. Pharma marketers must develop marketing strategies that differentiate their products and build brand loyalty among healthcare providers and patients.

Flagship Brand

A flagship brand is a primary or best-known product or brand associated with a business, typically producing the highest revenue and having greater brand recognition in the marketplace. A flagship brand can serve as both the face of the company as well a symbol for the values and mission of an enterprise.

A flagship brand in pharma marketing refers to any pharmaceutical product or brand that serves as an organization's primary focus of marketing efforts. A flagship brand can include any pharmaceutical product that has achieved substantial market share, earned strong brand recognition, or generated significant revenue. A flagship brand can also include innovative or effective treatments for specific medical conditions that distinguish it from competitors.

Pharmaceutical companies use marketing tactics to promote their flagship brands, including direct-to-consumer advertising, physician detailing services, digital channels, and sponsorship of medical conferences or events. By investing in these flagship brands, pharmaceutical companies can build brand equity among patients and healthcare professionals, and drive revenue and increase brand growth, and loyalty among both groups.

Flagship Brands in Pharma

Here are a few flagship pharmaceutical brands:

1. *Lipitor* (Atorvastatin) was Pfizer's flagship cholesterol-lowering medication, with annual revenues reaching nearly $14 billion at its peak. As one of history's best-selling pharma products, Lipitor had become synonymous with the company itself.
2. *Humira*: AbbVie's blockbuster drug Humira (Adalimumab), used for treating autoimmune conditions like rheumatoid arthritis and Crohn's disease, recorded worldwide sales exceeding $19 billion in 2020, becoming the best-selling pharmaceutical product worldwide.
3. *Botox*: Since 2002, Allergan's flagship aesthetic treatment brand, Botulinum toxin injection (Botox) has been used to address wrinkles, migraines, and muscle spasms. Botox is widely accepted and considered one of the premier aesthetic solutions available today.
4. *Nexium* (Esomeprazole), used to treat acid reflux and related conditions, was one of the top-selling pharmaceutical products worldwide during its peak years, generating annual revenues exceeding $6 billion and becoming one of the highest revenue generators for AstraZeneca.

These are some examples of iconic pharmaceutical industry brands. Each has been invaluable in driving revenue and growth for their respective companies while becoming highly recognized brands across global markets.

Flanker Brands

In pharmaceutical marketing, flanker brand is a strategy where a company introduces a new product similar to an existing product in its portfolio but with slight variations in formulation or positioning. The goal of the strategy is to capture additional market share by appealing to a different segment of the market by expanding the product used within the same segment. For example, a pharmaceutical company may introduce a new drug version formulated for a different age group or gender, indication, or disease state. Alternatively, the company may introduce a new product with a different dosage form, delivery system, or packaging that provides added convenience or value to the customer.

Depending on its usage context, a flanker brand strategy may be offensive or defensive. In some cases, a company may use a flanker brand strategy offensively to attack the market share of its competitors. By creating a new brand that competes directly with a competitor's product or targets a new market segment, a company can gain a foothold in a market where it previously had little or no presence.

Conversely, companies may defensively employ flanker brand strategies to defend their market share. Suppose an established brand begins losing market share to another product from competitors. In that case, a flanker brand strategy may provide the means for it to directly compete against these newcomers and protect itself from further loss in market share.

Flanker Brand Strategy: Key Points to Consider

Here are some key points to consider when implementing a flanker brand strategy in the pharmaceutical industry:

1. *Research and Development*: When designing a flanker brand strategy in pharmaceutical marketing, the initial step involves identifying an opportunity wherein a new brand could provide differentiated features or benefits in contrast with an existing brand. This may involve creating something with unique delivery mechanisms or dosage forms, or unique mechanisms of action, for instance. Research should therefore concentrate on producing differentiated products for this product line.
2. *Positioning*: Strategic positioning of a Flanker brand is key to its success. The product should complement an existing brand while offering unique benefits not present elsewhere. Marketing messaging must highlight the differences between products and the advantages of choosing the Flanker band over an established one.
3. *Intellectual Property*: The flanker brand strategy in pharma marketing must consider the intellectual property landscape in the pharmaceutical industry. Companies must ensure they are not violating patents or intellectual property rights when developing and marketing the Flanker brand.
4. *Marketing*: The marketing strategy for a flanker brand in pharma marketing should focus on the unique benefits and features of the product. The messaging should highlight the differences between the Flanker and existing brands while positioning the two products as complementary. Marketing efforts must also aim to inform healthcare providers and patients of the benefits of their new product.
5. *Distribution*: The distribution strategy for the Flanker brand should consider the existing distribution channels for the existing brand. Companies may also leverage relationships with wholesalers and pharmacies to distribute the Flanker brand. Alternatively, companies may develop their distribution network to sell the Flanker brand directly to healthcare professionals and patients.

Flanker Brands in Pharma: Some Examples

Here are a few examples of flanker brands in the pharmaceutical industry:

1. *Advil Liqui-Gels*: Pfizer introduced this product as a flanker brand to their popular pain reliever, Advil. The Liqui-Gels formulation was designed to provide faster relief of pain and fever by being absorbed more quickly than the traditional Advil tablets.
2. *Nexium 24HR*: AstraZeneca introduced this product as a flanker brand to their prescription heartburn medication, Nexium. The over-the-counter version, Nexium 24HR, is formulated at a lower dosage and is marketed to consumers who experience occasional heartburn rather than those who require daily treatment.
3. *Tylenol PM*: Johnson & Johnson introduced this product as a flanker brand to their popular pain reliever, Tylenol. Adding a sleep aid, diphenhydramine, allowed the company to target customers who experience pain and difficulty sleeping simultaneously.
4. *Claritin-D*: Schering-Plough introduced this product as a flanker brand to their allergy medication, Claritin. Adding the decongestant pseudoephedrine allowed the company to target customers who experience both allergy symptoms and nasal congestion.

These examples demonstrate how businesses leveraged their existing brand recognition and reputation to introduce products that met specific customer needs or preferences.

As previously discussed, flanker brand strategies can be offensive or defensive depending on a company's goals and the competitive environment in which it operates.

Flexible Pricing Models

Flexible pricing models in the pharmaceutical industry can be designed to accommodate diverse market conditions, patient needs, and regulatory environments. Here are some examples of flexible pricing models in pharma:

1. *Value-Based Pricing*: Tie the price of a pharmaceutical product to the value it delivers in terms of patient outcomes. This approach links pricing to the drug's effectiveness, potentially allowing higher prices for more successful treatments.
2. *Outcome-Based Pricing*: Set pricing based on predefined clinical outcomes. Pharmaceutical companies and payers agree on specific metrics, and if the treatment does not achieve the agreed-upon outcomes, there may be adjustments to pricing or reimbursement.
3. *Subscription-Based Models*: Introduce subscription-based pricing where healthcare providers or payers pay a fixed fee for access to a particular drug or a bundle of drugs over a specified period. This can help in budget predictability.
4. *Tiered Pricing*: Implement tiered pricing structures based on factors such as patient income levels, geographic regions, or the stage of the drug's lifecycle. This can address economic disparities and improve access in different markets.
5. *Dynamic Pricing*: Adjust pricing based on market demand, supply chain considerations, or real-time data. Dynamic pricing allows for agility in responding to changing market conditions.
6. *Risk-Sharing Agreements*: Collaborate with payers or healthcare systems to share financial risks. This could involve refund mechanisms, discounts, or rebates based on the drug's performance or the volume of usage.
7. *Patient Assistance Programs*: Establish programs to provide financial assistance to patients, ensuring affordability. This may involve discounts, co-pay assistance, or direct financial support for eligible patients.
8. *Bundled Pricing*: Package multiple pharmaceutical products together at a discounted rate. This can encourage complementary drugs and simplify the purchasing process for healthcare providers.
9. *Negotiate Discounts and Rebates*: Negotiate with healthcare payers to establish discounted prices or rebate agreements based on volume, market share, or formulary placement.
10. *Global Access Programs*: Develop pricing models that consider the economic conditions of different countries, allowing for affordability in low-income regions while sustaining profitability in high-income markets.

Implementing flexible pricing models requires careful consideration of local regulations, market dynamics, and the therapeutic landscape. Striking a balance between ensuring fair returns for pharmaceutical companies and enhancing patient access is crucial in developing effective pricing strategies in the pharmaceutical industry.

fMRI

Functional Magnetic Resonance Imaging (fMRI) is an imaging technique that tracks changes in blood oxygenation and flow related to neural activity. While traditionally utilized by medical and neuroscience research teams, its popularity is now also widespread within marketing research as a method to explore consumer behavior.

FMRI can give researchers insight into how marketing stimuli like product packaging, advertisements, and brand logos influence neural activity in the brain, providing researchers with more knowledge about consumer decision-making processes.

An fMRI study demonstrated that consumers exposed to brand logos associated with environmental friendliness experienced greater activation of brain regions related to positive emotions and social cognition; those shown advertisements featuring happy faces experienced increased activity in regions associated with reward processing.

Functional Magnetic Resonance Imaging (fMRI) can be an indispensable method for pharmaceutical marketing research to measure patients' neural responses to drug treatment. Researchers using fMRI can better understand how consumers perceive and process information related to a specific medication, which informs marketing strategies for that drug. Here are a few examples showing how pharmaceutical companies incorporate fMRI in their marketing plans:

1. Pfizer used functional Magnetic Resonance Imaging (fMRI) in pharmaceutical marketing research by studying patients suffering from depression who took different antidepressant medicines. Pfizer employed this tool to measure neural responses related to drug names or images presented to subjects during brain imaging sessions, with various medications

prompting different responses within patients' neural activity networks; results demonstrated different neural responses depending on which medication had been presented, suggesting personalized marketing strategies may be more successful at promoting certain antidepressant drugs.

2. Merck & Co conducted marketing research using functional magnetic resonance imaging (fMRI) on chronic pain patients to examine how neural responses differ to various painkillers; their study demonstrated how patients experienced different neural reactions for each medication studied, suggesting tailored marketing approaches may be more successful at promoting certain pain treatments.
3. Eli Lilly and Company used functional magnetic resonance imaging (fMRI) to study how patients with Alzheimer's responded to a potential drug candidate for Alzheimer's. Their researchers discovered that it improved neural activity in brain regions associated with memory and attention, informing Eli Lilly's marketing strategies accordingly.
4. GlaxoSmithKline utilized functional magnetic resonance imaging (fMRI) technology to assess patients with schizophrenia to antipsychotic medications. This led to insights about personalized marketing strategies that might prove more successful in targeting patients.

Although fMRI holds promise as an invaluable research method in marketing research, it should be remembered that its application in this area remains relatively new and may contain limitations. For instance, its costs and time commitment can make results difficult to interpret; furthermore, its external validity often comes under question because laboratory environments don't mimic real-life decision-making situations as closely. Therefore it should be combined with other research techniques like surveys or behavioral experiments to gain a holistic view of consumer behavior.

Focus Groups

Focus groups are an effective method of qualitative market research used in marketing to gather individual feedback on specific products or topics. Focus groups typically occur face-to-face or online and include participants chosen as target audiences' representatives.

Focus group sessions involve participants expressing their perspectives, thoughts, and experiences about a product or topic. Sessions are generally led by trained facilitators who ask open-ended questions encouraging participants to express their thoughts freely.

Focus groups offer insight into consumer behaviors, preferences, and attitudes regarding a product or service. Furthermore, focus groups provide the ideal environment to test new product concepts, marketing strategies, and advertising messages before moving them onto mass distribution channels.

Focus groups provide pharmaceutical marketers with an invaluable way to obtain feedback from patients, healthcare providers, and other stakeholders about pharmaceutical products and services. Focus groups may be utilized for gathering feedback regarding the effectiveness of new drug formulations, ease of use of medical devices, or the messaging and advertising strategy of pharmaceutical products.

Focus groups offer pharmaceutical marketers a tool for collecting qualitative feedback from a targeted group and using it to shape product development, marketing strategies, and advertising messages.

Conducting Focus Group Research

Focus group research for pharmaceutical marketing typically follows several steps:

1. *Establish Research Objectives*: The initial step of any successful research endeavor should be setting clear objectives. What purpose will the study serve, or what knowledge do participants wish to obtain through focus group sessions? This clear set of goals will guide all aspects of its implementation.
2. *Identification of Target Audience*: Next, Decide on your focus group audience. Consider who may benefit from using or purchasing your product or service. Consider who could impact the decision-making process through stakeholder interactions.
3. *Recruit Participants*: Once your target audience has been established, recruiting participants for your focus group should begin immediately. Working with an external recruitment agency may help accelerate this process, or reaching out directly through social media or email campaigns may yield better results.
4. *Develop the Discussion Guide*: A discussion guide outlines topics and questions to be covered during a focus group to encourage meaningful participant responses and gain insightful feedback from them.
5. *Conduct the Focus Group*: For optimal success, focus groups should take place in an inviting and neutral setting, with the facilitator introducing topics and questions and leading the dialogue so

all attendees have ample opportunity to voice their opinions and express themselves freely.

6. *Analyzing Data*: Following a focus group, all collected information must be evaluated carefully to uncover patterns and themes from the responses by participants. This may involve reviewing this meeting's transcripts, notes, and audio or video recordings.
7. *Report the Findings*: Once results have been uncovered, they should be presented clearly and succinctly to stakeholders via written report, presentation, or both. A good report should provide insights into target audience behavior and areas for improvement and recommend future marketing efforts.

Focus group research for pharmaceutical marketing requires careful planning, targeted recruitment, and skillful facilitation to gain useful insight into your target audience and create effective promotional plans for products or services. By following these steps successfully, you will gain invaluable information that could benefit both sides of the transaction chain.

Folksonomy

Folksonomy is an informal system for categorizing information found online by users, typically for personal or educational use. Users use Folksonomy as a collaborative tagging system where metadata such as keywords or tags are added to digital content such as photographs, videos, and articles by adding metadata tags (meta-tags).

Folksonomies differ from traditional taxonomies by being developed through collaborative intelligence from users who assign tags to content, making them much more adaptable, flexible, and open than their expert-generated counterparts as they quickly incorporate new terms as they emerge.

Folksonomies have gained prominence since the rise of social media and user-generated content. Folksonomies help users to organize information with tags that make sense to them, making finding and organizing online information much simpler for individuals. They are used across various contexts, including bookmarking sites, photo-sharing services, and online libraries and archives.

Folksonomy in Pharma Marketing

Folksonomies can play an essential part in pharmaceutical marketing for multiple reasons:

A. First and foremost, pharmaceutical product databases can help organize and classify information related to pharmaceutical products, such as clinical trial data, drug information, and patient education materials, making it easier for healthcare professionals and patients to locate relevant data while helping pharma companies promote their products more efficiently.

B. Folksonomies offer pharmaceutical companies another tool for understanding how their products are discussed online by analyzing tags and keywords associated with them on social media and other online platforms such as forums or review sites. By studying such data, companies can gain insights into product usage patterns; whether the patient needs are being met; any concerns that have been voiced— all information that can inform marketing and product development strategies and strategies moving forward.

C. Folksonomies can also support patient education efforts and engagement programs by enabling patients to tag and share information regarding their conditions and treatments, helping each learn from one another while encouraging engagement and empowerment among patients themselves. This allows companies to build stronger relationships with patients as trusted sources of information and assistance.

Folksonomies in pharmaceutical marketing are still relatively novel; however, their application promises to increase marketing effectiveness and foster patient engagement and education efforts.

Foot-in-the-Door Technique (FDIT)

The Foot-in-the-Door technique is an influential persuasion strategy to change people's behaviors and attitudes. The strategy begins by asking for something small in return, followed by larger requests or favors over time.

It works because people want their actions and decisions to remain consistent with past behaviors; by complying with something small, they show they're more willing to comply with additional ones that come their way. When people agree to comply with an initial request, they feel more committed to following through with what has already been agreed upon. They will likely comply with further ones in response to the promised.

Foot-in-the-Door Technique in Pharma Marketing

Pharma marketers employing the foot-in-the-door technique can involve sending sales representatives into healthcare professional (HCP) offices with small requests like asking if there is time available to discuss new medications before building rapport and engaging in conversation to make larger requests, such as asking them to prescribe those drugs to their patients.

The foot-in-the-door technique leverages cognitive consistency; people tend to agree more readily to larger requests if they've previously agreed to smaller ones.

Foot-in-the-door techniques are an effective pharma marketing tactic to establish relationships with healthcare professionals and increase prescription rates of certain drugs. Still, marketers must use this tactic ethically when employing this strategy involving healthcare practitioners' time and decision-making autonomy.

Forecasting

Forecasting in pharmaceutical marketing refers to anticipating trends and behaviors related to pharmaceutical sales volumes, market shares, and consumer behavior to make accurate predictions into future estimates, allowing pharma companies to make informed decisions regarding product development strategies, marketing tactics, and resource allocation.

Pharma marketing employs several forecasting strategies, including trend analysis, regression analysis, and simulation models, to forecast future performance accurately. These techniques rely on historical data and market trends to predict what may lie ahead for their success in future endeavors.

One important area of forecasting in pharma marketing involves forecasting new product success. To do this, market demand, competition, and regulatory requirements must be carefully considered when predicting how a drug or treatment may perform in market demand and regulatory consideration. Other areas may include:

- anticipating changes in market share
- estimating the effects of regulatory changes or patent expirations
- Predicting sales volumes for existing products

Forecasting Methods

Pharmaceutical professionals employ various forecasting methodologies with both benefits and drawbacks in mind. Consider the following, for example:

1. *Time Series Analysis*: Time-Series analysis involves reviewing past data to recognize patterns and trends that appear over time, for instance, by using historical sales trends as predictors for estimating future drug sales. Pharma companies might employ time series analysis in their forecasting operations by studying past sales patterns of specific drugs sold within their sales strategy to predict sales for any particular drug they sell now based on this forecasting method.
2. *Regression Analysis*: Regression analysis employs statistical models to detect relationships among variables and forecast outcomes, such as pharmaceutical sales volume projections. A company might use regression analysis when making pricing or advertising adjustments that impact sales volume directly or indirectly.
3. *Market Research Surveys*: These studies can gather consumer behavior and preferences data that can help predict demand for certain products; for instance, pharmaceutical companies might conduct such surveys to ascertain the prevalence and severity data of an illness to predict demand for new treatments in the future.
4. *Expert Opinions*: Pharma companies frequently consult industry insiders or key opinion leaders for predictions regarding future trends or outcomes, for instance, consulting healthcare providers on potential market demand for their new drug.
5. *Simulation Models*: Simulation models use mathematical algorithms to simulate various scenarios and predict outcomes, such as when used by pharmaceutical companies to predict patient outcomes and healthcare costs when testing new medications. Simulation models allow these companies to see exactly how an innovative new medicine might influence patient care and healthcare expenses before marketing it to customers.

However, the optimal forecasting technique will ultimately depend on your business needs, goals, and available data and resources.

Forecasting is an invaluable asset for pharmaceutical marketers looking to make informed decisions and plan for the future. By employing various approaches and regularly revising models, pharmaceutical firms can stay ahead of market trends while keeping an edge against rival businesses.

Foreign Corrupt Practices Act (FCPA)

The Foreign Corrupt Practices Act (FCPA) is a US statute prohibiting businesses from paying bribes to foreign officials to secure or maintain business with them. When applied to pharmaceutical marketing, FCPA poses several challenges to pharmaceutical firms operating in international markets.

Pharmaceutical companies face one key concern regarding third-party intermediaries such as distributors or consultants to facilitate relationships with foreign officials, for example, by providing gifts, entertainment, or hospitality in return for business opportunities or favorable treatment from these officials. Under FCPA laws, such activities could constitute illegal bribery even though no company provided bribes directly.

Pharmaceutical companies must exercise extreme care when engaging third-party intermediaries in international markets. They should implement strong anti-corruption policies and procedures to thwart fraudulent or unlawful behavior. This may involve performing due diligence on potential intermediaries, creating training programs for employees and intermediaries alike, and setting up monitoring mechanisms in case of potential violations. Under the FCPA, companies must maintain accurate and transparent accounting records documenting all international business activities resulting in transactions or payments. Pharmaceutical companies with global supply chains that utilize various third-party intermediaries often face difficulty meeting all required compliance obligations under the FCPA. However, failing to do so could incur serious fines and penalties under this legislation.

Foresight

Foresight is the ability to predict future events, trends, or possibilities using current information and analysis. It involves looking beyond immediate events to understand how current actions or decisions could influence future outcomes. It has applications across various fields, such as business, politics, technology, and social issues, and can aid strategic planning and decision-making processes. Individuals and organizations alike can utilize foresight methodologies in strategic planning processes to anticipate any looming challenges or opportunities and devise proactive plans to shape an improved future for themselves or others.

Foresight in Pharma Marketing

Pharma marketers understand the significance of foresight as an indispensable strategy in anticipating and adapting to changes within healthcare industries and market trends, particularly in pharmaceutical marketing. Proper foresight helps identify emerging health issues, understand patient requirements and preferences and remain ahead of competitors.

Pharma companies can leverage foresight to design innovative medicines to fill unmet medical needs and devise targeted marketing campaigns that resonate with patients and healthcare providers alike. Pharmaceutical firms can anticipate regulatory changes by monitoring market trends and patient information to align marketing strategies accordingly.

Foresight can also help pharma companies navigate the rapidly evolving digital landscape in healthcare. By staying ahead of emerging technologies and digital trends, pharma companies can develop effective digital marketing strategies that reach patients and healthcare providers where they are.

Foresight in pharma marketing is essential for companies to remain competitive and relevant in a constantly evolving industry. By anticipating changes and staying ahead of trends, pharma companies can serve patients, healthcare providers, and society as a whole better.

Formulary

In pharmaceutical marketing, a formulary refers to a list of medications and treatments approved for use and covered by a healthcare provider, insurance company, or pharmacy benefit manager (PBM). Formularies are essential in guiding prescribing decisions and determining which medications will be accessible and reimbursed for patients within a particular healthcare system or insurance plan.

Here is how formularies impact pharmaceutical marketing:

1. *Market Access*: Inclusion in a formulary is critical for pharmaceutical companies as it determines the availability and accessibility of their products to patients. Marketing efforts often focus on demonstrating medication's value, efficacy, and safety to secure a favorable formulary placement. This includes providing clinical data, comparative effectiveness research, and economic evidence to support the inclusion of their product in the formulary.
2. *Reimbursement and Pricing*: Formulary placement directly impacts reimbursement and pricing negotiations. Pharmaceutical companies

aim to secure favorable formulary positions that maximize reimbursement rates and minimize patient out-of-pocket costs. Marketing strategies may involve demonstrating cost-effectiveness, conducting health economic analyses, and offering discounts or rebates to secure favorable pricing and reimbursement terms.

3. *Promotional Strategies*: Pharmaceutical companies develop marketing campaigns targeting healthcare professionals to raise awareness of their products and promote their advantages. These efforts can include direct-to-physician advertising, medical education programs, and promotional materials. They highlight their medications' clinical benefits, safety profiles, and cost-effectiveness. Marketing messages often emphasize how a product aligns with formulary guidelines and meets the needs of specific patient populations.
4. *Market Differentiation*: In a competitive pharmaceutical landscape, formulary placement can differentiate a product from competitors. Companies highlight unique features, clinical advantages, or additional benefits of their medication to persuade healthcare professionals and formulary decision-makers to choose their products over alternatives. Marketing strategies often emphasize the specific attributes that set the medication apart and align with formulary preferences.
5. *Health Economics and Outcomes Research (HEOR)*: Health economic evaluations and outcomes research plays a crucial role in formulary decision-making. Pharmaceutical companies may conduct studies demonstrating their products' economic value and long-term outcomes. HEOR data, such as cost-effectiveness analyses, budget impact assessments, and real-world evidence, can support medication's value proposition and formulary consideration.
6. *Formulary Review and Updates*: Pharmaceutical companies must stay informed about formulary review cycles and updates. Regularly monitoring formulary changes allows companies to adapt their marketing strategies, address emerging formulary requirements, and ensure ongoing market access and reimbursement. Proactive engagement with formulary committees and decision-makers helps companies understand evolving needs and maximize formulary opportunities.
7. *Patient Assistance Programs*: In cases where medication is not included on a formulary or has limited coverage, pharmaceutical companies may develop patient assistance programs to help patients access and afford their medications. These programs can provide financial support, co-pay assistance, or patient access resources. Marketing efforts can inform healthcare professionals and patients about these programs and their eligibility criteria.

Understanding the formulary landscape, decision-making processes, and the specific needs of healthcare providers and payers is essential for effective pharmaceutical marketing; by aligning marketing strategies with formulary requirements, pharmaceutical companies can optimize market access, reimbursement, and utilization of their products.

Implications for Pharma Marketers

Formularies have significant implications for pharma marketers, shaping their strategies and tactics in several ways:

1. *Formulary Positioning*: Pharma marketers must prioritize securing favorable formulary positions for their products. This involves highlighting their medications' clinical benefits, safety profiles, and cost-effectiveness to formulary decision-makers. Marketing messages should focus on how the product meets the formulary criteria and addresses the needs of specific patient populations. Formulary positioning directly impacts market access, reimbursement, and utilization, making it a key consideration for marketers.
2. *Market Segmentation*: Understanding the formulary landscape allows marketers to segment their target audience effectively. Different formularies may have varying requirements and guidelines, influencing prescribing decisions by healthcare professionals. Marketers should tailor their messaging, educational materials, and promotional activities to align with healthcare providers' specific needs and preferences within each formulary.
3. *Value Communication*: Formularies prioritize medications that provide value to patients, healthcare systems, and payers. Pharma marketers must effectively communicate the value proposition of their products. This includes providing clinical evidence, health economic data, and outcomes research to demonstrate the positive impact of their medications on patient outcomes, cost savings, and overall healthcare value. Communicating the value proposition helps differentiate the product and gain formulary acceptance.
4. *Pricing and Contract Negotiations*: Formulary placement influences pricing and reimbursement negotiations. Pharma marketers must consider

the pricing and reimbursement policies of formulary expectations and reimbursement policies of formulary decision-makers. They may need to negotiate contracts, provide rebates, or offer pricing incentives to secure formulary inclusion and favorable reimbursement terms. Pricing strategies should align with the perceived value of the medication within the formulary context.

5. *Educational and Support Programs*: Pharma marketers can develop educational programs and support initiatives to assist healthcare professionals in navigating formulary requirements. These programs can provide training on formulary guidelines, reimbursement processes, and information on maximizing the product's benefits within a specific formulary. Marketers can also develop resources to help healthcare professionals communicate the product's value to their patients and navigate formulary-related challenges.
6. *Formulary Monitoring and Updates*: Formularies undergo periodic reviews and updates, impacting market access and reimbursement. Pharma marketers should closely monitor formulary changes and review cycles to adapt their marketing strategies accordingly. This includes staying informed about changes in formulary requirements, preferred medications, and therapeutic classes that may affect the positioning and marketing of their products.
7. *Collaborative Engagement*: Building relationships with formulary decision-makers, key opinion leaders, and other stakeholders is crucial. Engaging in dialogue, participating in formulary review and process, and providing relevant data and information can influence decisions. Collaboration and proactive engagement help marketers understand evolving formulary needs, demonstrate the value of their products, and influence formulary decisions in their favor.
8. *Real-World Evidence and Patient-Centric Outcomes*: Pharma marketers can leverage real-world evidence and patient-reported outcomes to support the value proposition of their products within formulary decisions. Collecting and analyzing data on their medications' effectiveness, safety, and patient-centered outcomes can contribute to formulary acceptance. Marketing efforts can highlight how the product positively impacts patient well-being, satisfaction, and quality of life, aligning with formulary goals of improving patient outcomes.

Understanding formulary dynamics, staying informed about formulary requirements, and tailoring marketing strategies to align with formulary goals are essential for pharma marketers. By effectively navigating the formulary landscape, marketers can optimize market access, reimbursement, and product utilization while ensuring the value and benefits of their medications are communicated to healthcare providers, payers, and patients.

How to Get Your Prescription Drug Brand into A Formulary

Including your brand in a formulary requires a strategic approach and collaboration with decision-makers. The following steps can help you increase the chances of including your products in a formulary:

1. *Understand the Formulary Landscape*: Familiarize yourself with the formulary landscape and the specific requirements of the formularies you target. Study the formulary guidelines, preferred drug lists, therapeutic class reviews, and specific criteria or restrictions.
2. *Evidence-Based Value Proposition*: Develop a strong value proposition for your product based on clinical evidence, safety profile, cost-effectiveness, and patient outcomes. Conduct robust clinical trials, health economic evaluations, and outcomes research to generate compelling data demonstrating your product's value compared to existing treatments.
3. *Comparative Effectiveness*: Compare your product to other treatments in the same therapeutic class, highlighting its advantage and superior outcomes. Comparative effectiveness research can provide evidence of improved efficacy, safety, patient satisfaction, or cost-effectiveness, strengthening your case for formulary inclusion.
4. *Engage with Key Stakeholders*: Establish relationships with key decision-makers, including formulary committees, healthcare providers, pharmacy benefit managers (PBMs), and payors. Attend conferences, industry events, and meetings where formulary decisions are discussed. Collaborate with healthcare professionals who influence formulary decision-making and engage in scientific exchange to gain support for your product.
5. *Provide Educational Resources*: Develop educational materials, such as clinical summaries, prescribing information, safety profiles, and patient support resources. Provide evidence-based information that supports the appropriate use and value of your product. Educational initiatives can help healthcare providers understand the benefits of your

product and increase its acceptance within the formulary.

6. *Health Economic Data*: Conduct health economic analyses, such as cost-effectiveness studies or budget impact assessments, to demonstrate the economic value of your product. Show how your product can reduce healthcare costs or improve patient outcomes while being cost-effective compared to alternative treatments.
7. *Communicate with Payors and PBMs*: Engage in discussions with payors and PBMs to understand their specific needs, formulary considerations, and budget constraints. Please provide them with the necessary data and information to support the case for including your product in the formulary. Understand their formulary review cycles and timelines to align your submissions and communications accordingly.
8. *Address Unmet Needs*: Highlight how your product addresses unmet medical needs or provides unique advantages over existing treatments. Emphasize the patient populations that can benefit the most from your product and how it fills a gap in current treatment options.
9. *Clinical Guidelines and Societal Recommendations*: Strive to have your product included in clinical guidelines and receive recommendations from professional societies and organizations. Clinical guidelines often influence formulary decisions. Recommendations from respected societies can add credibility to your product's value proposition.
10. *Stay Up-to-Date and Responsive*: Continuously monitor the formulary landscape for any updates or changes that may affect your inclusion. Stay responsive to formulary committee requests for additional information, data, or clinical support. Demonstrate your willingness to collaborate and address any concerns or questions raised during the formulary evaluation process.

Remember that the formulary inclusion process can be complex and time-consuming. It requires combining scientific evidence, effective communication, relationship-building, and understanding formulary decision-makers' specific needs and priorities. Collaboration, persistence, and a strong value proposition are key to increasing the chances of getting your brand included in a formulary.

Forum

Forums provide online platforms or communities where individuals can exchange ideas, explore subjects of mutual interest, and interact. Forums may be organized around specific topics or industries, while their moderation can range from moderated to unmoderated depending on user interest and preference.

Forums allow users to start new discussion threads about any subject matter, respond to existing threads, and converse with one another. Forums often utilize hierarchies in which different topics are organized into categories for easy navigation by users looking for pertinent discussions. Forums may feature either text, or multimedia discussions between registered users only, sharing texts, images, or videos between each post for mutual conversation and engagement between discussions that span numerous subjects ranging from politics and religion to music videos or any multimedia content shared between posts. Openness and registration can ensure discussions stay respectful on the topic while moderations keep discussions within acceptable parameters set forth.

Forums give businesses, organizations, and individuals a vital space to engage with their audiences or build communities around their products or services.

Forums in Pharma Marketing

Forums can play an integral part in pharma marketing by providing healthcare providers and patients an outlet to discuss health-related topics, share experiences, and offer feedback about products or services from pharmaceutical manufacturers. Here are just a few ways forums may be utilized in pharma marketing:

1. *Market Research*: Pharma companies can use forums to collect feedback about their products and services from healthcare professionals and patients, gathering valuable insight into consumer preferences, unmet needs, and market trends through monitoring forum discussions.
2. *Patient Education*: Pharma companies can use forums to educate patients on disease management, treatment options, and medication adherence. They can empower individuals to make educated healthcare decisions by sharing accurate and trustworthy information.
3. *Brand Awareness*: Pharma companies that actively engage in relevant forums can increase brand and product recognition among healthcare professionals and patients, engage in conversations about them and respond to

inquiries, demonstrating expertise while building trust with their target audiences.

4. *Thought Leadership*: Pharma companies can leverage forums to showcase their research and insights on healthcare topics while displaying thought leadership within the industry. By contributing meaningful dialogues and providing useful data, pharma firms can establish themselves as authoritative voices within healthcare conversations.

How Pharma Can Leverage Online Forums

Here are a few examples that demonstrate how pharmaceutical companies can leverage forums:

1. *PatientsLikeMe*: This platform connects those living with various health conditions with other patients who share similar experiences, providing pharmaceutical companies with valuable insights into patient perspectives while offering resources and support services directly to these users.
2. *Medscape Forums*: Medscape provides medical news and education content via an educational website with forums designed for healthcare professionals to discuss medical topics, ask questions, and exchange insights. Pharma companies may participate in these discussions to offer information to healthcare providers while building relationships.
3. *HealthUnlocked* is an online forum for patients and caregivers to discuss health-related topics and connect with others who share similar experiences. Pharmaceutical companies can utilize HealthUnlocked to engage patients and caregivers by offering information and support and to gain feedback for their products or services.
4. *DocCheck Community*: DocCheck Community provides healthcare professionals a platform to exchange ideas about medical topics and connect with colleagues worldwide. Pharma companies may participate in building relationships with healthcare professionals while sharing product or service details and offering education and other resources.
5. *Pharma Marketing Network*: This professional network allows pharma marketers to share knowledge, connect with colleagues, and discuss trends within the industry. Pharma companies may utilize this forum to build relationships amongst marketers while sharing expertise and gaining new perspectives into strategies and tactics employed for pharmaceutical marketing campaigns.

Overall, forums provide pharmaceutical companies with an effective tool for connecting with their target audiences and building relationships while gathering insights that inform marketing strategies.

Framing

Framing refers to how information is presented to influence its audience's perception of it or shaping how messages are distributed to alter how people understand and interpret them.

Framing can be used effectively across several areas, from politics and advertising campaigns to pharmaceutical products or disease marketing efforts. When applied within pharmaceutical marketing campaigns, framing may influence patients' and healthcare providers' views of any medication or condition.

For example, pharmaceutical companies might use positive framing when marketing new medications by emphasizing their benefits and efficacy in treating specific conditions. In contrast, negative framing emphasizes the risks or consequences of not treating specific ailments.

Framing techniques can enormously affect public perception of controversial issues in the pharmaceutical industry, including pricing or safety concerns surrounding medications. Pharma companies can craft messages and manipulate conversations around these subjects using framing.

Framing for Marketing, Advertising and Other Communications

Various framing techniques are used in marketing, advertising, and other communication contexts. Below are examples of common types of framing with their definitions:

1. *Positive Framing*: Positive framing draws attention to a message's benefits or positive aspects by emphasizing its ability to reduce pain or enhance the quality of life for people with certain conditions. Pharmaceutical companies might market a medication by emphasizing its ability to do just this.
2. *Negative Framing*: Negative framing emphasizes risks or negative ramifications associated with not following certain messages; for instance, pharma companies might market medications by emphasizing untreated symptoms that reduce the quality of life or raise risks of complications as possible consequences of not treating symptoms promptly.

3. *Statistical Framing*: This form of framing uses data or statistics to support a particular message, for instance, when marketing medications using clinical trial results that demonstrate effectiveness for treating specific conditions. A pharmaceutical company might do this when marketing new treatments by emphasizing this aspect of framing as evidence that their product works.
4. *Framing by Analogy*: Analogies are one form of framing that uses familiar or established analogies to portray messages clearly and understandably; for instance, a pharmaceutical company could market its drug by likening its mechanism of action with something popular such as pain relievers.
5. *Goal Framing*: Goal framing emphasizes reaching specific goals or outcomes; for instance, pharmaceutical companies could market medications by emphasizing how they help achieve particular health benefits such as increased mobility or enhanced quality of life for their target audiences.

Framing methods depend upon communication goals and target audience characteristics; different framing approaches can impact how an audience receives or comprehends particular messages.

Franchising

Franchising in pharmaceutical marketing refers to a business model in which pharmaceutical companies license the rights to use their name, products, and marketing strategies to independent individuals or companies (franchisees) in exchange for fees or royalties. Franchising can refer to any number of activities related to pharmaceutical marketing: from selling pharmaceutical products and providing healthcare services through franchising to running clinical trials through franchisees.

Franchising can give pharmaceutical companies several advantages in pharmaceutical marketing, including expanding their reach into new markets without incurring high startup and management costs for sales and marketing operations. Furthermore, by working alongside franchisees who better understand local markets, languages, cultures, etc., they can better adapt products and marketing strategies according to what works for the population there.

Of course, franchising in pharmaceuticals can present its own set of unique difficulties. Franchisees may fail to abide by company standards and guidelines, leading them into inconsistent or harmful practices; moreover, they could face regulatory or legal obstacles which damage the reputation or brand value of the companies they franchise for.

Franchising in Pharma Marketing

Pharma franchise marketing operations must adhere to various legal regulations based on where the franchisee operates. Here are a few regulations worth noting:

1. *Compliance Issues*: Pharmaceutical industries are heavily regulated, so all franchising activities must abide by various laws and regulations regarding drug development, manufacturing, marketing, distribution, and sale. Franchisees should receive training regarding these regulations to stay compliant.
2. *Intellectual Property Laws*: Franchisor agreements should include provisions regarding intellectual property rights such as trademarks, patents, copyrights, and trade secrets in their intellectual property clause. Franchisees should receive explicit instructions regarding how best to utilize and avoid unauthorized uses or infringements on this intellectual property owned by their franchisor.
3. *Disclosure Requirements*: Franchisors must often provide franchisees with certain disclosures, including financial data, operational manuals, and other important documents. Furthermore, in some countries, franchisors may be required to register their franchise offering with regulatory authorities before commencing sales activities.
4. *Antitrust Laws*: Franchisors must abide by antitrust regulations prohibiting anti-competitive behaviors and fostering fair market competition.
5. *Employment Laws*: Franchisees are expected to adhere to employment laws such as minimum wage, overtime payments, and labor regulations that differ by country and region.

Franchising in Pharma: Examples

Here are a few pharmaceutical companies using franchising to expand their business models:

1. *Novartis*: Novartis Pharmaceuticals Corporation operates an OTC franchise program in certain regions around the globe that allows local companies to distribute Novartis OTC products under franchise agreements with full branding and marketing support.
2. *Roche*, a Swiss multinational healthcare company, offers franchise agreements in certain regions worldwide for their diagnostic products. Through these programs, local companies may distribute Roche's diagnostic items under a

franchise agreement while receiving branding and marketing support from Roche.

3. *Pfizer*: Pfizer, an American multinational pharmaceutical corporation, offers its animal health products through a franchise program in certain regions around the globe. Local companies may access branding and marketing support provided by Pfizer when operating this agreement with local suppliers of Pfizer animal healthcare products under this franchise arrangement.
4. *GlaxoSmithKline (GSK)*: GSK is a British multinational pharmaceutical company that offers consumer healthcare franchise programs. Under these franchise agreements, local companies may distribute GSK consumer healthcare products with branding and marketing support provided by GSK.
5. *Sanofi*: Sanofi, the French multinational pharmaceutical company, operates a franchise program for certain world regions, allowing local companies to sell their pharmaceuticals with full branding and marketing support from Sanofi. This agreement grants these local distributors exclusive rights for product distribution by the franchisor.

Pharmaceutical companies often franchise their marketing and sales operations with other organizations, such as marketing agencies or sales representatives, including giving access to its marketing strategies and training on selling its products within legal and ethical parameters. This would entail providing franchisees access to company documents regarding this aspect of operation and ongoing support to meet compliance standards when selling these products.

Free Drug Coupons

Free drug coupons are a common promotional tactic used in pharmaceutical marketing to entice patients to try a particular medication, often offering discounts or free trials of specific prescription medicines to drive sales and build brand loyalty.

Utilizing free drug coupons as part of pharmaceutical marketing has advantages and drawbacks. The potential advantages include:

A. *Increased Patient Access to Medications*: Pharmaceutical companies can expand access for those without the means to afford prescription medicines by offering discounts or free coupons, helping reduce the financial strain of these prescription drugs.

B. *Improved Patient Adherence*: By helping lower medication costs, free drug coupons may encourage patients to adhere to treatment plans and stay with a particular drug over time.

C. *Increased Brand Loyalty*: Patients who experience positive results with their medication and benefit from discounts or free trials are likely to continue taking it, thus solidifying brand loyalty and encouraging future purchases from that pharmacy.

However, using free drug coupons has several potential drawbacks, such as:

1. *Increased Healthcare Costs*: Healthcare costs may increase if patients use free drug coupons to obtain more expensive medications than generic alternatives.
2. *Reduced Incentives for Cost Control*: Free drug coupons could diminish healthcare providers' incentives to pursue lower-cost solutions for decreasing patient medication costs.
3. *Limited Effectiveness*: Free drug coupons may drive short-term sales effectively. However, their impact on building long-term brand loyalty and increasing overall volume might not be significant enough.

Free Drug Coupons in Pharma Marketing

Here are a few examples of pharmaceutical companies using free drug coupons as promotional tactics in the United States:

1. Pfizer offers free drug coupons for medication such as Lyrica (Pregabalin) for treating pain and Chantix (Varenicline) to assist smokers who want to quit smoking cessation.
2. Eli Lilly offers free drug coupons for medications like Humalog (insulin lispro) for treating diabetes and Cialis (Tadalafil) to address erectile dysfunction.
3. Novartis Pharmaceuticals Corporation offers free drug coupons for Entresto (Sacubitril and Valsartan), used for treating heart failure, and Gilenya (Fingolimod), used for multiple sclerosis.
4. AstraZeneca provides free drug coupons for asthma medications Symbicort (Budesonide and Formoterol) and Crestor (Rosuvastatin).

However, using free drug coupons in pharmaceutical marketing must conform to regulations set out by regulatory bodies such as the Food and Drug Administration (FDA) or the Office of Inspector General (OIG).

Freemium

Freemium is a business model in which companies provide free and premium versions of a product or service for users to choose between. The free version often has limited features or functionality, while premium services typically add extra features at an extra charge. This model is popular among software and mobile application companies allowing users to download free basic versions before offering premium upgrades with more features or services within an app. This method has proven particularly successful among these platforms as users can simultaneously take advantage of both options.

Freemium services aim to give users a taste of what the product or service offers before encouraging them to upgrade to its premium version for additional features and functionalities.

Freemium in Pharm Marketing

Due to restrictions limiting promotion and advertising for prescription drugs, freemium business models have not become widespread within pharmaceutical marketing strategies. However, some companies have experimented with freemium strategies for over-the-counter (OTC) medications, health supplements, and medical devices.

Here are a few examples of freemiums in pharmaceutical marketing:

1. *Free Samples of OTC Drugs*: Pharmaceutical companies commonly give free samples of their OTC medications as part of an introduction strategy, like Proctor & Gamble's Crest toothpaste offering samples online to bring in new customers.
2. *Free Educational Content*: Some pharmaceutical companies provide healthcare professionals and patients educational content, including Pfizer's Medscape mobile app, which provides HCPs with drug information, medical news updates, and continuing education courses. Pfizer partners with Medscape to deliver education content via this app but does not own or run it directly; WebMD LLC owns it independently, so HCPs have access to an abundance of drug-related material and continuing education courses as part of this resource.
3. *Free Health Tracking Apps*: Pharmaceutical companies have recently developed free health tracking apps to aid patients in managing their medical conditions more easily, such as Sanofi's GoMeals mobile app for diabetes that tracks meals to manage blood sugar levels more effectively.
4. *Free Medical Device Demos*: Some medical device companies provide healthcare professionals with free demos of their products to assist in making a purchasing decision. Johnson & Johnson provides surgeons demos of its surgical robotics system before purchasing.

Notably, freemium strategies must abide by regulatory constraints in each country where they are sold or promoted.

Frequency

Frequency in pharmaceutical marketing refers to how often an advertisement or message is shown to its target audience within any given period. Repeated exposure increases its odds of being remembered and taken action upon by audiences, making frequency an integral component of advertising and promotion campaigns.

An advertising frequency could represent how often an advertisement airs per day; for instance, pharmaceutical companies could opt to air ads about new drugs on television at least ten times daily for one week; in such an example, its Frequency would equal 10.

Too much advertising frequency may lead to advertising wear-out, where your target audience quickly tires of seeing the same message repeatedly and tunes it out. Therefore, Frequency must be carefully balanced with other considerations, including reach and message variety, for an effective advertising campaign.

Free Standing Insert (FSI)

Free Standing Insert (FSI) ads can be an effective tool for pharmaceutical companies to promote their products and services to potential customers. Here are a few ways free-standing inserts (FSIs) are being utilized for pharmaceutical marketing:

1. *Product Information*: FSIs can provide valuable details about pharmaceutical companies' products, such as their features, benefits, and pricing information, to raise customer awareness and encourage purchases. This may help increase awareness while encouraging more people to buy these items from pharmaceutical manufacturers.
2. *Coupons and Discounts*: Pharmaceutical product FSIs may include coupons or discounts incentivizing consumers to try the products. Incentives such as these could provide

consumers with enough motivation and encouragement to try or purchase new pharmaceutical products.

3. *Cross-promotion*: Pharmaceutical companies can leverage FSIs to promote complementary products or services, such as vitamins or health supplements, that may increase sales and revenue.
4. *Direct Response*: FSIs can be utilized to encourage direct responses from consumers, such as calling a toll-free number or visiting an information website about an offering, which in turn creates leads and boosts sales.
5. *Geographic Targeting*: FSIs can target specific geographical regions to allow pharmaceutical companies to reach potential customers within that specific location or demographic group. This feature is especially helpful for pharmaceutical brands aimed at reaching specific audiences or regions or demographics.

Pharmaceutical companies can utilize FSIs as an effective promotional strategy to target audiences for their products and services. Companies can increase customer awareness through product promotion, coupons/discounts/cross-promotion while driving sales and revenue growth.

Free Website Promotion

Free website promotion refers to any method or technique employed to increase the visibility and traffic of a website without incurring costs associated with advertising it on various online platforms or channels to attract more visitors while increasing its search engine rank.

Here are a few free website promotion techniques you can utilize to attract more visitors and improve its online visibility:

1. *Search Engine Optimization (SEO)*: Utilizing techniques like content editing, meta tags optimization, and technical aspects optimization to increase its ranking within search engine results pages (SERPS).
2. *Social Media Marketing*: Using platforms such as Facebook, Twitter, and Instagram to market a website to increase awareness and attract additional visitors is the primary method for social media promotion.
3. *Content Marketing*: Producing informative blog posts, videos, infographics, and eBooks that target specific niche websites to increase visitor numbers and drive increased business success.
4. *Guest Blogging*: By writing guest blog posts for other blogs and including links to your website in their author bio, guest blogging can drive traffic and improve search engine rankings.
5. *Online Directories*: Submitting the website to localized search directories such as Yelp, Yellow Pages, and Google My Business can increase visibility and attract local customers.
6. *Email Marketing*: By building and sending subscribers regular newsletters or promotional emails, email marketers can increase engagement while driving more website visits.
7. *Forum Marketing*: Participating in online forums and discussion boards related to your site's niche can establish authority, create relationships and attract more visitors.

How Pharma Companies Utilize Free Website Promotion

Pharmaceutical firms must adhere to stringent marketing and promotion restrictions due to the highly sensitive nature of their products. Here are a few examples of how pharmaceutical firms advertise online:

1. *Social Media Marketing*: Pharmaceutical companies use social media outlets like Facebook, Twitter, and LinkedIn to reach audiences and market their products and services to potential clients. Novartis maintains an updated LinkedIn page featuring information regarding its offerings and company culture features to communicate this.
2. *Search Engine Optimization*: Pharmaceutical companies increasingly employ SEO tactics to increase visibility and drive website traffic. Pfizer, for instance, utilizes search engine optimization techniques so its products will appear first when people search online.
3. *Content Marketing*: Pharmaceutical companies create educational material like blog posts, white papers, and eBooks for their target audiences to learn about their products and services. GlaxoSmithKline (GSK) hosts an informative blog detailing research and development efforts and sharing updates via blog posts.
4. *Online Communities and Forums*: Some pharmaceutical companies utilize online communities and forums to engage their audience and respond to any inquiries or complaints it raises. Merck provides patients with a community forum to ask about specific discussions and connect with those suffering similar conditions.
5. *Email Marketing*: Pharmaceutical companies use email marketing to educate their audiences

about their products and services, like Sanofi, which sends subscribers regular newsletters that include information on Sanofi products and updates regarding company initiatives.

According to local regulations and laws, pharmaceutical companies must abide by stringent regulations when marketing their products and services in different countries. Marketing efforts should reflect such compliance efforts for optimal success.

Funnel

A marketing funnel or sales funnel is an illustration used in pharmaceutical marketing that depicts the customer journey from initial awareness of a product/service through consideration to purchase decision. The marketing 'Funnel' represents these steps of purchase decision process:

Here are the various steps of pharmaceutical marketing's marketing funnel:

1. *Awareness*: At this step, customers become aware of a product or service via various marketing channels, including advertisements, online searches, or word-of-mouth recommendations. Pharmaceutical companies may use social media advertising or content marketing techniques such as videos to raise awareness for new medications or specific conditions they treat; or partner with healthcare professionals in educating patients.
2. *Interest*: Once customers know a product exists, they will explore its features further and understand its benefits. At this stage, pharmaceutical companies might create educational content such as blog posts or infographics that outline how the medication works and its potential advantages; additionally, they might offer free samples directly to patients or healthcare professionals.
3. *Consideration*: At this stage, customers compare similar products. Pharma companies must convince potential customers that their medication is the superior option at this stage; to do this, they may provide detailed clinical trial data or patient testimonials that support this view; educational resources (webinars or events) could also help individuals and healthcare professionals better comprehend it. At this stage, customers have determined they wish to buy the product and are actively searching for the ideal offer, time, and date. During this stage, pharmaceutical companies might offer discounts, rebates, or free coupons to incentivize sales. Additionally, they may also work with insurance providers to ensure coverage for these mediations to improve access.
4. *Purchase*: At this final stage, customers purchase their medication through either an approved pharmacy or directly from the company, depending upon their distribution strategy.

Pharma companies can utilize the marketing funnel to devise an effective campaign that meets customers' needs at each funnel stage and ultimately increase brand recognition, customer engagement, and sales.

G

1. Gamification
2. Gap Analysis
3. Gate Keepers
4. GATT
5. GDPR
6. Generation X
7. Generation Y
8. Generation Z
9. Generational Marketing
10. Generative AI
11. Genomics
12. Genomic Mapping
13. Geo-Demographic Segmentation
14. Geo-fencing
15. Geo-targeting
16. Global Market
17. Global Marketing
18. Globalization
19. Glocal Market
20. Glocal Marketing
21. Goal
22. Good Distribution Practices
23. Good Management Practices
24. Good Manufacturing Practices (GMP)
25. Good Marketing Practices
26. Goodwill
27. Google
28. Go-to-Market Strategy
29. Go-to-Patient Strategy
30. Go-to-Patient Strategy Measurement
31. Global Positioning System (GPS)
32. Green Chemistry
33. Green Marketing
34. Greenwashing
35. Gresham's Law
36. Group Purchasing Organization (GPO)
37. Guerilla Marketing

Gamification

Gamification is a marketing method that employs game-like elements like points, badges, and leaderboards to engage and motivate consumers. Gamification in pharmaceutical marketing can promote healthy behaviors while teaching patients about their conditions while increasing medication adherence rates. Here are some examples:

1. *Health and Wellness Apps*: Pharmaceutical companies have created apps using gamification techniques to encourage healthy behaviors like exercising, eating healthily, and getting enough restful sleep. Such applications could offer rewards in the form of points or badges upon accomplishing certain tasks or meeting goals.
2. *Disease Management Programs*: Pharma companies have developed disease management programs using gamification techniques to educate patients on their medical conditions and encourage adherence to treatment regimens. Such programs could feature challenges, quizzes, or game elements designed to make learning about health conditions engaging and interactive for patients.
3. *Clinical Trials*: Some pharmaceutical companies have implemented gamification into clinical trial recruitment efforts, offering rewards, such as gift cards or other incentives in return for participating and completing certain tasks related to a trial.
4. *Medical Education*: Some pharmaceutical companies have developed gamified medical education programs targeted toward healthcare professionals (HCPs). Such programs often incorporate game elements like quizzes and challenges to make learning about treatments and medical conditions more engaging and interactive for HCPs.

Gamification can be an invaluable asset in pharmaceutical marketing, engaging and motivating patients and healthcare providers to learn about new treatments while actively taking charge of their health. Pharmaceutical companies must use it ethically and transparently. They should not unduly influence patient or healthcare professional behaviors with rewards or incentives that negatively affect individual behaviors or well-being.

Gap Analysis

Gap analysis in pharmaceutical marketing refers to identifying and assessing any differences between current and desired states for any marketing strategy or campaign. It involves evaluating the current marketing efforts of companies as well as opportunities and threats presented in their target markets to find places where improvements may be implemented.

Gap analysis seeks to establish where companies currently are relative to where they desire them to be regarding marketing goals, then devise plans to close any identified gaps. Such analysis helps businesses discover areas for expansion and areas they must improve to remain competitive within their marketplaces.

Key Steps

There are five essential steps involved in conducting a gap analysis for pharmaceutical marketing:

1. *Marketing Goals*: Decide on yourcompany's marketing goals; are they increasing market share or launching a new product/service? Once you decide on goals, then define success measures for each goal. Once goals have been defined for these, what success indicators exist on which success will depend?
2. *Examine Current Marketing Efforts*: Assess your company's current marketing efforts. This includes advertising, sales promotion, public relations, digital strategies and tactics, such as ads and promos and traditional marketing tactics like public relations or digital channels like SEO and PPC. Evaluate each tactic against its desired goal for effectiveness and its strengths and weaknesses to develop further plans.
3. *Analyze the Market*: Assess current market conditions, including competitors, customer needs, and industry trends, to identify opportunities or threats that might compromise company marketing efforts.
4. *Identify the Gap*: Evaluate how current marketing efforts compare to those intended by marketing goals, then pinpoint any gaps and areas for improvement.
5. *Create an Action Plan*: Develop an action plan to bridge the gap between current and desired states, such as revising marketing strategy or tactics or reallocating resources to focus on areas of weakness. This may require revising marketing strategy or tactics or reallocating resources towards areas with deficiencies.

Gap analysis can be an invaluable asset for pharmaceutical companies seeking to increase marketing efficiency and remain competitive in today's highly competitive pharmaceutical environment. By identifying gaps between their current marketing strategy and desired state, companies can develop an action plan to reach their goals and drive growth.

Gate Keepers

Gatekeepers in pharmaceutical marketing refer to individuals or organizations who regulate access to decision-makers and influencers, such as Healthcare Professionals (HCP), hospital administrators, or formulary committees within the healthcare industry who influence or make decisions related to pharmaceutical products or services.

Pharmaceutical companies rely on gatekeepers to enter into healthcare organizations' decision-making processes and better understand key stakeholder needs and preferences. Building relationships with these gatekeepers allows pharmaceutical firms to access these decision-makers quickly.

Gate Keepers in Pharma Marketing

Here are a few examples of gatekeepers in pharmaceutical marketing:

1. *Physicians*: Healthcare professionals like physicians are frequently the main gatekeepers in pharmaceutical marketing. They prescribe medicines, recommend products or services directly to patients, and can sway other healthcare professionals within their network.
2. *Hospital Administrators* often decide which products and services will be utilized within their facility, including pharmaceuticals. Their views and preferences often play a part in purchasing decisions. They are important gatekeepers for pharmaceutical companies promoting their products.
3. *Formulary Committees*: Formulary committees comprise healthcare professionals and administrators charged with selecting which medications will be included on an organization's formulary list. Their decisions have great sway over which pharmaceutical products are utilized within healthcare systems, and they serve as crucial gatekeepers to gain entry to key decision-makers.
4. *Insurance Providers*: Pharmaceutical companies seeking coverage under various health plans often need the support of insurers as intermediaries in proving the value and efficacy of their product to influence decision-makers to cover it. Companies often must demonstrate this via product demonstration.

Gatekeepers are indispensable in pharmaceutical marketing by controlling access to key decision-makers and influencers within healthcare industries. Therefore, developing relationships with gatekeepers can be an effective strategy for pharmaceutical companies seeking to promote their products or services and gain a competitive advantage in the marketplace.

GATT

The General Agreement on Tariffs and Trade (GATT) is an international treaty signed in 1947 to promote free trade among member countries. The GATT underwent several rounds of negotiations and revisions, and in 1995 it was replaced by the World Trade Organization (WTO).

GATT 1994, also known as the Final Act Embodying the Results of the Uruguay Round of Multilateral Trade Negotiations, was the eighth and final round of negotiations under the GATT. It represented a significant update to the GATT, focusing on expanding trade in services and intellectual property rights. GATT 1994 includes several key provisions, including the Most-Favored Nation principle, which requires WTO member countries to treat each other equally and not discriminate against anyone country in favor of another. It also includes the National Treatment principle, which requires WTO member countries to provide foreign companies the same treatment as domestic companies.

GATT 1994 and its successor, the WTO, have significantly promoted global trade and economic growth while ensuring that trade is conducted fairly and transparently between member countries.

Implications for Pharma Industry

The implications of GATT and the WTO for the pharmaceutical industry are significant. The WTO's Agreement to Trade-Related aspects of Intellectual Property Rights (TRIPS) has significantly impacted the pharmaceutical industry by setting minimum standards for protecting and enforcing intellectual property rights, including pharmaceutical patents.

One of the most significant impacts of TRIPS on the pharmaceutical industry is that it provides patent protection for a minimum of 20 years from the date of filing, giving pharmaceutical companies the exclusive right to manufacture, use and sell their inventions. This exclusivity incentivizes pharmaceutical companies to invest in research and development, leading to the discovery of new drugs and treatments.

However, there are concerns that the high costs of patented medicines make them unaffordable for many people in developing countries, leading to inadequate access to life-saving drugs. To address this concern, TRIPS allows developing countries to produce generic versions of patented medicines under certain circumstances, such as during public health emergencies.

The pharmaceutical industry has also been affected by WTO rules in areas such as:

1. *Trade in Goods*: The WTO has worked to reduce trade barriers and increase access to global markets, allowing pharmaceutical companies to expand their reach and sell their products in more countries.
2. *Settlement of Disputes*: The WTO's Dispute Settlement Body (DSB) provides a forum for resolving disputes related to trade in goods and services, including disputes related to intellectual property rights.

GATT: Implications for Pharmaceutical Marketing

The implications of GATT for pharmaceutical marketing are mainly related to intellectual property rights and trade agreements between countries. Here are some of the implications for pharma marketers:

1. *Patent Protection*: GATT and its successor, the WTO, provide a framework for protecting intellectual property rights, including patents for pharmaceutical products. Pharmaceutical marketers must comply with patent laws and regulations when promoting and selling their products in different countries.
2. *Market Access*: GATT and WTO agreements aim to reduce trade barriers and promote market access for goods and services, including pharmaceutical products. This means pharma marketers can access new markets and increase their reach through international trade agreements.
3. *Pricing and Reimbursement*: GATT and WTO agreements also affect drug pricing and reimbursement policies in different countries. For example, some countries may implement price controls or reimbursement restrictions that affect the profitability of pharmaceutical products. This can impact the marketing strategies and pricing decisions of pharmaceutical companies.
4. *Regulatory Harmonization:* GATT and WTO agreements encourage regulatory harmonization among member countries, which can impact pharma marketers. This means that pharmaceutical companies must comply with different regulatory requirements in different countries, which can affect their products' development, approval, and marketing. Regulatory harmonization will help pharmaceutical companies significantly as they must comply with one global standard instead of several as they do today.

GATT 1994 and the WTO implications for the pharmaceutical industry are complex and multifaceted, with benefits and challenges. While TRIPS has provided important protections for intellectual property rights and incentives for research and development, concerns about access to affordable medicine remain significant. Moreover, the WTO's efforts to reduce trade barriers and increase access to global markets have also been a mixed bag for the pharmaceutical industry.

GDPR

The General Data Protection Regulation (GDPR) is a comprehensive data protection and privacy regulation with significant implications for pharmaceutical marketing, just as it does for all industries. Here are some of the key implications of GDPR in the context of pharmaceutical marketing:

1. *Consent and Transparency*: Pharmaceutical companies need to obtain explicit and informed consent from individuals before collecting and processing their data. This applies to email marketing, patient information databases, and clinical trial recruitment. Transparency about data usage is crucial.
2. *Data Minimization*: The principle of data minimization under GDPR means that under GDPR means that only necessary data should be collected for a specific purpose in pharmaceutical marketing. This requires companies to collect and use only data directly relevant to their marketing efforts.
3. *Data Subject Rights*: GDPR grants individuals specific rights regarding other personal data, delete or port their data. Pharmaceutical companies must be prepared to facilitate these rights when requested by patients, healthcare professionals, or other data subjects.
4. *Security Measures*: Pharma marketing activities often involve handling sensitive medical information. GDPR mandates that companies implement appropriate security measures to protect this data from breaches and unauthorized access.
5. *Profiling and Automated Decision-Making*: If pharmaceutical marketing relies on profiling and automated decision-making processes (personalized recommendations based on patient data), GDPR imposes specific

requirements, including the right for individuals to contest automated decisions.

6. *International Data Transfers*: If data is transferred internationally, companies must ensure that the recipient country offers adequate data protection or establish alternative safeguards such as Standard Contractual Clauses (SCCs) or Binding Corporate Rules (BCRs).
7. *Data Protection Impact Assessments (DPIAs)*: Pharmaceutical companies may need to conduct DPIAs to assess and mitigate privacy risks for high-risk data processing activities.
8. *Accountability and Documentation*: GDPR requires organizations to maintain documentation of data processing activities, policies, and risk assessments. Companies in the pharma sector should be prepared to demonstrate compliance.
9. *Data Breach Notification*: In the event of a data breach, pharmaceutical companies must notify the relevant supervisory authority and, in some cases, data subjects within strict timeframes.
10. *Patient Recruitment for Clinical Trials*: Using patient data in recruitment efforts must align with GDPR requirements, ensuring patient consent and data protection.
11. *Data Protection*: Pharmaceutical direct marketing, including email and digital marketing, should adhere to GDPR requirements for consent and provide opt-out mechanisms.

The implications of GDPR in pharma marketing are significant, as the industry relies on extensive data collection and processing for various activities, including patient engagement, clinical trials, and healthcare professional relationships. Non-compliance with GDPR can result in substantial fines, damage to reputation, and legal consequences. Therefore, pharmaceutical companies should establish robust data protection and privacy practices, conduct regular audits, and ensure ongoing compliance with the regulation. Additionally, consulting with legal and privacy experts is essential to navigate the complex data protection landscape in the pharmaceutical sector.

Generation X

Generation X refers to people born between 1960 and 1984. It is an excellent target audience for pharmaceutical marketers as they enter their peak healthcare years, likely having more health concerns than younger generations.

Here are the key characteristics of Generation X that pharma marketers should keep in mind:

1. Generation X members often fall under the category of a sandwich generation because they care for elderly parents and children at once, leaving little time for themselves or their health maintenance. As such, Generation X often finds itself overburdened with care responsibilities while needing to devote attention to maintaining healthful lives for themselves and their family members.
2. Generation X tends to be less trusting of authority figures such as doctors or pharmaceutical companies than previous generations, which makes this generation somewhat skeptical of authority figures like politicians or pharmaceutical companies.
3. Generation X members may not be as tech-savvy as millennials; nevertheless, they remain more comfortable using modern devices to manage their health than previous generations.
4. Generation X values convenience and may often opt for mail-order pharmacies or telemedicine services to manage their health.

Pharma marketers should aim to meet Generation X's busy lifestyles by offering hassle-free solutions that fit effortlessly into their schedules, being open and honest in their marketing messages, engaging in two-way dialogue with consumers, and using multiple channels (email, social media, and targeted ads) to reach this demographic effectively.

Generation Y

Generation Y (millennials), or Gen Y, is an age group encompassing those born between 1980-1993 and an important target audience for pharmaceutical marketing as they enter their prime healthcare years and take more responsibility for managing their health than ever before.

Here are a few key characteristics of Generation Y that pharma marketers must keep in mind:

1. *Digital Natives*: Generation Y was raised with digital technologies around them, becoming familiar with and comfortable using various digital health management tools like apps, wearables, and telemedicine for themselves and their loved ones.
2. *Health Conscious*: *Gen Y'ers* tend to place greater value on wellness and prevention, taking an interest in natural and alternative remedies and seeking information online about their health status.

3. Generation Y tends to distrust traditional marketing approaches such as television commercials or print ads; they prefer receiving information directly from peers through social media channels such as Facebook.
4. Generation Y are generally socially aware, appreciating authenticity and transparency when making purchasing decisions, so they tend to favor companies that display transparency about their practices and dedication towards social or environmental causes.

Pharma marketers should utilize digital strategies like social media, mobile apps, and targeted email campaigns to reach Generation Y consumers. Furthermore, they must offer useful content tailored specifically for this demographic's health interests while being transparent and authentic when conveying marketing messages. They should be ready and willing to interact with consumers in two-way conversations.

Generation Z

Generation Z (post-millennial generation) includes individuals born between the late 1990s and 2010; it represents individuals born after 1995 becoming more involved with healthcare decisions as they mature, likely having different attitudes and behavioral habits from prior generations. Pharma marketing should consider targeting this demographic because healthcare is changing quickly with each passing year, and this generation may represent one of its greatest target markets for product advancement and brand messaging.

Here are a few key characteristics of Generation Z that pharma marketers should keep in mind:

1. *Digital Natives*: Generation Z was raised with digital technologies and is adept at using them to manage their health effectively. They are more likely than older generations to utilize apps and social media channels as sources of healthcare information.
2. *Socially Aware*: Generation Z tends to be socially aware and values transparency, authenticity, and sustainability in businesses they support; therefore, their choices align with these ideals.
3. *Visual Content Preference*: Generation Z prefers visual media such as videos and infographics over text-heavy texts; additionally, they respond positively to interactive experiences that offer them something extra!
4. *More Health Conscious*: Generation Z tends to be more health conscious than previous generations and is drawn toward natural and alternative remedies, curious about these forms of therapy, and more likely than any previous cohort to seek information online about their health issues.

Marketing to Generation Z

Gen Z was raised using social media as its main communication and information-gathering source, so pharmaceutical companies must adapt their marketing strategies to engage this generation on social media effectively. Here are a few tactics pharma companies can utilize when marketing to Gen Z:

1. *Use Social Media Platforms*: Generation Z spends significant time on popular social media platforms like Instagram, TikTok, and Snapchat. Pharma companies can take advantage of these channels by sharing engaging videos, infographics, and user-generated content. A pharmaceutical company could set up an Instagram account dedicated exclusively to this demographic that showcases before-and-after photos taken using their products; in addition, they could produce short TikTok videos to raise awareness for health conditions while advertising products or raising awareness on TikTok videos that increase brand recognition on these channels.
2. *Emphasize Convenience*: *Gen Z'ers* are busy individuals who prioritize convenience over all else, which pharma companies should keep in mind when offering products and services such as telemedicine or home delivery of medications.
3. *Socially Aware*: Gen Z is an extremely socially aware generation attracted to brands that align with their values, so pharma companies should promote social responsibility, sustainability, and ethical practices as part of their marketing. A company could do this through Eco-friendly packaging or by contributing a portion of profits toward environmental causes. Additionally, they could show transparency about their supply chains and manufacturing process.
4. *Authenticity*: Gen Z is known to appreciate authentic experiences. Pharma companies can tailor their messaging for this target demographic by using language they identify with while emphasizing the benefits associated with their products and services.
5. *Educational Content*: *Gen Z'ers* are known for their hunger for knowledge and desire for self-improvement, making Gen Z an excellent audience for pharmaceutical companies to offer educational material such as blog posts,

webinars, and e-books with information regarding health and well-being.

Pharma and Healthcare Companies Engage With Gen Z

Here are some examples of how pharmaceutical and healthcare companies have reached Gen Z through marketing:

1. Ro is an innovative digital health clinic providing telemedicine services that use social media channels like Instagram and TikTok to increase brand recognition among Gen Z consumers. They produce engaging videos about their services that capture Gen Z's attention.
2. Pfizer, the pharmaceutical company behind the COVID-19 vaccine, uses social media platforms such as YouTube to reach Gen Z and encourage them to get immunized against influenza. Influencers and celebrities have also joined Pfizer in spreading information on this new vaccination option and encouraging their followers to immunize against COVID.
3. GoodRx, the prescription drug price comparison website, has developed educational content on their blog to inform visitors about healthcare and prescription drugs. They have partnered with healthcare providers to offer telemedicine services and home delivery of medications, which appeals to Gen Z's preference for convenience.
4. Hims is an online telemedicine provider offering treatments for conditions including hair loss and erectile dysfunction, who has leveraged social media platforms, such as Instagram and Snapchat to reach Gen Z users through engaging content that uses humor and relatable messaging to raise awareness for their services.

Pharma marketers seeking to reach Generation Z effectively should create informative, visually attractive, and interactive content tailored specifically to its health concerns and interests. Marketing messages should also emphasize transparency and authenticity while emphasizing sustainability and social responsibility. Finally, multiple digital channels such as social media, mobile apps, and targeted advertisements must be utilized to reach this demographic effectively.

Generational Marketing

Generational Marketing in Pharma refers to tailoring marketing strategies and messages to different generations, such as Baby Boomers, *Gen X*, Millennials, and Gen Zs. Each generation possesses distinct characteristics, values, and preferences, influencing how they consume healthcare products and services.

Pharmaceutical companies can utilize generational marketing to tailor campaigns specifically to certain demographic groups and boost the success of their marketing initiatives. By understanding each generation's preferences and needs, companies can develop messages more likely to drive engagement and sales growth.

Here are a few examples of generational marketing in Pharma:

1. *Baby Boomers*: Baby Boomers are an expansive demographic group with significant healthcare needs, prioritizing health and well-being over longevity or vitality when seeking medical products and services. Pharmaceutical companies may target this audience by emphasizing how their products support healthy aging or maintain an active lifestyle for maximum effect.
2. *Gen X*: Gen X represents an independent demographic that values personal responsibility and self-care, so they tend to seek healthcare products and services that enable them to control their health and well-being. Pharmaceutical companies should target this group with products that emphasize effectiveness and convenience for an ideal user experience.
3. *Millennials*: Millennials are a tech-savvy demographic that places high importance on convenience and personalized experiences, preferring products and services easily accessible online or through mobile devices for healthcare use. Pharmaceutical companies may want to focus their marketing strategies on this group by emphasizing the digital features of their offerings as a key strategy to reach them.
4. *Gen Z*: Gen Z is an extremely diverse, socially aware demographic group emphasizing authenticity and transparency in healthcare products and services that reflect their values and promote sustainability and social responsibility. Pharmaceutical companies targeting this demographic should highlight ethical considerations within their products or services to reach this group effectively.

Generational marketing can be an effective strategy for pharmaceutical companies seeking to connect with specific demographic groups and increase sales of their products or services. By tailoring marketing messages specifically to each generation's needs and preferences, companies can develop more engaging campaigns that resonate with their target audiences.

Generative AI

Generative AI refers to artificial intelligence models capable of creating new data similar yet distinct from what they were trained on. Generative AI models like Open AI's GPT-4 learn to recognize patterns within data they are trained upon and apply this understanding towards creating original outputs. This concept offers many exciting applications in pharmaceutical marketing! For instance:

1. *Content Creation*: Generative AI can assist marketers by producing marketing content, such as blog posts, social media updates, or email campaigns. A model trained to analyze past marketing messages could create similar ones based on that past content to fit within your brand voice and messaging strategy.
2. *Personalized Marketing*: Generative AI models can be trained to predict future trends based on historical information. This makes generative AI ideal for market research, sales forecasting, identifying market opportunities, etc.
3. *Drug Discovery*: Generative AI has long been utilized as a powerful way to produce new potential drug molecules rapidly; for instance, AI firm *Insilico* Medicare employed GaN technology to produce an efficacious new medication within 46 days!
4. *Simulation*: Generative AI models can simulate various marketing strategies and predict their outcomes, helping marketers make data-driven decisions.
5. *Chatbots and Virtual Assistants*: Generative AI can power sophisticated chatbots and virtual assistants for customer service, lead generation, and patient engagement.
6. Pharmaceutical companies could utilize generative AI models to craft personalized email campaigns. Such models could consider recipients' past interactions with them, their medical history (with due regard for privacy and consent) and preferences when creating personalized messages that are likely to resonate.

Implications for Pharma Marketers

Generative AI technologies, specifically natural language generation (NLG) and image synthesis can have profound ramifications for pharmaceutical marketers. Leveraging deep learning algorithms and neural networks to produce content similar to what a human would produce can present new marketing challenges and opportunities in the pharmaceutical industry. Here are some key implications:

1. *Generativity*: AI can generate customized content for individual patients and healthcare professionals. Generative AI provides pharmaceutical marketers with a powerful solution for creating custom messaging by analyzing large datasets to analyze customer preferences and behavior while improving engagement and conversion rates.
2. *Drug Information and Education*: AI chatbots and virtual assistants can provide accurate, detailed, and up-to-date information about pharmaceutical products, their interactions, side effects, dosage instructions, patient education strategies, and patient adherence measures, thus improving health outcomes and patient experience.
3. *Content Automation*: Pharma marketers typically need to produce large volumes of content such as blog posts, articles, social media updates, and marketing materials. Generative AI offers marketers an efficient solution that saves time and resources by automating content production while creating a standardized message across various channels.
4. *Clinical Trial Recruitment*: AI can analyze patient data more effectively to match suitable candidates with clinical trials more efficiently and quickly. This results in faster recruitment times, reduced costs, and enhanced trial success rates.
5. *Compliance and Regulatory Considerations*: Before using AI to generate content for pharmaceutical marketers, marketers must ensure it conforms to all pertinent regulations and guidelines imposed by regulatory bodies. Content must be accurate, impartial, and follow their established rules and expectations.
6. *Addressing Language Barriers*: Generative AI can assist marketers with reaching global audiences more effectively by breaking through language barriers. AI translation tools create content in various languages to ensure essential information reaches diverse populations.
7. *Adverse Event Monitoring*: AI can quickly scan social media channels for mentions of adverse reactions related to pharmaceutical products. This allows marketers to respond swiftly and appropriately in case an issue arises.
8. *Reputation Management*: AI's content generation capability could play a pivotal role in helping marketers manage reputation more effectively and address negative opinions or misinformation in real-time.

Challenges

Though AI offers numerous benefits, there may also be challenges:

A. *Ethical Considerations*: AI-generated content should always disclose its source when conveying sensitive medical data.

B. *Quality Control*: Ensuring AI-generated content meets accuracy and quality criteria is essential to maintaining credibility.

C. *Data Privacy & Security*: Furthermore, data privacy & security requires adhering closely to regulations on handling patient information and sensitive medical records.

Generative AI offers pharmaceutical marketers incredible potential to improve content generation, personalization, and customer engagement. However, its use should always consider the well-being of patients and healthcare providers first and foremost.

Gene Therapy

Gene therapy is a medical intervention that alters your genes to treat or stop diseases within your cells, specifically to stop or cure genetic conditions such as cancer and Alzheimer's. Genes provide instructions to our cells on how they should operate and express certain traits. When these instructions become misdirected by a genetic mutation, genetic disorders arise.

Gene therapy treats diseases by inserting, replacing, or disrupting specific genes within a patient's cells. There are various types of gene therapy:

1. *Gene Augmentation Therapy*: Gene augmentation therapy involves injecting new copies of functioning genes into cells to replace one that either doesn't exist or doesn't function correctly, typically seen with diseases caused by single gene defects like cystic fibrosis or muscular dystrophy. This approach may provide some hope.
2. *Gene Inhibition Therapy*: Gene inhibition therapy involves injecting genetic material that blocks or suppresses an overactive gene and is frequently employed when treating cancer and similar disorders.
3. *Gene Editing* involves editing an individual's genetic code to repair defective or introduce beneficial genes into their genome, with CRISPR-CAS9 technology making this form of gene therapy increasingly accessible and feasible.

Gene therapy offers tremendous potential to treat and even cure genetic disorders that were once untreatable. Still, its practice can present numerous challenges, such as targeting therapy to the proper cells and long-lasting effects with no unintended repercussions like immune reactions or off-target effects.

Challenges

1. *Understanding the Science*: Gene therapy represents several challenges to pharma marketing strategy from an understanding of the science perspective. Marketers must learn about this rapidly developing field to communicate its benefits, risks, and mechanisms effectively with customers.
2. *Regulatory Landscape*: Gene therapy regulations continue to evolve rapidly across countries, making marketer navigation of this landscape essential. Marketers must tread cautiously as they navigate this terrain in their sales efforts.
3. *Price and Value*: Gene therapies tend to come with high price tags due to their potential ability to treat serious diseases and high research and development expenses, so marketers must effectively communicate the worthiness of such therapies to payers, providers, and patients alike.
4. *Education*: Healthcare providers and patients need to become better educated about gene therapy's potential advantages, risks, how it works, and what can be expected during treatment.
5. *Patient Satisfaction*: Gene therapies often target specific genetic mutations, making them only suitable for subsets of certain diseases. Marketers must therefore devise effective strategies for reaching and targeting these individuals with precision marketing.
6. *Post-MarketSurveillance*: Given the novelty and complexity of gene therapies, post-marketing surveillance to track their long-term effects will be crucial. Marketers could play an invaluable role in communicating the findings of such surveillance while supporting initiatives to collect relevant data.

Gene therapy is an exciting field revolutionizing medicine, offering immense potential to pharma marketers if managed well. But they must navigate this complex landscape carefully to take full advantage of its opportunities.

Generics

Generics are pharmaceutical products that are marketed without a brand name after the patent for the original branded product has expired. Generic drugs are sold at lower prices than their branded counterparts and have become increasingly popular in recent years due to their cost-effectiveness.

The rise of generic drugs has significant implications for pharma marketers, including the following:

1. *Increased Competition*: Generics have increased competition in the pharmaceutical market, making it more challenging for branded drugs to maintain their market share. This has forced pharma marketers to develop more effective marketing strategies to promote their products and differentiate them from their generic counterparts.
2. *Pricing*: Generics are typically sold at lower prices than branded drugs, which can impact the pricing strategy of branded products. This means that pharma marketers must consider the pricing of their products carefully and find ways to justify higher price points of their branded products.
3. *Brand Recognition*: With the availability of generic drugs, pharma marketers must work harder to build and maintain brand recognition for their branded products. This means that they must develop effective branding and advertising strategies that help to differentiate their products from generic alternatives.
4. *Market Segmentation*: Generics have created new market segments for pharma marketers, such as cost-conscious consumers willing to purchase generic drugs over branded drugs. Pharma marketers must effectively identify and target these new market segments to maintain their market share.
5. *Intellectual Property*: The availability of generic drugs has significant implications for the intellectual property of pharma marketers. They must work to protect their patents and trademarks and prevent generic manufacturers from infringing on their intellectual property.

Generics: Approval Process

The approval process for generic drugs varies by country and regulatory agency but generally follows a similar path. Here is a general overview of the process:

1. *Development and Testing*: The generic drug manufacturer develops and tests the drug to ensure it is safe and effective.
2. *Abbreviated New Drug Application (ANDA)*: The manufacturer submits an ANDA to the regulatory agency. This application includes the manufacturer's testing data and the original branded drug information.
3. *Bioequivalence Testing*: The regulatory agency mandates bioequivalence testing to compare the generic drug to the original branded drug. Bioequivalence testing ensures that the generic drug is similar in efficacy and safety to the branded drug.
4. *Review and Approval*: The regulatory agency reviews the ANDA and bioequivalence data to determine whether the generic drug is safe and effective.

It is important to note that the approval process can take several years and requires significant resources from the manufacturer. Additionally, the requirements for approval may vary by country and regulatory agency. For example, the FDA in the United States has specific requirements for the bioequivalence testing of generic drugs.

Generics: Marketing Strategies

Marketing strategies for generic drugs typically focus on cost-effectiveness, quality, and availability. Here are some common marketing strategies for generic drugs:

1. *Price*: The primary selling point for generic drugs is their lower price than branded drugs. Generic drug manufacturers often advertise their products as cost-effective alternatives to branded drugs, which can be especially appealing to cost-conscious consumers.
2. *Quality*: While generic drugs are typically sold at a lower price, they must meet the same quality standards as branded drugs. Generic drug manufacturers can highlight their quality standards in their marketing materials, emphasizing that their products are as safe and effective as branded drugs.
3. *Availability*: Generic drugs are often widely available in pharmacies and online, making them convenient for consumers. Marketing strategies can highlight the availability of generic drugs and make it easy for consumers to find and purchase them.
4. *Education*: Some generic drug manufacturers may provide educational resources to consumers and healthcare professionals to help them understand the benefits of generic drugs. This can include information about generic drugs' cost savings and quality and how to find and purchase them.

5. *Branding*: While generic drugs do not have a brand name, they may have a recognizable logo or packaging that helps differentiate them from other generic drugs. Marketing strategies may focus on building brand recognition for a specific generic drug or generic manufacturer.

In summary, marketing strategies for generic drugs tend to focus on affordability, quality, and availability. By emphasizing these benefits, generic drug manufacturers can successfully promote their products to consumers and healthcare professionals.

Genomics

Genomics, the study of all of a person's genes (the genome), including interactions between those genes and the person's environment, has played a pivotal role in the rise of precision medicine. With the growing understanding of genomics, we see more treatments targeting specific genetic mutations and variations.

The rise of genomics has several significant implications for pharmaceutical marketers:

1. *Understanding the Science*: The science of genomics is complex and evolving rapidly. Marketers must understand this science to effectively communicate genome-based therapies' benefits, risks, and mechanisms of action.
2. *Educational Role*: The intricacies of genomics mean a strong need to educate healthcare professionals and patients about genomic medicine. This includes how genetic testing works, the significance of specific genetic variants, and how these can affect treatment choices.
3. *Regulatory Compliance*: With the introduction of genomics into medicine, new regulatory aspects need to be considered, particularly around the use of genetic information. Marketers must ensure their campaigns comply with these regulations.
4. *Data-Driven Marketing*: Genomics is a data-intensive field, and marketers must be adept at handling, analyzing, and using genomic data to inform their strategies. This could involve understanding the prevalence of specific genetic variants, identifying key patient populations based on genomics, and personalizing marketing messages based on genomic information.
5. *Partnerships*: The integration of genomics into medicine often involves collaboration between different stakeholders, including diagnostic companies, genetic counselors, healthcare providers, and payors. Pharma marketers may need to foster partnerships with these groups to effectively promote their products.
6. *Ethics and Privacy*: The use of genetic information raises ethical and privacy considerations. Marketers must approach these sensitively and transparently to maintain trust with patients and healthcare professionals.
7. *Demonstrating Value*: Given that genomic-based therapies can be expensive, marketers must clearly demonstrate their value. This could involve gathering and using real-world evidence to show the effectiveness of these therapies in real-world settings.

In summary, the rise of genomics is transforming pharmaceutical marketing. It presents opportunities for more personalized and effective treatments. It also brings challenges that marketers need to navigate carefully.

Genome Mapping

Genome mapping, sometimes called genetic mapping, is a method used to identify the location of genes and other important biological sequences in the genome. Genomic mapping provides a skeleton of the genome, showing the relative positions of genes and other important landmarks. It is like a highway roadmap, indicating the cities (genes) and the distances between them.

There are two main types of genetic mapping:

A. *Physical Mapping*: This involves a direct study of the DNA molecule and gives a more detailed and accurate picture of the genome. The two common types of physical maps are *Restriction Maps* (which locate the positions of specific sequence motifs) and *Sequence Maps* (which provide the full genome sequence). Techniques such as *in-situ* hybridization, PCR (Polymerase chain Reaction), cloning, and DNA sequencing are often used in physical mapping.

B. *Linkage Mapping*: This type of mapping estimates the distance between genetic markers (specific sequence motifs with known locations) based on their tendency to be inherited together. Linkage mapping relies on the observation that the closer two markers are, the less likely they are to be separated during recombination in meiosis, which occurs during the production of eggs and sperm.

Implications of Genomic Mapping for Pharma Marketers

1. *Targeted Marketing*: Genomic mapping can lead to the discovery of disease-associated genes. This information can be used to develop targeted therapies. Pharmaceutical marketers can leverage this data to create campaigns focused on healthcare providers treating patients with these specific genetic disorders.
2. *Patient Stratification*: Genomic mapping can help identify populations likely to respond to a drug based on their genetic profiles. Marketers will need strategies to effectively reach these specific patient subgroups.
3. *Educational Campaigns*: Genomic mapping and its implications can be complex for patients and healthcare providers. Marketers may need to invest in educational campaigns to explain the benefits and risks of treatments that arise from these findings.
4. *Regulatory and Ethical Considerations*: Marketing campaigns will need to take into account regulatory and ethical considerations concerning genetic data. This includes protecting patient privacy and ensuring data is used responsibly.
5. *Value Communication*: Therapies derived from genomic data can be expensive due to the cost of research and development and the high value they bring. Marketers must effectively communicate this value to payers, providers, and patients.
6. *Collaborations*: Marketing initiatives may involve partnerships with various stakeholders, including research institutions, genetic counselors, patient advocacy groups, and regulatory bodies.

Genomic mapping provides significant opportunities for developing targeted therapies and personalized medicine. While it presents considerable potential for pharma marketers, genomic mapping also comes with challenges that need careful navigation.

Geo-Demographic Segmentation

Geo-demographic segmentation in pharmaceutical marketing divides populations into smaller subpopulations based on geographical and demographic considerations, including locational needs, age, gender, income level, education status, and lifestyle considerations. This approach uses this data to create targeted groups for marketing efforts.

Geo-demographic segmentation seeks to identify smaller groups of patients and healthcare providers with specific healthcare needs and preferences to help pharmaceutical companies develop more targeted marketing messages that resonate with these groups.

Geo-demographic segmentation offers several advantages when used for pharmaceutical marketing:

1. *Targeting*: Through the combination of geographic and demographic data, companies can better target smaller patient and healthcare provider groups with specific healthcare needs and preferences, creating more tailored marketing messages and campaigns that resonate with these groups.
2. *Increased Engagement*: Targeted messages can better engage patients and healthcare providers, increasing awareness, interest, and action taken against a disease or condition.
3. *Higher ROI*: Marketing campaigns designed specifically for pharmaceutical companies produce greater returns on their investment (ROI).
4. *Better Patient Outcomes*: Pharmaceutical companies can achieve improved patient outcomes and better overall health results by developing targeted marketing campaigns addressing patients' healthcare needs and preferences. By developing customer-centric campaigns, pharmaceutical companies can facilitate improved health outcomes and improve patient satisfaction levels.

Geo-demographic segmentation is an invaluable strategy in pharmaceutical marketing that allows pharmaceutical companies to identify smaller groups with specific healthcare needs and preferences more easily, thus engaging these segments through targeted messages and campaigns and improving patient outcomes for greater returns on investments.

Geo-fencing

Geo-fencing is a location-based marketing technique that involves setting up a virtual fence around a specific geographic area, such as a city or a store, using GPS (Global Positioning System) or RFID (Radio Frequency Identification) technology. When, a mobile device enters or exists in the defined area, it triggers a specific action or notification, such as a targeted advertisement or promotional offer.

In pharmaceutical marketing, geo-fencing can target specific audiences within a particular geographic location, such as patients or healthcare professionals attending a medical conference or visiting a hospital.

As a result, pharmaceutical companies can use geo-fencing to deliver targeted messages and promotional offers to these audiences, increasing the effectiveness of their marketing campaigns.

Here are some examples of how geo-fencing can be used in pharma marketing:

1. *Conference Targeting*: Pharmaceutical companies can use geo-fencing to target attendees of medical conferences with promotional offers or information about their products. This allows companies to connect with healthcare professionals interested in the latest developments in their field and are more likely to be receptive to marketing messages.
2. *Hospital Targeting*: Pharmaceutical companies can use geo-fencing to target patients or healthcare professionals visiting a hospital or medical facility. This can be particularly effective for promoting products or services relevant to patients' healthcare needs in a specific location.
3. *Pharmacy Targeting*: Pharmaceutical companies can use geo-fencing to target consumers near a pharmacy or drug store, delivering promotional offers or information about their products when customers are most likely to purchase.

Geo-fencing is a powerful marketing tool that pharmaceutical companies can use to reach specific audiences within a defined geographic area. By delivering targeted messages and promotional offers to these audiences, companies can increase the effectiveness of their marketing campaigns and drive more sales of their products or services.

Geo-targeting

Geo-targeting in pharma marketing refers to targeting specific geographical locations with marketing messages and campaigns. This can involve using location-based data to target audiences in specific regions or countries or even down to specific zip codes or neighborhoods.

Geo-targeting is a valuable strategy in pharma marketing because it allows companies to tailor their messaging and advertising to specific audiences based on location, culture, and healthcare needs. By understanding the unique healthcare challenges and preferences of different geographic locations, companies can develop more targeted and effective marketing campaigns that resonate with local patients and healthcare providers.

There are several ways that pharma companies can use geo-targeting in their marketing efforts:

1. *Digital Advertising*: Geo-targeted digital advertising can be used to reach audiences in specific regions or countries. Companies can use data from social media platforms, search engines, and other online sources to target specific geographic locations with ads and other marketing messages.
2. *Content Marketing*: Developing content tailored to specific geographic locations' needs and preferences can help build engagement and increase brand awareness. This can involve developing content that speaks to local patients' and healthcare providers' unique healthcare challenges and preferences.
3. *Local Events and Sponsorships*: Participating in local events and sponsorships can help build awareness and goodwill in specific locations. Companies can sponsor events, partner with local healthcare organizations, and participate in community initiatives to build relationships and increase brand awareness.
4. *Influencer Marketing*: Partnering with local influencers and thought leaders can help build credibility and increase engagement in specific locations. Companies can reach targeted audiences and build relationships with key regional opinion leaders by working with local influencers.

Geo-targeting is a valuable strategy in pharma marketing that can help companies to tailor their messaging and campaigns to specific geographic locations. By understanding different regions' unique healthcare challenges and preferences, companies can develop more targeted and effective marketing strategies that resonate with local patients and healthcare providers.

Global Market

The global pharmaceutical market refers to producing and selling drugs and medications globally. It includes both prescription and over-the-counter drugs, as well as biologic and biosimilar products.

The pharmaceutical industry significantly contributes to global health, providing treatments and medications for various illnesses and medical conditions. The market is highly regulated and competitive, with major global players like Pfizer, Novartis, and Roche dominating the industry.

Several factors, including technological advancements, growing demand for healthcare, and increasing prevalence of chronic diseases, drive the global pharma market. In addition, economic, political, and social factors, including government policies, trade agreements, and cultural attitudes toward medication, also influence the market.

Pharmaceutical companies must navigate a complex regulatory landscape to bring their products to market globally. They must also adapt their products and marketing strategies to meet each local market's needs and preferences.

Global Marketing

Global marketing in the pharmaceutical industry involves creating marketing strategies and promotional campaigns applicable to multiple regions or countries worldwide. Global marketing aims to develop a cohesive brand image, messaging, and strategy that can be used across different markets while adapting the strategy to meet local regulations and cultural norms.

Here are some examples of global marketing strategies in the pharmaceutical industry:

1. *Consistent Branding:* Pharmaceutical companies can use consistent branding strategies across different markets to create a strong and recognizable brand identity. This includes using the same brand names, logos, and packaging designs in different regions and ensuring that marketing messages and promotional materials are consistent across different markets.
2. *Global Product Launches:* Pharmaceutical companies can launch new products simultaneously across different markets to create a buzz and generate interest. This allows companies to leverage economies of scale and create consistent messages about the product's benefits and features.
3. *Global Marketing Campaigns:* Pharmaceutical companies can create global marketing campaigns that are applicable to multiple regions or countries. This can include using the same messaging and creative elements in different markets and adapting the campaign to meet local regulations and cultural norms.
4. *Global Partnerships:* Pharmaceutical companies can form partnerships with global organizations, such as the World Health Organization or global healthcare advocacy groups, to gain access to new markets and build trust with local communities. This can also help companies to gain insights into local healthcare needs and preferences and to develop more effective marketing strategies.
5. *Global Distribution:* Pharmaceutical companies can leverage their global distribution networks to ensure their products are available in different markets worldwide. This includes working with local distributors and wholesalers to ensure their products are available in local pharmacies and healthcare facilities.

Global marketing in the pharmaceutical industry involves creating a consistent brand image and messaging strategy that can be used across different markets. They also must adapt the strategy to meet local regulations and cultural norms. This allows companies to build a strong global presence and connect with customers in different regions worldwide.

Globalization

Globalization refers to the process of increasing interconnectedness and interdependence among people, businesses, and countries around the world. This process is driven by technological advancements, transportation, and communication, which have made it easier for people and goods to move across borders.

Globalization has led to greater economic integration, as countries trade goods and services and invest in each other's economies. It has also led to greater cultural exchange, as people from different countries share ideas, values, and traditions.

Implications for Pharma Marketers

Globalization has significantly impacted the pharmaceutical industry, including its marketing practices. Here are some implications of globalization for pharma marketers:

1. *Increased Competition*: Globalization has increased competition among pharmaceutical companies globally. Pharma marketers must develop more sophisticated marketing strategies to stand out from competitors and reach new markets.
2. *Diverse Customer Base*: Globalization has also led to a more diverse customer base for pharmaceutical products with different cultural, social, and economic backgrounds. Pharma marketers must develop campaigns tailored to specific regions and target audiences.
3. *Regulatory Challenges*: Globalization also presents regulatory challenges for pharma marketers, as regulations and guidelines vary widely from country to country. This means pharma marketers must stay current on

regulatory requirements in different countries and adapt their marketing strategies accordingly.

4. *Cultural Differences*: Cultural differences can also pose challenges for pharma marketers. For example, different cultures may have different attitudes towards healthcare, medicine, and illness, which can impact the effectiveness of marketing campaigns.
5. *Technology*: Globalization has led to the proliferation of digital technologies, which has significant implications for pharma marketers. Digital technologies allow pharma marketers to reach a global audience quickly and efficiently, but they also require new skills and knowledge to develop effective digital marketing campaigns.

Globalization has significant implications for pharma marketers, requiring them to develop more sophisticated marketing strategies tailored to specific regions and target audiences. Pharma marketers must also stay up-to-date on regulatory requirements and cultural differences to succeed in the global marketplace. They must be prepared to adapt their marketing strategies to changing market conditions and embrace new technologies to reach a global audience effectively.

Glocal Market

The term *Glocal* refers to the combination of *global* and *local*. For example, in the pharmaceutical industry, a glocal market would refer to a market that is global and yet considers local factors.

The pharmaceutical industry is a global industry that produces drugs and medications that are used by people all around the world. However, different regions of the world have different healthcare systems, regulatory requirements, and cultural attitudes toward medicine. Therefore, pharmaceutical companies must consider these local factors when developing and marketing their products.

For example, a popular medication in one country may not be as effective or well-received in another due to differences in the prevalence of certain medical conditions or cultural attitudes towards medication. Pharmaceutical companies must therefore adapt their products and marketing strategies to meet each local market's specific needs and preferences.

A glocal market in pharma refers to the intersection of global and local factors that pharmaceutical companies must consider when developing and marketing their products.

Glocal Marketing

The term *glocal* is a combination of the words *global* and *local*. In pharma marketing, a glocal market refers to a marketing approach that considers global and local factors when promoting a medication or healthcare product. Pharmaceutical companies must consider various factors when promoting their products in different regions worldwide, such as local regulations, cultural norms, and healthcare systems. A glocal marketing approach balances these global and local factors to develop a targeted and effective marketing strategy that resonates with local audiences.

Here are some examples of glocal marketing strategies in the pharmaceutical industry:

1. *Localization of Content*: Pharmaceutical companies can tailor their marketing materials to local languages, customs, and regulations to ensure their messaging is relevant and accurate. This includes translating product information and promotional materials into local languages and adapting promotional strategies to meet local cultural norms.
2. *Global Branding*: Pharmaceutical companies can maintain a consistent global branding strategy while adapting their branding to local markets. This can include using consistent brand names, logos, and packaging designs while tailoring marketing messages and promotional materials to local audiences.
3. *Regional Campaigns*: Pharmaceutical companies can develop targeted marketing campaigns that are specific to certain regions, taking into account local healthcare needs, cultural norms, and regulations. This allows them to connect with local audiences in a more meaningful way.
4. *Partnerships with Local Organizations*: Pharmaceutical companies can partner with local healthcare organizations and advocacy groups to gain insights into local healthcare needs and preferences and to build trust with local communities. These partnerships can also help companies access local distribution channels and networks.

The pharmaceutical industry's glocal marketing approach considers global and local factors, allowing companies to develop effective marketing strategies that resonate with local audiences while maintaining a consistent global brand identity.

Goal

The main goal of pharma marketing is to promote pharmaceutical products to healthcare professionals and consumers ethically, transparently, and effectively. The ultimate goal is to increase product sales and revenue for the pharmaceutical company.

However, there are several other important goals that pharmaceutical companies strive to achieve through their marketing efforts. These may include:

1. *Education*: Pharma marketing can help educate healthcare professionals (HCPs) and consumers about new treatments, disease states, and health conditions. By providing accurate and reliable information, pharma marketing can help improve patient outcomes and advance medical knowledge.
2. *Brand Awareness*: Building brand awareness is an important goal of pharma marketing. By creating a strong brand identity, pharmaceutical companies can differentiate themselves from competitors and establish themselves as leaders in the field.
3. *Relationship Building*: Pharma marketing can also be used to build and maintain relationships with healthcare professionals and consumers. Pharmaceutical companies can establish themselves as trusted partners in the healthcare industry by providing valuable information and resources.
4. *Compliance*: Pharmaceutical companies must adhere to strict regulatory requirements when promoting their product. Pharma marketing must ensure compliance with these regulations, avoiding potential legal and reputational issues.

Overall, pharma marketing aims to promote pharmaceutical products in a way that is ethical, effective, and compliant with regulatory requirements. By achieving these goals, pharmaceutical companies can improve patient outcomes, increase revenue, and establish themselves as leaders in their field.

Good Distribution Practices

Good Distribution Practices (GDP) in pharma marketing are guidelines and standards that ensure pharmaceutical products' quality, safety, and efficacy throughout the distribution chain. Good Distribution Practices are designed to ensure that pharmaceutical products are stored, transported, and handled in a manner that preserves their quality and efficacy and minimizes the risk of contamination or other quality issues. Here are some key elements of Good distribution practices in the pharmaceutical industry:

1. *Personnel*: GDP requires that all personnel involved in the distribution of pharmaceutical products are trained and qualified to handle and store products properly. This includes training in handling, storage, transport, and knowledge of relevant regulations and guidelines.
2. *Facilities*: Facilities used for storing and distributing pharmaceutical products must meet specific requirements. These include adequate space and security, appropriate storage conditions, temperature and humidity control, and proper sanitation and cleaning procedures.
3. *Proper Handling and Packaging*: Products must be packaged properly to prevent contamination or damage during transportation and storage.
4. *Transportation*: GDP requires that all products are transported in a manner that ensures their safety and quality. This includes appropriate packaging, temperature control during transport, and proper labeling and documentation. Pharmaceutical products must be stored and transported under appropriate conditions to ensure their quality and efficacy are not compromised during transportation.
5. *Documentation*: GDP requires creating and maintaining detailed records of all transactions in the distribution chain. This includes product receipts, shipment records, temperature, and other environmental conditions during transport and storage.
6. *Quality Control*: GDP requires implementing a robust quality control system to ensure the safety and efficacy of pharmaceutical products. This includes regular testing and monitoring of products to ensure they meet quality standards and measures to detect and correct any issues arising during the distribution process. In addition, if any deviations or issues are observed, they should be identified and resolved quickly.
7. *Traceability and Recall*: The distribution chain must be traceable, and measures must be in place to quickly and effectively recall any products that may be defective or unsafe.

GDP is essential to ensuring the safety and efficacy of pharmaceutical products throughout the distribution chain. By implementing robust guidelines and standards for personnel, facilities, transportation, documentation, and quality control, pharma companies can ensure that their products reach patients in the best possible condition without risk of contamination or other quality issues.

Good Management Practices

Marketing practices must be carefully managed and executed in the pharmaceutical industry to ensure compliance with regulations and ethical standards. Here are some good management practices that can help ensure successful and ethical pharmaceutical marketing:

1. *Comply with Regulations*: It is essential to be familiar with and comply with all relevant regulations, such as those set by the FDA and other regulatory bodies. This includes adhering to guidelines on advertising, labeling, and promotion.
2. *Prioritize Patient Safety and Health*: Patient safety and health should be top priorities in all marketing efforts. Marketing should not be designed to encourage the inappropriate use of medications or downplay potential risks.
3. *Be Transparent*: All marketing materials and communications should be truthful, accurate, and not misleading. Any potential conflicts of interest should be disclosed to patients and healthcare providers.
4. *Stay Up-to-date*: Marketing practices and regulations are constantly changing, and staying informed and up-to-date on the latest developments is important.
5. *Focus on Education*: Pharmaceutical marketing should educate healthcare providers and patients about the benefits and risks of medications and alternative treatments and disease management options.
6. *Respect for Patient Privacy*: Patient privacy should be respected at all times, and any patient information collected through marketing efforts should be protected and used only for legitimate purposes.
7. *Engage with Healthcare Professionals*: Building relationships with healthcare professionals is important in pharmaceutical marketing. However, interactions with healthcare professionals should be based on legitimate educational needs, not incentives or gifts.
8. *Clear and Effective Communication*: Managers should communicate clearly and effectively with their teams, ensuring everyone is on the same page and understands their roles and responsibilities.
9. *Strategic Planning*: Managers should develop and implement clear and well-defined strategies that align with the organization's goals and objectives.
10. *Effective Delegation*: Managers should delegate tasks and responsibilities appropriately, empowering their team members to take ownership and contribute to the organization's success.
11. *Performance Management*: Managers should regularly monitor and evaluate the performance of their teams and provide constructive feedback to help them improve continuously.
12. *Continuous Improvement*: Managers should continually look for ways to improve processes and procedures, seeking new ideas and best practices to optimize performance.

By following these good management practices, pharmaceutical companies can ensure that their marketing efforts are effective, ethical, and compliant.

Good Manufacturing Practices (GMP)

Good Manufacturing Practices (GMP) are guidelines and standards that ensure product safety, quality, and consistency throughout manufacturing. These practices are used in various industries, including pharmaceuticals, medical devices, food, and cosmetics.

In the pharmaceutical industry, adherence to Good Manufacturing Practices is crucial to ensure the safety and efficacy of drugs. Here are some of the key principles of GMP:

1. *Quality Management System*: Pharmaceutical companies must establish and maintain a robust quality management system to ensure that products are consistently produced and controlled to meet quality standards.
2. *Personnel*: Companies must ensure that personnel are appropriately trained, qualified, and competent to perform their assigned tasks and adhere to GMP standards.
3. *Facilities and Equipment*: Companies must ensure that facilities and equipment used in manufacturing are designed, constructed, and maintained to prevent contamination and ensure product quality.
4. *Materials Management*: Pharmaceutical companies must ensure that raw materials, components, and packaging materials are properly identified, stored, and handled to prevent contamination and ensure quality.

5. *Documentation and Records*: Companies must maintain complete and accurate documentation and records of all aspects of the manufacturing process, including production, testing, and quality control.
6. *Production and Process Controls*: Pharmaceutical companies must implement and maintain appropriate production and process controls to ensure that products meet quality standards and specifications.
7. *Validation and Qualification*: Companies must validate and qualify all equipment, processes, and procedures to ensure that they can consistently produce high-quality products.

By adhering to Good Manufacturing Practices, pharmaceutical companies can ensure their product's safety, quality, and consistency, improving patient outcomes and protecting public health. In addition, GMP compliance is required by regulatory agencies such as the US FDA the European Medicines Agency (EMA). Therefore, it is a crucial component of pharmaceutical quality assurance.

Good Marketing Practices

Marketing in the pharmaceutical industry involves promoting and advertising products and services to healthcare professionals and patients. Due to the pharmaceutical industry's unique nature, specific guidelines and regulations must be followed to ensure that marketing practices are ethical and effective. Here are some good marketing practices in the pharmaceutical industry:

1. *Honesty and Transparency*: Marketers must be honest and transparent about their products and services and avoid making false and misleading claims. This will help them build long-term relationships with all stakeholders.
2. *Customer Privacy*: Marketers must respect customer privacy and comply with applicable data protection laws.
3. *Targeting and Segmentation*: Marketers should target their marketing efforts to specific customer segments and avoid discrimination or bias.
4. *Informed Consent*: Marketers must obtain informed consent from customers before collecting or using their data for marketing purposes.
5. *Comply with Regulations*: the pharmaceutical industry is heavily regulated, and it is crucial to comply with all guidelines and regulations set by regulatory bodies. This includes adhering to advertising and labeling requirements, ensuring that all marketing materials are truthful and not misleading, and disclosing all relevant information about the product or service.
6. *Build Trust with Healthcare Professionals*: Building strong relationships with healthcare professionals is essential for successful marketing in pharma. This can be done by providing accurate and relevant information, being transparent about a product's benefits and risks, and addressing any concerns they may have.
7. *Educate Patients*: Patients are becoming more involved in their healthcare decisions, and educating them about the benefits and risks of a product or service is essential. Providing clear and concise information about the product, how it works, and its potential side effects can help patients make informed decisions.
8. *Provide Value*: Providing value to healthcare professionals and patients is critical in the pharmaceutical industry. This can be achieved by offering educational resources, patient support programs, and other services that add value to the healthcare ecosystem.
9. *Use Multiple Channels*: Pharma marketing should not rely solely on one channel or platform. A multichannel approach can include digital marketing, social media, traditional advertising, and direct mail. This can help reach a broader audience and ensure the right people receive the message.
10. *Measure Results*: Measuring the effectiveness of marketing campaigns is critical in the pharmaceutical industry. This can help determine which strategies are working and which are not and adjust marketing efforts accordingly.

By following these good marketing practices in pharma, companies can effectively promote their products and services while ensuring they remain ethical, transparent, and compliant with regulations.

Goodwill

Goodwill in pharma marketing refers to the reputation and perception of a pharmaceutical company within the healthcare industry among its stakeholders, including patients, healthcare professionals, and regulatory bodies. Goodwill can be earned through various activities, including high-quality research and development, effective communication, patient-centric approaches, and corporate social responsibility initiatives.

Goodwill is an important asset for pharmaceutical companies, as it can lead to increased brand loyalty, improved patient adherence, and positive relationships with healthcare providers and regulatory bodies. In addition, a company with strong goodwill is more likely to be trusted and respected by its stakeholders, which can lead to improved business outcomes and a more sustainable business model.

To build goodwill in pharma marketing, companies must focus on several key areas:

1. *Research and Development*: Developing high-quality, effective drugs is essential for building goodwill in the pharma industry. Companies that invest in research and development, prioritize patient needs, and work to develop innovative solutions to healthcare challenges are more likely to earn the trust and respect of their stakeholders.
2. *Communication*: Effective communication is critical for building goodwill in pharma marketing. Companies must communicate clearly and transparently with patients, healthcare providers, and regulatory bodies, providing accurate information about their products, research, and development activities.
3. *Patient-centricity*: Putting patients at the center of a pharma company's business is essential for building goodwill. Companies that prioritize patient needs and work to develop solutions that meet those needs are more likely to be trusted and respected by patients and healthcare providers.
4. *Corporate Social Responsibility*: Demonstrating a commitment to social responsibility and ethical business practices is another important way to build goodwill in pharma marketing. This can involve supporting community initiatives, engaging in sustainable business practices, and prioritizing ethical behavior in all aspects of the business.

Building goodwill in the pharmaceutical industry requires a long-term commitment to research and development, effective communication, patient-centricity, and corporate social responsibility. By prioritizing these areas, pharmaceutical companies can build a strong reputation and earn their stakeholders' trust and respect, leading to improved business outcomes and a more sustainable business model.

Google

Google is a multinational technology company founded in 1998 by Larry Page and Sergey Brin while they were Ph.D. students at Stanford University. Its headquarters are located in Mountain View, California. Google is known for several products and services billions of people use worldwide.

Here are some of the key products and services offered by Google:

1. *Google Search*: Google's most well-known product is its search engine, which processes billions of search queries daily.
2. *Google Ads*: This is an online advertising platform where advertisers pay to display brief advertisements, service offerings, product listings, and video content within the Google ad network to web users.
3. *Google Maps*: A popular mapping service that offers satellite imagery, street maps, Street View perspectives, and functions such as a route planner for traveling by foot, car, bicycle, or public transportation.
4. *Gmail*: A free email service with considerable storage and robust search features.
5. *Google Drive* is a file storage and synchronization service enabling user cloud storage, file sharing, and collaborative editing.
6. *Google Docs, Sheets, and Slides*: A suite of productivity software that allows users to create, edit, and share documents, spreadsheets, and presentations.
7. *YouTube*: A video-sharing platform where users can upload, share, and view videos. Google bought YouTube in November 2006.
8. *Google Chrome*: A fast, free web browser developed by Google.
9. *Android*: A mobile operating system developed by Google and used by several smartphone and tablet manufacturers.
10. *Google Cloud*: A suite of cloud computing services that runs on the same infrastructure that Google uses internally for its end-user products, such as Google Search and YouTube.

Google's mission is to organize the world's information and make it universally accessible and useful. This mission drives the company to continually innovate and offer new services.

Google in Pharma Marketing

Like businesses in other sectors, pharmaceutical companies can utilize Google's various tools and platforms for marketing and outreach. Here are some ways Google can be used in pharma marketing:

1. *Google Search Ads*: One of the most commonly used Google services. When someone searches

for a related keyword, your ad can appear at the top of the search results. This can particularly benefit drug manufacturers targeting doctors, pharmacists, or patients seeking specific medications or treatment options.

2. *Google Display Network*: This is a network of over two million websites where you can place banner ads. These ads can target specific demographics, locations, and even behaviors, making them an effective tool for reaching the right audience.
3. *Google My Business*: This tool allows businesses to manage their online presence across Google, including Search and Maps. Pharmaceutical companies can use this tool to ensure that their contact information, website, and hours of operation are accurate and easy to find.
4. *Google Trends*: Google Trends can provide insights into the popularity of search terms over time. Pharmaceutical marketers can use this tool to identify trending health topics or medication searches and tailor their marketing efforts accordingly.
5. *Google Analytics*: This is a powerful tool for understanding who is visiting your website, what they are doing once they are there, and how they found you in the first place. This data can be used to refine your marketing strategy and optimize your website.
6. *YouTube Ads*: As a Google-owned platform, YouTube can be a potent medium for video-based advertising. Educational videos, product ads, or testimonials can be effectively utilized in the pharma industry.
7. *Google SEO*: Search Engine Optimization (SEO) is key to increasing visibility in organic (non-paid) search results on Google. By optimizing website content and structure according to Google's algorithms, pharma companies can increase their visibility to potential customers or patients.

Remember that pharma marketing is heavily regulated, so it is important to comply with all relevant laws and regulations when advertising medications or treatments. This might include providing necessary disclaimers or restrictions on the type of claims that can be made.

Implications for Pharma Marketers

The digital transformation led by companies like Google has profound implications for pharma marketers. While their primary goal remains to educate healthcare professionals and patients about their products, digital technologies have significantly influenced marketing tactics and strategies. Here are some of the key implications:

1. *Multichannel Marketing*: Google's suite of products allows pharma marketers to engage with their audience through multiple channels, such as search engine marketing, email marketing (Gmail), video marketing (YouTube), and more. This requires marketers to develop an integrated multichannel strategy to reach their audience at the right time with the right message.
2. *Data-Driven Decisions*: Google provides powerful tools for data analytics, like Google Analytics, Google Data Studio, and more. These tools provide insights into how users interact with your digital assets. Pharma marketers can use these insights to make data-driven decisions and optimize their marketing efforts.
3. *Increased transparency and Compliance*: Since all activities on Google's platforms can be tracked and audited, it increases transparency. However, it also means pharma marketers must be extra careful to comply with all rules and regulations, as non-compliance can be easily detected and penalized.
4. *Need for Search Engine Optimization (SEO)*: Google's search engine drives most internal traffic. Pharma marketers must understand and implement SEO best practices to improve their visibility in search results and reach their target audience effectively.
5. *Improved Patient Engagement*: Google's platforms allow pharma companies to engage with patients directly. For example, YouTube can be used for patient education, or Google My Business for local business listings and reputation management. This requires pharma companies to rethink their communication strategies.
6. *Increased Competition*: As Google levels the playing field by providing the same tools to everyone, pharma marketers face increased competition. A unique value proposition and effective digital marketing strategies are needed to stand out.
7. *Privacy Considerations*: Given Google's widespread use, data privacy considerations become critical. Marketers must respect user privacy and comply with all relevant regulations like GDPR (General Data Protection Regulation), CCPA (California Consumer Privacy Act), etc.
8. *Need for Skill Development*: To use Google's tools effectively, pharma marketers must develop new skills or hire digital marketing experts. This might include understanding data analytics, SEO, video marketing, etc.

Remember, healthcare marketing has specific constraints in terms of regulatory and compliance issues. All marketing efforts should align with FDA and similar authorities' guidelines concerning direct-to-consumer advertising and promotion of prescription drugs.

Google's Foray into Healthcare and Implications for Pharma

Google has been making significant inroads into the healthcare and pharma industry. It uses its vast resources and technological expertise to create products and services that could revolutionize healthcare delivery, diagnosis, research, and even drug discovery. Here are some ways Google is entering the healthcare space:

1. *Google Health*: Launched in 2018, Google Health is a division within Google that aims to improve the quality, access, and understandability of health information. It uses technologies like artificial intelligence and machine learning to help manage diseases, aid research, and more.
2. *Google Cloud for Healthcare*: Google offers solutions designed specifically for the healthcare industry. These HIPAA-compliant solutions can help in everything from data storage to analysis, facilitating secure and efficient patient data management.
3. *Verily Life Sciences*: This Alphabet (the parent company of Google) subsidiary is focused on using technology to better understand health and manage disease. It works on several fronts, including studying specific diseases, developing hardware and software solutions for health monitoring, and more.
4. *DeepMind Technologies*: Another Alphabet subsidiary, DeepMind, has been making breakthroughs in using AI for health care. They developed an AI system that can predict the 3D shapes of proteins, a feat that could greatly aid drug discovery.
5. *Google Fit*: An app designed to help users track their fitness and health goals.
6. *Project Nightingale*: A collaboration with Ascension, one of the largest healthcare systems in the US, Project Nightingale involves transferring patient data to Google's cloud services to help healthcare providers better care.

Implications for Pharma Marketers

1. *Collaboration Opportunities*: The pharma industry can collaborate with Google and its subsidiaries on various projects, from clinical trials to drug discovery. For example, Verily has partnered with several pharma companies for research and clinical trials, providing innovative marketing opportunities.
2. *Data and Analytics*: The vast amount of health data that Google can collect and analyze could provide pharma marketers with valuable insights into patient behavior, treatment efficacy, and more.
3. *AI and Machine Learning*: Google's advancements in AI could lead to more efficient drug discovery, better diagnosis, and personalized medicine, opening new avenues for marketing.
4. *New Channels for Patient Engagement*: Platforms like Google Fit provide new communication channels for patients and healthcare providers. For example, Novo Nordisk partnered with Google Fit to launch a *Challenge* to help people with diabetes manage their condition.
5. *Cloud Solutions*: Google's cloud solutions for health care can be a boon for pharma marketers, providing efficient ways to manage and analyze data and facilitating personalized marketing.
6. *Evolving Regulations*: As Google forays into healthcare, it could influence regulations around health data, privacy, and more. Pharma marketers need to keep up with these evolving regulations to ensure compliance.

As always, all marketing activities must comply with the regulations the FDA and other authorities set forth. Google's entry into health care can provide exciting opportunities for pharma marketers, but it also brings challenges in terms of data privacy, security, and ethical considerations.

Go-to-Market Strategy

A Go-to-Market (GTM) strategy outlines how a company will bring a new product or service to the market and achieve a competitive advantage.

A Go-to-Market strategy in the pharmaceutical industry is essential for launching and commercializing new drugs, medical devices, or other healthcare products. Here are some key elements of a GTM strategy in Pharma:

1. *Conduct Market Research*: Before launching a new drug, pharmaceutical companies must conduct thorough market research to identify patient needs, treatment gaps, and potential competitors. The research helps to understand its target audience, the market size, and the market potential.

2. *Seek Regulatory Approvals*: Pharmaceutical companies must obtain regulatory approvals from government agencies like the FDA in the US, EMA in EU member States, or other regulatory bodies in their respective countries before launching a new drug. Obtaining these approvals requires meeting certain safety and efficacy standards.
3. *Define the Value Proposition*: Once the drug is approved, the company needs to define the product's value proposition. This includes understanding the clinical benefits of the drug, the patient population it is intended for, and the pricing strategy.
4. *Develop Sales Channels*: Pharmaceutical companies must develop a sales strategy with the right channels to reach their target audience. This may include direct-to-consumer marketing, healthcare providers, and hospitals.
5. *Build Relationships with Healthcare Providers*: Building strong relationships with healthcare providers is crucial for the success of a GTM strategy in pharma. This involves educating physicians and other healthcare providers about the drug, its clinical benefits, and its safety profile.
6. *Invest in Marketing*: To create awareness about the new drug, pharmaceutical companies must invest in marketing. This includes advertising, public relations, and other promotional activities.
7. *Develop a Pricing Strategy*: Set a price that reflects the value you deliver to your target audience and their willingness to pay.
8. *Create a Marketing Plan*: Determine how you will create awareness and generate prescription demand for your product. What channels will you use other than in-person visits by the sales force? Will you use social media, email marketing, and other digital advertising channels?
9. *Train Your Sales and Customer Support Teams*: Ensure your sales and customer support teams know your product or service thoroughly and are equipped to communicate effectively and deliver superior customer service.
10. *Measure Success*: Pharmaceutical companies need to measure the success of their GTM strategy by tracking sales data, patient and HCP feedback, and other metrics. This helps them refine their approach and improve results over time.

A well-executed GTM strategy in pharma is critical for successfully launching and commercializing new drugs, medical devices, and other healthcare products.

Go-to-Patient Strategy

A Go-to-Patient(GTP) strategy in Pharma involves a patient-centered approach to commercializing and promoting pharmaceutical products. This approach recognizes that patients are the ultimate users of drugs and other medical products and aims to engage them directly.

GTP Strategy: Key Elements

Here are some key elements of a GTP strategy in Pharma:

1. *Patient Research*: A GTP strategy starts with patient research to understand their needs, preferences, and experiences with the treated disease or condition. This research helps to develop a patient-centric value proposition.
2. *Patient Education*: A GTP strategy involves educating patients and caregivers about the disease or condition being treated, the benefits of the drug, and how it works. This education can be delivered through various channels, including patient support programs, social media, and websites.
3. *Support Programs*: GTP strategies involve developing patient support programs beyond traditional prescription refill reminders. These programs may include patient assistance programs, nurse support hotlines, and online communities.
4. *Multichannel Marketing*: GTP strategies use a multichannel approach to marketing, including digital and social media and traditional channels such as print and TV. This approach helps to reach patients where they are and provides them with relevant and timely information.
5. *Patient Advocacy*: GTP strategies involve partnering with patient advocacy organizations to raise awareness about the disease or condition and support patients and caregivers. These partnerships can help build trust and credibility with patients and provide valuable feedback on patient needs and preferences.
6. *Measuring Success*: GTP strategies include metrics to measure the program's success, such as patient engagement, adherence rates, and patient satisfaction. This feedback helps to refine the program and improve outcomes for patients.

A Go-to-Patient (GTP) strategy in pharma can help build strong relationships with patients and caregivers, improve adherence rates, and differentiate a drug from competitors. Pharmaceutical companies can improve patient outcomes and drive commercial success by focusing on patient needs and preferences.

Go-to-Patient Strategy Measurement

A Go-to-Patient strategy can be measured using various metrics that reflect its effectiveness and impact on patient engagement, satisfaction, and outcomes. Here are some possible ways to measure a Go-to-Patient strategy:

1. *Patient Engagement*: The level of patient engagement is a crucial factor in measuring the success of a Go-to-Patient strategy. This can be measured by the number of patients participating in the program, the frequency of their interactions, and their activities. This can be measured through surveys and patient feedback. For example, the healthcare organization can track the number of patients who enroll in the program, the frequency of their interactions with care team members, and the types of activities, such as telehealth visits, educational resources, and remote monitoring.
2. *Patient Satisfaction*: Another important metric is patient satisfaction. This can be measured through patient feedback surveys and ratings of their experiences with the Go-to-Patient strategy. For example, patients can be asked about the quality of communication with care team members, the ease of accessing healthcare services, and their overall satisfaction with the program.
3. *Patient Outcomes*: The impact of the Go-to-Patient strategy on patient outcomes can also be measured, such as the number of hospitalizations, readmissions, and emergency department visits. Additionally, patient outcomes can be tracked over time to measure improvements in health and wellness. For example, the organization can track the number of program participants' hospitalizations, readmissions, emergency department visits, and overall healthcare utilization rates.
4. *Cost Savings*: A Go-to-Patient strategy regarding cost savings for the healthcare organization can also be evaluated. This can include reduced costs associated with hospitalizations, fewer emergency department visits, and overall lower healthcare utilization rates. For example, the organization can track the reduction in costs associated with hospitalizations, emergency department visits, and overall healthcare utilization rates among program participants.
5. *Staff Satisfaction*: Staff satisfaction in implementing the Go-to-Patient strategy can also be evaluated through staff feedback surveys and by asking staff members to rate their experiences with the program. For example, staff members can be asked about the level of support they receive from the organization, the quality of communication with patients, and their overall satisfaction with the program.

In summary, a Go-to-Patient strategy can be measured by assessing patient engagement, satisfaction, outcomes, cost savings, and staff satisfaction. By evaluating these metrics, healthcare organizations can better understand the impact of their Go-to-Patient strategy and make informed decisions on optimizing it.

Global Positioning System (GPS)

GPS stands for Global Positioning System. It is a satellite-based navigation system that provides location and time information anywhere on or near the Earth's surface. The GPS consists of a network of orbiting satellites, ground control stations, and GPS receivers.

GPS works by measuring the time it takes for signals to travel between the GPS satellites and the receiver on the ground. The receiver calculates its distance from at least four GPS satellites to determine its location in three-dimensional space.

GPS is widely used in various applications, including navigation for vehicles, and ships, mapping and surveying, and tracking of objectives or people. In addition, it has become an essential technology for many industries and is widely used in personal devices such as smartphones, smartwatches, and fitness trackers.

GPS in Pharma Marketing

GPS technology can be used in pharmaceutical marketing in several ways. Consider the following, for example:

1. *Targeted Marketing*: GPS can track the location of healthcare providers and pharmacies, allowing pharmaceutical companies to target their marketing efforts more effectively. For example, companies can use GPS data to identify the locations of high-prescribing physicians and focus their marketing efforts on those areas. For

example, a pharmaceutical company can use GPS data to identify healthcare professionals (HCPs) who have prescribed a particular medication in the past and send targeted marketing messages to those HCPs when they are in the vicinity of a pharmacy.

2. *Sales Force Effectiveness*: GPS can help pharmaceutical companies optimize their sales force by providing real-time data on their sales representative's location, sales activity, and customer interactions. This data can be used to measure sales strategies' effectiveness and identify improvement areas. For example, a pharmaceutical company can track the location of its sales representatives and use that data to optimize their routes and schedules to ensure maximum coverage of healthcare providers.
3. *Patient Adherence*: GPS can also track patients' medication adherence. For example, some medication adherence apps use GPS technology to remind patients to take their medication when they are near their pharmacy or healthcare provider.
4. *Clinical Trial Recruitment*: GPS technology can also help recruit patients for clinical trials. For example, a pharmaceutical company can use GPS data to identify potential study participants based on their location and demographics and target them with recruitment messages.

GPS technology can provide valuable insights and data to pharma marketers, helping them to improve their marketing strategies and increase sales. However, it is important to note that the use of GPS data must comply with privacy laws and regulations to protect the privacy of patients and healthcare providers.

Green Chemistry

Green chemistry is the design and development of chemical processes and products that minimize the use and generation of hazardous substances. It is a field of chemistry focused on sustainability and reducing the impact of chemical processes on the environment.

There is a growing interest in incorporating green chemistry principles into the pharmaceutical industry, as it can potentially reduce the environmental impact of drug manufacturing and improve sustainability. Green chemistry can help pharmaceutical companies reduce the waste generated during drug production, lower energy consumption, and minimize the use of hazardous chemicals.

In pharmaceutical marketing, there is also an increasing focus on sustainability and social responsibility. In addition, many consumers are becoming more environmentally conscious and interested in supporting companies prioritizing sustainability. Therefore, pharmaceutical companies that incorporate green chemistry principles into their manufacturing processes may be able to use this as a selling point in their marketing efforts.

Green Chemistry Initiatives in Pharma

Here are some examples of green chemistry initiatives in the pharmaceutical industry and how they can be incorporated into pharma marketing:

1. *Solvent Substitution*: One way to reduce the environmental impact of drug manufacturing is by replacing hazardous solvents with safer alternatives. For example, Pfizer has developed a solvent-free process for producing a key intermediate in manufacturing a drug to treat HIV. This has resulted in a significant reduction in waste and energy consumption. Pfizer has highlighted this initiative in their sustainability report and website, showcasing their commitment to reducing their environmental footprint.
2. *Renewable Energy*: Another way to reduce the environmental impact of drug manufacturing is by using renewable energy sources. For example, Novo Nordisk's production facility in North Carolina uses a combination of solar panels and a biogas digester to generate electricity. This has resulted in a 35 percent reduction in greenhouse gas emissions compared to traditional fossil fuel-based energy sources. Novo Nordisk highlighted this initiative in its sustainability report and website, demonstrating its commitment to using sustainable energy sources.
3. *Lifecycle Assessment*: Lifecycle assessment (LCA) is a tool that can be used to assess the environmental impact of a product or process throughout its entire lifecycle. This can help pharmaceutical companies identify areas to reduce their environmental impact. For example, GlaxoSmithKline (GSK) used LCA to assess the environmental impact of their asthma inhaler, Ventolin. Based on the assessment results, they made changes to the design of the inhaler, resulting in a 25 percent reduction in its carbon footprint. GSK has highlighted this initiative in their sustainability report and on their website, showing how they are using LCA to reduce the environmental impact of their products.

Pharmaceutical marketers can highlight these green chemistry initiatives in sustainability reports, company websites, and marketing materials. For example, a pharmaceutical company could promote using renewable energy sources to reduce waste and greenhouse gas emissions as part of its marketing efforts. However, ensuring that credible data and transparent reporting back up any claims is important.

Green Marketing

Green marketing in the pharmaceutical industry refers to promoting medications or healthcare products and services that positively impact the environment or using environmentally sustainable practices in manufacturing and distributing these products. Green marketing in the pharmaceutical industry is a relatively new concept, but it is gaining popularity as consumers become more environmentally conscious and demand more sustainable products and services. There are several ways that pharmaceutical companies can engage in green marketing:

1. *Developing Environmentally Sustainable Products*: Pharmaceutical companies can develop medications and healthcare products made from environmentally sustainable materials that are biodegradable or recyclable.
2. *Using Environmentally Sustainable Manufacturing Processes*: Companies can use environmentally sustainable manufacturing processes to minimize waste, reduce energy consumption, and minimize their environmental footprint.
3. *Supporting Environmental Initiatives*: Pharmaceutical companies can support environmental initiatives, such as reforestation, recycling, or other green projects, to show their commitment to sustainability.
4. *Providing Education and Awareness*: Companies can educate patients and healthcare providers on properly disposing of medications, reducing waste, and adopting sustainable practices.
5. *Obtaining Third-party Certifications*: Companies can obtain third-party certifications, such as ISO 14001 or *Cradle to Cradle*, to demonstrate their commitment to sustainability and environmental practices.

Green marketing can benefit pharmaceutical companies, including increased consumer trust and loyalty, improved brand image, and a competitive advantage in the market. However, companies must ensure that their green marketing claims are accurate, supported by evidence, and not misleading or exaggerated. In addition, consumers are becoming increasingly savvy about greenwashing and will be turned off by any unsubstantiated environmental claims made by companies.

Greenwashing

Greenwashing is a deceptive practice where a company or organization exaggerates or falsely claims to be environmentally friendly to attract environmentally conscious consumers. It's a way for companies to present themselves as more sustainable or environmentally responsible than they actually are.

In the pharmaceutical industry, greenwashing could involve making misleading claims about the environmental impact of manufacturing processes, packaging, or a product's overall sustainability. For example, a pharmaceutical company might highlight a small environmentally friendly initiative while downplaying their operations' larger, less eco-friendly aspects.

The relevance of greenwashing in pharma lies in the growing demand for sustainable and ethical products. Consumers are increasingly concerned about their products' environmental and social impact, including pharmaceuticals. Greenwashing in this industry could lead consumers to choose based on false or exaggerated information, potentially undermining their efforts to support genuinely sustainable practices.

The implications of greenwashing in pharma are significant because it erodes trust. If consumers believe they support environmentally responsible companies and later discover they were misled, it can lead to losing trust in the industry. Additionally, it may divert attention and resources away from companies genuinely working towards sustainable practices.

In summary, greenwashing in the pharmaceutical industry can have serious consequences, both in terms of consumer trust and the overall effort to promote sustainable and ethical practices. Companies need to be transparent and accountable in their claims about environmental responsibility.

Gresham's Law

Gresham's law is a well-known economic principle that states that bad money drives out good. In 1858, the British economist Henry Dunning Macleod named the tendency for bad money to drive good money out of circulation after Sir Thomas Gresham, the financial agent of Queen Elizabeth I.

In pharmaceutical marketing, this principle can apply to the idea that misleading or dishonest marketing tactics can push out truthful and ethical marketing practices.

In the pharmaceutical industry, companies often compete to promote their products to healthcare providers and consumers. However, when companies engage in unethical and misleading marketing practices, it can undermine the industry's credibility and lead to a situation where honest companies struggle to gain a foothold.

For example, a pharmaceutical company makes false or exaggerated claims about the safety or effectiveness of its product. In that case, this may lead healthcare providers and patients to mistrust the entire industry. In addition, this could make it more difficult for other companies with genuinely effective products to gain the market's trust.

Gresham's Law and Pharma Marketing

Here are some examples of how Gresham's law can apply to pharmaceutical marketing:

1. *Over-promising on Product Benefits*: If a pharmaceutical company promotes its product by making unrealistic claims about its benefits or downplaying potential risks or side effects, it can create a situation where consumers lose trust in the company and the industry.
2. *Aggressive Sales Tactics*: If a pharmaceutical sales representative uses aggressive tactics, such as pressuring healthcare providers to prescribe their product or providing misleading information, it can damage the company's and the industry's reputation.
3. *Off-Label Marketing*: If a pharmaceutical company promotes its product for uses that regulatory agencies did not approve, it can create a situation where consumers are misled. Healthcare providers lose trust in the company and the industry.
4. *Paying Kickbacks to Healthcare Providers*: If a pharmaceutical company pays kickbacks to healthcare providers to prescribe their products, it can create a situation where patients receive unnecessary or ineffective treatments, and the industry suffers from a loss of trust.

These examples demonstrate how unethical or dishonest marketing practices can harm the pharmaceutical industry's reputation and create a situation where bad practices drive out good.

Applying Gresham's law to pharma marketing suggests that the industry benefits when companies prioritize honesty and transparency in their marketing efforts. By doing so, they can build trust with healthcare providers and consumers, leading to better health outcomes for patients and increased profits for the industry.

Group Purchasing Organization (GPO)

A Group Purchasing Organization (GPO) is an entity that helps various healthcare providers, such as hospitals, clinics, nursing homes, and physicians' offices, to collectively purchase medical supplies, equipment, pharmaceuticals, and other goods and services. GPOs are designed to leverage the collective purchasing power of their member organizations to negotiate better prices, terms, and conditions with suppliers and manufacturers. Here are key points about Group Purchasing Organizations:

1. *Collective Purchasing Power*: GPOs aggregate the purchasing needs of multiple healthcare providers, creating a larger and more powerful buying group. This increased volume of purchases allows GPOs to negotiate favorable deals with suppliers, often securing lower prices and better terms than individual providers could on their own.
2. *Membership-Based*: GPOs typically have a membership model, and healthcare facilities and providers become members to access the benefits of the group purchasing. These members can range from large hospitals to small physician practices.
3. *Diverse Categories*: GPOs cover various products and service categories, including medical and surgical suppliers, pharmaceuticals, medical devices, equipment, office supplies, facility maintenance, and more.
4. *Cost Savings*: The primary benefit of GPO membership is cost savings. By negotiating better prices, GPOs help healthcare providers reduce operational costs, lowering patients' healthcare costs.
5. *Efficiency and Convenience*: GPOs streamline procurement processes for healthcare providers. They offer a centralized platform for ordering supplies, managing contracts, and tracking spending, making purchasing more efficient and cost-effective.
6. *Quality Assurance*: Many GPOs work to ensure that the products and services they provide meet quality and safety standards. This can be particularly important in healthcare, where patient safety is paramount.

7. *Vendor Relationships*: GPOs maintain relationships with a network of approved suppliers and manufacturers. This allows healthcare providers to access a broad range of products and services from trusted sources.
8. *Compliance and Regulations*: GPOs are subject to regulations and compliance standards to ensure transparency, fair business practices, and adherence to legal requirements.
9. *Competitive Advantage*: GPOs enable smaller and medium-sized healthcare providers to compete more effectively with larger institutions by providing access to cost-effective procurement solutions.
10. *Diverse GPO Models*: There are various types of GPOs, including national, regional, and specialty GPOs, each focusing on specific markets or procurement categories.
11. *Revenue Model*: GPOs typically generate revenue by charging fees to suppliers for access to their member network rather than charging members for their services.

GPOs have become a significant part of the healthcare supply chain, helping providers reduce costs, improve supply chain efficiency, and focus on delivering high-quality patient care. They are critical in helping healthcare facilities manage their budgets and ensure access to essential medical supplies and services.

Implications for Pharma Marketers

Group Purchasing Organizations (GPOs) have implications for pharma marketers, particularly regarding the sale and distribution of pharmaceutical products to healthcare providers. Here are some of the implications for pharma marketers in their interactions with GPOs:

1. *Negotiations with GPOs*: Pharmaceutical companies often negotiate pricing, contracts, and terms with GPOs. Pharma marketers must work closely with their sales and account management teams to establish favorable agreements with GPOs to ensure their products are included in GPO contracts.
2. *Formulary Placement*: GPOs often establish formularies or preferred product lists. Pharma marketers need to engage with GPOs to secure a place on these formularies, which can significantly impact thc sales and distribution of their products.
3. *Competitive Bidding*: GPOs may conduct competitive bidding processes to include pharmaceutical products in their contracts. Pharma marketers need to participate in these processes and make compelling cases for the inclusion of their products.
4. *Price Negotiation*: GPOs negotiate prices with pharmaceutical companies, and pharma marketers may need to be involved. Pricing strategy and flexibility are key considerations in these discussions.
5. *Volume Discounts*: GPO contracts often include volume-based discounts. Pharma marketers should know these terms and their impact on pricing and profitability.
6. *Contract Compliance*: Ensuring compliance with GPO contracts is essential. Pharma marketers must work with their legal and compliance teams to meet contract requirements and obligations.
7. *Data Reporting*: GPO contracts may require pharmaceutical companies to provide product utilization and sales data. Pharma marketers need to ensure accurate and timely reporting to GPOs.
8. *Relationship Building*: Building and maintaining relationships with GPS representatives is crucial. Effective communication and collaboration with GPOs can influence the inclusion and promotion of pharmaceutical products.
9. *Formulary Positioning*: Achieving a favorable position on GPO formularies is important for pharma marketers. This can influence healthcare provider's prescribing decisions and product utilization.
10. *Market Access Strategies*: Pharma marketers must develop market access strategies that consider the role of GPOs in their distribution and purchasing of pharmaceutical products.
11. *Educational Initiatives*: Providing education and resources to healthcare providers within GPO networks can help raise awareness about pharmaceutical products' benefits and appropriate use.
12. *Post-Market Monitoring*: After GPO contracts are established, ongoing monitoring of product performance, utilization, and compliance with contract terms is crucial.
13. *Collaboration with Sales Teams*: Pharma marketers must collaborate closely with their sales and account management teams to ensure that GPO contracts and agreements are effectively communicated and implemented in the field.

Pharmaceutical companies must navigate the complex landscape of GPO interactions to ensure their products are accessible to healthcare providers and patients. Effective engagement with GPOs is essential for successful market access and distribution of pharmaceutical products.

Guerilla Marketing

Guerilla marketing is an advertising strategy that uses unconventional or unexpected tactics to promote a product or service. For example, guerilla marketing in the pharmaceutical industry can create buzz and generate interest in a medication or healthcare product.

Here are some examples of guerilla marketing tactics that pharmaceutical companies may use:

1. *Pop-up Events*: Pharmaceutical companies may organize events at public spaces, such as parks or shopping centers, to promote a new medication or healthcare product. These events can include interactive displays, free samples, and educational materials.
2. *Street Teams*: Street teams are groups of people who promote a product or service in public spaces. Pharmaceutical companies may hire street teams to distribute flyers, hand out samples, or engage with people to promote their medications or healthcare products.
3. *Stunts*: Pharmaceutical companies may organize attention-grabbing stunts, such as flash mobs or public demonstrations, to create buzz and generate interest in their products.
4. *Social Media Campaigns*: Pharmaceutical companies may use social media platforms like Twitter or Instagram to launch guerilla marketing campaigns involving creative or unexpected content to capture attention or generate engagement.
5. *Mobile Marketing*: Pharmaceutical companies may use mobile marketing strategies, such as branded vehicles or trucks, to promote their products or services in public spaces.

It's important to note that guerilla marketing tactics must comply with the regulations set by the pharmaceutical industry and government bodies, such as the FDA. Likewise, pharmaceutical companies must ensure that their marketing strategies are truthful, not misleading, and do not make false claims about their medications or healthcare products.

Guerilla marketing can be an effective way for pharmaceutical companies to create buzz and generate interest in their products. Still, it should be done responsibly and in compliance with industry regulations.

Guerilla Marketing in Pharma: Some Examples

1. *Pfizer's 'Chantix Challenge'*: Pfizer used a guerilla marketing campaign to promote its smoking cessation medication, Chantix. The campaign involved placing a *Chantix Challenge* kiosk in public spaces, such as malls, where smokers could take a quiz to see if they were ready to quit smoking. The kiosk also offered free samples of the medication and encouraged smokers to talk to their doctor about Chantix.
2. *Merck's 'Sleep Squad'*: Merck used a guerilla marketing campaign to promote its insomnia medication, Belsomra. The campaign involved a team of Sleep Squad members dressed in pajamas and carrying pillows, who visited public spaces such as parks and shopping centers to distribute samples of Belsomra and promote the medication's benefits for sleep.
3. *Roche's 'Cancer Arcade'*: Roche created a guerilla marketing campaign to raise awareness about cancer and promote its cancer medications. The campaign involved setting up a pop-up arcade in a public space where visitors could play games and learn about different types of cancer and cancer treatments.
4. *GlaxoSmithKline's 'Migraine Experience'*: GlaxoSmithKline used a guerilla marketing campaign to promote its migraine medication, Treximet. The campaign involved setting up a *Migraine Experience* booth at public events, where visitors could experience simulated migraines and learn about the benefits of Treximet.
5. *Novartis 'Heart to Heart*: Novartis used a guerilla marketing campaign to promote its heart failure medication, Entresto. The campaign involved setting up a booth at public events where visitors could learn about the benefits of Entresto and share their own experiences with heart failure.

These examples demonstrate how pharmaceutical companies have used guerilla marketing tactics to create buzz and generate interest in their medications and healthcare products. However, pharma marketers must ensure that their campaigns comply with industry regulations and that their marketing messages are truthful and not misleading.

H

1. H2H Marketing
2. Half-Life
3. Halo Effect
4. Hard Sell
5. Harvesting
6. HIPAA
7. Hashtag
8. Hatch-Waxman Act
9. Hawthorne Effect
10. Headline
11. Health Apps
12. Health Maintenance Organization (HMO)
13. Healthcare Professional (HCP)
14. Heat Maps
15. Health Economics and Outcomes Research (HEOR)
16. Hierarchy of Effects
17. Hierarchy of Needs
18. High Involvement Model
19. High Pressure Selling
20. Hologram
21. Hindsight
22. Holistic Health
23. HootSuite
24. Horizontal Diversification
25. Horizontal Integration
26. Horizontal Marketing System
27. HTML
28. Hybrid Model

H2H Marketing

H2H (Human-to-Human) marketing is a marketing approach that emphasizes the importance of building genuine, authentic relationships between businesses and their customers. This approach recognizes that people buy from people, not companies and that the key to successful marketing is creating meaningful connections with customers.

H2H marketing focuses on understanding individual customers' needs, wants, and motivations and tailoring marketing messages and strategies to meet those needs. The goal of H2H marketing is to build long-term, loyal customer relationships based on mutual trust, respect, and empathy. By treating customers as people rather than just consumers, businesses can create a more authentic and engaging brand experience that resonates with customers on a deeper level.

Several thought leaders and marketing experts have popularized the concept of H2H marketing, but no one individual can be credited with its invention or creation. However, the idea of humanizing marketing has been around for a long time, and H2H marketing can be seen as an evolution of that idea, emphasizing the importance of building genuine, one-to-one relationships with customers. Some of the leading proponents of H2H marketing include Bryan Kramer, Mark Schaefer, and Seth Godin.

More recently, in 2021, Philip Kotler, Waldemar Pfoertsch, and Uwe Sponholz wrote a book H2H Marketing: *The Genesis of Human-to-Human Marketing*, arguing that modern marketing has become too focused on data and technology and has lost sight of the human element that is at the heart of successful marketing. They offer a framework for H2H marketing that emphasizes five key principles: empathy, honesty, transparency, authenticity, and collaboration. In addition, the book provides practical guidance on implementing H2H marketing strategies in different industries and contexts.

H2H marketing presents an important contribution to the ongoing conversation about how to create more effective and ethical marketing practices that prioritize genuine human connections.

H2H Marketing in Pharma

H2H Marketing in pharma refers to developing personalized relationships between a pharmaceutical company, healthcare professionals (HCPs), and patients. H2H marketing aims to build trust, establish credibility, and provide value beyond the product. This approach focuses on creating a more human connection with HCPs and patients rather than relying solely on traditional marketing tactics.

H2H marketing is particularly relevant in the healthcare industry, where the human element is critical to the success of marketing efforts. In health care, the focus is on providing high-quality healthcare and improving patient outcomes, and H2H marketing can help pharmaceutical companies build trust and rapport with patients and healthcare providers.

H2H marketing involves using strategies that focus on the human element of marketing, such as:

1. *Building Relationships*: H2H marketing emphasizes building customer relationships rather than just promoting products and services. This involves understanding customers' needs, wants, and preferences and tailoring marketing efforts to meet those needs.
2. *Creating Emotional Connections*: H2H marketing recognizes the importance of creating emotional connections with customers through storytelling and empathy. By creating an emotional connection, marketers can build customer trust and loyalty.
3. *Providing Value*: H2H marketing focuses on providing value to customers through educational content, personalized recommendations, and exceptional customer service.
4. *Listening to Feedback*: H2H marketing involves listening to customer feedback and using it to improve products, services, and marketing efforts.

H2H marketing is about recognizing that marketing is a human-to-human interaction and that the success of marketing efforts depends on building genuine connections and relationships with customers.

H2H Marketing in Pharma: Some Examples

Here are some examples of H2H marketing strategies in pharma:

1. *Thought Leadership Content*: Developing high-quality content that showcases the company's expertise and thought leadership could help establish credibility and build trust with HCPs. This could include white papers, case studies, or blog posts that provide insights into disease management, treatment options, or patient care.
2. *Educational Programs*: Offering educational programs that help HCPs stay up-to-date with the latest medical advancements and best practices can effectively establish the company as a valuable partner in patient care. These programs could include webinars, workshops, or symposiums.
3. *Using Storytelling*: A hospital that shares patient stories on its website or social media channels

can create an emotional connection with its audience. The hospital can build trust and encourage others to seek care by sharing stories of patients who have had positive outcomes. Pharma companies, too, can follow the same strategy in their marketing efforts.

4. *Patient Support Programs*: Beyond the product, patient support programs can help build trust and loyalty. These programs could include disease management resources, personalized support from a nurse or counselor, or access to financial assistance programs.
5. *Personalized Communications*: Using targeted and personalized communications can help establish a more human connection with HCPs and patients. This could include personalized email campaigns or targeted direct mail pieces that provide relevant and timely information.
6. *Advocacy and Partnership*: Partnering with patient advocacy groups and professional associations can help establish the company as a trusted partner in the healthcare community. This could include sponsoring events or supporting advocacy initiatives that align with the company's values and mission.
7. *Exceptional Customer Service*: Pharmaceutical companies that go above and beyond to provide exceptional customer service can create a positive experience for patients and healthcare professionals and build loyalty.

H2H Marketing in pharma emphasizes the importance of building meaningful relationships with healthcare professionals and patients. Pharmaceutical companies can establish trust and credibility by focusing on providing value beyond the product, leading to long-term partnerships and improved patient outcomes.

Half-Life

In pharmacology, *Half-Life* refers to the amount of time it takes for the concentration of a drug in the bloodstream to decrease by half. In mathematical terms, after one half-life, 50% of the original amount of the drug remains in the body. After two half-lives, 25% remains, and so on.

The half-life of a drug has several implications:

1. *Dosing Frequency*: Drugs with short half-lives might need to be administered more frequently to maintain therapeutic levels in the body, whereas drugs with longer half-lives can be administered less frequently.
2. *Accumulation in the Body*: For drugs taken repeatedly (for example, daily), their levels can accumulate, especially if the dosing interval is shorter than the drug's half-life. This is crucial in ensuring the drug maintains its therapeutic effect without reaching the toxic level.
3. *Drug Withdrawal*: Drugs with shorter half-lives tend to be eliminated from the body more rapidly. This can lead to withdrawal symptoms for certain medications if they are not tapered off appropriately.
4. *Drug Interactions*: Knowing the half-life of drugs can help predict and prevent potential drug-drug interactions. Some drugs can alter the metabolism of others, which could impact their half-life and, consequently, their efficacy and safety.

Implications for Pharma Marketers

1. *Positioning and Branding*: A drug's half-life can be a unique selling proposition. For instance, if Drug A needs to be taken once a day and Drug B (which treats the same condition) needs to be taken three times a day, marketers might promote Drug A's convenience due to its longer half-life.
2. *Patient Adherence*: Drugs with longer half-lives and less frequent dosing might boast better patient adherence since they are more convenient for patients. This can be a selling point for physicians who want to ensure their patients adhere to their treatment regimen.
3. *Pricing Strategy*: Drugs with unique pharmacokinetic properties (like a long half-life) might command premium pricing, especially if this reduces the need for frequent dosing or offers better therapeutic outcomes.
4. *Educational Initiatives*: Marketers might need to invest in educational efforts to teach healthcare professionals and patients about the significance of drug half-life, how it impacts dosing, and its potential effects on efficacy and safety.
5. *Lifecycle Management*: For drugs going off-patent, companies sometimes develop extended-release formulations with a different half-life than the original product. This can provide a new marketing angle and prolong the product's market life.

In summary, the half-life of a drug is an essential pharmacokinetic property that impacts its clinical use. For pharma marketers, understanding and effectively communicating the implications of a drug's half-life can influence its positioning, adoption, and success in the market.

Halo Effect

The Halo effect is a cognitive bias in which our overall impression of a person, company, or product influences our perceptions of their specific qualities or characteristics. In other words, if we have a positive impression of something, we tend to attribute positive qualities to it even if there is no evidence to support them.

In pharma marketing, the halo effect can occur when a healthcare professional has a positive impression of a particular brand or company, influencing their perception of the brand's efficacy, safety, and overall value. For example, physicians may have had a positive impression of a pharmaceutical company because they have good experiences with their sales representatives or have attended a sponsored conference. This positive impression may lead them to prescribe that company's products more frequently.

However, the halo effect can work in reverse, leading to negative perceptions of a brand or company based on unrelated factors. For example, a physician who has had a negative experience with a sales representative from a particular company may be less likely to prescribe that company's products, even if they are effective and safe.

Pharmaceutical companies can mitigate the negative halo effect by ensuring their marketing and promotional activities are based on objective scientific evidence, not subjective impressions or perceptions. They can also focus on building strong, long-term relationships with healthcare professionals based on trust and transparency rather than short-term sales tactics.

Hard Sell

A hard sell is a sales strategy involving aggressive and persistent tactics to persuade potential customers to purchase or take a specific action. For example, in pharma marketing, hard-sell tactics may involve pressuring healthcare providers to prescribe a particular drug or making exaggerated claims about a product's efficacy or safety.

Hard sell tactics can be controversial in the pharmaceutical industry, as they may prioritize sales over patient welfare and can damage the reputation of both the salesperson and the company. In many cases, hard sell tactics are illegal, such as making false or misleading claims about a drug's benefits or downplaying potential side effects.

Pharmaceutical companies are subject to regulations and guidelines around marketing and advertising, including restrictions on the type of language and claims that can be made in marketing materials. As a result, most companies avoid hard sell tactics in favor of more educational and informative approaches to marketing their products.

Harvesting

In marketing, harvesting refers to maximizing profits from a product or service that has reached the end of its lifecycle. It involves reducing marketing and advertising expenditures and focusing on cost-cutting measures to maximize profits from existing customers while minimizing expenses.

Harvesting aims to generate as much revenue as possible from the product or service before it becomes obsolete or is replaced by a newer, more innovative product or service. This strategy is commonly used for products that have become mature or are in decline and where the costs of innovation or promotion may outweigh the benefits.

Harvesting in Pharma Marketing

In pharma marketing, harvesting can refer to maximizing profits from a drug that has reached the end of its lifecycle. This can happen when the patent for the drug expires, and generic versions become available, or when a new, more innovative drug is introduced that replaces the older drug.

To implement a harvesting strategy in pharma marketing, companies may reduce promotional activities for the drug, lower the price, and focus on cost-cutting measures to maximize profits from existing customers. This can involve reducing the drug's sales force, marketing, and advertising expenses.

However, it is important to note that pharma companies must comply with regulations regarding the promotion and marketing of drugs, even if they are in the harvesting phase of their lifecycle. In addition, companies must ensure that they provide accurate and balanced information to healthcare providers and patients and not make false or misleading claims about the drug's safety or efficacy.

Harvesting can be an effective strategy for maximizing profits for a drug that has reached the end of its lifecycle. Still, pharma companies must balance this strategy with ethical considerations and compliance with regulations.

HIPAA

The Health Insurance Portability and Accountability Act (HIPAA) is a US federal law that has significant implications for pharmaceutical marketing, particularly in the context of patient information and healthcare data. HIPAA primarily applies to healthcare providers, health plans, and healthcare clearinghouses, but its reach indirectly affects pharmaceutical marketing in the following ways:

1. *Protection of Patient Data*: HIPAA mandates strict rules for protecting patients' PHI (Protected Health Information). Pharmaceutical companies may contact PHI for research, clinical trials, or marketing activities. It is crucial to handle this information securely and ensure it remains confidential.
2. *Business Associates*: Pharmaceutical companies often collaborate with healthcare providers, such as doctors and hospitals, to promote their products. Pharmaceutical companies are classified as "business associates" under HIPAA when these collaborations involve sharing or accessing PHI. This means they must adhere to HIPAA regulations and safeguard patient data.
3. *Consent and Authorization*: When pharmaceutical companies want to use patient data for marketing research, they typically need the appropriate patient consent or authorization. HIPAA's Privacy Rule provides guidelines for obtaining valid patient consent.
4. *Marketing Communications*: HIPAA allows certain healthcare-related communications between pharmaceutical companies and providers without patient authorization. However, these communications must adhere to specific criteria and directly relate to the provider's current healthcare services.
5. *De-Identification*: HIPAA allows for the use of de-identified patient data for marketing research. To be considered de-identified, the data must not contain specific patient identifiers. This is a common approach in pharmaceutical marketing to protect patient privacy.
6. *Patient Rights*: Patients have specific rights under HIPAA, including the right to access their PHI and request restrictions on how their data is used. Pharmaceutical companies must comply with these requests and inform patients of their rights.
7. *Data Security*: HIPAA requires pharmaceutical companies to implement robust data security measures to protect patient information. This includes encryption, access controls, and policies to prevent data breaches.
8. *Marketing Authorization*: Pharmaceutical marketing efforts often use patient data to target specific populations. HIPAA mandates that pharmaceutical companies obtain valid marketing authorizations from patients before using their data for marketing purposes.
9. *Training and Education*: Personnel involved in pharmaceutical marketing must be trained and educated on HIPAA regulations to ensure they understand their obligations and responsible concerning patient data.

Non-compliance with HIPAA can result in significant penalties, fines, and legal actions. Therefore, pharmaceutical companies must establish clear HIPAA compliance policies and practices when dealing with patient data, whether for research, marketing, or other purposes. Compliance with HIPAA is essential for maintaining patient trust, respecting their privacy, and avoiding legal consequences.

Hashtag

A hashtag is a word or phrase preceded by the "#" symbol used on social media platforms to group and organize content around a specific topic or theme. When a user adds a hashtag to their post, it becomes clickable and searchable, allowing other users to find and join in on the conversation. For example, if a user posts a tweet about a new medication for migraines and includes the hashtag #migrainerelief, anyone searching for that hashtag can easily find the tweet and other posts related to migraine relief.

Hashtags are commonly used on platforms such as Twitter, Instagram, and Facebook to help users discover and engage with content that interests them. They can also be used to promote events, products, or campaigns and to increase brand awareness.

While hashtags can be a powerful tool in social media marketing, it is important to use them strategically and thoughtfully to ensure that they are being used in a relevant and compliant manner with industry regulations.

Hashtags in Pharma Marketing

Hashtags can be a valuable tool in pharmaceutical marketing, particularly in social media campaigns. Hashtags are keywords or phrases preceded by the "#" symbol, which makes them searchable and allows users to find and join conversations on a specific topic easily. Here are some tips for using hashtags in pharma marketing:

1. *Use Relevant and Specific Hashtags*: When creating a social media campaign, it is important

to use hashtags relevant to your content and specific to your target audience. This will help ensure that your content is seen by people interested in your products or services.

2. *Create Branded Hashtags*: Branded hashtags can be used to promote your company, products, or services. They should be unique and memorable to help your content stand out.
3. *Research and Analyze Hashtags*: Before using a hashtag in your campaign, it is important to research and analyze it to ensure that your target audience is using it and has a significant reach. You can use tools such as Hashtagify or Keyhole to analyze the performance of hashtags.
4. *Use Hashtags Consistently*: Using hashtags consistently across all your social media platforms can help build brand recognition and increase the visibility of your content.
5. *Follow Industry Regulations*: It is important to ensure that all marketing activities, including hashtags, comply with industry regulations and ethical standards.

Branded Hashtags

A branded hashtag is a hashtag that is specifically created and used by a company or organization to promote its brand, products, or services. It is usually unique to the company and is designed to help increase brand awareness and engagement on social media platforms. Branded hashtags can be used in a variety of ways, such as:

1. *Promoting a Product Launch or Campaign*: A company can encourage customers to share their experiences or photos using a branded hashtag.
2. *Creating a Social Media Contest*: A company can use a branded hashtag for a social media contest or giveaway.
3. *Building Brand Awareness*: Consistently using a branded hashtag can help increase brand recognition and awareness over time.

Creating a Branded Hashtag

The following steps are useful for creating a branded hashtag:

1. *Brainstorm Ideas*: Begin by brainstorming ideas for your branded hashtag. Think about your brand identity, target audience, and marketing goals. Your hashtag should be unique, memorable, and relevant to your brand.
2. *Research Existing Hashtags*: Once you have a few ideas, research existing hashtags to ensure that your chosen hashtag isn't already being used by another brand or for a different purpose. You can search for your proposed hashtag on social media platforms.
3. *Keep it Short and Simple*: Your branded hashtag should be easy to remember and spell. It is generally a good idea to keep it short and simple so that it is easy for people to use and share.
4. *Make it Unique*: Your branded hashtag should be unique to your brand and distinguishable from similar hashtags. This will help your content stand out and increase brand recognition.
5. *Promote Your Hashtag*: Once you have created your branded hashtag, promote it across all your social media channels. Encourage your followers to use the hashtag and share it with their networks.
6. *Monitor and Track Performance*: Monitor and track hashtag over time. Use analytics tools to track engagement and reach to see how your hashtag is performing and make adjustments as needed.

Branded Hashtags in Pharma: Some Examples

Here are a few examples of branded hashtags used in pharmaceutical marketing:

1. *#IBSrelief*: Ironwood Pharmaceuticals used the hashtag #IBSrelief to promote their drug, Linzess, which treats irritable bowel syndrome (IBS).
2. *#AskAboutAspire*: Astellas Pharma used the hashtag #AskAboutAspire to promote their drug, Xtandi (Enzalutamide), used to treat prostate cancer.
3. *#LetsTalkAD*: Biogen used the hashtag #LetsTalkAD to promote their drug, Aduhelm (Aducanumab), used to treat Alzheimer's disease.
4. *#LetsTalkPBC*: Intercept Pharmaceuticals used the hashtag #LetsTalkPBC to promote their drug, Ocaliva (Obeticholic acid), which treats Primary Biliary Cholangitis (PBC).
5. *#BreakTheStigma*: Janssen Pharmaceuticals used the hashtag #BreakTheStigma to promote its mental health awareness campaign, which aims to reduce the stigma around mental illness and encourage people to seek help.

It is important to note that pharmaceutical marketing is highly regulated, and companies must ensure that their marketing campaigns and branded hashtags comply with industry regulations and ethical standards.

Hatch-Waxman Act

The Hatch-Waxman Act, also known as the Drug Price Competition and Patent Term Restoration Act, is a federal law passed in the United States in 1984. The Act makes it easier for generic drug manufacturers to bring their products to market by allowing them to rely on the safety and efficacy data of the original brand-name drug.

The Hatch-Waxman Act establishes a process by which generic drug manufacturers can obtain approval from the Food and Drug Administration (FDA) to market their products. This process includes filing an abbreviated new drug application (ANDA) that demonstrates the generic drug is bioequivalent to the brand-name drug.

The Act also provides a mechanism for brand-name drug manufacturers to extend the patent life of their products. This is achieved by granting a patent term extension, which allows the brand-name drug manufacturer to recoup some of the costs associated with developing and marketing the drug. However, certain conditions, such as the following, apply for patent term restoration under the Hatch-Waxman Act.

Conditions for Patent Term Restoration Under Hatch-Waxman Act

- The patent must have been in force when the FDA approved the product.
- The FDA's approval of the product must have been delayed due to the FDA's regulatory review process, including any delay caused by a request for additional testing or data.
- The delay must not have been caused by the patent owner's actions or inactions.
- The patent owner must apply for restoration of the patent term within a specified time frame, generally within 60 days after the FDA approves the product.
- The total period of patent term extension cannot exceed five years beyond the original expiration date of the patent.
- The patent owner must pay an application fee to the USPTO (United States Patent and Trademark Office) and comply with other requirements and procedures outlined in the Hatch-Waxman Act and related regulations.

It is important to note that not all pharmaceutical patents are eligible for term restoration under the Hatch-Waxman Act. Only certain types of pharmaceutical-related patents, including patents for active ingredients, formulations, and methods of use, are eligible.

Hatch-Waxman Act's Impact on Pharma Industry

The Hatch-Waxman Act, introduced in 1984 to balance the competing interests of brand-name and generic drug manufacturers, significantly impacted the pharmaceutical industry in several ways. Consider the following, for example:

1. *Introduction of Generic Drugs*: The Act provided a streamlined approval process for generic drugs by allowing them to use data from the original drug's clinical trials, thus reducing the cost and time required to develop and bring a generic drug to market. This has led to increased competition and reduced prices for consumers.
2. *Patent Protection*: The Act extended patent protection for brand-name drugs by up to five years, allowing manufacturers to recoup research and development costs and maintain a monopoly on the market. This provided an incentive for pharmaceutical companies to invest in the development of new drugs.
3. *Drug Development*: The Act incentivized drug companies to invest in developing new drugs, offering an additional six months of market exclusivity for drugs approved for new uses or new formulations.
4. *Litigation*: The Act introduced a process for resolving patent disputes between brand-name and generic drug manufacturers, reducing costly and time-consuming court battles.

Overall, the Hatch-Waxman Act has profoundly impacted the pharmaceutical industry by balancing the interests of brand-name and generic drug manufacturers, incentivizing drug development, and increasing access to affordable medications for consumers.

Hawthorne Effect

The Hawthorne effect, also known as the observer effect, is a psychological phenomenon where individuals modify their behavior or performance in response to the awareness of being observed or studied. This effect was first observed during the Western Electric Hawthorne Works in Chicago experiments from the late 1920s to the early 1930s. The initial aim of these studies was to examine the relationship between working conditions and productivity, but researchers found that productivity increased regardless of changes in working conditions. They attributed this improvement to the fact that the workers knew they were being observed.

The Hawthorne effect can affect how healthcare professionals and patients respond to marketing activities in pharmaceutical marketing. Here are some examples of how the Hawthorne effect may manifest in pharma marketing:

1. *Clinical Trials and Drug Studies*: During clinical trials, participants might exhibit better adherence to the prescribed treatment or lifestyle changes due to the awareness that they are being monitored. This could lead to overestimating the drug's effectiveness when applied to the general population outside the trial setting.
2. *Sales Representative Visits*: Pharma sales representatives often visit healthcare professionals to promote their products. Suppose a healthcare professional knows they are being observed. In that case, they may respond more favorably to the sales pitch, positively leading to an artificial increase in prescription rates for the promoted drug.
3. *Physician Behavior*: Physicians may change their prescribing patterns when they know they are being monitored as part of a marketing campaign or post-marketing surveillance. This could distort the actual demand for a drug and may not reflect the real-world effectiveness or safety of the medication.
4. *Patient Compliance and Adherence*: Patients participating in patient support programs or receiving special attention from pharmaceutical companies may feel more motivated to adhere to their medication regimens. This could lead to inflated adherence rates compared to real-world conditions.

Implications for Pharma Marketers

1. *Awareness Bias*: Pharma marketers should know the Hawthorne effect when interpreting data from marketing initiatives. The observed behavior may not accurately reflect real-world behavior, and results might be inflated due to the temporary impact of the observation.
2. *Validating Real-World Data*: While clinical trials and controlled studies are essential for drug development and approval, pharma marketers should complement this data with real-world evidence to understand the impact of their products outside the study setting.
3. *Ethical Considerations*: Marketers should take ethical considerations seriously when conducting marketing research or monitoring physician and patient behavior. Manipulating behavior solely for marketing purposes can raise ethical concerns and may not lead to sustainable long-term otucomes.
4. *Balanced Marketing Strategies*: Rather than relying solely on the Hawthorne effect, pharma marketers should develop comprehensive marketing strategies that include robust evidence-based education, value-driven propositions, and transparent communication to foster trust and credibility among healthcare professionals and patients.

In conclusion, the Hawthorne effect can influence the behavior of healthcare professionals and patients in response to pharma marketing activities. Pharma marketers must be cautious about interpreting data influenced by this effect. They should strive for balanced and ethical marketing strategies to ensure their products' long-term success and trustworthiness in the pharmaceutical market.

Headline

A headline is a brief statement or title summarizing the main idea or key point of a news article, blog post, advertisement, or other written piece. It is usually placed at the top of the article or piece, often in a larger font or boldface type, to grab the reader's attention and give them a quick idea of the article. Headlines are an important aspect of journalism and writing, as they can influence whether or not a reader decides to read the article. Therefore, a good headline should be accurate, concise, and attention-grabbing while still conveying the essence of the story.

Headlines in Pharma Marketing

In pharmaceutical marketing, headlines play an important role in grabbing the attention of potential customers, such as doctors, healthcare providers, and patients. Therefore, the headline of a pharmaceutical advertisement or marketing material should be clear, concise, and informative while still engaging and compelling.

Pharmaceutical marketers often use headlines to highlight the benefits of their product, such as its effectiveness in treating a specific condition or its unique features compared to other products on the market. They may also use headlines to address common concerns or questions that potential customers may have about the product.

Types of Headlines in Pharma Marketing

Several types of headlines can be used in pharmaceutical marketing to grab the attention of potential customers and promote a product. Here are some examples:

1. *Benefit-focused Headlines*: These headlines focus on the benefits of the pharmaceutical

product, such as how it can improve health outcomes or provide relief from a particular symptom. An example is *Relieve Migraine Pain Fast with our new Triptan.*

2. *Problem-focused Headlines*: These headlines focus on a common problem or issue the target audience may face and position the pharmaceutical product as a solution. Example: *Tired of Dealing with Insomnia? Try Our New Sleep Aid.*
3. *News-Oriented Headlines*: These headlines use a news angle to promote a pharmaceutical product, such as announcing a breakthrough or clinical trial. Example: *New Study Shows Our Blood Pressure Medication is More Effective Than Competitors.*
4. *Educational Headlines*: These headlines provide information or education about a particular condition or disease and promote the pharmaceutical product as a treatment option. An example is *Understanding Diabetes: How Our Insulin Can Help You Manage Your Blood Sugar.*
5. *Urgency-focused Headlines*: These headlines use urgency to motivate potential customers to take action by highlighting the immediate need for treatment or limited product availability. An example is: *Don't let Psoriasis ruin your summer: Try Our Limited-Time Offer for Clearer Skin.*

It is important to note that pharmaceutical marketing is heavily regulated, and companies must ensure that their headlines and promotional materials comply with all relevant regulations and guidelines.

Health Apps

Health apps are mobile applications designed to help users manage their health and wellness. These apps can provide various features and functions, from tracking physical activity and nutrition to monitoring medical conditions and symptoms. There are many types of health apps available, such as:

1. *Fitness Apps*: These apps help users track their physical activity, such as steps taken, calories burned, and workouts completed. Examples of fitness apps include Fitbit, MyFitnessPal, and Nike Training Club.
2. *Nutrition Apps*: These apps help users track their food intake, log meals, and monitor their nutrition. Examples of nutrition apps include MyPlate by Livestrong, Calory, and Fooducate.
3. *Medical Apps*: These apps provide information and tools for managing medical conditions and symptoms, such as diabetes, asthma, and high blood pressure. Examples of medical apps include Glucose Buddy, AsthmaMD, and Blood Pressure Companion.
4. *Mental Health Apps*: These apps offer tools and resources for managing mental health conditions like anxiety and depression. Examples of mental health apps include HeadSpace, Calm, and MooFit.
5. *Women's Health Apps*: These apps focus on women's health and wellness, including menstrual cycle tracking, fertility tracking, and pregnancy tracking. Examples of women's health apps include Clue, Flo, and Ovia Pregnancy Tracker.

Health apps can be convenient and useful for managing one's health and wellness. Still, choosing reputable and trustworthy apps that protect user privacy and provide accurate information is important. Users should also consult with a healthcare professional before making significant changes to their health routine based on information from a health app.

Health Apps in Pharma Marketing

Health apps can be a valuable tool for pharmaceutical companies in their marketing efforts. By partnering with health app developers or creating their own health apps, pharmaceutical companies can provide users with valuable information and tools for managing their health conditions and promoting their products.

How Pharma Uses Health Apps

Here are some ways that health apps can be used in pharmaceutical marketing:

1. *Disease Education*: Health apps can provide information and resources for users about specific diseases or conditions, including symptoms, treatment options, and lifestyle management strategies. By providing disease education through a health app, pharmaceutical companies can raise awareness of their products and position themselves as trusted source of information.
2. *Treatment Management*: Health apps can help users manage their medications and treatment regimens, including tracking dosages and scheduling medication reminders. Pharmaceutical companies can encourage treatment adherence and improve patient outcomes by developing a health app that integrates with their product.

3. *Patient Support*: Health apps can offer tools and resources to support patients, such as symptom trackers, exercise routines, and diet logs. By providing these tools, pharmaceutical companies can improve patient engagement and satisfaction and promote their products as a part of an overall treatment plan.
4. *Data Collection*: Health apps can collect valuable data on user behavior and treatment outcomes, which can be used to inform future product development and marketing strategies. Pharmaceutical companies can gain insights into patient behavior and preferences by partnering with health app developers or creating health apps.

Pharmaceutical companies must ensure that any health apps they develop or partner with comply with regulatory guidelines and protect user privacy. Additionally, any marketing efforts within health apps should be transparent and provide accurate information to users. Pharmaceutical companies can use healthcare apps responsibly and ethically to improve patient outcomes and drive business success.

Health Maintenance Organization (HMO)

Health Maintenance Organizations (HMOs) are managed care organizations that provide comprehensive healthcare services to enrolled members. When it comes to implications for pharma marketers, here are some key points to consider:

1. *Limited Provider Network*: HMOs typically have a limited network of healthcare providers, including physicians, hospitals, and pharmacies. Pharma marketers should know the providers within an HMO's network to target their marketing efforts effectively. Building relationships with key prescribers within the network can be essential.
2. *Formulary Placement*: HMOs maintain formularies that list the medications covered by the organization. Pharma marketers should understand the formulary placement process of HMOs and strive to secure favorable positions for their products. Demonstrating their drugs' clinical and economic value compared to competitors is crucial to gaining preferred formulary status.
3. *Prior Authorization And Utilization Management*: HMOs often employ utilization management techniques, such as prior authorization, to control medication utilization and costs. Pharma marketers need to understand the prior authorization process and work closely with healthcare providers to ensure smooth and efficient approval of their medications.
4. *Focus on Cost-Effectiveness*: HMOs emphasize cost-effective healthcare delivery. Pharma marketers should consider the pricing and affordability of their products when targeting HMOs. Demonstrating their medications' cost-effectiveness and value proposition is crucial to gain favorable consideration from HMOs.
5. *Population Health Management*: HMOs often engage in population health management initiatives to improve the health outcomes of their members. Pharma marketers can align their marketing strategies with these initiatives by emphasizing the products' clinical benefits, safety, and efficacy and how they contribute to improved patient outcomes.
6. *Patient Education and Adherence*: HMOs emphasize patient education and adherence to promote better health outcomes and cost containment. Pharma marketers can support these efforts by providing HMO members with educational materials and support programs. Such initiatives can improve patients' understanding of their medications and encourage adherence, positively influencing HMOs' perception of the value of those medications.
7. *Value-Based Contracts*: Some HMOs may engage in value-based contracts with pharmaceutical manufacturers. These contracts link reimbursement to predefined outcomes or performance metrics. Pharma marketers should explore opportunities for value-based contracts and be prepared to provide evidence of their product's value in improved patient outcomes or cost savings.
8. *Collaboration with HMOs*: Building relationships and collaborating with HMOs is crucial for pharma marketers. This involves understanding the specific needs and priorities of HMOs, engaging in ongoing communication with key stakeholders, and demonstrating the value and benefits of their products in a way that aligns with the goals of the HMO.

Understanding the dynamics of HMOs, their formulary management, utilization management practices, and focus on cost-effectiveness is essential for pharma marketers to navigate this segment of the managed care market successfully. By aligning marketing strategies with the goals and priorities of HMOs, pharma marketers can optimize market access and the commercial success of their products.

Healthcare Professional (HCP)

Healthcare Professionals (HCPs), such as doctors, nurses, and other medical professionals, are an important target audience for pharmaceutical marketing. This is because HCPs are often the primary decision-makers when prescribing medications to patients. Therefore, pharmaceutical companies use marketing strategies to promote their products to HCPS and convince them of their value.

Pharmaceutical marketing to HCPs can take many forms, including in-person sales representative visits, direct mail, email marketing, and digital marketing. However, it is important to note that pharmaceutical marketing to HCPs is heavily regulated, and companies must comply with strict guidelines and regulations regarding promoting their products.

Effective pharmaceutical marketing to HCPs typically involves providing relevant and useful information about the product, such as its clinical data, safety profile, and indications for use. Marketers may also use product samples, patient education materials, and continuing medical education (CME) programs to engage HCPs and encourage them to consider their products for their patients.

However, pharmaceutical companies must maintain ethical and transparent practices when marketing to HCPs and avoid any practices perceived as unethical or misleading. This includes disclosing potential conflicts of interest, providing accurate information about the product, and avoiding any tactics that could be seen attempting to influence prescribing practices with financial incentives.

Building Strong Relationships with HCPs

Building strong relationships with healthcare professionals (HCPs) is key to the success of pharmaceutical companies. By establishing trust and rapport with HCPs, pharmaceutical companies can improve their chances of getting their products prescribed and gain valuable feedback and insights from HCPs that can help future product development.

Here are some ways that pharmaceutical companies can build strong relationships with HCPs:

1. *Provide Valuable Information*: HCPs want to stay up-to-date on the latest medical research, clinical data, and treatment guidelines. By providing HCPs with valuable information relevant to their practice, pharmaceutical companies can establish themselves as trusted sources of information and expertise.
2. *Offer Educational Opportunities*: Continuing medical education (CME) programs, webinars, and other educational opportunities can help HCPs stay informed about the latest developments in their field. In addition, pharmaceutical companies can demonstrate their commitment to supporting HCPs and improving patient outcomes by sponsoring or hosting these events.
3. *Be Responsive to Feedback*: HCPs often have valuable insights and feedback to inform product development and marketing strategies. By being responsive to HCP feedback and incorporating it into their products and services, pharmaceutical companies can show that they value HCPs' input and are committed to meeting their needs.
4. *Provide Patient Education Materials*: HCPs are often responsible for educating patients about their health conditions and treatment options. By providing high-quality patient education materials, such as brochures, videos, or online resources, pharmaceutical companies can support HCPs in this important role and improve patient outcomes.
5. *Maintain Ethical and Transparent Practices*: Maintaining ethical and transparent practices in all aspects of marketing and sales is essential to building trust with HCPs. This includes disclosing potential conflicts of interest, providing accurate product information, and avoiding tactics that could influence prescribing practices or financial incentives.

By implementing these strategies, pharmaceutical companies can build strong and mutually beneficial relationships with HCPs, improve patient outcomes and drive business success.

Heat Maps

A Heat Map in pharma marketing is a graphical representation of data that uses colors to indicate the intensity of a variable. The map is created by aggregating data into different regions and then assigning colors to represent the data. The colors typically range from light to dark, with the darkest color indicating the highest intensity of the measured variable.

In pharma marketing, heat maps can be used to visualize various data related to sales, customer demographics, prescribing patterns, and more. For example, a heat map could identify geographic areas with high prescribing rates for a particular drug or areas with a high concentration of a certain type of healthcare provider.

Heat maps can be a powerful tool for pharma marketers because they allow them to quickly identify trends and patterns in large amounts of data. By visualizing data in this way, marketers can quickly identify areas of opportunity and focus their efforts where they are most likely to have an impact.

Heat Maps in Pharma Marketing: Examples

Here are a few examples of how heat maps can be used in pharma marketing:

1. *Sales Heat Maps*: A pharma company can create a sales heat map to identify regions where a particular drug is selling well or not performing as expected. They can use this data to allocate sales resources more efficiently and tailor marketing efforts to improve sales in underperforming areas.
2. *Prescriber Heat Maps*: A pharma company can use prescriber heat maps to identify areas with high concentrations of healthcare providers prescribing their products. This can help the company to target its marketing efforts toward these providers and build stronger relationships with them.
3. *Patient Demographic Heat Maps*: A pharma company can create heat maps to identify areas with high concentrations of patients who would benefit from their products based on demographic data such as age, gender, or income. They can use this data to target their marketing efforts towards these patients and to tailor their messaging to better resonate with their needs.
4. *Adverse Event Heat Maps*: A pharma company can create adverse event heat maps to identify regions with high rates of adverse events associated with their products. This data can be used to identify potential safety issues and take appropriate corrective actions to address them.
5. *Competitive Intelligence Heat Maps*: A pharma company can create heat maps to visualize the competitive landscape in different regions. This can help them identify areas where their products face strong competition and adjust their marketing strategies accordingly.
6. However, it is important to note that heat maps should always be used with other data analysis techniques and should not be relied on as the sole source of information. Additionally, it is important to ensure that any data used to create heat maps is accurate and up-to-date to ensure that the resulting analysis is meaningful and actionable.

Health Economics and Outcomes Research (HEOR)

Health Economics and Outcomes Research (HEOR) examines the economic limitations of healthcare interventions, such as pharmaceuticals, medical devices, and various treatment protocols.s It aims to provide objective, evidence-based information to help make well-informed healthcare decisions that will maximize health benefits while optimizing the allocation of healthcare resources.

1. Importance in Pharma

- *Market Access*: HEOR studies help to inform payers (like insurance companies or government healthcare agencies) why a new drug or treatment protocol should be approved and subsidized.
- *Cost-Effectiveness:* By evaluating the cost-effectiveness of a new intervention compared to existing options, HEOR can demonstrate the value proposition of a new pharmaceutical product.
- *Budget Impact Models*: These models estimate the financial impact of adopting a new intervention. This is crucial for both payers and providers to understand the long-term implications of adopting a new technology or drug.
- *Clinical Guidelines*: HEOR can inform healthcare guidelines by integrating clinical efficiency with economic considerations.
- *Policy Making*: The evidence from HEOR can influence healthcare policy, especially in settings where limited resources must be allocated judiciously.
- *Patient Outcomes*: Beyond purely economic aspects, HEOR often includes evaluations of treatment effects on quality of life, morbidity, and other health-related quality of life aspects. This holistic view can help healthcare providers make better treatment Decisions.

2. Components of HEOR

- *Cost-Minimization Analysis*: Comparing the costs of two or more equivalent treatments.
- *Cost-Effective Analysis*: Comparing the cost and effectiveness (often measured in terms of life-years saved or quality-adjusted life-years) of different treatments.
- *Cost-Utility Analysis*: This is a more specific form of cost-effective analysis considering the patient's quality of life.

- *Cost-Benefit Analysis*: Compares the cost and benefits of different treatments but converts everything into a common monetary unit.
- *Real-World Evidence (RWE)*: Collection and analysis of data outside of controlled clinical trials to understand how a drug performs in everyday practice.

3. Challenges

- *Data Quality*: Real-world data can be messy and incomplete, making it challenging to draw strong conclusions.
- *Standardization*: With multiple stakeholders involved, a standard methodology is often lacking.
- *Ethical Considerations*: Cost-cutting based on HEOR could lead to ethical issues such as compromising the quality of care.
- *Interdisciplinary Expertise Required*: HEOR involves economics, statistics, medicine, and more, requiring a broad range of expertise for robust study and interpretation.

HEOR plays a pivotal role in the pharmaceutical industry, influencing everything from R&D decisions to pricing strategies and healthcare policy. As healthcare costs rise and the complexity of medical treatment increases, the role of HEOR is likely to grow even more critical in the future.

Implications for Pharma Marketers

For pharma marketers, Health Economics and Outcomes Research (HEOR) data can be an invaluable asset for positioning a product in the market, crafting persuasive messages, and strategically aligning the product within the healthcare ecosystem. Here are some of the implications for pharma marketers:

1. Creating a Value Proposition

- *Evidence-based Marketing*: HEOR provides rigorous data that can substantiate the value claims made in marketing materials. This is particularly important when trying to gain formulary access or secure reimbursement.
- *Targeting Decision-Makers*: Traditional pharma marketing often focuses on physicians. However, with the rise of managed care and value-based healthcare, stakeholders like payers, policymakers, and patients are becoming increasingly important. HEOR data can be tailored to address the specific concerns of each group.

2. Messaging and Communication

- *Clinical vs. Economic Value*: While the clinical efficacy of a drug is important, demonstrating its economic value (cost-effectiveness, budget impact, etc.) can often make a compelling case for adoption. This can be a key differentiator in a crowded market.
- *Patient-Centric Outcomes*: Marketers can leverage real-world evidence and quality-of-life studies from HEOR to create more patient-centric campaigns, appealing directly to end-users who are increasingly involved in healthcare decisions.
- *Transparency*: Utilizing peer-reviewed HEOR data in promotional articles can lend an added layer of credibility and transparency, a factor that is increasingly appreciated by healthcare professionals and payers alike.

3. Strategic Decision-Making

- *Product Lifecycle Management*: HEOR data can inform the launch strategy and lifecycle management decisions, helping to identify new use cases or patient segments where the product might be particularly beneficial.
- *Pricing Strategy*: Understanding a product's cost-effectiveness and budget impact can inform a more nuanced pricing strategy, potentially leading to higher market penetration and better negotiations with payers.
- *Global Markets*: HEOR can help tailor strategies for entering new markets by providing insights into local healthcare economics and treatment paradigms.

4. Challenges and Considerations

- *Regulatory Compliance*: It is essential to ensure that all marketing claims based on HEOR data comply with regulatory standards, which can vary significantly from one jurisdiction to another.
- *Data Interpretation*: HEOR data often involves complex statistical analyses, so having the expertise to interpret this data is crucial.
- *Ethical Boundaries*: Marketers must be cautious to avoid overstatement of economic claims that cannot be substantiated or could mislead healthcare providers and patients.

In a healthcare landscape that is increasingly focused on value-based care, the role of HEOR in pharma marketing is likely to grow in importance. Marketers who can effectively integrate and communicate the insights gained from HEOR are likely to have a competitive edge.

Hierarchy of Effects

The hierarchy of effects is a model used in marketing and advertising that describes the stages a consumer goes through when making a purchasing decision. The traditional hierarchy of effects model has six stages: Awareness, Knowledge, Liking, Preference, Conviction, and Purchase.

Hierarchy of Effects on Pharma Marketing

The hierarchy of effects model is also commonly used in pharmaceutical marketing to describe the stages patients and healthcare professionals go through in making decisions about medical treatments. Here are some examples of how the hierarchy of effects model can be applied in pharma marketing:

1. *Awareness*: In this stage, the patient or healthcare professional becomes aware of the medical condition and the available treatment options. For example, a patient might become aware of a new drug for treating diabetes through an advertisement in a magazine, or a healthcare professional might learn about a new treatment for cancer through a medical conference.
2. *Knowledge*: In this stage, the patient or healthcare professional seeks more information about the treatment options. For example, the patients might research the drug online, read the patient information leaflet, or consult with their doctor. Healthcare professionals might read medical journals, attend continuing education courses, or consult with colleagues.
3. *Liking*: In this stage, the patient or healthcare professional develops a positive attitude toward the treatment option. For example, the patient might like the drug to be available in a convenient once-daily pill or have fewer side effects. The healthcare professional might like that the treatment is effective in clinical trials or easy to administer.
4. *Preference*: In this stage, the patient or healthcare professional prefers the treatment option over others. For example, the patient might prefer the new drug over his current treatment because it is more effective or has fewer side effects. Likewise, the healthcare professional might prefer the new treatment over other options because it is more convenient or has a better safety profile.
5. *Conviction*: In this stage, the patient or healthcare professional strongly believes in the treatment option. For example, the patient might believe that the new drug is the best option for managing his diabetes and is willing to pay a higher price. The healthcare professional might believe that the new treatment is the best option for her patients and is willing to recommend it.
6. *Purchase*: In this stage, the patient or healthcare professional purchases or prescribes the treatment option. For example, the patient might ask his doctor to prescribe the new drug, or the healthcare professional might prescribe the new drug.

The hierarchy of effects model can be a useful framework for pharmaceutical marketers to understand the various stages of the decision-making process and to develop effective marketing and promotional strategies for each stage.

Hierarchy of Needs

The hierarchy of needs is a motivational theory in psychology proposed by Abraham Maslow in 1943. According to Maslow's theory, human needs can be categorized into five levels, each of which must be fulfilled before an individual can progress to the next level.

In pharma marketing, understanding the hierarchy of needs can be useful in developing marketing strategies that resonate with the target audience and address their specific needs and desires.

Here are some examples of how the hierarchy of needs can be applied in pharma marketing:

1. *Physiological Needs*: At this level, individuals require basic needs for survival, such as food, water, and shelter. Pharma marketing could include marketing campaigns for essential medicines and medical devices that help meet basic health needs.
2. *Safety Needs*: The next level in the hierarchy of needs is safety, including physical, financial, and emotional security. Examples of pharma marketing campaigns that address safety needs might include drugs and devices that reduce the risk of illness or injury or campaigns that emphasize the importance of preventive care.
3. *Love and Belonging Needs*: Individuals seek social connections and the community at this level. In pharma marketing, campaigns might focus on building relationships between patients and healthcare providers and promoting social support networks' benefits for managing chronic conditions.
4. *Esteem Needs*: This level encompasses the need for recognition, respect, and achievement. For example, pharma marketing campaigns that address esteem needs might include messaging that emphasizes the importance of self-care or the positive impact of treating a particular condition can have on a patient's quality of life.

5. *Self-Actualization Needs*: This level represents the highest human needs, including the desire for personal growth and fulfillment. In pharma marketing, campaigns might focus on helping patients achieve their goals and aspirations by managing their health and wellness.

Physicians' Hierarchy of Needs: Implications for Pharm Marketers

Physicians, like all individuals, have their hierarchy of needs, which can affect their behavior and decision-making processes. For example, physicians may focus on meeting their physiological and safety needs by earning enough money to provide for themselves and their families and avoiding malpractice suits. In addition, they may be motivated by higher-level needs such as a desire for professional recognition and respect from colleagues (belonging needs) and a desire to achieve their full potential as a healthcare provider (self-actualization needs).

The implications of the hierarchy of needs for pharma marketers are significant. First, marketers must understand what motivates physicians at each level of the hierarchy and tailor their marketing messages and tactics accordingly.

For example, marketing materials that emphasize the safety and efficacy of a particular drug may be more effective with physicians primarily concerned with meeting their patients' physiological needs, while marketing messages that focus on professional recognition and prestige may resonate more with physicians motivated by belonging needs.

Additionally, marketers may need to provide physicians with different information and support at each level. For example, physicians focused on meeting their physiological needs may be more interested in information about the cost-effectiveness of a particular drug. In contrast, those motivated by belongingness needs may be more interested in opportunities to participate in clinical research or attend professional conferences.

Thus, understanding the hierarchy of needs can help pharma marketers develop more effective campaigns that resonate with patients and healthcare providers and address their needs and desires.

High Involvement Model

A high involvement model is a marketing theory that suggests that certain products or services require a more in-depth decision-making process by the consumer. In this model, consumers are seen as actively seeking information and evaluating alternatives before purchasing.

High-involvement products or services are typically expensive, complex, and have a high degree of risk or consequences associated with their use. Examples of high-involvement products include automobiles, real estate, and healthcare services.

In a high-involvement model, consumers go through a series of steps in the decision-making process, including problem recognition, information search, evaluation of alternatives, and post-purchase evaluation. Therefore, marketers need to understand these steps and provide relevant information and resources to assist the consumer in making a decision.

The high involvement model contrasts with the low involvement model, which suggests that consumers make purchase decisions quickly and without much thought for low-cost, low-risk products such as household items like toothpaste or shampoo.

By understanding the high involvement model, marketers can develop strategies to engage consumers in decision-making and provide the information and resources needed to make informed decisions. This can lead to more successful marketing campaigns and improved customer satisfaction.

High Involvement Model in Pharma Marketing

The high involvement model can be particularly relevant in pharma marketing, where consumers (patients) may face complex medical conditions and treatments that significantly impact their health and well-being. Here are the steps involved in the high-involvement model in pharma marketing:

1. *Problem Recognition*: Patients recognize a health problem or condition that requires medical attention. For example, a patient with diabetes may recognize the need for medication to manage their blood sugar levels.
2. *Information Search*: Patients seek information about the condition and available treatment options. They may research online, speak with healthcare professionals, or consult with patient advocacy groups. For example, a patient with diabetes may research different types of insulin and their side effects.
3. *Evaluation of Alternatives*: Patients evaluate the available treatment options, considering factors such as effectiveness, side effects, and cost. They may also consider the brand reputation and recommendations from healthcare professionals. For example, a patient with diabetes may evaluate different insulin brands and choose one known for its effectiveness and has few side effects.

4. *Purchase Decision*: Patients decide which treatment option to pursue based on their evaluation of alternatives and recommendations from healthcare professionals. For example, a patient with diabetes may decide to use a particular brand of insulin their doctor has prescribed.
5. *Post-purchase Evaluation*: Patients evaluate their experiences with the treatment option, considering factors such as effectiveness, side effects, and overall satisfaction. This can impact future treatment decisions and brand loyalty. For example, if a patient experiences unpleasant side effects with a particular brand of insulin, they may switch to a different brand.

In pharma marketing, marketers can provide relevant information and resources to assist patients in decision-making. This can include providing educational resources about the condition and treatment options, patient testimonials, and access to healthcare professionals who can answer questions and address concerns. By supporting patients throughout the decision-making process, marketers can improve the chances of a successful treatment outcome and build brand loyalty.

High Pressure Selling

High-pressure selling in pharma marketing refers to the use of aggressive tactics by sales representatives to persuade healthcare professionals to prescribe a particular drug or medical device. This can involve excessive or misleading claims about the product's benefits, downplaying or omitting information about potential risks or side effects, and applying undue pressure or incentives to influence physicians' prescribing behavior.

Using high-pressure selling tactics is widely considered unethical in the pharmaceutical industry, as it can compromise patient safety and erode trust in healthcare professionals. As a result, many pharmaceutical companies have implemented strict codes of conduct and compliance programs to prevent such practices. In addition, regulatory bodies such as the FDA in the US, and EMA in the European Union closely monitor promotional activities to ensure they are truthful, balanced, and not misleading.

However, instances of high-pressure selling have been reported, and some companies have been fined or faced legal action for violating marketing regulations. For example, in 2012, GlaxoSmithKline paid a $3 billion fine to settle allegations of illegal promotion of certain drugs, including offering kickbacks and other incentives to healthcare providers. Similarly, in 2020, Purdue Pharma pleaded guilty to charges of misleading marketing of OxyContin and agreed to pay $8 billion in penalties.

High-pressure selling is unacceptable in pharma marketing and can have serious consequences for patients and the pharmaceutical industry.

Holistic Health

Holistic Health refers to an approach to health that considers the whole person and how they interact with their environment rather than just focusing on specific illnesses. This approach emphasizes the connection of mind, body, and spirit and recognizes that our physical, mental, emotional, and spiritual well-being are interconnected.

How is it Relevant to Pharma Marketing?

The relevance of holistic health to pharma marketing cannot be understated, especially in an age where consumers are increasingly informed and prioritize overall well-being. Here is a closer look at why a holistic perspective is relevant to pharma marketing:

1. *Changing Consumer Expectations*: Today's consumers are more informed about health and wellness and expect more from their healthcare providers and products. A holistic approach aligns with this shift in consumer expectations.
2. *Differentiation in a Competitive Market*: With so many products on the market, a holistic health approach can differentiate a product by focusing on overall wellness rather than just symptom alleviation.
3. *Building Trust*: Addressing patients' overall well-being and genuine concern for their holistic health can help pharma companies establish trust with their audience.
4. *Extended Engagement*: Focusing on holistic health allows for extended engagement with consumers. Instead of interacting only during illness, pharma brands can engage with consumers during their entire wellness journey.
5. *Comprehensive Solutions*: Holistic health can improve patient outcomes by focusing on prevention, early intervention, and comprehensive management. This approach can be more effective than merely addressing isolated symptoms.
6. *Regulatory Shifts*: There is a global trend in many healthcare regulatory bodies emphasizing patient-reported outcomes, quality of life, and other holistic health measures. This makes a holistic approach more aligned with regulatory shifts.

7. *Digital Revolution*: The rise of digital health platforms, apps, and wearables means that pharma companies have a wealth of data at their fingertips. This data can be used to gain a holistic view of a patient's health and create tailored marketing strategies.
8. *Opportunity for New Product Development*: A holistic understanding can reveal gaps in the market. For instance, if a particular group of patients has unmet needs regarding mental well-being associated with a physical ailment, it opens the door for developing complementary solutions.
9. *Sustainability and CSR*: Companies globally are being pushed to show their responsibility and sustainability. A holistic approach to health can be a strong component of a pharma company's corporate social responsibility (CSR) strategy.
10. *Improved Patient Adherence*: By understanding and addressing the holistic needs of patients, pharma companies can develop strategies that improve medication adherence. This can be through supportive apps, education, or ensuring mental and emotional well-being alongside physical health.

Integrating holistic health into pharma marketing can lead to better patient outcomes, increased trust, and a more substantial brand presence. It moves the conversation from solely about the product to a broader dialogue about overall well-being, fostering deeper connections with consumers.

Implications for Pharma Marketing

In pharmaceutical marketing, a shift towards a holistic health approach can have several implications:

1. *Patient-Centricity*: Instead of focusing solely on the drug or the disease, pharma marketing could shift towards understanding the entire patient journey. This includes understanding their lifestyle, beliefs, emotional well-being, and other factors influencing their health.
2. *Education and Awareness*: Marketing campaigns might focus more on educating patients about broader aspects of their health and well-being than just the specifics of a drug or treatment.
3. *Value-Based Outcomes*: The focus might shift from just selling pills to ensuring that the patient's overall health improves, leading to more value-based pricing and reimbursement strategies.
4. *Collaborations*: Pharma companies might collaborate with alternative medical practitioners, nutritionists, therapists, and others who focus on holistic health to provide a more comprehensive solution to patients.
5. *Digital Health and Wearables*: As pharma marketers tap into holistic health, there will be an increased emphasis on digital health solutions and wearables that monitor various aspects of a person's health, from sleep patterns to stress levels.
6. *Personalized Medicine*: Recognizing that each patient is unique, there will be a greater push towards personalized medicine, including treatments tailored to individual patients based on their genetic makeup, lifestyle, and other factors.
7. *Ethical Implications*: Pharma companies must ensure their push toward holistic health is not just a marketing gimmick. They must integrate these principles into their R&D, clinical trials, and other operations.
8. *Regulatory Scrutiny*: As pharma companies make claims about the holistic benefits of their products, they might face increased scrutiny from regulatory bodies to ensure that these claims are substantiated.

Implications for Pharma Marketers

1. *Skillset Shift*: Pharma marketers must understand the holistic health landscape and its players, from Yoga instructors to nutritionists. This requires a broader knowledge base than traditional pharma marketing.
2. *Engagement Platforms*: Instead of traditional advertising, pharma marketers might engage with patients on health and wellness platforms, online communities, apps, and other digital health tools.
3. *Content Strategy*: The content might shift from being heavily product-focused to offering broader health and wellness advice, insights, and solutions.
4. *Stakeholder Engagement*: Engaging with a broader set of stakeholders will become crucial. This includes doctors and other holistic health practitioners, patient advocacy groups, and more.

In summary, a holistic approach to health in pharmaceutical marketing means recognizing and addressing the broader spectrum of factors influencing a person's health. This can lead to a more comprehensive and effective approach to patient care and might require a significant shift in strategy and operations for pharma marketers.

Hindsight

Hindsight is the ability to understand and evaluate past events or situations, often with the benefit of hindsight bias, which is the tendency to believe that after an event has occurred, one would have predicted or expected the outcome. Hindsight involves looking back on a situation or event and analyzing what went right or wrong, what could have been done differently, and what lessons can be learned from the experience.

Hindsight is often used to evaluate and inform future decisions' effectiveness. It is also used in psychology and sociology to understand human behavior and decision-making processes.

While hindsight can be useful for learning from past experiences and making better decisions in the future, it is important to recognize that it is often influenced by bias and may not always accurately reflect the reality of the situation. Therefore, it is important to approach hindsight with a critical and objective mindset and to consider multiple perspectives and sources of information.

Hindsight in Pharma Marketing

In pharma marketing, hindsight can be used to evaluate the effectiveness of past marketing campaigns and strategies. By analyzing the outcomes of past campaigns and identifying what worked and what did not, pharma companies can make more informed decisions in future marketing efforts.

Hindsight can also be used to assess the success of previous drugs or therapies and identify improvement areas. Looking back on past launches, pharma companies can determine what factors contributed to success or failure and use this information to guide future product development and marketing efforts.

Additionally, hindsight can be valuable in understanding patients' and healthcare providers' changing needs and preferences. By analyzing data and feedback from past interactions, pharma companies can identify emerging trends and adjust their marketing strategies to better resonate with their target audience. However, it is important to note that hindsight bias can also be a risk in pharma marketing. Looking back on past events with the benefit of hindsight can lead to overconfidence in decision-making and a tendency to dismiss alternative perspectives or approaches. Therefore, it is important to approach hindsight with a critical and objective mindset and to seek out diverse perspectives and data sources to inform future decisions.

Hologram

Holograms are three-dimensional images that are created by using lasers to display objects. Holograms can create immersive and interactive experiences for healthcare professionals and patients in pharma marketing. In addition, holograms can be used to showcase a product's features, mechanism of action, and benefits in a visually stunning and memorable way.

For example, a pharmaceutical company may use a hologram to demonstrate the mechanism of action of a new drug. The hologram can display a three-dimensional image of the drug's molecular structure and interaction with the body to provide therapeutic benefits. This can be a powerful tool to educate healthcare professionals and patients about the drug's benefits and how it works.

Holograms can also be used to create virtual environments for training and education purposes. For example, a pharmaceutical company may use a hologram to create a virtual surgery room where healthcare professionals can practice surgical procedures using holographic models. This can be an effective way to train healthcare professionals in a safe and controlled environment.

Holograms in Pharma: 3 Examples

1. One example of a pharmaceutical company using hologram technology in marketing is Pfizer. In 2018, Pfizer launched a hologram experience at a medical conference to showcase its products and innovative technologies. The hologram allowed healthcare professionals to interact with virtual 3D models of Pfizer's products and see how they work in the body.
2. Another example is Novartis, which used a hologram display to promote its psoriasis drug, Cosentyx. The display was set up at a conference and allowed attendees to see the drug's mechanism of action visually and interactively.
3. Abbott Laboratories also used hologram technology in marketing their products. For example, they created a hologram of their laboratory to showcase their diagnostic testing technologies at medical conferences and events. The hologram allowed attendees to see the different components of the laboratory and learn more about Abbott's products and services.

Holograms have the potential to revolutionize pharma marketing by creating immersive and interactive experiences for healthcare professionals and patients.

Hootsuite

Hootsuite is a social media management platform used in pharma marketing to manage and analyze multiple social media accounts from a single dashboard. It allows pharma companies to schedule and publish posts, engage with followers, track social media metrics, and monitor their brand reputation.

Pharma companies can use Hootsuite to streamline their social media marketing efforts and ensure compliance with regulatory guidelines. For example, they can use Hootsuite's content approval workflow to ensure that all social media posts meet regulatory requirements before publication. They can also use Hootsuite's social listening tools to monitor social media for adverse events and other potential compliance issues. For example, global pharma majors like Novartis, Pfizer, and Roche use Hootsuite for social media management.

How Hootsuite Can Help Pharma Companies

As a social media management tool, Hootsuite can help pharma companies manage and monitor their social media presence across multiple platforms in one place. In addition, it can help pharma marketers to:

1. *Schedule and Publish Content*: Hootsuite allows pharma companies to schedule and publish content to their social media accounts in advance, helping maintain a consistent social media presence.
2. *Monitor Social Media Mentions*: The tool can monitor social media for mentions of the company or its products, allowing pharma companies to respond to customer complaints or inquiries quickly.
3. *Analyze Social Media Performance*: Hootsuite provides analytics that allows pharma companies to track the performance of their social media campaigns, including engagement rates, reach, and click-through rates.
4. *Collaborate with Team Members*: Hootsuite allows multiple team members to manage social media accounts and create content, making it easier for pharma companies to collaborate on social media campaigns.

Hootsuite can help pharma companies streamline their social media management process, improve their social media presence, and gain insights into the performance of their social media campaigns.

Horizontal Diversification

Horizontal diversification is a strategy businesses use to expand into new products or markets unrelated to their current products, services, or markets. It's different from vertical diversification, where a business expands within its existing supply chain or productline.

In the context of the pharmaceutical industry, horizontal diversification refers to companies branching out into unrelated healthcare or even non-healthcare sectors. Here is how horizontal diversification might look:

1. *Consumer Healthcare Products*: While prescription drugs are the core business of many pharmaceutical firms, many also have over-the-counter (OTC) consumer healthcare divisions. Examples include pain relievers, vitamins, cough, and cold remedies.
2. *Medical Devices*: Some pharma companies may diversify by investing in or developing medical devices, ranging from diagnostic equipment to implantable devices.
3. *Diagnostics and Testing*: Many pharmaceutical companies have ventured into diagnostics, especially as precision medicine and targeted therapies become more prominent. For example, developing tests that can identify genetic markers related to drug response.
4. *Digital Health Platforms and Solutions*: With the rise of telehealth, wearable technology, and health applications, some pharmaceutical companies are moving into the digital health space. This can include developing apps or platforms to monitor patient medication adherence, manage diseases, or provide information and resources to healthcare providers.
5. *Nutritional Supplements*: Some pharma companies have ventured into the nutritional sector, offering supplements that may complement their main product offerings.
6. *Cosmetics and Personal Care*: It is not uncommon for pharma companies to diversify into the skincare or cosmetic sectors, especially if they have expertise in dermatological treatments.
7. *Animal Health*: Some companies diversify into veterinary medicine, producing drugs, vaccines, and other health products for pets and livestock.

The rationale behind such diversification can be manifold:

1. *Risk Mitigation*: By diversifying product offerings, pharma companies can cushion the

impact of potential setbacks in their core operations, such as patent cliffs, regulatory challenges, or competition.

2. *Leveraging Brand and R&D*: A strong brand in the pharma space can be leveraged in related areas, and the company's R&D capabilities can be employed to innovate in the new sector.
3. *Maximizing Shareholder Value*: Diversification can lead to more stable revenue streams, potentially enhancing shareholder value.
4. *Utilizing Existing Sales and Distribution Channels*: A pharma company with a strong distribution network can introduce new products more efficiently.

However, horizontal diversification also comes with challenges, including potential dilution of the core business focus, difficulty in managing disparate business units, and risks associated with entering unfamiliar markets. It's crucial for pharma companies to carefully assess the potential benefits and risks when considering such a strategy.

Horizontal Integration

Horizontal integration refers to the process by which companies at the same stage in the production supply chain merge or acquire one another. It's a strategy to consolidate market share, achieve economies of scale, expand into new markets, or reduce competition.

In the pharmaceutical industry, horizontal integration would involve one pharmaceutical company merging with or acquiring another that operates at the same level. Here are some examples and reasons for horizontal integration in the pharma sector:

1. *Pfizer's Acquisition of Wyeth (2009)*: one of the world's leading biopharmaceutical companies acquired Wyeth for approximately $68 billion. The move expanded Pfizer's portfolio of consumer healthcare products and added several blockbuster drugs to its lineup. It also enhanced Pfizer's position in the biotech sector and provided access to Wyeth's vaccines.
2. *Merck & Co's Acquisition of Schering Plough (2009)*: Merck acquired Schering Plough in a deal valued at $41.1 billion. The merger expanded Merck's product portfolio, especially in cholesterol drugs, as both companies had previously collaborated on developing cholesterol medications Zetia and Vytorin.
3. *Actavis' Acquisition of Allergan (2015)*: In a deal worth over $70 billion, generic drug maker Actavis acquired specialty pharmaceutical company Allergan. This acquisition expanded Actavis' brand portfolio, especially with the addition of Allergan's star product, Botox.
4. *Takeda's Acquisition of Shire (2019)*: Japanese pharma company Takeda acquired Irish-based Shire in a deal valued at $62 billion, making it one of the biggest pharma mergers in history. This move strengthened Takeda's position in the global pharmaceutical market and expanded its portfolio, especially in rare diseases and plasma-derived therapies.

Reasons for horizontal integration in the pharma industry include:

1. *Portfolio Diversification*: Companies can acquire drugs in various stages of development, thus mitigating the risks associated with drug development.
2. *Economies of Scale*: Larger companies can often produce drugs more efficiently and at a lower cost.
3. *Market Expansion*: Merging with or acquiring a company can provide access to new markets, either geographically or therapeutically.
4. *Reduction of Competition*: A company can strengthen its position in specific therapeutic areas by acquiring a competitor.
5. *Knowledge and Technology Sharing*: Combining the R&D capabilities of two companies can accelerate drug discovery and development processes.
6. *Strategic Synergies*: Some mergers help achieve strategic benefits, such as complementary drug pipelines or expertise.

Despite the potential advantages, horizontal integration also presents challenges. Integration of two corporate cultures, potential layoffs, regulatory hurdles, and ensuring that the mergers create value are some potential difficulties. As with any business strategy, weighing the benefits against the potential drawbacks is essential.

Horizontal Marketing System

A horizontal marketing system (HMS) involves two or more companies at the same level in the supply chain joining forces for marketing benefits. This can be for a one-time collaboration or a longer-term joint venture. They collaborate to exploit a new market opportunity or share resources and competencies to achieve economies of scale or scope. In the context of the pharmaceutical industry, this collaboration usually takes the form of co-marketing or co-promotion agreements.

Here are a few examples of horizontal marketing systems in the pharma sector:

1. *Co-promotion Agreements*: Often, two pharmaceutical companies might decide to co-promote a drug. One company might have a robust drug but a weak sales force and a weak distribution network, while the other might have a strong sales force but a lack of innovative drugs in its pipeline. Together, they can market the drug more effectively than they would separately. For example, Eli Lilly and Boehringer Ingelheim co-promote diabetes drugs, including Jardiance, Trajenta, and Basaglar. This partnership leverages the strength of both companies to reach a broader patient base.
2. *Shared R&D Efforts*: Sometimes, pharmaceutical companies team up for research and development efforts to reduce costs, share expertise, or access specific technologies. Consider, for example, the collaboration between AstraZeneca and Daiichi Sankyo in 2019 to jointly develop and commercialize DS-1062, a trophoblast cell-surface antigen 2 (TROP2)-directed antibody-drug conjugate for multiple cancer types. This partnership helps share the high costs and risks associated with drug development.
3. *Joint Ventures*: Companies can create a separate entity or business unit to tap into new markets or consolidate resources for specific operations. For instance, GlaxoSmithKline and Pfizer combined their consumer health businesses into a joint venture in 2018. This joint venture brought together their portfolios of over-the-counter products under one umbrella.
4. *Collaboration for Expansion*: Companies might collaborate to enter markets where they lack a presence or expertise. For instance, a company with a strong presence in the US might collaborate with a local player in an emerging market to launch its products there. Consider another example where, Sanofi and Regeneron have entered multiple collaborations over the years, sharing the costs and profits of drugs they co-develop. These alliances have resulted in several approved products and a rich pipeline of investigational drugs.

Horizontal marketing systems can be beneficial because they leverage the strengths of multiple companies, but they can also be challenging to manage. Differences in corporate culture, conflicting interests, and decision-making processes can all pose hurdles. However, in the ever-competitive and high-stakes world of pharmaceuticals, such collaborations offer a strategic way to share risks, reduce costs, and increase market reach.

HTML

HTML stands for Hypertext Markup Language, the standard markup language used for creating web pages and applications. HTML provides a way to structure content on a web page, such as headings, paragraphs, images, links, and other elements.

HTML works by using tags to define the structure and content of a web page. A tag is a code snippet that starts with an opening angle bracket (<) and ends with a closing angle bracket (>). The content between the opening and closing tags is the data the tag represents.

HTML and Pharma Marketing

HTML is relevant to pharma marketing. It is the foundation of web pages and online content, which are important channels for reaching and engaging with customers in the pharmaceutical industry.

Pharmaceutical companies use HTML to create websites, landing pages, and other digital content providing information about their products, services, and research. HTML is also used to create email templates and newsletters for email marketing campaigns.

HTML is particularly important for creating mobile-friendly websites and content as more and more people use their smartphones and tablets to access the internet. Responsive web design, which uses HTML and CSS (Cascading Style Sheets) to automatically adjust the layout of a web page to different screen sizes, is essential for providing a seamless user experience across different devices. In addition, HTML is used for search engine optimization (SEO) to improve the visibility and ranking of pharmaceutical websites and content in search engine result pages. By using proper HTML tags and meta tags, pharmaceutical companies can help search engines understand the content of their web pages and improve their chances of being found by potential customers.

HTML is a foundational technology essential for creating and delivering digital content in the pharmaceutical industry, making it a critical tool for pharma marketing.

Hybrid Model

In marketing, a hybrid model refers to a business strategy combining different distribution and marketing methods to reach a wider audience and improve overall effectiveness. For example, a hybrid model may involve online and offline channels, such as a brick-and-mortar store and an e-commerce website, or direct and indirect sales, such as selling products through a company's sales force and intermediaries, such as wholesalers and retailers.

In digital marketing, a hybrid model may involve combining different types of advertising, such as social media ads and pay-per-click (PPC) ads, or using a combination of inbound and outbound marketing tactics to attract and engage customers.

A hybrid model allows companies to utilize the strengths of different marketing channels and approaches to optimize their reach, engagement, and sales.

Hybrid Model in Pharma Marketing

A Hybrid Model in pharma marketing refers to an approach that combines traditional marketing strategies with digital marketing tactics. This approach recognizes that customers (Healthcare professionals) and consumers (patients) increasingly use digital channels to access information and engage with pharmaceutical companies. Still, pharmaceutical marketing recognizes the continued importance of face-to-face interactions and other traditional marketing methods.

Here are some examples of how a hybrid model might work in pharma marketing:

1. *Multichannel Marketing*: A pharmaceutical company might use multiple channels to engage with customers, including traditional and digital. For example, a company might use print advertisements in medical journals, direct mail, and in-person sales visits with digital channels such as email campaigns, webinars, and social media outreach.
2. *Remote Detailing*: A company might use remote detailing (e-detailing) to connect with healthcare professionals virtually. This approach uses digital platforms such as video conferencing to deliver product information, answer questions, and provide product samples. This can be an efficient way to reach a large audience while reducing the need for in-person visits.
3. *Content Marketing*: A company might use content marketing to create and distribute high-quality content that is relevant and valuable to customers. This can include blog posts, white papers, case studies, and other content that provide insights into disease management, treatment options, or patient care.
4. *Digital Advertising*: A company might use digital advertising to reach customers through online channels such as search engines, social media platforms, and mobile apps. This can include targeted display ads, sponsored content, and paid search ads.
5. *Patient Engagement*: A company might use digital tools to engage with patients and provide support beyond the product. This can include patient education resources, disease management tools, and mobile apps that provide personalized support and information.

A Hybrid model in pharma marketing recognizes the need to use various marketing channels to reach customers where they are. By combining traditional and digital marketing tactics, companies can create a more effective and efficient marketing strategy that delivers value to customers and drives business results.

I

1. IBM
2. Icarus Paradox
3. Iceberg Principle
4. IFPMA
5. Image
6. Image Repositioning
7. Imitation Effect
8. Impact
9. Imperfect Competition
10. Import Substitution
11. Impression
12. Impulse Buying
13. Inclusivity
14. Integrative Solutions (Marketing)
15. Integrative Solutions (Medical)
16. Inbound Marketing
17. Incentives
18. Incentivized Traffic
19. Indian Patents Act 1970
20. Indirect Communications
21. Indirect Exports
22. Industrial Marketing
23. Inertia Selling
24. Inflation
25. Influencers
26. Influencer Marketing
27. Infographics
28. Infomediary
29. Infomercial
30. Informatics
31. Information Anxiety
32. Information Hierarchy
33. Informed Consent
34. Inherited Audience
35. In-licensing
36. Innovation
37. Instagram
38. Instant Gratification
39. Instant Messaging
40. Institutional Marketing
41. Intangibles
42. Intangible Repositioning
43. Integration
44. Integrated Marketing
45. Integration Strategies
46. Intellectual Capital
47. International Harmonization
48. International Marketing
49. International Marketing Planning
50. International Normalized Ratio (INR)
51. Internet Marketing
52. Intelligent Clinics
53. Internet of Things (IoT)
54. Interruption Marketing
55. Intrusive Marketing
56. Investigative New Drug (IND)
57. iPad Detailing

IBM

IBM, or International Business Machines Corporation, is an iconic American multinational technology company known for its wide range of offerings in computer hardware, software, and consulting services. Founded in 1911 as the Computing-Tabulating-Recording Company (CTR) and renamed IBM in 1924, the company has been at the forefront of technological and computing advancements for over a century.

IBM's Foray into Healthcare and Pharma

IBM's foray into healthcare and pharmaceuticals is marked by its endeavor to harness data analytics, artificial intelligence, and technological know-how to transform patient care, drug discovery, and healthcare operations. IBM Watson Health, a dedicated segment of IBM, embodies much of this effort. Here's an overview of IBM's involvement in healthcare and pharmaceuticals and the subsequent implications for pharma marketers:

IBM's Involvement

1. *IBM Watson Health*: This AI-powered entity was designed to assist in health data analysis. IBM has made several acquisitions to enhance Watson Health's capabilities, such as Truven Health Analytics, Phytel, and Explorys. Watson has been applied to various healthcare tasks, from aiding clinicians in cancer care to helping insurance companies analyze data for better decision-making.
2. *Drug Discovery*: IBM Watson for Drug Discovery was introduced as a cloud-based, AI-powered tool aimed at helping researchers identify novel drug candidates and new drug targets faster and more efficiently.
3. *Medical Imaging*: Watson Health has initiatives targeting medical imaging to assist radiologists in analyzing and diagnosing conditions from imaging data.
4. *Clinical Trial Matching*: Using AI, IBM Watson can help match patients to appropriate clinical trials, speeding up recruitment and potentially bringing drugs to market more swiftly.
5. *Genomics*: Partnering with institutes like Quest Diagnostics, IBM has used Watson to help oncologists analyze the genetic data of tumors and identify potential therapeutic routes.
6. *Electronic Health Records (EHR)*: IBM has been digitizing health records, and Watson can mine these records for insights into patient care and outcomes.

Implications for Pharma Marketers

1. *Personalized Marketing*: With AI's capacity to sift through vast amounts of patient and clinical data, pharma marketers can develop more targeted and personalized campaigns addressing specific patient segments and their unique needs.
2. *Evidence-based Campaigns*: The analytical power of tools like Watson can enable pharma marketers to back their strategies with solid clinical evidence, enhancing the credibility of their campaigns.
3. *Efficient Drug Launches*: Faster drug discovery and clinical trial recruitment can lead to swifter drug launches, demanding agile marketing strategies to capitalize on these new opportunities.
4. *Strategic Partnerships*: As IBM collaborates with various stakeholders in healthcare, there are ample opportunities for pharma companies to form strategic partnerships, leveraging IBM's technological prowess in their marketing endeavors.
5. *Enhanced Patient Engagement*: With deeper insights into patient behavior and treatment outcomes, marketers can craft campaigns that resonate more profoundly with patients, ensuring better engagement and adherence.
6. *Regulatory Compliance*: IBM's tools can help pharma marketers ensure that their campaigns comply with the constantly evolving regulatory landscape, especially concerning patient data privacy.
7. *Real-time Market Response*: Leveraging AI analytics, pharma marketers can adjust their strategies in real time based on market feedback and emerging trends, ensuring that their campaigns remain relevant and impactful.
8. *Educational Opportunities*: Pharma companies can collaborate with entities like IBM to offer training and educational sessions for healthcare professionals, informing them about the latest advancements in drug discovery and patient care, thus indirectly promoting their products.

In conclusion, IBM's venture into health care and Pharma, particularly with its emphasis on AI and data analytics, signifies a transformative era for the industry. It presents opportunities and challenges for pharma marketers, demanding a nuanced approach that balances technological advancements with patient-centric values.

Icarus Paradox

The Icarus Paradox is a concept developed by business author Danny Miller. It refers to the idea that companies can fail due to the same factors that led to their success. The metaphor is based on the Greek myth of Icarus, who flew too close to the sun with wings made of wax and feathers, causing his wings to melt and him to fall to his death. Miller argues that companies must balance their strengths with an awareness of their weaknesses and an openness to change.

In the pharmaceutical industry, the Icarus Paradox can manifest in several ways. For example, a company that experiences success with a particular drug may become complacent and fail to invest in research and development for new drugs, leading to a lack of innovation and a decline in market share. Additionally, a company that becomes too focused on maximizing profits may cut corners on drug safety and quality control, leading to negative patient outcomes and a damaged reputation.

To avoid the Icarus Paradox, companies in the pharma industry must maintain a balance between their strengths and weaknesses, stay vigilant in monitoring market trends and competition, and remain adaptable and open to change. This can involve investing in research and development, prioritizing patient safety and quality control, and cultivating a culture of innovation and continuous improvement.

Iceberg Principle

The Iceberg principle is a concept that suggests that the visible aspects of a situation or problem are only a small portion of the total reality, with the majority of the issue being hidden from view. This concept often describes complex problems or situations where underlying factors or root causes may not be immediately apparent.

The name Iceberg Principle comes from only a small portion of an iceberg visible above the water, while most of its mass is hidden beneath the surface. In the same way, only a small portion of a problem or situation may be visible to the naked eye, while most of the issue is hidden.

The iceberg principle is important in many areas, including business, management, and marketing. For example, in marketing, companies may only see the visible factors affecting their sales, such as pricing or advertising. Still, underlying factors, such as changes in consumer behavior or economic conditions, may drive sales trends. By understanding the iceberg principle, individuals and organizations can work to identify and address the underlying factors or root causes of a problem or situation rather than just addressing the visible symptoms. This can lead to more effective solutions and better outcomes in the long run.

Iceberg Principle in Pharma Marketing

The iceberg principle is also applicable in pharma marketing. In pharma marketing, the visible aspects of a situation might include sales data, customer feedback, and market trends. However, most of the reality of the situation may be hidden beneath the surface and not immediately apparent.

For example, a decline in sales of a particular drug may be attributed to factors such as increased competition or changes in the regulatory environment. In addition, however, there may be underlying factors that are not immediately visible, such as changes in prescribing behavior or negative perceptions of the drug among patients.

By applying the iceberg principle, pharma marketers can identify and address these underlying factors to improve sales and marketing effectiveness. This may involve conducting market research to understand better healthcare providers' and patients' attitudes and behaviors, developing targeted messaging and education campaigns, or engaging with key opinion leaders and other stakeholders to address concerns and build support for the drug.

The iceberg principle reminds us that the visible aspects of a situation or problem in pharma marketing may only be the tip. A deeper understanding of the underlying factors and root causes is often necessary to achieve success.

IFPMA

IFPMA stands for International Federation of Pharmaceutical Manufacturers and Associations. It is a global non-profit organization representing research-based pharmaceutical companies and associations worldwide. Founded in 1968, the IFPMA currently has 30 member companies and 67 national and regional associations.

The mission of the IFPMA is to promote and protect the research-based pharmaceutical industry and contribute to global health. The organization engages in various activities to achieve this mission, including advocacy, capacity building, knowledge sharing, and collaboration.

Some of the key initiatives and activities of the IFPMA include:

1. *Advocacy*: The IFPMA advocates for policies and regulations that support research and development of new medications that support research and development of new medicines, as well as policies that promote access to medicines and patient safety.
2. *Capacity Building*: The IFPMA works with its members to build their capacity to research and develop new medicines and navigate regulatory and policy environments worldwide.
3. *Knowledge Sharing*: The IFPMA facilitates knowledge sharing among its members, providing a platform for exchanging best practices, ideas, and information.
4. *Collaboration*: The IFPMA collaborates with various stakeholders, including governments, non-governmental organizations, and other industry associations, to advance its mission and promote global health.

The IFPMA is a key player in the pharmaceutical industry, working to promote and protect the interests of its members and contribute to global health.

Image

Image is an important component of pharmaceutical marketing, as it significantly shapes how stakeholders perceive pharmaceutical brands. In addition, a positive image can help to build trust and credibility with healthcare professionals (HCPs), patients, and other stakeholders, which can drive business success. Here are some ways the image can be used in pharma marketing:

1. *Branding*: Effective branding can help to create a strong and positive image for a pharmaceutical brand. This may involve developing a logo, brand identity, and messaging that reflects the company's values and mission.
2. *Reputation Management*: Reputation management is an important part of pharma marketing, as it involves monitoring and managing how stakeholders perceive the brand. This may involve addressing negative publicity or engaging with stakeholders to improve the brand's overall perception.
3. *Thought Leadership*: Positioning the company as a thought leader in the industry can help build a positive image and enhance stakeholder credibility. This may involve publishing articles, presenting at conferences, or engaging with key opinion leaders to share expertise and insights.
4. *Patient-centricMarketing*: Patient-centric marketing can help to build a positive image for a pharmaceutical brand by demonstrating a commitment to improving patient outcomes and experiences. This may involve developing educational materials, patient support programs, or other initiatives that help patients better understand and manage their conditions.

Image Repositioning

Image repositioning in pharmaceutical marketing refers to changing how a pharmaceutical brand is perceived by healthcare professionals, patients, and other stakeholders. This may involve altering the messaging, positioning, or branding of the product to better align with the needs and expectations of the target audience.

Image repositioning may be necessary if a drug is not performing as well as expected in the market or if negative perceptions or misconceptions about the product hinder its success. Repositioning may involve:

- Highlighting different benefits or attributes of the drug.
- Changing the target audience or market.
- Emphasizing different brand features.

The process of image repositioning in pharma marketing typically involves a range of activities, including market research, messaging and branding development, and communication and education campaigns targeted at healthcare professionals, patients, and other stakeholders. It may also involve engaging with key opinion leaders, patient advocacy groups, and other stakeholders to build support and address concerns.

How to Do it

Repositioning a pharmaceutical brand requires a well-planned and carefully executed marketing strategy. Here are some steps that can help you effectively reposition a pharmaceutical brand:

1. *Conduct Market Research*: The first step in repositioning a pharmaceutical brand is thoroughly understanding the target audience and market. This involves conducting market research to identify the needs, preferences, and behaviors of healthcare professionals, patients, and other stakeholders.
2. *Define the New Positioning*: Based on the market research findings, define the new positioning for the brand. This may involve emphasizing different benefits, changing the target audience, or rebranding the product.
3. *Develop a Messaging and Branding Strategy*: Once the new positioning is defined, develop a messaging and branding strategy that effectively communicates the new brand positioning to the target audience. This may involve creating new marketing materials, updating existing materials, or developing a new brand identity.
4. *Execute a Communication Plan*: A comprehensive communication plan that targets healthcare professionals, patients, and other stakeholders with the new messaging and branding. This may involve a mix of tactics, including advertising, public relations, social media, and educational campaigns.
5. *Monitor and Evaluate Results*: Monitor the results of the repositioning effort and evaluate its effectiveness. This involves tracking sales, brand awareness, and soliciting feedback from healthcare professionals, patients, and other stakeholders. Then, based on the results, adjust the strategy as needed to ensure continued success.

Image repositioning in pharma marketing is about improving the perception and acceptance of the brand among healthcare professionals, patients, and other stakeholders. Following these steps can effectively reposition your brand and improve its image and performance.

Imitation Effect

The imitation effect in pharmaceutical marketing refers to the phenomenon where the marketing tactics of one company are copied or imitated by competitors. This can occur when a marketing strategy is seen as successful, and other companies in the industry attempt to replicate that success by adopting similar strategies.

Here are some examples of the imitation effect in pharma marketing:

1. *Direct-to-Consumer Advertising*: When a pharmaceutical company launches a successful advertising campaign, other companies in the industry may imitate that campaign by using similar messaging or channels.
2. *Patient Support Programs*: Successful patient support programs, such as patient education or patient assistance programs, may be imitated by competitors in an attempt to replicate their success.
3. *Sales Force Tactics*: Sales representatives may observe competitors' successful sales tactics and imitate them in their interactions with healthcare professionals.

While imitation can be a strategy for success, it also presents some risks. For example, over-reliance on imitation may result in a lack of innovation and differentiation. In addition, it could lead to a me-too mentality where companies are not effectively distinguishing themselves in the market.

To avoid the negative effect, pharma marketers should focus on developing unique strategies and tactics tailored to their target audience and business objectives. By being creative and innovative, companies can stand out from their competitors and effectively engage with their audience.

Impact

'Impact' is a particular action or event's measurable or observable effects or consequences. It can refer to both positive and negative effects and is often used to evaluate the effectiveness or success of a particular initiative, program, or policy.

The impact can be measured in various ways, depending on the context of the goals of the initiative of the program. For example, in social programs, the impact might be measured in terms of the number of people who have been helped or the degree to which the program has achieved its goals. The impact might be measured in revenue, profit, or market share in the business context.

The impact can be direct and indirect and occur over short-term and long-term horizons. It can also be influenced by various factors, such as the context in which the action or event occurred, external factors, and individual and societal behavior.

The impact is a key concept in various fields, including business, public policy, and social and environmental advocacy. Measuring impact is essential for evaluating initiatives and programs' success and identifying areas for improvement and future investment.

Impact and Pharma Marketing

The impact of pharma marketing can be measured in various ways, depending on the marketing objectives and the target audience. In general, the impact of pharma marketing can be measured in terms of its effectiveness in achieving the desired outcomes, such as increasing awareness, brand perception, prescriptions, sales, and patient outcomes. Here are some key metrics used to measure the impact of pharma marketing:

1. *Reach*: Reach refers to the number of people exposed to the marketing message. Depending on the channel, it can be measured in terms of impressions, views, or clicks.
2. *Engagement*: Engagement measures how actively the target audience engages with the marketing message. It can be measured in terms of likes, shares, comments, or time spent on a website or social media page.
3. *Sales*: Sales are a key indicator of the impact of pharma marketing, as they reflect the effectiveness of the marketing efforts in driving revenue. Sales can be measured in revenue generated, units sold, or market share.
4. *Brand Awareness*: Brand awareness measures how well the target audience recognizes and remembers the brand. It can be measured through surveys or buy-tracking online brand mentions.
5. *Patient Outcomes*: In some cases, the impact of pharma marketing can be measured in terms of its impact on patient outcomes, such as adherence to treatment or improvement in health outcomes.

It is important to note that measuring the impact of pharma marketing can be complex. Factors such as the competitive landscape, regulatory environment, and patient preferences can influence the outcomes. Therefore, it is essential to use a combination of metrics and analyze the results in the context of the broader marketing strategy.

Imperfect Competition

Imperfect competition is a market structure when multiple companies operate in an industry but do not compete on a level playing field. In other words, some factors prevent competition from being perfect, such as barriers to entry, market power, and differentiation.

In the context of pharma marketing, imperfect competition can occur in many ways:

1. *Patents*: When a pharmaceutical company has a patent on a drug for a certain period, this gives them a significant market advantage and can limit competition.
2. *Brand Recognition*: Pharmaceutical companies that have strong brand recognition and reputation may be able to charge higher prices for their products and may have a larger market share than their competitors.
3. *Regulatory Barriers*: Regulations and requirements for drug approval can create barriers to entry for new companies, limiting competition.
4. *Physician Preference*: Physicians prefer certain drugs based on their own experiences or relationships with pharmaceutical companies, which can give certain companies an advantage.
5. *Insurance Coverage*: Insurance companies may have preferred drug lists or formularies, which can limit patient access to certain drugs and limit competition for those drugs.

Imperfect competition can negatively affect the industry, including higher drug prices, limited patient access to drugs, and decreased innovation. However, imperfect competition can also drive companies to innovate and differentiate themselves to stand out.

Import Substitution

Import substitution is an economic policy that promotes domestic production and self-sufficiency by replacing imported goods with locally produced ones. The policy involves reducing or eliminating imports of goods that can be produced domestically and replacing them with locally made products. This boosts the domestic economy, creates jobs, and reduces the country's import dependence.

Import substitution policies can take various forms, such as tariffs, quotas, subsidies, and other trade barriers that make foreign goods more expensive or difficult to import. Moreover, the policy can be applied to various products, from consumer goods to capital goods.

In pharma marketing, import substitution could refer to promoting domestically produced pharmaceutical products over imported ones. This could involve incentivizing local production of pharmaceuticals, reducing tariffs on domestically produced drugs, or other policies to encourage the development and growth of the domestic pharmaceutical industry. However, as with any economic policy, there are potential trade-offs and risks to consider, including the potential for reduced competition, increased prices for consumers, and decreased access to certain medications.

Impression

In pharmaceutical marketing, an 'Impression' refers to the number of times an ad or promotional message is displayed on a website or social media platform. It represents the total number of times the ad or message is seen by users, regardless of whether they interact with it or not.

Impressions are often used as a metric for evaluating the reach and exposure of a marketing campaign. They indicate how many people have been exposed to the message but do not necessarily reflect the campaign's level of engagement or effectiveness.

Impressions can be measured in various ways, depending on the marketing channel. For example, in digital advertising, impressions are typically measured by ad servers, which track the number of times an ad is displayed on a website or mobile app. In social media marketing, impressions are typically measured by the platform's analytical tools, which track the number of times a post or ad is displayed in a user's feed.

It is important to note that impressions alone do not provide a complete picture of the impact of a marketing campaign. Other metrics, such as clicks, engagement rates, and conversions, should also be considered to evaluate the campaign's effectiveness to optimize future marketing efforts.

Impulse Buying

Impulse buying refers to purchasing without prior planning or careful consideration. Responding to a strong emotional or psychological urge is often a spontaneous decision. Impulse buying can happen in various settings, including physical stores, online shopping platforms, and social media. Impulse buying can be driven by many factors, such as:

1. *Emotional Triggers*: Strong emotions like happiness, sadness, or excitement can drive people to make impulse purchases to improve their mood or reward themselves.
2. *Limited Availability*: When a product is scarce or only available for a limited time, customers may feel a sense of urgency to make a purchase, even if they had not planned to buy it.
3. *Social Influence*: When people see others buying or using a particular product, they may be more likely to buy it themselves.
4. *Marketing Tactics*: Advertising and marketing techniques, such as attractive packaging, sales promotions, or persuasive messaging, can encourage impulse buying behavior.

Impulse buying can have both positive and negative effects. On the one hand, it can lead to unexpected pleasures and a sense of excitement. But on the other hand, it can also result in regret, financial strain, and overconsumption.

Impulse Buying and Pharma Marketing

In pharmaceutical marketing, impulse buying can refer to patients making unplanned purchases of over-the-counter (OTC) medications or supplements without consulting their healthcare provider first.

Pharma companies may use marketing tactics to encourage impulse buying in certain circumstances. Here are some examples of strategies that may be used:

1. *Point-of-sale Promotions*: In a pharmacy or retail store, pharma companies may offer discounts or promotions on certain OTC medications or supplements at the point of sale. This can encourage customers to purchase immediately rather than considering their needs first.
2. *Product Placement*: Placing certain OTC medications or supplements in highly visible pharmacy or retail store areas can encourage impulse buying. For example, placing eye-catching packaging or displays near the checkout counter can prompt customers to make a last-minute purchase.
3. *Limited-time Offers*: Offering a limited-time discount or promotion on a certain product can create a sense of urgency for customers to purchase before the deal expires. This can encourage impulse buying behavior in customers who may not have considered purchasing the product.
4. *Celebrity Endorsements*: Using a celebrity to endorse a particular OTC medication or supplement can create a sense of trust and credibility among customers. This can prompt customers to purchase based on emotions rather than carefully considering their needs or budget.

It is important to note that impulse buying behavior can be problematic in pharma marketing if it leads patients to make uninformed or potentially harmful decisions about their health. As such, pharma companies should follow responsible marketing practices that prioritize patient safety and informed decision-making.

Inclusivity

Inclusivity in pharmaceutical marketing is a crucial element that focuses on ensuring that marketing efforts are accessible and considerate of all individuals, regardless of their backgrounds, abilities, or characteristics. Here are some key aspects and implications of inclusivity in pharma marketing:

1. *Representation*: Inclusive marketing aims to represent diverse groups of people in advertisements, promotional materials, and campaigns. This means featuring people of various races, ethnicities, ages, genders, abilities, and backgrounds to reflect the diversity of the patient population.
2. *Accessibility*: Inclusive marketing also involves making marketing materials accessible to disabled individuals. This includes providing alternative formats, such as braille or audio descriptions, and ensuring digital content complies with accessibility standards.
3. *Culturally Sensitive Messaging*: Inclusive marketing considers cultural nuances and avoids stereotypes or insensitivity. Messages should resonate with different cultural groups and respect their values and beliefs.
4. *Language Considerations*: Addressing language diversity is essential. Providing materials in multiple languages or utilizing interpreters and translated content can help reach non-English speaking communities.
5. *Health Literacy*: Pharma marketing should be designed with health literacy in mind, ensuring that information is clear, concise, and easy to understand for all patients, regardless of their education level.
6. *Awareness of Health Disparities*: Inclusivity in pharma marketing acknowledges and addresses healthcare disparities among different communities. It strives to provide information and access to healthcare solutions that can reduce these disparities.

The implications of inclusivity in pharmaceutical marketing include improved engagement with a wider patient base, enhanced trust and credibility, and compliance with regulations related to accessibility and diversity. Pharmaceutical companies can foster a more inclusive, equitable, and respectful healthcare environment by prioritizing inclusivity.

Integrative Solutions (Marketing)

Integrative solutions in pharmaceutical marketing refer to a holistic approach that combines various marketing strategies and channels to create a cohesive and effective marketing plan. This approach recognizes that modern marketing in the pharmaceutical industry is multifaceted and requires a combination of tactics to reach and engage healthcare professionals and patients. Here are some key components and implications of integrative solutions in pharmaceutical marketing:

1. *Multichannel Marketing*: Integrative solutions encompass multiple channels such as digital marketing, social media, print media, conferences, and direct sales to engage healthcare professionals and patients. It ensures the marketing message reaches the target audience through their preferred communication channels.
2. *Data-Driven Marketing*: Leveraging data analytics and customer insights is crucial for personalized and effective marketing. Integrative solutions involve collecting and analyzing data to tailor marketing strategies to the specific needs and preferences of the audience.
3. *Content Marketing*: Providing valuable and educational content is central to pharmaceutical marketing. Integrative solutions involve creating informative content, such as white papers, articles, webinars, and videos, to establish the company as a trusted source of information.
4. *Regulatory Compliance*: The pharmaceutical industry is highly regulated. Integrative solutions require a thorough understanding of the regulatory landscape to ensure that all marketing efforts comply with industry standards and legal requirements.
5. *Relationship Building*: Building strong relationships with healthcare professionals, opinion leaders, patient advocacy groups, and other stakeholders is vital. Integrative solutions focus on nurturing these relationships through various means, such as KOL (Key Opinion Leader) engagement and collaboration with healthcare organizations.
6. *Patient-Centric Approach*: Integrative solutions recognize the importance of putting patients at the center of marketing efforts. This involves understanding patient journeys, needs, and preferences and tailoring marketing strategies accordingly.

7. *Measuring and Optimization*: Continuous measurement of marketing efforts and the ability to adapt and optimize campaigns in real time are key elements of integrative solutions. This allows for improved ROI and effectiveness.

Implications of integrative solutions in pharma marketing include better engagement, more efficient use of resources, improved patient outcomes, and increased brand visibility and credibility. Combining various marketing approaches cohesively allows pharmaceutical companies to navigate the complex healthcare landscape and achieve their marketing goals more effectively.

Integrative Solutions (Medical)

Integrative solutions in medical treatment involve combining conventional medical therapies with Complementary and Alternative Medicine (CAM) approaches to provide a comprehensive and patient-centered healthcare experience. These approaches recognize the importance of addressing not only the physical aspects of health but also patients' mental, emotional, and social well-being. Integrative medicine can include acupuncture, herbal medicine, yoga, mindfulness, and nutrition alongside conventional treatments.

Pharmaceutical marketing can leverage integrative solutions in several ways:

1. *Education and Awareness*: Pharmaceutical companies can provide educational materials and resources highlighting the benefits of integrative medicine along with their medications. This can include information on how complementary therapies can enhance treatment outcomes and improve overall well-being.
2. *Partnerships*: Collaborating with complementary and alternative therapies providers can be a strategic move for pharmaceutical companies. Such partnerships can create synergies and offer patients a more holistic approach to their health. Pharma marketing can promote these partnerships and the benefits they bring.
3. *Patient Support Programs*: Pharma companies can offer patient support programs incorporating integrative medicine into the treatment plan. These programs can provide resources, counseling, and access to CAM therapies, enhancing patient experience.
4. *Content Marketing*: Creating content that highlights the value of integrative solutions and their positive impact on patient outcomes can be a part of marketing efforts. This can include case studies, patient testimonials, and expert interviews.
5. *Healthcare Professional Education*: Providing healthcare professionals with information and training on integrative medicine allows them to better advise patients on complementary therapies. Pharma marketing can support these educational initiatives.
6. *Digital Health Platforms*: Developing digital platforms and apps that offer integrative medicine resources and support can be a way to engage patients and healthcare professionals, especially in the growing field of digital therapeutics.
7. *Clinical Trials and Research*: Supporting and conducting research on the efficacy of integrative approaches can lend credibility to pharmaceutical products. Marketing efforts can communicate the results and benefits of these studies to the medical community and patients.

The key is to ensure that marketing efforts align with patient well-being and provide useful, evidence-based information. Pharma marketing can promote integrative solutions by focusing on patient-centered care, improving treatment outcomes, and enhancing the overall healthcare experience.

Inbound Marketing

Inbound marketing is a marketing strategy that creates valuable content and experiences that attract and engage potential customers. Inbound marketing aims to build customer relationships by providing useful information and resources to help them make informed purchasing decisions.

In contrast to traditional outbound marketing strategies, such as TV ads or cold calls, inbound marketing aims to pull customers through organic search traffic, social media, and other channels. By providing relevant and informative content, companies can establish themselves as thought leaders and trusted sources of information in their industry.

In the pharmaceutical industry, inbound marketing can provide patients and healthcare providers valuable information about drugs, treatments, and health conditions. For example, a pharmaceutical company might create a blog with articles on the latest research in a particular area or a website with patient resources and educational materials.

By providing useful content that helps patients and healthcare providers better understand their options, companies can build relationships with their target audience and position themselves as trusted partners in healthcare. This can lead to increased brand recognition and loyalty and improved patient outcomes.

Incentives

Incentives in pharma marketing refer to the various rewards or inducements that pharmaceutical companies offer to healthcare professionals, patients, or other stakeholders to encourage them to use or recommend their products. While incentives can be an effective way to promote pharmaceutical products, they are also subject to regulation. Therefore, they must be carefully managed to avoid conflicts of interest and maintain the integrity of the healthcare system.

Here are some examples of incentives that are commonly used in pharmaceutical marketing:

1. *Financial Incentives*: Pharmaceutical companies may offer financial incentives to healthcare professionals through consulting fees, speaker fees, or other forms of compensation in exchange for promoting their products. These incentives must be disclosed and comply with regulations to avoid potential conflicts of interest.
2. *Gifts and Samples*: Pharmaceutical companies may offer free samples of their products or other gifts to healthcare professionals, patients, or other stakeholders to introduce them to the benefits of their products. Gifts and samples are also subject to regulations and must be appropriate and within ethical guidelines.
3. *Educational Events*: Pharmaceutical companies may host educational events such as conferences, seminars, and webinars to educate healthcare professionals about their products. These events may include meals, travel, and other perks for attendees. However, even these are subject to regulations, and pharmaceutical companies must comply with the guidelines.
4. *Patient Support Programs*: Pharmaceutical companies may offer patient support programs, such as patient education materials, financial assistance, or access to healthcare providers, to help patients manage their conditions and encourage them to use their products.

Incentives are a common part of pharma marketing, but they must be carefully managed to avoid conflicts of interest and maintain the integrity of the healthcare system. Pharmaceutical companies must comply with regulations, be transparent about their marketing practices, and focus on building strong relationships with healthcare professionals, patients, and other stakeholders based on trust, mutual benefit, and ethical practices.

Incentivized Traffic

Incentivized traffic refers to website or mobile app visitors who are incentivized or rewarded for engaging with an advertiser's content, such as completing a survey, downloading an app, or watching a video advertisement. Incentives can take many forms, including virtual currency, points, exclusive content access, or real-world rewards like gift cards or discounts.

Incentivized traffic can be an effective way for advertisers to increase engagement and conversions, as users are more likely to engage with content if they receive a reward. However, incentivized traffic can also be of lower quality, as users may not be genuinely interested in the advertised product or service but only engage to receive the reward.

In pharmaceutical marketing, incentivized traffic may not be a suitable approach, as pharmaceutical advertising is subject to strict regulations and ethical considerations. For example, advertising prescription drugs or medical devices to the general public is heavily regulated or prohibited, and incentivizing users to engage with such content could be seen as unethical or potentially misleading. Additionally, pharmaceutical companies must ensure that any claims made in their advertising are truthful and not misleading, which can be difficult when incentivizing users to engage with content.

Indian Patents Act 1970

The Indian Patents Act of 1970 is a significant legislation that governs patents in India. It replaced the previous Patents Act of 1911 and introduced major changes to the Indian patent system.

One of the most significant changes introduced by the 1970 Act was the removal of product patents for pharmaceuticals and agricultural chemicals. Indian companies could produce and sell generic versions of patented drugs without fear of infringing on the original patent. This change significantly impacted the availability and affordability of medicines in India and made it easier for the Indian pharmaceutical industry to grow and become more competitive.

Another important change introduced by the 1970 Act was the introduction of a compulsory licensing provision. This provision allows the government to grant a licence to produce a patented invention to a third party without the patent holder's consent in cases where the invention is deemed necessary for public health or in the interest of national security.

The Indian government has used this provision to improve access to essential medicines. In addition, it allowed Indian companies to produce and sell generic versions of patented drugs at a lower cost, improving the affordability and availability of medicines for the Indian population. However, it has also been criticized by some patent holders and foreign governments, who argue that it has weakened patent protection and may discourage foreign investment in the Indian market.

Indirect Communication

Indirect communications in pharmaceutical marketing refer to marketing strategies and tactics that do not involve the direct promotion of a product or service. Instead, these strategies often create brand awareness, establish thought leadership, and build stakeholder relationships.

Here are some examples of indirect communications in pharmaceutical marketing:

1. *Content Marketing*: Creating and distributing informative and educational content, such as blog posts, white papers, and infographics, to engage and educate audiences.
2. *Social Media Marketing*: Leveraging social media platforms to share relevant content, engage with followers, and build relationships with key opinion leaders and patient advocates.
3. *Event Marketing*: Participating in industry events, conferences, and webinars to showcase thought leadership and engage with stakeholders.
4. *Public Relations*: Developing relationships with media outlets and journalists to secure coverage and generate positive publicity.
5. *Advocacy Marketing*: Collaborating with patient advocacy groups and other stakeholders to promote awareness and education about a disease or condition.

Indirect communications can effectively build credibility and trust with stakeholders without the perceived hard sell of traditional marketing tactics. However, measuring the impact of these strategies' ROI (Return on Investment) can be challenging, and they may require a longer-term investment to see results.

Indirect Exports

Indirect exporting refers to the process by which a company sells its products in a foreign market without handling the actual export process. Instead, it utilizes intermediaries to conduct these operations. In the pharmaceutical sector, indirect exports can be especially relevant due to the highly regulated nature of the industry and the complexities associated with ensuring compliance with different countries' health and safety standards. Here's how indirect exports typically work in the pharmaceutical industry:

1. *Intermediaries*: These could be export trading companies, intermediaries, or agents specializing in the pharmaceutical market. These intermediaries have the knowledge and networks to market and distribute pharmaceutical products in foreign markets effectively.
2. *Regulatory Compliance*: Many countries have stringent regulations surrounding the import and sale of pharmaceutical products. An intermediary will often have better knowledge of local regulations and can help ensure compliance.
3. *Distribution and Storage*: Certain pharmaceutical products, such as vaccines, require specialized storage conditions (like refrigeration) to maintain efficacy. Indirect exporters usually partner with local distribution chains to ensure products are stored and transported correctly.
4. *Marketing and Branding*: Local intermediaries have a deeper understanding of local market dynamics and consumer behavior. They can offer insights and strategies to position the pharmaceutical product effectively in the foreign market.
5. *After Sales Support*: Handling post-sales issues like product returns, adverse event reports, and other customer queries can be challenging in a foreign country. Intermediaries can manage this, providing a buffer between the manufacturer and the end consumer.
6. *Payment and Currency Handling*: Intermediaries handle the financial aspects of the transaction, including dealing with currency conversions, securing payments, and managing credit risks.

Benefits and Indirect Exports In Pharma

There are several benefits for pharmaceutical companies that choose the indirect export route. Consider the following, for example:

1. *Lowered Risk*: Companies can test the waters of a foreign market without committing extensive resources.
2. *Focused Resources*: The pharmaceutical company can concentrate on core activities like R & D and production, leaving the complexities of export to experts.
3. *Access to Local Expertise*: Intermediaries have local market knowledge, which can provide a competitive edge.
4. *Flexibility*: Companies can easily switch strategies or markets without significant investments.

Challenges

However, indirect exports in the pharmaceutical industry are not without challenges. Here are some of those:

1. *Lower Profit Margins*: Since intermediaries charge for their services, gross profit from sales may be reduced.
2. *Less Control*: The original manufacturer has less control over their product's marketing, branding, and final pricing.
3. *Dependency*: Over-reliance on intermediaries can lead to dependency, potentially causing issues if there's a disagreement about whether the intermediary should go out of business.

For pharmaceutical companies, indirect exporting can effectively expand their business globally, especially if they lack the resources or expertise to navigate foreign markets directly. However, as with all business strategies, weighing the benefits against potential challenges is essential.

Industrial Marketing

Industrial marketing, often referred to as B2B (Business-to-Business) marketing, pertains to selling products or services from one business to another.

This can be quite complex in the pharmaceutical industry, given the nature of the products, strict regulations, and the stakes associated with healthcare outcomes.

Here are some key aspects and considerations for industrial marketing in the pharmaceutical sector:

1. *Target Audience*: The primary audience in pharmaceutical B2B marketing includes hospitals, clinics, other pharmaceutical companies, research institutions, wholesalers, and government bodies.
2. *Regulations and Compliance*: The pharmaceutical industry is one of the most regulated sectors. Every marketing effort should comply with the country's regulations for promoting the product or service. This may include claims that can be made about a product, disclosures that need to be made, and the channels through which a product can be promoted.
3. *Relationship Building*: B2B relationships in the pharma industry are long-term in nature. Trust plays a significant role, especially in products affecting patient health. Building and nurturing relationships through customer service, transparency, and collaboration are crucial.
4. *Knowledge-based Marketing*: The pharma industry requires a deep understanding of the product's scientific background. Marketing efforts should often educate the potential buyer about the product's efficacy, safety, mechanism of action, and benefits.
5. *Customer Solutions*: Unlike B2C, where one product can cater to millions, B2B pharma often involves customized solutions for specific needs, like drug formulations for specific populations or API (Active Pharmaceutical Ingredient) supplies for particular drug production.
6. *Pricing and Contract Negotiations*: Pricing in B2B pharma deals can be complex. It might involve volume discounts, long-term contracts, and sometimes joint research or distribution partnerships. Negotiation skills are critical.
7. *Trade Shows and Conferences*: These are pivotal platforms for B2B marketing in Pharma. These events provide an opportunity to showcase products and innovations and establish direct face-to-face connections with potential clients.
8. *Digital Transformation*: Like many other industries, the pharma sector also increasingly leverages digital channels for B2B marketing. This includes webinars, online platforms for drug discovery collaborations, e-commerce

platforms for B2B sales, and utilizing AI and data analytics for demand forecasting.

9. *Supply Chain and Distribution*: Ensuring a seamless supply chain is essential. Delays or disruptions can seriously affect the seller's reputation and patients relying on these drugs.
10. *Ethics*: Ethical considerations are paramount. Any hint of impropriety, such as attempting to influence prescribing patterns or compromising patient safety for profit unduly, can have severe legal and reputational consequences.

In conclusion, industrial marketing in the pharma sector is about understanding the complex landscape of health care, regulatory environments, and scientific nuances while building long-term, trust-based relationships with business partnerships.

Inertia Selling

Inertia selling is a marketing strategy that automatically renews a customer's subscription or contract without explicit consent or agreement. This strategy relies on the customer's inertia or reluctance to take action to continue the subscription or contract.

Inertia selling can be controversial, as it may be seen as taking advantage of customers who may not be aware that their subscription or contract is being automatically renewed. In some cases, engaging in inertia selling may be illegal or against consumer protection laws.

Companies should be transparent with customers about their subscription or contract renewal policies to avoid negative consequences and maintain ethical business practices. This includes:

- Communicating the terms of the agreement
- Providing notice before any automatic renewals occur
- Providing customers with an easy way to opt out of automatic renewals

While using inertia selling may lead to short-term gains, it can damage the company's reputation and lead to long-term losses if customers feel they have been taken advantage of or deceived. Therefore, companies must weigh the potential benefits and risks before implementing such a strategy.

Inertia Selling: Is it Relevant to Pharma?

Inertia selling may be relevant to pharma marketing, particularly in cases where pharmaceutical companies offer subscription-based services or ongoing treatments. For example, some pharmaceutical companies offer prescription refill services that automatically renew a patient's prescription when it runs out. Similarly, some specialty pharmacies offer ongoing treatment services that automatically renew regularly.

However, in the pharmaceutical industry, there are often strict regulations and guidelines around marketing and advertising practices, which may prohibit or limit the use of inertia selling strategies. In addition, since pharmaceutical products often involve patient health and safety, companies must prioritize transparency and ethical business practices to maintain patient trust and comply with industry regulations

Inflation

Inflation is a sustained increase in the general price level of goods and services in an economy over time. Inflation can be measured by tracking the prices of a basket of goods and services over time and calculating the percentage increase in prices. Inflation can occur due to various factors, including an increase in the money supply, higher demand for goods and services, or a decrease in the supply of goods and services. When more money is in circulation, demand for goods and services increases, which can drive up prices. In addition, Inflation can also be affected by external factors, such as changes in exchange rates or the cost of raw materials.

Inflation can have both positive and negative effects on an economy. Moderate Inflation can signify a healthy economy, indicating a strong demand for goods and services. However, high or unpredictable Inflation can be detrimental to an economy, as it can erode the value of people's savings, reduce the purchasing power of wages, and increase the cost of borrowing.

In the pharmaceutical industry, Inflation can impact the cost of prescription drugs and healthcare services. As a result, pharmaceutical companies may need to adjust the prices of their products to keep up with Inflation, and healthcare providers may need to increase the cost of their services to cover rising costs. This can increase patient healthcare costs, which can concern governments and healthcare providers.

Influencers

In marketing, influencers have a significant following on social media platforms or other online channels and can influence their followers' opinions and purchasing decisions. Influencers can include celebrities, social media personalities, bloggers, and other online content creators.

In the pharmaceutical industry, influencers can be used to promote drugs, treatments, and other healthcare products to patients and healthcare providers. For example, a pharmaceutical company might partner with a healthcare influencer to promote a new drug or treatment on social media or to share information about a particular health condition or disease.

When selecting influencers to partner with, pharmaceutical companies must ensure they work with reputable individuals with a strong track record of promoting health and wellness. Additionally, companies must ensure that any promotional content adheres to industry regulations and guidelines, particularly about claims about drugs or treatments.

By partnering with trusted influencers with a loyal following, companies can tap into a broader network of potential customers and build relationships with patients and healthcare providers.

Influencer Marketing

Influencer marketing involves partnering with influential people or organizations to promote a brand, product, or service. In social media, influencers have a large following on platforms such as Instagram, YouTube, and TikTok and can engage their audience and influence their purchasing decisions.

In the pharmaceutical industry, influencer marketing can be used to promote drugs, treatments, and other healthcare products to patients and healthcare professionals. For example, a pharmaceutical company might partner with a healthcare influencer to promote a new drug or treatment on social media or to share information about a particular health condition or disease.

When selecting influencers to partner with, pharmaceutical companies must ensure they work with reputable individuals with a strong track record promoting health and wellness. Additionally, companies must ensure that any promotional content adheres to industry regulations and guidelines, particularly concerning claims about drugs or treatments.

How to Implement Influencer Marketing

Here are some general steps to follow for implementing an influencer marketing campaign in the pharmaceutical industry:

1. *Set Clear Goals and Objectives*: Determine what you hope to achieve with your influencer marketing campaign. For example: Are you looking to raise awareness of a particular health condition or disease? Are you promoting a new drug or treatment? Set clear goals and objectives that align with your overall marketing strategy.
2. *Identify Relevant Influencers*: Identify relevant influencers for your target audience and align them with your brand's values. For example, look for influencers with a large and engaged social media following who are known for promoting health and wellness.
3. *Develop a Partnership Strategy*: Work with your chosen influencers to develop a partnership strategy that aligns with your goals and objectives. Determine the type of content you would like them to create and how they will promote your brand on social media.
4. *Ensure Compliance with Regulations*: Ensure that any promotional content adheres to industry regulations and guidelines, particularly about claims made about drugs and treatments. Work closely with your legal and regulatory teams to ensure all content meets these standards.
5. *Track and Measure Results*: Use analytics tools to track the performance of your influencer marketing campaign. Monitor engagement rates, follower growth, and other key metrics to measure the success of your campaign and make adjustments as needed.

How Pharma Companies Use Influencer Marketing

Here are a few examples of how pharmaceutical companies have used influencer marketing:

1. Sanofi Genzyme partnered with professional athlete Kelly Olynyk to promote awareness of Gaucher disease, a rare genetic disorder for which the company develops treatments. Olynyk has a personal connection to the disease, as his granddaughter was diagnosed with Gaucher's disease as an infant. The company worked with Olynyk to create a video series that shared stories of patients and families affected by the disease and raised awareness of the importance of early diagnosis and treatment.
2. Novo Nordisk has partnered with several social media influencers to raise awareness of diabetes and promote its diabetes management products. For example, the company worked with popular fitness influencer Cassey Ho to promote its diabetes management app, which helps patients track their blood sugar levels and medication regimens.
3. Pfizer has partnered with several patient advocacy organizations and influencers to raise breast cancer awareness and promote its oncology products. For example, the company has partnered with the Breast Cancer Research Foundation to fund research into the disease and raise awareness of the importance of early detection and treatment. Pfizer has also worked with breast cancer survivors and advocates on social media to share stories of their experiences and promote the importance of patient education and support.
4. AbbVie worked with influencers and patient advocates to promote their drug, Skyrizi (Risankizumab), used to treat psoriasis. The company created a social media campaign called Skyrizi Squad, featuring influencers who shared their experiences with the drug and encouraged others to learn more.
5. Janssen Pharmaceuticals partnered with influencer and health advocate Carrie Hammer to raise awareness of psoriasis and encourage people to speak openly about their experiences with the condition. Hammer shared her personal experience with psoriasis on social media and encouraged her followers to join the conversation using the hashtag #psoriasisvisible.

Influencer marketing can effectively reach a wider audience and build awareness of your brand in the pharmaceutical industry. However, it is important to approach influencer marketing campaigns with care and attention to detail to ensure compliance with regulations and achieve the desired outcomes.

Infographics

An Infographic is a visual representation of information, data, or knowledge designed to convey complex ideas or concepts in an easy-to-understand and engaging format. Infographics typically use images, charts, graphs, and text to present information appealing visually, making it easy for the viewer to comprehend and remember.

Infographics are often used to present statistical data, research findings, and other complex information that may be difficult to communicate through text alone. Infographics can help break down complex concepts into simpler, more digestible information using visual elements such as icons, illustrations, and diagrams.

Infographics are used in marketing and advertising campaigns to convey key messages and promote products or services. They can be used on websites, social media platforms, other digital channels, and printed materials such as brochures and posters.

Infographics in Pharma Marketing

Infographics are a powerful marketing tool in the pharmaceutical industry, allowing companies to present complex information in a visually appealing and easy-to-understand format. Here are some ways in which infographics can be used in pharmaceutical marketing:

1. *Product Information*: Infographics can provide information about pharmaceutical products, including their indications, dosages, side effects, and contraindications. This can help healthcare professionals and patients better to understand the benefits and risks of different treatments and make more informed decisions about their healthcare.
2. *Disease Education*: Infographics can also educate healthcare professionals and patients about different diseases and conditions, including their causes, symptoms, and treatment options. This can help to raise awareness about important health issues and encourage patients to seek appropriate medical care.
3. *Clinical Trials Results*: Infographics can be used to present the results of clinical trials in a clear and concise format, making it easier for healthcare professionals and patients to understand the key findings and implications of the study.

4. *Marketing Campaigns*: Infographics can be used to promote pharmaceutical products and raise awareness about different health issues. They can be shared on social media, included in marketing materials, and used to engage with healthcare professionals and patients in various settings.

Infographics are a versatile and effective tool in pharma marketing, allowing companies to communicate complex information in a way that is engaging, accessible, and easy to understand. Using infographics to educate and inform healthcare professionals and patients, pharmaceutical companies can build trust, establish thought leadership, and drive business.

Infomediary

An infomediary is a third-party organization that collects, analyzes, and distributes information about consumers and their preferences to businesses. For example, in pharmaceutical marketing, an infomediary may collect data on healthcare providers and their prescribing habits, as well as on patients and their healthcare needs and preferences.

Pharmaceutical companies can use infomediaries to gather insights into their target audience and tailor their marketing efforts accordingly. By working with an infomediary, companies can gain access to data to help them identify key opinion leaders, understand patient preferences and needs, and optimize their marketing strategies.

Here are some of the ways pharmaceutical companies can use infomediaries in their marketing activities:

1. *Targeted Advertising*: Infomediaries can provide pharmaceutical companies with data that allows them to target their advertising to specific healthcare providers and patient populations.
2. *Customized Messaging*: Infomediaries can help pharmaceutical companies create customized messaging that resonates with their target audience.
3. *Data Analytics*: Infomediaries can use data analytics to identify trends and patterns in prescribing habits and patient behaviors, which can help pharmaceutical companies optimize their marketing strategies.
4. *Market Research*: Infomediaries can conduct market research on behalf of pharmaceutical companies, providing insights into patient preferences and needs and the competitive landscape.

Pharmaceutical companies operate in a highly regulated environment. Therefore, they must comply with all relevant regulations and guidelines when working with infomediaries.

Infomercial

An infomercial is a long-form television commercial providing detailed information about a product or service. Infomercials typically run for 30 minutes or longer and are designed to educate viewers about the features and benefits of the advertised product or service.

A. Infomercials often include:
B. Testimonials from satisfied customers
C. Demonstrations of the product in action
D. Explanations of how the product works

Infomercials are typically used for products that require more explanation or demonstration than can be provided in a traditional 30-second commercial.

Infomercials first gained popularity in the 1980s and 1990s and are used today in various industries. In addition to television, infomercials can be found online and in other digital formats.

Infomercials in Pharma Marketing

Infomercials can be used in pharmaceutical marketing to educate consumers about a product, its features, and its benefits. Pharmaceutical infomercials may be used to promote a specific medication or treatment. They can be particularly effective for conditions that are not widely understood or have a high degree of stigma. Here are a few ways pharmaceutical companies can use infomercials in their marketing efforts.

1. *Educate Customers*: Infomercials can educate consumers about a particular condition and the benefits of a specific medication or treatment. They can be particularly effective for poorly understood conditions or have a high degree of stigma.
2. *Build Brand Awareness*: Infomercials can build brand awareness and create a sense of trust with consumers. By presenting a clear and informative message about a product, pharmaceutical companies can create a sense of familiarity and trust with their target audience.
3. *Highlight Features and Benefits*: Infomercials can highlight the features and benefits of a particular medication or treatment. By presenting the information clearly and engagingly, companies can encourage consumers to consider their product a viable solution.

4. *Provide Testimonials*: Infomercials can include testimonials from satisfied customers or medical professionals, which can provide social proof and increase the perceived credibility of the product.

While infomercials can be an effective tool for pharmaceutical companies, they must be used responsibly and follow the regulations set forth by the governing bodies and the industry guidelines.

Informatics

Informatics is the study and application of information processing and computer technology to manage data, information, and knowledge. It is a multidisciplinary field that draws upon computer science, mathematics, statistics, and other disciplines to design, develop and implement information systems and tools that can be used to collect, store, process, analyze, and disseminate information.

Informatics is concerned with efficient and effective information management in various fields, including healthcare, finance, education, and business. In healthcare, for example, informatics plays an important role in developing and implementing electronic health records (EHRs), telemedicine, and clinical decision support systems.

Informatics in Pharma Marketing

Informatics plays an increasingly important role in pharma marketing. It refers to using information technology and data analysis to collect, manage, and interpret information related to marketing and sales activities in the pharmaceutical industry. Here are some ways in which informatics is used in pharma marketing:

1. *Market Research*: Informatics helps pharmaceutical companies to collect and analyze data about their target market, such as customer demographics, behavior, and preferences. This information can be used to develop more effective marketing strategies and identify new growth opportunities.
2. *Customer Relationship Management (CRM)*: Informatics is used to manage customer relationships by keeping track of customer interactions, preferences, and behaviors. This helps companies to personalize their marketing efforts and provide a better customer experience.
3. *Sales Force Automation*: Informatics automates sales processes, such as lead generation, tracking, and follow-up. This helps sales teams to be more productive and efficient, allowing them to focus on building customer relationships.
4. *Data Analytics*: Informatics is used to analyze large amounts of data to identify trends and patterns, which can be used to inform marketing strategies. This includes analyzing data on customer behavior, market trends, and sales performance.

Informatics is essential to pharmaceutical companies as it allows them to make data-driven decisions about their marketing and sales activities. By using informatics, companies can better understand their customers and target them more effectively, increasing sales and revenue.

Information Anxiety

Information anxiety in pharma marketing refers to feeling overwhelmed or anxious when trying to process and understand the large amounts of information that pharmaceutical companies often present to healthcare professionals and patients.

Pharmaceutical companies use a variety of marketing channels to communicate information about their products, including print and digital advertising, product brochures, clinical trial data, and scientific research papers. However, the sheer volume of information can be daunting for healthcare professionals and patients, who may struggle to keep up with the latest drug therapies and treatment developments.

This information overload can lead to anxiety, negatively affecting healthcare professionals and patients. For example, healthcare professionals may feel pressured to keep up with the latest research and developments, leading to burnout and stress. In addition, patients may feel overwhelmed by the amount of information available, which can lead to confusion and anxiety about their treatment options.

How Information Anxiety Can Arise in Pharma Marketing: Some Examples

Here are some examples of how information anxiety can arise in pharma marketing and some strategies that can be used to address it:

1. *Clinical Trial Data*: Pharmaceutical companies often present a large amount of clinical trial data to healthcare professionals to demonstrate the safety and efficacy of their products. However, the complexity of the data can be overwhelming, leading to information anxiety. One strategy to address this is to summarize the key findings that are easy to understand and relevant to the target audience.
2. *Digital Advertising*: Pharmaceutical companies use digital advertising channels to promote their

products to healthcare professionals and patients, including social media, search engines, and online forums. However, abundant information and competing messages can overwhelm patients, leading to information anxiety. One strategy to address this is to provide clear and concise messaging focused on the product's most important benefits and risks.

3. *Product Brochures*: Pharmaceutical companies often provide brochures to healthcare professionals to help them understand their products' key features and benefits. However, the amount of information in these brochures can be overwhelming, leading to anxiety. One strategy to address this is to provide brochures focused on the product's most important features and benefits organized clearly and concisely.

To address information anxiety in pharma marketing, pharmaceutical companies need to be mindful of the amount and type of information they present to healthcare professionals and patients. They should provide clear and concise information that is easy to understand and relevant to their target audience. They should also provide support and resources to help healthcare professionals and patients navigate the information and make informed decisions about their treatment options.

Addressing information anxiety in pharma marketing improves healthcare outcomes and builds trust between pharmaceutical companies, healthcare professionals, and patients.

Information Hierarchy

Information hierarchy is crucial to pharmaceutical marketing, ensuring that the most important information is presented clearly and prominently. Given the complexity of medical information, establishing a well-defined hierarchy helps healthcare professionals and patients navigate and understand the content effectively. Here are key considerations for information hierarchy in pharma marketing:

1. *Key Messages First*: Place the most critical information at the forefront. Whether it is the benefits of a drug, its unique selling points, or important safety considerations, ensure that this information is easily noticeable and understandable.
2. *Clear Headings and Subheadings*: Use clear and concise headings and subheadings to organize information. This aids in scanning and helps users locate specific details without having to read through large blocks of text.
3. *Visual Elements*: Incorporate visual elements such as icons, charts, and infographics to convey complex information more effectively. Visuals can enhance understanding and break up text, making it more digestible.
4. *Consistent Formatting*: Maintain consistency in formatting throughout marketing materials. This includes font styles, sizes, colors, and spacing. Consistency creates a cohesive and professional look, improving overall readability.
5. *Logical Flow*: Organize information in a logical flow, guiding the reader from general to specific details. This structure helps users build their understanding without feeling overwhelmed.
6. *Prioritize Patient-Centric Information*: For patient-focused materials, prioritize relevant and understandable information for patients. This may include dosing instructions, potential side effects, and tips for managing their health.
7. *Compliance Information*: Ensure compliance-related information, such as safety warnings and regulatory details, is present and visible. This is crucial for adhering to industry regulations.
8. *Call to Action (CTA)*: Include a clear and compelling call to action if applicable. The CTA should stand out if it encourages healthcare professionals to prescribe medication or prompts patients to consult their doctors.
9. *Responsive Design*: Consider the various platforms for viewing marketing materials, including print and digital. Ensure that the information hierarchy is effective across different mediums or devices.
10. *User Testing*: Conduct usability testing with representatives from the target audience to gather feedback on the information hierarchy. This feedback can be invaluable for refining the organization of content.

By establishing a thoughtful information hierarchy, pharmaceutical marketers can enhance communication, improve user understanding, and contribute to more effective engagement with healthcare professionals and patients.

Informed Consent

Informed consent is a foundational principle in healthcare and medical research. It is designed to ensure that individuals are fully aware of and understand the potential risks, benefits, and alternatives before they undergo a medical procedure, participate in research, or initiate a treatment regimen. In pharmaceuticals, informed consent becomes particularly important due to medication's potential side effects and risks.

Here's how informed consent relates to pharma marketing:

1. *Clinical Trials*: Before a patient can participate in a clinical trial, they must provide informed consent. They should be made aware of potential risks, benefits, the purpose of the study, and their rights as participants. Pharma companies must ensure transparency about these details and not overstate potential benefits or underplay risks in pursuing more trial participants.
2. *Direct-to-Consumer (DTC) Advertising*: Some countries, like the US, allow pharmaceutical companies to advertise directly to consumers. These advertisements need to include information about the risks associated with the drug. However, concerns arise when marketing tactics make benefits more salient than risks or when complex medical information is oversimplified.
3. *Product Labeling*: Pharmaceutical packaging often comes with patient information leaflets that detail the drug's uses, risks, and instructions. This information is essential for informed consent. Marketing should not deviate from or contradict these official product indications.
4. *Promotion to Healthcare Professionals*: Pharma representatives promote their products to doctors, nurses, and other healthcare professionals. It's essential that this promotion is accurate and doesn't omit significant risks or potential drug interactions, which could impair the healthcare professional's ability to secure informed consent from patients.
5. *Ethical Considerations*: Ethical marketing practices require pharmaceutical companies to ensure they are not using tactics that could be perceived as deceptive or as minimizing the potential dangers associated with their products. This is intertwined with the principle of informed consent.
6. *Regulations and Oversight*: In many countries, regulatory bodies oversee pharma marketing to ensure that it aligns with informed consent principles. For example, the US FDA oversees drug advertising to ensure it's not misleading and provides a balanced view of risks and benefits.
7. *Digital Marketing and Data Privacy*: With the advent of digital marketing, pharmaceutical companies have increased avenues to reach patients. However, they must be cautious about patient data privacy, ensuring patients understand how their data is used and not make claims online that they wouldn't in traditional media.

In summary, informed consent in pharma marketing is essential to ensure patients' rights to understand the full spectrum of potential risks and benefits associated with medications. As with other sectors, transparency, honesty, and ethical considerations should underpin all marketing efforts in the pharmaceutical industry.

Inherited Audience

Inherited audience refers to the audience a company inherits when it acquires or merges with another company. For example, in pharmaceutical marketing, the inherited audience can refer to the patient, healthcare professional, and other stakeholder audiences that a pharmaceutical company inherits when it acquires another company or merges with it.

Here are some considerations when dealing with an inherited audience in pharma marketing:

1. *Understand the Audience*: Understanding the inherited audience's characteristics and preferences is important to develop effective marketing strategies. This may involve conducting marketing research or analyzing data to gain insights into the needs and preferences of the inherited audience.
2. *Communicate Effectively*: When communicating with the inherited audience, it is important to use messaging and channels that are appropriate and relevant to them. This may involve adapting or developing new messaging that meets the inherited audience's needs and preferences.
3. *Manage Transitions Carefully*: When a company acquires or merges with another company, transitions or changes may affect the inherited audience. Therefore, managing these transitions carefully and communicating any changes or updates to the audience clearly and transparently is important.
4. *Build Relationships*: Inherited audiences may feel loyal to the previous company or brand. Building relationships with inherited audiences through effective communication, engaging initiatives, and patient-centric marketing can help build trust and credibility with them and drive business success.

An inherited audience can present both opportunities and challenges in pharma marketing. Pharmaceutical companies can successfully engage with the inherited audience and drive business success by understanding the audience, communicating effectively, managing transitions carefully, and building relationships.

In-licensing

In-licensing is a business strategy where a company acquires the rights to a product or technology from another company. For example, in the pharmaceutical industry, in-licensing refers to acquiring the rights to a drug or a technology related to drug development from another company or organization.

In-licensing can be a valuable strategy for pharmaceutical companies as it allows them to access new technologies or drugs they may not have been able to develop independently. This can help them to expand their product portfolio, enter new therapeutic areas, or strengthen their existing pipeline. In-licensing can also help reduce the time and costs associated with drug development, as the acquired product or technology may have already undergone some research and development.

The terms of an in-licensing agreement can vary widely depending on the specific product technology involved. Typically, the acquiring company will pay an upfront fee or royalty payment to the company that holds the rights to the product or technology. In addition, the agreement may include provisions related to intellectual property rights, regulatory approvals, and marketing and distribution arrangements.

In-licensing can be a valuable strategy for pharmaceutical companies looking to expand their product offerings and pipelines. However, it is important to carefully evaluate potential in-licensing opportunities and negotiate favorable terms to ensure the agreement benefits both parties.

In-licensing in Pharma: Some Examples

Here are some examples of in-licensing in pharma:

1. *Bristol-Myers Squibb and Bluebird Bio*: In 2019, Bristol-Myers Squibb (BMS) and Bluebird Bio announced that BMS would acquire exclusive rights to a gene-editing technology for sickle cell disease and beta-thalassemia. Under the agreement, BMS paid Bluebird Bio an upfront payment of $200 million and agreed to pay additional milestone payments based on the achievement of certain development and regulatory milestones.
2. *Novartis and Gilead Sciences*: In 2018, Novartis announced a licensing agreement with Gilead Sciences for the exclusive worldwide rights to develop and commercialize KITE-585, a CAR-T cell therapy for multiple myeloma. As part of the agreement, Novartis paid Gilead an upfront payment of $175 million and agreed to pay additional milestone payments based on the achievement of certain development and regulatory milestones.
3. *Sanofi and Regeneron*: In 2007, Sanofi and Regeneron partnered to develop and commercialize biologic drugs for various therapeutic areas, including cancer and inflammatory diseases. Under the agreement, Sanofi paid Regeneron an upfront payment of $640 million and agreed to pay additional milestone payments based on the achievement of certain development and regulatory milestones.

While in-licensing can benefit pharma companies, it can be complex and require careful consideration of financial, regulatory, and legal implications.

Innovation

Innovation is developing and implementing new ideas, methods, processes, products, or services that create value and lead to positive change. Innovation can occur in various fields, including technology, business, healthcare, and science.

Innovation often involves a combination of creativity, critical thinking, and problem-solving skills to identify new opportunities, improve existing processes, or create new solutions to meet unmet needs. It can involve incremental improvements to existing products or services or more radical changes that disrupt traditional ways of doing things.

Innovation is not limited to product development but can also apply to business models, organizational structures, and social and environmental initiatives. Moreover, it can occur at various levels, from individual entrepreneurs and small businesses to large multinational corporations and governments.

Innovation in Pharma Marketing

Innovation in pharma marketing refers to developing and implementing new and creative strategies, tools, and tactics to promote pharmaceutical products and engage with healthcare professionals and patients. It involves using novel approaches to reach target audiences, generate interest, and differentiate products from competitors.

Innovation in pharma marketing can take many forms, including using digital channels, social media, and mobile apps to deliver targeted messaging and educational content to healthcare professionals and patients. It can also involve using virtual reality and other emerging technologies to enhance medical education and improve patient engagement.

In addition, innovation in pharma marketing can also involve the development of new pricing and access models, such as value-based pricing and outcomes-based contracting, which focus on demonstrating the value and impact of pharmaceutical products on patient outcomes.

Innovation in Pharma Marketing: Some Examples

Here are some examples of innovation in pharma marketing:

1. *Use of Virtual Reality (VR)*: One example of innovation in pharma marketing is using virtual reality to educate healthcare professionals and patients. Companies like Pfizer and Takeda have used VR to create immersive experiences that showcase their products and educate users about specific conditions. For instance, Pfizer created a VR experience called *Rheumatoid Arthritis Unmasked* to help patients better understand the symptoms and impact of the disease.
2. *Digital Therapeutics*: Another example of innovation in pharma marketing is the development of digital therapeutics. These software-based interventions can treat various conditions, including substance abuse, mental health disorders, and chronic diseases. Companies like Pear Therapeutics and Akili Interactive have developed digital therapeutics approved by the FDA and marketed them as an alternative or complementary treatment to traditional medication.
3. *Outcomes-based Pricing*: Some pharma companies are innovating in the pricing model for their products by shifting from volume-based pricing to outcomes-based pricing. This involves setting the price of a product based on the health outcomes it delivers. For example, Novartis and Amgen have implemented outcomes-based pricing models for their products in certain markets.
4. *Social Media Campaigns*: Pharma companies increasingly use social media platforms like Twitter, Facebook, and Instagram to engage with patients and healthcare professionals. Some companies like Sanofi and Merck have launched social media campaigns to raise awareness of specific conditions, such as diabetes and cervical cancer. These campaigns often incorporate user-generated content and encourage followers to share their experiences with the condition.
5. *Wearables and Mobile Apps*: Pharma companies are also developing wearables and mobile apps to help patients manage their health and monitor their conditions. For instance, Johnson &Johnson has developed the Reveal LINQ wearable that monitors heart activity in atrial fibrillation patients. The company also offers a mobile app called *J&J Official 7 Minute Workout* that provides users with a personalized exercise routine.

Innovation in pharma marketing is about finding new ways to connect with customers and create value in a rapidly evolving healthcare landscape. By leveraging the latest technologies and strategies, pharma companies can better communicate the benefits of their products and improve patient outcomes while maintaining a competitive edge.

Instagram

Instagram is a social media platform that allows users to share photos and videos and interact with other users through likes, comments, and direct messages. It was launched in 2010 and quickly gained popularity, with millions of users worldwide. Facebook now owns Instagram, one of the world's most widely used social media platforms.

Instagram offers a range of features, including Stories, Reels, and IGTV. Stories are short-lived photos or videos that disappear after 24 hours, while Reels are short-form videos that are usually set to music. IGTV allows users to upload longer videos, up to 60 minutes.

In addition to personal use, businesses and organizations also use Instagram as a marketing tool to promote their products or services and engage with their audience. Instagram has various advertising options, including sponsored posts, stories, and shopping tags, that allow businesses to target specific audiences and drive businesses.

Instagram in Pharma Marketing

Pharmaceutical companies can use Instagram as a marketing tool to promote their products and engage with their target audience. Here are some ways pharmaceutical companies can use Instagram in their marketing efforts:

1. *Brand Awareness*: Instagram is a great platform to build brand awareness and showcase the company's values, mission, and vision. Pharmaceutical companies can use Instagram to showcase their products, services, and the benefits of their offerings.

2. *Influencer Marketing*: Pharmaceutical companies can use influencers to promote their products. They can collaborate with health and wellness influencers with a significant Instagram following to promote their products.
3. *Patient Education*: Instagram can be used to educate patients about health conditions and the treatments available. Pharmaceutical companies can create infographics, videos, and other educational content to help patients understand their conditions better.
4. *Behind-the-scenes Content*: Pharmaceutical companies can use Instagram to give a behind-the-scenes look at their research and development process. This can help build trust with their audience by showing how much effort goes into developing and testing new treatments.
5. *User-generated Content*: Pharmaceutical companies can encourage their followers to share their experiences with their products. User-generated content can be a powerful way to show how the products have helped people and can provide social proof to potential customers.

How Pharma Uses Instagram

Here are a few examples of how some pharmaceutical companies use Instagram to promote their products and engage with their audience:

1. *Pfizer*: Pfizer is a pharmaceutical company that produces vaccines and several other pharmaceutical products. Their Instagram page features images and videos related to their research and development process and educational content about their products.
2. *Novartis*: Novartis is a multinational pharmaceutical company that produces a wide range of pharmaceutical products. Their Instagram page features images and videos related to their products and educational content about various health conditions.
3. *Johnson & Johnson*: Johnson & Johnson is a global healthcare company that produces a wide range of products, including pharmaceuticals. Their Instagram page features images and videos related to products and educational content about various products.

It is important to note that pharmaceutical companies must comply with strict regulations regarding advertising and marketing their products. They must ensure their Instagram content is truthful, accurate, and not misleading. They must also include any necessary warnings and disclosures about their products.

Instant Gratification

Instant gratification refers to the desire for immediate satisfaction or reward without delay. It is the pleasure or feeling of pleasure that comes from receiving an immediate reward or fulfilling a desire at the moment. The concept of instant gratification is often associated with impulsiveness and a lack of self-control because the person seeks pleasure or reward without considering the long-term consequences.

Instant Gratification in Pharma Marketing

In pharmaceutical marketing, instant gratification can be used to engage with customers and incentivize them to take action.

Here are a few ways pharmaceutical companies can use instant gratification in their marketing efforts:

1. *RewardsPrograms*: Pharmaceutical companies can create rewards incentivizing customers to take specific actions, such as filing a subscription or signing up for a loyalty program. By offering immediate rewards, such as discounts or free samples, companies can encourage customers to take action and build loyalty.
2. *Instant Coupons*: Companies can offer instant coupons or discounts to customers who engage with their marketing campaigns. For example, they can offer a discount code to customers who sign up for a newsletter or follow them on social media.
3. *Instant Feedback*: Companies can use instant feedback mechanisms like surveys or polls to provide customers with immediate gratification. Companies can create a sense of engagement and satisfaction by giving customers real-time feedback on their opinions or experiences.
4. *Instant Content*: Pharmaceutical companies can use social media and other digital platforms to give customers instant access to informative and entertaining content. By providing customers with engaging content in real-time, companies can create a sense of community and encourage customers to stay engaged with their brand.

However, pharmaceutical companies must comply with strict regulations regarding the advertising and marketing of their product. They must also ensure their messaging is truthful, accurate, and not misleading. They must also include any necessary warnings and disclosures about their products.

Instant Messaging

Instant messaging can effectively allow pharmaceutical companies to communicate with their customers and engage them in real-time. Here are a few ways pharmaceutical companies can use instant messaging in their marketing efforts:

1. *Customer Support*: Pharmaceutical companies can use instant messaging to support their customers. They can set up a dedicated messaging channel where customers can ask questions, report side effects, and get help with their medication.
2. *Personalized Marketing*: Instant messaging allows companies to communicate with customers one-on-one. Pharmaceutical companies can use this opportunity to send personalized messages to their customers, such as reminders to take their medication, information about new products, or invitations to events.
3. *Chatbots*: Pharmaceutical companies can respond instantly to frequently asked questions and basic customer support. Chatbots can be programmed to answer specific questions and direct customers to the appropriate resources.
4. *Clinical Trial Recruitment*: Instant messaging can help pharma companies recruit patients for clinical trials. Pharmaceutical companies can send targeted messages to patients who meet the eligibility criteria for a specific trial and invite them to participate.
5. *Continuing Medical Education*: Instant messaging can help pharmaceutical companies provide continuing medical education (CME) to healthcare professionals. Pharmaceutical companies can use instant messaging to send healthcare professionals updates on new research, product information, and other educational materials.

It is important to remember that pharmaceutical companies must comply with strict regulations regarding the advertising and marketing of their products. They must also ensure their messaging is truthful, accurate, and not misleading. They must also include any necessary warnings and disclosures about their products.

Institutional Marketing

Institutional marketing refers to the strategies and activities a company undertakes to promote its brand and image among a particular group of stakeholders, such as institutions, organizations, or healthcare communities. Institutional marketing aims to establish the company's reputation and credibility within a specific market segment rather than directly selling products or services.

Institutional marketing typically involves developing a unique identity for the company that resonates with the target audience and differentiates it from competitors. This can include creating a consistent visual identity, messaging, and tone of voice that reflects the company's values, mission, and goals.

Institutional marketing can take many forms, such as sponsorships, corporate social responsibility initiatives, public relations activities, events, and advertising campaigns to build the company's reputation and relationship with the target audience. This can help establish the company as a trusted partner, improve brand loyalty, and drive sales.

Companies often use institutional marketing in industries that rely heavily on relationships and trust, such as financial services, healthcare, and education. However, it can be applied in any industry where building credibility and trust with key stakeholders is important.

Institutional Marketing in Pharma

Institutional marketing in the pharmaceutical industry involves promoting a pharmaceutical company's brand and products to healthcare institutions, such as hospitals, clinics, and physician groups, rather than directly to individual patients. The aim is to increase the company's visibility and reputation among healthcare providers, which can lead to increased sales of its products.

The marketing strategies used in institutional marketing may include educational programs for healthcare professionals, sponsored research studies, and partnerships with healthcare organizations to promote disease awareness and improve patient outcomes. These efforts can also involve providing information about a company's products and services, offering training programs, and supporting continuing medical education.

One important aspect of institutional marketing in the pharmaceutical industry is building relationships with key opinion leaders (KOLs) within the healthcare community. KOLs are respected and influential healthcare providers well-versed in the latest medical research and treatments. Pharmaceutical companies often collaborate with KOLs to promote their products and gain their endorsement.

It is worth noting that pharmaceutical companies must comply with strict regulations and guidelines when engaging in institutional marketing activities.

This includes adhering to codes of ethics and transparency when collaborating with healthcare providers, disclosing financial relationships with KOLs, and ensuring that all promotional materials are accurate and not misleading.

Intangibles in pharma marketing are important when developing marketing strategies and tactics. While they may be difficult to measure, they can significantly impact a company's success and long-term sustainability.

Intangibles

Intangibles in pharma marketing refer to the non-physical, non-monetary aspects of marketing that can significantly impact a pharmaceutical company's reputation, relationships, and overall success. These intangibles can be difficult to measure, but they are critical in building brand equity and creating a strong competitive advantage.

Some examples of intangibles in pharma marketing include:

1. *Brand Image and Reputation*: A company's image and reputation are intangible assets built over time through marketing efforts, product quality, and customer experiences. A strong brand image and reputation can increase loyalty, drive sales, and create a competitive advantage.
2. *Trust and Credibility*: Trust and credibility are essential intangibles in pharma marketing, as they can impact a customer's decision to purchase a product or service. Building trust and credibility requires transparency, ethical behavior, and a commitment to quality and safety.
3. *Relationships and Partnerships*: Building strong relationships and partnerships with key stakeholders, such as healthcare professionals, patient advocacy groups, and regulatory bodies, is an important intangible in pharma marketing. These relationships can help build trust and credibility, and provide access to new markets and opportunities.
4. *Innovation and R&D*: Innovation and research and development (R&D) are critical intangibles in pharma marketing, as they demonstrate a company's commitment to advancing health care and developing new treatments. Innovation and R&D can also help differentiate a company's products and services from its competitors.
5. *Corporate Social Responsibility*: Corporate social responsibility (CSR) is an intangible in pharma marketing that involves a company's commitment to positively impacting society and the environment. CSR efforts can enhance a company's brand image and reputation and attract customers who value socially responsible business practices.

Intangible Repositioning

Intangible repositioning in pharma marketing refers to changing how stakeholders perceive a pharmaceutical brand through intangible factors. These intangible factors may include emotional appeals, brand personality, values, and beliefs and may help to differentiate the brand from its competitors.

Here are some ways that intangible positioning can be used in pharma marketing:

1. *Emphasizing the Patient Experience*: Many pharmaceutical companies focus on patient-centric marketing, emphasizing patient experience and well-being. This involves marketing the product and highlighting how it can improve patients' lives and experiences.
2. *Creating a Brand Personality*: A brand personality can help to differentiate a pharmaceutical brand from its competitors and create a more emotional connection with stakeholders. This can involve using branding elements, such as logos, colors, and messaging, that reflect the personality of the brand and its values.
3. *Highlighting Social Responsibility*: Many pharmaceutical companies focus on social responsibility to differentiate their brands and appeal to stakeholders looking for socially responsible brands. This may involve supporting charitable causes or engaging in sustainable practices.
4. *Building Trust and Credibility*: Building trust and credibility with stakeholders is essential for success in the pharmaceutical industry. This can be achieved by providing accurate and transparent information, engaging with key opinion leaders and patient advocacy groups, and adhering to high ethical standards.

Intangible repositioning in pharma marketing can be a powerful tool for differentiating pharmaceutical brands, building emotional connections with stakeholders, and improving the brand's overall perception. By leveraging intangible factors, pharmaceutical companies can create a more compelling and differentiated marketing strategy that resonates with stakeholders and drives business success.

Integration

Integration in pharmaceutical marketing refers to combining multiple marketing channels and tactics to create a cohesive and effective marketing strategy. The integration allows pharmaceutical companies to reach their target audience through multiple touchpoints, providing a consistent message and a seamless experience across all channels.

Integrated marketing campaigns can include a combination of traditional marketing channels, such as print, television, and radio advertising, as well as digital channels, such as email marketing, social media, and search engine marketing. By combining these channels, pharmaceutical companies can create a comprehensive marketing strategy that reaches their target audience in various ways.

Here are some of the benefits of integration in pharma marketing:

1. *Increased Reach*: Integration allows pharmaceutical companies to reach their target audience through multiple channels, increasing the overall reach of their marketing campaigns.
2. *Consistent Messaging*: Integration ensures that the message communicated through each marketing channel is consistent, creating a cohesive and memorable brand experience for the target audience.
3. *Improved Efficiency*: Integration allows pharmaceutical companies to optimize their marketing efforts by identifying the most effective channels for reaching their target audience and allocating resources accordingly.
4. *Increased Engagement*: Integration can increase engagement with the target audience, as they are exposed to the brand message through multiple channels and touchpoints.

Integration is an important aspect of pharma marketing that can help pharmaceutical companies to create a comprehensive and effective marketing strategy that reaches the target audience in various ways.

Integrated Marketing

Integrated marketing is a marketing approach that involves creating a unified and seamless brand experience for customers across all channels and touchpoints. This approach recognizes that customers interact with brands through multiple channels, such as social media, email, website, events, and physical stores, and aims to create a consistent and cohesive brand message and experience across all these channels.

Integrated marketing involves coordinating and aligning different marketing channels and strategies to create a cohesive and integrated campaign. This may include integrating digital and traditional marketing channels, such as combining social media and TV advertising or coordinating offline events with online marketing campaigns.

Integrated Marketing in Pharma

In pharmaceutical marketing, the benefits of integrated marketing include:

A. A more consistent brand message and experience.

B. Improved customer engagement and loyalty.

C. Increased efficiency and effectiveness of marketing efforts.

D. Better measurement and optimization of marketing campaigns.

In pharmaceutical marketing, integrated marketing can be particularly important, as pharmaceutical companies often have complex products and services requiring a multi-channel approach to reach healthcare providers and patients effectively. In addition, integrated marketing can help pharmaceutical companies build strong relationships with their audiences, establish their brand as a thought leader, and drive sales and revenue.

Examples of integrated marketing in Pharma may include a coordinated advertising and social media campaign to promote a new drug launch, an email marketing campaign to educate healthcare providers about a new treatment option, or a combination of in-person events and direct mail to increase awareness of a specific health condition.

Implementing Integrated Marketing in Pharma

Implementing an integrated marketing strategy requires careful planning, coordination, and execution across multiple channels and tactics. Here are some steps to help you get started:

1. *Define Your Objectives*: Start by clearly defining your marketing objectives, such as increasing brand awareness, driving sales, or promoting a new product launch. This will help you determine which channels and tactics will more effectively achieve your goals.
2. *Understand Your Target Audience*: Conduct market research to understand better your target audience and their preferences, behaviors, and pain points. This will help you create a message that resonates with them and choose the right channels to reach them.

3. *Develop a Consistent Message*: Create a consistent and compelling message that speaks to your target audience and supports your marketing objectives. This message should be reflected across all channels and tactics to ensure a cohesive and unified approach.
4. *Choose the Right Channels and Tactics*: Consider which channels and tactics will most effectively reach your target audience and achieve your objectives. This may include a combination of advertising, social media, email marketing, direct mail, events, and content marketing.
5. *Plan and Coordinate Your Campaigns*: Develop a detailed plan for each campaign, outlining the objectives, message, channels, tactics, and timeline. Coordinate all campaigns and tactics to ensure a seamless and integrated approach.
6. *Monitor and Measure Results*: Track and measure all the results of each campaign and tactic to determine what is working and what needs improvement. Use this data to refine your approach and optimize your marketing efforts.

Implementing an integrated marketing strategy requires a holistic and coordinated approach across all channels and tactics, focusing on delivering a consistent and compelling message to your target audience. Following these key steps, you can create a successful integrated marketing campaign that achieves your objectives and drives results.

Integrated Strategies

Integration strategies in pharma marketing refer to how pharmaceutical companies combine multiple marketing tactics and channels to create a cohesive and effective marketing plan. Integration ensures all marketing efforts work together seamlessly to achieve the desired outcomes and objectives.

Here are some common integration strategies in pharma marketing:

1. *Multi-channel Marketing*: Using a combination of different channels, such as email, social media, direct mail, and events, to reach customers and promote products and services.
2. *Data Integration*: Integrating customer data from various sources, such as CRM systems, social media, and website analytics, to gain a holistic view of customer behavior and preferences.
3. *Content Integration*: Developing content that can be repurposed across multiple channels and formats, such as blogs, social media posts, and white papers, to reach customers at different stages of the customer journey.
4. *Sales and Marketing Alignment*: Aligning sales and marketing teams to ensure that all messaging and tactics are consistent and targeted towards the same goals and objectives.
5. *Customer Journey Mapping*: Mapping out the customer journey from initial awareness to post-purchase follow-up and identifying opportunities to integrate marketing tactics at each journey stage.
6. *Personalization*: Using customer data to personalize marketing messages and tactics, such as email campaigns and website content, to engage better and convert customers.

Integration strategies in pharma marketing can be complex and require coordination across multiple departments and channels. However, when executed effectively, they can result in a more effective and efficient marketing plan that better meets customers' needs and drives business growth.

Intellectual Capital

Intellectual capital refers to the intangible assets of an organization that are not reflected in its financial statements but contributes to its overall value and competitiveness. Intellectual capital can include many assets, such as knowledge, skills, expertise, technology, patents, trademarks, copyrights, databases, customer relationships, brand reputation, and organizational culture.

There are typically three categories of intellectual capital:

1. *Human Capital* refers to the knowledge, skills, and expertise of an organization's employees. It includes their education, training, experience, creativity, and ability to work together effectively.
2. *Structural Capital*: This refers to the non-human resources that an organization has at its disposal, such as its information systems, processes, patents, trademarks, copyrights, and other intellectual property.
3. *Relationship Capital*: This refers to the capital that an organization has with its customers, suppliers, partners, and other stakeholders. It includes the trust, loyalty, and goodwill an organization has built over time.

Intellectual capital is important because it can help an organization to create value, innovate and compete effectively. By leveraging its intellectual capital, an organization can develop new products and services, improve its processes, and build strong relationships with customers and other stakeholders. As a result, intellectual capital is a key driver of long-term growth and sustainability, enabling an organization to adapt to changing market conditions and stay ahead of the competition.

Intellectual Capital In Pharma Marketing

In pharmaceutical marketing, intellectual capital is crucial in developing effective marketing strategies and building strong relationships with stakeholders.

Pharmaceutical companies possess a wealth of intellectual capital from scientific expertise, clinical data, regulatory knowledge, and market insights. This intellectual capital can be leveraged to create value for the company and its stakeholders.

Here are some ways in which pharmaceutical companies can use their intellectual capital to improve their marketing efforts:

1. *Thought Leadership*: Pharmaceutical companies can position themselves as thought leaders in their respective therapeutic areas by sharing their scientific knowledge and expertise. This can be done through white papers, webinars, and other forms of content marketing.
2. *Education*: Pharmaceutical companies can educate healthcare professionals and patients about the latest scientific developments, treatment options, and disease management strategies. This can be done through training programs, online resources, and patient support programs.
3. *Collaboration*: Pharmaceutical companies can collaborate with healthcare providers, patient groups, and other stakeholders to share knowledge and expertise and to develop innovative solutions to unmet medical needs.
4. *Market Research*: Pharmaceutical companies can use their market insights to develop marketing strategies tailored to different stakeholders' needs. This can involve conducting market research, analyzing data, and monitoring trends in the market.
5. *Branding*: Pharmaceutical companies can use their intellectual capital to build strong brands associated with innovation, quality, and expertise. This can be done through effective branding strategies, such as developing a strong visual identity and messaging platform.

Thus, intellectual capital is a valuable resource that pharmaceutical companies can use to develop effective marketing strategies, build strong relationships with stakeholders, and create value for their customers and stakeholders.

International Harmonization

1. International harmonization in the context of pharmaceuticals refers to aligning regulations, standards, and guidelines related to drug development, manufacturing, and marketing across different countries and regions. International harmonization aims to provide consistency, reduce duplication of efforts, and facilitate the global movement of pharmaceutical products while ensuring patient safety and product quality. This has several implications for pharma marketers:
2. *Consistency in Regulatory Requirements*: Harmonization aims to create uniformity in regulatory requirements for drug approval and post-market surveillance. This can simplify obtaining marketing authorization in multiple countries, allowing pharma companies to plan their global marketing strategies more effectively.
3. *Efficiency in Drug Development*: When harmonizing regulatory requirements, drug development processes become more streamlined. Pharma marketers can benefit from reduced timelines for clinical trials and approvals, allowing them to bring new drugs to market faster and stay ahead of competitors.
4. *Global Marketing Strategy*: International harmonization enables pharma companies to develop standardized global marketing strategies. Instead of tailoring marketing materials and messages for each market's unique regulatory landscape, marketers can create consistent messages that resonate across different regions.
5. *Resource Optimization*: Harmonization reduces the need for redundant testing and documentation when seeking approval in multiple countries. This can lead to cost savings regarding resources, time, and finances, which can be allocated to other marketing initiatives.
6. *Access to Larger Markets*: With aligned regulations, pharma companies can more easily enter and operate internationally. This expanded market access provides more opportunities for pharma marketers to reach larger patient populations and expand their customer base.
7. *Standardized Safety and Efficacy Information*: International harmonization ensures that safety and efficacy information is presented

consistently across different markets. Pharma marketers can communicate this information effectively, ensuring that patients and healthcare professionals understand a particular drug's benefits and risks.

8. *Enhanced Reputation*: Aligning with international standards and adhering to harmonized regulations can enhance a pharma company's reputation. It demonstrates a commitment to high-quality products and patient safety, which can positively influence how healthcare professionals and patients perceive the company.
9. *Adaptation to Local Context*: While international harmonization promotes consistency, it's important to remember that there may still be some variations in local regulations and cultural factors. Pharma marketers must balance global strategies and localized tactics to cater to specific market needs.

It's worth noting that achieving complete international harmonization can be challenging due to differences in regulatory philosophies, healthcare systems, and cultural nuances among countries. Nevertheless, efforts toward harmonization continue, and pharma marketers can benefit from staying informed about evolving global regulatory trends and adapting their strategies accordingly.

International Marketing

International marketing refers to the practice of promoting and selling products or services in multiple countries or regions around the world. It involves adapting marketing strategies to meet different countries and regions' unique cultural, social, economic, and political environments. International marketing is important for companies looking to expand their customer base beyond their home country and tap into new markets. To succeed in international marketing, companies must develop a deep understanding of their target countries' cultural nuances, consumer preferences, and regulatory requirements. This often requires conducting market research, developing localized marketing campaigns, and establishing strong partnerships with local businesses and organizations.

Key challenges associated with international marketing include language barriers, cultural differences, regulatory requirements, and logistics. In addition, companies may need to adapt their products, packaging, pricing, and advertising to meet different markets' unique needs and preferences.

International marketing is an important component of global business strategy. Companies that can successfully navigate the challenges of international marketing can tap into new sources of revenue, expand their customer base, and strengthen their competitive position in the global marketplace.

International Marketing in Pharma

International marketing is an important component of the pharmaceutical industry, allowing companies to expand their reach beyond their home country and access new markets worldwide. Here are some key aspects of international marketing in pharma:

1. *Regulatory Compliance*: One of the key challenges of international marketing in pharma is navigating the complex regulatory environment in different countries. Each country has its own regulatory framework for drug approval and marketing, which can differ significantly from regulations in other countries. This requires pharmaceutical companies to develop a deep understanding of the regulatory landscape in each market they are targeting and ensure that they comply with local regulations.
2. *Localization of Marketing Campaigns*: To succeed in international markets, pharmaceutical companies must develop localized marketing campaigns considering different countries' unique cultural and social contexts. This may involve adapting advertising and promotional materials to local languages and customs and tailoring marketing messages to address different markets' specific needs and preferences.
3. *Pricing and Reimbursement*: Pricing and reimbursement policies can vary widely between countries, with some markets offering lower prices and others offering higher prices. Pharmaceutical companies must carefully consider the pricing and reimbursement landscape in each market they are targeting and develop strategies that maximize their revenues while ensuring their products remain accessible to patients.
4. *Partnerships and collaborations*: Establishing strong partnerships and collaborations with local businesses and organizations is essential for successful international marketing in pharma. This can help companies navigate local regulations, build brand awareness, and establish a strong presence in new markets.

International marketing is a key driver of growth and innovation in the pharmaceutical industry, allowing companies to expand their reach and access new sources of revenue. However, it requires careful planning, a deep understanding of local markets, and commitment to regulatory compliance and ethical business practices.

International Marketing Planning

International marketing planning is developing a marketing strategy tailored to consumers' unique needs and preferences in different countries or regions worldwide. It involves researching and analyzing various aspects of international markets, such as consumer behavior, market trends, competitive landscape, cultural differences, regulatory requirements, and other relevant factors.

International marketing planning aims to develop a comprehensive plan that outlines how a company will promote and sell its products or services in different countries or regions.

This may involve adapting marketing messages, product offerings, pricing strategies, distribution channels, and promotional activities to suit local market conditions better.

Key Steps

The steps involved in international marketing planning may vary depending on the specific company, industry, and target markets. However, some important general steps involved in international marketing planning are:

1. *Conduct a Market Analysis*: The first step is comprehensively analyzing the target market. This involves researching and analyzing consumer behavior, market trends, competition, and regulatory environments.
2. *Define Objectives and Goals*: Based on the market analysis, the company should define its objectives and goals for entering the international market. This may include market share, revenue targets, and brand recognition.
3. *Develop a Marketing Strategy*: The company should develop a marketing strategy that aligns with its objectives and goals. This may involve adapting marketing messages, product offerings, pricing strategies, distribution channels, and promotional activities to suit local market conditions better.
4. *Develop a Budget*: The company should develop a budget for its international marketing efforts, considering market entry costs, advertising expenses, and personal expenses.
5. *Implementation*: Once the marketing plan is in place, the company should implement the plan and begin executing marketing activities such as advertising, promotion, and sales.
6. *Monitor and Evaluate Results*: The company should continuously monitor and evaluate the results of its international marketing efforts and make adjustments as needed to optimize the plan's effectiveness.
7. *Adjust and Refine Strategy*: Based on the monitoring and evaluation results, the company should adjust and refine its marketing strategy to ensure that it continues to meet its objectives and goals in the international market.

Effective international marketing planning requires a deep understanding of the target market and a flexible and adaptable approach that can accommodate differences in culture, language, and other factors. It also involves careful coordination and communication between different departments within a company and external partners such as distributors, suppliers, and marketing agencies.

International Marketing Planning in Pharma

International marketing planning is critical for pharmaceutical companies to expand their reach beyond their home markets. Here are some key steps involved in the international marketing planning process, along with examples of how they are applied in the pharmaceutical industry:

1. *Market Research*: The first step in international marketing planning is to conduct market research to identify potential target markets and assess their viability. This includes analyzing market trends, consumer behavior, regulatory frameworks, and competitive landscapes. For example, Pfizer conducted extensive market research before launching its blockbuster drug Viagra in China, including surveys and focus groups to gauge consumer attitudes and preferences.
2. *Market Segmentation*: Once potential target markets have been identified, the next step is to segment them based on factors such as demographics, psychographics, and behavior. This helps pharmaceutical companies to tailor their marketing strategies to the specific needs and preferences of different market segments. For example, Novartis segments its international markets based on population size, GDP per capita, and disease prevalence to prioritize its marketing efforts in the most promising markets.

3. *Marketing Mix*: The marketing mix consists of the four Ps of marketing: product, price, promotion, and place. Pharmaceutical companies must develop strategies for these elements tailored to each target market's needs and preferences. For example, Merck & Co developed a unique pricing strategy for its diabetes drug Januvia in China, setting a lower price point than in other markets to compete with the lower-cost domestic brands.
4. *Regulatory Compliance*: International marketing in pharma requires a deep understanding of the regulatory environment in each target market, including the rules and requirements for drug approval, marketing, and distribution. For example, Sanofi's dedicated regulatory affairs team ensures compliance with local regulations in its international markets, working closely with local authorities and stakeholders to navigate the complex regulatory landscape.
5. *Partnerships and Collaborations*: Establishing strong partnerships and collaborations with local businesses and organizations is essential for successful international marketing in pharma. This can help companies to navigate local regulations, build brand awareness, and establish a strong presence in new markets. For example, GlaxoSmithKline has partnered with local pharmaceutical companies in China to develop and market drugs specifically for the Chinese market, leveraging the local company's expertise and knowledge of the market to gain a competitive advantage.

International marketing planning in pharma requires careful research, strategic planning, and a deep understanding of each target market's unique needs and preferences. By developing tailored marketing strategies that consider local regulations, consumer behavior, and the competitive landscape, pharmaceutical companies can expand their reach and access new sources of revenue.

International Normalized Ratio (INR)

The International Normalized Ratio (INR) is a laboratory test commonly used to monitor patients taking warfarin, an anticoagulant, or blood thinner. It is a standard way to measure the time it takes for blood to clot, and it helps healthcare providers ensure that patients are receiving the right dose of warfarin. Maintaining the INR within a specific range is crucial for balancing the benefits of preventing clots and the risks of causing excessive bleeding.

When discussing INR in pharma marketing, the implications are largely tied to anticoagulant medications and cardiovascular health.

Implications for Pharma Marketers

1. *Educational Campaigns*: One of the core responsibilities of pharma marketers, especially in anticoagulants, is to educate healthcare providers on the importance of monitoring INR. This ensures that the drug is used safely and effectively.
2. *Differentiation from Newer Agents*: Newer anticoagulant agents, often referred to as NOACs or DOACs (novel or direct anticoagulants) like Dabigatran, Rivaroxaban, and Apixaban, do not require routine INR monitoring. Marketers of these drugs might highlight the absence of frequent monitoring as a convenience and advantage over warfarin.
3. *Device Collaboration*: Companies producing INR monitoring devices could collaborate with pharma companies for joint monitoring efforts, especially if home INR monitoring is encouraged.
4. *Adherence Programs*: Warfarin requires strict adherence to ensure therapeutic INR levels. Pharma marketers might develop patient support programs to emphasize the importance of taking the medication regularly and attending routine INR checks.
5. *Safety Campaigns*: Given the risks of excessive bleeding with anticoagulants, marketers must emphasize the importance of maintaining therapeutic INR levels, recognizing signs of bleeding, and understanding drug and food interactions that can affect warfarin's efficacy.
6. *Direct-to-Consumer Advertising*: In regions where direct-to-consumer (DTC) advertising is allowed, marketers might emphasize the importance of INR monitoring when promoting warfarin, ensuring patients are informed about the need for regular checks.
7. *Healthcare Provider Training*: New medical staff or providers may need continuous training and educational materials on the importance of INR, its proper monitoring, and the interpretation of results.
8. *Digital Tools*: With the rise of digital health, pharma companies can develop support apps that help patients on warfarin track their INR levels, medication doses, and any related symptoms or side effects.

9. *Regulatory Oversight*: Any marketing materials or campaigns focused on anticoagulants and INR must adhere to regulatory guidelines, emphasizing benefits and risks.

While INR primarily serves a clinical purpose, it has several implications in pharmaceutical marketing, especially surrounding anticoagulant medications. If applicable, effective marketing strategies will emphasize patient safety, education, and the advantages of newer treatment options.

Internet Marketing

Internet marketing, or digital marketing, promotes products or services online using various digital channels and tactics. This includes search engine optimization (SEO), search engine marketing (SEM), social media marketing, email marketing, and content marketing. Internet marketing aims to reach and engage with a target audience online, drive website traffic, generate leads, and convert them into customers.

Some common tactics used in Internet marketing include:

1. *Search Engine Optimization (SEO)* involves optimizing your website and content to rank higher in search engine results pages (SERPs) for specific keywords and phrases relevant to your business.
2. *Pay-Per-Click (PPC) Advertising* involves placing ads on search engines, social media platforms, and other websites and paying each time someone clicks on your ad.
3. *Social Media Marketing involves* using social media platforms like Facebook, Twitter, and LinkedIn to engage with your target audience, promote your brand, and drive traffic to your website.
4. *Email Marketing* involves using targeted email campaigns to your subscribers and leads to build relationships, promote your products or services, and drive conversions.
5. *Content Marketing* involves creating and sharing valuable, informative content such as blog posts, videos, infographics, and ebooks to attract and engage with your target audience.

Internet marketing offers businesses a powerful way to reach and engage with their target audience online. By combining digital channels and tactics, businesses can increase their visibility, drive website traffic, generate leads, and grow their customer base.

Intelligent Clinics

Intelligent clinics, also known as smart clinics or AI-powered clinics, are healthcare facilities that integrate advanced artificial intelligence and automation technologies to enhance various aspects of patient care and medical operations. These clinics leverage cutting-edge technologies to improve efficiency and overall patient experience. Key features and components commonly found in intelligent clinics include:

1. *Artificial Intelligence and Machine Learning*: These technologies analyze vast medical data, including patient records, diagnostic images, and research papers. AI algorithms can assist in diagnosing medical conditions, predicting disease outcomes, and suggesting personalized treatment plans based on historical data and patterns.
2. *Robotics*: Intelligent clinics often employ robotic systems for automated sample collection, medication dispensing, and repetitive procedures, reducing human error and increasing efficiency.
3. *Telemedicine*: Telemedicine and remote patient monitoring technologies enable doctors to provide consultations and monitor patients remotely. Patients can access medical advice and care without physically visiting the clinic, making health care more convenient, especially for individuals in remote or underserved areas.
4. *Virtual Reality (VR): and Augmented Reality (AR)*: These technologies have applications in medical education, patient education, and surgical planning. Surgeons can use VR and AR to practice complex procedures, enhancing their skills and reducing the risk of errors during surgeries.
5. *Electronic Health Records (EHRs)*: Intelligent clinics utilize digital health record systems to securely store and manage patient information. EHRs enable healthcare providers to access patients' medical histories, test results, and treatment plans in real-time, promoting coordinated and comprehensive care.
6. *IoT Devices*: Internet of Things (IoT) devices, such as wearable health monitors and sensors, can be integrated into intelligent clinics to gather continuous patient data and enable remote monitoring of vital signs and health metrics.
7. *Self-Service Kiosks*: Some intelligent clinics may feature self-service kiosks for patient check-ins, data updates, and processes, reducing waiting times.

8. *Data Security*: Robust cybersecurity measures are crucial for protecting sensitive patient data and ensuring compliance with privacy regulations.

Intelligent clinics hold great promise in revolutionizing the healthcare industry by providing more efficient and accessible care while reducing costs and improving patient outcomes. However, as with emerging technology, there are challenges, including regulatory considerations, data privacy concerns, and the need to balance the human touch and technological advancements in patient care.

Implications for Pharma Marketers

The rise of intelligent clinics presents a transformative opportunity for pharma marketers. Here are the key implications:

1. *Precision Medicine and Personalization*: Intelligent clinics can harness patient data to pinpoint the best treatment options, and pharma marketers can use this to promote targeted drug therapies. Marketers can highlight their products' unique benefits and differentiation for specific patient groups.
2. *Real-time Data Analytics*: With the constant inflow of patient data, pharma marketers have an unprecedented view of how drugs perform in real-world settings. This can inform marketing strategies and enable better positioning of products based on actual patient outcomes.
3. *Virtual Health Engagement*: Intelligent clinics may use telehealth platforms or AI-powered chatbots to engage patients. Pharma marketers can collaborate with these platforms to offer patient support programs, medication reminders, or drug-specific information.
4. *Enhanced Clinical Trials*: With the capacity to gather and analyze vast amounts of data quickly, intelligent clinics can streamline the clinical trial process. This may speed up drug approvals and give marketers timely and robust data to leverage in their campaigns.
5. *A shift from Volume to Value*: Intelligent clinics prioritize treatments with the best outcomes. Pharma marketers will need to emphasize the value and effectiveness of their products rather than just volume sales or prescriptions.
6. *Improved Patient Adherence*: Through AI-driven reminders and tailored patient communication, intelligent clinics can boost medication adherence. Pharma marketers can work with these systems to create adherence programs and offer incentives to patients.
7. *Ethical Considerations*: With increased data collection, privacy concerns rise. Pharma marketers must ensure that collaboration with intelligent clinics upholds stringent data privacy standards to maintain patient trust.
8. *Educational Opportunities*: As intelligent clinics use advanced tools, there's a chance for pharma companies to provide educational content on how their products work in synergy with these technologies, addressing both healthcare providers and patients.
9. *Collaboration with Tech Companies*: Pharma companies can form alliances with these tech companies to create integrated solutions, making their products indispensable to the intelligent clinic ecosystem.
10. *Change in Sales Dynamics*: Given the tech-savvy nature of intelligent clinics, the traditional pharmaceutical sales model might evolve, with less emphasis on face-to-face interactions and more on digital engagement strategies.

By understanding the new ecosystem and aligning their strategies accordingly, pharma companies can form stronger ties with healthcare providers and patients, ensuring their products remain relevant and valuable in this rapidly changing landscape. However, with these opportunities come challenges, especially regarding data privacy and ethical considerations, which companies must address proactively.

Internet of Things (IoT)

IoT stands for Internet of Things. It refers to a network of physical devices, vehicles, home appliances, and other items connected to the Internet that can communicate. These devices are embedded with sensors, software, and other technologies that allow them to collect and exchange data over the Internet.

In pharmaceutical marketing, IoT can be used in many ways:

1. *Wearables Medical Devices*: IoT technology can be used in wearable medical devices like smartwatches or fitness trackers to collect patient health and wellness data. This data can be used to develop targeted marketing campaigns or personalized treatment plans.
2. *Remote Monitoring*: IoT technology can remotely monitor patients' health status and treatment adherence, allowing for more personalized and effective care.
3. *Supply Chain Management*: IoT technology can be used to track the movement of pharmaceuticals throughout the supply chain, ensuring that drugs are stored and transported

at the appropriate temperature and humidity levels.

4. *Smart Packaging*: IoT technology can be used in smart packaging to monitor the condition of drugs during shipping and storage, ensuring that they are not damaged or compromised.

IoT technology has the potential to revolutionize the pharmaceutical industry by providing real-time data on patient health, streamlining supply chain operations, and improving treatment outcomes.

Interruption Marketing

Interruption marketing is a traditional approach where advertisers interrupt people's activities to promote their products or services. This can include tactics such as television commercials, radio ads, print ads, pop-up ads, and telemarketing.

The key characteristic of interruption marketing is that it is intrusive and often unwelcome. The ads are inserted in the middle of people's activities, such as watching a TV show or browsing a website, and can be seen as interruptive.

In contrast to interruption marketing, inbound marketing focuses on creating valuable content that attracts and engages potential customers. This approach aims to build customer relationships and trust rather than interrupting them with ads.

While interruption marketing may still be effective in some contexts, such as during live events or sports games, it is becoming less effective in today's digital age. For example, many people use blockers or skip commercials, making it harder for advertisers to reach their target audience through traditional interruption marketing tactics. As a result, many businesses are shifting towards more targeted and personalized forms, such as content marketing and social media marketing.

Interruption Marketing in Pharma

Interruption marketing can be used in pharma marketing, but it is becoming less effective as people increasingly use ad blockers and skip ads. However, traditional interruption marketing tactics are still used in pharma marketing, such as television commercials, print ads in medical journals, and targeted online ads.

Pharma companies also use other forms of marketing, such as content marketing, social media marketing, and influencer marketing, to reach and engage with their target audience. These tactics aim to create valuable content that educates and informs potential customers about the benefits of their products and services rather than interrupting them with ads.

Pharmaceutical companies must balance traditional interruption marketing tactics and newer, more targeted, and personalized forms of marketing to reach and engage with their target audience effectively.

Intrusive Marketing

Intrusive Marketing is a term that refers to any form of marketing that is intrusive or interruptive to the user experience. This includes traditional marketing methods, such as pop-up ads, banner ads, email spam, telemarketing, and direct mail marketing.

Intrusive marketing tactics are often seen as annoying and unwelcome by the target audience. They can lead to a negative brand image and a reduction in customer trust and loyalty. In contrast, non-intrusive marketing tactics, such as content marketing, social media marketing, and influencer marketing, focus on creating valuable content that engages the target audience and encourages them to interact with the brand. These tactics aim to build customer relationships and establish a positive brand image.

In today's digital age, many people use ad-blockers or skip ads, making intrusive marketing tactics less effective. Therefore, businesses need to focus on more targeted and personalized forms of marketing to reach their target audience effectively.

Intrusive Marketing in Pharma

In pharma marketing, intrusive marketing tactics can be seen in traditional advertising methods such as television commercials, radio ads, billboards, and print ads in medical journals. However, in recent years, there has been a shift towards more targeted and personalized forms of marketing in the pharmaceutical industry, such as content marketing, social media marketing, and influencer marketing.

These non-intrusive marketing tactics aim to provide valuable information to patients, healthcare professionals, and other stakeholders rather than interrupting them with ads. For example, pharmaceutical companies might create educational videos or blog posts that inform patients about their medical condition and available treatment options. Social media platforms can create a community of patients sharing their experiences and supporting one another. Influencer marketing can be used to reach a specific audience and increase awareness.

While intrusive marketing tactics can still be effective in some cases, it is becoming increasingly important for pharma companies to focus on non-intrusive marketing methods that engage and educate their target audience.

Investigative New Drug (IND)

An Investigational New Drug (IND) application is critical in bringing a new pharmaceutical product, such as a drug or biologic, to market. It's a regulatory submission to the relevant health authority, such as the US Food and Drug Administration (FDA) in the United States or the European Medicines Agency (EMA) in the European Union. The IND application is submitted by a pharmaceutical company or sponsor that wishes to conduct clinical trials for a new drug. Here's how the IND application fits into the pharmaceutical marketing process:

1. *Preclinical Development*: Before a pharmaceutical product can be tested in humans, it undergoes preclinical testing. This phase involves laboratory and animal studies to assess the compound's safety, efficacy, and potential side effects.
2. *IND Application*: Once preclinical studies show promising results and the pharmaceutical company believes the compound is ready for human testing, they submit an IND application to the relevant regulatory agency. This application includes data from preclinical studies, manufacturing details, information on how the drug will be tested in humans, and plans for clinical trials.
3. *Clinical Trials*: Upon receiving the approval of the IND application, the pharmaceutical company can begin conducting clinical trials. These trials are conducted in three phases: *Phase 1*: Small-scale trials involving a small number of healthy volunteers to assess the safety and dosage; *Phase 2*: Larger trials involving a limited number of patients to evaluate safety and efficacy further. *Phase 3*: Large-scale trials involving a more extensive patient population to confirm safety, efficacy and monitor side effects.
4. *Marketing Approval*: If the results of the clinical trials are positive and demonstrate the drug's safety and efficacy, the pharmaceutical company can then submit a New Drug Application (NDA) or Biologics License Application (BLA) to seek marketing approval for the drug. The regulatory agency evaluates the application and decides based on the clinical data provided.
5. *Post-Marketing Activities*: After receiving marketing approval, the pharmaceutical company continues to monitor the drug's safety and effectiveness through post-marketing surveillance. They may also conduct additional studies to gather more data on the drug's long-term effects.
6. *Pharma Marketing:* Throughout these stages, pharmaceutical marketing plays a role in educating healthcare professionals, patients, and the public about the new drug. Marketing efforts often include developing promotional materials, conducting educational events, and raising awareness about the drug's benefits.
7. It is important to note that regulatory agencies like the FDA closely scrutinize IND applications and subsequent market approval applications to ensure the safety and efficacy of pharmaceutical products. The process balances the need for innovative new treatments with patient safety and public health considerations.

iPad Detailing

iPad detailing is a digital marketing strategy pharmaceutical companies use to promote their products to healthcare professionals. The iPad has become a popular tool for detailing because it allows sales representatives to showcase product information and educational content in a dynamic and interactive way.

Here are some ways that iPad detailing can be used in pharmaceutical marketing:

1. *Customized Presentations*: Sales representatives can create customized presentations based on the needs and interests of each healthcare provider they visit. This allows them to tailor the message to each customer's specific needs, which can improve engagement and help build trust.
2. *Interactive Content*: The iPad can display interactive content, such as videos, animations, and interactive graphics, which can be used to explain complex scientific concepts engagingly and memorably.
3. *Remote Detailing*: iPad detailing can be used for remote detailing, allowing sales representatives to connect with healthcare professionals they cannot meet in person. This can be particularly useful for reaching HCPs in remote or underserved areas.
4. *Real-time Feedback*: The iPad allows sales representatives to receive real-time feedback from healthcare professionals, such as questions or concerns, and build stronger relationships.

iPad detailing is a powerful tool for pharma marketing that allows sales representatives to engage with healthcare professionals more dynamically and interactively. By leveraging the capabilities of the iPad, pharmaceutical companies can create a more personalized and effective marketing experience for their customers.

J

1. Jargon
2. Joint Venture
3. Journal Advertising
4. Judgemental Sampling
5. Junkmail
6. Juxtaposition

Jargon

Jargon refers to specialized language or terminology used in a particular profession. Jargon can be technical or complex and often includes words or phrases not commonly used in everyday language. Jargon is used to communicate specific ideas or concepts within a particular field or community and is typically understood only by those familiar with that field or community.

Jargon can be found in many fields and professions, including law, medicine, engineering, finance, and technology. For example, medical jargon includes terms such as dyspnea (shortness of breath), hemiplegia (paralysis on one side of the body), and myocardial infarction (heart attack), which are not commonly used in everyday conversation but are necessary for clear and precise communication among healthcare professionals.

While jargon can help communicate technical information within a specific field, it can also be a barrier to communication outside that field. In addition, jargon can confuse or intimidate those unfamiliar with it and lead to misunderstandings or miscommunications. As a result, it is important to use jargon appropriately and to be aware of your audience when communicating technical information.

In pharmaceutical marketing, jargon is commonly used to describe technical terms, medical terminology, and regulatory language specific to the pharmaceutical industry. Some examples of pharmaceutical jargon include:

1. *Mechanism of Action (MOA)* refers to how a drug works in the body to achieve its therapeutic effect.
2. *Pharmacokinetics (PK)* studies how a drug is absorbed, distributed, metabolized, and eliminated by the body.
3. *Pharmacodynamics (PD)* refers to the study of how a drug affects the body at the molecular and cellular levels.
4. *A dosage Regimen* refers to a drug's dosing schedule and frequency based on age, weight, and medical history.
5. *Brand Name* is the trademarked name a pharmaceutical company gives its drug.
6. *FDA Approval*: The Food and Drug Administration (FDA) is a regulatory agency in the United States that approves drugs for use by the public. When a drug is FDA-approved, it has met certain safety and effectiveness standards.
7. *Indication*: This refers to the specific medical condition or disease a drug is approved to treat.
8. *Adverse Event (AE)* refers to any negative or unwanted effect that occurs while a patient takes a drug.
9. *Off-label Use*: This is the use of a drug to treat a condition not included in the drug's FDA-approved indications.
10. *Payer* refers to an entity that pays for healthcare services, such as an insurance company or government program.
11. *A Formulary* is a list of drugs a particular payer will cover for its beneficiaries.
12. *Market Access*: This refers to the ability of a drug to be sold and reimbursed by payers.

Pharmaceutical jargon can be difficult for patients and healthcare providers unfamiliar with the industry. Furthermore, too much jargon can be confusing or intimidating, leading to misunderstandings or miscommunications. Therefore, pharma marketers must use clear and concise language when communicating their products.

Joint Venture

A joint venture is a business arrangement between two or more companies or organizations that agree to work together on a specific project or enterprise. In a joint venture, each company contributes resources, expertise, and capital to the project or enterprise and shares profits and losses.

Joint ventures can take many forms, ranging from short-term projects to long-term strategic partnerships. Joint ventures can be established for various reasons, including entering a new market, sharing resources or expertise, reducing risk, or gaining access to new technologies or products.

Joint Ventures in Pharma Marketing

Joint ventures in pharmaceutical marketing are collaborations between two or more companies that agree to work together on a specific marketing initiative or product launch. Here are a few examples of joint ventures in pharma marketing:

1. *Co-promotion*: Two or more pharmaceutical companies partner to promote and sell a product jointly. For example, Prizer and Bristol-Myers Squibb formed a joint venture to market and sell the blood thinner Eliquis (Apixaban).
2. *Co-development*: Two or more pharmaceutical companies collaborate to develop and market a new drug. For example, Sanofi and Regeneron formed a joint venture to develop and commercialize biologics (biological drugs) for various diseases.

3. *Licensing Agreements*: A pharmaceutical company licenses the rights to a drug or technology from another company for use in its products. For example, Merck licensed the rights to develop and market the cancer drug Keytruda (Pembrolizumab) from a biotech company called Amgen.
4. *Research Partnerships*: Pharmaceutical companies partner with academic institutions or other research organizations to jointly fund and conduct research on a specific disease or medical condition. For example, Novartis partnered with the University of Pennsylvania to develop gene therapy for cancer.

Joint ventures in pharma marketing can provide significant benefits for all parties involved, including access to new technologies and expertise, shared research and development costs, and expanded market research. However, these collaborations also require careful planning and negotiation to ensure that each party's interests are protected and that the joint venture is successful.

Journal Advertising

Journal advertising is a common marketing strategy pharmaceutical companies use to promote their products to healthcare professionals, such as doctors, pharmacists, and nurses. These advertisements are typically placed in medical journals and publications that healthcare professionals read.

Medical and scientific journals are widely read by healthcare professionals, including physicians, nurses, and researchers, making them a valuable platform for companies to reach their target audience.

Journal advertising can take various forms, such as print ads, digital ads, or sponsored content. The content of journal ads typically includes information about the product or service being promoted, its benefits, indications, and side effects, as well as supporting clinical data or research.

Journal advertising can be an effective way for companies to increase awareness of their products or services among healthcare professionals. However, it can also be costly, as journal ad rates can be high, and companies must compete with other advertisers for readers' attention.

Journal advertising is subject to regulations and guidelines from organizations such as the Food and Drug Administration (FDA) and the International Committee of Medical Journal Editors (ICMJE), which aim to ensure that journal ads are accurate, fair, and balanced and do not mislead or deceive readers.

It is important for companies to carefully consider the content and format of their journal ads, as well as the journals in which they advertise, to ensure that their message is effectively communicated to their target audience.

It is important to note that pharmaceutical advertising, including journal advertising, is subject to strict regulations and guidelines in many countries, including the United States. These regulations are designed to ensure that all advertising is truthful, accurate, and not misleading and provides balanced information about the benefits and risks of the product. Companies must also disclose potential conflicts of interest or financial relationships with healthcare professionals who endorsed or recommended their products.

Judgemental Sampling

Judgmental sampling is a non-probability sampling technique used in market research and marketing. For example, in pharmaceutical marketing, judgmental sampling can be used to select a specific group of participants for a research study or to target a specific group of customers for a marketing campaign.

Judgmental sampling involves selecting participants or customers based on the researcher's or marketer's judgment rather than through a random selection process. For example, a pharmaceutical company might select a group of doctors to participate in a study based on their expertise in a particular medical field or their prescribing behavior for a particular medication.

While judgmental sampling can be useful in targeting a specific group of participants or customers, it is important to be aware of potential biases in the selection process. The researcher or marketer's judgment may be influenced by their own biases or preferences, which could lead to a non-representative sample.

How Pharma Can Use Judgmental Sampling

Here are a few examples of how judgmental sampling can be used in pharmaceutical marketing:

1. A pharmaceutical company is launching a new medication for a rare condition. The company selects a group of doctors specializing in treating this condition to participate in a study to evaluate the safety and effectiveness of the medication. The company uses judgmental

sampling to select doctors based on their expertise.

2. A pharmaceutical company is planning a marketing campaign for a new medication for arthritis. The company uses judgmental sampling to identify a target audience of patients diagnosed with arthritis who have a history of using similar medications. The company selects these patients based on their medication history, demographic information, and other relevant factors.
3. A pharmaceutical company is conducting market research to understand the preferences and needs of patients diagnosed with a specific type of cancer. The company uses judgmental sampling to select a group of patients who have received treatment for this type of cancer and have agreed to participate in the research study. The company selects these patients based on their medical history, treatment experience, and other relevant factors.

In each of these examples, the pharmaceutical company uses judgmental sampling to select a group of participants or customers for a research study or marketing campaign. By targeting a specific group of individuals, the company can better understand their needs, preferences, and behaviors and tailor their products and marketing efforts accordingly.

It is also important to note that the results of a study or marketing campaign based on judgmental sampling may not be generalizable to the broader population. Therefore, researchers and marketers must carefully interpret the results of their studies and campaigns within the context of the sample they have selected.

In summary, Judgmental sampling can be a useful tool in pharma marketing. Still, it should be used with other research methods and techniques to ensure a comprehensive and accurate understanding of the target audience.

Junkmail

Junk mail in pharmaceutical marketing refers to unsolicited marketing materials, such as letters, brochures, or promotional items, sent to individuals without their consent or request. Pharmaceutical companies often use junk mail to promote their products and services to healthcare providers, patients, and other stakeholders in the healthcare industry.

Junk mail in pharma marketing can effectively reach many individuals quickly and at a relatively low cost. However, it is also a controversial practice that has raised ethical concerns, particularly regarding patients' privacy and autonomy.

One of the main concerns with junk mail in pharma marketing is that it can be seen as intrusive and disruptive to patients dealing with sensitive medical issues. In addition, patients may feel uncomfortable or overwhelmed by the number of unsolicited marketing materials they receive, which could negatively impact their trust in the healthcare system and their willingness to engage in treatment.

In addition, junk mail in pharma marketing can be seen as a waste of resources, as many of these materials may go unread or be discarded without ever being opened. This can harm the environment, as well as the reputation of the pharmaceutical company.

Overall, while junk mail in pharma marketing can be an effective way to promote products and services, it is important for pharmaceutical companies to be mindful of potential ethical concerns and to ensure that their marketing practices are respectful of patients' privacy and autonomy. This may include obtaining consent from patients before sending them marketing materials or using alternative, less intrusive, and more targeted marketing methods.

Juxtaposition

Juxtaposition is a rhetorical technique where two contrasting elements are placed side by side to emphasize their differences. For example, in pharmaceutical marketing, Juxtaposition can be used to highlight the benefits of one medication over another or to emphasize the negative aspects of a competitor's product.

For example, a pharmaceutical company might use Juxtaposition in an advertisement by showing two patients with the same medical condition, one taking their medication and the other not. The patient taking the medication might be shown as healthy and active, while the patient not taking the medication might be shown as weak and bedridden. This type of comparison can effectively persuade patients to choose the company's medication over a competitor's.

However, Juxtaposition in pharma marketing can also be controversial, as it can be perceived as unfair or misleading. Regulators may scrutinize such claims to ensure they are accurate, truthful, and not misleading to patients. Therefore, it is important for pharmaceutical companies to use clear and objective language when making comparisons and to avoid making unsupported claims or overstating the benefits of their products.

Juxtaposition in Pharma Marketing: Examples

Here are a few examples that show how a pharmaceutical company might juxtaposition their advertisements:

1. A print ad for a pain reliever shows an image of a person in extreme pain on one side and an image of the same person smiling and enjoying an activity on the other. The headline reads, "Before and After (Brand Name)—The Pain Relief You Need to Get Back to Doing What You Love."
2. A TV commercial for an allergy medication shows a woman suffering from allergies who cannot enjoy time outside with her family. The commercial shows the woman happily playing with her family after taking the medication. The voiceover says, "Don't let Allergies Hold You Back. (Brand Name): Relief You Can Trust."
3. A website for a cholesterol-lowering medication compares their product to a competitor's. The website features a chart that shows the percentage of patients who experienced side effects while taking the competitor's medication and the percentage of patients who experienced side effects while taking the company's medication. The headline reads, "Choose (Brand Name): Fewer Side Effects, More Results."

In these examples, the advertiser uses Juxtaposition to highlight their product's benefits and compare it to a competitor's. However, it is important to note that such comparisons must be truthful, accurate, and not misleading for patients and follow the advertising regulations and conventions prevailing in that market.

K

1. Key Account
2. Key Account Management
3. Key Account Manager
4. Kanban
5. Key Opinion Leader (KOL)
6. Key Opinion Leader Engagement
7. Key Performance Indicators (KPIs)
8. Key Success Factors (KSFs)
9. Keywords
10. Keyword Marketing
11. Keyword Research
12. Kickbacks
13. Kiosk
14. Kirkpatrick Model
15. KISS principle

Key Account

A key account is a strategic customer or client important to a company's success. Key accounts represent a significant portion of the company's revenue and are often high-profile clients with complex needs or significant influence in their industry.

Companies may designate certain customers as key accounts based on some factors, including:

1. *Revenue*: Key accounts are often the customers who generate the most revenues for a company, either currently or with the potential for future growth.
2. *Strategic Importance*: Key accounts may be chosen because they are in a strategically important industry or market segment where the company wishes to expand or strengthen its presence.
3. *Relationship*: Key accounts are often long-term customers who have developed a strong relationship with the company and have demonstrated loyalty and a willingness to collaborate.
4. *Risk Management*: Key accounts may be chosen because they represent a significant risk to the company if the relationships deteriorate, either through lost revenue or damage to its reputation.

Managing key accounts requires a different approach than managing other customers or clients. Companies often assign dedicated account managers or teams to work with key accounts and provide them with specialized support, such as customized products or services, exclusive access to resources, or priority customer service. Effective key account management can help companies build strong, long-term relationships with their most important customers and achieve sustained business growth.

Key Accounts in Pharma Marketing

In pharma marketing, key accounts can refer to healthcare providers or institutions that are of strategic importance to the success of a pharmaceutical company. Here are some examples of key accounts in pharma marketing:

1. *Hospitals and Healthcare Systems*: Pharmaceutical companies often target large hospitals and healthcare systems as key accounts because they represent a significant portion of their sales revenue. These institutions often have formularies or purchasing committees that determine which medications are used, and pharmaceutical companies may work closely with these committees to ensure that their products are included.
2. *Pharmacy Benefit Managers (PBMs)*: PBMs are intermediaries between insurance companies and pharmacies, and they negotiate drug prices and formularies on behalf of their clients. Pharmaceutical companies may work with PBMs to ensure their products are included in formularies and accessible to patients.
3. *Key Opinion Leaders (KOLs)*: KOLs are healthcare providers with significant influence in their field and are often sought out for their expertise and opinions. Pharmaceutical companies may work with KOLs to develop and promote their products, as KOLs can provide valuable insights and recommendations to other healthcare professionals.
4. *Specialty Pharmacies*: Specialty pharmacies focus on medications that require specialized handling or administration, such as biologics or infusion therapies. Pharmaceutical companies may work with specialty pharmacies to ensure that their products are available and accessible to patients who need them.

Managing key accounts in pharma marketing requires a tailored approach that considers each account's unique needs and challenges. In addition, account managers may work closely with key account stakeholders to understand their priorities and develop strategies that support their goals. Effective key account management can help pharmaceutical companies build strong, long-term relationships with their most important customers and achieve sustained business growth.

Key Account Management

Key Account Management (KAM) is a strategic approach to managing relationships with a company's most important customers or clients, known as key accounts. KAM involves a range of activities aimed at identifying, understanding, and meeting the specific needs of these customers to build strong, long-term relationships and drive sustainable business growth.

Key account management typically involves a dedicated team or an individual managing each key account. These account managers work closely with the customer to understand their goals and priorities, identify opportunities for collaboration, and develop customized solutions that meet their specific needs.

Some common activities involved in key account management are:

1. *Account Planning*: Account managers work with key account stakeholders to develop a comprehensive plan that outlines the goals and objectives for the relationship, as well as the strategies and tactics that will be used to achieve them.
2. *Relationship Building*: Account managers establish and maintain strong relationships with key account stakeholders, such as decision-makers, influencers, and other relevant contacts.
3. *Cross-functional Collaboration*: Account managers work closely with other departments, such as sales, marketing, and product development, to ensure that the key account receives the support and resources they need.
4. *Performance Tracking*: Account managers regularly track and analyze the performance of the key account and the success of the KAM program overall and make adjustments as needed to ensure continued success.

Effective key account management requires a deep understanding of the customer's business and a commitment to providing high service levels, responsiveness, and value. By focusing on the needs of their most important customers, companies can build strong, long-lasting relationships that drive sustained growth and profitability.

Key Account Management in Pharma Marketing

In pharmaceutical marketing, Key Account Management (KAM) involves managing relationships with healthcare professionals, institutions, and other stakeholders strategically important to a pharmaceutical company. Here are some examples of key account management in pharma marketing:

1. *Hospitals and Healthcare Systems*: Key account managers for pharmaceutical companies may work closely with hospitals and healthcare systems to understand their needs and priorities, provide education and training on their products, and collaborate on research or other initiatives. They may also work with hospital formulary committees to ensure their products are included in formularies and accessible to patients.
2. *Pharmacy Benefit Managers (PBMs)*: PBMs negotiate drug prices and formularies on behalf of insurance companies and pharmacies, and they play a critical role in determining which medications are used in their healthcare plans. Key account managers for pharmaceutical companies may work with PBMs to ensure that their products are included in formularies and are accessible to patients.
3. *Key Opinion Leaders (KOLs)*: KOLs are healthcare professionals with significant influence and are often sought out for their expertise and opinions. Key account managers for pharmaceutical companies may work closely with KOLs to develop and promote their products, as KOLs can provide valuable insights and recommendations to other healthcare professionals.
4. *Specialty Pharmacies*: Specialty pharmacies focus on medications that require specialized handling or administration, such as biologics or infusion therapies. Key account managers for pharmaceutical companies may work with specialty pharmacies to ensure that their products are available and accessible to patients who need them.

Effective key account management requires a deep understanding of the customer's business and a commitment to providing high service levels, responsiveness, and value. By focusing on the needs of their most important customers, companies can build strong, long-lasting relationships that drive sustained growth and profitability.

Key Account Manager

A Key Account Manager (KAM) in pharmaceutical marketing manages relationships with a company's most important customers, typically large accounts or healthcare providers. Key account managers are responsible for creating and implementing account-specific strategies to maximize sales and profitability and to ensure that the company's products meet the needs of its customers.

In pharma marketing, KAMs work with healthcare providers to understand their needs and how their company's products can help meet them. They also work to maintain and strengthen relationships with customers by providing education and training on products and services, answering questions and concerns, and providing support for the use of their company's products.

KAMs in pharma marketing are also responsible for identifying new business opportunities and developing plans to increase sales and market share. They may work with other departments within their company, such as sales, marketing, and research and development, to develop and execute marketing campaigns, launch new products, and identify new market opportunities.

Key Account Managers in pharma marketing play a critical role in ensuring that their company's products are successful in the marketplace and that their customers are satisfied with their products and services.

KAM's Role, Tasks, and Responsibilities

The role of a Key Account Manager (KAM) in pharma is to develop and maintain strong relationships with key customers, such as hospitals, healthcare providers, and other large accounts. Their main responsibility is ensuring that the company's products and services meet customers' needs and drive revenue growth through these key accounts. Here are some common tasks and responsibilities of a KAM in pharma marketing:

1. *Building and Maintaining Relationships*: Key Account Managers must establish strong relationships with key customers. This involves developing an in-depth understanding of their needs, goals, and challenges and identifying ways the company's products and services can help them meet their objectives.
2. *Account Planning and Strategy*: Key Account Managers are responsible for developing account-specific strategies to drive sales and revenue growth. They must work closely with their customers to understand their goals and objectives and develop plans to help achieve them. This involves collaborating with other internal teams, such as sales, marketing, and product development.
3. *Business Development*: Key Account Managers are responsible for identifying new business opportunities and potential areas for growth. This may involve expanding product offerings, developing new services, or exploring new markets.
4. *Negotiation and Pricing*: Key Account Managers must negotiate pricing and contracts with key accounts and work to ensure that both parties are satisfied with the terms of the agreement.
5. *Sales Forecasting and Reporting*: Key Account Managers must track and report on sales performance and forecast future sales trends. They must also analyze market data and industry needs to identify growth opportunities.
6. *Cross-functional Collaboration*: Key Account Managers work closely with other internal teams, such as sales, marketing, and product development, to ensure that the company's products and services meet the needs of their key accounts.

Kanban

Kanban is a popular lean manufacturing and project management methodology that originated in Japan and has been widely adopted in many industries worldwide. Kanban systems use visual cues, such as cards or boards, to signal the need for action and to help teams manage workflow and inventory levels.

Kanban is a Japanese term that means a visual signal or card. The Kanban system was developed by Taichi Ohno, an industrial engineer at Toyota, to improve efficiency and reduce waste in the company's manufacturing processes.

In a Kanban system, each task or activity is represented by a card or other visual cue that indicates the status and priority of the task. The cards are placed on a board or other display that allows team members to quickly and easily see each task's status and the project's overall progress.

Kanban systems typically use a pull-based approach, in which work is only pulled into the system as needed rather than pushed through the system according to a predetermined schedule. This helps reduce waste and improve efficiency by ensuring that work is only done when needed and that resources are not wasted on unnecessary tasks.

Kanban systems are used in many industries, including manufacturing, software development, healthcare, and project management. Kanban boards and cards can be physical or digital, and many software tools are available to support Kanban-based project management.

Kanban in Pharma Marketing

Kanban methodology can be applied to various industries, including pharmaceutical marketing. Here are some examples of how Kanban can be used in pharmaceutical marketing:

1. *Content Development*: A Kanban board can be used to manage creating and approving marketing content, such as brochures, websites, or sales presentations. A card on the board can represent each piece of content, with columns indicating the status of each piece of content, such as in the process, waiting for review, approval, etc.
2. *Event Planning*: Kanban can be used to manage the planning and execution of events, such as conferences, trade shows, or product launches. Each task involved in the planning process, such as booking venues, designing exhibits, and preparing promotional materials. All these can be represented by a card on the board, with columns indicating the status of each task.

3. *Sales Tracking*: Kanban can be used to track sales activity and opportunities. Each potential customer or sales opportunity can be represented by a card on the board, with columns indicating the status of each opportunity, such as prospecting, negotiation, closed/won, and closed/lost.
4. *Product Development*: Kanban can be used to manage the development of new products or product updates. Each task involved in the development process, such as concept design, clinical trials, and regulatory approval, can be represented by a card on the board, with columns indicating the status of each task.

Kanban methodology can help pharma marketing teams improve their productivity and collaboration, reduce lead times, and improve the visibility of work in progress. By using Kanban boards, teams can quickly identify bottlenecks in the workflow and adjust their approach to improve efficiency and quality of work.

Key Opinion Leader (KOL)

KOL stands for Key Opinion Leader. A KOL is a healthcare provider recognized as an expert in their field and significantly influences other healthcare providers. KOLs may be physicians, researchers, academicians, or other healthcare professionals who are highly respected in their areas of expertise.

KOLs are often sought out by pharmaceutical companies and other healthcare organizations for their insights and opinions on new treatments, research findings, and other important developments in their field. KOLs may be invited to participate in advisory boards, clinical trials, or other industry collaboration activities.

In pharmaceutical marketing, KOLs are important in promoting new drugs or therapies. For example, KOLs may help educate other healthcare providers about the benefits and risks of a new drug, provide clinical insights and recommendations, or give talks at medical conferences or other events.

Effective Management of KOLs in Pharma

Effective management of KOLs (Key Opinion Leaders) is critical in pharma marketing, as KOLs play a significant role in shaping opinions and influencing prescribing behavior among healthcare providers. Here are some effective strategies for effective KOL management in pharma:

1. *Identify the Right KOLs*: Pharma companies should identify KOLs with a strong reputation, credibility, and influence. Companies should also consider the KOL's geographical location, specialty, and patient population to reach the right audience with their message.
2. *Build Strong Relationships*: Pharma companies should invest time and resources in building strong relationships with their KOLs. This may include regular communication, in-person meetings, and providing KOLs with access to company resources and expertise.
3. *Support and Resources*: Pharma companies should provide KOLs with the resources and support they need to succeed. This may include clinical data, educational materials, and new therapies or treatment protocol training.
4. *Collaborate on Research and Education*: Pharma companies can collaborate with KOLs on research studies, clinical trials, and other educational initiatives. By working together, companies and KOLs can develop new insights and generate data supporting the efficacy and safety of new therapies.
5. *Stay Compliant*: Pharma companies must ensure that all interactions with KOLs comply with relevant regulations and guidelines, including financial disclosures and conflicts of interest.

Effective management of KOLs in pharma requires a deep understanding of their needs and priorities, providing support and resources, and collaborating on research and education. In addition, pharma companies can gain valuable insights and recommendations from KOLs to help drive their product development and marketing strategies.

Key Opinion Leader Engagement

Key Opinion Leaders (KOLs) have been integral to pharmaceutical marketing and medical affairs strategies for several decades. They are highly influential figures within the medical community, with clinical expertise, research acumen, and the respect of their peers. KOL engagement in pharma marketing benefits companies and the broader healthcare community.

1. Understanding KOL Engagement

KOLs are typically well-regarded physicians but can also be pharmacists, nurses, or other healthcare professionals viewed as leading experts in their field. Engaging with KOLs allows pharmaceutical companies to gather insights, disseminate new information, and educate the medical community.

2. Key Areas of KOL Engagement In Pharma Marketing

- *Research Collaboration*: KOLs are often engaged in collaborative research projects as principal investigators for clinical trials or as contributors to real-world evidence studies.
- *Medical Education*: KOLs play a central role in educating peers about new therapies, either through continuing medical education (CME) programs, webinars, or speaking engagements at conferences.
- *Advisory Boards*: These are meetings where a group of KOLs provides feedback on product development, positioning, and potential challenges.
- *Publication Strategy*: KOLs collaborate with pharmaceutical companies to publish findings from clinical trials or other research initiatives.
- *Peer-to-Peer Programs*: KOLs can engage with their peers in smaller settings to provide insights into new products or treatment guidelines.

3. Benefits of KOL Engagement

- *Credibility*: KOLs lend credibility to the pharmaceutical company's products and messages.
- *Expert Insights*: Their expertise can provide valuable insights into product development, positioning, and market entry strategies.
- *Access*: KOLs can facilitate introductions and access to broader networks of healthcare professionals.
- *Education*: They play a vital role in educating the medical community about the latest advancements in treatments.

Ethical Considerations

Engaging with KOLs has come under scrutiny over the years during to potential conflicts of interest. Pharmaceutical companies need to ensure that engagements are transparent, ethical and centered around the primary goal of improving patient outcomes.

Evolving Landscape

With the rise of digital technology, how pharma engages with KOLs is evolving. Digital Opinion Leaders (DOLs) have significant online and social media influence and are becoming increasingly important. Engaging with these digital KOLs requires a different strategy, focusing on online content, social media platforms, and digital education forums. KOL engagement remains a cornerstone of pharma marketing and medical affairs strategies. Companies must approach these engagements ethically, focusing on improving patient outcomes. Adapting strategies to engage with traditional and digital KOLs will be vital for success in the evolving landscape.

Key Performance Indicators (KPIs)

Key Performance Indicators (KPIs) are metrics used to evaluate the effectiveness of a pharma marketing campaign. Here are some KPIs commonly used in pharma marketing:

1. *Sales Revenue*: This KPI measures the revenue generated by a drug or therapy. It can be broken down by region, product line, or sales rep. For example, a pharma company may track the sales revenue of a particular drug over time to evaluate the effectiveness of its marketing campaigns.
2. *Market Share*: This KPI measures the percentage of the total market that a pharma company controls. For example, a company may track its market share in a particular disease area to assess its competitive position.
3. *Return on Investment (ROI)*: This KPI measures the return on the investment made in a marketing campaign. For example, a pharma company may evaluate the ROI of a digital marketing campaign by comparing the cost of the campaign to the number of new prescriptions generated.
4. *Customer Satisfaction*: This KPI measures the level of satisfaction among customers, such as healthcare providers, patients, and payers. For example, a pharma company may survey customer satisfaction with a particular drug or therapy.
5. *Website Traffic*: This KPI measures the number of visitors to a company's website. For example, a pharma company may track website traffic to evaluate the effectiveness of its digital marketing campaigns.
6. *Social Media Engagement*: This KPI measures the level of engagement with a company's social media channels. For example, a pharma company may track the number of likes, shares, and comments on its social media posts to evaluate the effectiveness of its social media strategy.

Key Performance Indicators (KPIs) are important in measuring the effectiveness of pharma marketing campaigns. By tracking these metrics, companies can identify areas for improvement and adjust their strategies to maximize their impact.

Key Success Factors (KSFs)

Key Success Factors (KSFs) are the essential areas a pharma company must focus on to succeed in its marketing efforts. Here are some KSFs commonly used in pharma marketing:

1. *Understanding the Disease Area*: A pharmaceutical company must deeply understand its target area. This includes knowledge of the pathophysiology of the disease, the unmet needs of patients and healthcare professionals, and the competitive landscape. For example, a company targeting a particular type of cancer must thoroughly understand the cancer's biology, current treatment options, and patient and provider perspectives.
2. *Developing Innovative Therapies*: Pharma companies must develop innovative therapies that address unmet needs in the disease area. For example, a company may develop a therapy that targets a specific molecular pathway involved in a disease, providing a new treatment option for patients.
3. *Building Strong Relationships with KOLs*: Key Opinion Leaders (KOLs) are critical in shaping opinions and influencing prescribing behavior among healthcare providers. Pharma companies must build strong relationships with KOLs to gain their support and endorsement of their therapies. For example, a company may engage with leading researchers and clinicians in the disease area to collaborate on research studies and educational initiatives.
4. *Effective Market Segmentation*: Pharma companies must segment the market effectively to identify the most promising target segments and tailor their marketing efforts accordingly. For example, a company may identify a specific patient population with a high unmet need and develop a targeted marketing campaign to reach that population.
5. *Compliance with Regulations*: The pharma industry is highly regulated, and companies must comply with regulations related to clinical trials, marketing, and financial disclosures. Failure to comply with regulations can result in significant financial penalties and reputational damage.
6. *Measuring and Optimizing Performance*: Pharma companies must measure the performance of their marketing campaigns and optimize their strategies based on the results. This includes tracking KPIs such as sales revenue, market share, and customer satisfaction and adjusting marketing tactics to maximize their impact.

Key Success Factors (KSFs), thus, play a critical role in driving success in pharma marketing. By focusing on these essential areas, pharma companies can develop and market innovative therapies that address unmet needs in the disease area and drive growth for their business.

Keywords

Keywords are specific words or phrases representing a content piece's main ideas or topics, such as a web page, article, blog post, or video. These words and phrases are used by search engines to understand what a particular piece of content is about and to help users find relevant content when they perform a search.

For example, if someone is looking for information on how to lose weight, they might type that phrase into a search engine like Google. The search engine will then scan through its database of web pages and articles, looking for content that includes those keywords. The more relevant and useful the content is to the user's search query, the higher it will appear in the search results.

Choosing the right keywords is important for search engine optimization (SEO), as it helps increase the visibility and ranking of a piece of content in search results. It also helps content creators better understand and target their audience by knowing what keywords they are searching for.

Keywords and Pharma Marketing

Keywords in pharma marketing refer to specific terms or phrases commonly used to promote or advertise pharmaceutical products or services. These keywords are often used in online advertising, search engine optimization, and social media marketing to help pharmaceutical companies reach target audiences and increase brand awareness.

Here are some examples of common keywords in pharma marketing:

1. *Drug Names*: These are the specific names of pharmaceutical products companies want to promote or advertise, such as Advil, Lipitor, or Prozac.
2. *Medical Conditions*: These are the medical conditions or diseases that the pharmaceutical products are designed to treat, such as arthritis, diabetes, or depression.
3. *Side Effects*: These are the potential side effects of using a pharmaceutical product, such as nausea, dizziness, or fatigue.

4. *Treatment Options*: These are the different treatment options for a particular medical condition, such as medication, surgery, or therapy.
5. *Generic Drug Names*: These are the non-brand names of pharmaceutical products, such as ibuprofen instead of Advil or atorvastatin instead of Lipitor.

It is important to note that pharmaceutical companies must adhere to strict regulations when advertising their products, including guidelines on the use of keywords and claims about the efficacy and safety of their products.

Selecting the Right Keywords

Selecting the right keywords in pharma marketing is an important step in ensuring your content reaches its target audience and is visible to potential customers. Here are some tips for selecting keywords in pharma marketing:

1. *Identify Your Target Audience*: Before selecting keywords, it is important to identify your target audience and their language when searching for information related to your product or service. For example, think about the medical conditions, symptoms, and treatment options your target audience is interested in, and use these as a basis for selecting your keywords.
2. *Conduct Keyword Research*: Use online tools like Google's Keyword Planner or SEMrush to research and identify your target audience's most relevant and popular keywords. Look for keywords with high search volume and low competition, as these are more likely to lead to organic traffic to your website.
3. *Consider Long-tail Keywords*: Long-tail keywords are longer phrases that are more specific and targeted than general keywords. For example, instead of targeting the keyword diabetes, try targeting type 2 diabetes treatment options or diabetes medication side effects. Long-tail keywords can effectively reach a specific audience and drive conversions.
4. *Use Brand and Generic Drug Names*: Including your products' brand and generic names in your keywords can help increase brand recognition and drive targeted traffic to your website. Be sure to use the correct spelling and formatting for the drug names.
5. *Stay up-to-date with Industry Regulations*: Be aware of the regulations and guidelines that govern pharma marketing, and ensure that your keywords and content comply with these guidelines. Avoid making false or misleading claims about your products or their efficacy.

By following these tips, you can select relevant, targeted, and effective keywords to reach your intended audience in the pharma industry.

Keyword Marketing

Keyword marketing, also known as keyword advertising or pay-per-click (PPC) advertising, is a form of digital marketing where a company bids on specific keywords related to its products or services. Then, when a user searches for those keywords on a search engine, the company's ad will appear at the top of the search results.

In pharma marketing, keyword marketing can promote specific drugs or therapies to healthcare professionals or patients. For example, a pharma company may bid on keywords related to a specific disease or medical condition to target healthcare professionals searching for information on treatment options. They can also bid on keywords related to specific drugs or therapies to target patients searching for information on those treatments.

Keyword marketing can reach a highly targeted audience and drive traffic to a company's website. However, some regulations govern the advertising of prescription drugs, and pharma companies must ensure that their ads comply with these regulations. For example, they must include fair balance information, which presents both the benefits and risks of the drug, and avoid making unsupported claims or exaggerating the drug's effectiveness.

How to Do It

Here are some general steps to get started with keyword marketing in pharma:

1. *Identify Relevant Keywords*: Identify keywords related to the disease area or drug therapy you want to promote. Use tools like Google Adwords Keyword Planner or SEMrush to identify relevant keywords and estimate search volumes.
2. *Develop Ad Copy*: Create a compelling ad copy with relevant keywords and a clear call-to-action (CTA) that encourages users to click on the ad and learn more.
3. *Choose Targeting Options*: Choose your target audience and location. For example, for pharma marketing, you may want to target healthcare professionals (HCPs), patients, or both. You can also choose specific geographical locations to target.
4. *Set Your Bid*: Determine how much you are willing to pay for each click on your ad. This will depend on your budget and the level of competition for the keywords you are targeting.

5. *Monitor and Optimize*: Once your ads are live, monitor their performance and adjust your targeting and bid strategies. Use metrics like click-through rate (CTR) and cost per click (CPC) to track your performance and optimize your campaigns for maximum effectiveness.

It is important to note that pharma advertising is subject to strict regulations. For example, pharma companies must ensure that their ads comply with regulations related to fair balance, disclosure of side effects, and other requirements. Therefore, it is important to work closely with legal and regulatory teams to ensure compliance with these regulations.

Keyword marketing can be a valuable tool in pharma marketing when used effectively and in compliance with regulations. By targeting specific keywords related to their products or services, pharma companies can reach their target audience and drive website traffic.

Keyword Research

Keyword research is an important aspect of pharma marketing, as it can help pharmaceutical companies identify keywords and phrases that their target audience is searching for online. By understanding what patients and healthcare professionals (HCPs) seek, pharma companies can create relevant and useful content and optimize their websites for better search engine visibility.

Here are some steps that pharma companies can take to conduct keyword research for their marketing efforts:

1. *Identify Relevant Topics*: Start by brainstorming relevant topics related to your product or therapy area. This could include disease symptoms, treatment options, or lifestyle recommendations.
2. *Use Keyword Research Tools*: Many keyword research tools, such as Google Keyword Planner or SEMrush, can help pharma companies identify the most popular search terms related to their topic.
3. *Analyze Search Volume and Competition*: Once you have identified potential keywords, use the keyword research tool to analyze each keyword's search volume and competition level. Choose keywords that have a high search volume and low competition level.
4. *Optimize Content*: Once you have identified the relevant keywords, incorporate them into your website content, including titles, meta descriptions, headers, and body copy. This can help improve your website's search engine visibility and attract more traffic.
5. *Monitor and Adjust*: The keyword research should be ongoing, as search trends and competition levels can change over time. Therefore, monitor your website performance regularly and adjust your keyword strategy.

Conducting keyword research can help pharmaceutical companies better understand their target audience and create relevant and useful content, improving their marketing efforts and helping patients receive better care.

Kickbacks

Kickbacks refer to any financial incentive, gift, or other compensation given to an individual or organization in exchange for a particular action or favor. For example, in the pharmaceutical industry, kickbacks typically refer to situations where pharmaceutical companies offer physicians or other healthcare providers some financial or material benefit in exchange for prescribing their drugs.

Kickbacks in the pharmaceutical industry are illegal under the US Anti-Kickback Statute, which makes it illegal to offer, pay, solicit, or receive any form of compensation in exchange for referrals or business involving any service or items paid for by a federal healthcare program (such as Medicare or Medicaid).

Violations of the Anti-Kickback Statute can result in severe penalties, including hefty fines, exclusion from federal healthcare programs, and criminal prosecution.

Pharmaceutical companies can also run afoul of other laws and regulations prohibiting the exchange of kickbacks or other improper payments. For example, the Foreign Corrupt Practices Act (FCPA) makes it illegal to offer or pay bribes to foreign government officials or employees of state-owned companies in exchange for business or favorable treatment.

Kickbacks are considered unethical and illegal in the pharmaceutical industry, as they can compromise the integrity of medical decision-making and lead to inappropriate or unnecessary treatments. Therefore, pharmaceutical companies must adhere to strict ethical and legal guidelines to ensure their interactions with healthcare providers are transparent and focused on patients' best interests.

Kickbacks in Pharma

Here are some examples of kickbacks in the pharmaceutical industry:

1. Paying physicians or other healthcare providers to prescribe a particular drug or use a particular medical device or equipment.
2. Offering expensive gifts, trips, or other perks to physicians or other healthcare providers in exchange for their loyalty or business.
3. Providing funding for research studies, medical conferences, or other educational events in exchange for favorable treatment or promotion of a particular drug or medical product.
4. Offering funding for research studies, medical conferences, or other educational events in exchange for favorable treatment or promotion of a particular drug or medical product.
5. Offering rebates and discounts to healthcare providers in exchange for prescribing a particular drug over another that may be equally effective but less expensive.
6. Creating or sponsoring patient assistance programs that provide financial support to patients who use a particular drug in exchange for increased prescribing by physicians.

Kickbacks in Pharma: Some Examples

There have been several high-profile cases of kickbacks by pharmaceutical companies over the years. Here are a few examples:

1. In 2012, GlaxoSmithKline (GSK) agreed to pay $3 billion to settle charges that it had engaged in kickback schemes and some unethical marketing practices related to several drugs. The company was accused of paying doctors to prescribe its antidepressants and other drugs and promoting some for unapproved uses.
2. In 2019, Novartis agreed to pay $678 million to settle charges that it had paid illegal kickbacks to doctors to prescribe its drugs. In addition, the company was accused of using a speaker program to funnel money to doctors with little expertise in the drugs they were promoting.
3. In 2018, Pfizer agreed to pay $23.85 million to settle charges that it had violated the False Claims Act by paying kickbacks to Medicare patients who used its drugs. In addition, the company was accused of using a co-pay assistance program to induce patients to buy its drugs, violating federal anti-kickback laws.
4. In 2019, Insys Therapeutics founder John Kapoor was found guilty of racketeering charges related to his company's marketing of an opioid drug. The company was accused of using illegal kickbacks to induce doctors to prescribe the drug, which was highly addictive.

These are just a few examples of the many cases of kickbacks in the pharmaceutical industry. Therefore, it is important for pharmaceutical companies to ensure that their marketing practices are legal and ethical and to avoid any activities that could be perceived as offering kickbacks or other improper incentives.

However, it is important to note that not all financial or material incentives in the pharmaceutical industry are considered kickbacks, and many legitimate business practices are used to promote and sell drugs. However, the line between legal and illegal activities can be blurry. Therefore, pharmaceutical companies must carefully navigate the complex legal and ethical landscape to ensure their actions do not violate laws or regulations.

Kiosk

In pharmaceutical marketing, a Kiosk is a self-service interactive display typically placed in a high-traffic area, such as a hospital or pharmacy, to provide patients or healthcare professionals with information about a particular drug or disease. Kiosks can take various forms, from standalone devices to tablet-based displays, and may offer features such as touch screens, audio or video capabilities, and interactive quizzes or surveys. Here are some examples of how kiosks can be used in pharma marketing:

1. *Disease Education*: Kiosks can provide information about a particular disease or condition, including symptoms, treatment options, and lifestyle recommendations. This can help raise disease awareness and encourage patients to seek appropriate care.
2. *Drug Information*: Kiosks can also provide information about a particular drug, including its benefits, side effects, dosing instructions, and contraindications. This can help patients make informed decisions about their treatment options.
3. *Patient Support*: Kiosks can support patients throughout their treatment journey, track symptoms, or connect patients with support groups or resources.
4. *Market Research*: Kiosks can gather information about patients' opinions and preferences about a particular drug or disease. This can help pharma companies better understand their target audience's needs and refine their marketing strategies accordingly.

Kiosks can be a valuable tool in pharmaceutical marketing, providing patients and healthcare providers with convenient access to important information and support.

Kirkpatrick Model

The Kirkpatrick Model is a widely used framework for evaluating the effectiveness of training and development programs. It was developed by Donald L. Kirkpatrick and later expanded by his son, James D. Kirkpatrick. The model consists of four levels, each representing a different aspect of the evaluation process.

1. **Level 1: Reaction - How Did Participants Feel?**

- At this level, you assess participants' immediate reactions to the training program. This is often done through surveys or questionnaires.
- The focus is on measuring participants' satisfaction, engagement, and perception of the training experience.
- Example questions might include: "Did you find the training content engaging?" or "Was the instructor effective?'

2. **Level 2: Learning - What Did Participants Learn?**

- This level assesses the knowledge, skills, and attitudes gained by participants as a result of the training program.
- Evaluations can include quizzes, tests, or skill demonstrations to measure the extent of learning.
- Example questions could be: "Can participants demonstrate new skills learned?" or " Have participants acquired the knowledge conveyed in this training?"

3. **Level 3: Behavior - What Changes in Behavior Were Observed?**

- At this level, you evaluate whether participants are applying what they learned in their actual work or daily activities.
- Observations, performance assessments, and self-reports may be used to measure behavior change.
- Example questions might include: "Have participants incorporated new practices into their work routines?" or " Are they using the skills learned in their job tasks?"

4. **Level 4: Results - What Impact Did the Training Have on the Organization?**

- This level focuses on the broader impact of the training on the organization's goals and objectives.
- Evaluations consider increased productivity, improved quality, reduced costs, and overall impact on organizational performance.
- Example questions could include: "Did the training increase sales or revenue?" or "Did it reduce errors or accidents?"

It is important to note that while the Kirkpatrick Model is structured in four levels, not all training evaluations need to progress through each level. The choice of which levels to evaluate depends on the specific objectives of the training program and the resources available. Some organizations may focus on levels 1 and 2 for certain programs, while others may conduct evaluations at all four levels for more critical training initiatives.

The Kirkpatrick Model provides a systematic framework for assessing the effectiveness of training and development efforts, helping organizations improve their learning programs and achieve their performance goals.

KISS principle

The KISS principle, which stands for *Keep It Simple, Stupid*, is a widely used guideline in many industries, including pharmaceutical marketing. The principle suggests that the best approach is often the simplest and that overcomplicating things can lead to confusion and inefficiency.

In pharma marketing, the KISS principle can be applied in several ways. Here are a few examples:

1. *Clear and Concise Messaging*: When communicating with healthcare professionals (HCPs) or patients, it is important to use simple language and avoid jargon or technical terms that may be difficult to understand. This can help ensure that the intended message is received and retained.
2. *Streamlined Processes*: In complex industries like pharmaceuticals, many processes are involved in bringing a drug to market, from pre-clinical testing to regulatory approval. By simplifying and streamlining these processes where possible, pharma companies can reduce costs and speed up time to market.
3. *User-friendly Packaging*: The packaging should be designed to be as simple and user-friendly as possible for drugs administered by patients, such as self-injectable medications. This can include clear instructions, easy-to-use devices, and minimal steps required for administration.

The KISS principle can help pharmaceutical companies focus on what matters, delivering safe and effective treatments to patients while minimizing unnecessary complexity and confusion.

L

1. Label
2. Laddering
3. Laggard
4. Laissez-Faire
5. Landing Page
6. Late Majority
7. Latent Demand
8. Lateral Diversification
9. Lateral Thinking
10. Launch Strategy
11. Layout
12. Lead Generation
13. Lead Magnet
14. Leapfrogging
15. Learn-feel-buy Model
16. Lelly Triads
17. Leverage
18. Licensing
19. Lifecycle
20. Lifecycle Assessment (LCA)
21. Lifecycle Management
22. Lifestyle Marketing
23. Lifestyle Diseases
24. Lifestyle Research
25. Lifetime Value
26. Line Extension
27. LinkedIn
28. Linking Strategy
29. Lobbying
30. Localization
31. Logo
32. Long Tail
33. Long-range Planning
34. Longitudinal Research
35. Loss Leader
36. Low-Involvement Hierarchy
37. Low-Involvement Product
38. Loyalty
39. Loyalty Effect
40. Loyalty Marketing

Label

In pharmaceutical marketing, a label refers to the package insert or prescribing information accompanying a pharmaceutical product. It contains important information about the medication, including its indications, dosage, administration guidelines, contraindications, warnings, precautions, adverse reactions, and other relevant details.

The label is a regulatory requirement approved by the appropriate regulatory authority, such as the US Food and Drug Administration (FDA) in the United States. It provides comprehensive information about safe and effective medication use by healthcare professionals, such as doctors, pharmacists, and nurses.

The label plays a critical role in pharmaceutical marketing as it serves as a primary source of information for healthcare professionals and assists them in making informed decisions about prescribing and administering the medication. In addition, it ensures that healthcare providers have accurate and up-to-date information about the product, including its indications, contraindications, and potential risks.

In addition to the prescribing information, the label may also include other marketing elements, such as the brand name, product logo, and promotional claims, as allowed by regulatory guidelines. However, it is important to note that the marketing elements must be presented in a manner that is consistent with regulatory requirements and does not mislead or exaggerate the product's benefits.

Pharmaceutical companies must adhere to strict guidelines when developing and promoting the label in pharmaceutical marketing. The label must accurately reflect the scientific evidence, follow regulatory guidelines, and meet the specific market requirements where the product is being marketed.

The pharma marketing label is essential to ensure the safe and effective use of pharmaceutical products while providing healthcare professionals with the necessary information to make informed decisions about patient treatment.

Laddering

Laddering is a marketing research technique to uncover the underlying motivations and values that drive consumer behavior. It involves a structured questioning process that helps reveal the connections between the features and benefits of a product, the emotional needs that those benefits fulfill, and the core values and benefits that underlie those needs.

In Laddering, the interviewer asks the consumer about the specific features and benefits of the product or service. They then ask why those features or benefits are important to the consumer and continue to ask "why" questions to uncover deeper motivations and values. This process is repeated several times, with each answer laddering to a higher-level emotional need or core value.

For example, in pharmaceutical marketing, Laddering might be used to uncover the underlying motivations and values that drive a patient's decision to use a particular medication. First, the interviewer might start asking about the specific features and benefits of the medication, such as its efficacy and side effects. They might then ask why those features are important to the patient, leading to answers about the desire to manage symptoms or improve quality of life. Further questioning might reveal deeper emotional needs, such as the desire to feel in control of one's health or core values related to family or personal responsibility.

Laddering in Pharma Marketing

Laddering is a useful marketing research technique in the pharmaceutical industry to understand patient motivations and values that drive their healthcare decisions and medication choices. Here are some examples of how Laddering can be used in pharma marketing research:

1. *Understanding Why Patients Choose a Particular Medication*: The pharmaceutical company might ask patients why they chose a specific medication over others in the market. Laddering can help to reveal underlying values and motivations by asking 'why' questions repeatedly. For example, the patient may choose a medication because it effectively manages their symptoms, which may be linked to their desire to maintain their quality of life or sense of independence.
2. *Uncovering Emotional Needs and Values Associated with Medication Adherence*: Pharmaceutical companies may use Laddering to understand why patients adhere to their medication regimen. For instance, patients may indicate that they take their medication regularly because they want to be proactive in managing their health and be role models for their children. Laddering can help identify the core values of responsibility and family that underlie these emotional needs.
3. *Identifying Unmet Needs and Opportunities for New Products*: Using Laddering to understand patients' underlying needs and values, pharmaceutical companies can identify unmet needs and opportunities for new products. For

example, patients express a need for a medication that has fewer side effects or is more convenient. In that case, the pharmaceutical company might consider developing a new product that meets these needs.

How to Conduct Laddering Research

Here are the steps to conduct laddering in pharmaceutical marketing research:

1. *Define the Research Objectives*: The first step is clearly defining the research objectives. Next, determine what questions you want to answer and what goals you want to achieve through the laddering process.
2. *Recruit Participants*: Next, recruit participants who represent the target audience. You may use a sampling method, such as a random or purposive to identify participants who meet the inclusion criteria.
3. *Conduct Interviews*: Conduct one-on-one interviews with participants and use open-ended questions to explore the reasons behind their behavior and choices. Ask questions that elicit the features and benefits of the medication or treatment they are using, and follow up with "why" questions to uncover deeper motivations and values.
4. *Analyze the Data*: Once the interviews are complete, analyze the data to identify emerging patterns and themes. Look for commonalities among participants and the underlying motivations and values that drive their behavior.
5. *Develop Insights and Recommendations*: Use the data analysis to develop insights and recommendations for the pharmaceutical company. For example, identify areas of opportunity to improve the medication or treatment and develop strategies to address patients' underlying motivations and values.
6. *Communicate Findings*: Communicate the findings of the laddering research to stakeholders within the pharmaceutical company. Share the insights and recommendations and work with the team to develop strategies and tactics incorporating the findings.

How to Create Laddering Maps

Creating laddering maps is an effective way to visually represent the data obtained through the laddering process in pharma marketing research. Here are the steps to create laddering maps:

1. *Review Categorize the Data*: Review the interview data and categorize them into themes and sub-themes based on the responses received. This step helps in identifying the hierarchy of the themes and sub-themes, which will form the basis of the laddering maps.
2. *Create a Hierarchical Structure*: Starting with the broadest theme, identify the sub-themes that fall under it. Then, identify the motivations or values revealed in the interviews for each sub-theme. The hierarchy should be arranged from the most general to the most specific.
3. *Construct the Laddering Map*: Using the hierarchical structure, construct the laddering map. The top level of the map should represent the broadest theme, with sub-themes branching off from it. Below each sub-theme, list the motivations or values revealed through the laddering process. Finally, use lines to connect the sub-themes to the corresponding motivations or values.
4. *Analyze the Laddering Map*: Analyze the laddering map to identify patterns and relationships between the themes, sub-themes, motivations, and values. Look for commonalities and relationships that can inform marketing strategies and tactics.
5. *Share the Laddering Map*: Share the laddering map with stakeholders within the pharmaceutical company, including marketing teams, product development teams, and other relevant stakeholders. Use the map to inform marketing strategies and tactics and drive greater patient engagement and loyalty.

Laddering maps are useful for visually representing the data obtained through the laddering process in pharma marketing research. Following these steps, you can create effective laddering maps that help inform marketing strategies and drive greater patient engagement and loyalty.

How Pharma Companies Use Laddering

Several companies have used laddering in their marketing research to understand their patients' motivations and values better. Here are a few examples:

1. AstraZeneca used Laddering to understand the emotional drivers behind patient behavior regarding medication adherence. For example, they found that patients often felt overwhelmed and anxious about their condition, leading to non-adherence to medication. Based on these insights, AstraZeneca developed a support program that included educational materials, motivational messaging, and personalized reminders to help patients stay on track with their treatment.

2. Roche used Laddering to understand the patient's experience living with a specific type of cancer. They found that patients often felt isolated and disconnected from their support network, leading to emotional distress and difficulty coping with their condition. Based on these insights, Roche developed a patient support program that provided emotional support, counseling services, and support group connections.
3. Pfizer used Laddering to understand the patient's experience living with a rare genetic condition. They found that healthcare providers and society often misunderstood patients, creating frustration and isolation. Based on these insights, Pfizer developed an advocacy program that empowered patients to advocate for themselves and their community, providing them with resources to educate healthcare providers and the public about the condition.

Laddering is a powerful technique pharmaceutical companies use to gain insights into their patients' underlying motivations and values. By understanding these drivers, companies can develop more effective marketing strategies and tactics that drive greater patient engagement and loyalty.

Laggard

'Laggards' is a term often used in the context of the Diffusion of Innovations theory, which was developed by Everett Rogers in 1962. The theory is based on how, why, and at what rate new ideas and technology spread through cultures. In this theory, 'Laggards' is one of the five categories of adopters, each of which adopts innovations at different stages.

'Laggards' are the last sixteen percent of individuals to adopt an innovation. They have an aversion to change and are very traditional.

In pharmaceutical marketing, 'laggard' is a term that describes an individual or organization that is slow to adopt new technologies or innovations. Laggards are typically the last group of consumers to adopt new products or services, and they may be resistant to change or prefer to stick with what they know.

In pharma marketing, laggards may be slow to adopt new medications or treatment options, preferring to stick with traditional treatments or medications they are familiar with.

Laggards may also resist new marketing strategies or technologies, such as digital marketing or social media. Instead, they may prefer traditional marketing channels like print advertisements or direct mail.

Pharmaceutical companies may need to develop specific marketing strategies to target laggards and encourage them to adopt new products or treatment options. This may involve providing education and information about the benefits of the new medication or treatment and addressing any concerns or objections they may have. It may also involve using traditional marketing channels to reach laggards, such as print advertisements or targeted direct mail campaigns.

Thus, Laggards can be challenging for companies to promote new products or treatments in pharma marketing. However, by understanding their behavior and preferences and developing targeted marketing strategies, pharma companies can effectively reach and influence this group of consumers.

Laissez-Faire

Laissez-faire is an economic concept that originated in the 18th century and is derived from the French phrase *Laissez faire*, which means *let it be* or *leave it alone*. It is a policy or approach that advocates minimal interference by the government in economic affairs.

In a Laissez-faire system, the government refrains from imposing regulations, restrictions, or interventions on businesses and the free market. The belief is that individuals and businesses are best suited to make their own economic decisions based on their self-interest and that the market, when left to its own devices, will naturally reach an optimal state of equilibrium.

Proponents of laissez-faire argue that it promotes economic efficiency, innovation, and individual freedom. They contend that government intervention often leads to unintended consequences, market distortions, and inefficiencies. They believe that in a free market, competition and the pursuit of profit will drive economic growth and prosperity.

Critics of laissez-faire, on the other hand, argue that unregulated markets can result in monopolies, exploitation of workers, and income inequality. They contend that government intervention is necessary to protect consumers, ensure fair competition, and provide public goods and services.

It is important to note that in practice, pure laissez-faire is rare, and most economies have some level of government intervention and regulation. However, the degree of government involvement varies across countries and depends on their economic and political systems.

Laissez-faire in Pharma Marketing

Laissez-faire in pharmaceutical marketing refers to a minimal level of government regulation and intervention in the marketing practices of pharmaceutical companies. It implies allowing the industry to operate with a high degree of freedom in promoting and advertising its products. Here are a few examples of how laissez-faire principles can apply to pharma marketing:

A. *Direct-to-Consumer Advertising (DTCA)*: In some countries like the United States, pharmaceutical companies can advertise prescription drugs directly to consumers. This practice enables companies to promote their products through various channels, including television, print media, and online platforms, without extensive regulatory restrictions.

B. *Off-labelPromotion*: Laissez-faire principles may allow pharmaceutical companies to provide information to promote the off-label use of their products. Off-label use refers to using the drug for a purpose not specifically approved by regulatory authorities. While regulations and limitations are in place, allowing off-label promotion is an example of a hands-off approach.

C. *Marketing Strategies*: Laissez-faire in pharma marketing permits companies to develop and execute marketing strategies as they see fit, without excessive government interference. This includes decisions related to branding, pricing, product positioning, and promotional activities. Pharmaceutical companies have more leeway to create campaigns targeting healthcare professionals, highlighting the benefits of their products.

It is worth noting that the level of laissez-faire in pharma marketing can vary significantly between different countries and regions. Some nations may have more stringent regulations to ensure consumer protection, while others may adopt a more hands-off approach, allowing pharmaceutical companies greater freedom in their marketing practices.

Landing Page

In pharmaceutical marketing, a landing page is a standalone web page designed to capture visitors' attention and convert them into leads or customers. It is typically used in a targeted marketing campaign to drive traffic and encourage action, such as signing up for a newsletter, requesting more information, or purchasing. Here are some examples of landing pages in pharma marketing:

1. *Product Information Landing Page*: This type provides detailed information about a pharmaceutical product. It highlights key features, benefits, and indications and may include supporting clinical data, testimonials, and videos. The page may also include a call-to-action (CTA) to encourage visitors to request a sample, schedule a consultation, or speak with a healthcare professional.
2. *Disease Awareness Landing Page*: Disease awareness landing pages aim to educate visitors about a particular health condition or disease. They provide valuable information about symptoms, prevalence, risk factors, and treatment options. In addition, the page may include links to relevant resources, downloadable guides, or interactive tools for self-assessment. The goal is to raise awareness and guide visitors seeking appropriate medical advice.
3. *Event or Webinar Registration Landing Page*: These landing pages promote and facilitate registration for events, conferences, webinars, or educational sessions organized by a pharmaceutical company. They highlight the event's agenda, speakers, and key takeaways and provide a simple form for visitors to register. The page may also include testimonials or past event photos to generate interest.
4. *Patient Support Program Landing Page*: Pharmaceutical companies often offer patient support programs to provide resources, tools, or assistance to patients using their medications. A landing page for such programs can explain the benefits, eligibility criteria, and registration process. In addition, it may include testimonials from satisfied program participants and clear CTA to encourage patients to enroll.
5. *Clinical Trial Recruitment Landing Page*: Landing pages can be created especially to recruit participants for clinical trials. These pages provide information about the trial, eligibility criteria, and potential benefits to participants. In addition, they typically include a prominent call-to-action to encourage visitors to fill out a pre-screening form or contact the research team for further details.
6. *Email Subscription Landing Page*: Email subscription landing pages are designed to capture visitor contact information, such as email addresses, for future communication. These pages typically offer an incentive, such as exclusive content, discounts, or access to educational materials, in exchange for subscribing to the company's email list. In addition, the page may highlight the value of the

content subscribers will receive and assure privacy and data security.

7. *Medication Savings or Discount Page*: Landing pages can be dedicated to promoting medication savings programs or discounts. These pages highlight the potential cost savings and may include details on eligibility requirements, the enrollment process, and how to access the discount. The goal is to encourage visitors to take advantage of the savings opportunity and potentially become regular customers.

When creating a landing page in pharma marketing, it is important to have a clear objective, compelling content, an enticing offer or value proposition, and a strong call to action. The design should be user-friendly, visually appealing, and optimized for desktop and mobile devices. Additionally, landing pages should adhere to regulatory guidelines and ensure that any claims or information provided are accurate and supported by appropriate evidence.

Late Majority

The 'Late Majority' is a category within the Diffusion of Innovations theory developed by Everett Rogers. This theory aims to explain how, why, and at what rate new ideas and technology spread through cultures.

The Late Majority comprises individuals who adopt an innovation after innovators, early adopters and early majority. They make up about 34 percent of the population in the model. Here are some characteristics and aspects related to the Late Majority.

1. *Skepticism*: Individuals in the Late Majority are typically skeptical about the innovation and may only adopt it after most peers have already done so.
2. *Peer Pressure*: Their decision to adopt often comes from peer pressure rather than an intrinsic motivation to try the innovation.
3. *Economic Necessity*: The Late Majority might adopt the innovation out of economic necessity or increasing peer pressure rather than the perceived benefits of the innovation itself.
4. *Limited Social Networks*: Their social networks are more localized than those of the earlier categories and tend to rely on close-knit community connections.
5. *Lower Socio-economic Status*: They might not have immediate access to resources, so they wait until they are sure the innovation is beneficial, and the price is right.
6. *Interaction with Peers*: They tend to interact mostly with others in the Late Majority or Laggards and rely on them for information and insights.
7. *Need for Support*: They often require more support, such as infrastructure and training, to adopt the innovation successfully.

In marketing or policy implementation, understanding the characteristics of the Late Majority can be crucial. It helps tailor strategies to ensure the broadest possible uptake of a new product, idea, or practice.

In pharmaceutical marketing, the late majority refers to a segment of consumers who are typically slower to adopt new products or technologies. This group represents the second-to-last segment of consumers to adopt a new product or service, coming after the early adopters, the early majority.

The late majority tends to be skeptical of new products or technologies and is often more risk-averse than earlier adopters. They may wait before adopting a product or technology that has been tested and proven successful. In pharma marketing, the late majority may be slower to adopt new medications or treatment options, preferring to wait until they have been on the market for some time and have a proven track record.

Pharmaceutical companies may need to develop targeted marketing strategies to reach the late majority and encourage them to adopt new medications or treatment options. This may involve providing education and information about the new treatment's benefits and addressing any concerns or objections they may have. It may also involve using marketing channels known to be effective for reaching this group, such s print advertising or targeted direct mail campaigns.

Understanding the behavior and preferences of the late majority is an important part of pharma marketing, as it can help companies develop effective strategies to reach and influence this segment of consumers.

Latent Demand

Latent demand refers to existing, unfulfilled consumer needs or desires for a particular product or service. It represents the potential market demand not currently being met by available offerings. Latent demand exists when consumers desire a product or service but cannot fulfill that desire due to various reasons, such as product unavailability, limited access, affordability issues, or lack of awareness.

Latent Demand in Pharma Marketing

In pharmaceutical marketing, latent demand refers to the unfilled need or potential market demand for pharmaceutical products or healthcare solutions currently not being met by existing offerings. Here are some examples of latent demand in the pharmaceutical industry:

1. *Undiagnosed or Untreated Conditions*: Latent demand can arise when individuals have undiagnosed or untreated medical conditions. This can occur when people experience symptoms but are unaware of the underlying condition or delay seeking medical attention. For example, there may be latent demand for a specific diagnostic test for a currently under-diagnosed disease or not easily detectable through traditional methods.
2. *Unmet Treatment Needs*: Latent demand can exist when existing treatment options do not adequately address the needs of patients. This can occur in cases where available medications have limited efficacy, significant side effects, or are unsuitable for certain patient populations. For instance, there may be latent demand for more targeted therapies, or personalized medicine approaches for specific diseases or genetic profiles.
3. *Access and Affordability*: Latent demand can arise due to barriers related to access and affordability. In certain regions or populations, individuals may have limited access to healthcare facilities or face financial constraints that prevent them from obtaining necessary medications or treatments. This can create latent demand for affordable, accessible healthcare solutions.
4. *Innovative Delivery Methods*: Latent demand can emerge when there is a need for innovative delivery methods for pharmaceutical products. For example, individuals with chronic conditions requiring frequent injections may have latent demand for alternative delivery systems, such as wearable devices or needle-free medication options, to improve convenience and patient experience.
5. *Preventive Healthcare*: Latent demand can exist in the area of preventive healthcare. Many individuals may be unaware of the importance of preventivc measures, such as vaccinations, regular screenings, or lifestyle modifications. Therefore, there may be latent demand for educational campaigns and interventions that promote preventive healthcare practices.
6. *Pediatric Medications*: Latent demand can be present in pediatric medications. Children may have specific medical needs or require age-appropriate formulations not adequately addressed by existing products. This can create latent demand for pediatric-specific modifications of dosage forms.
7. *Dynamic Nature*: Latent demand is not static and can change over time. Factors like technological advancements, shifts in consumer preferences, or changes in market conditions can influence latent demand. Therefore, businesses must continuously monitor and adapt their strategies to meet evolving latent demand patterns.

Identifying and addressing latent demand in pharmaceutical marketing requires a deep understanding of patient needs, market research, and strategic decision-making. Pharmaceutical companies can leverage market insights, conduct surveys, engage with healthcare professionals, and collaborate with patient advocacy groups to uncover latent demand and develop innovative solutions that meet unmet needs. As a result, pharmaceutical companies can effectively target untapped market segments and enhance patient outcomes by recognizing and addressing latent demand.

Lateral Diversification

Lateral diversification in pharma marketing refers to expanding a pharmaceutical company's product portfolio into new, related product categories or therapeutic areas that differ from its current offerings. This type of diversification involves leveraging existing resources, capabilities, and knowledge to enter new markets and expand revenue streams. Here are some examples of lateral diversification in pharma marketing:

1. *Expanding into Related Therapeutic Areas*: A pharmaceutical company specializing in cardiovascular medications may diversify into diabetes or neurology medications.
2. *Developing Medical Devices or Diagnostic Tools*: A pharmaceutical company may diversify into developing medical devices or diagnostic tools that complement its existing product portfolio.
3. *Entering into Partnerships or Collaborations*: A pharmaceutical company may enter into partnerships or collaborations with other companies to co-develop new products or expand into new therapeutic areas.
4. *Acquiring Companies or Technologies*: A pharmaceutical company acquires other companies or technologies that complement its product portfolio or provide access to new markets or capabilities.

Lateral diversification can provide several benefits for pharmaceutical companies, including the potential for increased revenue and profitability, reduced risk through a diversified product portfolio, and the ability to leverage existing resources and capabilities to enter new markets. However, it also involves some risks, such as the potential for increased competition, regulatory challenges, and the need to manage a more complex product portfolio effectively.

Lateral Thinking

Lateral thinking is a problem-solving approach that involves thinking creatively and outside the box to find unconventional solutions. It was coined by Edward de Bono, a Maltese psychologist, and author, in his book *The Use of Lateral Thinking*, published in 1967.

Unlike traditional linear thinking, which follows a step-by-step logical progression, lateral thinking encourages the exploration of alternative perspectives, ideas, and possibilities. It involves breaking away from conventional or habitual thought patterns and considering fresh angles, connections, and viewpoints that may not be immediately obvious.

The key principles of lateral thinking include the following:

1. *Challenging Assumptions*: Lateral thinking questions the established assumptions and challenges preconceived notions. It encourages individuals to question why things are how they are and consider alternative perspectives.
2. *Generating Multiple Ideas*: Lateral thinking encourages generating multiple ideas, even if they initially seem impractical or unrelated. This quantity-over-quality approach opens up possibilities and allows for more creative solutions to emerge.
3. *Making Unexpected Connections*: Lateral thinking involves making connections between seemingly unrelated concepts, ideas, or domains. It seeks new relationships and associations that may lead to innovative solutions.
4. *Using Provocative Techniques*: Various techniques and tools can be employed in lateral thinking, such as random word association, reverse thinking, and challenging constraints. These techniques help break mental patterns and stimulate new ideas.
5. *Embracing Playfulness and Creativity*: Lateral thinking encourages a playful and imaginative mindset. It fosters a willingness to explore unconventional ideas, take risks, and think beyond the boundaries of traditional problem-solving approaches.

Lateral thinking is often used to overcome complex problems, encourage innovation, and promote creative problem-solving in various fields, including business, science, design, and art. By encouraging individuals to think differently and consider alternative possibilities, lateral thinking can lead to unique and inventive solutions.

Lateral Thinking in Pharma Marketing

Lateral thinking in pharma marketing involves applying creative and unconventional approaches to marketing strategies in the pharmaceutical industry. It encourages marketers to think outside the box and consider innovative ways to reach their target audience and promote their products. Here are a few examples of how lateral thinking can be applied in pharma marketing:

1. *Non-Traditional Channels*: Instead of relying solely on traditional marketing channels such as print ads or television commercials, pharma marketers can employ lateral thinking to explore non-traditional channels. For example, they could leverage social media platforms, online communities, or influencers to engage with patients and healthcare professionals in a more interactive and targeted manner.
2. *Gamification*: Lateral thinking can lead to gamification techniques in pharma marketing. By incorporating elements of games, such as challenges, rewards, and competition, marketers can create engaging experiences that educate patients or healthcare professionals about a particular disease or treatment. This approach can help increase knowledge retention and improve brand engagement.
3. *Collaboration and Partnerships*: Lateral thinking encourages pharma marketers to seek unconventional partnerships or collaborations. For example, partnering with patient advocacy groups or non-profit organizations working in related fields can help raise awareness, conduct joint campaigns, or develop educational materials that benefit both parties and the target audience.
4. *Personalized Marketing*: Applying lateral thinking can lead to personalized marketing strategies in the pharmaceutical industry. Marketers can gather insights about individual patients, healthcare providers, or specific target audience segments by utilizing data analytics and technology. This information can then be used to deliver tailored messages, customized

content, or targeted advertisements to enhance the relevance and impact of marketing efforts.

5. *Creative Content Formats*: Lateral thinking can inspire the creation of engaging and informative content in novel formats. For example, instead of relying solely on text-based materials, marketers can explore visual storytelling, interactive apps, animated videos, or virtual reality experiences to communicate complex medical information in a more accessible and memorable way.

These examples demonstrate how lateral thinking can inspire innovative marketing approaches in the pharmaceutical industry. By breaking away from traditional marketing methods and embracing unconventional strategies, pharma marketers can connect with their target audience more effectively, promote brand awareness, and communicate the value of their products in unique and compelling ways.

Launch Strategy

Launching a pharmaceutical product requires a well-planned marketing strategy to ensure a successful introduction into the market. Here are some key elements and examples of launch strategies in pharma marketing:

1. *Market Research*: Conduct comprehensive market research to identify the target audience, market size, competition, and unmet needs. This helps in developing a targeted launch strategy. For example, a pharmaceutical company developing a new medication for diabetes may conduct market research to understand the prevalence of the disease, patient demographics, and existing treatment options.
2. *Branding and Positioning*: Develop a strong brand identity and positioning for the product. This involves creating a unique brand name, logo, and visual identity that resonate with the target audience. For instance, a company launching a new oncology drug may focus on positioning the product as a breakthrough treatment with superior efficacy and fewer side effects.
3. *Key Opinion Leader (KOL) Engagement*: Engage with influential healthcare professionals and thought leaders in the therapeutic area to gain their support and endorsement. KOLs can help create awareness and build credibility for the new product. For example, a pharmaceutical company may organize advisory board meetings, scientific symposiums or sponsor educational programs to involve KOLs in the launch process.
4. *Multichannel Marketing*: Develop a comprehensive marketing plan that utilizes multiple channels to reach the target audience. This includes a mix of traditional marketing tactics, such as print advertising and direct mail, and digital channels, such as websites, social media, and email marketing. For example, a company launching a new respiratory medication may use digital advertising to reach patients through targeted online campaigns and print media to engage healthcare professionals.
5. *Patient and HCP Education*: Provide educational materials and resources to patients and healthcare professionals (HCPs) to create awareness and understanding of the product's benefits. This includes patient brochures, websites, educational videos, and continuing medical education (CME) programs for HCPs. For instance, a company launching a new medication for a rare disease may develop patient support programs, including disease education materials and access assistance.
6. *Market Access and Reimbursement*: Work closely with payers and reimbursement authorities to secure favorable coverage and reimbursement for the product. This involves demonstrating the product's clinical and economic value through health economic data and conducting pricing negotiations. For example, a company launching a new therapy for a chronic condition may engage in discussions with payers to ensure access and reimbursement coverage.
7. *Training the Sales Force*: Training the sales force in the launch strategy is critical to ensure they have the knowledge, skills, and tools necessary to execute the launch plan.
8. *Launch Events and PR*: Organize events and generate media coverage to create buzz around the new product. This includes press releases, media interviews, conference product presentations, and media partnerships. For example, a pharmaceutical company may host a launch event attended by key stakeholders, healthcare professionals, and patient advocacy groups.

It is important to note that each launch strategy should be tailored to the specific product, target market, and therapeutic area. Launching a pharmaceutical product requires careful planning, execution, and continuous monitoring to adjust the strategy based on market dynamics and stakeholder feedback.

Layout

In pharmaceutical marketing, layout refers to the arrangement and design of marketing materials, such as brochures, websites, advertisements, packaging, and other visual elements. The layout captures the target audience's attention, conveys information effectively, and creates a positive and engaging user experience. Here are some key considerations for layout in pharma marketing:

1. *Visual Hierarchy*: The layout should establish a clear visual hierarchy, prioritizing the most important information and guiding the viewer's attention. Important elements such as the product name, key benefits, and call-to-action should be displayed prominently, while secondary information can follow.
2. *Clear and Concise Communication*: The layout should facilitate clear, concise information communication. Use headings, subheadings, bullet points, and short paragraphs to organize and present information in a digestible format. Avoid cluttered designs and prioritize simplicity to enhance readability and comprehension.
3. *Brand Consistency*: The layout should adhere to the branding guidelines of the pharmaceutical company. Consistent use of brand colors, fonts, imagery, and log placement helps establish brand recognition and reinforces the company's identity. In addition, this consistency helps build trust and familiarity with the target audience.
4. *User-Friendly Navigation*: The layout should prioritize user-friendly navigation in digital marketing, especially on websites and mobile applications. Intuitive navigation menus, clear call-to-action buttons, and logical organization of content help users find information easily and engage with the desired actions, such as requesting more information or purchasing.
5. *Compliance with Regulatory Requirements*: Pharma marketing materials must comply with regulatory guidelines specific to the pharmaceutical industry. Ensure that the layout adheres to regulatory requirements regarding product claims, fair balance, safety promotion, and any specific regulations related to promotional materials.
6. *Mobile-Friendly Design*: With the increasing use of mobile devices, it is important to consider responsive and mobile-friendly design in the layout of pharma marketing materials. Optimize the layout to ensure a seamless user experience across different devices and screen sizes.
7. *Visual Appeal*: The layout should have visual appeal and aesthetics that align with the target audience and the pharmaceutical brand. Consider using high-quality images, graphics, and visually engaging elements to capture attention and create a positive impression.
8. *Testing and Iteration*: It is essential to test the effectiveness of different layouts through usability testing, focus groups, or A/B testing. You can refine the layout by gathering feedback and data to optimize its impact and effectiveness.

By carefully considering these aspects of layout design in pharma marketing, companies can create visually appealing, informative, and user-friendly marketing materials that effectively communicate their messages and engage the target audience.

Lead Generation

Lead generation in pharma marketing refers to identifying and attracting potential customers interested in a pharmaceutical company's products or services and capturing their contact information. Lead generation aims to build a database of leads that can be further nurtured through targeted marketing efforts to convert them into paying customers.

Here are some examples of lead-generation tactics in pharma marketing:

1. *Online Advertising*: Pharmaceutical companies may use online advertising, such as search engine marketing or special media advertising, to attract potential customers to their websites or landing pages.
2. *Content Marketing*: Companies may create informative content, such as blog posts, articles, or white papers, to attract potential customers and encourage them to provide their contact information in exchange for access to the content.
3. *Events and Conferences*: Companies may participate in or host events and conferences related to their products or therapeutic areas to connect with potential customers and capture their contact information.
4. *Direct Mail and Email Marketing*: Companies may use direct mail or email marketing campaigns to promote their products or services and capture leads through sign-up forms or landing pages.
5. *Referral Programs*: Companies may offer incentives or rewards for customers who refer new leads to their business.

Effective lead-generation strategies in pharma require a deep understanding of the target audience, the market, and the regulatory environment. It is also important for companies to ensure that their lead-generation tactics comply with all applicable regulations and guidelines.

Lead Magnet

In pharmaceutical marketing, a lead magnet is a content or information offered to potential customers for their contact information, such as their name and email address. The goal of a lead magnet is to attract potential customers and build a list of leads that can be further nurtured through targeted marketing efforts.

Here are some examples of lead magnets in pharma marketing:

1. *Educational Guides or eBooks*: Pharmaceutical companies may offer guides or eBooks that provide information about specific diseases or conditions, treatment options, or medications.
2. *Webinars or Online Events*: Companies may offer webinars or events that provide in-depth information about their products or treatment options or feature healthcare professionals discussing related topics.
3. *Quizzes and Assessments*: Companies may offer interactive quizzes or assessments providing insights or recommendations for specific diseases or conditions.
4. *Free Samples or Trial Offers*: Companies may offer free samples or introductory offers to induce trial.

Lead magnets can be an effective way for pharmaceutical companies to attract potential customers, build their email lists, and ultimately drive sales of their products through targeted marketing efforts. However, companies must first ensure that their lead magnets are relevant, high-quality, and comply with all regulatory guidelines and requirements.

Leapfrogging

Leapfrogging is a term used in business and economics to describe a situation where a developing country or region can bypass traditional development stages and move directly to advanced technologies or systems. This is often accomplished by using new technological developments or innovations to modernize and upgrade infrastructure, services, or products rapidly.

Leapfrogging in Pharma

Leapfrogging in pharma refers to adopting or implementing innovative technologies or business models that bypass traditional drug development, manufacturing, and distribution steps. This can be achieved by leveraging advanced technologies such as artificial intelligence, machine learning, and data analytics to improve the speed and efficiency of the drug development process, reduce costs, and enhance patient outcomes.

One example of leapfrogging in pharma is using digital technologies to conduct clinical trials remotely. This approach can significantly reduce the time and cost of traditional clinical trials, often requiring patients to visit research sites multiple times. Remote trials can also make it easier for patients to participate, particularly those who live in remote or underserved areas.

Another example of leapfrogging in pharma is 3D printing to produce personalized medicine. 3D printing allows drug manufacturers to create unique doses of medication tailored to an individual patient's specific needs, which can improve efficacy and reduce side effects.

Leapfrogging in pharma is becoming increasingly important as the industry faces pressure to develop new drugs faster, at lower costs, and with better patient outcomes. By adopting innovative technologies and business models, pharma companies can stay competitive and deliver better products and services to patients.

Learn-feel-buy-Model

The Learn-feel-buy Model in pharma marketing is a framework that describes the process that patients go through when making decisions about their healthcare. It consists of three stages:

A. *Learn*: In this stage, patients gather information about their condition, the available treatments, and options. This may involve researching online, talking to healthcare providers, and seeking advice from friends and family.

B. *Feel*: Patients develop emotional responses to their conditions and treatment options in this stage. Depending on their situation and the information gathered, they may experience fear, anxiety, or hope.

C. *Buy*: In this stage, patients decide which treatment plan to pursue. This may involve choosing between different medications, deciding whether to follow a certain course of treatment, or selecting a healthcare provider.

Pharmaceutical companies can use the *Learn-feel-buy* model to develop marketing strategies that target patients at each stage of the decision-making process. For example, in the *Learn* stage, companies can provide educational resources such as brochures, videos, or webinars that help patients understand their condition and treatment options. In the *Feel* stage, companies can develop messaging that speaks to patients' emotions and concerns, such as emphasizing the benefits of a particular treatment or addressing common fears or misconceptions. Finally, in the *Buy* stage, companies can provide information about pricing, insurance coverage, and access to medication, as well as offer support services such as patient assistance programs.

By understanding the *Learn-feel-buy* model and developing targeted marketing strategies, pharma companies can help patients make informed decisions about their healthcare and improve patient outcomes.

Leverage

Leverage is a term used in various contexts, including finance, business, and marketing, with slightly different meanings depending on the context. Generally, leverage refers to the strategic use of resources or techniques to amplify or enhance the outcome or impact of a particular action or situation.

In finance, leverage typically refers to using borrowed capital or debt to increase the potential return on investment. By utilizing borrowed funds, individuals or businesses can amplify their investment gains if the returns generated from the investment exceed the cost of borrowing. However, leverage also increases the risk, as losses can be magnified if the investment performs poorly.

In business, leverage can refer to using different resources, such as technology, relationships, intellectual property, or strategic partnerships, to gain a competitive advantage or achieve higher efficiency. For example, a company may leverage its existing customer base to launch new products or services, leverage technology to streamline operations or leverage a strong brand reputation to enter new markets.

In marketing, leverage refers to using various strategies and tactics to maximize the impact of marketing efforts and resources. This can include leveraging customer data and insights to personalize campaigns, leveraging social media influencers to reach a wider audience, leveraging partnerships for co-marketing initiatives or leveraging content marketing to enhance brand visibility and engagement.

Leveraging, thus, involves strategically utilizing available resources, assets, or techniques to achieve greater results or advantages. It often involves assessing the potential risks and rewards of the chosen approach and making calculated decisions to optimize outcomes.

Leverage in Pharma Marketing

In pharmaceutical marketing, leverage refers to the strategic use of various resources, tactics, and techniques to enhance the effectiveness and impact of marketing efforts. Here are a few ways leverage can be applied in pharma marketing:

1. *Key Opinion Leaders (KOLs)*: Leveraging the influence and expertise of healthcare professionals and key opinion leaders can significantly impact the reach and credibility of pharmaceutical marketing campaigns. Collaborating with respected KOLs can help generate awareness, build trust and influence healthcare providers' and patients' opinions and decisions.
2. *Data and Analytics*: Leveraging data and analytics can provide valuable insights into customer behaviors, preferences, and market trends. By analyzing data, pharmaceutical marketers can identify target segments, personalize messages, and optimize marketing strategies for better outcomes. Leveraging data can also help measure marketing campaigns' effectiveness and make data-driven decisions.
3. *Digital Marketing Channels*: Leveraging digital marketing channels, such as websites, social media platforms, email marketing, and search engine optimization, can expand the reach and engagement of pharmaceutical marketing initiatives. Digital platforms offer opportunities to target specific audiences, deliver personalized content, and track performance metrics, enabling marketers to refine their strategies for better results.
4. *Patient Advocacy Groups*: Collaborating with patient advocacy groups can provide a powerful leverage point in pharma marketing. These groups often have established networks, strong connections with patient communities, and credibility. Partnering with such groups can help raise awareness, educate patients, and enhance brand reputation through positive association with patient-centered initiatives.
5. *Thought Leadership Content*: Creating and disseminating thought leadership content, such as white papers and educational materials, can establish pharmaceutical companies as industry leaders. This content can help build trust, educate healthcare professionals and patients,

and position the company as a valuable resource in the therapeutic area.

6. *Strategic Partnerships*: Forming strategic partnerships with other companies or organizations in the healthcare ecosystem can provide mutual benefits and leverage each other's strengths. For example, a pharmaceutical company may partner with a diagnostic or medical device manufacturer to create joint marketing initiatives, integrated solutions, or co-promotions, enhancing the overall value proposition and market reach.

By strategically leveraging these resources and tactics, pharmaceutical marketers can maximize the impact of their campaigns, reach the right audiences, and create meaningful engagement with healthcare professionals, patients, and other stakeholders. The goal is to optimize marketing efforts and achieve better outcomes in terms of brand awareness, customer acquisition, and overall business growth

Licensing

Licensing in pharmaceutical marketing refers to granting or obtaining the rights to market and distribute pharmaceutical products developed by another company. It allows companies to leverage their marketing expertise and infrastructure to promote and sell products that other pharmaceutical companies have developed. This can benefit both the licensor and licensee, as it enables the licensor to expand the reach of their products while allowing the licensee to enhance their product portfolio.

Here are a few examples of licensing in pharmaceutical marketing:

1. *Licensing a Patented Drug*: A pharmaceutical company with a patented drug may license the marketing rights to another company, domestically or internationally. This allows the licensor to tap into the licensee's marketing capabilities and distribution networks to reach a broader market.
2. *Licensing of a Generic Drug*: Generic drug manufacturers often obtain licenses from the original brand-name pharmaceutical companies to market and distribute generic versions of their drugs. The licensor benefits from the additional revenue generated by the generic version, while the licensee gains access to an established drug with a recognized brand name.
3. *Co-promotion Agreements*: In some cases, two pharmaceutical companies may jointly enter a co-promotion agreement to market and distribute a specific drug. Each company contributes its marketing resources, expertise, and sales force to promote the product, sharing the revenues generated from its sales.
4. *Territory-specific Licensing*: Pharma companies may license the marketing rights to their products on a regional or country-specific basis. This allows them to benefit from the licensee's local market knowledge and distribution networks in each region.
5. *Over-the-counter Licensing*: Companies specializing in over-the-counter drugs may license the marketing rights to prescription drugs from pharmaceutical companies. They can modify the drug's formulation, packaging, and labeling to make it suitable for the OTC sale.

It is important to note that licensing agreements in pharmaceutical marketing involve complex legal and financial arrangements, including considerations such as royalties, exclusivity, intellectual property rights, and regulatory compliance. As a result, the specific terms and conditions of licensing agreements can vary widely depending on the companies involved, the products being licensed, and the geographical scope of the agreement.

Lifecycle

The lifecycle in pharmaceutical marketing refers to the various stages a pharmaceutical product goes through, from its development to its ultimate withdrawal from the market. These stages are:

1. *Research and Development (R&D)*: This is the initial phase where pharmaceutical companies invest in research to identify and develop new drugs or improve existing ones. This stage involves preclinical and clinical trials to test the safety and efficacy of the drug.
2. *Regulatory Approval*: Once the drug has completed clinical trials and demonstrated its safety and efficacy, the pharmaceutical company submits a New Drug Application (NDA) or Marketing Authorization Approval (MAA) to regulatory authorities such as the US Food and Drug Administration (FDA) or the European Medicines Agency (EMA). The authorities review the application and, if approved, grant marketing authorization for the drug.
3. *Launch*: After receiving the regulatory approval, the pharmaceutical company launches the product into the market. This involves creating marketing strategies, developing promotional materials, and training sales representatives to promote the drug to healthcare professionals.

4. *Growth*: The pharmaceutical company focuses on expanding the drug's market share at this stage. This may involve conducting additional clinical trials, obtaining approvals for new indications or patient populations, and increasing marketing efforts to reach a wider audience.
5. *Maturity*: The drug reaches its peak sales during the maturity phase. At this stage, competition from generic alternatives may emerge, and the pharmaceutical company may need to adjust its marketing strategies accordingly. For example, marketing efforts may focus on differentiating the drug from competitors, implementing pricing strategies, and maintaining strong relationships with healthcare professionals.
6. *Decline*: Over time, the drug may experience a decline in sales due to various factors, such as loss of patent protection, the emergence of newer and more effective drugs, or changes in clinical guidelines. The pharmaceutical company may consider discontinuing or withdrawing the product from the market at this stage.

Throughout the lifecycle, pharmaceutical companies engage in various marketing activities, including advertising, medical education programs, scientific publications, direct-to-consumer campaigns (where allowed), and interactions with healthcare professionals to promote their products and ensure their appropriate use. In addition, companies must comply with regulatory guidelines and ethical standards in their marketing practices.

Lifecycle Assessment (LCA)

Lifecycle Assessment (LCA) is a method used to assess the environmental impact of a product or service throughout its entire lifecycle, from the extraction of raw materials to its disposal. While LCA is commonly used in industries such as manufacturing and construction, it can also be applied to pharmaceutical marketing.

In pharmaceutical marketing, LCA can be used to evaluate the environmental impact of a drug product from its inception to its end-of-life disposal. This analysis can provide valuable information to pharmaceutical companies, healthcare providers, and patients about the potential environmental impact of medication and help identify opportunities to reduce that impact. Some of the key areas where LCA can be applied in pharma marketing are:

1. *Raw Materials*: Examining the environmental impact of sourcing and extracting raw materials used in drug production, such as plant-based or synthetic chemicals. A pharmaceutical company, for example, can conduct an LCA analysis to assess the environmental impact of sourcing raw materials used to produce medication. For example, if the medication contains plant-based ingredients, the LCA can evaluate the environmental impact of the farming practices used to grow those plants, including water usage, pesticide and fertilizer application, and carbon emissions associated with transportation.
2. *Manufacturing*: Assessing the energy usage, water consumption, and waste generation associated with the manufacturing process, including packaging materials. For example, the LCA analysis can examine energy consumption, greenhouse gas emissions, water usage, and waste generation associated with manufacturing.
3. *Distribution and Transportation*: Evaluating the environmental impact of transporting the drug from the manufacturing site to distribution centers and ultimately to healthcare providers or patients. This includes assessing the environmental impact of the transportation mode, such as by air, sea, or land, and the energy usage associated with transportation.
4. *Use and Disposal*: Analyzing the environmental impact of patients' use of the drug, including potential emissions or waste generated during the production of the drug and any disposal requirements after the drug has been used. An LCA can also assess the environmental impact of medication use, including emissions generated by the medication use and any waste generated when the medication is disposed of, such as packaging materials, empty medication containers, or unused medication.

Incorporating LCA into pharma marketing can help pharmaceutical companies make more informed decisions about the environmental impact of their products and identify opportunities to reduce that impact. For example, they may switch to more sustainable sourcing of raw materials, reduce the amount of packaging materials used, or implement energy-efficient manufacturing practices.

Lifecycle Management

Lifecycle management in pharmaceutical marketing refers to the strategic planning and execution of activities throughout the lifespan of a pharmaceutical product. It involves maximizing the product's value, extending its market presence, and adapting to changing market dynamics. Here are some key aspects and strategies involved in lifecycle management in pharma marketing:

1. *Product Development*: Lifecycle management begins during the product development stage. Companies may explore additional indications or formulations for an existing product to expand its market potential. For example, a company with a successful anti-inflammatory drug may conduct clinical trials to investigate its efficacy in treating a new indication.
2. *Market Expansion*: Identify opportunities to expand the product's market reach. This can involve launching the product in new geographic regions, targeting new patient segments, or pursuing additional regulatory approvals. For instance, a company may seek approval for pediatric use of a drug initially approved for adult patients only.
3. *Line Extensions*: Develop line extensions by introducing variations of the existing product. This can include different dosages and formulations, such as extended-release or combination products. Line extensions can help address specific patient needs, enhance convenience, and capture additional market share.
4. *Pricing and Access Strategies*: Adjust pricing and access strategies over time to align with market dynamics. This may involve periodic pricing evaluations, negotiations with payers, and exploring alternative pricing models. Companies may also consider strategies such as patient assistance programs or innovative reimbursement agreements to enhance access and affordability.
5. *Lifecycle Planning*: Develop a comprehensive lifecycle plan that outlines strategic initiatives and timelines for different stages of the product's lifecycle. The plan should consider factors such as patent expiration, competition, regulatory requirements, and market trends. Regularly review and update the plan as the product progresses through its lifecycle.
6. *Market and Competitive Intelligence*: Continuously monitor the market landscape and gather competitive intelligence to identify opportunities and challenges. Stay informed about changes in treatment guidelines, emerging therapies, and shifts in patient preferences. This information can guide decision-making and inform strategic planning for maintaining or enhancing the product's market position.
7. *Branding and Messaging*: Regularly assess and refine the product's branding and messaging to ensure alignment with the evolving market and target audience. Adjust the positioning and messaging to communicate the product's value proposition effectively and address any competitive or market changes.
8. *Lifecycle Marketing Campaigns*: Develop targeted marketing campaigns that leverage the product's lifecycle stage. This can include disease awareness initiatives, educational programs, or promotional activities tailored to specific patient populations or healthcare professionals. These campaigns aim to maintain or increase product awareness, drive adoption, and support continued usage.
9. *Post-Marketing Studies*: Conduct post-marketing studies and real-world evidence generation to demonstrate further the product's safety, effectiveness, and value. These studies can help expand the product's label, support health economic claims, and strengthen the evidence base for healthcare professionals, payers, and patients.
10. *Thought Leader Engagement*: Continue to engage with key opinion leaders (KOLs) and healthcare professionals throughout the product lifecycle. Collaborate with KOLs to generate scientific publications, conduct advisory board meetings, and support educational initiatives. KOL engagement helps maintain product visibility, credibility, and adoption within the medical community.

Effective lifecycle management in pharmaceutical marketing requires a proactive and adaptable approach. Companies can optimize the value and longevity of their pharmaceutical products by continuously assessing market dynamics, anticipating changes, and implementing appropriate strategies.

Lifecycle Marketing

Lifecycle marketing in the pharmaceutical industry refers to a strategic approach where pharmaceutical companies focus on managing their relationships with healthcare professionals, patients, and other stakeholders throughout the entire lifecycle of a product. This approach recognizes that these stakeholders' needs and behaviors can change at different stages of the product's life and tailors marketing efforts accordingly. Here are the key components of lifecycle marketing in the pharmaceutical industry:

1. *Pre-launch*: Before launching a product, pharmaceutical companies engage in activities to generate awareness and build anticipation among healthcare professionals and key opinion

leaders. This may involve educational initiatives, advisory board meetings, and scientific publications highlighting the product's benefits.

2. *Launch*: A comprehensive marketing strategy is implemented once the product is approved and ready to be introduced. This includes developing promotional materials, training sales representatives, and organizing launch events to educate healthcare professionals about the product's features, indications, and clinical benefits.
3. *Growth*: During the growth phase, the focus shifts to expanding market share and driving product adoption. Marketing efforts may involve targeted campaigns, continuing medical education programs, clinical trial support, and engagement with professional associations and patient advocacy groups to raise awareness and enhance the product's reputation.
4. *Maturity*: As the product matures, the marketing strategy may involve strategies to maintain market share, strengthen brand loyalty, and differentiate the product from competitors. This may include post-marketing studies, real-world evidence generation, health economics and outcomes research, and additional indications or formulations to extend the product's lifecycle.
5. *Decline*: Over time, the product may face challenges such as loss of patent protection, generic competition, or changing treatment guidelines. In this phase, the marketing focus may shift to managing transition, identifying opportunities for lifecycle extension, and planning to launch new products.

Throughout the lifecycle, pharmaceutical companies employ various marketing channels and tactics, including digital marketing, medical conferences, thought leader engagement, direct marketing, patient support programs, and relationship-building activities with healthcare professionals. Therefore, it is crucial to adhere to regulatory guidelines, comply with legal and ethical standards, and ensure that all marketing activities are evidence-based and transparent to maintain trust and credibility within and among stakeholders.

Lifestyle Diseases

Lifestyle diseases, or non-communicable diseases (NCDs), are chronic conditions often caused by unhealthy lifestyle choices and habits. These diseases are typically associated with modern, urbanized lifestyles, including diabetes, obesity, cardiovascular disease, cancer, and chronic respiratory diseases.

The primary risk factors for lifestyle diseases are often related to lifestyle choices such as physical inactivity, poor diet, smoking, excessive alcohol consumption, and stress. These risk factors can contribute to developing chronic diseases over time and exacerbate existing conditions.

Prevention and management of lifestyle diseases typically involve lifestyle modifications, such as regular exercise, healthy eating habits, smoking cessation, limiting alcohol consumption, and stress management. Early detection and treatment are also important for managing these conditions and preventing complications.

Pharmaceutical companies play an important role in preventing and managing lifestyle diseases by developing medications and treatments to help manage symptoms and prevent complications. However, it is important to note that lifestyle modifications and health habits are often the most effective ways to prevent and manage these conditions.

Implications for Pharma Marketers

The implications for pharma marketers related to lifestyle diseases are significant. Here are a few key points:

1. *Focus on Prevention*: Prevention is a key strategy for addressing lifestyle diseases, and pharma marketers should consider how they can help educate consumers on healthy lifestyle habits and promote the importance of early detection and management.
2. *Lifestyle-Focused Marketing*: Pharma marketers can take a lifestyle-focused approach to marketing, creating campaigns emphasizing healthy habits and encouraging consumers to make positive lifestyle changes.
3. *Collaboration with Healthcare Providers*: Collaboration with healthcare providers is important to ensure that patients receive the necessary care and support to manage lifestyle diseases. Pharma marketers can work with healthcare providers to create educational materials, patient support programs, and other initiatives to improve outcomes for patients with lifestyle diseases.
4. *Consideration of Regulatory Guidelines*: Pharma marketers need to consider regulatory guidelines related to promoting medications and treatments for lifestyle diseases. Marketers should ensure that their campaigns comply with regulatory requirements and focus on the benefits and risks of treatments while also providing information on lifestyle modifications.

Pharma marketers are important in addressing lifestyle diseases through education, promoting healthy habits, and collaborating with healthcare providers to improve patient outcomes.

Lifestyle Management

Lifestyle management refers to the process of making conscious choices in taking action to improve one's overall health and well-being by adopting healthy lifestyle habits. It involves various activities and interventions designed to prevent or manage chronic conditions, reduce risk factors for disease, and promote healthy behaviors.

Lifestyle management typically involves a combination of diet, exercise, stress management, sleep, hygiene, and other lifestyle factors that can impact health outcomes. It may also include preventive measures such as regular health screenings and vaccinations.

Lifestyle management aims to help individuals improve their physical, mental, and emotional health and achieve optimal well-being. By making positive lifestyle choices, individuals can reduce their risk of chronic diseases such as diabetes, heart disease, and cancer and improve their overall quality of life.

Several resources, including healthcare providers, nutritionists, fitness professionals, and mental health experts, may support lifestyle management. Additionally, many tools and resources, such as apps, websites, and wearable devices, can help track their progress and stay motivated to achieve their health goals.

Lifestyle Management in Pharma

Lifestyle management in pharma refers to using pharmaceutical products, lifestyle interventions, and behavioral changes to improve health outcomes and quality of life for patients with chronic diseases or conditions related to unhealthy lifestyle habits.

Pharmaceutical companies may offer a range of products, such as medications for diabetes, hypertension, and high cholesterol, that are designed to manage chronic conditions and prevent associated complications. However, lifestyle management in pharma goes beyond medication. It may also include support and resources to help patients adapt and maintain healthy lifestyle behaviors, such as exercise, diet, and stress management.

Pharmaceutical companies may offer programs and services that help patients learn about healthy lifestyle choices, set goals, track progress, and connect with support networks. For example, a company that produces diabetes medications may offer nutrition counseling, exercise programs, and educational materials to help patients manage their condition.

Lifestyle management in pharma can benefit both patients and pharmaceutical companies. Patients may experience improved health outcomes and quality of life. At the same time, pharmaceutical companies may benefit from increased patient loyalty, improved medication adherence, and a positive reputation as a provider of comprehensive healthcare solutions.

However, it is important to note that lifestyle management in pharma should be cautiously approached. Promoting healthy behaviors and lifestyle changes may be perceived as overreaching by some patients and could probably infringe on individual autonomy. The focus on lifestyle interventions may also obscure other factors contributing to health outcomes, such as social determinants of health and access to healthcare success.

Lifestyle Marketing

Lifestyle marketing in pharma refers to aligning pharmaceutical products or healthcare interventions with specific lifestyle choices, aspirations, or consumer behaviors. It involves understanding of target audience's lifestyle preferences, values, and habits and incorporating those insights into marketing strategies. Lifestyle marketing aims to position pharmaceutical products as not just treatments but as part of a broader lifestyle solution. Here are some key aspects and examples of lifestyle marketing in the pharmaceutical industry:

1. *Targeting Specific Lifestyle Segments*: Identify and target specific lifestyle segments that align with the therapeutic area or health condition addressed by the pharmaceutical product. For example, a medication targeting obesity may focus its marketing efforts on health-conscious individuals interested in fitness, healthy eating, and weight management.
2. *Lifestyle-Driven Messaging*: Craft marketing messages and campaigns that resonate with the target audience's lifestyle choices and aspirations. Highlight how the product can help individuals maintain or enhance their preferred lifestyle. For instance, a medication for migraine prevention may emphasize how it enables individuals to continue participating in activities they enjoy without frequent migraines interrupting.
3. *Partnerships with Lifestyle Influencers*: Collaborate with influencers, bloggers, or social media personalities who align with the target

audience's lifestyle preferences. These influencers can share their experiences with the product, provide lifestyle tips, and showcase how the product fits into their daily routines. This endorsement can help build trust and credibility among the target audience.

4. *Content Marketing and Educational Resources*: Create content and educational resources catering to the target audiences' lifestyle interests and needs. This can include lifestyle-focused articles, blogs, videos, and social media content that provide relevant information, tips, and insights. For example, a pharmaceutical company producing diabetes medications may develop content on healthy eating, exercise routines, and stress management.
5. *Patient Support Programs*: Develop programs beyond traditional medical support and provide lifestyle-related assistance. This can include access to nutritionists, fitness trainers, or wellness coaches who can help patients incorporate healthy lifestyle practices alongside their medication regimen. These programs can offer a holistic approach to managing health conditions.
6. *Wellness and Prevention Campaigns*: Focus on wellness and prevention as key aspects of lifestyle marketing. Emphasize the importance of early detection, routine check-ups, and healthy lifestyle choices to prevent or minimize the impact of certain health conditions. Pharmaceutical companies can align their products with preventive measures and position them as tools for maintaining overall well-being.
7. *Digital Health Tools and Apps*: Develop digital health tools and mobile applications that integrate with individual lifestyles and provide personalized support. These tools can help track health metrics, provide reminders for medication adherence, offer lifestyle recommendations, and connect patients with healthcare professionals. In addition, pharmaceutical companies can strengthen the lifestyle marketing approach by integrating the product into individuals' daily routines.

An important point. Pharmaceutical companies must ensure that lifestyle marketing strategies are ethical, responsible, and comply with relevant regulations and guidelines. The focus should be on providing accurate information, supporting patient needs, and promoting health and well-being along with the appropriate use of pharmaceutical products.

Lifestyle Research

Lifestyle research is a branch of research that focuses on understanding the lifestyle behaviors and habits of individuals and how they impact health outcomes. Lifestyle research typically involves collecting and analyzing data related to diet, physical activity, sleep, stress, and other lifestyle factors that can impact health.

Lifestyle research may be conducted in various settings, including academic institutions, government agencies, and private organizations. It may involve qualitative and quantitative research methods, including surveys, focus groups, interviews, and observational studies.

The findings of lifestyle research can be used to inform public health policies and interventions and to develop personalized lifestyle recommendations for individuals. For example, lifestyle research may help identify specific dietary patterns or physical activity levels associated with a lower risk of chronic diseases such as heart disease, diabetes, and cancer. This information can be used to develop evidence-based recommendations for healthy living and targeted interventions to promote healthy lifestyle behaviors.

Lifestyle Research in Pharma Marketing

Lifestyle research plays an important role in pharmaceutical marketing, as it helps pharmaceutical companies better understand the lifestyles and behaviors of their target patient populations and develop targeted marketing strategies and interventions that can improve health outcomes.

For example, lifestyle research can help identify the specific lifestyle factors that contribute to the development of certain chronic diseases, such as obesity, diabetes, and heart disease. This information can be used to develop educational materials, resources, and interventions tailored to the needs and preferences of patients with these conditions that can promote healthy lifestyle behaviors.

Lifestyle research can also help pharmaceutical companies develop marketing messages and campaigns that resonate with patients and promote healthy lifestyles. By understanding their target audience's values, beliefs, and motivations, companies can develop more engaging and persuasive messaging, inspiring patients to take action to improve their health.

In addition, lifestyle research can be used to evaluate the effectiveness of marketing interventions and campaigns and identify improvement areas. For example, by measuring changes in patient behavior and health outcomes over time, companies can determine which interventions most effectively promote healthy lifestyles and refine their marketing strategies accordingly.

Lifetime Value

Lifetime Value (LTV), or customer lifetime value (CLTV), is a business metric representing the total estimated value a customer brings to a company over their entire relationship or lifetime as a customer. Therefore, understanding the long-term profitability and value of acquiring and retaining customers is crucial.

The lifetime value calculation typically considers the revenue generated from a customer's purchases minus the cost of acquiring and serving that customer. By analyzing this metric, businesses can assess the financial impact of different customer segments and make informed decisions regarding marketing, customer retention strategies, and overall business growth.

The formula for calculating lifetime value may vary depending on the context and industry. However, a common approach involves multiplying the average purchase value by the average purchase frequency and multiplying that by the average customer lifespan. The resulting value estimates the total revenue a customer will likely generate over their entire relationship with the company.

It is important to note that lifetime value goes beyond a single transaction or immediate profitability. It considers the potential for repeat purchases, up-selling, cross-selling, and the customer's influence on others through referrals or brand advocacy. By focusing on customer retention and maximizing the lifetime value of each customer, businesses can build stronger relationships, increase profitability, and achieve long-term success.

Lifetime Value in Pharma Marketing

Lifetime value in pharma marketing refers to the estimated total value a pharmaceutical company derives from a customer over their entire relationship. It helps pharmaceutical marketers assess the long-term financial impact of acquiring and retaining customers. Here are some examples of how lifetime value is applied in pharma marketing:

1. *Patient Adherence Programs*: Pharmaceutical companies can implement patient adherence programs to improve medication compliance and long-term patient outcomes. By encouraging patients to use their medications as prescribed consistently, companies can increase customer lifetime value through continued product sales and potentially reduce the likelihood of disease progression or complications.
2. *Customer Loyalty and Retention Initiatives*: Developing loyalty programs or initiatives that reward ongoing customer engagement and product usage can help enhance customer lifetime value. For instance, offering discounts or exclusive benefits to loyal customers can incentivize them to continue using the company's products and potentially refer others to the brand.
3. *Targeted Communication and Engagement*: Using customer data and analytics, pharma marketers can identify high-value customers and personalize their communication and engagement efforts accordingly. By delivering targeted messaging, tailored content, and value-added services, companies can foster stronger relationships, enhance customer satisfaction, and potentially increase the lifetime value of those customers.
4. *Up-selling and Cross-selling Opportunities*: Pharma marketers can identify opportunities for up-selling and cross-selling by analyzing customer data and understanding their needs and preferences. For example, a customer is using a particular medication. In that case, the company can provide information about complementary products or medications that may benefit the customer's health condition, potentially increasing the customer's lifetime value.
5. *Disease Management*: Pharmaceutical companies can develop disease management and education programs that provide patients with ongoing support, information, and resources. By empowering patients to manage their health conditions effectively, companies can increase customer loyalty, long-term product usage, and the customer's lifetime value.

These examples illustrate how the concept of lifetime value can the applied in pharmaceutical marketing. By focusing on customer retention, loyalty, and personalized engagement, pharmaceutical companies can maximize the long-term financial value of their customer relationships while benefiting patients through improved health outcomes.

Line Extension

Line extension in pharmaceutical marketing refers to introducing variations or extensions of an existing pharmaceutical product. It involves leveraging an established product's success and brand equity to address new patient needs, expand market reach, or capture additional market share. Here are some examples of line extensions in pharma marketing:

1. *Dosage Variations*: Introducing different dosage strengths of an existing medication is a common line extension strategy. For example, a company may launch a drug's higher or lower dosage strength to cater to patients with different severity levels or to provide more flexibility in dosing options.
2. *Formulation Extensions*: Developing alternative drug formulations can be another line extension approach. For instance, a company may introduce an extended-release version of a medication that provides a sustained effect over a longer duration, offering patients a convenient dosing regimen and potentially improving medication adherence.
3. *Combination Products*: Combining two or more active ingredients into a single product is another line extension strategy. This can offer convenience to patients who require multiple medications for a specific condition. An example is the development of fixed-dose combination therapies for treating chronic diseases like hypertension, diabetes, or HIV.
4. *Indication Expansions*: Expanding the approved indications for an existing drug is a line extension tactic to capture new patient populations or medical conditions. This involves conducting additional clinical trials and seeking regulatory approvals for new indications. For instance, a medication initially approved for a specific type of cancer may later receive approval for use in a different type of cancer.
5. *Pediatric Extensions*: Developing pediatric formulations or adaptions of an existing drug is another line extension opportunity. Many medications may need specific formulations or dosing adjustments for pediatric patients. Creating age-appropriate formulations of dosage forms can address the unique needs of the pediatric population.
6. *Route Administration Extensions*: Introducing alternative routes of administration can be a line extension strategy. For example, a medication initially available in tablet form may be extended to include a sublingual formulation or a transdermal patch. This allows patients to have options based on their preferences or specific requirements.
7. *Brand Extensions*: Leveraging the established brand name of a product, pharmaceutical companies may extend the brand into related therapeutic areas. This involves launching new products under the same brand that target different conditions but share similarities regarding mechanisms of action or target patient population.

Line extensions in pharma marketing aim to meet diverse patient needs, expand market presence, and leverage the success of existing products. However, it is important for companies to carefully evaluate market demand, conduct appropriate research and development, and ensure regulatory compliance when pursuing line extension strategies.

LinkedIn

LinkedIn is a powerful platform for pharma marketing, offering numerous opportunities to connect with healthcare professionals, target specific audiences, and build brand awareness. Here are some key ways LinkedIn can be utilized in pharma marketing:

1. *Professional Networking*: LinkedIn provides a platform for pharmaceutical companies to connect and network with healthcare professionals, including doctors, pharmacists, researchers, and executives. Building relationships with key opinion leaders, physicians, and decision-makers can facilitate collaborations, partnerships, and opportunities for product promotion.
2. *Thought Leadership and Content Sharing*: Sharing valuable and informative content on LinkedIn can position pharmaceutical companies as thought leaders in their respective areas. Posting articles, white papers, case studies, and blog posts can demonstrate expertise, educate the audience, and generate engagement and discussions. This helps build brand credibility and attracts the attention of healthcare professionals.
3. *Targeted Advertising*: LinkedIn offers robust targeting options that allow pharmaceutical marketers to reach specific audiences based on job titles, industries, locations, and other relevant criteria. This enables precision targeting of healthcare professionals more likely to be interested in the company's products or services. In addition, sponsored content, Sponsored InMail, and display ads on LinkedIn can effectively reach the targeted audience.
4. *LinkedIn Groups*: Participating in relevant LinkedIn Groups or creating dedicated groups can provide a platform for engaging with healthcare professionals with a common interest or belonging to specific medical specialties.

Sharing relevant content, initiating discussions, and providing insights can help build relationships, gain visibility, and establish the company as a trusted resource in the field.

5. *Recruiting and Talent Acquisition*: LinkedIn is a valuable tool for pharmaceutical companies to recruit and acquire talent in various roles, including sales, marketing, research, and clinical development. Companies can showcase their company culture, job opportunities, and benefits and engage with potential candidates through LinkedIn's job postings, company pages, and targeted outreach.
6. *Event Promotion and Participation*: LinkedIn can be utilized to promote and participate in industry events, conferences, and webinars. Posting about upcoming events, sharing updates, and engaging with attendees can increase the company's visibility, generate interest in its products or services, and facilitate networking opportunities with relevant stakeholders.
7. *Company Branding and Reputation Management*: LinkedIn pages provide a dedicated space for showcasing a pharmaceutical company's brand, mission, values, and achievements. Regularly updating the company page with engaging content, sharing employee stories, and highlighting company milestones can enhance brand perception and manage the company's reputation among healthcare professionals and potential customers.

It is important to note that pharmaceutical marketing on LinkedIn should adhere to regulatory guidelines and legal requirements specific to the industry. Pharmaceutical companies must ensure compliance with relevant laws and regulations governing promotion and advertising in the healthcare sector.

LinkedIn offers many features and opportunities for pharmaceutical companies to connect with healthcare professionals, establish thought leadership, promote products or services, and build strong professional networks within the industry.

Linking Strategy

Linking Strategy in digital marketing involves systematically connecting different digital channels, tactics, and touchpoints to create a cohesive and effective marketing campaign. The goal is to provide a seamless customer experience and drive desired outcomes. Here are some examples of linking strategies in digital marketing:

A. *Cross-Channel Integration*: Integrating various digital channels such as websites, social media, email marketing, search engine optimization (SEO), search engine marketing (SEM), and display advertising. This ensures consistent messaging, brand identity, and a unified customer experience across different platforms. For example, a social media campaign can drive traffic to a website, where visitors can sign up for a newsletter or purchase.

B. *Content Marketing and SEO*: Developing valuable, informative, and engaging content to attract and engage the target audience. Linking this content with effective search engine optimization (SEO) practices helps improve organic search rankings and visibility. For example, creating blog posts or articles optimized with relevant keywords and internal links can drive organic traffic to a website and increase brand exposure.

C. *Email Marketing and Automation*: You can use email marketing campaigns to nurture leads, build customer relationships, and drive conversions. Linking email marketing with automation allows personalized and targeted messaging based on customer behavior and interests. For example, sending automated follow-up emails to prospects who have shown interest in a specific product or sending personalized recommendations based on previous purchases.

Linking Strategy in Pharma Marketing

In pharmaceutical marketing, linking strategies in digital marketing can be utilized to reach healthcare professionals, patients, and other stakeholders effectively. Here are some examples of how these strategies can be applied:

1. *Website and SEO*: Pharmaceutical companies can create informative websites with educational resources, product information, and patient support materials. By optimizing the website with relevant keywords and implementing the SEO best practices, they can improve organic search rankings and drive targeted traffic to their site. For example, a pharmaceutical company specializing in diabetes medication can create a website with valuable content about diabetes management, treatment options, and lifestyle tips to attract and engage healthcare professionals and patients searching for related information.
2. *Social Media and Influencer Marketing*: Pharma companies can establish a presence on social media platforms to engage with a target audience, share educational content, and raise awareness about specific health conditions or treatments. Partnering with healthcare

influencers, such as doctors or patient advocates, can help amplify the reach and credibility of their messaging. For instance, a pharmaceutical company focused on mental health may collaborate with a psychiatrist influencer to provide insights, answer questions, and share resources on social media platforms like Instagram or Twitter.

3. *Email Marketing and Automation*: Building a database of healthcare professionals and patients who have opted to receive communications allows pharmaceutical companies to send targeted email campaigns. These campaigns can include information about new product launches, clinical updates, disease management resources, or automated workflows that can be set up to deliver personalized content based on the recipient's preferences or actions. For example, an email marketing campaign could provide healthcare professionals with the latest clinical trial results for a particular drug, educational materials, and patient case studies.
4. *Online Continuing Medical Education (CME)*: Offering digital CME activities, such as webinars or e-learning modules, can help pharmaceutical companies engage healthcare professionals and provide them with valuable educational content. These digital channels can promote these activities, allowing healthcare professionals to access the content and earn CME credits conveniently. For instance, a pharma company specializing in cardiovascular drugs may develop an online CME course on the latest advances in managing heart disease, which cardiologists and other relevant healthcare professionals can access.
5. *Patient Support Apps and Tools*: Developing mobile applications or online tools that assist patients in managing their conditions or treatment can be an effective linking strategy. These apps can provide features like medication reminders, symptom trackers, or lifestyle tips. Pharma companies can promote these apps through digital marketing channels and healthcare providers to improve patient engagement and medication adherence. For example, a pharmaceutical company focusing on asthma treatment might create a mobile app that allows patients to track their symptoms, set reminders for medication doses, and access additional resources about asthma management.
6. *Data Analytics and Personalization*: Leveraging data analytics tools and customer insights can help pharmaceutical companies personalize their marketing efforts. They can segment their audience and deliver targeted messages by analyzing data such as prescription patterns, patient demographics, or online behavior. For instance, a pharma company specializing in oncology treatments may use data analytics to identify healthcare providers more likely to prescribe their drug based on patient profiles and treatment history. They can then create personalized marketing campaigns tailored to the needs and interests of those providers.

It is important to note that pharmaceutical marketing is subject to strict regulations, including privacy, data security, and advertising practices. Therefore, compliance with applicable laws and guidelines is essential.

Lobbying

Lobbying refers to attempting to influence decisions made by government officials, politicians, or other policymakers. In the pharmaceutical industry, lobbying typically involves efforts to shape legislation, regulations, or other policies related to healthcare or the pharmaceutical industry.

Pharmaceutical companies engage in lobbying to protect their interests and promote their agenda. Some common goals of pharmaceutical lobbying include:

1. Promoting Policies that support research and development of new drugs and medical technologies.
2. Influencing pricing and reimbursement policies to ensure that drugs are affordable and accessible to patients.
3. Advocating for policies that protect intellectual property rights and encourage innovation in the industry.
4. Shaping regulations related to drug safety, clinical trials, and marketing practices.
5. Opposing policies that could threaten the profitability of pharmaceutical companies, such as price controls or restrictions on direct-to-consumer advertising.

Pharmaceutical industry lobbying can take many forms, including directly lobbying policymakers, campaign contributions to political candidates, and participation in industry trade associations or other advocacy groups.

Lobbying is a controversial practice, as some argue it can lead to undue influence by powerful corporations over the political process. However, others argue that lobbying is a legitimate way for businesses to advocate for their interests and promote policies that benefit the industry and the public.

How Pharma Does Lobbying

Lobbying in the pharmaceutical industry can take many forms but typically involves efforts to influence policymakers at the federal, state, or local level. Some common strategies and tactics used in pharmaceutical lobbying include:

1. *Direct Lobbying*: This involves meeting with policymakers, lawmakers, or government officials to promote a particular policy or agenda. Pharmaceutical lobbyists may meet with members of Congress, regulators, or officials at government agencies such as the FDA (Food and Drug Administration) or CMS (Centers for Medicare & Medicaid Services).
2. *Grassroots Lobbying* involves mobilizing patients, healthcare providers, or other stakeholders for a particular policy or agenda. For example, pharmaceutical companies may encourage patients or patient advocacy groups to write letters or call their elected representatives to support specific legislation or policy proposals.
3. *Campaign Contributions*: Pharmaceutical companies may contribute money to political candidates who support their industry or policy agenda. These contributions may be made directly to individual campaigns or political action committees (PACs) that support specific candidates or parties.
4. *Industry Trade Associations*: Pharmaceutical companies may join industry associations such as PhRMA (Pharmaceutical Research and Manufacturers of America) or BiO (Biotechnology Innovation Organization) to advocate for policies supporting the industry collectively. These associations may also engage in lobbying activities for their member companies.
5. *Think Tanks and Policy Groups*: Pharmaceutical companies may fund or work with think tanks or policy groups that conduct research and advocacy related to healthcare policy. For example, these groups may publish reports, host events, or engage in other activities to influence policymakers and the public.

How Pharma Spends on Lobbying

Pharmaceutical companies and their trade associations are known to spend significant amounts of money on lobbying each year. According to the Center for Responsive Politics, which tracks lobbying spending by industry, the pharmaceutical and health products industry spent over $306 million on lobbying in 2020. This was the highest amount any industry spent, representing a slight decrease from the $313 million spent in 2019.

Individual pharmaceutical companies also spend large amounts on lobbying. For example, in 2020, Pfizer spent over $11 million on lobbying, while Johnson & Johnson spent over $9 million. Other top-spending pharmaceutical companies included Eli Lilly, Merck, and Novartis.

Pharmaceutical lobbying efforts typically focus on various issues related to healthcare policy and drug pricing, including efforts to influence legislation related to Medicare and Medicaid, drug safety and regulation, and intellectual property rights. Some critics argue that pharmaceutical lobbying can significantly influence public policy and may contribute to rising drug prices and other problems in the healthcare system. However, industry supporters argue that lobbying is a legitimate way to promote public policies that support innovation and improve patient access to new treatments.

Localization

Localization refers to adapting a product, service, or content to meet a particular target market or local cultural, linguistic, and functional requirements. It involves making modifications and adjustments to ensure that the product or content is well-received and effectively meets the needs and preferences of the local audience.

Localization goes beyond translation and considers various aspects of the target market, including language, cultural norms, local regulations, technical specifications, and user experience. It aims to create a seamless and natural experience for users in the target market, making the product or content feel like it was created for them.

The process of localization can include the following components:

1. *Language Translation*: Adapting written or spoken content, such as product labels, user interfaces, websites, marketing materials, or customer support, into the local language of the target market.
2. *Cultural Adaptation*: Considering cultural nuances, preferences, and sensitivities when adapting content is important. This includes adjusting images, symbols, colors, idiomatic expressions, and references to align with local culture.
3. *Formatting and Design*: Adjusting content layout, design, and formatting to align with local preferences and standards. This includes

considerations such as date formats, currency symbols, measurement units, and visual aesthetics.

4. *Localization of Images and Multimedia*: Replacing or modifying images, graphics, videos, or audio elements to suit the target market's cultural context, demographics, and sensitivities.
5. *Local Regulations and Compliance*: Ensuring the product or content meets local legal and regulatory requirements. This can involve adherence to privacy laws, labeling guidelines, product certifications, or industry-specific regulations.
6. *User Experience (UX)*: Adapting the user interface (UI) and user experience design to match the expectations and behaviors of the target market. This includes considerations for navigation, usability, user preferences, and accessibility requirements.

Localization is essential for successful market entry and expansion into new regions or countries. It allows companies to effectively communicate and engage with local customers, enhance user experience, build trust, and tailor their offerings to meet local market demands. By investing in localization efforts, businesses can increase their chances of market acceptance and success in diverse global markets.

Localization in Pharma Marketing

Localization in pharma marketing involves adapting marketing strategies and materials to reach and resonate with specific target markets or regions effectively. In addition, it ensures that the marketing efforts align with the intended audience's local culture, language, regulations, and preferences. Here are some examples of how localization can be applied in pharma marketing:

1. *Language Adaptation*: Localize marketing content, including brochures, websites, product labels, and packaging, by translating them into the local language. This ensures the information is easily understood and accessible to the target market.
2. *Cultural Sensitivity*: Adapt marketing messages and visuals to align with the local audience's cultural norms, values, and sensitivities. This includes considering aspects such as imagery, symbols, color choices, and content tone to resonate positively with the target culture.
3. *Regulatory Compliance*: Ensure all marketing materials and strategies comply with local regulations and guidelines. This includes adhering to specific rules regarding pharmaceutical advertising, product claims, or disclosure requirements in the target market.
4. *Market-Specific Campaigns*: Develop marketing campaigns tailored to the local market's needs, preferences, and healthcare systems. This may involve highlighting regional health concerns, showing local patient testimonials, or addressing the target audience's unique challenges.
5. *Local Key Opinion Leaders (KOLs)*: Collaborating with local healthcare professionals and KOLs to endorse and promote pharmaceutical products. Leveraging the influence and expertise of respected local experts can enhance credibility and trust among the target market.
6. *Patient Education and Support*: Localize patient education materials, support programs, and resources to address the specific healthcare practices, patient expectations, and cultural considerations of the target market. This ensures that patients receive relevant and accessible information that empowers them to make informed decisions about their healthcare.
7. *Digital Marketing Localization*: Adapting digital marketing strategies to the preferences and behavior of the local audience may involve optimizing websites for local search engines, using region-specific local media platforms, and leveraging local influencers to enhance brand visibility and engagement.

These examples demonstrate how localization is crucial in pharma marketing, allowing pharmaceutical companies to effectively communicate their message, build trust, and engage with their target audience in different regions or markets. In addition, by tailoring marketing efforts to local cultures, languages, and regulations, companies can increase the relevance and effectiveness of their campaigns and drive better market penetration and acceptance.

Logo

In pharmaceutical marketing, the logo is crucial in representing a pharmaceutical company or a specific pharmaceutical product. Here are some key considerations for the use of logos in pharma marketing:

1. *Brand Identity*: The logo serves as a visual representation of the brand identity of a pharmaceutical company or product. It should embody the brand's core values, mission, and unique attributes. The design, colors, and typography used in the logo should align with the overall brand positioning and messaging.

2. *Recognition and Credibility*: A well-designed logo helps create brand recognition and differentiation in a crowded marketplace. It should be distinctive and memorable, enabling customers and stakeholders to identify the brand or product easily. A unique and recognizable logo can help pharmaceutical companies stand out from competitors and build a strong brand presence.
3. *Trust and Credibility*: The logo plays a role in establishing trust and credibility. A professionally designed and visually appealing logo can convey a sense of professionalism, quality, and reliability. In addition, it should instill confidence in healthcare professionals, patients, and other stakeholders that the pharmaceutical company or product meets the highest safety and efficacy standards.
4. *Consistency*: Consistency in logo usage is essential for effective branding. The logo should be used consistently across all marketing materials, including packaging, promotional materials, websites, social media platforms, and other communication channels. Consistent use of the logo helps reinforce brand recognition and strengthens brand equity over time.
5. *Compliance*: In pharma marketing, logos must comply with regulatory requirements specific to the pharmaceutical industry. These regulations may dictate the logo's size, placement, and content, ensuring it does not mislead or exaggerate the product's benefits. Therefore, it is important to adhere to guidelines set by regulatory authorities to maintain compliance.
6. *Adaptability*: The logo should be adaptable to different formats and sizes without compromising its visual integrity. It should look clear and legible, whether displayed on large-scale advertisements, small packaging labels, or digital platforms. The logo should also be scalable to ensure optimal appearance across various mediums.
7. *Evolvability*: While logos provide consistency and brand recognition, they should also have the potential for evolution over time. As a pharmaceutical company or product evolves, the logo may need updates or modifications to reflect branding, messaging, or market positioning changes. However, it is important to carefully manage logo updates to maintain brand recognition and avoid confusing customers.

In summary, logos in pharmaceutical marketing visually represent a pharmaceutical company or product, embodying brand identity, differentiation, trust, and consistency. As a result, they play a critical role in building brand recognition, establishing credibility, and fostering a strong connection with healthcare professionals, patients, and other stakeholders in the pharmaceutical industry.

Long Tail

The Long Tail concept in economics and business describes the phenomenon of many niche products or services collectively making up a significant portion of total sales or demand, even though each product or service may sell in relatively small quantities.

Chris Anderson popularized the term Long Tail in his book *The Long Tail: Why the Future of Business is Selling Less of More*. Anderson argued that the rise of digital technologies and online marketplaces has made it easier and more cost-effective for companies to offer various niche products and services. This led to a shift away from focusing on blockbuster products and hit-driven business models.

The long tail is often visualized as a graph, with the head representing a small number of popular products that account for the majority of sales and the tail representing a large number of niche products that collectively account for a significant share of sales. In many cases, the tail may be longer than the head, meaning that the combined sales of niche products may exceed the sales of popular products.

The long tail has important implications for businesses, as it suggests that there may be significant opportunities to tap into niche markets and serve specialized customer needs. However, it also requires companies to adopt new business models and strategies better suited to serving these markets, such as using digital technologies to reach and engage niche audiences and offering personalized or customized products and services.

Long Tail in Pharma Marketing

The long tail in pharma marketing refers to targeting niche markets or rare diseases with specialized products and services. This approach is based on the idea that while the demand for mainstream healthcare products and services may be high, many smaller markets with unique needs and preferences can also be served profitably. Here are some examples of how the long tail strategy can be applied to pharma marketing:

A. *Rare Disease Medication*: Pharmaceutical companies that produce medications for rare diseases often use the long tail strategy to target niche markets with specialized needs. While the patient populations for these diseases may be small, the high cost of these medications and the lack of alternative treatments make them highly profitable.

B. *Personalized Medicine*: Personalized medicine involves tailoring treatments to individual patients based on their unique genetic or biological characteristics. This approach is based on the idea that one size does not fit all and that treatments can be more effective and efficient when customized to the individual. While personalized medicine is still in its early stages, it has the potential to revolutionize the pharma industry by targeting smaller patient populations with highly specific needs.

C. *Digital Health Solutions*: Digital health solutions, such as mobile apps, wearables, and telemedicine services, can target niche markets with specialized healthcare needs. For example, a company may develop a mobile app that tracks symptoms and provides personalized treatment recommendations for a specific condition or a telemedicine service that connects patients with specialized healthcare providers in remote or underserved areas.

The long tail strategy can be a powerful way for pharma companies to identify and target underserved markets with specialized needs. By developing products and services that meet the unique needs of these markets, companies can create value for patients and differentiate themselves from competitors. However, the long tail strategy also requires careful market research and product development and a willingness to take risks and invest in new markets with uncertain demand.

Long-range Planning

Long-range planning in pharmaceutical marketing refers to developing a strategic plan for the organization that covers several years, typically three to five years or longer. This type of planning involves setting long-term goals and objectives, identifying opportunities and threats in the market, and developing strategies to achieve the desired outcomes.

In pharma marketing, long-range planning may involve various activities, such as:

1. *Conducting a Market Analysis*: This involves gathering information about the market trends, competitive landscape, and customer needs and preferences. This information can help pharma companies identify opportunities and threats in the market and develop strategies to capitalize on them.
2. *Setting Long-term Goals*: Based on the market analysis, pharma companies can set long-term goals and objectives for the organization, such as increasing market share, launching new products, or expanding into new markets.
3. *Developing Marketing Strategies*: To achieve long-term goals, pharma companies must develop marketing strategies aligned with the overall strategic plan. This may involve developing promotional campaigns, pricing strategies, distribution strategies, or other tactics.
4. *Allocating Resources*: Long-range planning also involves allocating resources, such as budgets and personnel, to support marketing strategies and achieve long-term goals.
5. *Monitoring and Evaluation*: Finally, pharmaceutical companies need to monitor and evaluate the effectiveness of their marketing strategies and adjust them as needed to ensure they achieve the desired outcomes.

Long-range planning in pharma marketing is critical for ensuring the organization is well-positioned to achieve its goals and remain competitive in the marketplace over the long term. It requires a deep understanding of the market and customer needs and the ability to develop and execute effective marketing strategies aligned with the overall strategic plan.

Longitudinal Research

Longitudinal research is a type of research design that involves studying individuals or groups over an extended period. The goal of longitudinal research is to observe changes or patterns in behavior, attitudes, or other variables over time and to understand how these changes relate to other factors.

Longitudinal research may involve collecting data from individuals or groups at multiple time points, which allows researchers to track changes in behavior or other variables over time. This data can be collected through various methods, including surveys, interviews, observations, medical tests, or other measures.

One of the key advantages of longitudinal research is that it can provide insights into how variables are related over time and how they might interact with other factors. For example, longitudinal research may help identify risk factors for certain health conditions or track changes in health outcomes over time.

Longitudinal research can also help researchers understand the effects of interventions or treatments over time. By tracking individuals or groups over an extended period, researchers can determine whether interventions or treatments have a sustained effect or whether the effect diminishes over time.

Longitudinal research is a valuable tool for understanding how variables change or interact over time and evaluating the effects of interventions or treatments over an extended period. It is widely used in various fields, including healthcare, social sciences, and psychology.

Conducting Longitudinal Research

Conducting longitudinal research involves several steps, which may vary depending on the research question, study design, and data collection methods. However, here are some general steps to consider when conducting longitudinal research:

1. *Define the Research Question*: Define the research question you want to answer through the longitudinal study. This will help guide the study design and data collection methods.
2. *Develop the Study Design*: Decide on the study design, which may include collecting data from the same individuals or groups at different time points. You will also need to determine the frequency and duration of data collection and the methods you will use to collect the data.
3. *Select the Study Participants*: Identify the individuals or groups you will study. They should be representative of the population you want to generalize your findings to.
4. *Collect Baseline Data*: Collect baseline data at the start of the study, which will serve as a point of comparison for later data collection.
5. *Collect Follow-up Data*: Collect follow-up data at regular intervals, using the same or similar methods as the baseline data collection.
6. *Analyze the Data*: Use appropriate statistical methods like regression or time series analysis to analyze the data.
7. *Interpret the Results*: Consider any limitations or biases in the study design or data collection methods.
8. *Draw Conclusions and Make Recommendations*: Draw conclusions and recommendations for future research or practice based on the results.

Conducting longitudinal research requires careful planning, attention to detail, and rigorous data collection and analysis methods. It can be time-consuming and resource-intensive, but it can provide valuable insights into how variables change or interact over time and how interventions or treatments affect outcomes over an extended period.

Longitudinal Research in Pharma Marketing

Longitudinal research in pharma marketing refers to studying patients or other relevant populations over an extended period to understand changes in behavior, attitudes, or health outcomes. This type of research can provide valuable insights into the effectiveness of marketing interventions and the long-term impact of pharmaceutical products.

Longitudinal research in pharma marketing may involve collecting data from patients or other relevant populations over several months, years, or even decades. This can be done through various methods, including surveys, interviews, medical records, and other data sources.

One of the main advantages of longitudinal research is that it allows pharmaceutical companies to track changes in patient behavior and health outcomes over time and to evaluate the effectiveness of marketing interventions of pharmaceutical products over an extended period. For example, longitudinal research can help identify whether patients who receive certain pharmaceutical products experience better health outcomes over the long term than those who do not or whether targeted marketing campaigns sustain patient behavior.

Longitudinal research can also help pharmaceutical companies better understand the needs and preferences of their target patient populations and develop more effective marketing strategies and interventions tailored to their specific needs. By collecting data on patient behavior and health outcomes over time, companies can identify trends and patterns in patient behavior and preferences and use this information to develop more targeted marketing campaigns and interventions that better meet the needs of patients.

In summary, Longitudinal research is an important tool in pharma marketing, as it allows companies to track changes in patient behavior and health outcomes over time and to develop more effective marketing strategies and interventions tailored to their patient populations' needs.

Loss Leader

A loss leader is a pricing strategy in which a product is sold at a price lower than its cost or at a very low margin to attract customers to a store or business and stimulate the sales of other, more profitable products or services.

The idea behind a loss leader is that while the initial sale of the product may result in a loss, the increased traffic and sales generated by the promotion will ultimately result in a net gain for the business. For example, a grocery store may offer a deep discount on a popular product, such as milk or bread, to attract customers. While the store may lose money on the sale of the discounted product, it may make up for this loss by selling other products at higher margins to these customers. Loss leaders are often used in retail and e-commerce. Still, they can also be used in other industries, such as telecommunications, where companies may offer discounted or free products or services to attract customers and generate revenue from other services, such as data plans or additional features.

While using loss leaders can be an effective marketing strategy for businesses, it also carries some risks, such as the possibility of customers only buying discounted products and not purchasing other, more profitable products. Additionally, offering products at low prices for extended periods can erode profit margins and lead to financial difficulties for businesses.

Loss Leader: Is it Relevant to Pharma Marketing?

Loss leaders are not as common in pharma marketing as in retail or e-commerce, as pharmaceuticals are highly regulated, and pricing is often determined by factors such as production costs, R&D expenses, and market demand. However, there are certain ways in which loss leaders can be relevant to pharma marketing. Consider the following, for example:

A. *Patient Assistance Programs*: Patient assistance programs could be one way of a loss leader approach in pharma marketing. Pharmaceutical companies offer financial assistance or discounts to patients who cannot afford the full price of a medication. While these programs result in lower revenue per patient, they can help to build brand loyalty and generate positive PR (Public Relations) for the company.

B. *Clinical Trials*: In some cases, pharmaceutical companies may invest heavily in developing and testing a new medication or therapy, even if the likelihood of commercial success is uncertain. While the cost of developing and testing the product may exceed the revenue generated from its eventual sales, the company may see this investment as a loss leader that helps to establish its reputation as an innovator in the industry.

While the concept of loss leaders may not be as applicable to pharma marketing as it is to other industries, there are still ways in which pharmaceutical companies can use this strategy to build brand awareness, generate positive PR, and establish themselves as innovators in the industry.

Low-Involvement Hierarchy

The low involvement hierarchy in pharmaceutical marketing is a model that describes how patients make decisions about their healthcare when the decision-making process is not highly involved or emotionally charged. This model consists of three stages:

1. *Awareness*: In this stage, patients become aware of their condition and the available treatment options. This may be through general advertising or educational campaigns.
2. *Consideration*: In this stage, patients consider different treatment options and evaluate the benefits and drawbacks of each. This may involve researching online, talking to healthcare providers, or seeking advice from friends and family.
3. *Trial*: Patients try a treatment and evaluate its effectiveness in this stage. This may involve starting a new medication or undergoing a new treatment regimen.

In the low involvement hierarchy, patients are not highly invested in decision-making and may rely on shortcuts or heuristics to make decisions. These shortcuts may include choosing a well-known brand, a medication based on a healthcare provider's recommendation, or a medication with a lower price point.

Pharmaceutical companies can use the low involvement hierarchy to develop marketing strategies that target patients at each stage of the decision-making process. For example, in the awareness stage, companies can use advertising and educational campaigns to raise awareness of their products and the conditions they treat. Next, in the consideration stage, companies can focus on highlighting the benefits and features of their products and differentiating them from competitors. Finally, in the trial stage, companies can provide support services such as patient assistance programs to ensure patients can access and use their products correctly.

By understanding the low involvement hierarchy and developing targeted marketing strategies, pharma companies can effectively reach and influence patients who may be less invested in decision-making and improve patient outcomes.

Low-Involvement Product

In pharmaceutical marketing, low-involvement products are those that consumers do not spend a lot of time or effort researching or evaluating before making a purchase decision. Instead, these products may be perceived as routine or necessary, and consumers may rely on habit, familiarity, or convenience when choosing which products to purchase.

Examples of low-involvement products in pharma marketing include over-the-counter (OTC) medications, such as pain relievers, cold and flu remedies, and allergy medications. These products are widely available and do not require a prescription, so consumers may purchase them based on brand recognition, price, or other factors without spending much time researching or evaluating their options.

Pharmaceutical companies may use various marketing strategies to promote low-involvement products, such as offering discounts, eye-catching packaging, or emphasizing the convenience and accessibility of the product. They may also use advertising or promotional campaigns to increase brand awareness and familiarity, which can help consumers make purchasing decisions more quickly and easily.

Low-involvement products in pharma marketing may not require the same marketing effort or investment as high-involvement products, which may require more extensive education, demonstration, or clinical trial data to persuade consumers to try them. However, they can still be an important part of a pharma company's product portfolio and marketing strategy, as they can provide a steady stream of revenue and help build brand recognition and loyalty over time.

Loyalty

Loyalty in pharmaceutical marketing refers to the commitment of patients, healthcare providers, and other stakeholders to a particular pharmaceutical brand or company. It is the willingness of these individuals to continue to use a particular medication or product, despite the availability of alternatives.

Loyalty is an important factor in the pharmaceutical industry because it can drive revenue growth and improve patient outcomes. For example, patients loyal to a particular brand are more likely to continue using that medication over time, which can lead to increased sales and revenue for the pharmaceutical company. In addition, loyal patients may be more likely to adhere to their medication regimen and experience better health outcomes.

In pharma marketing, loyalty is created and maintained through various strategies and programs focusing on building strong relationships with patients and healthcare providers. These may include patient assistance programs, loyalty programs, educational initiatives, and other resources that support patients and improve their treatment experience.

Loyalty in pharma marketing is about creating positive experiences for patients and healthcare providers and building strong relationships that lead to a long-term commitment to a particular brand or company.

Loyalty Effect

The loyalty effect is that loyal customers are more profitable to a business than new customers. It refers to the positive impact that customer loyalty has on a company's revenue and profitability over time.

The loyalty effect is based on the idea that loyal customers are more likely to purchase from a company repeatedly and more likely to recommend the company's products or services to others. This can lead to increased sales and revenue for the company.

In addition, loyal customers lead to be more forgiving of occasional mistakes or errors made by the company, which can help to mitigate any negative impact on the company's reputation or sales.

The loyalty effect can be especially important in industries like pharmaceuticals, where competition is often high. As a result, customers may be likelier to stick with a particular brand or product over time. As a result, pharmaceutical companies can drive revenue growth and build a strong and sustainable business by building customer loyalty through programs and strategies designed to retain customers.

How to Improve Loyalty Effect

Creating and improving loyalty in pharma marketing involves developing strategies and programs that build strong relationships with patients, healthcare professionals, and other stakeholders in the healthcare ecosystem. Here are some specific steps that pharmaceutical companies can take to create and improve the loyalty effect in their marketing efforts:

1. *Focus on Patient Needs*: Pharmaceutical companies should focus on meeting the needs of patients by providing high-quality products, patient-centered services, and support programs that help patients manage their conditions.
2. *Provide Excellent Customer Service*: Excellent customer service can help build trust and loyalty with patients and healthcare providers. This includes responding to patient inquiries, providing clear and concise medication information, and offering support throughout treatment.
3. *Use Data to Personalize Marketing Efforts*: Pharmaceutical companies can use data analytics to understand patient preferences and behaviors and to personalize marketing efforts to meet their needs better.

4. *Build Relationships with Healthcare Providers*: Building strong relationships with healthcare providers can help drive prescriptions and referrals and improve patient outcomes. This can be achieved through educational initiatives, training programs, and other resources that support healthcare providers.
5. *Offer Patient Assistance Programs*: Patient assistance programs, such as co-pay cards, coupons, or other discounts, can help to make medications more affordable and accessible to patients. In addition, these programs can help to build loyalty by providing patients with financial support and reducing barriers to treatment.
6. *Use Loyalty Programs*: Loyalty programs incentivizing patients who continue to use a particular medication or brand can also help build brand loyalty. These programs can include rewards points, discounts, or other perks to encourage patients to stay loyal to a brand.

Pharmaceutical companies can create and improve the loyalty effect in their marketing efforts by creating a positive experience for patients and healthcare professionals and providing personalized support and assistance. This can help to drive revenue growth, improve patient outcomes, and build a sustainable business over the long term

Loyalty Marketing

Loyalty marketing in the pharmaceutical industry involves strategies and programs designed to retain existing customers and increase their loyalty to a pharmaceutical brand or company. The goal is to create a long-term relationship between the pharmaceutical company and its customers, leading to increased sales and revenue.

One common approach to loyalty marketing in pharma is using patient assistance programs (PAPs) that financially support patients who cannot afford their medications. These programs help build brand loyalty by making it easier for patients to access the needed medications. In addition to PAPs, pharmaceutical companies may also offer loyalty programs that provide initiatives and rewards to patients who continue to use their medications.

Another important aspect of loyalty marketing in pharma is providing excellent customer service. Pharmaceutical companies can differentiate themselves from competitors by offering superior customer service and support. This includes providing clear and concise medication information, promptly answering patient questions, and providing ongoing support throughout treatment.

Loyalty Marketing Strategies in Pharma: Some Examples

Here are some examples of loyalty marketing strategies in the pharmaceutical industry:

1. *Patient Assistance Program (PAP)*: Pharmaceutical companies may offer PAPs to provide financial assistance to patients who cannot afford their medications. This can include co-pay cards, coupons, or other discounts that help lower the medication cost and make it more accessible to patients.
2. *Loyalty Programs*: Pharmaceutical companies may also offer loyalty programs that incentivize and reward patients who continue to use their medications. These programs can include rewards points, discounts, or other perks to encourage patients to stay loyal to a brand.
3. *Educational Resource*: Pharmaceutical companies may provide educational resources to patients and healthcare professionals to help them better understand a particular condition or medication. This can include patient education materials, online resources, or educational events.
4. *Mobile Apps*: Some pharmaceutical companies have developed mobile apps that provide patients personalized support, medication reminders, and other resources to help them manage their condition. These apps can help build brand loyalty by providing patients with a convenient and easy-to-use tool to help them stay on top of their treatment.
5. *Patient Support Services*: Some pharmaceutical companies have dedicated teams that provide patient support services, such as nurse helplines, case management, or counseling services. These services can help build trust and loyalty with patients by providing personalized support throughout their treatment journey.

Loyalty marketing in pharma is about building strong relationships with patients, healthcare professionals, and other stakeholders in the healthcare ecosystem. As a result, pharmaceutical companies can increase customer loyalty, improve patient outcomes, and drive business growth.

M

1. 2x2 Matrix
2. Machiavellian Marketing
3. Machine Learning
4. Macro Segmentation
5. Macro-Environment
6. Mailing List
7. Managed Care
8. Managed Care Organization (MCO)
9. Management by Objectives (MBO)
10. Management Ratios
11. Many-to-One Communication
12. Marketing Assets
13. Marketing Collateral
14. Marketing Ethics
15. Marginal Analysis
16. Marginal Cost Pricing
17. Mark-up
18. Market
19. Market Acceptance
20. Market Access
21. Market Aggregation
22. Market Approval
23. Market Atomization
24. Market Attractiveness
25. Market Capitalization
26. Market Connection
27. Market Coverage
28. Market Cycles
29. Market Demand
30. Market Development
31. Market Dynamics
32. Market Ecology
33. Market Indicators
34. Market Lifecycle
35. Market Maps
36. Market Niche
37. Market Opportunity Analysis
38. Market Penetration
39. Market Positioning
40. Market Potential
41. Market Reach
42. Market Research
43. Market Segmentation
44. Market Share
45. Market Testing
46. Market Value
47. Marketing Audit
48. Marketing Authorization Application
49. Marketing Automation
50. Marketing Channels
51. Marketing Communications
52. Marketing Concept
53. Marketing Costs
54. Marketing Environmental Audit
55. Marketing History
56. Marketing Information System (MIS)
57. Marketing Intelligence
58. Marketing Intermediaries
59. Marketing Laws
60. Marketing Metrics
61. Marketing Mindset
62. Marketing Mix
63. Marketing Models
64. Marketing Myopia
65. Marketing Planning
66. Marketing Plans
67. Marketing Productivity Audit
68. Marketing Research
69. Marketing Strategy
70. Marketing Systems Audit
71. Markov Model
72. Mark-Up
73. MarTech
74. Mass Customization
75. Mass Marketing
76. Mechanism of Action (MOA)

77. Media
78. Media Mentions
79. Media Planning
80. Media Relations
81. Media Strategy
82. Medicaid
83. Medical Advertising
84. Medical Affairs
85. Medicalization
86. Medical Representative
87. Medical Science Liaison
88. Medicare
89. Medication Utilization
90. Medico-marketing
91. Memory Decay
92. Mergers and Acquisitions
93. Message
94. Message Management
95. Meta Tags
96. Meta Verse
97. Metcalfe's Law
98. Me-too
99. Micro Markets
100. Micro-marketing
101. Micro-segmentation
102. Microsites
103. Microsoft
104. MLR
105. Milking Strategy
106. Mission
107. Mission Statement
108. Mixed Reality
109. Mnemonics
110. Mobile Apps
111. Mobile Marketing
112. Modern Marketing Principles
113. Modular Content
114. Moments of Truth
115. Monitoring
116. Moore's Law
117. Motivation
118. Multichannel Marketing
119. Multidimensional Scaling
120. Multivariate Analysis

2 x 2 Matrix

A 2x2 matrix is a visual framework that analyzes and categorizes marketing strategies, products, or market segments based on two dimensions. It provides a simple and effective way to understand different aspects of a marketing situation or make strategic decisions. The dimensions used in a 2x2 matrix can vary depending on the specific context. Here are a few common examples:

1. *Market Attractiveness vs. Competitive Position*: This matrix assesses different market segments or products based on their attractiveness and competitive position. Market attractiveness may include size, growth rate, profitability, or customer demand. Competitive position refers to the company's ability to effectively compete within that market segment, considering factors like brand strength, market share, or competitive advantage. The matrix helps identify segments/products that are highly attractive and where the company has a strong competitive position (ideal), segments/products that are attractive but where the company is at a disadvantage (challenging), segments/products that are less attractive but where the company has a strong competitive position (niche opportunities), and segments/products that are both unattractive and where the company is at a disadvantage (least favorable).
2. *Customer Needs vs. Product Features*: This matrix focuses on understanding customer needs and how well a product or service meets those needs. Customer needs can be identified through market research and may include factors such as price, quality, convenience, performance, or innovation. Product features may refer to the attributes or characteristics of the offering. The matrix helps identify areas where the product aligns well with customer needs (sweet spot), areas where customer needs are not fully met (improvement opportunities), areas where customer needs are met but the product offers more than necessary (overkill), and areas where both customer needs and product features are not aligned (weak areas).
3. *Risk vs. Reward*: This matrix evaluates marketing strategies or investment opportunities based on risk levels and potential rewards. Risk can be assessed regarding financial, operational, or market-related uncertainties. Rewards can include revenue growth, market share gains, profitability, or brand equity. The matrix helps identify strategies or investments with high potential rewards and low risks (high-priority opportunities), high potential rewards but also high risks (strategic bets), low potential rewards but low risks (incremental improvements), and low potential rewards and high risks (caution or avoidance).

These are just a few examples of how a 2x2 matrix can be applied in marketing. In addition, the specific dimensions can be tailored to the marketing context or the problem being addressed, allowing marketers to gain insights and make data-informed decisions.

2x2 Matrix in Pharma Marketing

In pharmaceutical marketing, a 2x2 matrix can be used as a visual tool to categorize and analyze different aspects of marketing strategies or initiatives. It helps organize information and evaluate options based on two dimensions or criteria.

For example, in pharmaceutical marketing, a 2x2 matrix can assess marketing tactics based on their effectiveness and feasibility. The two dimensions can be defined as follows:

1. *Effectiveness*: This dimension measures a marketing tactic's potential impact or success in achieving its intended goals. It could include market reach, customer engagement, brand awareness, or sales impact.
2. *Feasibility*: This dimension evaluates the practicality and ease of implementing a marketing tactic. It considers available resources, time requirements, regulatory constraints, or internal capabilities.

Based on these dimensions, marketing tactics can be plotted in one of the four quadrants of the matrix:

1. *High Effectiveness, High Feasibility*: Highly effective and feasible tactics are considered top priorities and should be pursued enthusiastically. These tactics have a strong potential to drive results and can be implemented relatively easily.
2. *High Effectiveness, Low Feasibility*: Highly effective but less feasible tactics may require additional resources, planning, or collaboration. Strategies in this quadrant may require careful evaluation and consideration of the feasibility challenges before implementation.
3. *Low Effectiveness, High Feasibility*: Tactics that are feasible but less effective may be suitable for implementation with specific constraints or limitations. These tactics might not significantly impact marketing goals but can be considered for tactical or operational reasons.
4. *Low Effectiveness, Low Feasibility*: Tactics that are neither effective nor feasible should generally be avoided, as they are unlikely to contribute to marketing objectives and may consume unnecessary resources.

Using a 2x2 matrix, pharmaceutical marketers can visually assess and prioritize marketing tactics based on their potential impact and practicality, helping them make informed decisions and allocate resources effectively.

Machiavellian Marketing

Machiavellian Marketing refers to applying manipulative and cunning tactics in marketing strategies, taking inspiration from the ideas presented in Nicolò Machiavelli's book, *The Prince.*

Machiavelli was an Italian political philosopher who wrote about political power and the strategies leaders employ to gain and maintain control.

In marketing, Machiavellian tactics involve using calculated and often unethical means to achieve marketing goals, such as increasing sales, market share, or brand visibility. These tactics often prioritize short-term gains and may disregard ethical considerations or the long-term impact on customer relationships. Here are some examples of Machiavellian marketing tactics:

1. *Deception and Manipulation*: This involves intentionally misleading consumers through false advertising, exaggerated claims, or withholding important information to create a favorable perception of the product or brand.
2. *Exploiting Vulnerabilities*: Identifying and exploiting the weaknesses or insecurities of consumers to influence their purchasing decisions. This could create fear, guilt, or anxiety to drive sales or persuade consumers to purchase impulsively.
3. *Aggressive Competition*: Adopting ruthless and cutthroat tactics to eliminate competitors or gain a dominant position in the market. This may involve spreading false rumors, engaging in predatory pricing, or using legal maneuvers to hinder competitors.
4. *Influencer Manipulation*: Exploiting social media influencers or opinion leaders' influence and trust by offering undisclosed incentives or engaging in unethical practices to promote a product or brand.

Machiavellian tactics must be generally frowned upon and considered unethical and illegal in most professional and societal contexts. This is because they can lead to negative consequences such as damaged brand reputation, loss of customer trust, and potential legal repercussions. On the other hand, ethical marketing practices focus on building long-term relationships, providing value to customers, and maintaining transparency and integrity in all marketing activities.

Machiavellian Marketing in Pharma

In the pharmaceutical industry, the term Machiavellian marketing is not commonly used. However, it is important to note that the pharmaceutical industry, like any other industry, can face ethical challenges in marketing practices. Ethical marketing in the pharmaceutical industry emphasizes the importance of responsibly promoting products and services, with patients' well-being and safety as the top priority. The industry is heavily regulated to ensure that pharmaceutical companies adhere to ethical standards in their marketing efforts. However, there have been instances where unethical marketing practices have been observed in pharmaceutical marketing. Here are some examples:

1. *Off-labelPromotion*: Promoting a drug for uses that regulatory authorities have not approved can involve misleading or exaggerating the benefits of a drug or downplaying its potential risks.
2. *Direct-to-Consumer Advertising*: While direct-to-consumer advertising is legal in some countries, it can raise ethical concerns if the advertisements are misleading, present incomplete information, or overly promote the benefits without adequately addressing potential risks or side effects.
3. *Gifts and Incentives*: Providing gifts, trips, or financial incentives to healthcare professionals to influence their prescribing behavior. This can raise concerns about the objectivity and independence of medical practitioners and potentially compromise patient care.
4. *Disease Mongering*: Inflating the severity or prevalence of a disease to create a market for a particular drug. This can involve manipulating information or exaggerating symptoms to drive demand for pharmaceutical products.

Pharmaceutical companies must comply with ethical guidelines and regulations in their marketing practices. Many countries have regulatory bodies that monitor and enforce ethical standards in pharmaceutical marketing, such as the US Food and Drug Administration (FDA) in the United States or the European Medicines Agency (EMA) in the European Union. To maintain ethical marketing practices in the pharmaceutical industry, transparency, accurate information, and adherence to regulatory guidelines are essential. In addition, pharmaceutical companies should focus on providing healthcare professionals and patients with reliable and unbiased information about their products, ensuring that the benefits and risks are appropriately communicated.

Machine Learning

Machine Learning (ML) is a subset of artificial intelligence (AI) that focuses on developing algorithms that allow computers to learn from and make predictions or decisions based on data. Instead of being explicitly programmed to perform a specific task, these algorithms use statistical methods to improve performance as more data becomes available.

Here are some key points about machine learning:

1. Learning from Data:

Machine learning algorithms learn from data. The more data they are exposed to, the better their predictions or decisions typically become.

2. Types of Learning:

- *Supervised Learning*: The algorithm is provided with labeled training data, producing a model to make predictions based on that data. For example, given a dataset where houses and their sale prices are provided, an algorithm can predict the sale price of a new house based on its features.
- *Unsupervised Learning*: The algorithm is provided with unlabeled data and must find structures or patterns in the data independently. Clustering (grouping similar terms) and dimensionality reduction (reducing the number of variables under consideration) are common tasks.
- *Reinforcement Learning*: The algorithm learns by interacting with an environment and receiving feedback regarding rewards or penalties. This type of learning is used in areas like robotics and game playing.

3. Applications:

Machine learning has many applications, including recommendation systems (like those used by Netflix or Amazon), image and speech recognition, medical diagnosis, financial forecasting, etc.

Neural Networks and Deep Learning: Deep learning is a subfield of machine learning that focuses on algorithms based on artificial neural networks, particularly deep neural networks. The structure of the human brain inspires these models, and they are particularly good at processing complex data such as images and speech.

4. Overfitting and Generalization:

One challenge in machine learning is to ensure that models generalize well to new, unseen data. If a complex model learns the training data too closely (including its noise and outliers), it may perform poorly on new data.

5. Tools and Libraries:

There are several popular tools and libraries for machine learning, such as TensorFlow, Keras, PyTorch, and sci-kit-learn.

Machine learning is at the core of many of today's technological advancements and continues pushing the boundaries of what computers can achieve.

Machine Learning in Pharma Marketing

Machine learning can potentially revolutionize various aspects of the pharmaceutical industry, including drug discovery, clinical trials, and personalized medicine. In the context of pharmaceutical marketing, machine learning offers several benefits and applications:

1. *Customer Segmentation*: Machine learning can analyze vast data to identify and segment healthcare professionals or patient groups based on prescribing behaviors, treatment preferences, demographic data, and other relevant parameters. This segmentation allows for more targeted and personalized marketing campaigns.
2. *Predictive Analytics*: By analyzing historical data, machine learning can predict future drug sales, market demands, and potential market shifts, helping pharmaceutical companies better allocate resources and tailor marketing strategies.
3. *Sentiment Analysis*: Machine learning can analyze patient reviews, doctor feedback, and social media mentions of a specific drug or treatment. This helps companies gauge public sentiment and adjust their marketing messages or address concerns.
4. *Optimizing Marketing Channels*: With the help of machine learning, companies can determine which marketing channels (email, social media, medical journals, etc.) are most effective for different segments of their target audience and tailor their strategies accordingly.
5. *Chatbots and Virtual Assistants*: Machine learning-powered chatbots can provide instant information to healthcare professionals or patients about drugs, dosages, side effects, and other relevant data. This improves engagement and provides value-added services.
6. *Adverse Event Detection*: Monitoring social media or patient forums with machine learning can help detect potential adverse events or side effects of a drug, allowing companies to take swift action.
7. *Personalized Content Creation*: Based on user behavior, preferences, and feedback, machine learning algorithms can suggest or create

personalized content that will be more relevant and engaging for individual healthcare professionals or patients.

8. *Optimizing Sales Efforts*: Machine learning can analyze data to provide insights on which healthcare professionals are more likely to prescribe a certain drug, allowing for better allocation of sales representatives and resources.
9. *Forecasting*: Machine learning models can predict how new drugs will be received in the market, allowing companies to make informed decisions about production, distribution, and marketing.
10. *Clinical Trial Recruitment*: While this is more on the clinical side than direct marketing, ML can assist in identifying suitable candidates for clinical trials based on various data points. This can, in turn, speed up the drug approval process and its subsequent marketing.

In conclusion, machine learning offers pharmaceutical companies the tools to make their marketing efforts more efficient, targeted, and responsive to the needs and behaviors of their target audience. By harnessing the power of machine learning, pharmaceutical marketing can become more data-driven, personalized, and effective.

Macro Segmentation

Macro-segmentation in pharmaceutical marketing refers to dividing the target market into larger, distinct groups based on broad characteristics such as demographics, geography, or disease areas. It involves identifying and analyzing major segments within the market to develop marketing strategies that cater to each segment's unique needs and preferences. Here are some key aspects and examples of macro-segmentation in pharma marketing:

1. *Demographic Segmentation*: Demographic factors such as age, gender, income, and occupation are commonly used in macro-segmentation. For example, a pharmaceutical company may target a specific age group, like seniors or pediatric patients, with tailored marketing campaigns for drugs or healthcare services relevant to their specific needs.
2. *Geographic Segmentation*: Geographic segmentation involves dividing the market based on geographical locations, such as countries, regions, or local areas. This approach considers variations in healthcare systems, cultural factors, and regulatory environments. For instance, a pharmaceutical company may adapt its marketing strategy for a particular region based on differences in disease prevalence, treatment guidelines, or patient preferences.
3. *Disease Area Segmentation*: In pharmaceutical marketing, macro-segmentation based on disease areas involves targeting specific therapeutic categories or medical conditions. Different diseases may require distinct treatment approaches, and pharmaceutical companies may tailor their marketing efforts to healthcare professionals specializing in those disease areas. For example, a company focusing on oncology products would create specialized marketing campaigns targeting oncologists.
4. *Patient Journey Segmentation*: Macro-segmentation can also be based on the stages of the patient journey, from awareness to diagnosis, treatment, and post-treatment. This approach allows marketers to understand the patient experience at each stage and develop targeted messages and support programs. For instance, a company may develop educational materials for patients in the early awareness stage and provide adherence support for patients undergoing treatment.
5. *Channel-Based Segmentation*: Macro-segmentation can consider different channels through which pharmaceutical products are distributed or marketed. This includes segments such as hospitals, retail pharmacies, specialty clinics, or online pharmacies. Marketing strategies can be tailored to the specific channel, considering factors like procurement processes, decision-makers, and customer preferences.

By employing macro-segmentation, pharmaceutical companies can effectively allocate resources, develop targeted marketing campaigns, and enhance their understanding of diverse customer segments. In addition, it enables them to deliver tailored messages, services, and products that resonate with each segment's specific needs and characteristics, leading to improved customer engagement, satisfaction, and, ultimately, better patient outcomes.

Macro-Environment

In the pharmaceutical industry, the macro-environment refers to the broader external factors and influences that impact the industry. These factors are typically outside individual pharmaceutical companies' control but can significantly shape the industry's dynamic opportunities and challenges. Therefore, understanding the macro-environment is crucial for pharma companies to effectively adapt their strategies and navigate the external landscape.

Here are some key components of the macro-environment in pharma:

1. *Regulatory Environment*: The regulatory landscape, including laws, regulations, and policies, plays a vital role in the pharmaceutical industry. Government agencies, such as the US Food and Drug Administration (FDA) or the European Medicines Agency (EMA), oversee drug approvals, safety regulations, pricing controls, and marketing restrictions. Regulation changes or new guidelines can profoundly impact drug development, marketing practices, and market access.
2. *Economic Factors*: Economic conditions, including overall economic growth, healthcare expenditure, reimbursement policies, and pricing pressures, shape the pharma industry environment. Factors like healthcare budgets, insurance coverage, and affordability impact market dynamics and pharmaceutical companies' pricing and market access strategies of pharmaceutical companies.
3. *Technological Advancements*: Technological advancements, such as advances in biotechnology, genomics, artificial intelligence, and digital health, significantly impact the pharmaceutical industry. These innovations influence drug discovery, clinical research, manufacturing processes, and patient engagement. Pharma companies must stay abreast of emerging technologies and adapt their strategies to remain competitive.
4. *Social and Cultural Factors*: Social and cultural factors encompass societal attitudes, beliefs, values, and patient preferences. Changing demographics, patient empowerment, increasing focus on personalized medicine, and shifting perceptions of healthcare contribute to the evolving landscape of the pharma industry. Understanding patient needs and tailoring marketing efforts to cultural contexts and patient preferences is essential.
5. *Competitive Landscape*: The competitive environment, including the actions and strategies of rival pharmaceutical companies, impacts the macro-environment. Factors such as patent expirations, generic competition, mergers and acquisitions, and market consolidation shape the industry's dynamics and influence market access, pricing, and marketing strategies.
6. *Political Factors*: Political factors, such as government policies, trade agreements, intellectual property rights, and healthcare reforms, have a significant impact on the pharmaceutical industry. Political decisions and geopolitical events can influence market access, regulatory frameworks, research funding, and pricing regulations.

These components of the macro-environment interact and shape the overall landscape for pharmaceutical companies. Therefore, monitoring and understanding these external factors help pharma companies anticipate market changes, identify opportunities, and develop strategies to navigate challenges and deliver value to patients, healthcare providers, and other stakeholders in the industry.

Mailing List

A mailing list in pharma marketing refers to a database or collection of contact information, typically email addresses of individuals or organizations within the pharmaceutical industry or relevant target audience. Mailing lists are used for communication and outreach to share information, updates, promotion, and educational content related to pharmaceutical products, services, or events.

Here are some key aspects and considerations regarding mailing lists in pharma marketing:

1. *Building a Mailing List*: Pharmaceutical companies can build their mailing lists by collecting email addresses from various sources. This may include capturing email addresses through website sign-ups, online form submissions, trade show registrations, customer interactions, or collaborations with healthcare professionals or industry partners.
2. *Compliance with Regulations*: When collecting and utilizing email addresses for marketing purposes, it is crucial to comply with relevant data protection and privacy regulations in many countries, such as the General Data Protection Regulation (GDPR) in the European Union. According to these regulations, explicit consent is required from individuals to receive marketing communications. Ensure proper consent mechanisms are in place and subscribers can unsubscribe or manage their preferences.
3. *Targeted Segmentation*: To maximize the effectiveness of email marketing campaigns, pharmaceutical companies can segment their mailing lists based on relevant criteria. This may include factors such as healthcare professional type, specialty, geographical location, organization type, or specific interests within the pharmaceutical field. Segmentation allows for more personalized and tailored communications, delivering the right message to the right audience.

4. *Content Relevance*: When sending emails to the mailing list, providing valuable and relevant content to the recipients is essential. This can include educational materials, product updates, clinical trial information, industry news, or invitations to events or webinars. By delivering content that aligns with the interests and needs of the audience, pharmaceutical companies can engage subscribers and build stronger relationships.
5. *Email Automation and Analytics*: Email marketing platforms offer automation features that allow pharmaceutical companies to streamline their email campaigns. Automation can include welcome emails, drip campaigns, or triggered emails based on specific actions or milestones. Additionally, tracking and analyzing email metrics, such as open rates, click-through rates, and conversions, can provide insights into the effectiveness of campaigns and guide future optimizations.
6. *Compliance with Anti-Spam Laws*: It is crucial to adhere to anti-spam laws and regulations when conducting email marketing. Ensure that emails are sent to consented individuals and that appropriate opt-out mechanisms are in place. Complying with anti-spam laws helps maintain a positive reputation, prevents legal issues, and ensures ethical marketing practices.

A mailing list is a valuable communication tool in pharma marketing, allowing pharmaceutical companies to reach their target audience with relevant and engaging content directly. Building, managing, and utilizing the mailing list should be done in compliance with applicable regulations and ethical practices, prioritizing the interests and preferences of the recipients.

Managed Care

Managed care refers to a system of healthcare delivery in which insurance companies or other organizations play a significant role in managing and coordinating healthcare services. In pharmaceutical marketing, managed care has several implications for pharma marketers. Here are some key points to consider:

1. *Formulary Placement*: Managed care organizations (MCOs) typically maintain a formulary, a list of approved medications for coverage. Pharma marketers must understand the formulary placement process and strive to secure favorable product positions. This involves demonstrating their drugs' clinical and economic value compared to competitors to gain preferred formulary status.
2. *Cost Containment*: Managed care emphasizes cost-effective healthcare delivery. Pharma marketers should consider the pricing and affordability of their products when targeting MCOs. They must demonstrate their medications' cost-effectiveness and value proposition, highlighting improved patient outcomes, reduced hospitalizations, or lower overall healthcare costs.
3. *Market Access*: MCOs often negotiate contracts with pharmaceutical manufacturers to determine coverage and reimbursement for their members. Pharma marketers need to establish strong relationships with managed care account managers and payers to ensure their products gain access to the target patient population. Demonstrating their drug's value, safety, and efficacy becomes crucial during negotiations.
4. *Health Economic Data*: Managed care organizations increasingly demand health economic data, such as cost-effectiveness analyses and real-world evidence, to inform their coverage decisions. Pharma marketers should invest in generating robust data demonstrating their products' economic value. Such data can be used to support formulary placement discussions and reimbursement negotiations.
5. *Utilization Management*: Managed care often involves utilization management tools, such as prior authorization, step therapy, or quantity limits, to control medication utilization. Pharma marketers should understand these tools and be prepared to provide evidence supporting the appropriate use of their products. This may involve educating healthcare providers and MCOs about their medications' clinical benefits and appropriate patient populations.
6. *Patient Education and Support*: Managed care emphasizes patient outcomes and engagement. Pharma marketers can play a role in providing educational materials and support programs for patients using their products. This can help improve patient adherence, outcomes and overall satisfaction, which can influence MCO's perception of the value of the medication.
7. *Value-Based contracts*: In some instances, pharma marketers may enter into value-based contracts with managed care organizations. These contracts tie reimbursement to predefined outcomes or performance metrics. Pharma marketers must develop strategies to identify and measure relevant outcomes, collaborate with MCOs to establish appropriate contracts, and monitor and report outcomes effectively.

Navigating the managed care environment requires pharma marketers to understand the needs and priorities of MCOs, demonstrate the value of their products, generate robust health economic data, and establish strong relationships with key stakeholders. Adapting marketing strategies to align with managed care principles can help maximize market access and ensure the success of pharmaceutical products in this complex landscape.

Managed Care Organization (MCO)

Managed Care Organizations (MCOs) are crucial in managing and coordinating healthcare services for their members. These organizations typically work with health insurance companies, employers, or government programs to provide cost-effective and quality healthcare to their enrolled population. Here are some key aspects of Managed Care Organizations:

1. *Structure*: MCOs can take various forms, such as Health Maintenance Organizations (HMOs), Preferred Provider Organizations (PPOs), Point of Service (POS) plans, or Accountable Care Organizations (ACOs). Each type has its structure and approach to managing healthcare services and costs.
2. *Network of Providers*: MCOs establish networks of healthcare providers, including hospitals, clinics, physicians, specialists, and pharmacies. These networks form the primary source of care for their members. MCOs negotiate contracts with providers, often including discounted rates or predetermined reimbursement levels.
3. *Coverage and Benefits*: MCOs determine the scope of coverage and benefits for their members. This includes the drugs, treatments, and services included or excluded from coverage. MCOs typically maintain formularies that list approved medications and their coverage tiers.
4. *Utilization Management*: MCOs employ various utilization management techniques to control healthcare costs and ensure the appropriate use of services. These techniques may include prior authorization, step therapy, quality limits, or utilization review. These strategies aim to balance cost containment with providing quality care.
5. *Cost Containment*: Managed care organizations focus on cost containment and efficiency in healthcare delivery. They negotiate contracts with healthcare providers to secure favorable rates and use various cost-control mechanisms to manage utilization and expenses.
6. *Population Health Management*: MCOs often engage in population health management initiatives, aiming to improve the health outcomes of their members while minimizing costs. This involves proactive measures such as wellness programs, disease management, preventive care, and care coordination.
7. *Quality Performance Metrics*: MCOs establish quality and performance metrics to assess the effectiveness of healthcare delivery and providers. They may measure patient outcomes, satisfaction, adherence to clinical guidelines, and cost efficiency.
8. *Contracting with Payers*: MCOs enter into contracts with health insurance companies, employers, or government programs to provide healthcare services to their members. These contracts specify the terms, reimbursement rates, and performance expectations.
9. *Value-Based Contracts*: MCOs increasingly explore value-based contracts with healthcare providers and pharmaceutical manufacturers. These contracts tie reimbursement to predefined outcomes, such as improvements in patient health or reduced hospitalizations, fostering a focus on value and quality.
10. *Patient Engagement*: MCOs often promote patient engagement and education to empower their members to manage their health. They may provide resources, tools, and support programs to encourage healthier behaviors, medication adherence, and proactive healthcare decision-making.

Managed Care Organizations significantly influence healthcare delivery and reimbursement, making them essential stakeholders for pharmaceutical manufacturers, healthcare providers, and patients. Understanding the dynamics of managed care and collaborating with MCOs effectively can be critical for successful market access and commercialization strategies in the healthcare industry

Management by Objectives (MBO)

Management by Objectives (MBO) is a goal-setting and management approach that emphasizes establishing specific objectives for employees and aligning them with the organization's overall goals.

Peter Drucker introduced MBO in his 1954 book, *The Practice of Management*. The key principle of MBO is to ensure that individual and team goals are defined in a clear, measurable, and time-bound manner. This approach encourages managers' and employees' active participation and involvement in setting objectives, planning strategies, and evaluating performance. Here are the main components and steps involved in the MBO process:

1. *Goal Setting*: Managers and employees collaborate to set specific, measurable, achievable, relevant, and time-bound (SMART) objectives. These objectives should be aligned with the overall organizational goals and strategy.
2. *Cascading Objectives* are communicated and cascaded throughout the organization, ensuring employees understand how their goals contribute to the broader organizational objectives.
3. *Action Planning*: Once the objectives are set, employees and managers collaborate to develop action plans outlining the specific tasks, resources, and timelines required to achieve the objectives.
4. *Performance Monitoring*: Regular monitoring and tracking of progress toward objectives occur throughout the performance period. This may involve frequent check-ins, performance reviews, or progress reports to assess whether the objectives are being met.
5. *Performance Evaluation*: At the end of the performance period, a formal evaluation takes place to assess the degree to which the objectives have been achieved. This evaluation involves assessing individual and team performance against the established goals.
6. *Feedback and Development*: Feedback is provided to employees based on the evaluation results. It serves as a basis for recognizing achievements, identifying areas for improvement, and establishing development plans for future performance.

MBO promotes a results-oriented approach, encourages collaboration, and enhances employee engagement by providing a clear framework for goal setting and performance management. It gives employees greater ownership and accountability while aligning their efforts with the organization's strategic objectives.

MBO in Pharma Marketing

In pharmaceutical marketing, Management by Objectives (MBO) can be applied to set specific goals and measure the performance of marketing activities. Here are a few examples of how MBO can be implemented in pharmaceutical marketing:

1. *Increasing Market Share*: One objective could be to increase the market share of a particular pharmaceutical product within a specified timeframe. This objective would be measurable by tracking sales data and market research reports. The marketing team can develop strategies and tactics to achieve this goal, such as targeted promotional campaigns, pricing strategies, and market expansion initiatives.
2. *Launching a New Product*: When launching a new product, an objective could be to achieve a certain level of sales or market penetration within a specific period. This objective can be measured through sales data, prescription volume, and market research. The marketing team can set strategies for product positioning, market segmentation, physician engagement, and promotional activities to achieve the launch objectives.
3. *Enhancing Physician Awareness and Prescriptions*: An objective could be to increase awareness among healthcare professionals about a particular drug and subsequently increase the number of prescriptions. This objective can be measured by tracking prescription data and conducting surveys to assess physician awareness levels. Marketing strategies may include conducting medical education programs, organizing conferences, publishing research papers, and providing targeted educational materials to physicians.
4. *Improving Customer Satisfaction*: Another objective could be to enhance customer satisfaction levels and loyalty. This objective can be measured through customer feedback surveys, complaint resolution rates, and customer retention metrics. In addition, the marketing team can focus on developing customer-centric initiatives, such as patient support programs, improved customer service, and personalized communication, to achieve higher satisfaction levels.
5. *Expanding Geographical Reach*: If a pharmaceutical company aims to expand its geographical presence, an objective could be to enter new markets or increase market share in specific regions. This objective could be measured by tracking sales data and market share in targeted regions. Marketing strategies may include conducting market research, identifying key customer segments, establishing distribution networks, and developing localized marketing campaigns.

In each of these above examples, the key aspect of MBO is setting specific, measurable objectives aligned with the overall organizational goals and using performance tracking to assess progress and make data-driven decisions. The marketing team can regularly evaluate performance against the set objectives, make necessary adjustments to strategies, and ensure that the marketing efforts contribute to the pharmaceutical business's overall success.

Management Ratios

Management ratios, often known as financial or performance metrics, are tools managers, investors, and analysts use to evaluate a company's performance and stability. While many of these ratios are universal and can be applied across industries, some have particular relevance to the pharmaceutical industry, given its unique characteristics like high R&D costs, long product development cycles, and strict regulatory environments.

Here are some key management ratios relevant to the pharmaceutical sector:

1. *R&D Expenditure as a Percentage of Sales* measures the amount a company invests in research and development relative to its sales. For example, If a pharma company has sales of $1 billion and spends $200 million on R&D, the R&D expenditure as a percentage of sales is 20 percent.
2. *The Current Ratio* measures a company's ability to pay its short-term liabilities with its assets. For instance, if a company has assets of $500 million and liabilities of $250 million, the current ratio is 2:1.
3. *Quick Ratio (or Acid-Test Ratio)* is similar to the current ratio but excludes inventory from current assets, given that inventory might not be quickly converted to cash. This is especially relevant to pharma because of the potential for large inventories of drugs that may have limited shelf lives. For example, if a company's assets (excluding inventory) are $400 million and current liabilities are $250 million, the quick ratio is 1.6:1.
4. *Gross Margin* represents the percent of total sales revenue the company retains after incurring the direct costs of producing the goods/services sold. For instance, if a drug sells for $100 million and costs $60 to produce, the gross margin is 40 percent.
5. *Return on Investment for R&D* measures the profitability of investments in research and development. For example, if a company spends $100 million on R&D and earns $150 million from the developed products, the ROI is 50 percent.
6. *Debt-to-Equity Ratio* compares a company's total debt to its equity, indicating the relative proportions of equity and debt the company uses to finance its assets. For instance, if a pharma company has $400 million in debt and $600 million in equity, the debt-to-equity ratio is 0.67.
7. *Earnings Before Interest and Taxes (EBIT) margin* represents the company's profitability before accounting for interest and taxes. For example, if a company's EBIT is $50 million on sales of $500 million, the EBIT margin is 10 percent.
8. *Price-to-Earnings (P/E) Ratio* compares a company's stock price to its earnings per share, offering insight into how the market values the stock. For instance, if a pharma company's stock price is $100 and its earnings per share (EPS) is $5, the P/E ratio is 20.

With its blend of high-risk research, regulatory challenges, and potential for significant rewards, the pharmaceutical industry often experiences different dynamics than other sectors. As a result, while these ratios provide valuable insights, it is also essential to consider industry-specific factors and trends when interpreting them.

Many-to-One Communication

Many-to-one communication is a pattern where multiple individuals or entities interact or communicate with a single recipient or entity. This communication model flows information from many sources or participants toward a central point or receiver.

Typically, many-to-one communication occurs when there is a need to consolidate information, gather feedback, or make decisions based on input from multiple sources. It is commonly used in various settings, including organizations, educational institutions, community forums, and public meetings. Here are a few examples:

1. *Organizational Feedback*: In an organization, employees may provide feedback, suggestions, or reports to their managers or supervisors. The managers act as the central point of contact, receiving input from multiple employees and making decisions or taking actions based on the collective information received.

2. *Customer Service*: In customer service scenarios, many customers may contact a single support center or help desk with their inquiries, issues, or complaints. The support staff is the central point, receiving and addressing each customer's concerns individually.
3. *Public Meetings*: In public meetings or town hall events, community members gather to express their opinions, concerns, or suggestions to elected officials, community leaders, or representatives. The individuals in leadership positions receive input from multiple participants and respond to or address the issues raised.
4. *Educational Settings*: In classrooms or training sessions, students or participants may ask questions, share ideas, or provide input to the instructor or facilitator. The instructor acts as the central recipient, gathering information from the participants and guiding the learning process.

In many-to-one communication, the central recipient or entity plays a crucial role in managing and processing the information received from multiple sources. They need to listen, understand and respond appropriately to the input provided by the participants. Effective communication skills, active listening, and the ability to synthesize and make sense of diverse inputs are important for the central recipient in this communication mode.

In summary, many-to-one communication facilitates the consolidation of information, enables collective input, and supports decision-making processes by bringing together diverse perspectives and contributions from multiple sources toward a central point or recipient.

Many-to-One Communication in Pharma Marketing

In pharmaceutical marketing, many-to-one communication is significant in gathering feedback, insights, and opinions from various stakeholders and consolidating them for decision-making and strategy development. Here are some examples of its relevance in pharma marketing:

1. *Key Opinion Leader (KOL) Engagement*: Pharmaceutical companies often engage with healthcare professionals considered KOLs in their respective therapeutic areas. KOLs provide valuable insights, expertise, and feedback on products, clinical trials, and industry trends. The many-to-one communication model is employed when multiple KOLs communicate their perspectives and recommendations to the pharmaceutical company's marketing or medical affairs team. The company then synthesizes this input to define its marketing strategies, product positioning, and educational initiatives.
2. *Advisory Boards*: Pharmaceutical companies establish advisory boards comprising healthcare professionals, patient representatives, and industry experts. These boards serve as a platform for many-to-one communication, where diverse board members contribute their opinions, expertise, and experiences. The company can leverage this input to gain insights into market needs, unmet medical needs, and patient perspectives, ultimately shaping its marketing strategies and product development efforts.
3. *Customer Feedback and Market Research*: Pharma companies conduct surveys, focus groups, and other market research activities to gather feedback from healthcare professionals, patients, and other stakeholders. This many-to-one communication approach allows for collecting diverse opinions, experiences, and preferences. The company can then analyze and synthesize this feedback to identify market trends, understand customer needs, and tailor their marketing messages and campaigns accordingly.
4. *Sales Force Inputs*: Pharmaceutical sales representatives often act as intermediaries between the company and healthcare professionals. They interact with numerous physicians, pharmacists, and other stakeholders, collecting information about market dynamics, competitor activities, and customer preferences. The sales force provides many-to-one communication by relaying this information to the marketing team. The marketing team can then integrate these inputs to refine their targeting, messaging, and promotional strategies.
5. *Social Media Listening*: Many-to-one communication is relevant in the context of social media monitoring and engagement. Pharmaceutical companies monitor online conversations and discussions on social media platforms to gain insights into patient sentiments, experiences, and perceptions. Companies can identify emerging trends, detect potential issues, and develop targeted marketing initiatives or patient support programs by analyzing the collective input from numerous social media users.

In all these examples, many-to-one communication allows pharmaceutical companies to gather input and insights from multiple stakeholders, such as KOLs, advisory boards, customers, sales representatives, and online communities. By leveraging this diverse input, companies can make informed decisions, tailor their marketing strategies, and ensure their activities align with the needs and preferences of the target audience.

Marketing Assets

Marketing Assets in pharmaceutical marketing are the various tools, resources, and materials used to promote pharmaceutical products, engage healthcare professionals, educate patients, and build awareness. These assets are essential to creating effective campaigns in the pharmaceutical industry. Here are some common marketing assets:

1. Branding Materials

- *Brand Logo and Guidelines*: The pharmaceutical company's logo and brand guidelines ensure consistent visual identity across all marketing materials.
- *Brand Collateral*: Brochures, business cards, letterheads, and other print materials that showcase the company's brand.

2. Product Information and Detailing

- *Product Brochures*: Detailed brochures providing information about pharmaceutical products, including indications, dosage, side effects, and safety information.
- *Detail Aids*: Visual aids and presentations used by pharmaceutical sales representatives to detail healthcare professionals about products.

3. Digital Assets

- *Websites*: Pharmaceutical company websites provide product information, clinical data, patient resources, and contact details.
- *Social Media Profiles*: Profiles on social media platforms to engage with healthcare professionals and patients, share updates, and provide educational content.
- *Email Campaigns*: Email updates for marketing campaigns, newsletters, and updates.
- *Online Advertising*: Digital banners and advertisements for online promotion

4. Educational Materials

- *Patient Education Resources*: Materials to educate patients about their conditions and treatment options, including brochures, videos, and websites.
- *HCP Education*: Educational materials to healthcare professionals, such as clinical studies, treatment guidelines, and medical journals.

5. Event and Conference Materials

- *Trade Show Booths*: Booth design, banners, and promotional materials for pharmaceutical industry events and conferences.
- *Presentation Materials*: Slide decks and presentations for conferences and educational events.

6. Sales and Marketing Tools

- *Sales Presentations*: Tools for sales representatives to use during interactions with healthcare professionals.
- *CRM Systems*: Customer Relationship Management systems to manage interactions with healthcare providers and track sales efforts.

7. Regulatory Documentation

- *FDA and Regulatory Submissions*: Documents submitted to regulatory authorities, including drug applications and safety reports.

8. Advertising Materials

- *Print and Media Ads*: Materials for print, television, and digital advertising campaigns.
- *Outdoor Advertising*: Billboards and signage for promoting products

9. Market Research and Competitive Analysis

- Reports and data on market trends, competition, and consumer insights.

10. Patient Support Programs

- Materials related to patient assistance programs, including enrollment forms and educational resources.

11. Clinical Trial Materials

- Materials related to clinical trial recruitment and patient information.

12. Compliance Document

- Materials to ensure that all marketing activities adhere to industry regulations and guidelines, including compliance manuals and training materials.

13. Product Samples

- Samples of pharmaceutical products for healthcare professionals to evaluate and prescribe.

Pharmaceutical companies use these marketing assets to engage healthcare professionals, educate patients, promote their products, and maintain a strong brand presence in the highly regulated pharmaceutical industry. These assets are crucial for building trust, ensuring regulatory compliance, and delivering valuable information to healthcare providers and patients.

Marketing Collateral

In the pharmaceutical industry, marketing collateral refers to a collection of materials and tools pharmaceutical companies use to promote and communicate product information to healthcare professionals, patients, and other stakeholders. These materials convey pharmaceutical products' value, efficacy, and safety. Here are some common types of marketing collateral used in the pharmaceutical industry:

1. *Brochures and Flyers*: Printed materials that provide detailed information about a pharmaceutical product, including its indications, mode of action, dosage, side effects, and other relevant details. These are often distributed to healthcare professionals in clinics, hospitals, and during conferences.
2. *Detail Aids*: Visual aids or presentations used by pharmaceutical sales representatives during face-to-face meetings with healthcare professionals. Detail aids typically include graphics, charts, and key messages to communicate a product's benefits effectively.
3. *Product Monographs*: Comprehensive documents that contain detailed information about a pharmaceutical product. This includes clinical trial data, safety information, pharmacokinetics, and other technical details. Product monographs are often used for reference by healthcare professionals.
4. *Educational Materials*: Materials designed to educate healthcare professionals, patients, and the public about specific diseases, treatment options, and healthcare practices. These may include pamphlets, booklets, and online resources.
5. *Samples*: Actual product samples provided to healthcare professionals for trial purposes. Samples allow healthcare professionals to familiarize themselves with the product and assess its effectiveness.
6. *Conference Materials*: Materials prepared for pharmaceutical conferences and events, including posters, banners, and booth displays. These materials are designed to attract attention and communicate key messages to a targeted audience.
7. *Digital and Online Content*: With the increasing digitalization of marketing efforts, pharmaceutical companies use websites, social media platforms, and email campaigns to disseminate product information. This includes digital brochures, webinars, and interactive content.
8. *Patient Support Materials*: Materials created to support and educate patients about their conditions and prescribed medications. This may include patient brochures, instructional videos, and adherence tools.

It is important to note that marketing collateral in the pharmaceutical industry is subject to strict regulatory guidelines to ensure that the information provided is accurate, balanced, and complies with regulatory standards. The development and distribution of marketing collateral require close collaboration between pharmaceutical companies and regulatory bodies to maintain compliance.

Marketing Ethics

Marketing ethics in the pharmaceutical industry refers to the moral and ethical considerations that guide the marketing practices of pharmaceutical companies. Due to pharmaceutical products' critical role in public health, pharmaceutical marketers must uphold ethical standards and prioritize the well-being of patients and society. Here are some key aspects of marketing ethics in the pharmaceutical industry:

1. *Accuracy and Truthfulness*: Pharmaceutical marketers should provide accurate and truthful product information. This includes avoiding misleading or exaggerated claims, ensuring that promotional materials are supported by scientific evidence, and communicating the potential risks and benefits of the products.
2. *Patient Welfare*: Patient welfare should be the primary concern in pharmaceutical marketing. Marketers should ensure that their activities are in the best interest of patients and prioritize patient safety and health outcomes. In addition, ethical considerations should guide the promotion of appropriate and responsible use of medications.
3. *Compliance with Regulations*: Pharmaceutical marketing must comply with applicable laws, regulations, and industry guidelines. Marketers should adhere to regulations related to advertising, product labeling, promotion, and interactions with healthcare professionals.
4. *Transparency and Disclosure*: Pharmaceutical companies should be transparent in their

marketing practices and disclose potential conflicts of interest. This includes transparently reporting funding sources, disclosing financial relationships with healthcare professionals or organizations, and providing accurate and clear information about the benefits and risks of their products.

5. *Respect for Privacy and Confidentiality*: Marketers must respect patient privacy and confidentiality. They should handle patient data and personal information securely and responsibly, adhering to applicable data protection regulations.
6. *Fair Competition*: Pharmaceutical marketers should engage in fair competition and refrain from engaging in unethical practices that undermine fair market competition. This includes avoiding false or unfair comparisons with competitor products, respecting intellectual property rights, and refraining from engaging in anti-competitive behavior.
7. *Professionalism and Integrity*: Marketers should conduct themselves professionally and in their interactions with healthcare professionals, patients, and the public. This includes avoiding conflicts of interest, maintaining objectivity, and refraining from offering inappropriate incentives or gifts that may influence healthcare professionals' prescribing behavior.
8. *Compliance Programs and Training*: Pharmaceutical companies should establish comprehensive compliance programs to ensure employees know ethical standards and regulatory requirements. Regular training programs can help educate employees about marketing ethics, promote ethical decision-making, and ensure adherence to ethical guidelines.

Adhering to marketing ethics in the pharmaceutical industry is crucial for maintaining public trust, ensuring patient safety, and promoting responsible marketing practices. In addition, by upholding high ethical standards, pharmaceutical marketing contributes to the industry's integrity and patients' well-being.

Marginal Analysis

Marginal analysis is an economic concept that examines the incremental or additional changes in costs and benefits resulting from a particular decision of action. It focuses on studying the effects of small adjustments to existing conditions rather than considering the overall situation.

In marginal analysis, decision-makers evaluate the costs and benefits of producing or consuming one additional unit of a good or service. By comparing the marginal cost (MC) and marginal benefit (MB) of action, individuals, businesses, and policymakers can make informed decisions about resource allocation.

The basic principle of marginal analysis is rooted in the law of diminishing marginal returns, which states that as more units of a variable input are added to a fixed input, the marginal product's benefit or value of the variable input eventually diminishes.

For example, think about whether a manufacturing company will produce one more product unit. By analyzing the marginal cost of producing that additional unit (which includes factors like labor, materials, and energy costs) and comparing it with the marginal revenue generated from selling that unit, the company can determine whether it is economically beneficial to produce more.

If the marginal benefit (revenue) exceeds the marginal cost, it suggests that producing the additional unit will be profitable. Conversely, reducing production may be more efficient if the marginal cost exceeds the marginal benefit.

Marginal analysis is not limited to production decisions; it can be applied to various aspects of economics, such as pricing, investment, resource allocation, and public policy. Individuals and organizations can optimize their decision-making and achieve more efficient outcomes by considering the incremental changes resulting from different choices.

Marginal Analysis in Pharma Marketing

Pharmaceutical companies also can use marginal analysis to evaluate the costs and benefits of various marketing strategies and make informed decisions about resource allocation.

Here are a few ways marginal analysis can be applied in pharmaceutical marketing:

1. *Pricing Activities*: Pharmaceutical companies can analyze the marginal cost of producing and distributing an additional medication unit and compare it with the marginal revenue generated from selling that unit. This analysis helps determine the optimal price point for maximizing profits while considering production costs, competition, and demand elasticity.
2. *Promotional Activities*: By examining the marginal costs and benefits associated with different marketing channels and promotional campaigns, pharmaceutical companies can allocate their marketing budget effectively. They can evaluate the impact of each promotional activity on sales, customer acquisition, and

brand awareness to identify the most cost-effective strategies.

3. *Targeting and Segmentation*: Marginal analysis can assist in determining the incremental benefits of targeting specific patient segments or healthcare professionals. Companies can assess the additional revenue and market share gained by focusing their marketing efforts on specific demography or therapeutic areas and comparing it with the associated costs.
4. *Product Portfolio Decisions*: Pharmaceutical companies often have multiple products in their portfolio. They can evaluate the incremental costs and benefits of adding or removing products from their portfolio by conducting marginal analysis. This analysis helps optimize the product mix, focusing on resources on high-potential products and eliminating underperforming ones.
5. *Investment in Research and Development*: Pharmaceutical companies face decisions regarding investments in research and development (R&D) for new drugs or enhancements to existing drugs. Marginal analysis can be used to assess the expected additional benefits and costs of such investments considering factors like market potential, competitive landscape, and regulatory requirements.

Marginal analysis can be a valuable tool in pharmaceutical marketing, enabling companies to evaluate the costs and benefits of different marketing strategies, optimize resource allocation, and make informed decisions that maximize profitability and market effectiveness.

Marginal Cost Pricing

Marginal cost pricing is a pricing strategy where the selling price of a product or service is set equal to its marginal cost. This approach determines the price by considering the additional cost incurred in producing one more unit of the product or service.

The concept of marginal cost is based on the principle of economic efficiency. The marginal cost represents the cost of producing an additional unit, considering the variable costs, such as labor, raw materials, and energy. It does not include fixed costs, such as rent or equipment, or depreciation, as these costs do not change with the production of each additional unit.

Implementing marginal cost pricing can have several benefits:

1. *Efficiency*: Marginal cost pricing promotes economic efficiency by aligning the price with the actual cost of production. It helps prevent the underutilization of resources by ensuring that products or services are priced to cover the variable costs and contribute to optimal resource allocation.
2. *Cost Recovery*: By selling at prices equal to marginal costs, businesses can recover the direct costs of producing each unit. This approach ensures that the revenue generated from sales covers the immediate expenses incurred, allowing for cost recovery per unit.
3. *Competition*: Marginal cost pricing can enhance competition in the market. When prices are based on marginal costs, it reduces the possibility of firms using predatory pricing strategies to drive competitors out of the market. It creates a level playing field by preventing anti-competitive pricing practices.
4. *Price Transparency*: Pricing products or services based on marginal costs can provide transparency to customers and stakeholders. It allows customers to understand the direct cost components of the product and makes the pricing structure more transparent and understandable.

However, there are some considerations and limitations to marginal cost pricing:

1. *Fixed Costs*: Marginal cost pricing does not account for fixed costs, which are necessary for the long-term sustainability of a business. Therefore, it may not cover all costs and ensure overall profitability.
2. *Research and Development*: Marginal cost pricing may not adequately account for the costs associated with research and development (R&D) efforts. R&D costs are typically considered indirect and may not be fully recovered through marginal cost pricing alone.
3. *Market Demand*: Marginal cost pricing does not consider demand elasticity and customers' willingness to pay higher prices for certain products or services. It may overlook the value perception of the premium customers, who assign a premium to certain offerings, potentially leaving revenue on the table.

While marginal cost pricing has its merits, businesses often consider a combination of pricing strategies, considering both marginal costs and other factors such as market demand, competition and long-term profitability goals. This allows for a more comprehensive and balanced pricing approach.

Mark-up

Markup refers to the amount added to the cost price of a product or service to determine the selling price. It is typically expressed as a percentage of the cost price.

The markup covers various expenses and generates a profit for businesses. It considers the cost of producing or acquiring a product and additional costs associated with operations, such as overhead, marketing, distribution, and profit margin.

The formula for calculating markup is as follows:

Markup= (Selling Price - Cost Price) / *100

In this formula, the selling price is the final price at which the product or service is sold to customers, and the cost price is the price at which the product or service was acquired or produced. For example, a retailer purchases a product from a supplier for $50 and wants to apply a markup of 30%. The calculation would be as follows:

Markup = ($50*30%) / $50*100 = $15/$50 *100 = 30%

Markup is a common practice in various industries and is used to cover costs, generate profits, and ensure the sustainability of businesses. It is important for businesses to carefully consider factors such as market conditions, competition, and customer demand when determining the appropriate markup percentage set a competitive selling price while maintaining profitability.

Markup in Pharma Marketing

In pharmaceutical marketing, markup refers to the difference between the cost of producing or acquiring medication and the price at which it is sold to customers or healthcare providers. It represents the margin or profit that pharmaceutical companies earn on each unit of medication sold.

The markup in pharmaceutical marketing can vary depending on several factors, including:

1. *Research and Development Costs*: Pharmaceutical companies invest significant resources in research and development (R&D) to discover and develop new drugs. The costs incurred during the R&D process, including clinical trials, regulatory approvals, and intellectual property protection, are often factored into the markup.
2. *Manufacturing and Production Costs*: The costs associated with manufacturing, packaging, and distributing medications also contribute to the markup. These costs include raw materials, labor, equipment, quality control, and logistics.
3. *Marketing and Sales Expenses*: Pharmaceutical companies invest in marketing and sales activities to promote their medications and reach healthcare providers and patients. These costs, such as advertising, sales force salaries, promotional materials, and medical education programs, are typically incorporated into the markup.
4. *Distribution and Supply Chain Costs*: The markup may also cover the costs of distributing medications to various channels, such as pharmacies, hospitals, and wholesalers. These costs involve transportation, storage, inventory management, and compliance with regulatory requirements.
5. *Competitive Factors*: Market dynamics and competition influence the markup in pharmaceutical marketing. Pricing strategies, including positioning the medication as a premium or niche product, can impact the markup level. Pricing decisions also consider factors like the uniqueness of the medication, its perceived value, and market demand.

It is important to note that the markup in pharmaceutical marketing can vary significantly among different medications, therapeutic areas, and countries. Factors like patent protection, regulatory requirements, healthcare system dynamics, and government policies can influence the pricing and markup practices within a particular market.

Pharmaceutical companies must balance ensuring profitability to sustain research and development efforts covering production and marketing costs and maintaining accessibility and affordability for patients and healthcare systems. Pricing and markup decisions are complex and involve ethical, economic, and public health considerations.

Market

A Market is a physical or virtual space where products or services are exchanged. Buyers and sellers engage in transactions based on supply and demand dynamics in a market. It includes all the participants involved in the buying and selling process and the factors influencing the pricing, availability, and competitiveness of the exchanged products or services.

Market in Pharmaceutical Marketing

In pharmaceutical marketing, the market refers to the specific group of customers or target audience to whom pharmaceutical products or services are marketed. It encompasses the individuals, organizations, or healthcare professionals with a need or demand for pharmaceutical products and its potential consumers or influencers in the decision-making process. The pharmaceutical market is multifaceted and includes various segments and stakeholders. Some key components of the market in pharmaceutical marketing include:

1. *Patient Market*: Patients are an essential segment of the pharmaceutical market. They are the end-users of medications and often play a role in the decision-making process, directly or through their interactions with healthcare professionals. Understanding patient demographics, needs, behaviors, and preferences is crucial for developing effective marketing strategies and patient-centric healthcare solutions.
2. *Healthcare Professionals (HCP): Market*: Healthcare professionals, such as physicians, nurses, pharmacists, and other prescribers, represent an influential group within the pharmaceutical market. They have the authority to prescribe, recommend, or influence the use of pharmaceutical products. Targeting healthcare professionals through educational programs, scientific literature, and promotional activities is a common practice in pharmaceutical marketing.
3. *Institutional Market*: The institutional market includes hospitals, clinics, pharmacies, and other healthcare organizations that purchase and dispense pharmaceutical products. Building relationships with these institutions, understanding their procurement processes, and addressing their specific needs is important for successful pharma marketing.
4. *Payer Market*: Payers, such as insurance companies, government healthcare programs, and pharmacy benefit managers, play a significant role in the pharmaceutical market. Understanding the reimbursement landscape, formulary decisions, and pricing dynamics is crucial for pharmaceutical companies to navigate the payer market effectively.
5. *Regulatory and Policy Environment*: The pharmaceutical market is heavily regulated, with government agencies responsible for drug approvals, pricing regulations, and marketing guidelines. Staying informed about regulatory requirements, compliance standards, and policy changes is essential for pharmaceutical marketing strategies.
6. *Competitive Landscape*: The pharmaceutical market is competitive, with numerous companies developing and marketing similar products. Understanding the competitive landscape, monitoring competitors' activities, and differentiating products and services are vital aspects of pharma marketing.
7. *Market Dynamics and Trends*: The pharmaceutical market is influenced by various factors, including demographic shifts, disease prevalence, technological advancements, healthcare reforms, and patient empowerment. Keeping abreast of market trends and dynamics helps pharmaceutical companies identify opportunities and adapt their marketing strategies accordingly.

Pharmaceutical companies must conduct market research, gather data, and employ market segmentation techniques to understand the target market's needs, preferences, and behaviors. This understanding allows companies to develop effective marketing plans, product positioning, and communication strategies tailored to market segments.

In summary, the market in pharma marketing encompasses individuals, healthcare professionals, institutions, payers, and regulatory environments involved in the purchasing, prescribing, and use of pharmaceutical products. Understanding the dynamics, customer needs, and the competitive landscape is crucial for successful pharmaceutical marketing strategies.

Market Acceptance

Market acceptance in the pharmaceutical industry refers to the level of adoption and utilization of a pharmaceutical product or therapy by healthcare professionals, patients, and other stakeholders in the market. It reflects how much the market embraces and incorporates the product into clinical practice and patient care.

Market acceptance is influenced by several factors, including the following:

1. *Efficacy and Safety*: A pharmaceutical product's effectiveness and safety profile plays a significant role in its acceptance in the market. Healthcare professionals and patients must be confident in the product's ability to deliver the desired therapeutic outcomes while minimizing potential risks and side effects.
2. *Clinical Evidence*: Strong clinical evidence, such as data from well-designed clinical trials and real-world studies, can contribute to market acceptance. Robust evidence demonstrating the product's efficacy, safety, and comparative advantages over existing therapies helps build

trust among healthcare professionals and decision-makers.

3. *Guidelines and Recommendations*: Endorsement and inclusion in treatment guidelines, formularies, and reimbursement lists by authoritative bodies, such as medical societies, regulatory agencies, and payers, can greatly influence market acceptance. These recommendations guide healthcare professionals and improve the product's credibility and adoption.
4. *Competitive Landscape*: The competitive environment in the pharmaceutical market can impact market acceptance. Factors such as the availability of alternative therapies, perceived superiority over competing products, and pricing considerations can influence healthcare professionals' and patients' choices and affect the market acceptance of a specific pharmaceutical product.
5. *Market Access and Reimbursement*: The ability of patients to access and afford a pharmaceutical product is crucial for market acceptance and utilization in the market.
6. *Education and Awareness*: Adequate education and awareness among healthcare professionals, patients, and caregivers about the product's benefits, appropriate use, and potential impact on patient outcomes are essential for market acceptance. Educational initiatives, medical conferences, scientific publications, and promotional activities contribute to increasing awareness and understanding of the product.
7. *Patient Preferences and Adherence*: Patient preferences, convenience, and adherence to treatment regimens also influence market acceptance. Factors such as dosing frequency, administration route, ease of use, and patient support programs can impact patients' willingness to adopt and adhere to a specific pharmaceutical product.

Pharmaceutical companies employ strategies to drive market acceptance, including targeted marketing and promotional campaigns, scientific engagement with healthcare professionals, post-marketing studies, real-world evidence generation, and collaboration with key opinion leaders and patient advocacy groups.

Market acceptance is a dynamic process that evolves as new evidence emerges, clinical practices evolve, and patient needs change. Pharmaceutical companies must continually monitor market acceptance, engage with stakeholders, and adapt their strategies to ensure successful market adoption and utilization of their products.

Market Access

Market access in the pharmaceutical industry refers to ensuring that patients who need specific drugs can obtain them at a price that is both sustainable for the manufacturer and acceptable to the payer, whether the patient, a health insurance organization, or a government body. Here's a breakdown of the key elements and challenges in the field of market access for pharmaceuticals:

1. *Pricing*: This is a crucial factor determining a drug's commercial success or failure. It involves evaluating the potential economic impact of the new mediation, including costs avoided by preventing hospitalizations or other treatments.
2. *Reimbursement*: This concerns the policies set by health insurance providers or government bodies about which drugs they will cover and how much they will pay.
3. *Health Technology Assessment (HTA)*: Before a drug is approved for reimbursement by public health systems or insurance companies in some countries, its clinical and economic value may be assessed. HTAs evaluate the drug's effectiveness, costs, and impact on public health.
4. *Regulation*: In addition to regulatory approvals that drugs must receive to be marketed (e.g., from the FDA in the US or EMA in the European Union), there may be other regulations impacting market access, such as pricing regulations or mandatory rebates.
5. *Stakeholder Engagement*: Companies should engage with various stakeholders, from patient advocacy groups to policymakers, to understand and shape the environment in which their drugs are received.
6. *Value Demonstration*: With many health systems facing financial challenges, pharmaceutical companies must demonstrate the value of their products not just in clinical terms but in real-world, socio-economic terms.
7. *Distribution and Logistics*: In some markets, particularly in low-income countries, getting the drug to the patient can be a significant challenge. This could be due to a lack of infrastructure, regulatory hurdles, or economic issues.
8. *Patient Access Programs*: These programs are designed to ensure that patients can afford their medications, either through discounts, rebates, or other mechanisms. They can be especially important for high-priced drugs.

Challenges

1. *Cost-Containment*: Many health systems worldwide are under significant financial strain.

As a result, they may push back on high drug prices or deny coverage.

2. *Competition*: The rise of generic and biosimilar products can reduce the market share for innovative drugs.
3. *Diverse Stakeholders*: Each stakeholder, be it doctors, patients, payers, or policymakers, might have different concerns and priorities for drug value assessment and cost-effectiveness.
4. *Complex Decision-Making Frameworks*: Countries and regions within countries can have frameworks for assessing drug value and cost-effectiveness.

To navigate this complex environment, pharmaceutical companies typically employ or consult with market access experts who can develop strategies tailored to individual markets and products.

Implications for Pharma Marketers

Pharmaceutical marketers face a complex and evolving landscape shaped by regulatory frameworks, ethical considerations, changing consumer expectations, and scientific advancements. The implications for pharma marketers can be vast and multifaceted. Here are some key implications:

1. *Increased Focus on Real-world Evidence and Outcomes*: With the shift towards value-based care, payers and prescribers increasingly demand real-world data and outcomes to support drug usage. For example, a pharmaceutical company might engage in post-launch observational studies or use patient registries to collect data on how their drug performs in real-world settings.
2. *Rise of Digital Engagement*: Digital technology has transformed patient engagement, disease awareness, and the patient journey. Marketers need to optimize digital channels. For instance, Novartis launched the *ViaOpta* app, designed to help visually impaired individuals by utilizing smartphone capabilities to identify objects, read text, and navigate surroundings.
3. *Direct-to-Consumer Advertising Controversies*: DTC advertising, especially in the US, has sparked debates about its influence on drug prices and the medicalization of conditions. For example, the DTC advertisement for Humira (for conditions like arthritis) has faced criticism for perceived over-promotion and not adequately addressing risks.
4. *Heightened Regulatory Scrutiny*: Marketing messages, promotional activities, and communications must strictly adhere to regulatory guidelines, often differing across countries. For instance, in 2019, the FDA in the US issued a warning letter to Sanofi for omitting risk information in a promotional piece for its eczema drug Dupixent.
5. *Need for Transparency and Trust Building*: Trust in the pharmaceutical industry is vital. Marketers must emphasize transparency, especially regarding pricing, clinical trial data, and potential conflicts of interest. For example, Johnson & Johnson, amidst the opioid crisis, faced significant reputational and legal challenges due to allegations of misleading marketing of their opioid drugs.
6. *Patient-Centricity and Advocacy*: Modern patients are informed and active in their care decisions. Marketers must consider patient needs and perspectives, often involving patients in decision-making. For instance, Vertex, with its cystic fibrosis drug, Orkambi, worked closely with patient advocacy groups for awareness campaigns and to facilitate access programs.
7. *Market Access and Pricing Strategies*: Marketers must consider getting drugs approved and ensuring they are accessible and affordable. For instance, Gilead's hepatitis C drug, Sovaldi, faced criticism for its high price, leading to debates about drug pricing and market access.
8. *Emergence of Personalized and Precision Medicine*: The move toward targeted treatments requires marketers to consider niche audiences, personalized engagement strategies, and advanced educational efforts. For example, the marketing of Roche's cancer drug Herceptin is closely tied to diagnostic testing to identify patients with HER-2-positive breast cancer.

For pharma marketers, adapting to this multifaceted environment demands continuous learning, agility, and a focus on ethical considerations while navigating commercial objectives.

Market Aggregation

Market aggregation, in general, refers to the practice of viewing a market as a large homogenous group rather than breaking it down into distinct segments. This strategy can be contrasted with market segmentation, which divides the market into groups based on specific characteristics.

In the context of the pharmaceutical industry, market aggregation can have specific implications and uses:

1. *Broad Spectrum Medications*: Some drugs are developed for a wide range of symptoms or conditions; therefore, a broad market approach

can be employed. For example, pain relievers like ibuprofen or paracetamol have a wider user base and can be marketed to the general public without much segmentation.

2. *Mass Marketing*: When employing market aggregation strategies, pharmaceutical companies might use mass media advertising channels, such as television or national print campaigns, to reach a broad audience. Direct-to-consumer (DTC) advertising in countries that permit it, like the US, often uses this approach for certain drugs.
3. *Pricing*: In an aggregated market strategy, pricing is often uniform. The pharma industry, however, needs to be cautious due to varying healthcare systems, insurance provisions, and patient needs.
4. *Simplified Messaging*: Aggregation strategies rely on simpler, universally resonant messages rather than tailoring content to specific segments.
5. *Geographical Aggregation*: Sometimes, pharmaceutical companies view certain regions or countries as aggregated markets, especially when health demographics, regulatory conditions, and healthcare infrastructures are similar.

Challenges and Criticisms

However, there are challenges and criticisms associated with market aggregation in the pharma sector:

1. *Lack of Personalization*: Especially in an era where personalized medicine and treatments are gaining traction, an aggregated approach can seem out of touch with individual patient needs.
2. *Regulatory Differences*: Differences in regulatory environments across countries or regions can make a purely aggregated strategy untenable. What is permissible regarding marketing in one country might be illegal or frowned upon in another.
3. *Cultural and Demographic Differences*: Health needs, cultural beliefs related to health, and patient behaviors can vary widely, making a one-size-fits-all strategy inefficient in certain situations.
4. *Market Evolution*: With the rise of biologics, gene therapies, and precision medicine, there is an increasing move towards niche patient populations and specialized treatments. This shift requires a more segmented approach than aggregated.

In conclusion, while market aggregation can offer some advantages in simplifying marketing efforts and economies of scale, pharmaceutical companies must weigh these against the need for personalization, regulatory considerations, and the industry's evolving nature. The choice between aggregation and segmentation will largely depend on the specific drug in question, its target demographic, and the geographic markets in which a company operates.

Market Approval

Market approval in the pharmaceutical industry refers to the official authorization of regulatory authorities, allowing a drug or medical product to be marketed and sold to the public. This approval is granted after a rigorous review process where the drug's safety, efficacy, and quality are assessed based on data from preclinical and clinical trials.

The market approval process can vary from one country to another but usually involves the following steps:

1. Discovery and Development

- Research and identification of potential drug candidates
- Initial testing in laboratories and often on animal models to evaluate safety and potential effectiveness

2. Preclinical Research

- In-vitro (test tube or cell culture) and In-vivo (animal) testing to evaluate the safety, dosage, and potential benefits
- Determines whether the drug is safe to move to human testing

3. Clinical Trials (conducted in phases on human subjects

- *Phase 1*: Typically involves a small number of participants to evaluate safety, dosage, and side effects
- *Phase 2*: Larger group tested to evaluate drug efficacy and safe effects
- *Phase 3*: An even larger group is tested to confirm the effectiveness of monitoring side effects and compare with existing treatments
- *Phase 4*: Post-market surveillance to gather more information on the drug's risks, benefits, and optimal use

4. Submission to Regulatory Authorities

- The pharmaceutical company submits a comprehensive dossier, often called a New Drug

Application (NDA) in the US or a Marketing Authorization Application (MAA) in the European Union. The submission contains data from the drug development process, including results from all clinical trial phases.

5. Review

- The regulatory authority reviews the submission. This may involve independent experts assessing the data. They will decide whether the drug can be marketed and, if so, under what conditions.

6. Post-Market Surveillance

- Even after the drug is approved and on the market, companies must monitor and report any adverse reactions or long-term side effects. Regulatory agencies may sometimes demand post-approval studies or trials to assess certain outcomes.

Regulatory Agencies

A few notable regulatory agencies that grant market approval include:

- *US*: Food and Drug Administration (FDA)
- *European Union*: European Medicines Agency (EMA)
- *Canada*: Health Canada
- *Japan*: Pharmaceuticals and Medical Devices Agency (PMDA)
- *India*: Central Drugs Standard Control Organization (CDSCO)
- *China*: The National Medical Products Administration (NMPA)

It is worth noting that getting market approval is a lengthy, complex, and expensive process. Only a fraction of the drugs that enter the clinical trial phases receive final market authorization. Furthermore, market approval might come with certain conditions, like additional warnings on the label or the requirement for further studies.

Market Atomization

Market atomization is not a commonly used term within pharmaceutical or marketing literature; however, its usage suggests a breakdown or segmentation of markets into individual units that could exist on an even granular level.

Market atomization about pharmaceutical manufacturing might mean thinking of personalization and precision medicine, where treatments are targeted specifically toward patient populations based on genetic, environmental, and lifestyle considerations.

1. *Targeted Therapies and Market Atomization in Pharma*: As medications become more specialized, their patient populations narrow. For example, certain cancer drugs target only patients with certain gene mutations.
2. *Higher Drug Prices*: Drugs intended for specific patient populations might be priced higher due to limited customer numbers and the specific research conducted for them.
3. *Targeting Specific Patient Populations Can Improve Drug Efficacy*: Targeting specific patient populations can often yield better treatment results since targeted therapy will more precisely meet those groups' requirements.
4. *Advanced Diagnostics*: With more atomized markets emerging, advanced diagnostic tools could become necessary in identifying which patient group would best respond to specific medicines.
5. *Regulatory Challenges*: Regulators must adjust to accommodate drugs intended for specific, smaller populations that do not conform to traditional large-scale clinical trial methodologies.

Pharma companies must adapt their marketing tactics. Instead of broad-scale campaigns, more targeted approaches could reach clinicians, patients, and patient groups more efficiently.

Market Atomization in Pharma: Some Examples

1. *Cystic Fibrosis Treatments*: Vertex has introduced two medications, Orkambi and Kalydeco, designed to address mutations associated with cystic fibrosis; they should only be given to individuals exhibiting certain genetic profiles of cystic fibrosis patients.
2. *Oncology Therapies*: Many new cancer drugs focus on specific genetic mutations; for example, AstraZeneca's Tagrisso was specifically created for non-small cell lung carcinoma patients with certain EGFR mutations.
3. *Genetic Testing*: Companies such as 23andMe and AncestryDNA provide genealogical and health insights based on genetic markers that could lead to more personalized treatments. This data could even lead to genetic mapping.
4. *Rare Diseases*: Many orphan drugs have been developed specifically to meet the needs of rare conditions. Alexion Pharmaceuticals' Soliris (Eculizumab) was designed to meet this criteria, relieving paroxysmal nocturnal hemoglobinuria (PNH) and atypical hemolytic uremic syndrome (aHUS).

Although market atomization may not be a standard practice in the pharmaceutical industry, evidence points toward increasing specificity and personalization within this space, and this trend could have significant ramifications on drug research, development, regulation, and marketing efforts.

Market Attractiveness

Market attractiveness in the pharmaceutical industry refers to the overall desirability and potential of a specific market or segment within the pharmaceutical sector. It assesses the attractiveness of a market based on factors such as market size, growth rate, profitability, competitive landscape, regulatory environment, and other relevant market dynamics.

Here are some key factors to consider when evaluating market attractiveness in the pharma industry:

1. *Market Size*: The size of the target market, measured in terms of the patient population, the prevalence of the disease or condition, and potential market share, is a critical factor. Larger markets often offer more significant revenue potential and growth opportunities.
2. *Market Growth Rate*: The rate at which the market is expected to grow is an important indicator of market attractiveness. High-growth markets can offer substantial opportunities for pharmaceutical companies to expand their sales and market presence.
3. *Unmet Medical Needs*: Markets with significant unmet medical needs and limited treatment options are often considered attractive. Addressing unmet needs through innovative products or therapies can create a competitive advantage and market opportunities.
4. *Competitive Landscape*: Evaluating the competitive environment is crucial for determining market attractiveness. Assessing the number and strength of competitors, barriers to entry, intellectual property protections, and market share concentration help understand the level of competition and the potential for market success.
5. *Regulatory Environment*: The regulatory landscape, including the approval process, intellectual property protection, pricing and reimbursement policies, and compliance requirements, can significantly impact market attractiveness. Favorable regulatory conditions can facilitate market access and profitability.
6. *Healthcare Infrastructure*: The quality and accessibility of healthcare infrastructure, including hospitals, clinics, diagnostic facilities, and distribution networks, can influence market attractiveness. The adequate infrastructure supports efficient product distribution and patient access, enhancing market potential.
7. *Pricing and Reimbursement*: The pricing and reimbursement environment affects market attractiveness. Reimbursement policies, healthcare financing systems, insurance coverage, and pricing regulations can impact the affordability and profitability of pharmaceutical products.
8. *Technological Advancements*: Assessing the technological landscape and potential advancements in the market is crucial. Innovations like new drug delivery systems, personalized medicine, digital health solutions, and diagnostic tools can create opportunities and drive market attractiveness.
9. *Market Dynamics*: Understanding market dynamics, such as emerging trends, evolving patient preferences, healthcare system reforms, and shifts in disease patterns, helps gauge market attractiveness. Anticipating and adapting to these dynamics can provide a competitive edge.
10. *Market Risks and Challenges*: Evaluating the risks and challenges associated with a market, such as regulatory hurdles, intellectual property risks, pricing pressures, market volatility, and geographical factors, is important in assessing market attractiveness.

Assessing market attractiveness helps pharmaceutical companies prioritize their resources, identify growth opportunities, make informed investment decisions, and develop effective market entry strategies. However, Conducting thorough market research, gathering data, and considering multiple factors is essential to comprehensively understand a market's attractiveness before making strategic decisions.

Market Capitalization

Market capitalization, often referred to as a market cap, is a measure used to evaluate the size and value of a publicly traded company. It represents the total market value of a company's outstanding shares of stock.

To calculate market capitalization, the current market price per share of a company's stock is multiplied by the total number of outstanding shares. The result is the company's market cap, which represents the estimated total value of the company in the stock market.

Market capitalization categorizes companies into different segments and is commonly used by investors, analysts, and financial professionals to assess a company's relative worth and scale. Companies are typically classified into three main categories based on their market capitalization:

1. *Large-cap*: Large-cap companies have a market capitalization generally exceeding $10 billion. These are typically well-established companies with a significant market presence and are often considered more stable and mature.
2. *Mid-cap*: Mid-cap companies fall in the middle range, with market capitalization between $2 billion and $10 billion. These companies generally have moderate growth potential and may have established market positions in specific industries.
3. *Small-cap*: Small-cap companies have a market capitalization below $2 billion. They are generally smaller, less established companies with higher growth potential and risk. Small-cap stocks can offer greater growth opportunities but may also be more volatile.

Market capitalization indicates a company's size and reflects investors' perception of its value and potential. However, it is important to note that market capitalization is one factor when evaluating a company. Other metrics, such as revenue, earnings, debt, and industry dynamics, should also be analyzed to comprehensively understand a company's financial health and investment potential.

It is worth mentioning that market capitalization can fluctuate based on changes in stock prices and the number of outstanding shares. As a result, market cap values may change daily, reflecting shifts in investor sentiment and market conditions.

Market Capitalization in Pharma

Market capitalization in the pharmaceutical industry is a measure that reflects the market's perception of the company's worth and is influenced by factors such as financial performance, growth prospects, the pipeline of products, market share, and overall market conditions. Pharmaceutical companies can vary in market capitalization depending on their size, financial strength, and market position. The industry includes many companies, from large multinational pharmaceutical corporations to smaller biotech firms specializing in specific therapeutic areas.

1. *Large-Cap Pharmaceutical Companies* are typically multinational corporations with extensive product portfolios, established market presence, and significant market capitalization. Examples of large-cap pharmaceutical companies include Pfizer, Johnson & Johnson, Novartis, Merck & Co, and Roche. These companies often have diverse revenue streams, global operations, and substantial research and development (R&D) investments.
2. *Mid-Cap Pharmaceutical Companies* fall in the middle range regarding market capitalization. They may have a narrow focus on some therapeutic areas or niche markets. These companies can offer growth opportunities and may be involved in developing innovative drugs or technologies. Examples of mid-cap pharmaceutical companies include Jazz Pharmaceuticals, BioMarin Pharmaceuticals, and GW Pharmaceuticals (now part of Jazz Pharmaceuticals).
3. *Small-Cap Pharmaceutical Companies* have a relatively smaller market capitalization and may be focused on specialized therapeutic areas, drug development, or biotech research. These companies often have higher growth potential but may also carry higher risks due to factors such as clinical trial outcomes and regulatory approvals. Examples of small-cap pharmaceutical companies include Arena Pharmaceuticals, Innovia, and Portola Pharmaceuticals.

It is important to note that market capitalization can change over time due to various factors, including stock price fluctuations, financial performance, mergers and acquisitions, regulatory developments, and pipeline updates. The market capitalization of pharmaceutical companies is closely monitored by investors, analysts, and industry stakeholders as it provides insights into the overall valuation and market perception of a company's potential.

Market Connection

In pharmaceutical marketing, Market Connection refers to establishing and maintaining connections, relationships, and collaborations with various stakeholders in the market. It involves building networks and engaging with key players to facilitate the exchange of information, drive business growth, and support the successful commercialization of pharmaceutical products.

Here are some important aspects of market connection in pharma:

1. *Healthcare Professionals*: Establishing connections with healthcare professionals, such as physicians, specialists, pharmacists, and

nurses, is crucial. Pharmaceutical companies engage in various activities to build relationships with these professionals, including scientific and medical education programs, advisory boards, clinical trial collaborations, and providing updated product information.

2. *Key Opinion Leaders (KOLs)*: KOLs are influential medical community individuals with expertise and credibility in specific therapeutic areas. Building connections with KOLs can help pharmaceutical companies gain insights, gather expert opinions, and receive endorsements that influence prescription patterns and product adoption.
3. *Patient Advocacy Groups*: Connecting with patient advocacy groups can provide pharmaceutical companies valuable insights into patient perspectives, needs, and experiences. Collaborating with these groups can help develop patient-centered strategies, raise awareness about diseases and treatment options, and gather input from patients during drug development and commercialization.
4. *Payers and Reimbursement Authorities*: Connecting with payers, such as health insurance companies and government reimbursement authorities, is crucial for market access and success. Engaging in discussions, demonstrating the value and cost-effectiveness of pharmaceutical products, and understanding payer requirements and policies are essential for market connection.
5. *Regulatory Authorities*: Maintaining connections with regulatory authorities, such as the Food and Drug Administration (FDA) in the United States or the European Medicines Agency (EMA) in Europe, is vital. Companies need to stay updated on regulatory guidelines, provide required documentation, and engage in discussions to ensure compliance and timely approval of their products.
6. *Distributors and Supply Chain Partners*: Connecting with distributors and supply chain partners is important for efficient product distribution, ensuring the timely availability of pharmaceutical products to healthcare providers and patients. Collaborating with these partners helps optimize supply chain management, inventory control, and logistics, ensuring seamless product delivery.
7. *Market Research and Market Access Consultants*: Engaging market research firms and market access consultants can provide valuable insights into market dynamics, pricing strategies, competitive intelligence, and market entry requirements. These connections help companies gather critical information and develop effective commercialization plans.
8. *Digital and Online Platforms*: Utilizing digital and online platforms, such as social media, professional networking sites, and online communities, can enhance market connection. These platforms enable pharmaceutical companies to engage with healthcare professionals, patients, and other stakeholders conveniently and interactively, fostering communication and information exchange.

Successful market connection in the pharmaceutical industry requires a strategic and holistic approach. It involves understanding the needs and interests of different stakeholders, establishing trust and credibility, providing valuable information and support, and maintaining ongoing communication and collaboration. By fostering meaningful connections, pharmaceutical companies can better navigate the market landscape, gather insights, and drive the successful commercialization of their products.

Market Coverage

Market Coverage in pharmaceutical marketing refers to the extent to which a company's products or services are available and accessible to the target market. It involves the geographical areas, distribution channels, customer segments, and market segments a company reaches with its offerings. Market coverage strategies ensure that a company's products or services are effectively and efficiently distributed to reach the intended customers.

Here are some key aspects of market coverage:

1. *Geographical Coverage*: Market coverage involves determining the geographic areas where a company aims to operate and distribute its products or services. This may include local, regional, national, or international markets. The choice of geographic coverage depends on market size, growth potential, competition, infrastructure, and regulatory considerations.
2. *Customer Segments*: Market coverage involves identifying and targeting specific customer segments within the overall market. Customer segments may be defined based on demographic factors (age, gender, income, etc.), psychographic characteristics (lifestyle, attitudes, behavior, etc.), behavior (usage patterns, buying habits, etc.), or specific needs

and preferences. By understanding and targeting different customer segments, companies can tailor their marketing efforts to meet the specific needs of each segment.

3. *Distribution Channels*: Market coverage requires selecting and managing distribution channels through which the company's products or services will be available to customers. This may include direct sales teams, wholesalers, retailers, online platforms, or partnerships with other companies. The choice of distribution channels depends on factors such as customer preferences, product characteristics, competitive landscape, and cost efficiency.
4. *Market Segments*: Market coverage involves identifying and targeting specific market segments that offer the most potential for the company's products or services. Market segments may be defined based on industry size, growth rate, profitability, or specific customer needs. By focusing on relevant marketing segments, companies can allocate their resources more effectively and tailor their marketing strategies to address the specific requirements of each segment.
5. *Depth of Coverage*: Market coverage also considers the penetration depth within a target market. This refers to the extent to which a company's products or services are available to customers within a given market. It may involve ensuring widespread availability, convenient distribution, sufficient product assortment, and adequate customer support to meet the demand.
6. *Competitive Positioning*: Market coverage strategies also take into account the competitive landscape. This involves assessing the competitors' market coverage, distribution channels, customer, and market segments. By understanding the competitive positioning, companies can develop strategies to differentiate their offerings, target underserved segments, and gain a competitive advantage.

Market coverage strategies are developed based on market analysis, customer insights, competitive intelligence, and business objectives. It is important for companies to continuously evaluate and adjust market coverage strategies to align with the changing market dynamics, customer preferences, and business goals. Companies can increase their market share, reach more customers, and drive revenue growth by effectively covering the market.

Market Cycles

Market cycles, also known as business or economic cycles, refer to the recurring patterns of expansion and contraction in economic activity within a market or economy over time. These cycles reflect fluctuations in economic indicators such as GDP (Gross Domestic Product) growth, employment rates, consumer spending, investment levels, and business confidence. Market cycles are characterized by four distinct phases:

1. *Expansion/Recovery*: This phase marks the period of economic growth and increasing activity. It is characterized by rising GDP, low unemployment rates, increased consumer spending, and growing business investment. During this phase, businesses experience improved profitability and general optimism in the market. Monetary and fiscal policies often support this expansionary phase.
2. *Peak*: The peak represents the highest point of economic activity in a market cycle. It is characterized by the peak of economic indicators, such as high GDP growth, low unemployment rates, and robust consumer and business confidence. At this stage, the economy is operating at or near full capacity, and inflationary pressures may start to emerge. The peak phase often precedes a contraction or slowdown.
3. *Contraction/Recession*: The contraction phase represents a slowdown in economic activity. It is characterized by declining GDP growth, rising unemployment rates, decreased consumer spending, and reduced business investment. During this phase, businesses may experience declining profits, and economic indicators weaken. The contraction phase often leads to a recession, defined as a significant and prolonged decline in economic activity.
4. *Trough*: The trough represents the lowest point of the market cycle, indicating the end of the contraction phase. It is characterized by the bottoming out of economic indicators, such as low GDP growth, high unemployment rates, and reduced consumer and business confidence. At this stage, the economy may experience high levels of uncertainty and financial stress. The trough phase precedes the subsequent expansion phase, marking the beginning of a new market cycle.

Market cycles are influenced by various factors, including business investments, consumer spending, monetary and fiscal policies, technological advancements, geopolitical events, and global economic conditions. These factors interact, leading to the cyclical nature of markets.

It is important to note that market cycles can vary in duration and intensity. Some cycles may be shorter and milder, while others can be longer and more severe. Additionally, market cycles can differ across industries and countries due to specific economic and market conditions.

Understanding market cycles is important for businesses, investors, policymakers, and individuals to make informed decisions and manage risks. By recognizing the cycle's different phases, stakeholders can adjust their strategies, allocate resources effectively, and position themselves for success in different economic conditions.

Market Cycles and the Pharma Industry

Market cycles in the pharmaceutical industry refer to the recurring patterns of expansion and contraction in the pharmaceutical market over time. These cycles are influenced by various factors specific to the industry, including drug development and approval processes, patent expirations, regulatory changes, healthcare policies, market competition, and therapeutic advancements. Here are some key aspects of market cycles in the pharmaceutical industry:

1. *Research and Development (R&D) Phase*: The pharmaceutical market cycle begins with the research and development phase, where companies invest in discovering and developing new drugs or therapies. This phase involves extensive research, preclinical studies, and clinical trials to assess the safety and efficacy of potential pharmaceutical products. The R&D phase is characterized by high levels of investment, innovation, and scientific advancements.
2. *Launch and Growth Phase*: Once a new drug or therapy completes clinical trials and regulatory approvals, it enters the launch and growth phase. This phase is characterized by the commercialization and market introduction of the product. Companies focus on marketing efforts, building awareness among healthcare professionals and patients, and driving product adoption. During this phase, sales and market share typically experience significant growth.
3. *Patent Exclusivity and Peak Phase*: After the launch, pharmaceutical products often benefit from a period of patent exclusivity, during which the company holds exclusive rights to manufacture and sell the product. This period provides a competitive advantage and allows companies to generate substantial revenues. The peak phase represents the period of maximum sales and market share, typically driven by the success of patented products.
4. *Patent Expirations and Generic Competition*: As patents on pharmaceutical products expire, generic versions may enter the market, leading to increased competition. This phase is characterized by declining sales and market share of branded products as lower-cost generic alternatives become available. Companies may experience a contraction in revenue during this phase, especially if they heavily rely on sales of products with expiring patents.
5. *Lifecycle Management and Innovation*: To counter the impact of patent expirations, pharmaceutical companies engage in lifecycle management strategies and continue to innovate. They may introduce new formulations, dosage strengths, or new indications for existing products or develop entirely new ones. These efforts aim to extend product lifecycles, capture new market segments, and sustain growth.
6. *Regulatory and Reimbursement Changes*: Regulatory and reimbursement changes can significantly influence market cycles in the pharmaceutical industry. New regulations, pricing policies, or reimbursement adjustments imposed by healthcare systems or government authorities may impact market dynamics, pricing strategies, and market access for pharmaceutical products.
7. *Therapeutic Advancements and Market Shifts*: Advancements in therapeutic areas, such as introducing novel treatments, personalized medicine, or breakthrough therapies, can create market shifts within the pharmaceutical industry. Emerging treatment modalities or changing disease patterns may lead to new market opportunities and alter the competitive landscape.

Understanding market cycles in the pharmaceutical industry is essential for companies to anticipate and adapt to changing market dynamics. It helps them navigate patent expirations, generic competition, regulatory channels, and industry trends. By strategically managing their product portfolios, investing in R&D, and adapting to market cycles, pharmaceutical companies can position themselves for long-term success in an evolving market.

Market Demand

Market demand in the pharmaceutical industry refers to the number of pharmaceutical products or therapies that consumers and healthcare providers are willing and able to purchase at a given price and within a specific market or geographic area. It represents the aggregate demand for pharmaceutical products based on patient needs, disease prevalence, treatment options, healthcare access, and affordability. Here are some aspects of market demand in the pharmaceutical industry:

1. *Patient Needs and Medical Conditions*: Market demand is driven by patient needs and medical conditions that require pharmaceutical interventions. Diseases, disorders, and health conditions demand pharmaceutical products to prevent, diagnose, treat, or manage those conditions. The prevalence and severity of medical conditions influence the overall market demand for pharmaceutical products.
2. *Treatment Options and Efficacy*: Market demand is influenced by the availability and effectiveness of treatment options. When pharmaceutical products demonstrate clinical efficacy, have a favorable safety profile, and offer benefits over existing therapies, the demand for those products tends to increase. Patients and healthcare providers seek out effective treatments that can improve health outcomes.
3. *Healthcare Access and Affordability*: Market demand is also affected by healthcare access and affordability. Factors such as healthcare infrastructure, insurance coverage, reimbursement policies, and out-of-pocket costs can impact the ability of patients to access and afford pharmaceutical products. Limited access or high costs may reduce market demand, especially in markets with low healthcare coverage or high-income disparities.
4. *Market Demographics and Patient Characteristics*: Market demand considers the demographics and characteristics of the target patient population. Age, gender, geographic location, socioeconomic status, and cultural considerations can influence the demand for specific pharmaceutical products. Understanding different patient segments' diverse needs and preferences helps companies tailor their marketing strategies and product offerings.
5. *Regulatory Environment and Approvals*: Market demand is influenced by regulatory factors, including drug approvals and regulations governing pharmaceutical products. Regulatory approvals from authorities such as the FDA (Food and Drug Administration) in the United States or EMA (European Medicines Agency) in the European Union are necessary to market and sell pharmaceutical products. Regulatory requirements, such as safety and efficacy standards, can affect the availability and demand for specific products.
6. *Market Competition and Differentiation*: Market demand is shaped by competition among pharmaceutical companies. Companies strive to differentiate their products through innovation, unique features, pricing strategies, or therapeutic advancements. The competitiveness of the market and the perceived value of products can impact the demand for specific pharmaceutical offerings.
7. *Market Trends and Emerging Therapies*: Market demand is subject to market trends and emerging therapies. Scientific advancements, technological innovations, and evolving healthcare practices can drive changes in market demand. For example, the rising demand for personalized medicine or gene therapies reflects emerging trends and patient expectations for more targeted and precise treatments.

Understanding market demand is crucial for pharmaceutical companies to develop effective marketing strategies, allocate resources, and make informed business decisions. By analyzing patient needs, market dynamics, competitive landscape, and regulatory environment, companies can assess market demand and identify opportunities to meet the needs of patients and healthcare providers effectively.

Market Development

In pharmaceutical marketing, market development refers to the strategic expansion of a company's existing products or services into new markets or customer segments. It involves identifying untapped opportunities and creating strategies to enter and generate new markets to drive business growth.

Here are some key aspects of market development:

1. *Market Analysis*: Market development begins with thoroughly analyzing potential new markets or customer segments. This involves studying the market size, growth potential, customer needs and preferences, competition, regulatory considerations, and other relevant factors that may impact market entry and success.
2. *Target Market Identification*: Once potential markets are identified, companies need to define and target specific customer segments within those markets. This may involve demographic, psychographic, geographic, or behavioral segmentation to understand the characteristics and preferences of the target audience.

Companies can tailor their marketing strategies by identifying the most promising customer segments to effectively reach and engage those customers.

3. *Market Entry Strategies*: Companies must develop market entry strategies to establish a presence in new markets. These strategies may include various approaches such as direct sales, partnerships, distribution agreements, joint ventures, acquisitions, or licensing agreements. The choice of entry strategy depends on factors such as market complexity, entry barriers, resource availability, and the company's strategic goals.
4. *Product Adaptation or Customization*: To succeed in new markets, companies may need to adapt or customize their existing products or services to meet the specific needs and preferences of the target market. This could involve modifying product features, packaging, pricing, branding, or even developing new product variants tailored to the market requirements. By aligning the product offering with the new market's demands, companies can increase their chances of market acceptance.
5. *Marketing and Promotion*: Market development requires targeted marketing and promotion efforts to create awareness and generate demand in the new markets. This may involve developing marketing campaigns, advertising, public relations, digital marketing, and other promotional activities to reach the target audience and communicate the value proposition of the company's products or services. Effective marketing strategies help build brand recognition, establish credibility, and attract customers in new markets.
6. *Distribution and Sales Channels*: Market development often involves setting up or expanding distribution and sales channels in new markets. This includes identifying appropriate distribution partners, establishing relationships with retailers or wholesalers, or leveraging e-commerce platforms to ensure the availability and accessibility of the company's products or services to the target customers.
7. *Market Monitoring and Adaptation*: Once a company enters a new market, it is crucial to continuously monitor market dynamics, customer feedback, and the competitive landscape. This allows companies to adapt their strategies, fine-tune their offerings, and address any emerging challenges or opportunities in the market. Market development is an iterative process that requires ongoing assessment and adjustment based on market feedback and evolving market conditions.

Market development can be a valuable growth strategy for companies seeking to expand their customer base, reach new markets, and diversify their revenue streams. Companies can capitalize on untapped opportunities by effectively identifying and entering new markets, increasing market share, and achieving sustainable growth.

Market Dynamics

Market dynamics in the pharmaceutical industry refer to the factors and forces that influence the behavior, trends, and interactions within the pharmaceutical market. These dynamics shape the competitive landscape, pricing strategies, product demand, market entry barriers, and overall market conditions. Understanding market dynamics is crucial for pharmaceutical companies to make informed decisions and adapt to the changing market environment. Here are some key aspects of market dynamics in the pharmaceutical industry:

1. *Competitive Landscape*: The pharmaceutical market is highly competitive, with multiple companies vying for market share. Market dynamics include the presence and activities of competitors, such as their product portfolios, pricing strategies, marketing efforts, research and development capabilities, and regulatory compliance. The competitive landscape influences market positioning, market share, and the level of innovation within the industry.
2. *Patent Protection and Exclusivity*: Patents play a significant role in the pharmaceutical industry. Market dynamics are influenced by the duration of patent protection for innovative drugs, which grants exclusivity to the patent holder and limit competition. The expiration of patents allows generic drug manufacturers to enter the market, leading to increased competition and potentially lower prices.
3. *Regulatory Environment*: The pharmaceutical industry is subject to strict regulations governing drug development, testing, manufacturing, and marketing. Market dynamics are influenced by regulatory bodies such as the US Food and Drug Administration (FDA) or the European Medicines Agency (EMA), which oversee drug approvals, safety standards, labeling requirements, and post-marketing surveillance. Regulation changes can impact market entry, product development timelines, and market access.

4. *Healthcare Policies and Reimbursement*: Market dynamics in the pharmaceutical industry are closely linked to healthcare policies and reimbursement systems. Government healthcare programs, private insurance companies, and healthcare providers play a role in determining the availability and affordability of pharmaceutical products. Changes in reimbursement policies, formulary inclusion, or pricing regulations can significantly impact market demand and product accessibility.
5. *Technology and Innovation*: Advances in technology and innovation drive market dynamics in the pharmaceutical industry. New drug delivery systems, diagnostic tools, precision medicine, genetic therapies, and digital health solutions impact the development and commercialization of pharmaceutical products. Companies that embrace innovation and leverage emerging technologies often gain a competitive edge in the market.
6. *Market Segmentation and Patient Preferences*: Market dynamics are influenced by patient demographics, preferences, and behavior. Market segmentation helps identify patient subgroups with specific needs, treatment patterns, and preferences. Understanding patient preferences and tailoring product offerings can increase market demand and customer loyalty.
7. *Pricing and Market Access*: Pricing strategies and market access play a significant role in market dynamics. Pharmaceutical companies must navigate pricing considerations, including research and development costs, manufacturing expenses, healthcare affordability, and price negotiations with payers. Market access refers to securing reimbursement, formulary inclusion, and favorable market positioning for pharmaceutical products.
8. *Mergers, Acquisitions, and Partnerships*: Market dynamics can be influenced by mergers, acquisitions, and partnerships within the pharmaceutical industry. These activities shape the competitive landscape, impact market concentration, and drive consolidation. Collaborations between pharmaceutical companies, research institutions, or healthcare providers can facilitate research, development, and commercialization efforts.

Monitoring and analyzing market dynamics in the pharmaceutical industry is crucial for companies to identify market opportunities, assess competitive threats, and develop effective strategies. By staying informed about market trends, regulatory changes, patient needs, and competitive forces, pharmaceutical companies can adapt their approach, optimize their product offerings, and navigate the complex dynamics of the industry.

Market Ecology

Market ecology refers to the study and understanding of the interactions, relationships, and dynamics among various entities within a market. It involves analyzing the interdependencies and interconnections between market participants, their behaviors, strategies, and the overall market environment. Market ecology aims to gain insights into how different entities within a market, such as companies, customers, suppliers, competitors, and regulators, interact and influence each other. Here are some key aspects of market ecology:

1. *Market Participants*: Market ecology considers the diverse participants involved in a market, including companies, customers, suppliers, distributors, investors, and regulatory bodies. Each participant has a specific role and impact on the market. Understanding these participants' characteristics, motivations, and behavior is crucial to comprehend the market dynamics.
2. *Interactions and Relationships*: Market ecology examines the interactions and relationships between market participants. This includes analyzing the relationships between buyers and sellers, partnerships and collaborations among companies, supplier-customer relationships, and interactions with regulatory authorities. The nature and quality of these interactions shape market dynamics, competitiveness, and cooperation within the market.
3. *Competitive Dynamics*: Market ecology delves into the competitive dynamics among companies within a market. This includes analyzing market concentration, market share distribution, pricing strategies, product differentiation, competitive advantages, and barriers to entry. Understanding the competitive landscape helps identify opportunities and threats, assess market power, and anticipate competitive responses.
4. *Market Forces and Trends*: Market ecology studies the market forces and trends that influence the behavior and dynamics of participants. This includes technological advancements, regulatory changes, economic conditions, consumer preferences, industry trends, and social and environmental factors. These forces and trends shape market

conditions, opportunities, and challenges for market participants.

5. *Market Feedback and Adaptation*: Market ecology emphasizes the importance of market feedback and adaptation. Feedback from customers, suppliers, and other market participants provides valuable insights for companies to adapt their strategies, improve products or services, and meet evolving market demands. Adapting and responding to market feedback is crucial for long-term success and sustainability.
6. *Ecosystem Perspective*: Market ecology takes an ecosystem perspective, considering the interconnectedness and interdependence of various entities within the market. It recognizes that changes or disruptions in one part of the market can have ripple effects on its participants. For example, regulatory changes may impact access, affecting the strategies and behaviors of companies and customers. Considering the market as an ecosystem helps identify potential risks, dependencies, and opportunities.
7. *Market Evolution*: Market ecology acknowledges that markets are dynamic and constantly evolving. It considers the evolutionary processes of markets, including new technologies, shifts in consumer behavior, industry disruptions, and market transformation. Understanding market evolution helps companies anticipate future trends, adapt to changes, and seize emerging opportunities.
8. By studying market ecology, companies can gain insights into the complex dynamics of a market, make informed decisions, and develop effective strategies. It enables a deeper understanding of market participants' interactions, interdependencies, and influencers, leading to a more comprehensive and holistic approach to market analysis and business planning.

Market Ecology in Pharma

In the pharmaceutical industry, market ecology refers to the study of the interactions, relationships, and dynamics among various entities within the pharmaceutical market. It involves analyzing the interconnectedness and interdependencies of pharmaceutical companies, healthcare providers, patients, regulatory authorities, payers, and other stakeholders in the industry. Understanding the market ecology in pharma helps comprehend the complex dynamics that shape the development, manufacturing, marketing, and distribution of pharmaceutical products.

Here are some key aspects of market ecology in the pharmaceutical industry:

1. *Pharmaceutical Companies*: Market ecology considers the activities, strategies, and interactions among pharmaceutical companies. This includes understanding the competitive landscape, product portfolios, research and development efforts, marketing and sales strategies, partnerships, and collaborations among pharmaceutical companies. Companies' interactions and competitive dynamics influence market positioning, pricing strategies, and innovation within the industry.
2. *Healthcare Providers*: Market ecology examines the relationships and interactions between pharmaceutical companies and healthcare providers, such as hospitals, clinics, physicians, and pharmacists. Understanding how pharmaceutical products are prescribed, distributed, and administered by healthcare providers helps to identify many opportunities, assess the impact of healthcare policies and formulary decisions, and understand the factors that influence the adoption of specific pharmaceutical products.
3. *Patients and Consumers*: Market ecology considers the role of patients and consumers in the pharmaceutical market. This includes analyzing patient needs, behaviors, preferences, and treatment decision factors. Understanding patient perspectives and experiences helps pharmaceutical companies develop patient-centric approaches, tailor their marketing efforts, and effectively design products that meet patient needs.
4. *Regulatory Authorities*: Market ecology involves studying interactions between pharmaceutical companies and regulatory authorities responsible for drug approvals, safety regulations, and marketing guidelines. Understanding the regulatory environment, including the process of drug development, clinical trials, and post-marketing surveillance, is crucial for pharmaceutical companies to navigate the regulatory landscape and ensure compliance.
5. *Payers and Reimbursement Systems*: Market ecology in pharma considers the role of payers, such as insurance companies, government healthcare programs, and pharmacy benefit managers. Analyzing the reimbursement systems, formulary inclusion criteria, and pricing negotiation with payers helps pharmaceutical companies understand market access challenges and develop strategies to maximize reimbursement and market coverage for their products.

6. *Supply Chain and Distribution*: Market ecology examines interactions and relationships within the pharmaceutical supply chain, including manufacturers, wholesalers, distributors, and pharmacies. Understanding the dynamics of the supply chain helps pharmaceutical companies ensure the efficient and timely distribution of their products, maintain inventory levels, and optimize the availability and accessibility of pharmaceutical products to healthcare providers and patients.
7. *Market Trends and Healthcare Policies*: Market ecology considers the impact of market trends, healthcare policies, and emerging technologies on the pharmaceutical industry. This includes analyzing trends in personalized medicine, digital health, health outcomes research, value-based pricing, and regulatory reforms. Understanding the trends and policies helps pharmaceutical companies anticipate market shifts, adapt to changes, and align their strategies with evolving market dynamics.

Companies can gain insights into the complex interactions and dynamics among various stakeholders by studying market ecology in the pharmaceutical industry. This understanding enables better decision-making, identification of market opportunities, development of patient-centered strategies, and adaptation to the changing landscape of the pharmaceutical market.

Market Indicators

Market indicators are statistical measures or data points used to assess a specific market or economy's overall performance, trends, and conditions. These indicators provide valuable insights into the direction and health of the market, helping investors, analysts, and policymakers make informed decisions. Market indicators can vary depending on the specific market or industry being analyzed. Here are some commonly used market indicators:

1. *Stock Market Indicators*: Stock market indices, such as the S&P 500, Dow Jones Industrial Average, or NASDAQ (National Association of Securities Dealers Automated Quotations), represent the performance of a selected group of stocks listed on a particular exchange. These indices are benchmarks to gauge the stock market's performance and track trends.
2. *Bond Market Indicators*: Bond market indicators, such as yields on government bonds or corporate bond spreads, provide insights into the interest rates, credit quality, and investor sentiment within the fixed-income market. Bond market indicators assess borrowing costs, credit risk, and economic expectations.
3. *Economic Indicators*: Economic indicators reflect an economy's overall health and performance. Examples include Gross Domestic Product (GDP), inflation rates, unemployment rates, Consumer Price Index (CPI), Purchasing Managers' Index (PMI), and retail sales figures. These indicators help analyze economic growth, inflationary pressures, labor market conditions, and consumer spending patterns.
4. *Sector-Specific Indicators*: Different sectors within the economy may have specific indicators that are relevant to their performance. For example, indicators such as drug sales growth rates, research and development expenditure, clinical trial activity, or patent filings can provide insights into sector-specific trends and performance in the pharmaceutical industry.
5. *Consumer-Sentiment Indices*: Consumer sentiment indices measure consumers' confidence, optimism, and spending intentions. Examples include the Consumer Confidence Index (CCI) and the University of Michigan Consumer Sentiment Index. These indices reflect consumers' perception of the overall economy and their willingness to spend, which can impact various industries, including retail, hospitality, and consumer goods.
6. *Housing Market Indicators*: Housing market indicators include home sales, housing starts, average home prices, and mortgage interest rates. These indicators help gauge the strength of the real estate market and provide insights into consumer demand, housing affordability, and construction activity.
7. *Foreign Exchange Rates*: Foreign exchange rates, such as currency exchange rates between different countries, can have a significant impact on international trade, export/import competitiveness, and cross-border investments. Exchange rate fluctuations can affect various industries, including manufacturing, tourism, and global financial markets.
8. *Volatility Indices*: Volatility indices, such as VIX (CBOE Volatility Index), measure market volatility and investor sentiment. These indices reflect the market's expectation of future price fluctuations and can indicate periods of increased market uncertainty or potential market downturns.

These are just a few examples of market and other indicators used to assess specific markets or industries. By monitoring and analyzing market indicators, investors, analysts, and policymakers can gain insights into market trends, risks, and opportunities, enabling them to make more informed decisions. It is important to consider multiple indicators and their interrelationships to comprehensively understand market conditions.

Market Lifecycle

A market lifecycle refers to the stages a product, service, or industry goes through, from its introduction to its eventual decline. It provides a framework for understanding the various phases of a market's development and helps businesses and analysts make strategic decisions based on the characteristics of each stage. Typically, a market lifecycle consists of four stages:

1. *Introduction*: In this stage, a new product or service is introduced. There is limited customer awareness, and the product may face challenges in gaining acceptance. Companies often incur high research, development, and marketing costs during this phase. Profits are typically low or non-existent as companies focus on building brand recognition and customer adoption. The market is in its early stages and has limited customer awareness. Companies are trying to establish their presence and gain market share.
2. *Growth*: Once the product gains acceptance, it enters the growth stage. Demand and sales increase rapidly, and competitors may enter the market. This phase is characterized by expanding the customer base, improving economies of scale, and increasing profitability. Companies invest in marketing and product improvement to capture a larger market share. The market experiences rapid expansion as customer demand increases. New competitors may enter the market, and companies focus on capturing a larger share.
3. *Maturity*: The maturity stage is reached when the market becomes saturated with competitors and the growth rate slows. The focus shifts from customer acquisition to customer retention. Price competition may intensify as companies strive to maintain market share. Profit margins tend to stabilize, and companies may diversify their offerings or target new market segments to sustain growth.
4. *Decline*: Market saturation becomes more evident in the decline stage and sales decline. This can occur due to changing customer preferences, technological advancements, patent expirations, or the emergence of superior alternatives. Companies may discontinue the product or service, reduce investments, or focus on niche markets with loyal customers.

In summary, the market lifecycle focuses on the evolution of the market for the whole category, considering factors such as customer awareness, demand, competition, and profitability. It helps analyze the stages of development and maturity a market goes through, regardless of the specific product or industry.

The lifecycle looks at the broader market and the dynamics where many competing products operate. It includes the lifecycles of multiple products or services within the market and the interaction between competitors, customers, and other external factors.

Understanding the market lifecycle helps businesses anticipate and adapt to changes. Identify new opportunities and allocate resources effectively throughout each stage. It also highlights the importance of continuous innovation and diversification to remain competitive in evolving markets.

Market Maps

Market mapping is a strategic tool used in pharmaceutical marketing to visually represent a market's competitive landscape. It helps to identify the key players in the market, their strengths and weaknesses, and their relationships with each other.

A market map in pharmaceutical marketing typically involves identifying the different segments of the market and then mapping the various brands or products to those segments. This allows you to identify which brands compete for the same customers and which brands target different customer needs.

Here are the general steps involved in creating a market map in pharmaceutical marketing:

1. *Identify the Key Segments*: The first step is identifying market segments. This might include demographic segments, disease-based segments, or other relevant criteria.
2. *Collect Data*: Collect data on the various brands or products targeting each segment. This might include information on their clinical data, marketing tactics, pricing, and other relevant factors.
3. *Map the Brands*: Map the various brands or products to the relevant segments based on the data collected in step two. This might involve creating a visual map, such as a grid or chart,

representing the relationships between the brands and the segments.

4. *Analyze the Results*: Analyze the market map to identify areas of opportunity and potential threats. Look for areas where the market is underserved, and your brand may have opportunities to differentiate itself from competitors.
5. *Develop Strategies*: Based on your analysis, develop strategies to address the opportunities and threats identified. This might include optimizing your brand's targeting, developing new products, or improving marketing tactics.
6. *Monitor and Adjust*: Finally, monitor the market and adjust your strategies to stay competitive.

Market Maps: Some Examples

Here are a few examples of market maps in pharmaceutical marketing:

1. *Disease-based Market Map*: This market map plots pharmaceutical brands on two dimensions: the disease they treat and the severity of the disease. This market map can help identify which brands target which diseases and which have the greatest unmet need. For example, if a certain disease has a high severity rating, but there are no drugs available to treat it, there may be an opportunity for a new drug to enter the market.
2. *Customer Segment Market Map*: This market map plots pharmaceutical brands on two dimensions: the target customer segment and the features or benefits they offer. This market map can help identify which brands target customer segments and which are underserved. For example, if a certain customer segment values convenience and ease of use, a brand may be able to develop a product that meets those needs.
3. *Price-based Market Map*: This market map plots pharmaceutical brands on two dimensions: the drug's price and the features and benefits they offer. This market map can help identify which brands offer the best value for the price and which are overpriced. For example, if a certain brand is priced high but offers only moderate benefits, there may be an opportunity for a new brand to enter the market with a more affordable price and better benefits.

These are just a few examples of market maps in pharmaceutical marketing. The specific dimensions and brands plotted on the map will depend on your brand's specific goals and the competitive landscape in your market.

Market mapping can be complex and requires input from multiple stakeholders, including market research teams, brand managers, and sales teams. However, the insights gained from market mapping can be invaluable in developing effective pharmaceutical marketing strategies.

Market Niche

A market niche is a specialized segment or subset of a larger market. It represents a specific customer group with unmet needs, preferences, and characteristics that distinguish them from the broader market. In a market niche, businesses can focus on catering to the specific demands of these niche customers, providing tailored products or services to meet their requirements effectively. Here are some key points to consider about market niches:

1. *Targeted Customer Group*: A market niche targets a specific customer group or segment with distinct characteristics, such as demographics, behaviors, interests, or preferences. This customer group may have specific needs or challenges not adequately addressed by the general market offerings.
2. *Specialized Products or Services*: Businesses operating in a market niche develop specialized products or services tailored to meet the unique requirements of the niche customers. These offerings are designed to provide superior value or solve specific problems for the targeted customer group.
3. *Less Competition*: Market niches typically have fewer competitors than the broader market. By focusing on a narrow customer segment, businesses can establish a competitive advantage and differentiate themselves from more general competitors. This can result in higher customer loyalty and reduced price competition.
4. *Higher Profitability*: Due to reduced competition and specialized offerings, market niches are often more profitable for businesses. Niche customers are often willing to pay a premium for products that precisely meet their needs, allowing businesses to achieve higher profit margins.
5. *Niche Marketing and Positioning*: Effective niche marketing involves understanding the targeted niche customers' unique needs, preferences, and behaviors. Businesses can create tailored marketing messages and strategies to resonate with the nice audience and position themselves as experts or specialists in serving that particular market segment.

6. *Niche Expansion*: As businesses establish a strong presence and success within a specific market niche, they may consider expanding their offerings or targeting additional niche segments. This can help diversify their customer base and capture new market opportunities while focusing on specialized customer needs.
7. *Market Dynamics*: Market niches can evolve over time due to changes in customer preferences, technological advancements, or competitive forces. It is important for businesses operating in a market niche to continuously monitor the market dynamics and adapt their strategies to stay relevant and competitive.

Identifying and successfully serving a market niche requires thorough market research, an understanding of customer needs, and the ability to develop tailored offerings. By effectively addressing the unique requirements of a niche customer group, businesses can gain a competitive edge, establish customer loyalty, and achieve sustainable growth.

Market Niche in Pharma

In the pharmaceutical industry, a market niche refers to a specialized segment within the broader pharmaceutical market. It represents a specific area of focus where pharmaceutical companies target a particular group of patients, diseases, or therapeutic areas with their products or services. Here is a closer look at market niches in the pharmaceutical industry:

1. *Targeted Patient Population*: In a pharmaceutical market niche, companies focus on addressing the needs of a specific population with unique medical conditions or requirements. This could include rare diseases, specific demographic groups (pediatrics, geriatrics, etc.) or patients with specific genetic or physiological characteristics.
2. *Therapeutic Specialization*: Market niches in pharma often revolve around therapeutic specialization, where companies develop drugs or treatments for specific diseases or medical conditions. These niches can range from large therapeutic areas like oncology, cardiovascular health, or central nervous system disorders to more specialized areas such as orphan diseases or rare genetic disorders.
3. *Personalized Medicine*: With advances in genomics and personalized medicine, market niches have emerged in pharma that focus on tailoring treatments to individual patients based on their genetic profiles or other specific factors. These niches involve the development of targeted therapies or diagnostics that cater to the unique characteristics of patients, allowing for more precise and effective treatments.
4. *Biologics and Speciality Drugs*: Market niches can also be found in biologics and specialty drugs. These are typically complex, high-cost medications to treat specific diseases or conditions. They may require specialized manufacturing processes, distribution channels, or patient support programs, creating opportunities for companies to specialize in these niches.
5. *Orphan Drugs*: Orphan drugs target rare diseases that affect a small patient population. Due to the limited market size, companies that develop orphan drugs can benefit from regulatory incentives, market exclusivity, and higher pricing. This niche allows companies to focus on unmet medical needs and provide treatments for patients with rare conditions.
6. *Veterinary Pharmaceuticals*: Market niches can also exist within the veterinary pharmaceutical sector, where companies specialize in developing medications for specific animal species or health conditions affecting animals. These niches cater to veterinarians' and pet owners' unique needs and requirements.
7. *Niche Marketing and Positioning*: Effectively operating within a market niche in the pharmaceutical industry requires targeted marketing and positioning strategies. Companies need to understand the specific needs of the target patient population or disease area, engage with healthcare professionals, establish strong relationships with patient advocacy groups, and communicate the unique value proposition of their products or services.

Identifying and successfully serving a market niche in the pharmaceutical industry requires a deep understanding of patient needs, clinical research, regulatory considerations, and market dynamics. By focusing on a specialized segment, pharmaceutical companies can develop tailored therapies, establish their expertise, and address unmet medical needs in specific areas, ultimately driving growth and making a meaningful impact on patient outcomes.

Market Opportunity Analysis

Market opportunity analysis (MOA) identifies and evaluates opportunities within a specific market that a company can capitalize on. It involves assessing market conditions, customer needs, competition, and other factors to determine the viability and attractiveness of entering or expanding within a market. Market opportunity analysis aims to identify areas where a company can successfully meet customer demands and achieve sustainable growth. Here are the key steps involved in conducting a market opportunity analysis:

1. *Define the Market Scope*: Clearly define the boundaries and scope of the market you are analyzing. This includes identifying the target customer segments, geographical regions, and relevant product or service categories.
2. *Market Size and Growth Potential*: Determine the market's current size and assess its growth potential. This involves analyzing market trends, historical data, industry reports, and forecasts to understand the market's past and projected growth rates.
3. *Customer Needs and Preferences*: Gain a deep understanding of the target customer segments' needs, preferences, and pain points. This can be done through market research, surveys, interviews, and data analysis. Identify unmet needs or underserved areas where your company can provide value.
4. *Competitive Analysis*: Assess the competitive landscape within the market. Identify competitors' market share, strengths, weaknesses, and strategies. Evaluate how your company's offerings differ from competitors' products or services.
5. *Market Trends and External Factors*: Analyze the market trends, technological advancements, regulatory environment, and other external factors that may impact the market. Identify emerging trends, shifts in consumer behavior, or regulatory changes that could present opportunities and challenges.
6. *Market Segmentation and Target Market*: Segment the market based on relevant criteria such as demographics, psychographics, geographic location, or buying behavior. Identify the most attractive target market segments that align with your company's capabilities and competitive advantage.
7. *SWOT Analysis*: Conduct a SWOT analysis (strengths, Weaknesses, opportunities, Threats) to assess your company's internal strengths and weaknesses and external opportunities and threats in the market. Identify how your strengths can be leveraged to capitalize on market opportunities and mitigate potential threats.
8. *Financial Analysis*: Evaluate the financial viability of pursuing the market opportunity. Assess the potential revenue, profitability, and return on investment. Consider pricing, cost structure, sales projections, and investment requirements.
9. *Risk Assessment*: Identify and assess the risks associated with entering or expanding within the market. Evaluate factors such as market volatility, regulatory risks, competitive intensity, and potential barriers to entry.
10. *Decision-Making and Strategy Development*: Based on the analysis conducted, make informed decisions about pursuing the identified market opportunities. Develop a clear strategy and action plan that outlines how your company will position itself, differentiate its offerings, target customers, and allocate resources to capture the identified market opportunity.

Market opportunity analysis helps companies decide about entering new markets, launching new products or services, or expanding their existing offerings. It provides a structured approach to evaluate the potential benefits, risks, and market potential, enabling companies to focus their resources and efforts on the most promising opportunities.

Market Opportunity Analysis in Pharma

Market opportunity analysis in the pharmaceutical industry involves assessing potential opportunities for a company to enter or expand within specific market segments. Here are some key considerations for conducting a market opportunity analysis in pharma:

1. *Disease Prevalence and Unmet Needs*: Evaluate the prevalence of specific diseases or medical conditions and identify areas with significant unmet needs. Look for conditions where treatment gaps exist, side effects are high, or patient outcomes can be improved.
2. *Market Size and Growth Potential*: Determine the size of the target market segment and assess its growth potential. Analyze population demographics, epidemiological data, and market trends to understand the current and future demand.
3. *Competitive Landscape*: Assess the competition within the target market segment. Identify existing pharmaceutical products, therapies, or treatments that address the same medical conditions. Evaluate competitors' strengths, weaknesses, and market positions to identify potential gaps or areas where differentiation is possible.
4. *Regulatory Landscape*: Understand the regulatory environment governing the pharmaceutical industry, including approval processes, intellectual property protection, and reimbursement policies. Identify any regulatory

barriers or requirements that may impact market entry or expansion.

5. *Physician and Patient Preferences*: Gain insights into the preferences, prescribing patterns, and treatment guidelines followed by healthcare professionals within the target market segment. Understand patient preferences, including convenience, route of administration, dosage forms, or other specific advancements.
6. *Technology and Innovation*: Evaluate emerging technologies, scientific advancements, and innovative approaches within the pharmaceutical industry. Identify areas where new technologies or therapies can disrupt existing treatments or create opportunities for improved patient outcomes.
7. *Market Access and Distribution*: Assess the feasibility of gaining market access and establishing distribution channels within the target market segment. Consider factors such as healthcare infrastructure, reimbursement systems, distribution networks, and partnerships with healthcare providers or institutions.
8. *Pricing and Reimbursement*: Analyze the target market segment's pricing dynamics and reimbursement landscape within the target market segment. Evaluate factors such as healthcare budgets, payer policies, and the willingness of healthcare systems or insurers to cover new treatments or therapies.
9. *Patient Advocacy and Support*: Consider the presence of patient advocacy groups or support networks within the target market segment. These groups can raise awareness, influence treatment decisions, and advocate for improved treatment access.
10. *Risk Assessment and Mitigation*: Identify potential risks and challenges associated with entering or expanding within the target market segment. Evaluate clinical trial requirements, intellectual property risks, and potential market barriers.

Based on the market opportunity analysis findings, pharmaceutical companies can improve product development, market entry, pricing, distribution, and marketing strategies. By understanding the market dynamics, unmet needs, and competitive landscape, companies can position themselves to capture opportunities, address patient needs, and drive growth in the pharmaceutical industry.

Market Penetration

Market penetration is a business strategy aimed at increasing the market share of a product or service within an existing market. It involves capturing a larger portion of the target market by attracting new customers or encouraging existing customers to use the product/service more frequently or in greater quantities. Market penetration is typically pursued when there is still growth potential within the current market before considering expansion into new markets. Here are some key aspects of market penetration:

1. *Customer Acquisition*: Market penetration focuses on attracting new customers to the product or service. This can be achieved through various means, such as targeted marketing campaigns, advertising, promotions, or offering competitive pricing.
2. *Market Share Growth*: Market penetration aims to increase the market share of a product or service. By capturing a larger portion of the market, a business can solidify its position, gain a competitive advantage, and become a market leader.
3. *Customer Identification and Loyalty*: While market penetration involves attracting new customers, it also emphasizes retaining and increasing loyalty among existing customers. Strategies may include improving customer satisfaction, providing better customer service, or offering loyalty programs to incentivize repeat purchases.
4. *Competitive Pricing*: Pricing can be a significant factor in market penetration strategies. Offering competitive prices compared to competitors can attract new customers and encourage existing customers to switch from competitors' products.
5. *Product/Service Differentiation*: To penetrate the market successfully, businesses may focus on differentiating their products or services from competitors. This could be achieved through unique features, superior quality, better performance, or enhanced value propositions.
6. *Distribution and Sales Channels*: Effective distribution and sales channels are crucial in market penetration. Businesses must ensure their products or services are widely available and easily accessible to the target market. This may involve partnering with retailers, expanding distribution networks, or leveraging online sales channels.
7. *Market Research and Analysis*: Conducting thorough market research and analysis is essential in identifying market penetration

opportunities. This includes understanding customer needs, preferences, and behavior and evaluating competitors and market trends.

8. *Evaluation and Measurement*: Continuous evaluation and measurement of market penetration efforts are vital to assess the effectiveness of strategies. Monitoring market share growth, customer acquisition rates, customer retention rates, and other relevant metrics help businesses make data-driven decisions and refine their market penetration approach.

Market penetration strategies can be particularly useful when there is potential for growth within the existing market. By focusing on increasing market share, businesses can strengthen their position, drive revenue growth, and gain a competitive advantage. However, it is important to carefully assess market dynamics, competition, and customer demands to develop and execute market penetration strategies.

Market Positioning

Market positioning is the strategic process of establishing a distinctive perception of a product, brand, or company in the minds of the target market. It involves defining how your offering is unique, valuable, and differentiated from competitors. Effective market positioning helps create a favorable image, attract customers, and gain a competitive advantage. Here are key considerations and steps to achieve effective market positioning:

1. *Define Your Target Market*: Identify your target market segment or segments. Understand their needs, preferences, demographics, and psychographics to develop a focused positioning strategy.
2. *Understand Customer Needs and Perceptions*: Conduct market research and gather insights into customer needs, pain points, and perceptions. Understand how customers currently perceive your product or brand and how they perceive competitors.
3. *Identify Your Unique Value Proposition*: Determine the unique value proposition of your product, brand, or company. Identify the specific attributes, benefits, or features that set you apart from competitors and resonate with your target market. This could include quality, price, innovation, convenience, customer service, or sustainability.
4. *Conduct a Competitive Analysis*: Assess the competitive landscape and understand how competitors position themselves. Identify their strengths, weaknesses, and key messages to differentiate your positioning strategy. Identify opportunities to fill gaps and offer alternatives not currently available.
5. *Develop a Positioning Statement*: Craft a clear and compelling positioning statement summarizing your unique value proposition and differentiating factors. This statement should succinctly communicate your value to the target market and how you address their specific needs or solve their problems.
6. *Communicate Your Positioning*: Develop a consistent and cohesive marketing message that aligns with your strategy. Communicate your unique value proposition through various marketing channels such as advertising, branding, packaging, website content, social media, and customer interactions. Ensure that all communication channels consistently convey your desired positioning.
7. *Deliver on Your Promise*: Ensure that your product, brand, or company delivers on the promises made in your positioning strategy. Consistently provide a superior customer experience, deliver high-quality products or services, and exceed customer expectations. This helps build trust and credibility, reinforcing your desired positioning in the market.
8. *Monitor and Adapt*: Monitor market dynamics, customer feedback, and competitor activities. Regularly assess the effectiveness of your positioning strategy and make adjustments as needed to stay relevant, address market changes, and maintain a competitive edge.

Effective Market Positioning in Pharma

Effective market positioning in the pharmaceutical industry involves understanding the industry's unique characteristics and tailoring your approach accordingly. Here are some key considerations for achieving effective market positioning in the pharmaceutical sector:

1. *Understand Healthcare Professionals and Patients*: Gain a comprehensive understanding of the needs, preferences, and behaviors of healthcare professionals (physicians, pharmacists, and nurses) and patients within your target market. Identify their pain points, challenges, and desired outcomes to shape your positioning strategy.
2. *Focus on Therapeutic Areas*: Pharmaceutical companies often specialize in specific therapeutic areas. Position your products or services as experts in therapeutic areas by demonstrating deep knowledge, research, and

clinical evidence. Highlight how your offerings address specific patient needs or contribute to better patient outcomes.

3. *Emphasize Clinical Efficacy and Safety*: Pharmaceutical products are highly regulated, and healthcare professionals and patients prioritize clinical efficacy and safety. Position your products as evidence-based, supported by clinical trials, and with a favorable safety profile. Communicate the benefits and outcomes achieved through scientific data and compelling clinical evidence.
4. *Differentiate Based on Unique Features*: Identify and emphasize your products and services' unique features, characteristics, or benefits. This could include novel mechanisms of action, improved bioavailability, reduced side effects, patient-friendly formulations (once-daily dosing), or innovative delivery methods.
5. *Build Relationships with Key Opinion Leaders*: Key opinion leaders (KOLs) play a crucial role in shaping perceptions within the pharmaceutical industry. Engage with influential KOLs and thought leaders in your therapeutic area. Seek their endorsements, collaborate on research or educational initiatives, and leverage their expertise to strengthen your market positioning.
6. *Educate and Provide Value-Added Services*: Position your company as a valuable resource for healthcare professionals and patients. Provide educational materials, training programs, clinical guidelines, and other resources that support the appropriate use and understanding of your products. Offer value-added services such as patient support programs, adherence tools, or disease management resources.
7. *Tailor Messaging to Stakeholders*: Customize your messaging to stakeholders, including healthcare professionals, patients, payers, and regulatory authorities. Address their concerns, highlight the value proposition that resonates with each group, and emphasize how your products meet their unique needs and challenges.
8. *Stay Updated on Regulations and Guidelines*: Pharmaceutical marketing is subject to stringent regulations and compliance requirements. Ensure your marketing activities adhere to local regulations, industry guidelines, and ethical standards. Stay updated on any changes to regulations and adjust your positioning strategies accordingly.
9. *Leverage Digital Channels*: Utilize digital marketing channels to reach healthcare professionals, patients, and other stakeholders effectively. Leverage social media, online communities, professional networks, and digital platforms to share educational content, engage with your target audience and foster thought leadership.
10. *Continuously Monitor and Adapt*: Regularly assess the effectiveness of your market positioning efforts. Monitor market trends, competitor activities, customer feedback, and clinical developments. Continuously refine and adapt your positioning strategy based on insights gathered to stay ahead of the competition and address evolving market dynamics.

Effective market positioning requires a deep understanding of your target market, competitive landscape, and unique value proposition. It is an ongoing process that requires continuous evaluation, refinement, and adaptation to maintain a strong market position and meet evolving customer needs.

Market Potential

Market potential in the pharmaceutical industry refers to the maximum achievable sales or revenue generated by a pharmaceutical product or service within a specific market. It would represent the total demand for a product or service if all potential customers were to adopt it. Realizing the market potential involves identifying, targeting, and capturing a significant portion of that demand. Here are some steps to help you realize the market potential in the pharma industry:

1. *Market Research and Analysis*: Conduct market research to understand the target market's size, growth rate, and dynamics. Identify key trends, unmet needs, and emerging opportunities. Analyze market segments, patient populations, and healthcare provider preferences to assess the market potential for your products or service.
2. *Define Target Segments*: Define and prioritize specific customer segments within the larger market based on demographics, disease prevalence, healthcare infrastructure, and reimbursement landscape. Segment the market to understand better the needs, behaviors, and preferences of different groups of customers.
3. *Develop a Compelling Value Proposition*: Clearly articulate the unique value proposition of your product or service. Identify the specific benefits, features, or outcomes that differentiate your offering from competitors and resonate with the target market. Communicate how your product or service addresses their specific needs and challenges effectively.

4. *Regulatory Compliance*: Ensure compliance with regulatory requirements and obtain necessary approvals for marketing, sales, and distribution of pharmaceutical products or services. Familiarize yourself with local regulations and guidelines governing pharmaceutical marketing, product safety, labeling, and advertising to ensure full compliance.
5. *Product Development and Innovation*: Continuously invest in research and development to enhance your product or service offerings, address unmet needs, improve therapeutic outcomes, or differentiate from competitors. Leverage Technology advancements, explore new delivery methods, or develop additional indications to expand the market potential of your product.
6. *Build Relationships with Healthcare Professionals*: Forge strong relationships with healthcare professionals, key opinion leaders, and decision-makers within the target market. Engage with them through educational programs, medical conferences, and collaborative initiatives. Seek their input, establish trust, and gain endorsements to drive product adoption and realize market potential.
7. *Optimize Pricing and Reimbursement*: Develop pricing strategies that align with the perceived value of your product or service. Consider the competitive landscape, reimbursement policies, and cost-effectiveness of your offering. Collaborate with payers and reimbursement authorities to ensure favorable reimbursement coverage, which can significantly impact market potential.
8. *Implement Targeted Marketing and Promotional Campaigns*: Develop and execute targeted marketing and promotional campaigns to create awareness, educate healthcare professionals, and drive demand. Utilize channels such as digital marketing, direct-to-consumer advertising, physician detailing, and medical conferences to reach your target audience effectively.
9. *Establish Strategic Partnerships*: Partner with other organizations, research institutions, or healthcare providers to leverage their expertise, resources, and networks. Collaborate on research initiatives, co-marketing activities, or joint ventures to expand your reach, access new markets, and tap into additional market potential.
10. *Continuous Monitoring and Adaptation*: Monitor market dynamics, customer feedback, and competitor activities. Evaluate the effectiveness of your strategies, measure market penetration, and assess customer satisfaction. Make adjustments, refine your approach, and adapt to changing market conditions to realize the market potential fully.

Realizing the market potential in the pharmaceutical industry requires thorough market analysis, targeted strategies, product innovation, and effective marketing efforts. You can maximize your market potential and achieve sustainable growth by understanding the market, developing a compelling value proposition, building strong relationships, and adapting to and managing dynamics.

Market Reach

Market reach in the pharmaceutical industry refers to the extent to which a company or product can penetrate and engage with the target market. It measures the geographical coverage, customer segments, and distribution channels a pharmaceutical company effectively reaches and serves.

Maximizing market reach is crucial for expanding market share, increasing sales, and maximizing the impact of your products or services. Here are some strategies to maximize market reach in the pharmaceutical industry:

1. *Define Your Target Market*: Clearly define your target market segments based on demographics, disease prevalence, healthcare provider preferences, and patient needs. This helps you focus your efforts and resources on reaching the right audience.
2. *Develop a Multi-Channel Approach*: Utilize multiple channels to reach your target market effectively. This may include traditional channels such as visits by sales representatives, medical conferences, and print advertising, as well as digital channels such as websites, social media, email marketing, and online communities. Adopting a multi-channel approach ensures you reach healthcare professionals, patients, and stakeholders through their preferred communication channels.
3. *Build Relationships with Healthcare Professionals*: Forge strong relationships with healthcare professionals (physicians, pharmacists, nurses) who prescribe and recommend pharmaceutical products. Provide them with relevant information, educational resources, and support to build trust and encourage product adoption. Regularly engage

with them through conferences, seminars, and professional networking events.

4. *Engage with Patients and Advocacy Groups*: Directly engage with patients and patient advocacy groups to increase your products' awareness, education, and support. Develop patient-centric materials, online communities, and support programs that empower and educate patients. Collaborate with advocacy groups to amplify your reach and establish credibility among patient communities.
5. *Leverage Digital Marketing*: Embrace digital marketing strategies to maximize your market reach. Utilize targeted online advertising, search engine optimization (SEO), content marketing, and social media campaigns to reach a wider audience and drive engagement. Leverage online platforms to disseminate educational content, share success stories, and foster patient and healthcare professional interactions.
6. *Explore Partnerships and Collaborations*: Collaborate with other organizations, healthcare systems, hospitals, clinics, or specialty centers to expand your market reach. Establish joint partnerships to promote your products or services and research specialized care. Leveraging existing networks and relationships can help you access new customer segments and expand geographically.
7. *Optimize Distribution Channels*: Evaluate your distribution channels and ensure efficient and reliable product availability. Work closely with distributors, wholesalers, and pharmacies to ensure your products are readily accessible to healthcare professionals and patients. Streamline the supply chain to minimize barriers and improve market reach.
8. *Expand Geographically*: Assess opportunities for geographical expansion and market entry into new regions. Conduct market research to understand the local healthcare landscape, regulatory requirements, and patient needs. Tailor your marketing strategies and product offerings to suit the specific market dynamics of each region.
9. *Provide Value-added Services*: Offer value-added services that complement your products and enhance customer experience. This may include patient support programs, disease management resources, adherence tools, or patient education materials. You can differentiate yourself and maximize market reach by providing additional value beyond the product.
10. *Continuously Monitor and Adapt*: Regularly monitor market trends, customer feedback, and competitive activities to identify opportunities for improvement and refinement. Stay updated on new developments, emerging technologies, and evolving customer needs. Continuously adapt your strategies and offerings to maximize your market reach and stay ahead of the competition.

Maximizing market reach in the pharmaceutical industry requires a comprehensive and targeted approach. You can expand your reach, engage with stakeholders, and drive growth by identifying the right target market, utilizing multiple channels, building relationships, leveraging digital strategies, and continuously adapting to market dynamics.

Market Research

Market Research in the pharmaceutical industry refers to gathering and analyzing data and information about the market, customers, competitors, and other relevant factors. It helps pharmaceutical companies gain insights into market dynamics, customer needs, and competitive landscape, enabling informed decision-making and effective marketing strategies. Here are the steps to conduct market research effectively in the pharma industry:

1. *Define the Research Objectives*: Clearly define the research objectives and questions you want to answer. Determine the specific information you need, such as market size, customer preferences, unmet needs, or competitor strategies. This will guide your research approach and data collection methods.
2. *Identify Target Audience*: Determine the target audience for your research. This could include healthcare professionals, patients, caregivers, payers, or other stakeholders. It is vital to understand their characteristics, behaviors, and information needed to design research to provide meaningful insights.
3. *Choose Research Methods*: Select appropriate research methods based on your objectives and target audience. Common methods in pharmaceutical market research include surveys, interviews, focus groups, and secondary research. Consider both qualitative and quantitative approaches to gather a comprehensive understanding of the market.
4. *Conduct Primary Research*: If conducting primary research, design questionnaires, interview guides, or discussion topics that

address your research objectives. Ensure your questions are clear, unbiased, and relevant. Contact your target audience through appropriate channels, such as online surveys, phone interviews, or in-person focus groups. Collect data and responses systematically and maintain data confidentially.

5. *Analyze Data*: Once you have collected the data, use appropriate statistical or qualitative analysis techniques. Look for patterns, trends, and insights that answer your research questions. Use data visualization tools like charts or graphs to present findings effectively.
6. *Conduct Secondary Research*: Supplement your primary research with secondary research, which involves analyzing existing data and information from published sources, industry reports, scientific literature, and online databases. This helps to gather market statistics, competitor information, regulatory updates, and other relevant data.
7. *Validate Findings*: Validate your research findings by cross-referencing them with multiple sources and perspectives. Seek input from experts, colleagues, or industry professionals to ensure the accuracy and reliability of your findings.
8. *Interpret Findings and Draw Conclusions*: Interpret the research findings and draw meaningful conclusions based on the data analysis. Identify key insights, trends, opportunities, and challenges from the research. Relate the findings to your business objectives and marketing strategies.
9. *Develop Actionable Recommendations*: Based on your research conclusions, develop actionable recommendations for marketing strategies, product development, customer engagement, or other relevant areas. Ensure your recommendations are specific, realistic, and aligned with your company's goals and resources.
10. *Communicate and Disseminate Findings*: Prepare a comprehensive research report or presentation summarizing the research objectives, methodology, findings, and recommendations. Present the information clearly and concisely to stakeholders within your organization. Ensure the research findings reach the appropriate decision-makers who can act upon the insights.
11. *Monitor and Update*: Market research is an ongoing process. Continuously monitor market trends, customer preferences, and competitive dynamics to stay updated. Periodically conduct follow-up research to assess your strategies' impact and validate your actions' effectiveness.

Effective market research in the pharmaceutical industry requires rigorous data collection, thorough analysis, and actionable insights. By conducting comprehensive market research, pharmaceutical companies can make informed decisions, identify opportunities, mitigate risks, and optimize their marketing strategies to serve their target audience better.

Market Segmentation

Market segmentation in the pharmaceutical industry involves dividing the target market into distinct homogeneous groups based on specific characteristics, needs, or behaviors. Pharmaceutical companies can effectively tailor their marketing strategies, product offerings, and communication by segmenting the market to meet each segment's unique needs. Here are some steps to effectively conduct market segmentation in the pharma industry:

1. *Research and Data Collection*: Conduct thorough research to gather data on the target market. Utilize both primary and secondary research methods to collect demographic, psychographic, and behavioral data. This can include age, gender, income, lifestyle, treatment preferences, healthcare habits, and medication usage patterns.
2. *Identify Segmentation Variables*: Determine the key variables that will be used to segment the market. Common segmentation variables in the pharmaceutical industry include demographics (for example, age, gender, and others), geographic location, disease or medical condition, treatment history, healthcare provider preferences, and patient preferences.
3. *Analyze and Prioritize Segments*: Analyze the collected data to identify distinct segments within the target market. Look for similarities, differences, and patterns among the data points. Then, prioritize segments based on size, growth potential, profitability, and alignment with your company's strategic objectives.
4. *Create Detailed Personas*: Develop detailed personals for each identified segment. A persona represents a fictional but representative individual within a segment and includes demographic information, preferences, behaviors, goals, and challenges. This helps humanize the segment and enables better understanding and targeting.

5. *Define Segment Needs and Motivations*: Gain insights into each segment's needs, motivations, and pain points. Understand what drives their treatment decisions, challenges, and desired outcomes. This information will help in developing targeted marketing messages and product positioning.
6. *Tailor Marketing Strategies and Messages*: Develop customized marketing strategies and messages for each segment based on their unique characteristics and needs. Create compelling value propositions that address the specific pain points and provide solutions or benefits that resonate with each segment. Tailor your messaging, communication channels, and promotional activities to effectively reach and engage each segment.
7. *Adapt Product Offerings*: Modify or develop products or services to align with the needs and preferences of each segment. This could include variations in dosage forms, formulations, packaging, or delivery methods. Adapt the product attributes, features, or benefits to meet each segment's specific requirements better.
8. *Implement Targeted Communication Channels*: Select the most appropriate communication channels to reach each segment effectively. Utilize traditional and digital channels such as print media, medical journals, social media platforms, online communities, healthcare professional networks, and patient support groups. Ensure that the chosen channels align with the communication preferences of each segment.
9. *Continuous Monitoring and Refinement*: Monitor the market dynamics, segment preferences, and competitive landscape. Regularly collect feedback from each segment to evaluate the effectiveness of your segmentation and marketing efforts. Based on the insights gathered, refine your segmentation strategy, personas, and marketing approaches.
10. *Measure and Assess Segmentation Success*: Establish key performance indicators (KPIs) to measure the success of your segmentation strategy. Monitor market share, sales volume, customer satisfaction, and brand loyalty for each segment. Compare the performance of segmented marketing initiatives against non-segmented approaches to evaluate the impact of effective segmentation.

Effective market segmentation in the pharmaceutical industry requires a deep understanding of the target market, robust data collection and analysis, and the ability to tailor strategies and offerings to meet the unique needs of each segment. Pharmaceutical companies can enhance their market positioning, customer engagement, and overall business performance by implementing a well-defined segmentation strategy and consistently adapting to changing market dynamics.

Market Share

Market share in the pharmaceutical industry refers to the percentage of total sales or revenue generated by a company or product within a specific market. Improving market share involves increasing sales and capturing a larger portion of the market than your competitors. Here are some strategies to improve market share in the pharma industry:

1. *Understand the Market*: Conduct thorough market research to gain a deep understanding of the market dynamics, including customer needs, preferences, and behaviors. Identify market trends, competitor strategies, and areas of untapped opportunity.
2. *Competitive Differentiation*: Develop a unique value proposition that differentiates your products or services from competitors. Highlight the specific benefits, features, or outcomes that set you apart. Communicate how your offerings address unmet needs or provide superior value to healthcare professionals, patients, or other stakeholders.
3. *Product Innovation*: Continuously invest in research and development to enhance your product portfolio. Introduce innovative products that address unmet needs, offer improved efficacy, safety, or convenience, or target niche patient populations. Stay updated on emerging technologies, scientific advancements, and market trends to stay ahead of the competition.
4. *Targeted Marketing and Promotion*: Develop targeted marketing and promotional campaigns that effectively reach and engage your target audience. Utilize a mix of traditional and digital marketing channels to communicate your value proposition, educate healthcare professionals and patients, and drive demand. Customize your messaging and tactics based on the needs and preferences of different market segments.
5. *Strong Customer Relationships*: Build relationships with healthcare professionals, key opinion leaders, and patients. Provide educational resources, support programs, and personalized assistance, demonstrating your commitment to their success. Foster loyalty and advocacy through regular engagement, effective

communication, and exceptional customer service.

6. *Pricing and Reimbursement Strategies*: Develop pricing strategies that align with market expectations and the perceived value of your products. Consider the pricing dynamics within each market segment and adapt your pricing approach accordingly. Work closely with payers and reimbursement authorities to secure favorable coverage and reimbursement for your products, making them more accessible to patients.
7. *Distribution and Access*: Optimize your distribution channels to ensure easy access to your products. Collaborate with distributors, wholesalers, and pharmacies to streamline the supply chain and improve product availability. In addition, explore partnerships with healthcare systems, hospitals, or specialty centers to expand your reach and access to new customer segments.
8. *Continuous Improvement and Adaptation*: Monitor market trends, customer feedback, and competitor activities. Gather insights through market research, sales data analysis, and customer feedback mechanisms. Use the information to identify areas of improvement, refine your strategies, and adapt to changing market dynamics.
9. *Collaboration and Partnerships*: Seek opportunities for collaboration and partnerships with other organizations or stakeholders within the healthcare ecosystem. This could include research collaborations, co-marketing agreements, or joint ventures that leverage complementary expertise, resources, or networks to enhance market share.
10. *Measure and Track Performance*: Establish key performance indicators (KPIs) to measure and track your market share progress. Monitor sales growth, market penetration, customer satisfaction, and brand perception metrics. Regularly assess your performance against your competitors, and industry benchmarks to identify areas of strength and opportunities for improvement.

Improving market share in the pharmaceutical industry requires strategic planning, differentiation, customer focus, and continuous adaptation. You can improve your market share and drive business growth by understanding the market, differentiating your offerings, building strong relationships, and consistently delivering value.

Market Testing

Market testing in the pharmaceutical industry is the evaluation of a new product or service's potential success and market viability before its full-scale launch. It involves collecting feedback, assessing market demand, and making data-driven decisions to optimize the product and its marketing strategies. Here's how to effectively conduct marketing testing in the pharma industry:

1. *Define the Testing Objectives*: Clearly define the objectives of your market testing. Determine the specific insights or data you want to gather and the decisions you aim to inform through your testing process. This could include assessing market demand, understanding customer preferences, optimizing product features, or refining marketing strategies.
2. *Identify the Target Audience*: Define the target audience for your market testing. This could be healthcare professionals, patients, payers, or other relevant stakeholders, depending on the nature of your product or service. Ensure that the selected audience represents your intended market segment accurately.
3. *Design the Testing Methodology*: Determine the appropriate testing methodology based on your objectives and resources. Common methods in the pharmaceutical industry include surveys, focus groups, in-depth interviews, online feedback forms, and observational research. Consider using quantitative and qualitative research techniques to gain comprehensive insights.
4. *Develop Testing Materials*: Create the necessary testing materials, such as questionnaires, discussion guides, prototypes, or product samples. Ensure the materials are clear, concise, and relevant to the testing objectives. Tailor the materials to match the audience's level of understanding and engagement.
5. *Recruit Participants*: Identify and recruit participants who represent your target audience. Use various recruitment methods such as online communities or partnering with research agencies. Aim for a diverse and representative sample to ensure the validity of your findings.
6. *Conduct the Testing*: Execute the market testing according to the predetermined methodology. If conducting surveys or using online feedback forms, ensure they are easily accessible and user-friendly. If using focus groups or interviews, facilitate structured discussions or interviews to gather valuable insights. Record responses,

observations, and feedback accurately for later analysis.

7. *Analyze and Interpret Data*: Analyze the collected data to identify patterns, trends, and key insights. Look for common themes, preferences, or concerns expressed by the participants. Use statistical analysis or qualitative coding techniques to extract meaningful information. Interpret the findings about your objectives and make data-driven decisions.
8. *Adjust Product or Marketing Strategies*: Refine your product or service offerings based on the market testing results. Address any identified issues, optimize features, or modify marketing strategies based on the feedback received. This iterative process helps ensure your product aligns with market needs and preferences.
9. *Iterate and Retest if Necessary*: If significant changes are made based on the initial market testing, consider conducting additional testing rounds to validate the adjustments' effectiveness. This iterative approach allows for continuous improvement and refinement.
10. *Monitor and Track Performance*: Once the product or service is launched, monitor its performance closely. Track key performance indicators (KPIs) such as sales, market share, customer satisfaction, and adoption rates. Compare the actual outcomes with the expectations and learn from the market testing insights to make ongoing adjustments and optimize the product's performance in the market.

Market testing in the pharmaceutical industry provides valuable insights to guide decision-making, mitigate risks, and optimize product and marketing strategies. By effectively designing and executing market testing activities, pharmaceutical companies can increase the chances of success for their products, enhance customer satisfaction, and achieve better market penetration.

Market Value

Market value in the pharmaceutical industry is the financial worth of a company, product, or service within the market. It is determined by various factors such as revenue, profitability, brand equity, market share, and investor perception. Maximizing market value in the pharma industry involves implementing strategies to increase revenue, enhance profitability, strengthen the brand, and create long-term shareholder value. Here are some approaches to maximize market value in the pharma industry:

1. *Develop Innovative and Differentiated Products*: Invest in research and development to create innovative pharmaceutical products that address unmet medical needs, offer improved therapeutic outcomes, or provide unique features. Differentiation through innovation can help capture market share and command premium pricing, increasing market value.
2. *Strategic Portfolio Management*: Evaluate and optimize your product portfolio to focus on high-growth and profitability areas. Identify products with strong market potential and align investments and resources accordingly. Continuously assess the market dynamics, competitive landscape, and regulatory environment to make informed decisions about product acquisitions, divestitures, or collaborations.
3. *Market Expansion and Geographic Diversification*: Explore opportunities for market expansion by entering new geographic regions or target markets. Conduct thorough market research to identify regions with high growth potential, unmet medical needs, or favorable reimbursement environments. Develop strategies to adapt your products and marketing to suit the specific requirements of each target segment.
4. *Pricing and Reimbursement Optimization*: Implement pricing strategies that balance the perceived value of your products with market dynamics and affordability considerations. Conduct market research and assess the competitive landscape to determine optimal pricing levels. Then, work closely with payers, insurance companies, and reimbursement authorities to secure favorable coverage and reimbursement for your products, maximizing the value.
5. *Strategic Partnerships and Collaborations*: Partner with other organizations, research institutions, or healthcare providers. Collaborate on research and development initiatives, co-marketing, or joint ventures to leverage complementary resources, expertise, and networks. Strategic partnerships can expand market reach, access new markets, and enhance market value.
6. *Strong Brand Management*: Build and maintain a strong brand image through effective marketing, positioning, and communication. Develop a compelling brand identity that resonates with healthcare professionals,

patients, and other stakeholders. Invest in brand-building activities such as advertising, public relations, and thought leadership to increase brand recognition, loyalty, and market value.

7. *Regulatory Compliance and Quality Assurance*: Ensure compliance with regulatory requirements and maintain high-quality standards across all operations. Adhere to Good Manufacturing Practices (GMP), Good Clinical Practices (GCP), and other applicable regulations to ensure your products' safety, efficacy, and quality. A strong reputation for compliance and quality can positively impact market value.
8. *Continuous Research and Development*: Commit to ongoing research and development to drive innovation, improve existing products, and develop new therapeutic solutions. Stay abreast of scientific advancements, emerging technologies, and market trends. Continuously invest in research to expand your product pipeline and maintain a competitive edge, which can contribute to increased market value.
9. *Investor Relations and Financial Performance*: Communicate effectively with investors and stakeholders, providing transparent and timely information about your financial performance, growth strategies, and market outlook. Demonstrate strong financial management, profitability, and a clear vision for future growth. Building trust and credibility with investors can enhance the market value and attract potential investors.
10. *Talent Acquisition and Retention*: Attract and retain top talent in the pharmaceutical industry. Foster a culture of innovation, collaboration, and excellence. Invest in employee development, offer competitive compensation packages, and provide opportunities for career advancement. A skilled and motivated workforce can drive product innovation, operational efficiency, and market value.

Maximizing market value in the pharmaceutical industry requires a comprehensive approach encompassing product innovation, strategic decision-making, effective marketing, regulatory compliance, financial performance, and stakeholder engagement.

Marketing Audit

A *Marketing Audit* in the pharmaceutical industry comprehensively evaluates a company's marketing activities, strategies, and performance. It involves assessing the effectiveness of marketing efforts, identifying strengths and weaknesses, and determining areas for improvement. Conducting a marketing audit in the pharma industry helps identify opportunities, mitigate risks, and optimize marketing strategies. Here are some steps to effectively conduct a marketing audit in the pharmaceutical industry:

1. *Define Audit Objectives*: Clearly define the objectives of the marketing audit. Determine what specific aspects of the marketing function you want to evaluate, such as marketing strategies, customer segmentation, product positioning, promotional activities, or digital marketing effectiveness.
2. *Gather Relevant Information*: Collect comprehensive and relevant data to analyze and assess the marketing function. This can include market research data, sales data, customer feedback, competitive intelligence, marketing plans, and performance metrics. Use internal and external sources to gather a complete picture of the marketing landscape.
3. *Evaluate Marketing Strategies*: Assess the effectiveness of your marketing strategies in achieving your business objectives. Review your marketing goals, target audience, value proposition, and positioning strategies. Analyze the alignment of your strategies with market trends, customer needs, and competitive dynamics. Identify any gaps or areas for improvement.
4. *Analyze Customer Segmentation*: Evaluate your customer segmentation approach and its effectiveness. Assess how well you have identified and targeted the right customer segments. Review segmentation criteria, demographics, psychographics, and behavioral attributes. Determine if your segmentation strategy effectively addresses each segment's unique needs and preferences.
5. *Assess Your Product Positioning*: Evaluate how your products or services are positioned in the market. Analyze the perception of your brand and products among healthcare professionals, patients, and other stakeholders. Review how well your positioning differentiates you from competitors and resonates with the target audience. Identify opportunities for refining or strengthening your product positioning.
6. *Review Your Promotional Activities*: Assess the effectiveness of your promotional activities across various channels and mediums. Evaluate your advertising, sales promotion, public relations, digital marketing, and other communication strategies. Review your promotional efforts' messaging, creative

elements, targeting, and timing. Determine if they are reaching and engaging the intended audience effectively.

7. *Evaluate Digital Marketing Effectiveness*: Review your digital marketing initiatives, including website performance, social media presence, online advertising, and search engine optimization. Assess the effectiveness of your digital marketing channels in driving traffic, generating leads, and fostering engagement. Identify opportunities for optimizing your digital marketing strategies and improving online visibility.
8. *Analyze Competitive Landscape*: Conduct a thorough analysis of the competitive landscape in which your products operate. Identify key competitors, their marketing strategies, product offerings, market positioning, and promotional activities. Assess your competitive advantages and disadvantages. Identify areas where you can differentiate and outperform competitors.
9. *Identify Strengths and Weaknesses*: Evaluate the strengths and weaknesses of your marketing function and strategies. Identify areas where you excel and leverage those strengths. Also, identify weaknesses or gaps that need improvement. This could include inadequate resources, skill gaps, or areas where your marketing efforts are falling short.
10. *Develop an Action Plan*: Based on the findings from the marketing audit, develop a comprehensive action plan. Prioritize the identified areas for improvement and define specific strategies and tactics to address them. Set clear goals, timelines, and responsibilities for implementing the action plan. Continuously monitor progress and adjust strategies as needed.
11. *Regularly Review and Update*: A marketing audit should be conducted periodically to ensure ongoing evaluation and improvement. Review and update your marketing strategies, customer segmentation, positioning, and promotional activities based on changes in the market, competitive landscape, and customer preferences.

Conducting a marketing audit in the pharmaceutical industry provides valuable insights into your marketing efforts' effectiveness and helps identify improvement opportunities. In addition, regularly assessing and optimizing your marketing strategies can enhance customer engagement.

Marketing Authorization Application

In the pharmaceutical industry, an MAA, or Marketing Authorization Application, is a comprehensive dossier that a drug manufacturer submits to a regulatory authority to obtain marketing approval for a new drug. The implications of an MAA are significant and wide-ranging:

1. *Regulatory Approval*: The primary goal of an MAA is to secure regulatory approval for a new pharmaceutical product. This approval is granted by regulatory agencies such as the FDA in the United States or the EMA in the European Union.
2. *Market Access*: Successful approval through the MAA process allows the pharmaceutical company to introduce and market their product in the respective regions. This, in turn, opens up new markets and revenue streams.
3. *Patient Access*: Patients can gain access to potentially life-saving or life-improving medications due to successful MAAs. This is particularly important for individuals suffering from conditions for which there may be limited treatment options.
4. *Research and Development Investment*: The MAA process often culminates years of research and development efforts. A successful application validates the investments in discovering and developing a new drug.
5. *Competitive Advantage*: Obtaining marketing authorization can provide a competitive advantage for the pharmaceutical company. It allows them to differentiate their product from competitors and establish a foothold in the market,
6. *Economic Impact*: The approval of a new drug through the MAA process can have a significant economic impact. It can contribute to job creation, stimulate economic growth, and enhance the overall health of the pharmaceutical industry.
7. *Safety and Efficacy*: The MAA process ensures that a new drug meets rigorous standards for safety and efficacy. This is crucial for protecting public health and maintaining trust in the pharmaceutical industry.
8. *Post-Marketing Surveillance*: After approval, pharmaceutical companies are typically required to continue monitoring the safety and efficacy of their products through post-marketing surveillance. This ongoing evaluation is essential

for identifying and addressing any issues arising after a drug is on the market.

9. *International Collaboration*: For companies seeking global market access, successful MAAs in one region can facilitate the application process in other regions. International collaboration and recognition of approvals streamline the pathway for a drug to reach a broader patient population.
10. *Legal and Ethical Considerations*: The MAA process involves navigating complex legal and ethical considerations. This includes compliance with regulatory requirements, adherence to ethical standards in clinical trials, and transparency in reporting data.

In summary, the implications of an MAA are profound, impacting not only the company seeking approval but also patients, healthcare providers, and the broader community. It represents a critical step in bringing innovative and effective medications to the market.

Where are MAAs Applicable?

Marketing Authorization Application (MAA) is applicable in various countries worldwide, but the specific regulatory processes and agencies involved may differ from country to country. Here are some key regions and countries where the MAA or equivalent regulatory approval process is applicable:

1. *United States*: In the United States, the Food and Drug Administration (FDA) is responsible for reviewing and approving pharmaceutical products. The application process is known as the New Drug Application (NDA).
2. *European Union*: In the European Union, the European Medicines Agency (EMA) plays a central role in the approval process. Companies submit a Marketing Authorization Application (MAA) to the EMA.
3. *Canada*: Health Canada is the regulatory authority responsible for approving drugs in Canada. The submission process involves a New Drug Submission (NDS).
4. *Japan*: The Pharmaceuticals and Medical Devices Agency (PMDA) oversees the approval process in Japan. The application is called a New Drug Application (NDA) or a Marketing Authorization Application (MAA).
5. *China*: The China National Medical Products Administration (NMPA) is the regulatory agency in China. The application process involves submitting a New Drug Application (NDA).
6. *Australia*: The Therapeutic Goods Administration (TGA) is the regulatory authority in Australia. Companies submit a submission for the registration of a new medicine.
7. *Switzerland*: Swissmedic is the regulatory agency in Switzerland. The authorization process involves submitting a Marketing Authorization Application (MAA).
8. *United Kingdom*: While part of the European Union, the Medicines and Healthcare Products Regulatory Agency (MHRA) was involved. Post-Brexit, the MHRA continues to play a role in drug approvals in the UK.
9. *India*: In India, the Central Drugs Standard Control Organization (CDSCO) is responsible for the approval of pharmaceuticals. The application process involves submitting a New Drug Application (NDA).
10. *Brazil*: Brazil's National Health Surveillance Agency (ANVISA) is responsible for drug approvals. The application process involves submitting a registration dossier.

These are just a few examples, and many other countries have their own regulatory agencies and processes for approving pharmaceutical products. Global pharmaceutical companies must often navigate complex regulatory requirements to bring their products to global markets.

Marketing Automation

Marketing Automation in the pharmaceutical industry refers to using software and technology to streamline and automate marketing processes and tasks. It enables pharmaceutical companies to deliver personalized, targeted, and timely communications to healthcare professionals, patients, and other stakeholders. Here are some key aspects and benefits of marketing automation in the pharma industry:

1. *Lead Generation and Nurturing*: Marketing automation tools can capture and track leads from various sources, such as website forms, landing pages, or events. Leads can be segmented based on specialty, geographic location, or engagement level. Automated workflows can then nurture these leads with personalized content, automated emails, and follow-up communications to move them through the marketing and sales funnel.
2. *Email Marketing Campaigns*: Marketing automation platforms allow for the creation and execution of targeted email campaigns. Automated emails can be triggered based on specific actions or events, such as downloading educational materials or attending a webinar.

These automated campaigns help deliver relevant and timely information to healthcare professionals and patients, increasing engagement and conversion rates.

3. *Personalization and Segmentation*: Marketing automation enables the customization of messages and content based on the target audience's preferences, interests, and behaviors. By leveraging data and segmentation criteria, pharmaceutical companies can deliver personalized communications that resonate with individual healthcare professionals or patients. This personalization enhances engagement and builds stronger relationships.
4. *Multi-channel Marketing*: Marketing automation platforms support marketing efforts by integrating various communication channels such as email, social media, SMS, and website. This allows pharmaceutical companies to reach their target audience through their preferred channels and deliver consistent messaging across different touchpoints.
5. *Data Tracking and Analytics*: Marketing automation tools provide robust analytics and reporting capabilities. They track and measure various metrics, including open email rates, click-through rates, website visits, and conversions. These insights help evaluate marketing campaigns' effectiveness, identify improvement areas, and make data-driven decisions to optimize marketing strategies.
6. *Compliance and Regulatory Adherence*: The pharmaceutical industry operates under strict compliance regulations. Marketing automation platforms can incorporate compliance features to ensure marketing communications adhere to regulatory guidelines. This includes features such as opt-in and opt-out mechanisms, unsubscribe options, and data security measures to protect patient privacy.
7. *Improved Efficiency and Productivity*: Automating repetitive marketing tasks such as lead nurturing, email campaigns, and data tracking frees up valuable time and resources. Marketing teams can focus on strategic initiatives, content creation, and analyzing campaign performance rather than manual execution. This improves overall efficiency and productivity within the marketing function.
8. *Enhanced Customer Experience*: By delivering personalized and timely communications, marketing automation improves the customer experience for healthcare professionals and patients. It helps deliver relevant information, educational resources, and support throughout the customer journey, fostering engagement, loyalty, and advocacy.
9. *Workflow Automation and Collaboration*: Marketing automation platforms facilitate collaboration and streamline workflows across different teams and departments. They enable better coordination between marketing, sales, and other stakeholders, ensuring seamless communication and alignment of efforts.

When implementing marketing automation in the pharmaceutical industry, it is essential to consider factors such as data privacy, regulatory compliance, and customization based on the unique needs and preferences of the target audience. By effectivley leveraging marketing automation, pharmaceutical companies can improve lead generation, enhance customer engagement, drive conversions, and achieve better marketing results.

Implementing Marketing Automation

Here are some basic steps to follow for effectively implementing marketing automation in the pharmaceutical industry:

1. *Set Clear Goals*: Define your marketing objectives and determine how marketing automation can support those goals. Whether lead generation, nurturing, customer retention, or increasing conversions, having clear objectives will guide your implementation strategy.
2. *Choose the Right Marketing Automation Platform*: Research and select a marketing automation platform that aligns with your needs. Consider the factors such as ease of use, scalability, integration capabilities, compliance features, and customer support.
3. *Define Your Target Audience*: Identity and understand your target audience, including healthcare professionals, patients, and other stakeholders. Segment them based on specialty, location, interests, or behavior. This segmentation will guide your personalized and targeted campaigns.
4. *Build a Clean and Updated Database*: Ensure you have a clean and up-to-date contacts database. Eliminate duplicate or outdated information and ensure compliance with data privacy regulations.
5. *Create Personalized Content*: Develop relevant and engaging content tailored to the needs and preferences of your target audience segments. This includes educational materials, product information, case studies, and other resources that align with their interests and challenges.

6. *Set up Lead Nurturing Work Flows*: Create automated workflows that deliver targeted content to your leads based on their engagement level and interests. Design a series of automated emails triggered by specific actions to guide leads through the marketing funnel.
7. *Implement Lead-Scoring*: Assign scores to your leads based on their engagement and actions. This helps prioritize follow-up leads and identifies those most likely to convert into customers. Use lead scoring to trigger specific actions, such as notifying sales representatives when a lead reaches a certain score.
8. *Monitor and Analyze Data*: Track and analyze key metrics such as email open rates, click-through rates, conversion rates, and customer engagement. Use the insights to refine your marketing automation strategies and optimize campaign performance.
9. *Integrate with Other Systems*: Integrate your marketing automation platform with other systems, such as customer relationship management (CRM) software. This ensures seamless data-flow, better tracking of customer interactions, and more effective lead management.
10. *Train and Empower Your Team*: Provide training and support to your marketing team to ensure they understand how to use the marketing automation platform effectively. Empower them to create and manage campaigns, analyze data, and make data-driven decisions.
11. *Test and Optimize*: Continuously test different elements of your marketing automation campaigns, such as subject lines, content, and CTAs (Call-to-Actions). A/B testing can help you identify the most effective strategies. Use the data and insights gathered to optimize your campaigns and improve results.
12. *Ensure Compliance*: Given the regulated nature of the pharmaceutical industry, ensure compliance with data protection and privacy regulations. Familiarize yourself with regulations such as GDPR (General Data Protection Regulation) and HIPAA (Health Insurance Portability and Accountability Act) and implement necessary measures to protect patient information.

Successful marketing automation implementation requires a well-defined strategy, alignment with organizational goals, and continuous monitoring and optimization. Regularly review and adapt your marketing automation efforts based on feedback, performance data, and market dynamics to achieve optimal results.

What and How to Automate?

Several marketing processes and tasks can be automated in the pharmaceutical industry to improve efficiency and effectiveness. Here are some areas where automation can be beneficial and the technologies and applications commonly used:

1. *Email Marketing*: Automate creating, scheduling, and delivering personalized email campaigns to segmented audiences. Email marketing automation platforms like Mailchimp, HubSpot, or Marketo provide features for building email templates, segmenting contacts, setting up automated workflows, and tracking campaign performance.
2. *Lead Generation and Nurturing*: Automate lead capture from various sources, such s website forms, landing pages, or events. Use customer relationship management (CRM) platforms like Salesforce, HubSpot CRM, or Zoho CRM to manage and nurture leads through automated workflows and personalized communications.
3. *Social Media Management*: Use social media management tools like Hootsuite, Buffer, or Sprout Social to schedule and automate social media posts across multiple platforms. These tools also provide analytics to track engagement and measure the effectiveness of your social media campaigns.
4. *Content Management*: Utilize content management systems (CMS) like WordPress, Drupal, or Joomla to automate the publication and distribution of content. These platforms allow you to schedule content updates, manage workflows, and optimize content for search engines.
5. *Customer Relationship Management (CRM)*: Implement CRM software to automate customer data management, lead-scoring, and tracking interactions. Salesforce, Microsoft Dynamics 365, and HubSpot CRM are popular platforms offering automation capabilities for managing customer relationships and sales processes.
6. *Marketing Analytics*: Use analytics tools like Google, Adobe, or Mixpanel to automatically collect and analyze data from various marketing channels. These tools provide insights into website traffic, campaign performance, and user behavior to inform decision-making and optimize marketing strategies.
7. *Chatbots and AI-Powered Assistants*: Integrate chatbot technologies like Drift, Intercom, or Chatfuel on your website or social media

platforms to automate customer support, answer frequently asked questions, and capture lead information. AI-powered assistants like IBM Watson or Google Dialogflow can handle complex customer interactions and provide personalized recommendations.

8. *Marketing Campaign Tracking and Attribution*: Implement marketing attribution tools like Google Analytics, Marketo, or Bizible to track and measure the impact of marketing campaigns across multiple channels. These tools help attribute conversions and revenue to specific marketing efforts, enabling better campaign optimization.
9. *Marketing Automation Platforms*: Utilize comprehensive marketing automation platforms like Marketo, HubSpot, Pardot, or Eloqua. These platforms offer a range of automation features, including lead management, email marketing, campaign workflows, and analytics, all within a single integrated system.

When selecting technologies or applications for automation, consider factors such as scalability, ease of use, integration capabilities with existing systems, compliance with regulatory requirements, and customer support. Then, choose tools that align with your automation needs and seamlessly integrate with your existing marketing stack.

Always continually assess and optimize your automation strategies to align with your marketing goals and deliver the desired outcomes. Regularly review performance metrics, test different approaches, and adapt your automation processes to stay ahead in the dynamic pharmaceutical industry.

Marketing Channels

In the pharmaceutical industry, marketing channels refer to the various avenues for pharmaceutical companies to reach and communicate with their target audience. These channels help promote products, educate healthcare professionals and patients, and build brand awareness. Here are some common marketing channels and strategies used by pharmaceutical companies to optimize them:

1. Healthcare Professionals (HCPs)

- *Direct Sales Force*: Utilize a dedicated team of medical or sales representatives to establish direct relationships with HCPs. Train them to communicate the value of your products effectively, provide scientific information, and address HCP's concerns.
- *Medical Education Programs*: Organize medical education programs, conferences, and symposiums to educate HCPs about disease management, treatment guidelines, and the latest research. Ensure the content is evidence-based and relevant to their practice.
- *Key Opinion Leader (KOL) Engagement*: Identify influential KOLs in relevant therapeutic areas and engage them as advocates for your products. Collaborate with them on research, speaking engagements, or advisory boards to leverage their expertise and enhance credibility.
- *Digital Channels*: Optimize digital channels to engage HCPs, such as email newsletters, webinars, online portals, and virtual conferences. Provide valuable content, scientific updates, and opportunities for interaction to keep them informed and engaged.

2. Patients

- *Direct-to-Consumer (DTC) Advertising*: Develop DTC advertising campaigns to raise awareness about specific conditions or treatment options. To reach patients directly, use TV, Print, radio, digital, and social media. Ensure compliance with regulatory guidelines in DTC advertising.
- *Patient Support Programs*: Implement patient support programs to assist patients in accessing and adhering to medications. These programs can include educational materials, nurse helplines, mobile apps, and financial assistance programs.
- *Online Communities and Social Media*: Engage with patient communities and patient advocacy groups through online platforms. Provide accurate and reliable information, address patient concerns, and foster a supportive community environment.
- *Disease Awareness Campaigns*: Run awareness campaigns to educate the public about specific conditions, symptoms, and treatment options. Collaborate with patient advocacy groups, healthcare organizations, and influencers to amplify the reach and impact of these campaigns.

3. Payers and Insurers

- *Market Access Teams*: Develop specialized market access teams to engage with payers, insurers, and reimbursement authorities. Provide them with economic and clinical evidence to demonstrate the value of your products and negotiate favorable reimbursement terms.
- *Health Economics and Outcomes Research (HEOR)*: Conduct HEOR studies to generate data on your products' cost-effectiveness and patient outcomes. Use this evidence to support

reimbursement negotiations and value-based pricing discussions.

- *Market Access Digital Tools*: Develop online platforms or tools that provide payers and insurers access to relevant product information, health economic data, and formulary details. Simplify the process for accessing product information and submitting reimbursement requests.

4. Digtital Marketing Channels

- *Pharmaceutical Websites*: Optimize your company's website as a central hub for product information, educational resources, and news updates. Ensure the website is user-friendly, mobile-responsive, and compliant with regulations.
- *Search Engine Optimization (SEO)*: Implement SEO strategies to improve your website's visibility in search engine results. Focus on relevant keywords, create valuable content, and optimize meta tags and descriptions to attract organic traffic.
- *Content Marketing*: Develop and distribute valuable educational content through various digital channels. This can include blog articles, whitepapers, infographics, videos, and interactive tools. Tailor the content to address the needs and interests of your target audience.
- *Social Media Marketing*: Leverage social media platforms like LinkedIn, Twitter, and YouTube to engage with healthcare professionals, patients, and other stakeholders. Share informative content, participate in discussions, and respond to comments and queries.

Optimizing marketing channels in the pharmaceutical industry requires a deep understanding of the target audience, compliance with regulatory guidelines, and a data-driven approach. Continuously measure and evaluate the performance of each channel, track key metrics such as reach, engagement, and conversion rates, and adapt your strategies accordingly. By effectively utilizing various marketing channels, pharmaceutical companies can maximize their reach, build strong relationships and drive business outcomes.

Marketing Communications

Marketing Communications in the pharmaceutical industry refers to the strategies and tactics used to communicate with target audiences, including healthcare professionals, patients, payers, and other stakeholders. Effective marketing communications help build awareness, educate, and influence behavior. Here are some key considerations for effectively conducting marketing communications in pharma:

1. *Define Your Target Audience*: Identify the target audience for your communication efforts, such as healthcare professionals in a particular specialty or patients with a specific condition. Understand their characteristics, needs, and preferences to tailor your messages accordingly.
2. *Develop Clear Messaging*: Craft clear and concise messages highlighting your products' key benefits and differentiators. Emphasize clinical evidence, safety profiles, and patient outcomes. Ensure your messaging complies with regulatory guidelines and accurately represents the product attributes and benefits.
3. *Utilize Multiple Channels*: Mix channels to reach your target audience effectively. This may include:

- *Medical Literature and Scientific Publications*: Publish research articles, white papers, or case studies in relevant medical journals to establish credibility and reach healthcare professionals.
- *Sales Representatives and Medical Affairs Teams*: Train your sales and medical affairs teams to effectively communicate product information, address questions, and build relationships with healthcare professionals.
- *Digital Platforms*: Utilize digital channels, including websites, email marketing, social media, and mobile apps, to reach and engage your target audience. Share informative content, educational resources, and updates about your products.
- *Patient Education Materials*: Develop patient-centric educational materials, brochures, websites, and videos to help patients understand their condition, treatment options, and the benefits of your products. Provide information in a clear and accessible manner.
- *Conferences and Events*: Participate in medical conferences, trade shows, and other industry events to showcase your products, share research findings, and interact with healthcare professionals and stakeholders.
- *Tailor Messages for different Audiences*: Customize your messages based on the needs and interests of specific target audiences, such as healthcare professionals, patients, payers and insurers. For example:
- *Healthcare Professionals*: Focus on clinical data, efficacy, safety, and how the product can benefit patients. Provide resources like clinical trial results, prescribing information, and dosing guidelines.

- *Patients*: Use patient-friendly language and visuals to explain your products' benefits, potential side effects, and usage instructions. Empower patients to make informed decisions about their health care.
- *Payers and Insurers*: Highlight your products' economic value, cost-effectiveness, and outcomes data to demonstrate their value proposition and support reimbursement discussions.

4. *Ensure Compliance*: Adhere to regulatory guidelines and industry standards. Ensure that all marketing communications are accurate, fair, balanced and supported by scientific evidence.
5. *Measure and Optimize*: Continuously monitor and evaluate the performance of your marketing communications efforts. Track key metrics, such as reach, engagement, conversions and feedback to assess the effectiveness of your messages and channels. Use the insights gained to refine your strategies and improve future communications.

Marketing Concept

The Marketing Concept is a business philosophy that meets customers' needs and wants while achieving organizational goals. It is centered on understanding customer needs, developing products or services that fulfill them, and effectively promoting and delivering them to the target market. The marketing concept emphasizes customer orientation, integrated marketing efforts, and long-term relationship building. There are five key principles associated with the marketing concept:

1. *Customer Orientation*: The marketing concept places the customer at the center of all marketing efforts. It involves thoroughly understanding customer needs, preferences, and behaviors to develop products and services that provide value and satisfaction.
2. *Integrated Marketing Efforts*: The marketing concept emphasizes the coordination and integration of various marketing activities, including product development, pricing, distribution, and promotion. It recognizes that all marketing mix elements should work together to create a cohesive and consistent customer experience.
3. *Customer Value*: Providing value to customers is essential in the marketing concept. Value is not limited to price but encompasses the overall benefits and satisfaction customers derive from a product or service. Companies strive to deliver superior value to customers compared to their competitors.
4. *Long-term Customer Relationships*: The marketing concept emphasizes building and maintaining long-term customer relationships. It recognizes that customer retention and loyalty are key drivers of business success. Repeat customers contribute to ongoing revenue and serve as brand advocates and a source of referrals.
5. *Profitability*: While the marketing concept emphasizes meeting customer needs, it also acknowledges the importance of organizational goals and profitability. The ultimate objective is to generate profits by delivering value to customers sustainably and ethically.

In practice, the marketing concept involves conducting market research to understand customer needs, segmenting the market to identify target audiences, developing marketing strategies and tactics to reach those audiences, and continuously evaluating and adapting marketing efforts based on customer feedback and market dynamics.

By adopting the marketing concept, businesses aim to create customer-centric strategies that drive customer satisfaction, loyalty, and business growth.

Marketing Concept in the Pharmaceutical Industry

The marketing concept can be effectively applied in the pharmaceutical industry to ensure customer satisfaction, build long-term relationships, and achieve business goals. Here are some ways to apply the marketing concept in pharma:

1. *Customer Focus*: Place healthcare professionals (HCPs), patients, and other stakeholders at the center of your marketing efforts. Understand their needs, preferences, and challenges in managing diseases or healthcare decisions. Conduct market research, engage in dialogue, and continuously gather feedback to improve your understanding of their requirements.
2. *Product Development*: Develop products that address unmet medical needs and provide superior value to customers. Conduct thorough research and clinical trials to ensure efficacy, safety, and quality. Consider patient-centered design, convenient dosing, and formulations that improve compliance. Involve HCPs and patients in the development process to gain insights and refine products accordingly.
3. *Educational Initiatives*: Provide educational resources and programs that help HCPs and patients to stay informed about disease management, treatment options, and the latest

research. This can include medical education programs, continuing medical education (CME) courses, webinars, patient support materials, and online resources. Focus on delivering accurate, evidence-based information.

4. *Targeted Marketing*: Segment the market based on medical specialty, patient demographics, disease type, or treatment preferences. Tailor your marketing messages and strategies to specific segments, ensuring they are relevant, personalized, and resonate with the target audience. Leverage data analytics and digital tools to enhance targeting capabilities.
5. *Relationship Building*: Build strong relationships with HCPs and patients based on trust, transparency, and mutual respect. Establish regular communication channels, such as newsletters, email updates, and social media engagement, to provide valuable information and facilitate two-way communication. Offer platforms for feedback, and respond promptly to inquiries and concerns.
6. *Collaboration with Key Stakeholders*: Engage in partnerships and collaborations with HCPs, patient advocacy groups, professional organizations, and key opinion leaders (KOLs). Collaborate on research projects, participate in medical conferences, and contribute to scientific publications. Seek input from stakeholders to shape your strategies, understand their perspectives, and leverage their influence.
7. *Regulatory Compliance*: Ensure all marketing activities adhere to regulatory guidelines and comply with laws and industry standards. Maintain transparency and ethical practices in all HCPs, patients, and other stakeholder interactions. Stay up-to-date with evolving regulations and ensure that marketing materials are accurate, balanced and do not make unsupported claims.
8. *Continuous Evaluation and Improvement*: Regularly assess the effectiveness of your marketing strategies and tactics. Monitor key performance indicators, such as market share, customer satisfaction, prescribing patterns, and patient adherence. Gather feedback from HCPs and patients to identify areas for improvement and refine your marketing initiatives accordingly.

By applying the marketing concept in the pharmaceutical industry, companies can better understand customer needs, deliver products and services that provide value, and build strong relationships with healthcare professionals, patients, and other stakeholders. This customer-centric approach can drive business growth, foster brand loyalty, and improve patient outcomes.

Marketing Costs

Marketing costs in the pharmaceutical industry can vary significantly based on factors such as the company's size, product portfolio, target market, promotional strategies, and regulatory requirements. Here are some examples of marketing costs in pharma:

1. Advertising and Promotion

Pharmaceutical companies invest in various advertising and promotional activities to raise awareness, educate, and promote their products. Examples of marketing costs in this category include:

- *Direct-to-Consumer (DTC) Advertising* costs are associated with television, print, radio, and digital advertising campaigns, targeting consumers to create brand awareness and drive patient demand.
- *Healthcare Professional (HCP) Marketing* costs are related to promotional materials, sales representatives' salaries, benefits, samples, product detailing, conferences, and other activities to engage and educate HCPs about the company's products.
- *Digital Marketing* expenses include website development and maintenance, search engine optimization (SEO), pay-per-click (PPC) advertising, email marketing, social media campaigns, and content creation.

2. Market Research

Pharmaceutical companies conduct market research to understand customer needs, evaluate market potential, identify competitive landscapes, and assess the effectiveness of marketing campaigns. Market research costs may include:

- *Primary Research*: Expenses for conducting surveys, interviews, focus groups, and observational studies to gather insights directly from healthcare professionals, patients, and other stakeholders.
- *Secondary Research* costs are associated with purchasing or accessing syndicated market research reports, competitor analyses, industry trends, and other published data sources.

3. Regulatory Compliance

The pharmaceutical industry operates under strict regulatory guidelines. Compliance with regulations related to advertising, labeling, promotional materials, and interactions with healthcare professionals incurs costs. This may involve legal and regulatory consulting, review and approval processes, and monitoring activities to ensure adherence.

4. Medical Education and Scientific Engagement

These costs include investment in continuing medical education (CME) activities, symposiums, conferences, and advisory board meetings to educate healthcare professionals about disease management, treatment options, and the scientific evidence behind the company's products.

5. Market Access and Reimbursement

Market access costs are associated with market access activities, health economic assessments, payer negotiations, and pricing strategies to ensure reimbursement and formulary placement of products.

6. Digital Technologies and Infrastructure

The technology infrastructure costs include developing and maintaining digital platforms, websites, mobile apps, customer relationship management (CRM) systems, data analytics tools, and other technological infrastructure to support marketing initiatives and customer engagement.

7. Patient Support Programs

Investment in patient support programs includes patient education materials, nurse helplines, mobile apps, and financial assistance programs to support patient adherence and engagement.

8. Events and Sponsorships

These are costs associated with sponsoring and participating in medical conferences, trade shows, patient advocacy events, and other industry gatherings to showcase products, network, and engage key stakeholders.

Marketing Environmental Audit

Conducting an effective marketing environment audit in the pharmaceutical industry involves assessing various internal and external factors that impact a company's marketing activities. Here are some key steps to perform a comprehensive marketing environment audit in pharma:

1. Identify the Scope

Clearly define the scope of the audit, including the specific marketing functions, product lines, or geographic regions that will be assessed. This will help focus the audit and allocate resources effectively.

2. Internal Analysis

- *Organizational Capabilities*: Evaluate the company's internal resources, including human resources, infrastructure, technology, and marketing expertise. Assess the strengths and weaknesses of the marketing team and their ability to execute marketing strategies effectively.
- *Product Portfolio*: Analyze the company's product offerings, market positioning, lifecycle stage, and the extent to which they meet customer needs. Identify any gaps or opportunities for expansion.
- *Marketing Strategies and Tactics*: Review the company's marketing strategies and tactics. Assess their alignment with business goals, target audience needs, and regulatory requirements. Evaluate the effectiveness of current marketing campaigns and initiatives.
- *Marketing Metrics and Performance*: Key marketing metrics analyses include market share, sales growth, customer satisfaction, and brand perception. Identifying trends and patterns to evaluate the overall marketing performance requiring improvement.

3. External Analysis

- *Market and Competitive Landscape*: Assess the market dynamics, including market size, growth rate, trends, and competitive landscape. Identify key competitors, their market share, product offerings, marketing strategies, and pricing strategies. Understand the regulatory environment and any upcoming changes that may impact marketing activities.
- *Customer Analysis*: Gain insights into customer needs, preferences, and behaviors. Conduct market research through surveys and interviews with healthcare professionals, patients, and other stakeholders to understand their perceptions of the company, products, and marketing efforts.
- *Industry Trends and Innovations*: Stay ahead of industry trends, emerging technologies, and innovations in pharmaceutical marketing. Evaluate the potential impact of these trends on marketing strategies and identify opportunities for differentiating and gaining competitive advantage.
- *PESTEL Analysis*: Analyze the external macro-environmental factors affecting marketing activities. Consider political, economic, social, technological, environmental, and legal factors influencing the industry and marketing strategies.
- *SWOT Analysis*: Consolidate the findings from the internal and external analyses into SWOT (Strengths, Weaknesses, Opportunities, and Threats) analysis. Identify the company's strengths

and weaknesses, market opportunities, and potential threats to inform strategic decision-making.

4. Action Plan

Based on the audit findings, develop an action plan that outlines specific initiatives and strategies to capitalize on strengths, address weaknesses, seize opportunities, and mitigate threats. Set clear goals, objectives, and timelines for implementation.

- *RegularEvaluation and Monitoring*: Continuously evaluate and monitor the marketing environment to stay updated on changes and trends. Regularly review and update the marketing environment audit to ensure its relevance and effectiveness over time.

Pharmaceutical companies can gain valuable insights into the internal and external factors shaping their marketing activities by conducting a comprehensive marketing environment audit. This helps identify improvement areas, leverage marketing opportunities, and develop effective marketing strategies that align with customer needs and business goals.

Marketing History

Marketing History refers to the chronological development and evolution of marketing practices and concepts. It encompasses studying how businesses and organizations have approached marketing activities, strategies, and techniques throughout history.

The marketing field has undergone significant transformations influenced by technological changes, consumer behavior, economic factors, and societal trends. Studying marketing history provides the following:

- Insights into the evolution of marketing theory
- The emergence of new marketing concepts
- The adaptation of marketing practices to meet changing market dynamics

Some notable milestones and trends in marketing history include:

1. *Production Era*: In the early 20th century, businesses focused primarily on production and efficiency, assuming that if products were made available, customers would purchase them.
2. *Sales Era:* During the mid-20th century, businesses started adopting sales-oriented approaches to persuade consumers to buy their products through aggressive sales and promotional tactics.
3. *Marketing Concept Era*: In the late 1950s and 1960s, the marketing concept emerged, emphasizing the importance of understanding and meeting customer needs and preferences. This era marked a shift towards customer-centric marketing strategies.
4. *Relationship Marketing*: In the 1980s and 1960s, relationship marketing gained prominence, emphasizing building long-term customer relationships based on trust, loyalty, and mutual value creation.
5. *Digital Age*: The advent of the internet and digital technologies revolutionized marketing practices in the late 20th century. Digital marketing, including online advertising, social media marketing, and data-driven targeting, became integral to marketing strategies.
6. *Personalization and Customer Experience*: Recently, there has been a growing focus on personalized marketing and delivering exceptional customer experiences. Marketers use data analytics, customer segmentation, and automation to tailor marketing efforts to individual preferences and enhance customer satisfaction.
7. *Sustainability and Ethical Marketing*: Increasingly, businesses are incorporating sustainability and ethical considerations into their marketing strategies. Consumers are demanding brand transparency, social responsibility, and environmentally friendly practices.

Studying marketing history helps marketers understand the evolution of consumer behavior, marketing channels, and marketing strategies. It provides:

- A foundation for learning from past successes and failures
- Identifying industry trends
- Adapting marketing approaches to current market conditions

It also highlights the importance of continuously evolving marketing practices to meet consumers' ever-changing needs and expectations.

Marketing History in Pharma

The marketing history in the pharmaceutical industry reflects the evolution of marketing practices specific to the healthcare and pharmaceutical sectors. Here are some key aspects of marketing history in pharma:

1. *Early Pharmaceutical Marketing*: In the early days, pharmaceutical marketing primarily focused on disseminating scientific information to healthcare professionals (HCPs). Companies

relied on sales representatives who visited doctors' offices to provide product information, samples, and educational materials. The marketing efforts were centered on building relationships with HCPs and influencing their prescription decisions.

2. *Direct-to-Consumer (DTC) Advertising*: In the late Twentieth century, the pharmaceutical industry shifted towards direct-to-consumer advertising. Regulatory changes in some countries, such as the United States, allowed pharmaceutical companies to advertise prescription drugs directly to consumers through mass media. This led to the emergence of television, print, and digital advertisements targeting patients and creating awareness about specific medical conditions and available treatment options. However, DTC advertising of pharmaceutical products is not allowed in most countries.
3. *Pharmaceutical Sales and Promotion*: Sales and promotion activities have been a significant part of pharmaceutical marketing history. Companies invest in sales representatives, known as *detailers*, who visit healthcare professionals to provide information about their products, offer samples, and engage in product detailing. Promotional materials like brochures, branded merchandise, and medical education events are also used to support marketing efforts.
4. *Key Opinion Leader (KOL) Engagement*: Pharmaceutical companies have long engaged with KOLs, influential healthcare professionals, researchers, and experts in specific therapeutic areas. KOLs provide valuable insights, participate in advisory boards, conduct clinical trials, and endorse and disseminate information about pharmaceutical products.
5. *Regulatory Compliance*: Marketing in the pharmaceutical industry is subject to stringent regulations and compliance requirements due to the nature of healthcare products. Companies must ensure compliance with regulations related to product claims, promotional materials, advertising practices, and interactions with healthcare professionals. Compliance departments are established to monitor and enforce adherence to these regulations.
6. *Digital Marketing and Online Presence*: With the rise of digital technologies, pharmaceutical companies have increasingly embraced digital marketing strategies. Websites, social media platforms, email campaigns, and educational resources disseminate product information, engage patients and HCPs, and raise awareness about diseases and treatment options.
7. *Patient-Centric Marketing*: There has been a growing focus on patient-centric marketing in the pharmaceutical industry. Recognizing the importance of patient empowerment, companies are investing in patient education, support programs, and resources that provide valuable information and assistance to patients throughout their healthcare journey.
8. *Personal Medicine and Targeted Marketing*: Advances in genetics and personalized medicine have led to targeted marketing efforts in the pharmaceutical industry. Pharmaceutical companies increasingly tailor their marketing messages and strategies to specific patient populations based on genetic profiles, biomarkers, and disease characteristics.

As the pharmaceutical industry evolves, marketing practices will adapt to the changing healthcare landscape, technological advancements, regulatory requirements, and patient expectations. Effective marketing in pharma requires a balance between providing accurate information, meeting regulatory standards, and delivering value to patients and healthcare professionals.

Marketing Information Systems (MIS)

Marketing Information Systems (MIS) in the pharmaceutical industry refer to the tools, processes, and infrastructure used to gather, analyze, store, and distribute marketing-related data and information. MIS is crucial in supporting decision-making and strategic planning in pharmaceutical marketing. Here are some key components and functions of marketing information systems:

1. *Data Collection*: MIS collects relevant data from various sources, including market research, sales data, customer feedback, competitive intelligence, and digital analytics. This data can come from internal (sales reports, CRM systems) or external sources (syndicated market research reports and online databases).
2. *Data Analysis and Reporting*: MIS analyzes and processes the collected data to generate meaningful insights and reports. Statistical analysis, data visualization, and predictive modeling techniques are used to identify patterns, trends, and correlations. These insights help evaluate marketing performance, identify market opportunities, and support decision-making.
3. *Market Research*: MIS facilitates the planning, execution, and analysis of market research

studies. They assist in designing surveys, managing data collection, and analyzing research findings. This enables pharmaceutical companies to gain insights into customer needs, preferences, market trends, and competitive intelligence.

4. *Customer Relationship Management (CRM)*: MIS integrates with CRM systems to capture and manage customer information, including HCPs, patients, and other stakeholders. CRM data helps understand customer behavior, track interactions, manage relationships, and tailor marketing activities to specific customer segments.
5. *Competitive Intelligence*: MIS gathers and analyzes information about competitors, their products, pricing strategies, marketing activities, and market positioning. This helps pharmaceutical companies to monitor and respond to competitive threats effectively, identify market gaps, and develop differentiation strategies.
6. *Digital Analytics*: As digital marketing becomes increasingly important, MIS captures and analyzes data from various digital channels such as websites, social media, email campaigns, and mobile apps. This data provides insights into online user behavior, engagement metrics, conversion rates, and the effectiveness of digital marketing initiatives.
7. *Marketing Performance Measurement*: MIS tracks and measures key performance indicators (KPIs) related to marketing activities, such as market share, sales revenue, customer acquisition and retention rates, return on investment (ROI), and brand awareness. This enables companies to evaluate the effectiveness of marketing strategies and tactics and make data-driven decisions.
8. *Decision Support*: MIS provides decision support tools and dashboards that enable marketing executives and managers to access relevant information, monitor performance, and make informed decisions. This includes tools for scenario analysis, forecasting, budgeting, and strategic planning.
9. *Information Dissemination*: MIS distributes marketing information and reports to relevant organizational stakeholders, such as marketing teams, sales teams, senior management, and other departments. This ensures that the right information reaches the right people at the right time, enabling effective collaboration and decision-making.

Pharmaceutical companies leverage marketing information systems to gain insights, make informed decisions, and optimize marketing strategies. By utilizing MIS, they can improve customer targeting, enhance marketing effectiveness, identify growth opportunities, and respond to market dynamics promptly.

Marketing Intelligence

Marketing intelligence in the pharmaceutical industry refers to gathering, analyzing, and utilizing information and insights about the market, customers, competitors, and industry trends to make informed marketing decisions.

Pharmaceutical companies rely on marketing intelligence to:

1. *Understand Customer Needs and Preferences*: By collecting data and conducting market research, pharmaceutical companies can gain insights into the needs, preferences, and behaviors of healthcare professionals, patients, and other stakeholders. This information helps develop targeted marketing strategies, product positioning, and messaging that resonate with the intended audience.
2. *Identify Market Opportunities*: Through market intelligence, pharmaceutical companies can identify untapped market segments, emerging therapeutic areas, and unmet medical needs. This knowledge enables them to develop new products or repurpose existing ones to address these opportunities effectively.
3. *Monitor Competition*: Marketing intelligence helps pharmaceutical companies keep track of their competitors' activities, such as product launches, marketing campaigns, pricing strategies, and market share. This information allows companies to assess their competitive position, identify areas of differentiation, and develop strategies to stay ahead in the market.
4. *Assess Market Dynamics and Trends*: Pharmaceutical marketing intelligence involves monitoring market trends, regulatory changes, healthcare policies, and shifts in patient demographics. By staying informed about these factors, companies can proactively adapt their marketing strategies, product portfolios, and pricing approaches to align with market dynamics and meet evolving customer needs.
5. *Evaluate Marketing Effectiveness*: Marketing intelligence enables measuring and evaluating marketing efforts and their impact on business outcomes. By analyzing data on sales, market share, customer feedback, and campaign performance, pharmaceutical companies can assess the effectiveness of their marketing

initiatives and make data-driven adjustments to improve results.

6. *Support Decision-making*: Marketing intelligence provides the necessary data and insights to support strategic decision-making within pharmaceutical companies. Whether pricing decisions, product development, market entry strategies, or resource allocation, marketing intelligence helps executives and marketing teams make informed choices that maximize the return on investment and contribute to overall business success.

To gather marketing intelligence, pharmaceutical companies may employ various methods, including market research surveys, data analysis, competitive analysis, social media monitoring, sales data analysis, and engagement with key opinion leaders and healthcare professionals.

Marketing intelligence is vital in helping pharmaceutical companies understand the market landscape, make informed marketing decisions, and stay competitive in an evolving industry.

Marketing Intermédiaires

Marketing intermediaries in the pharmaceutical industry refer to the entities or organizations facilitating the distribution and promotion of pharmaceutical products between pharmaceutical companies and end customers, such as healthcare professionals, hospitals, pharmacies, and patients.

These intermediaries are crucial in connecting the manufacturers with the target market and ensuring the efficient and effective delivery of pharmaceutical products. Here are some examples of marketing intermediaries in the pharma industry:

1. *Wholesalers/Distributors*: Pharmaceutical wholesalers or distributors are intermediaries that purchase pharmaceutical products in bulk from manufacturers and then distribute them to retailers, pharmacies, hospitals, and other healthcare facilities. They handle logistics, inventory management, and transportation to ensure the availability of products across different locations.
2. *Retail Pharmacies*: Retail pharmacies are intermediaries that directly interact with patients and healthcare professionals. They stock and dispense pharmaceutical products prescribed by healthcare professionals and provide counseling and guidance on medication usage. Retail pharmacies also serve as an important source of information and education about pharmaceutical products for patients.
3. *Specialty Pharmacies*: Specialty pharmacies provide specialized medications and therapies for complex diseases and conditions. They often have expertise in managing complex treatment regimens, prior authorizations, and patient support services. Specialty pharmacies are intermediaries between manufacturers, healthcare providers, and patients, ensuring specialized medication delivery and comprehensive support.
4. *Group Purchasing Organizations (GPOs)*: GPOs negotiate contracts with pharmaceutical manufacturers for healthcare providers, such as hospitals, clinics, and long-term care facilities. These intermediaries leverage the collective purchasing power of their member organizations to secure favorable pricing and terms for pharmaceutical products.
5. *Pharmacy Benefit Managers (PBMs)*: PBMs are intermediaries that manage prescription drug benefits for health insurance plans, employers, and other payers. They negotiate drug pricing with manufacturers, administer prescription drug claims, implement formularies, and provide medication utilization management services. PBMs play a significant role in controlling costs and ensuring appropriate patient medication access.
6. *Medical Representatives/Sales Force*: Pharmaceutical companies employ medical or sales representatives as intermediaries between the company and healthcare professionals. They promote pharmaceutical products, provide information about their benefits and usage, and facilitate communication between the company and healthcare providers. Medical representatives are vital in educating healthcare professionals about new products, clinical trials, and scientific advancements.

These marketing intermediaries in the pharmaceutical industry help bridge the gap between pharmaceutical manufacturers and end customers, ensuring efficient distribution, accessibility, and appropriate usage of pharmaceutical products. They facilitate the exchange of information, provide support services, and contribute to pharmaceutical companies' overall marketing and sales efforts. Collaboration and effective communication with these intermediaries are crucial for successful pharmaceutical marketing and reaching the intended target market.

Marketing Laws

Marketing Laws generally refer to legal regulations and guidelines governing marketing activities to ensure fair competition, protect consumers, and maintain ethical standards. While the specific laws and regulations vary across countries and jurisdictions, here are some common marketing laws and regulations that businesses need to be aware of:

1. *Advertising Standards*: These laws regulate advertising practices to prevent false, misleading, or deceptive advertising. These laws typically require that advertisements be truthful, substantiated, and not misleading to consumers. They may also govern specific areas such as comparative advertising, endorsements, testimonials, and certain claims or disclaimers.
2. *Consumer Protection Laws*: Consumer protection laws protect consumers from unfair or deceptive practices. These laws prohibit fraudulent or misleading advertising, unfair pricing practices, false product claims, and other activities that may harm consumers' rights or interests. They may also cover product labeling, warranties, and customer refunds or returns.
3. *Privacy and Data Protection Laws* and regulations related to privacy and data protection govern businesses' collection, storage, and use of personal information. These laws typically require businesses to obtain consent for data collection, protect personal information from unauthorized access, and provide transparency regarding data handling practices. Examples include the General Data Protection Regulation (GDPR) in the European Union and the California Consumer Privacy Act (CCPA) in the United States.
4. *Intellectual Property Laws*: Intellectual property laws protect original creative works, trademarks, patents, and trade secrets. These laws prevent unauthorized use or infringement of intellectual property rights, and unauthorized use of trademarks, copyright-protected materials, or patented interventions. Marketers must ensure they do not infringe on the intellectual property rights of others in their marketing materials and campaigns.
5. *Anti-Spam Laws*: Anti-spam laws regulate electronic communications, such as email marketing and SMS marketing, to prevent unsolicited or deceptive communications. These laws typically require businesses to obtain consent from recipients before sending marketing messages and provide options for recipients to unsubscribe from future communications.
6. *Competition Laws*: Competition laws promote fair competition and prevent anti-competitive practices that harm consumers or restrict market competition. These laws prohibit price-fixing, collusion, abuse of dominant market position, and deceptive trade practices. They aim to maintain a level playing field and protect consumer choice.

Businesses must consult with legal professionals or regulatory bodies in their jurisdictions to ensure compliance with applicable marketing laws. Failure to comply with these laws can result in legal consequences, fines, reputational damage, and loss of consumer trust.

Marketing Laws in Pharma

In the pharmaceutical industry, marketing activities are subject to specific laws and regulations to ensure the safety and integrity of healthcare products and protect the interests of patients. Here are some key marketing laws and regulations in the pharmaceutical sector:

1. *Drug Approval and Regulation*: Pharmaceutical marketing must comply with drug approval, labeling, and advertising regulations. Regulatory agencies, such as the Food and Drug Administration (FDA) in the United States or the European Medicines Agency (EMA) in the European Union, oversee the approval process of pharmaceutical products. Marketers must adhere to the approved indications, contraindications, and safety information outlined in product labeling.
2. *Prescription Drug Promotion*: These Laws govern the promotion of prescription drugs to healthcare professionals (HCPs) and consumers (patients). Direct-to-Consumer (DTC) advertising regulations differ across countries, with some allowing DTC advertising and others strictly limiting or prohibiting it. Promotion to HCPs must be based on accurate and balanced information, ensuring that claims are supported by scientific evidence.
3. *Off-Label Promotion*: Off-label promotion refers to promoting a drug for use not approved by regulatory authorities. In many jurisdictions, it is illegal for pharmaceutical companies to market or advertise drugs for off-label uses. Marketers must adhere to regulations restricting off-label promotion and ensure that promotional materials accurately reflect the approved indications for a drug.

4. *Compliance with Anti-Kickback Laws*: Anti-Kickback laws prohibit pharmaceutical companies from providing unlawful incentives or inducements to healthcare professionals in exchange for prescribing their products. These laws aim to prevent improper financial relationships that could influence prescribing decisions. Marketers must ensure that their marketing activities and relationships with HCPs comply with these laws.
5. *Privacy and Data Protection*: Privacy laws such as the Health Insurance Portability and Accountability Act (HIPAA) in the United States or the General Data Protection Regulation (GDPR) in the European Union govern personal health information collection, use, and protection. Pharmaceutical marketers must handle patient data in compliance with these laws and obtain appropriate consent for data collection and use.
6. *Good Promotional Practices*: Pharmaceutical companies often establish internal policies and guidelines to ensure compliance with marketing laws and ethical standards. These practices outline principles for fair and responsible marketing, including guidelines for interactions with HCPs, promotional materials, and transparency in financial relationships.

Pharmaceutical companies must thoroughly understand their target markets' marketing laws and regulations. Compliance with these laws is essential to maintain regulatory compliance, protect patient safety, and uphold the company's reputation. Therefore, legal and regulatory teams are vital in ensuring marketing activities adhere to the applicable laws and guidelines.

Marketing Metrics

In the pharmaceutical industry, marketing metrics assess marketing efforts' effectiveness and efficiency and measure the impact on business performance. Here are some key marketing metrics commonly used in pharma:

1. *Sales Revenue*: Sales revenue is a fundamental metric that measures the total value of pharmaceutical products sold over a specific period. It provides an overall picture of marketing efforts' financial performance and success.
2. *Market Share*: Market share measures the percentage of total sales or prescriptions within a specific market captured by a pharmaceutical company or its products. It helps assess the company's position in the market relative to competitors.
3. *Prescription Volume*: Prescription volume tracks the number of prescriptions written for a specific pharmaceutical product. It provides insights into the product's adoption and usage by healthcare professionals and helps evaluate the market penetration.
4. *Return on Investment (ROI)*: ROI measures the profitability of marketing initiatives by comparing the gains or returns generated against the marketing expenses incurred. It helps determine the efficiency of marketing campaigns and the allocation of resources.
5. *Customer Engagement*: Customer engagement metrics measure how well a company engages with its customers, such as healthcare providers or patients. These metrics include website traffic, social media engagement, and open email rates. These metrics can help pharma companies understand how well their marketing campaigns resonate with their target audience.
6. *Customer Acquisition Cost (CAC)*: CAC calculates the cost of acquiring a new customer or prescription. It considers various marketing expenses, such as advertising, sales force, and promotional activities, and helps evaluate the cost-effectiveness of acquiring new customers.
7. *Customer Lifetime Value (CLTV)*: CLTV estimates the total value a customer contributes to the company over their entire relationship with the brand. It helps assess the long-term profitability of acquiring and retaining customers and supports customer segmentation and targeting decisions.
8. *Brand Awareness and Recognition*: Metrics related to brand awareness measure the extent to which a pharmaceutical brand is recognized and known among the target audience. This can include metrics such as brand recall, brand recognition, or aided and unaided brand awareness surveys.
9. *Digital Engagement Metrics*: With the increasing importance of digital marketing in the pharmaceutical industry, metrics related to digital engagement have become crucial. These include website traffic, social media engagement, email open rates, click-through rates, and conversions. These metrics help evaluate the effectiveness of digital marketing campaigns and the engagement level of the target audience.
10. *Key Performance Indicators (KPIs) by Channel*: Different marketing channels, such as sales representatives, digital advertising, medical conferences, and direct mail, may have specific

metrics associated with them. These KPIs assess the performance and effectiveness of each channel in terms of reach, engagement, conversions, or return on investment.

11. *Customer Satisfaction and Loyalty*: Customer satisfaction and loyalty metrics, such as Net Promoter Score (NPS) or customer satisfaction surveys, assess the level of satisfaction and loyalty among customers. These metrics help understand the overall customer experience, brand perception, and the likelihood of customers recommending the brand to others.

Pharmaceutical companies use these metrics to track performance, make data-driven decisions, and optimize marketing strategies and tactics. The specific metrics used may vary based on the company's goals, target audience, product portfolio, and marketing channels employed.

Marketing Mindset

Marketing Mindset refers to the way of thinking and approaching marketing activities. It encompasses the attitudes, beliefs, and perspectives guiding marketing professionals' strategic decisions and actions. A marketing mindset involves:

- A customer-centric Approach
- A focus on Value creation
- Adaptability to change.
- A continuous learning mentality

Here are some key aspects of a marketing mindset:

1. *Customer-Centricity*: A marketing mindset emphasizes understanding and meeting the needs of customers. It involves deeply understanding customer preferences, behaviors, and pain points to create targeted marketing strategies that deliver value and solve customer problems.
2. *Value Creation*: A marketing mindset recognizes that success comes from creating customer value. It involves identifying and communicating the unique value proposition of products or services, emphasizing how they address customer needs and provide benefits that differentiate them from competitors.
3. *Data-Driven Decision Making*: A marketing mindset emphasizes the importance of analytics in guiding marketing decisions. It involves using data to gain insights, measure performance, and optimize marketing strategies. Marketers with a data-driven mindset rely on evidence and objective analysis to make informed decisions and drive continuous improvement.
4. *Adaptability and Agility*: A marketing mindset acknowledges the dynamic nature of the marketplace and the need to adapt to changes. It involves being open to new ideas, embracing innovation, and quickly adjusting strategies in response to market trends, customer feedback, and the competitive landscape.
5. *Continuous Learning*: A marketing mindset embraces a culture of learning and personal growth. It involves staying up-to-date with industry trends, best practices, and emerging technologies. Marketers with a continuous learning mindset are open to new knowledge, seek out opportunities to expand their skills, and experiment with new strategies and tactics.
6. *Collaboration and Communication*: A marketing mindset values collaboration and effective communication. It involves working closely with cross-functional teams, such as sales, product management, and customer service, to align marketing efforts with overall business goals. Effective communication skills are essential for conveying messages to target audiences and building strong relationships with customers and stakeholders.
7. *Results Orientation*: A marketing mindset focuses on achieving measurable results and positively impacting business performance. It involves setting clear objectives, tracking key performance indicators, and evaluating the success of marketing initiatives based on their contribution to goals.

Developing a marketing mindset requires a combination of knowledge, skills, and willingness to embrace the core principles of marketing. In addition, it involves adopting a customer-centric perspective, leveraging data and analytics, embracing change, and continuously learning and adapting to new market realities.

Marketing Mindset in Pharma

In the pharmaceutical industry, a marketing mindset encompasses the specific attitudes and approaches relevant to marketing pharmaceutical products and services. While the core marketing principles apply across industries, the unique characteristics of the pharmaceutical sector shape the marketing mindset within this context. Here are some key aspects of a marketing mindset in pharma:

1. *Patient-Centricity*: Patient-centricity is the cornerstone of the marketing mindset in the pharmaceutical industry. It involves recognizing the importance of patients' well-being,

understanding their needs, and ensuring that marketing strategies and activities prioritize their health and quality of life. The focus is on delivering value to patients by providing effective, safe, accessible healthcare solutions.

2. *Regulatory Compliance*: Pharma marketers operate in a highly regulated environment due to the nature of healthcare products and must ensure patient safety. A marketing mindset in pharma involves deep knowledge and adherence to regulatory requirements related to drug approval, advertising, labeling, and compliance with laws such as the United States FDA regulations or the European Union's EMA regulations.
3. *Medical and Scientific Knowledge*: Pharma marketers must understand their products' medical and scientific aspects. This includes knowledge of the therapeutic area, disease states, treatment options, and clinical evidence supporting the efficacy and safety of the products. A marketing mindset in pharma involves continuous learning and staying updated with the latest medical advancements and research.
4. *Ethics and Integrity*: Pharma marketing must uphold high ethical standards due to its critical role in promoting healthcare products. The marketing mindset in pharma emphasizes the importance of integrity, honesty, and transparency in all interactions with healthcare professionals, patients, and other stakeholders. In addition, marketers must ensure that their promotional activities are accurate, evidence-based, and aligned with the approved labeling of the products.
5. *Collaborative Relationships*: In the pharmaceutical industry, successful marketing requires close collaboration and alignment with various stakeholders, including healthcare professionals, patient advocacy groups, regulatory authorities, and payers. A marketing mindset in pharma emphasizes building and maintaining strong relationships with these stakeholders based on trust, mutual respect, and shared goals.
6. *Evidence-Based Decision-Making*: A marketing mindset in pharma relies on evidence-based decision-making. It involves analyzing clinical data, real-world evidence, market research, and other relevant information to inform marketing strategies and tactics. Data-driven insights help guide promotional activities, target the right audience, and measure the impact of marketing initiatives.
7. *Patient Education and Support*: Pharma marketers educate patients about their healthcare options, treatment adherence, and disease management. A marketing mindset in pharma involves developing patient-centric educational materials, support programs, and digital tools that empower patients to make informed decisions about their health.

While these aspects of marketing mindset are important in the pharmaceutical industry, adapting and tailoring strategies based on specific regulations, therapeutic areas, and target audiences within the pharma sector is essential. Successful pharma marketers combine their marketing skills with understanding the healthcare landscape, patient needs, and regulatory framework to deliver meaningful and impactful marketing campaigns.

Marketing Mix

The 4 P's model of marketing, commonly referred to as the Marketing Mix, was proposed by E. Jerome McCarthy in his book *Basic Marketing: A Managerial Approach*, published in 1960. The four P's stand for:

1. *Product* refers to the goods, services, or ideas offered to customers. It includes decisions about product design, features, branding, and packaging.
2. *Price* relates to pricing decisions, including base price, discounts, and other pricing strategies.
3. *Place* deals with the distribution and how the product gets to the customer. This includes decisions related to distribution channels, logistics, and retail locations.
4. *Promotion* concerns how potential customers are informed about the product. It encompasses advertising, public relations, sales promotions, and personal selling.

This model has been fundamental in marketing for many years, providing a framework for marketers to develop, manage, and evaluate marketing strategies.

Marketing Mix in the Pharmaceutical Industry

In the context of the pharmaceutical industry, the marketing mix consists of the following components:

1. *Product*: The product element of the marketing mix refers to the pharmaceutical products or healthcare services offered by a company. This includes the formulation, dosage forms, packaging, branding, and any additional features or benefits in the pharma industry, and the

product may also include associated services such as patient support programs or educational materials.

2. *Price*: Price refers to the cost of the pharmaceutical product or service. Pricing strategies in pharma can vary depending on research and development costs, manufacturing expenses, market demand, competition, reimbursement considerations, and regulatory factors. Price can also be influenced by pricing models like value-based or differential pricing based on different markets or patient segments.
3. *Place* refers to the distribution channels and strategies used to make the pharmaceutical product available to customers. It is about deciding the most appropriate channels to reach healthcare professionals, pharmacies, hospitals, or direct-to-consumer distribution. It also includes considerations about inventory management, supply chain logistics, and ensuring product availability in the right locations.
4. *Promotion*: Promotion involves various marketing and communication activities to create awareness, generate interest, and persuade target audiences to choose the pharmaceutical product or service. Promotion strategies in pharma may include advertising, direct marketing, digital marketing, detailing by the sales force, promotion, public relations, medical conferences, and educational initiatives. However, compliance with regulatory requirements and ethical guidelines in all promotional activities is essential.

In the pharmaceutical industry, the marketing mix must consider the unique characteristics of healthcare products, the regulatory environment, and the ethical considerations involved. For example, marketing strategies must focus on accurate scientific and clinical information communication, adherence to regulatory guidelines, and drug promotion and advertising compliance laws. Additionally, the marketing mix should be tailored to specific therapeutic areas, patient populations, and market dynamics to effectively reach and engage the target audience.

It is important to note that the marketing mix is not a static concept but requires continuous evaluation and adjustment based on market dynamics, customer feedback, and competitive factors. Effective utilization of the marketing mix elements helps pharmaceutical companies promote their products, differentiate themselves from competitors, and meet the needs of healthcare professionals and patients.

Marketing Models

Marketing models are frameworks or theoretical constructs that help marketers understand, analyze, and make decisions about various aspects of marketing. These models provide a structured approach to studying consumer behavior, market dynamics, marketing strategies, and the impact of marketing efforts. Here are some commonly used marketing models:

1. *SWOT Analysis*: SWOT (Strengths, weaknesses, Opportunities, Threats) analysis is a framework that helps identify and evaluate the internal strengths and weaknesses of a company and external opportunities and threats in the market. It provides a comprehensive view of the company's competitive position and helps guide marketing strategies.
2. *STP*: STP stands for segmentation, Targeting, and Positioning. This model involves segmenting the market into distinct groups based on similar characteristics, selecting specific target segments to focus marketing efforts on, and positioning the product or service to differentiate it in the target audience's minds.
3. *Marketing Mix (4Ps)*: The marketing mix model consists of four elements—Product, Price, Place, and Promotion. It provides a framework for making marketing decisions by considering the product offering, pricing strategy, distribution channels, and promotional activities.
4. *AIDA Model*: AIDA (Attention, Interest, Desire, Action) is a model that describes the cognitive stages a consumer goes through when making a purchase decision. It outlines the steps in the consumer's journey, from becoming aware of a product to taking action and making a purchase.
5. *Customer Journey Mapping:* Customer journey mapping involves understanding and visualizing the various touchpoints and interactions a customer has with a brand throughout their buying journey. This model helps identify opportunities to engage customers, improve their experience, and build strong relationships.
6. *Product Life Cycle*: The product life cycle model represents the stages a product grows through, from introduction to growth, maturity, and eventual decline. It helps marketers understand the different marketing strategies and activities needed at each stage of the product's life cycle.
7. *Porter's Five Forces*: Porter's Five Forces model assesses an industry's competitive intensity and attractiveness. It examines the five forces—industry rivalry, the threat of new entrants, the threat of substitutes, the bargaining power of the

buyers, and the bargaining power of the suppliers - to analyze the overall competitiveness of the market.

8. *Branding Models*: Various branding models, such as brand equity models, brand positioning models, and brand personality models, help marketers understand and manage brand perceptions, customer loyalty, and brand value.
9. *Consumer Decision-Making Models*: These models, such as the Engle-Kollat-Blackwell model or Howard-Seth model, provide frameworks for understanding the psychological processes and factors that influence consumer decision-making, including problem recognition, information search, evaluation of alternatives, and post-purchase behavior.

These are just a few examples of marketing models, and many more specific models and frameworks can be applied in various marketing contexts. Marketers use these analytical models to gain insights, guide decision-making, and develop effective marketing strategies. It is important to note that the choice of a model depends on the specific marketing challenge or objective at hand.

Marketing Models in Pharma

Various marketing models are applied in the pharmaceutical industry to understand marketing dynamics and consumer behavior and develop effective marketing strategies. Here are some marketing models commonly used in the pharma sector:

1. *Segmentation, Targeting, and Positioning (STP)*: This model helps pharmaceutical companies identify specific patient or healthcare professional segments, target their marketing efforts towards those segments, and position their products or services to meet the unique needs of each segment.
2. *Physician and Patient Journey Mapping*: Similar to customer journey mapping, these models focus on understanding the touchpoints and experiences of physicians or patients throughout their interactions with the healthcare system. Mapping these journeys helps identify opportunities for engagement, education, and support at each stage of the process.
3. *Key Opinion Leader (KOL) Influence Models*: KOLs play a crucial role in the pharmaceutical industry by influencing healthcare professionals' prescribing behaviors and treatment decisions. Various models, such as network analysis and social influence models, are used to identify and leverage the influence of KOLs in targeted therapeutic areas.
4. *Health Economic Models*: Health economic models assess the cost-effectiveness and value proposition of pharmaceutical products or interventions. These models help evaluate the economic impact of treatments, pricing strategies, and reimbursement decisions.
5. *Diffusion of Innovation Model*: This model explores how new pharmaceutical products are adopted and diffused in the market. It examines the factors influencing the adoption rate, such as the innovativeness of the product, communication channels, and the characteristics of early and other adopter categories.
6. *Relationship Marketing Models*: Relationship marketing focuses on building and maintaining long-term relationships with healthcare professionals, patients, and other stakeholders. Models like customer lifetime value analysis and customer relationship management (CRM) help optimize customer interactions, personalize communication, and enhance customer loyalty.
7. *Market Access Models*: Market access models assess the market potential and barriers to entry for pharmaceutical products. They consider pricing, reimbursement, regulatory environment, and the competitive landscape to develop effective market access strategies.
8. *Digital Marketing and Analytics Model*: With the rise of digital marketing, various models related to digital channels, analytics, and customer engagement have become relevant in the pharmaceutical industry. These models help analyze digital campaigns, measure engagement, and optimize marketing efforts through data-driven insights.

It is important to note that the choice and application of marketing models in the pharmaceutical industry depend on the specific marketing objectives, target audience, therapeutic area, and regulatory considerations. Companies often employ a combination of models to gain a comprehensive understanding of the market, customers, and competitive landscape, enabling them to make informed marketing decisions and achieve their business goals.

Marketing Myopia

The concept of *Marketing Myopia* was proposed by Theodore Levitt, a renowned economist, and professor at Harvard Business School. Levitt first introduced the term *Marketing Myopia* in an article titled *Marketing Myopia* published in the Harvard Business Review in 1960. In his influential article,

Levitt argued that businesses often fail because they focus too narrowly on their products and internal operations rather than understanding and meeting customers' needs. He emphasized the importance of adopting a customer-centric mindset and recognizing the broader business opportunities beyond the immediate product offering. Levitt's article sparked significant discussion and has since become a foundational concept in marketing.

Marketing Myopia refers to a short-sighted and narrow focus on a company's products or services rather than understanding and meeting customers' broader needs. Myopia implies a lack of vision and an overemphasis on immediate product-centric goals, which can hinder long-term growth and sustainability.

Marketing Myopia in the Pharmaceutical Industry

In the context of the pharmaceutical industry, marketing myopia can manifest in several ways:

1. *Product-Centric Approach*: Companies may become too focused on their specific drugs or treatments to recognize the broader healthcare needs of patients and healthcare professionals. This narrow perspective can limit their ability to identify new opportunities, address unmet needs, or adapt to changing market dynamics.
2. *Rigid Definitions of Market*: Marketing myopia can occur when pharmaceutical companies define their market too narrowly, focusing solely on their existing therapeutic area or target patient population. They may miss potential growth opportunities by failing to explore adjacent or emerging markets.
3. *Ignoring Competitive Threats*: Companies experiencing marketing myopia may underestimate or overlook competitive threats from alternative therapies, generics, or disruptive innovations. They risk losing market share and relevance by failing to monitor the competitive landscape and adapting their strategies accordingly.
4. *Neglecting Customer Insights*: Marketing myopia can result in a lack of understanding of customers' evolving needs, preferences, and behaviors. Companies may fail to conduct market research, collect customer feedback, or adapt their marketing strategies based on these insights, leading to a disconnect between their offerings and customer expectations.

Overcoming Marketing Myopia in Pharma

To overcome marketing myopia in the pharmaceutical industry, companies can adopt several strategies:

1. *Customer-Centric Approach*: Shift the focus from products to understanding and meeting customers' needs. Conduct thorough market research, engage in customer dialogue, and develop a deep understanding of patients, healthcare professionals, and other stakeholders.
2. *Market Expansion*: Explore new therapeutic areas, patient segments, or geographical markets to uncover untapped growth opportunities. This may involve diversifying product portfolios, pursuing partnerships, or acquiring complementary businesses.
3. *Continuous Innovation*: Foster a culture of innovation and adaptability within the organization. Encourage cross-functional collaboration, embrace emerging technologies, and invest in research and development to stay ahead of market trends and evolving customer needs.
4. *Competitive Analysis*: Monitor the competitive landscape and proactively respond to emerging threats or market disruptions. Regularly assess competitors' offerings, market positioning, and strategies to identify areas where differentiation and improvement are necessary.
5. *Embrace Digital Transformation*: Leverage digital technologies and data analytics to enhance customer engagement, optimize marketing campaigns, and deliver personalized experiences. Embracing digital transformation can enable companies to understand better and serve their target audiences.

Marketing Planning

Marketing planning in the pharmaceutical industry involves developing a strategic roadmap to guide marketing activities and achieve business objectives. Effective marketing planning in pharma requires a thorough understanding of the market landscape, target audience, competitive dynamics, and regulatory considerations. Here are some key steps to create an effective marketing plan in the pharmaceutical industry:

1. *Set Clear Objectives*: Define specific and measurable marketing objectives aligning with the business goals. These objectives align with the overall business goals. These objectives could include increasing market share, launching a new product, expanding into new markets, or improving brand awareness. Clear objectives provide direction and serve as benchmarks for evaluating the success of marketing efforts.

2. *Conduct Market Research*: Gather comprehensive data and insights about the target market, including patient demographics, healthcare professionals, treatment trends, competitive landscape, and regulatory environment. Use market research techniques such as surveys, interviews, and data analysis to understand customer needs, preferences, and behavior.
3. *Define Target Segments*: Segment the market based on relevant criteria such as disease, indication, patient characteristics, healthcare provider preferences, or geographical factors. Identify the most attractive and viable target segments for your products or services. Each segment may require a tailored marketing approach and value proposition.
4. *Develop a Value Proposition*: Clearly articulate the unique value your product or service brings to the market and how it addresses the needs of the target segments. Highlight key differentiators, such as clinical efficacy, safety profile, patient outcomes, cost-effectiveness, or additional services. Craft compelling messaging that resonates with the target audience and differentiates your offering from competitors.
5. *Build a Marketing Strategy*: Based on the market research and target segments, develop a comprehensive marketing strategy that outlines the marketing mix elements (product, price, place, promotion) and channels to reach and engage the target audience effectively. Consider traditional and digital marketing channels, healthcare professional education initiatives, patient support programs, and other relevant tactics.
6. *Set Marketing Budget*: Allocate financial resources based on the marketing objectives, market potential, and the required marketing activities. Determine the appropriate budget for promotional activities, market research, sales force, digital marketing, and other initiatives. Regularly review and adjust the budget as needed throughout the planning period.
7. *Implementation and Execution*: Execute the marketing plan by implementing the identified marketing tactics, campaigns, and initiatives. Monitor and track the progress of marketing activities, measure their effectiveness, and make adjustments as necessary. Ensure compliance with regulatory guidelines and ethical considerations.
8. *Performance Measurement and Evaluation*: Continuously monitor key performance indicators (KPIs) to assess the success and impact of marketing efforts. Track metrics such as sales performance, market share, customer satisfaction, brand awareness, and return on investment (ROI). Regularly evaluate the marketing plan's effectiveness and make necessary refinements to improve results.
9. *Adaptability and Agility*: The pharmaceutical industry is dynamic, with evolving market trends, regulatory changes, and competitive dynamics. Maintain flexibility in the marketing plan to adapt to new insights and market developments. Continuously scan the market for emerging opportunities and challenges that may require adjustments to the marketing strategy.
10. *Collaboration and Cross-functional Alignment*: Effective marketing planning in the pharma industry requires collaboration and alignment across different functions, including marketing, sales, medical affairs, regulatory affairs, and market access. Foster cross-functional teamwork and communication to ensure a cohesive approach and optimize the use of resources.

Remember that marketing planning is interactive. Regular reviews and adjustments are essential to keep the plan relevant and effective. By following these steps and leveraging market insights, pharma companies can develop and implement marketing plans that effectively reach their target audience, differentiate their offerings, and achieve their business objectives.

Marketing Plans

Marketing Plans in the pharmaceutical industry outline the strategic approach and tactics to effectively promote pharmaceutical products or services. These plans are tailored to the unique characteristics of the pharma sector, including regulatory constraints, target audience considerations, and competitive landscape. Here are key components typically included in marketing plans in the pharma industry:

1. *Executive Summary*: Provide a concise overview of the marketing plan, including the objectives, target market, key strategies, and expected outcomes.
2. *Situation Analysis*: Conduct a thorough analysis of the internal and external factors that impact marketing efforts. This includes assessing the competitive landscape, market trends, regulatory environment, and relevant industry challenges and opportunities.
3. *Target Market Identification*: Define the specific target market segments for the pharmaceutical

product or service. Consider factors such as patient demographics, disease condition, healthcare professional preferences, and geographic considerations. Provide insights into the needs, behaviors, and characteristics of the target market segments.

4. *Competitive Analysis*: Evaluate the competitive landscape by identifying key competitors, their market share, product offerings, and positioning strategies. Assess the strengths and weaknesses of competitors and identify opportunities for differentiation,
5. *Value Proposition*: Define a compelling value proposition that communicates the unique benefits of the pharmaceutical product or service. Highlight the key features, clinical efficacy, safety profile, patient outcomes, and any additional value-added services.
6. *Marketing Objectives*: Set clear, measurable, and achievable marketing objectives that align with the overall business goals. These objectives may include increasing market share, launching new products, expanding into new markets, improving brand awareness, or enhancing customer loyalty.
7. *Marketing Strategies*: Develop a comprehensive set of strategies that outline how the marketing objectives will be achieved. These strategies may include product positioning, pricing, promotional activities, distribution channels, key opinion leader (KOL) engagement, and digital marketing initiatives.
8. *Tactical Implementation*: Outline the specific marketing tactics, such as advertising campaigns, professional education programs, patient support initiatives, digital marketing efforts, and participation in industry conferences or events. Define timelines, responsibilities, and budgets for each tactic.
9. *Regulatory Considerations*: Ensure compliance with applicable regulations and guidelines throughout the marketing activities. This includes adhering to regulations related to promotional materials, patient privacy, adverse event reporting, and compliance with industry codes of conduct.
10. *Performance Measurement and Evaluation*: Define the key performance indicators (KPIs) to monitor the effectiveness and impact of marketing efforts. Track metrics such as sales performance, market share, brand awareness, customer satisfaction, and return on investment (ROI). Regularly evaluate the marketing plan's performance, make data-driven adjustments, and refine strategies and tactics as needed.
11. *Budgeting*: Allocate financial resources to support the implementation of marketing activities. Develop a budget that covers various marketing expenses, including advertising, promotional materials, digital marketing campaigns, market research, and sales force support.
12. *Monitoring and Control*: Implement a system for ongoing monitoring, analysis, and control of marketing activities. Regularly review performance against targets, conduct market research, gather customer feedback, and monitor the competitive landscape. Make necessary adjustments to optimize marketing efforts and ensure alignment with business objectives.

Marketing plans in the pharmaceutical industry should be dynamic and adaptable to evolving market conditions and customer needs. Regularly review and update the marketing plan based on feedback, performance data, market changes, and emerging opportunities or challenges. Collaboration and coordination among cross-functional teams, including marketing, sales, medical affairs, and regulatory affairs, are crucial to execute the marketing plan effectively.

Marketing Productivity Audit

A Marketing Productivity Audit in the pharmaceutical industry involves assessing marketing activities' effectiveness and efficiency to identify improvement areas and enhance overall marketing performance. Here are the key steps to conduct a marketing productivity audit in pharma:

1. *Define Audit Objectives*: Clearly outline the objectives of the audit, such as identifying the bottlenecks, assessing resource allocation, evaluating ROI, or improving marketing effectiveness. These objectives will guide the audit process and help focus on specific areas of concern.
2. *Identify Key Performance Indicators (KPIs)*: Determine the KPIs that will be used to measure marketing productivity. These may include metrics such as sales revenue, market share, customer acquisition costs, marketing ROI, customer satisfaction, brand awareness, or engagement levels. Select KPIs that align with the audit objectives and provide meaningful insights into marketing performance.
3. *Gather Data*: Collect relevant data and information for analysis. This may include sales data, marketing expenditure data, customer data, market research findings, campaign

performance data, and any other relevant information that sheds light on marketing activities and their outcomes.

4. *Analyze Marketing Processes*: Assess the efficiency and effectiveness of marketing processes and workflows. Identify areas where processes may be inefficient, redundant, or prone to errors. Evaluate the alignment between marketing activities and overall business objectives. Analyze the effectiveness of marketing strategies, tactics, and campaigns in achieving desired outcomes.
5. *Evaluate Resource Allocation*: Review the allocation of marketing resources, including budget, personnel, and technology. Assess the effectiveness of resource allocation and identify areas where resources may be underutilized or misaligned with marketing objectives. Evaluate the effectiveness of marketing technology platforms and tools in supporting marketing activities.
6. *Assess Marketing Channels*: Evaluate the performance and effectiveness of marketing channels utilized in the pharmaceutical industry, such as digital marketing, traditional advertising, medical conferences, KOL engagements, or direct marketing. Analyze the channels' reach, engagement, conversion rates, and cost-effectiveness. Identify channels that deliver the highest returns and those that may require optimization or reallocation of resources.
7. *Review Marketing Messaging and Content*: Assess the quality, consistency, and relevance of marketing messaging and content. Evaluate the alignment of messaging with the target audience's needs and preferences. Review the effectiveness of marketing materials, including brochures, websites, digital content, and promotional materials.
8. *Benchmarking and Best Practices*: Compare marketing performance against industry benchmarks and best practices. Assess how the organization's marketing productivity compares to competitors or industry leaders. Identify opportunities to adopt successful strategies or tactics others use in the industry.
9. *Identify Improvement Opportunities*: Based on the audit findings, identify areas for improvement and develop actionable recommendations. Prioritize the recommendations based on their potential impact and feasibility of implementation. These recommendations may include process improvements, resource reallocation, technology enhancements, or marketing strategies or tactics changes.
10. *Implementation and Marketing*: Develop an action plan to implement the identified recommendations. Assign responsibilities, set timelines, and allocate necessary resources for implementation. Establish mechanisms to monitor and track the implementation progress and regularly evaluate the impact of improvements on marketing productivity.
11. *Continuous Improvement*: Recognize that marketing productivity is an ongoing process. Continuously monitor marketing performance, track key metrics, and conduct periodic audits to ensure marketing activities remain effective and aligned with business objectives.

Organizations can identify inefficiencies, optimize resource allocation, improve marketing strategies, and enhance marketing efforts' overall effectiveness and efficiency by conducting a marketing productivity audit in the pharmaceutical industry.

Marketing Research

Marketing Research in the pharmaceutical industry involves gathering and analyzing data to gain insights into market dynamics, customer behavior, competitor activities, and other factors influencing marketing strategies and decision-making. Here are the key aspects and steps involved in conducting marketing research in pharma:

1. *Define Research Objectives*: Clearly articulate the specific objectives of the research, such as understanding customer needs, assessing market potential, evaluating product positioning, or identifying market trends. Establishing clear objectives helps guide the research process and ensures the research outcomes align with the organization's goals.
2. *Determine Research Methodology*: Select the appropriate research methodology based on the research objectives, available resources, and time constraints. Common research methodologies in pharma include quantitative research (surveys, data analysis) and qualitative research (focus groups, interviews), market observation, secondary data analysis, and social listening through digital platforms.
3. *Identify Target Audience*: Define the target audience for the research, which may include healthcare professionals, patients, caregivers, payers, or other stakeholders relevant to the research objectives. Ensure that the sample size

and composition represent the target audience to draw accurate conclusions.

4. *Develop Research Instruments*: Create research instruments such as survey questionnaires, interview guides, or discussion guides. These instruments should be designed to collect data that aligns with the research objectives and provide actionable insights. In addition, consider incorporating validated scales or measures specific to the pharma industry, such as patient-oriented outcome measures (PROMs) or adherence scales.
5. *Data Collection*: Execute the research plan and collect data using the chosen research methods. This may involve conducting surveys, interviews, focus groups, or gathering data from secondary sources. Ensure data collection protocols adhere to ethical guidelines and data privacy regulations.
6. *Data Analysis*: Analyze the collected data using appropriate statistical or qualitative analysis techniques. Quantitative data may be analyzed using statistical software to uncover patterns, correlations, or statistical significance. Qualitative data can be analyzed through thematic analysis to identify key themes, opinions, or sentiments.
7. *Interpretation and Insights*: Interpret the research findings and derive meaningful insights that address the research objectives. Identify key trends, customer preferences, market opportunities, or challenges that can inform marketing strategies and decision-making. Draw connections between the research findings and the broader marketing context in the pharmaceutical industry.
8. *Reporting and Presentation*: Summarize the research findings in a clear and concise report or presentation. Present the insights in an easily understandable and actionable format for stakeholders. Include visualizations, charts, or graphs to enhance clarity and impact.
9. *Integration into Marketing Strategy*: Incorporate the research findings and insights into the overall marketing strategy. Use the insights to refine target audience segmentation, product positioning, messaging, communication channels, and other marketing elements. Ensure that the research findings are communicated effectively to relevant stakeholders within the organization.
10. *Continuous Research and Monitoring*: Recognize that market dynamics in the pharmaceutical industry are ever-changing. Continuously monitor the market, track customer preferences, and conduct periodic research to stay informed about evolving trends, competitor activities, and customer needs.

Marketing research in the pharmaceutical industry provides valuable insights that inform strategic decision-making, improve marketing effectiveness, and drive business growth. By conducting systematic and robust research, pharmaceutical companies can gain a deeper understanding of their target market, identify market opportunities, and make data-driven decisions to meet customer needs effectively.

Marketing Strategy

Marketing strategy in the pharmaceutical industry involves developing a comprehensive plan to promote pharmaceutical products or services, reach target audiences, and achieve business objectives. Here are the key components and considerations for developing an effective marketing strategy in pharma:

1. *Define Objectives*: Clearly articulate the marketing objectives, such as increasing market share, launching new products, expanding into new markets, improving brand awareness, enhancing customer loyalty, or driving sales revenue. Ensure the objectives are specific, measurable, attainable, relevant, and time-bound (SMART).
2. *Target Market Segmentation*: Identify and segment the target market based on patient demographics, disease indication, prescriber preferences, or geographic considerations. Understand each target segment's unique needs, behaviors, and characteristics to tailor marketing strategies accordingly.
3. *Product Positioning*: Determine how the pharmaceutical product or service will be positioned in the market relative to competitors. Define the key differentiators, value propositions, and benefits that differentiate the product. Align the positioning with the target audience's needs and preferences.
4. *Competitive Analysis*: Assess the competitive landscape by identifying key competitors, their market share, product offerings, and positioning strategies. Understand their strengths and weaknesses to identify opportunities for differentiation. Develop strategies to compete and gain a competitive advantage effectively.
5. *Branding and Messaging*: Develop a strong brand identity for the pharmaceutical product or service. Create compelling messaging communicating the value proposition, key benefits, and unique selling points. Ensure

consistent messaging across all marketing channels and touchpoints.

6. *Marketing Channels and Tactics*: Determine the most effective marketing channels and tactics to reach the target audience. This may include traditional marketing channels (salesforce, print, television, and direct mail) and digital channels (websites, social media, and email marketing). Select tactics such as advertising campaigns, KOL engagement, medical conferences, patient education programs, or online promotions based on the target audience's preferences and the desired outcomes.
7. *Digital Marketing and Technology*: Leverage digital marketing strategies and technologies to enhance reach, engagement, and measurement. Utilize online platforms, search engine optimization (SEO), content marketing, social media marketing, and data analytics to optimize marketing efforts and track performance.
8. *Regulatory Compliance*: Ensure compliance with regulations and guidelines specific to the pharmaceutical industry. Adhere to regulations related to promotional material, patient privacy, adverse event reporting, and compliance with industry codes of conduct.
9. *Measurement and Evaluation*: Establish key performance indicators (KPIs) to measure the effectiveness of the marketing strategy. Track sales performance, market share, brand awareness, customer satisfaction, and ROI. Then, regularly evaluate the performance, analyze data, and make data-driven adjustments to optimize marketing efforts.
10. *Collaboration and Alignment*: Foster collaboration and alignment across cross-functional teams, including marketing, sales, medical affairs, and regulatory affairs. Ensure marketing strategies align with broader business goals and coordinate with other functions to maximize impact.
11. *Continuous Improvement*: Monitor market trends, customer feedback, and competitive landscape continuously. Stay updated with industry developments, technological advancement, and evolving customer needs. Adapt marketing strategies and tactics to stay ahead of the competition and meet changing market dynamics.

Developing a well-defined marketing strategy in the pharmaceutical industry is crucial for effectively promoting pharmaceutical products or services, reaching target audiences, and achieving business objectives. It requires a deep understanding of the target market, competitive landscape, regulatory constraints, and evolving market trends. By implementing a robust marketing strategy, pharmaceutical companies can differentiate themselves in the market, build brand equity, and drive business growth.

Marketing Systems Audit

A Marketing Systems Audit in the pharmaceutical industry involves assessing the efficiency, effectiveness, and alignment of marketing systems and processes within an organization. It aims to identify strengths, weaknesses, and areas for improvement in the marketing systems to enhance overall marketing performance. Here are the key steps to conduct a marketing systems audit:

1. *Define Audit Objectives*: Clearly outline the objectives of the audit, such as evaluating the functionality of marketing systems, identifying process bottlenecks, assessing data accuracy and accessibility, or improving marketing automation. These objectives will guide the audit process and help focus on specific areas of concern.
2. *Assess Marketing Technology Infrastructure*: Evaluate the marketing technology stack used within the organization, such as customer relationship management (CRM) systems, marketing automation platforms, data analytics tools, content management systems, or digital marketing platforms. Assess these systems' functionality, integration, and usability to support marketing activities effectively.
3. *Review Data Management Processes*: Evaluate the processes for collecting, storing, and managing marketing data. Assess data accuracy, completeness, and accessibility. Review data governance practices, including data privacy, security, and compliance with relevant regulations such as GDPR (General Data Protection Regulation) or HIPAA (Health Insurance Portability and Accountability). Identify areas for improvement in data management and explore opportunities to enhance data-driven decision-making.
4. *Analyze Marketing Workflow and Processes*: Assess the efficiency and effectiveness of marketing workflows and processes. Identify areas where processes may be redundant, time-consuming, or prone to errors. Evaluate the alignment between marketing processes and overall business objectives. Look for opportunities to streamline processes, automate repetitive tasks, or eliminate bottlenecks.

5. *Evaluate Marketing Analytics Capabilities*: Review the organization's capabilities in gathering, analyzing, and leveraging marketing data for insights. Assess the availability and accuracy of marketing performance metrics, customer segmentation data, campaign effectiveness analysis, or ROI measurement. Identify gaps in analytics capabilities and explore ways to enhance data-driven decision-making.
6. *Assess Integration and Alignment*: Evaluate the integration and alignment of marketing systems with other key functions within the organization, such as sales, finance, or customer service. Assess the flow of information between departments and identify opportunities for better collaboration and data sharing. Ensure that marketing systems are aligned with broader business goals and strategies.
7. *Review Marketing Metrics and Reporting*: Assess the metrics and reporting mechanisms used to measure marketing performance. Evaluate the relevance, accuracy, and timeliness of marketing reports. Identify opportunities to enhance reporting capabilities and develop actionable insights from the data.
8. *Identify Improvement Opportunities*: Based on the audit findings, identify areas for improvement and develop actionable recommendations. Prioritize the recommendations based on their potential impact and feasibility of implementation. These recommendations may include systems upgrades, process improvements, training programs, or changes in data management practices.
9. *Implementation and Monitoring*: Develop an action plan to implement the identified recommendations. Assign responsibilities, set timelines, and allocate necessary resources for implementation. Establish mechanisms to monitor and track implementation progress and regularly evaluate improvements' impact on marketing system performance.
10. *Continuous Improvement*: Recognize that marketing systems audit is an ongoing process. Continuously monitor marketing system performance, track key metrics, and conduct periodic audits to ensure marketing systems remain effective, efficient, and aligned with business objectives.

By conducting a marketing systems audit in the pharmaceutical industry, organizations can identify areas of improvement in their marketing systems, optimize marketing processes, enhance data management practices, and ultimately improve overall marketing performance. In addition, it enables organizations to effectively leverage technology, data, and processes to drive business growth and serve customers better.

Markov Model

A Markov model is a mathematical framework that analyzes and predicts the probabilities of transitioning between different states over time. It is named after the Russian mathematician Andrey Markov and is widely applied in various fields, including finance, economics, health care, and marketing. For example, in marketing, Markov models are used to understand and predict customer behavior, such as the likelihood of purchasing or transitioning between different stages of the customer journey. The key concept in the Markov model is the Markov property, which states that the probability of transitioning to a future state depends only on the current state and is independent of the previous states. In other words, the future is predicted based on the current state without considering the history of how the system arrived at the current state. This property makes Markov modes particularly useful for modeling dynamic systems where past states may not significantly impact future states.

In marketing, a Markov model can be used to analyze and predict customer behavior throughout their journey. The different stages or states in the model represent various customer actions or behaviors, such as awareness, consideration, purchase, and loyalty. Transition probabilities are estimated based on historical data or expert knowledge to determine the likelihood of customers moving from one state to another.

By applying a Markov model in marketing, organizations can gain insights into customer behavior patterns, evaluate the effectiveness of marketing strategies and touchpoints, and optimize resource allocation. For example, a pharmaceutical company could use a Markov model to analyze the customer journey from initial medication awareness to prescription and adherence. The model can help identify potential barriers or bottlenecks in the customer journey and inform strategies to optimize marketing efforts and improve patient outcomes.

It is worth noting that Markov models are simplified representations of real-world systems and make certain assumptions, such as the Markov property and stationary transition probabilities. While they provide valuable insights, their accuracy, and effectiveness depend on the data quality, appropriate model assumptions, and the complexity of the modeled system.

Markov Model in Pharma

In pharmaceutical marketing, Markov models can analyze and predict customer behavior, providing insights into the customer journey and informing marketing strategies. Here are a few examples of how Markov models can be applied in pharma marketing:

1. *Patient Journey Analysis*: Markov models can be used to understand the journey from initial medication awareness to treatment initiation, adherence, and beyond. By modeling the different stages of the patient journey and estimating transition probabilities, pharmaceutical companies can identify critical touchpoints, potential drop-off points, and factors influencing patient behavior. This information can help optimize marketing strategies to improve patient engagement, adherence, and treatment outcomes.
2. *Marketing Automation*: Markov models can be employed to determine the contribution of different marketing channels or touchpoints to customer conversion and engagement. By modeling the customer journey and estimating transition probabilities between marketing touchpoints, pharmaceutical companies can attribute conversions or sales to specific marketing activities. This allows for data-driven decision-making on resource allocation, optimization of marketing budgets, and identification of the most effective marketing channels for driving customer engagement and conversion.
3. *Customer Segmentation*: Markov models can aid customer segmentation by grouping individuals based on their behavioral patterns and transition probabilities between different states. By identifying distinct customer segments, pharmaceutical companies can tailor their marketing strategies and messages to meet each segment's specific needs and preferences. This approach helps improve marketing effectiveness, customer engagement, and overall customer satisfaction.
4. *Lifecycle Marketing*: Markov models can be utilized to implement lifecycle marketing strategies in the pharmaceutical industry. By understanding the progression of customers through different stages of the product lifecycle, such as launch, growth, and maturity, pharmaceutical companies can design targeted marketing campaigns and interventions to drive customer retention, reactivation, or advocacy. Markov models enable the identification of critical moments in the product lifecycle and the development of personalized marketing approaches for each stage.

Markov models offer valuable insights into customer behavior and the effectiveness of marketing strategies in the pharmaceutical industry. They can help optimize marketing efforts, enhance patient engagement, improve treatment adherence, and drive better patient outcomes. However, It is important to note that the accuracy and reliability of the model depend on the quality and availability of data and the appropriate selection of model assumptions and parameters.

Mark-up

Markup refers to the amount added to the cost price of a product or service to determine the selling price. It is typically expressed as a percentage of the cost price.

The markup covers various expenses and generates a profit for businesses. It considers the cost of producing or acquiring a product and additional costs associated with operations, such as overhead, marketing, distribution, and profit margin.

The formula for calculating markup is as follows:

Markup= (Selling Price - Cost Price) / *100

In this formula, the selling price is the final price at which the product or service is sold to customers, and the cost price is the price at which the product or service was acquired or produced. For example, a retailer purchases a product from a supplier for $50 and wants to apply a markup of 30%. The calculation would be as follows:

Markup = ($50*30%) / $50*100 = $15/$50 *100 = 30%

Markup is a common practice in various industries and is used to cover costs, generate profits, and ensure the sustainability of businesses. It is important for businesses to carefully consider factors such as market conditions, competition, and customer demand when determining the appropriate markup percentage to set a competitive selling price while maintaining profitability.

Markup in Pharma Marketing

In pharmaceutical marketing, markup refers to the difference between the cost of producing or acquiring medication and the price at which it is sold to customers or healthcare providers. It represents the margin or profit that pharmaceutical companies earn on each unit of medication sold.

The markup in pharmaceutical marketing can vary depending on several factors, including:

1. *Research and Development Costs*: Pharmaceutical companies invest significant resources in research and development (R&D) to discover and develop new drugs. The costs incurred during the R&D process, including clinical trials, regulatory approvals, and intellectual property protection, are often factored into the markup.
2. *Manufacturing and Production Costs*: The costs associated with manufacturing, packaging, and distributing medications also contribute to the markup. These costs include raw materials, labor, equipment, quality control, and logistics.
3. *Marketing and Sales Expenses*: Pharmaceutical companies invest in marketing and sales activities to promote their medications and reach healthcare providers and patients. These costs, such as advertising, sales force salaries, promotional materials, and medical education programs, are typically incorporated into the markup.
4. *Distribution and Supply Chain Costs*: The markup may also cover the costs of distributing medications to various channels, such as pharmacies, hospitals, and wholesalers. These costs involve transportation, storage, inventory management, and compliance with regulatory requirements.
5. *Competitive Factors*: Market dynamics and competition influence the markup in pharmaceutical marketing. Pricing strategies, including positioning the medication as a premium or niche product, can impact the markup level. Pricing decisions also consider factors like the uniqueness of the medication, its perceived value, and market demand.

It is important to note that the markup in pharmaceutical marketing can vary significantly among different medications, therapeutic areas, and countries. Factors like patent protection, regulatory requirements, healthcare system dynamics, and government policies can influence the pricing and markup practices within a particular market.

Pharmaceutical companies must balance ensuring profitability to sustain research and development efforts covering production and marketing costs and maintaining accessibility and affordability for patients and healthcare systems. Pricing and markup decisions are complex and involve ethical, economic, and public health considerations.

MarTech

MarTech is a combination of the words Marketing and Technology. Marketing Technology, or MarTech, refers to using technology platforms and tools to automate and optimize marketing activities, including lead generation, customer engagement, analytics, and more. Using marketing technology in the pharmaceutical industry can help companies improve their marketing effectiveness, increase customer engagement and loyalty, and drive sales. Here are some examples of marketing technology in pharma:

1. *Customer Relationship Management (CRM) Systems*: CRM systems such as Salesforce, Microsoft Dynamics, and HubSpot can help pharmaceutical companies manage customer relationships and interactions. These systems allow companies to store customer data, track interactions, and deliver personalized marketing messages and content.
2. *Marketing Automation Platforms*: Marketing automation platforms such as Marketo, Eloqua, and Pardot can help pharma companies automate their marketing processes and workflows, including lead generation, lead nurturing, and email marketing.
3. *Digital Advertising Platforms*: Digital advertising platforms such as Google Ads, Facebook Ads, and LinkedIn Ads can help pharma companies target their advertising to specific audiences based on demographic, geographic, and behavioral data. These platforms allow companies to create and run highly targeted, personalized ad campaigns.
4. *Search Engine Optimization (SEO) Tools*: SEO tools help optimize website content and improve organic search visibility. They provide insights into keyword research, competitor analysis, on-page optimization, and link building. Pharma companies can use SEO tools to improve their website's search rankings and drive relevant traffic.
5. *Analytics and Reporting Tools*: Analytics and reporting tools such as Google Analytics, Adobe Analytics, and Tableau can help pharma companies track and analyze their marketing performance. These tools provide data on website traffic, engagement, and conversion rates, allowing companies to optimize their marketing efforts for better results. In addition, data tools, including data management platforms (DMPs) and customer data platforms (CDPs), enable the collection, integration, and analysis of customer data to drive targeted marketing strategies.

6. *Social Media Management Platforms*: Social media management platforms assist in managing and monitoring social media accounts, scheduling posts, engaging with audiences, and analyzing social media performance. They help pharma companies maintain an active presence on social media channels, comply with regulations, and listen to and respond to customer conversations.
7. *Mobile Marketing and App Development*: With the growing use of smartphones and mobile applications, pharma marketers can leverage mobile marketing strategies and develop health-focused apps. Mobile marketing tools and app development platforms help create engaging mobile experiences, deliver personalized messaging, and facilitate patient education and adherence.
8. *AdTech and Programmatic Advertising Platforms*: AdTech platforms and programmatic advertising tools enable pharma marketers to deliver targeted and personalized advertisements across various digital channels. These platforms use data and algorithms to automate ad buying and optimize placements, reaching the right audience at the right time.
9. *Virtual Events and Webinars*: Virtual event and Webinar platforms such as Zoom, GoToWebinar, and WebEx can help pharma companies engage with customers and healthcare professionals remotely. These platforms allow companies to host live webinars, virtual conferences, and other interactive events to share information and provide education.

These examples demonstrate how pharmaceutical companies use marketing technology to streamline their marketing processes, improve their targeting and personalization, and optimize their campaigns for better results. By leveraging technology platforms and tools, pharma companies can improve their marketing effectiveness and drive sales in a competitive marketplace.

Pharma marketers must select the appropriate MarTech tools that align with their needs, comply with industry regulations, and prioritize data privacy and security. Additionally, ongoing evaluation, training, and optimization of MarTech implementations are necessary to maximize the benefits and stay ahead in the dynamic marketing landscape.

Mass Customization

Mass customization in pharmaceutical marketing refers to tailoring marketing strategies and messages to individual healthcare professionals (HCPs) or patients on a large scale. It combines the efficiency of mass marketing with the personalization of individualized marketing. The goal is to create customized marketing experiences that resonate with each recipient and meet their unique needs and preferences. Here's how mass customization is applied in pharma marketing:

1. *Segmentation*: Pharmaceutical companies segment their target audience into distinct groups based on specialty, geographic location, prescribing patterns, or patient demographics. This segmentation allows for more targeted and relevant marketing efforts.
2. *Data-Driven Personalization*: By leveraging data, pharma marketers can personalize marketing messages and content to suit the specific interests and preferences of individual HCPs or patients. This can include personalized emails, website experiences, or targeted advertisements.
3. *Digital Communication Channels*: Digital channels provide opportunities for personalized marketing. Pharma companies can use email marketing, social media platforms, and websites to deliver personalized content and engage with HCPs or patients based on their interests and previous interactions.
4. *Customized Educational Materials*: Pharma marketers can develop educational materials, such as medical journals, brochures, or patient education resources, customized to the specific interests or needs of different HCPs or patient segments.
5. *Interactive Tools and Apps*: Pharma companies can develop interactive tools or mobile applications that allow HCPs or patients to customize information, such as dosing calculators, treatment decision support tools, or symptom trackers.
6. *Tailored Promotional Activities*: Mass customization can extend to promotional activities such as conferences, webinars, or symposiums. Pharma companies can tailor the content, speakers, and sessions to cater to different HCP segments' interests and needs.
7. *Direct Engagement*: Pharma sales representatives can use customer relationship management (CRM) systems to capture and track information about HCP preferences, prescribing habits, or feedback. This information

can be used to tailor future interactions and engagements.

By implementing mass customization in pharma marketing, companies can enhance customer engagement, improve the relevance of marketing messages, and build stronger relationships with HCPs and patients. It allows for a more personalized and targeted approach, increasing the likelihood of positive responses and better marketing outcomes. However, ensuring compliance with relevant regulations and privacy guidelines is important when utilizing personal data for customization.

Mass Marketing

Mass marketing in the pharmaceutical industry refers to targeting a broad audience with standardized marketing messages and strategies. It involves reaching many healthcare professionals (HCPs) or patients with the same marketing materials, campaigns, or promotional activities. Here are some key aspects of mass marketing in the pharmaceutical industry:

1. *Wide Audience Reach*: Mass marketing aims to reach a broad audience, often through traditional marketing channels such as television, print media, radio, or outdoor advertising. It focuses on maximizing exposure and creating awareness among many HCPs or patients.
2. *Standardized Messaging*: In mass marketing, the marketing messages and materials are typically standardized and generalized to appeal to a wide range of HCPs or patients. The content and communication are not personalized or tailored to individual preferences or needs.
3. *Branding and Product Awareness*: Mass marketing strategies emphasize building brand awareness and promoting specific pharmaceutical products. The goal is to create a recognizable brand identity and familiarize the target audience with the marketed products.
4. *Mass Media Advertising*: Mass marketing often involves utilizing mass media platforms to disseminate marketing messages. This includes television commercials, magazine or newspaper advertisements, radio spots, or billboards. These channels allow for broad exposure and reach many individuals simultaneously.
5. *Event Sponsorship*: Pharmaceutical companies may sponsor large-scale healthcare events, conferences, or exhibitions to gain visibility and reach a wide audience of HCPs. These events provide face-to-face interactions, product demonstrations, and brand promotion opportunities.
6. *Sales Force Engagement*: Mass marketing in pharma also involves using a sales force to promote products to HCPs on a wide scale. Sales representatives visit medical practices, hospitals, or clinics to present standardized promotional materials and product samples and engage in direct sales efforts.
7. *Mass Education Initiatives*: Pharmaceutical companies may develop mass educational initiatives, such as disease awareness campaigns or public health programs, to educate the general population or specific patient groups about particular diseases, treatment options, or health-related topics.

While mass marketing allows for broad audience reach and brand visibility, it may not offer the same personalization or targeted messaging as other marketing approaches. In recent years, the pharmaceutical industry has shifted towards more personalized and targeted marketing strategies to better engage with HCPs and patients. However, mass marketing still plays a role in creating initial awareness, generating brand recognition, and reaching a wide audience. It is often complemented by more targeted marketing efforts to drive deeper engagement and relationship-building with specific segments.

Mechanism of Action (MOA)

The Mechanism of Action (MOA) in pharmaceuticals refers to the specific biochemical interaction through which a drug substance produces its pharmacological effect. This can include how the drug binds to a particular protein, affects the transmission of signals in cells, or disrupts a pathogenic organism. Understanding the mechanism of action is crucial for drug development and regulatory approval. However, it also has significant implications for pharmaceutical marketing. Here are some ways the MOA plays a role in pharma marketing and its implications for marketers:

1. Educational Marketing

- *Implication*: Marketers can use the MOA as an educational tool to inform healthcare professionals about how a new drug works. This knowledge can increase physicians' confidence in prescribing the drug and help them explain its benefits and potential side effects to their patients.
- *Challenge*: The MOA can be complex, so marketers must find ways to communicate this information

clearly and concisely to ensure understanding without oversimplification.

2. Differentiation from Competitors

- *Implication*: A drug with a unique or novel MOA can differentiate it from other products in the market. Marketers can leverage this unique MOA as a selling point.
- *Challenge*: Competitors might highlight their unique MOAs, so the messaging must be compelling and evidence-based.

3. Targeted Marketing

- *Implication*: Understanding the MOA can help identify specific patient populations that might benefit most from the drug, enabling targeted marketing strategies.
- *Challenge*: Marketers must ensure that they don't overextend the drug's potential benefits beyond what is supported by clinical evidence.

4. Positioning in Treatment Protocols

- *Implication*: A drug's MOA can influence where it fits into treatment protocols or guidelines. If a drug addresses a previously untargeted mechanism, it might be a first-in-Class treatment or a combination therapy with existing drugs.
- *Challenge*: Changing established treatment protocols can be lengthy, requiring extensive data and convincing clinical evidence.

5. Regulatory and Reimbursement Implications

- *Implication*: Regulatory bodies may grant special designations (like *breakthrough therapy*) to drugs with novel MOAs that address unmet medical needs. This can speed up the approval process. Additionally, payers or insurance companies might be more willing to reimburse for a drug if its MOA offers benefits over existing treatments.
- *Challenge*: Marketers need to coordinate with regulatory and market access teams to ensure the drug's value proposition is clearly communicated and supported by evidence.

6. Risk Communication

- *Implication*: Understanding the MOA can help predict and communicate potential side effects or adverse reactions.
- *Challenge*: Marketers must ensure that risks are communicated transparently without downplaying them, which can lead to mistrust or legal challenges.

7. Lifecycle Management

- *Implication*: As the drug matures, new data about its MOA might emerge, leading to new indications and formulations. Marketers can use this information for lifecycle management strategies to extend the drug's patent life or market exclusivity.
- *Challenge*: There is a need to continuously invest in research and communicate evolving information transparently to the medical community and patients.

In summary, while the mechanism of action is a technical and scientific concept, its understanding is crucial for pharma marketers. It informs marketing strategies, provides opportunities for differentiation, and can be leveraged to communicate a drug's value proposition. However, this also comes with challenges, especially in ensuring accurate and transparent communication.

Media

Media plays a significant role in pharma marketing. It allows pharmaceutical companies to reach their target audience, raise awareness about their products, and educate healthcare professionals (HCPs) and patients about various health-related topics. Here are some key media channels commonly used in pharma marketing:

1. *Print Media*: This includes medical journals, magazines, newspapers, and brochures. Pharmaceutical companies often advertise their products in relevant medical publications to reach HCPs and inform them about new drugs, treatment guidelines, clinical studies, and other relevant information.
2. *Television and Radio*: Television and radio advertisements raise awareness of pharmaceutical products among a wide audience. These channels provide an opportunity to reach HCPs and consumers, especially for drugs, with direct-to-consumer (DTC) advertising. However, regulations and restrictions may apply to DTC advertising depending on the country.
3. *Digital and Online Media*: Digital media has become increasingly important in pharma marketing. Websites, online platforms, and social media channels offer opportunities for pharmaceutical companies to engage with HCPs, patients, and caregivers. Companies can provide educational content, product information, interactive tools, and patient support resources. Social media platforms like Facebook, Twitter,

and LinkedIn are utilized for targeted advertising, content sharing, and community engagement.

4. *Email Marketing*: Pharmaceutical companies often use email marketing campaigns to communicate with HCPs and provide them with relevant information about new products, clinical updates, educational resources, and promotional offers. Email newsletters and targeted email campaigns allow for personalized and direct communication.
5. *Webinars and Online Events*: Webinars and online events provide opportunities for pharmaceutical companies to conduct educational sessions, product presentations, and discussions with HCPs and other stakeholders. These virtual events allow convenient access to information, interactive participation, and knowledge sharing.
6. *Mobile Applications*: Pharma companies develop applications that provide valuable tools for HCPs and patients, such as medical calculators, dosage trackers, treatment guidelines, patient education materials, and medication reminders. These apps enhance engagement, convenience, and support in managing healthcare and medication-related needs.
7. *Direct Sales Force Communication*: While not strictly media, direct communication with HCPs through sales representatives is an important channel in pharma marketing. Sales representatives visit medical practices and hospitals to provide product information and samples and engage and discuss with HCPs.

Pharmaceutical companies must navigate regulatory guidelines and adhere to compliance standards when utilizing media channels for marketing. It is crucial to provide accurate and balanced information, ensure patient privacy and data protection, and comply with applicable advertising regulations and industry codes of conduct.

Media Mentions

Media mentions refer to mentions of a company, product, or service in news articles, blogs, social media posts, or other online or offline publications. Media mentions can be valuable for companies as they can increase brand awareness, credibility, and thought leadership with their target audience. Here are some examples of how pharmaceutical companies can use media mentions in their marketing efforts:

1. *Press Releases*: Pharmaceutical companies can issue releases to announce new product launches, clinical trial results, or other important news related to their product portfolio or disease areas. Media outlets may pick up these press releases, resulting in media mentions that can reach a wider audience.
2. *Thought Leadership*: Pharmaceutical companies can use media mentions to establish themselves as thought leaders in their respective fields. They can publish articles or blog posts on topics related to their product portfolio or disease areas and share them with relevant media outlets. These articles may result in media mentions that can increase the company's credibility and expertise in the eyes of its target audience.
3. *Influencer Marketing*: Pharmaceutical companies can partner with media outlets and journalists with a large following or influence in their target audience to promote their products or services. These partnerships may result in media mentions that can increase the company's reach and engagement with its target audience.
4. *Crisis Management*: Pharmaceutical marketing can use media mentions to manage crises or negative publicity related to their products or services. They can issue statements or responses to negative news articles or social media posts and use media mentions to ensure their side of the story is heard or understood by their target audience.
5. *SEO Optimization*: Pharmaceutical companies can use media mentions to improve their search engine optimization (SEO) rankings. Media mentions from reputable outlets can increase the company's online presence and domain authority, improving their search rankings and making it easier for their target audience to find it online.

Pharmaceutical companies must approach media mentions with a strategic and ethical mindset and ensure they comply with regulatory requirements governing pharmaceutical marketing. They should also monitor media regularly, ensuring they know how their brand is portrayed and respond appropriately to any negative or inaccurate portrayals.

Media Planning

Media planning in pharmaceutical marketing involves strategically selecting and scheduling media channels and placements to reach the target audience effectively, deliver the marketing messages, and achieve campaign objectives. Here are some steps to consider for effective media planning in pharma marketing:

1. *Define Campaign Objectives*: Start by clearly defining the goals and objectives of your marketing campaign. Are you aiming to raise awareness about a new drug, educate HCPs about a specific treatment, or promote a patient support program? Establishing clear objectives will guide your media planning efforts.
2. *Identify Target Audience*: Identify the specific healthcare professionals (HCPs) or patient segments you want to reach with your marketing message. Consider specialty, geographic location prescribing patterns, demographics, and psychographics. Understanding your target audience will help determine the most relevant media channels to reach them effectively.
3. *Conduct Market Research* to identify your target audience's media habits and preferences. This can include analyzing industry publications, healthcare websites, social media usage, and attending medical conferences or events. This research will help you determine which media channels will most likely reach your audience.
4. *Select Media Channels*: Select the most appropriate media channels to reach your audience effectively based on your target audience and market research. This could include medical journals, relevant websites, social media platforms, email newsletters, online forums, or industry-specific conferences and events. Consider each media channel's reach, engagement level, credibility, and cost-effectiveness.
5. *Set Budget and Allocate Resources*: Determine your budget for media planning and allocation. Allocate resources to different media channels based on their importance, effectiveness, and cost. Consider each media channel's potential reach, frequency, and impact to optimize your budget allocation.
6. *Plan Media Schedule*: Develop a media schedule that outlines the timing and duration of your marketing campaign across various media channels. Consider the optimal timing to reach your target audience, considering industry events, seasonality, or relevant healthcare milestones.
7. *Create Compelling Content*: Develop engaging and relevant content for each media channel that resonates with your target audience. Tailor your messages to address their needs, provide value, and support the campaign objectives. Ensure your content adheres to relevant regulatory guidelines and compliance requirements.
8. *Monitor and Optimize*: Continuously monitor the performance of your media placements and campaigns. Track key metrics such as reach, engagement, conversions, and return on investment (ROI). Analyze the data to identify areas for optimization and make necessary adjustments to your media and messaging.
9. *Measure Effectiveness*: Evaluate the effectiveness of your media planning efforts by assessing the achievement of your campaign objectives. Analyze the impact on brand awareness, HCP prescribing behavior, patient engagement, or other desired outcomes. Use these insights to inform future media planning and marketing strategies.

Remember, compliance with relevant regulations and guidelines is critical in pharma marketing. Ensure that your media planning and messaging comply with legal, ethical, and industry-specific requirements to maintain trust and integrity within the industry.

Media Relations

Media relations in pharma marketing involves building and maintaining relationships with media outlets and journalists to effectively communicate with the public and key stakeholders about pharmaceutical products, research, and related healthcare topics. It aims to shape positive perceptions, enhance brand reputation, and generate media coverage that reaches the target audience. Here are some key considerations for successful media relations in the pharmaceutical industry:

1. *Identify Target Media Outlets*: Define the media outlets most relevant to your target audience and strongly influence the healthcare industry. This may include medical journals, health publications, online healthcare news platforms, broadcast media, and trade publications. Research their editorial focus, readership, and coverage areas to ensure alignment with your messaging objectives.
2. *Build Relationships*: Establish and maintain relationships with journalists and key media contacts who cover health care and pharmaceutical topics. Attend industry conferences and events where journalists may be present, engage in professional networking, and participate in media briefings or press events. Building personal connections can increase the likelihood of media coverage and provide opportunities for ongoing collaboration.
3. *Develop Key Messages*: Clearly define the key messages you want to communicate to the media

and the public. Craft concise and compelling messages highlighting your pharmaceutical products' unique aspects, benefits, impact, clinical trials, research findings, or healthcare initiatives. Ensure your messages are accurate, credible, and aligned with your regulatory guidelines.

4. *Press Releases and Media Kits*: Create well-written press releases and media kits to disseminate newsworthy information to the media. Press releases should be informative, concise, and contain relevant details about your announcement or news. Media kits can provide additional background information, product images, key data, and spokesperson bios to support media coverage.
5. *Media Pitches*: Proactively pitch story ideas or interview opportunities to journalists that align with their interests and the topics they cover. Tailor your pitches to address the unique angles, trends, or perspectives relevant to their audience. Position yourself or your experts as valuable sources of information, insights, or expertise in the pharmaceutical field.
6. *Respond to Media Inquiries*: Promptly and professionally respond to media inquiries, whether they are seeking information, comments, or interviews. Provide accurate and balanced responses, being mindful of confidentiality or regulatory restrictions. Establish a designated spokesperson or media contact within your organization who can effectively handle media inquiries.
7. *Thought Leadership and Expert Opinions*: Position key executives, scientists, or experts within your organization as thought leaders in the pharmaceutical industry. Offer their insights, opinions, or expertise on relevant healthcare topics to the media through contributed articles, opinion pieces, or interviews. This can help credibility and generate media coverage.
8. *Media Training*: Provide media training to key spokespersons within your organization to ensure they are prepared to communicate with the media effectively. Training should cover message development, interview techniques, handling difficult questions, and maintaining consistency in messaging. This will help ensure your organization's key messages are effectively conveyed during media interactions.
9. *Monitor and Engage*: Monitor media coverage and engage with journalists through social media platforms or direct communication. Respond to media coverage, address any inaccuracies, and leverage positive coverage to enhance your brand reputation further and increase awareness of your pharmaceutical products or initiatives.

Effective media relations in pharma marketing require maintaining open lines of communication, transparency, and adherence to ethical standards. It is important to collaborate with legal, compliance, and regulatory teams to ensure that all media activities comply with relevant guidelines and regulations within the pharmaceutical industry.

Media Strategy

A media strategy in pharmaceutical marketing involves developing a comprehensive plan to effectively utilize various media channels and tactics to reach the target audience, convey key messages, and achieve marketing objectives. Here are some considerations for creating an effective media strategy in pharma marketing:

1. *Define Objectives*: Clearly define the objectives of your media strategy. These objectives could include increasing brand awareness, educating healthcare professionals and patients, promoting new products or treatments, driving website traffic, or generating leads. Setting clear objectives will guide your media planning and help measure the success of your strategy.
2. *Identify Target Audience*: Identify your target audience in terms of healthcare professionals, patients, caregivers, or other stakeholders. Consider their demographics, geographic locations, behaviors, and preferences to understand where and how best to reach them with your media efforts.
3. *Conduct Market Research* to understand your target audience's media habits and preferences. This may involve analyzing media consumption patterns, online behavior, social media usage, and industry-specific publications. This research will help identify the most relevant and impactful media channels to include in your strategy.
4. *Select Media Channels*: Select the media channels that align with your target audience and campaign objectives. These can include print media (medical journals, magazines, brochures), digital media (websites, online advertising, social media platforms), broadcast media (television and radio), conferences and events, and other relevant industry-specific channels. Consider the reach, effectiveness, and cost-efficiency of each channel.
5. *Allocate Budget*: Allocate your budget across different media channels based on their

importance, reach, and potential impact. Consider the cost of media placements, production costs for creative assets, and any associated fees or expenses. Optimize your budget allocation to maximize your reach and achieve the desired outcomes.

6. *Develop Key Messages*: Craft key messages relevant to your target audience and aligning with your campaign objectives. These messages should highlight the unique aspects and benefits of your pharmaceutical products or treatments. Ensure your messages are accurate, compliant with regulations, and resonate with your audience.
7. *Content Creation*: Develop compelling and engaging content that supports your key messages and is suitable for each media channel. This can include articles, blog posts, videos, infographics, case studies, testimonials, and interactive content. Tailor your content to each channel's format and audience preferences.
8. *Timing and Frequency*: Plan the timing and frequency of your media activities to ensure maximum impact. Consider the optimal times to reach your target audiences, such as during relevant conferences or key healthcare events. Determine the appropriate frequency of media placements to maintain visibility and reinforce your messages.
9. *Measurement and Optimization*: Establish metrics and KPIs to track the effectiveness of your media strategy. Monitor and analyze your data on media reach, engagement, website traffic, conversions, and other relevant metrics. Use this data to optimize your media strategy, adjust as needed, and improve future campaigns.
10. *Compliance and Regulations*: Ensure compliance with applicable regulations and guidelines, such as those set by regulatory authorities or industry's self-regulatory bodies. Pharma marketing is subject to specific regulations and restrictions, particularly when promoting prescription medications. Adhere to ethical standards and work closely with legal and compliance teams to ensure compliance throughout your media strategy.

Regularly evaluate and refine your media strategy based on performance data, market trends, and feedback from your target audience. Monitor the media landscape, industry developments, and emerging media channels to stay relevant and effective in your marketing efforts.

Medicaid

Medicaid is a government healthcare program in the United States that provides medical assistance to low-income individuals and families. As a pharma marketer, understanding Medicaid and its implications is crucial for navigating pharmaceutical marketing effectively. Here are some key implications of Medicaid for pharma marketers:

1. *Access and Formulary Placement*: Medicaid programs establish formularies and lists of drugs the program covers. Pharma marketers need to be aware of the formulary status of their products within each state's Medicaid program. Formulary placement can impact the accessibility and utilization of pharmaceutical products. It is important to understand the reimbursement policies, preferred drug lists, prior authorization requirements, and Medicaid coverage restrictions.
2. *Rebate Programs*: The Medicaid Drug Rebate Program requires pharmaceutical manufacturers to provide rebates to state Medicaid programs for their covered outpatient drugs. These rebates are based on the average manufacturer price (AMP) and the best price offered to other purchasers. Pharma marketers should ensure compliance with rebate program requirements and understand the financial implications of rebate calculations for their products.
3. *Price Negotiations*: Medicaid programs can negotiate drug prices with manufacturers. As a pharma marketer, it is important to understand the pricing dynamics and potential negotiations with Medicaid programs. This can include participating in discussions with state Medicaid agencies, understanding their cost containment strategies, and evaluating the potential impact on product pricing and profitability.
4. *Managed Care Organization (MCO)*: Many Medicaid beneficiaries receive healthcare services through managed care organizations. Pharma marketers should understand the contracting and reimbursement processes with these MCOs. It is important to establish relationships with key stakeholders within the MCOs, stay informed about their formulary decisions, and collaborate to ensure access to pharmaceutical products for Medicaid beneficiaries.
5. *Health Economic Outcomes Research (HEOR)*: Medicaid programs often prioritize cost-effectiveness and value-based healthcare. Conducting health economic outcomes research and generating real-world evidence can be

valuable for demonstrating the value and impact of pharmaceutical products on Medicaid programs. Pharma marketers should consider investing in studies that provide evidence of improved patient outcomes, reduced healthcare costs, and value to Medicaid populations.

6. *Patient Assistance Programs*: Medicaid beneficiaries may still face out-of-pocket costs, such as copayments or coinsurance. Developing patient assistance programs, such as copay assistance or patient savings programs, can help reduce financial barriers for Medicaid patients. Pharma marketers should consider implementing these programs to support patient product access.
7. *Compliance and Anti-Kickback Laws*: Pharma marketers must comply with anti-kickback laws and regulations when engaging with Medicaid programs. Avoiding any activities perceived as improper inducements to influence Medicaid's prescribing or reimbursement decisions is important.
8. *Advocacy and Education*: Engaging in advocacy efforts and providing educational resources to policymakers, Medicaid administrators, and healthcare providers can help shape policies and guidelines related to pharmaceutical products. By actively participating in discussions and providing relevant information, pharma marketers can influence decisions and promote an understanding of their product's value to Medicaid populations.

Understanding Medicaid and its implications is essential for pharma marketers to navigate the complex landscape of government-funded healthcare programs efficiently. Staying informed about the evolving policies, reimbursement structures, and formulary considerations can help optimize access, coverage, and utilization of pharmaceutical products within Medicaid populations.

Medical Advertising

Medical Advertising, a subset of medico-marketing, specifically focuses on promoting pharmaceutical products through various media channels. While the term encompasses many forms of promotion, it most commonly refers to campaigns aimed at healthcare professionals (HCPs) and, where permitted, direct-to-consumer (DTC) advertising.

Here is an overview of medical advertising in pharmaceutical marketing:

1. Objectives:

- Create awareness and recognition for a pharmaceutical product
- Educate HCPs and consumers about a product's benefits, dosing, and potential side effects
- Drive prescriptions and usage of the promoted product

2. Target Audiences:

- *Healthcare Professionals (HCPs)*: This includes doctors, nurses, pharmacists, and other medical professionals. Advertising to this group often focuses on clinical data, safety profiles, and comparative efficacy.
- *Consumers*: In regions where DTC advertising is allowed, campaigns target the general public or specific patient populations. These ads often emphasize the benefits of the drug and the conditions it treats and may include patient testimonials.

3. Channels and Tactics:

- *Print Media*: This can include advertisements in medical journals, magazines, newspapers, and brochures
- *Digital*: Websites, search engine marketing, social media campaigns, and email campaigns are now a significant part of pharma marketing. Many companies also use targeted ads on platforms frequented by HCPs.
- *Television and Radio*: These are primarily used for DTC advertising in countries where it is permitted.
- *Outdoor*: Billboards, posters, and transit ads can also be used, though they are more common for DTC campaigns.
- *Sales Representatives*: While not advertising in the traditional sense, pharma sales reps provide promotional materials, samples, and product information directly to HCPs.

4. Regulatory and Ethical Considerations:

- *Claims and Evidentiary Support*: Every claim made in an advertisement must be supported by robust scientific evidence. Misleading claims can lead to significant legal and financial consequences.
- *Disclosure*: Advertisements, especially DTC ones, must disclose potential side effects and contraindications. This is why many DTC ads have a long list of potential side effects mentioned.
- *Regulatory Bodies*: The Food and Drug Administration (FDA) oversees pharmaceutical advertising in the US. In the European Union, It is the European Medicines Agency (EMA), along

with individual country regulators. These bodies ensure that advertisements are accurate, not misleading, and in the best interests of public health.

- *Limitations* on DTC: Direct-to-consumer advertising of prescription drugs is allowed only in a few countries, most notably, the US and New Zealand. Even in these countries, strict regulations govern what can and cannot be said.

Medical Advertising: Examples

- *DTC Television Ad*: Many Americans are familiar with TV ads for drugs treating conditions ranging from rheumatoid arthritis to erectile dysfunction. These ads often have a memorable jingle, visuals of improved life after taking the drug, and a voiceover listing potential side effects.
- *Print Ads in Medical Journals*: A pharma company might place an ad in a cardiology journal for a new heart medication, highlighting its benefits over existing treatments backed by data from clinical trials.

In conclusion, medical advertising in pharma marketing is a critical tool for driving product awareness and usage. However, due to the sensitive nature of healthcare and the potential implications on patient health, it is also a heavily regulated area that demands a careful, evidence-based approach.

Medical Affairs

Medical Affairs is a crucial department within the pharmaceutical industry, acting as the bridge between the company and various stakeholders, especially regarding scientific and medical information. Here is an overview of its role in pharmaceutical marketing:

Medical Affairs teams consist of professionals, often with advanced scientific degrees (like MDs, PharmDs, or PhDs), who engage in scientific communications with external stakeholders, offer insights during product development, and support product launches and lifecycle management.

Primary Responsibilities

1. *Medical Science Liaison (MSL)*: MSLs are field-based scientific experts who engage with top healthcare professionals and researchers. Their primary role is communicating scientific information, answering medical inquiries, and facilitating research collaboration.
2. *Medical Information*: Medical Affairs provides scientifically accurate responses to inquiries from healthcare professionals and patients.
3. *Scientific Publications*: The Medical Affairs team is responsible for strategizing and disseminating scientific data, often through manuscripts in peer-reviewed journals or conference presentations.
4. *Clinical Trials*: The Medical Affairs teams may be involved in Phase IV trials, observational studies, or investigator-related trials.
5. *Health Economic and Outcomes Research (HEOR)* demonstrates a drug's economic value and real-world effectiveness.
6. *Education and Training*: The Medical Affairs team develops materials and programs to educate internal staff and external stakeholders about disease areas and products.

Role in Pharma Marketing

1. *Ensure Scientific Integrity*: Medical Affairs ensures that marketing initiatives are scientifically sound and compliant with regulations.
2. *Content Development*: They assist in developing content that communicates the scientific aspects of a drug, ensuring accurate and balanced information.
3. *Engage Key Opinion Leaders (KOLs)*: Through MSLs, Medical Affairs identifies and engages KOLs who can offer insights and become advocates.
4. *Support Product Launches*: The Medical Affairs team provides sales and marketing teams training, develops educational materials, and ensures medical accuracy in promotional content.
5. *Manage Post-Marketing Surveillance*: Medical Affairs tracks the safety and efficacy of drugs post-launch, gathering real-world evidence and feedback about the drug's efficacy and adverse reactions.
6. *Ethics and Compliance*: Medical Affairs is critical in ensuring that marketing practices are ethically sound, compliant with regulations, and focused on patient safety. They counterbalance the commercial pressures by primarily focusing on science and patient well-being.

Challenges

1. *Maintaining Independence*: There is a need to maintain a degree of independence from the commercial arms of the company to ensure unbiased scientific communication.
2. *Changing Landscape*: With the advent of digital health, data analytics, and real-world evidence, the role of medical affairs is rapidly evolving.

They must adapt to integrate new data sources and communicate in diverse digital platforms.

Future Trends

1. *Digital Transformation*: Virtual engagements, AI-driven insights, and telemedicine are changing how Medical Affairs interacts with stakeholders.
2. *Personalized Medicine*: As medicine becomes more tailored to individual patients, medical affairs will be critical in educating healthcare professionals about these nuances.

Medical Affairs is a critical link between pharmaceutical companies' scientific and commercial arms, ensuring that products are effectively developed, launched, and promoted with a solid scientific foundation. Their role in pharma marketing is essential in maintaining the credibility, ethics, and scientific integrity of the industry's interactions with healthcare professionals and patients.

Medicalization

Medicalization refers to the process by which human conditions, behaviors, or experiences come to be defined and treated as medical problems or disorders. It involves applying medical concepts, language, and interventions to areas of life that were previously not considered medical.

Medicalization of a particular issue typically involves several key elements:

1. *Definition*: A condition or behavior is framed as a medical problem, often a diagnosable disorder or disease.
2. *Pathologization*: The condition is considered abnormal or deviant from a perceived norm or standard, leading to the labeling of individuals experiencing it as patients.
3. *Medical Intervention*: Medical professionals and institutions become involved in diagnosing, treating, and managing the condition. This can include prescribing medication, performing surgeries, or providing other medical interventions.
4. *Institutionalization*: The issue becomes a part of the medical domain, leading to the establishment of medical specialties, professional associations, and research efforts focused on studying and addressing the condition.

Medicalization has both positive and negative implications. On the positive side, it can lead to increased understanding, research, and treatment options for previously overlooked conditions, potentially improving the lives of affected individuals. For example, the medicalization of mental health has led to advancement in psychiatric treatments and reduced stigma surrounding mental disorders.

However, medicalization also has potential downsides. It may lead to over-medicalization, where normal human variations or experiences are pathologized, potentially resulting in unnecessary medical interventions and the expansion of the pharmaceutical industry. Furthermore, medicalization can shift societal focus away from social, cultural, and environmental factors contributing to a particular issue, reducing the emphasis on non-medical solutions.

Medicalization is a complex and debated concept, and its impact varies depending on the context and specific conditions being discussed.

Medicalization and Pharma Marketing

Medicalization is how non-medical conditions or phenomena are defined and treated as medical problems. In pharmaceutical marketing, medicalization can affect how pharmaceutical products are marketed and positioned to healthcare professionals and consumers. Here are some key points to consider regarding medicalization and its relationship to pharma marketing:

1. *Expanding Indications*: Medicalization can lead to expanding indications for pharmaceutical products. Conditions previously considered part of normal human experience or unrelated to medical intervention may be redefined as medical conditions. Pharmaceutical companies may seize these opportunities to develop and market new products or promote existing products for these expanded indications.
2. *Disease Awareness Campaigns*: Medicalization often involves raising awareness about a particular condition and its impact on individuals. Pharmaceutical companies may engage in disease awareness campaigns to educate healthcare professionals and the public about the condition, its symptoms, and available treatment options. These campaigns can create demand for pharmaceutical products associated with the condition.
3. *Influencing Diagnostic Criteria*: Medicalization can influence the diagnostic criteria for certain conditions, potentially leading to increased diagnosis rates. Pharmaceutical companies may contribute to shaping these diagnostic criteria through research, funding medical conferences, or collaborating with medical societies. By influencing diagnostic guidelines,

pharmaceutical companies can create a market for their products by ensuring that more patients are diagnosed with the condition.

4. *Marketing to Healthcare Professionals*: Pharma marketers may target professionals who diagnose and treat medical conditions. This can involve promoting pharmaceutical products as treatment options during physician detailing, sponsoring medical education events, providing clinical evidence and data, and leveraging key opinion leaders to endorse the use of their products for medicalized conditions.
5. *Direct-to-Consumer Advertising*: Medicalization can increase direct-to-consumer advertising (DTCA) for pharmaceutical products. Pharmaceutical companies can create awareness and demand for their products by marketing directly to consumers. DTCA campaigns may include messaging about the condition, its symptoms, and how the pharmaceutical product can alleviate or manage it.
6. *Patient Advocacy and Support*: Medicalization can create opportunities for pharmaceutical companies to engage in patient advocacy and support initiatives. They may establish patient support programs, provide educational materials, and offer financial assistance programs for patients with the medicalized condition. These initiatives can build brand loyalty, increase patient adherence to treatment, and generate a positive public perception of the company and its products.
7. *Ethical Considerations*: The medicalization of certain conditions can raise ethical considerations. Pharma marketers need to ensure that their marketing practices align with ethical guidelines, provide accurate information, and avoid overmedication or promoting unnecessary medical interventions. Their marketing strategies should prioritize patient well-being, transparency, and ethical decision-making.

Pharma marketers need to be mindful of medicalization's potential impact and ethical implications. While medicalization can create opportunities for pharmaceutical companies, it is crucial to balance addressing genuine medical needs and avoiding the overmedicalization of normal human experiences. Responsible pharma marketing should focus on evidence-based information, ethical practices, and providing valuable solutions that improve patient outcomes.

Medical Representative

A medical or pharmaceutical sales representative plays a crucial role in pharma marketing. Their primary responsibility is to promote and sell pharmaceutical products to healthcare professionals, such as physicians, pharmacists, and hospitals. Here are some key aspects of the role of a medical representative in pharmaceutical marketing:

1. *Product Promotion*: Medical representatives promote pharmaceutical products to healthcare professionals. They provide information about the product's features, benefits, and clinical evidence. This involves delivering product presentations, distributing promotional materials, providing product samples, and answering questions to educate healthcare professionals about the product's efficacy, safety, and appropriate use.
2. *Building Relationships*: Medical representatives focus on building and maintaining relationships with healthcare professionals. They establish rapport, trust, and credibility to foster long-term partnerships. Developing strong relationships allows medical representatives to effectively communicate product information, address concerns, and influence prescribing decisions.
3. *Market Intelligence*: Medical representatives gather market intelligence and provide feedback to their company. They report on competitor activities, market trends, and healthcare professional preferences. This information helps the company understand the market landscape, identify opportunities, and make informed decisions about marketing strategies and product positioning.
4. *Territory Management*: Medical representatives are typically assigned specific territories or regions. They manage their territories efficiently by planning and organizing their schedules to maximize face-to-face interactions with healthcare professionals., managing appointments, and tracking interactions to ensure comprehensive coverage of the assigned territory.
5. *Continuing Education*: Medical representatives must stay updated on medical and scientific knowledge of their products and therapeutic areas. They participate in training programs their company provides to enhance their product knowledge, understand disease states, and keep abreast of the latest research and clinical studies. Continuous education enables them to effectively communicate the benefits and value of their products to healthcare professionals.

6. *Compliance*: Medical representatives must adhere to industry regulations, company policies, and ethical standards. They ensure that their promotional activities and interactions with healthcare professionals comply with legal and regulatory guidelines. This includes providing accurate and balanced information, avoiding off-label promotion, and appropriately documenting interactions.
7. *Customer Service*: Medical representatives are a resource and support for healthcare professionals. They address inquiries, provide timely responses, and offer assistance when needed. Medical representatives build trust and foster loyalty among healthcare professionals by delivering excellent customer service, increasing the likelihood of product recommendations and prescriptions.
8. *Territory Analysis and Reporting*: Medical representatives analyze their territories to identify and target healthcare professionals, understand market dynamics, and assess the effectiveness of their promotional efforts. They report their activities, sales metrics, and feedback to their managers, providing valuable insights for evaluating marketing strategies and adjusting tactics.

Effective medical representatives possess strong communication and interpersonal skills, a deep understanding of their products and therapeutic areas, and the ability to build and maintain relationships with healthcare professionals. They play a critical role in driving pharmaceutical sales, educating healthcare professionals about products, and contributing to the overall success of pharma marketing efforts.

Medical Science Liaison

MSL stands for Medical Science Liaison. In pharmaceutical marketing, an MSL is a field-based professional who bridges the company and the medical community, including healthcare providers, researchers, and opinion leaders. MSLs are responsible for building relationships and engaging in scientific discussions with healthcare professionals to support the company's products and therapeutic areas.

MSLs are typically highly educated with advanced degrees in scientific fields such as medicine, pharmacy, or life sciences. They deeply understand the company's products and therapeutic areas and the scientific literature and clinical trial data that support them.

MSLs use their scientific expertise and knowledge to engage with healthcare professionals in various settings, including medical conferences, scientific meetings, and one-on-one interactions. They provide scientific and medical information to healthcare professionals, answer their questions, and gather insights and feedback that can be used to inform the company's medical strategy and product development.

Overall, MSLs play a crucial role in pharma marketing by building relationships and engaging with healthcare professionals to support the company's products and therapeutic areas. They serve as a valuable resource for scientific information and help to ensure that healthcare professionals have access to the latest information about the company's products and their benefits.

MSL's Role In Pharma Marketing

Here are some key aspects of the role of an MSL in pharmaceutical marketing:

1. *Scientific Expertise*: MSLs possess deep scientific knowledge and expertise in specific therapeutic or disease areas. They stay up-to-date with their assigned therapeutic area's latest research, clinical data, and treatment guidelines. This enables them to provide accurate and credible scientific information to healthcare professionals.
2. *KOL Engagement*: MSLs focus on building and maintaining relationships with key opinion leaders (KOLs) in the medical and scientific community. They engage in scientific discussions, share clinical data, and exchange information with KOLs to gather insights, discuss research findings, and seek their expert opinions. These interactions help shape medical strategies and influence the perception of pharmaceutical products within the medical community.
3. *Medical Education and Training*: MSLs provide medical education and training to healthcare professionals. They conduct scientific presentations, organize advisory boards, and deliver educational programs to physicians, pharmacists, and other healthcare professionals. By providing accurate and up-to-date information, MSLs contribute to understanding disease states, treatment options, and the appropriate use of pharmaceutical products.
4. *Clinical Support*: MSLs support healthcare professionals by providing clinical support and addressing scientific inquiries related to pharmaceutical products. They help healthcare professionals understand clinical trial data,

navigate product profiles, and interpret complex scientific information. MSLs act as a resource for healthcare professionals to enhance their understanding of the scientific aspects of the products.

5. *Medical Information Exchange*: MSLs engage in scientific discussions and exchange medical information with healthcare professionals. They address questions related to product efficacy, safety, mechanism of action, and clinical studies. MSLs provide evidence-based information to support healthcare professionals in making informed treatment decisions and improving patient outcomes.
6. *Insights and Market Intelligence*: MSLs gather insights and market intelligence from interactions with healthcare professionals and KOLs. They report on emerging trends, clinical needs, and competitor activities. This information helps pharmaceutical companies understand the market landscape, identify unmet medical needs, and develop strategies to meet those needs effectively.
7. *Cross-Functional Collaboration*: MSLs collaborate with various internal stakeholders, including medical affairs, marketing, clinical development, and regulatory teams. They provide scientific input and expertise during the development and execution of medical and marketing strategies. MSLs work closely with cross-functional teams to ensure alignment between scientific activities and marketing objectives.
8. *Compliance and Ethics*: MSLs adhere to ethical and regulatory guidelines, including compliance with industry regulations and company policies. They ensure that their interactions with healthcare professionals are compliant, transparent, and driven by scientific integrity. MSLs are responsible for sharing unbiased and evidence-based information, avoiding off-label promotion, and following internal and external guidelines.

MSLs are crucial in establishing and maintaining scientific credibility and fostering collaborative relationships between pharmaceutical companies and healthcare professionals. They contribute to the success of pharma marketing efforts by providing scientific support, education, and insights that drive evidence-based decision-making and improve patient care.

Medicare

Medicare is a federal health insurance program in the United States that primarily provides coverage to individuals aged 65 and older and certain younger individuals with disabilities. As a government program, Medicare has implications for pharma marketers in several ways:

1. *Market Size*: Medicare serves a large population of seniors and individuals with disabilities, making it a significant market for pharmaceutical products. Pharma marketers must understand Medicare beneficiaries' specific needs and preferences to reach and engage this population effectively.
2. *Formulary Coverage*: Medicare operates different parts, such as Medicare Part D, which provides prescription drug coverage. Part D plans have formularies, which are lists of covered drugs. Pharma marketers need to ensure that their products are included in the formularies of Medicare Part D plans to ensure access for Medicare beneficiaries. Negotiating formulary placement and favorable reimbursement rates with Part D plan sponsors is crucial for market penetration.
3. *Reimbursement Considerations*: Medicare reimbursement policies and pricing regulations can impact pharmaceutical companies' revenue and profitability. Pharma marketers need to navigate Medicare's reimbursement structure, including understanding Medicare's Average Sales Price (ASP) reporting requirements, coverage criteria, and the impact of Medicare payment methodologies on drug pricing and market access.
4. *Health Technology Assessment (HTA)*: Medicare conducts health technology assessments to evaluate the clinical and cost-effectiveness of medical interventions, including pharmaceutical products. These assessments, performed by organizations like the Centers for Medicare and Medicaid Services (CMS), can influence coverage decisions and reimbursement rates. Pharma marketers should be aware of the health technology assessment processes and ensure that their products have the clinical evidence to support favorable evaluations and coverage decisions.
5. *Marketing to Healthcare Providers*: Pharma marketers often target healthcare providers who treat Medicare beneficiaries, such as physicians, nurse practitioners, and specialists. Understanding Medicare reimbursement policies, formulary coverage, and prescribing

patterns among Medicare providers is essential to tailor marketing strategies effectively. Providing healthcare professionals with evidence-based data, educational materials, and value propositions that align with Medicare guidelines can enhance product adoption and utilization.

6. *Patient Assistance Programs*: Pharma marketers may need to develop patient assistance programs specifically tailored to Medicare beneficiaries. These programs can help patients afford their medications by offering discounts, copay assistance, or patient support services. Pharma marketers should ensure compliance with Medicare guidelines and regulations when implementing such programs.
7. *Compliance and Anti-Kickback Laws*: Pharma marketers must adhere to stringent compliance requirements and anti-kickback laws when engaging with Medicare beneficiaries, healthcare providers, and Medicare-related programs. Marketing practices should comply with laws such as the Anti-Kickback Statute and the False Claims Act to avoid legal issues and penalties.

Navigating the Medicare landscape requires a deep understanding of the program's structure, regulations, and policies. Pharma marketers should closely monitor changes in Medicare policies, engage in strategic collaborations with healthcare providers and payers, and tailor marketing strategies to effectively target and serve the Medicare population while ensuring compliance with applicable regulations.

Medication Utilization

Medication utilization in pharmaceutical marketing refers to studying and analyzing how drugs are prescribed, dispensed, and consumed. This involves understanding patterns of drug use, including which drugs are used, by whom, in what quantities, and for what conditions. Medication utilization studies aim to optimize the safe, appropriate, and cost-effective use of drugs.

Here is a detailed look at medication utilization and its significance in the pharmaceutical industry:

1. Objectives:

- *Safety and Effectiveness*: Ensure that medications are being used safely and effectively in the broader population beyond the controlled environment of clinical trials.
- *Cost-Effectiveness*: Analyze the cost benefits of medications, ensuring that healthcare systems get value for money.
- *Identify Trends*: Detect overuse, underuse, or misuse of medications.
- *Inform Policy*: Aid health agencies in developing or modifying drug-related policies, guidelines, and reimbursement criteria.

2. Components of Medication Utilization Studies:

- *Descriptive Studies* describe the extent and nature of drug use in specific populations or settings.
- *Analytic Studies* examine factors associated with drug use or its outcomes, often focusing on the causes of specific utilization patterns.
- *Interventional Studies* assess the effects of strategies to modify drug use or its outcomes.

3. Key Metrics:

- *Prescription Frequency*: Number of prescriptions for a particular drug or class of drugs.
- *Defined Daily Dose (DDD)*: A standardized measure of drug consumption that can be used to compare drug usage between different drugs or health environments.
- *Days of Therapy (DOT)*: Total number of days a drug is administered.
- *Cost Analysis*: Financial implications of drug use, including direct costs (like drug acquisition) and indirect costs (like hospitalization due to side effects).

4. Significance in Pharma:

- *Pharmacovigilance*: Understand real-world side effects or adverse events associated with a drug.
- *Market Analysis*: For pharmaceutical companies, understanding how their products are used can inform marketing strategies, new product development, and post-launch strategies.
- *Health Economics and Outcomes Research (HEOR)*: Understand the broader impact of a drug on health and economics, which is increasingly important for pricing and reimbursement discussions.
- *Feedback Loop to R&D*: Drug utilization data can be fed back into the research and development process, influencing the development of new formulations, dosages, or entirely new products.

Medication Utilization: Two Examples

A. *Opioid Epidemic*: Medication utilization studies in the US highlighted the dramatic rise in prescriptions of opioid painkillers in the 2000s, leading to awareness of the opioid crisis and subsequent changes in prescription guidelines and practices.

B. *Antibiotic Resistance*: Studying the patterns of antibiotic prescription and consumption can help understand the development of antibiotic-resistant bacteria. This is critical in guiding policies around antibiotic stewardship.

In summary, medication utilization studies in pharma play a critical role in ensuring that drugs are used appropriately and effectively. They bridge the gap between clinical trials and real-world applications, providing a feedback mechanism for all stakeholders, from pharmaceutical companies to health policymakers.

Medico-marketing

Medico-marketing, often termed *Medical Marketing* or *Pharmaceutical Marketing*, refers to the strategies and tactics employed by pharmaceutical companies to promote their products to healthcare professionals (HCPs), patients, and other stakeholders. This type of marketing encompasses a range of activities, from educational efforts targeting physicians to direct-to-consumer (DTC) advertising. Here are some key aspects of medico-marketing:

1. Objectives:

- Increase awareness about a disease or condition
- Inform and educate HCPs about a drug's benefits, dosing, side effects, and other relevant information
- Encourage prescription and use of the company's products
- Build brand loyalty among HCPs and patients

2. Key Components and Tactics:

- *Detailing*: Pharmaceutical representatives, known as *detailers*, visit doctors to provide them with product information, samples, and sometimes educational materials. This one-on-one interaction allows in-depth discussions about the drug's benefits and applications.
- *Medical Education*: Companies may sponsor continuing medical education (CME) events, workshops, and seminars. These events can educate HCPs about diseases, treatments, and recent research findings.
- *Conferences and Trade Shows*: Participation in medical conferences allows pharmaceutical companies to showcase their products, distribute literature, and network with HCPs.
- *Patient Education*: Providing materials, websites, or apps to help patients understand their conditions and the benefits of specific treatments.
- *Direct-to-Consumer Advertising (DTCA)*: In countries where it is permitted (like the US and New Zealand), pharmaceutical companies might advertise directly to consumers through TV, radio, print, and online channels.
- *Digital Marketing* involves engaging HCPs and patients through websites, social media platforms, mobile apps, and email campaigns.
- *Publications*: Disseminating research findings and clinical trial results through scientific journals or other publications.
- *Market Access Strategies* involve engaging with payers, insurance companies, and health systems to ensure that drugs are accessible and affordable to patients.

3. Ethical and Regulatory Considerations:

Medico-marketing is highly regulated in many countries due to potential conflicts of interest and the high stakes associated with healthcare decisions. Here are some key considerations:

- *Transparency*: Companies need to be clear about the risks and benefits of their products, avoiding any misleading information.
- *Regulatory Compliance*: Many countries have strict rules about what can be said in pharmaceutical advertising, especially DTC advertising. Claims must be backed by scientific evidence.
- *Gifts and Incentives*: Offering gifts, financial incentives, or lavish entertainment to HCPs is controversial and, in many cases, regulated or banned to avoid undue influence on prescription behavior.
- *Data Privacy*: Especially when engaging patients directly, companies need to be cautious about how they collect, store, and use personal health information.

Medico-marketing: Two Examples

C. A pharmaceutical company launching a new drug for diabetes might organize a series of CME events for endocrinologists, distribute educational materials to general practitioners, create a patient-friendly app to track blood sugar levels and launch a DTC advertising campaign showcasing patient success stories.

D. Another company with a novel migraine medication might engage in digital marketing campaigns targeting neurologists and the general public, highlighting their drug's unique benefits and mechanism of action.

In summary, medico-marketing is a multidimensional discipline that requires a balance between commercial objectives, ethical considerations, and regulatory compliance. Effective medico-marketing can lead to informed HCPs, empowered patients, and successful product adoption.

Memory Decay

Memory decay, or forgetting or memory loss, refers to the gradual fading or weakening of stored information in memory over time. In marketing, memory decay refers to the decline in consumers' memory or recall of marketing messages, brand information, or advertising content. Here are some points to understand about memory decay in marketing:

1. *Limited Attention and Retention*: Consumers are exposed to many marketing messages and information daily. However, due to limited attention and cognitive capacity, not all information is fully processed and stored in memory. The forgetting curve suggests that memory retention decreases rapidly shortly after exposure to information, leading to memory decay.
2. *Forgetting Factors*: Several factors contribute to memory decay in marketing. These include the passage of time, interference from other information or experiences, lack of reinforcement of repetition, and the significance or relevance of the information to the individual. Marketing messages are more likely to be forgotten or decay over time without reinforcement or repetition.
3. *Impact on Brand Awareness and Recognition*: Forgetting marketing messages can affect brand awareness and recognition. If consumers do not remember a brand's message or identity, they may be less likely to consider the brand when making purchasing decisions. Maintaining a strong and consistent presence through repeated exposure and reinforcement can help combat memory decay and enhance brand recall.
4. *Frequency and Repetition*: To counteract memory decay, marketers often employ strategies that involve repeated exposure to marketing messages. Through consistent and frequent communication, marketers aim to reinforce brand information, product features, and key messages in consumers' minds. By increasing the frequency and repetition of marketing efforts, marketers can enhance memory retention and reduce the impact of memory decay.
5. *Enhancing Encoding and Retrieval*: Effective marketing strategies focus on optimizing memory encoding and retrieval processes. Encoding refers to how information is processed and stored in memory, while retrieval refers to the ability to access and recall that information. Marketers can employ various techniques, such as using compelling narratives, creating memorable brand experiences, employing visual and emotional appeals, and utilizing mnemonic devices to enhance coding and retrieval, thereby reducing memory decay.
6. *Reminder Strategies*: Marketers often use reminder strategies to combat memory decay and stimulate recall of brand information. This can include tactics such as remarketing campaigns, personalized communications, loyalty programs, and ongoing customer engagement. By providing timely reminders and reinforcement, marketers can help refresh consumers' memories and counteract the effect of memory decay.
7. *Long-Term Brand Building*: Building a strong and enduring brand requires ongoing efforts to combat memory decay. Marketers invest in long-term brand-building strategies involving consistent messaging, storytelling, associations, and positive brand experiences. By consistently reinforcing brand identity and value proposition, marketers aim to establish strong and persistent memory structures in consumers' minds, reducing the impact of memory decay over time.

Understanding memory decay in marketing allows marketers to develop effective strategies to enhance memory retention and counteract forgetting. By employing tactics such as repetition, reinforcement, reminder strategies, and consistent brand building, marketers can increase the chances of their marketing messages being remembered and positively impacting consumers' purchasing decisions.

Implications for Pharma Marketers

Memory decay, or forgetting, can affect pharma marketers in several ways. Here are some key considerations:

1. *Product Information*: Pharma marketers often communicate important product information to healthcare professionals (HCPs), such as efficacy, safety, dosing, and indications. Memory decay can impact HCPs' recall of this information, potentially leading to misinterpretation or incomplete understanding

of the product. Marketers should employ strategies to reinforce key messages over time and provide easily accessible resources for reference.

2. *Brand Awareness*: Pharma marketers strive to build brand awareness among HCPs and patients. However, memory decay can affect the recall and recognition of a brand name logo or key attributes. Marketers should invest in consistent branding efforts and repeated exposure to ensure their brand is remembered and associated with the desired attributes and values.
3. *Promotional Messages*: Pharma marketers create promotional messages to communicate the value of their products to HCPs and patients. However, their impact may diminish if these messages are not effectively retained in memory. Marketers should consider repetition and reinforcement strategies, such as multichannel marketing campaigns, to combat memory decay and increase message recall.
4. *Adherence and Education*: Pharma marketers often provide educational materials and resources to promote patient adherence to prescribed medications. Memory decay can hinder patients' recall of important instructions, dosing schedules, or potential side effects. Marketers should develop patient support programs with reminder systems, clear instructions, and accessible educational materials to overcome memory decay and improve patient adherence.
5. *Continuing Medical Education(CME)*: Pharma marketers often engage in CME activities to provide HCPs with up-to-date medical knowledge. However, memory decay can impact HCPs' retention of the information presented during CME sessions. Marketers should leverage reinforcement strategies such as follow-up materials, online resources, and interactive platforms to help HCPs retain and apply the knowledge gained from CME activities.
6. *Key Opinion Leader (KOL) Influence*: KOLs play a crucial role in pharma marketing by endorsing and advocating for specific products. However, memory decay can weaken the impact of KOL recommendations over time. Marketers should ensure regular engagement with KOLs, provide updated information, and support their ongoing education to maintain their influence and combat memory decay.
7. *Regulatory and Safety Information*: Pharma marketers must ensure that important regulatory and safety information about their products is effectively communicated to HCPs and patients. Memory decay can affect the recall of these critical details, potentially leading to medication errors or non-compliance. Marketers should use clear and concise communication channels, repetition, and reinforcement to ensure that essential safety information is retained and readily accessible.

To address the implications of memory decay, pharma marketers should adopt strategies that focus on repetition, reinforcement, and consistent messaging. Multichannel marketing approaches, ongoing education and support programs, and engaging communication tools can help combat memory decay and enhance the retention of important information among HCPs and patients. Regular evaluation and assessment of the effectiveness of marketing efforts can also guide adjustments and improvements to counteract memory decay.

Mergers and Acquisitions

Mergers and Acquisitions (M&A) in pharmaceutical marketing refer to the strategic transactions where pharmaceutical companies acquire or combine with other companies to expand their market presence, product portfolio, capabilities, or resources. Here are some key points to understand about M&A in pharma marketing:

1. *Market Expansion*: M&A activities in pharma marketing allow companies to expand their market reach and presence. Pharmaceutical firms can access new geographical markets, customer segments, or therapeutic areas by acquiring or merging with other companies. This expansion enables companies to increase their customer base and market share.
2. *Portfolio Diversification*: M&A transactions allow pharmaceutical companies to diversify their product portfolios. Pharmaceutical firms can expand their offerings and address a broader range of healthcare needs by acquiring companies with complementary products or technologies. This diversification helps companies reduce reliance on a single product or therapeutic area and mitigate risks associated with pipeline failures or patent expirations.
3. *Synergies and Cost Savings*: M&A transactions in pharma marketing can lead to synergies and cost savings. Consolidating operations, eliminating redundancies, and leveraging shared resources can result in economies of scale and improved operational efficiencies. These

synergies and cost savings can enhance profitability and create a competitive advantage in the market.

4. *Access to Intellectual Property*: M&A activities can provide pharmaceutical companies access to valuable intellectual property (IP) assets. This includes patented drugs, proprietary technologies, research capabilities, or manufacturing processes. Acquiring companies with strong IP portfolios can strengthen a company's competitive position, enable the development of innovative therapies, and enhance the protection of its products.
5. *Enhanced R&D Capabilities*: M&A transactions can bolster a company's research and development (R&D) capabilities. Pharmaceutical firms can accelerate their drug discovery and development efforts by acquiring companies with advanced R&D pipelines, expertise, or specialized technologies. This allows for faster market entry of new products and strengthens the company's innovation capabilities.
6. *Competitive Advantage*: M&A activities in pharma marketing can provide companies with a competitive advantage in the market. By combining resources, expertise, and market knowledge, pharmaceutical firms can create a stronger presence, enabling them to compete better with other industry players. M&A transactions can result in increased market power, improved bargaining position, and enhanced ability to negotiate with payers, providers, and regulatory bodies.
7. *Integration Challenges*: M&A transactions in pharma marketing come with integration challenges. Combining different corporate cultures, integrating operations, harmonizing marketing strategies, and aligning product portfolios can be complex and time-consuming. Successful integration requires careful planning, effective communication, and strong project management to ensure a smooth transition and maximize the value of the transaction.

Pharmaceutical companies engage in M&A activities as part of their strategic growth initiatives. These transactions provide opportunities for market expansion, portfolio diversification, synergies, cost savings, access to IP, enhanced R&D capabilities, and competitive advantage. However, companies need to conduct thorough due diligence, assess the potential risks and benefits, and develop effective integration plans to ensure the success of the M&A transaction in the dynamic and highly regulated pharma industry.

Message

In pharmaceutical marketing, the message refers to the core content or information that pharmaceutical companies communicate to their target audience, including healthcare professionals (HCPs), patients, and other stakeholders. An effective message conveys a pharmaceutical product or service's value, benefits, and differentiation. Here are some key considerations when developing messages in pharma marketing:

1. *Clear and Concise*: Messages in pharma marketing should be clear, concise, and easy to understand. Complex scientific information should be translated into simple language that the intended audience can easily grasp. Avoid jargon and technical terms that may confuse or overwhelm the recipients.
2. *Differentiation*: Messages should highlight the pharmaceutical product or service's unique selling position and differentiating factors. What sets it apart from competitors? How does it address unmet needs or provide superior outcomes? Communicate the value proposition to help the product over alternatives.
3. *Benefit-focused*: Emphasize the benefits of the pharmaceutical product or service to the target audience. How does it improve patients' health or quality of life? How does it address specific medical conditions or symptoms? Highlight the positive impact and outcomes that can be achieved using the product.
4. *Evidence-based*: Support messages with relevant and credible scientific evidence. Provide data from clinical trials, studies, or real-world evidence demonstrating the product's efficacy, safety, and quality. Clear and transparent communication of the evidence builds trust and credibility among HCPs, patients, and other stakeholders.
5. *Patient-Centricity*: When crafting messages, consider patients' needs, preferences, and perspectives. Highlight how the product addresses patients' concerns, improves their well-being, and enhances their treatment experience. Use patient testimonials or stories to create emotional connections and demonstrate the impact of the product on individuals' lives.
6. *Regulatory Compliance*: Ensure that messages adhere to regulatory guidelines and requirements. Pharma marketing is subject to strict regulations to ensure accurate and ethical communication. Messages should not make false claims, exaggerate benefits, or promote off-label use. Compliance with regulatory frameworks is

crucial to maintaining the pharmaceutical brand's integrity and trustworthiness.

7. *Tailored for Audience*: Customize messages to resonate with different target audiences. HCPs may require more technical and scientific information, while patients may need simplified explanations and practical instructions. Tailor messages to address each audience segment's specific needs, concerns, and knowledge levels.
8. *Consistency*: Consistency is key in pharma marketing messages. Ensure the messages align with brand positioning, marketing strategy, and communication efforts. Consistent messaging across various channels and touchpoints reinforces the brand identity and helps build stakeholder recognition and trust.
9. *Adaptable and Dynamic*: Pharma marketing messages should be adaptable and flexible to accommodate evolving scientific knowledge, market dynamics, and regulatory changes. Regularly review and update messages to reflect the latest research, market trends, and regulatory guidelines.
10. *Multichannel Approach*: Distribute messages through various channels, including digital platforms, print media, conferences, sales representatives, and patient education materials. Adopt a multichannel approach to reach and engage with the target audience effectively.

Effective messages in pharma marketing are tailored, evidence-based, patient-centric, compliant with regulations, and aligned with the brand strategy. They communicate the value, benefits, and differentiation of the pharmaceutical product or service clearly and compellingly to drive awareness, understanding, and adoption among the target audience.

Message Management

Message management in pharmaceutical marketing refers to strategically developing, organizing, and controlling the messages used to communicate with various stakeholders in the pharmaceutical industry. It ensures consistency, accuracy, and effectiveness in delivering messages across different channels and touchpoints. Here are key aspects of message management in pharma marketing:

1. *Message Development*: The first step in message management is the development of key messages. This involves identifying the core content, value proposition, and differentiation points that must be communicated. Messages should be aligned with the overall marketing strategy and tailored to specific target audiences, such as healthcare professionals (HCPs), patients, payers, or regulatory authorities.
2. *Message Framework*: Establish a message framework to maintain consistency and coherence in communication. Provide guidelines for structuring messages, defining the key points, and addressing common questions and objections. The framework serves as a reference for all stakeholders involved in delivering the messages, including marketing teams, sales representatives, and customer support staff.
3. *Content Creation*: Content creation involves translating the key messages into various formats, such as written materials, visual assets, presentations, videos, or online resources. The content should be engaging, informative, and tailored to the specific communication channels and target audiences. It should convey the value proposition, address the needs and concerns of stakeholders, and adhere to regulatory guidelines.
4. *Message Distribution*: Effective message management includes a strategic distribution plan to ensure messages reach the intended audience through appropriate channels. This may include digital marketing, print media, conferences, sales representatives, websites, social media platforms, or direct mail. The distribution plan should consider the preferences and behaviors of the target audience and leverage channels that provide maximum reach and impact.
5. *Message Consistency*: Consistency is crucial in message management to avoid confusion and build a strong brand identity. Messages should be consistent across communication channels, touchpoints, and geographical regions. This includes maintaining consistent language, tone, visual elements, and core content across all marketing materials and interactions.
6. *Message Monitoring and Evaluation*: Continuously monitoring and evaluating the effectiveness of messages is essential for message management. This involves tracking key metrics, such as message reach, engagement, understanding, and impact on target audiences. Feedback from stakeholders, market research, or customer surveys can provide valuable insights to refine and improve the messages over time.
7. *Training and Alignment*: Message management requires all stakeholders involved in delivering the messages to be well-trained and aligned with the messaging strategy. This includes providing training programs to sales representatives, customer support staff, and other relevant teams

to ensure they effectively communicate the messages and respond to inquiries and objections.

8. *Regulatory Compliance*: Message management in pharma marketing should always comply with relevant regulations, such as those set by regulatory authorities or industry guidelines. This includes avoiding false or misleading claims, adhering to labeling requirements, and accurately representing the product's benefits and limitations.
9. *Adaptability and Agility*: The pharma industry is dynamic, with new scientific discoveries, market trends, and regulatory changes. Effective message management requires the ability to adapt and update messages accordingly. This involves regularly reviewing and revising messages to incorporate new information, address emerging needs, and comply with evolving regulations.

By effectively managing messages in pharmaceutical marketing, companies can ensure consistent and impactful communication with stakeholders, enhance brand reputation, drive awareness and understanding of products, and ultimately achieve their marketing objectives.

Meta Tags

Meta tags are snippets of HTML code that provide information about a webpage to search engines and website visitors. Meta tags may not directly impact pharma marketing, but play a role in optimizing the visibility and relevance of pharmaceutical websites in search engine results. Here are two types of meta tags commonly used in pharma marketing:

1. *Meta Title Tag*: The meta title tag appears as the clickable headline in search engine results and is important in determining a web page's relevance. In pharma marketing, the meta title tag should accurately and concisely describe the web page's content while incorporating relevant keywords. For example, a meta title tag for a webpage about a specific medication could be "*Product Name: Uses, Dosage, Side Effects: Pharma Company.*"
2. *Meta Description Tag*: The meta description tag briefly summarizes the webpage's content that appears below the meta title in search engine results. While it doesn't directly impact the search engine rankings, it influences the click-through rate and can affect user engagement. In pharma marketing, the meta description tag should provide a compelling and concise overview of the web page's content, highlighting key information and benefits. For example, a meta description tag for a webpage about a medication could be " Learn about the uses, dosage instructions, and potential side effects of the product (name). Trust the expertise of (Pharma Company Name) for safe and effective treatment.

It is important to note that while meta tags are important for search engine optimization, they should accurately represent the webpage's content and avoid deceptive practices. Compliance with regulatory guidelines is crucial in pharma marketing, and meta tags should not make false claims, exaggerate benefits, or promote off-label use.

In addition to meta tags, other elements such as well-structured URLs, Header tags (H1, H2, etc.), and relevant keywords with the webpage's content can also contribute to optimizing the visibility and relevance of pharmaceutical websites in search engine results. It is recommended to follow best practices in search engine optimization (SEO) and consult with SEO specialists or digital marketing professionals to ensure compliance and effectiveness in pharma marketing efforts.

Meta Verse

Metaverse is a virtual reality space where users can interact with a computer-generated environment and other users in real-time. It is often depicted as a collective virtual shared space accessible through the Internet or other digital platforms.

The metaverse concept has been popularized in science fiction, particularly in novels like *Snow Crash* by Neal Stephenson and *Ready Player One* by Ernest Cline. In these fictional portrayals, the metaverse is a fully immersive and interactive digital universe that extends the real world, allowing users to engage in various activities such as socializing, working, playing games, and conducting business. The real-world implementation of the metaverse is still evolving. Still, it typically involves virtual reality (VR) and augmented reality (AR) technologies, along with advancements in artificial intelligence, blockchain, and other emerging technologies. The goal is to create a seamless and immersive digital environment that transcends the limitations of traditional two-dimensional screens and offers a more engaging and interconnected experience.

Various companies and tech giants are actively exploring the development of the metaverse. These efforts include the creation of virtual worlds, social platforms, and online marketplaces where users can create and trade digital assets, participate in virtual events, and connect with others from around the world. The metaverse is envisioned to have many applications, spanning entertainment, education, communication, e-commerce, and beyond.

Implications for Pharma Marketing

While the full realization of the metaverse is still in development, its potential implications for pharmaceutical marketing can be considered. Here are some possible implications of the metaverse for pharma marketers:

1. *Virtual Conferences and Events*: The metaverse can offer opportunities for pharma companies to host virtual conferences, symposiums, or educational events. It can provide an immersive and interactive environment for healthcare professionals, researchers, and stakeholders to exchange knowledge, attend presentations, and engage in discussions.
2. *Virtual Rep Presentations*: Pharma marketers can utilize the metaverse to create virtual representations of their sales representatives. This allows for more personalized and interactive engagement with healthcare professionals and other stakeholders. Virtual reps can provide product information, answer questions, and showcase the benefits of pharmaceutical products in a simulated environment.
3. *Patient Education and Support*: The metaverse can create virtual environments facilitating patient education and support. Pharmaceutical companies can develop immersive experiences that help patients understand their medical conditions, treatment options, and medication adherence. Virtual support groups and communities can also be established to provide patients with a sense of connection and shared experiences among patients.
4. *Virtual Product Launches*: Pharma companies could organize launch events within the metaverse to showcase new medications or medical devices to healthcare professionals and consumers. This could involve interactive presentations, virtual demonstrations, and opportunities for attendees to ask questions and provide feedback.
5. *Disease Awareness Campaigns*: Pharmaceutical companies could use the metaverse as a platform to raise awareness about specific diseases and medical conditions. They could create virtual experiences or games that educate users about the symptoms, risks, and available treatment options, thereby increasing disease awareness and promoting early diagnosis and treatment.
6. *Virtual Product Demonstrations*: Pharma marketers can leverage the metaverse to provide virtual product demonstrations. This allows healthcare professionals and other stakeholders to explore pharmaceutical products' features, mechanisms of action, and benefits in a simulated environment. Virtual demonstrations can enhance understanding and create memorable experiences.
7. *Digital Advertising and Branding*: As the metaverse evolves, pharmaceutical companies could have opportunities to advertise and build their brand within virtual environments. This could involve placing virtual billboards, sponsored virtual events, or even integrating branded products into virtual worlds.
8. *Clinical Trials and Research*: The metaverse can be utilized for virtual clinical trials, where participants can interact with virtual environments to simulate real-world scenarios. This can enhance the efficiency and accessibility of clinical research, potentially accelerating the development and testing of pharmaceutical products.
9. *Virtual Pharmacies and Retail Spaces*: With the metaverse, pharma marketers can create virtual pharmacies or retail spaces where users can explore and purchase pharmaceutical products. Virtual pharmacies can provide information on product availability, dosage instructions, and potential interactions while offering a convenient and personalized shopping experience.
10. *Data Collection and Analysis*: The metaverse can generate vast amounts of data on user behavior, preferences, and interactions. Pharma marketers can leverage this data to gain insights into customer preferences, refine marketing strategies, and personalize marketing efforts based on user behavior within the metaverse.

It is important to note that the metaverse is still an evolving concept, and its full implementation and adoption in pharma marketing may take time. Additionally, privacy and security considerations must be addressed when utilizing virtual environments and collecting user data within the metaverse. Pharma marketers should closely monitor the development of the metaverse, explore opportunities for engagement, and carefully assess the value and impact it can bring to their marketing strategies. Collaborating with technology experts, virtual reality developers, and digital marketing professionals can help ensure the utilization of the metaverse effectively in pharma marketing efforts.

Metcalfe's Law

Metcalfe's Law, named after Robert Metcalfe, the co-inventor of Ethernet and founder of 3COM Corporation, states that *the value of a network is proportional to the square of the number of connected users in the network.*

In simpler terms, this means that as more users join a network, the value of a network increases exponentially. The value of the network is not just determined by the number of users but also by the interactions and connections between them. More connections lead to more opportunities for communication, collaboration, and exchange of information.

Metcalfe's Law is often applied in the context of telecommunications and computer networks, where the value of a network, such as the Internet, grows as more people and devices are connected. It highlights the concept of network effects, where the value of a network is influenced by the number of participants and their level of interaction.

Implications of Metcalfe's Law for businesses, including pharmaceuticals, can include:

1. *Network Growth*: To maximize the value of a network, businesses should focus on expanding their user base and increasing the number of connections between users. This can involve strategies to attract more customers, engage with them effectively, and encourage interactions within the network.
2. *Collaboration and Partnerships*: Building partnerships and collaborating with other businesses can help expand the network and create synergistic effects. By connecting with complementary businesses, pharma marketers can leverage shared resources, expertise, and reach to enhance the value and impact of their marketing efforts.
3. *User Engagement and Retention*: User engagement and retention are crucial in a network. Creating a positive user experience, providing valuable content, and fostering a sense of community can encourage users to remain active and attract new users through positive word-of-mouth.
4. *Data and Insights*: As the network grows, more data is generated, providing opportunities for data analysis and insights. By leveraging the data within the network, businesses can gain a deeper understanding of user behavior, preferences, and trends, enabling them to make informed marketing decisions and personalize their offerings.
5. *Viral Marketing Amplification*: Metcalfe's Law suggests that network effects can lead to viral growth. If a message or content resonates with users within the network, it can spread rapidly, reaching a larger audience and increasing the network's value. Pharma marketers can use this amplification effect by creating compelling and shareable content.

In summary, Metcalfe's Law emphasizes the value of networks and the exponential growth potential that comes with increased connectivity and interactions. Pharma marketers can consider these implications when developing strategies to expand their networks, foster collaboration, engage users, analyze data, and leverage viral marketing opportunities.

Me-too

In marketing, *Me-too* refers to a product or service that closely imitates or emulates a competitor's offering. It refers to a strategy where a company introduces a similar product or service in response to the success or popularity of a competitor's existing offering. Me-too is derived from the idea that the company follows another player's lead in the market.

Me-too products or services are typically positioned as alternatives to the original, with similar features, benefits, and target audiences. The me-too strategy intends to capture a market share by offering a comparable option to consumers who may be attracted to the original product but are open to alternatives.

Me-too in Pharma Marketing

In pharma marketing, me-too refers to developing and marketing drugs similar to existing drugs in terms of their therapeutic class, mechanism of action, or indications. The me-too drugs are introduced into the market by pharmaceutical companies to compete with existing drugs that have already established a strong presence.

The motivation behind me-too drugs in the pharmaceutical industry can vary. It may be an attempt to capitalize on an existing drug's success and market share by offering a product. The hope is to attract a portion of the market by providing an alternative option, often with minor differentiating factors such as dosage form, dosing regimen, or delivery system.

However, Me-too drugs in pharma marketing can face challenges due to the stringent regulatory requirements and the need to demonstrate comparative effectiveness and safety. Regulatory authorities often require new drugs to undergo clinical trials to establish their efficacy and safety, even if similar drugs are already available. This can result in additional costs and time required for development and approval.

From a marketing perspective, promoting me-too drugs can be challenging due to the need to differentiate them from existing drugs and convince healthcare practitioners (HCPs) to adopt the new option. Companies may employ strategies to differentiate their me-too drugs, such as emphasizing slight advantages in efficacy, safety profile, patient compliance, effectiveness, or cost. Effective communication and education to HCPs about the specific advantages and appropriate patient populations for the me-too drug are crucial.

It is important to note that introducing me-too drugs can contribute to therapeutic competition and offer additional options for patients and healthcare providers. However, It is also essential for pharmaceutical companies to continue investing in research and development to bring innovative and breakthrough drugs to the market, addressing unmet medical needs and providing substantial clinical benefits.

Micro Markets

In the pharmaceutical industry, micro markets refer to specific segments or submarkets within the larger pharmaceutical market. These micro markets are characterized by their unique dynamics, customer profiles, and product requirements. Here are a few examples of micro markets within the pharmaceutical industry:

1. *Therapeutic Areas*: Micro markets can be defined based on specific therapeutic areas or medical conditions. For instance, there are micro markets for cardiovascular drugs, oncology drugs, neurology drugs, and so on. Each therapeutic area has its own set of drugs, treatment protocols, and target patient populations.
2. *Demographics*: Micro markets can also be based on demographic factors such as age, gender, or ethnicity. Certain pharmaceutical products may be specially developed for children, elderly individuals, women, or particular ethnic groups. These products cater to the unique needs and characteristics of these demographic segments.
3. *Specialty Drugs*: Micro markets for specialty drugs developed to treat rare diseases or conditions can exist. These drugs are often expensive and require specialized distribution channels, healthcare providers, and patient support systems. The micro market for specialty drugs differs from the broader market for common pharmaceutical products.
4. *Geographical Regions*: Micro markets can be defined based on specific geographic regions. Pharmaceutical companies may focus on regions or countries with high demand for specific drugs or favorable regulatory environments. The dynamics and market characteristics can vary significantly across different geographical micromarkets.

In summary, micro markets in the pharmaceutical industry refer to specific segments or submarkets within the larger pharmaceutical market. Each micro-market has unique dynamics and requirements based on therapeutic areas, demographics, specialty drugs, or geographical regions.

Micro-marketing

Micro marketing in pharma refers to tailoring marketing efforts to very specific and targeted segments within the pharmaceutical market. It involves identifying and understanding these micro-segments' unique needs, preferences, and characteristics and developing customized marketing strategies to reach and engage them effectively. Here are some key aspects and implications of micro-marketing in the pharmaceutical industry:

1. *Targeted Segmentation*: Micro marketing starts with precisely segmenting the market into smaller, well-defined micro-segments. These segments can be based on various factors such as demographics, geographic location, disease state, treatment preferences, or even genetic profiles. By dividing the broader market into specific micro-segments, pharma marketers can focus on reaching the right audience with relevant messages and offerings.
2. *Personalized Messaging*: Micro marketing allows for highly personalized and targeted messaging. By understanding each micro-segment's specific needs and preferences, pharma marketers can craft messages that resonate with audiences individually. This can involve addressing their unique challenges, highlighting the benefits of specific treatments or therapies, and emphasizing the value proposition tailored to their specific circumstances.
3. *Customized Offerings*: Micro marketing enables pharma companies to develop customized offerings for different micro-segments. This can involve developing specialized formulations, dosage forms, or treatment protocols that cater

to the unique needs of specific patient populations. By tailoring their products and services to address the specific requirements of micro-segments, pharma companies can differentiate themselves in the market and enhance patient satisfaction.

4. *Precision Targeting*: Micro marketing allows for precisely targeted promotional activities and marketing channels. By understanding each micro-segment's preferred communication channels and media consumption habits, pharma marketers can optimize their marketing spend and focus on the most effective channels for reaching and engaging the target audience. This includes digital platforms, social media, targeted advertising, and even direct outreach to healthcare professionals or patient support groups.
5. *Relationship Building*: Micro marketing emphasizes building relationships with key stakeholders within each micro-segment. This can involve engaging with healthcare professionals, patient advocacy groups, or specialized healthcare organizations catering to the micro segment's special needs. By establishing strong relationships, pharma marketers can gain insights, build trust, and collaborate with these stakeholders to serve the target audience better.
6. *Data-Driven Insights*: Micro marketing relies on data collection and analysis to understand the characteristics and behavior of each micro-segment. By leveraging data analytics, market research, and real-world evidence, pharma marketers can gain valuable insights into each micro segment's preferences, treatment responses, and outcomes. These insights help refine marketing strategies, optimize resource allocation, and identify areas for innovation.

Micro marketing in pharma requires a deep understanding of the target audience, careful segmentation, and a tailored approach to marketing strategies. By focusing on the unique needs of specific micro-segments, pharma marketers can enhance the relevance, engagement, and success of their marketing.

Micro-segmentation

Micro-segmentation in pharma refers to dividing the pharmaceutical market into small, distinct segments based on specific criteria or characteristics. It involves identifying homogeneous groups of customers within the broader market and tailoring marketing strategies and tactics to meet the unique needs and preferences of each micro-segment. Here are some key aspects and implications of micro-segmentation in the pharmaceutical industry:

1. *Precise Targeting*: Microsegmentation allows pharma marketers to target specific groups of patients or healthcare professionals precisely. By understanding the demographics, behaviors, attitudes, or medical conditions of each microsegment, marketers can customize their marketing efforts to address the specific needs and interests of the target audience.
2. *Personalized Messaging*: Microsegment enables pharma marketers to develop personalized and relevant messages for each microsegment. By understanding the pain points, treatment preferences, or challenges each group faces, marketers can create tailored messages that resonate with the audience individually. This personalization enhances the effectiveness of communication and increases the likelihood of engagement.
3. *Customized Offerings*: Microsegmentation allows for the customization of products, services, or treatment solutions to meet the unique requirements of each microsegment. By understanding the specific needs, treatment protocols, or medication preferences of different patient populations or healthcare professionals, pharma companies can develop specialized formulations, delivery systems, or packaging options that cater to the specific demands of each microsegment.
4. *Targeted Channel Selection*: Microsegmentation helps select the most appropriate marketing channels for each microsegment. Different groups of customers may have varying preferences for information sources, communication channels, or digital platforms. By understanding these preferences, pharma marketers can optimize their channel selection to ensure the right message reaches the right audience through the most effective channels.
5. *Enhanced Customer Experience*: Microsegmentation enables pharmaceutical companies to provide a personalized and tailored customer experience for each microsegment. By understanding different customer groups' specific needs and preferences, marketers can design customer support programs, educational materials, or patient assistance initiatives that address their unique requirements. This enhances customer satisfaction, loyalty, and overall patient experience.

6. *Improved Resource Allocation*: Microsegmentation helps allocate marketing resources more efficiently and effectively. By focusing on the most promising microsegments that offer the highest potential return on investment, pharma marketers can optimize their marketing spend and allocate resources to initiatives more likely to generate desired outcomes.
7. *Market Insights and Innovation*: Microsegmentation provides valuable market insights that can drive innovation. By closely analyzing each microsegment and its specific needs, marketers can identify unmet needs, gaps in existing solutions, or emerging trends within the market. This knowledge can inform the development of new products, treatment approaches, or healthcare services that cater to the unique requirements of each microsegment.

Microsegmentation in pharma requires a deep understanding of the target audience, robust data analytics capabilities, and effective market research. By dividing the market into smaller, more targeted segments, pharma marketers can develop strategies and initiatives that align with each microsegment's specific needs and preferences, leading to improved engagement, customer satisfaction, and business success.

Microsites

Microsites in pharmaceutical marketing refer to small, dedicated websites created to provide targeted information about a specific drug, therapeutic area, or medical condition. These sites are distinct from the main corporate website and are designed to deliver focused content to a particular audience. Here are some key aspects and advantages of using microsites in pharma marketing:

1. *Focused Information*: Microsites allow pharmaceutical companies to provide detailed and targeted information about a specific drug or therapeutic area. This focused approach ensures visitors find the necessary information without navigating through extensive content.
2. *Patient Education*: Microsites are effective tools for patient education. They can offer in-depth information about a particular medical condition, treatment options, and resources to support patients in understanding their health and managing their conditions.
3. *HCP Engagement*: Healthcare professionals (HCPs) can benefit from microsites that offer detailed data on drug efficacy, safety profiles, clinical trial results, and dosing information. This targeted approach helps in engaging and informing medical professionals.
4. *Product Launches*: Microsites are commonly used during product launches. They provide a platform to showcase the benefits of a new drug, share clinical trial data, and communicate key messages directly to healthcare professionals, patients, and other stakeholders.
5. *Interactive Features*: Microsites often incorporate interactive features like quizzes, videos, and patient testimonials. These elements enhance engagement and provide a more dynamic and user-friendly experience.
6. *Compliance and Regulatory Control*: By creating separate microsites, pharmaceutical companies can maintain better control over content related to specific drugs, ensuring compliance with regulatory guidelines. This is crucial in an industry where accurate and transparent communication is paramount.
7. *Event Support*: Microsites can be created to support specific events, such as medical conferences or educational seminars. They are centralized platforms for event-related information, speaker details, and downloadable resources.
8. *Responsive Design*: Microsites can be optimized for various devices, ensuring a seamless user experience across desktops, tablets, and smartphones. Responsive design is essential for reaching a diverse audience of healthcare professionals, patients, and caregivers.
9. *Data Collection and Analytics*: Microsites allow for collecting specific data related to user engagement and interactions. Analytics tools can provide insights into how visitors navigate the microsite, helping marketers understand the effectiveness of their content.
10. *Call-to-Action*: Microsites often include clear and specific calls-to-action, guiding visitors to take desired steps such as contacting a healthcare professional, signing up for updates, or accessing additional resources.

Microsites play a valuable role in pharmaceutical marketing by offering focused and targeted information, supporting patient education, and providing a platform for effective communication during product launches or specific events. Their flexibility and ability to deliver tailored content make them a valuable tool in the pharmaceutical industry's digital marketing strategy.

Microsoft

Microsoft is a multinational technology company headquartered in Richmond, Washington, USA. Founded by Bill Gates and Paul Allen on April 4, 1975, the company has become one of the world's most valuable and influential tech corporations. As stated by the company, Microsoft's primary mission is *to empower every person and organization to achieve more*.

Microsoft has been making several moves into the healthcare sector, leveraging its technological prowess to create solutions and platforms that cater to the healthcare industry. Here are some key areas and initiatives where Microsoft has made inroads:

1. *Microsoft Cloud for Healthcare*: Announced in 2020, this integrated cloud solution offers capabilities tailored for the healthcare sector, allowing organizations to coordinate care, manage health data, and integrate systems across the health ecosystem.
2. *Acquisition of 'Nuance'*: In 2021, Microsoft announced its plans to acquire Nuance Communications for nearly $20 billion. Nuance is best known for its voice recognition software, but it also offers products for healthcare providers, including solutions that help digitize patient records and facilitate telehealth appointments.
3. *Microsoft Teams for Healthcare*: The tech giant enhanced its Teams platform to provide special features to healthcare professionals (HCPs), such as secure messaging and meetings, electronic health record (EHR) integration, and virtual visits.
4. *Microsoft Healthcare Bot*: Microsoft introduced a cloud service that empowers healthcare organizations to create AI-powered virtual health assistants and chatbots. These bots can answer symptom questions, update outpatient appointments, and assist in other patient interactions.
5. *Research Collaborations*: Microsoft Research has been involved in various collaborations in the biotech and healthcare sectors. They have worked on everything from machine learning models that predict patient readmission to algorithms that can analyze radiology images to technologies that can understand the complexities of cancer biology.
6. *Project Hanover*: An initiative by Microsoft Research aimed at using machine learning to help oncologists find the most up-to-date treatments for cancer by sifting through biomedical papers.
7. *AI for Health*: A program aimed at empowering researchers and organizations with AI to improve the health of people and communities worldwide. The program focuses on areas like disease prevention, diagnosis, and treatment.
8. *Healthcare NexT*: This initiative aimed to accelerate healthcare innovation through artificial intelligence and cloud computing, working with partners to create innovative solutions.

While these are some of the significant forays, it is essential to note that the landscape is continuously evolving. Like other tech giants, Microsoft recognizes the vast potential and critical nature of healthcare and is likely to deepen its involvement in this sector further.

Implications for Pharma Marketers

Integrating technology giants like Microsoft into the healthcare and pharma sectors has various implications for pharma marketers. Here are some potential effects and considerations:

1. *Data Accessibility and Analysis*: With companies like Microsoft providing cloud and AI solutions, pharma marketers can access vast amounts of data. This data can be used to glean insights into patient behaviors, treatment efficacy, and market trends, allowing for more targeted and effective campaigns.
2. *Personalized Marketing*: Leveraging AI and machine learning, pharma marketers can craft campaigns tailored to individual patient needs and preferences. Personalized marketing can lead to improved patient engagement and better outcomes.
3. *Digital Engagement Platforms*: Microsoft's push into healthcare, especially with tools like *Teams*, provides new platforms for pharma marketers to engage with healthcare professionals and patients. These platforms can be used for educational webinars, virtual product launches, and more.
4. *Compliance and Security*: Microsoft's entry ensures higher data security and compliance standards, given its experience with enterprise-level security solutions. This is crucial for pharma marketers who deal with sensitive patient data and must adhere to strict regulations.
5. *Integrated Patient Experience*: As tech solutions make patient care more integrated and seamless, pharma marketers must think holistically. The patient journey, from diagnosis to treatment to

follow-up, can be mapped and addressed in marketing strategies.

6. *Voice and Chatbot Solutions*: With Microsoft's acquisition of Nuance and the push for healthcare bots, pharma marketers can leverage voice and chatbot solutions for patient engagement, medication reminders, and answering common queries.
7. *Collaboration with Tech Giants*: As Microsoft deepens its footprint in health care, opportunities for partnerships and collaborations will increase. Pharma companies can work with Microsoft to co-create solutions, platforms, or campaigns that benefit both parties.
8. *Shift in Budgets and Priorities*: As digital platforms and tools become more prevalent, pharma marketing budgets might shift from traditional channels to these new avenues. There could be increased investment in digital marketing skills, tools, and platforms.
9. *Direct-to-Consumer (DTC) Possibilities*: Advanced tech solutions can empower patients to take charge of their health, providing pharma marketers with more avenues for direct-to-consumer marketing. However, this must be approached with caution and in compliance with regulations.
10. *Educational Opportunities*: Pharma marketers can leverage platforms like Teams or AI-driven content to provide healthcare professionals with educational materials, product information, or Continuing Medical Education (CME) opportunities.

Microsoft's foray into healthcare and pharma provides pharma marketers with many opportunities but also presents challenges in adjusting to new platforms and ways of engagement. As always, understanding the audience (patients, healthcare professionals, or other stakeholders) and ensuring the delivery of valuable, compliant content will remain paramount.

MLR

MLR stands for Medical, Legal, and Regulatory review in the pharmaceutical industry. MLR is a crucial process that pharmaceutical companies follow to ensure compliance with medical, legal, regulatory, and ethical standards when creating promotional materials, such as advertisements, websites, brochures, and sales aids.

The MLR process involves reviewing and approving marketing and promotional materials by cross-functional teams consisting of individuals from medical, legal, and regulatory departments within the pharmaceutical company. These teams assess the materials for accuracy, scientific validity, fair balance, compliance with regulations and guidelines, and adherence to the company's policies and procedures.

The medical reviewers evaluate the scientific and medical content of the materials, ensuring that the claims are supported by clinical data and aligned with approved indications and labeling. The legal reviewers focus on assessing the materials for compliance with applicable laws, regulations, and industry guidelines, addressing potential legal risks. The regulatory reviewers ensure the materials meet regulatory requirements and are consistent with the approved product labeling.

The MLR process is essential to ensure that promotional materials accurately represent the pharmaceutical product, provide balanced and evidence-based information, and comply with the complex legal and regulatory landscape governing pharmaceutical marketing. It helps safeguard patient safety, maintain ethical standards, and minimize legal and regulatory risks for the pharmaceutical company.

Milking Strategy

A milking strategy is a short-term strategy to generate revenue by snatching the largest possible revenue and profit from a particular product or service in the shortest time, regardless of the product's future possibilities of generating revenue. However, milking strategy is not a well-defined term in a general sense. However, in certain contexts, it may refer to a strategy that involves extracting maximum value or profit from a particular situation or resource. Here are a few examples of how the term milking strategy could be interpreted or how implementing a milking strategy could be interpreted in different contexts:

1. *Financial Markets*: In investment or trading, a milking strategy could refer to a technique where an investor or trader aims to extract consistent profits from a specific asset or market condition by taking advantage of short-term pricing fluctuations.
2. *Gaming*: In the gaming industry, a milking strategy might refer to releasing additional content or expansions over an extended period to monetize the game and its player base beyond the initial purchase price. This could include selling downloadable content (DLC), in-game items, or subscriptions.

3. *Business*: In business, a milking strategy could be seen as a short-term approach where a company focuses on maximizing profits from its existing customer base or products rather than investing in innovation or long-term growth. This might involve increasing prices, reducing costs, or minimizing investments in research and development.
4. *BCG Matrix*: The BCG matrix is a strategic tool for portfolio analysis and product management. It categorizes a company's products or business units into four quadrants based on their market growth rate and relative market share: stars, cash cows, question marks, and dogs. While the milking strategy is not specifically associated with the BCG matrix, it might be loosely associated with the Cash Cow Quadrant. Cash Cows are products or business units with a high market share in a low-growth market. These entities generate significant cash flow and profit, which can be milked or harvested to support other business areas or invest in new ventures. So, while the milking strategy is not explicitly mentioned in the BCG matrix framework, the concept of milking can be related to the cash cow quadrant within the context of the matrix.

Mission

In the pharmaceutical industry, the *Mission* refers to a pharmaceutical company's purpose or overarching goal. It represents the company's fundamental existence and outlines its intended impact on the healthcare industry and patients' lives. The mission statement is a guiding principle for all marketing activities and influences strategic decisions and priorities. Here are key aspects related to the mission in pharma marketing:

1. *Patient-Centric Focus:* The mission in pharmaceutical marketing often centers around improving patient outcomes, enhancing the quality of life, and addressing unmet medical needs. It reflects the company's marketing commitment to prioritizing patients' well-being and health.
2. *Ethical Responsibility*: The mission emphasizes ethical conduct and compliance with regulations and industry standards. Pharma companies are responsible for ensuring the safety, efficacy, and appropriate use of their products, and the mission statement reflects a commitment to ethical behavior in marketing practices.
3. *Scientific Advancement*: Pharma's marketing missions often underscore the commitment to scientific innovation, research and development, and the pursuit of breakthrough therapies and treatments. This focus on scientific advancement positions the company as a leader in the industry and reinforces its dedication to advancing medical knowledge and improving patient care.
4. *Stakeholder Engagement*: The mission may highlight the importance of building strong relationships with healthcare professionals, patient advocacy groups, and other stakeholders. Effective collaboration and engagement with key stakeholders are crucial to achieving marketing goals and fulfilling the company's mission.
5. *Brand Identity and Differentiation*: The mission statement can communicate the company's unique value proposition and positioning in the market. It reflects the brand identity and the distinctive attributes that set the company apart from competitors, whether through product innovation, patient support programs, or other strategic initiatives.

Crafting an effective mission statement in the pharmaceutical industry requires careful consideration of the company's values, market positioning, and long-term objectives. It should be clear and concise and inspire all stakeholders, including employees, healthcare professionals, patients, and investors, to align with the company's purpose and work towards its fulfillment. The mission statement is a compass for decision-making, resource allocation, and developing marketing strategies supporting the company's mission and vision.

Mission Statement

A mission statement in pharmaceutical marketing is a concise and clear declaration of the purpose and goals of a pharmaceutical company's marketing efforts. It outlines the company's commitment to improving healthcare outcomes, meeting customer needs, and achieving business success. A well-crafted mission statement in pharma marketing should reflect the company's values, target audience, and long-term objectives. Here is an example of a mission statement in pharma marketing:

Our mission is to empower patients and healthcare professionals with innovative, safe, and effective pharmaceutical solutions. We are dedicated to improving global health outcomes by delivering breakthrough therapies that address unmet medical needs. Through collaborative partnerships, ethical practices, and patient-centric approaches, we strive to enhance the quality of life and create a healthier future for individuals and communities worldwide.

In this example, the mission statement highlights the key elements of a pharma marketing mission:

1. *Patient Focus*: The Mission underscores the company's dedication to improving patient health and well-being as the primary objective of its marketing efforts.
2. *Innovation*: The company emphasizes its commitment to scientific excellence and developing innovative pharmaceutical products that address unmet medical needs.
3. *Ethics and Compliance*: The mission statement reflects the company's adherence to ethical conduct and regulatory compliance in all marketing practices.
4. *Collaboration*: The Mission acknowledges the importance of collaborating with healthcare professionals, patient advocacy groups, and other stakeholders to ensure patient outcomes.
5. *Global Reach*: The Mission indicates the company's ambition to impact patients worldwide, suggesting a global perspective in its marketing endeavors.

A well-crafted mission statement guides the company's marketing strategies, activities, and decision-making processes. It helps align the entire organization and its stakeholders toward a common purpose and provides a framework for assessing the effectiveness and impact of marketing initiatives.

Mission Statements of Some Pharma Companies

1. *Johnson & Johnson*: We blend heart, science, and ingenuity to profoundly change humanity's health trajectory.
2. *Pfizer*: We strive to improve global health through innovative medicines and breakthrough discoveries significantly.
3. *Novartis*: Our mission is to discover new ways to improve and extend people's lives, leveraging science-based innovation and a deep understanding of disease pathways.
4. *Merck*: We are committed to improving health and well-being worldwide by providing innovative medicines, vaccines, and solutions.
5. *GlaxoSmithKline (GSK)*: We are dedicated to helping people do more, feel better, and live longer by researching and developing innovative medicines and healthcare products.
6. *AstraZeneca*: Our mission is to push the boundaries of science to deliver life-changing medicines that transform patients' lives and address global healthcare challenges.
7. *Sanofi*: We work passionately every day to understand and solve the healthcare needs of people worldwide by developing innovative solutions and providing accessible healthcare.

These mission statements highlight the companies' focus on improving health outcomes, advancing medical knowledge, and positively impacting individuals and communities.

Mixed Reality

Mixed Reality (MR) combines the physical and virtual worlds to create immersive and interactive experiences. It combines Augmented Reality (AR) and Virtual Reality (VR) to enable users to interact with digital content in real-world environments. In pharmaceutical marketing, mixed reality offers unique opportunities to engage healthcare professionals, patients, and other stakeholders in innovative ways. Here are some potential implications and applications of mixed reality in pharma marketing:

1. *Product Demonstrations*: Mixed reality can provide virtual demonstrations of pharmaceutical products, allowing healthcare professionals to visualize a drug's mechanism of action (MOA), mode of administration, and potential benefits. It enhances understanding and engagement by providing an immersive experience beyond traditional brochures and videos.
2. *Medical Education and Training*: Mixed reality can be utilized for medical education and training, enabling healthcare professionals to practice procedures, surgical techniques, or patient interactions in a realistic virtual environment. It offers a safe and controlled space for learning and skill development.
3. *Patient Education*: Mixed reality can be leveraged to educate patients about their medical conditions, treatment options, and medication adherence. It can provide interactive and visually engaging experiences that simplify complex medical concepts and enhance patient understanding.
4. *Virtual Tours and Simulations*: Pharma companies can use mixed reality to offer virtual tours of manufacturing facilities, research labs, or clinical trial sites, providing a behind-the-scenes look at their operations. Additionally, it can simulate patient experiences or clinical scenarios to help healthcare professionals gain insights into specific disease states or treatment pathways.
5. *Conference and Event Engagement*: Mixed reality can enhance pharma marketing at

conferences and events by creating immersive and interactive experiences. Companies can use virtual booths or showcases to demonstrate products, engage with attendees, and deliver presentations more engagingly and memorably.

6. *Disease Awareness Campaigns*: Mixed reality can support disease awareness campaigns by creating interactive and immersive experiences that convey the impact of a particular disease on patients' lives. It can help raise awareness, empathy, and understanding among healthcare professionals, patients, and the general public.

Implementing mixed reality in pharmaceutical marketing requires a thoughtful approach and collaboration with experienced technology partners. It is important to consider the target audience, objectives, and desired outcomes when designing mixed reality experiences. Additionally, ensuring compliance with regulatory requirements and maintaining data privacy and security are crucial when using mixed reality technologies in the pharma industry.

Mnemonics

Mnemonics are memory aids used to help remember information. In pharmaceutical marketing, mnemonics can be especially useful because of the complex nature of drug names, mechanisms of action, indications, and side effects. Utilizing mnemonics can assist healthcare professionals in recalling critical information about a drug, enhancing patient safety, and improving therapeutic outcomes. Here are a few ways in which mnemonics might be used in pharma marketing:

1. *Drug Names*: Many drug names can be difficult to pronounce and remember. A mnemonic that relates the drug's name to its primary use or key characteristic can be helpful. Consider a fictional drug named *Cardioxin that treats heart disease, for example. Cardio (relating to the heart) + Xin (medicine).*
2. *Mechanism of Action*: Knowing how a drug works can be vital. For example, a drug that inhibits enzyme X for cholesterol reduction. The mnemonic could be: *X marks the spot where cholesterol stops.*
3. *Indications*: Remembering what a drug is used for is crucial. For example, an asthmatic mediation can use a mnemonic: *A Breath of Fresh Air.*
4. *Side Effects*: Mnemonics can help in recalling side effects. For instance, in a drug category where side effects like nausea, headache, and dizziness are common, you have a product that minimizes these side effects; the mnemonic could be: *NHD– Not Having Delightful Day?*
5. *Dosing Schedule*: If a drug needs to be taken, say twice daily. The mnemonic could be *Sunrise and Sunset for optimal effect* for a twice-daily drug.
6. *Interactions with Other Drugs*: Remembering drug interactions can prevent adverse effects. For example, if a drug interacts with alcohol, you could say: *Avoid the bottle with this pill.*
7. *Contraindications*: Mnemonics can help remember who should not take the medication. For instance, you could say for a drug contraindicated in pregnancy: *Not for moms-to-be.*
8. *Drug Classes*: Grouping drugs by their class can help in recalling similar drugs. For instance, SSRIs (Selective Serotonin Reuptake Inhibitors) like Prozac, Zoloft, etc., can be remembered as *SSRIs are Soothing for Sadness.*
9. *Product Differentiation*: Mnemonics can help differentiate a product from its competitors. You could highlight the differentiators of your drug by saying: Only our drug provides A, B, and C benefits.

Pharmaceutical companies should be cautious when creating mnemonics to ensure they are accurate and do not mislead. Misinformation can lead to inappropriate drug use or missed therapeutic opportunities. It is always crucial for healthcare professionals to validate and update their knowledge through trusted and reliable sources.

How to Create Effective Mnemonics

Creating effective mnemonics in pharma marketing requires a blend of creativity, accuracy, and relevance. Here are some steps and tips to help design impactful mnemonics:

1. *Understand the Key Information*: Determine the core information you want to communicate. Is it the drug's mechanism of action, side effects, dosing, or something else?
2. *Keep it Simple*: The best mnemonics are short and easy to recall. Avoid overly complicated mnemonics that defeat the purpose.
3. *Make it Relevant*: The mnemonic should directly connect to the drug or the message you want to convey. This enhances recall and relevance.
4. *Utilize Familiar Concepts*: If the mnemonic relates to something healthcare professionals are already familiar with, they are more likely to remember it.
5. *Use Rhymes or Alliteration*: *Beta-blockers block the beat faster.* Rhyming and alliteration can

make the mnemonic catchy and more memorable.

6. *Incorporate Humor*: Mnemonics that make people smile or laugh are often more memorable. However, be cautious about being respectful and not making light of serious issues.
7. *Visual Mnemonics*: Creating a memorable image or associating the drug with a strong visual can help recall. Visual aids can be particularly effective when used in combination with verbal mnemonics.
8. *Engage the Senses*: If you can engage more than one sense (visual, auditory, kinesthetic), the mnemonic becomes more effective.
9. *Test Your Mnemonic*: Before finalizing a mnemonic, test it among a small group. If they find it easy to remember and useful, it is likely that a broader audience will as well.
10. *Repetition is Key*: Repetition enhances memory. Repeat the mnemonic in various marketing materials, presentations, and communications.
11. *Stay Ethical and Accurate*: Always ensure that your mnemonics are accurate and not misleading. They should align with regulatory guidelines and not oversimplify to the point of being incorrect.
12. *Customize for the Audience*: Consider the primary audience for the mnemonic. A pharmacist's mnemonic might differ from one for a nurse or physician.
13. *Incorporate Feedback*: If healthcare professionals provide feedback about a mnemonic, consider it. If they find it confusing or misleading, it is essential to revisit and revise.
14. *Evolve with Time*: As new information or guidelines come up, updating or changing mnemonics may be necessary. Stay flexible and ready to evolve.

By focusing on the target audience's needs and ensuring accuracy and creativity, you can create effective mnemonics in pharma marketing that aid memory and improve understanding.

Mobile Apps

A mobile app in pharmaceutical marketing refers to a software application specifically designed for use on mobile devices such as smartphones and tablets. It is a digital platform for pharmaceutical companies to engage with healthcare professionals, patients, and other stakeholders, providing valuable information, resources, and services related to healthcare and pharmaceutical products. Here are some key aspects and potential functionalities of a mobile app in pharmaceutical marketing:

1. *Product Information*: The app can offer comprehensive and up-to-date information about pharmaceutical products, including indications, dosages, contraindications, side effects, and safety profiles. It can serve as a convenient reference tool for healthcare professionals and patients.
2. *Disease Education*: The app can provide educational content about specific diseases, symptoms, diagnoses, and treatment options. It can help raise awareness, improve health literacy, and support disease management.
3. *Patient Support*: A mobile app can offer patient support resources, such as medication reminders, adherence trackers, symptom diaries, and lifestyle tips. It can enhance patient engagement, self-care, and treatment compliance.
4. *Continuing Medical Education (CME)*: Pharmaceutical companies can develop CME modules within the app to provide healthcare professionals with educational content and activities, contributing to their professional development and knowledge enhancement.
5. *Adverse Event Reporting*: The app can include a feature that allows healthcare professionals and patients to report adverse events associated with using pharmaceutical products. This facilitates pharmacovigilance and ensures prompt reporting and monitoring of safety concerns.
6. *Product Ordering and Samples*: Some apps may enable healthcare professionals to place product orders directly or request samples, streamlining the ordering process and enhancing convenience.
7. *Health Tracking*: A mobile app can integrate with wearable devices or utilize smartphone sensors to track health-related data, such as fitness activities, sleep patterns, or vital signs. This data can be used to provide personalized recommendations and insights.
8. *Patient Engagement and Communication*: The app can facilitate two-way communication between pharmaceutical companies, healthcare professionals, and patients. It can include messaging features, appointment scheduling, or telehealth capabilities for remote consultations.

Pharmaceutical companies must ensure compliance with applicable regulations, such as data privacy, GDPR (General Data Protection Regulation), and pharmaceutical advertising and promotion guidelines when developing and promoting medical apps in pharmaceutical marketing.

Mobile Marketing

Mobile marketing in the pharmaceutical industry refers to mobile devices, such as smartphones and tablets, as a platform to promote pharmaceutical products for engaging with healthcare professionals and patients and deliver relevant healthcare information. It leverages the widespread use of mobile devices and the accessibility they provide to reach target audiences effectively. Here are some key aspects and strategies of mobile marketing in the pharmaceutical industry:

1. *Mobile Optimized Websites*: Pharmaceutical companies create responsive and optimized websites for mobile devices. These websites provide information about their products, services, and resources in a mobile-friendly format, ensuring a seamless user experience for healthcare professionals and patients.
2. *Mobile Apps*: Developing mobile applications tailored for healthcare professionals and patients allows pharmaceutical companies to deliver specific functionalities, such as product information, disease education, patient support, CME modules, etc. Mobile apps offer users a personalized and interactive experience, enhancing engagement and convenience.
3. *SMS and Push Notifications*: Pharmaceutical companies utilize SMS (Short Messaging Services) and push notifications to deliver timely and relevant information to healthcare professionals and patients. These notifications can include updates on new product launches, medical conferences, educational resources, and patient support programs.
4. *Targeted Advertising*: Mobile advertising platforms enable pharmaceutical companies to target specific audiences based on demographics, location, interests, and behavior. This allows for more precise targeting and delivery of personalized messages to the right individuals, maximizing the impact of marketing efforts.
5. *Mobile Video and Multimedia Content*: Mobile devices are ideal for delivering engaging and interactive content, such as videos, animations, and infographics. Pharmaceutical companies can create educational and promotional content optimized for mobile devices to educate healthcare professionals and patients about their products, disease management, treatment options, and more.
6. *Mobile Surveys and Feedback*: Mobile devices provide a convenient platform for conducting surveys, gathering feedback, and collecting real-time data from healthcare professionals and patients. This data can be valuable for market research, product development, and improving customer experiences.
7. *Location-Based Services*: Mobile marketing can leverage location-based services to provide location-specific information, such as nearby pharmacies, healthcare facilities, clinical trials, or events. This can be particularly useful for patients seeking immediate medical assistance or healthcare professionals seeking local resources.

Pharmaceutical companies should ensure compliance with regulatory guidelines, such as those related to pharmaceutical advertising and data privacy when implementing mobile marketing strategies. Respecting user privacy and obtaining proper data collection and communication consent is essential.

Modern Marketing Principles

Modern marketing principles encompass a set of guiding principles that reflect the evolving landscape of marketing in the digital age. These principles emphasize customer-centricity, data-driven decision-making, and the use of digital technologies to engage with target audiences effectively. While the specific principles may vary depending on the industry and context, here are some commonly recognized modern marketing principles:

1. *Customer-Centricity*: Putting the customer at the center of marketing strategies and activities is paramount. Understanding customer needs, preferences, and behaviors to deliver personalized experiences and build lasting relationships is vital for achieving customer-centricity.
2. *Data-Driven Insights*: Utilize data analytics, market research, and consumer insights to inform marketing decisions. Leverage data to understand customer behavior, optimize campaigns, and drive continuous improvement.
3. *Personalization*: Deliver tailored and relevant customer experiences based on their preferences, behaviors, and demographics. Utilizing data and technology to create personalized messaging, content, and offers drive personalization,
4. *Multichannel Marketing* is about engaging customers through multiple online and offline channels to meet them at different touch points in their buyer's journey. Creating integrated and

cohesive experiences across various platforms and devices is crucial for multichannel marketing success.

5. *Content Marketing*: Create valuable and engaging content to attract, educate, and engage target audiences. Provide relevant information, solve problems, and build trust to establish thought leadership and drive customer loyalty.
6. *Digital Transformation*: Harness digital technologies and platforms to reach and engage customers effectively. Embrace automation, artificial intelligence (AI), social media, mobile marketing, and other digital tools to enhance marketing efforts.
7. *Relationship Building*: Foster long-term customer relationships through personalized communication, exceptional customer service, and ongoing engagement. Build trust, loyalty, and advocacy by consistently delivering value and addressing customer needs.
8. *Agile and Iterative Approach*: Embracing an iterative and adaptable mindset to continuously test, measure, and refine marketing strategies. Embrace agile methodologies to respond quickly to changing market dynamics and customer feedback.
9. *Social Responsibility and Sustainability*: It is about Aligning with ethical values, addressing societal issues, and demonstrating a commitment to corporate social responsibility.
10. *Collaboration and Partnerships*: Collaborate with strategic partners, influencers, and complementary brands to extend reach, leverage expertise, and create mutually beneficial marketing initiatives.

These modern marketing principles reflect the shift towards customer empowerment, digital transformation, and the use of data and technology to drive marketing strategies. By adopting these principles, businesses can adapt to the changing marketing landscape and effectively connect with their target audiences in a meaningful and impactful way.

Modern Marketing Principles in the Pharmaceutical Industry

Modern marketing principles in the pharmaceutical industry reflect the evolving landscape of digital technologies, changing consumer behavior, and the increasing importance of patient-centricity. Here are some key principles that characterize modern marketing in pharma:

1. *Patient-Centric Approach*: Modern marketing in pharma emphasizes placing the patient at the center of all strategies and activities. It involves understanding patient needs, preferences, and experiences to develop personalized communication and support programs. Patient engagement, education, and empowerment are prioritized to improve health outcomes and enhance patient satisfaction.
2. *Multichannel Marketing*: Modern pharma marketing recognizes the importance of reaching audiences through multiple channels. It utilizes a combination of traditional and digital channels, such as websites, mobile apps, social media, email marketing, content marketing, and search engine optimization (SEO), to engage with healthcare professionals, patients, and other stakeholders. Integrated multichannel campaigns ensure consistent messaging across platforms and enhance customer experiences.
3. *Data-Driven Insights*: With abundant data, modern pharma marketing can leverage data analytics and insights to make informed decisions and optimize marketing strategies. Data-driven approaches enable targeted segmentation, personalization, and measurement of marketing efforts. Pharmaceutical companies can leverage real-time data to understand customer behavior, track campaign performance, and adapt strategies for better results.
4. *Digital Engagement and Education*: Modern marketing in pharma recognizes the value of digital technologies in engaging healthcare professionals and patients. It utilizes digital platforms, such as websites, mobile apps, webinars, podcasts, and virtual conferences, to provide educational resources, scientific information, and continuing medical education (CME) opportunities. Interactive and engaging content is developed to enhance learning experiences and drive engagement.
5. *Influencer Marketing*: Influencer marketing has gained prominence in pharma marketing as trusted opinion leaders play a vital role in shaping perceptions and influencing decisions. Collaborating with healthcare professionals, patient advocates, and key opinion leaders (KOLs) helps pharmaceutical companies establish credibility, expand reach, and foster trust among target audiences.
6. *Ethical and Transparent Communication*: Modern pharma marketing strongly emphasizes ethical practices and transparent communication. Pharmaceutical companies adhere to marketing materials regulations and guidelines and provide accurate, balanced, evidence-based information about products, benefits, risks, and appropriate uses. Clear

disclosures and transparency in relationships with healthcare professionals and influencers are maintained to build trust and credibility.

7. *Real-Time Customer Engagement*: Modern marketing leverages technology for real-time customer engagement and support. Chatbots, live data features, and social media monitoring allow prompt responses to customer inquiries, concerns, and feedback. This fosters a customer-centric approach, enhances customer satisfaction, and strengthens relationships with healthcare professionals, patients, and other stakeholders.

These modern marketing principles reflect the industry's shift towards a more patient-focused, data-driven, and digitally enabled approach. By embracing these principles, pharmaceutical companies can effectively navigate the evolving marketing landscape and meet their target audience's changing needs and expectations.

Modular Content

Modular content is a strategy used in pharmaceutical marketing to create content that can be easily adapted and repurposed for various channels and formats. The idea is to create a modular set of content components that can be combined and customized to create multiple pieces of content that are tailored to the needs of specific channels or audiences. Here are some aspects of modular content in pharma marketing to consider:

1. *Efficiency*: Modular content can save time and resources by allowing marketers to create a set of reusable content components that can be quickly assembled into new pieces of content for different channels and formats.
2. *Customization*: Modular content allows marketers to create content tailored to the needs of specific channels or audiences. Mixing and matching different content components allows marketers to create more engaging and relevant content for their target audience.
3. *Consistency*: Modular content can help ensure consistency across different channels and formats. Marketers can use the same content components to ensure the messaging and branding are consistent across all channels.
4. *Compliance*: Modular content can help ensure compliance with regulatory guidelines by creating pre-approved content components that can be assembled into new pieces of content while maintaining compliance.
5. *Analytics*: Modular content can provide valuable analytics and insights by tracking the performance of individual content components and measuring how they perform in different channels and formats.

Modular content can be an effective strategy in pharmaceutical marketing to create efficient, customizable, and compliant content that is tailored to the needs of specific channels and audiences. By creating a modular set of content components, pharma marketers can save time and resources while ensuring consistency and compliance across different channels and formats.

Modular Content in Pharma: Some Examples

Here are some examples of modular content in pharmaceutical marketing:

1. *Pfizer*: Pfizer created a modular content library for their breast cancer drug, Ibrance. The library included pre-approved content components, such as images, videos, and text, that could easily be customized and assembled into new pieces of content for different channels and formats.
2. *Novartis*: Novartis created a modular content toolkit for their migraine drug, Aimovig. The toolkit included pre-approved content components, such as videos, social media posts, and website content, that could easily be customized and assembled into new content for different channels and audiences.
3. *Merck*: Merck created a modular content platform called *Better Nights Better Days* to promote their sleep disorder drug, Belsomra. The platform included pre-approved content components, such as articles, videos, and social media posts, that could be customized and shared by patients, caregivers, and healthcare providers.
4. *Sanofi*: Sanofi created a modular content platform called *GoInsulin* to support people with diabetes. The platform included pre-approved content components, such as videos, articles, and social media posts, that could be customized and shared by patients, caregivers, and healthcare providers.

These examples show pharmaceutical companies are using modular content to create efficient, customizable, and compliant content that is tailored to the needs of specific channels and audiences. By creating a set of pre-approved content components that can easily be customized and assembled into new pieces of content, pharma marketers can save time and resources while ensuring consistency and compliance across different channels and formats.

Moments of Truth

Moments of truth in marketing refer to critical touch points or interactions between a customer and a brand that significantly influence the customer's perception and experience. These moments can potentially share customer satisfaction, loyalty, and advocacy. The concept was popularized by Jan Carlzon, the former CEO of Scandinavian Airlines, who emphasized the importance of these interactions in delivering exceptional customer experiences. Here are three key moments of truth in marketing:

1. *Pre-Purchase Moment of Truth* occurs when a potential customer becomes aware of a brand or product and begins considering a purchase. It includes interactions such as online research, reading reviews, seeking recommendations, and comparing options. The quality of a brand's website, the effectiveness of marketing messages, and the availability of relevant information can greatly influence a customer's decision to purchase.
2. *A Purchase Moment of Truth* occurs when a customer decides and completes the transaction. It involves the entire buying process, including interactions with sales representatives, ease of purchase, payment options, and overall customer service. A positive experience with the product, including its performance, creates reliability and overall satisfaction, while a negative experience can result in lost sales and damage the brand's reputation.
3. *Post-Purchase Moment of Truth* occurs after customers purchase and use the product or service. It encompasses the customer's experience with the product, including its performance, reliability, and overall satisfaction. Positive post-purchase experiences can lead to customer loyalty, repeat purchases, and positive word-of-mouth referrals. On the other hand, if the product does not meet the expectations of the customer or the customer encounters issues, it can result in dissatisfaction, negative reviews, and potential loss of future business.

Marketers must understand and optimize these moments of truth to create positive and memorable customer experiences. By delivering exceptional experiences at these critical touchpoints, brands can build customer loyalty, enhance brand reputation, and drive long-term success.

Moments of Truth in Pharma Marketing

In pharmaceutical marketing, moments of truth refer to critical touchpoints or interactions between healthcare professionals, patients, and pharmaceutical brands that significantly impact their perception, engagement, and decision-making. Here are three key moments of truth in pharma marketing:

1. *Healthcare Professional-Patient Interaction:* The interaction between healthcare professionals (HCPs) and patients is a crucial moment of truth in pharma marketing. It can occur during clinical consultations, patient education sessions, or interactions at healthcare events. Effective communication, provision of accurate and relevant information, and empathetic support during these interactions can greatly influence patient adherence, satisfaction, and overall treatment outcomes.
2. *Access to Information and Resources*: This moment of truth involves the availability and accessibility of information and resources provided by pharmaceutical companies to HCPs and patients. This includes digital platforms, medical websites, mobile apps, face-to-face or virtual detailing sessions with pharmaceutical sales representatives, educational materials, and scientific publications. Offering comprehensive and up-to-date resources, including clinical trial data, safety profiles, and educational content, contributes to building trust, enhancing knowledge, and supporting informed decision-making.
3. *Adverse Event Reporting and Pharmacovigilance*: Adverse event reporting and pharmacovigilance is a critical moment of truth in pharma marketing. Prompt and effective communication channels for reporting adverse events associated with pharmaceutical products ensure patient safety, compliance with regulations, and brand trustworthiness. Streamlining the reporting process and providing clear guidelines to HCPs and patients helps identify potential safety concerns and take appropriate actions.

Pharmaceutical companies should prioritize these moments of truth to ensure that their interactions, resources, and processes align with ethical guidelines and regulations. By delivering valuable information, fostering strong relationships, and prioritizing patient safety and satisfaction, pharmaceutical companies can establish credibility, build trust, and drive positive outcomes in their marketing efforts.

Monitoring

Monitoring is crucial in pharma marketing to ensure compliance, assess campaign effectiveness, and gather insights for strategic decision-making. Here are some important aspects of monitoring in pharma marketing:

1. *Regulatory Compliance*: The pharmaceutical industry is highly regulated, and marketers must adhere to guidelines set by regulatory authorities such as the Food and Drug Administration (FDA) in the United States or the European Medicines Agency (EMA) in the European Union. Monitoring ensures that marketing activities, including advertising materials, websites, and promotional campaigns, comply with these regulations, avoiding misleading or inaccurate claims about pharmaceutical products.
2. *Adverse Event Monitoring*: Monitoring systems are essential for tracking and reporting adverse events associated with pharmaceutical products. Adverse event monitoring involves collecting and analyzing data on any harmful or unintended effects experienced by patients using specific medications. This information helps pharmaceutical companies promptly identify and address safety concerns, ensuring patient safety and regulatory compliance.
3. *Social Media and Online Monitoring*: Monitoring social media platforms, online forums, and review websites is crucial for pharmaceutical companies to track public sentiment, identify emerging trends, and address customer concerns. Monitoring online conversations helps marketers gain insights into the perception of their brands, products, and services, enabling them to respond proactively and engage with customers effectively.
4. *Key Performance Indicators (KPIs)*: Monitoring KPIs allows pharma marketers to assess the effectiveness of their marketing campaigns. Common KPIs include website traffic, click-through rates, conversion rates, engagement metrics (likes, shares, comments), lead generation, and sales figures. Regular monitoring of these metrics helps identify areas of improvement, optimize marketing strategies, and make data-driven decisions.
5. *Competitive Monitoring*: Keeping an eye on competitors' marketing activities is crucial for staying informed about industry trends, benchmarking performance, and identifying opportunities. Monitoring competitor campaigns, messaging, product launches, and promotional strategies can provide valuable insights for refining your marketing approach and maintaining a competitive edge.
6. *Market Research and Customer Insights*: Monitoring involves conducting market research and gathering customer insights to understand their preferences, behaviors, and needs. Surveys, focus groups, and interviews help gather valuable data for marketing strategies, product development, and customer targeting.

It is important to note that monitoring should always be conducted in compliance with data protection and privacy regulations. Patient privacy and confidentiality should be respected, and data should be handled securely throughout the monitoring process.

Moore's Law

Moore's law is an observation and prediction made by Gordon Moore, one of the co-founders of Intel Corporation, in 1965. It states that the number of transistors on a microchip doubles approximately every two years while technology costs decrease. In other words, Moore's law suggests that the computing power of microchips tends to double every couple of years, leading to advancements in performance, speed, and capabilities.

Moore's Law has been a guiding principle in the semiconductor industry and has played a significant role in the rapid advancement of technology. It has fueled the development of more powerful and efficient computers, mobile devices, and electronic devices.

While Moore's Law has been held for several decades, there has been debate about its long-term sustainability as transistors approach physical limits, and challenges arise regarding power consumption and heat dissipation. Nonetheless, Moore's Law serves as a reference point for the industry and a catalyst for innovation and research in microchip technology.

Its Relevance to Pharma Marketing

Moore's law, specifically related to doubling transistors on microchips, is not directly applicable to pharma marketing. However, technological advancement and innovation principles can indirectly impact pharmaceutical marketing. The continuous evolution of technology, including computing power, data analytics, artificial intelligence (AI), and digital platforms, transformed marketing strategies in various industries, including pharmaceuticals.

Pharma marketing can leverage technological advancements to enhance customer engagement, personalize messaging, optimize data analytics, and deliver targeted marketing campaigns. The increased computing power enables more complex data analysis, facilitating a better understanding of customer behavior, preferences, and market trends.

Moreover, the rise of digital platforms, mobile apps, telemedicine, and wearable devices has expanded opportunities for pharma companies to engage with healthcare professionals and patients. These advancements enable remote communication, personalized healthcare experiences, and the delivery of educational resources.

While Moore's Law itself may not directly apply to pharma marketing, the underlying principles of technological progress and innovation can significantly influence the strategies, tools, and approaches used in the industry. Staying updated with the latest technologies and leveraging them effectively can be instrumental in driving successful marketing initiatives in the pharmaceutical industry.

Motivation

Motivation in pharmaceutical marketing is critical to drive sales and promote pharmaceutical products effectively. Motivated marketing teams can overcome the industry's unique challenges, including regulatory constraints, ethical considerations, and competition. Here are some ways to foster motivation in pharma marketing:

1. *Clear and Ethical Purpose*: Communicate the ethical and social importance of the marketed pharmaceutical products. Emphasize how they can improve patient health and well-being. A sense of purpose can be a strong motivator.
2. *Training and Education*: Invest in ongoing training and education for marketing teams. Keeping them updated on scientific advancements, product knowledge, and regulatory changes can boost confidence and motivation.
3. *Recognition and Rewards*: Implement performance-based incentive programs and recognition schemes. Recognizing and rewarding achievements can motivate sales representatives and marketing professionals.
4. *Goal Setting*: Establish clear, achievable, and measurable goals for marketing teams. Individuals are motivated to perform when they have a sense of purpose and achieve targets.
5. *Personal Development*: Encourage and support personal and professional development for team members. This could include offering opportunities for skill-building, career advancement, and leadership training.
6. *Feedback and Communication*: Regularly provide feedback on performance and recognize accomplishments. Open lines of communication allow employees to share their ideas and concerns, fostering a sense of involvement.
7. *Team Collaboration*: Encourage collaboration and teamwork. In the pharmaceutical sector, cross-functional collaboration is often essential to success.
8. *Adaptability*: Equip teams with the flexibility to adapt to changes in the industry, such as shifts in regulatory requirements, market dynamics, and emerging technologies.
9. *Ethical Leadership*: Ensure that leaders within the organization set a positive example of ethical conduct. Ethical leadership fosters trust and a sense of moral purpose among team members.
10. *Autonomy*: Allow team members a degree of autonomy in decision-making. Autonomy can motivate employees to take ownership of their responsibilities.
11. *Performance Metrics*: Esbalish clear and relevant performance metrics that enable employees to see the impact of their work. This provides a sense of accomplishment and motivation to improve.
12. *Professional Growth Opportunities*: Offer opportunities for career advancement and growth within the company. Knowing that they can progress in their careers can be a strong motivator for marketing professionals.
13. *Wellness Initiatives*: Promote work-life balance and wellness programs to support employees' physical and mental health. A healthy and happy workforce is more motivated and productive.
14. *Innovative Marketing Tools*: Provide marketing teams with innovative tools and technology to streamline their efforts and enhance productivity.
15. *Market Feedback*: Encourage marketing professionals to gather feedback from healthcare professionals and patients. Positive feedback can be a powerful motivator.

Motivation in pharmaceutical marketing goes beyond financial incentives. It involves aligning the team's values and goals with the ethical and social mission of improving health and delivering valuable pharmaceutical products. Creating a supportive, ethical, and growth-oriented work environment is essential for maintaining high motivation in this industry.

Multichannel Marketing

Multichannel marketing in pharma refers to the use of multiple channels, both online and offline, to promote pharmaceutical products and engage with healthcare professionals (HCPs) and patients. Multichannel marketing aims to reach HCPs and patients most likely to consume information and provide them with relevant and personalized content across multiple touchpoints. Here are some key elements of multichannel marketing in pharma:

1. *Diverse Channels*: Multichannel marketing involves using a variety of channels, including email, social media, search engines, mobile apps, and other digital channels, as well as traditional channels such as print and face-to-face meetings. This allows pharma companies to reach a broader audience and engage with HCPs and patients in the most relevant and effective way.
2. *Personalization*: Multichannel marketing involves delivering personalized content and messages tailored to the specific needs and preferences of individual HCPs and patients. This can include customized messaging based on their specialty, patient population, past behavior, and personalized content such as educational materials or clinical data.
3. *Integration*: Multichannel marketing requires the integration of different channels and touchpoints to deliver a seamless and consistent experience for HCPs and patients. This involves ensuring that messaging and content are consistent across different channels and that data is integrated and shared across different touchpoints.
4. *Customer-Centric Approach*: Multichannel marketing focuses on understanding customer behavior, preferences, and needs. By gathering insights into customer preferences and behavior across different channels, marketers can tailor their messages and offerings to specific customer segments. This customer-centric approach enhances engagement and improves the overall customer experience.
5. *Analytics and Optimization*: Multichannel marketing ensures ongoing measurement and optimization to ensure that messaging and content resonate with HCPs and patients and that the channels effectively reach and engage with them. This involves analyzing engagement and behavior data and using this data to optimize messaging, content, and channel mix.
6. *Compliance*: Multichannel marketing must comply with all relevant laws and regulations governing the promotion of pharmaceutical products. This includes ensuring that messaging and content are accurate, not misleading, and consistent with approved labeling.
7. *Testing and Optimization*: Multichannel marketing allows marketers to test and optimize different channels and messaging to find the most effective combination for reaching their target audience. A/B testing, analyzing engagement metrics, and gathering customer feedback refine strategies and improve campaign performance over time.

Multichannel marketing in pharma is an effective strategy for reaching HCPs and patients in a personalized, relevant, and engaging way. By leveraging multiple channels and touchpoints and using data-driven insights to deliver personalized content and messages, pharma companies can build stronger relationships with HCPs and patients and drive better outcomes for both.

Multichannel Marketing in Pharma

Multichannel marketing in the pharmaceutical industry involves various communication channels to engage healthcare practitioners (HCPs), patients, and other stakeholders. Here are some examples of how multichannel marketing is applied in pharma:

1. *Digital Advertising*: Pharmaceutical companies utilize digital advertising channels such as search engine advertising, display ads, and social media advertising to raise awareness about their products and reach their target audience. These channels allow for precise targeting based on demographic segmentation and online behavior.
2. *Websites and Online Portals*: Pharmaceutical companies develop dedicated websites and online portals to provide information about their products, disease states, treatment options, and patient support programs. These platforms serve as valuable resources for HCPs and patients seeking medical information and facilitate engagement through interactive content, educational materials, and user forums.
3. *Email Marketing*: Email marketing is a widely used channel in pharma marketing to communicate with HCPs and patients. Pharmaceutical companies send targeted emails to provide updates on new research, product information, medical conferences, and educational opportunities. Personalization and segmentation are employed to ensure relevant content delivery.
4. *Mobile Applications*: Mobile apps play a significant role in pharma multichannel marketing. Pharma companies develop apps to provide medication reminders, track health

parameters, offer patient support resources, and facilitate communication between patients and healthcare professionals. These apps enhance patient engagement and adherence to treatment plans.

5. *Social Media Engagement*: Pharmaceutical companies engage with HCPs, patients, and advocacy groups through social media platforms like Twitter, LinkedIn, and Facebook. They share educational content, research updates, and disease awareness campaigns and engage in discussions to build relationships and increase brand visibility.
6. *Virtual Events and Webinars*: Pharma companies organize virtual events and webinars to educate HCPs and patients on therapeutic areas, treatment guidelines, and new product launches. These interactive sessions allow real-time engagement, question-and-answer sessions, and networking opportunities.
7. *Point-of-Care Tools*: Pharma companies develop point-of-care tools such as mobile apps or digital platforms that provide HCPs with immediate access to clinical guidelines, drug interaction checkers, dosing calculators, and treatment decision support. These tools help HCPs make informed treatment decisions and enhance patient care.
8. *Direct Mail and Print Media*: While digital channels dominate pharma marketing, direct mail, and print media are still utilized. Direct mail can send targeted educational materials, samples, or patient support resources to HCPs and patients. Print media, such as medical journals and magazines, are used to publish scientific research, clinical studies, and product advertisements.
9. *Virtual Key Opinion Leader (KOL) Engagements*: Pharma companies leverage video conferencing, webinars, and virtual platforms to engage with KOLs and expert physicians. These interactions enable companies to seek expert insights, share research findings, and gather feedback on their products or marketing strategies.

These are just a few examples of how multichannel marketing is applied in the pharmaceutical industry. The key is strategically integrating these channels, tailoring messages to specific audiences, and leveraging data and analytics to measure effectiveness and optimize marketing efforts.

Multidimensional Scaling

Multidimensional scaling (MDS) is a statistical technique to visualize and analyze the similarities or dissimilarities between objects or observations. It is primarily used in market research, psychology, and other fields where it is important to understand and present complex relationships between items or entities.

The goal of multidimensional scaling is to create a visual representation of the data in a lower-dimensional space (typically two or three dimensions) while preserving the relative distances or dissimilarities between the objectives as accurately as possible. In other words, MDS transforms high-dimensional data into a simplified visual form that can be easily interpreted.

The MDS Process

The process of multidimensional scaling involves the following steps:

1. *Distance Measurement*: A similarity or dissimilarity measure is computed for each pair of objects in the dataset. This could be based on metrics such as Euclidean distance, correlation, or rank order.
2. *Configuration*: MDS aims to find a configuration of points in a lower-dimensional space that best represents the distances between the objects. Initially, the points are randomly placed in the space.
3. *Iterative Optimization*: The positions of the points are adjusted iteratively to minimize the discrepancies between the distances in the lower-dimensional space and the original dissimilarity matrix. Different optimization algorithms can be used, such as gradient descent or stress minimization.
4. *Visualization*: Once the optimization process converges, the final configuration of points is plotted in a lower-dimensional space (scatter plot). The relative positions of the points reflect the underlying similarities or dissimilarities between the objects.

The resulting visual representation from MDS provides insights into the relationships and structures within the dataset. Objects close together in the plot are considered more similar or related, while far-apart objects are considered more dissimilar. The plot can help identify clusters or groups of similar items, uncover patterns, and aid decision-making.

Multidimensional scaling can be applied to various domains, such as customer segmentation, brand positioning, product similarity analysis, and preference mapping. By reducing the complexity of high-dimensional data into a more interpretable form, MDS allows researchers and analysts to gain valuable insights into the relationships and structure of the data.

MDS in Pharma Marketing

Multidimensional scaling (MDS) can be applied in pharmaceutical marketing to understand and analyze various market aspects, customer perceptions, and product positioning. Here are a few applications of MDS in pharma marketing:

1. *Perceptual Mapping*: MDS can create perceptual maps that visualize the positioning of pharmaceutical products or brands in customers' minds. By measuring and analyzing customer perceptions of various attributes or characteristics of products, MDS can help identify how products are perceived relative to each other. This information can inform marketing strategies, product differentiation, and competitive positioning.
2. *Patient Segmentation*: MDS can aid in patient segmentation by analyzing and visualizing the similarities and differences among patient groups based on their attitudes, behaviors, or preferences. By clustering patients into segments using MDS, pharmaceutical companies can gain insights into distinct patient groups and tailor their marketing messages and strategies accordingly.
3. *Preference Mapping*: MDS can be used to understand and map patient preferences for different product features or attributes. By collecting data on patient preferences and using MDS to analyze the data, pharmaceutical companies can identify which attributes are most important to patients and how different products or formulations are perceived in terms of these attributes. This information can guide product development, marketing messaging, and targeting strategies.
4. *Brand Image and Perception*: MDS can help evaluate and visualize the perception and image of pharmaceutical brands in the market. By measuring customer perceptions and analyzing them with MDS, companies can identify the unique positioning of their brand relative to competitors. This information can be used to refine brand messaging, enhance brand positioning, and develop targeted marketing campaigns.
5. *Market Segmentation*: MDS can assist in market segmentation by analyzing the similarities and differences between market segments based on various variables, such as demographics, behavior patterns, or treatment preferences. MDS can help identify distinct market segments and understand the underlying factors that drive customer preferences and decision-making.

Multidimensional scaling can provide valuable insights into the complex relationships and structures within the pharmaceutical market. By visualizing and analyzing data in a simplified and interpretable form, MDS can support strategic decision-making, target marketing efforts, and enhance understanding of customer perceptions and preferences in pharma marketing.

How to Do It

Performing multidimensional scaling (MDS) involves several steps. Here is a general overview of the process:

1. *Define the Objective*: Clearly define the objective of your MDS analysis. Determine what you want to achieve or understand, such as brand positioning, customer segmentation, or preference mapping.
2. *Data collection*: Collect the data you need for your analysis. This could involve surveying customers or gathering data on customer perceptions, preferences, or product attributes. Ensure that your data is appropriate for conducting MDS, typically in a dissimilarity or similarity matrix.
3. *Select MDS Method*: Choose the appropriate MDS method based on your data and objective. Commonly used MDS techniques include classical MDS, non-metric MDS, or correspondence analysis. Each method has assumptions and requirements, so select the best method with your data and analysis goals.
4. *Distance Measurement*: Calculate the dissimilarity or similarity measure between the objects in your dataset. This measure quantifies the relationships between the objects based on the attributes or variables you are considering. Different distance measures, such as Euclidean distance, correlation, or rank order, can be used.
5. *Configuration*: Initialize the configuration of points in the MDS space. This involves placing the points randomly or using an existing configuration if available. The number of dimensions in the MDS space is typically two or three, allowing easy visualization.
6. *Iterative Optimization*: Optimize the configuration of points to minimize the discrepancies between the distances in the MDS space and the original dissimilarity matrix. This optimization process typically involves iterations

of adjusting the positions of points to improve the fit.

7. *Visualization*: Plot the final configuration of points in the lower-dimensional space. This visualization could be a scatter plot or other suitable representation. The distances between points reflect the dissimilarities or similarities between the objects. Consider using different colors or symbols to represent different groups or categories within the data.
8. *Interpretation and Analysis*: Interpret the MDS plot and analyze the results. Look for patterns, clusters, or trends in the data. Analyze the positioning of objects about each other and interpret their meaning within the context of your objective. This analysis can provide insights into market segments, brand positioning, or customer preferences.
9. *Validation and Iteration*: Validate your MDS results by comparing them to your original objective and considering additional analyses or statistical tests. Iterate and refine your analysis to improve the interpretation or address any limitations if necessary.

It is important to note that performing MDS can be complex and requires a solid understanding of statistical analysis techniques. Consider seeking assistance from a qualified researcher or statistician if you are new to MDS or your analysis requires advanced methodologies.

Many Methods

Multidimensional scaling (MDS) encompasses several methods that can be used to analyze and visualize data in a lower-dimensional space. Here are some commonly used MDS methods:

1. *Classical MDS*: Classical MDS, or metric MDS, is the most straightforward and widely used method. It seeks to find a configuration of points in the MDS space that best reproduces the pairwise dissimilarities or similarities between objects. Classical MDS assumes that the dissimilarities/similarities are metric, meaning that the distances between points in the MDS space correspond to the dissimilarities/similarities in the original data.
2. *Non-Metric MDS*: Non-metric MDS is used when the dissimilarities /similarities between objects are only ordinal or rank-ordered, meaning that the exact distance between points is not meaningful. This method aims to find a configuration of points that preserves the rank order of the dissimilarities/similarities. Non-metric MDS is often employed when the exact measurement of distances is not feasible or reliable.
3. *Procrustes Analysis*: Procrustes analysis is a technique used to compare two or more MDS configurations. It aligns and superimposes the configurations to evaluate their similarity. This method is useful when comparing results from different analyses or assessing the stability of the MDS solution.
4. *Correspondence Analysis*: While not strictly MDS, correspondence analysis is a related technique for analyzing categorical or frequency data. It can visualize relationships between categories or variables in lower-dimensional space. Correspondence analysis is often employed when dealing with contingency tables or analytical data with categorical variables.
5. *Individual Differences Scaling*: Individual differences scaling, also known as INDSCAL or Asymmetric MDS, is used when individual differences are considered in the analysis. It aims to identify subgroups or individual variations in the data. This method is suitable when there are variations in how individuals perceive or evaluate the objects in the analysis.
6. *Generalized Procrustes Analysis (GPA)*: Generalized Procrustes Analysis is a technique used to combine multiple MDS configurations into a single consensus configuration. It aligns the configurations by minimizing their differences and generates a representative solution. GPA is used when integrating data from multiple sources or when multiple analysts provide separate MDS solutions.

These are some of the commonly used methods in MDS. The choice of method depends on the nature of the data, the type of dissimilarities/similarities, and the specific objectives of the analysis. It is important to select the appropriate method that aligns with the characteristics and requirements of your data to obtain meaningful results.

Which Method to Choose

When choosing a multidimensional scaling (MDS) method in pharmaceutical marketing, it is important to consider the nature of your data, the measurement scale of your variables, and the specific objective of your analysis. Here are some considerations and examples to help you choose the appropriate MDS method in pharma marketing:

1. *Data Type*: Determine the type of data you have. Classical MDS is a suitable choice if your data consists of metric measurements, such as ratings on a Likert Scale. However, non-metric MDS may be more appropriate if your data only

provides ordinal rankings or categories. For example, you have survey data where healthcare professionals rank different drug attributes on a Likert scale, in which case classical MDS would be suitable for analyzing and visualizing their perceptions and attributes.

2. *The Scale of Measurement*: Consider the scale of measurement of your variables. Classical MDS assumes metric data, meaning that the distances between points in the MDS space correspond to the dissimilarities/similarities in the original data. Non-metric MDS, on the other hand, is used when only the order of the dissimilarities/similarities matters. For instance, if you have data on the preference rankings of pharmaceutical products by patients (1st, 2nd, 3rd, etc.), non-metric MDS can be employed to analyze and visualize the relative rankings of the products.
3. *Research Objective*: Clarify your specific research objective. Different MDS methods may be better suited for different objectives. For example, if you want to compare and align multiple MDS configurations from different sources or analysts, Procrustes analysis or Generalized Procrustes Analysis (GPA) can be employed. For instance, you want to compare the perceptual maps different pharmaceutical market research agencies created. In this case, Procrustes analysis can help align and compare the configurations to identify similarities and differences.
4. *Individual Differences*: Consider whether individual differences or subgroups are important in your analysis. Individual Differences Scaling (INDSCAL) may be appropriate to identify and analyze these subgroup variations if there are variations in how individuals perceive or evaluate the objects. For instance, if you want to investigate how different patient segments perceive the effectiveness of different medications, INDSCAL can help identify subgroups within the data and their distinct perceptions.
5. *Data Structure*: Analyze the structure of your data. If you have categorized or frequency data, such as responses to multiple-choice questions, Correspondence Analysis may be more suitable for visualizing relationships between categories or variables. For instance, you want to analyze the relationship between different symptoms patients report. Correspondence Analysis can be employed to visualize symptom associations and identify potential patterns.

Ultimately, the choice of the MDS method depends on the specific characteristics of your data and the research objective at hand. It is recommended to consult with a statistician or data analysis expert to determine the most appropriate MDS method for your pharmaceutical study.

How Pharma Can Use MDS

While specific examples of pharmaceutical companies utilizing multidimensional scaling (MDS) may be limited to the proprietary nature of their research and data, MDS techniques have been widely employed in the pharmaceutical industry for various applications. Here are some general examples of how pharma companies can apply MDS:

1. *Brand Positioning*: Pharmaceutical companies often use MDS to understand how their brands are positioned relative to competitors in the minds of healthcare professionals, patients, or other target audiences. By collecting data on perceptions of different brands and applying MDS, companies can visualize and analyze the relative positioning of their brand in terms of attributes such as efficacy, safety, convenience, or price.
2. *Product Preference Mapping*: MDS can help pharmaceutical companies identify and map patient preferences for different product attributes. By measuring patient preferences and applying MDS techniques, companies can provide insights into the relative importance of these attributes. This information can guide product development, marketing strategies, and segmentation approaches.
3. *Customer Segmentation*: MDS is valuable for segmenting customer groups based on perceptions, behaviors, or preferences. Pharmaceutical companies can collect data on different customer segments (physicians, patients) and apply MDS to visualize the similarities and differences among these groups. The resulting segmentation can inform targeted marketing strategies and communication efforts.
4. *Product Positioning and Differentiation*: MDS can assist in identifying and visualizing the unique positioning and differentiation of pharmaceutical products. By collecting data on product attributes and applying MDS techniques, companies can understand how their products are perceived compared to competitors. This information can guide marketing messaging, communication strategies, and product positioning efforts.
5. *Adverse Event Analysis*: MDS can be applied to analyze adverse event data reported by patients or healthcare professionals. Pharmaceutical

companies can identify patterns, clusters, or associations among adverse events by measuring the similarities and dissimilarities between adverse events and applying MDS. This information can support pharmacovigilance efforts, risk assessment, and safety monitoring.

It is important to note that while these examples highlight potential applications of MDS in the pharmaceutical industry, the specific methodologies and techniques employed may vary based on the research objectives, data availability, and analysis approach chosen by each company.

Multivariate Analysis

Multivariate Analysis is a statistical technique that involves analyzing multiple variables simultaneously to identify relationships and patterns between them. In pharmaceutical marketing, multivariate analysis can identify factors influencing patient and healthcare provider behavior, which can help companies develop more effective marketing strategies. Here are some examples of how multivariate analysis can be used in pharma marketing:

1. *Market Segmentation*: Multivariate analysis can segment the market based on patient and healthcare provider characteristics, such as demographics, health status, or treatment history. Pharmaceutical companies can develop more targeted marketing strategies by identifying patient and healthcare provider groups and their needs.
2. *Product Positioning*: Multivariate analysis can identify factors that influence the positioning of a pharmaceutical product in the market. For example, by analyzing factors such as patient preferences, product efficacy, and safety, a pharmaceutical company can identify the optimal positioning for its product and develop marketing messages highlighting its strengths.
3. *Sales Forecasting*: Multivariate analysis can be used to forecast sales of a pharmaceutical product based on different factors, such as market size, pricing, and promotion. Using this information, pharmaceutical companies can adjust their marketing strategies to optimize sales and market share.
4. *Ad Targeting*: Multivariate analysis can be used to identify factors that influence the effectiveness of advertising campaigns. By analyzing factors such as patient demographics, advertising messages, and advertising channels, pharmaceutical companies can develop more effective marketing strategies that are more likely to resonate with patients and healthcare providers.
5. *Outcomes Analysis*: Multivariate analysis can identify factors influencing patient otucomes, such as adherence to medication or treatment efficacy. By analyzing these factors, pharmaceutical companies can develop marketing messages and resources more likely to improve patient outcomes.

The multivariate analysis provides a powerful tool for pharmaceutical companies to identify factors influencing patient and healthcare provider behavior and develop more effective marketing strategies. Leveraging multivariate analysis allows pharmaceutical companies to improve patient care and outcomes while optimizing sales and market share.

References

1. Lea Prevel Katsanis, Global Issues in Pharmaceutical Marketing, Routledge, Taylor & Francis Group, New York and London, 2016
2. Sean McDade, PhD, Pharma Customer Experience: 20 Secrets to 10X and Boost Patient Outcomes, Lioncrest Publishing, 2021
3. Key Account Management Excellence in Pharma and Medtech, Edited by Mike Moorman, Routledge, New York and London, 2022
4. Tony Ellery and Neal Hansen, Pharmaceutical Lifecycle Management: Making the Most of Each and Every Brand, John Wiley & Sons, Kindle Edition, 2012
5. Markus Saba, Hilary Gentile, Brand Plan Rx: The Marketers Guide to Building a Thriving Health and Wellness Brand, Kindle Edition, 2022
6. Martin Voet, The Generic Challenge: Understanding Patents, FDA and Pharmaceutical Lifecycle Management, Fifth Edition, Brown Walker Press, Boca Raton, 2016
7. Osman Daggezen, Omnichannel Customer Engagement in Pharma, Independently Published, Kindle Edition
8. Ira J. Haimowitz, PhD, Healthcare Relationship Marketing: Strategy, Design, and Measurement, Gower Publishing Limited, England, 2011
9. Hervé Basset, David Stuart and Denise Silber, From Science 2.0 to Pharma 3.0: Semantic search and social media in the pharmaceutical industry and STM publishing, Chandos Publishing, Oxford, UK, 2012
10. Brain D. Smith, Brand Therapy: 15 Techniques for Creating Brand Strategy in Pharma and Medtech, Pragmedic, 2018
11. Leonard Lerer and Mike Piper, Digital strategies in the pharmaceutical industry, Palgrave Macmillan, New York, 2003
12. Eric Topol, Deep Medicine: How Artificial Intelligence Can Make Healthcare Human Again, Basic Books, Kindle Edition, 2019
13. Kamal Biswas, Pharma's prescription: How the right technology can save the pharmaceutical business, Kindle Edition, Academic Press, 1st edition, October 21, 2013
14. Faisal Ahmed, and Paul Tunnah, Digital Unlocked: A beginner's guide to Digital Pharma, Kindle Edition, PM Society, February 2013, Bloomsbury, USA, January 2018
15. Miles Young, Ogilvy on advertising in the digital age, Bloomsbury, USA, January 2018
16. Daniel Ghinn, Can you feel my pain; Pfizer with European Patient groups, Creation Knowledge, https://creation.co/knowledge/hes-cyfmp-pfizer/
17. Jan Zimmerman, Deborah Ng, Social media marketing All-in-one for dummies, 4th Edition, John Wiley & Sons Inc, NJ, USA, 2017
18. Eric Topol, The Patient Will See You Now: The Future of Medicine is in Your Hands, Basic Books, New York, 2016
19. Harley Manning, Josh Bernoff, Forrester Research, Outside In: The Power of Putting Customers At the Center of Your Business, New Harvest, 2012
20. Sean McDade, Listen or Die: 40 Lessons That Turn Customer Feedback into Gold, LionCrest Publishing, 2018
21. Charlene LI Josh Bernoff, Groundswell: Winning in A World Transformed by Social Technologies, Harvard Business School Press, Boston, MA, USA
22. Letizia Affinito, Empowering the Connected Physician in the E-Patient Era: How Physician's Empowerment on Digital Health Tools Can Improve Patient Empowerment and Boost Health (Care) Outcomes, Routledge, Taylor & Francis Group, New York, 2019
23. Edouard Demeire, KICCASS Pharma: Keep it Customer Centric, Agile & Strategically Simple in Pharma & Diagnostics Management, 2020
24. Jordi Bernal-Figo and Joaquin Bernal-Fuertes, Pharma 2027: Evolve or Disappear, Published by Jordi Bernal-Figo, 2013
25. Paul Hellman, You've Got 00:00:08 Seconds: Communication Secrets for a Distracted World, AMACOM, American Management Association, 2017
26. Philip Kotler, Hermawan Kartajaya, Iwan Setiawan, Marketing 5.0: Technology for Humanity, Wiley, 1st Edition, April 2021
27. Philip Kotler, Waldemar Pfoertsch, Owe Sponholz, H2H Marketing: The Genesis of Human-To-Human Marketing, Springer, 1st Edition, 2021
28. Sean McDade, Pharma Customer Experience: 20 Secrets to 10X Your CX and Boost Patient Outcomes, Lion Crest Publishing, 2021
29. Ernest Hemingway, The Sun Also Rises, Simon & Schuster Classic Edition, 1996
30. Paul Hudson, Pharma needs to stop chasing shiny objects and start embracing practical technology, Fortune, January 7, 2020, https://fortune.com/2020/01/07/pharma-health-tech-digitization-sanofi/

31. Mike DeLone, Vice Chairman, US Life Sciences Leader, Deloitte LLP, The COVID-19 Pandemic Could Forever Change Biopharma, Deloitte Blog: Health Forward, April 7, 2020, https://www2.deloitte.com/us/en/blog/health-care-blog/2020/covid-19-pandemic-could-forever-change-biopharma.html

32. Greg Reh, Jonathan Fox, Christine Chang, Tacking Digital Transformation: How Biopharma Companies Can Realize, the Power of Digital and Prepare for a New Reality, deloitte.com, July 17, 2019, https://www2.deloitte.com/us/en/insights/industry/life-sciences/biopharma-company-of-the-future.html

33. Gaurav Agarwal, Hemant Ahlawat, and Martin Dewhurst, Winning Against COVID-19: The Implications for Biopharma, McKinsey & Company, April 15, 2020, https://www.mckinsey.com/industries/pharmaceuticals-and-medical-products/our-insights/winning-against-covid-19-the-implications-for-biopharma

34. David Bell,The Wharton Business School, Brian Fox, McKinsey&Co, Ryan Olohan, Google, Pharma 3D: Rewriting the Script for Marketing in a Digital Age, http://www.pharma3d.com/#chapter-856435

35. Blue Latitude Strategic Marketing Consultancy, Customer Experience: The Essential Guide for Pharma, http://cdn2.hubspot.net/hub/230479/file-645840154-pdf/Blue_Latitude_Customer_Handbook__March_2014_.pdf?t=1397045610220

36. Mohanbir Sawhney, Northwestern University, Re-imagining Pharma Marketing, December 2016, http://www.mohansawhney.com/wp-content/uploads/2016/12/ReimaginingMarketing_v4.pdf

37. Sarah Armstrong, Dianne Esber, Jason Heller, Björn Timelin, Modern Marketing: What it is, What it isn't and How to Do it, mckinsey.com, March 2, 2020, https://www.mckinsey.com/business-functions/marketing-and-sales/our-insights/modern-marketing-what-it-is-what-it-isnt-and-how-to-do-it

38. Erin Fitzgerald, SERMO, Today's Healthcare Professionals are Leveraging Social Media Conversations for Collaboration, Global Reach, and Real-Time Learning, Health IT Outcomes, November 15, 2018, https://www.healthitoutcomes.com/doc/today-s-healthcare-professionals-are-leveraging-social-media-conversations-for-collaboration-global-reach-and-real-time-learning-0001

39. Suzanne Gamwell, Breaking from Tradition—Social Media at Medical Congresses, PMLive, July 8, 2019, http://www.pmlive.com/pharma_intelligence/Breaking_from_tradition_-_social_media_at_medical_congresses_1292138

40. Life Sciences, How to Reach HCPs on Social Media: Are You Missing Out? March 6, 2020, https://lifesciences.stickyeyes.com/how-to-reach-hcps-on-social-media-are-you-missing-out/

41. Life Sciences, How Pharma Can Harness the Influence of Digital Opinion Leaders, February 17, 2020, https://lifesciences.stickyeyes.com/how-pharma-can-harness-the-influence-of-digital-opinion-leaders/

42. Sarah Morgan, HCPs—They are Just Like Us! InTouch Solutions, August 1, 2017, https://www.intouchsol.com/blog/hcps%E2%80%8B-theyre-just-like-us/

43. Jonathan Catley, Study Shows Patient Influencers Turn to Social Media Over HCPs, MDConnect, May 16, 2019, https://www.mdconnectinc.com/medical-marketing-insights/patient-influencers-turn-to-social-media-over-hcps

44. Alessandro Di Fiore, Kendra West and Andrea Segnalini, Why Science-Driven Companies Should Use Agile, Harvard Business Review, November 4, 2019, https://hbr.org/2019/11/why-science-driven-companies-should-use-agile

45. Paul Tunnah, Eye-on-Innovation: Can 'Design Thinking' Revolutionize Pharma's Culture? Pharmaphorum, May 3, 2018, https://pharmaphorum.com/views-and-analysis/can-design-thinking-revolutionise-pharmas-culture/

46. Sascha Lehmann, Nils Liedtke, Phyllis Rothschild, Eloy Trevino, The Future of Brand Strategy: It's Time to 'Go Electric,' McKinsey & Company, May 27, 2020, https://www.mckinsey.com/business-functions/marketing-and-sales/our-insights/the-future-of-brand-strategy-its-time-to-go-electric

47. Linda Watts, 10 Reasons to Build Healthcare Journey Maps, Perficient Healthcare, August 15, 2020, https://blogs.perficient.com/2020/08/15/10-reasons-to-build-healthcare-journey-maps/

48. PM 360 Staff, The Keys to Delivering Superior Digital Customer Experience, PM360, June 21, 2018, https://www.pm360online.com/the-keys-to-delivering-superior-digital-customer-experience/

49. J. Clement, Percentage of Mobile Device Web Traffic Worldwide from 1st Quarter 2015 to 2nd Quarter 2020, Statista, July 21, 2020, https://www.statista.com/statistics/277125/share-of-website-traffic-coming-from-mobile-devices/

50. Madeline Good, How Customer Centricity is Changing Pharmaceutical Customer Experience, PeopleMetrics, January 19, 2018, https://www.peoplemetrics.com/blog/the-patient-experience-how-customer-centricity-is-changing-the-pharmaceutical-industry

51. Pete Gale and Will Myddleton, Customer Experience for Pharma Companies, PMLiVE, March 21, 2013, http://www.pmlive.com/pharma_thought_leadership/customer_experience_for_pharma_companies_468166

52. Victoria Summers and Vijay Unnikrishnan, While Telehealth Continues to Evolve, Pharma Needs to Keep an Eye on the Future, zs.com, August 3, 2020, https://www.zs.com/insights/telehealth-continues-to-evolve-pharma-keeps-an-eye-on-the-future

53. Kevin Dolgin, Digital— Teaching An Old Dog New Tricks: Car Maker Tesla Has Few Lessons for Pharma On Truly Putting Digital First, Reuters Events, March 20, 2017, https://www.reutersevents.com/pharma/column/digital-teaching-old-dog-new-tricks
54. George Underwood, Beyond 'beyond the pill,' PharmaTimes Magazine, January, 2018, http://www.pharmatimes.com/magazine/2018/janfeb/beyond_beyond_the_pill
55. Robin Robinson, Moving Beyond The "Beyond The Pill" Conversation, PharmaVoice, March 2018, https://www.pharmavoice.com/article/2018-03-beyond-the-pill/
56. Chris Round, How Merck Is Stepping Up For Patients, Pharmaphorum, May 8, 2018, https://pharmaphorum.com/views-analysis-patients/how-merck-is-stepping-up-for-patients/
57. DMI Blog, Ethics, Regulation & Customer Experience in the Pharma Industry: Why It Matters, digitalmarketinginstitute.com, https://digitalmarketinginstitute.com/blog/ethics-regulations-customer-experience-in-the-pharma-industry
58. Dr. Nicola Davies, Design Thinking: A Human-Centered Approach for Pharma, Reuters Events: Pharma, September 15, 2015, Design Thinking: A Human-Centered Approach for Pharma
59. Lucy Fulford, Design: Pharma's Next Frontier, Reuters Events Pharma, September 16, 2019, https://www.reutersevents.com/pharma/patients-and-medical/design-pharmas-next-frontier
60. Marcia Angell, M.D, The Truth About the Drug Companies: How They Deceive Us and What To Do About It, Random House, New York, 2004
61. Joel Lexchin, MD, Doctors in Denial: Why Big Pharma and the Canadian Medical Profession are Too Close for Comfort, Kindle Edition, James Lorimer & Company Ltd, Toronto, 2017
62. Melody Petersen, Our Daily Meds: How the Pharmaceutical Companies Transformed Themselves into Slick Marketing Machines and Hooked the Nation on Prescription Drugs, Picador, First Edition, 2009
63. Katherine Eban, Bottle of Lies: The Inside Story of the Generic Drug Boom, Kindle Edition, Ecco, Reprint Edition, 2020
64. Stephen Sheller, Sidney Kirkpatrick, Pharmageddon: A Nation Betrayed: A National Trial Lawyer Reveals an Industry Spinning out of Control, Kindle Edition, Cape Cedar Media, 2016
65. Jerome P. Kassirer, MD, On The Take: How Medicine's Complicity With Big Business Can Endanger Your Health, Oxford University Press, 2005
66. John L. LaMattina, Devalued and Distrusted: Can the Pharmaceutical Industry Restore its Broken Image, 1st Edition, Kindle Edition, Wiley, 2012
67. Robert Yoho, MD, Butchered By "Healthcare": How Doctors and Corporations Try to Kill you For The Money and How To Survive Anyway, Amazon Kindle Edition, 2021
68. Gerald Posner, Pharma: Greed, Lies and The Poisoning of America, Simon & Schuster,
69. Christopher Lane, Shyness: How Normal Behavior Became a Sickness, 1st Edition, Kindle Edition, Yale University Press, 2007
70. Alison Bass, Side Effects: A Prosecutor, a Whistleblower, and a Bestselling Antidepressant on Trial, Kindle Edition, Algonquin Books, 2008
71. Dr. Arun Gadre, and Dr. Abhay Shukla, Dissenting Diagnosis: Voices of Conscience from the Medical Profession, Random House India, 2016
72. Edited by Samiran Nundy, Keshav Desiraju, Sanjay Nagral, Healers or Predators? Healthcare Corruption in India, Oxford University Press, 2018
73. John Abramson, Overdosed America: The Broken Promise of American Medicine, Harper Collins Publishers Inc, 2008
74. Atul Gawande, The Checklist Manifesto: How to Get Things Right, Profile Books, London, 2010
75. Linda Banks, Applying Closed Loop Pharma Marketing in Pharma, pharmaphorum.com, September 9, 2014, https://pharmaphorum.com/views-and-analysis/applying-closed-loop-marketing-in-pharma/
76. Ramon Chen, Data Driving Metamorphosis of Pharma Marketing, pharmaphorum.com October 26, 2016, https://pharmaphorum.com/views-and-analysis/data-driving-metamorphosis-of-pharma-marketing/
77. Robin Robinson, Marketing Using Data Analytics, pharmavoice.com, March 1, 2018, https://www.pharmavoice.com/news/2018-03-analytics/612645/
78. Farris, Paul W., Neil T. Bandle, Phillip E. Pfeifer, and David J Reibstein, Marketing Metrics: The Definitive Guide to Measuring Marketing Performance, Second Edition, Pearson Education Inc, 2010
79. Amy Gallo, Analytics And Data Science: A Refresher on A/B Testing, Harvard Business Review, https://hbr.org/2017/06/a-refresher-on-ab-testing
80. Jason Gordon, Always Be Closing (Sales Strategy) — Explained, The Business Professor Blog, Updated December 15, 2021, https://thebusinessprofessor.com/en_US/sales/always-be-closing-sales-strategy-definition
81. Dan Tyre, It's Time to Move From 'Always Be Closing' to This New Sales Mantra, HubSpot Blog, January 3, 2023, https://blog.hubspot.com/sales/always-be-closing-is-dead-how-to-always-be-helping-in-2015
82. About dynamic remarketing: Show ads tailored to your site and app...https://support.google.com/google-ads/answer/3124536?l=en

83. Justin Grossman, CEO & Partner at Meltmedia, Is Agile the Key to Mastering Journey Orchestration in Pharma Marketing, PharmaLive.com, February 13, 2019, https://www.pharmalive.com/is-agile-the-key-to-mastering-journey-orchestration-in-pharma-marketing/
84. Raquel Alberdi, What is Igor Ansoff's Growth Matrix? The Full Guide, The Power Business School Blog, https://www.thepowermba.com/en/blog/ansoff-growth-matrix
85. The Investopedia Team, Reviewed by Charles Potters and Fact Checked by Skylar Clarine, Absolute Advantage: Definition, Benefits, and Example, investopedia.com, Updated January 11, 2023, https://www.investopedia.com/terms/a/absoluteadvantage.asp
86. Aruna Pattam, Artificial Intelligence, In Simple Terms, LinkedIn Blog, June 27, 2021, https://www.linkedin.com/pulse/artificial-intelligence-simple-terms-aruna-pattam/?trk=public_profile_article_view
87. Nick Taylor, Getting Multichannel Marketing Right, PMLiVe, June 2, 2018, https://www.pmlive.com/pharma_intelligence/Getting_multichannel_marketing_right_1236340
88. Jay Baer, Content Marketing: 47 Tactics to Atomize Your Content Marketing, Convince&Convert, https://www.convinceandconvert.com/content-marketing/atomize-your-content-marketing/
89. Sakshi Sharma, Brand Valuation— Approaches and Methods, Mondaq: Blog, December 19, 2016, https://www.mondaq.com/india/advertising-marketing--branding/553838/brand-valuation--approaches-and-methods
90. Julie Wilkinson, Barcelona Principles 3.0, AMEC (International Association for the Measurement and Evaluation of Communication), July 9, 2020, https://amecorg.com/2020/07/barcelona-principles-3-0/
91. Diffusion of Innovations, WikipediA: The Free Encyclopedia, https://en.wikipedia.org/wiki/Diffusion_of_innovations
92. Kayla Carmicheal, How to Explain Banner Ads to Anyone, HubSpot, December 1, 2020, https://blog.hubspot.com/marketing/banner-ad-clicks
93. Adam Hayes, Barriers to Entry: Understanding What Limits Competition, Investopedia, December 30, 2022, https://www.investopedia.com/terms/b/barrierstoentry.asp
94. Adam Hayes, Bayes' Theorem: What It Is, the Formula, and Examples, Investopedia, Updated March 1, 2022, https://www.investopedia.com/terms/b/bayes-theorem.asp
95. Conniekroskin, How to Write a Brand Positioning Statement That is Benefit Oriented, CKC: Connie Kroskin Consulting, May 29, 2018, https://conniekroskin.com/how-to-write-a-brand-positioning-statement-that-is-benefit-oriented/
96. Wallstreetmojo Team, Brand Personality, Brand Personality, https://conniekroskin.com/how-to-write-a-brand-positioning-statement-that-is-benefit-oriented/
97. Hitesh Bhasin, What is Brand Character? Marketing91, December 17, 2019, https://conniekroskin.com/how-to-write-a-brand-positioning-statement-that-is-benefit-oriented/
98. How to Identify Your Brand's Values? SILBER Consulting, December 26, 2022, https://silber-consult.com/how-to-identify-your-brands-values/
99. Blitzkrieg, History Channel, Updated December 12, 2022, https://www.history.com/topics/world-war-ii/blitzkrieg
100. What is a Blog? Definition, Types, Benefits and Why You Need One? WiX Blog, Updated December 6, 2022, https://www.wix.com/blog/2020/02/what-is-a-blog/?utm_source=google&utm_medium=cpc&utm_campaign=12188669214%5E114296906861&experiment_id=%5E%5E530595868227%5E%5E_DSA&gclid=CjwKCAiAmJGgBhAZEiwA1JZollsqKppU-tdS_nJ225bosjS_xWbwCisQ7A07NYiUtN-kYgps8bp22xoC7PEQAvD_BwE
101. David Chapin, 10 Situations in Which Archetypes Give You A Distinct Sales Advantage in the Life Sciences, Biotech, and Drug Development, Forma Life Science Marketing, Volume 7, Number 10, https://www.formalifesciencemarketing.com/white-papers/10-situations-where-archetypes-increase-life-science-sales/
102. Patrick Nycz, Brand Psychology: 5 Valuable Takeaways for Marketers and Entrepreneurs, Forbes, August 31, 2022, https://www.forbes.com/sites/forbesagencycouncil/2022/08/31/brand-psychology-5-valuable-takeaways-for-marketers-and-entrepreneurs/?sh=6123f4ba24ad
103. David Kreutter (Pfizer), interviewed by David Kiron and Rebecca Shockley, How Pfizer Uses Tablet PCs and Click-Stream Data to Track Strategy, MIT Sloan Management Review, August 25, 2011, https://sloanreview.mit.edu/article/how-pfizer-uses-tablet-pcs-and-click-stream-data-to-track-its-strategy-2/
104. Kendra Cherry, What Are the Jungian Archetypes, VeryWellMind, Updated on March 11, 2023, https://www.verywellmind.com/what-are-jungs-4-major-archetypes-2795439
105. Jeremy Wagstaff, As Sensors Shrink, Watch As 'Wearables' Disappear, Reuters, April 30, 2015,

https://www.reuters.com/article/us-tech-wearables/as-sensors-shrink-watch-as-wearables-disappear-idINKBN0NK2KV20150430

106. Stuart Karten, Invisibles, Not Wearables, Will Profoundly Change Healthcare, Fast Company, March 10, 2014, https://www.fastcompany.com/3036554/invisibles-not-wearables-will-profoundly-change-healthcare

107. Sabrina Ortiz, What is ChatGPT And Why Does It Matter? Here is What You Need to Know, ZDNET, March 23, 2023, https://www.fastcompany.com/3036554/invisibles-not-wearables-will-profoundly-change-healthcare

108. Timothé Cynober, 5 Ways Pharma Can Benefit From the Metaverse, LinkedIn Blog, June 21, 2022, https://www.linkedin.com/pulse/5-ways-pharma-can-benefit-from-metaverse-timothé-cynober-pharm-d-/?trk=pulse-article

109. Md Kawser Hossain, Milking Strategy, LinkedIn Blog, August 5, 2020, https://www.linkedin.com/pulse/milking-strategy-md-kawser-hossain/

110. Types of Demand in Marketing: 8 Types of Demands with Examples, LAPAAS, https://lapaas.com/types-of-demand-in-marketing/

111. Category Development Index (CDI): What it is and How to Calculate it? buildd website, https://buildd.co/marketing/category-development-index

112. Stephanie Glen, "About/Contact" From StatisticsHowTo.com: Elementary Statistics for the rest of us! https://www.statisticshowto.com

113. Glossary/Lexicon, Dependent Variable, Psychology-Lexicon, https://www.psychology-lexicon.com/cms/glossary/37-glossary-d/78-dependent-variable.html

114. Connie D. Stapleton, Factor Analysis and Construct Validity: Basic concepts on Exploratory Analysis (EFA) as a Tool to Evaluate Score Validity— A Right Brain Approach, Texas A&M University, January 1997, http://ericae.net/ft/tamu/Efa.htm

115. Smith, W. (2017, January 1). Brave New World is Closer Than You Think. Human Life Review, 43(1), 47.

116. NIH Tech Day | RackTop. https://www.racktopsystems.com/event/nih-tech-day/

117. 7 Effective Digital Marketing Services That Drive Results. https://www.bsnstoday.com/blog/7-effective-digital-marketing-services-that-drive-results-3-1

118. What is SEO? -. https://www.keenweb.net/what-is-seo/

119. Content Marketing - Best Digital Marketing Company in Noida - Vindhya Process Solutions. https://www.vindhyaprocess.com/category/contentmarketing/

120. The impact of AI on the economy: How artificial intelligence is transforming business and industry – The Hatchet. https://thewhshatchet.org/the-impact-of-ai-on-the-economy-how-artificial-intelligence-is-transforming-business-and-industry/

121. What is Online Reputation Management (ORM) in digital Marketing. https://www.bigtrunk.co.in/what-is-online-reputation-management/

122. The 6 Most Important Digital Marketing KPIs (and How to Track Them). https://veneratedigital.com/the-6-most-important-digital-marketing-kpis-and-how-to-track-them/

123. The Importance of Online Marketing for Small Businesses - moviesb4u. https://moviesb4u.com/the-importance-of-online-marketing-for-small-businesses/

124. Understanding How Google Pagespeed Impacts Your Business | Locally. https://www.locally.net.au/post/understanding-how-google-pagespeed-impacts-your-business

125. Complete Guide to Brand Performance [6 key metrics included]. https://locobuzz.com/blogs/brand-performance-complete-guide/

126. Digital Marketing Agency | Search Engine optimization - Techgeen. https://techgeen.com/digital-marketing/

127. 5 Consequences Of Not Updating Your Computer's Software Regularly | Geek Culture Podcast: The most important news.. https://geekculturepodcast.com/5-consequences-of-not-updating-your-computers-software-regularly/

128. Responsive Web Design and how it affects user experience? - Extended Web. https://www.extwebtech.com/blog/responsive-web-design-and-how-it-affects-user-experience/

129. 5 Real-World Operational Excellence Examples To Inspire Your Business. https://www.glendalecommunity.ca/19111/operational-excellence-examples/

130. Maximizing Survey Response Rates - Part 2: 10 Tips to Achieve Your Goal - CX Journey™. https://cx-journey.com/2012/01/maximizing-survey-response-rates-part-2.html

131. What Is DTC Marketing? | Crystallize. https://crystallize.com/answers/marketing-stuff/what-is-dtc-marketing

132. How to demonstrate the ROI of your marketing with research | Attest. https://www.askattest.com/events/how-to-blend-research-digital-marketing-tactics-to-improve-your-campaigns

133. What is SERPs: Ultimate Guide | SiteGuru. https://www.siteguru.co/seo-academy/what-is-serps-search-engine-results-page

134. Search Engine Optimization | St. Louis SEO Company | SEO Services. https://www.elitewebstl.com/internet-marketing/search-engine-optimization.html

135. SEO vs PPC: Which Is Better for Your Business?. https://wf.traktion.ai/blog/seo-vs-ppc

136. How to Improve Your Website Ranking | Masterpiece Web Designs. https://masterpiecewebdesigns.com/how-to-improve-your-website-ranking/

137. The School of Public Health < Brown University. https://bulletin.brown.edu/public-health/

138. Understanding the Statistical Properties of the Normal Distribution - dummies. https://www.dummies.com/article/academics-the-arts/math/statistics/understanding-the-statistical-properties-of-the-normal-distribution-169627/

139. Lombardo, Veronica Andrea, et al. "Morphogenetic Control of Zebrafish Cardiac Looping by Bmp Signaling." 2019, https://doi.org/10.1242/dev.180091.

140. The Ultimate Guide to Sales Funnel Optimization - CC | Website Design and Custom Web Development Atlanta. https://codeconspirators.com/the-ultimate-guide-to-sales-funnel-optimization/

141. Marketing Strategies for a Successful Pensacola Tree Removal Business – CLC Marketing. http://clc-marketing.com/marketing-your-pensacola-tree-removal-business/

142. Why is planned obsolescence used? – Wise-Advices. https://yourwiseadvices.com/why-is-planned-obsolescence-used/

143. Data Protection. https://www.kahun.com/data-protection

144. Informed Consent | Bill Petrie. https://www.deepinsightscoaching.com/informed-consent

145. Probability Sampling Overview - Statistics By Jim. https://statisticsbyjim.com/basics/probability-sampling/

146. What Does ADR Stand For In Drug Safety? - Meds Safety. https://medssafety.com/what-does-adr-stand-for-in-drug-safety

147. Navigating the World of Programmatic Advertising - California Digitals. https://californiadigitals.com/navigating-the-world-of-programmatic-advertising/

148. Precision Medicine | List of High Impact Articles | PPts | Journals | Videos. https://www.scitechnol.com/scholarly/precision-medicine-journals-articles-ppts-list.php

149. Can Pharma Defy Gravity at the Patent Cliff?. https://www.pharmtech.com/view/can-pharma-defy-gravity-patent-cliff

150. Davies, B., McHugh, M., Elgheriani, A., Kolias, A., Tetreault, L., Hutchinson, P., Fehlings, M., & Kotter, M. (2016). Reported Outcome Measures in Degenerative Cervical Myelopathy: A Systematic Review. PLoS One, 11(8), e0157263.

151. Short-Form Health Survey - Hypersomnia Foundation. https://www.hypersomniafoundation.org/glossary/sf-36/

152. The role of stability testing in pharmaceutical manufacturing - Seqens. https://www.pcisynthesis.com/how-to-know-when-to-toss-your-prescription-drug-or-refrigerate-it/

153. Strict regulatory compliance - Acadia Software. https://www.acadia-software.com/case-studies/ensuring-strict-regulatory-compliance-in-cultivation-wholesale-and-dispensary-operations

154. Sidra Condron, How Search Engines Work: A Guide to Search Engine Algorithms, SpyFu Blog, Technical SEO, SEO, June 12, 2023, https://www.spyfu.com/blog/how-do-search-engines-work/

155. How Search Engines Work: A Guide to Google and Bing Algorithms. https://www.spyfu.com/blog/how-do-search-engines-work/

156. Alicia Raeburn, SWOT Analysis: Examples and Templates, asana, November 6, 2023, https://asana.com/resources/swot-analysis#:~:text=Facebook%2C%20and%20Instagram.-,Threats,change%20in%20the%20competitive%20landscape.

157. Sherry Baker & David Martinson, The TARES Test: Five Principles for Ethical Persuasion, Journal of Mass Media Ethics, 16 (2-3):148-175 (2001)

158. Gavin Wright, Ivy Wigmore, VUCA (Volatility, Uncertainty, Complexity, and Ambiguity), WhatIs.com, https://www.techtarget.com/whatis/definition/VUCA-volatility-uncertainty-complexity-and-ambiguity#:~:text=VUCA%20use%20and%20history,The%20Strategies%20for%20Taking%20Charge.

159. HOW IS WEB ACCESSIBILITY BENEFICIAL? - General Tops. https://generaltops.com/how-is-web-accessibility-beneficial/

160. Annamarie Hanlon, How to Use the BCG Matrix Model, Smart insights.com, January 7, 2022, https://www.smartinsights.com/marketing-planning/marketing-models/use-bcg-matrix/#:~:text=The%20Boston%20Consulting%20group%27s%20product,as%20the%20Growth%2FShare%20Matrix.

About the Author

Subba Rao Chaganti

Has a master's in business administration and over fifty-five years of experience in pharmaceutical marketing, covering the whole gamut and all facets of the industry from selling to sales management product management to heading the total marketing activity. His experience covers domestic and international marketing and Indian and multinational sectors.

He also taught for a few years a course on Advertising and Brand Management at Gitam Institute of Foreign Trade (now part of Gitam University) at Visakhapatnam as an adjunct professor. Also, he taught a course on Marketing at Jawaharlal Nehru Technological University (JNTU), Hyderabad as a visiting faculty.

He lives in Hyderabad and can be reached at subbarao.chaganti@gmail.com

Here is a list of his publications:

1. Pharmaceutical marketing in India: Concepts, Cases, Strategy
2. Game Plans for Post-Gatt Era: Action Agenda of Indian Pharmaceutical Industry
3. Compete or Forfeit: Strategies for Sustainable Competitive Advantage in Pharma Product Patents Era
4. Pharmaceutical Marketing in India for Today and Tomorrow - 25th Anniversary Edition
5. Bullseyes and Blunders: Lessons from 100 Cases in Pharma Marketing
6. Digital Pharma Marketing Playbook: Winning With the New Rules of Engagement
7. Cracking the Generics Code: Your Single-Source Success Manual for Winning in Multi-Source Product Markets
8. Reimagine Pharma Marketing: Make It Future-Proof!
9. Brand Positioning in Pharma
10. Transactional to Transformational Marketing in Pharma: The Art of Why and the Science of How!

www.ingramcontent.com/pod-product-compliance
Lightning Source LLC
Chambersburg PA
CBHW080535250926
51846CB00016B/965